Frommer's®

FLORIDA
FROM $60 A DAY

Here's what the critics say about Frommer's:

"Amazingly easy to use. Very portable, very complete."
—*Booklist*

♦

"Complete, concise, and filled with useful information."
—*New York Daily News*

♦

"Hotel information is close to encyclopedic."
—*Des Moines Sunday Register*

♦

"The only mainstream guide to list specific prices. The Walter Cronkite of guidebooks—with all that implies"
—*Travel & Leisure*

Other Great Guides for Your Trip:

Frommer's®

2nd Edition

FLORIDA
FROM $60 A DAY

The Ultimate Guide to
Comfortable Low-Cost Travel

by Bill Goodwin,
Victoria Pesce Elliott & Mary Meehan

MACMILLAN • USA

ABOUT THE AUTHORS

Bill Goodwin began his career as an award-winning newspaper reporter before becoming legal counsel and speechwriter for two U.S. senators. A full-time travel writer since 1984, he also is the author of *Frommer's South Pacific* and *Frommer's Virginia,* and he compiled and edited Frommer's USA.

Victoria Pesce Elliott is a freelance journalist and native of Miami. She returned there after nearly a decade in New York City, where she graduated from the Columbia University Graduate School of Journalism. She is also the author of *Frommer's Miami & the Keys.*

From opening day at Universal Studios to that first plunge down the Tower of Terror, **Mary Meehan** has an insider's view of the best things to see and do in Central Florida. She is an Orlando-based writer whose work has appeared in regional and national publications.

MACMILLAN TRAVEL

A Simon & Schuster Macmillan Company
1633 Broadway
New York, NY 10019

Find us online at **www.frommers.com**

ISBN 0-02-862256-1
ISSN 1090-2317

Editor: Kelly Regan, Jeff Soloway, Matthew Garcia
Production Editor: Mark Enochs
Design by Michele Laseau
Digital Cartography by John Decamillis
Page Creation by Jena Brandt, Carrie Allen, Natalie Evans, and Ellen Considine

SPECIAL SALES

Bulk purchases (10+ copies) of Frommer's and selected Macmillan travel guides are available to corporations, organizations, mail-order catalogs, institutions, and charities at special discounts, and can be customized to suit individual needs. For more information write to Special Sales, Macmillan General Reference, 1633 Broadway, New York, NY 10019.

Manufactured in the United States of America

Contents

7 The National Parks of South Florida: The Everglades & Beyond 223

by Victoria Pesce Elliott

8 The Gold Coast 245

by Victoria Pesce Elliott

9 The Treasure Coast 301

by Victoria Pesce Elliott

10 Southwest Florida 327

by Bill Goodwin

14 **Northeast Florida 610**

by Bill Goodwin

List of Maps

AN INVITATION TO THE READER

In researching this book, we discovered many wonderful places—hotels, restaurants, shops, and more. We're sure you'll find others. Please tell us about them, so we can share the information with your fellow travelers in upcoming editions. If you were disappointed with a recommendation, we'd love to know that, too. Please write to:

Frommer's Florida from $60 a Day
Macmillan Travel
1633 Broadway
New York, NY 10019

AN ADDITIONAL NOTE

Please be advised that travel information is subject to change at any time—and this is especially true of prices. We therefore suggest that you write or call ahead for confirmation when making your travel plans. The authors, editors, and publisher cannot be held responsible for the experiences of readers while traveling. Your safety is important to us, however, so we encourage you to stay alert and be aware of your surroundings. Keep a close eye on cameras, purses, and wallets, all favorite targets of thieves and pickpockets.

WHAT THE SYMBOLS MEAN

✪ Frommer's Favorites

Our favorite places and experiences—outstanding for quality, value, or both.

The following abbreviations are used for credit cards:

AE	American Express	EURO	Eurocard
CB	Carte Blanche	JCB	Japan Credit Bank
DC	Diners Club	MC	MasterCard
DISC	Discover	V	Visa

FIND FROMMER'S ONLINE

Arthur Frommer's Outspoken Encyclopedia of Travel (www.frommers.com) offers more than 6,000 pages of up-to-the-minute travel information—including the latest bargains and candid, personal articles updated daily by Arthur Frommer himself. No other Web site offers such comprehensive and timely coverage of the world of travel.

The Best of Florida from $60 a Day

Every year more than 40 million visitors escape bleak northern winters to bask in Florida's warmth, lured to the Sunshine State by the promise of clear skies and 800 miles of spectacular sandy beaches. A host of kid-pleasers, from Busch Gardens to Walt Disney World, make this the country's most popular year-round family vacation destination.

Here you can choose from a wide array of accommodations, from deluxe resorts to mom-and-pop motels. You can visit remote little towns like Apalachicola or a megalopolis like Miami. Devour fresh seafood, from amberjack to oysters—and work off those calories in such outdoor pursuits as bicycling, golf, or kayaking. Despite overde-velopment in many parts of the state, Floridians have maintained thousands of acres of wilderness areas, from the little respite of Clam Pass County Park in downtown Naples to the magnificent Everglades National Park, which stretches across the state's southern tip.

Choosing the "best" of all this is a daunting task, and the selections in this chapter are only a rundown on some of the affordable high-lights. You'll find numerous other outstanding resorts, hotels, destina-tions, activities, and attractions—all described in the pages of this book. With a bit of serendipity you'll come up with some bests of your own.

And the real best of Florida: You can see it, do it, and eat it on a budget.

1 The Best Beaches

Many of Florida's best beaches are in its state parks and recreation areas. Admission to most of them is $3.25 per vehicle with up to eight occupants, $2 for a vehicle with one occupant, or $1 per pedestrian or bicyclist. Given the quality of what you'll see, that's one of Florida's best bargains.

- **Bill Baggs Cape Florida State Recreation Area** (Key Biscayne, Miami): At the very tip of Key Biscayne and only minutes from downtown Miami is a natural wonder. Consistently voted one of the best in the country, this secluded bend of beach juts out into the Atlantic Ocean, surrounded by sand dunes, sea oats, towering palms, and palmettos. Its centerpiece is a recently restored light-house and small museum. Next door is an outfit that rents boating equipment and lounge chairs, and a large casual beach bar serving good, cheap Cuban specialties. Just watch out for the raccoons. See chapter 5.

- **Crandon Park Beach** (Key Biscayne, Miami): A well-equipped, active beach, Crandon Park has 3 miles of oceanfront and nearly 500 acres of grassy grounds that sport barbecue grills, soccer and softball fields, and a public 18-hole championship golf course. Families and young soccer players scatter throughout the area on weekends, while more relaxed visitors walk along nature trails and take in the view of Miami Beach across the Bay. See chapter 5.

- **South Beach** (South Beach, Miami): This miniature metropolis at southern the tip of Miami Beach is wild and wonderful. The actual beach that edges this decadent town is certainly not like any others in this country. The sand, grayish and a bit course, is nothing to marvel at, but the people are. Boys who like boys hang out near 12th Street, a popular pick-up spot, showing off bodies like you have never seen. Further north are scores of topless women from the world over. Models preen for catalogue or commercial shoots, bikers and bladers race by on the board-walk, volleyball players compete, aging snowbirds look for shells, families settle in for elaborate picnics, and food vendors hawk their homemade Latin meat pastries and sodas. This daily carnival is set against a backdrop of a pastel colored skyline made up of the now-famous art deco hotels that date from the '30s and '40s. See chapter 5.

- **Sebastian Inlet** (North Hutchinson Island): At the tip of North Hutchinson Island, Sebastian Inlet is where surfers find the biggest swells. Nonsurfers come for the flat sandy beaches and miles of shaded walkways; facilities include kayak, paddleboat, canoe rentals, picnic tables, and a snack shop. See chapter 9.

- **Lover's Key–Carl E. Johnson State Recreation Area** (Fort Myers Beach; ☎ 941/463-4288): There are bathhouses with outdoor showers, a snack shop, and canoe and kayak rentals at the parking lot; but access to this unspoiled, shell-strewn beach is restricted to footpaths or a tractor-pulled tram through a bird-filled forest of mangroves and casuarinas. See chapter 10.

- **Cayo Costa Island State Park** (off Captiva Island): These days, deserted tropical islands with great beaches are scarce in Florida, but this 2,132-acre barrier strip of sand, pine forests, mangrove swamps, oak hammocks, and grasslands provides a genuine get-away-from-it-all experience. The only nonnative residents are wild pigs and a lone park ranger. This is one of the more expensive state parks to visit since access is by boat from nearby Gasparilla, Pine, and Captiva Islands. See chapter 10.

- **Clam Pass County Park** (Naples): Although Clam Pass sits in a developed part of Naples, a free tram takes you along a 3,000-foot boardwalk winding through mangrove swamps and across a back bay to this fine white-sand beach. It's a strange sight, what with high-rise condos standing beyond the mangrove-bordered backwaters, but this miniature wilderness actually boasts some 6 miles of canoe and kayak trails, a multitude of birds, and the occasional alligator. See chapter 10.

- **Naples Beach** (Naples): Many Florida cities and towns have beaches, but few are as lovely as the gorgeous strip that runs in front of Naples's famous Millionaires' Row. You don't have to be rich to wander its length, peer at the mansions, and stroll on historic Naples Pier to catch a sunset over the gulf. See chapter 10.

- **Caladesi Island State Park** (Clearwater; ☎ 813/469-5942): Even though it's in the heavily developed Tampa Bay area, 3½-mile Caladesi Island has a lovely, relatively secluded beach with soft sand edged in sea grass and palmettos. Dolphins cavort in offshore waters. In the park itself, there's a nature trail, and you might see one of the rattlesnakes, black racers, raccoons, armadillos, or rabbits that live here. The park is accessible only by ferry from Honeymoon Island State Recreation Area off Dunedin. See chapter 11.

- **Fort Desoto Park** (St. Pete Beach; ☎ **813/866-2662**): At the very mouth of Tampa Bay, this group of five connected barrier islands is a 900-acre bird, animal, and plant sanctuary. Watch dolphins play in the gulf off of one of the nation's best white-sand beaches, and there's a Spanish-American War–era fort, fishing piers, a large playground for kids, and trails for in-line skaters, bicyclists, and joggers. See chapter 11.

- **Gulf Islands National Seashore** (Pensacola; ☎ **850/934-2600**): You could argue that all of Northwest Florida's gulf shore is one of America's great beaches—an almost uninterrupted stretch of pure white sand that runs the entire length of the Panhandle, from Perdido Key to St. George Island. The Gulf Islands National Seashore preserves much of this natural wonder in its undeveloped state. Countless terns, snowy plover, black skimmers, and other birds nest along the dunes topped with sea oats. East of the national seashore and equally as beautiful are Grayton Beach State Recreation Area near Destin, St. Andrews State Recreation Area in Panama City Beach, and St. Joseph Peninsula and St. George Island state parks near Apalachicola. See chapter 13.

- **Canaveral National Seashore** (Cape Canaveral; ☎ **407/267-1110**): Midway between the crowded attractions at Daytona Beach and the Kennedy Space Center is a protected stretch of coastline 24 miles long, backed by cabbage palms, sea grapes, and palmettos. Wooden boardwalks lead from a free parking lot to the huge expanse of soft brown sand and a few well-spaced picnic tables. Their neighbor is the 140,000-acre Merritt Island National Wildlife Refuge (☎ **407/ 861-0667**), home to hundreds of Florida birds, reptiles, alligators, and mammals. See chapter 14.

- **Fort Clinch State Park** (Amelia Island; ☎ **904/277-7274**): You'll find a wide, gray sand beach here, but the best part is that the coast curves here, which gives the feeling of being in a private cove. Boardwalks lead from the parking area through lush dunes to the beach. A jetty and a pier at its north end are popular with anglers. See chapter 14.

2 The Best Destinations for Low-Cost Vacations

- **The Middle and Lower Keys:** With all the hype about Key West, it seems the other keys get neglected by tourists who race through en route to the wild tip of the continental United States. Thank goodness. The string of islands that are far enough from Miami to dissuade day-trippers are a virtual treasure trove for active travelers who enjoy biking, boating, fishing, bird watching, snorkeling, or just plain old relaxing. Areas like Conch Key, Grassy Key, Marathon, Big Pine Key, and Sugarloaf are dotted with lush parks, simple fish houses, and modest accommodations. There is the National Key Deer Refuge, home to hundreds of nearly extinct miniature golden deer, Bahia Honda State Park, where Florida's unusual plant and animal life thrive for all to see. And of course, these keys are surrounded by some of the country's most incredible underwater attractions, including a living reef system that divers flock to from all over the world. See chapter 6.

- **Hollywood:** For about half what you'd spend in trendy South Beach, near by Holly-wood offers wide beaches, plenty of outdoor activities, lively night-spots and some real bargain hotels. Plus, you can drive half an hour in either direction to visit Ft. Lauderdale's elegant restaurants, and tourist attractions or head south to Miami Beach to partake in some of its outrageous activity. See chapter 8.
- **Lake Okeechobee:** Head inland to Clewiston on Lake Okeechobee for a real feel of Old Florida. This is a popular spot for RVs and anglers. Everything from food to lodging is reasonably priced. You can stay in the nicest spot in town for about $40 a person. And while you're on the lake, why not catch your own dinner. See chapter 9.
- **Fort Myers Beach:** Just a few miles from trendy Sanibel and Captiva Islands, Fort Myers Beach offers just as much sun, sand, and shells—and at much less expensive prices—as its more affluent neighbors. It has always had a more Coney Island–like reputation, but its busy "Times Square" has been spiffed up in recent years, and the rest of Estero Island offers some very comfortable accommodations at reasonable rates, even in the winter high season. And the gorgeous Lovers Key–Carl E. Johnson State Recreation Area is just across the bridge. See chapter 10.
- **Naples:** For a town with residents who possess industrial-strength money, charming and friendly Naples offers some surprising bargains on accommodations and restaurants. During winter you'll have to book far in advance and perhaps stay a week or more, but the historic district's apartment motels are among the best deals in Florida. And admission to Naples's great beach and historic pier is free. See chapter 10.
- **The St. Pete and Clearwater Beaches:** The 20 miles of sand between St. Pete Beach and Clearwater have been a vacation mecca for a century, and they attract vacationers across the economic spectrum. Here is one of Florida's finest and most expensive grand old resorts, but you can also choose from many comfortable and inexpensive motels and condos, too. Granted, some four million guests a year can crowd this area at times, but there's a multitude of activities to keep them, and you, busy without breaking the bank. See chapter 11.
- **Bradenton and Anna Maria Island:** Although they sit next door to affluent Sarasota and expensive Longboat Key, Bradenton and its offshore counterpart, Anna Maria Island, are down-to-earth in both lifestyle and prices. They have fine beaches and a host of cost-conscious activities—and you only have to drive a few miles south to dine and shop on St. Armands Key, or to enjoy Sarasota's fine performing arts scene. See chapter 11.
- **The Beaches of Northwest Florida:** Many visitors to Pensacola Beach, Fort Walton Beach, Destin, and Panama City Beach are working-class families, couples, and singles from Alabama and Georgia. They don't have all the money in the world to spend. As a result, the Panhandle has a multitude of inexpensive accommodations and restaurants. And there's plenty to keep everyone busy here, from touring historic Pensacola to trying your luck in Destin, "The World's Luckiest Fishing Village." The only problem: The Panhandle can get cold in winter. See chapter 13.
- **Daytona Beach:** Like the Panhandle, Daytona Beach attracts a working-class clientele—not to mention stock-car fans and bikers who make pilgrimages to this "World Center of Racing." Accordingly, you'll find many low-cost places to stay and dine here. In addition to its famous racetrack, the area sports a beach so wide and hard-packed that you can drive on it. See chapter 14.

3 The Best Experiences You Can Have for Free (or Almost)

- **See the Boys of Spring** (statewide): Although Florida has the big-league Florida Marlins in Miami and the Tampa Bay Devil Rays in St. Petersburg, the whole state goes baseball crazy during spring training from mid-February through March. Great seats close to the action are a bargain compared to what you'll pay when the Boys of Spring get home. See the box in chapter 2.

- **Watch the Sunset Over Miami's Downtown Skyline** (Miami): Driving west over the Julia Tuttle Causeway is a great vantage point to catch the lights of the buildings and the bursts of aqua, pink, and orange from the sky. Head back the other direction and catch the glowing, neon necklaces that decorate a cluster of towering palms. See chapter 5.

- **Walk Along Ocean Drive** (Miami): In impossibly trendy South Beach, check out the parade of well-toned bodies, skaters, and gawking tourists. The show can keep you busy for hours. And for the price of a beer or a carrot juice, you can have a front-row view. See chapter 5.

- **Experience the Caribbean on U.S. Soil** (Miami): Stroll down Little Havana's Calle Ocho, 8th Street, to get a flavor of Hispanic culture. Stop by Maximo Gomez Park, at 801 SW 15th Ave., where the *viejitos* (old men) play dominoes from morning until sunset. Watch expert cigar rollers make hand-made stogies at one of the many cigar factories. Then have a potent *cafecito* at the take-out window at Versailles. See chapters 4 and 5.

- **Take the Metrorail Over Downtown Miami** (Miami): For 25¢, you can tour the city from above and get an overview of the bustling metropolis. The best part is you can enjoy it all sitting down in the cool comfort of air-conditioned cars. See chapter 5.

- **Catch the "Green Flash" at Sunset** (Key West and the Gulf Coast Beaches): Key West and the beaches of Southwest Florida and the Tampa Bay Area face due west, thus providing glorious sunsets over the Gulf of Mexico and a chance to see the elusive "green flash"—a quick burst of green light just as the top of the sun dips below the horizon. It costs not a cent to wander down to the shore and keep a sharp eye peeled. Or for a few bucks, grab a drink from a beachside restaurant or gulf-front bar. See "The Best Places for Sunset Cocktails," below, and chapters 6, 10, and 11.

- **Walk or Ride Along Wildlife Drive** (Sanibel Island): The mangrove swamps, winding waterways, and uplands of Sanibel Island's **J. N. (Ding) Darling National Wildlife Refuge** (☎ 941/472-1100) are great places to see alligators, raccoons, otters, and hundreds of species of birds. You can see many of the creatures from the 5-mile, one-way Wildlife Drive, which costs $4 per vehicle or $1 per pedestrian or biker. A naturalist will explain what you're seeing on a 2-hour narrated tram tour—a very good value at $8 for adults, $4 for children 12 and under. See chapter 10.

- **Stoop for Shells** (Sanibel Island): Okay, you'll have to pay a $3 toll to get here and a small fee to park your car (or lock your bike to a tree for nothing), but you can stroll Sanibel Island's world-famous shelling beaches as long as you want for free. After a few hours hunched over in the "Sanibel stoop," you're sure to go home with a prize find or two. See chapter 10.

- **Stroll Among the Millionaires** (Naples): Olde Naples residents love to stroll out on their ancient city pier to fish, catch a sunset, or look at Millionaires' Row, a string of magnificent mansions along the town's lovely beach. Now a state historic site, the pier is open 24 hours a day and is free, although it will cost you a few quarters to park in the nearby municipal lots. When you're done ogling the wealthy from the Naples Pier, you can walk among them while window-shopping in the ritzy 3rd Street district nearby. Naples is so midwestern-friendly that nobody will care if you maxed your credit cards just to get here. See chapter 10.

- **Poke Through a Dusty Museum Dedicated to Sponges** (Tarpon Springs): The highlight of any stroll along the carnival-like Sponge Docks in Tarpon Springs is the rickety **Spongeorama** (☎ 813/943-9509), a dusty museum dedicated to sponges and sponge divers. You can buy a wide variety of fresh-from-the-gulf sponges here and watch a 30-minute video about sponge-diving. Admission is free. The docks also have a host of inexpensive restaurants featuring authentic Greek cuisine brought here by the town's sponge-diving settlers. See chapter 11.

- **See What the Big Top Bought** (Sarasota): Adults pay $8 or $9 to get in, but you'll have three "rings" to visit at the **Ringling Museums** in Sarasota (☎ 941/359-5700 or 941/351-1660 for recorded information), which house the phenomenal collections of circus master John Ringling. A pink Italian Renaissance villa is filled with over 500 years of European and American art, including one of the world's most important collections of grand 17th-century baroque paintings. The Ringling's 30-room winter residence displays their personal mementos. And the Circus Galleries are devoted to memorabilia from The Greatest Show on Earth. See chapter 11.

- **Skip the Theme Parks in Lieu of Culture on the Cheap** (Orlando): Almost every arts festival—and there are many in Central Florida, especially in the spring—offers free entertainment ranging from clogging to jazz bands. The **Cathedral Church of St. Luke's** (☎ 407/849-0680) in downtown Orlando offers a series of free concerts. There is also a lunchtime series, Bach's Lunch, in the spring that provides an hour of music, plus lunch from a downtown restaurant, for about $4 per person. Check Friday's "Calendar" section of the *Orlando Sentinel* to find out about arts festivals or concerts, or check the paper's Web site at www.orlandosentinel.com. See chapter 12.

- **OD on Sports at a Disney Resort** (Orlando): Walt Disney's Wide World of Sports has a deal that sports fans will appreciate. For an $8 admission price, you can tour the facility and watch whatever sporting events are taking place that day. The complex also has shops and the All-Star Cafe. A family of four could spend the day at Wide World of Sports for the cost of one ticket to the parks. See chapter 12.

- **Visit a Park So Nice They'll Let You in Twice** (Orlando): Universal Studios regularly runs second-day free promotions in order to compete with Walt Disney World. It's a phenomenal deal for the family and even more so once Islands of Adventure, with its Seuss Island and other kid-focused attractions, opens. See chapter 12.

- **Hit a Talcumlike Beach** (Northwest Florida): Admission is free to most of the 100-plus miles of powdery, snow-white beaches that make the Panhandle special, but a few bucks will let you into the Gulf Islands National Seashore at Pensacola, the Henderson Beach and Grayton Beach state recreation areas at Destin, the St. Andrews State Recreation Area at Panama City Beach, and the St. Joseph Peninsula and St. George Island state parks near Apalachicola. You won't soon forget the time you spend on these protected sands and dunes, all consistently ranked among the nation's finest beaches. See chapter 13.

- **Visit the Blue Angels and Top Guns** (Pensacola and Fort Walton Beach): Next to the Smithsonian Institution's National Air and Space Museum in Washington, D.C., the next best places to see our nation's warplanes on display are at the **National Museum of Naval Aviation** in Pensacola (☎ **850/452-3604**) and at the **U.S. Air Force Armament Museum** in Fort Walton Beach (☎ **850/882-4062**). Admission to both is free. They cost a few dollars, but the naval museum's IMAX films will make you believe you're flying in a Blue Angel's cockpit. See chapter 13.
- **Take a Giant Leap for Mankind** (Cape Canaveral): You can see some of the exhibits at the visitors center of the **John F. Kennedy Space Center** in Cape Canaveral (☎ **407/452-2121**) for free, but bus tours of the complex are well worth $10 for adults, $7 for children 3 to 11 (they're free for children 2 and under). You'll see the Complex 39 Space Shuttle launch pads and the massive Vehicle Assembly Building, the impressive Apollo/Saturn V Center, and the original pads where the moon walkers were launched into space. Also worth the price of admission are the IMAX films which bring the program to life on a huge screen. See chapter 14.
- **Stroll the Streets of America's Oldest City** (St. Augustine): Older than Jamestown, Plymouth Rock, or Pensacola, St. Augustine's restored Spanish Quarter offers a look back to America's very beginnings. You'll have to pay a few dollars to enter sites such as the nation's oldest store and oldest jail, but you can freely stroll these narrow streets for hours, poking your head into antique shops, peering into lush yards surrounding ancient buildings, and watching the boats out on the Matanzas River. See chapter 14.
- **Visit a New Breed of National Park** (Jacksonville): The Timucuan Ecological and Historic Preserve isn't one chuck of land; instead, it's a vast, intriguing system of sites on both sides of the St. Johns River. The prime attraction is the **Fort Carolina National Memorial** (☎ **904/641-7155**), the site of a 16th-century French Huguenot settlement. It's on the edge of the 600-acre Theodore Roosevelt Area, a beautiful, undisturbed wood- and marshland rich in history and wildlife. On the north side of the river, the **Zephaniah Kingsley Plantation** (☎ **904/251-3537**) was an early 19th-century manse owned by Zephaniah Kingsley, a white man who married a Senegalese woman he once owned and then moved his family to Haiti to escape racism at home. Admission is free to all the park's attractions. See chapter 14.

4 The Best-Value Package Deals

- **The Biltmore Hotel** (Coral Gables, Miami; ☎ **800/727-1926** or 305/445-1926): This Mediterranean palace offers great deals for those who don't mind coming to Miami in the slow and hot summer months. Even during holidays, you may be able to find package deals that include breakfasts, free use of the fitness center, free local calls, and a complimentary daily newspaper. Golfers especially will benefit from packages that might include early morning tee times and room upgrades at prices up to 35% lower than the standard winter rates. See chapter 4.
- **Biscayne National Park** (Miami; ☎ **305/230-1100**): Scuba divers should consider a trip to Biscayne National Park where the local outfitter will set up superaffordable 2-day dive trips to the largest underwater national park in the world for under 100 bucks. Here, huge clusters of living coral reef formations attract an amazing array of colorful, tropical fish and other sea life. See chapter 7.

- **The Breakers** (Palm Beach; ☎ **800/833-3141** or 561/655-6611): Unless you are part of one of the many conventions or retreats that often book large blocks of rooms, there's no way to get out of paying at least $150 for a room here, even in the steamy summer months. Still, package deals in these posh surroundings are a great value. Offering more than a dozen package deals, this most elegant of elegant hotels probably has something for you. Consider, for example, one of the cheapest deals, the 2-night, 3-day "Oceanfront Getaway." Offered Sunday through Wednesday in 1998 from late May through September, this little advertised special is especially worthwhile for active travelers who would otherwise be blowing a big wad on pricey sports facilities. For $149, two guests and children under 16 could stay in a basic room and take advantage of a generous credit of $200 to pay for tennis, golf, bicycle rental, or other activities. For less than $8 an hour, kids from 3 through 12 can join a fun day of activities that might include horseshoes, shell hunts, nature walks, or swimming. The "Coconut Crew Camp" is staffed by college-educated child care experts and is another good reason to splurge on a stay at the Breakers. See chapter 8.
- **South Seas Resorts** (Fort Myers Beach, Sanibel and Captiva Islands, Marco Island; ☎ **800/554-5454**): Based in Fort Myers, this company owns or manages several family oriented properties in Southwest Florida, including Sundial Beach Resort on Sanibel, South Seas Plantation Resort & Yacht Harbor on Captiva, and the Best Western Pink Shell Resort in Fort Myers Beach. Most are expensive during the winter months, but a variety of packages aimed at families and sports enthusiasts can bring them within the affordable range, especially off-season. See chapter 10.

5 The Best Adventure Trips

- **Swim with the Dolphins** (Grassy Key/Marathon): You've heard how smart these water-dwelling mammals are. Find out for yourself. For an unforgettable adventure, make a date to swim with the dolphins at the Dolphin Research Center in Grassy Key. This unique experience is as exciting as it is educational. See chapter 6.
- **Everglades National Park:** Whether hiking or biking, canoeing or kayaking, a trip through the bizarre landscape of the Everglades is sure to be an adventure. Where else do you share suntanning space with an alligator? Throughout the millions of acres of federally protected lands, canoers will see manatees, dolphins, the endangered key deer, alligators, reptiles, and hundreds of species of birds. To the north are the Big Cypress National Preserve and the Big Cypress Swamp. See chapter 7.
- **Jonathan Dickinson State Park** (Hobe Sound): You can rent a canoe and explore a scenic route that winds through a variety of botanical habitats. You may see a gator, a variety of reptiles, and even an occasional manatee. See chapter 9.
- **Bird Watching by Canoe or Kayak** (Sanibel Island): Naturalist, avid environmentalist, and former Sanibel mayor Mark "Bird" Westall (☎ **941/472-5218**) takes visitors on guided canoe trips through the J. N. (Ding) Darling National Wildlife Refuge and on the Sanibel River. They aren't cheap at $35 for adults, $15 for children under 18, but you won't soon forget this experience. On Captiva Island, naturalist **Brian Houston** leads similar kayaking trips for $35 per person for his morning and midday trips, $25 for a shorter version leaving at 4pm (make your reservations at Tarpon Bay Recreation on Sanibel (☎ **941/ 472-8900**). See chapter 10.

- **Primitive Camping in Collier Seminole State Park** (Marco Island; ☎ 941/394-3397): This inviting, 6,423-acre preserve on the edge of Big Cypress Swamp, 12 miles east of Marco Island, offers a host of activities, including canoeing over a 13-mile loop with primitive camping. Canoes can be rented, but the park has only four campsites along the canoe trails, so book early. For the more civilized, narrated boat tours wander through these winding waterways daily. See chapter 10.
- **Canoeing in Blackwater River State Park** (Milton, near Pensacola; ☎ 850/953-5363): The little town of Milton is the official "Canoe Capital of Florida" (by act of the state legislature, no less). It's a well-earned title, for the nearby Blackwater River, Coldwater River, Sweetwater Creek, and Juniper Creek are all perfect for canoeing, kayaking, tubing, rafting, and paddleboating. The Blackwater is considered one of the world's purest sand-bottom rivers and has retained its primordial, backwoods beauty. See chapter 13.
- **Trying Yours at the "World's Luckiest Fishing Village"** (Destin): Billing itself as the "World's Luckiest Fishing Village," Destin has Florida's largest charter-boat fleet, with more than 140 vessels. Rates for private charters range from about $360 to $900 per boat, depending on length of voyage, but a less-expensive way to try your luck is on a larger group-oriented party boat—about $25 to $30 per person, including gear, bait, and fishing license. See chapter 13.
- **Jeanni's Journeys** (Apalachicola; ☎ 850/927-3259): From her base in Apalachicola, Jeanni McMillan of Jeanni's Journeys leads informative nature cruises to the offshore barrier islands, including mountain bike excursions to the pristine St. Vincent National Wildlife Refuge, and on canoe trips in the creeks and streams of the Apalachicola River basin. Her very reasonable prices range from $15 to $70, including equipment. See chapter 13.

6 The Best Family Attractions

- **Miami Seaquarium** (Key Biscayne, Miami): Children and adults seem to love the dramatic performances by killer whales and dolphins. Come early and plan to spend the day at this lively and interesting animal park that has been here for nearly 50 years. Two-for-one discount coupons are available in the Entertainment book. See chapter 5.
- **Miami Metrozoo** (Miami): This completely cageless zoo offers such star attractions as a monorail "safari" and a petting zoo. Kids love the elephant rides. See chapter 5.
- **Mel Fisher Maritime Heritage Museum** (Key West): Especially since the success of the film *Titanic*, this museum full of doubloons, pieces of eight, emeralds, and solid-gold bars has fascinated visitors intrigued with shipwrecks. See chapter 6.
- **Key West Aquarium** (Key West): The oldest attraction on the island, this modest but fascinating exhibit is a great place for curious children. Touch tanks and feeding exhibitions get kids involved. See chapter 6.
- **Playmobil Fun Park** (Palm Beach Gardens): It's the only Playmobil park outside of Germany and it's a ball. This indoor fantasy world offers more than 17,000 square feet filled with thousands of toys. The best part? It's free. See chapter 8.
- **Edison and Ford Winter Estates** (Fort Myers; 941/334-3614): Inventor Thomas Alva Edison and his friend, automobile magnate Henry Ford, built side-by-side winter homes on the banks of the Caloosahatchee River in Fort Myers. Today these Victorian cottages serve as memorials to the two men, and especially

to Edison. The museum will show the kids how we got the lightbulb, the phonograph, and hundreds of other Edison inventions. Tours of both estates cost $10 adults, $5 children 6 to 12, free for children 5 and under. See chapter 10.

- **Caribbean Gardens** (Naples; ☎ 941/262-5409): Owned and operated by the family of noted animal trainer Larry Tetzlaff, this zoo features a variety of animals and birds, including a fascinating community of primates living free on their own island. Larry's son, David Tetzlaff, himself a talented trainer, puts lions and tigers through their paces in his Big Cat Show. For kids, there's a Petting Farm, elephant rides, and a playground. You can easily spend a day here for $13.95 adults, $8.95 children 4 to 15, free for children 3 and under. See chapter 10.

- **Teddy Bear Museum** (Naples; ☎ 800/681-2327 or 941/598-2711): More than 3,000 examples of stuffed teddy bears from around the world are cleverly displayed descending from the rafters in hot-air balloons, attending board meetings, sipping afternoon tea, celebrating a wedding, reading in the "Li-bear-y," even doing bear things like hibernating. Kids can even buy their own bear to take home. Admission is $6 adults, $4 seniors, $2 children 4 to 12, free for children under 4. See chapter 10.

- **Busch Gardens Tampa Bay** (Tampa; ☎ 813/987-5283): Although the thrill rides, live entertainment, shops, restaurants, and games get most of the ink at this 335-acre family theme park, Busch Gardens ranks among the top zoos in the country, with several thousand animals living in naturalistic environments. If you can get them off the roller coasters, the kids can find out what all those wild beasts they've seen on the Discovery Channel look like in person. You can save a few bucks off admission by buying your tickets outside the main gate. See chapter 11.

- **Florida Aquarium** (Tampa; ☎ 813/273-4000): This major aquarium will introduce you and the kids to more than 5,300 aquatic animals and plants that call Florida home. There's an "Explore a Shore" playground to educate the kids, a deepwater exhibit, and a tank housing moray eels. The Cafe Ray serves snacks and light meals. See chapter 11.

- **Museum of Science and Industry (MOSI)** (Tampa; ☎ 813/987-6300): One of the largest educational science centers in the Southeast, MOSI has more than 450 interactive exhibits in which the kids can experience hurricane-force winds, defy the laws of gravity, cruise the mysterious world of microbes, explore the human body, and much more. They can also watch stunning movies in MOSIMAX, Florida's first IMAX dome theater. See chapter 11.

- **The Magic Kingdom & Disney-MGM Studios** (Orlando): Of the four Disney parks, these two are the most fun for families with young children, with opportunities to meet and greet the famed characters, and rides to delight young and old alike. Yes, it can be prohibitively expensive, but with a little know-how and a lot of planning, you can have a memorable Disney experience without breaking the bank. For tips and advice, see chapter 12.

- **Universal Studios Florida, Sea World, and Wet 'n Wild** (Orlando): These three non-Disney parks have joined forces to fight the Mouse's multipark pass system. For one price you can visit any of the three during either a 7- or 10-day period. An added bonus: The 10-day pass includes Busch Gardens in Tampa, just a few hours drive from the Orlando area. See chapter 12.

- **Kennedy Space Center** (Cape Canaveral; ☎ 407/452-2121): The nation's spaceport is a must-see. There is plenty to keep kids and parents busy for at least a full day, including interactive computer games, IMAX films, and dozens of informative displays on the space program. Try to schedule a trip during a real launch; there are more than a dozen each year. See chapter 14.

- **Daytona USA** (Daytona Beach): Opened in late 1996 on Daytona International Speedway grounds, this huge state-of-the-art interactive attraction is an exciting and fast-paced stop even for nonrace fans. Kids can see real stock cars, go-carts, and motorcycles, and even participate in a pit stop on a NASCAR Winston Cup race car. See chapter 14.

7 The Best Offbeat Travel Experiences That Won't Cost a Fortune

- **South Beach's Free Drag Show** (South Beach, Miami): Stop by Lucky Cheng's for a wild floor show most evenings after 9:30 when over-the-top drag queens strut their stuff for all to see. Save the cover and drink fees and watch from the steamed up windows on the corner. See chapter 4.
- **Coral Castle** (Homestead; ☎ 305/248-6344): Truly a mystery to modern science, these massive stone structures have been around for more than 75 years. This prehistoric-looking, roofless "castle" was built as a monument to a young beauty by a crazed Latvian with a bad case of unrequited love. See chapter 5.
- **Houseboating** (Everglades National Park): Cruising the shallow waterways of the Everglades on your own is an exciting way to explore the region by day and by night. These spacious motorized houseboats let you get lost for days (or just overnight). You'll fall asleep to the sounds of frogs, crickets, and the lapping waves. See chapter 7.
- **Ride a Swamp Buggy with Babcock Wilderness Adventures** (Fort Myers; ☎ 800/500-5583 or 941/338-6367): Experienced naturalists lead "swamp buggy" tours through the Babcock Ranch, including the mysterious Telegraph Swamp where alligators lounge in the sun. Although the Babcock Ranch is the largest cattle operation east of the Mississippi (with bison and quarter horses, too), it is a major wildlife preserve inhabited by countless birds and other creatures. You'll get your money's worth at $17.95 for adults, $9.95 for children 3 to 12. See chapter 10.
- **Swim with the Manatees** (Homosassa Springs, north of Clearwater): Some 300 manatees spend the winter in the Crystal River, and you can swim, snorkel, or scuba with them in the warm-water natural spring of Kings Bay, about 7 miles north of Homosassa Springs. It's not uncommon to be surrounded in the 72°F water by 30 to 40 "sea cows," which nudge and caress you as you swim with them. See the box in chapter 11.
- **Swim with the Dolphins** (Orlando; ☎ 407/351-3600): At Sea World, it costs about $125 for a chance to interact with the dolphins under the watchful eyes of their trainers. For adults only; call ahead for information. See chapter 12.
- **Check out Disney—Literally** (Orlando): The Orlando Public Library, located downtown, has a complete collection of Disney books, even a collection of company press releases. Here, you can find out everything you have ever wanted to know about the Magic Kingdom, and then some. Best of all, it's free. See chapter 12.
- **Think About Skinny Dipping at Playalinda Beach** (Cape Canaveral): It isn't legal anymore, but you'll feel like stripping it all off on beautiful and deserted Playalinda Beach, in the Canaveral National Seashore (☎ 407/267-1110), a protected 13-mile stretch of barrier island beach backed by cabbage palms, sea

grapes, palmettos, marshes, and Mosquito Lagoon. The seashore and the adjacent Merritt Island National Wildlife Refuge (☎ **407/861-0667**) also are great places to see herons, egrets, ibis, willets, sanderlings, turnstones, terns, and other birds, plus giant sea turtles nesting from May to August. See chapter 14.

- **Surf Down the Waves** (Cocoa Beach): You can either try surfing yourself, or just watch for free from the Cocoa Beach Pier (☎ **407/783-7549**), surfing capital of the East Coast. The rustic, seemingly slapped-together pier was built in 1962 and has 842 feet of fishing, shopping, food, and drinks overlooking a wide, sandy beach. See chapter 14.

- **Vroom Around Daytona International Speedway** (Daytona Beach): You can't really drive your own race car around Daytona Beach's world center of racing, but the next best thing is action-packed IMAX film Daytona USA (☎ **904/947-6800**). You'll think you're in the winner's seat of the Daytona 500. You also can participate in a pit stop on a NASCAR Winston Cup stock car, see the actual winning car still covered in track dust, talk via video with favorite competitors, and play radio or television announcer by calling the finish of a race. Compared to admissions to other Florida theme parks, Daytona USA charges a reasonable $12 for adults, $10 for seniors, and $6 for children 6 to 12. Kids 5 and under get in free. See chapter 14.

- **Get Up Close and Personal to 1,000 Gators** (St. Augustine): You can't leave Florida without seeing at least one real live gator, and there are more than 1,000 of them on display at the century-old St. Augustine Alligator Farm and Zoological Park (☎ **904/824-3337**). In fact, it houses the world's most complete collection of alligators, crocodiles, caimans, gavials, and other crocodilians. Admission is $10.95 adults, $9.95 seniors 65 and over, $6.95 children 3 to 10, free for children under 3. See chapter 14.

8 The Best Golf Courses with Greens Fees That Won't Break Your Budget

- **Crandon Park Golf Course** (Key Biscayne, Miami): Formerly known as the Links of Key Biscayne, this stunning and famous course was ranked the number-one municipal course in the state and one of the top five in the country. Located on a posh residential island, it's one of the few courses remaining in South Florida not surrounded by development. Golfers enjoy pristine vistas of hammocks and stretches of water, with a glimpse of Miami's dramatic skyline to the north. See chapter 5.

- **Doral Golf Resort & Spa** (Miami): There are four championship courses here, including the famous Blue Monster, which is the site of the annual Doral-Ryder Open. The Gold Course, recently restored by golf great Raymond Floyd, has water on every hole. Look in the *Miami Herald* sports section for special discounts and coupons or call for twilight specials starting at $25 per person. See chapter 5.

- **Haulover Park** (Miami): The longest hole on this par-27 course is 125 yards in a pretty bay-side location. Golfers here are patient with beginners and greens fees start at a remarkable $5 per person in winter. See chapter 5.

- **The Boca Raton Municipal Golf Course** (Boca Raton): This 18-hole, par-72 course covers approximately 6,200 yards. With greens fees starting at $11 for 9 holes, this is a superior deal. See chapter 8.

- **Emerald Dunes Golf Course** (West Palm Beach): This beautiful Tom Fazio championship course features 60 acres of water, including a waterfall, and great views of the Atlantic. Prime weekend times are pricey, but it is one of the only great courses open to the public in this area of ritzy resorts. Twilight prices from Monday through Thursdays are a mere $35. See chapter 8.

- **"Golf-A-Round"** (Gold Coast): From May to October or November, about a dozen private courses open their greens to visitors staying in Palm Beach County hotels. This "Golf-A-Round" program is free or severely discounted (carts are additional), and reservations can be made through most major hotels. Or contact the **Palm Beach County Convention and Visitors Bureau** (☎ **561/ 471-3995**). See chapter 8.
- **Orangebrook Golf Course** (Hollywood): Built in 1937, this 18-holer is one of the state's oldest courses and one of the area's best bargains. Morning and noon rates range from $17 to $32. After 3pm, prices go down to about $15. See chapter 8.
- **PGA National Resort & Spa** (Palm Beach Gardens): The headquarters of the Professional Golfers Association of America, PGA National is the granddaddy of Florida golf venues. The five tournament courses were designed by George and Tom Fazio, Arnold Palmer, and Karl Litten. The Fazio-designed Champion was redesigned by Jack Nicklaus in 1990; his 15th, 16th, and 17th holes are called "The Bear Trap" to honor their 1992 induction into the "Ten Toughest Holes on the Seniors Tour." Call for specials in the off-season. See chapter 8.
- **Babe Zaharias, Rocky Point, and Rogers Park Courses** (Tampa): With three fine municipal courses charging just $26 to $34, Tampa is a great place for affordable golf. The **Babe Zaharias Municipal Golf Course** (☎ **813/ 631-4374**) is the shortest, but small greens and narrow fairways present ample challenges. Water presents obstacles on 12 of the 18 holes at **Rocky Point Municipal Golf Course** (☎ **813/673-4316**). On the Hillsborough River, the **Rogers Park Municipal Golf Course** (☎ **813/673-4396**) has a lighted driving and practice range. Lessons and club rentals are available. See chapter 11.
- **Mangrove Bay Golf Course** (St. Petersburg; ☎ **813/893-7797**): One of the nation's top 50 municipal courses, these 18-hole, par-72 links hug the inlets of Old Tampa Bay. Facilities include a driving range; lessons and golf-club rental are also available. Fees are about $22, $32 including a cart in winter, slightly lower off-season. The city also operates the challenging, par-3 **Twin Brooks Golf Course,** 3800 22nd Ave. S. (☎ **813/893-7445**), charging the same fees. See chapter 11.
- **Bobby Jones Golf Complex** (Sarasota; ☎ **941/365-GOLF**): Sarasota's municipal facility has two 18-hole championship layouts—the American (par 71) and British (par 72) courses—and a 9-hole executive course (par 30). Greens fees range from $25 to $31, including cart rental, a bargain in this affluent area. See chapter 11.
- **Buffalo Creek Golf Course** (Bradenton; ☎ **941/776-2611**): Locals love to play this 18-hole, par-72 municipal course on the north side of the Bradenton River. At well over 7,000 yards, it's the longest in the area, and lots of water and alligators will keep you entertained. Wintertime greens fees are about $34 with cart, $24 without. They drop to about $18 and $16, respectively, during summer. See chapter 11.
- **Dubsdread Golf Course** (Orlando; ☎ **407/246-2551**) With greens fees that range from $22 to $27, this course, owned by the city of Orlando, is a real steal. Availability varies so call as soon as possible for tee times. See chapter 12.
- **The Moors** (Pensacola; ☎ **800/727-1010** or 850/995-4653): Pot bunkers make you think you're playing in Scotland at this course which has greeted the Nike

Tour and is home to the Emerald Coast Classic, a PGA seniors event. Greens fees here are about $30 without cart. The Moors also has a lodge with eight luxury rooms. See chapter 13.

- **Hilaman Park Municipal Golf Course** (Tallahassee; ☎ **850/891-3935**): Another outstanding municipal course, Hilaman Park has 18 rolling, par-72 holes, a driving range, racquetball, squash courts, and a swimming pool. The park also includes the Jake Gaither Municipal Golf Course, with a 9-hole, par-35 fairway and a pro shop. Greens fees are a steal: $25 on weekdays, $30 on weekends, including cart, or just $12 and $17, respectively, if you walk. See chapter 13.

- **Cocoa Beach Country Club** (Cocoa Beach; ☎ **407/868-3351**): This fine municipal course has 27 holes of championship golf and 10 lighted tennis courts set on acres of natural woodland, rivers, and lakes. Greens fees are about $38 in winter, dropping to about $32 in summer, including cart. Nearby, **The Savannahs at Sykes Creek** (☎ **407/455-1377**) has 18 holes over 6,636 yards bordered by hardwood forests, lakes, and savannas inhabited by a host of wildlife. You'll have to hit over a lake to reach the seventh hole. Fees with cart are $35 in winter, less in summer. See chapter 14.

- **Pelican Bay Country Club** (Daytona Beach; ☎ **904/788-6494**): The South Course of this semiprivate club is one of the area's favorites, with fast greens to test your putting skills. With-cart fees are $40 in winter, less in summer (no walking allowed). See chapter 14.

9 The Best of Natural Florida

- **National Key Deer Refuge** (Big Pine Key): With patience and a bit of luck you may catch a glimpse of these delicate creatures in their natural habitat; with the country's largest herd (only about 300), the tiny, protected island of Big Pine Key is worth a stop. See chapter 6.

- **Exploring the Everglades:** It's not as majestic as the Rockies, but the swampy expanse of the Everglades is full of beautiful wildlife. From egrets to orchids and gators to frogs, these quiet grounds are peaceful and intriguing. See chapter 7.

- **Lover's Key–Carl E. Johnson State Recreation Area** (Fort Myers Beach; ☎ **941/463-4288**): Just south of Fort Myers Beach, this gorgeous state preserve provides respite from the hustle and bustle of its busy neighbor. A highway runs the length of the island, but otherwise Lover's Key is totally undeveloped. Access through a mangrove forest to a truly fine beach is by foot or by a tractor-pulled tram driven by park rangers, who take a dim view of anyone leaving trash behind. See chapter 10.

- **J. N. (Ding) Darling National Wildlife Refuge** (Sanibel Island; ☎ **941/472-1100**): Preserving most of the mangrove forests and winding waterways on Sanibel Island's north side, this famous 5,000-acre refuge is rich in such barrier-island wildlife as roseate spoonbills, ospreys, shorebirds, white pelicans, ducks, loons, and mangrove cuckoos. Visitors can hike, bike, or canoe on their own or be escorted by experts such as former Sanibel Mayor Mark "Bird" Westall. See chapter 10.

- **Cayo Costa State Park** (off Captiva Island; ☎ **941/964-0375**): A huge variety of sea- and shorebirds congregate on this state preserve, which encompasses one of the northernmost of Southwest Florida's Ten Thousand Islands. This uninhabited island is only accessible via boat. See chapter 10.

- **Corkscrew Swamp Sanctuary** (Naples; (☎ **941/348-9151**): Maintained by the National Audubon Society, this 11,000-acre bald cypress wilderness is a favorite wood-stork nesting ground. It's also home to herons, bald eagles, and a host of other birds and wildlife, plus ferns and colorful orchids. Some of North America's oldest trees are here. See chapter 10.

- **Briggs Nature Center** (Marco Island; ☎ **941/775-8569**): Operated by The Conservancy and part of the Rookery Bay National Estuarine Research Reserve, this refuge is a pristine example of Florida's disappearing scrublands, home to the threatened scrub jays and gopher tortoises. There's a self-guided canoe trail and canoes for rent during winter. You can also canoe through The Conservancy's smaller Nature Center in Naples. See chapter 10.

- **Harry P. Leu Gardens** (Orlando; ☎ **407/246-2620**): This 50-acre botanical garden, on the shores of Lake Rowena near downtown Orlando, offers a serene respite from theme-park razzle-dazzle. See chapter 12.

- **St. Vincent National Wildlife Refuge** (Apalachicola; ☎ **850/653-8808**): There are no facilities whatsoever on this 12,358-acre barrier island, which has been left in its natural state by the U.S. Fish and Wildlife Service. The local chamber of commerce will arrange a boat to get you here. Then you can walk through pine forests, marshlands, ponds, dunes, and beaches. In addition to native species like the bald eagle and alligators, the island is home to a small herd of sambar deer from Southeast Asia, and red wolves are bred here for reintroduction to other wildlife areas. See chapter 13.

- **St. Marks National Wildlife Refuge** (Tallahassee; ☎ **850/925-6121**): On the gulf due south of Tallahassee, this 65,000-acre preserve is home to more species of birds than anyplace else in Florida except the Everglades. Built of limestone blocks 4 feet thick at the base, the 80-foot-tall St. Marks Lighthouse has marked the harbor entrance since 1842. The nearby Apalachicola National Forest is another good spot. See chapter 13.

- **Apalachicola National Forest** (Tallahassee; ☎ **850/926-3561**): The largest of Florida's three national forests, this huge preserve encompasses 600,000 acres of woodlands, rivers, streams, lakes, and caves populated by a host of wildlife. There are picnic facilities with sheltered tables and grills, canoe and mountain-bike trails, campgrounds with tent and RV sites, and a number of other facilities, some of them especially designed for the physically disabled. See chapter 13.

10 The Best of Underwater Florida

- **John Pennekamp Coral Reef State Park** (Key Largo): This 188-square-mile park is the nation's first undersea preserve, established to protect the only living coral reef in the continental United States. The water throughout much of the park is shallow, so it's an especially great place for snorkelers to see tree-sized elkhorn coral, giant brain coral, colorful sea fans, hundreds of rainbow-colored fish, and a sunken statue, Christ of the Deep. See chapter 6.

- **Looe Key National Marine Sanctuary** (off Big Pine Key): Voted the number-one dive spot in North America by *Skin Diver* magazine, Looe Key has some of the most beautiful underwater scenery in the country, including more than 150 varieties of hard and soft coral—some centuries old. Most every type of tropical fish, including the gold and blue parrot fish, moray eels, barracudas, French angels, and tarpon, call this dense and diverse reef home. See chapter 6.

- **Biscayne National Park:** The clear, warm waters of Biscayne National Park are packed with colorful tropical fish that swim in the offshore reefs. Glass-bottom boats allow visitors a glimpse into the exciting underwater world of more than 180,000 acres. For an up-close look, get in the water. Snorkeling and scuba gear is rented and sold at Convoy Point for about the same price as Miami outfits. Snorkel tours depart daily and last about 4 hours. See chapter 7.

11 The Best Affordable Spas

- **Doral Golf Resort & Spa** (Miami; ☎ 800/22-DORAL, 800/71-DORAL, or 305/592-2000): Voted among the top spas by Zagat and *Condé Nast Traveler*, this 650-acre resort has something for every family member. Room rates may be out of this world, but just 1 day at the spa is an affordable luxury. For about $125, you can enjoy full use of the huge spa, unlimited exercise classes, an upper body massage, an aromatherapy facial and a choice of a body wrap, body scrub, or pedicure. The ambience is pure luxury—marble, crystal, formal gardens, and soft-spoken white-clad therapists. The healing muds and minerals come from ancient volcanic pools. Besides the great golf, tennis, swimming, and spa services, you'll find gourmet food and a variety of packages for those who want a taste of luxury. See chapter 4.

- **The Eden Roc Resort & Spa** (Miami Beach; ☎ 800/327-8337): For $35 you can use the resort's up-to-date facilities including saunas, steam rooms, pools, aerobics classes, weight machines and cardio equipment. It's the only place in town where you can work out while drinking in a sweeping view of the ocean. Day packages start at $85. See chapter 4.

- **PGA National Resort & Spa** (Palm Beach Gardens; ☎ 800/633-9150 or 561/627-2000): Known primarily as a golf destination, this sprawling resort also has a top-rated Mediterranean-style spa with unique offerings for pregnant guests—specialized exercise and nutrition classes, custom-designed massage tables, and more. In addition, the resort has nine pools and a private lake where you can ski or sail, as well as six restaurants and lounges (including one with a surprisingly delicious spa menu). See chapter 8.

- **Safety Harbor Resort and Spa** (Safety Harbor, near St. Petersburg; ☎ 800/BEST-SPA or 813/726-1161): The only full-service spa in Florida with mineral springs, this tranquil, waterfront retreat on Old Tampa Bay offers pampering from massages to hydrotherapy and a full menu of fitness classes from boxercise to yoga. The Phil Green tennis and Quinzi golf academies are based here. The least expensive way to enjoy all this is via the spa's basic fitness package, which starts at $209 per person single occupancy, $134 per person double occupancy, but that includes accommodation, meals, and unlimited use of spa facilities, fitness classes, and daytime tennis. A 2-night minimum stay is required. See chapter 11.

- **The Spa at the Disney Institute** (Orlando; ☎ 407/827-4455): This spa offers five different types of body therapy, massage therapy, aroma therapy; half-day packages start at $171. But à la carte services allow for facials, massages, and various therapies for under $100. See chapter 12.

12 The Best Affordable Accommodations

- **Hotel Leon** (South Beach, Miami; ☎ 305/673-3767): This classy little hotel in the very hippest part of South Beach is beautifully maintained and fantastically practical. Although there are no fancy grounds or facilities, this has to be one of the best deals on the beach. See chapter 4.

- **Bay Harbor Inn** (Bay Harbor Island, Miami; ☎ 305/868-4141): On an exclusive island in Miami Beach, this gem offers charm and value in an area that has precious little of either. See chapter 4.

- **Indian Creek Hotel** (Miami Beach; ☎ 800/491-2772 or 305/531-2727): It's modest but full of character, and so close to South Beach. Modest rooms are brightly outfitted in period furnishings, and many overlook the pretty pool and garden. For the price, there's no competition. See chapter 4.
- **Conch Key Cottages** (Marathon; ☎ 800/330-1577 or 305/289-1377): Right on the ocean, this little hideaway offers rustic but clean and well-outfitted cottages that are especially popular with families. Each has a hammock, barbecue grill, and kitchen. See chapter 6.
- **The Grand** (Key West; ☎ 888/947-2630 or 305/294-0590): There's no better value than this newish little hotel that is slightly out of the way, but still within walking distance of Duval Street. All of the clean and quaint rooms have private baths, air-conditioning, telephones, and private entrances for under $100. Suites are slightly more expensive but worth it if you want to save some money on food; the large two-room units come with complete kitchens. See chapter 6.
- **Beachcomber Apartment Motel** (Palm Beach; ☎ 800/833-7122 or 561/585-4646): This simple pink motel sits right on the ocean just a few miles from the superhigh-priced accommodations that make Palm Beach, well, Palm Beach. No fancy frills here, but rooms are pleasant and clean. See chapter 8.
- **Harborfront Inn Bed & Breakfast** (Stuart; ☎ 800/294-1703 or 561/288-7289): Located riverfront and within walking distance of the restaurants and shops of downtown Stuart, this handsome, highly recommended B&B offers private rooms with their own entrances. See chapter 9.
- **Island House Motel** (Fort Myers Beach; ☎ 941/463-9282): Sitting on stilts in the Old Florida fashion, but with modern furnishings, this clapboard-sided establishment enjoys a quiet location across the street from the beach and within walking distance of busy Times Square. You'll have screened porches, kitchens, ceiling fans, an open-air lounge with a small library, a small pool and sundeck area, a guest laundry, beach chairs, and free local calls. Book as early as possible for February and March, when rooms cost $99. Off-season they drop to $49. Weekly rates available. See chapter 10.
- **Palm Terrace Apartments** (Fort Myers Beach; ☎ 800/320-5783 or 941/765-5783): Many Europeans stay in these comfortable, well-maintained apartments about midway down Fort Myers Beach. The smaller, less-expensive units are on the ground level, with sliding glass doors opening to a grassy yard, but even they have cooking facilities including microwave ovens. There's beach access across Estero Boulevard, and Anthony's on the Gulf and the Junkanoo Beach Bar are 3 short blocks away. Winter rates range from $82 to $125 per apartment, dipping to $48 to $80 off-season. Weekly rates available. See chapter 10.
- **Palm View Motel** (Sanibel Island; ☎ 941/472-1606): In a quiet residential area less than a block from the beach, this is the jewel of Sanibel's few inexpensive accommodations, offering one hotel room and a few spacious, well-ventilated one- and two-bedroom apartments. Originally from Germany, the owners have lived on the premises since 1979 and keep their grounds groomed and their units clean and very well maintained. Winter rates range from $80 to $150 per unit, dropping to $45 to $90 off-season. See chapter 10.
- **Cabbage Key Inn** (Cabbage Key, off Sanibel and Captiva Islands; ☎ 941/283-2278): You never know who's going to get off a boat on this 100-acre islet and walk unannounced into the funky, rustic house built in 1938 by the son and daughter-in-law of mystery novelist Mary Roberts Rinehart. Singer and avid yachtie Jimmy Buffett likes Cabbage Key so much that it inspired his hit song *Cheeseburger in Paradise*. The inn has six rooms and six cottages, all with original

1920s furnishings, private baths, and air conditioners. Four of the cottages have kitchens, and one room reputedly has its own ghost. Rates are $65 for single or double rooms, $145 to $200 for cottages. See the box in chapter 10.

- **Olde Naples Inn & Suites** (Naples; ☎ **800/637-6036** or 941/262-5194): Some of Naples's best values can be found at its apartment motels, such as this dated but extraordinarily well-maintained apartment hotel with an eclectic combination of rooms, efficiencies, and one- and two-bedroom suites. It's just 2 blocks from the beach and 4 blocks from the tony 3rd Street South shopping area. Winter rates are $99 to $179 single or double, but they drop to as little as $55 off-season, including continental breakfast. See chapter 10.

- **Tides Inn of Naples** (Naples; ☎ **800/438-8763** or 941/262-6196): There's a very good reason why this immaculate two-story motel stays heavily booked during the winter months: It's right on the beach, just one door removed from the super-expensive Edgewater Beach Hotel, and on the edge of Millionaires' Row and Olde Naples. Winter rates start at $105 for a single or double room, with off-season rooms going for $65 to $130. The suites and efficiencies must be reserved for at least a month in winter; otherwise, ask for a room and pray for a cancellation. See chapter 10.

- **Budgetel Inn** (Tampa; ☎ **800/428-3438** or 813/930-6900): Fake banana trees and a parrot cage welcome guests to this comfortable motel, just down the street from Busch Gardens Tampa Bay. Like other members of the fine Budgetel chain, all rooms are spacious and have amenities such as ceiling fans, desks, phones with long cords, and coffeemakers. Local calls and Danish pastries or a blueberry muffin and juice (in containers hung on your doorknob before dawn) are free. There's an unheated swimming pool with plenty of space for sunning, a game room, and coin laundry. Rooms are reasonable at $77 single or double in winter, $57 off-season. See chapter 11.

- **Beach Haven** (St. Pete Beach; ☎ **813/367-8642**): Fax 813/360-8202. These low-slung, pink-with-white-trim structures were built in the 1950s but have been completely renovated and now have bright tile floors, vertical blinds, pastel tropical furniture, and many modern amenities, including TVs, VCRs, refrigerators, and coffeemakers. There's an outdoor heated pool surrounded by a white picket fence, plus a sunning deck with lounge furniture by the beach. It's in the heart of the hotel district, so lots of restaurants are just steps away. Rooms are $75 to $125 single or double in winter, $50 to $108 off-season. See chapter 11.

- **Island's End Resort** (St. Pete Beach; ☎ **813/360-5023**): This little all-cottage hideaway on the southern tip of St. Pete Beach is a wonderful respite from the maddening crowd, and a great bargain to boot. You can step from the six contemporary cottages right onto the beach. They have dining areas, living rooms, VCRs, and kitchens, and the one three-bedroom unit also has its own private pool. The cottages cost $82 to $175 in winter, $61 to $175 off-season, and weekly rates are available. See chapter 11.

- **Catalina Beach Resort** (Bradenton Beach; ☎ **941/778-6611**): In a shady spot across the street from the beach, this 2-story Spanish-style motel offers exceptional value, with well-kept units equipped with modern furnishings and adorned with bright Florida colors. Most are one- and two-bedroom suites with kitchenettes. Facilities include a restaurant, outdoor solar-heated swimming pool, barbecue grills, shuffleboard courts, guest laundry, fishing and boating dock, and water-sports rentals. Winter rates range from $81 for a single or double room, $112 to $184 for a suite. Off-season, $49 to $57 for a room, $69 to $125 suite, and weekly rates are available. See chapter 11.

- **Disney's Dixie Landings** and **Port Orleans Resort** (Orlando; ☎ 407/ W-DISNEY): These magnificently designed resorts bring a touch of the Old South to Orlando—one is modeled after the folksy homes of Cajun country, one after the stately townhomes of turn-of-the-century New Orleans. Amid the gurgling fountains and lush landscaped grounds are the kind of extensive facilities and thoughtful extras that normally warrant much higher prices. See chapter 12.

- **Quality Inn on Lake Cecile** (Kissimmee, near Orlando; ☎ 800/228-1828 or 407/396-4455): Of the non-Disney accommodations, this Quality Inn offers both excellent value and a lovely setting. The basic, clean rooms (ranging from $59 to $79) overlook 223-acre Lake Cecile, and the hotel offers both water-ski and jet-ski rental. An excellent budget choice for singles and young couples. See chapter 12.

- **Five Flags Inn** (Pensacola Beach; ☎ 850/932-3586): This friendly motel looks like a jail from the road, but big picture windows look out to the swimming pool and gorgeous white-sand beach, which comes right up to the property. Although the accommodations are small, the rates are a bargain for well-furnished, gulf-front rooms: $85 single or double in summer, $49 to $69 off-season. Packages are available, too. See chapter 13.

- **A Highlands House Bed & Breakfast** (Santa Rosa Beach, near Destin; ☎ 850/ 267-0110): This comfortable B&B is styled after the luxurious 18th-century plantation homes in the South Carolina low country. A path leads from an extrawide front porch to the beach. Inside, you'll find four-poster rice beds, comfy wingback chairs, and antique accoutrements. One unit has a fireplace; another, a whirlpool tub. Rates start at $70 single or double, including full breakfast. See chapter 13.

- **Gibson Inn** (Apalachicola; ☎ 850/653-2191): Built in 1907 as a seaman's hotel, this brilliant, cupola-topped example of Victorian architecture is listed on the National Register of Historic Inns. No two guest rooms are alike—some still have the original sinks in the sleeping area—but all are richly furnished with period reproductions. Grab a drink from the oak bar and relax in one of the high-back rockers on the old-fashioned veranda. All this charm goes for $65 to $80 single or double. See chapter 13.

- **Kenwood Inn** (St. Augustine; ☎ 904/824-2116): Rooms in this Victorian wood-frame house with graceful verandas are larger and more private than most other accommodations in converted single-family homes. Everything from the carpeting to the linens to the china is first class. There's an outdoor swimming pool, a lushly landscaped sundeck, and a secluded garden courtyard complete with a fish pond and neat flower bed under a sprawling pecan tree. Rates start at $85 single or double, including continental breakfast, sherry, tea, and coffee. See chapter 14.

- **Beachside Motel Inn** (Amelia Island; ☎ 904/261-4236): The only motel beside the beach on this otherwise upscale island, this inexpensive property is clean and well maintained by its resident owners. The rooms, many with ocean views, are spacious. Many long-term visitors return each season to stay in the efficiencies with fully equipped kitchens. An outdoor pool is surrounded by lounge chairs and a spacious deck overlooking the ocean. Rates are $65 to $103 single or double for rooms, $79 to $139 efficiency, including coffee and store-bought pastries each morning. Weekly discounts are available. See chapter 14.

13 The Best Family Accommodations for Parents Who Don't Want to Blow the Kids' College Fund

- **Riviera Inn** (Coral Gables; ☎ **800/368-8602** or 305/665-3528): Built in 1954, this family-owned motel is a super value option in this otherwise pricey area. There are no special facilities for children, but the pool and canal out back provide some diversion. See chapter 4.
- **Lago Mar Resort and Club** (Ft. Lauderdale; ☎ **800/255-5246** or 954/523-6511): This family owned and family-oriented resort is a bit high end but well worth it. When you consider the amenities, waterfront location, restaurants, and supervised activities for children, rates are actually quite reasonable. Most accommodations are suites, with plenty of room for the kids. Each has a private balcony and full kitchen, or at least a microwave and a refrigerator. See chapter 8.
- **Palm Beach Hotel** (Palm Beach; ☎ **800/536-7161** or 561-659-7794): The best deal in town for those who want the convenience of a private apartment and don't need all the fancy extras of a full-service resort. A well-outfitted kitchenette means you don't have to rely on overpriced room service; you can always have milk, juice, and snacks on hand. A pool and sundeck, plus a coin laundry, all for less than the price of most Holiday Inns, make this a real steal. See chapter 8.
- **Best Western Pink Shell Beach Resort** (Fort Myers Beach; ☎ **800/554-5454** or 941/463-6161): Although it requires a real splurge in winter, this popular, family-oriented establishment's hotel rooms, suites, one- and two-bedroom apartments, and beach cottages can be affordable off-season, especially if you opt for a package deal or weekly rate. The gulf beach side of the property has watersports equipment to rent, three heated swimming pools, a kiddie pool, and a chickee hut (covered wooden platforms on stilts) bar. Sailboats and nature and sightseeing cruises pick up guests at the bay-side marina, which rents boats. Facilities also include a coin laundry, store for buying victuals, lighted tennis courts, and rental bikes. Every unit has cooking facilities, but the Hungry Pelican Café, on a deck overlooking the channel, serves breakfast, lunch, and dinner. Off-season rates are $119 to $155 for a room, with condos and cottages starting at $135. See chapter 10.
- **Sundial Beach Resort** (Sanibel Island; ☎ **800/237-4184** or 941/472-4151): A games area, kiddie pool, playground, a small ecology center with a touch tank, and a fine children's recreation program make this large condo complex attractive to families. VCRs and movies can be rented, too. The one- to three-bedroom units have screened balconies overlooking the beach or tropically landscaped gardens. There are several dining options plus extensive recreational facilities. Winter rates at $275 to $575 per condo require a real splurge, but you can get in here for as little as $145 off-season, even less on package deals. See chapter 10.
- **TradeWinds Resort** (St. Pete Beach; ☎ **800/237-0707** or 813/367-6461): A maze of brick walkways, patios, and lily ponds connected by a quarter mile of streams gives the kids plenty of exploring to do at this large, employee-owned resort. The guest units have up-to-date kitchens or kitchenettes, and there's a supervised program to keep the children busy. A number of food outlets include an Italian bistro, a casual family restaurant, a Pizza Hut outlet, and an ice-cream parlor. Rates start at $195 per unit, $135 off-season, but summer packages are a big hit with families from around the world, attracting lots of Europeans. See chapter 11.
- **Disney's All-Star Resorts** (Orlando; ☎ **407/W-DISNEY**): When the third All-Star Resort opens, the total number of discount rooms at Walt Disney World will

jump to about 6,000. The rooms may be small, but at $74 to $89 a night, it's the least-expensive way to take advantage of all the perks of being a Disney resort guest. See chapter 12.

- **Larson's Lodge Main Gate** (Lake Buena Vista, near Orlando; ☎ **800/ 327-9074** or 407/396-6100): With a water park next door, an on-site playground, and poolside picnic tables, Larson's is an excellent family choice. Room rates begin at $59 for a double, and all units have a microwave and refrigerator, which will save on meal costs (a supermarket is nearby). Children under 18 stay free in parents' room. Good package deals are available. See chapter 12.

- **Holiday Inn Sunspree Resort Lake Buena Vista** (Lake Buena Vista, near Orlando; ☎ **407/239-4500**): It doesn't get more child-friendly than this—kids "check in" at their own pint-size desk and receive a free fun bag containing a video-game token coupon, a lollipop, and a small gift. "Camp Holiday" activities are available for a minimal charge for kids 2 to 12. And if you're renting a second room for the little ones, ask about the themed "kidsuites," decorated as igloos, spaceships, and so on. Rooms average $89 to $129 for up to four people. See chapter 12.

- **The Resort at Sandestin** (Destin; ☎ **800/277-0800** or 850/267-8000 in the U.S., or 800/933-7846 in Canada): One of Florida's best sports-oriented resorts, this luxurious hotel/condo complex sprawls over 2,300 acres complete with a spectacular beach. While the adults choose from 63 holes of championship golf, the kids can keep busy at three wading pools, a playground, in a summer children's program (ages 3 to 13), or tennis camp (ages 12 to 18). Rates start at $145 in summer, $75 off-season, but they include health club, bicycle, boogie board, canoe, and kayak use, 1 hour of tennis daily, and discounts on other amenities. See chapter 13.

14 The Best Places to Stay on a Shoestring

- **Banana Bungalow** (Miami Beach; ☎ **800/7-HOSTEL** or 305/538-1951): This youth hostel-ish hotel is across the street from a popular beach and only 6 or 7 blocks from the best shops, clubs, and restaurants. Rooms are fully equipped and a cheap restaurant and bar also operate in season. See chapter 4.

- **Clay Hotel & Hosteling International** (South Beach, Miami; ☎ **305/ 534-2988**): Housed in a gorgeous Mediterranean building at the corner of bustling and historic Española Way. This is the South Beach's best budget find. See chapter 4.

- **Key West International Hostel** (Key West; ☎ **800/51-HOSTEL** or 305/ 296-5719): Whether you are renting a bed in one of the supercheap dorm rooms or a pricier, private motel room, if you can get a spot at this well-run hostel you have found one of the best deals in Key West. Motel rooms come with cooking facilities, a real plus in a town where overpriced tourist restaurants dominate the scene. Cheap eats are prepared on the premises. See chapter 6.

- **Jabour's Trailer Court** (Key West; ☎ **305/294-5723**): Rent an old mobile home, a room in a guest house, or a campsite just a few blocks from Mallory Square. Rooms in Walden House are sparse but do offer private entrances, color television, and air-conditioning. Especially if you have the kids and/or the pets along, the trailers make sense. See chapter 6.

- **Floyd's Youth Hostel/Crew House** (Ft. Lauderdale; ☎ **954/462-0631**): Fort Lauderdale's best place to crash is Floyd's, offering what every backpacker and international traveler wants: safety and good, warm fellow travelers. See chapter 8.

- **The Sea Downs (and the Bougainvillea)** (Hollywood; ☎ **954/923-4968**): On a relatively quiet but convenient stretch of Hollywood beach, these ocean-side properties offer a heated pool, barbecue grills, picnic area, laundry facilities, sundeck, and many units with kitchens for very reasonable rates. See chapter 8.
- **Sun West Beach Motel** (Clearwater Beach; ☎ **813/442-5008**): Overlooking the bay and yet only a 2-block walk from the beach, this well-maintained 1-story motel has a heated pool, fishing/boating dock, sundeck, shuffleboard court, and guest laundry. All units have contemporary resort-style furnishings. Four motel rooms have small refrigerators, while 10 efficiencies have kitchens. Rates are to $61 to $79 single or double in winter, just $40 to $48 off-season. See chapter 11.
- **Super 8 Motel** (Orlando; ☎ **800/325-4348** or 407/847-6121): There's nothing fancy about this newly renovated place (formerly the Colonial Motor Lodge), but the surroundings are pretty and the rooms are clean. See chapter 12.
- **Flamingo Motel** (Panama City Beach; ☎ **800/828-0400** or 850/234-2232): Evoking Key West, this well-maintained, family-owned motel takes great pride in its gorgeous tropical garden surrounding a heated swimming pool and a large sundeck overlooking the gulf. The brightly decorated rooms have either full kitchens or refrigerators and microwave ovens, and they can sleep two to six people, some in separate bedrooms. Forget spending spring break here unless you're a family or couple. Rates start at $66 in summer, $32 off-season. See chapter 13.
- **Beach House** (Daytona Beach; ☎ **800/647-3448** or 904/788-7107): The nicely landscaped exterior and the furnishings and appointments inside are excellent for a property in this price range. All accommodations have front lawns with umbrella tables overlooking the ocean, and all but two have full kitchens. There are barbecue grills and a heated swimming pool. Rates are $28 to $59 single or double room, $50 to $69 for an ocean-view suite, and weekly rates are available. See chapter 14.

15 The Best Camping

Florida's state parks offer a variety of camping facilities, from primitive sites without even running water to full hookups for RVs. The sites cost between $10 and $20 a night, depending on the season, and all state parks accept camping reservations up to 11 months in advance.

- **Everglades National Park:** Although they recently instituted a $10 fee for back country permits, the Everglades still has some of the most affordable and scenic camp sites around. Choose from beachfront sites, rough ground sites inland, or chickees, large wooden platforms built over water. The chickees, which have toilets, are the most civilized and unusual. Be prepared for the bugs! See chapter 7.
- **Boca Chita Key** (Biscayne National Park): Recently reopened after a thorough clean up, Boca Chita offers rustic campsites which are only accessible by boat. Enjoy the calm and quiet with no noisy generators to drown out the gentle sound of waves lapping against the shore. See chapter 7.
- **Koreshan State Historic Site** (Fort Myers; ☎ **941/992-0311**): The shady sites here are near the gardens and some of the buildings erected by the Koreshan Unity Movement, a sect which believed that humans lived *inside* the earth, who established a self-sufficient settlement on these 300 acres on the narrow Estero River in 1894. Nature and canoe trails (rentals available) wind downriver to

Mound Key, an islet made of the shells discarded by the Calusa Indians. See chapter 10.

- **Collier Seminole State Park** (Marco Island; ☎ **941/394-3397**): You'll be on the edge of the Everglades in this state preserve 12 miles east of Marco Island. The shady sites are organized around screened-in activities buildings. RV and tent campers are segregated here. The park has a multitude of nature-oriented activities to keep you busy. See chapter 10.
- **Fort DeSoto Park** (St. Pete Beach; ☎ **813/866-2662**): The 230 sites in this 900-acre bird, animal, and plant sanctuary sit on an island by themselves and all have water and electricity hookups. They usually are sold out, however, especially on weekends, and you must appear *in person* and pay for your site no more than 30 days in advance at the campground office. If you can go to this trouble, you'll pay $18.76 a night. See chapter 11.
- **Disney's Fort Wilderness Resort and Campground** (Orlando; ☎ **407/ W-DISNEY** or 407/824-2900): This woodsy 780-acre camping resort—shaded by towering pines and cypress trees and crossed by fish-filled streams, lakes, and canals—is ideal for family vacations. Among the attractive extras are nightly campfire programs with Chip 'n' Dale, trail rides, pony rides, and a petting farm. See chapter 12.
- **Fort Pickens Area, Gulf Islands National Seashore** (Pensacola; ☎ **800/ 365-2267**): You'll be near one of Florida's finest beaches at these 200 sites (135 with electricity) in a pine forest beside Santa Rosa Sound. Nature trails lead from the camp through Blackbird Marsh and to the beach. A small store sells provisions. Sites cost $15 a night without power, $20 a night with it. Golden Age and Golden Access cardholders get a 50% discount. You can make reservations up to 5 months in advance here. See chapter 13.
- **St. Andrews State Recreation Area** (Panama City Beach; ☎ **850/233-5140**): This preserve of dazzling white sand and dunes has RV and tent sites beautifully situated in a pine forest right on the shores of Grand Lagoon. If you can't get a waterfront site here, you might at nearby **Magnolia Beach RV Park** (☎ **850/235-1581**), with great views of Panama City from an idyllic setting under magnolias and moss-draped oaks. The latter also accepts pets. See chapter 13.
- **Anastasia State Recreation Area** (St. Augustine; ☎ **904/461-2033**): You'll be near 4 miles of sandy beach bordered by picturesque dunes, as well as a lagoon flanked by tidal marshes, at this urban park. Anastasia is one of Florida's most popular tate facilities for camping, with its 139 wooded sites in high demand all year. They have picnic tables, grills, and electricity. Campsite reservations are required. See chapter 14.

16 The Best Affordable Restaurants

- **Shells** (statewide): You'll see Shells restaurants all over Florida, and with good reason, for this casual, award-winning chain consistently provides excellent value, especially if you have a family to feed. Starting at just $6, main courses range from the usual fried seafood platters to pastas and charcoal-grilled shrimp, fish, steaks, and chicken. They all have the same prices and menu, including a children's menu.
- **San Loco** (Miami; ☎ **305/538-3009**): This eatery serves the freshest and best Mexican favorites and such popular specials as fried catfish tacos and superior guacamole. See chapter 4.
- **Stephan's Gourmet Market & Cafe** (South Beach, Miami; ☎ **305/674-1760**): Enjoy a cheap and filling meal upstairs in a tiny loft used to store wine bottles,

out on the sidewalk, or delivered to your hotel. Choose the chalkboard special for two, usually a pasta dish with some kind of chicken or fish. It's served with salad, garlic bread and a bottle of decent wine for around $25. (Other locations: 2 NE 40th St., ☎ 305/571-4070; and 19495 Biscayne Blvd. [One Turnberry Pl.], ☎ 305/932-8885.) See chapter 4.

- **La Cibeles Café** (Miami; ☎ **305/577-3454**): Service is a little slow, but the food and the prices can't be beat. Daily specials, like grilled red snapper, fried pork chop, a half-baked chicken with sautéed onions and tomatoes, ropa vieja, or the grilled trout are served with rice and beans, or potatoes, fried plantains, or salad. See chapter 4.

- **Versailles** (Little Havana, Miami; ☎ **305/444-0240**): This is the place where Miami's Cuban power brokers meet over *café con leche* and pastries. The homey food is plentiful and cheap, if not always gourmet quality. See chapter 4.

- **Thai Spice** (Ft. Lauderdale; ☎ **954/771-4535**): Worth trying just for the supercheap lunch specials, this tiny storefront is a great find in Ft. Lauderdale's often overpriced and uninspired dining scene. See chapter 8.

- **Tom's Place** (Boca Raton; ☎ **561/997-0920**): An institution in otherwise exorbitantly priced Boca Raton, this successful barbecue joint offers expertly grilled meats paired with well-spiced sauces. See chapter 8.

- **Farmers Market Restaurant** (Fort Myers; ☎ **941/334-1687**): The retail Farmers Market next door may be tiny, but the best of the cabbage, okra, green beans, and tomatoes end up here at this simple eatery, frequented by everyone from business executives to truck drivers. The specialties of the house are Southern favorites like smoked ham hocks with a bowl of black-eyed peas. See chapter 10.

- **Greco's Italian Deli** (Fort Myers Beach; ☎ **941/463-5634**): Wonderful aromas of baking pizza, calzone, cannoli, bread, and cookies will lure you to this Italian deli, where you can take "heat-and-eat" meals of spaghetti, lasagne, eggplant parmigiana, manicotti, and ravioli back to your hotel or condo oven. See chapter 10.

- **Hungry Heron** (Sanibel Island; ☎ **941/395-2300**): There's something for everyone on the huge, tabloid-size menu at Sanibel's most popular family restaurant—from hot and cold "appiteezers" and overstuffed "seawiches" to pasta and steamed shellfish. And even though this is an affluent island, main courses range from just $8 to $15. To keep the kids occupied, video cartoons run all the time, and a magician circulates among the tables from 5 to 9pm every day except Tuesday. An all-you-can-eat breakfast buffet on Saturday and Sunday in winter is an excellent value. See chapter 10.

- **Sanibel Café** (Sanibel Island; ☎ **941/472-5323**): Be sure to call for preferred seating at Sanibel's most popular breakfast spot, whose tables are museum-like glass cases containing delicate fossilized specimens from the Miocene and Pliocene epochs. Fresh-squeezed orange and grapefruit juice, Danish Havarti omelettes, and homemade muffins and biscuits highlight the breakfast menu, while lunch features specialty sandwiches; shrimp, Greek and chicken-and-grape salads made with a very light, fat-free dressing; and a limited list of main courses such as grilled or blackened chicken breast. See chapter 10.

- **Jam's Italian Restaurant** (Boca Grande; ☎ **941/964-2002**): President Bush may have hobnobbed with the rich and famous when he vacationed at Boca Grande, but he had at least one meal with his White House staffers at this pleasant Italian restaurant, whose motto is "More food for less lira." See chapter 10.

- **First Watch** (Naples; ☎ **941/434-0005**); and Sarasota (☎ 941/954-1395): These little restaurants are everyone's favorite spots for breakfast, late brunch, or a midday meal in Naples and Sarasota. They are anything but diners: You get classical music and widely spaced tables topped with pitchers of lemon-tinged ice water. The identical menus lean heavily on healthy selections, but you can get your cholesterol from a sizzling skillet of fried eggs served over layers of potatoes, vegetables, and melted cheese. Lunch features large salads, sandwiches, and quesadillas. See chapters 10 and 11.
- **Silver Spoon Café** (Naples; ☎ **941/591-2123**): In the swanky Waterside Shops complex, this chic bistro flaunts sophisticated black-and-white high-tech decor and has large window walls overlooking the mall action. But you'll pay anything but swanky prices for thick sandwiches served either with french fries, spicy pecan rice, or black beans; luscious tomato-dill soup; gourmet pizzas and pasta dishes; and main courses such as orange Dijon chicken. See chapter 10.
- **Mel's Hot Dogs** (Tampa; ☎ **813/985-8000**): Just outside Busch Gardens, Tampa Bay, this red-and-white cottage offers everything from "bagel-dogs" and corn dogs to a bacon/Cheddar Reuben. Even the decor is dedicated to wieners: The walls and windows are lined with hot-dog memorabilia. See chapter 11.
- **Carmine's Restaurant & Bar** (Tampa; ☎ **813/248-3834**): A great variety of patrons gather at this noisy corner cafe, one of Ybor City's most popular hangouts. For lunch or dinner, you can order a genuine Cuban sandwich—smoked ham, roast pork, Genoa salami, Swiss cheese, pickles, salad dressing, mustard, lettuce, and tomato on a crispy submarine roll. There's a vegetarian version, too, and the combination half sandwich and bowl of Spanish soup made with sausages, potatoes, and garbanzo beans makes a hearty meal for just $4. See chapter 11.
- **Yoder's** (Sarasota; ☎ **941/955-7771**): It's worth driving about 3 miles east of downtown Sarasota to this award-winning Amish restaurant evoking the Pennsylvania Dutch country. The simple dining room displays handcrafts, photos, and paintings celebrating the Amish way. You'll get plain, made-from-scratch meat loaf, baked and Southern-fried chicken, country-smoked ham, and fried fillet of flounder. Burgers, salads, soups, and sandwiches are also available. Leave room for traditional shoo-fly pie. Another good, inexpensive Amish choice is **Miller's Dutch Kitchen** in Bradenton (☎ **941/746-8253**). See chapter 11.
- **Gulf Drive Café** (Bradenton Beach; ☎ **941/778-1919**): The coral and green dining room of this inexpensive gem opens to a beachside patio with tables shaded by a trellis. The breakfast fare is led by sweet Belgian waffles, which are available all day. You can also order salads, sandwiches, and burgers anytime here, with quiche du jour, Mediterranean seafood pasta, and regular seafood platters coming on line after 4pm. See chapter 11.
- **Romano's Macaroni Grill** (Orlando; ☎ **407/239-6676**): Sure, it's a chain restaurant, but the ambience is warm and inviting, and the Northern Italian food is fresh and first rate. Especially scrumptious are the pizzas, fired in a oak-burning oven. A children's menu offers small-scale entrees for under $5. And beyond that, the prices are low, low, low. See chapter 12.
- **Boatwright's Dining Hall** (in Disney's Dixie Landings Resort; ☎ **407/WDW-DINE**): The interior resembles an 1800s boat-building factory (complete with fishing boat suspended from the beamed ceiling). And the Cajun food satisfies kids and adults alike; standouts include the sourdough/sweet-potato French toast for breakfast, and the blackened seafood pasta for dinner. Breakfast items are

under $8, sandwiches are under $10, and main courses range from $10 to $20. See chapter 12.

- **Bonfamille's Cafe** (in Disney's Port Orleans Resort; ☎ **407/WDW-DINE**): Welcome to the French Quarter, complete with Dixieland jazz soundtrack. The American Creole dishes here are both tasty (beignets and café au lait for breakfast, a zesty crayfish and andouille sausage skillet for dinner) and affordable (most meals are under $15). See chapter 12.

- **Hopkins' Boarding House** (Pensacola; ☎ **850/438-3979**): There's a delicious peek into the past at this Victorian boardinghouse, surrounded by ancient trees and a wraparound porch with old-fashioned rocking chairs. Everyone eats family style—at your elbow could be the mayor or a mechanic, for everyone in town dines here. Platters are piled high with seasonal Southern-style vegetables from nearby farms. In true boardinghouse fashion, guests bus their own dishes. See chapter 13.

- **Gypsy Cab Co.** (St. Augustine; ☎ **904/824-8244**): Billing itself as a temple of "urban cuisine," this high-energy establishment offers the likes of Shrimp Buena Vista, a concoction featuring gulf shrimp, linguine, Canadian bacon, green peas, and onions in a white-wine sauce. The menu changes daily, but the hearty black-bean soup is a constant. See chapter 14.

- **Biscotti's** (Jacksonville; ☎ **904/387-2060**): This brick-walled little neighborhood gem might have come out of New York's East Village, San Francisco's downtown, or Washington, D.C.'s Georgetown. A young and hip wait staff is pleasant and well informed. Daily specials, like pan-seared salmon or pork loin, are always fresh and beautifully presented, and huge and inventive salads are especially good. See chapter 14.

- **The Homestead** (Jacksonville Beach; ☎ **904/249-5240**): There's a good reason for the greasy atmosphere at this log-cabinesque restaurant, for the big draw here is Southern-fried chicken served in a skillet with homemade buttermilk biscuits and fresh honey, coleslaw, black-eyed peas, rice and gravy, creamed peas, and a choice of daily vegetables. Other favorites, like the saucer-sized chicken dumpling, are served with thick gravy and all the fixings. See chapter 14.

17 The Best Seafood Restaurants

- **Fishbone Grille** (Miami; ☎ **305/530-1915**): It isn't scenic and it isn't where the tourists go, but this stellar little fish restaurant has some of the area's best seafood. In addition to an excellent ceviche, the stews, crab cakes, and starters are all superb. If you like Caribbean flavor, try the daily special with jerk seasoning. See chapter 4.

- **Grillfish** (South Beach, Miami; ☎ **305/538-2203**): A limited menu of only the freshest and simplest seafood is served in a relaxed but upscale atmosphere. It's remained popular in an area where many others have failed because of its excellent food and trendy atmosphere but reasonable prices. See chapter 4.

- **Monty's Bayshore Restaurant** (Coconut Grove and South Beach, Miami; ☎ **305/858-1431**): You can spend three times as much money and four times as long in line at Joe's. Or, try this multifaceted seafood restaurant that serves all-you-can-eat stone crabs in season, with prices way below those of their South Beach neighbor. Other good seafood and continental specialties are available, including a large and fresh salad bar. See chapter 4.

- **Marker 88** (Islamorada; ☎ **305/852-9315**): A legend in the Keys, this dark, romantic restaurant has standard fare as well as a winning version of nouvelle cuisine. You'll find the area's largest selection of seafood, including lobster from the Keys, conch from The Bahamas, frog legs from the Everglades, stone crabs from the Florida Bay, and shrimp from the West Coast, among other dishes. See chapter 6.

- **Monte's** (Summerland Key; ☎ 305/745-3731): It's cash only at this restaurant/ fish market where plastic place settings rest on plastic-covered picnic-style tables in a screen-enclosed dining patio. Monte's has survived for more than 20 years because the food is very good and incredibly fresh. See chapter 6.

- **Capt. Charlie's Reef Grill** (Juno Beach; ☎ 561/624-9924): The cooking is imaginative and mouthwatering. A wide range of ever-changing selections include a Caribbean chili, a sizable tuna spring roll, and an enormous Cuban crab cake. Ask for suggestions, and enjoy this, one of the area's best-kept secrets, hidden behind a tiny strip mall. See chapter 8.

- **Harbortown Fish House** (Fort Pierce; ☎ 561/466-8732): This rustic, open-air fish house looks like a tourist trap, but last time I checked it was still serving the area's best seafood at reasonable prices. See chapter 9.

- **Channel Mark** (Fort Myers Beach; ☎ 941/463-9127): Every table looks out on a maze of channel markers on Hurricane Bay, and a dock with palms growing through it makes this a relaxing place for a waterside lunch. The atmosphere changes dramatically at night, when the relaxed tropical ambience is ideal for kindling romance. Congenial owners Mike McGuigan and Andy Welsh put a creative spin on their seafood dishes, and their delicately seasoned crab cakes are tops. See chapter 10.

- **Timbers** (Sanibel Island; ☎ 941/472-3128): This casual, upstairs restaurant, with bamboo railings, oversized canvas umbrellas, and paintings of tropical scenes through faux windows, is Sanibel's best place for the freshest fish available. The chef will charcoal-grill or blacken it to order. See chapter 10.

- **Fourth Street Shrimp Store** (St. Petersburg; ☎ 813/822-0325): The outside of this place looks like it's covered with graffiti, but it's actually a gigantic drawing of people eating. Inside, murals on two walls seem to look out on an early 19th-century seaport (one painted sailor permanently peers in to see what you're eating). This is the best and certainly the most interesting bargain in St. Petersburg. See chapter 11.

- **Crabby Bill's** (St. Pete Beach; ☎ 813/360-8858): The least-expensive gulf-side dining on St. Pete Beach, this member of a small local chain is a great place to bring the kids, especially after 5:30pm Tuesday, when they eat free and are entertained by games and contests. There's little room for al fresco dining here, but big glass windows look out on the gulf. Picnic tables are equipped with rolls of paper towels and buckets of saltine crackers, the better to eat the Alaskan, snow, golden, and stone crabs which are the big draws here. The creamy smoked fish spread is a delicious appetizer, and you'll get enough to whet at least two appetites for just $4. See chapter 11.

- **Lobster Pot** (Redington Shores, near St. Pete Beach; ☎ 813/391-8592): If you can afford a splurge, owner Eugen Fuhrmann supplies the finest seafood dishes on the St. Pete and Clearwater beaches. Among his amazing variety of lobster dishes is one flambéed in brandy with garlic, and the bouillabaisse—as authentic as any you'll find in the south of France. See chapter 11.

- **Seafood & Sunsets at Julie's** (Clearwater Beach; ☎ 813/441-2548): A Key West–style tradition takes over Julie Nichols's place at dusk as both locals and visitors gather to toast the sunset over the beach across the street. The best seats are in the tiny upstairs dining room. The menu features mahimahi charcoal-broiled with sour cream, fresh Florida grouper, and stuffed flounder. See chapter 11.

Aphrodisiacs from Apalachicola

Seafood is a major culinary draw all across Florida. Some waterfront restaurants even operate their own fishing boats, so you're guaranteed super-fresh offerings. You'll dine on snapper, swordfish, amberjack, triggerfish, pompano, grouper, clams, gulf shrimp, blue crab, and sweet deep-sea scallops.

Some seafood specialties may be new to your palate. The clawless tropical **lobsters** are smaller and sweeter than the cold-water Maine variety, with all of their meat concentrated in the tail. You should also try **conch,** a chewy shellfish that's often served in deep-fried fritters, in chowder, or in a spicy salad marinated in lime juice. You're sure to fall in love with the taste of Florida's succulent **stone crab claws** (the crustacean is thrown back into the sea to grow another hand), and you won't soon forget the sweet, slightly briny taste of **Apalachicola oysters** (which reputedly have aphrodisiac properties).

- **Hemingway's** (St. Armands Circle, Sarasota; ☎ 941/388-3948): A laid-back, friendly Key West ambience prevails at this casual upstairs spot above ritzy St. Armands Circle. An eclectic "Floribbean" menu stars healthy mariner's shrimp: The crustaceans are perfectly charcoal-grilled, basted with a light teriyaki sauce, and served over rice with fresh asparagus and baby carrots. See chapter 11.
- **Staff's Seafood Restaurant** (Fort Walton Beach; ☎ 850/243-3526): Staff's started as a hotel in 1913 and moved to this barnlike building in 1931. Among the display of memorabilia are an old-fashioned phonograph lamp and a 1914 cash register. All main courses are served with heaping baskets of hot, home-baked wheat bread from a secret 70-year-old recipe. The tangy seafood gumbo also has gained fame for this casual, historic restaurant. See chapter 13.
- **Back Porch** (Destin; ☎ 850/837-2022): The food isn't gourmet at this cedar-shingled shack, whose long porch offers glorious beach and gulf views, but this is where charcoal-grilled amberjack originated. Today, you'll see it on menus throughout Florida. Other fish and seafood, as well as chicken and juicy hamburgers, also come from the coals. See chapter 13.
- **Marina Café** (Destin; ☎ 850/837-7960): Jim Altamura's establishment provides a classy atmosphere with soft candlelight, subdued music, and formally attired waiters. The outdoor balconied deck overlooks Destin Harbor. The creative chef prepares pizzas and pastas with a special emphasis on light, spicy fare. Menu highlights include fettuccine combined with andouille sausage, shrimp, crawfish tails, and a piquant tomato-cream sauce. See chapter 13.
- **Shuckums Oyster Pub & Seafood Grill** (Panama City Beach; ☎ 850/235-3214): "We shuck 'em, you suck 'em" is the motto of this extremely informal pub, which became famous when comedian Martin Short tried unsuccessfully to shuck oysters here during the making of an MTV spring-break special. The original bar is virtually papered over with dollar bills signed by old and young patrons who have been flocking here since 1967. See chapter 13.
- **Chef Eddie's Magnolia Grill** (Apalachicola; ☎ 850/653-8000): Chef Eddie Cass's pleasant restaurant occupies a small bungalow built in the 1880s, and is still in possession of the original black cypress paneling in its central hallway. Nightly specials emphasize fresh local seafood and New Orleans–style sauces. He received more than 2,000 orders for his spicy seafood gumbo at a recent Florida Seafood Festival. See chapter 13.

- **The Boss Oyster** (Apalachicola; ☎ **850/653-9364**): This rustic, dockside eatery is a good place to see if what they say about the aphrodisiac properties of Apalachicola oysters is true. The bivalves are served raw, steamed, or under a dozen toppings ranging from capers to crabmeat. They'll even steam three dozen of them and let you do the shucking. Dine inside or at picnic tables on a screened dockside porch. Everyone in town eats here, from bankers to watermen. See chapter 13.
- **Down the Hatch** (Daytona Beach; ☎ **904/761-4831**): This 50-year-old fish camp on the Halifax River serves up fresh fish and seafood from its shrimp boat docked outside. You can start your day here with a bagel or a country-style breakfast while taking in the scenic views of boats and shorebirds through the big picture windows—you might even see dolphins frolicking. In summer, light fare is served outside on an awninged wooden deck. Portions are large. See chapter 14.
- **Salt Water Cowboy's** (St. Augustine Beach; ☎ **904/471-2332**): Another turn-of-the-century fish camp-like establishment, Salt Water Cowboy's enjoys a spectacular view of the sun setting over a saltwater marsh. The rambling restaurant has a mix of rustic dining areas ranging from intimate booths to an outdoor plant-filled deck shaded by live oaks and lit by tiki torches. Order up a half-dozen oysters or perhaps some gator bits while you peruse the menu. See chapter 14.
- **Singleton's Seafood Shack** (Jacksonville Beach; ☎ **904/246-4442**): This rustic restaurant has kept up with the times by offering fresh fish in more ways than just battered and fried. Yet, they have retained the charming casualness of a riverside fish camp. Even if you don't want seafood, this spot is worth stopping in just for a feel of Old Florida. See chapter 14.

18 The Best Deals for Serious Shoppers

- **The Keys Factory Shops** (Florida City) have a manageable 60 or so stores including Nike Factory Store, Bass Co. Store, Levi's, OshKosh, and Izod. Although it is not well publicized, any customer at the mall is welcome to pick up a valuable "Come Back Pack," from the customer service desk. The square red packet contains dozens of coupons good for significant discounts. See chapter 6.
- **Half Buck Freddie's** (Key West) stocks out-of-season bargains and "rejects" from the main store. See chapter 6.
- **Lord & Taylor** (Ft. Lauderdale): This old department-store standby has a little-known clearance center where discounts on new clothing for women, kids, and men can be as high as 75%. If you can handle open dressing rooms, overstuffed racks, and obnoxious sales help, it's a great find just west of Ft. Lauderdale. See chapter 8.
- **The Fort Lauderdale Swap Shop:** These guys claim to be one of the world's largest flea markets. In addition to endless acres of vendors, there's a mini amusement park, a 13-screen drive-in movie theater, weekend concerts, and even a free circus complete with elephants, horse shows, high-wire acts, and clowns. See chapter 8.
- **Sawgrass Mills** (Sunrise, Ft. Lauderdale) is the monster of all outlet malls with more than 300 shops, kiosks, and restaurants in nearly 2.3 million square feet covering 50 acres. Look for discount coupon books at the information booth. They are good for substantial savings at dozens of mall stores. See chapter 8.
- **ABC Carpet & Home** (Delray Beach) displays gorgeous antique and new high-end furniture and flooring. Even with discounts of up to 40%, prices are still

high. Go for inspiration or some super specials offered during big sales. See chapter 8.

- **The Shell Factory** (Fort Myers; ☎ 941/995-2141): Dating back more half a century, this institution carries one of the world's largest collections of shells, shell jewelry, shell lamps, corals, sponges, and fossils. Many items here cost under $10, some under $1. See chapter 10.

- **Fleamasters** (Fort Myers; ☎ 941/334-7001): One of the largest of Florida's numerous flea markets, the weekend Fleamasters has more than 800 busy booths offering bargains on antiques, crafts, fashions, and fresh produce. It has snack bars and entertainment, too. See chapter 10.

- **Shells and Nature Toys** (Sanibel Island): If you have no luck scouring Sanibel Island's beaches for shells, head for **Sanibel Sea Shell Industries** (☎ 941/472-1603), with more than 10,000 shells in stock; to one of the two locations of **She Sells Sea Shells** (☎ 941/472-6991 or 941/472-8080); or to **Neptune's Treasures Shell Shop** (☎ 941/472-3132), which also has a good collection of fossils. Also on Sanibel, **Toys Ahoy!** (☎ 941/472-4800) carries fascinating toys, games, and stuffed animals, and **The Cheshire Cat** (☎ 941/472-3545) offers nature toys and other unique items for kids. See chapter 10.

- **Anything for a Dollar** (Orlando): The Orlando area branches of this national chain of discount stores sometimes end up with last year's hot Disney merchandise. It's not a guarantee, so don't go out of your way. But if you come across one of their stores in your travels, it's worth a look. See chapter 12.

- **Silver Sands Factory Stores** (Destin): One of the largest outlet malls in Florida, Silver Sands has the upscale likes of Anne Klein, Donna Karan, J. Crew, Jones New York, Brooks Brothers, Hartman Luggage, Coach leathers, Bose electronics, and so many more you'll have to drive from one end to the other to spot your favorite brands. There's even a food court with a branch of Destin's Harbor Docks Restaurant. See chapter 13.

- **Ron Jon Surf Shop** (Cocoa Beach; ☎ 407/799-8888): Hundreds of billboards will lure you to this glaring, 24-hour surf shop, where you'll find boards, wax, and everything else you need to look like a surfer. The shelves and racks hold souvenirs of every description and a wide array of beachwear. See chapter 14.

- **Dunn Toys & Hobbies** (Daytona Beach; ☎ 904/253-3644): This 18,000 square-foot emporium carries one of the country's largest selection of toys, games, art supplies, puzzles, model kits, costumes, collectibles, and other diversions for kids of all ages. In fact, Pres. Bill Clinton did a little shopping here during a 1996 campaign visit. Dunn's also has family activities, especially on Friday night. Upstairs you can browse through Dunn's Antique Mall. See chapter 14.

19 The Best Places for Sunset Cocktails

Any beachside restaurant, swimming pool bar, or pub on Florida's west coast will supply cocktails as the sun sets brilliantly over the Gulf of Mexico. All you have to do is go west. Here are a few places that stand out.

- **Harbor View Restaurant at the Pier House Resort and Caribbean Spa** (Key West; ☎ 305/296-4600): This otherwise undistinguished patio restaurant offers a great vantage point to see the nightly sunset. Sip a frozen drink under an umbrella and enjoy the view. See chapter 6.

- **Louie's Backyard** (Key West; ☎ **305/294-1061**): Nestled amid blooming bougainvillea on a lush slice of the gulf, this spot—a rear deck that juts out over the water—personifies romance. See chapter 6.
- **Mallory Square on Duval Street** (Key West): Join the circus that is Mallory Square at dusk. If the spectacular colors of the sun dropping into the sea aren't dramatic enough for you, take in performing cats, jugglers, mimes, and a crowd of tourists from all over the world. It's all free and good fun. See chapter 6.
- **Seven-Mile Bridge** (Lower Keys): For a free and quiet view of the sunset, stop at the Seven-Mile Bridge between MM 40 and 47. The old "ghost bridge" is the perfect place to watch the sun set, especially if you have had enough of the bars. See chapter 6.
- **Anthony's on the Gulf and the Junkanoo Beach Bar** (Fort Myers Beach; ☎ **941/463-2600**): The party never ends in the Junkanoo Beach Bar, underneath Anthony's on the Gulf Italian restaurant. The Junkanoo's bar and Anthony's large windows and appropriately named Sunset Terrace are two of the better places on Estero Island for sundowners. A casual, unpretentious tropical ambience prevails. See chapter 10.
- **Mucky Duck** (Captiva Island; ☎ **941/472-3434**): The one place on Captiva with beachside dining, this lively, British-style pub has picnic tables on the sand. Order a drink from the bar inside and bring it out before the "green flash" occurs as the sun slips below the horizon. See chapter 10.
- **Vanderbilt Inn on the Gulf** (Naples; ☎ **800/643-8654** or 941/597-3151): Right on the gulf, the "chickee" bar at this beachside motel about 4 miles north of Naples's historic district reduces the price of drinks during its daily happy hours—which the Naples Beach Hotel & Golf Club's bar doesn't (see below). Both of these establishments are jammed when bands play on Sunday. See chapter 10.
- **Naples Beach Hotel & Golf Club** (Naples; ☎ **800/237-7600** or 941/261-2222): Since this charming, Old Florida–style resort predates the strict historic district zoning laws, it has the only restaurants and bars directly on the beach in historic Olde Naples. Wedged between the beach and an Olympic-size pool, the Sunset Beach Bar is one of the region's most famous beachside chickee bars and is always crammed as the sun sets over the gulf. It's hopping on Sunday afternoons during the winter season, when live bands perform. See chapter 10.
- **South Beach** (Boca Grande; ☎ **941/964-0765**): The only place in ritzy Boca Grande where you can dine or have a sunset cocktail by the gulf, this casual establishment has a covered patio with plastic chairs and tables right by the white sand. The "help" likes to hang out here, lending a relaxed, don't-give-a-hoot atmosphere. See chapter 10.
- **Days Inn Island Beach Resort** (St. Pete Beach; ☎ **800/544-4222** or 813/367-1902): Situated in St. Pete Beach's hotel district, this motel boasts Jimmy B.'s beach bar, where happy "hour" actually runs from noon to 7:30pm daily. You can stick around for evening entertainment, including beachside bonfires on Saturdays in winter. See chapter 11.
- **Sandbar** (Anna Maria Island, off Bradenton; ☎ **941/778-0444**): Sitting on the site of the former Pavilion, built in 1913 when people from Tampa and St. Pete took the ferry here, this popular restaurant is right on the beach overlooking the gulf. The action is under the umbrellas on the lively beachside deck, with a snack menu and live music weeknights and on weekend afternoons. See chapter 11.

- **TradeWinds Resort** (St. Pete Beach; ☎ **800/237-0707** or 813/367-6461): The Flying Bridge, a Florida cracker-house–style beachside bar, actually floats on one of the lily ponds at this large resort. You can take your drink out to the sands as the "sun goes to bed," as the French say. See chapter 11.

20 The Best Bars & Nightspots

- **Cafe Nostalgia** (Little Havana, Miami; ☎ **305/541-2631**): They start with films from the old country and follow up with the hot sounds of Afro-Cuban jazz. It's become popular with a few non-Hispanics and lots of sentimental exiles. Plans are in the works to open a second Nostalgia in Miami Beach. See chapter 5.
- **The Clevelander** (South Beach, Miami; ☎ **305/531-3485**): On one of Ocean Drive's busiest corners, there's always a mixed crowd gathered around the large outdoor pool area drinking brightly colored concoctions and ogling the lively sidewalk parade. See chapter 5.
- **Liquid** (South Beach, Miami; ☎ **305/532-9154**): If you can get past the velvet ropes you'll experience one of South Beach's hippest and most enduring night spots where G-string-clad dancers take to the stage and no one notices. The music is pounding and after midnight, the place is packed. Go early for a better chance of getting in. See chapter 5.
- **Tobacco Road** (Miami; ☎ **305/374-1198**): Open every day of the year since 1912, Tobacco Road is a Miami institution. No matter who is playing, this two-story dive bar is worth a visit. From homegrown blues to nationally known jazz acts to poetry readings, you'll find the best live music and atmosphere at "The Road." Plus there are nightly dinner specials like complete lobster dinners on Tuesdays for $9.95 or a 14-ounce T-bone with all the fixings for $7.99 on Thursdays. Any night after midnight you can get a steak dinner for only $6. See chapter 5.
- **Washington Avenue** (South Beach, Miami): On any Saturday night, you'll find the sidewalks packed from 6th Street to Española Way. There's no way to keep track of the many bars and clubs that go in and out as quickly as cars in a parking lot. See chapter 5.
- **Duval Street** (Key West): The partying-est strip this side of Bourbon Street is home to literally dozens of bars and dance spots. Explore them for yourself. See chapter 6.
- **Epoch** (Key West; ☎ **305/296-8521**): Formerly known as The Copa, this warehouse-style dance club made famous by its colorful gay patrons is right on Duval Street. They play everything from techno to house to disco and welcome anyone. See chapter 6.
- **Woody's Saloon and Restaurant** (Islamorada; ☎ **305/664-4335**): This raunchy bar has live bands almost every night, but it is the house band you want to see. Big Dick and the Extenders is headed by a 300-pound Native American who does a lewd, rude, and crude routine of jokes and songs guaranteed to offend everyone in the house. He usually shows some time after 9pm, Tuesdays through Sunday. Despite a small cover charge, drink specials, contests, and the legendary Big Dick keep this place packed until 4am almost every night. See chapter 6.
- **Clematis Street** (West Palm Beach): This newly gentrified area has some of the area's best (and only) nightlife. Just over the bridge from stodgy Palm Beach, this

5-block area, from Flagler Drive to Rosemary Avenue, has everything from late-night bookshops and wine bars to dance clubs and outdoor cafes. See chapter 8.

- **O'Hara's Pub and Jazz Cafe** (Hollywood/Ft. Lauderdale; ☎ **954/925-2555**): Kitty Ryan owns two of South Florida's best spots for live music. On Las Olas Boulevard in Ft. Lauderdale, there is always a crowd enjoying smoking music. The newer Hollywood spot is swinging every night with live jazz and blues and good food, too. See chapter 8.
- **Las Olas Boulevard** (Ft. Lauderdale): This wide, scenic street, dotted with good clubs and late-night shopping, is especially popular with a more mature local crowd and European visitors. See chapter 8.
- **The Leopard Lounge in the Chesterfield Hotel** (Palm Beach; ☎ **561/659-5800**): This is a popular hangout, especially for older locals who come for live music, a great happy hour and no cover charge. A generous spread of hot and cold appetizers, plus two for one drink specials, keep the blue blazer crowd happy every evening starting at 5pm. See chapter 8.
- **E. R. Bradley's Saloon** (Palm Beach; ☎ **561/833-3520**): Better known as just Bradley's, this big, old bar attracts a fun. loud, crowd of young professionals and serious older drinkers. Come for the generous happy-hour buffets. See chapter 8.
- **Shooters Waterfront Café USA** (Fort Myers; ☎ **941/334-2727**): A setting right on the river makes this Fort Myers's most popular watering hole. There's live music every night, and the place is absolutely packed after work on Friday and Saturday. See chapter 10.
- **Junkanoo Beach Bar** (Fort Myers Beach; ☎ **941/463-2600**): Away from the crowds of Fort Myers Beach's busy Times Square, the Junkanoo attracts a more affluent crowd for its constant Bohemian-style beach parties with live reggae and other island music. A concessionaire rents beach cabanas and water-sports toys, making it a good place for a lively day at the beach. See chapter 10.
- **Dock at Crayton Cove** (Naples; ☎ **941/263-9940**): Right on the City Dock, this lively pub is a perfect place for an open-air meal or a libation while watching the action on Naples Bay. See chapter 10.
- **Frankie's Patio Bar & Grill** (Tampa; ☎ **813/249-3337**): All you have to do is stroll along 7th Avenue East, between 15th and 20th streets, in Tampa's Ybor City to find a club or bar to your liking. Frankie's stands out for its exposed industrial pipes—a stark contrast to the Spanish-style architecture prevalent here. There's seating indoors, on a large outdoor patio, or on an open-air balcony over-looking the action on the street. Pick up a calendar at the reception desk: There's that much live jazz, blues, reggae, and rock here. See chapter 11.
- **Pleasure Island** (Orlando): A $20 admission gets you into an wide array of clubs—an exceptionally good deal. Drinks here are expensive; but if you pace yourself you'll get more than your money's worth. And if you hang around till midnight, they'll throw in the fireworks for free. See chapter 12.
- **Church Street Station** (Orlando; ☎ **407/422-2434**): Though not part of Disney World, this downtown shopping/dining/nightclub complex operates on a principle similar to Pleasure Island. Less than $17 gets you into five show-rooms. The best deals? Every Wednesday from 6:30 to 7:30pm is Nickel Beer Night (well, *Hour*) at **Phineas Phogg's.** And on Thursdays from 4:30 to 7:30pm, at **Cheyenne Saloon,** longneck beers are $1 and barbecue sandwiches are $2. (The Cheyenne also holds free dance lessons on Sunday from 2 to 5:30pm.) See chapter 12.
- **Hathaway's Landing** (Panama City Beach; ☎ **850/230-0409**): There's live entertainment nightly and on Saturday and Sunday afternoons from March to

September under one of the largest thatch pavilions in Florida. The emphasis is on Jimmy Buffet–style music, reggae, and some country and western. While the young crowd hoots the night away over by the gulf, Hathaway's draws lots of customers on the far side of 30. See chapter 13.

- **Seville Quarter** (Pensacola; ☎ 850/434-6211): In Pensacola's Seville Historic District, this restored antique brick complex with New Orleans–style wrought-iron balconies contains pubs and restaurants whose names capture the ambience: Rosie O'Grady's Goodtime Emporium, Lili Marlene's Aviator's Pub, Apple Annie's Courtyard, End o' the Alley Bar, Phineas Phogg's Balloon Works (a dance hall, not a balloon shop), and Fast Eddie's Billiard Parlor (which has electronic games for kids, too). Live entertainment ranges from Dixieland jazz to country and western. See chapter 13.
- **Flora-Bama Lounge** (Perdido Key, near Pensacola; ☎ 850/492-0611): This slapped-together gulf-side pub is almost a shrine to country music, with jam sessions from noon until way past midnight on Saturday and Sunday. Flora-Bama is the prime sponsor and a key venue for the Frank Brown International Songwriters' Festival during the first week of November. Take in the great gulf views from the Deck Bar. See chapter 13

Planning an Affordable Trip to Florida

2

by Bill Goodwin

Most visitors go to Florida to see Orlando's theme parks or to relax on the beach. Choosing Walt Disney World as your destination is easy, but how do you pick a beach when Florida has some 800 miles of them?

Indeed, the Sunshine State has so much vying for your attention that planning a trip can seem overwhelming. But Florida's size and diversity also means that it has bargains galore for the traveler who knows where to go, when to go, and how to mine for discounts.

The great money-saving tips in this chapter will tell you where and how to look for the best deals. Also here is information and advice about transportation, seasons and special events, taking care of your special needs, and picking among the myriad types of accommodations—always with an eye to saving you money.

Don't just rely on this chapter, however. We've captured Florida's many personalities, attractions, and specific bargains in the chapters that follow. Peruse each one to see which destinations offer the activities you're looking for and the prices that fit your budget. If you pick the right place and go at the right time of year, you can have a terrific trip to Florida without feeling forced into bankruptcy.

THE $60-A-DAY PREMISE

With careful planning, two people can travel in Florida from $60 a day, combining their money for accommodation and at least two meals a day. That is, we assume you have at least $120 a day between the two of you for room and board, less drinks and tip. The costs of sightseeing, outdoor activities, transportation, and entertainment are all extras, but don't worry: We'll provide tips on saving money in those areas as well.

1 50 Money-Saving Tips

IN GENERAL

1. Avoid traveling during the high seasons, especially in southern Florida; hotel rates can more than double from mid-December to April. For example, the least expensive room on Sanibel Island costs about $90 a night, including tax, during winter, but that same room drops to $60 during spring, summer, and fall. Keep in mind also that many airlines have deep-discount promotional

fares to Florida during the off-seasons. Central Florida sees less of a seasonal difference in prices, given its somewhat cooler winters and the year-round clientele visiting its theme parks. In northern Florida, even during its high summer season, you can survive on $60 a day.

2. Always ask about discounts: corporate, students, military, auto club, senior citizen, and so on. Most airlines, car-rental firms, accommodations, attractions, and even some restaurants offer such price breaks but don't necessarily volunteer the information. Be sure to bring identification or your group membership card with you. Most Florida activities and attractions offer discounts, but you'll need a valid ID to qualify for the bargain rates.

3. Use any coupons you can get your hands on. The ubiquitous give-away booklets (such as *Florida on the Go*) you'll see in racks at the tourist information offices and elsewhere may look like junk mail, but they're loaded with discount coupons you can use at hotels, motels, restaurants, and attractions throughout the state. Other, more comprehensive coupon books are for sale. In business since 1961, **The Entertainment Publication** (☎ **800/374-4464**) offers particularly well-stocked versions for Miami and the Keys and Orlando. Their books usually cost between $28 and $48, depending on the locale, but the Miami and the Keys edition for 1999 sells for just $20. You can make that back with one trip to the Seaquarium, where one adult admission normally costs $19.95. In Orlando, the *Entertainment 99* costs less than $40 and has lots of restaurant coupons, including some fine-dining establishments. Over at the St. Pete and Clearwater beaches, the **Gulf Beaches of Tampa Bay Chamber of Commerce** (☎ **800/944-1847** or 813/360-6957) sells a book with discounts at many area restaurants, attractions, and other establishments for $30. You can recoup more than the cost of these books if you stay for more than a week and use them religiously.

AIR TRAVEL

4. Ask for the cheapest airfare, not just the coach fare. As the tips below illustrate, there are many options.

5. Buy your ticket well in advance. Most airlines offer deep discounts on tickets purchased 7, 14, or 21 days before the departure date—and the cheap seats sell out first. Always ask about restrictions such as staying over a Saturday night. Tickets are usually nonrefundable if you must cancel your trip, but even if you have to pay an extra fee if you alter your plans later, you'll get substantial savings over the regular fare.

6. On the other hand, you can often benefit by buying at the last minute. You do run the risk of being stuck with a really expensive ticket—or no ticket at all—but when a flight is only half-sold, the airlines may offer deep, deep discounts to fill seats that aren't sold 72 hours before take-off. The airline Web sites listed in the "Cyberdeals for Net Surfers" box, below, are good sources for finding out about last-minute fares. This is a better strategy in the off-season, when flights are more likely to have empty seats.

7. Be flexible in your schedule. Flying on Tuesday, Wednesday, or Thursday can save you money with some airlines; the prime Friday through Monday flights are often priced higher. Also inquire about night flights; the red-eye may leave you bleary, but if it's substantially cheaper, it might be worth it—you can make up the sleep later.

8. Surf the Internet and save. There are lots of Web pages and on-line services designed to clue you in on discounted airfares, accommodations, and car rentals; see the "Cyberdeals for Net Surfers" box in this chapter for some sites worth checking out.

9. If you don't have access to the Internet, consult a travel agent. They can get on their machines and find you the cheapest airfares, room rates, package deals, and other travel bargains that you could never find. You're under no obligation to buy, and it will cost you nothing, since most travel agents work on commissions paid by the airlines, hotels, car-rental companies, and tour operators.

10. Ask a travel agent about charter flights. Several airlines, such as Canada 3000, have charter flights to Florida during winter. They can offer great savings over commercial airline fares, but make sure you book with a reputable firm and inquire about all restrictions before you pay.

11. Check out consolidators (also known as "bucket shops"). These wholesalers buy tickets directly from the airlines in bulk at heavy discounts, and then resell them. Many consolidators also book charter as well as commercial flights. The tickets are usually heavily restricted (ask about all the details), but you may save a bundle—usually 20 to 35%. See "Getting There," below, for the names of reputable consolidators.

12. Check the travel ads in your local newspaper. Airlines, consolidators, and charter and tour companies love to advertise package deals and promotions in weekend travel sections around the country. Just remember: If you're dealing with a new company, or one that you're unfamiliar with, it's a good idea to check with the Better Business Bureau to make sure they're legit.

13. Take local shuttle services to and from the airports. They usually are less expensive than taxis. Some hotels will even pick you up at the airport for free, so be sure to ask if they have airport transportation when you book your room.

CAR RENTALS

14. Reserve your rental in advance, especially during the high seasons when cars, especially the small, least expensive models, can be in heavy demand. Not only will you have a car waiting, you'll avoid paying top dollar for a vehicle that's larger than you need.

15. Call all the major car-rental firms and compare rates (see "Getting Around," below, for their toll-free numbers). Always ask for their cheapest rates. Even after you've made your reservations, call again and check rates a few days or weeks later—you may stumble upon a cheaper rate.

16. If you'll be visiting for a week or more, ask for a long-term rate. Most Florida firms offer substantial discounts for weekly rentals, especially during the off-season.

17. Be sure to ask for discounts if you belong to a national organization such as AAA, AARP, Costco, or USAA, which negotiate special rates for their members. But be wary: Some of these specials may be more expensive than the rental companies' weekly rates or promotional deals, so ask about all possibilities.

18. Keep in mind that Florida has a $1.05-per-day state highway fund surcharge, and that state and local sales taxes will be added to your bill. The car-rental companies don't include these taxes when they quote rates, so before you hang up, be sure to ask how much your entire bill will be.

19. If there are only one or two of you traveling, reserve the least expensive subcompact or compact (sometimes called economy cars). You'll also save money on fuel and have an easier time parking. But be careful: Some reservations agents may tell you that all their least expensive cars are booked; this may be a ploy to get you to upgrade, so thank them and call another company. On the other hand, if you arrive with a valid reservation with a confirmation number, the agents are obligated to honor the rate you were quoted, even if they have to give you an upgrade. Make them stick to their original quote.

Florida

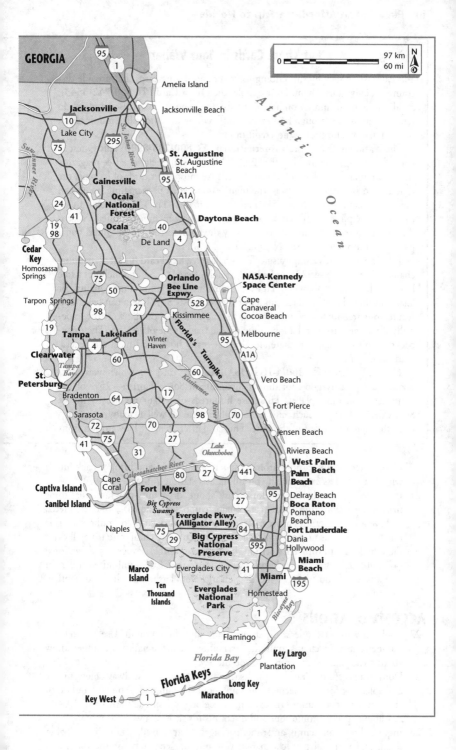

Put These Cards in Your Wallet

You can save money by subscribing to credit and dining cards that provide discounts when you use them. For example, the **Quest Card** (☎ 800/742-3543), good for discounts mostly on hotels but also for some airfare, cruises, and condo rentals, is available through hundreds of different organizations like motor clubs, professional organizations, and credit unions.

The **National Travel Club International** (☎ 800/285-8900) sells Quest as part of a package membership for $29.97. Membership includes a free magazine subscription and travel accident insurance. Like most other cards of its type, the Quest Card is not much help in the high season, when participating hotels can decline the card if they have 75% percent occupancy. The Quest's helpful customer service phone staff may be able to locate a new member willing to accept the card even in the busiest season. To buy the book directly from Quest, you'll pay a premium, $99. Try the National Travel Club first.

The **Traveler's Advantage** also offers a half-price hotel card for many national chains (☎ 800/479-4523). A 3-month trial is offered for $1 and includes a free hotel night stay at Ramada, Howard Johnson, La Quinta Inn, Quality, or Clarion caliber hotel. The remainder of the year costs $59. If you can be sure to secure your free night before enrolling for the card, this can be worth it, especially if you plan to spend a long time on the road in the off-season. The drawbacks of this plan are that there are not that many hotels and most are generic roadside chains.

The **IGT Card** (☎ 800/4-IGT-USA), a credit card for which you must qualify, is especially good for dining discounts in South Florida—25% of the entire check in most places. There are hundreds of restaurants mostly in the South Beach, Miami Beach, and Coral Gables areas, as well as many more scattered throughout the rest of the state. They also offer 25% off Howard Johnsons

20. Never agree to buy gasoline from a car-rental company, and bring it back full. It will always be less expensive if you fill up at a station in town.
21. If you don't mind driving to Florida, ask about "drive out" programs that some firms use to reposition their fleets. Major companies like Avis, Budget, Hertz, and National sometimes move their cars from northern cities to southern Florida for the winter season, and you could get a ridiculously cheap rate if you'll drive the vehicles south (or back north in the warmer months). For example, National (☎ 800/227-7368) recently offered a midsize rental with unlimited miles for $89 a week if you picked it up in Newark, New Jersey, and dropped it off in Miami.

ACCOMMODATIONS

22. Book early to get the least expensive room, and shop around. Use the toll-free numbers; at some chains, only the reservationists at the national number know about package deals that can save you money.
23. Don't just accept the "rack" or published rate—there's almost always a lower price available. Ask for the cheapest rate and about discounts for seniors, families, or any national organizations that you might belong to (especially AAA and AARP). Ask about special promotions and discounts for stays of a week or more.
24. Inquire about golf, tennis, and other packages. Many Florida establishments offer them, and you will pay less than if you ante up separately for the room and

nationwide and a number of upscale hotels as well. Regular membership price is $48 a year. But, if you mention this Frommer's guide, you'll get a free 6-month trial membership. It's an especially good deal for northeasterners since you can use the card at home, too. A majority of the participating establishments are in the tristate area of New York, New Jersey, and Connecticut. Be sure to order several weeks before your trip so they can check your credit. Even free trial members must pass a credit check.

Like The IGT card, the **Gusto Card** (☎ **888/464-8786**) has quite a few restaurant members in South Florida, especially in South Miami. If you subscribe to one of more than a dozen Florida newspapers, from the *Miami Herald* to the *The Boca News,* you can get the card for free. Call for details. Depending on the plan you choose, you can get from 20% to 35% discounts at participating establishments. If you pay for the card, from $29 to $39 a year, it may not be worth it. Unfortunately, the customer service department is difficult to reach by phone and some establishments are reluctant to honor the card.

Although not as widely accepted, **Transmedia** (☎ **800/422-5090**) offers 20% discounts on meals, including drinks. A one-time membership fee of $4.95 is good forever. They have fewer participating establishments, but many more card holders—1.3 million in the United States. The advantage of Transmedia is its very low price and that it's very seldom declined in restaurants that do accept it.

Even if you use these cards, you'll still have to pay the sales tax, and remember to tip 15% to 20% on the whole check, not on the discounted amount.

Restaurants go on and off these programs, so it's a good idea to call the restaurant in advance to see if they accept the card you have.

—Victoria Pesce Elliott

activities. Sometimes you can even get a rental car thrown in. We've mentioned the hotels and resorts that regularly offer package deals in the accommodations listings in this book. Their offers change frequently, however, so you'll have to ask.

25. Choose a hotel or motel that offers free continental breakfasts. The savings could enable you to afford better meals at lunch and dinner. The accommodations listings in this book indicate the properties that offer free breakfasts.

26. Choose a hotel or motel a block or more from the beach, since these usually are less expensive than those directly facing the sand. And in places where the prime resorts are on islands, mainland hotels and motels usually cost less than their off-shore brethren (they also are more likely to offer discounted weekday or weekend rates). And even if you elect a beachfront hotel, rooms with bay or garden views normally are less expensive than those directly facing the ocean or gulf.

27. If you're traveling with children, check to see if they can stay in your room for free. Or better yet, consider getting a one-bedroom suite with a pullout sofa in the living room; one suite is usually cheaper than two hotel rooms, and you'll still have privacy.

28. Get a room with cooking facilities. Many Florida establishments have units with at least kitchenettes. They cost a bit more than regular rooms, but preparing your own breakfast and lunch could slash your food costs in half. And it makes life a lot easier, especially if you're traveling with kids.

Cyberdeals for Net Surfers

It's possible to get some great deals on airfare, hotels, and car rentals via the Internet. So go grab your mouse and start surfing before you hit the real waves—you could save a bundle on your trip. The Web sites highlighted below are worth checking out, especially since all services are free.

In addition, most Florida tourist information offices have informative Web sites (see "Orientation" or "Essentials" in the following chapters for their addresses), and you can find out about packages and other special deals at the sites maintained by many hotels, resorts, and condo rental agencies (see the "Accommodations You Can Afford" sections).

Microsoft Expedia (www.expedia.com)   The best part of this multipurpose travel site is the "Fare Tracker": You fill out a form on the screen indicating that you're interested in cheap flights from your hometown, and, once a week, they'll e-mail you the best airfare deals. The site's "Travel Agent" will steer you to bargains on hotels and car rentals, and you can book everything, including flights, right on-line. This site is even useful once you're booked: Before you go, log on to Expedia for oodles of up-to-date travel information, including weather reports and foreign exchange rates.

Preview Travel (www.reservations.com and www.vacations.com) Another useful travel site, "Reservations.com" has a "Best Fare Finder," which will search the Apollo computer reservations system (a huge database used by travel agents worldwide) for the three lowest fares for any route on any days of the year. Say you want to go from Chicago to Orlando and back between December 6th and 13th: Just fill out the form on the screen with times, dates, and destinations, and within minutes, Preview will show you the best deals. If you find an airfare you like, you can book your ticket right on-line—you can even reserve hotels and car rentals on this site. If you're in the preplanning stage, head to Preview's "Vacations.com" site, where you can check out the latest package deals around the world by clicking on "Hot Deals."

Travelocity (www.travelocity.com)   This is one of the best travel sites out there. In addition to its "Personal Fare Watcher," which notifies you via e-mail of the lowest airfares for up to five different destinations, Travelocity will track the three lowest fares for any routes on any dates in minutes. You can book a flight right then and there, and if you need a rental car or hotel, Travelocity will find you the best deal via the SABRE computer reservations system (another

---

29. If you're staying for a week or more, consider a condominium unit, apartment, or cottage, especially if you're traveling with children. Condos usually have a sleeper sofa as extra bedding, a kitchen that lets you prepare some of your own meals, and the complexes usually have a pool and often tennis courts and other recreational facilities. Most have weekly rates that are less than paying by the night at hotels. Do note, however, that you'll usually have to pay extra for daily maid service.

30. Choose a hotel or motel that lets you make local calls for free. Most charge 50¢ or more per local phone call, and some even hit you with a fee on credit-card calls. Use the pay phone down in the lobby instead. Many hotels also tack on hefty surcharges for laundry, dry cleaning, and other services. You can cut these costs by choosing one with a guest laundry and washing your own clothes, and you can easily find dry cleaners on your own.

huge travel agent database). Click on "Last Minute Deals" for the latest travel bargains, including a link to "H.O.T. Coupons" (**www.hotcoupons.com**), where you can print out electronic coupons for travel in the United States and Canada.

Trip.Com (www.thetrip.com)   This site is really geared toward the business traveler, but vacationers-to-be can also use Trip.Com's valuable fare-finding engine, which will e-mail you every week with the best city-to-city airfare deals on your selected route or routes.

Discount Tickets (www.discount-tickets.com)   Operated by the European Travel Network (ETN), this site offers discounts on airfares, accommodations, car rentals, and tours. It deals in flights between the United States and other countries, not domestic U.S. flights, so it's most useful for foreign travelers.

E-Savers Programs   Several major airlines, most all of which service Florida, offer a free e-mail service known as **E-Savers,** via which they'll send you their best bargain airfares on a weekly basis. Here's how it works: Once a week (usually Wednesday), subscribers receive a list of discounted flights to and from various destinations, both international and domestic. Here's the catch: These fares are only available if you leave the very next Saturday (or sometimes Friday night) and return on the following Monday or Tuesday. It's really a service for the spontaneously inclined and travelers looking for a quick getaway. But the fares are cheap, so it's worth taking a look. If you have a preference for certain airlines (in other words, the ones you fly most frequently), sign up with them first.

Here's a list of airlines and their Web sites, where you can not only get on the e-mailing lists, but also book flights directly:

- **American Airlines:** www.americanair.com
- **Continental Airlines:** www.flycontinental.com
- **TWA:** www.twa.com
- **Northwest Airlines:** www.nwa.com
- **US Airways:** www.usairways.com

One final caveat: You'll get frequent-flier miles if you purchase one of these fares, but you can't use miles to buy the ticket.

—Jeanette Foster

31. If you show up without a reservation, bargain at the front desk. This usually won't work during the high seasons, when most hotels are nearly full, but you might be able to strike a very favorable off-season deal. If you try this, arrive in late afternoon or early evening, when the majority of the guests with reservations have already checked in, and rooms that aren't yet occupied are likely to stay empty for the night. If the front-desk clerk is unhelpful, ask to speak to the hotel manager, who may be the only employee who can discount rooms.

DINING

32. Take advantage of Florida's usually fine weather by planning daytime and romantic sunset picnics. Many towns and cities have shops purveying gourmet picnic fare, and most of the large supermarkets such as Publix, Albertson's, and Winn-Dixie have deli sections with good selections of meats, cheeses, breads, and salads.

33. Look for happy-hour specials at restaurants and cocktail lounges. They signal reduced prices on drinks, and sometimes appetizers. You can grab a free meal, for example, at the happy-hour buffet at Chadwick's Restaurant & Lounge, on otherwise expensive Capitva Island (see chapter 10).

34. If you don't mind dining before 6pm, take advantage of the early bird specials offered by many restaurants. The selections may be limited, but they are a less-expensive way to sample the fine fare at otherwise expensive establishments. We've pointed many of them out in the dining listings in this book.

35. If you're traveling with the kids, inquire about children's menus or discounts. Most restaurants offer them—and at resort-restaurant prices, they can be a real boon to your budget.

36. Look for fixed-price menus at the pricier restaurants, or splurge on a special meal at lunch rather than dinner. You'd be surprised at the difference between lunch and dinner prices at some of the finer restaurants.

37. The Friday Calendar section of *The Orlando Sentinel* sometimes includes two-for-one dinner special coupons and other discounts to entertainment. It will also list cultural events and concerts throughout central Florida, some of them free or for a small price.

SIGHTSEEING & ACTIVITIES

38. Bring your own golf clubs, tennis rackets, snorkeling and scuba gear, and other equipment. In addition to saving the rental costs, your gear will fit correctly and be in top condition.

39. The best way to find a good deal to Orlando's many golf courses is to look in the sports section of the local newspaper, *The Orlando Sentinel,* for discount coupons and otherwise unadvertised specials.

THE MAJOR THEME PARKS

40. Stick with the Value Pass over the Park Hopper when buying multiday tickets to the Walt Disney parks in Orlando. Both options permit visits to multiple parks over 4 days, but the Park Hopper pass allows you to visit more than one park during a single day. This can take considerable effort and time, so it's better to stick to the Value Pass, especially if you are traveling with children. And the 4-day Value Pass will save you about $17 per person.

41. Buy a combined pass to Universal Studios Florida, Sea World, and Wet 'n Wild in Orlando. You pay one price to get into all three over either a 7- or a 10-day period. The combined passes cost more up front, but you'll save in the long run.

42. Look for discount tickets to Sea World and Universal Studios Florida on 2-liter bottles of Pepsi products. These discounts are usually available during Halloween Horror Night at Universal.

43. Buy "bottomless souvenir cups" at some Walt Disney parks. They allow you unlimited drinks at the hotel food courts—a significant savings if you and the kids consume a lot of coffee or soda.

44. Take food and drink with you into the parks. Grocery stores and discount drug-stores tend to be a little more expensive in tourist areas, but filling coolers or backpacks with snacks, lunch basics, sodas, bottled water, juices, and other drinks will save you a bundle over the cost inside the parks.

45. Invest in inexpensive plastic rain ponchos for the entire family before you leave home. All major parks include water rides, and it's miserable to walk around wet all day, even in the summer. Plus, they will come in handy during summer storms, which can come up quickly. They cost twice in the parks than what you'll pay at home.

46. If you have young children, bring lightweight, easy-to-carry strollers, since rentals inside the parks can add up. Don't bring your Cadillac of kiddie carriers: It could be stolen.

47. Think twice about items such as souvenir cups or fanny packs that some hotels leave in your room. These are not complimentary: If you use them, you will be charged.

48. The Disney parks have outdoor carts selling things such as turkey legs, baked potatoes, and fresh fruit. These can easily make a simple meal, and are cheaper than any restaurant.

49. Buy your tickets to Busch Gardens Tampa Bay at Tampa Bay Visitor Information Center, across the street from the main entrance (☎ 813/985-3601). You'll save a few dollars, and the staff is expert at advising you on how to maximize your time in the park. Many area hotels and motels have packages with include free or discounted admission.

NIGHTLIFE

50. Check out the local newspapers for free concerts and other entertainment in municipal parks. The Friday newspapers usually have entertainment sections listing activities for the upcoming weekend.

2 Visitor Information

Once you've chosen a specific destination in Florida, your best sources of detailed information are the **local visitor information offices.** They're listed under "Orientation" or "Essentials" in the following chapters. Most of them have Web sites on the Internet (we've included their addresses throughout this book), and you can call or write for brochures.

For general information about the state, contact **Visit Florida,** P.O. Box 1100, Tallahassee, FL 32399-1100 (☎ **800/7-FLA-USA;** www.flausa.com), which will send you its *Florida Vacation Guide* and an official state highway map.

Visit Florida also has offices in:

Canada: 121 Bloor St. East, Suite 1003, Toronto M4W 3M5 (☎ **416/928-3139;** fax 416/928-6841).

United Kingdom: Roebuck House, Palace Street, London SW1E 5BA (☎ **171/ 630-6602;** fax 171/630-7703).

Germany: Schillerstrasse 10, 60313 Frankfurt/Main (☎ **69/131-0092;** fax 69/ 131-0647).

Japan: Belevedere Kudan Bldg., no. 204, 2-15-5, Fujimi, Chiyoda-Ku, Tokyo 102 (☎ **35276-0260;** fax 35276-0264).

Visit Florida also has **welcome centers** on I-10 west of Pensacola, I-75 north of Jennings, I-95 north of Yulee, and U.S. 231 at Campbellton. There's also a walk-in information office in the west foyer of the New Capitol Building in Tallahassee (see chapter 13).

3 When to Go

To a large extent, the timing of your visit will determine how much you'll spend, and how much company you'll have, once you get here. That's because room rates can more than double during the high seasons, when countless visitors migrate to Florida.

The weather determines the high seasons (see "Climate," below). In subtropical southern Florida, it's during the winter, from mid-December to mid-April. On the

The Boys of Spring (Training)

Major-league baseball fans can watch the Florida Marlins in Miami and the Tampa Bay Devil Rays in St. Petersburg throughout their seasons from April through September, but the entire state is a baseball hotbed from late February through March when many other teams tune up for the regular season with "Grapefruit League" exhibition games.

Most of Florida's spring training stadiums are relatively small, so fans can see their favorite players up close, maybe even to get a handshake or an autograph. Also, tickets are priced from $5 to $12, a bargain when compared to regular season games. Many games sell out by early March, so don't wait until you're in Florida to buy tickets.

The teams tend to move around from season to season, but you can contact the **Florida Sports Foundation,** 1319 Thomaswood Dr., Tallahassee, FL 32312 (☎ **850/488-8347**), or the main office of **Major League Baseball,** 350 Park Ave., New York, NY 10022 (☎ **212/339-7800**), to find out the schedules and to make sure of where your favorite teams will be playing.

Here's where the teams played in 1998, with their ticket office phone numbers. See the outdoor activities sections in subsequent chapters for specifics.

Atlanta Braves, Orlando (☎ 407/939-8600); **Baltimore Orioles,** Fort Lauderdale (☎ 800/236-8908 or 954/776-1921); **Boston Red Sox,** Fort Myers (☎ 941/334-4799); **Cincinnati Reds,** Sarasota (☎ 941/954-4101); **Cleveland Indians,** Winter Haven (☎ 941/291-5803); **Detroit Tigers,** Lakeland (☎ 941/688-9589); **Florida Marlins,** Melbourne (☎ 407/633-9200); **Houston Astros,** Kissimmee (☎ 407/839-6500); **Kansas City Royals,** Davenport (☎ 941/424-7211); **Los Angeles Dodgers,** Vero Beach (☎ 407/569-4900); **Minnesota Twins,** Fort Myers (☎ 800/338-9467 or 941/768-4200); **Montreal Expos,** Jupiter (☎ 561/775-1818); **New York Mets,** Port St. Lucie (☎ 561/871-2100); **New York Yankees,** Tampa (☎ 813/875-7753); **Philadelphia Phillies,** Clearwater (☎ 813/442-8496); **Pittsburgh Pirates,** Bradenton (☎ 941/747-3031); **St. Louis Cardinals,** Jupiter (☎ 561/775-1818); **Tampa Bay Devil Rays,** St. Petersburg (☎ 813/822-3384); **Texas Rangers,** Port Charlotte (☎ 813/625-9500); **Toronto Blue Jays,** Dunedin (☎ 813/733-9302).

other hand, you'll be rewarded with incredible bargains if you can stand the heat and humidity of a South Florida summer between June and early September. In northern Florida, the reverse is true: Tourists flock here during the summer, from Memorial Day to Labor Day.

Presidents' Day weekend in February, Easter week, Memorial Day weekend at the end of May, the Fourth of July, Labor Day weekend at the start of September, Thanksgiving, Christmas, and New Year's are busy throughout the state, and especially at Walt Disney World and the other Orlando area attractions, which can be packed anytime school's out (see chapter 12).

Both northern and southern Florida share the same "shoulder seasons"—April and May and from September to November, when the weather is pleasant throughout Florida and hotel rates are considerably less than during the high seasons. If price is a consideration, then these months of pleasant temperatures and fewer tourists are the best times to visit.

See the accommodations sections in the chapters that follow for specifics about the local high, shoulder, and off-seasons.

CLIMATE   Northern Florida has a temperate climate, and even in the warmer southern third of the state, it's subtropical, not tropical. Accordingly, Florida sees more extremes of temperatures than, say, the Caribbean islands.

Spring sees warm temperatures throughout Florida, but it also brings tropical showers, and May contributes the first waves of summertime humidity.

Summer runs from May to September in Florida, when it's hot and *very* humid throughout the state. If you're in an inland city during these months, you may not want to do anything too taxing when the sun is at its peak. Coastal areas, however, reap the benefits of sea breezes. Severe afternoon thunderstorms are prevalent during the summer heat (there aren't professional sports teams here named Lightening and Thunder for nothing), so schedule your activities for earlier in the day, and take precautions to avoid being hit by lightening during the storms.

Fall is a great time to visit—the really hottest days are gone, and the crowds have thinned out a bit. August through November, however, is hurricane season—you may remember Hurricanes Andrew and Opal in 1992 and 1995, respectively, which caused billions of dollars' worth of damage to South Florida and to the Panhandle. Fortunately, the National Weather Service closely tracks hurricanes and gives ample warning if there's any need to evacuate coastal areas.

Winter can get a bit nippy throughout the state, and sometimes downright cold in northern Florida. Although snow is rare, a flake or two has been known to fall as far south as Miami. The "cold snaps" usually last only a few days in the southern half of the state, however, and daytime temperatures quickly return to the 70s.

For up-to-the minute forecasts, tune in to cable TV's **Weather Channel,** or click on its Web site: www.weather.com.

Average Temperatures (°F) in Selected Florida Cities

	Jan	Feb	Mar	Apr	May	June	July	Aug	Sept	Oct	Nov	Dec
Key West	69	72	74	77	80	82	85	85	84	80	74	72
Miami	69	70	71	74	78	81	82	84	81	78	73	70
Tampa	60	61	66	72	77	81	82	82	81	75	67	62
Orlando	60	63	66	71	78	82	82	82	81	75	67	61
Tallahassee	53	56	63	68	72	78	81	81	77	74	66	59

FLORIDA CALENDAR OF EVENTS

January

- **Orange Bowl,** Miami. Two of the year's toughest college teams do battle at Pro Player Stadium, preceded by King Orange Jamboree Parade (see December listing, below). Tickets are available starting March 1 of the previous year through the Orange Bowl Committee. Call ☎ **305/371-4600** for details. January 1 (but note that dates of this and the other college bowl games mentioned below may vary to accommodate TV schedules).

- ✪ **CompUSA Florida Citrus Bowl,** Orlando. Two more of the year's best college teams duke it out on the gridiron. Downtown parade a few days before the game features dozens of marching bands, parade units, and a few floats. New Year's Eve extravaganza at Sea World (see December listing, below). Game tickets go on sale in late October or early November. Call ☎ **407/423-2476** for information; 407/839-3900 for tickets. January 1.

- **Gator Bowl,** Jacksonville. Yet two more of the country's better college football teams battle it out in Alltel Stadium. Call ☎ 904/798-1700 for information on tickets and postgame festivities. January 1.

- **Outback Bowl,** Tampa. Two top college teams kick off at Houlihan's Stadium, preceded by weeklong series events. Call ☎ **813/874-2695** for schedule and tickets. January 1.
- **Art Miami,** Miami. This fine-art fair features more than 100 galleries from all over the world. International, modern, and contemporary works are featured at this annual event, attracting thousands of visitors and buyers to the Coconut Grove Convention Center. For information and ticket prices, call ☎ **561/220-2690.** Early January.
- **Three Kings Parade, Miami.** Since Cuban Pres. Fidel Castro outlawed this religious celebration more than 25 years ago, Cuban Americans in Little Havana have put on a bacchanalian parade winding through Calle Ocho from 4th Avenue to 27th Avenue, with horse-drawn carriages, native costumes, and marching bands. Call WQBA at ☎ **305/447-1140** for the exact date during the first week of January.
- **Epiphany Celebration,** Tarpon Springs. After morning services at St. Nicholas Cathedral, young folks dive for the Epiphany cross in Spring Bayou. For information, call ☎ **813/937-3540.** First Saturday in January.
- ✪ **Art Deco Weekend,** South Beach, Miami. Held along the beach between 5th and 15th streets, this festival—with bands, food stands, antique vendors, artists, tours, and other festivities—celebrates the whimsical architecture that has made South Beach one of America's most unique neighborhoods. Call ☎ **305/672-2014** for details. Usually held on Martin Luther King weekend.
- **Martin Luther King Day Parade,** Miami. This parade along NW 62nd Avenue, north of downtown, honors Dr. King. For information, call ☎ **305/636-1924.** Second weekend in January.
- **International Circus Festival and Parade,** Sarasota. Circus acts, clowns, and rides for kids honor the city's rich circus heritage. Call ☎ **941/351-8888** for schedule. Day after Christmas through January.
- ✪ **Royal Caribbean Classic,** Key Biscayne. World-renowned golfers compete for more than $1 million in prize money at Crandon Park Golf Course, formerly known as The Links. Lee Trevino is a two-time winner of this championship tournament. Call ☎ **305/374-6180** for more information. Late January.
- **Palm Beach Antique Show,** Palm Beach. Dealers from around the world attract collectors and regular shoppers alike to this international art and antique show, which features museum-quality art, antique furniture, jewelry, tapestries, books, porcelain, and much more. Call ☎ **561/220-2690.** Late January to early February.
- ✪ **Walt Disney World Marathon,** Orlando. This 26.2-mile marathon winding through the resort and theme-park areas is open to all, including travelers with disabilities. The $50 entry fee is included in room price with some Disney resort packages. Preregistration is required. Call ☎ **407/824-4321** for details.
- ✪ **Zora Neale Hurston Festival,** Eatonville. This 4-day celebration in Eatonville, the first incorporated African American town in America, highlights the life and works of author Zora Neale Hurston. Eatonville is about 25 miles north of the theme parks. Call ☎ **800/352-3865** for details. Usually last weekend in January.
- **Taste of the Grove Food and Music Festival,** Miami. This fund-raiser in the Grove's Peacock Park is an excellent chance for visitors to sample menu items from some of the city's top restaurants and sounds from international and local performers. Call ☎ **305/444-7270** for details. Mid-January.
- **The Key Biscayne Art Festival,** Key Biscayne. Really one of the finest in the country, this art festival, held in Cape Florida State Park, offers hundreds of

artists, craftspersons, and lots of great international food for a high-quality, juried fine art show, all for charity. Call ☎ **305/361-0049** for details. Last weekend in January.

- **Goodland Mullet Festival,** Marco Island. Stan Gober's Idle Hour Seafood Restaurant in Goodland is mobbed during a massive party featuring the Buzzard Lope dance and the Best Men's Legs Contest. Call ☎ **941/394-3041** for details. Sunday before Super Bowl.

- **Winter Antique Show,** Miami Beach. Antique glasswork, coins, jewelry, furniture, and more fill 800 booths and two halls at the mammoth Miami Beach Convention Center. Call ☎ **305/754-4931** for details. Late January to early February.

February

✪ **Edison Pageant of Light,** Fort Myers. The spectacular Parade of Lights tops off arts-and-crafts shows, pageants, and a 5km race. Call ☎ **800/237-6444** or 941/334-2550. First 2 weeks in February.

✪ **Everglades Seafood Festival,** Florida City. As many as 75,000 people show up each year for this two day eating festival in the quaint old town of Florida City. Florida delicacies like stone crab and gator tails are dished up from shacks and food booths on the outskirts of town. Friday night is family night where a carnival and craft fair attract the kids. No admission charge. Call ☎ **941/695-4100** for more details. First full weekend in February.

- **Winter Gayla,** Ft. Lauderdale. More than 10,000 gay men and women turn out for this 10-day pride festival with parties, games, vendors, and displays. Call ☎ **954/561-2020** for details. Early February.

✪ **Gasparilla Pirate Fest,** Tampa. Hundreds of boats and rowdy "pirates" invade the city, then parade along Bayshore Boulevard, showering crowds with beads and coins. For information, call ☎ **813/273-6495.** Early February.

- **Artigras,** Palm Beach Gardens. This 3-day event featuring local and national artists was named 15th best art show in the nation. It boasts local and regional musicians and entertainers, kids and seniors activities, and international foods. Call ☎ **561/748-8844** for details. Presidents' Day weekend.

✪ **Speedweeks,** Daytona. This features 19 days of events with a series of races that draw the top names in NASCAR stock-car racing, all culminating in the **Daytona 500.** All events take place at the Daytona International Speedway. Especially for the Daytona 500, tickets must be purchased even a year in advance. They go on sale January 1 of the prior year. Call ☎ **904/253-7223** for ticket information. First 3 weeks of February.

✪ **Miami Film Festival.** This 10-day festival has made an impact as an important screening opportunity for Latin American cinema and American independents. It's relatively small, well priced, and easily accessible to the general public. Contact the Film Society of Miami at ☎ **305/377-FILM.** Early February.

✪ **Coconut Grove Art Festival,** Miami. This is the state's largest art festival and the favorite annual event of many locals. More than 300 artists are selected from thousands of entries to show their works at this prestigious and bacchanalian fare. Almost every medium is represented during this outside festival, including the culinary arts. Call ☎ **305/447-0401** for details. Presidents' Day weekend.

- **Florida State Fair,** Tampa. Despite all its development, Florida still is a major agricultural state, which status it celebrates at this huge annual exposition. Judged competitions, botanical gardens, crafts building, carny rides, nationally known entertainers. Call ☎ **800/345-FAIR** for details. Mid-February.

- **Mardi Gras at Universal Studios,** Orlando. Started in the mid-1990s, this evening event has become more elaborate each year. Authentic parade floats from New Orleans, stilt walkers and doubloons and beads thrown to the crowd add to the fun. Special entertainment is also part of the fun. Included in the price of admission to the park. For information call ☎ **407/363-8000.** Mid-February.
- ✪ **Miami International Boat Show,** Miami. This show draws almost a quarter of a million boat enthusiasts to the Miami Beach Convention Center and surrounding locations to see the megayachts, sailboats, dinghies, and accessories. It's the biggest anywhere. Call ☎ **305/531-8410** for more information and ticket prices. Mid-February.
- **Palm Beach Seafood Festival,** West Palm Beach. This festival at Currie Park features arts and crafts, kiddie rides, and of course, stone crabs, lobster, and more. Call ☎ **561/832-6397** for the word on the day's catch. Mid-February.
- ✪ **Silver Spurs Rodeo,** Kissimmee. The rodeo featuring real cowboys in contests of calf roping, bull and bronco riding, barrel racing, and more is a celebration of the area's rural, pre-Disney roots. It's held at the Silver Spurs Arena, 1875 E. Irlo Bronson Memorial Hwy. (U.S. 192) in Kissimmee. Call ☎ **407/847-5000** for details. Tickets $15. Third weekend in February.
- **St. Lucie County Fair,** Fort Pierce. Agricultural youth and livestock fair that features an impressive country music lineup. Stars like Loretta Lynn, Brenda Lee, Mark Chestnut, and Johnny and June Carter Cash have performed in recent years. Call ☎ **561/464-2910** for more details. End of February.
- **Doral-Ryder Golf Open,** Miami. One of the county's most prestigious annual tournaments. Call ☎ **305/477-GOLF** for more information. Late February to early March.
- **Medieval Fair,** Sarasota. Knights in shining armor and fair maidens in flowing gowns on the grounds of the Ringling Museum. For information, call ☎ **941/ 351-8497.** Late February to early March.

March

- **Bike Week,** Daytona Beach. An international gathering of motorcycle enthusiasts draws a crowd of more than 200,000. In addition to major races held at Daytona International Speedway (featuring the world's best road racers, motocrossers, and dirt trackers), there are motorcycle shows, beach parties, and the Annual Motorcycle Parade, with thousands of riders. Call ☎ **800/854-1234** or 904/255-0981, or on-line at www.officialbikeweek.com. First week in March.
- **The Central Florida Fair.** This 11-day fair, held at the Central Florida Fairgrounds, 4603 W. Colonial Dr., features rides, entertainers, 4-H and livestock exhibits, a petting zoo, and food booths. Adults pay $6, children 6 to 10 are charged $3, and children 5 and under enter free. Call ☎ **407/295-3247** for details. Early March (some years beginning late February).
- **Winter Party,** Miami. The Dade Human Rights Foundation hosts this gay and lesbian weekend-long party that features several activities at clubs around town and culminates in a huge all-day dance fest on the beach on Sunday. For more information on specific events and ticket prices, call ☎ **305/538-5908** or check out their Web site at www.winterparty.com. Early March.
- **Florida Strawberry Festival,** Plant City. Country music's brightest stars entertain and overdose on strawberry shortcake in the "Winter Strawberry Capital of the World." Call ☎ **813/752-9194.** First weekend in March.
- **Kissimmee Bluegrass Festival,** Kissimmee. Major bluegrass and gospel entertainers from all over the country perform at this 4-day festival at the Silver Spurs

Arena, 1875 E. Irlo Bronson Memorial Hwy. Tickets are $12 to $20; multiday packages are available. Call ☎ **800/473-7773** for details. Begins first weekend in March.

- **Renaissance Festival,** Largo. Knights jousting for honor, arts and crafts, entertainment, rides, plus medieval food and drink. Call ☎ **813/586-5423.** Weekends March to mid-April.

- ✪ **Sanibel Shell Fair,** Sanibel and Captiva islands. A show of shells from around the world and the sale of unusual shell art. Call ☎ **941/472-2155.** Begins first Thursday in March.

- **Grand Prix of Miami.** An auto race that rivals the big ones in Daytona. This high-purse, high-profile event attracts the top Indy car drivers and large crowds. For information and tickets, contact Homestead Motorsports Complex at ☎ **305/230-5200.** First week of March.

- ✪ **Calle Ocho Festival,** Miami. A salsa-filled blowout that marks the end of a 10-day extravaganza called Carnival Miami. One of the world's biggest block parties held along 23 blocks of Little Havana's Southwest 8th Street between 4th and 27th avenues. Call ☎ **305/644-8888** for more information. Early to mid-March.

- **The Italian Renaissance Festival,** Miami. Stage plays, music, and period costumes complement Villa Vizcaya's neo-Italian architectural style. Call ☎ **305/250-9133** for more information. Mid-March.

- **Miami Gay & Lesbian Film Festival,** Miami. A 10-day festival of short and feature-length films and videos by gay filmmakers at South Beach's Colony Theater on Lincoln Road and other smaller venues. For details, call Robert Rosenberg ☎ **305/532-7256.** Mid-March.

- ✪ **Bay Hill Invitational,** Orlando. Hosted by Arnold Palmer, and featuring some Orlando-based golfers like Tiger Woods, this PGA Tour event is held at the Bay Hill Club, 9000 Bay Hill Blvd. Daily admission is Tuesday to Wednesday $18; Thursday to Sunday $28; weeklong admission, $50 for grounds-only access; $70 for clubhouse access. Call ☎ **407/876-2888** for details. Mid-March.

- **Indian River County's Firefighter's Fair,** Vero Beach. To really get the local flavor of the Treasure Coast, spend a day watching the cattle judging and steer auction. Call ☎ **561/562-2974** to find out more about the fair, which features down-home cooking and carnival rides, too. Third Friday of March.

- **Artsfest,** Stuart. Arts and crafts share the spotlight with real blues, jazz, and classical music as well as food from the best local restaurants. Call the **Council on Arts** at ☎ **561/287-6676** for more information. Mid- to late March.

- **Spring Break,** Daytona Beach, Miami Beach, Panama City Beach, Key West, and other beaches. College students from all over the United States and Canada flock to Florida for endless partying, wet T-shirt and bikini contests, free concerts, volleyball tournaments, and more. Tune into Music TV if you can't be here. Call the local visitor information offices. Three weeks in March.

- **Lipton Championships,** Miami. One of the world's largest tennis events hosted at the lush Tennis Center at Crandon Park on Key Biscayne. Call ☎ **305/446-2200** for details. Mid- to late March.

- **Blues Festival,** Miami. Mozart Stub restaurateur Harald Neuweg hosts this all-day street fest featuring down-home blues tunes as well as great food and lots of beer. Call ☎ **305/446-1600** for more details or see "Oktoberfest" listing below. Third weekend in March.

- **Sidewalk Art Festival,** Winter Park. Central Park exhibition draws artists from all over North America during the third full weekend in March. The festival is consistently named one of the best in the nation by the national magazine *Sunshine Artist.* Call ☎ **407/623-3234** or 407/644-8281 for details. Admission is free, although you may have to pay for parking.

- **Players Championship,** Ponte Vedra Beach. A major golf event held at the Tournament Player's Club, the toughest course on the PGA tour. Call ☎ **904/ 285-7888** for details. Late March.
- **Spring Speedway Spectacular,** Daytona. A car show and swap meet at the Daytona International Speedway featuring a wide variety of collector vehicles. Admission is charged. Call ☎ **904/255-7355** for details. Late March or early April.
- **The Spring Flower Festival,** Cypress Gardens. More than 30,000 brightly colored bedding plants and flowers create beautiful topiaries shaped as butterflies, birds, and animals. You have to pay admission to the park to get into the festival: adults $29.50, children 6 to 12 $19.50, seniors $24.50. Call ☎ **941/324-2111** for details. March to May.

April

- **Springtime Tallahassee,** Tallahassee. One of the South's largest celebrations welcomes abundant azaleas, camellias, and other other blossoms. Call ☎ **850/224-1373.** Runs 4 weeks from late March.
- **Festival of States,** St. Petersburg. Since 1921 one of the South's largest civic celebrations sees national band competition, three parades, concerts, sports, and more. Call ☎ **813/898-3654.** First full week in April.
- **Highland Games and Festival,** Dunedin. Scottish band contests and Highland dancing, piping, and drumming celebrate Dunedin's Scottish heritage. Call ☎ **813/733-6240.** First full week in April.
- **Miller Lite Professional Men's Beach Volleyball Tournament,** Clearwater Beach. One of the largest pro beach volleyball events is nationally televised. Call ☎ **813/461-0011.** Second weekend in April.
- **PGA Seniors Golf Championship,** Palm Beach Gardens. Held at the PGA National Resort & Spa, it's the oldest and most prestigious of the senior tournaments. Call ☎ **561/624-8400** for the lineup. Mid-April.
- **World Cup Polo Tournament,** Palm Beach. Join royalty at the Palm Beach Polo and Country Club to see the best in international polo circles as the season closes. Call ☎ **561/793-1440** for details. Mid-April.
- ✪ **Fringe Festival,** Orlando. More than 100 diverse acts from around the world participate in this eclectic event, held for 10 days at various stages in downtown Orlando. Everything from sword swallowers to actors doing a 7-minute version of *Hamlet* perform on outdoor stages available to Fringe goers for free after they purchase a festival button for under $5. Ticket prices vary, but individual performances are generally under $12. Call ☎ **407/648-1333** for details.
- **Easter Sunday,** Orlando. Mickey and friends celebrate with an old-fashioned parade and early opening/late closing throughout Easter week. Call ☎ **407/ 824-4321** for details. Also, an interdenominational service, with music, is presented at the Atlantis Theatre at Sea World, 7007 Sea World Dr. It is hosted by a well-known person each year, most recently Elizabeth Dole. Admission is free. Call ☎ **407/351-3600** for details.
- **Easter Surfing Festival,** Cocoa Beach. More than 250 surfers ride the waves at the "Surf Capital of the East Coast," while Brazen Bikini Contests liven things up ashore. Call ☎ **800/936-2326** for details. Easter weekend.
- **World's Largest Easter Egg Hunt,** Bradenton. The city tries to break into the *Guinness Book of World Records* by burying 200,000 eggs in the sand of Coquina Beach. Call ☎ **941/746-7117.** Easter week.

- **Underwater Easter Egg Hunt,** Destin. Certified divers scour East Pass for colored golf balls and $10,000 in prizes. Call ☎ 800/322-3319 for details. Easter weekend.
- **Beach Goes Pops,** St. Pete Beach. The Florida Orchestra and Florida Opera perform on the gulf shore, with restaurateurs serving dinner at tables on the sand. Call ☎ 813/360-6957. Last Saturday in April.
- **Sunfest,** West Palm Beach. A huge party happens on Flagler Drive in the downtown area with four stages of continuous music, a craft marketplace, a juried art show, a youth park, and fireworks. Call ☎ 561/659-5992 for details. Late April to early May.

May

- **Epcot International Flower and Garden Festival,** Orlando. A monthlong event with theme gardens, topiary characters, special floral displays, speakers, and seminars.
- **Arabian Nights Festival,** Opa-Locka. This yearly event commemorates the distinctive Moorish architecture in the heart of Opa-Locka. Historical tours, street festivals, live music, and food booths are part of the fun. For details, call ☎ 305/688-4611. Early May.
- **Turtle Time Festival,** Juno Beach. Swing by the Marine Center at Loggerhead Park and help the locals celebrate the beginning of sea-turtle nesting season. Kids can learn about the marine environment with arts and crafts and children's activities including stage shows. Call ☎ 561/627-8280 for more information. A Saturday in early to mid-May (Mother's Day).
- **Texaco/Hemingway Key West Classic.** Hailed as the top fishing tournament in Florida, this catch-and-release competition offers $50,000 in prizes to be divided between the top anglers in three divisions: sailfish, marlin, and light tackle. Call ☎ 305/294-4440 for more information. Mid-May.
- **Coconuts Dolphin Tournament,** Key Largo. The largest fishing tournament in the Keys, offering $5,000 and a Dodge Ram pickup truck to the person who breaks the record for the largest fish caught. The competition is fierce! Call ☎ 305/451-4107 for details. Mid-May.
- **Cajun/Zydeco Crawfish Festival,** Fort Lauderdale. Spend 3 days at Mills Pond Park dancing to Cajun music—if you don't know how, sign up for free lessons. Can you peel? If so, enter the crawfish-eating contest. Call the Crazee Crawfish 24-hour hotline at ☎ 954/761-5934. Early May.
- **Shell Air and Sea Show,** Fort Lauderdale. A spectacular display of aeronautics featuring the Blue Angels and aquatic demonstrations by the navy guaranteed to evoke oohs and aahs. Call ☎ 954/527-5600 for details. Early May.
- **Grayton Beach Fine Arts Festival,** South Walton County. With artists from the artsy community of Seaside participating, this is one of the state's finest fine arts festivals. Music and good food, too. Call ☎ 850/267-3511. Early May.
- **Mayfest,** Destin. Upscale arts and crafts festival attracts more than 20,000 people to look, buy, and sample fine cuisine at the Panhandle's ritziest resort. Call ☎ 850/837-6241. Third full weekend in May.
- **The Great Sunrise Balloon Race & Festival,** Homestead. Dozens of multicolored balloons rise up over Homestead Air Reserve Base as sky divers fall from the sky. The race is celebrated on the ground with a variety of food, music, arts, and crafts. For information, call ☎ 305/275-3317. Memorial Day weekend.

June

- **Walt Disney World All-American College Orchestra and College Band.** The best collegiate musical talent in the country performs at Epcot and the Magic Kingdom throughout the summer. Call ☎ **407/824-4321** for details.
- **Fiesta of Five Flags,** Pensacola. Extravaganza commemorates the Spanish conquistador Tristan de Luna's arrival in 1559. Call ☎ **850/433-6512** for information. First week in June.
- **Billy Bowlegs Festival,** Fort Walton Beach. A fleet of modern-day pirates captures the Emerald Coast in a rollicking, weeklong bash honoring notorious buccaneer William Augustus Bowles. Treasure hunt, parade, and carnival, too. Call ☎ **800/322-3319.** First week of June.
- **Gay Weekend,** Orlando. The first weekend in June has become known for attracting tens of thousands of gay and lesbian travelers to Central Florida. In 1997, Universal City Travel offered a "Gay Weekend" tour package including tickets to Universal Studios, Sea World, and Church Street Station. This has all grown out of "Gay Day," which has been held unofficially at Walt Disney World for about 5 years, drawing upward of 40,000 folks. Special events throughout the weekend cater to gay and lesbian travelers throughout Central Florida. **Universal City Travel** offers special packages (☎ **800/224-3838** for information). Also get information on the Internet by accessing www.gayday.com.
- **Walt Disney World Wine Festival,** Orlando. More than 60 wineries from all over the United States participate. Events include wine tastings, seminars, food, and celebrity-chef cooking demonstrations at Disney's Yacht and Beach Club Convention Center. Call ☎ **407/827-7200** or 407/824-4321 for details.
- **Super Boat Racing Series,** Key West. A day of food, fun, and powerboat racing in downtown Key West. Call ☎ **305/296-8963** for details. Early June.
- ✪ **Coconut Grove Goombay Festival,** Miami. Bahamian bacchanalia with dancing in the streets of Coconut Grove and music from the Royal Bahamian Police marching band. This bash is one of the country's largest black-heritage festivals. The food and music draw thousands to an all-day celebration of Miami's Caribbean connection. It's lots of fun if the weather isn't scorching. Call ☎ **305/ 372-9966** for festival details. Early June.
- **Spanish Night Watch Ceremony,** St. Augustine. Actors in period dress lead a torchlight procession through historic St. Augustine and reenact the closing of the city gates with music and pageantry. Call ☎ **800/OLD-CITY** for details. Third Saturday in June.
- **International Hemingway Festival,** Sanibel Island. Moved from Key West in 1997, literary conferences have replaced beery Ernest look-alike contests as highlights of this highbrow festival organized by the author's family. Call ☎ **800/ 533-4753.** Third weekend in July.
- **Soulfest,** West Palm Beach. Celebrate African American culture with cuisine, arts and crafts, and entertainment, as well as children's activities. Call the Suncoast Chamber of Commerce at ☎ **561/842-7146** for details.

July

- **Dodger Home Stadium Fireworks Display,** Vero Beach. A day of all-American fun centered around some hometown baseball as well as a barbecue and fireworks. Call ☎ **561/569-4900** for more information. July 3.
- **Independence Day**, Orlando. Walt Disney World's Star-Spangled Spectacular brings bands, singers, dancers, and unbelievable fireworks displays to all the Disney parks, which stay open late. Call ☎ **407/824-4321** for details. Sea World also features a dazzling laser/fireworks spectacular; call ☎ **407/351-3600**

for details. There is also a free fireworks display in downtown Orlando at Lake Eola Park. For information call ☎407/246-2827.

- **Independence Day,** Miami. Celebrate July 4th on the beach, where parties, barbecues, and fireworks flare all day and night. For a weekend's worth of events on Key Biscayne, call ☎ 305/361-5207. You can also find one of the wildest parties around complete with fireworks and top-notch festivities at Bayfront Park, 301 N. Biscayne Blvd. For more on this free event call ☎ 305/358-7550.

- **Miccosukee Everglades Music and Crafts Festival,** Miami. Native American rock, Razz (reservation jazz), and folk bands perform down south while visitors gorge themselves on exotic treats like pumpkin bread and fritters. Watch the hulking old gators wrestle with Native Americans. Call ☎ 305/223-8380 for prices and details. Late July.

- ✪ **Lower Keys Underwater Music Fest,** Looe Key. At this outrageous celebration, boaters go out to the underwater reef of Looe Key Marine Sanctuary off Big Pine Key, drop speakers into the water, and pipe in music. It's entertainment for the fish and swimmers alike! A snorkeling Elvis can usually be spotted. Call ☎ 800/872-3722 for details. Second Saturday of July.

- **Space Week Celebration,** Cape Canaveral. Kennedy Space Center celebrates man landing on the moon. Science fairs, space art, space station design competition. Call ☎ 407/452-2121 for details. Mid-July.

- ✪ **Fourth of July Festivities,** Delray Beach. You can attend a celebration featuring art and jazz on Atlantic Avenue and Fla. A1A and enter a sand-sculpting contest, fly a kite, and sample fare from Delray's neighborhood restaurants. Call ☎ 561/278-0424 for more information. July 4.

- **Pepsi 400,** Daytona. A race marking the halfway point in the NASCAR Winston Cup Series for stock cars. Held at the Daytona International Speedway at 11am. Call ☎ 904/253-7223 for details. July 4.

- **World's Richest Tarpon Tournament,** Boca Grande. Some $175,000 is at stake in the great tarpon waters off Southwest Florida. Call the event hot line at ☎ 800/237-6444 or 941/964-2995. Second Wednesday and Thursday in July.

- **Blue Angels Air Show,** Pensacola. World-famous navy pilots do their aerial acrobatics just 100 yards off the beach. Call ☎ 800/874-1234 for schedule.

- **Wine and All That Jazz,** Boca Raton. A great way to quench your thirst on a sweltering summer day. It's one of the largest wine-tasting parties in the state; sample your choice from more than 100 wines and vintages while listening to a little live jazz. For details, call ☎ 561/395-4433. Friday night at the end of July or beginning of August.

August

- **Boca Festival Days,** Boca Raton. A month-long, city-wide event for the summer-weary featuring everything from baby contests to swim meets. One of the best events is the food-and-wine-tasting thrown by the Hospice-by-the-Sea. Dozens of Palm Beach county's best chefs turn out succulent dishes for the black-tie-optional affair. Add to that booth upon booth of the world's most renowned vintners serving sips of fine wine and a silent auction, and this could be one of the year's finest, and most accessible, benefits. Call ☎ 561/395-4433 for details.

- **Miami Reggae Festival,** Miami. Jamaica's best dance-hall and reggae artists turn out for this 2-day festival. Burning Spear, Steel Pulse, Spragga Benz, and Jigsy King participated recently. Call Jamaica Awareness at ☎ 305/891-2944 for more details. Early August.

September

- **Labor Day Pro-Am Surfing Festival,** Cocoa Beach. One of the largest surfing events on East Coast draws pros and amateurs from around the country. Rock-and-roll bands and swimsuit contests are among the activities. Call ☎ **800/ 936-2326** for details. Labor Day weekend.
- **Festival Miami.** A 4-week program of performing arts featuring local and invited musical guests. Centered in the University of Miami School of Music and Maurice Gusman Concert Hall. For a schedule of events, call ☎ **305/284-4940.** Mid-September to mid-October.
- ✪ **Columbus Day Regatta,** Miami. Find anything that can float, from an inner tube to a 100-foot yacht, and you'll fit right in. Yes, there actually is a race, but who can keep track when you're partying with a bunch of seminaked crazies in the middle of Biscayne Bay? It's free and it's wild. Rent a boat, jet-ski, or sailboard to get up close. Be sure to secure a vessel early, though—everyone wants to be there. Check local newspapers for exact date and time. Columbus Day weekend.
- **Night of Joy,** Orlando. One weekend in September, the Magic Kingdom hosts a festival of contemporary Christian music featuring top artists. This is a very popular event; obtain tickets early. Each year performers make a personal appearance at Long's Christian Bookstore in nearby College Park, about 20 minutes north of Disney. Admission to the concert is about $25 to $30 per night. Exclusive use of Magic Kingdom attractions is included. Call ☎ **407/824-4321** for details about the concert. For information about the free appearance at Long's, call ☎ **407/ 422-0293.**

October

- **Destin Seafood Festival,** Destin. The "World's Luckiest Fishing Village" cooks its bountiful catch in every style of cuisine imaginable. Also arts, crafts, and music. Comes right after **Destin Fishing Rodeo,** with 450 angler awards, giant dock parties. Call ☎ **850/837-6241.** First full weekend in October.
- **Biketoberfest,** Daytona. Road-racing stars compete at the CCS Motorcycle Championship at Daytona International Speedway, plus parties, parades, concerts, and more. Call ☎ **904/253-7223** for race ticket information, or 800/854-1235 for other activities. Mid-October.
- ✪ **Walt Disney World Oldsmobile Golf Classic.** Top PGA tour players compete for a total purse of $1 million at WDW golf courses in October's major golf event. Transplanted local golf phenom Tiger Woods is usually among the players. Daily ticket prices range from $8 to $15. The event is preceded by the world's largest golf tournament, the admission-free **Oldsmobile Scramble.** Call ☎ **407/824-4321** for details.
- **Walt Disney World Village Boat Show.** Central Florida's largest in-the-water boat show, featuring the best of new watercraft. At the Village Marketplace, over a 3-day weekend. Call ☎ **407/824-4321** for details. Early October.
- **Oktoberfest,** Miami. They close the streets for this German beer and food festival thrown by the Mozart Stub Restaurant in Coral Gables. You'll find loads of great music and dancing at this wild party. Call owner Harald Neuweg at ☎ **305/446-1600** to find out where and when. See www.mozartstub.com for more details.
- ✪ **Fantasy Fest,** Key West. It might feel as if the rest of the world is joining you if you're in Key West for this insane, world-famous Halloween festival, Florida's version of Mardi Gras. Crazy costumes, wild parades, and even more colorful revelers gather for an opportunity to do things Mom said not to do. Definitely leave the kids at home! Call ☎ **305/296-1817** for information. Last week of October.

- ⊙ **Goombay Festival,** Key West. Sample Caribbean dishes and purchase art and ethnic clothing in this celebration with a Jamaican flair that coincides with Fantasy Fest (see above).
- • **SunTrust Sunday Jazz Brunch at Riverwalk,** Fort Lauderdale. This year-long music and food gig kicks off on the banks of the historic New River, promising leisurely afternoons of great live jazz and tasty food in the company of fellow music lovers. Call ☎ **954/761-5363** for details. First Sunday of every month.
- ⊛ **Fort Lauderdale International Boat Show.** Your chance to meet fellow boating enthusiasts and look over more than 1,400 boats and every imaginable variety of marine paraphernalia. Call ☎ **800/940-7642** for details. Late October to early November.
- • **Clearwater Jazz Holiday,** Clearwater. Top jazz musicians play for 4 days and nights at bay-front Coachman Park in this free musical extravaganza. Call ☎ **813/363-7866** for schedule. Mid-October.
- ⊙ **Halloween Horror Nights,** Orlando. Universal Studios Florida transforms its studios and attractions for several weeks before and after Halloween, with haunted attractions, live bands, a psychopath's maze, special shows, and hundreds of ghouls and goblins roaming the studio streets. The studio essentially closes at dusk, reopening in a new macabre form a few hours later. Special admission is charged. Call ☎ **407/363-8000** for details.
- • **Guavaween,** Tampa. Ybor City's Latin-style Halloween celebration begins with the "Mama Guava Stumble," a wacky costume parade. All-night concerts from rock to reggae. For information, call ☎ **813/248-3712.** October 31.
- • **Amelia Heritage Festival,** Amelia Island. Civil War reenactments, tours of Fernandina Beach historic district, and more. Call ☎ **800/2-AMELIA.** Late October.
- ⊙ **John's Pass Seafood Festival,** Madeira Beach. Tons of fish, shrimp, crab, and other seafood go down the hatch at one of Florida's largest seafood festivals. Call ☎ **813/391-7373.** Last weekend in October.
- ⊙ **Jacksonville Jazz Festival.** This free weeklong, nonstop music event in Metropolitan Park features major artists. Call ☎ **904/353-7770** for details. Late October or early November.

November

- • **Frank Brown International Songwriters' Festival,** Pensacola. Composers gather at the infamous Flora-Bama Lounge and other beach venues to perform their country-music hits. Call ☎ **850/492-4660** for information. First week in November.
- ⊙ **Florida Seafood Festival,** Apalachicola. Book a room at the Gibson Inn 5 years in advance of this huge chow-down in Florida's oystering capital. Call ☎ **850/653-9419** for details. First Saturday in November.
- • **Mum Festival,** Cypress Gardens. November's monthlong flower festival at Cypress Gardens features millions of mums, their colorful flowers displayed in beds, "blooming" gazebos, poodle baskets, and bonsais. Call ☎ **941/324-2111** for details.
- ⊙ **Walt Disney World Festival of the Masters,** Orlando. One of the largest art shows in the South takes place at Disney's Village Marketplace for 3 days, including the second weekend in November. The exhibition features top artists, photographers, and craftspeople—winners of juried shows throughout the country. Free admission. Call ☎ **407/824-4321** for details.
- ⊛ **Mercury Outboards Cheeca/Redbone Celebrity Tournament,** Islamorada, in the Upper Keys. Curt Gowdy from *American Sportsman* hosts this tournament,

whose proceeds go to finding a cure for cystic fibrosis. The likes of Wade Boggs, actor James B. Sikking, and Gen. Norman Schwartzkopf compete almost yearly. Call ☎ **305/664-2002** for details. This event is followed by the **George Bush Cheeca Lodge Bonefish Tournament.** Call ☎ **305/743-7000** for more information. Second and third weekends of November.

- **The Jiffy Lube Miami 300 weekend of NASCAR,** Miami. Here's more world-class racing at the recently constructed 344-acre motor sports complex. For information and tickets contact Homestead Motorsports Complex, One Speedway Blvd., Homestead (☎ **305/230-5200**). Mid-November.
- **Chili Cook-Off,** Miami. Sample some of the nation's best chili as the area's "hottest" restaurants compete for the glory of being the best. For details, call ☎ **305/441-6677.** Mid-November.
- **Blues Festival at Riverwalk,** Fort Lauderdale. Receive a blues infusion during this weekend-long festival that features several live music stages scattered throughout area clubs. You can buy individual event tickets, but a 3-day pass is definitely worthwhile. Call ☎ **954/489-3256** for more details. Mid-November.
- ✪ **White Party Week,** Miami. This weeklong AIDS fund-raiser begins with a series of events in Miami Beach nightclubs and leads up to the Sunday night gala, where Miami's gay community comes out to celebrate at the Renaissance mansion Vizcaya. Since this gala always sells out, make sure to buy your tickets as soon as they go on sale October 1. Call ☎ **305/759-6181** for details. Thanksgiving weekend.
- **Walt Disney World Doll and Teddy Bear Convention,** Orlando. The top doll and teddy-bear designers from around the world travel to WDW for this major November event. Call ☎ **407/824-4321** for details.
- ✪ **Fort Lauderdale International Film Festival.** Showcases 3 week's worth of international, independent, and student film competition winners. Also, don't forget about the star-studded parties hosted by the festival. Call ☎ **954/563-0500** for details. Mid-November.
- ✪ **Miami Book Fair International.** An event that draws hundreds of thousands of visitors, including foreign and domestic publishers and authors from around the world, with great lectures and readings by world-renowned authors. Call ☎ **305/237-3258.** Mid-November.
- ✪ **Daytona Beach Fall Speedway Spectacular.** Featuring the Annual Turkey Rod Run, this is the Southeast's largest combined car show and swap meet, with thousands of street rods and classic vehicles on display and for sale. It takes place at the International Speedway. Call ☎ **904/255-7355** for details. Thanksgiving weekend.
- **Blue Angels Homecoming Air Show,** Pensacola. World-famous navy pilots do their aerial acrobatics just 100 yards off the beach. Call ☎ **800/874-1234** or 850/452-2583 for information. Second weekend in November.
- **Sarasota French Film Festival,** Sarasota. Acclaimed French films, directors, and celebrities come for premiere screenings. For information, call ☎ **941/351-9010.** Second weekend in November.
- **Fort Myers Beach Sand Sculpting Contest,** Fort Myers Beach. Some 50,000 gather to sculpt or see the world's finest sand castles. Call ☎ **800/782-9283** or 941/463-6451. First weekend in November.
- **The Ramble,** Miami. Old-time Floridians love this yearly event at the Fairchild Tropical Gardens. Here you can buy antiques, exotic orchids, or vintage clothes. If you're not shopping, it's still worth strolling around the lush park where you

can learn about various botanical miracles. For more information, call ☎ 305/
667-1651. Mid-November.

- **Poinsettia Festival,** Cypress Gardens. A spectacular floral showcase of more than
40,000 red, white, and pink poinsettia blooms (including topiary reindeer) highlight this flower festival. This is actually one of the best ways to view the park.
Call ☎ 941/324-2111 for details. Late November to mid-January.

✪ **Jolly Holidays Dinner Shows,** Orlando. From late November to mid-
December these all-you-can-eat events are offered at the Contemporary Resort's
Fantasia Ballroom. A cast of more than 100 Disney characters, singers, and
dancers performs in an old-fashioned Christmas extravaganza. Call ☎ 407/
W-DISNEY for details and ticket prices.

December

✪ **Edison/Ford Winter Homes Holiday House,** Fort Myers. Thousands of lights
and Christmas music hail the holiday season. At the same time, candles create a
spectacular Luminary Trail along the full length of Sanibel Island's Periwinkle
Way. Call ☎ 941/275-1088 for information. First week of December.

- **Captiva Sea Kayak Classic,** Captiva Island. Sea kayaker and surf skiers from
around the nation depart from beach in front of 'Tween Waters Inn for a series
of races. Call ☎ 941/472-5161. First weekend in December.

- **JC Penney Mixed Team Golf Classic,** Tarpon Springs. Westin Innisbrook
Resort hosts mixed-gender teams of top pro golfers. Call ☎ 813/942-2000, ext.
5393. First week in December.

- **Burger King Classic Half-Marathon and Hooter's 5K Run,** Orlando. This
annual race, early in December, takes place in downtown Orlando, beginning at
8am at Church Street Market, 200 S. Orange Ave. Anyone can participate. An
entry fee is charged. The event kicks off the Citrus Bowl season. Call ☎ 407/
423-2476 for information.

- **Winterfest Boat Parade,** Fort Lauderdale. A hundred boats decorated with
lights cruise up the Intracoastal Waterway from Port Everglades to Lake Santa
Barbara. There's no better way to get into the Christmas spirit. Call ☎ 954/
767-0686 for details. Second weekend in December.

- **City Link Music Fest,** Fort Lauderdale. The largest 1-night music fest in the
state of Florida. More than 100 local bands play jazz, blues, and rock at different
nightclubs throughout Fort Lauderdale. Call ☎ 954/356-4943 for details. Mid-
December.

✪ **Grand Illumination Ceremony,** St. Augustine. A torchlight procession from
Government House through the Spanish Quarter. Kicks off a month of
Christmas festivities: reenactments of British colonial customs, encampments,
18th-century music, crafts demonstrations, cannon firings, caroling, an 18th-
century bazaar, a performance of Handel's *Messiah,* parade, and more. Call
☎ 800/OLD-CITY for details. First Saturday in December.

✪ **Christmas at Walt Disney World,** Orlando. Main Street is lavishly decked out
with lights, holly, 80-foot tree, and carolers greet visitors. Resorts offer special
embellishments and entertainment, including Mickey's Very Merry Christmas
Party, an after-dark ticketed event ($25). Magic Kingdom has traditional
Christmas parade and breathtaking fireworks display. Candlelight procession at
Epcot features hundreds of candle-holding carolers, a celebrity narrator telling
the Christmas story, and a 450-voice choir. Call ☎ 407/824-4321 for events, or
407/934-7639 to inquire about hotel/events packages. Most of December.

- **Christmas at Sea World,** Orlando. Sea World features a special Shamu show and a luau show called *Christmas in Hawaii.* The 400-foot sky tower is lit like a Christmas tree nightly. Call ☎ 407/351-3600 for details.
- **World Karting Association Enduro World Championships,** Daytona. The biggest go-carting event in the country takes place between Christmas and New Year's at the Daytona International Speedway. Call ☎ 904/253-7223 for details.
- **Annual Tour of Homes,** Boca Raton. Exclusive mansions in Old Floresta open their doors to visitors (thanks to a little arm twisting on the part of the Boca Raton Historical Society). Space is limited, so be sure to call ☎ 561/395-6766 and reserve early. End of December or January.
- **King Mango Strut,** Coconut Grove, Miami. This fun-filled march encourages everyone to wear wacky costumes and join the floats in a spoof of the King Orange Jamboree Parade, held the following night. Runs from Commodore Plaza to Peacock Park in Coconut Grove. Comedians and musical entertainment follow in the park. Call ☎ 305/444-7270 for details. December 30.
- **Walt Disney World New Year's Eve Celebration,** Orlando. For 1 night the Magic Kingdom is open until 2am for a massive fireworks exhibition. Other New Year's festivities in the WDW parks include a big bash at Pleasure Island featuring music headliners, a special *Hoop-Dee-Doo Musical Revue* show, and guest performances by well-known musical groups at Disney-MGM Studios and Epcot. Call ☎ 407/824-4321 for details.
- ✪ **Citrus Bowl Parade,** Orlando. On an annually selected date in late December, the parade features lavish floats and high school bands for a nationally televised event. Reserved seats in the bleachers are $12. Call ☎ 407/423-2476 for details.
- **CompUSA Florida Citrus Bowl New Year's,** Orlando. The official New Year's Eve celebration of the CompUSA Florida Citrus Bowl takes place at Sea World. Events include headliner concerts, a laser and fireworks spectacular, a countdown to midnight, and special shows throughout the park. Admission is charged. Call ☎ 407/423-2476 for details.
- ✪ **King Orange Jamboree Parade,** Miami. The world's largest nighttime parade is followed by a long night of festivities leading up to the Orange Bowl football game (see January listing, above). Runs along Biscayne Boulevard. For information and tickets (which cost $7.50 to $13), contact the Greater Miami Convention and Visitors Bureau at ☎ 305/539-3063. Usually December 31.

4　Health & Insurance

Florida doesn't present any unusual health hazards for most people. Folks with certain medical conditions such as liver disease, diabetes, and stomach ailments, however, should avoid eating raw **oysters,** which can carry a natural bacterium linked to severe diarrhea, vomiting, and even fatal blood poisoning. Cooking kills the bacteria, so if in doubt, order your oysters steamed, broiled, or fried.

Florida has millions of **mosquitoes** and invisible biting **sand flies** (known as "no-see-ums"), especially in the coastal and marshy areas. Fortunately, neither insect carries malaria or other diseases. Keep these pests at bay with a good insect repellent.

It's especially important to protect yourself against **sunburn.** Don't underestimate the strength of the sun's rays down here, even in the middle of winter. Limit the amount of time you spend in the sun, especially during the first couple of days of your trip and always from 11am to 2pm. Use a sunscreen with a high protection factor and apply it liberally. And children need more protection from the sun than adults do.

Pack any **prescription medications** you need to take in your carry-on luggage. Also bring along copies of your prescriptions in case you lose your pills or run out.

If you have a serious condition or allergy, consider wearing a Medic Alert identification bracelet; contact the **Medic Alert Foundation,** P.O. Box 1009, Turlock, CA 95381-1009 (☎ **800/432-5378**). If you have dental problems, a nationwide referral service known as **1-800-DENTIST** (☎ **800/336-8478**) will give you the name of a nearby dentist or clinic.

INSURANCE   Many travelers buy insurance policies providing health and accident, trip-cancellation and -interruption, and lost-luggage protection. The coverage you should consider will depend on how you're getting to Florida and how much protection is already contained in your existing health insurance or other policies. Some credit- and charge-card companies may insure you against travel accidents if you buy plane, train, or bus tickets with their cards. Before purchasing additional insurance, read your policies and agreements over carefully. Call your insurers or credit/charge-card companies if you have any questions.

Here are some American firms offering travel insurance:

Worldwide Assistance (☎ 800/821-2828 or 202/347-2025); **Travel Guard International** (☎ 800/782-5151 or 715/345-0505); **Access America** (☎ 800/284-8300 or 804/285-3300); or **Mutual of Omaha** (☎ 800/228-9792). The **Divers Alert Network (DAN)** (☎ 800/446-2671 or 919/684-2948) insures scuba divers.

5 Tips for Travelers with Special Needs

FOR TRAVELERS WITH DISABILITIES   **Walt Disney World** and **Universal Studios** do everything possible to facilitate disabled guests. Disney's many services are detailed in the *Guidebook for Guests with Disabilities.* To obtain a free copy, contact Guest Letters, P.O. Box 10040, Lake Buena Vista, FL 32830-0040 (☎ **407/824-4321**). For information about Universal Studios, CityWalk, and Islands of Adventure, contact Universal Studios Florida, 1000 Universal Studios Dr., Orlando, FL 32816 (☎ **407/393-8080**).

A free copy of the *Florida Planning Companion for People with Disabilities* is available from the **Florida Governor's Alliance,** 345 S. Magnolia Dr., Suite D-11, Tallahassee, FL 32301 (☎ **850/487-2223** or 850/487-2222 TTD).

Nationwide resources include **Mobility International USA** (☎ **503/343-1284**), which offers its members travel-accessibility information and has many interesting travel programs for people with disabilities; the **Travel Information Service** (☎ **215/456-9600**); **AccessAbility Travel** (☎ **800/645-0001** or 617/661-9200); and the **Society for the Advancement of Travel for the Handicapped** (☎ **212/447-7284**). In addition, **Twin Peaks Press,** P.O. Box 129, Vancouver, WA 98666 (☎ **360/694-2462**), publishes travel-related books for people with disabilities.

Companies offering tours for those with physical or mental disabilities include **Accessible Journeys** (☎ **800/TINGLES** or 610/521-0339); **Flying Wheels Travel** (☎ **800/535-6790** or 507/451-5005); **The Guided Tour** (☎ **215/782-1370**); and **Wilderness Inquiry** (☎ **800/728-0719** or 612/379-3858).

In addition, both **Amtrak** (☎ **800/USA-RAIL;** www.amtrak.com) and **Greyhound** (☎ **800/752-4841;** www.greyhound.com) offer special fares and services for travelers with disabilities. Call at least a week in advance of your trip for details.

The **National Park Service** issues free "Golden Access Passports," which waive admission fees into national parks, forests, and wildlife refuges for a disabled person and a companion. Get them at park entrances.

FOR SENIORS   With one of the largest retired populations of any state, Florida offers a wide array of activities and benefits for senior citizens. Don't be shy about asking for discounts, but always carry some kind of identification, such as a driver's license, that shows your date of birth.

Also, mention the fact that you're a senior citizen when you first make your travel reservations. For example, both **Amtrak** (☎ **800/USA-RAIL;** www.amtrak.com) and **Greyhound** (☎ **800/752-4841;** www.greyhound.com) offer discounts to persons over 62. And many hotels offer seniors discounts, including the **Choice Hotels** (Clarion Hotels, Quality Inns, Comfort Inns, Sleep Inns, Econo Lodges, Friendship Inns, and Rodeway Inns), which give 30% off their published rates to anyone over 50, provided you book your room through their nationwide toll-free reservations numbers (that is, not directly with the hotels or through a travel agent).

Members of the **American Association of Retired Persons (AARP),** 601 E St. NW, Washington, DC 22049 (☎ **800/424-3410** or 202/434-2277), get discounts not only on hotels but on airfares and car rentals, too.

The **National Park Service** issues "Golden Access Passports," admitting senior citizens, or a disabled person and companion into a national park, forest, or wildlife refuge for free. Buy them at park entrances.

Other helpful organizations include the nonprofit **National Council of Senior Citizens,** 1331 F St. NW, Washington, DC 20004 (☎ **202/347-8800**), part of whose magazine is devoted to travel tips. **Mature Outlook,** 6001 N. Clark St., Chicago, IL 60660 (☎ **800/336-6330**), offers discounts at ITC-member hotels and savings on selected auto rentals and restaurants. **Golden Companions,** P.O. Box 5249, Reno, NV 89513 (☎ **702/324-2227**), helps travelers 45-plus find compatible companions through a personal voice mailbox service. Contact them for more information.

Companies specializing in seniors travel include **Grand Circle Travel,** 347 Congress St., Suite 3A, Boston, MA 02210 (☎ **800/221-2610** or 617/350-7500); and **SAGA International Holidays,** 222 Berkeley St., Boston, MA 02115 (☎ **800/ 343-0273**).

FOR FAMILIES   Florida is a great family destination, with most of its hotels and restaurants willing and eager to cater to families traveling with children. Many hotels and motels let children 17 and under stay free in their parents' room (be sure to ask when you reserve).

At the beaches, it's the exception rather than the rule for a resort not to have a children's activities program (some will even mind the youngsters while the parents enjoy a night off!). Even if they don't have a children's program of their own, most will arrange baby-sitting services.

If you call ahead before dining out, you'll see that most restaurants have some facilities for children, such as booster chairs and low-priced kids' menus.

FOR STUDENTS   It's worth your while to bring along your valid high school or college identification. Presenting it can open the door to discounted admission to museums and other attractions. And remember, alcoholic beverages cannot be sold in Florida to anyone who is under 21, so if you're eligible and intend to imbibe, bring your driver's license or another valid photo identification showing your date of birth.

FOR GAY & LESBIAN TRAVELERS   According to the editors of *Out and About,* a gay and lesbian newsletter, Miami's **South Beach** is the "hippest, hottest, most happening gay travel destination in the world." For many years that could also be said of **Key West,** which still is one of the country's most popular destinations for gays.

The popularity of **Orlando** with gay and lesbian travelers is highlighted with Gay Weekend in early June, which draws as many as 40,000 participants and includes events at Disney World, Universal Studios, and Sea World. **Universal City Travel**

> ## ❷ Did You Know?
>
> - Ponce de León, the Spanish conquistador who discovered Florida in 1513, had earlier sailed with Columbus.
> - Movie star Burt Reynolds played defensive back for Florida State University's Seminoles football team.
> - Pres. Teddy Roosevelt once fought all day to land a 30-foot manta ray at Sanibel Island. It took some 50 steel-jacketed bullets to kill the huge "devil-fish."
> - Although it looks like a marsh, the Everglades in reality is a river some 40 miles wide and 6 inches deep.
> - The 800 buildings in Miami Beach's Art Deco District were the first 20th-century structures to be included in the National Register of Historic Places.
> - The old Tarzan movies starring Johnny Weissmuller were filmed at Wakulla Springs, near Tallahassee.
> - Now surviving only in Florida, manatees were once common from the Carolinas to Texas.

(☎ 800/224-3838), offers a "Gay Weekend" tour package including tickets to Universal Studios, Sea World, and Church Street Station. For information about events for that weekend, or throughout the year, contact the **Gay & Lesbian Community Services of Central Florida,** 714 E. Colonial Dr., Orlando, FL 32804 (☎ 407/425-4527). You can get information on the Worldwide Web at www.gayday.com.

Florida is not without its intolerant contingent, but there are active gay and lesbian communities in most other cities here.

The **International Gay Travel Association (IGTA),** P.O. Box 4974, Key West, FL 33041 (☎ 800/448-8550, or 305/292-0217 for voice mailbox), links travelers with the appropriate gay-friendly service organization or tour specialist. Contact the IGTA for a list of its member agencies, who will be tied into IGTA's information resources.

In addition to its editor's choices, *Out and About,* 8 W. 19th St., Suite 401, New York, NY 10011 (☎ 800/929-2268), profiles the best gay or gay-friendly hotels, gyms, clubs, and other places and destinations throughout the world. *Our World,* 1104 N. Nova Rd., Suite 251, Daytona Beach, FL 32117 (☎ 904/441-5367), is a magazine devoted to options and bargains for gay and lesbian travel worldwide.

6 Getting There

BY PLANE

Many major domestic airlines fly to and from Florida, including **American** (☎ 800/433-7300), **Continental** (☎ 800/525-0280), **Delta** (☎ 800/221-1212), **Northwest** (☎ 800/225-2525), **TWA** (☎ 800/221-2000), **United** (☎ 800/241-6522), and **US Airways** (☎ 800/428-4322).

Several so-called no-frills airlines—low fares but no meals or other amenities—fly to Florida. The biggest, best, and most reliable is ✪ **Southwest Airlines** (☎ 800/435-9792), which has flights from many U.S. cities to Fort Lauderdale, Jacksonville, Orlando, and Tampa. An arm of the popular cruise line, **Carnival Air** (☎ 800/824-7386) flies from New York and Washington, D.C. to Fort Lauderdale. **AirTran**

(☎ 800/AIR-TRAN) flies from several Northeast, Midwest, and Southern cities to its hub in Orlando and several other Florida cities.

Others flying to Florida include **Delta Express,** a branch of Delta Airlines ☎ 800/ 325-5205); **Eastwind** (☎ 800/644-3592); **Kiwi International** (☎ 800/538-5494); **MetroJet,** an arm of U.S. Airways (☎ 800/428-4322); **Midway** (☎ 800/ 44-MIDWAY); **Midwest Express** (☎ 800/452-2022); **Pan Am** (☎ 800/359-7262); **Spirit** (☎ 800/722-7117); **SunJet** (☎ 800/478-6538); **Tower Air** (☎ 800/ 348-6937); and **Vanguard** (☎ 800/826-4827).

There's no shortage of **discounted and promotional fares** to Florida. November, December, and January often see fare wars that can result in savings of 50% or more. Watch for advertisements in your local newspaper and on TV, or call the airlines.

Ask the airlines for their lowest fares, and ask if it's cheaper to book in advance, fly in midweek, or stay over a Saturday night. Don't stop at the 7-day advance purchase; ask how much the 14- and 30-day plans cost. Decide when you want to go before you call, since many of the best deals are nonrefundable.

Many **charter flights** go to Florida, especially during the winter season. They cost less than regularly scheduled flights, but they are very complicated. It's best to go to a good travel agent and ask him or her to find one for you and to explain the problems as well as the advantages.

You might also get a low fare by calling a "consolidator" such as **Cheap Tickets** (☎ 800/377-1000 or 212/570-1179); **Smart Traveller** (☎ 800/448-3338 or 305/448-3338); **TFI Tours International** (☎ 800/745-8000 or 212/736-1140); **1-800-FLY-CHEAP** (www.websrus.com/flycheap); and **1-800-FLY-4-LESS** (e-mail fly4less@juno.com). These firms serve as clearinghouses for unused seats. A travel agent can tell you more about consolidators, and they will shop among them to find their best deals. "Rebators" such as **Travel Avenue** (☎ 800/333-3335 or 312/ 876-1116) refund part of their commissions to you. Look in your local newspaper's Sunday travel section for rebators' usually tiny advertisements.

Another possibility is travel clubs such as **Moment's Notice** (☎ 718/234-6295) and **Sears Discount Travel Club** (☎ 800/433-9383, or 800/255-1487 to join), which supply unsold tickets at discounted prices. You pay an annual membership fee to get the club's hot line number. Of course, you're limited to what's available, so you have to be flexible.

If you live overseas, see "Getting to & Around the U.S.," in chapter 3.

BY CAR

Florida is reached by **I-95** along the east coast, **I-75** from the central states, and **I-10** from the west. **Florida's Turnpike,** a toll road, links Orlando, West Palm Beach, Fort Lauderdale, and Miami (it's a shortcut from Wildwood on I-75 north of Orlando to Miami). **I-4** cuts across the state from Cape Canaveral through Orlando to Tampa.

See "Getting Around," below, for more information about driving in Florida and the car-rental firms operating here.

If you're a member, your local branch of the **American Automobile Association** **(AAA)** will provide a free trip-routing plan. AAA also has nationwide emergency road service (☎ 800/AAA-HELP).

BY TRAIN

Amtrak (☎ 800/USA-RAIL; www.amtrak.com) offers train service to Florida from both the East and West coasts. It takes some 26 hours from New York to Miami, 68 hours from Los Angeles to Miami, and Amtrak's fares aren't much less than many deals offered by the airlines.

Amtrak's *Silver Meteor* and *Silver Star* each run twice daily between New York and either Miami or Tampa, with intermediate stops along the East Coast and in Florida. Amtrak's Thruway Bus Connections are available from the Fort Lauderdale Amtrak station and Miami International Airport to Key West, and from Tampa to St. Petersburg, Treasure Island, Clearwater, Bradenton, Sarasota, and Fort Myers. Depending on date of travel, the round-trip fare between New York and Miami for midweek travel ranges from about $150 to $400. The highest fares are between mid-June and mid-August.

From the West Coast, the *Sunset Limited* runs three times weekly between Los Angeles and Orlando. It stops in Pensacola, Crestview (Fort Walton Beach and Destin), Chipley (Panama City Beach), and Tallahassee. Round-trip coach fares between Los Angeles and Miami range from about $300 in low season to $550 in summer. Sleeping accommodations are available for an extra charge.

If you intend to stop off along the way, you can save money with Amtrak's **Explore America** (or All Aboard America) fares, which are based on three regions of the country. At press time, you could stop three times in the eastern states for about $318 in summer, $258 during the off-season.

Amtrak's **Auto Train** runs daily from Lorton, Virginia (12 miles south of Washington, D.C.), to Sanford, Florida (just northeast of Orlando). You ride in a coach while your car is secured in an enclosed vehicle carrier. Round-trip fares at press time ranged from $110 to $170 for each passenger, plus $220 for your car. You should make your train reservations as far in advance as possible.

7 Package Deals

Travel agents offer hundreds of package tour options to the Sunshine State. Quite often a package tour will result in savings not just on airfares but on hotels and other activities as well. You pay one price for a package that varies from one tour operator to the next. Airfare, transfers, and accommodations are always covered, and sometimes meals and specific activities are thrown in. The specifics vary a great deal, so consult your travel agent to find out the best deals at the time you want to travel.

There are some drawbacks: The least expensive tours may put you up at a bottom-end hotel. And since the lower costs depend on volume, some more expensive tours could send you to a large, impersonal property. And since the tour prices are based on double occupancy, the single traveler is almost invariably penalized.

Ask your travel agent to find the best package tours to Florida. Many are offered by subsidiaries of the major airlines, including American, Continental, Delta, Northwest, and TWA. **American Express** (☎ 800/241-1700) also has several tours available.

In Orlando, the **Walt Disney World Central Reservations Office** (☎ 407/W-DISNEY) and **Universal City Travel Co.** (☎ 800/224-3838) both have numerous packages including air, hotel, and discounted admissions.

Premier Cruise Lines (☎ 800/726-5678) and **Disney Cruise Line** (☎ 407/939-7787) offer 3- and 4-night luxury ocean cruises to The Bahamas in conjunction with 3- or 4-day Orlando theme-park package vacations. Cruises depart from and return to Port Canaveral, 45 minutes east of Walt Disney World.

In addition to these all-inclusive tours, many Florida hotels and resorts and even some motels offer **golf and tennis packages,** which bundle the cost of room, greens and court fees, and sometimes equipment into one price. These deals usually don't include airfare, but they do represent savings over paying for the room and golf or tennis separately. See the accommodations sections in the following chapters for hostelries offering special packages to their guests.

8 Getting Around

Having a car is the best and easiest way to see Florida's sights, or just to get to and from the beach. Public transportation is available only in the larger metropolitan areas, and even there it may provide infrequent or even inadequate service. When it comes to getting from one city to another, cars and planes are the ways to go.

BY CAR Jacksonville is about 350 miles north of Miami and 500 miles north of Key West, so don't underestimate how long it will take you to drive all the way down the state. The speed limit is either 65 m.p.h. or 70 m.p.h. on the rural interstate highways, so you can make good time between cities. Not so on U.S. 1, U.S. 17, U.S. 19, U.S. 41, and U.S. 301; although most have four lanes, these older highways tend to be heavily congested, especially in built-up areas.

Every major car-rental company is represented here, including **Alamo** (☎ 800/ 327-9633), **Avis** (☎ 800/331-1212), **Budget** (☎ 800/527-0700), **Dollar** (☎ 800/ 800-4000), **Enterprise** (☎ 800/325-8007), **Hertz** (☎ 800/654-3131), **National** (☎ 800/227-7368), **Thrifty** (☎ 800/367-2277), and **Value** (☎ 800/GO-VALUE).

If you decide to rent a car, shop around and ask a lot of questions; the rental firms certainly aren't going to tell you how to save money. You may have to try different dates, different pickup and drop-off points, and different discount offers yourself to find the best deal. It changes constantly. Also, if you're a member of any organization (AARP or AAA, for example), check to see if you're entitled to discounts.

Be prepared to have local taxes of 10% or more added to your rental bill, plus $1.05 a day state use taxes.

Most of the companies pad their profits by selling loss-damage waiver (LDW) insurance. You may already be covered by your insurance carrier and credit- or charge-card companies, so check with them before succumbing to the hard sell. Also, the rental companies will offer to refill your gas tank at "competitive" prices when you return, but fuel usually is less expensive in town.

Most also require a minimum age, ranging from 19 to 25, and some also set maximum ages. Others deny cars to anyone with a bad driving record. Ask about rental requirements and restrictions when you book to avoid problems later. You must have a valid credit card to rent a vehicle.

Many packages are available that include airfare, accommodations, and a rental car with unlimited mileage. Compare these prices with the cost of booking airline tickets and renting a car separately to see if these offers are good deals.

BY PLANE Most major Florida cities are connected by both the major commuter airlines (see "Getting There," above) and smaller intrastate airlines such as **Gulf Stream International** (☎ **800/992-8532**) which has an in-state network; **Cape Air** (☎ **800/352-0714**), which flies between Key West, Fort Myers, and Naples; and **Sky America** (☎ **800/368-2307**), which links Key West to St. Petersburg and Sarasota. Fares for these short hops tend to be reasonable.

BY TRAIN You'll find that train travel from destination to destination isn't terribly feasible in Florida, and it's not a great deal less expensive than flying. See "Getting There," above, for Florida towns served by **Amtrak** (☎ **800/USA-RAIL;** www. amtrak.com).

9 The Active Vacation Planner

Florida will keep active vacationers very busy. Bird watching, boating and sailing, camping, canoeing and kayaking, fishing, golfing, tennis—you name it, the Sunshine

State has it. In fact, you'll find them almost everywhere you go. Of course, beach lovers and water sports enthusiasts can indulge their passions almost anywhere along the state's lengthy coastlines. Merely head east or west, and you'll easily find plenty to do—or viewed another way, Florida's multitudinous water-sports operators will find you.

These and other activities are described in the outdoor activities sections of the following chapters, but here's a brief overview of some of best places to move your muscles, with tips on how to get more detailed information.

The **Florida Sports Foundation,** 1319 Thomaswood Dr., Tallahassee, FL 32312 (☎ 850/488-8347), publishes free brochures, calendars, schedules, and guides to outdoor pursuits and spectator sports throughout Florida. I've noted some of its specific publications in the sections below.

For excellent color maps of state parks, campgrounds, canoe trails, aquatic preserves, caverns, and more, contact the **Florida Department of Environmental Protection,** Office of Communications, 3900 Commonwealth Blvd., Tallahassee, FL 32399 (☎ 850/488-6327). Some of the department's publications are mentioned below.

ACTIVITIES A TO Z

BICYCLING & IN-LINE SKATING   Florida's relatively flat terrain makes it ideal for riding bikes and skating on blades. You can bike right into the **Everglades National Park** along the 38-mile Main Park Road, for example, and bike or skate from St. Petersburg to Tarpon Springs on the 47-mile converted railroad bed known as the **Pinellas Trail.** Many towns and cities have designated routes for cyclists, skaters, joggers, and walkers, such as the paved pathways running the length of **Sanibel Island,** the lovely Bayshore Boulevard in **Tampa,** and the bike lanes from downtown **Sarasota** out to St. Armands, Lido, and Longboat keys. We've detailed all the many options in the following chapters.

Florida Outback Bike & Boat Tours (☎ 888/269-1169 or 407/518-9311) has biking and kayaking excursions to the Everglades. The national companies **Vermont Bicycle Touring** (☎ 800/537-3850 or 802/453-4811) and **Backroads Bicycle Touring** (☎ 800/462-2848 or 510/527-1555; www.backroads.com) sometimes offer Florida bike tours for cyclists of all fitness levels.

BIRD WATCHING   With hundreds of both land- and sea-based species, Florida is one of America's best places for bird watching. We've picked the best places in chapter 1, but birds are everywhere in Florida—if you're not careful, pelicans will even steal your picnic lunch on the historic **Naples Pier.** The **J. N. "Ding" Darling National Wildlife Refuge** is great for watching, and it shares Sanibel Island with luxury resorts and fine restaurants.

The Florida Audubon Society manages four exceptional sites: **Corkscrew Swamp Sanctuary** near Naples, **Madalyn Baldwin Center for Birds of Prey** in Maitland, **Turkey Creek Wildlife Sanctuary** in Palm Bay, and **Sabal Point Wildlife Sanctuary** on the Wekiva River in Central Florida.

Many of the state's wildlife preserves have gift shops that carry books about Florida's birds, including the *Florida Wildlife Viewing Guide,* in which authors Susan Cerulean and Ann Morrow profile 96 great parks, refuges, and preserves throughout the state.

BOATING & SAILING   With some 1,350 miles of shoreline, it's not surprising that Florida is a boating and sailing mecca. In fact, you won't be near the water very long before you see flyers and other advertisements for rental boats and for cruises on sailboats. Many of them are mentioned in the following chapters.

The Moorings, the worldwide sailboat charter company, has its headquarters in Clearwater and its Florida yacht base nearby in St. Petersburg (☎ **800/437-7880** or 813/530-5424; www.moorings.com). From St. Pete, experienced sailors can take its bareboats as far as the Keys and the Dry Tortugas, out in the Gulf of Mexico.

Key West has gained prominence as a world sailing capital. Yachting magazine sponsors the largest winter regatta in America here each January, and smaller events take place regularly.

Even if you've never hauled on a halyard, you can learn the art of sailing at **Steve and Doris Colgate's Offshore Sailing School** headquartered at the South Seas Plantation Resort & Yacht Harbour on Captiva Island, and at the prestigious **Annapolis Sailing School,** which has bases in St. Petersburg and on Marathon in the Keys.

If you don't want to do any real work on the water, you can rent a houseboat along the St. John's River in the northeastern part of the state; contact the **Hontoon Landing Marina,** 2317 River Ridge Rd., Deland (☎ **904/734-2474**). In the Everglades, houseboat rentals are available through the **Flamingo Lodge** (☎ **800/ 600-3813,** 813/695-3101, or 305/253-2241). You might also try **Houseboat Vacations of the Florida Keys,** Mile Marker 85.9, Islamorada (☎ **305/664-4009**). Book everything well in advance.

The free *Florida Boater's Guide* has tips about safe boating in the state, available from the **Florida Marine Patrol,** 3900 Commonwealth Blvd., Tallahassee, FL 32399-3000 (☎ **850/488-5600**). The annual *Florida Cruising Directory* is a treasure trove of charts and tables, coast guard customs and regulations, locations of marinas, hotels, and resorts, marine products and services, and more—in magazine format. It's sold in bookstores and marinas all over the state.

CAMPING   Florida is literally dotted with RV parks (if you own such a vehicle, it's the least expensive way to spend your winters here). But for the best tent camping, look to Florida's national preserves and 110 state parks and recreation areas. Options range from luxury sites with hot-water showers and cable TV hookups to primitive island and beach camping with no facilities whatsoever.

Primitive camping in **St. Joseph Peninsula State Park** near Apalachicola, in fact, is a bird-watcher's dream, and you'll be on one of the nation's most magnificent beaches. Great, too, are the sands at **St. Andrews State Recreation Area** in Panama City Beach (with sites right beside the bay). Other top spots are **Caladesi Island State Park** off Clearwater, the remarkably preserved **Cayo Costa Island State Park** between Boca Grande and Captiva Island in Southwest Florida, **Canaveral National Seashore** near the Kennedy Space Center, **Anastasia State Recreation Area** in St. Augustine, **Fort Clinch State Park** on Amelia Island, and **Bill Baggs Cape Florida Recreation Area** on Key Biscayne in Miami. Down in the Keys, the ocean-side sites in **Long Key State Recreation Area** are about as nice it gets.

Many sites are accessible only by boat, such as the chickee huts (covered wooden platforms on stilts) in Everglades National Park and the backcountry sites in Caladesi Island State Park off Clearwater and **Collier Seminole State Park** near Marco Island.

These all are popular campgrounds, so reservations are essential, especially in the high seasons. All of Florida's state parks take bookings up to 11 months in advance.

The **Florida Department of Environmental Protection,** Division of Recreation and Parks, Mail Station 535, 3900 Commonwealth Blvd., Tallahassee, FL 32399-3000 (☎ **850/488-9872**), publishes an annual guide of tent and RV sites in Florida's state parks and recreation areas. For private campgrounds, the **Florida Association of RV Parks & Campgrounds,** 1340 Vickers Dr., Tallahassee, FL 32303 (☎ **850/ 562-7151;** fax 850/562-7179), issues an annual *Florida Camping Directory* with locator maps and details about its member establishments throughout the state.

CANOEING & KAYAKING From picturesque rivers to sandy coastlines to gigantic Lake Okeechobee, from the marshes of northern and Central Florida to the mangroves of the southwest, canoers and kayakers have almost limitless options here. We've picked the best in chapter 1, which generally are exceptional trails through parks and wildlife preserves, including **Everglades National Park,** the **J. N. "Ding" Darling National Wildlife Refuge** on Sanibel Island, and **Collier Seminole State Park** and the **Briggs Nature Center,** both on the edge of the Everglades near Marco Island.

Another local favorite is **Myakka River State Park** near Sarasota, Florida's largest state park with some 28,000 acres of pure backcountry.

According to the Florida state legislature, however, the state's official "Canoe Capital" is the Panhandle town of **Milton,** on U.S. 90 near Pensacola. Up there, the Blackwater River, Coldwater River, Sweetwater Creek, and Juniper Creek are perfect for tubing, rafting, and paddleboating as well as canoeing and kayaking.

Many conservation groups throughout the state offer half-day, day, and overnight canoe trips. For example, **The Conservancy of Naples** (☎ 941/262-0304) has a popular series of moonlight canoe trips through the mangroves, among other programs.

Based during the winter at Everglades City, on the park's western border, **North American Canoe Tours** (☎ 941/695-4666 November through April, or 860/739-0791 May through October), offers 4-day and weeklong guided expeditions via canoe through the Everglades, as well as 1-day excursions. **Florida Outback Bike & Boat Tours** (☎ 888/269-1169 or 407/518-9311) also has kayaking excursions to the Everglades.

Some 36 creek and river trails, covering 950 miles altogether, are itemized in the excellent free **"Canoe Trails" booklet** published by the Florida Department of Environmental Protection, Office of Communications, 3900 Commonwealth Blvd., Tallahassee, FL 32399 (☎ 850/488-6327).

Specialized guidebooks include *A Canoeing and Kayaking Guide to the Streams of Florida: Volume 1, North Central Florida and Panhandle,* by Elizabeth F. Carter and John L. Eearch, and *Volume II, Central and Southern Peninsula,* by Lou Glaros and Dough Sphar. Both are published by Menasha Ridge Press.

FISHING In addition to the amberjack, bonito, grouper, mackerel, mahimahi, marlin, pompano, redfish, sailfish, snapper, snook, tarpon, tuna, and wahoo running offshore and in its inlets, Florida has countless miles of rivers and streams, plus some 30,000 lakes and springs stocked with more than 100 species of native freshwater fish. Indeed, Floridians seem to fish everywhere: off canal banks and old bridges, from fishing piers and fishing fleets. You'll even see them standing alongside the Tamiami Trail (U.S. 41) that cuts across the Everglades, one eye on their line, the other watching for alligators.

We picked the best places to fish in chapter 1, but nearly every marina in Florida harbors captains and their charter boats. You don't have to pay them a small fortune to try your luck, for most ports also have "party" boats that take groups out to sea. You'll have lots of company, but their rates are reasonable, they provide the gear and bait, and you won't need a fishing license.

Anglers age 16 and older need fishing licenses for any other kind of saltwater or freshwater fishing, including lobstering and spearfishing. Licenses are sold at bait and tackle shops.

The **Florida Department of Environmental Protection,** 3900 Commonwealth Blvd., Tallahassee, FL 32399-3000 (☎ 850/488-7326), publishes an annual *Fishing Lines,* a free magazine with a wealth of information about fishing in Florida, including regulations and licensing requirements. It also distributes free brochures with annual freshwater and saltwater limits. And the **Florida Sports Foundation** (see the introduction to this section) publishes *Florida Fishing*, another treasure trove of information.

HIKING   There are thousands of beautiful hiking trails in Florida. The ideal hiking months are October through April, when the weather is cool and dry and mosquitoes are less evident. Some trails are gentle and short; others are challenging—some trails in the Everglades require you to wade waist-deep in water!

If you're venturing into the backcountry, watch out for alligators, and never try to feed them or any other wild animal. You risk getting bitten (they can't tell the difference between the food and your hand). You're also upsetting the balance of nature, since animals fed by humans lose their ability to find their own food. Most Florida snakes are harmless, but a few have deadly bites, so avoid them all.

The **Florida Trail Association,** P.O. Box 13708, Gainesville, FL 32604 (☎ 800/ 343-1882 or 352/378-8823), maintains a large percentage of the public trails in the state and puts out an excellent book packed with maps, details, and color photos.

For a copy of *Florida Trails,* which outlines the many options, contact Visit Florida (see "Visitor Information," above). Another resource is *A Guide to Your National Scenic Trails,* Office of Greenways and Trails, Department of Environmental Protection, 3900 Commonwealth Blvd., Tallahassee, FL 32399 (☎ 850/ 487-4784). You can also contact the office of **National Forests in Florida,** Woodcrest Office Park, 325 John Knox Rd., Suite F-100, Tallahassee, FL 32303 (☎ 850/ 942-9300). And *Hiking Florida,* by M. Timothy O'Keefe (Falcon Press), details 132 hikes throughout the state, with maps and photos.

The **Florida Conservation Foundation,** 1191 Orange Ave., Winter Park, FL 32789 (☎ 407/644-5377), publishes information about the state's ecology, including *Common Florida Natural Areas,* an illustrated brochure explaining what you'll find in each ecosystem.

GOLF   Florida has more golf courses than any other state. We picked the best in chapter 1, but suffice it to say that you can play almost anytime and anywhere in Florida. The highest concentrations of excellent courses are in Southwest Florida around Naples and Fort Myers (some 1,000 holes!), the Orlando area (Disney alone has 99 holes open to the public), and in the Panhandle around Destin and Panama City Beach. And it's a rare town in Florida that doesn't have a municipal golf course—even Key West has 18 great holes.

Greens fees and other costs usually are much less at the municipal courses than at privately owned clubs. Whether public or private, greens fees tend to vary greatly depending on the time of year. You could pay $100 or more at a private course during the high season, but only half that when the tourists are gone. The fee structures vary so much that it's best to call ahead and ask. And you should always reserve a tee time as far in advance as possible.

You can learn the game or hone your strokes at several excellent golf schools. David Ledbetter has teaching facilities in Orlando and Naples. Fred Griffin is in charge of the Grand Cypress Academy of Golf at Grand Cypress Resort in Orlando. You'll find Jimmy Ballard's school at the Ocean Reef Club on Key Largo. The Westin Innisbrook Resort at Tarpon Springs has its Innisbrook Golf Institute, Amelia Island near Jacksonville is home to Amelia Island Plantation Golf School, and Saddlebrook Resort north of Tampa hosts the Arnold Palmer Golf Academy.

You can get information about most Florida courses, including current greens fees, and reserve tee times through **Tee Times USA,** P.O. Box 641, Flagler Beach, FL 32136

(☎ **800/374-8633,** 888/465-3567, or 904/439-0001; fax 904/439-0099). This company also publishes a vacation guide that includes many stay-and-play golf packages.

Fairways in the Sunshine, published by the **Florida Sports Foundation** (see the introduction to this section), lists every course in Florida. *Golfer's Guide* magazine publishes monthly editions covering most regions of Florida; it is available free in racks at the local visitor centers and in hotel lobbies, or you can contact the magazine at P.O. Box 5926, Hilton Head, SC 29938 (☎ **800/864-6101** or 803/842-7878; fax 803/842-5743; www.homes.com). Northwest Florida is covered by *Gulf Coast Tee Time,* published by Tee Time LLC, 3 W. Garden St., Pensacola, FL 32501 (☎ **888/ 520-4300** or 850/435-4858; fax 850/435-7383; www.teetimeweb.com).

You also can get more information from the **Professional Golfers' Association (PGA),** 100 Ave. of the Champions, Palm Beach Gardens, FL 33418 (☎ **407/ 624-8400**); or the **Ladies Professional Golf Association (LPGA),** 2570 Volusia Ave., Suite B, Daytona Beach, FL 32114 (☎ **904/254-8800**).

SCUBA DIVING & SNORKELING Divers love the Keys, where you can see magnificent formations of tree-sized elkhorn coral and giant brain coral, as well as colorful sea fans and dozens of other varieties, sharing space with 300 or more species of rainbow-hued fish. Reef diving is good all the way from Key Largo to Key West, with plenty of tour operators, outfitters, and dive shops along the way. Particularly worthy are **John Pennekamp Coral Reef State Park** at Key Largo and **Looe Key National Marine Sanctuary** off Big Pine Key. *Skin Diver* magazine picked Looe Key as the number-one dive spot in North America. Also, the clearest waters in which to view some of the 4,000 sunken ships along Florida's coast are in the Middle Keys and the waters between Key West and the Dry Tortugas. Snorkeling in the Keys is particularly fine between Islamorada and Marathon.

In Northwest Florida, the 100-fathom curve draws closer to the white, sandy Panhandle beaches than to any other spot on the Gulf of Mexico. It's too far north here for coral, but you can see brilliant-colored sponges, fish, and Timber Hole, an undersea "petrified forest" of sunken planes, ships, even a railroad car. And the battleship USS *Massachusetts* lies in 30 feet of water just 3 miles off Pensacola. Every beach town in Northwest Florida has dive shops to outfit, tour, or certify visitors.

In the Crystal River area, north of the St. Petersburg and Clearwater beaches, you can dive with the manatees as they bask in the warm spring waters of Kings Bay.

The "cave-diving capital of the world" is in northern Florida between High Springs and Branford. The two most renowned spots are in crystal-clear Ginnie Springs, on the Santa Fe River, and in Ichetucknee Springs State Park, a few miles farther north. The **Ginnie Springs Resort,** 7300 NE Ginnie Springs Rd., High Springs (☎ **800/ 874-8571** or 904/454-2202), is a 200-acre campsite park along the Santa Fe River with dive packages, canoe rentals, and other recreation. Underwater explorers have found artifacts from the native tribes that once inhabited the region around Ichetucknee, and topside explorers often sight limpkin, wood duck, otter, and beaver. This 2,241-acre state park also offers camping, nature trails, canoeing, and tubing. The **Steamboat Dive Inn,** U.S. 27 at U.S. 129, Branford, FL 32008 (☎ **904/ 935-DIVE**), on the Suwannee River, has its own on-site, full-service diving center with certified instructors for every level. Also in Branford, the **Branford Dive Center,** U.S. 27 and the Suwannee River, Branford, FL 32008 (☎ **904/935-1141**), offers guides, air, rentals, accessories, and instruction.

If you want to keep up with what's going on statewide, you can subscribe to *Florida Scuba News,* a monthly magazine published in Jacksonville (☎ **904/783-1610;**

www.scubanews.com). You might also want to pick up a specialized guidebook. Good ones include *Coral Reefs of Florida,* by Gilbert L. Voss (Pineapple Press), and *The Diver's Guide to Florida and the Florida Keys,* by Jim Stachowicz (Windward Publishing).

TENNIS   Sunshine and year-round playing make Florida a tennis paradise. There are some 7,700 places to play, from municipal courts to exclusive resorts. Even some of the municipal facilities—Cambier Park Tennis Center in Naples leaps to mind— are equal to those at expensive resorts, and they are either free or next to free.

If you can afford it, you can learn from the best in Florida. **Nick Bollettieri** has sports academies in Bradenton and at the Westin Innisbrook Resort in Tarpon Springs. The Saddlebrook Resort in Wesley Chapel north of Tampa is home to the **Phil Green Tennis Program.** Amateurs can hobnob with the superstars at **ATP Tour International Headquarters** in Ponte Vedra Beach, near Jacksonville. **Peter Burwash International** has a tennis program at Doral Golf Resort & Spa in Miami. And **Chris Evert, Robert Seguso, and Carling Basset** have their own center in Boca Raton.

Other top places to learn as well as play are **Amelia Island Plantation** on Amelia Island; **Colony Beach and Tennis Resort** on Longboat Key off Sarasota (which *Tennis* magazine picked as the number-two tennis resort in the nation); **Sanibel Harbour Resort & Spa** in Fort Myers, whose 5,500-seat stadium has hosted Davis Cup matches; **South Seas Plantation Resort & Yacht Harbour** on Captiva Island; **The Registry Resort** in Naples (it will have changed names by 1999); and **World Tennis Center Resort & Club** in Naples, where the World Tennis Academy is headed by renowned tennis psychologist and coach Roland Carlstedt.

ECOTOURS   If you don't want to do it yourself, some organizations offer excursions to observe Florida's flora and fauna and to have a little adventure while you're at it.

The Florida chapter of the **Nature Conservancy** has purchased and protects more than 700,000 acres of natural lands throughout Florida. Most of its properties are closed to the public, but you can pay small fees to go on its field trips, and you can participate in its preservation work parties for free. Both will give you a chance to learn about the state's ecosystems. For details, contact the Nature Conservancy, Florida Chapter, 222 S. Westmonte Dr., Suite 300, Altamonte Springs, FL 32714 (☎ **407/ 682-3664;** fax 407/682-3077; www.tnc.org).

The **Sierra Club,** America's oldest and largest grassroots environmental organization, offers exceptional ecoadventures through its Florida chapters. You can go canoeing or kayaking through the Everglades, hiking the Florida Trail in America's southernmost national forest, camping on a barrier island, or exploring the sinkhole phenomenon in north-central Florida. You do have to be a Sierra Club member, but you can join at the time of the trip. Contact the national office at Department J-319, P.O. Box 7959, San Francisco, CA 94120 (☎ **415/923-5653**), for a current outings magazine and local chapter contacts.

Soft ecoadventure experiences are available at **Silver Springs,** a 350-acre nature theme park near Ocala (☎ **800/234-7458** or 352/236-2121). It has been conducting ecotours since before the term was invented. You can take a sunrise breakfast cruise to photograph great blue herons, white-tail deer, and other wildlife; or you can take a "Jungle Cruise" or "Jeep Safari" to get a feeling of the ecosystem without getting your feet dirty.

10 Tips on Accommodations

Florida has a vast array of accommodations, from rock-bottom roadside motels to some of the nation's finest resorts. Whether you spend a pittance or a bundle depends on your budget and your tastes. To repeat a well-worn phrase, you can enjoy "champagne on a beer budget"—if you plan carefully.

The **Florida Hotel & Motel Association,** P.O. Box 1529, Tallahassee, FL 32302 (☎ 850/224-2888), publishes a directory listing all of its member establishments. This is a handy booklet to have if you're taking your animal along, since it tells which properties accept pets. For a copy, send a check for $2 if you live in the U.S., $4 if you live elsewhere. The association also has a free **reservation service** (☎ 800/847-4835) covering the entire state.

Inn Route, P.O. Box 6187, Palm Harbor, FL 34684 (☎ 800/524-1880 or 281/499-1374; fax 281/403-9335; www.florida-inns.com; e-mail: innroute@worldnet.att.net), publishes the *Inns of Florida,* which lists inns and bed-and-breakfasts throughout the state. Inn Route inspects each property, thus ensuring quality and cleanliness of its members.

At the inexpensive end, **Hostelling International/American Youth Hostels,** 733 15th St. NW, Suite 840, Washington, DC 20005 (☎ 800/444-6111 or 202/783-6161), offers low-cost accommodations in Miami Beach, Key West, Fort Lauderdale, and Orlando.

MONEY-SAVING TIPS

The rates quoted in this book are "rack" or "published" rates; that is, the highest regular rates charged by a hotel or motel. Not long ago the rack rate was what you paid, unless you were part of a tour group or had purchased a vacation package. Today most hotels give discounts to corporate travelers, government employees, senior citizens, automobile club members, active duty military personnel, and others.

Most hotels usually don't advertise these discounted rates or even volunteer them at the front desk, but you can take advantage of them by asking politely if there's a special rate which applies to you. One company that does advertise a major discount is **Choice Hotels** (see "For Seniors" under "Tips for Travelers with Special Needs," above).

Computerized reservations systems also have permitted many larger properties to adjust their rates on an almost daily basis, depending on how much business they anticipate having. Even if they don't officially reduce their rates, they may drop them rather than having beds go empty. Don't hesitate to ask if a less expensive rate is available on the days you plan on being there.

Most rack rates include commissions of 10% to 25% or more for travel agents, which many hotels will knock off if you make your own reservations and bargain a little.

Downtown hotels catering to business travelers during the week usually have big discounts on Friday and Saturday nights. If you're staying over a weekend in an off-beach city such as Tampa, always ask about a special rate or package deal. Weekend rates don't apply in the resort areas, nor in college towns like Tallahassee, but you should ask there about weekday or weeklong vacation packages.

Many Florida hotels and motels offer weekly rates, which as a general rule will knock off the price of 1 night if you stay for 7.

Most also have free self-parking, but fees can run up the cost at some downtown and beachfront hotels. We've indicated in the listings if a hotel or resort charges for parking; if no charge is given, parking is free. And many hotels jack up the price of long distance phone calls made from your room. Accordingly, always inquire about the costs of parking, and use a pay phone if the hotel tacks a hefty surcharge on calls.

CONDOS, HOMES & COTTAGES

It may seem at first impression that many Florida beaches are lined with great walls of high-rise condominium buildings. That's not much of an overstatement, for the state literally has thousands upon thousands of condo units. People actually live in many of them year-round, but others are for rent on a daily, weekly, or monthly basis. In addition, there are many private homes and cottages for rent throughout Florida.

Some of the resorts listed in this book actually are condo complexes operated as full-service hotels, but usually you'll have to without such hotel amenities as on-site restaurants, room service, and even daily maid service. On the other hand, almost every condo, home, and cottage has a fully equipped kitchen, and many have washers, dryers, and other such niceties of home, which means they can represent significant savings, especially if you're traveling with children or are sharing with another couple or family.

We have pointed out a few of the best condo complexes in the "Accommodations You Can Afford" sections of the following chapters, and we have named some of the reputable **real estate agencies** that have inventories of condos, private homes, and cottages to rent.

If you think a condo will meet your needs, your best bet is to contact the rental agencies well in advance and request a brochure describing all the properties they represent, and their rates.

FAST FACTS: Florida

American Express   There are a number of American Express offices in Florida. Call Cardmember Services (☎ **800/528-4800**) for the location nearest you.

Banks   Banks are usually open Monday to Friday from 9am to 3 or 4pm, and most have automated-teller machines (ATMs) for 24-hour banking. You won't have a problem finding a Cirrus or PLUS machine. Of the national banks, **First Union Bank** and **NationsBank** have offices throughout Florida. **Barnett** and **Sun** are the largest in-state banks.

Car Rentals   See "Getting Around," earlier in this chapter.

Climate   See "When to Go," earlier in this chapter.

Currency Exchange   See "Money" under "Preparing for Your Trip," in chapter 3.

Emergencies   Call **911** anywhere in the state to summon the police, the fire department, or an ambulance.

Liquor Laws   You must be 21 to purchase or consume alcohol in Florida. This law is strictly enforced, so if you look young, carry some photo identification that gives your date of birth. Minors can usually enter bars where food is served.

Newspapers/Magazines   Most cities of any size have a local daily paper, but the well-respected *Miami Herald* is generally available all over the state, with regional editions available in many areas.

Safety   Whenever you're traveling in an unfamiliar city, stay alert. Be aware of your immediate surroundings. Always lock your car doors and the trunk when your vehicle is unattended, and don't leave any valuables in sight. See "Safety" under "Preparing for Your Trip" in chapter 3 for more information.

Taxes   The Florida state sales tax is 6%. Many municipalities add 1% or more to that, and most levy a special tax on hotel and restaurant bills. See "Accommodations You Can Afford" in the following chapters for details.

Time   The Florida peninsula observes eastern standard time, but most of the Panhandle west of the Apalachicola River is on central standard time, 1 hour behind the rest of the state.

Tourist Information   See "Visitor Information," earlier in this chapter, for the tourist office serving the entire state. For local offices, which will have more detailed information on your particular destination, see "Orientation" or "Essentials" in the following chapters.

3 For Foreign Visitors

American fads, fashions, and television may have spread across the world so much that the United States may seem like familiar territory, but there are still many peculiarities and uniquely American situations that you likely will encounter while here. This chapter points out many of the differences that you may not expect, and explains some of the more confusing aspects of daily life in the United States.

1 Preparing for Your Trip

ENTRY REQUIREMENTS

DOCUMENT REGULATIONS Immigration laws have been a hot political issue in the United States in recent years, so it's wise to check at any U.S. embassy or consulate for current information and requirements. You can also plug into the U.S. State Department's Internet site at www.state.gov.

Canadians may enter the United States without passports or visas; you need only proof of residence.

The U.S. State Department has a **Visa Waiver Program** allowing citizens of the United Kingdom, Australia, New Zealand, Japan, and most western European countries to enter the United States without a visa for stays of up to 90 days. If you're from one of these countries, you will need only a valid passport and a round-trip air or cruise ticket in your possession upon arrival. Once here, you may then visit Mexico, Canada, Bermuda, and/or the Caribbean islands and return to the United States without needing a visa. Further information is available from any U.S. embassy or consulate.

If you're from any other country, you must have (1) a valid **passport** with an expiration date at least 6 months later than the scheduled end of your visit to the United States; and (2) a **tourist visa,** which may be obtained without charge from the nearest U.S. consulate.

To obtain a visa, submit a completed application form with a 1½-inch square photo and demonstrate binding ties to your residence abroad. If you cannot go in person, contact the nearest U.S. embassy or consulate for directions on applying by mail. Your travel agent or airline office may also be able to provide you with the visa application forms and instructions. The U.S. embassy or consulate where you apply will determine whether you receive a multiple- or single-entry visa and any restrictions regarding the length of your stay. This may take a few days or even weeks, so apply well in advance.

Foreign **driver's licenses** are recognized in Florida, but you may want to get an international driver's license if your home license is not written in English.

MEDICAL REQUIREMENTS   No inoculations are needed to enter the United States unless you are coming from, or have stopped over in, areas known to be suffering from epidemics, particularly cholera or yellow fever.

CUSTOMS REQUIREMENTS   Every adult visitor may bring in free of duty: 1 liter of wine or hard liquor; 200 cigarettes *or* 100 cigars (but no cigars made in Cuba) *or* 3 pounds of smoking tobacco; and $100 worth of gifts. You must spend at least 72 hours in the United States and must not have claimed the exemptions within the preceding 6 months. It is altogether forbidden to bring into the country foodstuffs (particularly cheese, fruit, cooked meats, and canned goods) and plants (vegetables, seeds, tropical plants, and so on). Foreign tourists may bring in or take out up to $10,000 in U.S. or foreign currency with no formalities; larger sums must be declared to Customs upon entering or leaving.

Penalties are severe for smuggling illegal narcotics into the United States, so if you have a disease requiring treatment with medications containing narcotics or drugs (especially those administered by syringe), carry a valid signed prescription from your physician to allay any suspicions that you are smuggling drugs.

INSURANCE   There is no national health system in the United States, and the cost of medical care here is extremely high; therefore, we strongly advise that you secure health insurance coverage before setting out. You may want to take out a comprehensive travel policy that covers sickness or injury costs (medical, surgical, and hospital), as well as loss or theft of your baggage, trip-cancellation costs, guarantee of bail in case you are arrested, and costs of accident, repatriation, or death. See "Health & Insurance" in chapter 2 for more information. Packages such as Europ Assistance in Europe are sold by automobile clubs and travel agencies at attractive rates. **Worldwide Assistance Services** (☎ **800/821-2828** or 202/347-2025) is the agent for Europ Assistance in the United States.

Canadians should check with their provincial health plan offices or call **Health-Canada** (☎ **613/957-3025**) to find out the extent of their coverage and what documentation and receipts they must take home in case they are treated in the United States.

MONEY

The U.S. monetary system has a decimal base: one American dollar ($1) = 100 cents (100¢). Notes come in $1 ("a buck"), $5, $10, $20, $50, and $100 denominations (the last two are not welcome when paying for small purchases and are not accepted in taxis or at subway ticket booths). There are also $2 bills, but you are unlikely to see one since Americans consider them to be unlucky. There are six denominations of coins: 1¢ (one cent, known here as "a penny"), 5¢ (five cents or "a nickel"), 10¢ (ten cents or "a dime"), 25¢ (twenty-five cents or "a quarter"), 50¢ (fifty cents or "a half dollar"), and the rare $1 piece.

Changing foreign currency in the United States is a hassle, so leave any currency other than U.S. dollars at home—it will prove more of a nuisance than it's worth. Even banks here may not want to change your home currency into U.S. dollars. The exceptions are the currency exchange desks in the Miami, Orlando, Tampa, and Fort Myers airports, and **Thomas Cook Foreign Exchange,** which changes foreign currency and sells commission-free foreign and U.S. traveler's checks, drafts, and wire transfers. Thomas Cook has offices in Miami, Fort Lauderdale, Orlando, and Fort Myers. Call ☎ **800/287-7362** for its branch locations and hours.

Walt Disney World Services for International Visitors

Walt Disney World, which welcomes thousands of foreign visitors each year, has numerous services designed to meet their needs. Unless otherwise indicated, call ☎ 407/W-DISNEY for details. Services include:

- A special phone number (☎ 407/824-7900) to speak with someone in French, Spanish, German, and other languages.

- Personal translator units (in French, German, and Spanish) to translate narration at some shows and attractions.

- Detailed guidebooks to the three major parks in Spanish, French, German, Portuguese, and Japanese (available at any guest relations location).

- Currency exchange (see below).

- World Key Terminals at Epcot that offer basic park information and assistance with dining reservations in Spanish.

- Resort phones equipped with software that expedites international calls by allowing guests to dial direct to foreign destinations.

Traveler's checks denominated in U.S. dollars are readily accepted at most hotels, motels, restaurants, and large stores. Do not bring traveler's checks denominated in other currencies. Sometimes a passport or other photo identification is necessary.

Credit and charge cards are the most widely used form of payment in the United States: Visa (Barclaycard in Britain), MasterCard (EuroCard in Europe, Access in Britain, Chargex in Canada), American Express, Diners Club, Discover, and Carte Blanche. You must have a credit or charge card to rent a car. Widespread in Florida, some automated-teller machines (ATMs) will allow you to draw U.S. currency against your bank and credit cards. Check with your bank before leaving home, and remember that you will need your personal identification number (PIN) to do so.

SAFETY

GENERAL   While tourist areas are generally safe, crime is on the increase everywhere, and U.S. urban areas tend to be less safe than those in Europe or Japan. You should always stay alert. This is particularly true of large U.S. cities. It is wise to ask your hotel front desk staff or the city's or area's tourist office if you're in doubt about which neighborhoods are safe.

Remember also that hotels are open to the public, and in a large hotel, security may not be able to screen everyone entering. Always lock your room door—don't assume that once inside your hotel you are automatically safe and no longer need be aware of your surroundings.

DRIVING   Recently more and more crime has involved vehicles, so safety while driving is particularly important. Question your rental agency about personal safety, or ask for a brochure of traveler safety tips when you pick up your car. Obtain written directions, or a map with the route clearly marked, from the agency showing how to get to your destination. And if possible, arrive and depart during daylight hours.

If you drive off a highway into a doubtful neighborhood, leave the area as quickly as possible. If you have an accident, even on the highway, stay in your car with the doors locked until you assess the situation or until the police arrive. If you are bumped from behind on the street or are involved in a minor accident with no injuries and the situation appears to be suspicious, motion to the other driver to follow you. *Never* get out of your car in such situations. You can also keep a premade sign in your car that reads: PLEASE FOLLOW THIS VEHICLE TO REPORT THE ACCIDENT. Show the sign to the other driver and go directly to the nearest police precinct, well-lighted service station, or all-night store.

If you see someone on the road who indicates a need for help, do *not* stop. Take note of the location, drive on to a well-lighted area, and telephone the police by dialing ☎ 911.

Park in well-lighted, well-traveled areas if possible. Always keep your car doors locked, whether attended or unattended. Look around you before you get out of your car, and never leave any packages or valuables in sight. If someone attempts to rob you or steal your car, do *not* try to resist the thief/carjacker—report the incident to the police department immediately.

Also, make sure that you have enough gasoline in your tank to reach your intended destination, so that you're not forced to look for a service station in an unfamiliar and possibly unsafe neighborhood, especially at night.

2 Getting to & Around the United States

GETTING TO THE UNITED STATES

A number of U.S. airlines offer service from Europe and Latin America to Florida, including American, Delta, Northwest, and United. Many of the major international airlines, such as **British Airways, KLM Royal Dutch Airlines,** and **Lufthansa** also have direct flights from Europe to various Florida cities, either in their own planes or in conjunction with an American "partner" airline (KLM and Northwest, to name one partnership). Call the airlines' local offices or contact your travel agent, and be sure to ask about promotional fares and discounts.

Attractive values are offered by **Virgin Atlantic Airways** (☎ 800/662-8621 in the U.S., or 01/293-74-77-47 in the U.K.), which has cut-rate fares on its flights from London and Manchester to Miami and Orlando. The same is true with **Laker Airways** (☎ 888/525-3724 in the U.S., or 011-44-129-377-2020 in the U.K.), which flies from London to Fort Lauderdale, and with the Belgian airline **CityBird** (☎ 888/637-4985 in the U.S.), which flies from Brussels to Miami and Orlando. **LTU International** (☎ 800/888-0200 in the U.S.) frequently has reduced fares from Frankfurt, Munich, and Dusseldorf in Germany to Miami, Orlando, and Fort Myers.

You should always ask about **advance purchase excursion (APEX) fares,** which represent substantial savings over regular fares. Most require tickets to be bought 21 days before departure. **British Airways** has a 90-day advance purchase plan with fares about $100 lower than its 21-day APEX program.

Canadians should check with **Air Canada** (☎ 800/776-3000), which offers service from Toronto and Montréal to Miami, Tampa, West Palm Beach, Fort Lauderdale, and Fort Myers. Also ask your travel agent about **Canada 3000** (☎ 800/993-4378), which has wintertime charter flights to several Florida destinations.

On the Worldwide Web, the European Travel Network (ETN) operates a site at **www.discount-tickets.com**, which offers low rates on international airfares to the United States, accommodations, car rentals, and tours. Another site to click for current discount fares worldwide is **www.etn.nl/discount.htm#disco**.

No matter at which airport you land, getting through immigration control may take as long as 2 hours on some days, especially summer weekends. Accordingly, you should make very generous allowances for delay in planning connections between international and domestic flights.

In contrast, travelers arriving by car or by rail from Canada will find border-crossing formalities streamlined to the vanishing point. And air travelers from Canada, Bermuda, and some places in the Caribbean can sometimes go through Customs and Immigration at the point of departure, which is much quicker.

For further information, see "Getting There," in chapter 2.

GETTING AROUND THE UNITED STATES

BY AIR   The United States is one of the world's largest countries, with vast distances separating many of its key sights. From New York to Miami, for example, is more than 1,350 miles (2,173km) by road or train. Accordingly, flying is the quickest and most comfortable way to get around the country.

Ask your travel agent or local airline office about a **Visit USA** discount ticket sold by some large American airlines (for example, American, Delta, Northwest, TWA, and United) to travelers on their transatlantic or transpacific flights. It allows travel between many U.S. destinations at minimum rates. They must be purchased before you leave your foreign point of departure. The conditions attached to these discount tickets can be changed without warning.

BY TRAIN   Long-distance trains in the United States are operated by **Amtrak** (☎ **800/USA-RAIL;** www.amtrak.com), the national rail passenger corporation. Be aware, however, that with a few notable exceptions (for instance, the Northeast Corridor line between Boston and Washington, D.C.), intercity service is not up to European standards. Delays are common, routes are limited and often infrequently served, and fares are seldom significantly lower than discount airfares. Thus cross-country train travel should be approached with caution.

International visitors can buy a **USA Railpass,** good for 15 or 30 days of unlimited travel on Amtrak. The pass is available through many foreign travel agents, and with a foreign passport, you can also buy them at some Amtrak offices in the United States, including Boston, Chicago, Los Angeles, Miami, New York, San Francisco, and Washington, D.C. The prices are based on a zone system: eastern, central, and western United States. At press time, a 15-day pass good in the eastern third of the country ranged from $205 to $250, depending on the time of travel, while 30-day passes ranged from about $255 to $310. The highest prices are in summer and at holidays. Reservations are generally required and should be made for each part of your trip as early as possible.

If you'll be traveling in both the United States and Canada, Amtrak and VIA, the Canadian railway system, offer a joint **North American Rail Pass,** good for unlimited travel over 30 consecutive days anywhere the two systems go. One key restriction: You must travel by rail in both the United States and Canada. At press time, these cost $645 from June to mid-October, $450 the rest of the year.

See "Getting There," in chapter 2, for more information about Amtrak's services to and within Florida.

BY BUS   Although it's the least expensive way to get around the country, long-distance bus service here can be both slow and uncomfortable, so it's not for everyone. The only national bus company is **Greyhound** (☎ **800/231-2222** in the U.S.; www.greyhound.com), which offers an **Ameripass** for unlimited travel anywhere on its system. In 1998, prices for a 7-day pass started at $199; 15 days at $299; 30 days at $409; and 60 days at $599. Senior citizens get a discount ranging from $20 to $60.

BY CAR   Traveling by car gives you the freedom to make, and alter, your itinerary to suit your own needs and interests. And especially in Florida, it offers the possibility of visiting some of the off-the-beaten-path locations, places that cannot be reached easily by public transportation. For information on renting cars in the United States, see "Getting Around," in chapter 2, and "Automobile Organizations" and "Automobile Rentals" in "Fast Facts: For the Foreign Traveler," below.

Please note that in the United States we drive on the **right side of the road** as in Europe, not on the left side as in the United Kingdom, Australia, and New Zealand.

3 Shopping Tips

Our federal government charges very low duties when compared to the rest of the world, so you could get some excellent deals here on imported electronic goods, cameras, and clothing. Of course, it all depends on the value of your home currency versus the dollar, and how much duty you'll have to pay on your purchases when you get home.

The national "discount" chain stores consistently offer some of the best shopping deals. For televisions, VCRs, radios, camcorders, computers, and other electronic goods, go to **Best Buy, Circuit City,** and **Radio Shack.** Best Buy also has a wide selection of music. **CompUSA, Computer City,** and **Micro Center** specialize in computer hardware, accessories, and software. **Service Merchandise** is one of our best chains for cameras, and it also has electronics, jewelry, and many other items.

Many computers and other electronic equipment sold here use only 110- to 120-volt AC (60 cycles) electricity. You will need a transformer to use them at home if your power is 220 to 240 volts AC (50 cycles). Be sure to ask the salesperson if an item has a universal power adapter.

Major U.S. department store chains are **Sears, Macy's, Saks Fifth Avenue, Lord & Taylor,** and **JC Penney.** In Florida, you'll also find **Burdines, Jordan Marsh,** and **Dillard's** anchoring many shopping malls. You get real deals in department stores only during sales, when selected merchandise is marked down 25% or more. The **Marshall's** and **TJ Maxx** chains carry name-brand clothing at department-store sale prices, but their stock tends to vary greatly.

Outlet malls are another source, in which manufacturers operate their own shops, selling directly to the consumer. Sometimes you can get very good buys at the outlets, especially when sales are going on. Most lingerie and china outlets have good prices when compared to department stores, but that's not necessarily the case with designer clothing. In addition, some manufacturers produce items of lesser quality so they can charge less at their outlets, so inspect the quality of all merchandise carefully. The main advantage to outlet malls is that if you are looking for a specific brand—Levi's jeans, for example—the company's outlet will have it.

You'll find national chain stores, department stores, and outlet malls throughout Florida; many are listed under "Shopping" in the following chapters. You can also look under their names in the White Pages of the local telephone directory for addresses and phone numbers, or under subjects such as computer dealers, television and radio dealers, stereo and hi-fi dealers, department stores, and discount stores in the Yellow Pages directory.

FAST FACTS: For the Foreign Traveler

Automobile Organizations   Auto clubs will supply maps, suggested routes, guidebooks, accident and bail-bond insurance, and emergency road service. The **American Automobile Association (AAA)** is the major auto club in the United States. If you belong to an auto club in your home country, inquire about AAA reciprocity before you leave. You may be able to join AAA even if you're not a member of a reciprocal club; to inquire, call AAA (☎ **800/222-4357**). AAA is actually an organization of regional auto clubs; in Florida, look under "AAA Automobile Club South" in the White Pages of the telephone directory. AAA has a nationwide emergency road service telephone number (☎ **800/AAA-HELP**).

Automobile Rentals See "Getting Around," in chapter 2.

Business Hours See "Fast Facts: Florida," in chapter 2.

Currency & Currency Exchange See "Entry Requirements" and "Money" under "Preparing for Your Trip," above.

Electricity Like Canada, the United States uses 110 to 120 volts AC (60 cycles), compared to 220 to 240 volts AC (50 cycles) in most of Europe, Australia, and New Zealand. If your small appliances use 220 to 220 volts, you'll need a 110-volt transformer and a plug adapter with two flat parallel pins to operate them here. Downward converters that change 220 to 240 volts to 110 to 120 volts are difficult to find in the United States, so bring one with you.

Embassies & Consulates All embassies are located in the national capital, Washington, D.C. Some consulates are located in major U.S. cities, and most nations have a mission to the United Nations in New York City.

The embassy of **Australia** is at 1601 Massachusetts Ave. NW, Washington, D.C. 20036 (☎ **202/797-3000**). There are consulates in New York, Honolulu, Houston, Los Angeles, and San Francisco.

The embassy of **Canada** is at 501 Pennsylvania Ave. NW, Washington, D.C. 20001 (☎ **202/682-1740**). There's a Canadian consulate in Florida at 200 S. Biscayne Blvd., Suite 1600, Miami, FL 33131 (☎ **305/579-1600**). Other Canadian consulates are in Atlanta, Buffalo (New York), Chicago, Cleveland, Dallas, Detroit, Los Angeles, Minneapolis, New York, and Seattle.

The embassy of the **Republic of Ireland** is at 2234 Massachusetts Ave. NW, Washington, D.C. 20008 (☎ **202/462-3939**). Irish consulates are in Boston, Chicago, New York, and San Francisco.

The embassy of **New Zealand** is at 37 Observatory Circle NW, Washington, D.C. 20008 (☎ **202/328-4800**). New Zealand consulates are in Los Angeles, Salt Lake City, San Francisco, and Seattle.

The embassy of the **United Kingdom** is at 3100 Massachusetts Ave. NW, Washington, D.C. 20008 (☎ **202/462-1340**). In Florida, there's a full-service British consulate in Miami at Suite 2110, Brickell Bay Office Tower, 1001 S. Bayshore Dr. (☎ **305/374-1522**), and a vice consulate for emergency situations in Orlando at the Sun Trust Center, Suite 2110, 200 S. Orange Ave. (☎ **407/426-7855**). Other British consulates are in Atlanta, Boston, Chicago, Cleveland, Dallas, Houston, Los Angeles, and New York.

Emergencies Call ☎ **911** to report a fire, call the police, or get an ambulance anywhere in the United States. This is a toll-free call (no coins are required at public telephones).

If you encounter traveler's problems, check the local telephone directory to find an office of the **Traveler's Aid Society,** a nationwide, nonprofit, social-service organization geared to helping travelers in difficult straits. Their services might include reuniting families separated while traveling, providing food and/or shelter to people stranded without cash, or even emotional counseling. If you're in trouble, seek them out.

Gasoline (Petrol) Petrol is known as gasoline (or simply "gas") in the United States, and petrol stations are known as both gas stations and service stations.

Gasoline costs about half as much here as it does in Europe (about $1.20 per gallon at press time). One U.S. gallon equals 3.8 liters or .85 Imperial gallons. A majority of gas stations in Florida are now actually convenience grocery stores with gas pumps outside; they do not service automobiles. All but a very few stations have self-service gas pumps.

Holidays   Banks, government offices, post offices, and many stores, restaurants, and museums are closed on the following legal national holidays: January 1 (New Year's Day), the third Monday in January (Martin Luther King Day), the third Monday in February (Presidents' Day, Washington's Birthday), the last Monday in May (Memorial Day), July 4 (Independence Day), the first Monday in September (Labor Day), the second Monday in October (Columbus Day), November 11 (Veterans' Day/Armistice Day), the last Thursday in November (Thanksgiving Day), and December 25 (Christmas). Also, the Tuesday following the first Monday in November is Election Day and is a federal government holiday in presidential-election years (1996 was the most recent, 2000 is the next).

Legal Aid   The foreign tourist will probably never become involved with the American legal system. If you are "pulled over" for a minor infraction (for example, of the highway code, such as speeding), never attempt to pay the fine directly to a police officer; this could be construed as attempted bribery, a much more serious crime. Pay fines by mail, or directly into the hands of the clerk of the court. If accused of a more serious offense, say and do nothing before consulting a lawyer, since here the burden is on the state to prove a person's guilt beyond a reasonable doubt, and everyone has the right to remain silent, whether they are suspected of a crime or actually arrested. Once arrested, a person can make one telephone call to a party of his or her choice. Call your embassy or consulate.

Mail   If you aren't sure what your address will be in the United States, mail can be sent to you, in your name, **c/o General Delivery** at the main post office of the city or region where you expect to be. You must pick it up in person and must produce proof of identity (driver's license, passport).

Generally to be found at intersections, **mailboxes** are blue with a red-and-white stripe and carry the inscription U.S. MAIL. If your mail is addressed to a U.S. destination, don't forget to add the five-digit postal code, or ZIP code, after the two-letter abbreviation of the state to which the mail is addressed (FL for Florida).

The U.S. postal service is expected to raise its rates in 1999, but at press time domestic **postage rates** were 20¢ for a postcard and 32¢ for a letter. Airmail postcards to Canada cost 30¢, while letters were 46¢. Airmail letters to other countries were 60¢ for the first half ounce.

Newspapers/Magazines   All over Florida, you'll be able to purchase the *Miami Herald,* one of the most highly respected dailies in the country. Every city has its own daily paper.

Safety   See "Safety" in "Preparing for Your Trip," above, and in "Fast Facts: Florida," in chapter 2.

Taxes   In the United States there is no value-added tax (VAT) or other indirect tax at the national level. Every state, county, and city has the right to levy its own local tax on all purchases, including hotel and restaurant checks, airline tickets, and so on. For Florida's sales taxes, see "Fast Facts: Florida," in chapter 2. Florida's hotel tax varies from county to county; we give the rates in the accommodation sections of the chapters that follow.

Telephone, Telegraph, Telex & Fax   The telephone system in the United States is run by private corporations, so rates, especially for long-distance service and operator-assisted calls, can vary widely. Generally, hotel surcharges on long-distance and local calls are astronomical, so you're usually better off using a **public pay telephone,** which you'll find clearly marked in most public buildings and private establishments as well as on the street. Convenience grocery stores and gas stations always have them. Many convenience groceries and packaging services sell prepaid calling cards in denominations up to $50; these can be the least expensive way to call home. Many public phones at airports now accept American Express, MasterCard, and Visa credit cards. Local calls made from public pay phones in most locales in Florida cost 35¢.

Most **long-distance and international calls** can be dialed directly from any phone. For calls within the United States and to Canada, dial 1 followed by the area code and the seven-digit number. For other international calls, dial 011 followed by the country code, city code, and the telephone number of the person you are calling.

Calls to area codes 800, 888, and 877 are toll-free. However, calls to numbers in area codes 700 and 900 (chat lines, bulletin boards, "dating" services) can be very expensive—usually a charge of 95¢ to $3 or more per minute, and they sometimes have minimum charges that can run as high as $15 or more. For **reversed-charge** or **collect calls,** and for **person-to-person calls,** dial 0 (zero, *not* the letter O) followed by the area code and number you want; an operator will then come on the line, and you should specify that you are calling collect, or person-to-person, or both. If your operator-assisted call is international, ask for the overseas operator.

For local **directory assistance** ("information"), dial 411; for long-distance information, dial 1, then the appropriate area code and 555-1212.

Telegraph and telex services are provided primarily by Western Union. You can bring your telegram into the nearest Western Union office (there are hundreds across the country) or dictate it over the phone (☎ **800/325-6000**). You can also telegraph money or have it telegraphed to you, very quickly over the Western Union system, but this service can cost as much as 15% to 25% of the amount sent.

Most hotels have **fax** machines available for guest use (be sure to ask about the charge to use it), and many hotel rooms are even wired for guests' fax machines. A less expensive way to send and receive faxes may be at stores such as **Mail Boxes Etc.,** a national chain of packing service shops (look in the Yellow Pages directory under "Packing Services").

There are two kinds of telephone directories in the United States. The so-called **White Pages** lists private and business subscribers in alphabetical order. The inside front cover lists emergency numbers for police, fire, ambulance, the coast guard, poison-control center, crime-victims hot line, and so on. The first few pages will tell you how to make long-distance and international calls, complete with country codes and area codes. Government numbers usually are on pages printed on blue paper. Printed on yellow paper, the so-called **Yellow Pages** lists all local services, businesses, industries, and churches and synagogues by type of activity, with an index at the front or back. The Yellow Pages also includes city plans or detailed area maps, often showing postal ZIP codes and public transportation routes.

Time   The continental United States is divided into four **time zones:** eastern standard time (EST), central standard time (CST), mountain standard time

(MST), and Pacific standard time (PST). Alaska and Hawaii have their own zones. For example, noon in New York City (EST) is 11am in Chicago (CST), 10am in Denver (MST), 9am in Los Angeles (PST), 8am in Anchorage (AST), and 7am in Honolulu (HST). Most of Florida observes eastern standard time, though the Panhandle west of the Apalachicola River is on central standard time (1 hour earlier than Tallahassee, Orlando, and Miami).

Daylight saving time is in effect from 1am on the first Sunday in April through 1am the last Sunday in October. Daylight saving time moves the clock 1 hour ahead of standard time.

Tipping   Tipping is so ingrained in the American way of life that the annual income tax of tip-earning service personnel is based on how much they should have received in light of their employers' gross revenues. Accordingly, they may have to pay tax on a tip you didn't actually give them.

Here are some rules of thumb: bartenders can be tipped 10% to 15% of the check; bellhops, at least 50¢ per bag, or $2 to $3 for a lot of luggage; cab drivers, 10% of the fare; chambermaids, $1 per day; checkroom attendants, $1 per garment; hairdressers and barbers, 15% to 20% of the bill; waiters and waitresses, 15% to 20% of the check; valet parking attendants, $1 per vehicle; rest room attendants, 25¢. We do not tip theater ushers, gas station attendants, or the staff at cafeterias and fast-food restaurants.

Toilets   You won't find public toilets (referred to here as "rest rooms") on the streets in most U.S. cities, but they can be found in hotel lobbies, bars, restaurants, museums, department stores, railway and bus stations, or service stations. Note, however, that restaurants and bars in resort or heavily visited areas may reserve their rest rooms for the use of their patrons.

4 Settling Into Miami

by Victoria Pesce Elliott

Arriving in Miami—whether by plane, bus, or train—it's easy to feel like you've touched down in the Caribbean. Gritty, sunny, and glamorous, the city boasts a diversity that is its very essence—a bouillabaisse of colors, sounds, and scents. From the bustling airport to the palm-lined beachfront, you'll hear Miamians all around you speaking Creole, French, Italian, Portuguese, Yiddish, patois, and, of course, Spanish. And speaking Spanish is a real asset in an area where more than 60% of the population considers it their first language.

This is Miami. Really, the city is a sprawling metropolis made up of more than 30 cities and countless neighborhoods within or near Miami-Dade County. The actual city of Miami is home to only 350,000 residents out of a county population of more than 2 million. And though this young city, which celebrated its 100th birthday in 1996, has become a major commerce center and trendy resort destination, it's had more than its share of growing pains.

A spate of tourist murders in the early 1990s catapulted Miami into the headlines, where it became known as one of the nation's murder capitals. Also well publicized was the surge of undocumented immigrants from nearby Haiti and Cuba who landed by rafts on local beaches.

In 1997, after a series of corruption scandals and a huge fiscal deficit made the papers, fed-up citizens even introduced an unsuccessful referendum to abolish the city of Miami. That same year, Miami Beach again made news when Andrew Cunanan gunned down fashion designer Gianni Versace on the steps of Versace's beachfront mansion—a building that, sadly, has become a new, gruesome tourist attraction.

Although still a real concern, Miami's crime rate is down overall—the result of increased police presence and stricter sentencing for crimes against tourists. And erratic Mayor Xavier Suarez was ousted in March 1998, after CBS's *60 Minutes* uncovered proof of voter fraud and mismanagement. Even El Niño—the notorious weather system that made the winter of 1997–98 one of the wettest and windiest on record—didn't put a damper on the city's tourism.

Don't get me wrong; it's not all disquietude down Miami way. South Beach, that trendy resort area, continues to be a fixture in glossy style magazines for its glitzy nightlife, innovative cuisine, exuberant architecture, and celebrity sightings. It's become the colorful backdrop for hundreds of fashion shoots and major movies (most recently *There's Something About Mary* and *Wild Things*). And in 1997, the Florida Marlins became the youngest expansion team ever to win the World Series.

Through Miami's ups and downs, two characteristics have remained constant: the city's predictable year-round warmth and its location—a lush peninsula surrounded by deep, clear waters pointing emphatically toward the Caribbean and the rest of the Americas.

Waves of eager people have come seeking a new life ever since the Spanish first colonized the area in the 16th century. They continue to arrive from all over the world for leisure, business (primarily banking and shipping), the excellent cuisine, and the varied cultural offerings. More and more are visiting every year—about 10 million in 1997 alone.

Though an expensive city, Miami is a real, working city, which means there are plenty of ways to avoid the tourist traps and save some serious money here.

1 Tips for Saving Money in Miami

Long a haven for retirees, Miami offers **senior citizens** discounts on almost everything from dinners to attractions. In addition to the numerous early bird dinner specials (see "Cheap Eats: The Early Bird Gets the Bargain," on page 123), most places will honor American Association of Retired Persons (AARP) membership as well. Carry a driver's license or other official proof of age to ensure you get a senior discount.

Students, too, can get a price break at most attractions and some restaurants, especially near the local colleges in downtown Miami and Coral Gables. Carry your student ID and ask at all attractions before buying your ticket.

When it comes to snagging hotel discounts, the words to live by are, it can't hurt to ask. Many hotels will give discounts (usually 5% to 10%) for **AAA membership.** For details on membership and fees, call AAA at ☎ **800/926-4222.** A **military ID** can also come in handy at many hotels.

Always inquire about corporate rates at hotels. Even if you don't work for IBM, you may be able to get the special rate, which is usually about 10% to 15% off the posted rates. Also ask about promotions and packages. Reservation agents don't volunteer this information unless you inquire.

Airlines fight perpetual price wars to woo tourists to the Sunshine State. In fact, airfares are so competitive that, unless you're driving in from an adjacent state, flying to Miami will almost always be your most economical option. But take a look at your alternatives. Greyhound/Trailways offers several types of bus passes, and Amtrak offers a host of rail services to Miami. See "Arriving," below, for more information.

Other good sources for coupons are the local papers. Check the *Miami Herald,* especially the "Neighbors" section, and *New Times* for coupons and specials at restaurants, nightclubs, and attractions.

2 Orientation

ARRIVING

BY PLANE Carved out of scrubland in 1928 by Pan American Airlines, **Miami International Airport (MIA)** (☎ **305/876-7000**) has emerged as one of the busiest airports in the world. Approximately 37 million people passed through this huge structure in 1996. Unfortunately, it's undergoing major reconstruction to expand its capacity, which means it can feel like a maze of inadequate signage and surly employees, many of whom speak limited English.

The airport is about 6 miles west of downtown, and about 12 miles from the beaches. You can usually get from the airport to a hotel room anywhere in Miami-Dade County in less than an hour. If you're arriving from an international destination, however, you'll have to go through customs and immigration, a process that can double your time in the airport.

Once past customs, look for a tourist information booth—they are located on the lower levels of Concourses B, D, E, and G. You can pick up maps and brochures and arrange for transportation to your lodging.

To change money or use your Honor or PLUS System ATM card, head for the airport branch of Barnett Bank of South Florida. One is located on the fourth level in Concourse B and another is on the second level in Concourse C.

Virtually every major car-rental company has a desk at Miami airport. (For phone numbers, see "Getting Around," in chapter 2.) But no matter which firm you rent from, you'll have to take a (free) shuttle to the rental site. Buses and vans, clearly marked with rental-car logos, circle the airport every few minutes.

GETTING INTO THE CITY　At the airport's exit, bright-orange sunbursts point the way to tourist-friendly zones, but getting into the city can still be confusing. Be sure to have available 25¢ in change, or at least small U.S. bills, to get past the tolls leading to the highways.

Taxis line up in front of a dispatcher's desk outside the airport's arrival terminals. Some companies offer flat rates to tourist zones; others charge by the meter. In either case, prices should average $14 to Coral Gables, $24 to Miami Beach, $26 to South Beach, and $30 to Key Biscayne. You may have to pay the tolls on the way (between 25¢ and $1.25). Tip 10% to 15%, plus a few dollars extra if the driver helps with your bags.

You'll save almost half the fare with **SuperShuttle** if you are traveling solo. Outside the first-floor baggage claim area, look for the royal blue vans with the words SuperShuttle written in yellow. Or call (☎ **305/871-2000**), if you want to arrange your pick up (or drop-off) in advance. You'll pay a flat fee ranging from $12 to $28 per person, for door-to-door service in any part of the county. The fare to South Beach should be $14. A uniformed dispatcher can summon a van if you don't see one with your destination displayed above the front windshield. The best part is, SuperShuttle operates 24 hours a day and accepts major credit cards.

Public transportation, though notoriously inefficient, is available and cheap. As a rule, expect a bus trip to take about three times as long as a drive. Buses heading downtown leave the airport from the arrivals level only once every half-hour or 40 minutes. Bus no. 7 to downtown departs every 40 minutes Monday to Friday from 5:30am to 8:30pm and Saturday and Sunday from 7am to 7pm. Bus J heads south to Coral Gables every 30 minutes from about 6am to 7:30pm, and east to Miami Beach every 30 minutes from about 4:30am to 11:30pm. Bus no. 42 goes to Coconut Grove hourly from 5:30am to 7:15pm. All city buses cost $1.25 for adults and 60¢ for seniors and children who are taller than the bus fare box. For detailed schedule information or a map, call ☎ **305/638-6700** weekdays from 6am to 10pm, or weekends from 9am to 5pm.

BY BOAT　If you enter the country on a craft weighing less than 5 tons, the craft must proceed to designated marinas and call U.S. Customs to come by (☎ **800/ 432-1216**). The **Haulover Marine Center,** 15000 Collins Ave., Miami Beach (☎ **305/945-3934**), and the **Watson Island Marina,** 1050 MacArthur Causeway, Miami (☎ **305/579-6955**), are two sanctioned marinas in Greater Miami. If you are arriving from a domestic port, simply dock at any of the area's many marinas and then taxi into town. You can save dockage fees by docking at a local restaurant, like Sundays' in Key Biscayne. For the price of lunch or dinner, you've got yourself a spot for the day.

BY BUS   Greyhound (☎ **800/231-2222**) buses pull into a number of stations around the city, including 4111 NW 27th Ave. (near the airport), 700 Biscayne Blvd. (downtown), and 16560 NE 6th Ave. (North Miami Beach).

BY CAR   No matter where you start your journey, chances are you'll reach Miami by way of I-95. This north-south interstate is the city's lifeline and an integral part of the region; it connects the city's larger neighborhoods on the mainland and crosses all other major roads that go to the beaches and airport. Unfortunately, many of Miami's road signs are completely confusing and notably absent when you need them. Take time out to study a map before getting on the highway. You'll notice the far left lane of the interstate is labeled HOV (high-occupancy vehicles). Solo drivers are prohibited from driving in the "fast" lane during rush hours. Exceeding the speed limit by 10 to 15 miles per hour usually won't draw the attention of highway troopers; however, dri-

---

Driving Alert

Miami's signage, especially at or near I-95, is utterly inadequate. Make sure you get a free map and clear directions to your destination before you leave the car-rental desk. Better yet, take a taxi or shuttle to your hotel, and then arrange to rent a car nearer to your lodging. Many agencies will deliver a vehicle right to your hotel. And many have offices throughout Miami, especially in the beach areas. It's a safer proposition; the area surrounding the airport is plagued with thieves preying on lost tourists.

---

ving in the restricted lane will almost certainly get you an expensive ticket and points on your license.

Seat-belt laws are also enforced, but only if you are pulled over for another infraction. Anyone in the front seat of a moving car must be buckled in. Children under the age of 4 must be in a car seat, whether they are seated in the front or back seat.

For a more detailed description of the city's main arteries and streets, see "City Layout," below.

BY TRAIN   If you're traveling to Miami by train, you'll pull into Amtrak's Miami terminal at 8303 NW 37th Ave. (off 79th Street; ☎ **305/835-1206**). Unfortunately, none of the major car-rental companies have an office at the train station; you'll have to go to the airport, about 7 miles from the train station (see "Getting Around," below). Hertz (☎ **800/654-3131**) will reimburse your cab fare up to $10 if you rent from them.

Taxis meet each Amtrak arrival. Depending on traffic, the fare to downtown should run about $23; to South Beach, about $35. Either trip should take less than 30 minutes.

SAFETY

Although recently improved, Florida suffers one of the highest crime rates in the nation. You can, however, take specific steps to lessen your chances of being victimized. When driving around Miami, always know where you're going before getting in the car. Don't walk alone at night, and be extra wary when walking or driving through areas in and around downtown. There has been an increase in muggings, car break-ins, and pickpocketing in the bustling center of Coconut Grove. You are better off paying higher parking fees to a valet or guarded lot than parking at meters a few blocks away from your destination.

When arriving in Miami late in the evening, consider shuttling to your hotel by taxi or shared van and then renting a car the next day when you have the time to get your bearings. Many rental agencies will deliver a vehicle directly to your hotel. Plus, many have offices throughout Miami, especially in the beach areas.

Be cautious when changing money or using credit cards. Scammers and muggers may be lurking looking for an easy target. If you have used a credit card to purchase goods, be sure to tear up the copy and to check the amount column before signing. Some unscrupulous shopkeepers may add a few zeros to your purchase price.

If you are in an accident or have been robbed or assaulted in Miami, call **Advocates for Victims** (☎ **305/758-2546**), an organization that specializes in helping distressed travelers.

VISITOR INFORMATION

The **Greater Miami Convention and Visitors Bureau,** 701 Brickell Ave., Suite 2700, Miami, FL 33131 (☎ **800/283-2707** or 305/539-3063; www.miamiandbeaches.

com; e-mail: gmcvb@miamiandbeaches.com), is the best source of information for tourists intending to travel to any of the many regions that are collectively known as Miami. For recorded information in French, Spanish, or English. call ☎ **800/ 22-SUNNY.** Even if you don't have a specific question, you may want to phone ahead for the free magazine, *Greater Miami and the Beaches Visitor's Guide,* which includes several good, clear maps and details on sports, attractions, and events. The office is open Monday to Friday from 8:30am to 5pm.

Greater Miami's various chambers of commerce also can send maps and details about their particular regions. These include the **Coconut Grove Chamber of Commerce,** 2820 McFarlane Rd., Miami, FL 33133 (☎ 305/444-7270; fax 305/ 444-2498); the **Coral Gables Chamber of Commerce,** 50 Aragon Ave., Coral Gables, FL 33134 (☎ 305/446-1657; fax 305/446-9900); the **Key Biscayne Chamber of Commerce,** 328 Crandon Blvd., Suite 217, Key Biscayne, FL 33149 (☎ 305/361-5207; fax 305/361-9411); the **Florida Gold Coast Chamber of Commerce,** 1100 Kane Concourse (Bay Harbor Islands), Miami, FL 33154 (☎ 305/ 866-6020), which represents Bal Harbour, Sunny Isles, Surfside, and other North Dade waterfront communities; the **Greater Miami Chamber of Commerce,** Omni International, 1601 Biscayne Blvd., Miami, FL 33132 (☎ 800/283-2707 or 305/ 350-7700; fax 305/374-6902); and the **Miami Beach Chamber of Commerce,** 1920 Meridian Ave., Miami Beach, FL 33139 (☎ 305/672-1270; fax 305/538-4336; sobe.com/miamibeachchamber), which represents South Beach. The Miami Beach chamber operates a conveniently located information center at Meridian Avenue and Dade Boulevard, just a few blocks from Lincoln Road and across the street from the Holocaust Memorial. They are staffed from 9am to 5pm weekdays and from 10am to 4pm on Saturday.

CITY LAYOUT

The area commonly called Miami actually includes dozens of cities and many more distinctive neighborhoods in and around Dade County (which was renamed Miami-Dade County in 1997 in an attempt to allay confusion).

Geographically, Miami is divided into two main sections: the mainland and the adjacent barrier islands to the east (the largest is Miami Beach and includes South Beach at its tip). These two parts are connected by a series of causeways that hopscotch across the many islands dotting Biscayne Bay. Miami's international airport and towering city center are located on the mainland. Coconut Grove and Coral Gables, two of the city's most popular neighborhoods, sit more or less adjacent to one another, a short drive south of the center. The working-class streets of Little Havana are immediately west of downtown, and Little Haiti is immediately north.

The main barrier island is divided crosswise into the communities of South Beach, Miami Beach, Surfside, Bal Harbour, and Sunny Isles—areas that, collectively, are simply referred to as Miami Beach.

Weather Tips: Tan, Don't Burn!

A very real danger in Miami is **sunburn.** Many visitors who are unfamiliar with the scorching tropical sun and eager to get a golden tan here, don't bother with sunscreen. Do yourself a favor. Take the sun exposure slow and *wear protection.* Many people end up hospitalized or wretchedly ill from sun poisoning. Take it from me: A flaming red glow with peeling skin doesn't look, or feel, very attractive.

Area Code Alert

Thanks to the proliferation of fax machines, modems, and cellular phones, Miami has nearly run out of phone numbers. As of July 1, 1998, all *new* telephone numbers assigned within Miami-Dade County will use the area code 786 (SUN). After that time, to reach any local number (even one with a 305 area code), you will have to dial all 10 digits. For example, to call for a reservation at the Italian place that's just around the corner, you will still have to dial 305/123-4567. If you're calling the new little bistro on the corner which opened in time for the Fourth of July, you will call 786/456-7890. Either call still will be billed as a local call.

FINDING AN ADDRESS   Street finding on the mainland is infinitely easier once you learn how the city's numbering system works. The city of Miami is divided into quadrants—NE, NW, SE, and SW—by the intersection of Flagler Street and North Miami Avenue. These two otherwise unremarkable roads meet in the city center, and are colored dark red on most city maps. Building numbers (along with places, courts, terraces, lanes, streets, and avenues) increase from this intersection. The streets of Hialeah, a middle-class residential suburb northwest of the city center, are exceptions to this pattern, and are listed separately in map indexes.

In most cases you can determine the cross street of an address by lopping off the last two digits. For example, 12301 Biscayne Blvd. is located at 123rd Street. It's also helpful to remember that avenues generally run north-south, while streets go east-west.

The city of Miami Beach consists of 16 narrow islands. The largest is only 7 miles long and 1½ miles wide and is the main area referred to throughout the book. Here, street numbering starts with 1st Street, near Miami Beach's southern tip (South Pointe), and increases to 192nd Street, in the northern part of Sunny Isles. Named streets intersect and are usually clearly marked. Collins Avenue (Fla. A1A) makes the entire journey from head to toe.

You should know that the numbered streets in Miami Beach are not the geographical equivalents of those on the mainland, but they are close. For example, the 79th Street Causeway leads into 71st Street on Miami Beach, and the 125th Street exit on I-95 brings you to 96th Street on the beach.

MAPS   A reliable map is essential. If you aren't planning on exploring extensively, the maps located inside the tourist board's free publication *Greater Miami and the Beaches Visitor's Guide* are adequate. If you really want to get to know the city, invest in one of the small, accordion-fold maps available at most gas stations and bookstores. Rand McNally's **Easy Finder** is a colorful accordion that gives great details of most of Miami-Dade County with the exception of some of West and South Miami.

NEIGHBORHOODS IN BRIEF

A region that has long attracted sun-seekers, retirees, immigrants, international businesses, and drifters, Miami has spawned many diverse and interesting communities.

SOUTH BEACH/THE ART DECO DISTRICT   The revitalization that began in the early 1980s and made South Beach famous continues today, peppering the beautiful skyline with cranes and scaffolding. Really just a 15-block strip at the southern tip of Miami Beach, South Beach happens to have more art deco architecture than any other place in the world. The colorful, whimsical shapes that define this 1920s style are evident on almost every building in the neighborhood. Once known as "God's waiting room," because of the legions of retirees who settled here, South Beach is now home to models, photographers, musicians, world-renowned writers, and a large gay contingency that fell in love with the climate and the excitement inherent in a burgeoning community.

By the way, never refer to this area as "SoBe." Only tourists and public relations people use this abbreviation.

MIAMI BEACH   This is the area used to describe the central and northern parts of Miami Beach situated north of South Beach—generally considered to begin at 24th Street. To tourists in the 1950s, Miami Beach was Miami. Extravagant resort hotels offered northerners everything under one roof and hosted major performers like Frank Sinatra and Jackie Gleason. In the 1960s and 1970s many failing hotels converted to condominiums, resulting in the nickname "Condo Canyon." In the late 1980s, the mammoth hotels that survived the slow years renovated their properties to accommodate the huge numbers of tourists returning to the area, and Miami Beach proper is once again a destination in its own right.

Surfside, Bal Harbour, and Sunny Isles lie in the northern part of Miami Beach. Collins Avenue (Fla. A1A), Miami Beach's most active thoroughfare, links these neighborhoods together seamlessly.

Surfside, packed with moderately priced "resort" motels, is very popular with European and ultraconservative Jewish tourists, who return year after year. **Bal Harbour,** a shopping mecca, is the highest net worth zip code in South Florida. Elegant bay-front homes are clustered on small islands that are part of the city. **Sunny Isles,** at the far north end of the beach, is for budgeteers. With some outstanding exceptions, the farther north you go on Miami Beach, the cheaper lodging and eating becomes.

KEY BISCAYNE   Located south of Miami Beach, off the shores of Coconut Grove, **Key Biscayne** is protected from the troubles of the mainland by the long Rickenbacker Causeway and a $1 toll (which the city has debated raising). For the most part, the island is an exclusive residential community with million-dollar homes enjoying priceless views. For tourists, this key offers great beaches, a spectacular golf course, a top resort hotel, and a couple of good restaurants.

DOWNTOWN   Downtown's high-tech buildings perched on the water's edge and neon-lighted monorail system make the area visually stunning, but is better enjoyed from afar. The downtown area is segmented and more easily explored by car than on foot. Some great shopping and a few excellent restaurants cater primarily to the nine-to-five crowd and cruise-boat passengers who usually don't get farther than the Bayside marketplace. Plans are in the works to revitalize the area with a new waterside arena, entertainment complex, and retail shops. Also showing signs of life is the area known as the Design District, in the northern part of downtown. Suddenly little cafes, galleries, and clubs are popping up just west of Biscayne Boulevard starting at about 36th Street. Here you can get some great bargains on high-end home furnishings and fabrics.

LITTLE HAVANA   Miami's original Cuban center is still the city's most vibrant ethnic enclave. Southwest 8th Street, referred to locally as "Calle Ocho," is a one-way street lined with car-repair shops, tailors, electronics stores, cafeterias, and bodegas; it's the region's main thoroughfare. Old men in guayaberas suck on stogies over their daily games of dominoes. Despite some shabby-looking buildings, the neighborhood is unusually safe for visitors at any hour.

LITTLE HAITI   During a brief period in the late 1970s and early 1980s almost 35,000 Haitians arrived in Miami. The influx continues today. Most of the new refugees settle in a decaying 200-square-block area north of downtown. Extending from 41st to 79th streets and bordered by I-95 and Biscayne Boulevard, Little Haiti, as it is known, is a relatively depressed neighborhood with at least 60,000 residents, more than half of whom were born in Haiti. Unfortunately, gangs and petty theft make this area unsafe even in the daytime.

COCONUT GROVE There was a time when the heart of Coconut Grove was populated by artists and intellectuals, hippies and radicals. But these days, gentrification has pushed most alternative types out, leaving in their place a multitude of cafes, boutiques, and nightspots. The Grove's hub is the intersection of Grand Avenue, Main Highway, and McFarlane Road. Around this center are dozens of shops and eateries that attract businesspeople, students, and loads of foreign tourists—especially at night, when the Grove becomes a colorful parade of people.

Don't wander far from your destination. Unfortunately, much of the property surrounding the Grove's active center is an impoverished residential area plagued by drugs and crime.

CORAL GABLES Built in the early 1920s, the Gables was one of the country's first planned developments and one of Dade County's oldest neighborhoods. Modest and beautiful houses were built in a Mediterranean style along lush tree-lined streets that open onto fountained plazas. Many businesses, especially Latin American companies and some foreign embassies, are based in the large modern office buildings that have been integrated into the unique cityscape. Coral Gables offers visitors some of the city's best restaurants, shopping, and top hotels, within 5 minutes of the airport—but no ocean or beach.

SOUTH MIAMI To locals, South Miami is both a specific area, southwest of Coral Gables, and a general region that encompasses all of southern Dade County and includes Kendall, Perrine, Cutler Ridge, and Homestead. For clarity, this book has grouped all these southern suburbs under the category "South Miami." Similar attributes unite the communities: They're heavily residential, and all are packed with strip malls as well as rapidly diminishing acres of farmland. Few tourists stay in these parts as there is no beach and few cultural offerings. But South Miami does contain some worthwhile attractions, making it likely that you'll spend some time here during your stay.

NORTH DADE This suburban area across the Biscayne Bay from Miami Beach has a number of excellent restaurants and good shopping, but very little else to interest most visitors. With the exception of the Turnberry Resort, there are no major hotels here. The areas include Aventura, North Miami, and North Miami Beach (a misleadingly named residential area on the mainland near the Dade-Broward county line).

3 Getting Around

BY CAR

Unless you're going to spend your entire vacation at a self-contained resort, on pedestrian-friendly South Beach, or are traveling directly to the Port of Miami for a cruise, a car is a necessity in this sprawling metropolis. See "Safety," under "Orientation," earlier in this chapter, for special driving tips.

Unfortunately, the public transportation system in Miami is not very efficient. The most elaborate system, the Metrorail and the Metromover, inexplicably do not service the beaches or the airport. However, if you want to tour downtown, these Disneyesque rails are a great and inexpensive way to see the city.

RENTALS   Every major car-rental company has at least one office in Miami. Because of such competition, the city is one of the cheapest places in the world to rent a car. Many firms regularly advertise prices in the neighborhood of $180 per week for their bottom-of-the-line tin can, and one can often be had even cheaper. Rates vary seasonally; see "Getting Around," in chapter 2, for a list of national car-rental companies. One growing and recommendable company is **Enterprise** (☎ **800/325-8007** or 305/534-9037), which rents cars from dozens of well-placed locations throughout the city and offers extremely competitive rates.

PARKING   Especially in South Beach and Coconut Grove, parking is just a hassle. On beach-perfect weekends it's close to impossible, especially on Ocean Drive. A good parking lot to know about is the one on 13th Street, between Collins Avenue and Ocean Drive, and the one on 6th Street, between Collins Avenue and Ocean Drive. The charge is usually $1 per hour and $8 per day (more on weekends).

If you find a vacant metered spot, be sure to have plenty of quarters. Depending on the area, they are enforced daily, including Sunday and holidays, usually from 9am to 9pm, and sometimes until midnight. A quarter buys you as little as 15 minutes or as much as an hour.

What most people (even locals) don't realize is that on weekdays you can park for free in the residential zones on South Beach. Wordy and confusing signs posted on many blocks, especially west of Washington Avenue, look ominous. But the gist is that anyone can park there between the hours of 9am and 6pm. The spots are reserved for residents who have stickers in their car windows at all other times.

Valet service at restaurants and nightclubs is commonplace. Expect to wait for your car and to pay $5 to $15 in Coconut Grove and on South Beach's Ocean Drive on busy weekend nights. Don't leave any valuables in your car since they are usually left unattended on the street. Also, valets have been known to look in glove compartments and change-holders for a little extra compensation.

SPECIAL DRIVING RULES   In Miami, you can make right turns at red lights, as long as you come to a complete stop first. Anyone sitting in the front seat of a moving car must be buckled up. Children under the age of 4 must be in a car seat, whether they are seated in the front or back seat.

BY PUBLIC TRANSPORTATION

Notoriously inefficient, Greater Miami's mass transit system is operated by the **Metro-Dade Transit Agency,** 360 NE 185th St., Miami, FL 33179 (☎ **305/654-6586** or 305/638-6700 for route information). Free schedules, maps, and a "First-Time Rider's Kit" are available at Government Center Station, 111 NW 1st St. (1 block from Flagler Street), in downtown Miami, or by mail from the address above.

One tiny and popular innovation was introduced in 1998 in South Beach. In an effort to alleviate the chronic traffic problem, the city has charged up six electronic shuttle buses which take passengers east from 5th Street, up Washington Avenue (just 2 blocks from the ocean), and across 17th Street before turning around at Alton Road to follow the same route back again. The free shuttles run every day, making 29 stops along the way including, the Miami Beach Marina, the Sanford L. Ziff Jewish Museum, the Art Deco Welcome Center, Lincoln Road Mall, City Hall, The Jackie Gleason Theater, the Holocaust Memorial, and the Miami Beach Chamber of Commerce. Waiting time is usually less than 15 minutes. Weekdays, the shuttles operate from 8am until 2am, Thursdays through Saturdays until 4 am and on Sunday and holidays from 10am until 2am. The funky painted vehicles are air-conditioned and fully handicap accessible. Look for small rectangular white signs along the route indicating a stop, or call ☎ 305/843-9283 for more information. The drivers, though not tour guides, will try to answer any questions you have about the area. And the windows are superwide, which allow for great sightseeing. Also on South Beach is a free tram that runs up and down Lincoln Road mall, where no other vehicles are permitted, from Washington Avenue to Alton every day from 9am until 5pm.

BY RAIL   Two rail lines, operated by the Metro-Dade Transit Agency (☎ **305/ 638-6700**), run in concert with each other. **Metrorail,** the city's modern high-speed commuter train, is a 21-mile elevated line that connects Miami's northern and southern suburbs to downtown and each other. If you're staying in Coral Gables or Coconut Grove, you can park your car at a nearby station and ride the rail downtown. Unfortunately for visitors, the line's usefulness is limited. The trains simply don't go most places that tourists go. Metrorail operates daily from 6am to midnight; trains run every 7½ minutes during rush hours and every 15 minutes at other times. The fare is $1.25.

Metromover, a 4½-mile elevated line, circles the city center in two big loops, and connects with Metrorail at Government Center and Brickell Station. Riding on rubber tires, the single-train car winds past 21 stations and through some of the city's most important business and retail locations, including the Omni International Mall and the Brickell Financial District. At 25¢ a ride, the Disneyesque Metromover is one of Miami's best sightseeing bargains. Service runs daily from 6am to midnight about every 5 minutes. Transfers to Metrorail are $1.

BY BUS   Miami's suburban layout is not conducive to getting around by bus. **Metrobus** provides service with widely varying frequency. Stops are sometimes marked by green-and-blue signs that should be (but often aren't) accompanied by route information. Standard bus fare is $1.25, though some express routes charge $2.75, and exact change is required. Transfers cost 25¢. Most buses are wheelchair accessible. Disabled passengers, students, and those over 65 pay only 60¢ (10¢ per transfer).

BY TAXI   If you're not planning to travel any great distance, an occasional taxi is a good alternative to renting a car. Especially if you plan to spend most of your holiday in South Beach's Art Deco District, you'd be wise to avoid the parking hassles and expense that come with a car. Consider renting a car only for the days you choose to venture onto the mainland or to some other city.

The meter starts at $1.10 for the first one-seventh of a mile and increases at the rate of $1.75 for each additional mile. Major cab companies include **Metro** (☎ **305/ 888-8888**) and **Yellow** (☎ **305/444-4444**). On Miami Beach, the reigning cab company is **Central** (☎ **305/532-5555**). A flat-rate schedule is in place only for rides to the airport and prices range from $22 to $46.

BY BICYCLE   The sprawling nature of Miami makes distance bicycling both difficult and dangerous, but if you're staying in South Beach or Coral Gables, cycling to neighborhood spots makes sense. See "More Places to Play, Both Indoors & Out," in chapter 5, for details.

ON FOOT   With the exception of a few areas in Coconut Grove and South Beach, Miami is not a walker's city. Most attractions are too far apart from each other to make walking feasible. Like the citizens of Los Angeles, most Miamians get into their cars even when going just a few blocks.

FAST FACTS: Miami

American Express   For travel arrangements, traveler's checks, currency exchange, and other member services, Miami offices include 330 Biscayne Blvd., downtown (☎ **305/358-7350**); 9700 Collins Ave., Bal Harbour (☎ **305/ 865-5959**); and 32 Miracle Mile, Coral Gables (☎ **305/446-3381**). Offices are open Monday to Friday from 9am to 5pm and Saturday from 10am to 4pm. Bal Harbour also keeps hours on Sunday from noon to 5pm.

To report lost or stolen traveler's checks, call ☎ **800/221-7282.**

Camera Repair   The following are shops known for reliable repair work: **Dan's Camera Clinic,** 5142 Biscayne Blvd., downtown (☎ **305/759-2541**); **World Wide Photo,** with various locations in Miami, including 219 7th St., South Beach (☎ **305/672-5188**); and **Aberbach's of Miami Beach,** 441 41st St., Miami Beach (☎ **305/532-5446**).

Car Rentals   See "Getting Around," earlier in this chapter, and in chapter 2.

Convention Center   A high-tech "new-deco" facade fronts over a million square feet of exhibition space at the **Miami Beach Convention Center,** 1901 Convention Center Dr., Miami Beach, FL 33139 (☎ **305/673-7311**), the venue for many annual huge shows, including the world's largest boat show (See "Florida Calendar of Events," in chapter 2).

Curfew   The city of Miami enforces a curfew for teenagers 18 or younger out without a legal guardian after 11pm on weekdays and midnight on weekends.

Doctors   In an emergency, call an ambulance by dialing ☎ **911** from any phone. No coins are required.

The **Dade County Medical Association** sponsors a Physician Referral Service (☎ **305/324-8717**), open Monday to Friday from 9am to 4:30pm.

Health South Doctors' Hospital, 5000 University Dr., Coral Gables (☎ **305/666-2111**), is a 285-bed acute-care hospital with a 24-hour physician-staffed emergency department.

Emergencies   To reach the police, ambulance, or fire department, dial ☎ **911** from any phone. No coins are needed.

Emergency hotlines include **Crisis Intervention** (☎ **305/358-4357** or 305/ 358-HELP); **Poison Information Center** (☎ **800/282-3171**); and **Rape Hotline** (☎ **305/585-5185**).

Gratuities   Many area restaurants and bars automatically add a 15% gratuity to bar and food checks without telling customers. Read the check carefully and make it a habit to ask your server if a tip has already been included before paying any bill. Some unscrupulous servers count on being double tipped by unwary customers.

Information   Always check local newspapers for special things to do during your visit. See "Newspapers/Magazines," below. For a complete list of tourist boards and other information sources, see "Visitor Information" under "Orientation," earlier in this chapter.

Liquor Laws   Only adults 21 or older may legally purchase or consume alcohol in the state of Florida. Minors are usually permitted in bars that serve food. Liquor laws are strictly enforced; if you look young, carry identification. Beer and wine are also sold in most supermarkets and convenience stores. Liquor stores in the City of Miami Beach and most of Miami are open 7 days a week, but can't sell alcohol until after noon on Sunday.

Luggage Storage/Lockers   Miami International Airport no longer offers baggage checks because of bomb threats. However, most hotels offer luggage-storage

A Note on Smoking

Unless I note otherwise, hotels in this chapter offer no-smoking rooms. Inquire before booking.

facilities. If you're taking a cruise from the Port of Miami (see chapter 5), bags can be stored in your ship's departure terminal.

Newspapers/Magazines   The well-respected *Miami Herald* is the city's only English-language daily. It's especially known for its Latin American coverage and its excellent Friday "Weekend" entertainment guide. The most useful alternative weekly is the well-respected tabloid *New Times. Ocean Drive* a large-format free monthly is the best source for the scoop on local goings-on. Look for it especially in South Beach boutiques and restaurants. *Miami-Metro,* on sale at newsstands, is the area's trendy glossy with articles and listings to keep local readers up on events. *TWN* is a gay publication distributed free in Miami in purple boxes. Other gay publications can be found at neighborhood gyms.

Pharmacies   **Walgreens** pharmacies are all over town, including 8550 Coral Way, Coral Gables (☎ **305/221-9271**); 1845 Alton Rd., South Beach (☎ **305/531-8868**); and 6700 Collins Ave., Miami Beach (☎ **305/861-6742**). The branch at 5731 Bird Rd., at Southwest 40th Street (☎ **305/666-0757**), is open 24 hours. **Eckerd Drugs** at 1825 Miami Gardens Dr. (at Northeast 185th Street), North Miami Beach (☎ **305/932-5740**), is open until midnight.

Police   For emergencies, dial ☎ **911** from any phone. No coins are needed. For other matters, call ☎ **305/595-6263** to find the precinct nearest you.

Post Office   The main post office, 2200 NW 72nd Ave. (☎ **305/470-0222**), is located west of Miami International Airport. Conveniently located post offices include 1300 Washington Ave., South Beach (☎ **305/599-1787**), and 3191 Grand Ave., Coconut Grove (☎ **305/599-1750**).

Safety   Miami has been plagued by a spate of bad press, and there are some dangers here. In general, however, visitors are safe in the beach areas and in the daylight hours. For more specifics, see "Safety" under "Orientation," earlier in this chapter.

Taxes   A 6% state sales tax plus 0.5% local tax, for a total of 6.5%, is added on at the register for all goods and services purchased. In addition, most municipalities levy special taxes on restaurants and hotels. In Surfside, hotel taxes total 10.5%; in Bal Harbour, 9.5%; in Miami Beach (including South Beach), 11.5%; and in the rest of Miami-Dade County, 12.5%. Combined, these taxes can add 16% to 19% to your hotel bill—a hefty sum to keep in mind.

In Miami Beach, Surfside, and Bal Harbour, the resort (hotel) tax also applies to hotel restaurants and restaurants with liquor licenses.

Taxis   See "Getting Around," earlier in this chapter.

Transit Information   For **Metrorail** or **Metromover** schedule information, phone ☎ **305/638-6700.** See "Getting Around," earlier in this chapter, for more information.

Weather   For an up-to-date recording of current weather conditions and forecast reports, dial ☎ **305/229-4522.**

4 Accommodations You Can Afford

There are literally hundreds and hundreds of places to stay in and around Miami. And accommodations come in every price range. The best deals are to be had in the summer season. Although Miami is a business city as well as a resort destination, the warm summer months attract fewer vacationers and conventioneers.

South Florida's tourist season is fairly well defined, beginning in mid-November and lasting until about Easter. Hotel prices escalate until about March, after which they begin to decline. You can get some great rates during the off-season and the shoulder season, when hotel rates are typically 30% to 50% lower than their winter highs.

But timing isn't everything. In many cases, rates will also depend on your hotel's proximity to the beach and how much ocean you can see from your window. Small motels a block or two from the water can be up to 40% cheaper than similar hostelries right on the sand. When a hotel is right on the beach, its oceanfront rooms will usually be significantly more expensive than similar accommodations in the rear.

TIPS ON FINDING THE ROOM THAT'S RIGHT FOR YOU

Many of the old hotels from the 1930s, 1940s, and 1950s (when most Miami resorts were constructed) have been totally overhauled; others have survived with occasional coats of paint and new carpeting, which some owners like to call renovation. Be sure to ask about what work has been done, since, especially on the ocean, sea air and years of tourist wear can result in musty, paint-peeled rooms. Also, be sure to find out if the hotel you're booking (or one of its neighbors) is undergoing reconstruction while you're there. There's nothing worse than the sounds of jackhammers over breakfast. I've omitted the more worn hotels and tried to list only those that have been fully upgraded recently. But it is hard to keep up. There are dozens of properties always under renovation on South Beach, where most of Miami's tourists spend their time.

In addition to hotels, there are some great guest houses in Miami Beach. They may not offer all the amenities of the high-priced resorts, but they're generally intimate, clean, and well run by hospitable hosts.

An even better deal can be had at condos or homes that rent by the week or month. I've listed sources below to help you find the right place.

If you can't get a room after inquiring at the places listed in this guide (an extremely unlikely prospect), look along Miami Beach's Collins Avenue, especially between 70th and 195th streets and 3rd to 40th streets. Also check on Abbot Avenue between 78th and 95th streets. There are dozens of hotels and motels, in all price categories, on this strip; many of them are slated for renovation, so there's bound to be a vacancy.

I've selected several good chain hotels in each area—all the big ones are here—and included contact information in the introduction to each section.

A NOTE ABOUT PRICES For the sake of simplicity, the rates have been broken down into broad categories: winter (usually between November and March or April) and off-season (usually May to August). The months in between, the shoulder season, should fall somewhere in between the highs and lows. These prices given should be considered a guideline, not as a guarantee.

The prices listed below are based on 1998 rates and don't include state and city taxes, which, in some parts of Miami, are as high as 12.5%. Some hotels, especially those in South Beach, also tack on an additional service charge.

Prices are based on published rates (or rack rates) for standard single and double rooms. Check with the reservations agent, since many rooms are also available above and below the category ranges listed. And always ask about packages, since it's almost always possible to get a better deal than these "official" rates.

LONG-TERM STAYS If you plan to visit Miami for a week, a month, a season, or more, think about renting a room in a condominium apartment. Long-term accommodations (also known as short-term rentals, meaning less than a year) exist in every price category from budget to deluxe and in general are extremely reasonable, especially during the off-season. A short note to the chamber of commerce in the area in which you're interested will be answered with a list of availabilities. Also check with the reservation services and real estate agents below.

Call Bill Squire at **Florida Sun Break** (☎ **800/786-2732** or 305/532-1516; fax 305/781-1312), one of the only specialists in short-term rentals with properties from Jupiter to Key West. Rates for South Beach condos range from $450 to $900 per week. An oceanfront one-bedroom with a balcony and full kitchen recently rented for $700 weekly. You get about double the space of a typical hotel room in this price range, plus all the convenience and privacy of your own apartment. **Renter's Connection** at 1680 Meridian Ave., Miami Beach 33139 (☎ **305/538-7368;** fax 305/538-7473), also offers daily, weekly, or monthly condos from Miami Beach to Ft. Lauderdale.

Also, **Majestic Properties** (☎ **305/674-0202;** fax 305/674-0704), has a few South Beach homes and condos for rent.

RESERVATION SERVICES One of the country's largest hotel consolidators, **Hotel Reservations Network** (☎ **800/964-6835;** www.180096hotel.com), can secure discounts of up to 50% on some properties in South Florida. For example, in mid-March, they offered a rate of $169 at Miami Beach's Eden Roc down from $230—a savings of more than 25%.

Central Reservations (☎ **800/950-0232** or 305/274-6832; www.reservation-services.com; e-mail: rooms@america.com) works with many of Miami's hotels. The service can often secure discounts of up to 40% off for otherwise unyielding hotels and offer advice on the specific locales, especially in Miami Beach and downtown. The **South Florida Hotel Network** lists more than 300 hotels throughout Palm Beach to Miami and the Keys (☎ **800/538-3616** or 305/538-3616).

SOUTH BEACH

South Beach's hotels were mostly built in the late 1930s, just after the Depression, in an area originally planned as an affordable destination for middle-class northeasterners. Therefore, none of the hotels were really luxurious—they just happened to be situated on one of the most beautiful strips of beach in the country and built in a whimsical style that later became famous. Large resorts like the Fountainebleu were built later, 20-plus blocks north of South Beach, to cater to celebrities and jet-setters.

But after many years of transition, South Beach gained national recognition for its unique art deco architecture. The area is now South Florida's number-one tourist destination and home to many of the city's best restaurants and nightclubs.

The most expensive rooms are on Ocean Drive or Collins Avenue, just across the street from the beach. Thankfully, for at least most of South Beach, new buildings cannot be built directly on the sand and cannot exceed three stories. Remember, with a few notable exceptions, the art deco hotels generally are small and have tiny bathrooms and few services and facilities.

Some very well located chain hotel options include the **Days Inn** (☎ **800/325-2525** or 305/538-6631) at 100 21st St. (off Collins Avenue) or **Holiday Inn** (☎ **800/327-5476** or 305/534-1511) at 2201 Collins Ave. Both are at the north edge of the historic district and are within walking distance to the scene. Both hotels play

South Beach Accommodations & Dining

Accommodations:
Avalon Hotel 34
Banana Bungalow 1
Bayliss Guesthouse 19
Brigham Gardens 12
The Cavalier 21
The Chesterfield 32
Clay Hotel &
  Hostelling International 18
The Delano 10
Essex House 25
The Franklin Hotel 30
The Governor Hotel 3
Hotel Astor 28
Hotel Continental Riande 4
Hotel Leon 33
The Kent 23
Marseilles Deco Beach Hotel 5
Mermaid 31
Miami Beach International
  Travellers Hostel 29
Park Washington Hotel 26
The Tides 22
The Tudor 24
Villa Paradiso 14

Dining:
David's Cafe II 8
Grillfish 13
Joe's Stone Crab
  Restaurant 37
La Provence 11
La Sandwicherie 15
Macarena 20
Mama Vieja 2
Monty's 36
Mrs. Mendoza's 27
San Loco 16
Smith & Wollensky 38
Sport Cafe 35
Stephan's Gourmet
  Market & Cafe 17
Van Dyke Cafe 9
World Resources 7
Yuca 6

NA-0024

up the tropical look and offer standard chain-hotel-style rooms. Also, each has its own pool, sundeck, and pool bar and is directly on the ocean. The Holiday Inn has larger, more lushly landscaped grounds hidden behind an Eckerd's drugstore and lots of amenities, including a private beach and water-sports equipment rentals. Both usually offer rooms for under $90 even in season.

SUPER-CHEAP SLEEPS

✪ **Banana Bungalow.** 2360 Collins Ave., Miami Beach, FL 33139. ☎ **800/7-HOSTEL** or 305/538-1951. Fax 305/531-3217. E-mail: MIAMIres@bananabungalow.com. 60 private units, all with bathroom; 30 shared units, with shared bathroom. A/C TV TEL. Winter $13–$16 per person in shared units; $60–$67 single; $72–$78 single or double. Off-season $12–$14 per person in shared units; $40–$50 single; $56–$63 double. Maximum stay is 20 days. In shared rms. if you pay for 7 days, you'll get the 8th free. MC, V. Free parking.

Opened in late 1996, this youth hostel-like hotel is the most recent and recommendable addition to the South Beach budget scene. Situated across the street from a popular beach and only 6 or 7 blocks from the best shops, clubs, and restaurants, this redone 1950s 2-story newcomer surrounds a pool and deck complete with shuffleboard, a small alfresco restaurant, and a tiki bar where young European travelers hang out.

Private rooms are like a very hip Holiday Inn with painted floors and cool furnishings. Many have a fridge; ask for one. If one happens to be available, you can use it at no extra charge. The best rooms face a narrow canal where motorboats and kayaks are available to rent for a small charge. In general, rooms are clean and well kept despite a few rusty faucets and chipped Formica furnishings. Guests in shared rooms need to bring their own towels.

All rooms have telephones, televisions, and air conditioners. It's also one of the only hotels in this price range with a private pool. In addition, guests can enjoy free nightly movies, sightseeing tours, discounts at local clubs, and a great community spirit.

Bayliss Guesthouse. 504 14th St., South Beach, FL 33139. ☎ **888/3054683** or 305/531-3755. Fax 305/532-3755. www.nassausuites.com. E-mail: SouthBComber@worldnet.com. 21 units, all with bathroom (some with shower only). A/C TV TEL. Winter $60–$75 single or double, $75–$100 efficiency or 1-bedroom. Off-season $45–$65 single or double, $65–$80 efficiency or 1-bedroom. AE, DISC, MC, V. Street parking may be difficult to find nearby.

From small but sparkling clean guest rooms to sunny and spacious efficiencies, this understated guest house is a perfect antidote to the high-priced accommodations in Miami Beach. On a conveniently located side street, this 2-story 1939 apartment house has been converted into a modest, gay-friendly hotel with comfortable, well-outfitted rooms. In addition to telephones, televisions, and air conditioners, all rooms also have cable, refrigerators, ceiling fans, and voice mail. Others offer full kitchens and living rooms. Although it has no pool or recreation on the premises, this simple and private hotel is an excellent choice for those eager to explore the many facets of this bustling neighborhood, just 3 blocks from the ocean. A school across the street makes it quiet on weekends and in the evening, but a bit raucous around lunchtime. The owners also manage three other recommendable properties on South Beach, but they are slightly higher priced.

✪ **Brigham Gardens.** 1411 Collins Ave., South Beach, FL 33139. ☎ **305/531-1331.** Fax 305/538-9898. 19 units, all with bathroom. A/C TV TEL. Winter $85–$130 single or double. Off-season $60–$110 single or double. Extra person $5. Pets stay for $6 a night, and young children stay in parents' room free. 10% discount on all stays of 1 week or longer. AE, MC, V.

When you enter the tropically landscaped garden, you'll hear macaws and parrots chirping and see cats and lizards running through the bougainvillea. The tiny but lush grounds are framed by the quaint Mediterranean buildings that are pleasant, though in need of some sprucing up. Thanks to the fact that most rooms have full kitchens, you'll find many people staying for longer than a weekend. You may, too. You can make your own coffee and do your own laundry on the premises. All rooms have at least microwaves and coffeepots. This happy spot is managed by a mother and daughter who go out of their way to see that their guests and their pets are well cared for. There is no pool, restaurant, or bar, but you'll find the funky, central setting a homey, affordable respite from the neighborhood's crazy pricing and overcommercialization. Like most other small properties on South Beach, parking can be a pain. Consider ditching the car.

The Chesterfield Hotel. 855 Collins Ave., South Beach, FL 33139. ☎ **800/244-6023** or 305/531-5831. www.southbeachgroup.com. 49 units, all with bathroom. A/C TV TEL. Introductory rates winter 1998, from $79 single or double. Weekly $395. Rates include continental breakfast. MC, V.

A number of cheap hotels started springing up between 8th and 9th streets on Collins Avenue in late 1997. Three are owned by the South Beach Group, which does a decent job on rehabbing old deco buildings on a shoestring. All are relatively clean and just 1 block to the hippest boutiques in town and 2 blocks to the most popular beach. With a funky decor, inexpensive sidewalk cafe, and large lobby, The Chesterfield is the most recommendable. Like those in most other deco hotels, the rooms here are not particularly large, but are outfitted with all the necessary comforts such as TV, phone, and central air-conditioning. The decor is a budget interpretation of the safari look with cool animal print fabrics and sleek black and wood furniture. It's not luxurious, but it is a good deal, especially for the neighborhood. With rates of less than $80, all the hotels are worth considering. Stay for a week and pay about $400, which is like getting 2 nights free.

✪ Clay Hotel & Hosteling International. 1438 Washington Ave. (at Española Way), South Beach, FL 33139. ☎ **305/534-2988.** Fax 305/673-0346. 200 beds, all with bathroom. A/C. $40–$50 single; $60–$70 single or double; $14–$16 dorm beds. Taxes are included. Sheets and towels for dorm rooms are $2 extra. Pay for 6 nights in advance and get 7th night free. Bring Frommer's guide to the desk for an additional 10% off. JCB, MC, V.

A member of the International Youth Hostel Federation, the Clay occupies a beautiful 1920s-style Spanish Mediterranean building at the corner of historic Española Way. Like other IYHF members, this hostel is open to all ages and is a great place to meet like-minded travelers. The usual smattering of Australians, Europeans, and other budget travelers makes this Miami's best clearinghouse of "insider" travel information. Even if you don't stay here, you might want to check out the ride board, walk through the garden, or mingle with fellow travelers over a beer at the sidewalk cafe. It is, by far, the nicest hostel in town.

A thorough renovation in 1996 and 1997 made this hostel an exceptional value and an attractive budget alternative even for those who may be reluctant to stay in a hostel. The rates even include the local 12.5% tax, which most places in town tack on. Still, don't expect nightly turndown service or chocolates. You'll find a self-serve Laundromat, satellite TV, occasional movie nights, and a tour desk with car rental available. You will be charged 50¢ per local phone call. Advanced reservations are essential for private rooms year-round. They are superclean and simply furnished. Private rooms have phones and televisions. Be sure to ask for a room off the main drag where the street noise won't be too loud. Don't bother with a car in this congested area.

The Franklin Hotel. 860 Collins Ave., South Beach, FL 33139. ☎ **305/531-5541.** Fax 305/673-4112. 48 units, all with bathroom. A/C TV TEL. Winter $75–$125 single or double. Off-season $50–$65 single or double. AE, DC, MC, V. Rate includes continental breakfast. Parking at nearby municipal pay lot.

This impressive Mediterranean hotel occupies a bustling corner in the hub of South Beach's Art Deco District. Yearly refurbishments brought the stunning 3-story building back to its original 1934 splendor. In the grand tile and wood lobby you'll find a subdued bar where some young trendy guests usually hang out. The rooms, though not at all charming or fancy, are large and clean. Unfortunately, while the lobby and hallways have stunning wood floors, the guest rooms are covered with dark, depressing carpet. Still, the place is thoroughly recommendable. You may want to ask for a room on the top floor away from the street. On a Saturday night the sidewalks of this corner are loud and wild.

Miami Beach International Travellers Hostel. 236 9th St., Miami Beach, FL 33139. ☎ **800/978-6787** or 305/534-0268. Fax 305/534-5862. 12 private units, all with bathroom; 16 hostel units (with 3 or 4 bunk beds) with shared bathroom. A/C. $50 single or double; $12 hostel bed for members, $14 for nonmembers. MC, V.

Although not a member of any national or international hostel organization, this family run addition to the hostel scene on Miami Beach is worthwhile for superbudget travelers and does give discounts to members. It couldn't be in a better spot. Only 2 blocks from the beach, the old building has been tidied up for the droves of young backpackers and explorers who find their way here to stay in simple rooms, some with wooden-planked bunkbeds and others with plain but adequate single beds. There are no more than four beds per room.

The helpful staff is always available to help plan trips and give tips on what's happening in town. Though not as well maintained or as popular as the Clay, this friendly little South Beach crash pad is a good second choice. As in other hostels, be particularly careful with your valuables.

✪ Park Washington Hotel. 1020 Washington Ave., South Beach, FL 33139. ☎ **305/532-1930.** Fax 305/672-6706. 36 units, all with bathroom. A/C TV TEL. Winter $79–$99 single or double; $129 suite. Off-season $59–$69 single or double; $99 suite. Rates include self-serve coffee and Danish. Extra person $20. Children stay free in parents' room. AE, MC, V.

The Park Washington is a large, refurbished hotel that offers some of the best values in South Beach. Located 2 blocks from the ocean, this hotel has made a name for itself by offering good-quality accommodations at incredible prices. Designed in the 1930s by Henry Hohauser, one of the beach's most famous architects, the Park Washington reopened in 1989. Most of the rooms have original furnishings and well-kept interiors, and some have kitchenettes.

You'll also enjoy a decent-sized outdoor heated pool with a sundeck, bikes for rent, and access to a nearby health club.

The same owners run the adjacent Taft House and Kenmore hotels. All three attract a large gay clientele, and all offer privacy, lush landscaping, a great pool and sundeck, consistent quality, and a value-oriented philosophy. There is no parking on the premises, but there is a public garage at 7th Street, less than 3 blocks away.

For a Few Bucks More

Avalon Hotel. 700 Ocean Dr., South Beach, FL 33139. ☎ **800/933-3306** or 305/538-0133. Fax 305/534-0258. 106 units, all with bathroom. A/C TV TEL. Winter $120–$180 single or double. Off-season $65–$145 single or double. Rates include continental breakfast, full breakfast off-season. Extra person $10. Children 11 and under stay free in parents' room. 10% discount for stays of 7 days or more. AE, CB, DC, DISC, MC, V. Valet parking $14.

Classic art deco digs right on the beach, occupying a pretty parcel of land that wraps around the corner of 7th Street, the hotel is striking both inside and out. The rooms are well decorated in traditional 1930s style. A casual restaurant occupies the modest lobby; it's best for lunch either inside or on the breezy outdoor patio. The experienced management, known for its excellent inns in Newport, Rhode Island, runs this hotel with an even hand.

If the Avalon is full, don't hesitate to accept a room in its other hostelry, the **Majestic,** located across the street. Room service, free coffee, refreshments, and breakfast are also available.

Cavalier. 1320 Ocean Dr., South Beach, FL 33139. ☎ **800/OUTPOST** or 305/604-5000. Fax 305/531-5543. 44 units, all with bathroom. A/C MINIBAR TV TEL. Winter $150–$195 single or double; $275–$350 suite. Off-season $95–$155 single or double; $230–$250 suite. Extra person $15. Children 11 and under stay free in parents' room. AE, DC, DISC, MC, V. Valet parking $14, self-parking $6.

Like Island Outpost's other recommendable properties, the Cavalier, a hip, well-priced hotel, is kept in shape by yearly refurbishments. You can't beat this oceanfront location, which is adjacent to shops and restaurants. Palm trees brush the ceilings of the modest lobby, where young trendy guests make their way to their rooms. Funky prints cover the walls, which are the colors of a tequila sunrise. A young, competent staff waits on guests and offers lots of good advice about local clubs, restaurants, and shopping. Rooms come equipped with CD players and discs. You can also use a VCR and rent videos. Considering it's on Ocean Drive, most rooms are relatively quiet.

✪ **Essex House.** 1001 Collins Ave., South Beach, FL 33139. ☎ **800/55-ESSEX** or 305/534-2700. Fax 305/532-3827. 79 units, all with bathroom. A/C TV TEL. Winter $155–$195 single or double; $255–$300 suite. Off-season $99–$139 single or double; $199–$245 suite. Rates include deluxe continental breakfast. Minimum stay 2 nights on weekends in season, 3 nights on holidays. Extra person $10. AE, CB, DC, DISC, MC, V. Valet parking $14. Nearby parking available for $4 weekdays, $6 weekends and holidays.

This art deco landmark is one of South Beach's gems, especially since the $3 million renovation completed in 1998. A new, very small pool is just one of the many additions here. On-line is a new martini bar and piano lounge. The Essex House is a gorgeous textbook example of streamline moderne style, complete with large porthole windows, original etched glasswork, ziggurat arches, and detailed crown moldings. Suites feature minibars, coffeemakers, and VCRs. Ask for a room with a refrigerator, since more than a dozen standard rooms do have them. The Essex also features 24-hour reception, a high-tech piano in the lobby/lounge, and a state-of-the-art security system. Located 1 block from the ocean, this hotel is spick-and-span, almost too much like a chain. But the staff is extremely pleasant and helpful.

The Governor Hotel. 35 21st St., Miami Beach, FL 33139. ☎ **800/542-0444** or 305/532-2100. Fax 305/532-9139. 125 units, all with bathroom. A/C TV TEL. Winter $89–$125 single or double. Off-season $69–$89 single or double. Children under 18 stay free. AE, DC, DISC, MC, V. Free parking.

This reasonably priced hotel on the northernmost border of South Beach is frequented by conventioneers who until recently had no real hotel to stay in. The Governor is nothing special, but the rooms are decent enough and the rates are pretty cheap. There is also a medium-sized pool and small cafe and bar.

As an example of art deco architecture, this hotel is one of the most stylish in the area. It has streamlined details from the checkerboard floor tiles to the steel marquee and looming flagstaffs. But don't expect too much inside. A recent revamping improved the slightly tacky decor and introduced some more service-oriented staff to the place. You'll want to drive to the beach since it's a few long blocks through a not-so-scenic neighborhood of mostly unrenovated hotels serving as residences to a pretty seedy set.

✪ **Hotel Continental Riande.** 1825 Collins Ave., South Beach, FL 33139. ☎ **800/RIANDE-1** or 305/531-3503. Fax 305/531-2803. 251 units, all with bathroom. A/C MINIBAR

TV TEL. Winter $135–$160 single or double. Off-season $105–$135 single or double. Extra person $10. Children 11 and under stay free in parents' room. Frommer's readers get a 20% discount. AE, DC, DISC, MC, V. Valet parking $8.

Catering to a largely Latin and European clientele, the Riande has become quite well known with its simple formula for success. The rooms and lobby areas are clean and well cared for but not too fussy. The hotel overlooks the ocean and is just 2 blocks from The Delano hotel (see below) and the best of South Beach. Also, a large outdoor pool and sundeck are just out back. There's a restaurant/coffee shop with both buffet and menu service. Also, room service is available daily for breakfast and dinner. The Riande is just the ticket if you want value and convenience right on South Beach.

✪ **Hotel Leon.** 841 Collins Ave., South Beach, FL 33139. ☎ **305/673-3767.** Fax 305/673-5866. E-mail: hotel-leon@travelbase.com. 17 units, 1 penthouse, all with bathroom. A/C TV TEL. Winter $125 single or double, $165–$215 suite, $375 penthouse. Off-season $100 single or double, $135–$185 suite, $315 penthouse. Extra bed $10. Valet parking $14. AE, DC, MC, V.

A true value, this stylish sliver of a property has won the loyalty of fashion industrialists and romantics alike. The very central location—1 block from the sea and in the heart of shopping and dining—means a car isn't necessary. Unfortunately there is no pool. The spacious, well-renovated rooms are sparkling clean and warmly appointed. Gleaming wood floors and simple pale furnishings are appreciated in a neighborhood where many others overdo the art deco motif. Each room has two phones, sunken oval tubs and robes, and CD players and CDs. A meeting room and business center make this a fine choice for business trips. In the standard rooms there are no minibars or fridges, but you can order room service anytime. In the morning enjoy a moderately priced breakfast ($8.50) of croissants, fresh rolls, ham, cheese, and eggs cooked to order. The young German owners, Eric and Angela Gabriel, are committed to providing excellent service with a distinctly personal touch.

✪ **The Kent.** 1131 Collins Ave., South Beach, FL 33139. ☎ **800/OUTPOST** or 305/604-5000. Fax 305/531-0720. www.islandlife.com. E-mail: outpost800@aol.com. 54 units, all with bathroom. A/C MINIBAR TV TEL. Winter $150–$195 single or double; $275 suite. Off-season $95–$155 single or double; $230 suite. Extra person $15. Children 11 and under stay free in parents' room. AE, DC, DISC, MC, V. Valet parking $14, self-parking $6.

When the other Island Outpost hotels are full, you are likely to find a spot at this property. The prices are same as their beachside hotels, the Cavalier and the Leslie, but the rooms tend to be less noisy. The staff includes an eager-to-please group of Caribbeans, and they cater to a clientele largely made up of the fashion industry. Frequent shoots are coordinated in the lobby and conference room, where full office services are available. Thanks to a vacant lot in the backyard (for now), some rooms in the rear offer nice views of the ocean. The decor is modest but tasteful. CD players are standard, as are bright and whimsical furnishings. VCRs are available, and video rentals can be delivered. For the price, this is an excellent value right in South Beach's active center. There is no pool or sundeck, but you are only a block from the beach. By all means, accept a room in any of the other Island hotels if this is booked up.

Marseilles Hotel. 1741 Collins Ave. South Beach, Fl 33139. ☎ **800/327-4739** or 305/538-5711. Fax 305/673-1006. www.marseilleshotel.com. E-mail: peter@marseilleshotel.com. 116 units, all with bathroom. A/C TV TEL Winter $115–$135 single or double; $180 suite. Off-season $79–$99 single or double; $145 suites. Frommer's readers get 10% discount in winter and 20% off in the off-season. AE, DC, DISC, MC, V. Valet parking $10.

The Marseilles is a full-service, classic art deco hotel located right on the beach, making it one of the very best deals in this supertrendy area. It's three doors from the Delano and near the best of everything. Still, it's a little worn around the edges, despite a recent sprucing up. But owners Lloyd and Clara Mandell are continuing to make improvements. It's got a million-dollar location, the right price, a pleasant staff, a very recommendable restaurant and bar, and a thoroughly tasteful decor. With only about 100 units, it is more intimate than the larger Riande, a few doors away. The bar and restaurant are popular with budget-seeking locals. The suites (three of which have Jacuzzis at no extra charge) are an exceptionally good deal if you want to spend a lot of time in your room. (You'll find a telescope for spying on naked sunbathers below.) The rooms are on the small side but clean and comfortable. All have small refrigerators and bottled water upon check-in. When Marseilles is full, the staff may suggest the nearby **Dorchester** (also owned by the Mandells). It's cheaper and decent but not nearly as recommendable.

✪ **The Mermaid.** 909 Collins Ave., Miami Beach, FL 33140. ☎ and fax **305/538-5324.** 8 units, all with bathroom. A/C TEL. Winter $105–$115 single or double; $200 suite. Off-season $75–$95 single or double; $175 suite. Extra person $10. Small children stay free in parents' room. Rates include continental breakfast. Discounts for longer stays and when it is not too busy. AE, MC, V.

There's something magical about this little hideaway tucked behind tropical gardens in the very heart of South Beach. You won't find the amenities of the larger hotels, but this 1-story guest house offers charm and hospitality that keeps people coming back. Plus, it's smack in the middle of the hottest part of South Beach and less than 2 blocks from the ocean. In 1996 the new owners, Ana and Gonzalo Torres, did a thorough clean-up, adding brightly colored fretwork around the doors and windows and installing phones in each room. Also, the wood floors have been stripped or covered in straw matting, one of the many Caribbean touches that make this place so cheery. There are no TVs so guests tend to congregate in the lush garden in the evenings. The owners sometimes host free impromptu dinners for their guests and friends. Also new in 1998 is live Latin music on the patio two or three nights a week.

Tudor Hotel. 1111 Collins Ave., South Beach, Fl 33139. ☎ **800/843-2934** or 305/ 534-2934. Fax 305/531-1874. 85 units, all with bathroom. A/C TV TEL. Winter from $99 single or double. Off-season from $79 single or double. AE, MC, V. Book through Sobe Discount Rooms (1059 Collins Ave., no. 205, Miami Beach, FL 33139; ☎ 305/538-8171; e-mail: sobedisc@netrox.net), which owns 9 units, and get a significantly lower rate (about 20% less) and free airport transportation with a stay of 3 days or longer.

This superbly situated hotel occupies a busy and attractive corner in the middle of the Art Deco District. Built in 1939, this classic deco charmer has been cleaned up, but not completely gutted. The curvaceous 3-story hotel still sports its original jalousie windows, but its tiny bathrooms have been redone in white basic tiles. Though small, the rooms are clean and bright. Most offer a small refrigerator and microwave. Some even have full kitchens at no extra cost. You won't find a view or any fancy amenities, but this property is a real value.

✪ **Villa Paradiso.** 1415 Collins Ave., Miami Beach, FL 33139. ☎ **305/532-0616.** Fax 305/ 673-5874. E-mail villap@gates.net. 17 units, all with bathroom. A/C TV TEL. Winter $100– $145 apt. single or double. Off-season $79–$105 apt. single or double. Weekly rates are 10% less. Extra person $5–$10. Frommer's readers get 10% discount on rack rates weekdays from June to September, except for holidays. AE, DC, MC, V.

This guest house, like Brigham Gardens, is more like a cozy apartment house than a hotel. There's no elegant lobby or restaurant, but rather amicable hosts, Lisa and Pascal Nicolle, who are happy to give you a room key and advice on what to do. The apartments are simple, but the style is fine for the beach, since you'll be spending most of your time outside anyway. Plus, the spacious apartments are quiet considering their location, smack in the middle of the bustling area, a few blocks from Lincoln Road and all of Miami Beach's best clubs. Most also have Murphy beds or foldout couches for extra friends. One big advantage here is that most units have a full kitchen, which saves money when it comes to eating out. There are also laundry facilities on the premises and free local phone service.

WORTH A SPLURGE

The Delano. 1685 Collins Ave., South Beach, FL 33139. ☎ **800/555-5001** or 305/672-2000. Fax 305/532-0099. 209 units, all with bathroom. A/C MINIBAR TV TEL. Winter $310–$415 single or double; $475 loft; $700 suite; $800 bungalow; $1,850 two-bedroom; $2,200 penthouse. Off-season $180–$265 single or double (weekend rates for single or double same as winter rates); all other unit rates same as winter rates. Extra person $35. Children 17 and under stay free in parents' room. AE, DC, DISC, MC, V. Valet parking $16.

The opening of the Delano (pronounced like FDR's middle name) in 1995 made the front page of nearly every architecture and style magazine in the country. The design is whimsical and elegant; look for a huge hedge with a simple blue arched door in its center, or look up for a rocketlike fin (an original 1947 detail) sprouting from the top of the all-white building. Owner Ian Shrager, of Studio 54 fame, brought in designer Philippe Starck, who went wild with an impossible decor of 40-foot sheer white curtains hanging outside, mirrors everywhere, white billowing curtains, Adirondack chairs, and fur-covered beds.

If you absolutely have to tell your friends you stayed here, go ahead. The prices are out of this world, not only for rooms but for drinks, food, and services. So to cover the bases you may want to just splurge on a meal or a drink. An elegant bar attracts curious beautiful people nightly. The **Blue Door** (owned in part by Madonna) is known more as a place to be seen than it is for its great cuisine; the food and service are inconsistent. The thatched **Beach Bar** restaurant serves pricey gourmet sandwiches and salads. The guest rooms are all white; a perfectly crisp green Granny Smith apple is the only dose of color. It may sound antiseptic, but it's not: It's sexy and sophisticated. The poolside cabanas are the most desirable rooms because of their huge size, but they can be noisy since they are on an active poolside walkway. Unfortunately, the model-gorgeous staff is often aloof or simply unavailable. But the location is ideal; it's just north of the Art Deco District strip of bars and restaurants, away from the noisy street traffic but close enough to walk to hopping Lincoln Road Mall. And of course, it is right on the ocean.

✪ **Hotel Astor.** 956 Washington Ave., South Beach, FL 33139. ☎ **800/270-4981** or 305/531-8081. Fax 305/531-3193. 40 units, all with bathroom. A/C MINIBAR TV TEL. Winter $145–$200 single or double; $275–$320 suites. Off-season $115–$190 single or double; $245–$290 suites. Astor suite $420–$600. Extra person $30. Valet parking $14.

If you book enough in advance, you may actually be able to procure one of the three standard rooms, which rent for less than $150 in season. Otherwise, rates for this elegant and modern hotel are nearly double. It won't be easy, since the Astor is a small property that attracts many loyal return guests. Originally built in 1936, the renovation in 1995 made this simple 3-story gem into an overnight sensation. Although not waterfront, there is a small lap pool and a beautiful waterfall outside the sleek lobby bar area. And all the details are pure luxury, like swivel stands for the large screen TVs, ministereo systems, Belgian linens and towels, and funky custom lighting with dimmer switches. The hotel staff is known for bending over backwards in a town where service can fall flat. For the price (about half The Delano), this is a great option for those who like intimate but terribly hip accommodations. This is definitely a place for those in the know. **Astor Place** is one of Miami's best restaurants. The Florida-style menu is diverse and delicious (see listing under "Great Deals on Dining," below). Sunday brunch is one of the best in town.

✪ **The Tides.** 1220 Ocean Dr., South Beach, FL 33139. ☎ **800/OUTPOST** or 305/604-5000. Fax 305/672-6288. www.islandlife.com. E-mail: outpost800@aol.com. 45 units, all with bathroom. A/C MINIBAR TV TEL. Winter single or double $275 superior, $350–$425 suite; $900–$2,000 penthouse suite. Off-season single or double $150 superior, $200–$275 suite, $600–$1,100 penthouse suite. Extra person $20. Rates includes continental breakfast. AE, CB, DC, DISC, MC, V. Valet parking $15.

It will cost you a bundle, but the views alone might be worth it just for a night or two. Opened in late 1997 to rave reviews, this 12-story art deco masterpiece is one of the tallest buildings on this strip of Ocean Drive. It is the latest addition the Deco Hotel Chain owned by Chris Blackwell and his Island Outpost group, which includes the Cavalier and the Kent (reviewed in this section) and others. As in most of Outpost's hotels, there are VCRs and CD/cassette stereos as well as an eclectic collection of CDs in each room. Rooms are similar to those at The Delano, meaning they are starkly white but luxurious and fully equipped. The advantage here is the warm staff and more central location. Plus, rates for the cheapest rooms are about 30% less than the more famous Delano. Also, all rooms are large and have ocean views. Amenities include terraces, exercise facilities, a lobby lounge with live entertainment, a heated, freshwater pool on the rear mezzanine, and two superb alfresco restaurants featuring Mediterranean cuisine and fresh local seafood.

MIAMI BEACH/KEY BISCAYNE

The area just north of South Beach encompasses Surfside, Bal Harbour, and Sunny Isles. Unrestricted by zoning codes throughout the 1950s, 1960s, and especially the 1970s, area developers went nuts, building ever-bigger and more brazen structures, especially north of 41st Street, which is now known as "Condo Canyon." Subsequently, there's now a glut of medium-quality condos, with a few scattered holdouts of older hotels and motels that front the ocean casting shadows over the sand by afternoon.

Miami Beach, as described here, runs from 24th Street to 192nd Street, a long strip that varies slightly from end to end. The southern section, from 24th to 42nd streets, is really an extension of South Beach and can be a great deal if you want to pay slightly lower rates for your lodging while enjoying the scene in South Beach. Bal Harbour and Bay Harbour are at its center and retain their exclusivity and character. The neighborhoods north and south of here, like Surfside and Sunny Isles, have nice beaches and some shops, but seem a little worn around the edges.

There are only a couple of hotels on Key Biscayne, and both their rates are uniformly high. There are no budget listings here, but if you can afford it, Key Biscayne is a great place to stay. The island is far enough from the mainland to make it feel like a secluded tropical paradise yet close enough to downtown to take advantage of everything Miami has to offer.

Just north of South Beach is the **Days Inn** (☎ **800/325-2525** or 305/673-1513) at 42nd Street and Collins Avenue. It is right on the ocean and is very well kept. The **Howard Johnson** (☎ **800/446-4656** or 305/532-4411) at 4000 Alton Rd., just off the Julia Tuttle Causeway (I-95), is a generic 8-story building on a strip of land near a busy road. But it is convenient to the beach, by car or bike. Rooms, renovated in 1995, are clean and spacious, and some have pretty views of the city and intracoastal waterways. Farther north in Miami Beach, on an uncrowded stretch of beach, there is an oceanfront **Ramada Inn** (☎ **800/272-6232** or 305/865-8511), at 6701 Collins Ave., and a Howard Johnson (☎ **800/446-4656** or 305/868-1200), at 6261 Collins Ave.

SUPER-CHEAP SLEEPS

Compostela Motel. 9040 Collins Ave., Miami Beach, FL 33154. ☎ **305/861-3083.** Fax 305/861-2996. 20 units, all with bathroom (some with shower only). A/C TV TEL. Winter from $75 suite; from $65 one-bedroom apt., $55 efficiency. Off-season from $65 suite; $55 one-bedroom apt., $45 efficiency. Extra person $10. Children 17 and under stay free in parents' room. AE, MC, V. Free parking.

The owners of the Compostela have recently set to renovating their three buildings, all within walking distance of the exclusive Bal Harbour Shops and many good shopping and dining areas. Although the buildings were run-down efficiencies for many years, the new interiors are really quite nice. All are carpeted and most have full kitchenettes, a bonus when you're on a budget. There's no fancy lobby, no doorman to greet you as you enter, and no amenities to speak of, save an outdoor pool and laundry facilities. But the area is safe and the staff courteous, although at some hours only Spanish speakers are available. Best of all, you're across the street from a great beach. You get a lot of space and a great location for a low price.

✪ **Dezerland Surfside Beach Hotel.** 8701 Collins Ave., Miami Beach, FL 33154. ☎ **800/ 331-9346** in the U.S., 800/331-9347 in Canada, or 305/865-6661. Fax 305/866-2630. 225 units, all with bathroom. A/C TV TEL. Winter $85–$115 single or double. Off-season $60–$75 single or double. Extra person $8. Children 18 and under stay free in parents' room. Special packages and group rates available. AE, CB, DC, DISC, MC, V. Self-parking.

Designed by car enthusiast Michael Dezer, the Dezerland is a unique place—part hotel and part 1950s automobile wonderland. Visitors, who include many European tourists, are welcomed by a 1959 Cadillac stationed by the front door, one of a dozen mint-condition classics around the grounds and lobby.

While it isn't luxe, the place is clean, and constant renovations improve it every year. Some rooms contain fully-equipped kitchenettes. Dezerland is located directly on the beach and features a mosaic of a pink Cadillac at the bottom of its surf-side pool.

Other amenities include a Jacuzzi, adjacent tennis courts and jogging track, Windsurfer and jet-ski rental, game room, launderette, car-rental and tour services desk, and an antique shop featuring 1950s memorabilia. There is also a restaurant and a lobby lounge with all-you-can-eat buffets and nightly entertainment.

Don't hesitate to accept a room in any of the other hotels owned by the Dezer family. The Colonial, Driftwood, and Chateau are slightly cheaper and located north on the beach.

Ocean Roc Resort Motel. 19505 Collins Ave., Miami Beach, FL 33160. ☎ **800/327-0553** or 305/931-7600. Fax 305/866-5881. 90 units, all with bathroom. A/C TV TEL. Winter $58–$79 single or double. Off-season $48–$70 single or double. $7 additional for efficiency. Extra person $7. Special rates for long stays. AE, CB, DC, MC, V. Free self-parking.

This place could use more than just a coat of paint to bring it up to snuff, but you certainly can't beat the price. Considering that it's got its own large pool, is situated directly on the ocean, and has private terraces and refrigerators in almost every room, you've found yourself a deal. The faded exterior, peeling paint, and chipped tile of this 3-story 1950s relic may not signify quality, but it doesn't seem to trouble the aging snowbirds who make a winter of it here. Many play cards in the common area or lounge on the concrete deck. Lounge chairs at the large pool rent for $2.75 a day or $15 for the week. There's also a budget diner on the lobby level overlooking the ocean and pool deck. Breakfast and lunch are served daily. Full dinners including coffee and dessert cost from $7 to $10 and are served every Friday and Saturday night. At press time, a huge condo tower was under construction. You may want to check to see if it's finished when you book a room, otherwise the construction noise and dust could be unbearable.

Miami Beach Accommodations & Dining

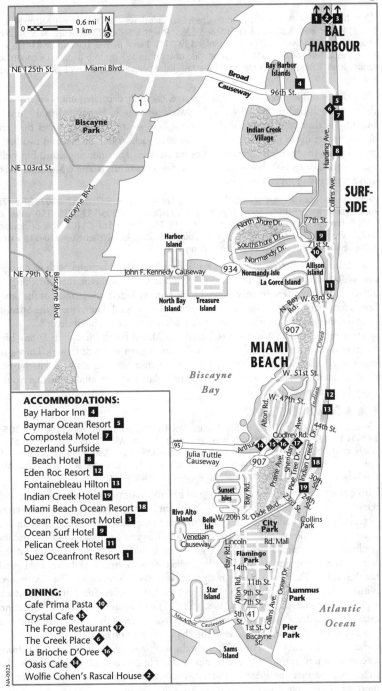

ACCOMMODATIONS:
Bay Harbor Inn 4
Baymar Ocean Resort 5
Compostela Motel 7
Dezerland Surfside
 Beach Hotel 8
Eden Roc Resort 12
Fontainebleau Hilton 13
Indian Creek Hotel 19
Miami Beach Ocean Resort 18
Ocean Roc Resort Motel 3
Ocean Surf Hotel 9
Pelican Creek Hotel 11
Suez Oceanfront Resort 1

DINING:
Cafe Prima Pasta 10
Crystal Cafe 15
The Forge Restaurant 17
The Greek Place 6
La Brioche D'Oree 16
Oasis Cafe 14
Wolfie Cohen's Rascal House 2

✪ **Pelican Creek Hotel.** 6580 Indian Creek Dr. (1 block west of Collins Ave.), Miami Beach, FL 33141. ☎ **800/588-7918** or 305/868-2285. Fax 305/868-3392. 46 units, all with bathroom (some with two). A/C TV TEL. Winter $89–$110 1 to 4 people; townhouse $145 up to 6 people. Off-season $65–$80 1 to 4 people; townhouse $99 up to 6 people. Discounts for longer stays. Rates include continental breakfast. Extra person $10. AE, DC, DISC, MC, V. Free parking.

This former condominium now rents its large, tastefully decorated units—many with fully-outfitted kitchenettes—by the day, week, or month. Renovated in 1996, the building is clean and bright. The best deals here are the two-level suites that can accommodate up to six people using a fold-out couch. A full kitchen and two bathrooms make this an ideal vacation choice for families. The undistinguished but well-maintained 2-story building is only 2 blocks from the ocean (about a 5-minute walk) and near many shops and restaurants.

Suez Oceanfront Resort. 18215 Collins Ave., Sunny Isles, FL 33160. ☎ **800/327-5278** (reservations from 9am to 5pm only), or 305/932-0661. Fax 305/937-0058. 150 units, all with bathroom (some with shower only). A/C TV TEL. Winter $67–$110 single or double; $175 suite. Off-season $39–$67 single or double; $125 suite. Kitchenettes $10–$15 extra. Extra person $15. AE, DC, MC, V. Free parking.

Guarded by an undersize replica of Egypt's famed Sphinx, this motel, with its orange-and-yellow motif, is more reminiscent of a fast-food restaurant than anything in ancient Egypt. It offers brightly colored rooms on the beach, where most of the other hotels have gone condo. The thatched umbrellas over beach lounges and the Spanish Mediterranean–style fountains in the courtyard add to the confused decor.

However, it's on the ocean and technically in Miami Beach (though its Sunny Isles location is closer to Hallandale in Broward County than to South Beach). There's an outdoor heated pool and a free launderette—perfect for long stays. A kitschy but pleasant lounge offers good prices and a palm-lined area reminds you that you're indeed in a tropical paradise.

FOR A FEW BUCKS MORE

✪ **Bay Harbor Inn.** 9601 E. Bay Harbor Dr., Bay Harbor Island, FL 33154. ☎ **305/868-4141.** Fax 305/867-9094. 24 units, all with bathroom. A/C TV TEL. Winter from $139 single or double; $149 suite; $199 penthouse suite. Off-season $60 single or double; $70 suite; $90 penthouse suite. Extra person $25. Children 12 and under stay free in parents' room. Rates include continental breakfast. AE, MC, V. Free parking.

This quaint little inn looks as if it ought to be in Vermont or somewhere woodsy and remote. But it's just moments from the beach, fine restaurants, and some of the city's best shopping. Actually the inn comes in two parts; the more modern section sits squarely on a little river, or "the creek" as it's called, and overlooks a heated outdoor pool and a boat named *Celeste* where guests eat breakfast. On the other side of the street is the cozier, antique-filled portion, where glass-covered bookshelves hold good beach reading. The rooms have a hodgepodge of wood furnishings, like oak-framed mirrors, canopied beds, Victorian chairs, and modern vanities. Some of the rooms are slightly larger (like no. 301, 305, 308, and 311) and boast an extra half bath at no extra cost. You do at times smell the aroma of cooking from the restaurant below, but you might find that this only adds to the charm of this homey inn.

Adjacent to the hotel is **The Palm,** a clubby steak-and-lobster house. Students from a nearby culinary institute run a restaurant and bar in the creekside building across the street, and a deluxe continental breakfast is served on a yacht. Try the restaurant for lunch or dinner, too. Prices are great and so is the service.

Baymar Ocean Resort. 9401 Collins Ave., Miami Beach, FL 33154. ☎ **800/8-BAYMAR** or 305/866-5446. Fax 305/866-8053. 106 units, all with bathroom. A/C TV TEL. Winter

$115–$125 single or double; $125–$135 efficiency; $150–$235 suite. Off-season $85–$95 double; $95–$105 efficiency; $125–$185 suite. Extra person $10. Children 11 and under stay free in parents' room. AE, DISC, MC, V. Parking $5.

A full renovation in 1996 did wonders for this little hotel on the strip just south of Bal Harbour, which makes it extremely popular with conservative religious groups and budget-conscious travelers.

Depending on what you're looking for, this could be one of the beach's best buys—assuming prices hold at their current level. The hotel is right on the ocean, with a low-key beach that attracts few other tourists, and offers all the modern conveniences, including some kitchenettes and large closets. You won't flip over the decor, but it's pleasant enough and all brand new. There isn't much within walking distance from this spot (much of the rest of the area is run-down or has been converted into condos), but you aren't far from anything you could possibly want to drive to. It may not be worth it to pay more for the oceanfront rooms since they tend to be smaller than the others. Rooms overlooking the large pool and sundeck area could get loud on busy days. You do get nice shared balcony space on the first-floor ocean-view rooms.

A small restaurant serving basic American fare and a tiki bar are popular with guests.

✪ **Indian Creek Hotel.** 2727 Indian Creek Dr., Miami Beach, FL 33140. ☎ **800/491-2772** or 305/531-2727. Fax 305/531-5651. 61 units, all with bathroom. A/C TV TEL. Winter from $130 single or double; $220 suite. Off-season $90 single or double; $150 suite. Extra person $10. Group packages available. AE, CB, DC, DISC, MC, V. Limited parking available on street.

Slightly north of South Beach is this small hotel where every detail of the 1936 building has been meticulously restored, from one of the beach's first operating elevators to the period steamer trunk in the lobby. The modest rooms are outfitted in art deco furnishings with pretty tropical prints and all the modern amenities. Just 1 short block from a good stretch of sand, the hotel is perfectly situated away from the hectic scene on South Beach, yet close enough to walk to most activities there. A landscaped pool area is a great place to lounge in the sun. The hotel also offers a small fitness center and conference facilities but not much else in the way of amenities.

Miami Beach Ocean Resort. 3025 Collins Ave., Miami Beach, FL 33140. ☎ **800/550-0505** or 305/534-0505. Fax 305/534-0515. 243 units, all with bathroom. A/C TV TEL. Winter $170–$200, 1 to 4 people; $220–$600 suite. Off-season $140–$170, 1 to 4 people; $200–$550 suite. AE, DC, MC, V.

Popular with tour groups and Europeans, this oceanfront resort reopened in 1995 and is a great choice for those who want a quiet place on the ocean in close proximity to South Beach and the mainland. The vast, elegant lobby is done up in Mexican tile, wood fretwork, and pleasing furnishings. Rooms are basic but very tastefully decorated with new wicker and rattan furnishings. A giant outdoor area is landscaped with palms and hibiscus and has a large heated pool as its centerpiece. It faces the large beach where water-sports equipment is available. The resort is a giant step above a good Holiday Inn at comparable prices. Plus, it boasts a decent restaurant that serves a breakfast and dinner buffet of simple but good Caribbean and international cuisine to many who choose MAP programs. À la carte offerings and lunch are also available. A patio garden offers cake and coffee and a pool bar serves snacks and drinks. A colorful indoor/outdoor lounge features cocktails and live music most nights. Another real benefit is the vast array of amenities like a game room, self-service Laundromat, currency exchange, tour desk, conference rooms, car-rental desk, beauty salon, and boutique all on the premises.

✪ **Ocean Surf Hotel.** 7436 Ocean Terr. (just east of Collins Ave.), Miami Beach, Fl 33141. ☎ **800/555-0411** or 305/866-1648. Fax 305/866-1649. www.oceansurf.com. E-mail:

oceansurf@oceansurf.com. 49 units, all with bathroom. A/C TV TEL. Winter $89–$94 single or double; $104–$134 with large shared balcony. Off-season $64–$69 single or double; $79–$89 balcony. AE, DC, DISC, MC, V. Rates include self-serve continental breakfast. Extra person $4–$6. Free street parking.

Ocean Surf is a great find amid this little pocket of hotels just east of Collins Avenue. By far the most thorough renovation I have seen in the midbeach, this intimate, family owned deco jewel is worth a visit just to see the fine details that have been brought back to life by devoted second-generation owners Brian and Tamara Kraus. The wide porthole windows look directly out to sea and the many balconies are wide and edged with decorative railings. In the true spirit of art deco, this hotel resembles an ocean liner more than a hotel. But a hotel is what it is and a very impressive one at that, considering its modest scale. With larger rooms than most built in this era, the decor is tasteful and sparkling clean, if a little stark. Ask for a fridge; if one is available, there is no extra charge. You'll be thankful for the cold sodas and juice upon your return from the large, underpopulated beach just out the door. Plenty of restaurants and shopping are within a few blocks. Travelers with disabilities will particularly appreciate the thoroughly accessible lobby, rooms, and common areas.

WORTH A SPLURGE

✪ **Eden Roc Resort and Spa.** 4525 Collins Ave., Miami Beach, FL 33140. ☎ **800/327-8337** or 305/531-0000. Fax 305/674-5568. 350 units, all with bathroom. A/C TV TEL. Winter $195–$350 single or double; $275–$1,500 suite. Off-season $120–$250 single or double; $175–$1,000 suite. Extra person $15. Children 16 and under stay free in parents' room. Weekend, spa, and honeymoon packages available. AE, CB, DC, DISC, MC, V. Valet parking $12.

Originally opened in 1956 and located just next door to the mammoth Fontainebleau Hotel, this flamboyant, large hotel seems almost intimate by comparison. Luckily, because of the hotel's size, you should be able to negotiate a good rate unless there's a big event going on. The accommodations here are a bit gaudy, but hey, this *is* Miami Beach. The amenities by far make up for the ostentation. The huge, modern spa has excellent facilities and exercise classes, including yoga and ballet. An even more impressive sports complex offers squash, racquetball, and basketball courts as well as a rock-climbing arena all overlooking a gorgeous swath of beachfront and pool decks.

The big, open, and airy lobby is dressed in solid tropical colors, diamond-pattern carpeting, and fleur-de-lis wallpaper; wander around and you'll no doubt run into a gaggle of name-tagged conventioneers. The rooms, uniformly outfitted with purple and aquatic-colored interiors and retouched 1930s furnishings, are unusually spacious.

A steakhouse serves exceptionally good Angus beef and seafood. From **Jimmy Johnson's,** the poolside sports bar, patrons can watch swimmers through an underwater "porthole" window. And the lobby lounge and bar has occasional jazz.

Fontainebleau Hilton. 4441 Collins Ave., Miami Beach, FL 33140. ☎ **800/HILTONS** or 305/538-2000. Fax 305/674-4607. Telex 519362. 1,266 units, all with bathroom. A/C MINIBAR TV TEL. Winter $310–$340 single or double; $525–$725 suite. Off-season $205–$310 single or double; $475–$675 suite. Extra person $30. Children under 18 stay free in parents' room. Weekend and other packages available. AE, CB, DC, DISC, MC, V. Overnight valet parking $10.

The most famous hotel in Miami, the Fontainebleau (pronounced *fountain-blue*) has built its reputation on garishness and excess. For most visitors, this spectacle is more tourist attraction than hotel; you really shouldn't miss seeing the incredible lagoon-style pool and waterfall. Since opening its doors in 1954, the hotel has hosted presidents, pageants, and movie productions—including the James Bond thriller *Goldfinger.*

The sheer size of the Fontainebleau, with its full complement of restaurants, stores, and recreational facilities, plus more than 1,100 employees, makes this a perfect place for conventioneers. Unfortunately, the same recommendation cannot be extended to individual travelers. It's easy to get lost here, both physically and personally. The lobby is terminally crowded, the staff is overworked, and lines are always long. Still, this is the one and only Fontainebleau, and in many ways it's the quintessential Miami hotel. Renovations to the rooms in 1995 and 1996 freshened up the decor with new furnishings and pastel accents. No matter if it suits your tastes, this is one place you'll never forget.

Seven different eateries are located throughout the hotel. The Steak House serves dinner until 11pm and a continental restaurant serves a huge Sunday buffet brunch. Additionally, there are five other cafes and coffee shops (including two by the pool), as well as a number of cocktail lounges, including the Poodle Lounge, which offers live entertainment and dancing nightly. Another features a Las Vegas–style floor show with dozens of performers and two orchestras.

Silver Sands Oceanfront. 301 Ocean Dr., Key Biscayne, FL 33149. ☎ **305/361-5441.** Fax 305/361-5477. 56 units, all with bathroom. A/C TV TEL. Winter $149–$179 minisuite; $300 cottage; $385 oceanfront suite. Off-season $109–$129 minisuite; $200 cottage; $385 oceanfront suite. Extra person $30. Children 14 and under stay free in parents' room. Weekly rates available. AE, DC, MC, V. Free parking.

If Key Biscayne is where you want to be and you don't want to pay the prices of the next-door Sonesta, consider this quaint, 1-story motel where everything is crisp and clean and a pleasant staff will help with anything you may need, including baby-sitting. The well-appointed rooms are very beachy, sporting a tropical motif and simple furnishings; extras include microwaves, refrigerators, and coffeemakers. Oceanfront suites have the added convenience of full kitchens with stoves and pantries. You'll sit poolside with an unpretentious set of Latin American families and Europeans who have come for a long and simple vacation—and get it.

DOWNTOWN

Most downtown hotels cater primarily to business travelers, but tourists with a reason to stay downtown can get well-located, good-quality accommodations, too.

Although business hotels are expensive and seasonal markdowns are hard to find, quality and service are also of a high standard. Look for weekend discounts and packages, when offices are closed and rooms often go empty. After dark there's virtually nothing outside of the hotels; the streets are often deserted and crime can be a problem.

In downtown Miami, the **Wyndham** (☎ **800/227-6963** or 305/374-0000), at 1601 Biscayne Blvd., located above the Omni Mall, offers a perfect option for the thrifty business traveler. It offers a full business center as well as a heated rooftop pool. Also, it is just a few minutes away from Bayside and Miami Beach.

SUPER-CHEAP SLEEPS

Everglades Hotel. 244 Biscayne Blvd., Miami, FL 33136. ☎ **800/327-5700** or 305/379-5461. Fax 305/577-8445. 371 units, all with bathroom. A/C TV TEL. Year-round $92 single or double; $115 suite. Extra person $10. Children 4 and under stay free in parents' room. AE, DC, DISC, MC, V. Parking $7.

This hotel has been around forever on downtown's most active street, Biscayne Boulevard. Though the lobby and rooms are in sore need of renovation, you're in a great location and have access to a multitude of services (including a bank) in the building. Many traveling business types and Latin American families stay here because of its convenient location, low rates, and many services. Also, it's one of the only downtown hostelries with a pool. The location is quite safe and near to the highways, Metrorail, and great shopping across the street at Bayside Marketplace.

Royalton Hotel. 131 SE 1st St. (between 1st and 2nd aves.), Miami, FL 33131. ☎ **305/374-7451.** Fax 305/358-5842. 125 units, all with bathroom. A/C TV TEL. Year-round $43 single, $50 double, $58 triple. AE, DC, MC, V. Nearby parking garage $9.

This very basic downtown hotel caters largely to Caribbean and Latin American tourists who are in town to shop. The modest rooms and common areas are clean and well maintained. Just blocks from Bayside and Metrorail, its location and its supercheap prices are its best assets.

FOR A FEW BUCKS MORE

✪ **Miami River Inn.** 118 SW South River Dr., Miami, FL 33130. ☎ **305/325-0045.** Fax 305/325-9227. E-mail: miami100@ix.netcom.com. A/C TV TEL. 40 units, 38 with bathroom. Winter $89–$120 single or double. Off-season $69–$89 single or double. Rates include continental breakfast. Extra person $15. Children 11 and under stay free in parents' room. AE, CB, DC, DISC, MC, V. Free parking.

A great deal for those who want to be in a central location, close to the highway, public transportation, downtown eateries, and museums. Extras include a small outdoor pool, Jacuzzi, and complimentary coffee and wine in the lobby. Although many predict that the riverfront area will soon undergo a renaissance, for now the area is still a bit seedy. Don't venture too far out of the enclave, unless you want to see the ugly underside of Miami.

Five buildings make up this compound of historic Florida on the trade-laden Miami River. Some of the buildings date from as early as 1910 and have since been well restored by careful and loving hands. The rooms are nicely furnished with a mix of antiques from all eras and gentle wallpaper prints. In the common area is a collection of books about old Miami, with histories of this land's former owners, Julia Tuttle, William Brickell, and Henry Flagler. The low year-round rates make this an attractive option for those who appreciate old things. There's a small outdoor pool on the premises and a Jacuzzi.

Riande Continental Bayside. 146 Biscayne Blvd., Miami, FL 33132. ☎ **800/RIANDE-1** or 305/358-4555. Fax 305/371-5253. 250 units, all with bathroom. A/C MINIBAR TV TEL. Winter $115–$175 single or double. Off-season $85–$155 single or double. Frommer's readers get a 20% discount. Children stay free in parents' room. AE, DC, MC, V. Parking $7.50.

Like its sister hotel in South Beach, this Riande caters to a Latin American crowd that descends on downtown in droves to shop for clothes and electronics. The location is ideal, only steps away from Bayside shopping center, many great ethnic restaurants, and a Metrorail stop. The rooms come with extras such as 10-channel Spectravision. The reasonable prices and helpful staff are reason enough to consider staying here if you want to be right in downtown Miami.

Sheraton Brickell Point Miami. 495 Brickell Ave., Miami, FL 33131. ☎ **800/325-3535** or 305/373-6000. Fax 305/374-2279. Telex 6811701. 598 units, all with bathroom. A/C TV TEL. Winter $129–$169 single or double; $305–$375 suite. Off-season $129–$159 single or double; $275–$375 suite. Extra person $10. Children 18 and under stay free in parents' room. Senior discounts and weekend and other packages available. AE, CB, DC, DISC, MC, V. Parking $12.

This downtown hotel's waterfront location is its greatest asset. Nestled between Brickell Park and Biscayne Bay, the Sheraton is set back from the main road and surrounded by a pleasant bay-front walkway.

In case you want to see the world.

At American Express, we're here to make your journey a smooth one. So we have over 1,700 travel service locations in over 120 countries ready to help. What else would you expect from the world's largest travel agency?

do more

AMERICAN EXPRESS

Travel

http://www.americanexpress.com/travel

In case you want to be welcomed there.

We're here to see that you're always welcomed at establishments everywhere. That's why millions of people carry the American Express® Card – for peace of mind, confidence, and security, around the world or just around the corner.

do more ®

Cards

In case you're running low.

We're here to help with more than 118,000 Express Cash

locations around the world. In order to enroll, just call

American Express before you start your vacation.

do more

Express Cash

And just in case.

We're here with American Express® Travelers Cheques and Cheques *for Two*.® They're the safest way to carry money on your vacation and the surest way to get a refund, practically anywhere, anytime.

Another way we help you...

do more

Travelers Cheques

Just as clean and reliable as other hotels in the Sheraton chain, Brickell Point has a pretty location and good water views from most of the rooms. In addition, you get all the amenities you'd expect from a hostelry in this class, like car-rental and tour desk, a small gift shop, room service, and several good restaurants and lounges. Besides a few popular restaurants that cater to the business set, there isn't much to do in the area, but you are within a short drive to anything Miami has to offer.

WORTH A SPLURGE

✪ **Hotel Inter-Continental Miami.** 100 Chopin Plaza, Miami, FL 33131. ☎ **800/ 327-3005** or 305/577-1000. Fax 305/577-0384. Telex 153127. 644 units, all with bathroom. A/C MINIBAR TV TEL. Winter $209–$289 single or double; $325–$450 suite. Off-season $159–$259 single or double; $325–$450 suite. Extra person $20. Weekend and other packages available. AE, CB, DC, DISC, MC, V. Valet parking $12.

Especially since the $5 million renovation of all its guest rooms and some common areas, the Inter-Continental is downtown's swankiest hotel. It boasts more marble than a mausoleum (both inside and out), but it's warmed by colorful, homey touches like fresh flowers, plants, palm trees, and brightly colored wicker furniture. The 5-story lobby features a marble centerpiece sculpture by Henry Moore and is topped by a pleasing skylight. Brilliant downtown and bay views add luster to already posh rooms that are outfitted with every convenience known to hoteldom, including VCRs and eight-channel Spectravision selection. Some suites have fully-equipped kitchenettes. There are three fine restaurants covering all price ranges and two popular lounges— but really, why eat in the pricey hotel? The gleaming tower is also steps from many great ethnic cafes and fast-food outlets. The best part is that even in this downtown location there is plenty of opportunity for exercise. You can work out in the health spa or jogging track, relax on the large sundeck, and cool off in the Olympic-size heated outdoor pool.

COCONUT GROVE/CORAL GABLES

The intimate enclave known as "the Grove" hugs the shores of Biscayne Bay just south of U.S. 1 and about 10 minutes from the beaches. It's a great place to stay, offering ample nightlife, excellent restaurants, and beautiful surroundings. Unfortunately, all the hotels here are expensive. By late 1999, Ritz Carlton will have added a $60 million, 250-room luxury hotel to the landscape. Values in Coconut Grove come in the way of a bed-and-breakfast or a single chain, the Hampton Inn.

Coconut Grove eases into Coral Gables, which extends north toward Miami International Airport. "The Gables," as it's known, was one of Miami's original planned communities and is still one of the city's prettiest. It means being close to the shops along the Miracle Mile and the University of Miami. Two popular and well-priced chains are a **Holiday Inn** (☎ **800/327-5476** or 305/667-5611) at 1350 S. Dixie Hwy. and a **Howard Johnson** (☎ **800/446-4656** or 305/665-7501) at 1430 S. Dixie Hwy., both located across the street from the University of Miami.

A CHEAP SLEEP

✪ **Riviera Inn.** 5100 Riviera Dr. (on U.S. 1), Coral Gables, FL 33146. ☎ **800/368-8602** or 305/665-3528. 31 units, all with bathroom. A/C TV TEL. Winter $68 single or double; $78 efficiencies. Off-season $55 single or double; $78 efficiencies. AE, CB, DC, DISC, MC, V.

Besides the newly renovated Holiday Inn down the road, this family owned motel is the best discount option in this otherwise pricey area. Built in 1954, this comfortable and clean 2-story property has a small pool and is set back from the road so that the rooms are quiet. Vending machines are your only choice for refreshments, but you are near many great dining spots. Or, you may choose to stay in an efficiency, all of which have fully stocked kitchens. Popular with friends and families of students at nearby University of Miami, this enduring relic of Old Florida is a real find.

FOR A FEW BUCKS MORE

✪ **Coconut Grove Bed & Breakfast.** 4286 Douglas Rd. (between Matheson and Stewart aves.) ☎ **800/339-9430** or 305/665-2274. Fax 305/666-1186. www.kwflorida.com/coconut.html. E-mail: cocobandb@aol.com. 3 units, all with bathroom. A/C TV TEL. Winter $135–$175. Off-season $115–$150. Rates include full breakfast. AE, MC, V. To find it, take I-95 south to U.S. 1; turn left at Le Jeune Rd. (42nd Ave.); turn left again at Ingram Hwy. and then take your first right on Edgewater Dr. and first left onto Douglas Rd. (37th Ave.). You'll see the house about 5 blocks ahead on the left side of the road. There is no sign.

Not only is this the only real full-time bed-and-breakfast in town, it is also the only moderately priced option you'll find for miles. Plus, you're only a block from the bay and the home of historian and conservationist Marjory Stoneman Douglas. Downtown Coconut Grove is less than a 15-minute walk. All rooms/suites have large private sitting alcoves with desks, and two have their own marble bathroom with shower. The very large banyan suite is so named because it looks out over an 80-foot-high tree, the second largest of its kind in state of Florida. You'll be treated to a true gourmet breakfast, which will include fresh ground Colombian coffee, fresh squeezed orange juice, and such entrees as three-egg omelettes, blackberry Belgian waffles, or strawberry pancakes. An added privilege is guest membership to a nearby island resort where there is swimming, tennis, and a gym. Opened in September 1997, this 1913 private home is one of Miami's oldest. Owners Annete Rawlings and Bill Grier live in the carriage house in the back. Smoking is permitted only outside and on the verandas.

Hampton Inn Hotel. 2800 SW 28th Terr. (between 27th Ave. and U.S. 1), Coconut Grove, FL 33133. ☎ **800/HAMPTON** or 305/448-2800. Fax 305/ 305/442-8655. E-mail: HICG4MIAMI@AOL.com. 137 units, all with bathroom. A/C TV TEL. Winter $109–$129 single; $119–$139 single or double. Off-season $99–$119 single. Rates include continental breakfast buffet. AE, DC, DISC, MC, V.

This very standard chain hotel is a welcome reprieve in an area otherwise known for having only very pricey accommodations. The rooms are nothing exciting, but the freebies, like local phone calls, parking, in-room movies, breakfast buffet, and hot drinks around the clock, make this chain choice a real steal. Rooms are brand new and have large TVs, voice mail phones, plus, you can request a refrigerator and microwave if you like. A large outdoor pool and Jacuzzi is an added bonus in this generic but recommendable hotel.

WORTH A SPLURGE

✪ **Biltmore Hotel Coral Gables.** 1200 Anastasia Ave., Coral Gables, FL 33134. ☎ **800/727-1926**, 305/445-1926, or Westin at 800/228-3000. Fax 305/442-9496. 275 units, all with bathroom. A/C TV TEL. Winter $259 single or double; $379–$479 suite. Off-season $189 single or double; $309–$409 suite. Extra person $20. Children 17 and under stay free in parents' room. Special packages available. AE, CB, DC, DISC, MC, V. Valet parking $9.

Although this is one of the most elegant hotels in Coral Gables, you can sometimes find very reasonable package rates. In the weeks before and after Easter for example, you can get a deluxe room for $189 including full American breakfast for two, unlimited use of the fitness center, free local calls, and daily local newspaper. Even if you don't stay here, consider a tour or at least a drink in the piano bar of this historic landmark. The Biltmore is the oldest Coral Gables hotel and a city landmark—one of only two operating hotels in Florida to be granted official historic status from the National Register. Rising above the Spanish Mediterranean–style estate is a majestic 300-foot copper-clad tower, modeled after the original Giralda bell tower in Seville and visible

Coral Gables, Coconut Grove, Downtown Miami & Key Biscayne

Accommodations:
Biltmore Hotel 17
Coconut Grove
  Bed & Breakfast 20
Everglades Hotel 4
Hampton Inn 21
Hotel Intercontinental
Miami International
  Airport Hotel 1
Miami River Inn 2
Riande Continental Bayside 6
Riviera Inn 19
Royalton Hotel 8
Sheraton Brickell Point
  Miami 5
The Wyndham 7
KEY BISCAYNE
Silver Sands Oceanfront 33

Dining:
At's A Nice 16
Cafe Abbracci 25
Cafe Tu Tu Tango 27
Caribbean Delite 3
Cocowalk 21
Daily Bread 9
Fishbone Grille 11
Gables Diner 15
The Globe 24
Hy-Vong 10
Kaleidoscope 26
La Cibeles Café 14
Monty's 18
Norman's 13
Señor Frogs 23
Versailles 12
KEY BISCAYNE
Bayside Seafood Restaurant 30
La Boulangerie 31
The Oasis Cafe 32
Sundays On the Bay 29

119

throughout the city. Having been through many incarnations, including being used as a VA hospital after World War II and a dorm for the University of Miami, the Biltmore is now back to its original 1926 splendor and a common site of black-tie weddings and other celebrations. Always a popular destination for golfers, including President Clinton, it is situated on a lush rolling 18-hole course that is as challenging as it is beautiful. Take a look at the enormous 21,000-square-foot swimming pool surrounded by arched walkways and classical sculptures is the largest hotel pool in the country. There is also a state-of-the-art health club, full-service spa, sauna, and 10 lighted tennis courts.

WEST MIAMI/AIRPORT AREA

If you've got an early morning flight to catch, by all means stay near the airport. If not, why not spend a few dollars to get to the beach, less than 10 miles away. You'll have a lot more options and will get a better value for your money.

If you must stay near the airport, consider any of the dozens of moderately priced chain hotels. You'll find one of the cheapest options at either **Days Inn,** at 7250 NW 11 St. (☎ **800/325-2525** or 305/261-4230) or 4767 NW 36th St. (☎ 305/888-3661), each 2 miles from the airport.

The larger property on 36th Street offers slightly cheaper rates with singles starting at $49. The 11th Street locale may charge more for weekends, but prices usually start at $80. There is no single rate. Prices include free transportation from the airport.

The **Sheraton Gateway,** at 3900 NW 21st St. (☎ **800/933-1100**), has corporate rates in season starting at $149.

Miami International Airport Hotel. P.O. Box 997510, NW 20th St. and Le Jeune Rd., Airport Terminal Concourse E., Miami, FL 33299-7510. ☎ **800/327-1276** or 305/871-4100. Fax 305/871-0800. 260 units, all with bathroom. A/C TV TEL. Winter $135–$185 single or double; $250–$650 suite. Off-season $150–$170 single or double; $250–$265 suite. Extra person $10. Up to two children under 12 stay free in parents' room. AE, CB, DC, EURO, JCB, MC, V. Parking $9.

I don't know of a nicer airport hotel and this one couldn't be more convenient—the hotel is actually *in* the airport, at Concourse E. The hotel also has every amenity of a first-class tourist destination, including a large rooftop pool, health club, Jacuzzi, sauna, sundeck, racquetball courts, jogging track, small business center, conference room, a beauty salon, eight-channel Spectravision, Laundromat, tour desk, boutiques, and several cocktail lounges and restaurants. You'd think you'd be deaf from the roar of the planes, but all of the rooms have been soundproofed and allow in very little noise. In addition, the hotel is extremely safe with modern security systems.

The rooms are modern and spacious with industrial-grade carpeting and nondescript furnishings, but clean and tasteful. If you need to be at the airport and want excellent service this is your best bet.

WORTH A SPLURGE

✪ **Doral Golf Resort and Spa.** 4400 NW 87th Ave., Miami, FL 33178. ☎ **800/22-DORAL,** 800/71-DORAL, or 305/592-2000. Fax 305/594-4682. 681 units in the resort and at the spa. A/C MINIBAR TV TEL. Winter $225–$315 double; $315–$945 suite; $350–$1,280 spa suite. Off-season $95–$275 double; $175–$380 golf suite; $350–$825 spa suite. Extra person $35. One or 2 children 15 and under stay free in parents' room. 18% service charge added. Golf and spa packages available. AE, CB, DC, DISC, MC, V. Valet parking $8.50.

By no means a budget option, the Doral epitomizes the luxury resort in Florida. While the pampering in the spa attracts worldwide attention, the next-door golf resort hosts world-class tournaments and is home to the Blue Monster Course—rated one of the top 25 in the country. The season is booked well in advance by those who have been here before or have just read about the fantastic offerings on this 650-acre resort, which is surrounded only by warehouses and office buildings. However, it's just moments from the Miami airport and about a 20-minute drive to Miami Beach.

No matter: There's no reason to leave the grounds. The spacious lobbies and dining areas shimmer with polished marble, mirrors, and gold. The rooms, too, are luxuriously large and tastefully decorated; large windows allow views of the tropical gardens or golf courses below.

The Spa restaurant serves delicious low-fat cuisine, including reduced-calorie desserts. Various other dining options include a cafe with super Italian sandwiches, salads, and pasta. A sports bar at the golf club has excellent club fare.

Besides the renowned golf courses and spa, this top-rated destination has all the amenities you could ask for, including an Olympic-size outdoor heated pool, a jogging track, bicycle rentals, game rooms, children's programs during the holidays, a business center, a car-rental desk, sundeck, 15 outdoor tennis courts, a tour and activities desks, beauty salon, and boutiques.

5 Great Deals on Dining

Regional cuisine in Miami is hard to define. It encompasses the varied tastes of the Caribbean (especially Cuba), as well as an old-time rural Florida influence. The chefs who pioneered what has been dubbed "Floribbean" have fused these many influences into an ever-changing style that's limited only by the imagination of those preparing or eating the food.

It's a blend of Caribbean and American fare accented with dashes of Latin American, Spanish, Asian, and western European. In general, the result is spectacular, although it can be overambitious and pretentious at times. Think mango-infused oils dotted on tuna tartare with jicama slaw served in a cracked coconut. It's not for the xenophobic or the meat-and-potatoes crowd.

And you can always find ethnic cuisine—from Cuban to Haitian to Jamaican to Vietnamese. For real bargains, check out any of the hundreds of little take-out bodegas serving fresh hot lunches and dinners. You can usually see the stews cooking behind a glass partition and choose what looks best. Roast pork, *asado lechon,* roast chicken, pollo asado, shredded beef stew, ropa vieja, and toasted Cuban sandwiches are some of the great and cheap choices. I've reviewed a few of these spots below, but there are way too many to mention. You may also want to try a tasty empanada from one of the many vendors who wander the beaches selling the homemade meat-filled pastries.

Also, a number of chains that originated here are worth trying when you want a quick, inexpensive bite. Try **Pollo Tropical,** a Cuban fast-food chain serving delicious moist chicken, rice and beans, and garlic-drenched yuca (a potato-like root vegetable). Locations include 18710 S. Dixie Hwy. (at 186th Street), South Miami (☎ **305/ 225-7858**); 1454 Alton Rd., Miami Beach (☎ **305/672-8888**); and 11806 Biscayne Blvd., North Miami (☎ **305/895-0274**). Check the phone book for others. **Miami Subs Grill** is also popular since it serves basic fast-food favorites like burgers and fries, but also offers a selection of salads, grilled chicken, beer and wine, as well as key lime pie and frozen yogurt. Locations include 351 Lincoln Rd. (off Washington Avenue), South Beach (☎ **305/538-9044**), and 3030 Grand Ave., Coconut Grove (☎ **305/ 567-0041**).

To help you choose where to eat, the restaurants below are divided first by neighborhood, then by price.

SOUTH BEACH

With the largest concentration of restaurants in South Florida, South Beach offers something for every palate and pocketbook. Unfortunately, service is often rude and inefficient.

There is a pizza joint or Cuban diner on nearly every block of South Beach. Take your pick. One of the best is **Pucci's,** with two locations on Washington Avenue, one just north of Española Way and the other between 6th and 7th streets (☎ **305/ 673-8133**). Ask for coupon specials. The extra flyers are usually kept behind the counter and are good for free sodas, free toppings, or other giveaways. Also see the box below, "The Best Dinner (or Lunch) Show in Town: Strolling Lincoln Road," for great dining options on Lincoln Road.

SUPER-CHEAP EATS

David's Cafe II. 1654 Meridian Ave. (north of Lincoln Rd.). ☎ **305/ 672-8707.** Sandwiches $2–$5, main courses $7–$11. Breakfast and lunch all-you-can-eat buffets from $5–$6. MC, V. Daily 7am–11pm. Sometimes later on weekends. CUBAN.

From grilled sandwiches, roast pork, and rice and beans, to fried plantains and *cafecitos* (tiny cups of thick Cuban espresso), David's bright and airy cafe serves hearty, standard Cuban fare at good prices. Though not as well known as the now famous **Puerto Sagua** at 700 Collins Ave. (☎ **305/673-1115**), David's is typical of the cheap Cuban diners in the area and much better priced, especially for the lunch and brunch buffets. Choose from nearly a dozen dishes at a long steam table piled high with daily specials that might include *ropa vieja* (shredded beef stew), *arroz con pollo* (rice and chicken), or sautéed fish and vegetables. The homemade soups are always recommendable (go for the black bean or the chicken noodle). The regular à la carte menu is not as great a bargain, but prices are fair and the service at least cordial. Waitresses struggle a bit with English, but they are well used to gringos, so persevere.

La Provence. 1627 Collins Ave. (just south of Lincoln Rd.). ☎ **305/538-2406.** Sandwiches $5–$6, pastries $2–$3, quiches and lunch croissants $2.50–$4. No credit cards. Daily 7am– 8pm. FRENCH BAKERY.

Don't miss a stop into this authentic French bakery for a croissant or piece of quiche. Large sandwiches on fresh baguettes are also delectable. This is the perfect spot to pick up breakfast or picnic supplies for a day at the beach. Or, sit at any of the dozen or so tables in this completely undistinguished storefront for a killer coffee and pastry experience. The small handmade baguettes, a bargain at 95¢, are a potential addiction.

La Sandwicherie. 229 14th St. (east of Washington Ave., behind the Amoco Station). ☎ **305/532-8934.** Sandwiches and salads $4.50–$7. No credit cards. Daily 10am–5pm. Delivery daily 10am–6pm. FRENCH SNACK BAR.

If you want the most incredible gourmet sandwich you've ever tasted, stop by the green-and-white awning that hides this fabulously French lunch and snack counter. Choose pâté, salami, prosciutto, turkey, tuna, ham, roast beef, or any of the perfect

A Note on Tipping

Be aware that many Miami Beach restaurants, especially along Ocean Drive and Lincoln Road, automatically add a 15% service charge to every bill. When this is the case, the restaurant's policy should be written on the menu. It is often written in very small letters. No matter, be sure to look *and* ask. Many unscrupulous waiters "forget" to mention this, and will deliver your credit- or charge-card receipt with the tip space left open. Don't tip twice unless you mean to.

Cheap Eats: The Early Bird Gets the Bargain

Long before its sidewalks were crowded with cafe tables and long-legged models, a decidedly less glamorous Miami was home to budget-conscious retirees from around the nation. And though Miami, and especially Miami Beach, now attracts more jet-setters and celebrities than pensioners, the area still offers outstanding dining values. But that doesn't mean you have to settle for meat loaf and mashed potatoes on a plastic tray, either. With a bit of planning, you can sample the very best cuisine from the city's most elegant restaurants for a fraction of regular menu prices—that is, if you don't mind eating dinner before the sun goes down.

In the hopes of drawing a crowd before the usual "crunch time," many establishments offer what is most commonly known as the Early Bird Special. Alternately, a prerush menu might be described as a "Twilight," "Sunset," "Pretheater," "Pre-Event," or "Beat the Clock" dinner. These specials, usually offered on weekday evenings after 5pm and until 6 or 7pm, may consist of an abbreviated menu with a choice of entrees. They are served with soup or a salad, dessert, and coffee for a fixed price—one usually less than the entree price from the à la carte menu.

One of the best deals around can be found at **Islands Café,** 9601 Bay Harbor Dr., in the Bay Harbor Inn (☎305/868-4141). Here students from a well-known cooking school turn out an impressive selection of dinner specials for around $10, including starters, desserts, and coffee. Advanced students (supervised by a veteran staff) run the whole operation. You're likely to get not only great food, but also good service, since the staff is graded on its work. And **Macarena,** 1334 Washington Ave., on South Beach (☎ 305/531-3440), entices an earlier seating several nights a week (between 6 and 8pm) with huge meals of paella or chicken and soup or salad for less than $10.

A few hip Italian restaurants have added a novel twist to the classic early bird called "Beat the Clock." Meals are priced in a graduated scale depending on the time of day. At South Beach's **Tiramesu,** at 721 Lincoln Rd. (☎ 305/532-4538), early diners, who arrive after 5:30pm, can choose from three pastas with prices corresponding to the time the order is placed. For example, if you order at 5:30, your meal costs $5.30. At 6:15, the same dish is $6.15, and so on until 7:30, when the regular menu goes in effect. A similar deal is offered at ✪ **Stephan's Gourmet Market & Cafe** from 4 until 7pm, at three locations: the Aventura store, at 19495 Biscayne Blvd. (☎ 305/932-8885); the South Beach location, at 1430 Española Way (☎ 305/674-1760); and in Miami Beach, at 6345 Collins Ave (☎ 305/861-8060).

I've highlighted many of Miami's best bargains in this chapter, but I also recommend taking a look at the local papers. The *New Times,* a giveaway available in red boxes throughout Miami-Dade, and the "Neighbors" section of the *Miami Herald* often feature new specials, coupons, and fixed-price promotions.

cheeses (Swiss, mozzarella, Cheddar, or provolone). You could make a meal of the optional sandwich toppings alone (black olives, pickles, cucumbers, lettuce, onions, green or hot peppers, tomatoes) that are included in the sandwich price. The fresh French bread has a golden crust and is just thick enough to hold all you'll want to have stuffed into it.

Mrs. Mendoza's Tacos al Carbon. 1040 Alton Rd. ☎ **305/535-0808.** Main courses $3–$5; side dishes 80¢–$3. No credit cards. Mon–Thurs 11am–10pm, Fri–Sat 11am–11pm, Sun noon–10pm. FAST FOOD/MEXICAN.

Popular with locals and those who work in the area, this hard-to-spot storefront eatery is a godsend. It's the only fresh California-style Mexican joint in town where the steak and chicken are grilled as you wait and then stuffed into homemade flour or corn wrappings. You order at the tile counter and pick up your dish on a plastic tray in minutes. One of my favorites is the chicken burrito, which includes rice, black beans, cheese, lettuce, and guacamole doused in tomato salsa. They offer three types of salsa, from mild to superhot. The chips are hand-cut and flavorful but a bit too coarse. Skip them and enjoy an order of the rich and chunky guacamole with a fork.

Another branch is located at Doral Plaza, 9739 NW 41st St. (☎ 305/477-5119).

✪ **San Loco.** 235 14th St. (between Washington and Collins aves.). ☎ **305/538-3009.** Burritos and tacos $1.50–$6.25; salads and guacamole $2–$6. No credit cards. Mon–Thur, 11am–5am and Fri–Sat 11am–6am. MEXICAN/FAST FOOD.

Renowned as the beach's best spot for tacos and burritos, this tiny joint is especially popular with vegetarians and fans of real hot sauce. The menu is pretty extensive, especially considering that the place has only space enough to sit a dozen people. Try a fish taco, made with sautéed catfish or the huge, overstuffed burrito loco filled with your choice of chicken, beans, beef (or fish) and cheese, onions, thick meat or chicken chili, sour cream, guacamole, lettuce, tomato and jalapeños. You get a side of refried beans and rice, too. It's a lot of food. For lighter meal, try a simple fresh taco or the heavenly guacamole, served in a fried flour tortilla basket. In this case, the portion is small but oh so good.

✪ **Sport Cafe.** 538 Washington Ave. ☎ **305/674-9700.** Reservations accepted only for parties of 4 or more. Main courses $7–$10; sandwiches and pizzas $4.50–$7. AE, MC, V. Daily 11am–1am (sometimes open earlier for coffee). RUSTIC ITALIAN.

Inside the decor is dark and smoky, with a beautiful wooden bar and a large-screen TV that dominates the small dining room. But don't expect to see the latest football or baseball aired here; soccer and bicycle races are more popular with the European crowd. The Sport Cafe is owned by brothers Tonino and Paolo Doino from Rome, and the food is really made by their mother, Rosa. Prices are so low that you often have to wait for a seat, especially at the sidewalk tables.

The simple menu lists only three entrees and a few pizzas. Ask for the day's specials and go for one of them. Always good is the penne with salmon served with a pink sauce. Rosa also makes the very best eggplant parmigiana I've had (except for my mother's). The vegetable disks are lightly sautéed without any heavy breading and then layered in a rich tomato sauce with lots of sweet mozzarella. Though not on the menu, this dish is available almost every day. Ordering from the newly arrived Italian waiters can be a challenge.

Also try the sister restaurant, **Rosinella,** at 525 Lincoln Rd. (☎ 305/672-6777).

✪ **Stephan's Gourmet Market & Cafe.** 1430 Washington Ave. (at Española Way). ☎ **305/674-1760.** Reservations not necessary. Main courses $6–$12; daily dinner special for two with salad and a bottle of wine $24.95 5–11pm. AE, MC, V. Sun–Thurs 8am–midnight; Fri–Sat 8am–2am; dinner special served daily 5:30–11pm. DELI/ITALIAN.

This deli, which could be in New York's Little Italy, sells a huge assortment of fresh pastas, breads, and salads as well as cold cuts, cheeses, and grocery items. But upstairs in a tiny loft used to store wine bottles is a cozy dining room with space for about 10 couples. Dinner is also served out on the sidewalk or delivered to your hotel.

A chalkboard displays the chef's special, usually a pasta dish with some kind of chicken or fish. One of my favorites is the linguine Alfredo with tender pieces of chicken breast mixed into the light and cheesy sauce. While you wait, you'll want to eat baskets and baskets full of the garlicky garlic bread and get started on the bottle of wine that comes with the daily special. The red is an excellent full-bodied Italian Merlot. However, I find the white undrinkable. If the special doesn't strike you, consider any of the other moderately priced dishes like rotisserie chicken with potatoes and vegetables, ziti, sausage and peppers, or eggplant parmigiana. Also good are the hummus and olive salads. Other locations: 2 NE 40th St. (☎ 305/571-4070) and 19495 Biscayne Blvd. (One Turnberry Pl.; ☎ 305/932-8885).

Van Dyke Cafe. 846 Lincoln Rd. ☎ **305/534-3600.** Reservations recommended for evenings. Main courses $6–$14. AE, DC, MC, V. Daily 8am–1am; Fri–Sat 8am–3am. AMERICAN.

Owned by the same group that owns the successful News Café, the Van Dyke has used the same formula to guarantee its longevity on Lincoln Road. The smart, upscale decor inside and European sidewalk cafe outside are always crowded due to the diner-like prices and fast, friendly service.

There is nothing too ambitious on the menu, which offers basic sandwiches and salads, and best of all, breakfast all day long. The pastas are decent, though not too exciting. House specialties include an excellent smoked salmon on thick, rustic black bread and a smooth and lemony hummus with pita chips. Also, since you are in Miami Beach, you may want to consider a nice hot bowl of cure-all chicken soup with matzoh balls. In the evenings the sounds of a talented jazz band waft down from the dark and elegant club upstairs.

✪ **World Resources.** 719 Lincoln Rd. ☎ **305/535-8987.** Main courses $6–$8; sushi hand rolls $3–$4. AE, DC, MC, V. Daily noon–11:30pm. JAPANESE/THAI.

World Resources is a popular little cafe and sushi bar masquerading as an Indonesian furniture and bric-a-brac store. Local hippie types and Euros frequent this downright cheap hangout instead of cooking at home. Offerings include some of the freshest and most innovative sushi and many Thai specialties. The portions are generous and the cooking simple. The basil chicken, for example, is a tasty combination of white meat sautéed in a coconut sauce with subtle hints of basil and garlic. The Thai salad is heaped with fresh vegetables including cauliflower, sprouts, and cucumbers. Although you can get better Thai food at a number of spots on the beach, you can't beat the atmosphere. Dozens of outside tables surround a tiny pond and stage where musicians perform a variety of styles, from African drumming to Indian sitar playing.

FOR A FEW BUCKS MORE

✪ **Grillfish.** 1444 Collins Ave. (corner of Española Way). ☎ **305/538-2203.** Reservations recommended on weekends. Main courses $8–$13. AE, DC, MC, V. In season daily 6pm–midnight; off-season daily 6–11pm. SEAFOOD.

From the beautiful Byzantine-style mural and the gleaming oak bar that runs the length of the corner storefront of stylish Española Way, you'd think you were eating in a much more expensive restaurant. No doubt Grillfish manages to pay the exorbitant South Beach rent because the restaurant has a loyal following of locals, who come for the fresh and simple seafood in a relaxed but upscale atmosphere. As the name implies, fish, fish, and fish is what you'll get.

The waiters are friendly and know the limited menu well. The barroom seafood chowder is full of chunks of shellfish as well as some fresh white fish filets in a tomato broth. The small ear of corn, included with each entree, is about as close as you'll get to any type of vegetable offering besides the pedestrian salad. Still, at these prices, it's worth a visit to try some local fare including Mako shark, swordfish, tuna, marlin, and wahoo. They'll grill it or sauté it. Also, choose the spicy red sauce on the pasta as a great complement to this rustic, Italian-inspired seafood fare.

✪ **Macarena.** 1334 Washington Ave. ☎ **305/531-3440.** Reservations suggested for late-night weekends. Tapas $2.50–$8; main courses $8–$14. AE, DC, MC, V. Daily 7pm–midnight (drinks, dancing, and a limited menu until 3am). SPANISH/TAPAS.

Like an ancient tavern in Madrid, this lively little cafe in the heart of South Beach packs them in after 10pm. Before that however, the place is empty. It seems gringos haven't quite caught on yet (to bring people in, they're offering early evening specials; see "The Early Bird Gets the Bargain," above). The food is outstanding and the sangria as good. You can make a meal of the perfectly creamy and rich paella, which is more like an Italian risotto than the famous Spanish classic. This golden saffron rice dish, loaded with chunks of chicken, sausage, seafood, peppers, and peas, is even better. It's the signature dish, and an incredible bargain. Order a tapas portion when available or get a whole dish to share.

Flamenco shows are Wednesday, Friday, and Saturday at 10pm and midnight. A more mellow experience is on Thursday when a classical guitarist plays acoustic music after 9pm.

✪ **Mama Vieja.** 235 23rd St. (just west of Collins Ave.). ☎ **305/538-2400.** Reservations accepted, but not necessary. $7–$18 main courses. AE, CB, DC, DISC, MC, V. Daily noon–midnight. COLOMBIAN/INTERNATIONAL.

This funky Colombian hangout is a real find serving supremely fresh national specialties in a setting that might well be the backdrop for a Latin American spaghetti Western. Brightly painted walls and elevated porches look out onto a large screen TV showing music videos from the old country. The walls and ceilings are decorated with hundreds of hats that have been donated by customers and signed in exchanged for a free meal. Bring in an interesting hat and mention it to the server before placing your order so he or she can bring you to the attention of the owner.

Start with an avocado salad and rich meat-filled empanadas served with spicy sauce or a creamy fish soup and green plantains stuffed with mixed seafood with large chunks of shellfish and fresh fillets. The best dishes are those from the sea. An outrageous seafood dish is Pargo Rojo Estofado à la Mama Vieja. This stuffed red snapper is stuffed with a supercreamy and delicate seafood sauce in a rice base. It's made for two ($29.95), but if you order the Corvina à la Mama Vieja for one ($12.95), you can try the same rich stuffing in a slightly smaller fish for much less money. All the dishes here are worth trying and so reasonably priced it's easy to order a lot. Try to save room for the milky sweet desserts and a good strong coffee. You'll need it if you want to dance all night. Next door is a popular disco and nightclub, Studio 23 (see "Miami After Dark," in chapter 5).

WORTH A SPLURGE

Joe's Stone Crab Restaurant. 227 Biscayne St. (at the corner of Washington Ave.). ☎ **305/673-0365.** Reservations not accepted. No shorts allowed. Market price for stone crabs varies but averages $10–$18 per claw. Other main courses $6–$26. AE, CB, DC, DISC, MC, V. Sun–Mon 5–10pm, Tues–Thurs 11:30am–2pm and 5–10pm, Fri–Sat 11:30am–2pm and 5–11pm. SEAFOOD. Closed mid-May to mid-October.

Open since 1913 and steeped in tradition, this restaurant is famous in Florida and beyond, as evidenced by the long lines of people waiting to get in. A full menu is available, but to order anything but stone crabs is unthinkable—the restaurant is only open when the stone crabs are in season. Service is brusque and pushy. It used to be that only men worked as servers, but in the aftermath of a huge lawsuit, a few women have joined the elite cadre of Joe's wait staff. Even after the $5 million renovation, which more than doubled the size of the place, the lines are ridiculously long—sometimes more than 3 hours. If you have to say you were there, brave it and enjoy drinks in the newly renovated oak bar. Otherwise, try the take-out bar next door for a slightly lower price and much less hassle. The claws here are pricier than at other local restaurants, but you're paying for history. Consider Monty's only a few doors away (see listing below) and avoid the wait and the attitude. Or, go and splurge on the superfresh claws as an appetizer and have one of the amazingly cheap entrees like the Spanish mackerel for $5, the fried catfish for $7.50, or the half spring chicken for $4.95. You'll have to pay for any side dishes on top of that. The superrich creamed garlic spinach is worth a taste. With careful ordering and only one glass of wine, you can get away with a truly affordable meal. The servers won't be happy, but you will have done Joe's on the cheap.

✪ Monty's Stone Crab/Seafood House. 300 Alton Rd. ☎ **305/ 673-3444.** Reservations recommended. Main courses $20–$37. AE, DC, MC, V. Sun– Thurs 5:30–11pm, Fri–Sat 5:30pm–midnight. SEAFOOD.

Many seafood fans have long been enamored of Monty's various menus in the Grove and in Boca. Now, Monty's has moved into South Beach, burnished the rustic oak floor, set up a raw bar outside around a large swimming pool, and opened the doors for business. The best deal in town is still the all-you-can-eat stone crabs—about $40 for the large ones and $35 for the mediums. At Joe's, located 2 blocks away, you'll pay that for just three or four claws. (But don't order stone crabs in summer; they serve frozen ones then.) Enjoy the incredible views and off-season fish specialties, including the Maryland she-crab soup—rich and creamy without too much thickener in evidence. Year-round, you can enjoy the saffron and tomato-base bouillabaisse; it's always worth a trip.

✪ Smith & Wollensky. 1 Washington Ave. (in South Pointe Park). ☎ **888/ 517-8325** or 305/673-2800. Reservations suggested. Main courses $20–$30. DC, DISC, MC, V. Daily noon–midnight. The Grill, 3pm–1am. STEAK/AMERICAN.

This pricey New York steakhouse opened its doors in late 1997 and was packed from the start. The handsome, clubby atmosphere is enhanced by views of the intercoastal waterway that leads to the Port of Miami. The expensive menu is pretty basic, almost austere, with a few chicken and fish choices and beef served about a dozen ways. The classic is the sirloin seared lightly and is served naked. Also good is the filet mignon, a thick and buttery cut also served unadorned. Delicious side dishes like asparagus, baked potato, onion rings, creamed spinach, and hash browns are sold à la carte. Ask for advice from the wine steward, since the vast and impressive menu can be over- whelming. Service here unlike so many other South Beach restaurants is actually pro- fessional and polite. Desserts are superb, too. For a taste of the renowned steaks for a lot less money, reserve a seat in the more casual Grill. A smaller menu offers similar entrees for about 30% less than in the main restaurant. Portions are slightly smaller, but that just means no doggie bags. It's still more than enough food.

Yuca. 501 Lincoln Rd. (corner of Drexel Ave.). ☎ **305/532-9822.** Reservations required. Main courses $19–$32. AE, CB, DC, MC, V. Tues–Sun noon–4pm and 6pm–midnight; Mon 6–11pm. NOUVELLE CUBAN.

Don't give yourself away as a gringo by calling it *Yuck*-a. It's *Yoo*-ka, and is a double entendre, being the name of a staple root vegetable as well as an acronym for young upscale Cuban Americans. The point is, it's known for its superb reinvention of

The Best Dinner (or Lunch) Show in Town: Strolling Lincoln Road

The strip of Lincoln Road, one block north of 16th Street between Washington Avenue and Alton Road, is home to dozens of restaurants. Most places offer outdoor seating, so it's some of the best people-watching you'll ever encounter. In-line skaters whoosh by with dogs in the lead; old eccentrics shuffle past with possession-laden grocery carts; buff body-builders promenade in muscle shirts; graceful models smile demurely at admiring stares; and young lovers (of all sexual persuasions) wander hand in hand along a pedestrian stretch of road lined with towering palms.

In early 1997, an 18-month construction project was completed at a cost of more than $16 million, and this became the hottest spot for locals and visitors alike.

I've reviewed my very favorite spots elsewhere in this chapter, including **Yuca, Norma's,** and **World Resources,** but I'd also recommend the following.

If you like your spring rolls with a little extra spice, try **Lucky Cheng's** in its new location, at 600 Lincoln Rd. (☎ **305/672-1505**). This New York import serves up mediocre Asian specialties and some of the most beautiful transvestites in town. If you come for the risqué drag shows at dinner, be prepared to participate; these "waitresses" know no boundaries. Just across the road is **Le Bistro,** at 639 Lincoln Rd. (☎ **305/672-1799**), an unassuming French bistro with simple and delicious salads, pastas, and sandwiches.

Locals either love or hate **Pacific Time,** 915 Lincoln Rd., between Jefferson and Michigan avenues (☎ **305/534-5979**). The focus is seafood done in a Pacific Rim style. Plates are small but beautiful, and usually delicious, though some complain about the high prices and slow service.

Van Dyke, 846 Lincoln Rd. (☎ **305/534-3600**), is a casual but elegant diner in one of Lincoln Road's most beautiful buildings. They serve burgers, salads, and many healthful entrees, and there's free jazz music nightly.

Balans, a British import at 1022 Lincoln Rd. between Lenox and Michigan aves. (☎ **305/534-9191**), has something for everyone—upscale atmosphere, sidewalk seating, international menu, tasty vegetarian dishes, great pastas, and a good wine selection.

On Sunday from 10am to 3pm, from late November through April, the **Lincoln Road Farmers Market** sells fresh greens, exotic fruits, homemade cheeses, and baked goods, along the road between Euclid and Meridian avenues.

Cuban comfort food. Cofounded by Douglas Rodriguez, who went on to open Patria in New York, this pricey but particularly Miami experience is worth a splurge.

It's an especially good deal for lunch, when the whole meal is discounted 35%. Or order lightly at brunch, when a lively band plays. All of the large and exotic appetizers are tempting and beautifully displayed. Try the lobster medallions with sautéed spinach and a portobello mushroom stuffed with vegetarian paella. The pieces of lobster tail are expertly grilled and served over wilted greens. The mushroom is deliciously rich, though the paella can be a bit pasty. For a main course, the pork tenderloin will steal the show. It must be marinated for days and can be cut with a butter knife. The addition of a hearty congri, a mash of red beans and rice, and a mango salsa is a perfect balance. The menu is badly translated, so don't be shy about asking for a waiter who is proficient in English if you don't *habla Español.*

MIAMI BEACH/KEY BISCAYNE

The dining scene in Miami Beach runs the gamut. Many old steak and seafood shops and bagel joints are popular with locals and seasonal condo-dwellers. Some of the most formal restaurants on the beach are here. A growing number of low-priced Italian places have sprouted up in recent years, too.

There are surprisingly few great restaurants on "the Key," considering how many wealthy visitors vacation in this pristine enclave each year. For good take-out, try **La Boulangerie,** 328 Crandon Blvd., in the Eckerd's shopping mall (☎ **305/361-0281**). You'll find luscious sandwiches and salads, vegetarian omelettes, and dangerous desserts. Also good is **The Oasis,** at 19 Harbor Dr., on the corner of Crandon Blvd. (☎ **305/361-5709**), a rugged little shack where everyone, from the city's mayor to the local handymen, meet for Cuban coffees, delicious paella, or good Cuban sandwiches. It's a little dingy, but the food is good and cheap.

SUPER-CHEAP EATS

Bayside Seafood Restaurant and Hidden Cove Bar. 3501 Rickenbacker Causeway, Key Biscane. ☎ **305/361-0808.** Reservations accepted only for parties of more than 15. Salads and sandwiches $4.50–$6; platters $7–$13. AE, MC, V. Sun–Thurs 11:30am–11pm (later on weekends). SEAFOOD.

Known by locals as "the Hut," this ramshackle restaurant and bar is a laid-back outdoor tiki hut and terrace that serves pretty good sandwiches and fish platters on paper plates. A chalkboard lists the latest catches, which can be ordered blackened, fried, broiled, or in a garlic sauce. I prefer blackened, which is supercrusty and spicy. The fish dip is wonderfully smoky and moist, if a little heavy on mayonnaise.

Weekdays you'll find a great happy hour. On weekends the Hut features live reggae or disco until as late as 4am. They sometimes charge a cover of $5. Bring bug spray or ask the servers for some (they usually keep packets behind the bar) because this place is always plagued by mosquitoes. Local fishers and yacht owners share this rustic outpost with equal enthusiasm and loyalty.

✪ **The Greek Place.** 233 95th St. (between Collins and Harding aves.), Surfside. ☎ **305/866-9628.** Main courses $5–$6. No credit cards. Mon–Fri 10am–6pm. GREEK.

The only drawback of this tiny hole in the wall is that it's open only on weekdays. It's a little diner with sparkling white walls and about 10 wooden stools that serves fantastic Greek and American diner-style food. Daily specials like pastitsio, chicken alcyone, and roast turkey with all the fixings are the big draws for the locals working in the area who crowd the place at lunchtime. Every variety of salad and typical Greek dishes like shish kebab, souvlakis, and gyros are cooked to perfection as you wait. Even the hamburger, prime ground beef delicately spiced and fresh grilled, is exemplary.

✪ **La Brioche D'Oree.** 4017 Prairie Ave. (just off 41st St.), Miami Beach. ☎ **305/538-4770.** Sandwiches and salads $6–$8. No credit cards. Mon–Fri 7:30am–5pm, Sun 7:30am–2pm. FRENCH BAKERY.

You won't find better croissants anywhere but Paris—and even then, *maybe*. Sandwiches and salads are good, too, since they are served on deliciously crusty French bread or, of course, the aforementioned killer croissants. Sit at one of the four outdoor tables or cram inside the tiny storefront to enjoy a real French treat for breakfast or lunch.

Wolfie Cohen's Rascal House. 17190 Collins Ave., Sunny Isles. ☎ **305/947-4581.** Omelettes and sandwiches $4–$6; other dishes $5–$14. AE, MC, V. Daily 24 hours. JEWISH/BAKERY/DELICATESSEN.

Opened in 1954 and still going strong, this culinary extravaganza is a Miami Beach institution. Simple tables and booths, packed with plenty of patrons, fill the airy 425-

seat dining room. The menu is as huge as the portions; try the corned beef, schmaltz herring, brisket, kreplach, chicken soup, or other authentic Jewish staples. Some dishes are overpriced, but this is a favorite for those seeking authentic New York–style deli food. Take-out and delivery is available.

FOR A FEW BUCKS MORE

Café Prima Pasta. 414 71st St. (just west of Collins Ave.), Miami Beach. ☎ **305/ 867-0106.** Main courses $12–$14; pastas $7–$9. No credit cards. Sun–Thurs 5pm–midnight, Fri–Sat 5pm–1am, Sat 1pm–midnight. ITALIAN.

This popular pasta joint has an early bird special, but it's pretty skimpy. Served for only 1 hour from Monday through Thursday, you get a pasta with marinara sauce, soup or salad, coffee or tea, and tiramisu. Even without a special, it's pretty reasonably priced, serving phenomenal homemade noodles with good old Italian sauces like carbonara, Bolognese, puttanesca, and pomodoro. With only 30 seats, the restaurant feels a bit cramped, but it's not usually a problem squeezing in with this young, laid-back crowd. The stuffed agnolotti—with pesto, spinach, and ricotta or tomato—are incredibly delicate and flavorful. Try the apple tart with golden caramel sauce; ask for it à la mode.

✪ **Islands Café in the Bay Harbor Inn.** 9601 Bay Harbor Dr., Bay Harbor Islands. ☎ **305/867-8883** or 305/868-4141. Reservations accepted for parties of 5 or more. Main courses $13–$18, sandwiches $5–$7. Early bird specials 4:30–6:30pm. AE, MC, V. Mon lunch only 11:30am–2:30pm, Tues–Sat 11:30–10pm, Sun 11:30am–6pm. Sun brunch $16. London Tavern open from 1pm Sun and later on weekend nights. AMERICAN/CONTINENTAL.

Run by a prestigious cooking school, Johnson & Wales, this sunny waterfront restaurant represents a great value in the pricey Bal Harbour area. The sunset specials are especially recommended when full meals are offered for $7 to $12. Entrees might include a half rack of baby back ribs, grilled New York strip with red wine sauce, grilled salmon with a tropical glaze, or pasta primavera. Entrees come with soup or salad, potatoes and vegetables, and a choice of dessert. Prices are comparable to the old-fashioned Morrison's cafeteria, but the atmosphere is casually elegant and full service. Meals are sometimes served aboard the floating yacht docked behind the bay-side dining room. You can be sure that all meals are made from scratch; the kitchen is the classroom and there is no cheating. So far, the place has earned straight A's for consistently pleasant service, superbly executed dishes and generous portions. Happy hour at the adjacent London bar is also popular with visitors and locals. Enjoy large martinis for $4 and free homemade finger food like Mexican nachos, vegetable dips, hot dogs, and other bar snacks.

WORTH A SPLURGE

✪ **Crystal Cafe.** 726 41st St. ☎ **305/673-8266.** Reservations recommended Sat–Sun. Main courses $13–$22. AE, MC, V. Tues–Sun 5–11pm. CONTINENTAL/NOUVELLE.

The decor is black and white, with Lucite salt-and-pepper grinders and a bottle of wine as the only centerpiece on each of the 15 or so tables. Chef Klime (pronounced *Klee*-me), with the help of his affable wife and a superb service staff, has created a neighborhood bistro that attracts stars and locals alike. With something like 30 entrees and a dozen side dishes from which to choose with each order, it's amazing that each comes out perfectly prepared, with some unexpected addition that was not mentioned in the unpretentious menu. The shrimp cake appetizer, for example, is the size of a bread plate and rests on top of a small mound of lightly sautéed watercress and mushrooms. Surrounding the delicately breaded disk are concentric circles of beautiful sauces—tomato and a basil mayonnaise. The osso buco is gaining renown among

Miami foodies, and with good reason. The tender, almost buttery meat is steeped in chicken broth and is piled high with an assortment of vegetables. Desserts are tempting but hard to commit to after such generous portions. If you're able, consider the crepe stuffed with warm berry compote with a nutty topping.

The Forge Restaurant. 432 Arthur Godfrey Rd. (at 41st St.). ☎ **305/538-8533.** Reservations required. Main courses $18–$35. AE, DC, MC, V. Sun–Thurs 4pm–midnight, Fri–Sat 5pm–3am. STEAK/AMERICAN.

English oak paneling and Tiffany glass suggest high prices and haute cuisine, and that's exactly what you get at the Forge. Each elegant dining room possesses its own character and features high ceilings, ornate chandeliers, and high-quality European artwork. The Forge's huge American menu has a northern Italian bias, evidenced by a long list of creamy pasta appetizers. Equal attention is given to fish, veal, poultry, and beef dishes, many prepared on the kitchen's all-important oak grill. Look for appetizers like oak-grilled tomatoes with mozzarella. The Forge has one of Miami's biggest wine lists. Ask the very knowledgeable and affable head wine steward, Gino Santangelo, for a tour of the cellar. No matter what your budget, stop in for a drink at least to see the magnificent interior and some of the most stylish Miamians.

Sundays on the Bay. 5420 Crandon Blvd. ☎ **305/361-6777.** Reservations accepted; recommended for Sun brunch. Main courses $15–$24; Sun brunch $18.95. AE, CB, DC, MC, V. Mon–Sat 11:30am–11:30pm, Sun 10:30am–11:30pm. AMERICAN.

Although the food is fine, Sundays is really a fun tropical bar that features an unbeatable view of downtown, Coconut Grove, and the Sundays marina. The menu features local favorites—grouper, tuna, snapper, and good shellfish when in season. Competent renditions of such classics as oysters Rockefeller, shrimp scampi, and lobster fra diablo are also recommendable. Sunday brunches are particularly popular, when a buffet the size of Bimini attracts the city's late-rising in-crowd.

The lively bar stays open all week until 2:30am, with a deejay spinning Thursday to Sunday from 9pm. Some legal trouble put the owners in hot water in 1995, leaving the future of this reggae scene up in the air.

DOWNTOWN

A number of inexpensive and fantastic ethnic options are available throughout the densely packed streets of downtown Miami, including great Cuban, Brazilian, and Peruvian lunch counters and sit-down restaurants. Check out the food court in the **Galeria International Mall,** hidden at East Flagler Street between Northeast 2nd Avenue and Northeast 1st Court; or at Bayside's second-floor food court, you'll find lots of great and inexpensive choices. You many want to try **Las Tapas** (☎ **305/372-2737**), at the entrance, for delicious Spanish samplings. Also nearby are a tourist-friendly **Hard Rock Cafe** (☎ **305/377-3110**), and a number of more elegant restaurants overlooking the bay.

Caribbean Delite. 236 NE 1st Ave. (across the street from Miami-Dade Community College). ☎ **305/381-9254.** Full meals $5.50–$9. AE, MC, V. Daily 8:30am–7:30pm. Closed some Sundays. JAMAICAN.

You'd never see this tiny storefront diner from the one-way street it stands on, though you might smell it from the sidewalk. The aroma of succulent jerk chicken and pork beckons regulars from all over. Try Jamaican specialties like the curried goat, tender and tasty pieces of meat on the bone in a spicy yellow sauce, or oxtail stew. The kitchen can be stingy with the spectacular sauces, so consider asking for an extra helping on the side. They're happy to oblige. For breakfast, ask for the national dish of Jamaica, ackee, and saltfish, a rare and delicious find in this country.

✪ **Fishbone Grille.** 650 S. Miami Ave. (at SW 7th Ave., next to Tobacco Rd.). ☎ **305/ 530-1915.** Reservations recommended Fri–Sat. Main courses $7–$16. AE, DC, MC, V. Mon–Thurs 11:30am–10pm, Fri 11:30am–11pm, Sat 5:30–11pm. SEAFOOD.

Located in a small strip center it shares with Tobacco Road (see "The Club & Music Scene," in chapter 5), this sensational and casual fishery prepares dozens of outstanding specials daily. The atmosphere is nothing to speak of, though there's a good table where you can stare into a lively fish tank. This is by far Miami's best and most reasonably priced seafood restaurant. Try the excellent ceviche; there's just enough spice to give it a zing but not enough to overwhelm the fresh fish flavor. The stews, crab cakes, and all the starters are superb. If you like Caribbean flavor, try the jerk corvina or one of the excellent dolphin specialties.

✪ **La Cibeles Café.** 105 NE 3rd Ave. (1 block east of Biscayne Blvd.). ☎ **305/ 577-3454.** Main courses $4.75–$10. No credit cards. Mon–Sat 8am–8pm. CUBAN/SPANISH/ BRAZILIAN.

Suits and day laborers wait in line for a seat at this tiny, bustling lunch spot serving fantastic fresh specialties for great discount prices. Choose from more than a dozen daily specials like grilled red snapper, fried pork chop, or half a baked chicken with sautéed onions and tomatoes. Try the ropa vieja or the grilled trout when available. Served with rice and beans, or potatoes, fried plantains, or salad, this is one of the best deals in town. You can also get good breakfast sandwiches and superior coffee. A large selection of wines and beers as well as many good desserts make this an ideal choice for any time of day.

LITTLE HAVANA

If you don't speak Spanish, you'll want to pick up a Spanish dictionary to help you get along in Little Havana. More and more restaurants, however, have started providing English-language menus. If not, you may have to find a young patron or employee to help translate. The following is but a tiny sampling of the area's best eateries and includes an aberration, one of the city's only Vietnamese restaurants.

Hy-Vong. 3458 SW 8th St. (between 34th and 35th aves.). ☎ **305/446-3674.** Reservations not accepted. Main courses $8–$12. No credit cards. Tues–Sun 6–11pm. Closed 2 weeks in Aug. VIETNAMESE.

Although rumor has it that the talented Vietnamese chef has split, Hy-Vong is still popular. Expect to wait for hours for a table and don't even think of mumbling a complaint. If you do, the crabby owner/waitress will be sure to forget to stop by your small wooden table to refill your glass or take an order. Enjoy the wait with a traditional Vietnamese beer and lots of company. Outside this tiny storefront restaurant you'll meet interesting students, musicians, and foodies who come for the large and delicious portions, not for the plain wood-paneled room or painfully slow service. It's worth it. The Vietnamese food at Hy-Vong is elegantly simple and superspicy. Appetizers include small, tightly packed Vietnamese spring rolls and kimchee, a spicy, fermented cabbage. Star entrees include pastry-enclosed chicken with watercress/cream-cheese sauce and fish in tangy mango sauce.

✪ **Versailles.** 3555 SW 8th St. ☎ **305/444-0240.** Main courses $5–$8. DC, MC, V. Mon–Thurs 8am–1:30am, Fri–Sat 8am–3:30am, Sun 9am–1:30am. CUBAN.

Versailles is the place where Miami's Cuban power brokers meet daily over *café con leche*. A glorified diner, the place sparkles with glass, chandeliers, murals, and mirrors meant to evoke its French namesake. There's nothing fancy here—nothing French either, just straightforward food from the home country. The menu is a veritable survey of Cuban cooking and includes specialties like *Moros y Cristians* (flavorful black beans with white rice), *ropa vieja* (a Cuban beef stew), and fried whole fish.

COCONUT GROVE

The Grove's biggest tourist draw is Cocowalk, a cluster of shops, theaters, restaurants, bars, and cafes that provide all the entertainment and dining options for any taste or budget. Especially recommendable here is **The Cheesecake Factory** (☎ 305/447-9898), a newish franchise that is flourishing because of its varied and sophisticated menu. Expect a wait. **Cafe Tu Tu Tango** (☎ 305/529-5222) is another great option. This artsy cafe serves appetizer-sized portions from an extensive and ethnically varied menu. Just up the block at Mayfair House is **Planet Hollywood** (☎ 305/445-7277), or on Grand Avenue is **Johnny Rockets** (☎ 305/444-1000), for burgers and fries.

SUPER-CHEAP EATS

Cafe Tu Tu Tango. 3015 Grand Ave. (on the second floor of Cocowalk). ☎ **305/529-2222.** Reservations not accepted. Tapas $3–$8. AE, MC, V. Sun–Wed 11:30am–midnight, Thurs 11:30am–1am, Fri–Sat 11:30am–2am. SPANISH/INTERNATIONAL.

In the bustling microcosm of Cocowalk, this second-floor restaurant is designed to look something like a disheveled artist's loft. Dozens of original paintings, some only half-finished, hang on the walls and studio easels. Seating at sturdy wooden tables and chairs is either inside, on wooden floors among the clutter, or outdoors, overlooking the Grove's main drag.

Flamenco and other Latin-inspired tunes complement a menu with a decidedly Spanish flare. Hummus spread on rosemary flat bread and baked goat cheese in marinara sauce are two recommendable starters. The large and varied menu has something for everyone. Take note, however, of how much you're ordering; it is easy to spend more than you think when getting tiny, inexpensive plates. They do add up.

FOR A FEW BUCKS MORE

At's a Nice. 2779 Bird Ave. (off SW 27th Ave.). ☎ **305/441-9119.** Pizza pies $6–$16; entrees $9–$16. AE, MC, V. Tues–Sun 4–11pm. ITALIAN.

A welcome addition to the Coconut Grove dining scene, this Italian eatery has won immediate fans for its superb pizza and good pastas, too. The setting is as casual as you can get, with a wood deck and plastic patio furniture the setting for the half a dozen tables overlooking a busy street.

Kaleidoscope. 3112 Commodore Plaza (1 block from Main Hwy.). ☎ **305/446-5010.** Reservations recommended. Main courses $14–$20; pastas $12–$15. AE, CB, DC, DISC, MC, V. Mon 6–11pm, Tues–Sun 11:30am–3pm and 6–11pm, Fri–Sat 6pm–midnight, Sun 5:30–10pm. NEW AMERICAN.

Kaleidoscope is an unusually low-key and elegant restaurant in the heart of Coconut Grove. It's conveniently located slightly off the main drag and perched on a second-floor terrace assuring privacy and a good view. The dishes are well prepared, and the pastas, topped with sauces like seafood and fresh basil or pesto with grilled yellowfin tuna, are especially tasty. The linguine with salmon and fresh dill is perfection. Although there's no specially priced before-theater dinner, many locals stop in at this always reliable and reasonable spot for dinner before a show at the Coconut Grove Playhouse, a few blocks away.

✪ **Monty's Bayshore Restaurant.** 2560 S. Bayshore Dr. ☎ **305/858-1431.** Reservations recommended upstairs Sat–Sun. Main courses $19–$35; sandwiches $6–$8; platters $7–$12. AE, CB, DC, MC, V. Daily 11:30am–midnight. Call for hours of each of the three restaurants; some are open later. SEAFOOD.

Starbucks, Schmarbucks:
Miami Does Coffee the Cubano Way

Forget those cookie-cutter coffeehouses that have sprouted up all over the country. A few of the national chains *have* made it this far south with their pricey, frothy blends. But for a *real* taste of Florida, head to where the locals go: Miami's got its own brew, and it is some serious Joe!

Cuban coffee is a staple on the Miami restaurant scene. You'll find it served from take-out windows at hundreds of *cafeterias* or *luncherias* around town. Depending on where you are and what you want, you'll spend between 40¢ and 95¢ per cup. And to partake, you'll just have to learn how to ask for it *en español.*

The best *café cubano* has a rich layer of foam on top, formed when hot espresso shoots from the machine into the sugar below. The result is a caramelly, potent concoction that is a local favorite.

The most commonly ordered take-out coffee is the *colada.* This large cup of sweet black coffee is served in a Styrofoam cup with five or six thimble-size plastic cups on top; it's meant to be shared with friends or coworkers.

If you are alone, ask for a *café* or *cafecito,* a thimble-size cup of the same thick black espresso with lots of sugar. It's usually swallowed in one quick gulp. Unless you ask for it to go (*para llevar*), you'll probably get it in a miniature ceramic cup and saucer. Don't be fooled by the size; caffeine-wise, one shot of this stuff is equal to two or three mugs of the American version.

For the less brave, there is the *cortado* or *cortadito,* the same dose cut with a little steamed milk. Even more mild is the *café con leche,* a large cup of steamed milk with a single shot of coffee mixed into it. It's especially popular at breakfast, and is often eaten with *pan tostada,* a long hunk of grilled, flattened, and buttered bread that is dunked in the cup, donut-style. You can request it *oscuro* (dark) or *claro* (light), but count on it being sweet.

In fact, unless you ask for your coffee *sin azúcar* (without sugar), or *con poco azúcar* (with a little sugar), you'll get the standard cloyingly sweet coffee. Even when you request an unsweetened version you'll have to be vigilant. It's an automatic motion for the person behind the counter. Ask twice and watch closely.

These days, coffee vendors are used to odd requests. Artificial sweetener is usually available—ask for *azúcar de dieta.* Although not usual, you can even find decaffeinated coffee, *café descafeínado,* in some shops. Café Bustelo, the most ubiquitous brand of Cuban coffee, has marketed a neutered version of its famous espresso with some success. It's not bad, but it doesn't have the same effect as the real stuff. Likewise, low-fat or skim milk is an anomaly.

Finally, if you insist, you can usually find a cup of American coffee, *café americano,* in a Latin restaurant—though the fact that it's referred to colloquially as *agua sucia* (dirty water) should be an indication of what it will taste like. I'd stick with the real stuff. But watch out, it can be habit forming. Remember, you're supposed to *relax* in Miami.

This branch of the well-known seafood chain (see also listing in South Beach, above) comes in three parts: a lounge, a raw bar, and a restaurant. Among them, Monty's serves everything from steak and seafood to munchies like nachos, potato skins, and Buffalo chicken wings. This is a fun kind of place, usually with more revelers and drinkers than diners. At the outdoor dockside bar there's live music nightly and all day on weekends. Upstairs is an upscale dining room that serves one of the city's best Caesar salads and respectable stone crab claws in season. However, do not order the claws from May to October, since the local product is out of season; they'll serve you imported ones that simply don't compare. In season, however, splurge on the all-you can-eat jumbo claws for $40 to $50. That's about the same price as three or four claws at Joe's (see above).

Señor Frogs. 3480 Main Hwy. (across from the Barnacle). ☎ **305/448-0999.** Reservations recommended on weekends. Full meals $9–$15. AE, CB, DC, DISC, MC, V. Mon–Sat 11:30am–2am, Sun 11:30am–1am. MEXICAN.

Filled with a college-student crowd, this restaurant is known for a raucous good time, its mariachi band, and especially its powerful margaritas. The food at this rocking cantina is a bit overly cheesy, but tasty, if not exactly authentic. The mole enchiladas, with 14 different kinds of mild chiles mixed with chocolate, is as flavorful as any I've tasted. Almost everything is served with rice and beans in quantities so large that few diners are able to finish. Consider some of the generous appetizers like the Quesadilla Tia Esther, a sandwich of tortillas piled with shredded beef, lots of cheese and beans, and guacamole.

CORAL GABLES & ENVIRONS
SUPER-CHEAP EATS

Daily Bread. 2400 SW 27th St. (on U.S. 1). ☎ **305/856-0363** or 305/856-0366. Sandwiches and salads $3–$6. Mon–Sat 8:30am–7pm. MC, V.

At press time this budget institution was moving from its very modest digs on 17th Avenue into an impressive, new Mediterranean building worthy of its fine food. Not only is there great take-out food and homemade breads, but also backgammon and water pipes are for sale. The falafel and gyro sandwiches are large, fresh, and filling. Spinach pie for less than $1 is also recommended, though short on spinach and heavy on pastry. Salads, including luscious tabouli, hummus, and eggplant, are also worth a go. To take in or eat out, the Middle Eastern fare here is a real treat, especially in an area so filled with fancy French and Cuban fare.

The Globe. 377 Alhambra Circle (just off Le Jeune Rd.). ☎ **305/445-3555.** Reservations only for more than 6. Salads $4–$10; pizzas and sandwiches $7–$11. AE, DISC, MC, V. Mon–Fri 11:30am–midnight, Sat 6:30pm–2am. INTERNATIONAL/CASUAL.

This funky coffee shop/travel agency is an odd addition to a neighborhood dominated by fancy eateries and hotels. Take advantage of the hip surroundings and enjoy the quite recommendable food. Especially good are the pizzas and salads. In addition to an extensive list of wines and specialty beers, there are many interesting nonalcoholic choices. More importantly, sample some of the excellent live music every weekend.

FOR A FEW BUCKS MORE

Gables Diner. 2320 Galiano Dr. (between Ponce de León Blvd. and 37th Ave.). ☎ **305/567-0330.** Main courses $9–$16; pastas $10–$12; burgers and sandwiches $7–$9; salads $8–$10. AE, DC, DISC, MC, V. Daily 8am–10pm. AMERICAN.

This upscale diner serves an eclectic mix of comfort food and nouvelle health food. From meat loaf to Chinese chicken salad, there is a moderately priced option for everyone. My favorite is the chicken pot pie, a homemade flaky crusted pie filled with large chunks of white meat, pearl onions, peas, and mushrooms. Also good are the large burgers with every imaginable condiment. Vegetarians can find a few good choices including pastas, bean soups, pizzas, a vegetable stir-fry and some hearty salads. All the ingredients are fresh and crisp. No need to dress up here, though you will find a clean and almost romantic setting that is as appropriate for families as it is for first dates.

WORTH A SPLURGE

✪ **Caffè Abbracci.** 318 Aragon Ave. (between Le Jeune Rd. and Miracle Mile). ☎ **305/ 441-0700.** Reservations recommended for dinner. Main courses $16–$24; pasta $13–$20. AE, CB, DC, MC, V. Mon–Fri 11:30am–3pm and 6pm–midnight. NORTHERN ITALIAN.

You'll be greeted with a hug by Nino, owner and maître d', who oversees this wonderful spot as only an Italian could. The food is remarkable, and the place is packed on weekends by those in the know. It's hard to get beyond the appetizers here, all of which are so good that you could order a few and be satisfied. My favorite is the shrimp with a bright pesto sauce that has just enough garlic to give it a kick, but not so much you won't get a kiss later. The risottos are excellent and can be served in half portions so that you'll have room for the indescribable fish dishes. You're guaranteed perfect service in a pretty wood-and-marble setting—the only drawback is the unfortunately loud dining room.

Norman's. 21 Almeria Ave. (between Douglas and Ponce de León Blvd.). ☎ **305/ 446-6767.** Reservations highly recommended. Main courses $25–$32. AE, DC, MC, V. Mon– Fri noon–2pm and 6–10:15pm, Sat 6–10:45pm. NEW WORLD CUISINE/REGIONAL.

Master chef and one of the originators of what has become known as New World cuisine, Norman Van Aken reemerged after a 2-year break from the restaurant biz to open what he has called his "culmination." The result is an open kitchen where a handful of silent and industrious chefs prepare Asian- and Caribbean-inspired dishes for the well-dressed patrons. The atmosphere is comfortable and subdued with hand-painted walls, marble floors, and an upstairs gallery. Eating here is an experience where the food is the main focus of attention. It's difficult not to let the exotic-sounding list of ingredients on the menu be the topic of conversation. Some think it's pretentious and overwrought; I think there's plenty to enjoy, like the pizzas and pastas with a good glass of wine.

The staff is adoring and professional, and the atmosphere is tasteful without being too formal. You'll want to try some of the wacky desserts like mango ice cream served with Asian pears and crushed red pepper (the pepper really just adds color to the plate); like the restaurant, it's hot but very approachable.

NORTH MIAMI BEACH/NORTH DADE

The area is mostly residential, with lots of condos filled with seasonal visitors. And though there are no real attractions here, except the Spanish Monastery (see chapter 5 for details), this cluster of neighborhoods has some of Miami's very best restaurants and shopping.

SUPER-CHEAP EATS

The Lagoon. 488 Sunny Isles Blvd. (163rd St.), North Miami Beach. ☎ **305/947-6661.** Reservations accepted. Main courses $12–$22; lobster special $13.95 or two for $23.95 ($3 more on weekends and holidays). AE, CB, MC, V. Daily 4:30–11pm; early bird dinner 4:30–6pm. SEAFOOD/CONTINENTAL.

This old bay-front fish house has been around since 1936. Major road construction that makes it nearly impossible to find should have guaranteed its doom years ago, but the excellent view and incredible specials make it a worthwhile stop.

Yes, it's true! Lobster lovers can get two 1¼-pounders for $23.95 or one for $13.95. Broiled is best with a light buttery seasoned coating. This dish is not only inexpensive but incredibly succulent, too. Complimentary side dishes include pickled vegetables, bread, and a huge baked potato, stuffed or plain. The salads are good but come with too much commercial-tasting dressing. I've tried a few and all are disappointing. To be safe, ask for oil and vinegar on the side. Actually, I recommend skipping all the accoutrements to save room for the lobster.

The bathrooms could use a good cleaning, as could the whole cavernous restaurant. Disregard that and the nonchalant service and you'll find the best-priced juicy Maine lobsters around. An impressive early bird menu features all kinds of great seafood dinners like salmon or dolphin for less than $12.

Laurenzo's Cafe. 16385 West Dixie Hwy. (at corner of 163rd St.), North Miami Beach. ☎ 305/945-6381. Main courses and two side dishes $8–$15; pastas $4–$5; salads $2–$5. AE, MC, V (credit cards for take-out only). Mon–Sat 11am–7pm, Sun 11am–4pm. SOUTHERN ITALIAN CAFETERIA.

This little cafeteria-style counter in the middle of a chaotic grocery store serves delicious buffet lunches and dinners to the *paesanos* and loyal Jewish neighbors. A meeting place for the growing Italian population in Miami, the store has been open for more than 40 years. Daily specials usually include a lasagna or eggplant parmigiana and two or three salad options. Evening options are more extensive with choices of a dozen pastas, meats, and seafood specials, too. Prices have gone up recently, but the food is as good as ever.

Choose a wine from the vast selection and take your meal to go or sit in the trellis-covered seating area amid busy shoppers buying their evening's groceries. You'll get to eavesdrop on some great conversations over your plastic tray of real Southern-style Italian cooking.

FOR A FEW BUCKS MORE

The Gourmet Diner. 13951 Biscayne Blvd. (between NE 139th and 140th sts.), North Miami Beach. ☎ **305/947-2255.** Reservations not accepted. Main courses $10–$17. No credit cards. Mon–Fri 11am–11pm, Sat 8am–11:30pm, Sun 8am–10:30pm. BELGIAN/ FRENCH.

This retro 1950s-style diner serves plain old French fare without pretensions. The atmosphere is a bit brash and the lines are often out the door. You'll want to get here early anyway to taste some of the house specialties—beef burgundy, trout amandine, and frogs' legs Provençal, which tend to sell out quickly. Check the chalkboard (which, depending on where you're seated, can be hard to see) for the salads and soups all prepared to order. Even a simple hearts-of-palm salad becomes a gourmet treat under the tangy vinaigrette. A well-rounded wine list with reasonable prices makes this place a standout and a great deal. The homemade daily pastries are also delicious.

Here Comes the Sun. 2188 NE 123 St. (west of the Broad Causeway), North Miami. ☎ **305/893-5711.** Reservations recommended in season. Main courses $10–$14; early bird special 4–6:30pm, $7.95; sandwiches and salads $5–$7.50. AE, DC, DISC, MC, V. Mon–Sat 11am–8:30pm. AMERICAN/HEALTH FOOD.

One of Miami's early health-food spots, this bustling grocery-store-turned-diner serves hundreds of plates a night, mostly to blue-haired locals. It's noisy and hectic, but worth it. In season, all types pack the place for a $7.95 special, served between 4 and 6:30pm, which includes one of more than 20 choices of entrees, soup or salad, coffee or tea, and a small frozen yogurt. Fresh grilled fish and chicken entrees are reliable and served with a nice array of vegetables. The miso burgers with "sun sauce" are a vegetarian's dream.

SOUTH MIAMI

This mostly residential area has a few good dining spots and every possible chain restaurant you can imagine, most scattered along U.S. 1. The fast-food Cuban chain,

Pollo Tropical, is a good quick stop if you are heading to one of South Miami's attractions. One of the old favorites that must be mentioned is listed below.

Shorty's. 9200 S. Dixie Hwy. (between U.S. 1 and Dadeland Blvd.), South Miami. ☎ **305/ 670-7732.** Main courses $5–$9. MC, V. Daily 11am–11pm (later on weekends). BARBECUE.

A tradition in Miami since 1951, this hokey log cabin is still serving some of the best ribs and chicken in South Florida. People line up for the smoky slow-cooked meat, so tender it wants to jump off the bone into your mouth. The secret, however, is to ask for your order with sweet sauce—the regular stuff tastes bland and bottled. All the side dishes, including coleslaw, corn on the cob, and baked beans, look commercial, but you really need to try them to complete the experience. This is barbecue with a neon *B*.

What to See & Do in Miami

by Victoria Pesce Elliott

5

Unlike the theme-park landscape of Central Florida, Miami is more attractive for its natural resources than for its large entertainment complexes. Head for the natural treasures here, like the incredibly diverse beaches and sea life, or check out the places that locals built for their own enjoyment, like Villa Vizcaya and Coral Castle.

But don't discount the human-made attractions altogether. Miami was, and still is, designed to court visitors (and their dollars) from around the world, and many of these efforts make for fantastic entertainment. Some of the city's older animal attractions, like Monkey Jungle, Parrot Jungle, and the Seaquarium for example, make for great diversions and are popular with locals and visitors alike. With professional hockey, baseball, football, and basketball teams based here, you are sure to find a game almost anytime. In addition, you'll find a new wave of world-class exhibitions, theater, dance, a plethora of sports- and water-related activities, the country's largest cruise-ship port, impressive shopping, and an unbelievably varied and wild nightlife, especially in hip South Beach.

1 Beaches

There are more than 35 miles of beachfront in Miami-Dade County and most are open to the public. The character of Miami's many beaches is as varied as the city's population. Some are shaded by towering palm trees, while others are darkened by the shadows of formidable condominium complexes. Some beaches attract families or old-timers; some have an active singles scene. Still others are crowded with topless Europeans and models. In short, there are two major distinct beach alternatives: Miami Beach and Key Biscayne. It's all explained below. You can bring picnics, but no alcohol or glass bottles, to most beaches. Most also forbid dogs.

Have fun, but also be sure to check warning signs posted at beaches to avoid powerful rip currents and rough seas.

MIAMI BEACH

This long barrier island, which includes the much-photographed South Beach area at its tip, has something for everyone. Collins Avenue and Ocean Drive front nearly a dozen miles of gray-sand beach and blue-green waters from 1st to 192nd streets. Although most of this stretch is lined with a solid wall of hotels and condos, beach access is plentiful, and you're free to frolic along the entire strip. Granted, finding a parking spot can be a challenge. There are lots of amenities on the public beaches here, including lifeguards, toilet facilities, concession stands, and metered parking (bring lots of quarters). Miami Beach's beaches are generally wide and well maintained. Except for a thin strip close to the water, most of the sand here is hard-packed—the result of a $10 million Army Corps of Engineers Beach Rebuilding Project meant to protect buildings from the effects of eroding sand.

You'll find the beaches on this barrier island become less crowded the farther north you go. A wooden boardwalk runs along the hotel side of the beach from 21st to 47th streets (about 1½ miles), offering a terrific sun-and-surf experience without getting sand in your shoes. Aside from the "Best Beaches" listed below, Miami Beach's lifeguard-protected public beaches include **Lummus Park,** between 6th and 14th streets, where whimsical lifeguard stands don't look like anything you've ever seen on *Baywatch.* Instead, they are turned into a bed, a rocket ship, a Japanese Shinto-style temple, and other fanciful shapes. Lifeguard stands are also located at the following streets: 1, 3, 6, 8, 10, 12, 13, 14, 17, 21, 29, 35, 46, 53, 64, 72, 74, 79, 81, and 83. For safe swimming try the following: 21st Street, at the beginning of the boardwalk; 35th Street, popular with an older crowd; 46th Street, near the popular Jimmy Johnson's Sports bar in the Eden Roc hotel and the Fontainebleau Hilton; 53rd Street, a narrower, more sedate beach; 64th Street, one of the quietest strips around; and 72nd Street, a local old-timers' spot.

I've highlighted the best spots below:

The ultrachic ✪ **Lummus Park Beach,** which runs along Ocean Drive from about 6th to 14th streets in South Beach, is the best place to go if you're seeking entertainment as well as a great tan. On any day of the week you might spy models primping for a photo shoot or topless sunbathers wearing sunglasses larger than their bikini bottoms.

The **85th Street Beach,** along Collins Avenue, is the best place to swim away from the crowds. It's one of Miami's only stretches of sand with no condos or hotels looming over sunbathers. A shady green park complete with a fitness track and a small playground offers a refuge from the sun. Lifeguards patrol the area throughout the day.

You'll find plenty of colorful shells at **Bal Harbour Beach,** Collins Avenue at 96th Street, just a few yards north of Surfside Beach. There's also an exercise course and good shade, but no lifeguards.

Although the state has been trying to outlaw nudity, there is a small, secluded beach in the southern portion of **Haulover Beach,** just north of the Bal Harbour border at about 106th Street, which attracts nudists from around the world. It has created something of a boom for area businesses that cater to them.

KEY BISCAYNE

If Miami Beach isn't private enough for you, **Key Biscayne** might be more of what you have in mind. Crossing Rickenbacker Causeway ($1 toll) is almost like crossing into The Bahamas. The 5 miles of public beach here are blessed with softer sand and are less developed and more laid-back than the hotel-laden strips to the north.

Below are some of the highlights on "The Key." Though not known for world-class surfing, Miami does get its share of decent swells. Head to Haulover Beach/Harbor House, just north of Miami Beach on Collins Avenue at about 108th Street. This otherwise undistinguished beach seems to get the area's only real curls. Go early and avoid the rush of young locals who wish they were on Maui.

On Key Biscayne, **Crandon Park Beach,** on Crandon Boulevard, has 3 miles of oceanfront beach, 493 acres of park, 75 grills, three parking lots, several soccer and softball fields, and a public 18-hole championship golf course. This beach is

Attractions in South Miami–Dade County

Coral Castle **7**
Fairchild Tropical Gardens **2**
Miami Metrozoo **4**
Monkey Jungle **5**
Parrot Jungle **1**
Preston B. Bird and Mary Heinlein
  Fruit and Spice Park **6**
Week's Air Museum **3**

particularly wide and the water here so clear you can usually see to the bottom. Admission is $2 per vehicle. It's open daily from 8am to sunset.

2 The Art Deco District/South Beach

Located on the southern tip of Miami Beach, the **Art Deco District** is a whole community made up of outrageous and fanciful 1920s and 1930s architecture. The Art Deco District is roughly bounded by the Atlantic Ocean on the east, Alton Road on the west, 6th Street on the south, and Dade Boulevard (along the Collins Canal) on the north. This approximately 1-square-mile area is the first of its kind to be listed on the National Register of Historic Places. Most of the finest examples of this whimsical style are concentrated along three parallel streets—Ocean Drive, Collins Avenue, and Washington Avenue—from about 6th to 23rd streets.

After years of neglect and calls for the wholesale demolition of its buildings, South Beach got a new lease on life in 1979. That year, this 800-building area was granted a listing on the National Register of Historic Places, thanks in large part to the leadership of Barbara Baer Capitman, a dedicated crusader for the art deco region and the Miami Design Preservation League. Long-lost architectural details were highlighted with soft sherbets of peach, periwinkle, turquoise, and purple. Developers soon moved in, and the full-scale refurbishment of the area's hotels got under way.

Today, dozens of new hotels, restaurants, and nightclubs are undergoing renovation. You'll see cranes and bulldozers on almost every block.

Cheap Thrills: What to See & Do for Free (or Almost) in Miami

- **Watch the Sun Set Over Downtown.** Driving west over the Julia Tuttle Causeway (S.R. 112), you can catch the best views in the city. Bursts of aqua, pink, and orange lights explode behind a cluster of skyscrapers, and the surrounding water reflects it all. Head back in the other direction, and catch the glow of neon decorating a cluster of towering palms.
- **Feast on Ocean Drive's Eye Candy.** All along South Beach's Ocean Drive, well-toned and tanned bodies abound. Scantily clad boys and girls, leggy models, in-line skaters, and gawking tourists alike parade along the wide promenade, with a backdrop of cotton-candy colored art deco buildings on one side and the glistening ocean on the other. If you're around in winter, you're almost guaranteed to find a preview fashion shoot in progress. Stake out a front row seat at any of the sidewalk cafes lining the strip where, for the price of a soda or a glass of wine, you'll be amused for hours.
- **Taste Some Latin Flavor in Little Havana.** To experience a little slice of Cuba on U.S. soil, stroll down Calle Ocho (8th Street) and stop into any of the shops catering to the huge exile population. Visit Maximo Gomez Park, at 801 SW 15th Ave. where *viejitos* (old men) face off over chess boards from morning until sunset. Between 15th and 13th avenues is the street of *estrellas,* where stars like Celia Cruz have their names etched in the sidewalk, Hollywood style. Visit a cigar factory, and then savor a *cafe con leche* at a local diner like Versailles (See "Great Deals on Dining," in chapter 4). There's no better way to get a feel for this city. (And if you don't *habla Español,* bring along a phrase book.)
- **Tour Downtown from the Metro-Rail.** For 25¢, you can get a spectacular overview of Miami's bustling metropolis. The best part is, you can enjoy it all seated in the cool comfort of air-conditioned cars. It's like the monorail at Disney, but without the commentary.
- **Swim, Stroll, and Lounge on the Beach.** Most of Miami's beaches are entirely free, though some in park areas do charge a fee for vehicles. You can enjoy miles of wide sandy beaches all along Miami Beach where the water is calm and warm. South Beach between 5th and 20th streets has the most characters, from topless Europeans to super buffed body-builders.
- **Walk Through the Lobby of The Delano Hotel.** The Delano is a wild and wonderful art deco eyeful, with a gorgeous staff that competes for attention with the outlandish Philippe Starck decor. Check out the overflowing pool, out-of-proportion chess set, and the funky gift shop. Splurge on a $10 drink poolside, and settle in for a few hours of celeb-spotting and people watching. You won't be disappointed.
- **Sample the Flavor of South Beach at Its Most Venerated Gourmet Store.** A bunch of tomatoes might cost you 5 bucks at **Epicure** (☎ **305/672-1861**), but if you can resist the temptation of buying the high-ticket items, this is a great place to browse and nosh. On most days, a busy booth offers samples of anything from salsa to olive oils. Stop by the cheese department and taste a wedge of something exotic or familiar. The deli folks will happily share a forkful of chicken salad or a generous slice of nova to anyone who asks for a nibble.

If you're exploring on your own, start at the **Art Deco Welcome Center,** 1001 Ocean Dr. (☎ **305/531-3484**), which has several informative giveaways, including maps and art deco architecture information. Art deco books (including the *Art Deco Guide,* an informative compendium of all buildings here), T-shirts, postcards, mugs, and other items are sold. It's open Monday to Saturday from 9am to 6pm, sometimes later.

Among the highlights to seek out are the **Essex House,** 1001 Collins Ave., at 10th Street, an excellent example of nautical moderne, complete with porthole windows and sleek racing stripes along its sides. Along Ocean Drive, between 6th and 8th streets there's the **Park Central,** the **Imperial, Majestic,** and **Colony** hotels. At 1020 Ocean Dr., the **Clevelander** is one of the few hotels in the area with an original swimming pool and a deco-style sundeck area that now hosts a popular bar scene. (See "Miami After Dark," below).

Other particularly memorable areas for strolling include Lincoln Road (see box in "Great Deals on Dining," in chapter 4), which is lined with galleries, cafes, and funky art and antique stores. The **Community Church,** at the corner of Lincoln Road and Drexel Avenue, is the neighborhood's first church and, built in 1921, one of the oldest surviving buildings.

For informative walking and biking tours of the area, including a self-guided audio tour, see "Sightseeing Cruises & Organized Tours," below.

3 Animal Parks

Kids of all ages will enjoy Miami's animal parks, which feature everything from dolphins and lions to parrots and alligators. And, of course, what is a trip to Florida without having seen at least one gator?

✪ **Miami Metrozoo.** SW 152nd St. and SW 124th Ave. ☎ **305/251-0403.** Admission $8 adults, $4 children 3–12. Daily 9:30am–5:30pm (ticket booth closes at 4pm). From U.S. 1 south, turn right on SW 152nd St. and follow signs about 3 miles to the entrance.

It's about a 35-minute drive from the beaches to this huge 290-acre cageless complex (the animals are kept at bay by cleverly designed moats). If you are with children, this is definitely worth an afternoon. Mufasa and Simba (of Disney's *Lion King* fame) were modeled on Metrozoo lions, still in residence today. Plus, there are two rare white Bengal tigers, a Komodo dragon, rare koala bears, a monorail safari, and a petting zoo. You can even take a ride on an elephant.

Miami Seaquarium. 4400 Rickenbacker Causeway (south side), Key Biscayne. ☎ **305/ 361-5705.** Admission $19.95 adults, $13.95 seniors over 55, $15.95 children 3–9. Daily 9:30am–6pm (ticket booth closes at 4:30pm). I-95 south to exit no. 1, the Rickenbacker Causeway, left through the toll booth. Look right for Seaquarium.

You'll want to arrive early to experience all of this fun and educational attraction. It takes about 4 hours to tour the 35-acre oceanarium and see all four daily shows starring the world's most impressive ocean mammals. Trained dolphins, killer whales, and frolicking sea lions play with trainers and very brave visitors.

Monkey Jungle. 14805 SW 216th St., South Miami. ☎ **305/235-4253.** Admission $11.50 adults, $9.50 seniors and active-duty military, $6 children 4–12. Daily 9:30am–5pm (tickets sold until 4pm). Take U.S. 1 south to SW 216th St or from Florida Turnpike Exit 11.

See rare Brazilian golden lion tamarins. Watch skin-diving Asian macaques. Yes, it's a primate paradise! With no cages to restrain their antics, the monkeys here swing, chatter, and play their way into your heart. Screened-in trails wind through acres of jungle, and daily shows feature the talents of the park's most talented residents. You've got to love primates to get over the heavy smell of the jungle; this attraction has been here for more than 60 years.

Parrot Jungle and Gardens. 11000 SW 57th Ave., Greater Miami South. ☎ **305/ 666-7834.** Admission $12.95 adults, $11.95 seniors, $8.95 children 3–10. Daily 9:30am– 6pm. Cafe opens at 8am. Take U.S. 1 south, turn left at SW 57th Ave. or exit Kendall Dr. from Turnpike and turn right on U.S. 1.

Parrot Jungle is loud and silly, but it's fun. In addition to parrots, hundreds of magnificent macaws, peacocks, cockatoos, and flamingos occupy this 22-acre park. Continuous shows in the Parrot Bowl Theater star roller-skating cockatoos, card-playing macaws, and more stunt-happy birds than you ever thought possible. Alligators, tortoises, and iguanas are also on exhibit. Other attractions include a wildlife show focusing on indigenous Florida animals, an area called the "Primate Experience," a children's playground, and a petting zoo.

After 50 years at this location, Parrot Jungle is planning to move to its own island midway between downtown Miami and the beaches in 1999.

4 Miami's Museum & Art Scene

Miami's museum scene has always been quirky and interesting, though inconsistent at best in terms of quality. Recently, with the reinvention of the Wolfsonian, the reincarnation of the Museum of Contemporary Art (MOCA), and the increased daringness of the Miami Art Museum, the scene has improved dramatically. It's now safe to say that Miami has world-class art exhibitions. Listed below is a selection of the valuable treasures that have become a part of the city's diverse cultural heritage.

Art lovers should take a look at "Sightseeing Cruises & Organized Tours," below, for listings of free scheduled gallery walks, and "Shopping" for highlights of a few of the best galleries.

The best days to schedule your museum visits are Tuesdays or Thursdays, when many local museums, like the Miami Art Museum and the Wolfsonian, welcome contributions in any amount for admission. The Bass Museum is open on a volunteer donation basis on alternate Wednesday evenings.

THE TOP MUSEUMS & MEMORIALS

✪ **Bass Museum of Art.** 2121 Park Ave. (just west of Collins Ave.), South Beach. ☎ **305/ 673-7530.** Admission $5 adults, $3 students with ID and senior citizens, free for children 6 and under; second and fourth Wed of the month by donation from 5–9pm. Tues–Sat 10am–5pm, Sun 1–5pm (every second and fourth Wed open 1–9pm). Closed Mon and major holidays.

An important and growing visual arts museum in Miami Beach, Bass displays European paintings, sculptures, and tapestries from the Renaissance, baroque, rococo, and modern periods as part of their small permanent collection. Temporary exhibitions alternate between traveling shows and rotations of the Bass's stock, with themes ranging from 17th-century Dutch art to contemporary architecture.

Built from coral rock in 1930, the Bass sits in the middle of 6 tree-topped, landscaped acres. Make sure to wander the grounds to enjoy the changing outdoor sculpture exhibits before the heavy construction starts—a 12-acre expansion is due in 1998.

The Wolfsonian. 1001 Washington Ave., South Beach. ☎ **305/531-1001.** Admission $5 adults; $3.50 senior citizens, students, and children 6–12; $5 tour-group members; free on Thurs evenings. Children under 6 and members free. Tues–Sat 11am–6pm, Sun noon–5pm, and Thurs 6–9pm.

Culture for Less: Soaking Up Miami's Art Scene on a Shoestring

Miami's art world is diverse and dynamic, and you don't have to be rolling in the dough to get a taste of it. One of the best ways to save money is to save your museum visits for days when admission is free or on a donate-what-you-wish basis. South Beach's quirky **Wolfsonian-FIU** stays open late on Thursday, and requires only a meager donation. Admission to the **Miami Art Museum** is free on Thursday evenings from 5 until 9pm. In addition, the second Saturday of every month is free for families, and every Tuesday is contribution day. The **Bass Museum** likewise welcomes visitors on a pay-what-you-wish basis on the second and fourth Wednesday of every month.

Another way to expand your cultural horizons without deflating your wallet is to take a **free gallery tour.** More than 20 galleries in Coral Gables (and a sizable number in Miami Beach as well) participate in these programs; typically, you meander from one gallery to the next, sipping wine and pondering the art. For specifics, see the "Sightseeing Cruises & Organized Tours" section of this chapter.

Mitchell Wolfson Jr., an eccentric collector of late 19th- and 20th-century art and other paraphernalia, was spending so much money storing his booty he decided to buy the warehouse that held the more than 70,000 items, including glass, ceramics, sculptures, paintings, and photographs. Now this incredibly diverse and controversial collection is on display in the former storage facility retrofitted with such painstaking detail that it's the envy of curators around the world. In 1997, he donated the collection to a local college that continues to run the exhibition space.

✪ **Holocaust Memorial.** 1933 Meridian Ave. (at Dade Blvd.), South Beach. ☎ 305/538-1663. Free admission. Daily 9am–9pm.

This heart-wrenching memorial of the genocide that took place in 1940s Europe is hard to miss and would be a shame to overlook. The powerful centerpiece is a bronze statue by Kenneth Treister that depicts millions of people crawling into an open hand to freedom. You can walk through an open hallway lined with photographs and the names of concentration camps and their victims. From the street, you'll see the outstretched arm, but do stop and tour the sculpture at ground level. Hidden behind the beautiful stone facade is an extremely moving museum.

IN & NEAR DOWNTOWN

Florida Museum of Hispanic and Latin American Art. 4006 Aurora St., Coral Gables (between Bird Rd. and Ponce de Leon). ☎ **305/444-7060.** Free admission. Tues–Fri 11am–5pm, Sat 11am–4pm. Closed Aug and major holidays.

In addition to the permanent collection of contemporary artists from Spain and Latin America, this museum hosts monthly exhibitions of works from Latin America and the Caribbean Basin. Usually the group shows focus on a theme, such as International Women or Surrealism. Run by an impressive staff, the small museum is a real slice of Miami.

Miami Art Museum at the Miami-Dade Cultural Center. 101 W. Flagler St., Miami. ☎ **305/375-1700** or 305/375-3000. Admission $5 adults, $2.50 senior citizens and students with ID, free for children 11 and under, Tues is contribution day. Tues–Wed and Fri 10am–5pm; Thurs 10am–9pm; Sat–Sun noon–5pm. Closed Mon and major holidays. From I-95 south, exit at Orange Bowl–NW 8th St. and continue south to NW 2nd St.; turn left at

Miami Area Attractions & Beaches

Amelia Earhart Park **4**

American Police Hall of
Fame and Museum **7**

The Barnacle **20**

Bayside Marketplace
& Bayfront Park **11**

Biltmore Hotel **16**

CocoWalk **21**

Florida Museum of Hispanic
and Latin American Art **18**

Hialeah Racetrack **5**

Miami-Dade
Cultural Center
(Miami Art Museum &
The Historical Museum
of Southern Florida) **10**

Miami Jai-Alai Fronton **6**

Miami Museum of Science
and Space Transit
Planetarium **12**

Miami Seaquarium **14**

Miami Youth Museum **15**

Museum of Contemporary
Art **3**

Orange Bowl **9**

Pro Player Stadium **1**
Scott Rakow Youth Center **8**
Spanish Monastery
Cloisters **2**
University of Miami **19**
Venetian Pool **17**
Villa Vizcaya **3**

SOUTH BEACH
Lummus Park Beach
Collins Ave.
Alton Rd.
5th St.
Fisher Island

Atlantic Ocean

Crandon Park Beach
Bill Baggs Cape Florida State Park
Crandon Blvd.
KEY BISCAYNE
Virginia Key

MacArthur Causeway A1A
Port of Miami

Brickell Ave. **11**
South Miami Ave.
395
95 **10**
41
8th St.
1
Rickenbacker Causeway
14

Biscayne Bay

SW 12th Ave. **9**
SW 17th Ave.
SW 1st St.
SW 7th St.
836
Beacom Blvd.
SW 27th Ave.
DOWNTOWN
SW 22nd St. **12**
S. Bayshore Dr.
13
US 1 South Dixie Highway

NW 7th St.
West Flagler St.
Tamiami Trail
SW 37th Ave.
Ponce de Leon Blvd.
Miracle Mile **15**
17
16
Bird Ave.
COCONUT GROVE **20**
21
Douglas Rd.

SW 42 Ave.
Le Jeune Rd.
836
41
CORAL GABLES
Coral Way
Bird Rd. (SW 40th St.) **18**
19
Hardee Ave.
Ponce de Leon Blvd.
SW 57th Ave.
SW 72nd Ave. (Sunset Rd.)
Red Rd.

LEGEND
Airport
Beach

See also more detailed map of Attractions in South Miami–Dade County

N
0   2 mi
    3.2 km

147

NW 2nd St. and go 1½ blocks to NW 2nd Ave., turn right, and park at the Metro-Dade Garage. Bring the parking ticket to the lobby for validation.

The recently renamed Miami Art Museum (it was called the Center for the Fine Arts until 1996) features an eclectic mix of modern and contemporary works by such artists as Eric Fischl, Max Beckman, Jim Dine, and Stuart Davis. Rotating exhibitions span the ages and styles and often focus on Latin American or Caribbean artists. The shows are almost always superbly curated and installed, although sometimes subject to controversy in the ultrapolitical Cuban community.

The Miami-Dade Cultural Center, where the museum is housed, is an oasis for those seeking cultural enrichment during their trip to Miami. In addition to the world-acclaimed Miami Art Museum, the center houses the main branch of the Miami-Dade Public Library, which sometimes features art and cultural exhibits, and the Historical Museum of Southern Florida, which highlights the fascinating history of Florida and, in particular, the state's southern region.

American Police Hall of Fame and Museum. 3801 Biscayne Blvd., Miami. ☎ **305/ 573-0070.** Admission $6 adults, $4 seniors over 62, $3 children 11 and under, free for police officers worldwide. Daily 10am–5:30pm. Drive north on U.S. 1 from downtown until you see the building on the right near 38th St. with the real police car affixed to its side.

This odd museum appeals mostly to those fascinated with police and their gadgetry. Inside the car-bedecked block building is a combination of reality and fantasies that's part thoughtful tribute, part Hollywood-style drama. Just past a car featured in the motion picture *Blade Runner* is a mock prison cell, in which visitors can take pictures of themselves pretending they're doing 5 to 10. Also on display are execution devices including a guillotine and an electric chair. In the entryway there is a touching memorial to the more than 3,000 police officers who have lost their lives in the line of duty.

The Rubell Family Collection. Call for address, just north of Miami Design Center, downtown Miami. ☎ **305/573-6090.** Open by appointment only, 11am–5pm Fri–Sat.

The Rubell Family Collection is open for art lovers or students only by appointment. More than 100 works are displayed in a dilapidated warehouse that was once used by the U.S. Drug Enforcement Agency. The pieces, many of which are too big or too daring for your average museum, reveal the Rubell's taste for the strange, humorous, or irreverent. Included in this diverse and shocking menagerie are works by some of the best-known artists of the last half century: Keith Haring, Jean-Michel Basquiat, Charles Ray, Cindy Sherman, Paul McCarthy, and Beverly Semme. If you don't know these names, skip this stop. It's not for young children either.

✪ **Museum of Contemporary Art (MOCA).** 770 NE 125th St., North Miami. ☎ **305/ 893-6211.** Admission $4 adults, $2 seniors and students with ID, free for children 12 and under. Tues–Sat 11am–5pm, Sun noon–5pm. Closed major holidays.

MOCA recently acquired a new 23,000-square-foot space in which to display its impressive collection of internationally acclaimed art. You can see works by Jasper Johns, Roy Lichtenstein, Larry Rivers, Duane Michaels, and Claes Oldenberg. Guided tours are offered in English, Spanish, French, Creole, Portuguese, German, and Italian.

A new screening facility allows for film presentations that will complement the exhibitions. Although the $3.75 million project was built in an area that is otherwise an uncharted tourist destination, MOCA is well worth a drive to view an important contemporary art collection in South Florida.

IN CORAL GABLES & COCONUT GROVE

Miami Museum of Science and Space Transit Planetarium. 3280 S. Miami Ave., Coconut Grove. ☎ **305/854-4247** for general information, or 305/854-2222 for planetarium show times. Museum of Science $6 adults, $4 seniors and children 3–12, free for children 2 and under. Planetarium $5 adults, $2.50 children and seniors. Combination ticket $9 adults, $5.50 children and seniors. Twilight price 4:30–6pm weekdays is half-price. Museum of Science daily 10am–6pm; call for planetarium show times. Closed major holidays. Metrorail: Vizcaya station. Or take I-95 south to Exit 1 and follow the signs.

The Museum of Science features more than 140 hands-on exhibits that explore the mysteries of the universe. Live demonstrations and collections of rare natural history specimens make a visit here fun and informative. Two or three major traveling exhibits are usually on display as well.

The adjacent Space Transit Planetarium projects astronomy and laser shows as well as interactive demonstrations of upcoming computer technology and cyberspace features. Plan to spend at least 3 or 4 hours exploring the fascinating exhibits and displays here.

Miami Youth Museum. On Level B of Paseos, 3301 Coral Way, Coral Gables. ☎ **305/ 446-4FUN.** Admission $4 anyone over 1 year old. Mon–Thurs 10am–5pm, Fri 10am–9pm, Sat–Sun 11am–6pm.

This interactive museum is almost like a theater since it's a place where kids can explore their interests in the grown-up world. If you're in the Gables and want to placate (and educate) the kids, check out this place, which has a great selection of hands-on exhibits, including a minigrocery store complete with cashier and stock boy assignments for role-playing. The kids can pretend to be Dr. Smiles, the dentist, or publish their own newspaper from the "Hot off the Press" exhibit. Tours are offered in English and Spanish.

5 Fantastic Feats of Architecture

Not all the great buildings in Miami are in South Beach's Art Deco District. You'll also find many other exciting enclaves filled with Mediterranean gems and eclectic wonders, especially in Coral Gables. Even if you aren't staying there, check out the Biltmore Hotel (see "Accommodations You Can Afford," in chapter 4) and the stunning Congregational Church across the street.

Villa Vizcaya. 3251 S. Miami Ave. (just south of Rickenbacker Causeway), North Coconut Grove. ☎ **305/250-9133.** Admission $10 adults, $5 children 6–12, free for children 5 and under. Villa daily 9:30am–5pm (ticket booth closes at 4:30pm); gardens daily 9:30am–5:30pm. Closed Christmas. Take I-95 south to Exit 1 and follow the signs.

Sometimes referred to as the "Hearst Castle of the East," this magnificent villa is the setting for many society weddings and galas. It was built in 1916 as a winter retreat for James Deering, cofounder and former vice president of International Harvester. The industrialist was fascinated by 16th-century art and architecture, and his ornate mansion—which took 1,000 artisans 5 years to build—became a celebration of these designs. Most of the original furnishings, including dishes and paintings, are still intact.

This spectacularly opulent villa wraps itself around a central courtyard and includes lush formal gardens. Accented with statuary, balustrades, and decorative urns, the gardens front an enormous swath of Biscayne Bay, neighboring the homes of Sylvester Stallone and Madonna.

The Barnacle State Historic Site. 3485 Main Hwy. (1 block south of Commodore Plaza), Coconut Grove. ☎ **305/448-9445.** Open Fri–Sun 9am–4pm. Admission $1. Tours Fri–Sun at 10am, 11:30am, 1pm, and 2:30pm from the main house porch. From downtown Miami, take U.S. 1 south to South Bayshore Dr., continue to where it becomes McFarlane Rd. Follow McFarlane to Main Highway and turn left at traffic light. The museum is 2 blocks ahead on the left.

The former home of naval architect and early settler Ralph Middleton Munroe is now a museum in the heart of Coconut Grove. The house's quiet surroundings, wide porches, and period furnishings illustrate how Miami's privileged class lived in the days before skyscrapers and luxury hotels. Enthusiastic and knowledgeable state park employees offer a wealth of historical information to those interested in quiet, low-tech attractions like this one.

✪ **Coral Castle.** 28655 S. Dixie Hwy., Homestead. ☎ **305/248-6344.** Admission $7.75 adults, $6.50 seniors, $5 children 7–12. Daily 9am–6pm. Closed Christmas. Take U.S. 1 south to SW 286th St.

There's plenty of competition, but Coral Castle is probably the strangest attraction in Florida. In 1923, so the story goes, a crazed Latvian suffering from unrequited love immigrated to South Miami and spent the next 25 years of his life carving huge boulders into a prehistoric-looking, roofless castle. It seems impossible that one man could have done all this, but there are scores of affidavits on display from neighbors who swear it happened. Apparently experts have studied this phenomenon to help figure out how the Great Pyramids and Stonehenge were built.

Listen to the audio tour to learn about this bizarre spot, now on the National Register of Historic Places. The commentary lasts about 25 minutes and is available in four languages. Although Coral Castle is a bit overpriced and undermaintained, it is worth a visit when you're in the area.

✪ **Spanish Monastery Cloisters.** 16711 W. Dixie Hwy. (at NE 167th St.), North Miami Beach. ☎ **305/945-1461.** Admission $4.50 adults, $2.50 seniors, $1 children 11 and under. Mon–Sat 10am–4pm, Sun noon–4pm.

Did you know that the oldest building in the Western Hemisphere dates from A.D. 1141 and is located in Miami-Dade County? The Spanish Monastery Cloisters were first erected in Segovia, Spain. Centuries later newspaper magnate William Randolph Hearst purchased and brought the Cloisters to America in pieces. The carefully numbered stones were quarantined for years until they were finally reassembled on the present site in 1954. Visitors are free to explore; you'll want to spend about an hour touring the cold, ancient structure, the beautiful grounds, and the gift shop.

Venetian Pool. 2701 DeSoto Blvd. (at Toledo St.), Coral Gables. ☎ **305/460-5356.** Admission $5 adults, $4 teens, $2 children 3–12 and under (children under 36 months not allowed in the water). June–Aug, Mon–Fri 11am–7:30pm, Sat–Sun 10am–4:30pm; Apr–May and Sept–Oct, Tues–Fri 11am–5:30pm, Sat–Sun 10am–4:30pm; Nov–Mar, Tues–Fri 10am–4:30pm, Sat–Sun 10am–4:30pm.

Miami's most beautiful and unusual swimming pool, dating from 1924, is hidden behind pastel stucco walls and is honored with a listing in the National Register of Historic Places. Underground artesian wells feed the free-form lagoon, which is shaded by 3-story Spanish porticos and features both fountains and waterfalls. Though it can be cold in the winter months, during the summer the pool's 800,000 gallons of water are drained and refilled nightly, ensuring a cool, clean swim. Visitors are free to swim and sunbathe here, just as Esther Williams and Johnny Weissmuller did decades ago. For a modest fee, you or your children can learn to swim during special summer programs.

6 Nature Preserves, Parks & Gardens

The Miami area is a great place for outdoors-minded visitors, with beaches, parks, and gardens galore. Plus, South Florida is the country's only area with two national parks; see chapter 7 for coverage of the Everglades and Biscayne National Park.

BOTANICAL GARDENS & A SPICE PARK

In Miami the **Fairchild Tropical Gardens,** 10901 Old Cutler Rd. (☎ **305/ 667-1651**), feature a veritable rain forest of rare and exotic plants on 83 acres. Palmettos, vine pergola, palm glades, and other unique species create a scenic, lush environment. It's well worth taking the free hourly tram to learn what you always wanted to know about flowers and trees on a 30-minute narrated tour.

Admission is $8 for adults, free for children 12 and under accompanied by an adult. Open daily from 9:30am to 5pm. Take I-95 south to U.S. 1, turn left onto Le Jeune Road, and follow it straight to the traffic circle; there, take Old Cutler Road 2 miles to the park.

A testament to Miami's unusual climate, the **Preston B. Bird and Mary Heinlein Fruit and Spice Park,** 24801 SW 187th Ave., Homestead (☎ **305/247-5727**), is home to a variety of rare fruit trees that cannot survive elsewhere in the country.

Definitely ask for a guide. If a volunteer is available, you'll learn some fascinating things about this 30-acre living plant museum where the most exotic varieties of fruits and spices, including ackee, mango, ugly fruit, carambola, and breadfruit, grow on strange-looking trees with nearly unpronounceable names.

The best part? You're free to take anything that falls to the ground. You'll also find samples of interesting fruits and jellies made from the park's bounty in the gift store. Cooks who like to experiment should visit the park store, which carries exotic ingredients and cookbooks.

Admission to the spice park is $2 for adults and 50¢ for children under 12. Open daily from 10am to 5pm. Closed major holidays. Tours are $1.50 for adults and $1 for children on Saturday and Sunday at 1 and 3pm. Take U.S. 1 south, turn right on SW 248th Street, and go straight for 5 miles to SW 187th Avenue.

MORE MIAMI PARKS

The **Amelia Earhart Park,** 401 E. 65th St., Hialeah (☎ **305/685-8389**), has five fishing lakes stocked with bass and brim. It also has playgrounds, picnic facilities, and a big red barn with cows, sheep, and goats for petting and ponies for riding. There's a country store and dozens of old-time farm activities like horseshoeing, sugarcane processing, and more. On weekdays parking is free and on weekends $3.50 per car. Open daily from 9am to sunset. To drive here, take I-95 north to the NW 103rd Street exit, go west to East 4th Avenue, and then turn right. Parking is 1½ miles down the street.

At the very tip of Key Biscayne, the historic **Bill Baggs Cape Florida State Recreation Area,** 1200 Crandon Blvd. (☎ **305/361-5811**), features a recently reopened lighthouse. You can explore the unfettered wilds and enjoy some of the most secluded beaches in Miami. A rental shack has bikes, hydrobikes, kayaks, and other water toys. It's a great place to picnic, and a newly constructed restaurant serves authentic Latin food, including great fish soups and sandwiches. Just be careful that the raccoons don't get your lunch, because the furry black-eyed beasts are everywhere. Admission is $4 per car with up to eight people. Open daily from 8am to sunset. A tour of the recently renovated lighthouse, lightkeeper's quarters, and kitchen costs $1 to $2.

Tropical Park, 7900 SW 40th St. (☎ **305/226-0796**), has it all. Enjoy a game of tennis or racquetball for a minimal fee or swim and sun yourself on the secluded little lake. You can use the fishing pond for free, and they'll even supply you with fishing rods and bait. If you catch anything, however, you're on your own. Open daily from sunrise to sunset.

7 Especially for Kids

The **Scott Rakow Youth Center,** 2700 Sheridan Ave. (☎ **305/673-7767**), is a hidden treasure on Miami Beach. This 2-story facility boasts an ice-skating rink, bowling alleys, a basketball court, gymnasium equipment, and full-time supervision for kids. Call for a complete schedule of organized events. The only downside is that it's only open to adults on Sunday. Admission is $1.50 per day for visiting children 9 to 17. Open daily from 2 to 8:30pm.

Following is a roundup of other attractions kids will especially enjoy. Details on each one can be found earlier in the chapter.

Amelia Earhart Park   This is the best park in Miami for kids. They'll like the petting zoos, pony rides, and a private island with hidden tunnels.

Miami Metrozoo   This completely cageless zoo offers such star attractions as a monorail safari and a petting zoo. Kids love the elephant rides.

Miami Museum of Science and Space Transit Planetarium   At the Planetarium, kids can learn about space and science by watching entertaining films and cosmic shows. The space museum also offers child-friendly explanations for natural occurrences.

Miami Seaquarium   Kids can get a kiss from a dolphin and watch exciting animal performances.

Miami Youth Museum   Here children can dabble in fantasy land, playing at careers they're interested in. It's one huge game of "what do you want to be when you grow up?"

8 Sightseeing Cruises & Organized Tours

Always call ahead to check prices and times. Reservations are usually suggested.

BOAT & CRUISE-SHIP TOURS

Gondola Adventures. Docked at Bayside Marina, at the Biscayne Market Place, 401 Biscayne Blvd., Miami. ☎ **305/358-6400.** Rates from $5 and up.

A real gondola ride in Miami? While it may not be the canals of Venice, with a little imagination the Bayside Marina will do for a fun time. You can go on a simple ride around Bayside for $5, or splurge on your own private and cozy sunrise island cruise.

Heritage Miami II Topsail Schooner. Bayside Marketplace Marina, 401 Biscayne Blvd., downtown. ☎ **305/442-9697.** Tickets $12 adults, $7 children 12 and under. Sept–May only. The 2-hour tours leave daily at 1:30, 4, and 6:30pm, and on weekends also at 9, 10, and 11pm.

More adventure than tour this relaxing ride aboard Miami's only tall ship is a fun way to see the city. The 2-hour cruises pass by Villa Vizcaya, Coconut Grove, and Key Biscayne and put you in sight of Miami's spectacular skyline. Call to make sure the ship is running on schedule.

Lady Lucille. 4441 Collins Ave. (docked across from the Fontainebleau Hotel), Miami Beach. ☎ **305/534-7000.** Tickets $15 adults, $6 children. The 3-hour cruise leaves daily at 11am and 2pm.

Set your sights and sails on Miami's human-made beauty: Millionaires' Row. You can cruise along Biscayne Bay and check out Gloria Estefan's or Fitipaldi's mansion from the comfort of an air-conditioned 150-passenger boat, complete with snacks and two full bars.

SPECIALIZED TOURS

Miami Design Preservation League. The Art Deco Welcome Center, 1001 Ocean Dr., South Beach. ☎ **305/672-2014.** Walking tours $10 per person. Self-guided audio tours also available 7 days a week for $5. Call ahead for updated schedules.

On Thursday evenings and Saturday mornings the league sponsors walking tours that offer a fascinating inside look at the city's historic Art Deco District. Tour-goers meet for a 1½-hour walk through some of America's most exuberantly designed architecture. The Design Preservation League led the fight to designate this area a National Historic District and shares the splendid results with visitors on Saturday at 10:30am and on Thursday at 6:30pm. For half the price, you can do your own tour whenever you want. Rent the do-it-yourself audio tour and enjoy a leisurely walk.

Art Deco Cycling Tour. 601 5th St., South Beach. ☎ **305/674-0150.** $10 per person, plus another $5 if you rent a bike. Tours depart every other Sun at 10am from the Miami Beach Bicycle Center.

Since the bicycle seems to be the most efficient mode of transportation through the streets of South Beach, what better way to view the historic Art Deco District than perched on the seat of a two-wheeler? If you'd rather bike or in-line skate than walk around the area, call to reserve a spot and catch this fun Sunday morning tour.

Biltmore Hotel Tour. 1200 Anastasia Ave., Coral Gables. ☎ **305/445-1926.** Free admission. Tours depart on Sun at 1:30, 2:30, and 3:30pm. Call to reserve.

Enjoy the hotel's beautiful grounds by taking advantage of these free walking tours offered on Sundays. The Biltmore is chock-full of history and mystery, including a few ghosts; it's out there so go uncover it.

Coral Gables Art and Gallery Tour. Various locations in Coral Gables. For more information, call Richard Arregui (☎ **305/447-3973**) or stop by any of the galleries in the area. Free. First Fri of the month 7–10pm.

Vans shuttle art lovers to more than 20 galleries that participate in Gables Night in the gallery section of Coral Gables. Viewers can sip wine as they take in American folk art as well as photography and even African, Native American, and Latin art. Most galleries are on Ponce de León Boulevard, between SW 40th and SW 24th streets. The vans run every 15 minutes from 7 to 10pm.

Lincoln Road Gallery Walk. 924 Lincoln Rd. ☎ **305/674-8278.** Free. Second Sat of every month.

Meet at the Art Center, one of Miami's most popular galleries, at 7pm to tour the artist's studios and the many galleries along "the Road." This really is a unique opportunity to see and meet some up and coming talent. You'll even be treated to free glasses of inexpensive wine in some of the galleries.

9 Water Sports

BOATING & SAILING   You can rent sailboats and catamarans through the beachfront concessions desk of several top resorts, such as the **Doral Ocean Beach Resort, Sheraton Bal Harbour Beach Resort,** and **Dezerland Surfside Beach Hotel** (see "Accommodations You Can Afford," in chapter 4).

Private rental outfits include **Beach Boat Rentals,** 2400 Collins Ave., Miami Beach (☎ **305/534-4307**), where 50-horsepower, 18-foot powerboats rent for some of the best prices on the beach. Rates are $61.25 for an hour, $165.13 for 4 hours, and $225.70 for 8 hours. All rates include taxes and gas. A $250 cash or credit-card deposit is required. Cruising is exclusively in and around Biscayne Bay—ocean access is prohibited. Renters must be over 21. The rental office is at 23rd Street on the inland waterway in Miami Beach, and it's open from 9am to 6pm (weather permitting) during the high season and 9am to 8pm during the summer.

   Club Nautico of Coconut Grove, 2560 S. Bayshore Dr., Coconut Grove (☎ **305/858-6258**), rents high-quality powerboats for fishing, waterskiing, diving, and cruising in the bay or ocean. All boats are coast guard equipped with VHF radios and safety gear. Rates range from $199 for 4 hours and $299 for 8 hours to as much as $419 on weekends. Club Nautico is open daily from 9am to 5pm (weather permitting). Other locations include the **Crandon Park Marina,** 4000 Crandon Blvd., Key Biscayne (☎ 305/361-9217), with the same rates as the Coconut Grove location; and the **Miami Beach Marina,** Pier E, 300 Alton Rd., South Beach (☎ **305/673-2502**), where rates are $229 for 4 hours and $299 for 8 hours to rent a 20-foot boat. A 24-footer will run you $259 for half a day and $359 for a full day. Nautico on Miami Beach is open daily from 9am to 5pm.

   If speedboats aren't your style, **Sailboats of Key Biscayne Rentals and Sailing School,** in the Crandon Marina (next to Sundays on the Bay), 4000 Crandon Blvd., Key Biscayne (☎ **305/361-0328** days, or 305/279-7424 evenings), offers a slightly more subdued ride. A 22-foot sailboat can be rented for $27 an hour, or $81 for a half day. A Cat-25 or J24 is available for $35 an hour or $110 for a half day. If you've always had a dream to win the America's Cup but can't sail, Sailboats will get you started. It offers a 10-hour course over 5 days for $250 for one person or $350 for you and a buddy; $50 for each additional person.

   Shake a Leg, 2600 Bayshore Dr., Coconut Grove (☎ **305/858-5550**), is a unique sailing program for disabled and able-bodied people alike. The program pairs up sailors for day and evening cruises and offers sailing lessons as well. Consider a moonlight cruise (offered monthly) or a race clinic. Shake a Leg members also welcome able-bodied volunteers for activities on and off the water. It costs $60 for nonmembers to rent a boat for 3 hours; free for volunteers. Open on Wednesday through Sunday from 9am to 5pm.

JET-SKIS/WAVE RUNNERS   Many beachfront concessionaires rent a variety of these popular water scooters. The latest models are fast and smooth. Don't miss a chance to tour the islands on the back of your own little watercraft. Try **Tony's Jet Ski Rentals,** 3601 Rickenbacker Causeway, Key Biscayne (☎ **305/361-8280**), one of the city's largest rental shops, located on a private beach in the Miami Marine Stadium lagoon. Jet-skis rent for about $38 for a half hour and $64 for an hour. Wave Runners rent for $45 for a half hour and $70 for an hour. Tony's is open daily from 10:30am to 6:30pm.

KAYAKS   The laid-back **Urban Trails Kayak Company** rents boats from 10800 Collins Ave., Miami Beach (☎ **305/947-1302**). It offers scenic routes through rivers with mangroves and islands as your destination. Most of the kayaks are sit-on-tops, which are what they sound like. Most boats are plastic, though there are some fiberglass ones available too. Rates are $8 an hour, $20 for up to 4 hours ($25 for over 4 hours). Tandems are $12 an hour, $30 for up to 4 hours, $35 for the day. Open daily from 9am to 5pm.

   Urban Trails gives interested explorers a map to take with them and quick instructions on how to work the paddles and boats. If you want a guided tour, you'll need at least four people and will pay $35 per person for half a day. This is a fun way to experience some of Miami's unspoiled wildlife, and it is good exercise, too.

SCUBA DIVING   In 1981 the government began a wide-scale project designed to increase the number of habitats available to marine organisms. One of the program's major accomplishments has been the creation of nearby artificial reefs, which have attracted all kinds of tropical plants, fish, and animals. In addition, Biscayne National Park (see chapter 7) offers a protected marine environment just south of downtown.

Several dive shops around the city offer organized weekend outings, either to the reefs or to one of over a dozen old shipwrecks around Miami's shores. Check "Divers" in the Yellow Pages for rental equipment and for a full list of undersea tour operators.

Divers Paradise of Key Biscayne, 4000 Crandon Blvd. (☎ 305/361-3483), offers two dive expeditions daily to the more than 30 wrecks and artificial reefs off the coast of Miami Beach and Key Biscayne. Take a 3-day certification course for $399, which includes all the dives and gear. If you already have your C-card, a dive trip costs about $90 for those with no equipment and only $35 if you show up with your own gear. It's open Monday to Friday from 10am to 6pm and Saturday and Sunday from 8am to 6pm. Call ahead for times and locations of dives. This is the best way to see Miami.

WINDSURFING   Many hotels rent Windsurfers to their guests. If yours doesn't have a water-sports concession stand, head for Key Biscayne, the area's best spot for windsurfing.

Sailboards Miami, Rickenbacker Causeway, Key Biscayne (☎ 305/361-SAIL), operates out of big yellow trucks on Hobie Beach, the most popular windsurfing spot in the city. For those who've never ridden a board but want to try their hand at it, Sailboards Miami offers 2-hour, $39 lesson that's guaranteed to turn you into a wave warrior or your money back. After that, you can rent a windsurf board for $20 an hour, or $37 for 2 hours. If you want to make a day of it, a 10-hour card costs $130. Open daily from 10am to 5:30pm. Make the first right after the tollbooth to find the outfitters.

10 More Places to Play, Both Indoors & Out

BIKING & SCOOTERS   The cement promenade on the southern tip of the island is a great place to ride. Biking up the beach is great for surf, sun, sand, exercise, and people watching. You may not want to subject your bicycle to the salt and sand, but there are plenty of oceanfront rental places here. Most of the big beach hotels rent bicycles, as does the **Miami Beach Bicycle Center,** 601 5th St., South Beach (☎ 305/674-0150). This shop rents bicycles for $5 per hour or $14 per day. It's open Monday to Saturday from 10am to 7pm and Sunday from 10am to 5pm.

Cyclists can also enjoy more than 130 miles of paved paths throughout Miami. The beautiful and quiet streets of Coral Gables and Coconut Grove seem to beg for the attention of bicyclists. Old trees form canopies over wide, flat roads lined with grand homes and quaint street markers. Several bicycle trails are spread throughout these neighborhoods.

In Key Biscayne the terrain is perfect for biking, especially along the park and beach roads. If you don't mind the sound of cars whooshing by, Rickenbacker Causeway is also fantastic since it is one of the only bikeable inclines in Miami from which you get fantastic elevated views of the city and waterways.

Key Cycling, 61 Harbor Dr., Key Biscayne (☎ 305/361-0061), rents mountain bikes for $5 an hour or $15 for the day. They're open Monday through Friday from 10am to 7pm, Saturday from 10am to 6pm, and Sunday from 11am to 4pm.

If you want to avoid the traffic altogether, head out to Shark Valley in the Everglades National Park—one of South Florida's most scenic bicycle trails and a favorite haunt of city-weary locals. See chapter 7 for more details.

Cool Rides Rental and Sales, at 642 6th St. on South Beach (☎ 305/672-7375), is one of the only scooter-rental places in town. Be careful; drivers here are nuts.

Several outfits rent Harleys and sell all the black fringed gear you could possibly want. Call **Rolling Thunder** at ☎ **305/441-0952** or **Budget Rent A Car** at 3901 NW 28th St., (☎ **305/871-1040,** www.budgetharley.com) to rent bikes by the hour, day, or week.

FISHING   One of the least expensive and fun ways to fish is off one of the bridges that arch over the many waterways throughout the county. You'll see locals with poles over most every bridge. Drive around to see where they are biting. The south side of the Julia Tuttle Causeway or the MacArthur are good places to check.

Some of the best surf casting in the city can be had at Haulover Beach Park, at Collins Avenue and 105th Street, where there's a bait-and-tackle shop right on the pier. South Pointe Park, at the southern tip of Miami Beach, is another popular fishing spot and features a long pier, comfortable benches, and a great view of the ships passing through Government Cut.

If you are willing to spend a few bucks, you can do some deep-sea fishing. One bargain outfitter, the **Kelley Fishing Fleet,** at the Haulover Marina, 10800 Collins Ave. (at 108th Street), Miami Beach (☎ **305/945-3801**), has half-day, full-day, and night fishing aboard diesel-powered party boats. The fleet's emphasis on drifting is geared toward trolling and bottom fishing for snapper, sailfish, and mackerel, but it also schedules 2- and 3-day trips to The Bahamas. Half-day and night fishing trips are $21 for adults and $14.50 for children; full-day trips are $33 for adults and $26.50 for children; rod and reel rental is $5. Daily departures are scheduled at 9am, 1:45pm, and 8pm; reservations are recommended.

Also at the Haulover Marina is the charter boat *Helen C,* 10800 Collins Ave., Haulover (☎ **305/947-4081**). Although there's no shortage of private charter boats here, Capt. Dawn Mergelsberg is a good pick, since she likes to put individuals together to get a full boat, which can cut your cost by more than half. Her *Helen C* is a twin-engine 55-footer, equipped for big-game fish like marlin, tuna, dolphin, shark, and sailfish. The cost is $70 per person, and sailings are scheduled for 8am to noon and 1 to 5pm daily; call for reservations. Private charters and transportation are also available. Children are welcome.

Key Biscayne offers deep-sea fishing to those willing to get their hands dirty and pay a lot. The competition among the boats is fierce, but the prices are basically the same no matter which boat you choose. The going rate is about $400 to $450 for a half day and $600 to $700 for a full day of fishing. These rates are usually for a party of up to six, and the boats supply you with rods and bait as well as instruction for first-timers. Some will take you out to Key Biscayne and even out to the Upper Keys if the fish aren't biting in Miami.

Although pricier, you might consider the following boats, all of which sail out of the Key Biscayne marina and need reservations: *Sunny Boy III* (☎ **305/361-2217**); *Queen B* (☎ **305/361-2528**); and *L & H* (☎ **305/361-9318**).

GAMBLING   Although it is technically illegal to gamble in Miami, plenty of loopholes allow for offshore casinos, bingo, dominoes, jai-alai, card rooms, horse races, and dog races. One good thing about these popular outfits is the free food and drinks. Many offer low-priced or free refreshments to attract would-be gamblers. If you can keep your head as you fill your stomach, you'll come out ahead.

Especially popular is the huge outpost west of Miami, **Miccosukee Indian Gaming,** 500 SW 177th Ave., west of Miami (☎ **800/741-4600** or 305/222-4600). This glitzy casino isn't Vegas, but you can play slots, all kinds of bingo, and even poker (with a $10 maximum pot). Supercheap specials like $10 lobster dinners are worth the drive.

One of many gambling cruises to nowhere is the *Sea Kruz.* It departs daily and most evenings from 1280 5th St. (Mac Arthur Causeway), South Beach. (☎ **800/ 688-PLAY** or 305/538-8300). Tickets are $15 but you can usually find a discount coupon for admission or free chips. Or just ask when booking. For an extra $5 on the lunch cruise there's an all-you-can-eat soup-and-salad bar, and for an additional $9 on the dinner cruise there's an all-you-can-eat dinner with a carving station. The food isn't gourmet, but there is always plenty of it. Throw in a little dancing with a live band and the trip is complete.

Casino Miami (☎ **305/577-7775**) sails every day but Mondays and most evenings from the Dupont Plaza Hotel in downtown Miami. Admission is the same as *Sea Kruz* ($15), but this boat is slightly newer and the crowd a little more subdued.

The game of dominoes is also popular in Miami and is played at **Flagler Dog Track,** 401 NW 38th Ct. (☎ **305/649-3000**), and at Miami Jai Alai (see below). Poker rooms are also available.

Check "Spectator Sports," below, for races and other pari-mutuel outlets.

GOLF   There are more than 50 private and public golf courses in the Greater Miami area. Contact the **Greater Miami Convention and Visitors Bureau** (☎ **800/ 283-2707** or 305/539-3063) for a complete list of courses and costs. Some of the area's best and most expensive are at the big resorts, many of which allow nonguests to play. The Doral Blue Course at the Doral Resort and Spa in West Miami and the Biltmore in Coral Gables allow day passes. See "Accommodations You Can Afford," in chapter 4, for more details.

Otherwise, the following public courses represent some of the area's best values. **Crandon Park Golf Course,** formerly known as The Links, 6700 Crandon Blvd., Key Biscayne (☎ **305/361-9129**), is the number-one ranked municipal course in the state and one of the top five in the country. The park is situated on 200 bay-front acres and offers a pro shop, rentals, lessons, carts, and a lighted driving range. The course is open daily from dawn to dusk; greens fees (including cart) are about $90 per person during the winter and $45 per person during the summer. Special twilight rates starting at $50 are available.

Known as one of the best in Miami, the **Golf Club of Miami,** 6801 Miami Gardens Dr., at NW 68th Avenue (☎ **305/829-8456**), has three 18-hole courses of varying degrees of difficulty. You'll encounter lush fairways, rolling greens, and some history. The west course, designed in 1961 by Robert Trent Jones and updated in the 1990s by the PGA, was where Jack Nicklaus played his first professional tournament and Lee Trevino won his first professional championship. The course is open daily from 6:30am to sunset. Cart and greens fees are $45 to $75 per person during the winter, $20 to $34 per person during the summer. Special twilight rates are available.

Amateurs still perfecting their game or golfers on a budget looking for some cheap practice time will appreciate **Haulover Park,** 10800 Collins Ave., Miami Beach (☎ **305/940-6719**). The longest hole on this par-27 course is 125 yards in a pretty bay-side location. The course is open daily from 7:30am to 5:30pm during the winter, until 7:30pm during the summer. Greens fees are $5 per person during the winter, $4 per person during the summer. Hand carts cost $1.40.

HEALTH CLUBS   Although many of Miami's full-service hotels have fitness centers, you can't count on them in less upscale establishments or in the small Art Deco District hotels. Several health clubs around the city will take in nonmembers on a daily basis. If you're already a member at the megahealth club chain **Bally's Total Fitness,** dial ☎ **800/777-1117** to find the clubs in the area. There are no outlets on the beaches; most are in South Miami.

There are many other clubs that welcome walk-in guests, including **Crunch Fitness,** 1253 Washington Ave., South Beach (☎ 305/674-8222), where you might work out on top-of-the-line equipment with Cindy Crawford, Madonna, or any of a number of supermodels when they're in town.

IN-LINE SKATING　Miami's consistently flat terrain should make in-line skating easy but the heavy traffic and construction make it tough to find long routes. Still, blading is one of the most popular ways to get around South Beach. Remember to keep a pair of sandals or sneakers with you since many shops won't allow you inside wearing skates. The following rental outfits can help chart an interesting course and provide you with all the necessary gear.

In Coral Gables, **Extreme Skate & Sport,** 7876 SW 40th St. (☎ **305/261-6699**), is one of South Florida's largest in-line skate dealers. Even if you know nothing about this trendy new sport, a knowledgeable sales staff and a large selection to choose from ensure that you can't go wrong.

In South Beach, **Fritz's Skate Shop,** 726 Lincoln Rd. Mall (☎ **305/532-1954**), rents top-quality skates, including safety pads, for $7.50 per hour, $22.50 per day, and $14 overnight. If you're an in-line skate virgin, an instructor will hold your hand for $25 an hour. The shop also stocks lots of gear and clothing.

Also in South Beach, **Skate 2000,** at 1200 Ocean Dr. (☎ **305/538-8282**) and 650 Lincoln Rd. (☎ 305/538-9491), will help you keep up with the beach crowd by renting in-line skates and safety accessories. Their rates are the best in town: $8 an hour and $24 a day plus $100 deposit, credit card or cash. Plus, whether you rent from them or not, you can show up at either store for a 2-hour free lesson from a certified instructor every Sunday at 10am.

SWIMMING　Most hotels have pools. If not, there is plenty of water around, including the vast and mild Atlantic Ocean. Except for a few weeks in winter when the water is a bit frigid, you can swim year-round. See "Beaches" and also the Venetian Pool under "Fantastic Feats of Architecture," above, for descriptions of good swimming options.

TENNIS　Hundreds of tennis courts in South Florida are open to the public for a minimal fee. Most courts operate on a first-come, first-served basis, and are usually open from sunrise to sunset. For information and directions to one of the free public courts near where you're staying, call one of these government offices: the **City of Miami Beach Recreation, Culture, and Parks Department** (☎ 305/673-7730) or the **City of Miami Parks and Recreation Department** (☎ 305/575-5256).

The three hard courts and seven clay courts at the **Key Biscayne Tennis Association at the Crandon Park Golf Course,** located at 6702 Crandon Blvd. (☎ **305/361-5263**), get crowded on weekends since they're some of Miami's most beautiful and well-priced courts. You'll play on the same courts as Lendl, Graf, Evert, McEnroe, and other greats since this the venue for one of the world's biggest annual tennis events, the Lipton Championship (see "Florida Calendar of Events," in chapter 2). There's a pleasant, if limited, pro shop, plus many good pros. Only four courts are lit at night, but if you reserve at least 48 hours in advance, you can usually take your pick. It costs $4 to $5 per person per hour. The courts are open daily from 8am to 9pm.

11 Spectator Sports

Check the *Miami Herald*'s sports section for a daily listing of local events and the paper's Friday "Weekend" section for comprehensive coverage and in-depth reports. For last-minute tickets, call the stadium directly since many season ticket holders sell singles and return unused tickets. Expensive tickets are available from brokers or individuals, listed in the classified sections of the local papers. Some tickets are also available through **Ticketmaster** (☎ **305/358-5885**).

BASEBALL   Once ecstatic over the **Florida Marlins'** 1997 World Series win, fans have since been disappointed over the team's revolving-door roster and ongoing squabbles over moving the stadium. For current information about home games and ticket prices, contact **Ticketmaster** (☎ **305/538-5885**).

BASKETBALL   The Miami Heat, now coached by Pat Riley, made its NBA debut in November 1988. Predictably, it's also one of Miami's hottest tickets. The season of approximately 41 home games lasts from November to April, with most games beginning at 7:30pm. Plans are in the works to build a new arena on the waterfront near the Seaport, but for now games are played at the **Miami Arena,** 721 NW 1st Ave. (☎ **305/577-HEAT**) in downtown Miami. Seats are $14 to $44. Box office hours are Monday to Friday from 10am to 4pm (until 8pm on game nights); tickets are also available through Ticketmaster.

FOOTBALL   Miami's golden boys are the **Miami Dolphins,** the city's most recognizable team in turquoise and orange uniforms, followed by thousands of "dolfans." Coached by Jimmy Johnson, the team plays at least eight home games during the season, between September and December, at the Pro Player Stadium, 2267 NW 199th St., North Miami Beach (☎ **305/626-7426** or 305/623-6100). Tickets cost about $30 and can be tough to come by. The box office is open Monday to Friday from 10am to 6pm; tickets are also available through **Ticketmaster** (☎ **305/350-5050**).

HORSE RACING   Wrapped around an artificial lake, **Gulfstream Park,** at U.S. 1 and Hallandale Beach Boulevard, Hallandale (☎ **305/931-7223**), is both pretty and popular. Large purses and important races are commonplace at this suburban course, and the track is often crowded. Call for schedules. Admission is $3 to the grandstand, $3 to the clubhouse; parking is free. January 3 to March 15, post times are Wednesday to Monday at 1pm.

You've seen the pink flamingos at **Hialeah Park,** 2200 E. 4th Ave., Hialeah (☎ **305/885-8000**), in the opening credits for *Miami Vice,* and indeed, this famous colony is the largest of its kind. This track, listed on the National Register of Historic Places, is one of the most beautiful in the world, featuring old-fashioned stands and acres of immaculately manicured grounds. Admission is $1 to the grandstand and $2 to the clubhouse weekdays; and weekends $2 and $4, respectively. Children 17 and under enter free with an adult. Parking starts at $2. Races are held mid-March to mid-May, but the course is open year-round for sightseeing Monday to Saturday from 9am to 5pm. Call for post times.

ICE HOCKEY   The young **Florida Panthers** (☎ **954/768-1900**), have already made history. In the '94–'95 season they won the Eastern Championships and played in the Stanley Cup finals. The Panthers actually play in Broward County; see the section on Ft. Lauderdale in chapter 8 for more information.

JAI ALAI   Jai alai, sort of a Spanish-style indoor lacrosse, was introduced to Miami in 1924 and is regularly played in two Miami-area frontons. Although the sport has roots stemming from ancient Egypt, the game as it's now played was invented by Basque peasants in the Pyrenees mountains during the 17th century.

Players use woven baskets, called *cestas,* to hurl balls (*pelotas*), at speeds that sometimes exceed 170 miles per hour. Spectators, who are protected behind a wall of glass, place bets on the evening's players.

The **Miami Jai Alai Fronton,** 3500 NW 37th Ave., at NW 35th Street (☎ **305/ 633-6400**), is America's oldest jai alai fronton (arena), dating from 1926. It schedules 13 games per night. Admission is $1 to the grandstand, $5 to the clubhouse. It's open year-round. There are games Monday and Wednesday to Saturday at 7pm, with matinees on Monday, Wednesday, and Saturday at noon.

12 Shopping

A mecca for hard-core shoppers from Latin America, the Caribbean, and the rest of the state, Miami has everything you could ever want and things you never dreamed of. This shopping capital has strip malls, boutiques, and enclosed malls in every conceivable nook and cranny of the city, which makes for lots of competition among retailers and good bargains for those who like to hunt.

For unadvertised discounts, look for coupon books at hotels, rest stops, and at the airport. The Bayside Marketplace, for example, offers a free booklet called *Miami Passport* with dozens of coupons good for discounts of 10% to 25% off purchases at the rambling outdoor mall. If you don't find the booklet at your hotel, call ☎ **305/ 577-3344** to find out where to pick one up. The *Miami Herald* often publishes coupons good for discounts at local department stores like Burdines, Macy's, and Bloomingdale's.

THE SHOPPING SCENE
THE MALLS

The Aventura Mall, 19501 Biscayne Blvd. (☎ **305/935-4222**), is an enclosed mall with more than 200 shops, a varied food court, an enormous Bloomingdale's, and a Macy's. The high-end **Bal Harbour Shops,** 9700 Collins Ave. (☎ **305/866-0311**), has the big names: Bulgari, Chanel, Hermès, Versace, Tiffany & Co., Neiman Marcus, Polo/Ralph Lauren, Saks Fifth Avenue, Fendi, Rodier, Gucci, Brooks Brothers, Cartier, Tourneau, and a well-dressed shopping crowd.

The **Bayside Marketplace,** 401 Biscayne Blvd., downtown (☎ **305/577-3344**), consists of 16 beautiful waterfront acres along Biscayne Bay with lively and exciting shops, kiosks, restaurants, and bars. You'll find high-tech electronics, designer clothing, jewelry, and trinkets galore. A food court, popular with office workers in the area, offers dozens of choices from Chinese to Cuban and even a Hard Rock Cafe.

The **Dadeland Mall,** 7535 N. Kendall Dr., Kendall (☎ **305/665-6226**), is the granddaddy of Miami's suburban mall scene, featuring more than 175 specialty shops, anchored by five large department stores. **The Falls,** 8888 Howard Dr., Kendall area (☎ **305/255-4570**), is an outdoor shopping center set among tropical waterfalls, with dozens of upscale shops, including Bloomingdales.

The newly renovated **Streets of Mayfair,** 2911 Grand Ave., Coconut Grove (☎ **305/448-1700**), is a grand open-air complex, just across the street from Cocowalk, with several top-quality shops, restaurants, movies, art galleries, and nightclubs. Finally there is **Sawgrass Mills,** 12801 W. Sunrise Blvd., Sunrise (☎ **954/ 846-2300**), which is actually located in Broward County, west of Ft. Lauderdale. This mall is a phenomenon worth mentioning—it's a behemoth with more than 270 shops and kiosks in nearly 2½ million square feet covering 50 acres (see "Shopping & Browsing," in chapter 8, for more details). Call **Classic Lines Bus Service** (☎ **800/ 533-7755** or 305/887-6223) to ride to the mall for only $10 round-trip. Buses depart daily from locations at the beach and downtown.

GREAT SHOPPING AREAS

For real deals, avoid the enclosed malls and check out the thrift stores and boutiques instead. Ocean Drive on South Beach has no bargains, but head a few blocks west for the same selection at lower prices.

COCONUT GROVE   Downtown Coconut Grove is one of Miami's few pedestrian-friendly zones. Centered on Main Highway and Grand Avenue and branching onto the adjoining streets, the Grove's wide, cafe- and boutique-lined sidewalks provide hours of browsing pleasure. Look for dozens of avant-garde clothing stores, funky import shops, and excellent sidewalk cafes, especially in Cocowalk and Mayfair.

CORAL GABLES/MIRACLE MILE   Located at the end of Coral Way (SW 22nd St.), this central shopping street, which is really only half a mile, was an integral part of George Merrick's original city plan. Today the strip still enjoys popularity for its bridal shops, but also for its old-fashioned ladies' shops, haberdashers, shoe stores, and gift shops. The Miracle Mile, which terminates at the Mediterranean-style City Hall rotunda, also features several good and unusual restaurants and is worth a stop on your tour of Coral Gables.

SOUTH BEACH/LINCOLN ROAD   This luxurious pedestrian mall just north of 16th Street between Washington Avenue and Alton Road underwent a multimillion-dollar renovation in 1997 that added new lighting, more than 500 palm trees, and necessary repairs to the infrastructure. Here shoppers can find an array of clothing and art and a collection of South Beach's finest restaurants. Enjoy an afternoon of gallery hopping and be sure to look into the open studios of the Miami City Ballet. Monthly gallery tours, periodic jazz concerts, and a weekly Farmer's Market are just a few of the offerings on "The Road."

Further south many cool boutiques like Armani, ABS, Banana Republic, Versace, Urban Outfitters, and Kenneth Cole are concentrated on and around 8th Street and Collins Avenue.

DOWNTOWN MIAMI   This is the place for discounts on all types of goods, from watches and jewelry to luggage and leather. But watch out for a handful of unscrupulous businesses trying to rip you off. Look around Flagler Street and Miami Avenue for all kinds of cluttered bargain stores. Most of the signs around here are printed in both English and Spanish for the benefit of locals and tourists alike.

HOURS & TAXES

Most stores around the city maintain shopping hours Monday to Saturday from 10am to 6pm and Sunday from noon to 5pm. Many stay open late (usually until 9pm) one night of the week (usually Thursday). Shops in trendy Coconut Grove are open until 9pm Sunday through Thursday and even later on Friday and Saturday nights. Department stores and shopping malls keep longer hours, staying open from 10am to 9 or 10pm Monday to Saturday and noon to 6pm on Sunday.

The 6.5% state and local sales tax is added to the price of all nonfood purchases.

SHOPPING A TO Z
ART & ANTIQUES

There are hundreds of small consignment stores and upscale stores selling art of every description. To list only a few would be unfair. You'll have to check them out yourself.

The best hunting grounds are scattered in small pockets around Miami. Many are in North Miami on NE 123rd Street between West Dixie Highway and NE 6th Avenue.

Several top galleries have moved into trendy Lincoln Road on South Beach. But the majority of the art and antique dealers are in Coral Gables, mostly along Ponce de León Boulevard, extending from S. Dixie Highway (U.S. 1) to Bird Road. See "Sightseeing Cruises & Organized Tours," above, for details on walking tours of these areas. Or pick up the Coral Gable's Gallery Guide at the Greater Miami Visitor's Bureau, the Coral Gables Chamber of Commerce, or any of the more than 20 galleries in the area. One of the largest is the **Engman Gallery,** at 2111 Ponce de León Blvd., across from the Hotel Place St. Michel, near Alcazar Avenue (☎ **305/445-5125**).

Many funky galleries and antique stores are also sprouting up in and around NE 40th Street, west of Biscayne Boulevard in the newly trendy Design District. Here you'll find old-fashioned fabric and wallpaper shops and many newer stores selling stunning hand-carved Indonesian furnishings and decorations.

BEACHWEAR/SURFING GEAR

As you'd expect, there's a plethora of beachwear stores in Miami. However, if you want to get away from the cookie-cutter styles available at any local mall and in the resort areas, here are a few notable stores that will surely make you stand out while you're basking on the beach or giving the waves a workout.

Alice's Day Off. 5900 SW 72nd St., South Miami. ☎ **305/284-0301.**

Alice's comes out season after season with pretty and flattering patterns. If an itsy-bitsy bikini is not your style, Alice's has a range of more modest cuts that won't make you look like one of the local retirees.

Bird's Surf Shop. 250 Sunny Isles Blvd., North Miami Beach. ☎ **305/940-0929.**

If you're a hard-core surfer, head to Bird's Surf Shop. Although Miami doesn't regularly get huge swells, if you're here during the winter and one should happen to hit, you'll be ready. The shop carries more than 150 boards.

Call their surf line (☎ **305/947-7170**) before going out, to find the best conditions, from South Beach to Cape Hatteras and even The Bahamas and Florida's west coast.

Ritchie Swimwear. 800 Ocean Dr. ☎ **305/538-0201.**

With several outlets, including this one, Ritchie has some of the sexiest suits for women and the biggest selection.

Up Wind Watersports. 238 Biscayne Blvd., downtown Miami. ☎ **305/374-5321.**

This pleasant spot across the street from Bayside is run by a young set of very helpful water fanatics who cater to surfers. If they haven't got it, they will find it. From a full selection of sunglasses and wet suits to boards and bikinis.

X-Isle Surf Shop. 437 Washington Ave., South Beach. ☎ **305/534-7873.**

Prices are slightly high at this beach location, but the young staff is knowledgeable.

BOOKS

✪ **Books & Books.** 933 Lincoln Rd., South Beach. ☎ **305/532-3222.**

This is Miami's literary mecca. Writers and readers converge daily for readings, coffee, and conversation. If you need a good beach book, an art tome, an obscure biography, or any title about Florida or the Caribbean, stop here. Also ask for a schedule of free readings. Nobel Prize winners, cookbook authors, and mystery writers make appearances all the time. In the South Beach store there's also an active indoor/outdoor cafe filled with bookworms. Dial ☎ **305/444-POEM** to hear a poem read by a local poet. There's another location at 296 Aragon Ave. (1 block north of Miracle Mile, on the corner of Salzedo Avenue), in Coral Gables (☎ **305/442-4408**).

Borders Book Stop. 2905 S. Dixie Hwy., Kendall. ☎ **305/665-8800.**

Although all three Borders (see below) have cafes on the premises, only the Coconut Grove and North Miami Beach locations have extensive music sections. You can browse through your selection while eating a bagel at the cafe and listening to the live music Borders offers to its customers. Borders also schedules lots of readings, discussions, and other events. Call for schedules. Other locations in Miami include Borders Books and Music Cafe at 19925 Biscayne Blvd., North Miami Beach (☎ **305/935-0027**), and 3390 Mary St., Coconut Grove (☎ **305/447-1655**).

Grove Antiquarian. 3318 Virginia St., Coconut Grove. ☎ **305/444-5362.**

One of very few bookstores in Miami that carries out-of-print books, the Grove Antiquarian specializes in Florida and the Caribbean, but also boasts a large selection of out-of-print cookbooks, sci-fi, and first editions.

Cuba Art and Books. 2317 Le Jeune Rd., Coral Gables. ☎ **305/567-1640.**

This shop specializes in old books about Cuba and some prints and paintings by Cuban artists. Most titles are in Spanish and focus on art and politics.

Kafka's Used Book Store and Kafe. 1460 Washington Ave., South Beach. ☎ **305/673-9669.**

Open most days until 10pm, this stunning wood and glass corner shop is well organized and well stocked. There is a little bit of everything here, including a cozy cafe serving sandwiches and coffees, all at very reasonable prices.

CIGARS/SMOKE SHOPS

Although it's illegal to bring Cuban cigars into this country, somehow Cohibas show up at every dinner party and nightclub in town. Not that I condone it, but if you hang around the cigar smokers in town, no doubt one will be able to tell you where you can get some of the highly prized contraband. Be careful, however, of counterfeits.

Some of the following stores sell excellent hand-rolled cigars made with domestic and foreign-grown tobacco. Many of the *viejos* (old men) got their training in Cuba working for the government-owned factories in the heyday of Cuban cigars.

Ba-balú. 500 Española Way (at Drexel Ave.), South Beach. ☎ **305/538-0679.**

Including an extensive collection of Cuban memorabilia from pre-1959 Cuba, Ba-balú offers a taste of Cuba, selling not only their hand-rolled cigars (they do about 1,000 a week) but also T-shirts, baseball caps, Cuban coins, bills, postcards, stamps, and coffee. Enjoy live bongo music nightly and ask Herbie Sosa, the owner, for a free shot of Cuban coffee.

La Gloria Cubana. 1106 SW 8th St., Little Havana. ☎ **305/858-4162.**

This tiny storefront shop employs about 45 veteran Cuban rollers who sit all day rolling the very popular torpedoes and other critically acclaimed blends. They've got back orders until next Christmas, but it's worth stopping in. They will sell you a box and show you around.

Mike's Cigars. 1030 Kane Concourse (at 96th St.), Bay Harbor Island. ☎ **305/866-2277.**

Recently moved to this location, Mike's is one of the oldest in Miami. Since 1950 Mike's has been selling the best of Honduras, the Dominican Republic, and Jamaica as well as the very hot local brand, La Gloria Cubana. Most say they've got the best prices, too.

CITRUS/FRUIT BASKETS

There was a time when it seemed as though almost every other store was shipping fruit home for tourists. Today such stores are a dying breed. **Todd's Fruit Shippers** (☎ 305/448-5215) will send the best quality fruit anywhere in the country. Boxes are sold by the bushel or fractions thereof and start at about $20 (orders are only taken by phone).

ELECTRONICS

Many people travel to Miami from South America and other parts of the world to buy playthings and gadgets. Although there are many electronics stores around, a trip to downtown Miami is both amazing and overwhelming when you're shopping around for a good Walkman or television. The streets of downtown are littered with bargain electronics stores. Bargain! But beware—make sure any equipment comes with a warranty. It would be wise to charge instead of paying cash. Otherwise, try:

Sound Advice. 1220 SW 88th St., Kendall. ☎ **305/273-1225.**

An audio junkie's candy store, Sound Advice features the latest in high-end stereo equipment, as well as TVs, VCRs, and telephone equipment. Techno-minded, but sometimes pushy salespeople are on hand to educate.

   Other locations in Miami include 17641 Biscayne Blvd. (☎ 305/933-4434), and 1222 S. Dixie Hwy., Coral Gables (☎ 305/665-4434).

FASHIONS FOR MEN, WOMEN & CHILDREN

In addition to the many clothing stores in the malls and shopping areas listed above, more than 100 retail outlets are clustered in Miami's mile-square **Fashion District** just north of downtown. Surrounding Fashion Avenue (NW 5th Avenue) and known primarily for swimwear, sportswear, children's clothing, and glittery women's dresses, Miami's fashion center is second in size only to New York's. The district features European- and Latin-influenced designs with tropical hues and subdued pastels. Most stores offer medium-quality clothing at a 25% to 70% discount, as well as on-site alterations. Most stores are open only weekdays from 9am to 5:30pm. A discount favorite is **Loehmann's** at 18703 Biscayne Blvd. (Fashion Island), North Miami Beach (☎ **305/932-4207**). If you don't mind fighting other zealous shoppers and communal dressing rooms, you'll find some great deals here on everything from bathing suits to evening wear.

   In addition to the many designer shops in Bal Harbour, you'll find that other boutiques are scattered throughout town especially on trendy South Beach's Lincoln Road and around 8th Street. The best shoe stores are in Coconut Grove around Cocowalk and Mayfair.

GOLF

Alf's Golf Shop. 524 Arthur Godfrey Rd., Miami Beach. ☎ **305/673-6568.**

The best pro shop on the beach, Alf's can sell you balls, clubs, gloves, and instructional videos—plus, the neighboring golf course offers discounts to Alf's clients.

   Another Miami location is 15369 S. Dixie Hwy., Miami (☎ 305/378-6086).

Edwin Watts Golf Shops. 15100 N. Biscayne Blvd., North Miami Beach. ☎ **305/944-2925.**

This full-service golf retail shop has it all, including clothing, pro-line equipment, gloves, bags, balls, videos, and books. Ask the pros for advice, and ask for coupons for discounted greens fees for various courses.

Nevada Bob's. 7930 NW 36th St., at NW 79th Ave., Miami (near the airport). ☎ **305/593-2999.**

Discounted Greg Norman and Antigua clothing, pro-line equipment, steel-shafted conventional clubs to the high-tech Yonex clubs—with more than 6,000 square feet of store, this place has everything for golfers. Practice your swing at an indoor driving range with a radar gun. No commission salespeople here—they're a laid-back crew and very up on the latest in soft and hard equipment.

GOURMET GROCERS

The best produce is found at the traveling Farmer's markets in Coral Gables and Miami Beach. Check the papers or call the chambers of commerce for details.

There are a number of ethnic grocery stores in and around Miami. You can find Indian selections at **Bombay Bazaar,** 2008 NE 164th St., North Miami Beach (☎ **305/948-7258**), Caribbean at **Kingston Miami Trading Company,** 280 NE 2nd St., downtown (☎ **305/372-9547**), and Italian at **Laurenzo's Italian Supermarket and Farmer's Market,** 16385 and 16445 W. Dixie Hwy., North Miami Beach (☎ **305/945-6381** and 305/944-5052). Many Cuban, Nicaraguan, and Peruvian outposts are also in the area. Check the phone book for those in your neighborhood. And check out these gourmet markets listed below for a variety of food specialties.

Epicure. 1656 Alton Rd., South Beach. ☎ **305/672-1861.**

Fancy produce here includes portobello mushrooms the size of a yarmulke, as well as pineapples, cherries, and salad greens like you can't imagine. You can get great prepared foods as well, including chicken soup and smoked fish at this landmark Jewish deli and gourmet shop combined into one.

Gardner's Market. 7301 Red Rd., South Miami. ☎ **305/271-3211.**

This place is a tradition in South Miami, with anything a gourmet or novice cook could desire—the freshest and best from fish to cheese.

Scotty's Grocery. 3117 Bird Ave., Coconut Grove. ☎ **305/443-5257.**

A vast selection of wines, fresh fish, meats, and superb prepared goods, Scotty's will tempt any food lover. From racks of fresh endive to fantastic salads and fresh-cut steaks, you will find it all here.

JAMES BOND GADGETS

Spy Shops International. 350 Biscayne Blvd. (across from Bayside Marketplace), downtown. ☎ **305/374-4779.**

Where else could you find electronic surveillance equipment, day and night optical devices, stun guns, minisafes, doorknob alarms, and other anticrime gadgets?

A second branch is located at 2900 Biscayne Blvd. (☎ 305/374-4779).

JEWELRY

International Jeweler's Exchange. 18861 Biscayne Blvd. (in the Fashion Island), North Miami Beach. ☎ **305/931-7032.**

This is the place with the city's best prices, especially on gold and diamonds. More than 50 jewelers hustle their wares from individual counters at one of the city's most active jewelry centers. Haggle your brains out for excellent prices on timeless antiques from Tiffany's, Cartier, or Bulgari, or unique designs you can create yourself. Closed Sunday and early on Friday.

The Seybold Building. 36 NE 1st St., downtown. ☎ **305/377-0122.**

Jewelers of every assortment gather here daily to sell their diamonds and gold. The glare is blinding as you enter this multilevel retail marketplace. You'll see a huge variety of handsome and up-to-date designs, but unless you know your stuff, don't expect too many bargains here.

MUSIC

Blue Note Records. 16401 NE 15th Ave., North Miami Beach. ☎ **305/940-3394.**

New, used, and discounted CDs and old vinyl too—this place has hard-to-find progressive and underground music and a good bunch of music aficionados who can tell you a thing or two.

Their quaint Blue Note Jazz Cafe offers pastries, coffee, and the occasional live show.

Casino Records. 1208 SW 8th St., Little Havana. ☎ **305/856-6888.**

Here you'll find the largest selection of Latin music in Miami, including pop icons like Willy Chirino, Gloria Estefan, Albita, and local boy Nil Lara. Its slogan translates to, "If we don't have it, forget it." Believe me, they've got it.

CD Warehouse. 13150 Biscayne Blvd., North Miami. ☎ **305/892-1048.**

Buy, sell, or trade your old CDs at this eclectic music hut.

Specs Music. 1655 Washington Ave., South Beach. ☎ **305/534-6533.**

Call to find out who is playing at this megamusic mall. In addition to a great collection of multicultural sounds, you'll find a lively scene most weekends. Also, there is a coffee bar with donuts and pastries and live performances.

SEAFOOD

Head to the south side of the MacArthur Causeway, near the Miami Beach marina, to get the freshest daily catch. Local fishers sell their shrimp, tuna, mahimahi, and whatever else they have at the best prices in town. The best time to go is when the boats arrive between 3 and 6pm.

Miami's most famous restaurant, **Joe's Stone Crab,** 227 Biscayne St., South Beach (☎ **800/780-CRAB** or 305/673-0365), makes overnight air shipments of stone crabs to anywhere in the country from October to May. It's pricey, but they are the best. You can also get it to go from the fancy take-out counter next-door (☎ 305/673-4611).

East Coast Fisheries. 330 W. Flagler St., downtown. ☎ **305/577-3000.**

This retail market and restaurant has shipped millions of pounds of seafood from its own fishing fleet around the world. It's equipped to wrap and send 5- or 10-pound packages of stone crab claws, Florida lobsters, Florida Bay pompano, fresh Key West shrimp, and a variety of other local delicacies to your door via overnight mail.

13 Miami After Dark

Miami nightlife is as varied as its population. On any night, you'll find world-class opera or dance as well as grinding rock and salsa. Restaurants and bars are open late and many clubs, especially on South Beach, stay open past dawn.

South Florida's after-hours scene is abuzz, too, with South Beach at the center of the scene. The Art Deco District has been the spawning ground for top international musicians and DJs, such as Latin artist Julio Iglesias; Cuban diva Albita; controversial rappers 2 Live Crew; jazz man Nestor Torres; and rockers The Mavericks, Nil Lara, and, of course, Gloria Estefan. It's no secret that Cuban and Caribbean rhythms are extremely popular, and the sounds of the salsa and the conga, inextricably incorporated into Miami's club culture, make dancing irresistible. So do some of the world's best DJs like David Padilla, JoJo Odyssey, Junior Vazquez, and David Knapp, who mix at top clubs in the area.

One of the most striking aspects of the city is the recent growth of world-class music, dance, and theater. Miami boasts a top opera company and symphony orchestra, as well as respected ballet and modern dance troupes.

The one thing Miami seems to have trouble sustaining is consistently good live music. In the past few years Miami has watched more than half a dozen music clubs shut their doors. By the time this book comes out more will surely have followed suit. Some blame the lack of community support, others say it's Miami's remote geographic location, which is too far a drive for bands to include on their circuit, still others claim promoters in town don't work hard enough to get the word out. The truth is that there are some excellent venues for live music, especially popular spots for jazz and Latin music. I hope these clubs will endure.

For up-to-date entertainment listings, check the *Miami Herald*'s "Weekend" section, which runs on Fridays, or the more comprehensive listings in *New Times,* Miami's free alternative weekly. Available each Wednesday, this award-winning paper prints articles, previews, and advertisements on upcoming local events. Several telephone hotlines—many operated by local radio stations—give free recorded information on current events in the city. These include **Love 94 Concert** hot line (☎ **305/ 770-2511**), the **Planet Radio Concert Hotline** (☎ **305/770-2513**), the **Zeta Concert Hotline** (☎ **305/770-2515**), and the **UM Concert Hotline** (☎ **305/ 284-6477**). Other information-oriented telephone numbers are listed under the appropriate headings below.

Tickets for many performances are handled by **Ticketmaster;** call ☎ **305/ 358-5885** to charge tickets. For sold-out events, you might try **Ultimate Travel & Entertainment,** 3001 Salzedo, in Coral Gables (☎ **305/444-8499**). This well-known ticket broker is open Monday to Friday from 9am until 6pm, Saturday from 10am until 4pm.

BARS

There are countless bars in and around Miami with the highest concentration on trendy South Beach. Many are in the lobbies of trendy hotels or restaurants. Keeping track of them all would be a full-time job. And not a bad one at that. Still the selection below is a mere sample. On the beach, you'd do best to walk along Ocean Drive and especially Washington Avenue below 10th Street to see what's hot. In Coconut Grove, check out the retail complexes Cocowalk and Mayfair next door. None of the bars listed below impose cover charges.

China Grill. 404 Washington Ave., South Beach. ☎ **305/534-2211.**

Don't bother with the food, but do stop in this neon-decorated restaurant for an overpriced drink and some superb people watching. The dinner and bar crowd arrive decked out as if going to a disco, and from the look-over you get on the way in, you get the idea that the front-door staff would like to hang a velvet rope outside. Dress in your slinky, sexy black best.

✪ **The Clevelander.** 1021 Ocean Dr., South Beach. ☎ **305/531-3485.**

This old standby is always a sure bet. On one of Ocean Drive's busiest and most spacious corners, you'll find a casual crowd gathered around the large outdoor pool area up until 5am. Cheap drinks in plastic cups complete the beachy atmosphere in this spring-breaky bar.

The Delano. 1685 Collins Ave., South Beach. ☎ **305/672-2000.**

I'm surprised they haven't started charging admission to this spectacular attraction. In the lobby is the Rose Bar, one of the best spots in South Beach to see beautiful people decked out in trendy splendor. Lounge on a cushy sofa or in any of the plump beds (yes, *beds,* covered with furs and pillows) that are casually arranged throughout the lobby and backyard, and grab an expensive drink. This is a good place to start the evening before heading out to the more lively clubs in the area. Note: Don't valet park your car here. Not only will you pay about $15 for the privilege, but you will also wait forever for the valets to retrieve your car.

Mac's Club Deuce. 222 14th St. (between Collins and Washington aves.), South Beach. ☎ **305/673-9537.** No cover. Open daily 8am–5am.

Housed in a squat, neon-covered deco building, this old dive bar is popular with bikers, barflies, and pool players who love the dark and smoky scene. A real local's favorite for those who like to slum it. Here you'll no doubt catch a great conversation, some old tunes on the jukebox, or a good scene out the front picture window that faces a busy all-night tattoo parlor.

Molly Malone's. 166 Sunny Isles Blvd. (just west of Collins Ave.), North Miami Beach. ☎ **305/948-3512.**

Open all day and into the next, Molly's is a divey Irish pub that is popular with drinkers and folk lovers alike. There's a pool table, darts, occasional Irish rock or acoustic music from all over, and, of course, a selection of good ales and lagers.

Murphy's Law Irish Pub. 2977 McFarlane Dr., Coconut Grove. ☎ **305/446-9956.**

This wood- and brass-decorated Irish pub is for those who want to escape the more antiseptic night scene at CocoWalk down the road. Though a big-screen TV shows sporting events, otherwise it's you and a pint sharing the bar with old-timers, grungers, and young professionals.

Wet Willies. 760 Ocean Dr., South Beach. ☎ **305/532-5650.**

This upstairs deck right on the main drag is one of the prime spots for watching the hectic parade that defines Ocean Drive. From up here you can see the ocean and the spectacle of folks who walk the strip night and day. After just one Wet Willie frozen concoction, you may not be able to see much of anything. Watch out: These drinks taste like soda pop but bite like a mad dog.

THE CLUB & MUSIC SCENE
LIVE MUSIC & JAZZ

Despite the spotty success of local music, South Florida's jazz scene is very much alive with traditional and contemporary performers. Keep an eye out for guitarist Randy Bernsen, vibraphonist Tom Toyama, or flutist Nestor Torres, all young performers who lead local ensembles. The **University of Miami** has a well-respected jazz studies program in its **School of Music** (☎ **305/284-6477**) and often schedules low- and no-cost recitals. Additionally, many area hotels feature live music of every assortment. Schedules are listed in the newspaper entertainment sections.

Churchill's Hideaway. 5501 NE Second Ave., Miami. ☎ **305/757-1807.** Cover usually $3, but depends on band.

It's a dive and in a rough neighborhood, but if you want to sample Miami's local music scene, Churchill's is the place to go see a fledgling band before they make it big. The

Learn to Salsa in Six Easy Lessons

If you're feeling shy about hitting a Latin club because you have two left feet, it might be a good idea to take a few lessons before tripping the light fantastic. Several dance companies and dance teachers around the city offer individual and group lessons to Anglos or bad dancers of any origin willing to learn. The following folks make it their mission to teach meringue, flamenco, and more to gringo wannabes or Latin left-foots.

Ballet Flamenco La Rosa, at the PAN (Performing Arts Network) building, 555 17th St., South Beach (☎ 305/672-0552), will teach you how to flamenco, salsa, or meringue with the best of them. This is the only professional flamenco company in the area, and you'll hear those castanets going. Private lessons are $50 if you're feeling shy, or $10 an hour will allow you to learn the art of the dance with a group of other beginners.

Nobody salsas like **Luz Pinto** (☎ 305/868-9418), and she can help you master the basics with patience and humor. She charges between $45 and $50 for a private lesson for up to four people and $10 per person for a group lesson. A good introduction is her multilevel group class, at 7pm Sunday evening at the PAN building. Though she teaches everything from ballroom to meringue, her specialty is Casino-style salsa, popularized in the 1950s in Cuba, Luz's homeland. A mix between disco and country square dancing, Casino-style salsa is all the rage in Latin clubs in town. If you are a very good student, you may be able to talk Luz into chaperoning a trip to a nightclub to show off your moves. She'll work out a fee based on the number of participants and their ability.

Angel Arroya has been teaching salsa to the clueless out of his home at 16464 NE 27th Ave., North Miami Beach (☎ 305/949-7799), for the past 10 years. Just $10 will buy you an hour's time in his school. He traditionally teaches Monday and Wednesday nights, but call ahead to check for any schedule changes.

---

theme is a British pub (hence the name Churchill's) where you can snack on rustic shepherd's pie and good English brew. And for those homesick Brits craving a good game of rugby, Churchill's is probably the only place that broadcasts English sports via satellite. Call ahead for information on upcoming bands and open hours.

The Globe. 377 Alhambra Circle (at Le Jeune), Coral Gables. ☎ 305/445-3555. No cover.

This odd little cafe is attached to a travel agency. On weekends, a red curtain transforms a corner into a stage where you'll find decent jazz and good food.

The Hungry Sailor. 3426 Main Hwy., Coconut Grove. ☎ 305/444-9359. Cover Fri–Sat $5–$10.

This small English-style wood-paneled pub has Watney's, Bass, and Guinness on draught and reggae regularly on tap. The club attracts an extremely mixed crowd. High-quality live reggae and soca music are featured Thursday through Saturday. Other nights include an open-mike night and dance music provided by a DJ. Closed Monday.

South Beach Pub. 717 Washington Ave., South Beach. ☎ 305/532-PUB-1. Cover for back room varies from $3 to $8.

This hole-in-the-wall offers a run-of-the-mill bar up front with a small live music room in the back. Local bands as well as national touring bands pack them in at this tiny venue. Watch local papers for special Latin rock nights, where Miami's flavor is infused with some good old rock and roll.

Stella Blue. 1661 Meridian Ave. (just north of Lincoln Rd.), South Beach. ☎ **305/ 532-4788.** Cover $5–$15.

This hot little spot features live music almost every night. From rock to folk to gospel, it is usually very good stuff. There are also pool tables in the back and a pretty decent menu, too.

✪ **Tobacco Road.** 626 S. Miami Ave. (over the Miami Ave. Bridge near Brickell Ave.), Downtown. ☎ **305/374-1198.** Cover varies none–$8.

This Miami institution is a must-see. It's been around since 1912 doing more in the back room than just dancing. These days you'll find a good bar menu along with the best live music anywhere—blues, zydeco, brass, jazz, and more. Some regulars include the Dirty Dozen Brass band from New Orleans, which plays a mean mix of zydeco and blues with an actual dozen brass players; Bill Warton and the Ingredients, which makes a pot of gumbo while up on stage; Monkey Meet; Iko Iko; Chubby Carrier and his band; and many more. On Friday and Saturday nights, the music is played upstairs, and people dance like crazy, even though it's packed and there's no real dance floor. Monday, of course, is reserved for the blues. Escape the smoke and sweat in the backyard patio where air is a welcome commodity. The downright-cheap dinner specials, like a $10 lobster dinner, are quite good and served until 2am.

Van Dyke Cafe. 846 Lincoln Rd., Miami Beach. ☎ **305/534-3600.** No cover.

Live jazz is on tap 7 nights a week until midnight, and it's free! In an elegant little upstairs lounge, the likes of Eddie Higgins, Mike Renzi, and some locals, like Don Wilner, play for a well-dressed crowd of jazz enthusiasts. You can have a drink or two at the pristine oak bar or enjoy some snacks from the bustling patio seats below.

Dance Clubs

In addition to quiet cafes and progressive poolside bars, Miami Beach pulsates with one of the liveliest night scenes in the city. Also check out "Latin Clubs" listings later in this chapter for more places to dance.

A popular trend in Miami's club scene are one-off nights—events organized by a promoter and held in established venues on irregular schedules. Word of mouth, local advertising, and listings in the free weekly *New Times* are the best way to find out about these hot events, or ask a waitperson at a hip South Beach eatery.

Bash. 655 Washington Ave., South Beach. ☎ **305/538-2274.** www.BarBashClub.com. Cover $10 weeknights, $15 weekends.

Worth a mention of its own since this place has been around longer than most and is still pretty hot. Open every night but Monday from 10pm to 5am, Bash gets going late and features an eclectic mix of music and special events including Eurodance, disco, and funk nights as well as occasional funky fashions shows. The crowd is Eurohip and supertrendy.

Bermuda Bar and Grill. 3509 NE 163rd St., North Miami. ☎ **305/945-0196.** Cover none–$10. No cover before 9pm.

This huge suburban "danceteria" specializes in ladies' nights, charging no cover for women on Wednesdays and Thursdays. Plus, it hosts cash-prize contests for women who dare to wear the skimpiest outfits. And everybody loves the high-energy music that packs the dance floor every night but Monday and Tuesday. Thursday is Latin night and Friday is happy hour from 5 to 8pm. Saturday is the biggest night when all the goings-on are broadcast live on a local radio station. This place usually stays open until the sun comes up.

Cafe Iguana. 8505 Mills Dr. (in the Kendall Town & Country Mall on the corner of 88th St. and 117th Ave.), Miami. ☎ **305/274-4948.** Cover none–$10.

This tropical-theme bar and dance club may be a bit much for low-key club goers, but for those looking for a high-energy party, this is the place to be. Everything from male and female hot body contests to a raving Latin night are incorporated into this nightspot.

Club St. Croix. 3015 Grand Ave., Coconut Grove (CocoWalk). ☎ **305/446-4999.** Cover none–$15.

How many bodies can fit in one club? Club St. Croix has made it its mission to find out. If you're not blinded by the pulsating disco lights and shocking Caribbean decor, and you love loud dance music and scantily clad bodies, you'll enjoy the bar scene here. The Voodoo Lounge cigar bar inside the club is quiet by comparison. The club normally opens at 9pm and closes at 5am except on Thursday and Friday, when the party starts at 4pm for happy hour. Open Wednesday to Sunday.

821. 821 Lincoln Rd., South Beach. ☎ **305/531-1188.** No cover.

On most nights it's more gay than straight. It's something between a neighborhood bar and a nightclub, with a DJ or a live music show every night. Thursday night is for women only and usually features a cabaret singer. Friday night is all boys and they do party hard. Offering a good mix of music and people, this hot spot is a Lincoln Road staple that's open daily from 3pm until 3 or 5am.

Groove Jet. 323 23rd St. (next to the Fina gas station), South Beach. ☎ **305/532-2002.** Cover $10–$20.

This fantastic hidden spot north of the South Beach scene has been through many incarnations. Its most recent, Groove Jet, has three distinct areas, including a breezy outdoor patio, playing totally different music. Deep house, jungle, and trance tunes are usually heard in the front room with more experimental music in the back rooms. A very hip young crowd hangs in this out-of-the-way scene, which gets going late, Thursday to Sunday 11pm to 5am.

Howl at the Moon Saloon. 3015 Grand Ave. (on the second level of CocoWalk), Coconut Grove. ☎ **305/442-8300.** Cover $5–$10.

This spot is unusual in that it has a popular college night, every Thursday during the school year. And 19 to 20 year olds, though not allowed to drink, are always welcome. If you are over 21 and have a college ID, you can skip the cover and enjoy cheap buckets of beer. Tuesday night women drink free. Drink specials are a regular fixture on Sunday when beers are $1.75 a pop, and on other nights throughout the week, except Monday, when the Moon is dark.

✪ Liquid and The Lounge. 1439 Washington Ave., South Beach. ☎ **305/532-9154** for table reservations, or 305/532-8899. Cover $10–$15.

Liquid is reminiscent of the '80s New York club scene, so you can expect to wait at the ropes until a disdainful bouncer chooses you. Don't dare to wear the usual casual South Beach attire, as they are looking for something more chic. Once inside, you'll find a cavernous space with up-to-the-minute dance music and two beautiful bars, VIP seating in a cozy back area, a hip-hop side room, and a downstairs lounge playing jazz and funk. Sunday night is gay. Madonna sightings are not unusual. The club opens its doors at 11pm, but the action starts late (around 2am).

Living Room at the Strand. 671 Washington Ave., South Beach. ☎ **305/532-2340.** Cover $5–$15.

This very Euro hot spot is the place to mix and mingle with South Beach's slightly older, and much more sophisticated, crowd. The popular restaurant is one of the longest-surviving success stories on South Beach and is still good. It's been around more than a dozen years. Models and moguls alike converge here to drink and relive the art of conversation at one of the many tightly packed VIP tables. You'll spend a few hundred dollars to buy a bottle and set up, but otherwise don't expect a seat.

Marsbar. 8505 Mills Dr. (in the Kendall Town & Country Mall on the corner of 88th St. and 117th Ave.), Miami. ☎ **305/271-6909.** Cover $5–$10.

After closing down for a while, this alternative dance club is back with a vengeance and it's all about the '70s and '80s. The retro-only format caters to young and old alike, with youngsters and hipsters packing it in from neighboring South Miami and Kendall.

✪ **Shadow Lounge.** 1532 Washington Ave. ☎ **305/531-9411.** Cover $10–$15.

Opened in December 1997, this massive dance club with two levels, two VIP areas, and a bunch of bars plays house and techno music to a wild but well-dressed crowd.

Tantra. 1445 Pennsylvania Ave. (at Española Way), South Beach. ☎ **305/672-4765.**

When this supersexy restaurant/lounge opened in late 1997, it was scorching hot and continues to be the place for the beautiful-in-black crowd. Dinner reservations are hard to get and, if you come after 11pm, a spot at the bar is even tougher. The place looks like some ultraluxurious opium den in Marrakech. You'll step into a small entryway that is covered with real grass. Continue on to the lounge with sod underfoot and find a stone waterfall, huge Indian sculptures, smoky lanterns, and low curtained tables. This is the place to check out Miami's hippest residents. A small dance floor gets going late. Plus, the pricey food (which is said to have aphrodisiacal properties) is excellent. You're not in Kansas anymore, Dorothy.

A STRIP CLUB

Just for the record: No, Madonna, the original Material Girl, does not own a nightclub in South Beach. The club that uses her name on its oversized billboard at 1527 Washington Ave. is a strip joint, one of a handful on South Beach that features completely nude dancing (☎ **305/534-2000**).

GAY & LESBIAN CLUBS & BARS

The gay and lesbian scene is particularly active in South Beach. Not only are there many clubs, but there's a thriving network of gay-owned businesses. Most hotels and restaurants are gay-friendly, and many of the gay clubs are hetero-friendly as well. There are quite a few gay organizations ready to offer any information (see "Tips for Travelers with Special Needs," in chapter 2). A very open lifestyle here allows for open displays of affection among gay male or female visitors. Many of the normally straight clubs also have gay nights. Both Liquid and 821 host these parties. Another particularly good one can be found in the form of the Sunday afternoon tea dance at **Amnesia** (136 Collins Ave., South Beach; ☎ **305/531-5535**), where buffed boys parade around in minuscule outfits while dance music plays in the background. These parties change nights and locations from month to month so be sure to call ahead of time.

Loading Zone. 1426 Alton Rd., Miami Beach. ☎ **305/531-5623.** No cover.

The town's only leather bar, complete with hot men, sexy videos, and, in case you forgot something, a leather shop in back.

Salvation. 1771 West Ave. (just West of Alton Rd.), South Beach. ☎ **305/673-6508.** Cover varies.

Probably the largest gay dance party in the state, with pumping dance music and some of South Beach's most recognized, and wildest, drag queens. It's a weekly party at a huge place and it goes on until the sun comes up.

Twist. 1057 Washington Ave., South Beach. ☎ **305/53-TWIST.** No cover.

One of the beach's most popular cruise bars, Twist attracts mostly male clientele but has an open-door policy.

Warsaw Ballroom. 1450 Collins Ave., South Beach. ☎ **305/531-4555.** Cover $10–$15.

One of Miami's oldest and most fun nightclubs, Warsaw hosts various theme nights and some of the best dance music in town. After all these years, regulars still line the sidewalk, waiting to get in and dance until 5am. The new owners may be slipping a bit, but it's worth checking out.

West End. 942 Lincoln Rd., South Beach. ☎ **305/538-9378.** No cover.

A mellow bar and pool hall, this Lincoln Road standby is a favorite hangout for women and men. Enjoy a relaxed atmosphere and a good place to meet people. Open 2pm to 5am on weekdays and noon to 5am on weekends.

LATIN CLUBS

Considering that Hispanics make up the majority of Miami's population and there's a huge influx of Spanish-speaking visitors, it's no surprise that there are some great Latin nightclubs in the city. What's interesting is that in recent years, many new clubs have opened and are attracting a mix of curious Anglos and Europeans as well. Plus, with the meteoric rise of the international music scene that's based in Miami, many international stars come through the offices of MTV Latino, SONY International, and a multitude of Latin TV studios based in Miami, and look for a good club scene on weekends.

Because of the increased competition, some of Miami's older Latin clubs have gone into decline. Thankfully, however, there are still many authentic clubs to check out. If you don't already know how to dance to Latin music, consider taking a salsa class and then head out to one of the following Anglo-friendly clubs.

✪ **Alcazaba.** 50 Alhambra Plaza (in the Hyatt Regency Coral Gables), Coral Gables. ☎ **305/441-1234.**

The Hyatt's Top-40 lounge plays an eclectic mix of music but exudes a decidedly Mediterranean atmosphere that mixes fantasy with reality. Cool out with some tropical drinks and authentic tapas in between songs. Happy hour—Wednesday and Friday from 5 to 7pm and Saturday from 9 to 11pm—offers half-price beer, wine, and drinks, plus a free buffet.

✪ **Cafe Nostalgia.** 2212 SW 8th St. (Calle Ocho), Miami. ☎ **305/541-2631.** Cover $10 Fri–Sat.

As the name implies, Cafe Nostalgia is dedicated to reminiscing about old Cuba. After watching a Celia Cruz film, you can dance to the hot sounds of Afro-Cuban jazz. With pictures of old and young Cuban stars smiling down on you and a live band celebrating Cuban heritage, Cafe Nostalgia is very popular. Be prepared, it's packed after midnight and dance space is mostly between the tables. Open Thursday to Sunday from 9pm to 4am. Films are shown from 10pm to midnight, followed by live music.

Casa Panza. 1620 SW 8th St. (Calle Ocho), Miami. ☎ **305/643-5343.** No cover.

Clap your hands or your castanets if you have them. Every Tuesday and Thursday night, Casa Panza, in the heart of Little Havana, becomes the House of Flamenco, with shows at 8 and 11pm. Patrons of the restaurant can enjoy a flamenco show or don their own dancing shoes and participate in the celebration. Enjoy a fantastic dinner before the show or have a few drinks before you do some stomping.

Mango's. 900 Ocean Dr., South Beach. ☎ **305/673-4422.** Cover $6–$15.

If you want to dance to a funky, loud Brazilian beat till you drop, check out Mango's on the beach. They feature nightly live Brazilian and some Latin music on a little patio bar. When you need refreshment, you can choose from a schizophrenic menu of Caribbean, Mexican, vegetarian, and Cuban specialties. Open daily from 11am to 5:30pm.

Studio 23. 247 23rd St. (adjacent to Mama Vieja Restaurant between Collins Ave and Pinetree Dr.), South Beach. ☎ **305/538-1196.** Cover $5–$10.

You've heard of salsa, perhaps? Well, this is where it thrives, along with son, cumbia, merengue, vallenato, and house music. This neighborhood Latin disco and nightclub gets going after hours with a wild strobe-lit atmosphere. If you don't know how to do it, just wait. You'll have plenty of willing teachers on hand. Open Friday to Sunday from 8pm to 4am.

Yuca. 501 Lincoln Rd., South Beach. ☎ **305/532-9822.** Cover $25, plus 2-drink minimum for the Albita performance Fri–Sat nights at 11pm.

One of the city's best restaurants (see "Great Deals on Dining," in chapter 4) also serves up hot music in an upstairs club. If Albita is playing, don't miss her. The bill will be high and you'll be squeezed into a table no bigger than a cocktail napkin, but it is worth it for some of the highest-energy dance music, including traditional sol, salsa, and son from the old country. No matter who is playing, you are bound to have fun at this super authentic Latin hot spot. If you don't speak Spanish, sign language works here, too.

THE PERFORMING ARTS

The **New World Symphony,** at 541 Lincoln Rd. in South Beach (☎ **305/673-3331;** e-mail: ticketsenws.org), is a stepping stone for gifted young musicians seeking professional careers. Led by artistic advisor Michael Tilson Thomas, the orchestra specializes in ambitious, innovative, energetic performances and often features guest soloists and renowned conductors. The symphony season lasts from October to May. Tickets cost $30 to $40. Student and senior discounts are available. For a real deal, call to find out when dress rehearsals are scheduled. Usually held monthly on a Saturday morning from September through May, these full 3-hour sessions are open to the public for a mere $10.

THEATER

Miami has an active and varied selection of dramas and musicals throughout the year. Thanks to the support of many loyal theater aficionados, season subscriptions are common and allow the theaters to survive. Some traveling Broadway shows make it to

---

Cheap Thrills

A little-publicized, but very popular weekly event is held from February through April along Biscayne Bay at Bayfront Park. See the stunning sculptures designed by Isamu Noguchi. Local musicians and dancers perform free starting at 7:30pm. In 1998, performances were held on Thursdays, but the future schedules have not been set yet. For details, call ☎ **305/358-7550.**

---

town, as do revivals. In South Beach, many are shown at the **Jackie Gleason Theater of the Performing Arts,** 1700 Washington Ave. (☎ **305/673-7300**), or the **Colony Theater,** on Lincoln Road (☎ **305/674-1026**).

Some theaters are dark in the summer or show a limited schedule. Call the following recommended venues to see what's coming up.

The **Actors' Playhouse,** at the newly restored Miracle Mile Theater in Coral Gables (☎ **305/444-9293**), is a grand 1948 art deco movie palace with a 600-seat main theater as well as a smaller theater/rehearsal hall.

The **Coconut Grove Playhouse,** 3500 Main Hwy. in Coconut Grove (☎ **305/442-4000**), was also a movie house, built in 1927 in an ornate Spanish rococo style. Today this respected venue is known for its original and innovative staging. The more intimate Encore Room is well suited to alternative and experimental productions.

The **Florida Shakespeare Theatre,** at the Biltmore Hotel, on Anastasia Avenue in Coral Gables (☎ **305/446-1116**), stages at least one Shakespeare play, one classic, and one contemporary piece a year. In addition, this well-regarded theater usually tries to get the rights to a national or local premiere. Tickets cost $20 and $22, $12 and $17 for students and seniors.

New Theater, 65 Almeria Ave., Coral Gables (☎ **305/443-5909**), prides itself on showing world-renowned works from America and Europe. As the name implies, you'll find mostly contemporary plays, with a few classics thrown in for variety. Performances are staged Wednesday to Sunday year-round. Tickets are $20 weekdays, $25 weekends. They don't widely advertise it, but on most weekdays you can get a second ticket for half price. Students always pay half price.

CLASSICAL MUSIC & OPERA

Although it looked as though classical music was in trouble for a while in Miami, the influx of international music lovers to the area has revitalized the classical scene. Most companies still suffer from economic problems, and the musicians tend to be underpaid, but there are many offerings, especially in the fall and winter.

In addition to a number of local orchestras and operas, which regularly offer high-quality music and world-renowned guest artists, each year brings a slew of special events and touring artists. One of the most important and longest-running series is produced by the **Concert Association of Florida** (CAF), 555 17th St., South Beach (☎ **305/532-3491**). Known for almost 25 years for its high-caliber, star-packed schedules, CAF regularly arranges the best serious music concerts for the city. Season after season the schedules are punctuated by world-renowned dance companies and seasoned virtuosi like Itzhak Perlman, Andre Watts, and Kathleen Battle. Performances are usually scheduled in either the Dade County Auditorium or the Jackie Gleason Theater of the Performing Arts. The season lasts from October to April, and ticket prices range from $20 to $60.

Florida Grand Opera, 1200 Coral Way, Coral Gables (☎ **800/741-1010** or 305/854-1643), is South Florida's oldest arts organization. It has been featuring top

Late-Night Bites

If you want a quick bite after clubbing and you find that it's 4am, don't fret! There are a vast number of pizza places lining Washington Avenue in South Beach that are open past 6am. Especially good is Pucci's, with several locations including one at 651 Washington Ave. (☎ **305/673-8133**). **La Sandwicherie,** 229 14th St. (behind the Amoco station; ☎ **305/532-8934**), serves up a great late-night sandwich until 5am. Another place of note for night owls is the **News Cafe,** 800 Ocean Dr. (☎ **305/538-6397**), and one in Coconut Grove at 2901 Florida Ave. (behind Mayfair; ☎ **305/774-6397**), a trendy and well-priced cafe with an enormous menu offering great all-day breakfasts, Middle Eastern platters, fruit bowls, or steak and potatoes.

If you've just left a Latin club, stop in at **Versailles,** 3555 SW 8th St. (☎ **305/444-0240**). What else but a Cuban *medianoche* (midnight sandwich) will do? They may not be open all night, but their hours extend until about 2am, catering to gangs of revelers young and old.

American and European singers for nearly 60 years. All productions are sung in their original language and staged with projected English supertitles. Tickets become scarce when Placido Domingo or Luciano Pavarotti (who made his American debut here in 1965) come to town. The opera's season runs roughly from November to April, with five performances each week.

The **Florida Philharmonic Orchestra,** 169 E. Flagler St., Miami (☎ **800/226-1812** or 305/930-1812), is South Florida's premier symphony orchestra, under the direction of James Judd. It presents a full season of classical and pops programs interspersed with several children's and contemporary popular music dates. The Philharmonic performs downtown in the Gusman Center for the Performing Arts or the Jackie Gleason Theater of the Performing Arts, and puts on children's concerts at the Dade County Auditorium.

An inexpensive alternative to the high-priced classical venues is the **Miami Chamber Symphony,** 5690 N. Kendall Dr., Kendall (☎ **305/858-3500**). Renowned international soloists regularly perform with this professional orchestra. The symphony performs October to May and most concerts are held in the Gusman Concert Hall, on the University of Miami campus. Tickets are $12 to $30.

DANCE

Several local dance companies train and perform in the greater Miami area. In addition, top traveling troupes regularly pass through the city, stopping at the venues listed above. Keep your eyes open for special performances, like those by **Ballet Flamenco La Rosa** (☎ **305/672-0552**), a local Flamenco and Afro-Caribbean dance troupe that really puts the heat in Latin dance.

Miami City Ballet. Office and rehearsal studios, Lincoln Road Mall at Jefferson, South Beach. ☎ **305/532-4880,** or 305/532-7713 box office. Tickets $17–$54.

Headquartered in a storefront in the middle of the Art Deco District's popular pedestrian mall, this Miami company has quickly emerged as a top troupe, performing both classical and contemporary works. This artistically acclaimed and innovative company, directed by Edward Villella, has premiered more than 30 ballets, and has a repertoire of more than 75 works, many by George Balanchine. Stop by most afternoons to watch rehearsals through the large storefront window. Plans are in the works to move to a bigger studio by 2000. The City Ballet season runs from September to April, with performances in South Beach at the Jackie Gleason Theater of the Performing Arts and other venues around the state.

14 Cruises & Quick Flights to the Caribbean & Other Islands

Most of the Caribbean-bound ships sailing out of the Port of Miami are relatively inexpensive, can be booked without advance notice, and make for excellent excursions.

Home to more than 20 cruise ships from all around the world, the Port of Miami is the world's busiest, with a passenger load of close to three million people annually. All the cruises are well equipped for gambling, and casinos open as soon as the ship clears U.S. waters—typically 45 minutes after leaving port. Usually, four full-size meals are served daily, with portions so huge they're impossible to finish. Games, movies, and other onboard activities ensure that you're always busy. Passengers can board up to 2 hours before departure for meals, games, and cocktails.

There are dozens of cruise options, from a 1-day excursion to a trip around the world. Pick up the Passport to Adventure, an up-to-date list of cruises sailing from the port, from the **Metro-Dade Seaport Department,** 1015 N. America Way, in Miami (☎ **305/371-7678**), open Monday to Friday from 8am to 5pm. It's just off NE 5th Street and Biscayne Boulevard, near the Bayside Marketplace. Also, see "More Places to Play, Both Indoors & Out," above, for details on gambling "cruises to nowhere."

Most of the big lines listed below offer 3- and 4-day excursions to The Bahamas, Key West, and other islands in the Atlantic. Cruise ships usually depart Miami on Friday night and return on Monday morning. If you want more brochures or other information, contact the **Bahamas Tourist Office,** 19495 Biscayne Blvd., Suite 809, in Aventura (☎ **800/422-4262** or 305/932-0051). All passengers must travel with a passport or proof of citizenship for reentry into the United States.

Carnival Cruise Lines, 35201 Blue Lagoon Dr., Miami (☎ **800/327-9501** or 305/599-2200), sails the Ecstasy on 3- to 4-night cruises to Nassau, usually departing on Friday at 4pm and returning on Monday at 7am. The cost starts at $519, but discounts are available if you book well in advance. Carnival also sails one of the largest cruise ships in the world, the *Destiny*. It made its debut in November of 1996 with lots of publicity. Several swimming pools, game rooms, and lounges surround a spectacular multistory foyer that has quickly made the Destiny the centerpiece of Carnival's fast-growing fleet. The 101,000-ton ship can accommodate up to 3,400 passengers.

Norwegian Cruise Line, 95 Merrick Way, Coral Gables (☎ **800/327-7030** or 305/436-0866), offers 3- and 4-day trips. Departures are on Friday and Monday at 5pm. Bookings start at $349 ($639 including airfare). A more intimate ship, the 950-passenger *Leeward,* spends a full day in Nassau or Key West and Cozumel. As on other Caribbean-bound ships, you can choose to disembark at any destination, or you can stay on board for food, drinks, and games.

Royal Caribbean Cruise Line, 1050 Caribbean Way, Miami (☎ **800/327-6700** or 305/539-6000), now sails its old *Sovereign of the Seas* on 3- and 4-night cruises to Nassau, Key West, and Coco Cay (the cruise line's private island), departing on Friday and Monday at 5pm, with fares that start at around $600, including airfare from most major U.S. cities. Beautifully renovated in 1996, this stylized ship offers a huge youth center for kids and treats its 2,000-plus passengers to some pampering. For brochures, call ☎ 800/ALL-HERE.

Note that port charges are additional and can be more than $70 per person, depending on the destination. Ask before booking.

If you want a quick getaway to the Caribbean without the experience of cruising, many airlines and hotels team up to offer extremely affordable weekend packages.

Competitively priced packages are available from American Flyaway Vacations, operated by American Airlines (☎ **800/321-2121**); Bahamas Air (☎ **800/ 222-4262**); Pan Am Bridge (☎ **305/359-7980**); the slightly run-down Princess Casino in Freeport (☎ **305/359-9898**); and US Airways Vacations (☎ **800/ 455-0123**). Call for rates, since they vary dramatically throughout the year and depend on the type of accommodations you choose.

Finally, for more in-depth information on cruises to the Caribbean, consult *Frommer's Caribbean Cruises and Ports of Call.*

The Florida Keys   6

by Victoria Pesce Elliott

As if the very tip of Florida's peninsula had shattered into hundreds of wayward fragments, the islands of the Keys are scattered across the sea like the loose beads of an exotic coral necklace. Each of the more than 400 islands that make up this 150-mile chain has a distinctive character. While some are crammed with strip malls and tourist traps, most are dense with unusual species of tropical plants, birds, and reptiles. Surrounded by calm blue waters and graced by year-round warmth, all offer a fascinating experience for travelers.

Despite the intriguing landscape, the stark, rocky coast hardly looks inviting from the bow of a ship. When Spanish explorers Juan Ponce de León and Antonio de Herrera sailed amid these craggy and dangerous rocks in 1513, they and their men dubbed the string of islands "Los Martires" (The Martyrs), because they thought the rocks looked like men suffering in the surf. It wasn't until the early 1800s that the larger islands were settled by pirates who amassed great wealth by salvaging cargo from ships that wrecked at sea—wrecks often caused by the "salvagers" who occasionally moved and removed vital markers in the sea.

Wars, fires, hurricanes, mosquitoes, and the Depression took their toll on these resilient islands in the early part of this century, causing wild swings between fortune and poverty. In 1938, the spectacular Overseas Highway (U.S. 1) was finally completed atop the ruins of Henry Flagler's railroad; this opened the region to tourists who previously had never been able to drive to this sea-bound destination.

These days, that narrow highway connects more than 30 of the populated islands in the Keys. The hundreds of small, undeveloped islands that surround these "mainline" keys are known locally as the "backcountry" and are home to dozens of exotic animals and plants. To get to them, you must take to the water—a vital part of any Keys trip.

The sea and the myriad life beneath it are the main attractions here. Warm, shallow waters nurture living coral that supports a complex and delicate ecosystem of plants and animals—sponges, anemones, jellyfish, crabs, rays, sharks, turtles, snails, lobsters, and thousands of types of fish. This vibrant underwater habitat thrives on one of only two living tropical reefs in the entire North American continent (the other is off the coast of Belize). As a result, anglers, divers, snorkelers, and water-sports enthusiasts of all descriptions come to explore. The heavy traffic has taken its toll on this fragile ecoscape, however, and efforts are now underway to protect this unique resource.

Although the atmosphere throughout the Keys is that of a low-key beach town, don't expect to find many impressive beaches here. Once you head south of Miami, with the exception of a few private beachfront resorts and the small, sandy beaches in Bahia Honda State Park and in Key West, there are no wide natural beaches to speak of. To appease visitors, some hoteliers have imported Caribbean sand to create tiny beaches near the sea.

For the purposes of this chapter, I have divided the Keys into three sections. The **Upper and Middle Keys** are closest to the Florida mainland and therefore are popular with weekend warriors who come by boat or car to fish, drink, or relax in towns like Key Largo, Islamorada, and Marathon. Further south you'll find the **Lower Keys,** a small, unspoiled swath of islands teeming with wildlife. In this protected region you're most likely to catch sight of such endangered animals as eagles, egrets, or Key deer. Also, keep an eye out for alligators, turtles, rabbits, and a huge variety of birds.

Key West, literally at the end of the road, is the most popular destination in the Florida Keys. Made famous by the Nobel Prize–winning rogue Ernest Hemingway, this "Conch Republic" has been overrun with cruise-ship passengers, day-trippers, franchises, and T-shirt shops. Still, you'll find here a tightly knit community of permanent residents who cling fiercely to their live-and-let-live attitude—an atmosphere that has made Key West famously popular with gay travelers.

VISITOR INFORMATION   For general information on the Keys, contact **Florida Keys & Key West Visitor Bureau,** P.O. Box 1147, Key West FL 33041 (☎ **800/ FLA-KEYS;** www.flakeys.com).

International visitors who have any questions or difficulties can call ☎ **800/ 771-KEYS** to speak with multilingual operators who can help with problems at any hour.

1 Exploring the Keys by Car

Once you have left the turnpike and started along U.S. 1 (see "Getting There," below), you'll have no trouble negotiating these narrow islands. U.S. 1, also known as the Overseas Highway, is the only main road connecting the Keys. Although some find the long, straight drive from Miami to Key West tedious, it can be enjoyable if you linger to explore the region's diverse towns and islands. If you have the time, I recommend allowing at least 3 days to work your way down to Key West.

Most of U.S. 1 is a narrow, two-lane highway, with some wider passing zones along the way. The speed limit is usually 55 miles per hour (35 to 45 m.p.h. on Big Pine Key and in some commercial areas). Residents and government planners have fought over the years over whether or not to widen the highway in order to facilitate an evacuation in case of a hurricane or other emergency. So far, residents have held strong. Even on the narrow road, you can usually get from downtown Miami to Islamorada within an hour. If you're determined to drive straight through to Key West, allow at least 3½ hours. No matter what, avoid driving *anywhere* in the Keys on Friday afternoons or Sunday evenings, when the roads are jammed with weekenders from the mainland.

To find an address in the Keys, don't bother looking for building numbers; most addresses (except in Key West and parts of Marathon) are delineated by mile markers (MM), small green signs on the side of the road that announce the distance from Key West. The markers start at number 126, just south of the Florida mainland. The zero marker is in Key West, at the corner of Whitehead and Fleming streets. Addresses in this chapter are accompanied by a mile marker (MM) designation when appropriate.

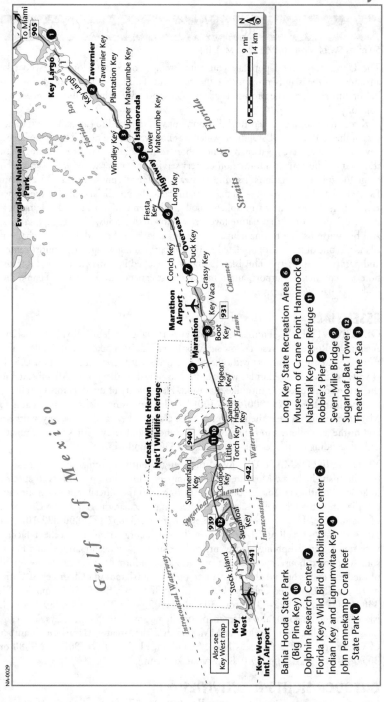

The Florida Keys

NA-0029

N

0   9 mi
    14 km

To Miami
905

1 Key Largo

Key Largo

2 Tavernier
Tavernier Key
Plantation Key

3 Upper Matecumbe Key
Islamorada

4 5 Lower Matecumbe Key
Windley Key

Everglades National Park

Florida Bay

Gulf of Mexico

Fiesta Key

6 Overseas Highway
Long Key

Conch Key
7 Duck Key
Grassy Key
Key Vaca
931

Marathon Airport

8 Boot Key
Marathon

Hawk Channel

9 Pigeon Key

Spanish Harbor Key

11 10 Little Torch Key
940
Summerland Key
Cudjoe Key
942

Great White Heron Nat'l Wildlife Refuge

Sugarloaf Channel
Intracoastal Waterway

939
12 Sugarloaf Key

941 Stock Island

1 Key West

Key West Intl. Airport

Also see Key West map

Straits of Florida

Bahia Honda State Park (Big Pine Key) 10
Dolphin Research Center 7
Florida Keys Wild Bird Rehabilitation Center 2
Indian Key and Lignumvitae Key 4
John Pennekamp Coral Reef State Park 1

Long Key State Recreation Area 6
Museum of Crane Point Hammock 8
National Key Deer Refuge 11
Robbie's Pier 5
Seven-Mile Bridge 9
Sugarloaf Bat Tower 12
Theater of the Sea 3

2 The Upper & Middle Keys: Key Largo to Marathon

50 miles SW of Miami (MM 127 to MM 48)

The Upper Keys are a popular, year-round refuge for South Floridians who take advantage of the islands' proximity to the mainland. This is the fishing and diving capital of America, and the profusion of outfitters and advertising billboards never lets you forget it.

Key Largo was once called Rock Harbor, but was renamed to capitalize on the success of the 1948 Bogart/Bacall film, which was not even filmed here. This is the largest key and is more developed than its neighbors to the south. Dozens of chain hotels, restaurants, and tourist information centers service the many water enthusiasts who come to explore the nation's first underwater park, John Pennekamp Coral Reef State Park, and its adjacent marine sanctuary. Islamorada, the unofficial capital of the Upper Keys, offers the area's best atmosphere, food, fishing, entertainment, and lodging. It is in these "purple isles" that nature lovers can enjoy hiking trails, historic explorations, and big-purse fishing tournaments. Marathon, smack in the middle of the chain of islands, is one of the most populated Keys. It is part fishing village, part tourist center, and part nature preserve. This island's highly developed infrastructure includes resort hotels, a commercial airport, and a highway that expands to four lanes. Thankfully, high-rises have yet to arrive.

ESSENTIALS

GETTING THERE   From the Miami airport, take Le Jeune Road (NW 42nd Avenue) to Route 836 west. Follow signs to the Florida Turnpike (about 7 miles). The turnpike extension connects with U.S. 1 in Florida City. Continue south on U.S. 1. If you're coming from Florida's west coast, take Alligator Alley to the Miami exit and then turn south onto the turnpike extension. Have plenty of quarters for the tolls.

American Eagle (☎ **800/433-7300**) has daily nonstop flights from Miami to Marathon, which is near the midpoint of the chain of keys and at the very southern end of the area referred to here as the Upper and Middle Keys. Fares range dramatically depending on the season, from $88 to $336 round-trip.

VISITOR INFORMATION   Avoid the many "Tourist Information Centers" that dot the main highway. Most are private companies hired to lure visitors to specific lodgings or outfitters. You are better off sticking with the official, not-for-profit centers that are extremely well located and staffed. In particular, the **Key Largo Chamber of Commerce,** U.S. 1 at MM 106, Key Largo, FL 33037 (☎ **800/822-1088** or 305/451-1414; fax 305/451-4726; www.floridakeys.org), runs an excellent facility with free direct-dial phones and plenty of brochures. Now headquartered in a handsome clapboard house, the chamber operates as an information clearinghouse for all of the Keys and is open daily from 9am to 6pm. The **Islamorada Chamber of Commerce,** in the Little Red Caboose, U.S. 1 at MM 82.5 (P.O. Box 915), Islamorada, FL 33036 (☎ **800/322-5397** or 305/664-4503; fax: 305/664-4289; e-mail: islacc@ix.netcom.com), also offers maps and literature on the Upper Keys. You can't miss the big blue visitor's center at MM 53.5. It is the **Greater Marathon Chamber of Commerce,** 12222 Overseas Hwy., Marathon, FL 33050 (☎ **800/842-9580** or 305/743-5417; fax: 305/289-0183; www.flakeys.com).

OUTDOOR SIGHTS & ACTIVITIES

One of this area's only beaches, **Anne's Beach** (at MM 73.5) is really more of a picnic spot than a full-fledged beach. Still, die-hard suntanners congregate on this tiny strip of coarse sand. Others enjoy the wide wooden boardwalk, which connects a dozen or so chickee huts (raised wooden platforms) or venture off the walkways into the mangroves. This minipark was dedicated to Anne Eaton, a local naturalist. Parking is free, and there are clean, safe bathrooms at the park's northern end.

Indian Key and Lignumvitae Key. Off Indian Key Fill, Overseas Hwy., MM 79. ☎ **305/ 664-4815.**

If you are interested in seeing the Keys in their natural state, before modern development, you should really venture off the Highway and take to the water. Two backcountry islands that offer visitors a glimpse of the "real" Keys are **Indian Key** and **Lignumvitae Key.**

Named for the *lignum vitae* ("wood of life") trees found there, **Lignumvitae Key** supports a virgin tropical forest, the kind that once thrived on most of the Upper Keys. Over the years, shortsighted developers have imported "exotic" plants and animals to the Keys, irrevocably changing the botanical makeup of many backcountry islands and threatening much of the indigenous wildlife. Over the past 25 years, the department of natural resources has successfully removed most of the exotic vegetation, leaving this 280-acre site much as it existed in the 18th century.

Indian Key, a much smaller island on the Atlantic side of Islamorada, was occupied by Native Americans for thousands of years before European settlers arrived. The 10-acre historic site was also the original seat of Dade County before the Civil War. You can see the ruins of the prior settlement and tour the lush grounds on well-marked trails.

If you want to see both islands, plan to spend half a day relaxing and enjoying the lush hammocks and colorful birds that call these islands home. To get there, you can rent your own boat at **Robbie's Rent-A-Boat** (U.S. 1 at MM 77.5 on the bay side). Rates range from $60 for a 14-foot boat for half a day to $155 for an 18-foot boat for a full day. It's then a $1 admission fee to each island, which includes an informative hour-long guided tour by park rangers. This is a good option if you are a confident boater. However, I recommend taking Robbie's ferry service for $15, which includes the $1 park admission. Trips to both islands cost $25 per person. Not only is the ferry more economical, but it is easier to enjoy the natural beauty of the islands when you're not negotiating the shallow reefs along the way. If you are only planning to visit one island, make it Lignumvitae, which has a historic house built in 1919 and has survived numerous storms and major hurricanes. The runabouts, which carry up to six people, depart from Robbie's Pier Thursday to Monday at 9am and 1pm for Indian Key, and at 10am and 2pm for Lignumvitae Key. In the busy season, you may need to book as early as 2 days before departure. Call ☎ **305/664-4815** for information from the park service or ☎ **305/664-9814** for Robbie's.

✪ **Tropical Crane Point Hammock.** 5550 Overseas Hwy. (MM 50), Marathon. ☎ **305/ 743-9100.** Admission $7.50 for adults, $6 for seniors over 64, $4 for students and free for children 6 to 12. Mon–Sat 9am–5pm, Sun noon–5pm.

Crane Point Hammock is a little-known but very worthwhile stop, especially for those interested in the rich botanical and archaeological history of the Keys. This privately owned 64-acre nature area is considered one of the most important historical sites in the Keys. Although Crane Point Hammock is surrounded by shopping centers and condominiums, it contains what is probably the last virgin thatch palm hammock in North America. Also, an archaeological dig site contains evidence of pre-Colombian and prehistoric Bahamian artifacts.

Now headquarters for the Florida Keys Land and Sea Trust, the hammock's small nature museum has simple and informative displays of the Keys' wildlife, including a

Cheap Thrills: What to See & Do for Free (or Almost) in the Keys

- **Take in the view from Seven-Mile Bridge.** Getting weary on that road trip south? Get out and stretch your legs at Seven-Mile Bridge, between MM 40 and 47 on U.S. 1. Its apex is the highest point in the pancake-flat Keys, which makes it an excellent place to admire the watery panorama. Alongside sits the old "ghost bridge," the ruins of oil magnate Henry Flagler's incredible Overseas Railroad. This scenic, 4-mile stretch is rife with bikers, joggers, and fishers trolling for barracuda, yellowtail, and dolphin. Come evening, it's a peaceful spot to watch the sunset.

- **Feed some giant fish at Robbie's Pier.** In the shallow waters off this Islamorada pier (at MM 77.5), scores of jumbo, valiant tarpon loiter, waiting for a snack or two from benevolent passersby. For $1 admission and a $2 bucket of fish, you can feed these oversized, prehistoric-looking fish, some of which can grow up to 200 pounds. If you want to get even more up-close and personal, embark on one of the newly instituted kayak tours.

- **Soak up the sunset and the scene at Mallory Square.** In what has become an evening ritual, artists, acrobats, food hawkers, and animal acts gather for some end-of-the-day revelry at Mallory Square, ground zero for Key West's eccentric set. Nab a spot on the docks (at the westernmost end of Duval Street) to take it all in. For a bird's-eye view of the mayhem, kick back at the Hilton's **Sunset Deck** (☎ **305/294-4000**), a luxurious bar on top of their restaurant at the intersection of Front and Greene streets.

- **Explore one man's inventive whimsy: the Sugarloaf Bat Tower.** Developer Clyde Perkey hated mosquitoes—so much so that in 1929 he built a 45-foot-high wooden, flat-topped pyramid to lure bug-eating bats to the region. Alas, despite a pervasive bat aphrodisiac, the critters never materialized. Now empty

walk-through replica of a coral-reef cave and life-size dioramas with tropical birds and Key deer. A single-room children's museum is very popular with kids who can play with a miniature railway station, walk though a Native American thatched hut, and touch a variety of sea creatures in a small saltwater touch tank.

Outside, visitors are encouraged to wander through the museum's quarter-mile nature trail amid species of exotic plants that grow nowhere else in the country.

✪ **Seven-Mile Bridge.** Between MM 40 and 47 on U.S. 1. ☎ **305/289-0025.**

A stop at the Seven-Mile Bridge is a rewarding and relaxing break from the drive south. Built alongside the ruins of oil magnate Henry Flagler's incredible Overseas Railroad, the new Seven-Mile Bridge (between MM 40 and 47) is still considered an architectural feat. Completed in 1982 at a cost of more than $45 million, the wide arched span is impressive; its apex is the highest point in all of the Keys. The new bridge, and especially its now-defunct neighbor, provides an excellent vantage point from which to view the surrounding waters. Take a few minutes or spend a few hours to appreciate this free attraction. The old "ghost bridge" is the perfect place to watch the sunset, more so if you have tired of the bar scene. In the daytime, you may want to jog, walk, or bike along the scenic 4-mile stretch—or join local anglers on this, "the longest fishing pier in the world." They use shrimp as bait to catch barracuda, yellowtail, and dolphin (mahimahi). To get there from the south-bound lane of the and deserted (and devoid of any explanatory signage), the Sugarloaf Bat Tower (at MM 17) is the only human-made attraction in the Lower Keys. Admission is free; it's worth a quick detour, if only to admire Perkey's quirky ingenuity.

- **Go wild—with the birds, that is.** The Florida Keys Wild Bird Rehabilitation Center (at MM 94, in Tavernier) serves as a hospital for the many native species of birds found here. Narrow wooden walkways, overhung by dense mangrove canopies, will take you past broad-winged hawks, great blue and white herons, roseate spoonbills, white ibis, cattle egrets, and a variety of pelicans. Come at feeding time (usually about 2pm) and see the dedicated staff feed the hundreds of those hungry beaks. This not-for-profit center doesn't charge admission, but does request donations.

- **Reef madness: snorkel an underwater state park.** John Pennekamp Coral Reef State Park is the nation's first undersea preserve, and the only living coral reef in the continental United States. So to experience this park, get in the water, which is shallow enough to make the 40 species of corals and more than 650 species of fish more than accessible to divers, snorkelers, and glass-bottom-boat passengers (though divers and boaters are putting a strain on the already fragile ecosystem). The park rents snorkeling and diving equipment, several types of boats, Windsurfers, and canoes. But best of all, mention this guide at **Hall's Dive Center & Career Institute,** U.S. 1 at MM 48.5, Marathon (☎ **305/743-5929**), and you'll get special discounted rates for snorkeling and diving. Park admission is $2.50 per vehicle for one occupant; for two or more, it is $4 per vehicle, plus 50¢ per passenger; $1.50 per pedestrian or bicyclist. Call ☎ **305/451-1621** for information.

Overseas Highway, slow down just before the bridge and turn right, off the road, into the unpaved parking lot at the foot of the bridge.

Recently opened to the public, **Pigeon Key,** at the curve of the old bridge, is an intriguing historical site that has been under renovation since late 1995. It was once the camp for the crew that built "Flagler's Folly" in the early part of the century. From here your vista includes both bridges, many old wooden cottages, and a truly tranquil stretch of lush foliage and sea. The key is open every day except Monday from 9am to 5pm. Admission is $2 and free for children under 8. Shuttle service is provided for visitors who don't want to walk or bike the 2-mile trail to the 5-mile island. Cars cannot drive on the old bridge. Parking is available at the Knight's Key end of the bridge, at MM 48, or at the Visitor's Center at the old train car across the highway.

VISITING WITH THE ANIMALS

✪ **Dolphin Research Center.** U.S. 1 at MM 59 (on the bay side), Marathon/Grassy Key. ☎ **305/289-1121.** Swim with the Dolphins, $90 per person. Children 5–12 must be accompanied by paying adult. Advanced reservations are essential. Call on the first or 15th of the month to book for the following month. Dolphin encounter $75 per person. Educational walking tours five times every day: 10am, 11am, 12:30pm, 2pm, and 3:30pm. Admission $12.50 adults, $10 seniors, $7.50 children 4–12, free for children 3 and under. MC, V. Daily 9:30am–4pm. Look for the 30-foot statue of a dolphin.

Don't miss this experience. If you've always wanted to touch, swim, or play with dolphins, this is the most respected place to do it. Of the three such centers in the continental United States (all located in the Keys), the Dolphin Research Center is the most organized and informative. The group's main goal is to protect the mammals and educate the public about these unusually smart beasts.

Although some people argue that training dolphins is cruel and selfish, the knowledgeable trainers at the Dolphin Research Center will tell you that the dolphins need stimulation and enjoy human contact. They certainly seem to. They nuzzle and seem to smile and kiss the lucky few who get to swim with them in the daily program. The "family" of 15 dolphins swims in a 90,000-square-foot, coral, natural saltwater pool carved out of the shoreline.

The procedure for making reservations is quite unbending. Call ☎ **305/289-0002.** If you can't book your choice of dates, don't despair. You can still take a walking tour or maybe get into a half-day class to learn hand signals and to feed the dolphins from docks.

Florida Keys Wild Bird Rehabilitation Center. U.S. 1 at MM 94, Tavernier. ☎ **305/852-4486.** Fax 305/852-3186. Donations suggested. Daily 8:30am–6pm. Heading south on U.S. 1, look right for the wooden bird sculptures to point the way.

Wander through lush canopies of mangroves on narrow wooden walkways to see some of the Keys' most famous residents—the large variety of native birds, including broadwing hawks, great blue and white herons, roseate spoonbills, white ibis, cattle egrets, and a variety of pelicans. This not-for-profit center operates as a hospital for the many birds that have been injured. If you have the stomach for it, ask to see naturalist Laura Quinn at work removing a fish hook from a bird's throat or untangling fishing line from a broken wing. Or come at feeding time (usually about 2pm) when you can watch the dedicated staff feed the hundreds of hungry beaks. Keep alert: The bigbilled pelicans often poke their heads down from the low structures just to check out who is visiting.

✪ **Robbie's Pier.** U.S. 1 at MM 77.5, Islamorada. ☎ **305/664-9814.** Admission $1. Bucket of fish $2. Daily 8am–5pm. Look for the Hungry Tarpon restaurant sign on the right after the Indian Key channel.

One of the best and definitely one of the cheapest attractions in the Upper Keys is the famed Robbie's Pier. Here, steely tarpons, a fierce fighting fish and a prized catch for backcountry anglers, have been gathering for the last 20 years. You may recognize these prehistoric-looking giants that grow up to 200 pounds. Many are displayed as trophies and mounted on some local restaurant walls. To see them live, head to Robbie's Pier, where tens and sometimes hundreds of these behemoths circle the shallow waters waiting for you to feed them. New kayak tours promise an even closer glimpse.

Theater of the Sea. U.S. 1 at MM 84.5, Islamorada. ☎ **305/664-2431.** Fax 305/664-8162. Admission $15.25 adults, $8.75 children 3–12; Swim with the Dolphins and Trainer for a Day program by reservation, $85 and $75 per person, respectively. Daily 9:30am–4pm.

Established in 1946, the Theater of the Sea is one of the world's oldest marine zoos. Although the facilities could use some sprucing up, the dolphin and sea lion shows are entertaining and informative, especially for children who can also see sharks, sea turtles, and tropical fish. The price is a bit steep for the rather limited resources here. Still, if you want to swim with the dolphins and you haven't booked well in advance, this is the place you may be able to get in with just a few hours' or days' notice as opposed to the more rigid Dolphin Research Center in Grassy Key (see above). After an hour's orientation session where you'll learn everything you'd ever want to know about these incredible swimming mammals—from their food preferences to their mating habits—you can climb into one of the three lagoons to touch and frolic with the playful beasts. Though the water is murky and individual time with the animals is short, for those who have dreamed of swimming beside these clever creatures, this is a great experience. Cat lovers will be thrilled to learn that the facility also serves as a haven for dozens of strays who have free run of the entire grounds and gift shop. Those who are allergic or sensitive to cat fur and smells should skip this stop.

TWO EXCEPTIONAL STATE PARKS

One of the best places to discover the diverse ecosystem of the Upper Keys is in its most famous park, ✪ **John Pennekamp Coral Reef State Park,** located on U.S. 1 at MM 102.5, in Key Largo (☎ **305/451-1202**). Named for a former *Miami Herald* editor and conservationist, the 188-square-mile park is the nation's first undersea preserve. It's a sanctuary for part of the only living coral reef in the continental United States. The original plans for Everglades National Park included this part of the reef within its boundaries, but opposition from local homeowners made its inclusion politically impossible.

Because the water is extremely shallow, the 40 species of corals and more than 650 species of fish are particularly accessible to divers, snorkelers, and glass-bottom-boat passengers. Unfortunately, the reef is a little too accessible, and the ecosystem is showing signs of stress from a steady stream of divers and boaters.

You can't see the reef from shore. To experience this park, visitors must get in the water. Your first stop should be the visitor center, which is full of demonstrative fish tanks and a mammoth 30,000-gallon saltwater aquarium that re-creates a reef ecosystem. At the adjacent dive shop, visitors can rent snorkeling and diving equipment and join one of the boat trips that depart for the reef throughout the day. They also rent motorboats, sailboats, Windsurfers, and canoes. The 2-hour glass-bottom-boat tour is the best way to see the coral reefs if you refuse to get wet.

Canoeing around the park's narrow mangrove channels and tidal creeks is also popular. You can go on your own in a rented canoe or in winter sign up for a tour led by a local naturalist. Hikers have two short trails to choose from: a boardwalk through the mangroves and a dirt trail through a tropical hardwood hammock. Ranger-led walks are usually scheduled daily from the end of November through April. Phone for schedule information and reservations.

Park admission is $2.50 per vehicle for one occupant; for two or more, it is $4 per vehicle, plus 50¢ per passenger; $1.50 per pedestrian or bicyclist. Call ☎ **305/451-1621** for information. On your way into the park, ask the ranger for a map. Glass-bottom boat tours cost $13 for adults and $8.50 for children 11 and under. Snorkeling tours are $23.95 for adults and $18.95 for children 17 and under, including equipment. Sailing and snorkeling tours are $28.95 for adults, $23.95 for children 17 and under, including equipment but not tax. Canoes rent for $8 per hour, or $28 for 4 hours. Reef boats (powerboats) rent for $25 to $45 per hour; call ☎ **305/451-6325.** Open daily from 8am to 5pm; phone for tour and dive times. Also, see below for more options on diving, fishing, and snorkeling these reefs.

✪ **Long Key State Recreation Area,** U.S. 1 at MM 68, Long Key (☎ **305/664-4815**) is situated atop the remains of an ancient coral reef. The 965-acre park is one of the best places in the Middle Keys for hiking, camping, and canoeing. At the entrance gate, ask for a free flyer describing the local trails and wildlife.

Railroad builder Henry Flagler created the Long Key Fishing Club here in 1906, and the waters surrounding the park are still popular with game fishers. In summer, sea turtles lumber onto the protected coast to lay their eggs.

You can hike along two nature trails. The Golden Orb Trail is a 1-mile loop around a lagoon that attracts a large variety of birds. Rich in West Indian vegetation, the trail leads to an observation tower that offers good views of the mangroves. Layton Trail, the only part of the park that doesn't require an admission fee, is a quarter-mile shaded loop that goes through a tropical hammock before opening onto Florida Bay. The trail is well marked with interpretive signs; you can easily walk it in about 20 minutes.

The park's excellent 1½-mile canoe trail is also short and sweet, allowing visitors to loop around the mangroves in about an hour—it couldn't be easier. You can rent canoes at the trailhead for about $4 per hour. Long Key is also a great spot to stop for a picnic if you get hungry on your way to Key West.

Admission is $3.25 per car plus 50¢ per person (except for the Layton Trail, which is free). Open daily from 8am to sunset.

WATER SPORTS FROM A TO Z

There are literally hundreds of outfitters in the Keys who will set up all kinds of water activities from cave dives to parasailing. If those recommended below are booked up or unreachable, ask the local chamber of commerce for a list of qualified members.

BOATING   In addition to the rental shops in the state parks, you will find dozens of outfitters along U.S. 1 offering a range of runabouts and skiffs for boaters of any experience level. **Captain Pip's,** U.S. 1 at MM 47.5, Marathon (☎ **800/707-1692** or 305/743-4403), rents 18.5–24 foot motorboats with 90- to 225-horsepower engines for $110 to $170 per day.

Robbie's Rent-a-Boat, U.S. 1 at MM 77.5, Islamorada (☎ **305/664-9814**), rents 14- to 27-foot motorboats with engines ranging from 15 to 200 horsepower. Boats cost $60 to $205 for a half day and $80 to $295 for a whole day.

CANOEING/KAYAKING   I can think of no better way to explore the uninhabited, shallow backcountry than by kayak or canoe. You can reach places big boats just can't get to because of their large draft. Sometimes manatees will cuddle up to the boats, thinking them another friendly species.

For a more enjoyable time, ask for a sit-inside boat—you'll stay drier. Also, a fiberglass (as opposed to plastic) boat with a rudder is generally more stable and easier to maneuver. Many area hotels rent kayaks and canoes to guests, as do the outfitters listed here. **Florida Bay Outfitters,** U.S. 1 at MM 104, Key Largo (☎ **305/451-3018**), rents canoes and sea kayaks for use in and around John Pennekamp Coral Reef State Park for $20 to $30 for a half day and $35 to $50 for a whole day. Canoes cost $25 for a half day and $35 for a whole day. At **Coral Reef Park Co.,** on U.S. 1 at MM 102.5, Key Largo (☎ **305/451-1621**), you can rent canoes and kayaks for $8 per hour, $28 for a half day—most canoes are sit-on-tops.

DIVING & SNORKELING   The **Florida Keys Dive Center,** on U.S. 1 at MM 90.5, Tavernier (☎ **305/852-4599;** fax 305/852-1293), takes snorkelers and divers to the reefs of John Pennekamp Coral Reef State Park and environs every day. PADI training courses are also available for the uninitiated. Tours leave at 8am and 12:30pm and cost $25 per person to snorkel (including mask, snorkels, and fins) and $40 per person to dive, plus an extra $30 if you need to rent all the gear.

At **Hall's Dive Center & Career Institute,** U.S. 1 at MM 48.5, Marathon (☎ **305/743-5929;** fax 305/743-8168), snorkelers and divers can choose to dive at Looe Key, Sombrero Reef, Delta Shoal, Content Key, and Coffins Patch. Tours are scheduled daily at 9am and 1pm. If you mention this guide, you will get a special discounted rate of $30 per person to snorkel (including equipment) and $40 per person to dive. Choose from a wide and impressive array of equipment. Rental is extra.

With **Snuba Tours of Keys Largo** (☎ 305/451-6391), you can dive down to 20 feet attached to a comfortable breathing apparatus that really gives you the feeling of scuba diving without having to be certified. You can tour shallow coral reefs teeming with hundreds of colorful fish and plant life, from sea turtles to moray eels. Reservations are required; call to find out where and when to meet—usually in the late afternoon from the Westin or the Cheeca Lodge. A 2- to 3-hour underwater tour costs $70, including all equipment. If you've never dived before, you may require a 1-hour lesson in the pool, which costs an additional $40. The best part is you can bring the kids, as long as they are at least 8 years old.

FISHING **Robbie's Partyboats & Charters,** on U.S. 1 at MM 84.5, Islamorada (☎ 305/664-8070 or 305/664-9184), located at the south end of the Holiday Isle Docks (see "Accommodations You Can Afford," below), offers day and night deep-sea and reef fishing trips aboard a 65-foot party boat. Big-game-fishing charters are also available, and "splits" are arranged for solo fishers. Party-boat fishing costs $25 for a half day, $40 for a full day, and $30 at night. Charters run $400 for a half day, $600 for a full day; splits begin at $65 per person. Phone for information and reservations.

Bud n' Mary's Fishing Marina, on U.S. 1 at MM 79.8, Islamorada (☎ 800/742-7945 or 305/664-2461; fax 305/664-5592), one of the largest marinas between Miami and Key West, is packed with sailors offering guided backcountry fishing charters. This is the place to go if you want to stalk tarpon, bonefish, and snapper. If the seas are not too rough, deep-sea and coral fishing trips can be arranged. Charters cost $400 to $500 for a half day, $600 to $800 for a full day, and splits begin at $125 per person.

The **Bounty Hunter,** 15th Street, Marathon (☎ 305/743-2446), offers full- and half-day outings. For years, Capt. Brock Hook's huge sign has boasted no fish, no pay. You're guaranteed to catch something. Choose your prey from shark, barracuda, sailfish, or whatever else is running. Prices are $350 for a half day, $375 for three-quarters of a day, and $450 for a full day. Rates are for groups of no more than six people.

SHOPPING

Perhaps the most exciting shopping experience comes before you officially enter the Keys. On the drive down south of Homestead and north of Key Largo, you'll pass a large outlet center, the **Keys Factory Shops** (☎ 305/248-4727), at 250 E. Palm Dr. (where the Florida Turnpike meets U.S. 1), in Florida City, with more than 60 stores including Nike Factory Store, Bass & Co. Store, Levi's, OshKosh, and Izod. They are open every day until 9pm except for Sunday, when the stores close at 6pm. Although it is not well publicized, any customer at the mall is welcome to pick up a valuable "Come Back Pack" from the customer service desk. The square red packet contains dozens of coupons good for significant discounts. Last winter, for example, Nine West outlet was giving a 20% discount on any purchase of two or more pairs of shoes and Corning Revere offered $5 off any purchase over $25.

Once in the Keys, you'll see that there is no shortage of tacky tourist shops selling shells and T-shirts and other hokey souvenirs. But for real Keys-style shopping, check out the weekend flea markets. One of the best is held every Saturday and Sunday bay side at MM 103.5 (☎ 305/451-0677). Dozens of vendors open their stalls from 9am until 4 or 5pm selling every imaginable sort of antiques, T-shirts, plants, shoes, books, toys, and games, as well as a hearty dose of good old-fashioned junk.

A mecca for fishing and sports enthusiasts is the **World Wide Sportsman** (☎ 305/664-4615), opened in late 1997 at MM 81.5. It's not only the largest fishing store in the Keys, but also a meeting place for anglers from all over the world. This spiffy 25,000 square foot specialty store stocks every possible gizmo and gadget, plus T-shirts, hats, books, and cute gift items. Unlike many other Keys servicepeople, here the staff seems knowledgeable and eager to help. Travel specialists can even arrange for charter trips and backcountry tours. The store is open daily from 7am until 8:30pm. If you want to call for free weather and travel data, ask for the tackle department, which is where the weather station operates.

ACCOMMODATIONS YOU CAN AFFORD

For the best value in the Keys, plan your trip in the off-season. That doesn't necessarily mean the scorching days of summer. Try September or May for great deals; midweek specials abound year-round as well. But be sure to check that your trip doesn't coincide with a major holiday, fishing tournament, or festival.

U.S. 1 is lined with chain hotels in all price ranges. In the Upper Keys the best moderately priced options are the **Holiday Inn Key Largo Resort & Marina,** U.S. 1 at MM 99.7 (☎ **800/THE-KEYS** or 305/451-2121), and right next door, at MM 100, the **Ramada Limited Resort & Casino** (☎ **800/THE-KEYS** or 305/ 451-3939). Both hotels share three pools and a casino boat; however, the Ramada is cozier and offers slightly cheaper rates. Also, the **Best Western Suites at Key Largo,** 201 Ocean Dr., MM 100 (☎ **800/462-6079** or 305/451-5081), is just 3 miles from John Pennekamp Coral Reef State Park. Another good option in the Upper Keys is **Islamorada Days Inn,** U.S. 1 at MM 82.5 (☎ **800/DAYS-INN** or 305/664-3681). In the Middle Keys, the **Howard Johnson** at 13351 Overseas Hwy., MM 54 in Marathon (☎ **800/321-3496** or 305/743-8550), also offers reasonably priced ocean-side rooms. Rates are competitive and generally start at around $90 in the off-season (summer) and about $150 in high season.

Since the real beauty of the Keys lies mostly beyond the highways, there is no better way to see this area than by boat. Why not stay in a floating hotel? Especially if you're traveling with a group, houseboats can be economical. To rent a houseboat, call Ruth and Michael Sullivan at **Smilin' Island Houseboat Rentals** (MM 99.5), Key Largo, FL (☎ **305/451-1930**). Rates are from $750 to $1,350 for 3 nights. Rates sound high, but realize that boats accommodate up to six people. Plus, when you are on the water, it's hard to spend money on incidentals.

Super-Cheap Sleeps

✪ **Bay Harbor Lodge.** U.S. 1 at MM 97.7 (off the southbound lane of U.S. 1), Key Largo, FL 33037. ☎ **305/852-5695.** 16 units, all with bathroom. A/C TV TEL. Year-round $58–$78 single or double; $78–$98 efficiency; $85–$125 cottage. AE, MC, V.

A small, simple retreat that's big on charm, the Bay Harbor Lodge is an extraordinarily welcoming place. The lodge is far from fancy, and the differing accommodations are not all created equal. The motel rooms are small in size and ordinary in decor, but even the least expensive is recommendable. The efficiencies are larger motel rooms with fully equipped kitchenettes. Some have private terraces. The oceanfront cottages are larger still, have minikitchens, and represent one of the best values in the Keys. The vinyl-covered furnishings and old-fashioned wallpapers won't win any design awards, but elegance isn't what the "real" Keys are about. The 1½ acres of lush grounds are planted with banana trees and have an outdoor heated pool and several small barbecue grills. Guests are free to use the rowboats, paddleboats, canoes, kayaks, and snorkeling equipment. Bring your own beach towels.

Bonefish Resort. 58070 Overseas Hwy., MM 58 (ocean side), Grassy Key, FL 33050. ☎ **305/743-7107.** Fax 305/743-3073. www.bonefishresort.com. E-mail: bonefishgk@ aol.com. 13 units, all with bathroom (some with shower only). A/C TV TEL. Winter $39–$95 single or double. Off-season $29–$89 single or double. Rates include use of nonmotorized boats. DISC, MC, V.

This bare-bones accommodation is popular with anglers and boaters. The quality improved greatly when the Moir family took over in 1996; they bought new furniture and did some landscaping. Rates are extremely reasonable, considering that the price includes free use of canoes, rowboats, or paddleboats. All of the modest rooms are different; some have futons and a potpourri of art on the wall, sent from around the world by loyal return guests. All the essentials are present, and the pricier rooms come with kitchenettes and private decks. There's a gas grill on the property, as well as a friendly pot-bellied pig named Willie.

Faro Blanco Marine Resort. 1996 Overseas Hwy., U.S. 1 at MM 48.5, Marathon, FL 33050. ☎ **800/759-3276** or 305/743-9018. Fax 305/743-2918. 154 units, all with bathroom (some with shower only). A/C TV TEL. Winter $65–$150 cottage, single or double; $99–$200 houseboat, single or double; $185 lighthouse; $240 condo for up to six. Off-season $55–$125 cottage, single or double; $79–$150 houseboat; $150 lighthouse; $210 condo for up to 6. AE, DISC, MC, V.

Spanning both sides of the Overseas Highway and all on waterfront property, this huge, two-shore marina and hotel complex offers something for every taste. Free-standing, camp-style cottages with a small bedroom are the resort's least expensive accommodations, but are in dire need of rehabilitation. Old appliances and a musty odor also make these the least desirable units on the property. There are some larger apartments with modern furniture and cleaner bathrooms and kitchens.

The houseboats are the best choice and value. Permanently tethered in a tranquil marina, these white rectangular boats look like floating mobile homes and are uniformly clean, fresh, and recommendable. They have colonial American-style furnishings, fully equipped kitchenettes, front and back porches, and water, water everywhere. The boats are so tightly moored, you hardly move at all, even in the roughest weather.

Finally, there are two unusual rental units located in a lighthouse on the pier; circular staircases, unusually shaped rooms and showers, and nautical decor make this quite a unique place to stay, though some guests may find it claustrophobic. Guests in any of the accommodations can enjoy the Olympic-size pool, any of the four casual restaurants, a fully equipped dive shop, barbecue/picnic areas, and a playground.

Holiday Isle Resort. U.S. 1 at MM 84, Islamorada, FL 33036. ☎ **800/327-7070** or 305/664-2321. Fax 305/664-2703. 199 units, all with bathroom (some with shower only). Winter $85–$425 single or double. Off-season $65–$350 single or double. AE, CB, DISC, MC, V.

A huge resort complex encompassing five restaurants, lounges, and shops, and four distinct (if not distinctive) hotels, the Holiday Isle is one of the biggest resorts in the Keys and attracts a spring-break kind of crowd year-round. Their Tiki Bar claims the invention of the rum runner drink (151-proof rum, blackberry brandy, banana liquor, grenadine, and lime juice), and there's no reason to doubt it. Hordes of partiers are attracted to the resort's nonstop merrymaking, live music, and beachfront bars. As a result, some of the accommodations can be noisy.

Rooms can be bare-bones-budget to oceanfront luxury, as reflected in the broad range of prices. Even the nicest rooms could use a good cleaning. El Captain and Harbor Lights, two of the least expensive hotels on the property, are both austere and basic. Like the other hotels here, rooms could use a thorough rehab. Howard Johnson's, another Holiday Isle property, is a little farther from the action and a shred more civilized. If you plan to be there for a few days, choose an efficiency or suite; both have kitchenettes. Guests can choose between two outdoor heated pools and a kids' pool. They also offer water-sports equipment rental, gift boutiques, and a shopping arcade.

Lime Tree Bay Resort Motel. U.S. 1 at MM 68.5 in Layton, Long Key, FL 33001. ☎ **800/723-4519** or 305/664-4740. Fax 305/664-0750. 30 units, all with bathroom (some with shower only). A/C TV TEL. Winter $105–$135 motel rm. or efficiencies, $115–$250 cottages. Off-season $80–$110 motel rm. or efficiencies, $115–$150 cottages. AE, DC, DISC, MC, V.

The Lime Tree Bay Resort is the only hotel in the tiny town of Layton (pop. 183). Midway between Islamorada and Marathon, the hotel is only steps from Long Key State Recreation Area. Motel rooms and efficiencies have tiny bathrooms with standing showers, but are clean and well maintained. The best deal is the two-bedroom bay-view apartment. The large living area with new fixtures and furnishings leads out to a large private deck where you can enjoy a view of the gulf from your hammock. A full kitchen and two full bathrooms make this a comfortable space for six people.

This affordable little hideaway has all the amenities you could want, among them shuffleboard, tennis, a small pool, water sports, and a little cafe with a small but decent menu. It's situated on a very pretty strip of waterfront graced with hundreds of mature palm trees and lots of other tropical foliage.

FOR A FEW BUCKS MORE

Banana Bay Resort & Marina. U.S. 1 at MM 49.5, Marathon, FL 33050. ☎ **800/BANANA-1** or 305/743-3500. Fax 305/743-2670. 60 units, all with bathroom. A/C TV TEL. Winter $95–$195 single or double. Off-season $75–$125 single or double. Rates include breakfast. Children 4 and under stay free in parents' room. Weekend and 3- and 7-night packages available. AE, DC, DISC, MC, V.

It doesn't look like much from the sign-cluttered Overseas Highway, but once you enter the lush grounds of Banana Bay you will realize that you're in for one of the most bucolic and best-run properties in the Upper Keys. Built in the early 1950s as a fishing camp, the resort is a puzzle of pink-and-white 2-story buildings hidden among banyans and palms. Guest rooms are very similar, but those with better views are more expensive. The rooms are moderately sized, and many have private balconies where you can enjoy complimentary coffee and newspapers every morning.

The restaurant serves breakfast, lunch, and dinner by the pool or in a kitschy old dining room. A waterfront tiki bar offers great sunset views. Head down to the marina to sign up for charter fishing, sailing, and diving. Kids will enjoy the small game room and free use of bicycles.

✪ **Conch Key Cottages.** Near U.S. 1 at MM 62.3 (RR 1, Box 424), Marathon, FL 33050. ☎ **800/330-1577** or 305/289-1377. Fax 305/743-8207. 12 units, all with bathroom (some with shower only). A/C TV. Winter $100 efficiency; $126–$194 1-bedroom apt. or cottage, single or double; $202–$249 2-bedroom cottage, up to 4. Off-season $74 efficiency; $115–$135 1-bedroom apt. or cottage, single or double; $147–$215 2-bedroom cottage, up to 4. DISC, MC, V. Weekly rates available.

Occupying its own private micro-island just off of U.S. 1, Conch Key Cottages is a unique and comfortable hideaway run by live-in owners Ron Wilson and Wayne Byrnes, who are constantly fixing and adding to their unique property. Request one of the new two-bedroom cottages, completed in 1997—especially if you are traveling with the family. These are the most spacious and well designed, practically tailor-made for couples or families. This is a place to get away from it all; the cottages aren't close to much, except maybe one or two interesting eateries. The cabins, which were built at different times over the last 40 years, overlook their own stretch of natural, but very small, private beach and have screened-in porches and cozy bedrooms and baths. Each has a hammock and barbecue grill. On the other side of the pool are a handful of efficiency apartments that are similarly outfitted, but enjoy no beach frontage. All have fully equipped kitchens. There's also a small heated freshwater pool.

✪ **Kona Kai Resort & Gallery.** 97802 Overseas Hwy., U.S. 1 at MM 97.8 Key Largo, FL 33037. ☎ **800/365-7829** or 305/852-7200. Fax 305/852-4629. E-mail: KonaKai@aol.com. 11 units, all with bathroom. Winter $141–$165 single or double; $175–$400 suite. Off-season $94–$145 single or double; $117–$205 suite. Three- to 4-night minimum stay usually required. AE, DISC, MC, V.

No one seems to get quite as thrilled over the Florida Keys' low-key beauty as the transplanted city folk. The garrulous proprietor of Kona Kai, Joe Harris, is the quintessential New Yorker and an enthusiastic tour guide. Former TV executives with NBC, he and his partner, Ronnie Farina, have created a peaceful haven in the overcommercialized upper Keys. They bend over backward to accommodate a guest's every need—it's all about personal service. It's also about 2 acres of tropical fruits, like carambola, passion fruit, banana, key limes, guava, Florida pistachios, and more. A small tennis court, pool, Jacuzzi, Ping-Pong, volleyball, and all kinds of water sports are available for those who want a physical workout. For the adventurous, Joe and Ronnie will organize excursions to the Everglades, the backcountry, or wherever. The fact that there are no phones in the rooms and that there is a 4-day minimum stay required in the winter makes relaxing imperative. The rooms, all very private and simply furnished, are spaced out and protected by low walls of tropical trees. An impressive art gallery doubles as the property's office and lobby. Photos by renowned local artist Clyde Butcher will inspire even the most tender-footed to explore the natural wonders of the Keys.

WORTH A SPLURGE

✪ **Cheeca Lodge.** U.S. 1 at MM 82 (P.O. Box 527), Islamorada, FL 33036. ☎ **800/327-2888** or 305/664-4651. Fax 305/664-2893. 267 units, all with bathroom. A/C MINIBAR TV TEL. Winter $240–$610 single or double; $315 suite. Off-season $160–$425 single or double; $275 suite. AE, CB, DC, DISC, MC, V.

One of the better places to stay in the Upper Keys, Cheeca has been hosting celebrities, royalty, and politicians since its opening in 1949. This lodge offers all the amenities of a world-class resort in a very laid-back setting. You may not feel compelled to leave the sprawling grounds, but it's good to know the hotel is conveniently situated near the best restaurants and nightlife. Located on 27 acres of beachfront property, this rambling resort is known for its excellent sports facilities, including diving and snorkeling programs and one of the only golf courses in the Upper Keys.

Although rooms are not particularly plush, all are spacious and have small balconies. The nicer ones overlook the ocean and have large marble bathrooms. Privacy is at a premium here; almost all rooms have entrances accessible from open-air hallways, and guests can park their cars in private spots near their rooms. The staff is always available, but not overly visible.

The **Atlantic's Edge** restaurant is one of the best in the Upper Keys. A pool bar and comfortable lounge offer more casual options throughout the day and evening, and free coffee and refreshments are available in the lobby.

Among the other amenities on hand are kitchenettes, VCRs and video rentals, three outdoor heated pools, a kids' pool, five hot tubs, access to nearby health club, bicycle rental, a 9-hole par-3 golf course, children's nature programs, car-rental desk, sundeck, six lighted tennis courts, water-sports equipment rental, tour desk, and a nature trail.

✪ **Hawk's Cay Resort.** U.S. 1 at MM 61, Duck Key, FL 33050. ☎ **800/432-2242** or 305/
743-7000. Fax 305/743-5215. 176 units, all with bathroom. A/C TV TEL. Winter $220–$350
single or double; $400–$850 suite. Off-season $160–$250 single or double; $300–$750 suite.
AE, DC, DISC, MC, V.

Located on its own 60-acre island just outside of Marathon in the Middle Keys,
Hawk's Cay is a sprawling and impressive resort encompassing a marina as well as a
saltwater lagoon that's home to a half dozen dolphins. It's especially popular with families who appreciate the many activities and reasonably priced diversions. It's also more
casual than other resorts, like Cheeca Lodge, which offers many of the same amenities. The manicured grounds are dotted with handsome 2- and 3-story flamingo-
colored buildings. The guest rooms within are all quite similar—the views account for
the differences in price. All are large and have Caribbean-style bamboo furnishings
padded with colorful fabrics, walk-in closets, small refrigerators, and a sliding glass
door that opens onto a private balcony. If you want to splurge, the top-floor suites
have separate seating areas with pull-out sofas and large wraparound terraces with
spectacular views.

Three good restaurants and a lounge have a wide range of food, from Italian to
seafood. A well-stocked ship's store has snacks and basic groceries. A popular lounge
features live music every evening and most weekend afternoons.

An Underwater Hotel

Jules' Undersea Lodge. 51 Shoreland Dr. (P.O. Box 3330), Key Largo, FL 33037. ☎ **305/
451-2353.** Fax 305/451-4789. 1 unit. A/C TV TEL. Year-round $195–$295 per person.
Rates include breakfast and dinner as well as all equipment and unlimited scuba diving in the
lagoon. AE, DISC, MC, V. From U.S. 1 south, at MM 103.2, turn left onto Transylvania Ave.,
across from the Central Plaza shopping mall.

Originally built as a research lab in the 1970s, this small underwater compartment
now operates as a single-room hotel. As expensive as it is unusual, Jules' is most popular with diving honeymooners. The lodge rests on pillars on the ocean floor. To get
inside, guests swim under the structure and pop up into the unit through a 4-by-6-
foot "moon pool" that gurgles soothingly all night long. The 30-foot-deep underwater
suite consists of a bedroom and galley, and sleeps up to six. There is a television and
VCR. Also, room service will bring breakfast, lunch, and daily newspapers in waterproof containers at no extra charge. Needless to say, this novelty is not for everyone.

CAMPING

John Pennekamp Coral Reef State Park. U.S. 1 at MM 102.5 (P.O. Box 487), Key Largo,
FL 33037. ☎ **305/451-1202.** 47 campsites. Phone or in-person camping reservations only.
$24–$26 per site. MC, V.

One of Florida's best parks (see above), Pennekamp offers 47 well-separated campsites;
half are available by advance reservation, and the rest distributed on a first-come, first-
served basis. The car-camping sites are small but well equipped with bathrooms and
showers. A little lagoon nearby attracts many large wading birds. Reservations are held
until 5pm, and the park must be notified of late arrival by phone on the check-in date.
Pennekamp opens at 8am and closes around sundown. No pets.

Long Key State Recreation Area. U.S. 1 at MM 67.5 (P.O. Box 776), Long Key, FL 33001.
☎ **305/664-4815.** 60 campsites. $24–$26 per site for 1 to 4 people. MC, V.

The Upper Keys' other main state park is more secluded than its northern neighbor
and more popular. All sites are located ocean-side and are surrounded by narrow rows
of trees and nearby toilet and bathroom facilities. Reserve well in advance, especially
in winter.

GREAT DEALS ON DINING

Although not known as a culinary hot spot, the Upper and Middle Keys do offer some excellent restaurants, many of which specialize in seafood. Often visitors (especially those who fish) take advantage of accommodations that have kitchen facilities and cook their own meals. Also, most restaurants will clean and cook your catch for a nominal charge.

SUPER-CHEAP EATS

✪ Henry's Bakery and Gourmet Pizza Shop. U.S. 1 at MM 82.5 (adjacent to Days Inn), Islamorada. ☎ **305/664-4030.** Pastas $7–$9.50; pizzas $8–$18; sandwiches and salads $4.50–$8. Mon–Sat 6am–10pm (sometimes later on weekends). No credit cards. BAKERY/ PIZZERIA.

It would be easy to drive right past this tiny storefront bakery, which serves the best pizzas and sandwiches in town. My favorite is freshly sliced turkey on homemade warm French bread, with a splash of superb tangy vinaigrette. Most days Henry bakes fresh multigrain, semolina, and Italian bread, too. Stop by early for delicious pastries and croissants. If you want pizza, consider the decadent Sublime Pie with lobster tail, roasted bell peppers, and sun-dried tomatoes. The crust has the perfect texture—just a bit chewy, but not too doughy.

Islamorada Fish Company. U.S. 1 at MM 81.5 (up the street from Cheeca Lodge), Islamorada. ☎ **800/258-2559** or 305/664-9271. Main courses $8–$20. Mon–Sat 8am–9pm, Sun 9am–9pm. DISC, MC, V. SEAFOOD.

The original Islamorada Fish Company has been selling seafood out of its roadside shack since 1948. It's still the best place to pick up a cooler of stone crab claws in season (October through early April). Enjoy spectacular views from picnic tables on the store's bay-side dock while munching on their famous (and fattening) Islamorada fish sandwich, served with melted American cheese, fried onions, and coleslaw.

A few hundred yards up the road is the newer Islamorada (MM 81.6, ☎ 305/ 664-8363), which looks like an average diner, but has a selection of fantastic seafood and pastas. It's also the place to eat breakfast. Locals gather for politics and gossip as well as delicious grits, oatmeal, omelettes, and homemade pastries (the fresh donuts are great dunked in coffee).

FOR A FEW BUCKS MORE

Key Largo's Crack'd Conch. U.S. 1 at MM 105.5 (ocean side). ☎ **305/451-0732.** Main courses $9–$13; sandwiches $5–$7. AE, MC, V. Thurs–Tues noon–10pm. SEAFOOD.

This colorful little shack looks appealing from the road and actually isn't a bad place to stop, especially if you like beer. More than 100 imported and domestic lagers, porters, stouts, and ales are available. Food choices, on the other hand, are not as varied or as predictable. The Crack'd Conch will deliver decent baskets of fried clams, shrimp, chicken, and, of course, conch. Soups are okay, but certainly not made from scratch. The zesty conch salad and the messy po' boy sandwiches are the best options. Prices are higher than they ought to be, considering the quality and atmosphere, but it won't break your bank.

Lazy Days Oceanfront Bar and Seafood Grill. U.S. 1 at MM 79.9, Islamorada. ☎ **305/ 664-5256.** Main courses $11–$20. AE, DISC, MC, V. Tues–Sun 11:30am–10pm. SEAFOOD/ AMERICAN.

Opened in 1992, the Lazy Days quickly became one of the most popular restaurants around, mostly because of the large portions and lively atmosphere. Meals are pricier than the casual dining room would suggest, but the food is good enough and the menu varied. Steamed clams with garlic and bell peppers make a tempting appetizer. The menu focuses on—what else?—seafood, but you can find Italian dishes. Most main courses come with baked potato, vegetables, a tossed salad, and French bread, making appetizers redundant.

✪ **Lorelei Restaurant and Cabana Bar.** U.S. 1 at MM 82, Islamorada. ☎ **305/664-4656.** Reservations not usually required. Main courses $9–$22. AE, DC, DISC, MC, V. Daily 7am–10pm. Outside bar serves lunch menu 11am–9pm. Bar closes at midnight. SEAFOOD/BAR FOOD.

Don't resist the siren call of the enormous, sparkling, roadside mermaid—you won't be dashed into the rocks. This big old fish house and bar is a great place for a snack, a meal, or a beer. Inside, a good-value menu focuses mainly on seafood. When in season, lobsters are the way to go. For $20 you can get a good-sized tail—at least a 1-pounder—prepared any way you like. Other fare includes the standard clam chowder, fried shrimp, and doughy conch fritters. Salads and soups are hearty and satisfying. For those tired of fish, the menu does offer a few beef selections. The outside bar has live music every evening, and you can order snacks and light meals from a limited menu that is satisfying and well priced. Enjoy the live entertainment every night.

WORTH A SPLURGE

✪ **Marker 88.** U.S. 1 at MM 88 (bay side), Islamorada. ☎ **305/852-9315.** Reservations not usually required. Main courses $14–$29. AE, DC, DISC, MC, V. Tues–Sun 5–11pm. SEAFOOD/REGIONAL.

An institution in the Upper Keys, Marker 88 has been pleasing locals, visitors, and critics since it opened in the early 1970s. Chef-owner Andre Mueller has created a "gourmet" restaurant in a tropical-fish house setting that serves a wide range of standard fare that's tinged with his take on nouvelle cuisine. Taking full advantage of his island location, Andre offers dozens of seafood selections, including Keys lobster, Bahamas conch, Everglades frogs' legs, Florida Bay stone crabs, Gulf Coast shrimp, and an impressive variety of fish from around the country. Once you've figured out what kind of fish to have, you can choose from a dozen styles of preparation. The Keys' standard is meunière, which is a subtle and tasty sauce of lemon and parsley. I love the more dramatic Rangoon, with currant jelly, cinnamon, and fresh tropical fruits, including bananas and mangos. Though everything looks tempting, don't overorder—portions are huge. The wait staff, who are pleasant enough, require a bit of patience, but the food is worth it.

✪ **Morada Bay.** U.S. 1 at MM 81.6, Islamorada. ☎ **305/664-0604.** Reservations recommended for large groups. Main courses $16–$22; sandwiches $7–$8. AE, MC, V. Mon–Thurs 11:30am–10pm. Fri–Sun 11am–11pm. CARIBBEAN/AMERICAN.

This lovely bay-side bistro provides a great setting for its superfresh and innovative seafood as well as some more basic offerings like chicken fajitas, hamburgers, and salads. Salads like the Sunshine Salad are large and generously lavished with slices of avocado, mango, and tomato. When in season raw oysters are imported from Long Island, and they're delicious. Fish dishes are always fresh. I like mine jerked with a peppery coating and nearly black finish. For those who can't decide, share a few items from the tapas menu: jumbo shrimp cocktails, fried calamari, conch fritters, smoked fish dip, or a charcuterie of sausages and hams on country bread.

THE UPPER & MIDDLE KEYS AFTER DARK

Nightlife in the Upper Keys tends to start before the sun goes down, since most people—visitors and locals alike—are on vacation. Partying starts at noon. Also, many anglers and sports-minded folk go to bed early. It's not that they're a puritanical lot;

it's just many have been drinking all day and need to crash by midnight in order to be able to get up and do it again.

Opened in the early '90s by some young locals who were tired of tourist traps, **Hog Heaven,** at MM 85.3 just off the main road on the ocean side in Islamorada (☎ **305/ 664-9669**), is a welcome respite from the neon-colored cocktail circuit. This white-washed biker bar offers a waterside view and diversions that include big-screen TVs and video games. The food isn't bad either. The atmosphere is cliquish since most patrons are regulars, so start up a game of pool or skeet to break the ice.

No trip is complete without a stop at the Tiki Bar at the **Holiday Isle Resort,** U.S. 1 at MM 84, Islamorada (☎ **800/327-7070** or 305/664-2321). Hundreds of revelers stop at this ocean-side spot for drinks and dancing any time of day, but the live rock music starts at 8:30pm.

In the afternoon and early evening (when everyone is either sunburned, drunk, or just happy to be alive and dancing to live reggae), head for **Kokomo's,** just next door to the thatched-roof Tiki Bar. Kokomo's closes at 7:30pm on weekends, so get there early.

Locals and tourists mingle at the outdoor cabana bar at **Lorelei** (see "Great Deals on Dining," above). Most evenings after 5, you'll find local bands playing on a thatched roof stage—mainly rock and roll, Caribbean, and sometimes blues.

✪ **Woody's Saloon and Restaurant,** on U.S. 1 at MM 82, Islamorada (☎ **305/ 664-4335**), is a lively, wacky, raunchy place serving up mediocre pizzas and live bands almost every night. The house band, Big Dick and the Extenders, showcases a 300-pound Native American who does a lewd, rude, and crude routine of jokes and songs starting at 9pm, Tuesday through Sunday. He is a legend. There is a small cover charge most nights. By the way, don't think you're lucky if you are offered the front table: It's the target seat for Big Dick's haranguing. Avoid the lame karaoke performance on Sunday and Monday evenings. Drink specials, contests, and the legendary Big Dick keep this place packed until 4am almost every night.

For a more subdued atmosphere, try the handsome wood bar at **Zane Grey's** (on the second floor of World Wide Sportsman at MM 81.5). Outside, enjoy a view of the calm waters of the bay or inside soak up the history of some real old anglers. Original manuscripts and photographs are displayed in mahogany cases. You feel like a real swell in this stained-glass, clubby atmosphere. It is open from 11am to 11pm and later on weekends. But call to find out who is playing on weekends (☎ **305/664-4244**) when there is live entertainment and no cover charge.

3 The Lower Keys: Big Pine Key to Coppit Key

127 miles SW of Miami (MM 31 to MM 10)

Big Pine, Sugarloaf, Summerland, and the other Lower Keys are less developed and more tranquil than the Upper Keys. If you're looking for haute cuisine and a happening nightlife, look elsewhere. But if you're looking to commune with nature or adventure in solitude, you've come to the right place. Unlike their neighbors to the north and south, the Lower Keys are devoid of rowdy spring-break crowds, boast few T-shirt and trinket shops, and have almost no late-night bars. What they do offer are the very best opportunities to enjoy the vast natural resources—on land and water—that make the area so rich. Stay overnight in the Lower Keys, rent a boat, and explore the reefs—it might be the most memorable part of your trip.

ESSENTIALS

GETTING THERE   See "Essentials" for the Upper and Middle Keys. Continue South on U.S. 1. The Lower Keys start at the end of the Seven-Mile Bridge.

VISITOR INFORMATION   The **Lower Keys Chamber of Commerce,** ocean side of U.S. 1 at MM 31 (P.O. Box 430511), Big Pine Key, FL 33043 (☎ **800/872-3722** or 305/872-2411; fax 305/872-0752; e-mail: lkchamber@aol.com), is open Monday through Friday from 9am to 5pm and Saturday from 9am to 3pm. The pleasant staff will help with anything a traveler may need. Call, write, or stop in for a comprehensive and detailed information packet.

ENJOYING THE OUTDOORS

The centerpiece of the Lower Keys and its greatest asset is ✪ **Bahia Honda State Park,** U.S. 1 at MM 37.5, Big Pine Key (☎ **305/872-2353**), which has one of the most beautiful coastlines in South Florida and one of the only natural beaches in the Keys. Bahia Honda is a great place for hiking, bird watching, swimming, snorkeling, and fishing. The 524-acre park encompasses a wide variety of ecosystems, including coastal mangroves, beach dunes, and tropical hammocks. There are miles of trails packed with unusual plants and animals and a small white beach. Although the beach is never wider than five feet even at low tide, this is one of the Keys' best beach areas. Shaded seaside picnic areas are fitted with tables and grills.

True to its name (*Bahia Honda* is Spanish for "deep bay"), the park has relatively deep waters close to shore that are perfect for snorkeling and diving. Head to the stunning reefs at Looe Key where the coral and fish are more vibrant than anywhere else in the United States. Snorkeling trips depart daily from March through September and cost $22 for adults, $18 for youths 6 to 14, and free for children 5 and under. Call ☎ **305/872-3210** for a schedule.

Admission to the park is $4 per vehicle (and 50¢ per person), $1.50 per pedestrian or bicyclist, free for children 5 and under. Open daily from 8am to sunset.

NATIONAL KEY DEER REFUGE

The most famous residents of the Lower Keys are the tiny Key deer. Of the estimated 300 existing in the world, two-thirds live on Big Pine Key's National Key Deer Refuge. To get your bearings, stop by the ranger's office, at the Winn-Dixie Shopping Plaza near MM 30.5 off U.S. 1. They'll give you an informative brochure and map of the area. It is open Monday through Friday from 8am to 5pm.

If the office is closed, head out to the Blue Hole, a former rock quarry that's now filled with the fresh water that's vital to the deer's survival. To get there, turn right at Big Pine Key's only traffic light onto Key Deer Boulevard (take the left fork immediately after the turn), and continue 1½ miles to the observation site parking lot, on your left. The half-mile Watson Hammock Trail, located about a third of a mile past the Blue Hole, is the refuge's only marked footpath. Try coming out here in the early morning or late evening to catch a glimpse of these gentle, dog-sized deer. Refuge lands are open daily from half an hour before sunrise to half an hour after sunset. Whatever you do, do not feed them—it will threaten their survival. Call the park office (☎ **305/872-2239**) to find out about the infrequent, free tours of the refuge, scheduled at different times throughout the year.

THE ONLY HUMAN-MADE ATTRACTION IN THE LOWER KEYS

Sugarloaf Bat Tower. Off U.S. 1 at MM 17 (next to Sugarloaf Airport on the bay side). Free admission.

In a vain effort to battle the ubiquitous and troublesome mosquitoes in the Lower Keys, developer Clyde Perkey built this odd structure to lure bug-eating bats. Despite his alluring design and a pungent bat aphrodisiac, his guests never showed. Since 1929, this wooden, flat-topped pyramid has stood empty and deserted, except for the occasional tourist who stops to wonder what it is. There is no sign or marker to commemorate this odd remnant of ingenuity. It's worth a 5-minute detour to see the odd 45-foot-high tower. To reach the tower, turn right at the Sugarloaf Airport sign, then right again, onto the dirt road that begins just before the airport gate; the tower is about 100 yards ahead.

AFFORDABLE OUTDOOR ACTIVITIES FROM A TO Z

BICYCLING   If you have your own bike, or your lodging offers rentals (many do), the Lower Keys is a great place to get off busy U.S. 1 to explore the beautiful back roads. On Big Pine Key, cruise along Key Deer Boulevard (at MM 30)—those with fat tires can ride into the National Key Deer Refuge.

BIRD WATCHING   Bring your birding books. A stopping point for migratory birds on the eastern flyway, the Lower Keys are populated with many West Indian bird species, especially during spring and fall. The small, vegetated islands of the Keys are the only nesting sites in the United States for the great white heron and the white-crowned pigeon. It's also one of a very few breeding places for the reddish egret, the roseate spoonbill, the mangrove cuckoo, and the black-whiskered vireo. Look for them in Bahia Honda and the many uninhabited islands nearby.

BOATING   Dozens of shops rent powerboats for fishing and reef exploring. Most also rent tackle, sell bait, and have charter captains available. **Bud Boats,** at the Old Wooden Bride Fishing Camp and Marina, MM 30 in Big Pine Key (☎ **305/ 872-9165**), has a wide selection of well-maintained boats. Depending on the size, rentals will cost between $70 and $250 for a day; between $50 and $130 for a half day. Another good option is **Jaybird's Powerboats,** U.S. 1 at MM 33, Big Pine Key (☎ **305/872-8500**). They rent only for full days. Prices start at $127 for a 19-footer.

CANOEING & KAYAKING   The Overseas Highway (U.S. 1) only touches on a few dozen of the many hundreds of islands that make up the Keys. To really see the Lower Keys, rent a kayak or canoe, perfect for these shallow and exciting waters. **Reflections Kayak Nature Tours,** operating out of Parmer's Place Resort Motel, on U.S. 1 at MM 28.5, Little Torch Key (☎ **305/872-2896**), offers fully outfitted backcountry wildlife tours, either on your own or with an expert. A former U.S. Forest Service guide, Mike Wedeking, keeps up an engaging discussion describing the area's fish, sponges, coral, osprey, hawks, eagles, alligators, raccoons, and deer. The 3-hour tours cost $45 per person and include spring water, fresh fruit, granola bars, and use of binoculars. Bring a towel and sea sandals or sneakers.

FISHING   Generally cheaper than Key West or the Upper Keys, fishing in the lower Keys, either in the shallow backcountry or in the deep sea, is a great way to assure yourself a fresh fish dinner. Or release your catch and appreciate the challenge. **Larry Threlkeld's Strike Zone Charters,** U.S. 1 at MM 29.5, Big Pine Key (☎ **305/ 872-9863**), is one of the area's best chartered boats in either the deep sea or the backcountry. Prices start at $250 to $400 for a half day. Especially if you have enough anglers to share the price, it isn't too steep. They may be able to match you with other interested visitors. Call a day or two in advance to see. Reef fishing trips are also offered by **Scandia-Tomi,** U.S. 1 at MM 25, Summerland Key (☎ **305/745-8633;** fax 305/872-0520). There's a six-passenger maximum.

HIKING   You can hike throughout the flat and marshy Keys, on both marked trails and meandering coastlines. The best places to trek through nature are Bahia Honda State Park (at MM 29.5) and National Key Deer Refuge (at MM 30). Bahia Honda Park has a free brochure describing an excellent self-guided tour along the Silver Palm Nature Trail. You'll traverse hammocks, mangroves, sand dunes, and cross a lagoon.

You can do the walk (which is less than a mile) in less than half an hour, and can explore a great cross section of the natural habitat in the Lower Keys. See "Enjoying the Outdoors," above.

SNORKELING/DIVING　Snorkelers and divers should not miss the Keys' most dramatic reefs at the **Looe Key National Marine Sanctuary.** Between 2 and 30 feet under water you'll see more than 150 varieties of hard and soft coral, some centuries old. Also, every type of tropical fish, including the gold and blue parrot fish, moray eels, barracudas, French angels, and tarpon, call this dense and diverse reef home. **Looe Key Dive Center,** U.S. 1 at MM 27.5, Ramrod Key (☎ **305/872-2215**), offers a mind-blowing 2½-hour tour aboard a 45-foot catamaran with two shallow 1-hour dives for snorkelers and scuba divers. Snorkelers pay $30, and divers with their own equipment pay $65. Good-quality rentals are available. (See "Bahia Honda State Park," above, for other diving options.)

SHOPPING

Certainly not known for great shopping, the Lower Keys do happen to be home to many good visual artists, particularly those who specialize in depicting their natural surroundings. The **Artists in Paradise Gallery,** on Big Pine Key in the Winn-Dixie Shopping Plaza, near MM 30.5 one block north of U.S. 1 at the traffic light (☎ **305/872-1828**), displays an ever-changing selection of watercolors, oils, photos, and sculptures. This cooperative gallery displays the work of more than a dozen artists who share the task of watching the store. Usually hours are daily from 10am to 6pm. Even more impressive is the ✪ **Gallery at Kona Kai** (see "For a Few Bucks More," under section 2, above), which shows dramatic black-and-white photos, oil and watercolors, and more.

ACCOMMODATIONS YOU CAN AFFORD

There are a number of cheap fish shacks along the highway for those who want bare-bones accommodations. See also "Camping," below, for inexpensive options in fully equipped cabins or rented trailers. Thankfully, there are no national hotel chains in the Lower Keys—yet.

SUPER-CHEAP SLEEPS

✪ **Big Pine Key Fishing Lodge.** P.O. Box 513, MM 33, Big Pine Key, FL 33043. ☎ **305/872-2351.** 16 units, all with bathroom (showers only). A/C TV. Year-round $73–$89 single or double; $89–$95 loft rm., for 1 to 4 people; $24–$31 campsites for tent or with full hookup. Discounts for stays longer than a week. Extra person $10. DISC, MC, V.

This superaffordable and well-maintained property is a favorite of campers and boaters. With more than 6 acres of lush ocean-side land and separate tenting areas, the rustic fishing lodge is a true bargain. Help yourself to coffee in the mornings. Most rooms have full kitchenettes or at least microwaves and refrigerators. There are no phones in the rooms, but there are plenty of pay phones conveniently located. A large heated pool with a sundeck and lounge chairs is a plus, especially since there isn't any real beach here. A tiny swath of artificial beach suffices for determined sand lovers. A 24-hour coin laundry room, a game room, recreation room, convenience store, gift shop, and marina make this an incredibly recommendable site.

✪ **Parmer's Place Cottages.** Barry Ave. (P.O. Box 430665), near MM 28.5, Little Torch Key, FL 33043. ☎ **305/872-2157.** Fax 305/872-2014. 41 units, all with bathroom (some with shower only). In winter and during festivals from $77 single or double; from $93.50 efficiency. Off-season $55–$65 single or double; from $75 efficiency. AE, DISC, MC, V. Turn right onto Barry Ave. Resort is a ½ mile down on the right.

This downscale resort offers modest but comfortable cottages. Every unit is different: Some face the water, while others are a few steps away; some have small kitchenettes, others just a bedroom. Room 26, a one-bedroom efficiency, is especially nice, with a small sitting area that faces the water. Room 6, a small efficiency, has a little kitchenette and an especially large bathroom. The rooms have linoleum floors, dated 1970s-style painted rattan furnishings, fake flowers, and thrift-store art. They're very clean, and many can be combined to accommodate large families. Facilities include a horseshoes court and boat ramp, plus a heated swimming pool. Parmer's, a fixture here for more than 20 years, is well known for its charming hospitality and helpful staff.

FOR A FEW BUCKS MORE

Barnacle Bed & Breakfast. 1557 Long Beach Dr. (P.O. Box 780), Big Pine Key, FL 33043. ☎ **800/465-9100** or 305/872-3298. Fax 305/872-3863. 4 units, all with bathroom. A/C TV TEL. Winter $95–$125 single or double. Off-season $85–$125 single or double. No children under 16. Rates include breakfast. DISC, MC, V. From U.S. 1 south, turn left at the Spanish Harbor Bridge (MM 33) onto Long Beach Rd. Look left for the stone wall and signs to the house on the left.

Joan Cornell, the Barnacle's owner, was once an innkeeper in Vermont; she knows what amenities travelers are looking for and goes out of her way to accommodate. Her Big Pine Key home has only four bedrooms, each with its own character. Two are located upstairs in the main house—their doors open into the home's living room, which contains a small Jacuzzi-style tub. For privacy, the remaining two rooms are best; each has its own entrance and is out of earshot of the common areas. The Cottage Room, a freestanding, peak-topped bedroom, is best, outfitted with a kitchenette and pretty furnishings. The accommodations are standard, not luxurious. All rooms have small refrigerators and private baths. The property has its own private sandy beach where you can float all day on the inn's rafts, rubber boat, or kayak. Beach towels, chairs, bicycles, and coolers are available at no charge. Neither children nor pets are welcome.

Deer Run Bed and Breakfast. Long Beach Dr. (P.O. Box 431), Big Pine Key, FL 33043. ☎ **305/872-2015.** Fax 305/872-2842. E-mail: deerrunbb@aol.com. 3 units, all with bathroom (some with shower only). Winter $110–$135 single or double. Off-season $75–$95 single or double. Rates include full American breakfast. No credit cards. From U.S. 1 south, turn left at the Big Pine Fishing Lodge (MM 33); continue for about 2 miles.

Located directly on the beach, Sue Abbott's small, homey, smoke-free B&B is a real find. One upstairs and two downstairs guest rooms are comfortably furnished with queen-size beds, good closets, and touch-sensitive lamps. All rooms have satellite TV. Rattan and 1970s-style chairs and couches furnish the living room, along with 13 birds and three cats. Breakfast, which is served on a pretty, fenced-in porch, is cooked to order by Sue herself. The wooded area around the property is full of deer, often spotted on the beach as well. Ask to use one of the bikes to explore nearby nature trails. The owner prefers adults and mature children over 16 only.

CAMPING

Bahia Honda State Park, 36850 Overseas Hwy. (MM 37), Big Pine Key, FL 33043, offers some of the best camping in the Keys. See "Enjoying the Great Outdoors," above, or call ☎ **305/872-2353.** It is as loaded with facilities and activities as it is with campers. However, don't be discouraged by its popularity—this park encompasses more than 500 acres of land. There are 80 campsites and 6 spacious and comfortable cabin units. If you're lucky enough to get one, the park's cabins represent a very good value. Each holds up to eight guests and comes complete with linens, kitchenettes, and utensils. Ask for a cabin overlooking the bay, which offers the best views and most privacy. You'll enjoy the wraparound terrace, barbecue pit, and rocking chairs.

Camping costs about $25 per site for one to four people without electricity and $26 with electricity. Depending on the season, cabin prices change: From December 15 to September 14 it's about $125 per cabin for one to four people; from September 15 to December 14 it's about $98 per cabin. Additional people (over four) cost $6. Master-Card and Visa are accepted.

Another excellent value can be found at the **KOA Sugarloaf Key Resort,** near MM 20. This ocean-side facility has 200 fully equipped sites that rent for about $53 a night (sites with no hookups cost about $36). Or pitch a tent on the 5 acres of lush waterfront property. They also rent out travel trailers. The 22-foot *Dutchman* sleeps six and is equipped with eating and cooking utensils. The cost is about $100 a day. More luxurious trailers go for $160 a day. They take all major credit cards. For details, contact them at P.O. Box 420469, Summerland Key, FL 33042 (☎ **800/562-7731** or 305/745-3549; fax 305/745-9889; e-mail: sugarloaf@koa.net).

GREAT DEALS ON DINING

There aren't many fine dining options in the Lower Keys. There's decent food for the motorists passing through—but nothing too fancy. The following are worth a stop.

SUPER-CHEAP EATS

✪ **Coco's Kitchen.** 283 Key Deer Blvd. (in the Winn-Dixie Shopping Center), Big Pine Key. ☎ **305/872-4495.** Main courses $5–$12; lunch $2–$5; breakfast $1–$4.50. No credit cards. Mon–Sat 7am–7:30pm. Turn right at traffic light near MM 30.5. Stay in the left lane. CUBAN/NICARAGUAN.

This tiny storefront has been dishing out black beans and rice and shredded beef to Cuban food fans for more than 10 years. The owners, who actually hail from Nicaragua, cook not only superior Cuban food but also some local specialties, Italian food, and Caribbean food. The best bet is the daily special, which may be roasted pork or fresh grouper, served with rice and beans or salad and crispy fries. Top off the huge, cheap meal with a rich caramel-soaked flan.

No Name Pub. ¼ mile south of No Name Bridge on N. Watson Blvd., Big Pine Key. ☎ **305/872-9115.** Pizzas $8–$18; subs $5. MC, V. Daily 11am–11pm. Turn right at Big Pine's only traffic light (near MM 30.5) onto Key Deer Blvd. Turn right on Watson Blvd. At stop sign, turn left. Look for a small wooden sign on the left marking the spot. PUB FOOD/PIZZA.

No Name Pub is a funky old bar out in the boonies that serves snacks and sandwiches until 11pm on most nights and drinks until midnight. Pizzas are tasty—thick crusted and supercheesy. Try one topped with local shrimp. Also consider a bowl of the hearty, cheap chili with all the fixings, or the very decent smoked fish dip. Everything is served on paper plates. Locals hang out at the rustic bar (one of the oldest in the Keys), drinking beer and listening to a jukebox that's heavy with '80s selections. The decor—if you can call it that—is basic. Walls and ceilings are plastered with thousands of autographed dollar bills. Ask the waitress for a stapler to affix yours. At sunset, look outside, and you may see one of the famed Key deer.

FOR A FEW BUCKS MORE

✪ **Mangrove Mama's Restaurant.** U.S. 1 at MM 20, Sugarloaf Key. ☎ **305/745-3030.** Main courses $13–$19; lunch $2–$9; brunch $5–$7. MC, V. Daily 11:30am–10pm (11am in season). SEAFOOD/CARIBBEAN.

As dedicated locals who come daily for happy hour will tell you, Mangrove Mama's is a true Lower Keys institution and a dive in the best sense of the word. The restaurant is a shack that used to have a gas pump as well as a grill. Now, guests share the property with some miniature horses (out back) and stray cats. A handful of simple tables, inside and out, are shaded by banana trees and palm fronds. Fish is, not surprisingly, the menu's mainstay, though soups, salads, sandwiches, and omelettes are also good. Grilled teriyaki chicken and club sandwiches are tasty alternatives to fish, as are the meatless chef's salad and spicy barbecued baby back ribs.

✪ **Monte's.** U.S. 1 at MM 25, Summerland Key. ☎ **305/745-3731.** Main courses $10–$14; lunch $3–$8. No credit cards. Mon–Sat 9:30am–10pm, Sun 10am–9pm. SEAFOOD.

Nobody goes to this restaurant/fish market for its atmosphere: Plastic place settings rest on plastic-covered picnic-style tables in a screen-enclosed dining patio. Monte's has survived for more than 20 years because the food is very good and incredibly fresh. The day's catch may include shark, tuna, lobster, stone crabs, or shrimp.

Montego Bay. US. 1 at MM 30.2, Big Pine Key. ☎ **305/872-3009.** Reservations suggested. $8–$15 main courses. AE, MC, V. Mon–Thurs 11am–1pm, Sun 10am–10pm. Brunch 10am–3pm. CARIBBEAN/SEAFOOD.

Known more as a drinking place than a fine dining spot, Montego Bay does host a fine and filling Sunday brunch. With a huge room full of buffet trays of hot and cold specials like carved meats, salad, seafood, lox, bagels and cream cheese, pastas, eggs to order, and coffee drinks, the brunch is a deal at $12.95. A dark, old-fashioned dining room is often half full of locals enjoying bar snacks and Caribbean fare. Stick to the basics like fish and soups for the most success.

THE LOWER KEYS AFTER DARK

The mellow islands of the Lower Keys aren't exactly known as a haven for wild nightlife; however, there are a number of friendly bars and restaurants where locals and tourists gather to hang out and drink.

One of the most scenic is **Sandbar** (☎ **305/872-9989**), a wide open breezy wooden house built on slender stilts and overlooking a wide channel on Barry Avenue (near MM 28.5). It attracts an odd mix of bikers and blue-hairs daily from 11am until 11pm. Pool tables are the main attraction, but there is also live music some nights. The drinks are reasonably priced, and the food isn't too bad either. For a fun bar scene, see **No Name Pub** in "Super-Cheap Eats," above.

4 Key West

155 Miles SW of Miami

The locals, or "conchs" (pronounced *conks*), and the developers have long been at odds—for years, in fact. Finally, the developers have won. There's no denying the fact that this once low-key island has been thoroughly commercialized; a Hard Rock Cafe sits smack in the middle of Duval Street, Sloppy Joe's has opened franchises around the country, and thousands of cruise-ship passengers descend on Mallory Square each day. This is definitely not the seedy town Hemingway and his cronies once called their own.

Laid-back Key West does still exist, but it's now found in the backyard of a popular guest house, in an art gallery, in a secret garden, in the hip hangouts of Bahama Village, and, of course, on the sea.

The heart of town offers a more wild time. There are some good restaurants, lively bars, live music, rickshaw rides and lots of shopping. Don't bother with a jacket, stockings, a tie, or even a watch. This is the home of the perennial vacation.

ESSENTIALS

GETTING THERE See "Essentials" for the Upper and Middle Keys. Continue south on U.S. 1. When entering Key West, stay in the far-right lane onto North Roosevelt Boulevard, which becomes Truman Avenue in Old Town. Continue for a few blocks and you'll find yourself on Duval Street, in the heart of the city. If you stay to the left, you'll also reach the city center after passing the airport and historic houseboat row, where a motley collection of boats makes up one of Key West's most interesting neighborhoods. Unfortunately, the houseboats may be gone by the end of the decade, since state regulators have long been trying to drive out boat owners.

Several regional airlines fly nonstop from Miami to Key West; fares are about $120 to $300 round-trip. **American Eagle** (☎ **800/443-7300**) and **US Airways Express** (☎ **800/428-4322**) land at Key West International Airport, South Roosevelt Boulevard (☎ **305/296-5439**), on the southeastern corner of the island.

GETTING AROUND With limited parking, narrow streets, and congested traffic, the best way to get around Key West is by bicycle. The island is small and as flat as a board, which makes it easy to negotiate, especially away from the crowded downtown. More tourists choose to cruise by moped, an option that can make navigating the streets risky, especially since there are no helmet laws in Key West. Spend the extra money and rent a helmet; there are hundreds of serious accidents each year.

Rates for simple one-speed cruisers start at about $6 per day (from $30 per week). Tacky, pink mopeds start at about $25 per day and $100 per week. The best shops include **The Bike Shop,** 1110 Truman Ave. (☎ **305/294-1073**); the **Moped Hospital,** 601 Truman Ave. (☎ **305/296-3344**); and **Tropical Bicycles & Scooter Rentals,** 1300 Duval St. (☎ **305/294-8136**).

VISITOR INFORMATION The **Florida Keys and Key West Visitors Bureau,** P.O. Box 1147, Key West, FL 33041 (☎ **800/FLA-KEYS**), offers a free vacation kit that's packed with useful information. The **Key West Chamber of Commerce,** 402 Wall St., Key West, FL 33040 (☎ **800/527-8539** or 305/294-2587), also offers general as well as specialized information. The lobby is open daily from 8:30am to 6pm; phones are answered 8am to 8pm. The Key West Visitor's Center also provides information on accommodations, goings-on, and restaurants; the number is ☎ **800/LAST-KEY.** They're open weekdays from 8am to 5:30pm and weekends from 8:30am to 5pm.

ORIENTATION A mere 2-by-4-mile island, Key West is simple to navigate, even though there is no real order to the arrangement of named streets and avenues. As you enter town on U.S. 1 (also called Roosevelt Boulevard), you will see most of the moderately priced chain hotels and fast-food restaurants. The better restaurants, shops, and outfitters are crammed onto Old Town's main thoroughfare, Duval Street. On surrounding streets are the many inns and lodges in picturesque Victorian/Bahamian homes. On the southern side of the island is the coral beach area and some of the larger resort hotels.

SEEING THE SIGHTS

✪ Audubon House & Tropical Gardens. 205 Whitehead St. (between Greene & Caroline sts.). ☎ **305/294-2116.** www.audubonhouse.com. Admission $7.50 adults, $3.50 children 6–12. Daily 9:30am–5pm (last admission at 4:45).

This well-preserved home dating from the early–19th century stands as a prime example of early Key West architecture and life. Named after the renowned painter and bird expert, John James Audubon, who was said to have visited the house in 1832, the graceful 2-story home is a peaceful retreat from the bustle of nearby Duval Street

Accommodations
Abaco Inn 18
Angelina Guesthouse 23
Big Ruby's 24
The Brass Key 4
Blue Lagoon Resort 1
Caribbean House 22
Chelsea House 13
The Grand 5
Island City House Hotel 7
Jabour's Trailer Court 11
Key West International Hostel 14
La Pensione 10
Marquesa Hotel 12
Oasis 8
Rainbow House 15
South Beach Oceanfront Motel 17
Southernmost Point Guest House 16
Wicker Guesthouse 19

Attractions
Aquarium 29
Audubon House & Tropical Gardens 26
Cemetery 9
Chamber of Commerce 30
East Martello Museum and Gallery 2
Ernest Hemingway Home and Museum 20
Fort Zachary Beach 25
Higgs Beach 6
Lighthouse Museum 21
Mallory Square 28
Mel Fisher Maritime Heritage Museum 27
Smathers Beach 3

and Mallory Square. Included in the price of admission is a self-guided audiotape tour that lasts just under half an hour. With voices of several characters from the house's past, the tour never gets boring—though it is at times a bit hokey. See rare Audubon prints, gorgeous antiques, historical photos, and lush tropical gardens, and, while you are at it, learn a little about the island's colorful history. Even if you don't want to spend the time and money to explore the grounds and home, check out the impressive gift shop, which sells a variety of fine mementos at reasonable prices.

Ernest Hemingway Home and Museum. 907 Whitehead St. (between Truman Ave. and Olivia St.). ☎ **305/294-1575** or 305/294-1136. Admission $6.50 adults, $4 children. Daily 9am–5pm.

One-time Key West resident Ernest Hemingway has become somewhat of a touristic icon down here; the novelist's gruff image is emblazoned on T-shirts and mugs and is used to sell everything from beer to suntan lotion. Hemingway's particularly handsome stone Spanish Colonial house was built in 1851 and was one of the first on the island to be fitted with indoor plumbing and a built-in fireplace. The author lived here

---

A Secret Refuge

Perhaps the most perfect retreat for any weary traveler is **Nancy's Secret Garden,** a peaceful shade garden nestled amid Key West's busy downtown. Nancy Forrester opened her haven to the public in 1994 in an effort to raise money to keep up the maintenance on this 1-acre miracle. She calls the site, which includes a small gallery and gift shop, a work of "installation art." There are no explanatory signs or recorded descriptions. This is a place for people who aren't looking to be educated, entertained, or enlightened. With the help of dedicated volunteers, she keeps the place open from 10am until 5pm every day. For a fee of $6, picnickers, nature lovers, or tourist-weary travelers can escape to the serene spot. To get there, walk down Duval Street, away from Mallory Square. Turn left on Fleming, and after 1 long block, turn right onto Simonton Street (just behind the Marquesa Hotel). On your left there will be a tiny alley named Free School Lane. The garden is just beyond the swinging wooden gates. There may or may not be a sign—Nancy can't decide.

---

from 1928 until 1940 along with about 50 six-toed cats, whose descendants still roam the walled-in premises. It was during those years that the Nobel Prize winner wrote some of his most famous works, including *For Whom the Bell Tolls, A Farewell to Arms,* and "The Snows of Kilimanjaro." Fans may want to take the optional half-hour tour. It's interesting and included in the price of admission.

Key West Cemetery. Entrance at Margaret and Angela sts. Free admission. Daily dawn to dusk. Tours can be arranged by calling **305/294-WALK.**

Epitomizing the quirky Key West image, this funky and picturesque cemetery is as irreverent as it is humorous. Many tombs are stacked several high, condominium style—the rocky soil made digging 6 feet under nearly impossible for early settlers. And pets are often buried beside their owners. Many of the memorials are emblazoned with nicknames—a common Key West informality that's literally taken to the grave. Look for headstones labeled "The Tailor," "Bean," "Shorty," and "Bunny." Other headstones also reflect residents' lighthearted attitudes toward life and death. "I Told You I Was Sick" is one of the more famous epitaphs, as is the tongue-in-cheek widow's inscription "At Least I Know Where He's Sleeping Tonight."

East Martello Museum and Gallery. 3501 S. Roosevelt Blvd. ☎ **305/296-3913.** Fax 305/296-6206. Admission $6 adults, $2 children 8–12, free for children 7 and under. Daily 9:30am–5pm (last admission is at 4pm).

Adjacent to the airport, the East Martello Museum is located in a Civil War–era brick fort that itself is worth a visit. The museum contains a bizarre variety of exhibits that, collectively, do a thorough job interpreting the city's intriguing past. Historical artifacts include ship models, a deep-sea diver's wooden air pump, a crude raft from a Cuban "boat lift," a supposedly haunted doll, a Key West–style children's playhouse from 1918, and a horse-drawn hearse. Exhibits illustrate the Keys' history of wrecking, sponging, and cigar making. And if all that's not enough, the museum also exhibits modern works by local artists. After seeing the galleries, climb a steep spiral staircase to the top of a lookout tower for good views over the island and ocean.

✪ **Key West Aquarium.** 1 Whitehead St. (at Mallory Square/Front St.). ☎ **305/296-2051.** Admission $8 adults, $4 children 4–12, free for children under 4. Tickets are good for 2 consecutive days (a bonus for kids with short attention spans). Look for discount coupons from local hotels, Duval Street kiosks, and from trolley and train tours. Daily 10am–6pm.

The oldest attraction on the island, the Key West Aquarium is a modest but fascinating exhibit. A long hallway of eye-level displays showcase dozens of varieties of fish and crustaceans. See delicate sea horses swaying in the backlit tanks. Kids can touch sea cucumbers and sea anemones in a shallow touch tank in the entryway. If you can, catch one of the free guided tours offered daily at 11am, 1, 3, and 4pm. Then you'll witness the dramatic feeding frenzy of the sharks, tarpon, barracudas, stingrays, and turtles.

Key West Lighthouse Museum. 938 Whitehead St. ☎ **305/294-0012.** Admission $6 adults, $2 children 7–12, free for children 6 and under. Daily 9:30am–5pm (last admission at 4:30pm).

When the Key West Lighthouse was opened in 1848, many locals mourned. Its bright warning to ships signaled the end of a profitable era for wreckers, pirate salvagers who looted reef-stricken ships. The story of this, and other Keys lighthouses, is illustrated in a small museum that was formerly the keeper's quarters. When radar and sonar made the lighthouse obsolete, it was opened to visitors as a tourist attraction. It's worth mustering the energy to climb the 88 claustrophobic steps to the top, where you'll be rewarded with magnificent panoramic views of Key West and the ocean.

✪ **Mel Fisher Maritime Heritage Museum.** 200 Greene St. (at Whitehead St.) ☎ **305/294-2633.** Fax 305/294-5671. Admission $6.50 adults, $2 children 6–12, free for children 5 and under. Open daily 9:30am–5pm.

This museum honors local hero Mel Fisher, who, along with a crew of other salvagers, found a multimillion-dollar treasure trove in 1985 aboard the wreck of the Spanish galleon *Nuestra Señora de Atocha*. The admission price is steep, but if you're into diving, pirates, and the mystery of sunken treasures, check out this small and informative museum, full of doubloons, pieces of eight, emeralds, and solid-gold bars. A dated but informative film provides a good background of Fisher's incredible story. The museum also features a new exhibit entitled "Battleship" about the USS *Maine*.

ORGANIZED TOURS

TROLLEY-BUS TOURS   Yes, it's more than a bit hokey to sit in these red cars, but worth the embarrassment. The city's whole story is packed into a neat, 90-minute package on the **Conch Tour Train,** which covers the island and all its rich, raunchy history. The "train's" engine is a propane-powered jeep disguised as a locomotive. Tours depart from both Mallory Square and the Welcome Center, near the intersection of U.S. 1 and North Roosevelt Boulevard, on the other side of the island. For more information, contact the Conch Train at 1 Key Lime Sq., Key West (☎ **305/294-5161;** fax 305/292-8993). The cost is $15 for adults, $7 for children 4 to 12, and free for children 3 and under. Daily departures are every half hour from 9am to 4:30pm.

The other option to get a good perspective on this history-packed island is the **Old Town Trolley.** Drivers maintain a running commentary as the open-air tram loops around the island's streets past all the major sights. The main advantage of this 90-minute tour is that riders can get off at any of 14 stops, explore a museum or visit a restaurant, and then reboard later at will. Trolleys depart from Mallory Square and other points around the island. For details, contact them at 1910 N. Roosevelt Blvd. (☎ **305/296-6688**). Tours are $16 for adults, $7 for children 4 to 12, and free for children 3 and under. Departures are daily from 9am to 4pm.

AIRPLANE TOURS   Proclaimed by the mayor as "the official air force of the Conch Republic," **Island Airplane Tours,** at Key West Airport, 3469 S. Roosevelt Blvd. (☎ **305/294-8687** for reservations), offers windy rides in its open-cockpit 1940

Waco biplanes over the reefs and around the islands. Thrill seekers—and they only—will enjoy a spin in the company's S2-B aerobatics airplane that does loops, rolls, and sideways figure eights. Company owner Fred Cabanas was "decorated" in 1991, after he spotted a Cuban airman defecting to the United States in a Russian-built MiG fighter. Sightseeing flights cost $50 to $200, depending on the duration.

BOAT TOURS ✪ The *Pride of Key West/Fireball,* at 2 Duval St. (☎ 305/296-6293; fax 305/294-8704), is a 58-foot glass-bottom catamaran that goes on both day and evening coral-reef tours and sunset cruises by evening. Reef trips cost $20 per person; sunset cruises are $25 per person and include snacks, sodas, and a glass of champagne.

The Wolf, at Schooner Wharf, Key West Seaport (☎ 305/296-9653; fax 305/294-8388), is a 44-passenger topsail schooner equipped with a cannon that sets sail daily for daytime and sunset cruises around the Keys. Key West Seaport is located at the end of Greene Street. Day tours cost $25 per person; sunset sails cost $30 per person and include champagne, wine, beer, or soda, and live music.

OTHER TOURS For a lively tour of Key West, try a 2-hour tour of Key West's five most famous pubs daily at 2:30. The tour takes 1½ hours, costs $21, and includes four drinks. Another fun and interesting tour for those into the paranormal is the nightly ghost tour that takes you to haunted hotels, pubs, and guest houses. Cost is $18 for adults and $10 for children. Guests report sightings periodically. Both are offered by **Key West Tour Association** (☎ 305/294-WALK). New in 1998 is a cemetery tour at 10:30am.

HITTING THE BEACH

At the end of the chain of Keys are finally a few beaches, though they do not compare to the state's natural and wide wonders up the coast. If you want to go to the beach, here are your options: **Smathers Beach,** off South Roosevelt Boulevard west of the airport; **Higgs Beach,** along Atlantic Boulevard between White Street and Reynolds Road; and **Fort Zachary Beach,** located off the western end of Southard Boulevard.

Although there is an entrance fee ($3.75 per car, plus more for each passenger), Fort Zachary is the most recommendable of the beaches, since it also includes a great historical fort, a Civil War museum, and a large picnic area with tables, barbecue grills, bathrooms, and showers.

GREAT GOLF THAT WON'T BREAK YOUR BUDGET & OTHER OUTDOOR ACTIVITIES

BICYCLING & MOPEDING A popular mode of transportation for locals and visitors, bikes and mopeds are available at many rental outlets in the city (see "Getting Around," above). Escape the hectic downtown scene and explore the island's scenic side streets. Head away from Duval Street to South Roosevelt Boulevard and the beach-side enclaves along the way.

DIVING One of the area's largest scuba schools, **Dive Key West,** 3128 N. Roosevelt Blvd. (☎ 800/426-0707 or 305/296-3823; fax 305/296-0609; www.divekeywest.com; e-mail: divekeywest@flakeysol.com), offers instruction on all levels. Dive boats take participants to scuba and snorkel sites on nearby reefs.

Wreck dives and night dives are two of the special offerings of **Lost Reef Adventures,** 261 Margaret St. (☎ 800/952-2749 or 305/296-9737). Regularly scheduled runs and private charters can be arranged. Phone for departure information.

FISHING Any fisher will tell you, there is no fishing like Keys fishing. From bone fish to tarpon to dolphin (mahimahi) and tuna, grouper to cobia and sharks, too, Key

West has it all. Besides diving and snorkeling, fishing is probably the most popular outdoor activity in the Keys and the most expensive, especially if you don't have your own boat. It is on the little open skiffs that you can find incredible diversity of fishing experiences in the same day. In the morning you can fish offshore for sailfish or dolphin and then by afternoon get a quick shot close to shore to pick up tarpon, permit, grouper, or snapper. Here in Key West you can probably find more cobia—one of the best fighting and eating fish around—than you will anywhere else in the world.

For another challenge, try tarpon, one of the most agile and acrobatic fighters in the sea. As soon as it's hooked, you'll see it do a dramatic walk on water called the "tail walk." Shark fishing is also popular.

For a look at real competition, watch the charter captains and their bookers in and around Mallory Square. Booking through one of the kiosks in town is usually the most costly way to go. Realize that most bookers earn 20% of a captain's fee per person in addition to an additional monthly fee. So you can usually save yourself some money by booking directly with a captain or going straight to one of the docks. You can negotiate a good deal at **Charter Boat Row,** at 1801 N. Roosevelt Ave. (across from the Shell station), home to more than 30 charter fishing and party boats. Whichever you are looking for, just show up to arrange your outing, or call **Garrison Bite Marina** (☎ 305/292-8167) for details.

The advantage of the more expensive but smaller charter boats is that you can call the shots, ask to go where you want, and catch what you want. These "light tackles" are easier to maneuver, which means you and one or two others can go to backcountry spots for tarpon and bonefish as well as out into the open ocean for tuna and dolphin. You'll really get to feel the fish and get some good fights.

Larger boats, which can carry up to six or seven people, work out to be cheaper and are best for catching kingfish, billfish, and sailfish.

Consider Jim Brienza's 27-foot *Sea Breeze,* docked at 25 Arbutus Dr. (☎ 305/294-6027), if you want a light tackle experience. Or, for a larger boat, try Capt. Henry Otto's 44-foot *Sunday,* docked at the Hyatt in Key West (☎ 305/294-7052).

The huge commercial party boats are more for sightseeing than serious angling, although you can get lucky and get a few bites at one of the fishing holes. One especially good deal is the *Gulfstream II* (☎ 305/296-8494). This all-day charter goes out daily from 9:30am until 4pm. You'll pay $30, plus $3 for a rod and reel. This 65-foot party boat usually has at least 30 other anglers. Bring your own cooler or buy snacks on the boat. Beer and wine are allowed.

However, for serious anglers, nothing compares to the light tackle boats that go out from **Oceanside Marina** (☎ 305/294-4676) in Stock Island, at 5950 Peninsula Avenue, 1½ miles off U.S. 1. It's a 20-minute drive from Old Town on the Atlantic side. Here there are more than 30 light tackle guides, which range from flatbed, backcountry skiffs to a 28-foot open fisherman. There are also a few larger charters and a head or party boat that goes to the Dry Tortugas. Call the dockmaster for details.

For the light tackle experience of your life, call Capt. Bruce Cronin at ☎ 305/294-4929 or Capt. Kenny Harris at ☎ 305/294-8843, two of the more popular and good-humored captains still working these docks.

Expect to pay from $450 to $500 for a full day, usually about 8am until 4pm and from $200 to $350 for half a day.

GOLF   One of the area's only courses is **Key West Golf Club,** an 18-hole course located just north of the island of Key West at MM 4.5 (turn onto College Road to the course entrance; ☎ 305/294-5232). Designed by Rees Jones, the course has plenty of mangroves and water hazards on its 6,526 yards. It's open to the public, and there's a new pro shop. Call ahead for tee-time reservations.

SHOPPING

Like any tourist destination, Key West has an abundance of tacky tourist shops. They also happen to have a wide variety of fantastic antique stores, designer boutiques, art galleries, and bookstores.

On Duval Street, T-shirt shops outnumber almost any other business. If you must get a wearable memento, be careful of unscrupulous salespeople. Despite efforts to curtail the practice, many shops have been known to rip off unwitting shoppers. A few too many Rum Runners sometimes result in some very expensive souvenirs. It pays to check the prices and the exchange rate before signing any sales slips. You are entitled to a written estimate of any T-shirt work before you pay for it.

At Mallory Square is the **Clinton Street Market,** an over-air-conditioned mall of kiosks and stalls designed for the many cruise-ship passengers who never venture beyond this extremely commercial zone. Amid the dreck are some delicious coffee and candy shops and some high-priced hats and shoes. There is also a free and clean rest room.

Once the main industry of Key West, cigar making is enjoying renewed success at the handful of factories that survived the slow years. Stroll through "Cigar Alley," between Front and Greene streets, where you will find *viejitos*—little old men rolling fat stogies just as they used to do in their homeland across the Florida Straits. Stop at the **Key West Cigar Factory,** at 308 Front St. (☎ 305/294-3470), for an excellent selection of imported and locally rolled smokes, including the famous El Hemingway. Remember, buying or selling Cuban-made cigars is illegal. Shops advertising "Cuban Cigars" are usually referring to domestic cigars made from tobacco grown from seeds that were brought from Cuba decades ago.

If you are looking for local or Caribbean art, you will find nearly a dozen galleries and shops clustered on Duval Street between Catherine and Fleming streets. You'll also find some excellent shops scattered on the side streets. One worth seeking out is the ✪ **Haitian Art Co.,** 600 Frances St. (☎ **305/296-8932**), where you can browse through room upon room of original paintings from well-known and obscure Haitian artists in a range of prices from a few dollars to a few thousand. Also, check out **Cuba, Cuba!** at 814 Duval St. (☎ **305/295-9442**). Here you will find paintings, sculpture, and photos by Cuban artists.

A favorite stop in the Keys is the deliciously fragrant **Key West Aloe.** Since 1971, this shop has been selling a simple line of bath products, including lotions, shampoos, and soothing balms for those who have spent too much time in the hot tropical sun. Sweet aromas waft from the several outlets in town. At the main shop (open until 8pm) you can find great gift baskets, tropical perfumes, and candies and cookies, too. In addition to frangipani, vanilla, and hibiscus scents, sample a fragrance called Key West for Men, a unique and alluringly musky best-seller. Stop by 524 Front St. (between Simonton and Duval streets), or call for a catalogue (☎ **305/ 294-5592**).

Literature buffs will appreciate the many book shops and record stores on the island. **Flaming Maggie's** at 800 Caroline St. carries a wide selection of gay books (☎ **305/294-3931**). **Key West Island Bookstore,** at 513 Fleming St. (☎ **305/ 294-2904**), carries new, used, and rare books and specializes in fiction by Key residents, including Hemingway, Tennessee Williams, Shel Silverstein, Ann Beattie, Richard Wilbur, and John Hersey. Both are open daily.

For anything else, from bed linens to candlesticks to clothing, go to downtown's oldest and most renowned department store, **Fast Buck Freddie's,** 500 Duval St. (☎ **305/294-2007**); it's open daily from 10am to 6pm in season, 11am to 7pm in the summer, and until 10pm most Saturdays and some evenings in season. For the same merchandise at more reduced prices, try ✪ **Half Buck Freddie's,** 726 Caroline St. (☎ **305/294-6799**). Here you can shop for out-of-season bargains and "rejects" from the main store. Half Buck is open on Thursday through Sunday only, from 11am to 5pm.

ACCOMMODATIONS YOU CAN AFFORD

You'll find a wide variety of places to stay in Key West, from resorts with all the ameni-ties to seaside motels, quaint bed-and-breakfasts, and clothing-optional guest houses. Unless you're in town during Key West's most popular holidays—Fantasy Fest (around Halloween), Hemingway Days (in July), Christmas and New Year's Eve—or a big fishing tournament, you can almost always find a place to stay at the last minute. However, you may want to book early, especially in the winter, when prime properties fill up and many require 2- or 3-night minimums. For real savings, try planning your Key West portion of your trip during the week.

Try Reservation Hotline of Key West, one of the most pleasant reservation services in town, to help you sort out the many small lodgings that couldn't all be reviewed here or to find a private home or condo. Rita Logan can help you find the perfect place; call ☎ **800/546-5397** or 305/745-9977 between 9am and 6pm, Monday through Saturday. During high season this service is open on Sunday, too. The **Key West Innkeepers Association,** P.O. Box 6172, Key West, FL 33041 (☎ **800/ 492-1911** or 305/292-3600), can also help find lodging in any price range from its dozens of members and affiliates.

Most major hotel chains have at least one location in Key West; many are clustered on North Roosevelt Boulevard (U.S. 1). Moderately priced options include **Howard Johnson,** 3031 N. Roosevelt Blvd. (☎ 800/942-0913 or 305/296-6595); the **Ramada Inn,** 3420 N. Roosevelt Blvd. (☎ 800/330-5541 or 305/294-5541); the **Econo Lodge,** 3820 N. Roosevelt Blvd. (☎ 800/553-2666 or 305/294-5511); the **Holiday Inn Beachside,** 3841 N. Roosevelt Blvd. (☎ 800/292-7706 or 305/ 294-2571); and the **Quality Inn,** 3850 N. Roosevelt Blvd. (☎ 800/228-5151 or 305/294-6681). The Howard Johnson and the Holiday Inn are the only hotels with gulf-view rooms; the other hotels listed are just across the street. You can drive or taxi to Duval Street in less than 5 minutes.

However, if you want to be closer to Key West's historic section and you like the idea of staying at a national chain, you might want to try **Holiday Inn La Concha Hotel** at 430 Duval St. (☎ **800/745-2191**). It is centrally located but room rates are high for a mediocre room (from $160 in-season). Like much of Key West, service here can be brusque. Avoid the Best Western Hibiscus Hotel, located at 1313 Simonton St. The property is in bad shape, management is rude, and prices are high.

Note that parking in Old Town is severely limited. There is a well-placed municipal parking lot at Simonton and Angela streets just behind the firehouse and police sta-tion. You may want to stash your car there while you enjoy the very walkable down-town section of Key West.

GAY-FRIENDLY ACCOMMODATIONS

Gay travelers will want to call the **Key West Business Guild** (☎ 305/294-4603), which represents more than 50 guest houses and B&Bs in town as well as many other gay-owned businesses. Ask for their 52-page color brochure. Or, try **Good Times Travel** (☎ 305/294-0980), which will set up package tours on the island.

One of the most elegant and popular gay guest houses is **Big Ruby's** (☎ 800/ 477-7829 or 305/296-2323) at 409 Applerouth Lane (a little alley just off Duval Street). A low cluster of buildings surround a lushly landscaped courtyard where a hearty breakfast is served each morning and wine is poured at dusk. The mostly male guests hang out by a good-sized pool tanning in the buff. Also popular is **Oasis** at 823 Fleming St. (☎ **305/296-2131**). It's superclean and friendly. Guests can enjoy a central location and a 14-seat hot tub.

Another luxurious property is **The Brass Key** at 412 Frances St. (☎ **305/ 296-4719**), which is more romantic and traditionally decorated and welcomes many lesbian travelers as well. *Out and About* gave them a five-star rating. For women only, the **Rainbow House** at 525 United St. (☎ **800-74/WOMYN** or 305/292-1450) is a large, gorgeous guest house with lots of amenities including two pools and two hot tubs.

If you're uncomfortable with nudity, be sure to ask if your accommodation is like most gay guest houses, which have a clothing-optional policy.

SUPER-CHEAP SLEEPS

Abaco Inn. 415 Julia St. (half a block from Duval St.), Key West, FL 33040. ☎ **800/ 358-6307** or 305/296-2212. Fax 305/295-0349. www.abaco-inn.com. E-mail: stay@ abaco-inn.com. 3 units, all with bathroom (showers only). A/C TV TEL. Winter $99 single or double. Off-season $59 single or double. Three-day minimum stay in season. Extra person $15. AE, DISC, MC, V.

This tidy little guest house is situated on a secluded lane just off Duval Street and offers all the conveniences of a larger and more expensive property. You'll find a hair dryer, iron and ironing board, little refrigerator, microwave, and coffeemaker and coffee and tea in each of the three simple rooms. Once the home of a cigar maker, the house dates from the early 1900s. Now, it is owned and operated by George Fontana, a smart and knowledgeable tour guide and writer. Look for his column on local characters in the *Key West Citizen*. Enjoy his gracious hospitality and lovely home. Smoking is not permitted on the property.

Angelina Guest House. 302 Angela St. (at the corner of Thomas St.) Key West, FL 33040. ☎ **305/294-4480.** Fax 305/294-0621. E-mail: gftk37a@prodigy.com. 15 units, 11 with bathroom (showers only). Winter $65–$70 single or double without bathroom; $79–$150 single or double with bathroom. Suite $175 for up to 6 people. Off-season $39–$49 single or double without bathroom; $49–$79 with bathroom; $95–$125 studio with kitchenette for up to 6 people. DISC, MC, V.

This youth hostel–looking guest house is well run by Robbie Byer, a bright-eyed refugee from Chicago and longtime Keys resident. His two historic buildings in the middle of Caribbean Village are about the cheapest in town and are conveniently located near a hot "hippie" restaurant called **Blue Heaven** (see "Great Deals on Dining," below) and also in a neighborhood known for occasional drug busts. Still, it is generally safe and full of character. The rooms are all furnished differently in a modest style. There are no televisions or telephones since Robbie believes guests should be out exploring Key West, not sitting in their rooms. "I don't even put chairs in the rooms," he explained. "I've even considered confiscating cell phones and beepers." Only six of the 15 rooms have air-conditioning, something to keep in mind on sweltering summer days. A good cross breeze and ceiling fans do cool the rooms considerably, though. It's sparse, but the Angelina is a good place to crash if you are on the cheap. During slow times, Robbie will negotiate rates.

Blue Lagoon Resort. 3101 N. Roosevelt Blvd., Key West, FL 33040-4118. ☎ 305/ 296-1043. Fax 305/296-6499. 72 units, all with bathroom (some with shower only). A/C TV TEL. Winter $80–$240 single or double. Off-season $50–$110 single or double. MC, V.

More than half of the rooms at this funky ocean-side resort rent for less than $100 year-round—an all-too-unusual occurrence in Key West, especially for full-service resorts. The pricier waterfront rooms aren't really worth the extra money (although some do include a jet-ski ride). The rooms, furnished in heavy cedar wood, are basic and a bit run-down but still decent—along the lines of a Howard Johnson or other budget accommodation. Second-floor rooms are generally quieter. Guests tend to be young college-aged kids looking for a wild time. Although pretty far from Old Town, the resort is convenient by scooter and car. And it is literally surrounded by WaveRunners, boats, parasailing, and diving fun.

Caribbean House. 226 Petronia St., Key West, FL 33040. ☎ **800/543-4518** or 305/296-1600. Fax 305/296-9840. 10 units, all with bathroom (shower only). Winter and special holidays, $69 single or double, $79–$89 cottage or penthouse. Off-season $49 single or double, $59 cottage or penthouse. Rates include continental breakfast. Extra person free. 1-night deposit by cashier's check required in advance. MC, V.

For the really budget-conscious, Key West offers a funky inn with 10 modest but brightly decorated rooms and two separate cottages. The walls behind the beds in the tiny but clean rooms have been painted with likenesses of elaborately styled headboards, and the rich turquoise and shocking pinks are reminiscent of a quaint Bahamian fish-shack—appropriate to this gingerbread home's location in the largely untouristed Bahama Village. The ghettolike neighborhood is what disturbs some visitors. Here you'll run into European backpackers, descendants of Bahamian immigrants, and local bohemians who share the streets with roosters, stray dogs, and the occasional wobbling drunk. The hospitable Jamaican hosts are happy to welcome a third guest to any room and will even provide an extra futon. Across the street is Blue Heaven and Blue Heaven Bakery, a hip and fantastically popular restaurant (see "Great Deals on Dining," below).

✪ **The Grand.** 1116 Grinnell St. (between Virginia and Catherine sts.), Key West. FL 33040. ☎ **888/947-2630** or 305/294-0590. www.conch.net/~thegrand/. E-mail: thegrand@conch. net. 10 units, all with bathroom (some with shower only). A/C TV TEL. Year-round $58–$98 single or double; $118 suite. AE, DISC, MC, V.

Don't expect locals to know about this gem. Opened in 1997, this little-known guest house wasn't even in the phone book its first or second year. Lucky for you! It's got everything you could want including a very moderate price tag. All rooms have private baths, air-conditioning, telephones, and private entrances. The floors are painted in bright colors and beds are dressed in light tropical prints. It's run by another one of those happy-to-be-alive Northeastern transplants, Elizabeth Rose, who goes out of her way to provide any and all services for her appreciative guests. Room no. 2 on the back side of the house is the best deal. And although it's small, it also has a porch and the most privacy. Suites are a real steal, too. The large two-room units come with a complete kitchen, which is outfitted with dishes and utensils. The house is in a modest residential section of Old Town, only about 7 blocks from Duval Street. With the exception of the youth hostel/motel, other accommodations in this price range tend to be in Caribbean Village, a more seedy part of Key West. This is without a doubt the best bargain in town.

✪ **Jabour's Trailer Court.** 223 Elizabeth St., Key West, FL 33040. ☎ **305/294-5723.** 30-plus mobile homes, all with bathroom; 6 units, 4 with bathroom (some with shower only). Winter $40–$55 camping spots; $105 single or double guest rm. with bathroom, $90 guest rm. without bathroom; $140–$200 mobile home for 1 to 4 people. Off-season $38–$50 camping spots; $65–$70 guest rm. without bathroom, $85 guest rm. with bathroom; $100–$150 mobile home for 1 to 4 people. Extra person $5–$20. Minimum stay required in season. MC, V.

It's so very Key West to have a trailer park in the middle of the most expensive real estate in town. This run-down spot offers a camping ground, a guest house, and a trailer park, all within steps to Mallory Square and Duval Street. You can rent large or small mobile homes and spots to park your camper, or you can pitch your own tent. The most recommendable accommodations here are in the quaint 2-story Walden House. Rooms are sparse but do offer private entrances, color television, and air-conditioning. The nicest and priciest have private bathrooms. The mobile homes vary in condition, but most are older and a bit threadbare. Still, all have full cooking facilities and are outfitted with linens and towels. Especially if you have the kids and/or pets in tow, the mobile homes can be a good option. You're bound to meet some real characters here. Especially during spring break (from March through April), this place is full of rowdy, economizing college students.

✪ **Key West International Hostel.** 718 South St., Key West, FL 33040. ☎ **800/ 51-HOSTEL** or 305/296-5719. Fax 305/296-0672. 86 beds, with shared bathroom (shower only) and 14 private motel rooms, all with bathroom (some with shower only). A/C TV. Winter $17 for IYHF members, $20 for nonmembers dorm beds; $75–$105 motel rm., single or double. Off-season from $15 for IYHF members, from $18 for nonmembers dorm beds; $50–$85 motel rm., single or double. DISC, MC, V.

This well-run hostel is a 3-minute walk to the beach and to Old Town. It's not the Ritz, but it's cheap. Very busy with European backpackers, this is a fine place to spend a few nights and a great place to meet people. The dorm rooms are dark and sparse but clean enough. The higher priced motel rooms are a good deal, especially those that are equipped with full kitchens. Facilities include a pool table under a tiki-hut roof and bicycle rentals for $6 per day. There is also cheap food available for breakfast, lunch, and dinner. As in all community living arrangements, you should keep an eye on your valuables. There are minisafes in each room.

FOR A FEW BUCKS MORE

Chelsea House. 707 Truman Ave., Key West, FL 33040. ☎ **800/845-8859** or 305/ 296-2211. Fax 305/296-4822. 20 units, all with bathroom (some with shower only). A/C TV TEL. Winter $128–$195 single or double; $360 apt. Off-season $75–$125 single or double; $250 apt. Rates include breakfast. Pets $10. AE, CB, DC, DISC, MC, V.

Despite its decidedly English name, the Chelsea House is "all American," a term that in Key West isn't code for "conservative." Chelsea House caters to a mixed gay/straight clientele with a liberal philosophy that exhibits itself most demonstratively on the clothing-optional sundeck.

One of only a few guest houses in Key West that offers TVs, VCRs, coffeemakers, and kitchenettes on request at no extra charge, Chelsea House has a large number of repeat visitors. The apartments come with full kitchens and a separate living area, as well as a palm-shaded balcony in back. The baths and closets could be bigger, but both are adequate and serviceable.

When weather permits (which is almost always), breakfast is served outside by the pool. There is private parking. However, note that children 14 and under are not permitted here.

Island City House Hotel. 411 William St., Key West, FL 33040. ☎ **800/634-8230** or 305/ 294-5702. Fax 305/294-1289. 24 units, all with bathroom (some with shower only). A/C TV TEL. Winter $165 studio, single or double; $195–$225 1-bedroom suite, single or double; $255–$285 2-bedroom suite, 1 to 4 people. Off-season $95 studio, single or double; $125–$155 1-bedroom suite, single or double; $165–$190 2-bedroom suite, 1 to 4 people. Rates include breakfast. AE, CB, DC, DISC, MC, V.

A little resort unto itself, the Island City House consists of three separate and unique buildings that share a common junglelike patio and pool. The Island City House shares its property name with one of the buildings on it, making descriptions more complicated. The Island City House building is a historic 3-story wooden structure with wraparound verandas that allow guests to walk around the entire edifice on any floor. The warmly dressed old-fashioned interiors include wood floors and many antique furnishings. Many rooms have full-size kitchens, queen-size beds, and sumptuous floral window treatments. The tile bathrooms could use more counter space, and the room lighting isn't always perfect, but eccentricities are part of this hotel's charm. The unpainted wooden Cigar House's particularly large bedrooms are similar in ambience to those in the Island City House. Most rooms are furnished with wicker chairs and king-size beds and enjoy big bathrooms that also suffer from a lack of counter space. As with the Island City House, rooms facing the property's interior courtyard are best. There, you'll find an outdoor heated pool and Jacuzzi. The hotel's Arch House is the least appealing of the three buildings, but still very recommendable. Built of Dade County pine, the Arch House's cozy bedrooms are furnished in wicker and rattan and come with small kitchens and bathrooms. Enjoy free coffee in the lobby.

✪ **La Pensione.** 809 Truman Ave. (U.S. 1 between Windsor and Margaret sts.), Key West, FL 33040. ☎ **800/893-1193** or 305/292-9923. Fax 305/296-6509. 9 units, all with bathroom (most with shower only). A/C TEL. Winter from $158 single or double with Frommer's discount. Summer from $98 single or double with Frommer's discount. Rates include large continental breakfast and represent a 10% discount for readers who mention this guide. AE, DC, DISC, JCB, MC, V.

This classic bed-and-breakfast in the 1891 home of a former cigar executive distinguishes itself from other similar inns by its extreme attention to details. The friendly and knowledgeable staff treats the stunning home and the guests with extraordinary care. Rooms, which are comfortable, all have air-conditioning, ceiling fans, king-size beds, and private bathrooms. Many have French doors opening onto spacious verandas. Although the rooms have no phones or televisions, you'll find the distractions of Duval Street, only steps away, keep you adequately occupied during your visit. Breakfast, which includes made-to-order Belgian waffles, fresh fruit, and a variety of breads or muffins, can be taken on the wraparound porch or at the communal dining table. No children are allowed.

South Beach Oceanfront Motel. 508 South St. (at the Atlantic Ocean), Key West, FL 33040. ☎ **800/354-4455** or 305/296-5611. Fax 305/294-8272. 50 units, all with bathroom (some with shower only). A/C TV TEL. Winter $105–$199 single or double. Off-season $69–$140 single or double. AE, MC, V.

This standard 2-story motel is located directly on the ocean, within walking distance of Duval Street. Because it is built perpendicular to the water, however, most of the rooms overlook a pretty Olympic-size swimming pool rather than a wide swath of beach. The best, and by far most expensive, rooms are those lucky two on the end (nos. 115 and 215) that are beachfront.

All rooms share similar aging decor and include standard furnishings. The smallish bathrooms could also use a makeover. At least most have tubs and showers. There's a private pier, an on-site water-sports concession, and a laundry room available for guest use. When booking, ask for a room that's as close to the beach (and as far from the road) as possible. If you'll be there a while, ask for one of the rooms with a kitchenette; there is no restaurant on the premises but plenty are nearby.

Southernmost Point Guest House. 1327 Duval St., Key West, FL 33040. ☎ **305/294-0715.** Fax 305/296-0641. 6 units, all with bathroom (some with shower only). A/C TV TEL. Winter $95–$175 single or double; $150 suite. Off-season $55–$125 single or double; $95 suite. Rates include breakfast. AE, MC, V.

One of the only inns that actually welcomes children and pets, this romantic and historic inn is a real find. Kids will enjoy the swings in the backyard and the pet rabbits.

The B&B's antiseptically clean rooms are not as fancy as the house's ornate 1885 exterior. Each room has basic beds and couches and a hodgepodge of furnishings, including futon couches, high-back wicker chairs, and plenty of mismatched throw rugs. Each room is different. Room 5 is best; situated upstairs, it has a private porch, an ocean view, and windows that let in lots of light. Every room has a refrigerator and a full decanter of sherry. Mona Santiago, the hotel's kind and laid-back owner, provides chairs and towels that can be brought to the beach, which is just a block away. Plus, guests can help themselves to wine as they soak in the new 14-seat hot tub.

Wicker Guesthouse. 913 Duval St., Key West, FL 33040. ☎ **800/880-4275** or 305/296-4275. Fax 305/294-7240. 18 units, 12 with bathroom (some with shower only). Winter $85–$95 single or double without bathroom, $155–$205 single or double with bathroom. Off-season $63 single or double without bathroom, $79–$89 single or double with bathroom. Rates include continental breakfast. Extra person $15 in winter, $10 off-season. AE, CB, DC, DISC, MC, V.

Occupying six separate buildings, one overlooking busy Duval Street, the Wicker offers some of the best-value accommodations in Key West (even since a recent boost in rates). The cheapest rooms are in the front of the complex. These have shared bathrooms and are predictably sparse, with no telephones, TVs, or even closets. The guest rooms get nicer, quieter, and more expensive the farther back on the property you go. Way back, beyond a kidney-shaped, heated swimming pool, are the guest house's top accommodations, each furnished with two double beds, cable TVs, and the ubiquitous wicker furnishings that give this house its name. Some have small kitchenettes. A few two-bedroom apartments are also available, a rare find in Key West guest houses. Three connected units share a living room and stoveless kitchen, and are particularly recommended for families and small parties. There's a communal kitchen for guests' use and a pay phone by the pool.

WORTH A SPLURGE

✪ **Marquesa Hotel.** 600 Fleming St. (at Simonton St.), Key West, FL 33040. ☎ **800/869-4631** or 305/292-1919. Fax 305/294-2121. 40 units, all with bathroom. A/C MINIBAR TV TEL. Winter $215–$325 single or double. Off-season $135–$235 single or double. AE, DC, MC, V.

One of my very favorite properties in Florida, the Marquesa offers all the charm of a small historic hotel with the amenities of a large resort. The Marquesa encompasses four different buildings, two adjacent swimming pools (one heated), and a three-stage waterfall that cascades into a lily pond. Two of the hotel's houses are luxuriously restored Victorian homes with rooms outfitted with extraplush antiques and oversize contemporary furniture. The rooms in the two newly constructed buildings are even richer, some of which include four-poster wrought-iron beds with bright floral spreads. The green-marble baths are lush and spacious. The decor is simple, elegant, and spotless. It is the only hotel room I have ever seen that I would like my home to resemble. An adjacent restaurant is pricey and popular. No children under 12 are allowed.

GREAT DEALS ON DINING

Key West offers a vast and tempting array of food. You'll find most every ethnicity represented, from Thai to Cuban, plus the usual drive-through franchises (mostly up on Roosevelt Boulevard). There is even a Hard Rock Cafe on Duval Street. Wander Old Town and browse menus after you have exhausted the list below. Or, if you don't feel like venturing out, you can call **We Deliver** (☎ 305/293-0078), a service that for a small fee (between $3 and $6) will bring you anything you want from any area restaurants or stores. We Deliver operates between 3 and 11pm. **Fausto's Food Palace,** operated since 1926, will deliver groceries, beer, wine, or snacks to stock your fridge (☎ **305/294-5221** or 305/296-5663). Fausto's has a $25 minimum.

For a quick bite or a beach picnic, take out some freshly fried chicken from **Dion's Quick Mart,** at 1127 Truman Avenue 9 ☎ **305/294-7572.** This gas station/minimart serves fresh hot chicken pieces for between 45¢ and $1.40. Full meals are less than $3.

SUPER-CHEAP EATS

The Deli. 926 Simonton St. (corner of Truman), Key West. ☎ **305/294-1464.** Full meals $5–$13. sandwiches, $2–$7. DISC, MC, V. Daily 7:30am–9:30pm. DINER/AMERICAN.

Here since 1950, this family owned corner eatery has kept up with the times. It's really more of a diner than a deli and has a vast menu with all kinds of hearty options from meat loaf to yellowtail snapper, plus more healthful options like salads and pastas. Avoid the lobster sandwich, which is fried and a bit greasy. Other seafood options, however, are good. A daily selection of more than a dozen vegetables includes the usual diner choices of beets, corn, and cole slaw, with some distinctly Caribbean additions like rice and beans and fried plantains. Most dinners include a choice of two vegetables and homemade biscuits or corn bread. Breakfasts, too, are made to order and attracts a loyal following of locals. Plus, you can get great ice-cream sundaes and gourmet coffees.

✪ **El Siboney Restaurant.** 900 Catherine St. (at Margaret St.). ☎ **305/296-4184.** Main courses $5–$13. No credit cards. Mon–Sat 11am–9pm. CUBAN.

For good, cheap Cuban food, stop at this corner dive that looks more like a gas station than a diner. Be prepared however, to wait like the locals for succulent roast pork, Cuban sandwiches, grilled chicken, and ropa vieja, all served with heaps of rice and beans. This tiny storefront is a worthwhile and very affordable choice in a town with lots of glossy tourist traps.

PT's Late Night. 920 Caroline St. (at the corner of Margaret St.). ☎ **305/296-4245.** Main courses $5–$14; lunch $5–$12. DISC, MC, V. Daily 11am–4am. AMERICAN.

This place is worth knowing about not only because it's one of the only places in town serving food past 10pm, but because it also happens to serve good food at extremely reasonable prices. The sports-bar atmosphere might make you wonder, but I've never been disappointed. Service can be a bit slow and brusque, but let's say it's 1am, you're starving, and you've just parked your bike outside—you'll be ecstatic when that heaping plate of nachos arrives. Fajitas are served sizzling hot with a huge platter of fixings, including beans, rice, lettuce, jalapeños, and tomatoes. Superfresh salads are so big they can be a meal in themselves. There are nightly specials, like corned beef and cabbage on Monday and roast turkey with all the trimmings on Thursday. This place is worth knowing about at any time of day.

FOR A FEW BUCKS MORE

✪ **Blue Heaven.** 729 Thomas St. (at the corner of Petronia St., in Bahama Village). ☎ **305/ 296-8666.** Reservations not accepted. Main courses $9–$23; lunch $5.25–$12; breakfast $3–$8.50. DISC, MC, V. Mon–Sat 8am–3:30pm and 6–10:30pm, Sun 8am–1pm and 6–10:30pm. SEAFOOD/AMERICAN/NATURAL.

You'll wait in line forever at this little hippie-run gallery and restaurant, which has become the place to be in Key West—and with good reason. This ramshackle Mediterranean Revival house serves up some of the best food in town, especially for breakfast. In this former bordello, where Hemingway was said to hang out watching cockfights, you can enjoy homemade granolas, huge tropical fruit pancakes, and seafood Benedict. Dinners are just as good and run the gamut from just-caught fish dishes to

Jamaican-style jerk chicken, curried soups, and vegetarian stews. But if you are a neat freak, don't bother. The dirt floors and roaming cats and birds put off some people. A bakery/coffeehouse has opened next door and has proved a big hit.

Mangia, Mangia. 900 Southard St. (at Margaret St.). ☎ **305/294-2469.** Reservations not accepted. Main courses $9–$14.50. AE, MC, V. Daily 5:30–10pm. ITALIAN/AMERICAN.

A low-key Italian trattoria, Mangia, Mangia is one of Key West's best values. Locals appreciate that they can get inexpensive and good food here in a town of so many tourist traps. Off the beaten track, in a little corner storefront, you'll find this great Chicago-style pasta place serving some of the best Italian food in the Keys. The family-run restaurant offers superb homemade pastas of every description, including one of the tastiest marinaras around. The simple grilled chicken breast that's brushed with olive oil and sprinkled with pepper is a tasty dish, too. You wouldn't know it from the glossy glass front room, but there's a fantastic little outdoor patio dotted with twinkling chile pepper lights and lots of plants. There's often a wait for one of the tables outside when the weather permits, so relax out back with a glass of one of their excellent wines or homemade beer while you wait.

✪ **Mangoes.** 700 Duval St. (at Angela St.). ☎ **305/292-4606.** Reservations recommended for parties of 6 or more. Main courses $12–$24; pizzas $10–$12; lunch $7–$14. AE, CB, DC, DISC, MC, V. Daily 11am–midnight, pizza until 1am. Upstairs bar, Limbo, 7pm–4am. AMERICAN/REGIONAL.

The restaurant's large brick patio draped with greenery, directly on Duval, is so seductive to passersby that it's packed most every night of the week. The food and service are some of the best in the Keys. Mangoes enjoys a good buzz among locals, and even competitors envy the restaurant's servers, who are some of the best on Duval. Appetizers include conch chowder laced with sherry, lobster dumplings with tangy key lime sauce, and grilled shrimp cocktail with spicy mango chutney. Spicy sausage with black beans and rice, crispy curried chicken, and local snapper with passion fruit sauce are typical among the entrees, but Mangoes' outstanding individual-size designer pizzas are the best menu items by far. They're baked in a Neapolitan-style oven that's fired by buttonwood.

✪ **Pepe's.** 806 Caroline St. (between Margaret and Williams sts.). ☎ **305/294-7192.** Main courses $11–$20; lunch $5–$9; breakfast $2–$9. DISC, MC, V. Daily 6:30am– 10:30pm. AMERICAN.

This old dive has been serving good, basic food for nearly a century. Steaks and Apalachicola Bay oysters are the big draw for regulars who appreciate the rustic barroom setting and historic photos on the walls. See original scenes of Key West in 1909, when Pepe's first opened. If the weather is nice, choose a seat on the patio under a stunning mahogany tree. Burgers, fish sandwiches, and standard chili satisfy hearty eaters. Buttery sautéed mushrooms and rich mashed potatoes are the best comfort food in Key West. Stop by early for breakfast when you can get old-fashioned chipped beef on toast and all the usual egg dishes. In the evening enjoy reasonably priced cocktails on the deck.

Turtle Kraals Wildlife Grill. 213 Margaret St. (at Caroline). ☎ **305/294-2640.** Main courses $12–$18. DISC, MC, V. Mon–Thurs 11am–1am, Fri–Sat 11am–2am. SOUTHWESTERN/ SEAFOOD.

You'll join lots of locals in this out-of-the-way converted warehouse that serves innovative seafood at great prices. Try the twin lobster tails stuffed with mango and crabmeat or any of the big quesadillas or fajitas. Kids will like the wildlife exhibits and the very cheesy menu. Be careful not to double tip. Like some other local spots, a 15% tip is already included on the tab. Greedy servers have been known to double dip. Blues bands play most nights. There's never a cover.

WORTH A SPLURGE

Antonia's. 615 Duval St. Key West. ☎ **305/294-6565.** Reservations suggested. Main courses $17–$24; pastas $12–$15. Daily 6–11pm. AE, DC, MC, V. NORTHERN ITALIAN.

The food is great but the atmosphere a bit fussy for Key West. If you don't have a reservation in season, don't bother. The management is less than accommodating. Still, if you are organized and don't mind paying high prices for dishes that elsewhere go for much less, try this old standby. From the perfectly seasoned homemade focaccia to an exemplary crème brûlée, this elegant little standout is amazingly consistent. The menu, a small selection of classics like zuppa di pesce, rack of lamb in a rosemary sauce, and veal marsala never disappoint. But the way to go is with the nightly specials. If offered, try the flaky and tender mutton snapper served with a light anchovy cream sauce (or your choice). The presentation is simple but elegant; the sauce, perfectly subtle. You can't go wrong with either fresh pastas or beef dishes.

✪ **Bagatelle.** 115 Duval St. ☎ **305/296-6609.** Reservations recommended. Main courses $16–$24; lunch $5–$12. AE, DC, DISC, MC, V. Daily 11:30am–3pm and 5:30–10pm. SEAFOOD/TROPICAL.

Reserve a seat at the elegant second-floor veranda overlooking Duval Street's mayhem. From the calm above enjoy any of the selections from this large menu. You may want to start your meal with the excellent herb-and-garlic stuffed whole artichoke or the sashimi-like seared tuna rolled in black peppercorns. One of the best pastas is a lightly creamy garlic-herb pasta topped with gulf shrimp, Florida lobster, and mushrooms. The best chicken and beef dishes are given a tropical treatment, grilled with papaya, ginger, and soy.

✪ **Louie's Backyard.** 700 Waddell Ave. ☎ **305/294-1061.** Reservations highly recommended. Main courses $25–$30; lunch $8–$15. AE, CB, DC, MC, V. Daily 11:30am–3pm and 6–10:30pm. CARIBBEAN CONTEMPORARY.

Louie's, once known as Key West's most elegant restaurant, has lost its luster. Still nestled amid blooming bougainvillea on a lush slice of the gulf, the spot remains one of the most romantic on earth. Unfortunately, the gorgeous real estate doesn't improve the uneven food, sluggish service, and snooty attitude. Part of the problem seems to be that the kitchen doors seem to be constantly swinging. Depending on who is cooking, you may or may not have an interesting or tasty meal. Try the weekend brunches, which tend to be more reliable than dinners. Or, to be assured of a satisfying splurge, just sit at the dockside bar and enjoy a cocktail and bar snacks and watch the glorious sunset over the sea.

KEY WEST AFTER DARK

Duval Street is the Bourbon Street of Florida. Amid the T-shirt shops and clothing boutiques you'll find bar after bar serving stiff drinks to revelers who bounce from one to another. Bands and crowds vary from night to night and season to season. Your best bet is to start at Truman Avenue and head up Duval to check them out for yourself. Cover charges are mostly unheard of, so stop in at a dozen and see which you like.

One of Duval's largest entertainment complexes, **Durty Harry's,** 208 Duval St. (☎ **305/296-4890**), features live rock bands almost every night. You can wander to one of the many outdoor bars or head up to **Upstairs at Rick's,** an indoor/outdoor dance club that gets going late. For the more racy singles or couples, there is the **Red**

Garter, a pocket-size strip club popular with bachelor and divorced parties. The hawker outside reminds couples, "The family that strips together sticks together."

You'll have to stop into **Sloppy Joe's,** at 201 Duval St. (☎ **305/294-5717**), just to say you did. Scholars and drunks debate whether this is the same Sloppy Joe's that Hemingway wrote about, but there's no argument that this classic bar's turn-of-the-century wooden ceiling and cracked tile floors are Key West originals. The popular and raucous bar is crowded with tourists almost 24 hours a day, and there's almost always live music.

Named after another Key West legend, **Jimmy Buffett's Margaritaville Cafe,** at 500 Duval St. (☎ **305/292-1435**), is another worthwhile stop. Although Mr. Buffett moved to glitzy Palm Beach years ago, his name is still attracting large crowds. This kitschy restaurant/bar/gift shop features live bands every night—from rock to blues to reggae and everything in between. The touristy cafe is furnished with plenty of Buffett memorabilia, including gold records, photos, and drawings. The margaritas are high priced but tasty. The cheeseburgers, however, aren't worth singing about.

Just around the corner from Duval's beaten path is **Captain Tony's,** 428 Greene St. (☎ **305/294-1838**), which is about as authentic as you'll find. The smoky old wooden bar comes complete with old-time regulars who remember the island before cruise ships docked here; they say Hemingway drank, caroused, and even wrote here. Owner Capt. Tony Tarracino, a former and controversial Key West mayor, has recently capitalized on the success of this once-quaint tavern by franchising the place.

Limbo, a secret little hideaway above the well-known restaurant **Mangoes** (see "Great Deals on Dining," above), is a great bar with all kinds of music ranging from house/techno to calypso, rock 'n' roll, jazz, blues, and classical guitar; they boast, "We've had it all." Cozy individual booths allow patrons to talk while catching a great view of the crowd that sometimes dances in the small space near the outside deck.

THE GAY SCENE

In Key West, the best music and dancing can be found at the predominantly gay clubs. While many of the areas other hot spots are geared toward tourists who like to imbibe, the gay clubs are for those who want to rave—mostly locals (or at least, recent transplants). None of the spots described here discriminate—anyone open-minded and fun is welcome.

The gay nightlife was once dominated by The Copa. However, an arsonist put an end to the former legend in 1995. Back and better than ever in its place at 623 Duval St. is a bigger, more modern club called ✪ **Epoch** (☎ **305/296-8521**). The music is still an eclectic mix, with everything from techno to house to disco. But with a bigger dance floor, a huge outside deck overlooking Duval Street, and a new state-of-the-art sound system, this is a better choice than ever for people of any orientation who appreciate a good dance club. Another popular late-night spot is **One Saloon,** 524 Duval St. (☎ **305/296-8118**), featuring great drag and lots more disco. A mostly male clientele frequents this hot spot from 9pm until 4am. Escape to the outdoor garden bar if it gets too steamy inside.

Sunday nights are fun at two local spots. **Tea by the Sea,** on the pier at the Atlantic Shores Motel, 510 South St. (☎ **305/296-2491**), attracts a faithful following of regulars and visitors alike. Show up after 7:30pm. Better known around town as La-Te-Da, **La Terraza,** at 1125 Duval St. (☎ **305/296-6706**), is a great spot to gather poolside for the best martini in town—but don't bother with the food.

5 The Dry Tortugas

70 miles W of Key West

As long as you've come this far, you might as well take a trip to the Dry Tortugas, especially if you are into bird watching, which is the primary draw of these seven small islands. Because of their remoteness, few people realize that Florida's Keys don't end at Key West.

Ponce de León, who discovered this far-flung cluster of coral keys in 1513, named them "las Tortugas" because of the many sea turtles, which still flock to the area during the nesting season in the warm summer months. Oceanic charts later carried the preface "dry" to warn mariners that fresh water was unavailable here.

Modern intervention has made drinking water available, but little else. Now, rustic campers come for the very lack of amenities that these islands offer.

Popular with serious bird watchers, these islands are nesting grounds and roosting sites for thousands of tropical and subtropical oceanic birds.

A stopping point for migratory birds on the eastern flyway, these keys are populated with many West Indian bird species, especially during spring and fall. The small vegetated islands of the Keys are the only nesting sites in the United States for the great white heron and the white-crowned pigeon. The islands are also one of a very few breeding places for the reddish egret, the roseate spoonbill, the mangrove cuckoo, and the black-whiskered vireo.

These underdeveloped islands make a great day trip for any travelers interested in seeing the truly natural anomalies of the Florida Keys. You'll find a historical fort, snorkeling, good fishing, and terrific snorkeling around shallow reefs.

GETTING THERE   The **Yankee Fleet,** based in Key West (☎ **800/634-0939** or 305/294-7009), offers day trips from Key West for sightseeing, snorkeling, or both. Cruises leave daily from the Land's End Marina, at Margaret Street at 7:30am, and breakfast is served onboard. The journey takes 3 hours. Once on the island, you can join a guided tour or explore Garden Key on your own. Boats return to Key West by 7pm. Tours cost $85 per person, including breakfast; $50 for children 16 and under; $70 for seniors, students, and military personnel. Snorkeling equipment rental is free. Phone for reservations.

The best option for air service from Key West to the Dry Tortugas is **Seaplanes of Key West,** based at Key West Airport (☎ **800/950-2FLY** or 305/294-0709). Flights, departing at 8am, 10am, noon, and 2pm, are almost twice as fast as the competitors. The 40-minute flight at about 500 feet offers a great introduction to these little-known islets. Fares for adults start at $159 for half-day trips and $275 for full-day excursions that include snorkeling equipment and a cooler for use on the island. Rates for kids under 12 are discounted by about 30%. Call for detailed rate schedules and flight plans.

EXPLORING THE DRY TORTUGAS

Fort Jefferson, a huge six-sided 19th-century fortress, is built almost to the water's edge of Garden Key, giving the appearance that it floats in the middle of the sea. The monumental structure is surrounded by formidable 8-foot-thick walls that rise up from the sand to nearly 50 feet. Impressive archways, stonework, and parapets make this 150-year-old monument a grand sight. With the invention of the rifled cannon, the fort's masonry construction became obsolete, and the building was never completed. For 10 years, from 1863 to 1873, Fort Jefferson served as a prison, a kind of "Alcatraz East." Among its prisoners were four of the "Lincoln Conspirators," including Samuel A. Mudd, the doctor who set the broken leg of fugitive assassin John Wilkes Booth. In 1935 Fort Jefferson became a national monument administered by the National Park Service.

BIRD WATCHING　Bring your binoculars and your bird books. This is the reason to visit this little cluster of tropical islands that are tagged onto the southernmost tip of the United States. The islands, uniquely situated in the middle of the migration flyway between North and South America, serve as an important rest stop for the more than 200 winged varieties that pass through here annually. The season peaks from mid-March to mid-May, when thousands of birds—including thrushes, orioles, boobies, swallows, noddy, and snooty terns—show up. In season, a continuous procession of migrant birds fly over or rest at the islands. About 10,000 terns nest here each spring, and many other species from the West Indies can be found here year-round.

DIVING & SNORKELING　The warm, clear, and shallow waters of the Dry Tortugas combine to produce optimum conditions for snorkeling and scuba diving. Four endangered species of sea turtles—the green, leatherback, Atlantic ridley, and hawksbill—can be found here, along with myriad marine life. The region just outside the seawall of Garden Key's Fort Jefferson is excellent for underwater touring; an abundant variety of fish, corals, and more live in just 3 or 4 feet of water.

FISHING　Snapper, tarpon, grouper, and other fish are common, and fishing is popular. A saltwater fishing permit is mandatory and costs $7 for 3 days and $17 for 7 days. No bait or boating services are available in the Tortugas, but there are day docks on Garden Key as well as a cleaning table. Waters are roughest during winter, but the fishing is excellent year-round. Outfitters from Key West can arrange day charters to the islands (see "Great Golf That Won't Break Your Budget & Other Affordable Outdoor Activities," above). Or contact **Florida Fish Finder,** 8262 NW 58th St., Miami, FL 33166 (☎ **305/513-9955;** fax 305/513-9955), specializing in 2- and 3-day fishing trips to the Dry Tortugas. The rugged 115-foot fishing boat leaves from Stock Island, MM 5 (about 5 miles north of Key West). Two-day trips leave Friday night, return Sunday afternoon, and cost $200 per person. The price includes sleeping accommodations in bunk beds, bait, and tackle, but not food. For an extra fee, you can purchase breakfast, lunch, and dinner, or bring your own cooler of food and snacks. Three-day trips leave the last Friday morning of every month, return the following Sunday afternoon, and cost $240 per person. Phone for reservations. Bring a towel, your camera, a cooler, and a bathing suit. This is real ocean adventure.

CAMPING

The rustic beauty of tiny Garden Key is a camper's dream. You won't be sharing your site with noisy RVs or motor homes; they can't get here. This is the most isolated spot in Florida. The abundance of birds doesn't make it quiet, but camping here—literally a stone's throw from the water—is as picturesque as it gets. Campers are allowed to pitch tents only on Garden Key. Picnic tables, cooking grills, and toilets are provided, but there are no showers. All supplies must be packed in and out. Sites are free and are available on a first-come, first-served basis. No stoves are permitted. For more information about Fort Jefferson and the Dry Tortugas, call the National Park Service (☎ **305/242-7700**).

The National Parks of South Florida: The Everglades & Beyond

by Victoria Pesce Elliott

Within an hour's drive of downtown Miami are two of the country's largest and most valuable natural resources: Everglades National Park and Biscayne National Park. These full-fledged, federally designated national parks make Miami-Dade County the only county in United States to contain two such parks. Also nearby is Big Cypress National Preserve, a remote, enormous expanse of land set aside for the benefit of the surrounding parklands; consequently, the preserve is slightly less accessible for visitors.

The largest and oldest of the parks, Everglades National Park was described poetically as the "river of grass" by the late conservationist Marjory Stoneman Douglas. And she was right; the Everglades is actually a shallow, 40-mile-wide, slow-moving river. Rarely more than knee-deep, the water is the lifeblood of this wilderness. Subtle shifts in water level dictate the life cycle of plants and animals. Most folks viewed it as a worthless swamp until Ms. Douglas focused attention on the area with her moving, insightful book *The Everglades: River of Grass,* published in 1947.

It was that same year that 1.5 million acres—less than 20% of Everglades wilderness—were established as Everglades National Park. At that time, few lawmakers understood how neighboring ecosystems relate to each other: You can't just chop off a chunk of a much larger wilderness and expect it to survive. The land is intimately affected by its surroundings; it's the butt end that suffers for every environmental insult occurring upstream.

Indigenous wildlife has been on the decline here, but the Everglades remains one of the few places where you can see dozens of endangered species in their natural habitat, including the swallowtail butterfly, American crocodile, leatherback turtle, southern bald eagle, West Indian manatee, and Florida panther. In addition to the hundreds of species of mammals, reptiles and amphibians, more than 300 species of birds, 120 species of trees, and 25 types of orchids coexist in a rugged landscape of murky swamps, freshwater marshes, and mangrove forests.

The slow and subtle splendor of this exotic terrain may not be immediately appealing to kids raised on video games and rapid-fire commercials, but they'll certainly remember the experience and no doubt thank you for it later.

Meanwhile, you'll find plenty of dramatic diversions around the park, like airboat rides, alligator wrestling, and biking to keep the kids satisfied for at least a day. For most families and others who aren't especially intrigued with nature, 1 day is probably plenty of time to spend in and around the park.

Less accessible but equally important to the fragile and bruised ecosystem that makes up South Florida, Biscayne National Park is a paradise for snorkelers and divers who have access to this 181,500-acre underwater preserve. Several islands, informative boat tours, primitive camping, and an abundance of sea life make it a destination for anyone interested in spending a day in this uncommercialized, exotic place.

Before taking off, be sure to note some of the dangers particular to these wild playgrounds. Also, familiarize yourself with the park rules by picking up a Park newspaper available at any of the visitor centers. See "Just the Facts," below.

1 Everglades National Park

35 miles SW of Miami

In the 1800s, before the southern Everglades was designated a national park, the only inhabited piece of this wilderness was a quiet fishing village called Flamingo. Accessible only by boat and leveled every few years by hurricanes, the mosquito-infested town never grew very popular. When the 38-mile road from Florida City was completed in 1922, many of those who did live here fled to someplace either more or less remote. Today, Flamingo is a center for visitor activities and the main jumping-off point for backcountry camping and exploration. Flamingo is now home to employees of the National Park Service and the concessionaires and their families.

Everglades National Park's northern Shark Valley entrance and the eastern approaches described in this section are the most accessible from Miami and the rest of Florida's east coast. You'll find many diversions along the way, like Indian villages, alligator farms, and boat rides. An excellent tram tour goes deep into the park along a trail that's also terrific for biking. This is also the best way to reach the park's only accommodation (and full-service outfitters), the Flamingo Lodge.

There are hiking trails also from Everglades City, the western gateway to Everglades National Park. This entrance provides access to a maze of islands and swamps that can be reached only by boat and is home to a number of recommendable boat tours of the area. For more information on the town of Everglades City, including lodging and dining options there, see section 2 of this chapter.

JUST THE FACTS

GETTING THERE & ACCESS POINTS   Everglades National Park has four entrances. The three described below are the most popular and the ones most convenient to visitors from Florida's east coast, including Miami. No matter which part of Miami you start in, the drive should take no longer than an hour. However, if you're traveling during rush hour—between 8 and 9:30am or from 4 until 6pm—the roads, especially S.R. 836, will be backed up, and your driving time could be doubled. If you're coming from Florida's west coast, use the fourth entrance in Everglades City. See section 2 of this chapter for details.

The **main entrance,** in Homestead on the park's east side, is located 10 miles southwest of Florida City. From Miami, take S.R. 836 west to the Florida Turnpike south until it ends in Florida City. Signs will point you southwest onto the road that leads into the park, S.R. 9336. The main entrance's Park Ranger Station is open 24 hours.

The **Shark Valley entrance,** on the park's north side, is located on the Tamiami Trail (U.S. 41), about 35 miles west of downtown Miami. From Miami, take S.R. 836 west to the Florida Turnpike south; exit on Tamiami Trail (U.S. 41), and go west for approximately 30 miles. The park will be on your left side. Shark Valley is known for its 15-mile trail loop that's used for biking, walking, and an excellent interpretive tram tour. This entrance is open daily from 8:30am to 5:30pm, with some seasonal variation. Call ahead to make sure it's open when you want to go.

Chekika, popular with day visitors, picnickers, and campers, is located halfway between the two entrances above in the northeast section of the park. Chekika can be reached from Miami as if going to Shark Valley (see above). After exiting on Tamiami Trail (Highway 41), head west 5 miles to Krome Avenue (177th Avenue); turn left, then proceed to SW 168th Street (Richmond Avenue) and head west (left) until you reach a stop sign. Turn right; the entrance will be on the left side. There are picnic facilities and a 20-site campground here. You can enter at Chekika from 8:30am until sundown.

VISITOR CENTERS & INFORMATION   General inquiries and specific questions should be directed to **Everglades National Park Headquarters,** 40001 S.R. 9336, Homestead, FL 33034 (☎ **305/242-7700**). Ask for a copy of *Parks and Preserves,* a free newspaper that's filled with up-to-date information on goings-on in the Everglades. Headquarters are staffed by helpful phone operators daily from 8:30am until 4:30pm.

Note that all hours listed are for the high season, generally November through May. During the slow summer months, many offices and outfitters keep abbreviated hours.

The Flamingo Lodge, Marina and Outpost Resort, in Flamingo (☎ **800/ 600-3813** or 941/695-3101), is the one-stop clearinghouse and the only option for in-park accommodations, equipment rentals, and tours.

Especially since its recent expansion, the **Ernest F. Coe Visitor Center,** located at the park's main entrance, is the best place to stop to gather information for your trip. In addition to free brochures outlining trails, wildlife and activities, and information on tours and boat rentals, you will also find state-of-the-art educational displays, films, and interactive exhibits. A gift shop sells postcards, film, unusual gift items, the best selection of books about the Everglades, and your most important gear: insect repellent. It is open from 8am until 5pm daily.

The **Royal Palm Visitor Center,** a small nature museum located 3 miles past the park's main entrance, is a smaller information center at the head of the popular Anhinga and Gumbo-Limbo trails and is open daily from 8am until 4pm.

The **Shark Valley Information Center** at the park's northern entrance and the **Flamingo Visitor Center** are also staffed by knowledgeable rangers who provide brochures and personal insight into the goings-on in the park. They are open from 8:30am until 5pm.

ENTRANCE FEES, PERMITS & REGULATIONS   Permits and passes can be purchased at either the main park entrance, the Chekika entrance, or the Shark Valley entrance stations only.

Even if you are just visiting Everglades National Park for an afternoon, you'll need to buy a 7-day permit, which costs $10 per vehicle. Pedestrians and cyclists are charged $5 each and $4 at Shark Valley.

An **Everglades Park Pass,** valid for a year's worth of unlimited entrances, is available for $20. U.S. citizens may purchase a 12-month **Golden Eagle Passport** for $50, which is valid for entrance into any U.S. national park. U.S. citizens aged 62 and older pay only $10 for a **Golden Age Passport** that's valid for life. A **Golden Access Passport** is available free to U.S. citizens with disabilities.

Permits are required for campers wanting to stay overnight either in the backcountry or in primitive campsites. See "Camping & Houseboating in the Everglades," in "Accommodations You Can Afford," below.

Everglades National Park

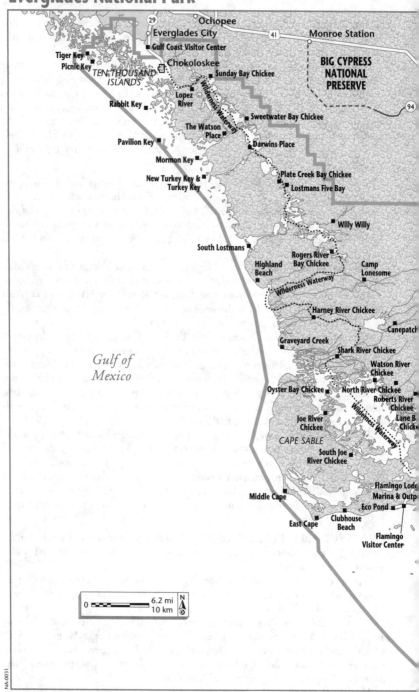

Ochopee
Everglades City
29
Gulf Coast Visitor Center
41
Monroe Station
Chokoloskee
Tiger Key
Picnic Key
TEN THOUSAND ISLANDS
Sunday Bay Chickee
BIG CYPRESS NATIONAL PRESERVE
94
Lopez River
Rabbit Key
Sweetwater Bay Chickee
The Watson Place
Pavilion Key
Darwins Place
Mormon Key
Plate Creek Bay Chickee
New Turkey Key & Turkey Key
Lostmans Five Bay
Willy Willy
South Lostmans
Rogers River Bay Chickee
Camp Lonesome
Highland Beach
Wilderness Waterway
Gulf of Mexico
Harney River Chickee
Canepatch
Graveyard Creek
Shark River Chickee
Watson River Chickee
Oyster Bay Chickee
North River Chickee
Roberts River Chickee
Lane B Chick
Joe River Chickee
Wilderness Waterway
CAPE SABLE
South Joe River Chickee
Flamingo Lodg
Marina & Outp
Middle Cape
Eco Pond
East Cape
Clubhouse Beach
Flamingo Visitor Center

0   6.2 mi
     10 km
N

NA-0031

226

Tamiami Trail

27
997
826
112
836

Miami

Miccosukee
Indian
Village

Shark Valley
Information Center

Tram Tour

41

Florida's Turnpike
874
1

Chekika — Richmond Dr.

Krome Ave.

997

BISCAYNE
NATIONAL
PARK

Pay-Hay-Okee
Overlook

Homestead

SW 137th
Ave.

North Canal Dr.
SW 328th St.

Convoy Point
Visitor Center

ELLIOTT KEY

9336

Florida City

Long Pine Key

Main Visitor
Center

Royal Palm
Visitor Center

Palm Dr.

Card Sound Rd.

Old
Ingraham

Ernest Coe

Hell's Bay
Canoe Trail

Nine Mile Pond
Canoe Trail

Noble Hammock
Canoe Trail

KEY LARGO

North
Nest
Key

JOHN PENNEKAMP
CORAL REEF
STATE PARK

THE
FLORIDA
KEYS

Florida Bay

1

Atlantic Ocean

Safety Alert

Especially in the hot summer months, **insects** are the most common enemy you'll encounter here. Be sure to bring bug repellent and wear long sleeves and pants. **Poisonous snakes** also inhabit the marshy areas of the parks. Keep alert. It's a good idea to wear boots or sneakers and socks when walking along the water's edge and in heavy brush.

Despite action movies that would have you believe otherwise, **alligators** almost never attack humans who are minding their own business. There are plenty of these prehistoric-looking creatures roaming the brackish, shallow waters in and around the park. Keep your distance and don't feed them. Doing so is extremely dangerous to them and may be to you as well. Besides the other obvious risks, you could get arrested.

Those who want to fish without a charter captain must obtain a standard State of Florida saltwater **fishing license.** These are available in the park at Flamingo Lodge or any tackle shop or sporting goods store nearby. Nonresidents will pay $17 for a 7-day license and $7 for 3 days. Florida residents can get a fishing license good for the whole year for $14. Snook and crawfish licenses must be purchased separately at a cost of $2.

Charter captains carry **vessel licenses** that cover all paying passengers. Ask to be sure. Freshwater fishing licenses are available at various bait and tackle shops outside the park at the same rates. A good one close by is **Don's Bait & Tackle** located at 30710 S. Federal Hwy. in Homestead right on U.S. 1. (☎ **305/247-6616**). Most of the area's freshwater fishing, limited to murky canals and artificial lakes near housing developments, is hardly worth the trouble when so much good saltwater fishing is available.

Firearms are not allowed anywhere in the park.

SEASONS   There are two distinct seasons in the Everglades: high season and mosquito season. High season is also dry season, lasting approximately from late November to May. Despite the bizarre cold and wet weather patterns that El Niño brought in 1998, most winters here are warm, sunny and breezy—a good combination to keep the bugs away. This is the best time to visit, as low water levels attract the largest variety of wading birds and their predators. As the dry season wanes, wildlife follows the receding water, and by the end of May, the only living things you are sure to spot will cause you to itch. The worst, called "no see-ums," are not even swat-able. If you choose to visit during the buggy season, be sure to be vigilant in applying bug spray.

Also, realize that many establishments and operators either close or curtail offerings in the summer, so always call ahead to check schedules.

RANGER PROGRAMS   More than 50 ranger programs, free with admission, are offered each month during high season and give visitors an opportunity to gain an expert's perspective. Some programs occur regularly, such as **Glade Glimpses,** a walking tour during which rangers point out flora and fauna and discuss issues affecting the Everglades' survival. These tours are scheduled at 10:15am, noon, and 3:30pm daily. The **Anhinga Ambles,** a similar program that takes place on the Anhinga Trail, starts at 10:30am, 1:30pm, and 4pm.

A more interesting program, the **Slough Slog,** is offered occasionally. On this journey, participants wade into the park and through the muck, stopping at an alligator hole, which is a particularly interesting and vital ecological community unto itself. Lace-up shoes and long pants (preferably ones you don't care about) are required on this walking trip. On Saturday and Sunday rangers can choose programs they want to offer in some time slots.

Park rangers tend to be helpful, well informed, good-humored, and happy to answer questions. Since times, programs, and locations vary from month to month, check a schedule, available at any of the visitor centers (see above).

SAFETY There are dangers inherent in this vast wilderness area. Always let someone know your itinerary before you set out on an extended hike. It's mandatory that you file an itinerary when camping overnight in the backcountry. When on the water, watch for weather changes; severe thunderstorms and high winds often develop very rapidly. Swimming is not recommended because of the presence of alligators, sharks, and barracudas. Watch out for the region's four indigenous poisonous snakes: diamondback and pygmy rattlesnakes, coral snakes (identifiable by their colorful rings), and water moccasins (which swim on the surface of the water). And bring insect repellent to ward off mosquitoes and biting flies.

First aid is available from park rangers. The nearest hospital is in Homestead, 10 miles from the park's main entrance.

SEEING THE HIGHLIGHTS

Shark Valley provides a fine introduction to the wonder of the Everglades, but visitors shouldn't expect to spend more than a few hours there. Bicycling or taking a guided tram tour can be a satisfying experience, but neither fully captures the wonders of the park. Likewise, boaters who choose to explore via the Everglades City entrance to the park are likely to see a lot of mangroves and not much else.

If you want to see a greater array of plant and animal life, make sure that you venture into the park through the main entrance, pick up a trail map, and dedicate at least a day to exploring from there.

Stop first along the **Anhinga** and **Gumbo-Limbo trails,** which start right next to one another, 3 miles from the park's main entrance. These trails provide a thorough introduction to Everglades flora and fauna and are highly recommended to first-time visitors. There's more water and wildlife here than in most parts of the Everglades, especially during dry season. Alligators, turtles, river otters, herons, egrets, and other animals abound, making this one of the best trails for seeing wildlife. Arrive early to spot the widest selection of exotic birds; like the Anhinga Trail's namesake, a large black fishing bird that is so used to humans that many of these birds build their nests in plain view. Others travel deeper into the park during daylight hours. Take your time—at least an hour is recommended. If you treat the trails and modern boardwalk as pathways to get through quickly, rather than destinations to experience and savor slowly, you'll miss out on the still beauty and hidden treasures that await.

Those who love to mountain bike, and who prefer solitude, might check out the infrequently traveled **Old Ingraham Highway.** This dirt road delves deeper into the Glades and isn't used by most visitors. Since this pathway is sometimes closed, check at the visitor center when you arrive.

Also, it's worth climbing the observation tower at the end of the quarter-mile-long **Pa-hay-okee Trail.** The panoramic view of undulating grass and seemingly endless vistas gives the impression of a semiaquatic Serengeti. Flocks of tropical and semitropical birds traverse the landscape, alligators and fish stir the surface of the water, small grottoes of trees thrust up from the sea of grass marking higher ground, and the vastness of the hidden world you've entered seems unparalleled.

If you want to get closer to nature, a few hours in a canoe along any of the trails
allows paddlers the chance to sense the park's fluid motion, and to become a part of
the ecosphere. Visitors who choose this option end up feeling more like explorers than
merely observers. (See "Affordable Outdoor Activities in the Everglades," below.)

No matter which option you choose (and there are many), I strongly recommend
staying for the 7pm program, available during high season at the Long Pine Key
Amphitheater. This talk by one of the park's rangers, along with the accompanying
slide show, gives a detailed overview of the park's history, natural resources, wildlife,
and threats to its survival.

AFFORDABLE OUTDOOR ACTIVITIES IN THE EVERGLADES

BIKING   The relatively flat 38-mile paved Main Park Road is excellent for bicycling, as are many park trails, including Long Pine Key. Cyclers should expect to spend
2 to 3 hours along the path.

If the park isn't flooded from excess rain (which it often is, especially in spring),
Shark Valley in Everglades National Park is South Florida's most scenic bicycle trail.
Many locals haul their bikes out to the Glades for a relaxing day of wilderness-trail
riding. You can ride the 17-mile loop with no cars in sight. Instead, you'll share the
flat paved road only with other bikers and a menagerie of wildlife. Don't be surprised
to see a gator lounging in the sun or a deer munching on some grass. Otters, turtles,
alligators, and snakes are common companions in the Shark Valley area.

You can rent bikes at the **Flamingo Lodge, Marina and Outpost Resort** (see
"Accommodations You Can Afford," below) for $17 per 24 hours, $14 per full day,
$8.50 per half day (any 4-hour period), and $3 per hour. Bicycles are also available
from **Shark Valley Tram Tours,** at the park's Shark Valley entrance (☎ **305/
221-8455**), for $3.25 per hour; rentals can be picked up any time after 8:30am and
must be returned by 4pm.

BIRDING   More than 350 species of birds make their homes in the Everglades.
Tropical birds from the Caribbean and temperate species from North America can be
found here, along with exotics that have blown in from more distant regions. Eco and
Mrazek ponds, located near Flamingo, are two of the best places for birding, especially
in early morning or late afternoon in the dry winter months. Pick up a free birding
checklist from a visitor center (see "Just the Facts," above), and ask a park ranger what's
been spotted in recent days.

BOATING   Motorboating around the Everglades seems like a great way to see plants
and animals in remote habitats. However, environmentalists are taking stock of the
damage motorboats (especially airboats) inflict on the delicate ecosystem (see "Airboat
Tours," below). If you choose to motor, remember that most of the areas near land are
"no wake" zones, and for the protection of nesting birds, landing is prohibited on most
of the little mangrove islands. There's a long list of restrictions and restricted areas, so

get a copy of the park's boating rules from National Park Headquarters before setting out (see "Just the Facts," above).

The Everglades' only marina—accommodating about 50 boats with electric and water hookups—is the **Flamingo Lodge, Marina and Outpost Resort,** located in Flamingo. The well-marked channel to Flamingo is accessible to boats with a maximum 4-foot draft and is open year-round. Reservations can be made through the marina store (☎ **941/695-3101,** ext. 304). Skiffs with 15-horsepower motors are available for rent. These low-power boats cost $90 per day, $65 per half day (any 5-hour period), and $22 per hour. A $50 deposit is required.

CANOEING   The most intimate view of the Everglades comes from the humble perspective of a simple low boat. From a canoe, you'll get a closer look into the park's shallow estuaries where water birds, sea turtles, and endangered manatees make their homes.

Everglades National Park's longest "trails" are designed for boat and canoe travel, and many are marked as clearly as walking trails. The **Noble Hammock Trail,** a 2-mile loop, takes 1 to 2 hours, and is recommended for beginning canoers. The **Hell's Bay Trail,** a 3- to 6-mile course for hardier paddlers, takes 2 to 6 hours, depending on how far you choose to go. Park rangers can recommend other trails that best suit your abilities, time limitations, and interests.

Canoes can be rented at the **Flamingo Lodge, Marina and Outpost Resort** (see "Accommodations You Can Afford," below) for $40 for 24 hours, $32 per full day, $22 per half day (any 4-hour period), and $8 per hour. They also have family canoes that rent for $12, $30, $40, and $50, respectively. A deposit is required. Skiffs, kayaks, and tandem kayaks are also available. The concessionaire will shuttle your party to the trailhead of your choice and pick you up afterward. Rental facilities are open daily from 6am to 8pm.

FISHING   About one-third of Everglades National Park is open water. Freshwater fishing is popular in brackish Nine-Mile Pond (25 miles from the main entrance) and other spots along the Main Park Road, but because of the high mercury levels found in the Everglades, freshwater fishers are warned not to eat their catch. Before casting, check in at a visitor center, as many of the park's lakes are preserved for observation only. Fishing licenses are required. See "Just the Facts," above.

Saltwater anglers will find that snapper and sea trout are plentiful. Charter boats and guides are available at Flamingo Lodge, Marina and Outpost Resort (see "Accommodations You Can Afford," below). Phone for information and reservations.

ORGANIZED TOURS

AIRBOAT TOURS   Shallow-draft, fan-powered airboats were invented in the Everglades by frog hunters who were tired of poling through the rushes. And though it is the most efficient way to get around, airboats are not permitted in the park. Just outside the boundaries are many outfitters offering rides. These shallow-bottom runabouts tend to inflict severe damage on the animals and plants there. If you choose to ride on one, you may consider bringing earplugs; these high-speed boats are also *loud.* Airboat rides are offered at the **Miccosukee Indian Village,** just west of the Shark Valley entrance on U.S. 41, the Tamiami Trail (☎ **305/223-8380**). Native American guides will take you through the reserve's rushes at high speed and stop along the way to point out alligators, native plants, and exotic birds. Prices are just $7.

Also, the **Everglades Alligator Farm,** 4 miles south of Palm Drive/S.R. 9336 and on SW 192 Ave. (☎ **305/247-2628**), offers half-hour guided airboat tours from 9am until 6pm daily. The price, which includes admission to the park, is $12 for adults, $6 for children.

MOTORBOAT TOURS   Both Florida Bay and backcountry tours are offered at the **Flamingo Lodge, Marina and Outpost Resort** (see "Accommodations You Can Afford," below). Both are available in 1½- and 2-hour versions that cost an average of $16 adults, $8 children, under 6 free. There are also charter-fishing and sightseeing boats that can be booked through the main reservation number (☎ 941/695-3101). Florida Bay tours cruise nearby estuaries and sandbars, while six-passenger backcountry boats visit smaller sloughs. Tours depart throughout the day, and reservations are recommended.

TRAM TOURS   At the park's Shark Valley entrance, open-air tram buses take visitors on 2-hour naturalist-led tours that delve 7½ miles into the wilderness. At the trail's midsection, passengers can disembark and climb a 65-foot observation tower that offers good views of the Glades. The tour offers visitors considerable views that include plenty of wildlife and endless acres of saw grass. Tours run November to April only, daily from 9am to 4pm, and are sometimes stalled by flooding or particularly heavy mosquito infestation. Reservations are recommended from December to March. The cost is $8 for adults, $4 for children 12 and under, and $7 for seniors. For further information, contact the Shark Valley Tram Tours at ☎ 305/221-8455.

SHOPPING

Florida City is home to the **Keys Factory Shops,** an outlet mall. See "Shopping" for the Upper and Middle Keys in chapter 6 for details.

A necessary stop and good place for a refreshment is one of Florida's best-known fruit stands, **Robert Is Here** (☎ 305/246-1592). Robert has been selling homegrown treats for nearly 40 years at the corner of SW 344th Street (Palm Drive) and SW 192nd Avenue. You'll find the freshest and biggest pineapples, bananas, papayas, mangos, and melons anywhere, as well as his famous shakes in unusual flavors like key lime, coconut, orange, and cantaloupe. Exotic fruits, bottled jellies, hot sauces, and salad dressings are also available. This is a great place to pick up culinary souvenirs and sample otherwise unavailable goodies. Open daily 8am until 7pm.

Along Tamiami Trail there are several roadside shops hawking Indian handicrafts including one at the **Miccosukee Indian Village** (☎ 305/223-8380) just west of the Shark Valley entrance. At nearly every one you'll find the same stock of feathered dream-catchers, stuffed alligator heads and claws, turquoise jewelry, and other trinkets. However, do note the unique and colorful handmade cloth Miccosukee dolls.

ACCOMMODATIONS YOU CAN AFFORD

The only lodging in the park proper is the Flamingo Lodge, a fairly priced and very recommendable option. However, here are a few slightly better priced hotels just outside the park, near the entrances and highways.

Though bugs can be a major nuisance, especially in the warm months, camping is really the way to go in this very primitive environment. There are dozens of campsites and chickee platforms (see below for details) for tenters. In addition to the rooms, cottages, houseboats, and campsites described below, the town of Everglades City at the western edge of the park has more lodging options, including the historic Rod & Gun Lodge. See section 2 of this chapter for more information.

IN & AROUND EVERGLADES NATIONAL PARK

✪ **Flamingo Lodge, Marina and Outpost Resort.** 1 Flamingo Lodge Hwy., Flamingo, FL 33034. ☎ **800/600-3813** or 941/695-3101. Fax 941/695-3921. 127 units, all with bathroom (some with shower only). A/C TV TEL. High season $95–$135 single or double;

$135–$145 cottage or suite for 1 to 4 people. Off-season $65–$99 single or double; $99–$110 cottage or suite for 1 to 4 people. Rates include continental breakfast from May through October. Children under 18 stay free. AE, DC, DISC, MC, V. The lodge is 35 miles southwest of the main entrance to the park.

The Flamingo Lodge is the only lodging actually located within the boundaries of Everglades National Park. This woodsy, sprawling complex offers rooms overlooking the Florida Bay in either a 2-story simple motel or the lodge.

Either option is very much like being at summer camp, except there are a few more amenities. VCRs and videos are available for guests in the regular rooms or in the suite, but not in more primitively outfitted cottages. Still, the cottages are an especially good choice if you plan to stay more than a night or two, because they come with small kitchens equipped with dishes and flatware (though no televisions). The cottages are also larger and more private, almost romantic.

Facilities on the premises include a waterside bar and restaurant, a freshwater swimming pool, convenience store, gift shop, coin laundry, bike, canoe and kayak rental, and full-service marina. The hotel is open year-round, although the restaurant (see "Great Deals on Dining in & Around the Park," below) closes in the summer. Reservations are accepted daily from 8am to 5pm. Guests are treated to free coffee in the lobby.

CAMPING & HOUSEBOATING IN THE EVERGLADES

Campgrounds are available in Flamingo and Long Pine Key, where more than 300 campsites are on hand for tents and RVs. They have level parking pads, tables, and charcoal grills, but no electrical hookups, and showers are cold water. Private ground fires are not permitted, but supervised campfire programs are conducted during winter months. Reservations may be made in advance through **Destinet** at ☎ **800/365-CAMP.** Campsites are $14 per night with a 14-day consecutive stay limit, 30 days a year maximum.

Camping is also available in the backcountry year-round on a first-come, first-served basis, and is only accessible by boat, foot, or bicycle. Campers must register in person or by telephone no more than 24 hours prior to the start of their trip. Permits must be obtained at ranger stations in either Flamingo or Everglades City. Campers can use only designated campsites, which are plentiful and well marked on visitor maps.

Many backcountry sites are **chickees,** covered wooden platforms on stilts. They're accessible only by canoe and can accommodate freestanding tents (without stakes). Ground sites are located along interior bays and rivers, and beach camping is also popular. In summer especially, mosquito repellent is necessary gear.

Houseboat rentals are one of the park's best-kept secrets. Available through the Flamingo Lodge, Marina and Outpost Resort, motorized houseboats make it possible to explore some of the park's more remote regions without having to worry about being back by nightfall. You can choose from two different types of houseboats. The first, a 40-foot pontoon boat, sleeps six to eight people in a single large room that's separated by a central head (bathroom) and shower. There's a small galley (kitchen) that contains a stove, oven, and charcoal grill. Prices aren't cheap unless you're in a good-sized group. It rents for between $340 and $475 for 2 nights (there's a 2-night minimum in high season).

The newer, sleeker Gibson fiberglass boats sleep six; each has a head and shower, air-conditioning, and electric stove. They also come with full rooftop sundecks. These rent for $575 for two nights (with a 2-night minimum). With either boat, the 7th night is free when renting for a full week.

If you choose this option, boating experience is helpful, but not mandatory; the boats only cruise up to 6 miles per hour and are surprisingly easy to use. In-season reservations should be made months in advance; call **Flamingo Lodge, Marina and Outpost Resort** (☎ **800/600-3813** or 941/695-3101).

NEARBY IN HOMESTEAD & FLORIDA CITY

Homestead and Florida City are about 35 miles south of Miami and 10 miles from the park's main entrance along U.S. 1, these somewhat rural towns offer several budget lodging options, including a handful of chain hotels. Among them are a very recommendable **Days Inn** (☎ **305/245-1260**) in Homestead and a **Hampton Inn** (☎ **800/426-7866** or 305/247-8833) right off the turnpike in Florida City.

Super-Cheap Sleeps

✪ **Best Western Gateway to the Keys.** 1 Strano Blvd. (U.S. 1), Florida City, FL 33034. ☎ **800/528-1234** or 305/246-5100. Fax 305/242-0056. 114 units, all with bathroom. A/C TV TEL. Winter from $84 single or double; from $99 suite. Off-season from $70 single or double; from $95 suite. Rates include continental breakfast. During races and very high season there may be a 3-night minimum. AE, DC, DISC, MC, V.

Opened in late 1994, this 2-story, pink-and-white Best Western offers contemporary style and comfort about 10 miles from the park's main entrance. A decent-sized pool and a small spa are especially attractive. Each identical standard room has bright, tropical bedspreads and oversize picture windows. The suites offer convenient extras like a microwave, coffeemaker, an extra sink, and a small fridge. Overall, this business-oriented hotel is well priced and well maintained, and is the best choice in the area. The only drawback is that in season, there is often a 3-day minimum-stay requirement. You'd do best to call the local reservation line instead of the toll-free number. On several occasions, the hotel made an exception to the rule while the central reservation line was not able to.

Everglades Motel. 605 S. Krome Ave., Homestead, FL 33030. ☎ **305/247-4117.** 14 units, all with bathroom (some with shower only). A/C TV TEL. Winter $39 single, $43 double. Off-season $29 single, $32 double. Additional person $5. AE, DISC, MC, V.

This 1-story hotel is probably the cheapest option you can find in Homestead, but certainly not the greatest. There is a small swimming pool, coin laundry and free coffee in the lobby. Though not thoroughly fluent in English, the East Indian staff is accommodating and friendly. Rooms are modest in size and decor, but could use a good scrubbing. Nonetheless, the place is safe, very affordable and perfectly fine for 1 or 2 nights. Make your local calls from here; they're free.

GREAT DEALS ON DINING IN & AROUND THE PARK

You won't find fancy nouvelle cuisine in this suburbanized farm country, but there are plenty of fast-food chains along U.S. 1, and a few old favorites worth a taste. For dining options in the western part of the park, see section 2 of this chapter.

Here for nearly a quarter of a century, **El Toro Taco,** 1 S. Krome Ave., near Mowry Drive and Campbell Drive (☎ **305/245-8182**), opens daily at 9:30 am and stays crowded until at least 9pm most days. The fresh grilled meats, tacos, burritos, salsas, guacamole, and stews are mild and delicious. No matter how big your appetite, it's hard to spend more than $12 per person at this Mexican outpost. You'll have to bring your own beer or wine.

Housed in a squat, 1-story, windowless stone building that looks something like a medieval fort, the **Capri Restaurant,** 935 N. Krome Ave., Florida City (☎ **305/ 247-1542**), has been serving hearty Italian American fare since 1958. Great pastas and salads complement a full menu of meat and fish dishes. Portions are big. They serve lunch and dinner every day (except Sunday) until 11pm.

Another landmark is **Potlikker's,** 591 Washington Ave. (at the corner of NE 6th Street), in Homestead (☎ **305/248-0835**), featuring fried fish and shrimp baskets, along with barbecued chicken and ribs, roast pork, grilled fish, and lots of local veggies. It's good, unadulterated Southern feed at popular prices. Full meals cost from $6 to $16. The kitchen is open every day from 7am until 9pm.

The **Miccosukee Restaurant** (☎ **305/223-8380**), just west of the Shark Valley entrance on the Tamiami Trail (U.S. 41), serves authentic pumpkin bread, fry bread, fish, and not-so-authentic Native American interpretations of tacos and fried chicken. This interesting spot is worth a stop for brunch, lunch or dinner, served daily from 8am until 3pm. Meals cost from $5 to $14.

Once inside the Everglades, you may want to try the only restaurant within the boundaries of this huge park. The **Flamingo Restaurant** (☎ **941/695-3101**), in the Flamingo Lodge (see "Accommodations You Can Afford," above), is a very civilized and affordable restaurant; the large, airy dining room has a spectacular view of Florida Bay and a few of the Keys. The large menu has something for everyone but focuses on fresh fish, including my very favorite, mahi-mahi. Also on hand are basic and very tasty sandwiches, pastas, burgers, and salads. A kid's menu has several standard choices like hot dogs, grilled cheese, or fried shrimp for less than $6. Prices are surprisingly moderate, with full meals starting at about $11 and going no higher than $22. You may need reservations for dinner, especially in season.

2 Everglades City: The Western Gateway to the Everglades

The brainchild of advertising magnate Barron Collier, who funded the completion of the Tamiami Trail from Miami to Naples, Everglades City was conceived as a major center of activity on Florida's west coast.

While building the highway in the 1920s, Collier dredged a channel through the Ten Thousand Islands and created a new island with the spoil, upon which he laid out Everglades City. Although it became a popular hunting and fishing destination for the rich and famous, Everglades City never became the metropolis he had hoped for. In 1947, Everglades National Park took in most of the land and bays around the town.

Everglades City is an isolated little town with one school, a post office and a bank as well as a dozen or so seafood restaurants, some motels and B&Bs and a few tourist shops. It lies in the Ten Thousand Islands area, and the Wilderness Waterway twists and turns 99 miles from here all the way to Flamingo at the southwestern edge of the Everglades. This makes the town a perfect starting point for canoe or boat explorations of the area.

ESSENTIALS

GETTING THERE   Take I-75 or U.S. 41 east to S.R. 29 and turn south to Everglades City. S.R. 29 runs through town and then over a causeway along beautiful Chokoloskee Bay to Chokoloskee Island, an old Calusa shell mound that's the highest point in the Everglades.

VISITOR CENTERS & INFORMATION   The National Park's **Gulf Coast Visitor Center,** on S.R. 29 at the south end of Everglades City (☎ **941/695-3311;** fax 941/695-3621), offers information and advice to visitors during the high season from 8:30am to 4:30pm, and intermittently in the summer.

The **Everglades City Area Chamber of Commerce,** P.O. Box 130, Everglades City, FL 34139 (☎ **941/695-3941;** fax 941/695-3919), provides information on tours and outfitters operating near the park's northwestern entrance, at the intersection of U.S.

41 and S.R. 29. See section 1 of this chapter for information sources within the national park. They are open every day from 9am until 5pm.

AFFORDABLE OUTDOOR ACTIVITIES NEAR EVERGLADES CITY

BIKING   In Everglades City, a 4-mile paved bike path runs from town across a picturesque causeway to Chokoloskee Island. The **Ivey House Bed & Breakfast,** 107 Camellia St., 1 block behind the Circle K store (☎ **941/695-3299**), rents bikes during the winter months for $3 per hour or $15 for the day November to May. It's open from 8:30am to 4:30pm.

BIRDING   Pick up a free brochure on area birds at the visitor center. (Also, see "Boat Tours," below.)

CANOEING   Canoes are one of the best ways to cruise through these shallow waters, frequented by gators, manatees, and dolphins. The vessels are available at Everglades City, near the Park Ranger Station at the Everglades' western entrance; and from **North American Canoe Tours,** 107 Camelia St., Everglades City (☎ **941/695-4666** November to April, or 860/739-0791 May to October; fax 941/695-4155 November to April). The 17-foot aluminum canoes can be rented with or without camping equipment, a personal guide, or fully outfitted tour. Canoes cost $20 per day. Canoes with camping supplies cost $50 per person per day.

For information about boat tours, hiking, canoeing, boating, fishing, and other outdoor activities in the park, see section 1 of this chapter.

SEEING THE SIGHTS BY WATER

You can wander a few trails and relax in this pristine park and visit the simple attractions below, but most of the sights in this region are accessible only after you leave land. Try at least one of the tours below for a look at the beautiful natural wilderness.

AIRBOAT TOURS   Flat-bottom, airplane propeller-driven airboats can take two people to large groups speeding across the waterways. They operate on privately owned property, since they're not allowed in the national park or other nearby federal preserves.

The most advertised and touristy operator is **Wooten's Everglades Adventure,** on U.S. 41, two miles east of S.R. 29 (☎ **800/282-2781** or 941/695-2781). This large operation has airboat and swamp-buggy rides, an alligator farm, gift shop, and snack bar. Buggy and boat rides cost $13.25 each. Admission to the alligator farm is $6.36 (free for children 6 and under). Combined tickets for both rides and a visit to the farm are about $30. Wooten's is open daily from 8:30am to 5pm. Discount coupons are available from the visitor center.

In town on S.R. 29, **Jungle Erv's Airboat World** (☎ 800/432-3367 or 941/695-2805) has a large airboat tour charging $12.50 for adults and $8 for children. Private rides in small boats cost $30 per person. A jungle tour by pontoon boat costs $12.50. **Eden's Jungle Boat Tours** (☎ 800/543-3367 or 941/695-2800) has a nature tour by large pontoon boat as well as private airboat rides for the same prices.

BOAT TOURS   Tours from Everglades City are offered by **Everglades National Park Boat Tours** (☎ 800/445-7724 in Florida, or 941/695-2591). The "Mangrove Wilderness Tour" explores the Glades' inland rivers and creeks at high tide. White ibis, cuckoos, egrets, herons, and other animals can often be seen through the thick mangroves. The "Ten Thousand Islands Cruise" navigates through the mangrove estuaries of the Gulf Coast. The endangered manatee can often be spotted, along with dozens of species of birds, including the southern bald eagle. Tours depart daily, every half hour from 9am to 5pm (less frequently off-season), last about 90 minutes, and cost

$11 for adults, $5.50 for children 6 to 12. Reservations are not accepted. Tours depart from the Park Docks, on Chokoloskee Causeway (Fla. 29), half a mile south of the traffic circle by the ranger station.

Everyone raves about the narrated tours given by naturalists Frank and Georgia Garrett of ○ **Majestic Everglades Excursions** (☎ 941/695-2777). They take up to six passengers on 4-hour excursions through the islands on their covered-deck boat and explain the bird, marine, animal, and plant life. The trips cost $65 for adults, $35 for children 11 and under. Reservations are required; pickup is at the Seas Store and Deli in Everglades City.

If you are up for an intriguing all-day tour, **Everglades Excursions** (☎ 800/592-0848 or 941/598-1050) offers full-day guided trips to Everglades City from both Naples and Marco Island, which include a nature cruise, an airboat ride, and a visit to Ted Smallwood's store (described below). The trips cost $79 for adults and $64 for children; they also stop for an Old Florida–style lunch of seafood and other fare at a neighborhood restaurant (the cost is included in the price of the trip).

One-hour boat tours leave from the dock of **Ted Smallwood's Store,** at the south end of Mamie Street on Chokoloskee Island (see "Seeing the Sights on Land," below, for more information). You'll see where Ed Watson, reputed murderer of the notorious female outlaw Belle Star, was gunned down. Boat tours cost $15 per person.

CANOE TOURS   David Harraden and sons, Jason and Jeremy, of **North American Canoe Tours** (☎ 941/695-4666 November to April, or 860/739-0791 May to October; fax 941/695-4155 November to April) have been leading canoe expeditions into the Everglades every winter since 1978, offering trips ranging from a day to a week. The 1-day trips cost $40 per person.

SEEING THE SIGHTS ON LAND

For an overview of this watery region, climb the **E. J. Hamilton Observation Tower,** opposite the visitor center. It is not part of the national park, but for $1 you can rise above the trees and see for miles across the islands and saw grass plains.

Plan to take at least a half-hour break at **Smallwood's Store Museum** (☎ 941/695-2989), at the south end of Mamie Street on Chokoloskee Island. Looking almost exactly as it did in pioneering days, this former trading post dates from 1906 and operated continuously as a store, post office, and voting place until 1982. Some 90% of the stock still on its shelves was there when it closed. That stuff is not for sale, but there is a well-stocked gift shop selling books, gator heads, T-shirts, and Native American dolls. The museum is open daily from 10am to 5pm during winter, hours vary the rest of the year. Admission is $2.50 for adults, $2 for seniors, and free for children 11 and under. See "Seeing the Sights by Water," above, for details on the boat tour from Smallwood's.

Midway between Everglades City and the Shark Valley entrance to the park is **Big Cypress Gallery** (☎ 941/695-2428) at 52388 Tamiami Trail, where the renowned local photographer Clyde Butcher displays his monumental depictions of the area landscape. See "Big Cypress National Preserve," in section 3 of this chapter.

ACCOMMODATIONS YOU CAN AFFORD
SUPER-CHEAP SLEEPS

Captain's Table Lodge & Villas. 102 E. Broadway (P.O. Box 530), Everglades City, FL 34139. ☎ **800/741-6430** or 941/695-4211. Fax 941/695-2633. 56 units. A/C TV TEL. Winter $55–$75 single, $75–$95 double. Off-season $36–$52 single, $55–$70 double. DISC, MC, V. Take I-75 to Exit 14A, which is S.R. 29, to Everglades City. Follow S.R. 29 to the front door.

Stone Crab City, or Where to Find the "Filet Mignon of the Ocean"

If you haven't tasted them, don't bother making comparisons. No, they aren't like blue crabs, snow crabs, soft-shelled crabs, Alaskan kings, or even lobster. These meaty limbs are whiter, juicier, and sweeter than any other crustacean I've ever tasted. It was these tender morsels that James Bond devoured in *Goldfinger*—the same delicacy that drew the normally reclusive duke and duchess of Windsor out for their only public meal in Miami when they visited in 1941.

Made famous in the 1920s by a Miami Beach institution called Joe's Stone Crab Restaurant (see "Great Deals on Dining," in chapter 5), this popular delicacy has since been the object of cravings for locals and visitors alike.

Demand is so high, in fact, that most Florida stone crab claws never make their way out of the state. Fish stores and restaurants report a brisk business in overnight shipping, but with Joe's alone serving nearly 500,000 pounds of the stuff each year, there's hardly enough to export commercially. Thousands more are consumed at the **Everglades City Seafood Festival** each February (See "When to Go," in chapter 2, for details).

Thankfully, stone crabs face no real threat to their survival. Unlike most commercially harvested crustaceans, these sweeties are cultivated only for their luscious claws, which actually regenerate in little over a year.

It's estimated that more than two-thirds of Florida's claws come from the waters surrounding Everglades City. So swing into town any evening from mid-October through early May, and watch the trappers hauling in their catch and you'll witness a tradition that has kept these fishing families profitable and popular for decades.

Located in the heart of town, this collection of rooms, suites, and villas is a condo development, so the units are furnished and decorated in each owner's tastes. Some have kitchens. The rooms and suites are in a main building, while the villas are built on stilts and have a cottagelike feel. A swimming pool sits by canal-like Lake Placid along the property's eastern flank. Bicycle rentals are also available here.

Ivey House Bed & Breakfast. 107 Camellia St. (P.O. Box 5038), Everglades City, FL 34139. ☎ **941/695-3299** Nov–Apr, or 860/739-0791 May–Oct. Fax 941/695-4155. www. iveyhouse.com. E-mail: sandee@iveyhouse.com. 11 units, 10 with shared bathrooms (shower only), 1 with bathroom (shower only). A/C. During Seafood Festival (Feb) and Christmas holidays $70 single or double with shared bathroom; $120 cottage. $50 single or double $85 single or double, cottage ($15 for extra person up to four). Two-night minimum during high season. Rates include continental breakfast. MC, V. Closed May–Oct.

This wooden structure once was operated by a Mrs. Ivey as a boardinghouse for men working on the Tamiami Trail in the 1920s. Today, canoe specialist David Harraden and his clan run the place during the winter months. Guests share separate men's and women's bathrooms, and a center hallway separates the simple rooms. There are two decks and a large living room for relaxation. A cottage next door has two bedrooms with bathrooms, a screened porch, and antiques. Breakfasts and dinners are served in a spacious kitchen at the rear of the main house (dinners cost $10 to $15 per person, and outsiders are welcome by reservation). Guests have free use of bicycles but have to

Most every local restaurant serves the tender flesh in season, but you can save some money by buying direct from the fish markets. They're sold precooked and ready to crack and dunk in some tangy mustard sauce (see the recipe below).

There are several reputable vendors in town. Make a stop at **Everglades Fish Corp.** at 208 Camellia St. (☎ **941/695-3241**). They're open every day and sell the very freshest claws, as well as some excellent fresh smoked fish. They also take most major credit cards. **Triad Fish Co.**, at 410 School Dr. (☎ **941/695-2662**), also sells claws at reasonable prices—along with Mrs. Hilton's famous mustard sauce. Perhaps the area's oldest purveyor is **Ernest Hamilton's**, 100 Hamilton Lane, on Chokoloskee Island (☎ **941/695-2771**). To get there, take S.R. 29 to Chokoloskee; after the post office, turn right (across the street from JT's grocery store); go straight and look for the bright yellow building.

Bargain hunters may be lured roadside with promises of cheap claws. If prices are less than $8 or $9 a pound, you can be sure these are the castaways from the more reputable traders. The seconds are waterlogged and less meaty than their superfresh counterparts. You can tell the difference by feeling the weight in the palm of your hand. A good fresh claw of any size should feel solid and hefty; the second-rate ones are "light as a hawk's feather," according to one local trapper. Any visible meat should not look shriveled or as if it is shrinking away from its shell. Open one before committing to more.

And no matter what anyone tells you, size *does* count. Claws are usually graded in four categories: medium, large, jumbo, and colossal. One pound of mediums usually contains between six and eight claws; colossals can weigh nearly three-quarters of a pound each. Get the biggest claws you can afford, and ask the vendor to crack them for you. Digging into those hard shells is tough work, but someone's got to do it.

---

pay to use the coin laundry. They can smoke and drink on the decks, but not in the house. All of the bed-and-breakfast rooms have numerous 1900 to 1920 antiques—a wood washing machine and 1918 Hoosier apple-green-speckled enamelware, for example. Plans are in the works for an additional building with private bathrooms and a hot tub. Full-day and half-day guided adventures and kayak rentals are available.

Rod & Gun Lodge. Riverside Dr. and Broadway (P.O. Box 190), Everglades City, FL 34139. ☎ **941/695-2101.** 17 units, all with bathroom (some with shower only). A/C TV. Winter $85 single or double. Off-season $65 single or double. No credit cards.

This rustic, old white clapboard house has plenty of history and all kinds of activities for sports enthusiasts, including a swimming pool, bicycle rentals, tennis center, tennis courts, nearby boat rentals, and private fishing guides. This famous outpost on the banks of the sleepy Barron River was originally built as a private residence nearly 170 years ago, but Barron Collier turned it into a cozy hunting lodge in the 1920s. Pres. Herbert Hoover vacationed here after his 1928 election victory, and Pres. Harry S. Truman flew in to sign Everglades National Park into existence in 1947. Other guests have included Richard Nixon, Burt Reynolds, and Mick Jagger. The public rooms are beautifully paneled and hung with tarpon, wild boar, deer antlers, and other trophies. Rooms in this single-story building are unfussy but perfectly comfortable. Out by the swimming pool and riverbank, a screened veranda with ceiling fans offers a pleasant place for a libation. The dining room serves breakfast, lunch, and dinner.

GREAT DEALS ON DINING

Everglades City has no gourmet restaurants, but you can get your fill of fresh seafood at several local eateries. Since the town produces about two-thirds of Florida's crab catch, most have fresh-off-the-boat claws from mid-October through mid-May. If you are in town on a weekend, swing by the Shell station at S.R. 29 and U.S. 41 to sample another local favorite, boiled peanuts. "Goobers," as the old-timers call them, are sold in paper bags from a colorful trailer. These soggy, spicy nuts are a real treat for some. I don't get the appeal, but hey, they've been around a lot longer than I have.

Do stop and have a chat with the friendly Joan of **Joan's Quik Stop,** at 39395 U.S. 41, in Ochopee (☎ **941/695-2682**). This pleasant little eatery serves a great breakfast from when it opens at 9am until close at 5pm. A favorite is the Indian breakfast of eggs on flat bread with sautéed vegetables like zucchini, eggplant, and broccoli. Lunch specials include lots of fried seafood like gator nuggets, fritters, and shrimps. Take a free postcard and send one back when you get home. It'll join the hundreds of others on the walls of this quaint and inexpensive diner. Most dishes are under $7, but be sure to have cash or traveler's checks, because no checks are accepted.

The **Oyster House,** on S.R. 29 opposite the Everglades National Park visitor center (☎ **941/695-2073**), also specializes in seafood. Main courses range from $12 to $17; sandwiches are $4.50 to $9.50. A narrow, screened front porch here is a fine place to sip a drink while watching the sunset over the Everglades. Open daily from 11am to 9pm. On some weekends you may find live music and dancing, too.

The down-home **Oar House Restaurant,** 305 Collier Ave. (Fla. 29), in town (☎ **941/695-3535**), offers "cooters, legs, and tails" (turtles, frogs' legs, and alligator tails) as specialties. Main courses range from $8 to $16, and sandwiches and seafood baskets run $2 to $8. Open daily from 6am to 9pm.

3 Big Cypress National Preserve

50 miles W of Miami, 22 miles E of Naples

In Big Cypress, northwest of the Florida Everglades, "big" refers not to the size of the trees, but to the vastness of the stands. More than half a million acres of parkland were acquired by the National Park Service in 1974, and the Big Cypress National Preserve Addition Act of 1988 is gradually adding 146,000 more acres.

The preserve is intentionally lean on visitor facilities and contains few marked trails of any kind. As a result, Big Cypress feels plenty big and remote. If you are looking for a true wilderness experience, you'll want to spend an afternoon exploring here. Just be sure you have snacks, water, and a full tank of gas before entering—there are no gasoline stations or food services in the preserve.

Camping is available throughout the preserve. It's free, but there are no facilities: no fresh water, no toilets, no picnic tables, no grills.

To see one artist's incredible renderings of the area, stop at **Big Cypress Gallery** (☎ **941/695-2428**) at 52388 Tamiami Trail (less than 1 mile east of the Oasis Visitor Center). This museum/gallery showcases Clyde Butcher's award-winning black-and-white photographs of his backyard—the vast expanse that is the Everglades. Many have been featured in television specials and magazines throughout the world. His landscape prints are huge—some spread 4 by 7 feet across—allowing you to focus into the quiet beauty of the Everglades. It's worth a drive. The gallery is open daily 9:30am to 5pm.

JUST THE FACTS

Entrance is free to Big Cypress National Preserve. Contact **Big Cypress National Preserve Headquarters,** P.O. Box 110, Ochopee, FL 33943 (☎ **941/695-4111** or 941/695-2000), for a map and specialized information on the preserve.

On-site information is dispensed at the **Oasis Visitor Center,** at the preserve's main entrance, on the Tamiami Trail (U.S. 41) in Ochopee, 37 miles west of Florida City and 22 miles east of Naples. During the winter months, information is also available at Preserve Headquarters, on the Tamiami Trail, about 18 miles west of Oasis. The visitor centers are staffed daily from about 8:30am to 4:30pm.

EXPLORING THE PRESERVE

Big Cypress is a sprawling expanse that was designated as a national preserve primarily to help protect the ecosystem of the Everglades. There's little to attract tourists except for die-hard walkers sure to enjoy more than 30 miles of flat trails. Pick up a free trail map from the visitor center before heading out. Otherwise, there is nothing you will see here that you won't find in the main park area.

If you want to explore, start on the Florida Trail, the preserve's main hiking trail. It stretches northwest (with significant gaps) all the way into the Florida Panhandle. The part of the trail that's inside Big Cypress is about 30 miles long and runs north from the Oasis Visitor Center. Hikers should be prepared for wet areas that are ankle- to waist-deep in the rainy season. There are two primitive campsites but no potable water on the trail.

4 Biscayne National Park

35 miles S of Miami and 21 miles E of Everglades National Park

This unusual and underappreciated park celebrated its 30th birthday in 1998, when park rangers offered many free programs in order to entice more locals to visit. With only about 500,000 visitors each year (mostly boaters and divers), it is one of the least crowded parks in the country. Biscayne National Park is a little more difficult than most to access—more than 95% of its 182,00 acres are underwater.

Its significance was first formally acknowledged in 1968 when, in an unprecedented move, Pres. Lyndon Johnson signed a bill to conserve the barrier islands off South Florida's east coast as a national monument—a protected status that's one rung below national park. After being twice enlarged, once in 1974 and again in 1980, the waters surrounding the northernmost coral reef in North America became a full-fledged national park, the largest of its kind in the country

Think of Biscayne more as a preserve than a destination. I suggest using your time here to explore underwater life—but most of all, come here to relax.

The park's greatest dry attraction is the 29-acre island known as **Boca Chita Key,** once an exclusive haven for wealthy yachters. It was closed after 1992's devastating Hurricane Andrew wiped out much of the tiny park. Six years and nearly $2 million were spent to restore the quaint island, which is especially popular with boaters. Now, visitors can tour the island's newly restored historic buildings, including the county's second-largest lighthouse and a tiny chapel.

Also popular is **Elliott Key,** one of the park's 44 little mangrove-fringed islands. Located about 9 miles from Convoy Point, Elliott Key contains a visitor center, hiking trails, and a campground.

The park's small mainland mangrove shoreline and 41 keys are best explored by boat. Its extensive reef system is extremely popular with divers and snorkelers. The concessionaire at Convoy Point rents canoes, runs dive trips, and offers popular glass-bottom-boat tours.

JUST THE FACTS

GETTING THERE & ACCESS POINTS   The park's mainland entrance is Convoy Point, located 9 miles east of Homestead. To reach the park from Miami, take the Florida Turnpike to the Speedway Boulevard (Exit 6). Turn left, heading south 4½ miles, then left again at North Canal Drive (SW 328th Street), and follow signs to the park. If you're coming from U.S. 1, whether you're heading north or south, turn east at North Canal Drive (SW 328th Street).

As mentioned earlier, most of Biscayne National Park is accessible only to boaters. Mooring buoys abound, since it's illegal to anchor on coral. When no buoys are available, boaters must anchor on sand or on the new docks surrounding the small harbor off Boca Chita, where boats can stay overnight for $15. Even the most experienced boaters should carry updated nautical charts of the area, which are available at Convoy Point. The waters are often murky, making the abundant reefs and sandbars difficult to detect—and there are more interesting ways to spend a day than waiting for the tide to rise. There's a boat launch at adjacent Homestead Bayfront Park, and 66 slips on Elliott Key, available free on a first-come, first-served basis.

Transportation to and from the visitor center costs $21 per person. Call for seasonal schedules (☎ **305/230-1100**).

VISITOR CENTERS & INFORMATION   For information on park activities and tours, contact **Biscayne National Underwater Park**, P.O. Box 1270, Homestead, FL 33030 (☎ **305/230-1100;** fax 305/230-1120; www.nps.gov/bisc; e-mail captsaw@bellsouth.net). The center is open daily from 8:30am to 5pm and later in winter.

The **Convoy Point Visitor Center,** 9700 SW 328th St., at the park's main entrance (☎ **305/230-7275;** fax 305/230-1190), is the natural starting point for any venture into the park. In addition to providing comprehensive information on the park, rangers will show you a short video on request. Open Monday to Friday from 8:30am to 4:30pm and Saturday and Sunday from 8:30am to 5pm. The permanent visitor center opened in early 1997, and museum exhibits were installed during summer 1997 at the cost of $5 million.

ENTRANCE FEES & PERMITS   Entrance is free to Biscayne National Park. At press time, backcountry permits were also free and available at the visitor center.

SEEING THE HIGHLIGHTS

Since Biscayne National Park is primarily underwater, the only way to truly experience it is with snorkel or scuba gear. You can rent a speedboat in Miami and cruise south for about 1½ hours, but a better idea would be to take one of the organized tours offered every day from the main visitor center. (See "Organized Tours," below.) Beneath the surface, the aquatic universe pulses with multicolored life: Brilliant parrot and angelfish, gently rocking sea fans, and coral labyrinths abound. Before entering the water, be sure to apply waterproof sunblock, or wear a T-shirt; once you begin to explore, it's easy to lose track of time, and the Florida sun is brutal, even in the winter.

Afterward, take a picnic out to Elliott Key and taste the crisp salt air blowing off the Atlantic. Or head to Boca Chita, an intriguing island that was once the private playground of wealthy yachters.

AFFORDABLE OUTDOOR ACTIVITIES IN BISCAYNE NATIONAL PARK

CANOEING/KAYAKING   Biscayne National Park offers excellent canoeing, either along the coast or across open water to nearby mangroves and artificial islands that dot the longest uninterrupted shoreline in the state of Florida. Since tides can be strong, only experienced canoeists should attempt to paddle far from shore. If you plan to go far, first obtain a tide table from the visitor center (see "Just the Facts," above) and paddle with the current. Free ranger-led canoe tours are scheduled for most weekend mornings; phone for information. You can rent a canoe at the park; rates are $8 an hour or $22 for four hours. Kayakers will have to bring their own boats but are welcome to explore the same quiet routes.

FISHING   Ocean fishing is excellent year-round; many people cast their lines right from the breakwater jetty at Convoy Point. A fishing license is required (see "Entrance Fees, Permits & Regulations," under "Just the Facts," in section 1, for complete information). Bait is not available in Biscayne, but is sold in adjacent Homestead Bayfront Park. Stone crabs and Florida lobsters can be found here, but you're only allowed to catch these on the ocean side when they're in season. There are strict limitations on size, season, number, and method of take (including spear fishing) for both fresh- and saltwater fishing. The latest regulations are available at most marinas, bait and tackle shops, and at the park's visitor centers. Or you can contact the **Florida Game and Fresh Water Fish Commission,** Bryant Building, 620 S. Meridian St., Tallahassee, FL 32399-1600 (☎ **904/488-1960**).

HIKING/EXPLORING   Since the majority of this park is underwater, hiking is not the main attraction here, but there are some interesting sights and trails. At **Convoy Point** you can walk along the 370-foot boardwalk, and along the half-mile jetty that serves as a breakwater for the park's harbor. From there you can usually see brown pelicans, little blue herons, snowy egrets, and a few exotic fish.

Elliott Key is accessible only by boat, but once you're there, you have two good trail options. True to its name, the **Loop Trail** makes a 1½-mile circle from the bay-side visitor center, through a hardwood hammock and mangroves, to an elevated oceanside boardwalk. It's likely that you'll see purple and orange land crabs scurrying around the mangrove roots.

Restored in 1998 after a devastating hurricane in 1992, Boca Chita Key is a great island to explore. Once the playground for wealthy tycoons, it still offers the peaceful beauty that attracted elite fishers from cold climates. Many of the historical buildings are still intact, including an ornamental lighthouse that was thankfully never put into use. Since it was built on the western side of the island in the path of shallow reefs, boaters would have followed the beacon, only to go aground.

Take advantage of the tours, usually led by an interpretative park ranger and available every Sunday at 1pm. Including the 45-minute boat trip and the 45-minute return, the tour will take about three hours The price for adults is $19.95 and $9.95 for children. However, call in advance to see if the sea is calm enough for the boat trip. Rough seas often mean boats cannot reach the island safely. Also call to see if any free tours are being offered. In 1998, in order to increase awareness of this little-known destination, the park service sponsored a series of free outings

SNORKELING & SCUBA DIVING   The clear, warm waters of Biscayne National Park are packed with colorful tropical fish that swim in the offshore reefs. If you don't have your own gear, or don't want to lug it to the park, you can rent or buy snorkeling and scuba gear at the full service dive shop at Convoy Point. Rates are in line with dive shops on the mainland.

The best way to see the park is to take a snorkel tour. **Biscayne National Underwater Park** (☎ **305/230-1100**) operates daily tours that last about 4 hours and cost $27.95 per person. A full-gear package is only $37. They also run two-tank dives for certified divers and provide instruction for beginners. The price is $35.50 per person. The shop is open daily from 8am to 5:30pm. Two-tank dives depart on Wednesday,

A Scuba Deal in Biscayne

For a real bargain, consider a **money-saving package** that includes accommodations. A winter special in 1998 consisted of lodging for 1 night at a nearby Hampton Inn (a 15-minute drive to the park) and 2 days of diving for less than $100. Each day takes you on two different and beautiful boat dives. You'll have to rent the equipment if you don't have your own, but still, this is a steal, considering that 2 days of diving alone would cost well over $100 at most resorts. Contact **Biscayne National Underwater Park** (☎ 305/230-1100) for details.

Saturday, and Sunday at 8:30am. Make reservations a few days in advance. No matter what your choice, if you are planning to get in the water, you *must* know how to swim.

SWIMMING   You can swim at the protected beaches of Elliott Key, Boca Chita Key, and adjacent Homestead Bayfront Park, but none of these beaches match the width or softness of other South Florida beaches. Check the water conditions before heading into the sea. Strong currents make this a popular destination for windsurfers and sailors, but it can be dangerous even for strong swimmers.

WINDSURFING/SURFING   Strong and steady winds provide an excellent venue for windsurfers. Feel free to bring your own board and take on some of South Florida's best waves.

ORGANIZED TOURS

The best way to see the sites without getting wet is on the glass-bottom boat tour. **Biscayne National Underwater Park** (☎ 305/230-1100) offers daily trips to view some of the country's most beautiful coral reefs and tropical fish. Boats depart year-round from Convoy Point at 10am and stay out for about 3 hours. At $19.95 for adults, $17.95 for seniors, and $9.95 for children 12 and under, the scenic and informative tours are well worth the price. Boats carry fewer than 50 passengers, so reservations are almost always necessary. The company also offers guided canoe, scuba, and snorkeling reef trips led by underwater naturalists. See "Affordable Outdoor Activities in Biscayne National Park," above.

ACCOMMODATIONS YOU CAN AFFORD

There are no facilities available for overnight guests to this watery park. Most visitors come for an afternoon on their way to the Keys and stay overnight in nearby Homestead where there are many national chain hotels and other affordable lodgings. See "Accommodations You Can Afford," in section 1 of this chapter.

CAMPING

Although you won't find hotels or lodges in Biscayne National Park, you will find some of the state's most pristine campsites. Since they are completely inaccessible by motor vehicle, you'll be sure to avoid the mass of RVs so prevalent in so many of the state's other campgrounds. Sites are on **Elliott Key** and **Boca Chita,** and can only be reached by boat. If you don't have your own vessel, call ☎ 305/230-1100 to arrange a drop-off. Transportation to and from the visitor center costs $21 per person. The best facilities are on the northeast side of newly reopened Boca Chita, where there are brand-new showers, solar-powered rest rooms, and drinking fountains, as well as barbecue grills and picnic tables. With a backcountry permit, available from the ranger station, you can pitch your tent somewhere even more private. Ask for a map at the visitor center. And be sure to bring plenty of bug spray.

The Gold Coast   8

by Victoria Pesce Elliott

The cities along Florida's southeast coast have been growing at an explosive rate, especially over the last decade. Many newcomers have relocated from neighboring Miami, where a number of circumstances—the influx of Caribbean immigrants, a drastic increase in violent crime, and a devastating 1992 hurricane—caused many old-timers to head north to the cities and suburbs of Broward and Palm Beach counties.

As a result, a building boom is underway in the region, one of which extends westward into the swampy areas of the Everglades. Another by-product is the successful revitalization of several once-depressed downtown areas in Hollywood, Ft. Lauderdale, and West Palm Beach. Now spruced up, these vibrant hubs attract more young travelers and families than ever before. Of course, there's the exclusive island of Palm Beach, where a staggering number of the world's superrich reside. In fact, according to the *Palm Beach Post,* the city was home to more than half of the homes in America that sold for more than $10 million in 1996.

The dozens of gorgeous beaches, of course, have always drawn a steady stream of sun worshipers and water-sports enthusiasts. Beyond the sands, the Gold Coast offers fantastic shopping, entertainment, clubbing, boating, golfing, tennis, and just plain old relaxing.

Active travelers in particular enjoy the array of facilities available year-round in this beautiful region. With some of the country's most famous golf courses and even more tennis courts, this area attracts big-name tournaments in both sports (see "Florida Calendar of Events," in chapter 2).

Like its neighboring regions to the south, parts the Gold Coast can be prohibitively expensive during the winter high season, and prohibitively hot and buggy in the summer. However, the good news is that bargains abound in these slow months (between May and October), and many take advantage of discounts offered at the uncrowded resorts, especially in the Hollywood and Ft. Lauderdale area.

EXPLORING THE GOLD COAST BY CAR

The Gold Coast consists of a section of Florida's mainland and an adjacent strip of barrier islands. You'll have to consult a map to keep track of the many bridges that allow access to the islands where most of the tourist activity is centered. Interstate 95, which runs north-south, is the area's main highway. Farther west is the Florida Turnpike, a toll road that can be worth the expense, since the speed limit is higher and it is often less congested than I-95. Also on the mainland is U.S. 1, which generally runs parallel to I-95 (to the east) and is a narrower thoroughfare mostly crowded with strip malls and seedy hotels.

I recommend taking Fla. A1A, a slow ocean-side road that connects the long, thin islands along Florida's entire east coast. Though the road is narrow, it is the most scenic, and forces you into the ultrarelaxed atmosphere of these resort towns.

1 Broward County: Hallandale & Hollywood to Fort Lauderdale

23 miles N of Miami

With more than 23 miles of beachfront and 300 miles of navigable waterways, Broward County is a great destination for lovers of the outdoors. Scattered amid the tacky shopping malls, gaudy condos, and glitzy tourist areas are hundreds of lovely parks, as well as golf courses and tennis courts. With year-round temperatures of 77° and a growing industrial base, the area attracts more than six million visitors each year. Some 1.3 million people reside in the more than 28 cities and dozens of towns that make up Broward County.

Like many small American towns, the quaint city of Hollywood has been trying to redevelop its downtown area for years. Finally, it seems, the effort has paid off. A spate of redevelopment has made the pedestrian-friendly center—along Hollywood Boulevard and Harrison Street east of Dixie Highway—a popular destination for travelers and locals alike. Some predict Hollywood will be South Florida's next big destination—South Beach without the attitude, traffic jams, and parking nightmares. Prices are a fraction of other tourist areas, and a true artsy image is apparent in the galleries, clubs, and restaurants that dot the new strip. But its gritty undercurrent still makes it more popular with the boho-and-backpacker crowd than with society-page regulars.

Fort Lauderdale and its well-known strip of beaches, restaurants, bars, and souvenir shops have also undergone a major transformation. Once especially famous (or infamous) for the annual mayhem it hosted each spring when hedonistic college students descended from all over the country, the town is now attracting a more upscale, mainstream crowd.

In addition to beautiful wide beaches, the city includes more than 300 miles of navigable waterways and innumerable canals that permit thousands of residents to anchor boats in their backyards. Boating isn't just a hobby here; it's a lifestyle. It's the reason many choose to live in this area, which is known, along with a string of other evocative names, as the "yachting capital of the world." Visitors can easily get on the water, too, by renting a boat, or simply by hailing a moderately priced water taxi (see "More than a Boat Tour," below).

Huge cruise ships also take advantage of Florida's deepest harbor, Port Everglades. It is the second-busiest cruise-ship base in Florida (after Miami) and one of the top five in the world. If you're interested in cruising, call Port Everglades at ☎ **954/523-3404.** Their Web site (www.co.broward.fl.us/port.htm) lists all cruise ships and their schedules, too. Or, call ☎ **800/22-SUNNY** for the numbers of Lauderdale-based cruise lines. For great land packages, ask for "A Shore Thing" brochure.

ESSENTIALS

GETTING THERE   If you're driving up or down the Florida coast, you'll probably reach Hollywood and Fort Lauderdale on I-95. Visitors on their way to or from Orlando should take the Florida Turnpike.

Fort Lauderdale Area Attractions & Accommodations

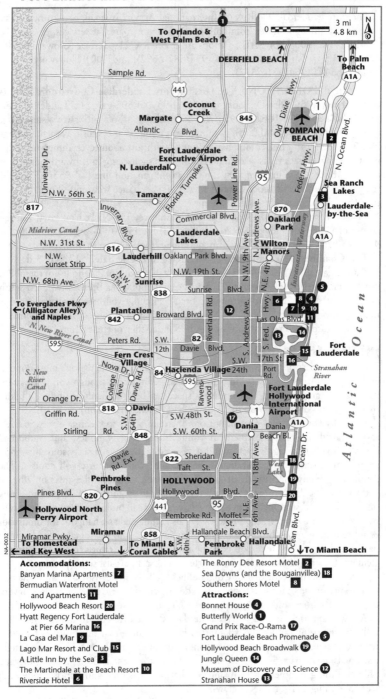

Accommodations:

Banyan Marina Apartments **7**

Bermudian Waterfront Motel
and Apartments **11**

Hollywood Beach Resort **20**

Hyatt Regency Fort Lauderdale
at Pier 66 Marina **16**

La Casa del Mar **9**

Lago Mar Resort and Club **15**

A Little Inn by the Sea **3**

The Martindale at the Beach Resort **10**

Riverside Hotel **6**

The Ronny Dee Resort Motel **2**

Sea Downs (and the Bougainvillea) **18**

Southern Shores Motel **8**

Attractions:

Bonnet House **4**

Butterfly World **1**

Grand Prix Race-O-Rama **17**

Fort Lauderdale Beach Promenade **5**

Hollywood Beach Broadwalk **19**

Jungle Queen **14**

Museum of Discovery and Science **12**

Stranahan House **13**

The Fort Lauderdale/Hollywood International Airport is small, easy to negotiate, and located just 15 minutes from both of the downtown areas it services.

Amtrak (☎ **800/USA-RAIL**) stations are at 200 SW 21st Terrace (Broward Boulevard and I-95), Fort Lauderdale (☎ **954/587-6692**), and 3001 Hollywood Blvd., Hollywood (☎ **954/921-4517**).

VISITOR INFORMATION   The **Greater Fort Lauderdale Convention & Visitors Bureau,** 1850 Eller Dr., Suite 303 (off I-95 and 595 east), Ft. Lauderdale, FL 33316 (☎ **800/356-1662** or 954/765-4466; fax 954/765-4467; www.sunny.org; e-mail: gflcvb@co.broward.fl.us), is an excellent resource in Spanish, French, or English. Call them for a free comprehensive guide with just about everything you could want to know about events, accommodations, and sightseeing in Broward County. In addition, once you're in town, you can call an information line (☎ **954/527-5600**) to get easy-to-follow directions, travel advice, and assistance from multilingual operators who staff a round-the-clock help line.

The **Greater Hollywood Chamber of Commerce,** 330 N. Federal Hwy. (on the corner of U.S. 1 and Taylor Street), Hollywood, FL 33020 (☎ **954/923-4000;** fax 954/923-8737), is open Monday through Friday from 8:30am to 5pm.

The **Chamber of Commerce of Greater Ft. Lauderdale,** 512 NE 3rd Ave., Ft. Lauderdale, FL 33301 (☎ **954/462-6000**) will provide maps and list of members, but you may do better at the official visitors center at 600 Sea Breeze Blvd., just south of Las Olas Blvd., and across from the beach. Friendly volunteers will give advice, maps, transportation schedules, and any other details you may need. It's open Monday through Saturday from 9am until 6pm. On Sunday they open at 11am.

HITTING THE BEACH

The southern part of the Gold Coast, Broward County, has the region's most popular and amenities-laden beaches. Most do not charge for access, though you will pay for parking. Beware, however, that finding a space can be as difficult as finding a bikini that fits. Here's a rundown on the county's best beaches from south to north.

✪ **Hollywood Beach,** stretching from Sheridan Street to Georgia Street, is a real carnival, with its odd assortment of young hipsters, big families, and sunburned French Canadians dodging cyclists and skaters along the rows of tacky souvenir shops, game rooms, snack bars, beer stands, hotels, and even miniature golf courses. The 3-mile-long Hollywood Beach **Broadwalk** is notable as one of the area's only beach paths where the diversions are right on the beach, separated from the sand and sea by only a thin paved strip instead of a busy highway and tall buildings. Popular with runners, skaters, and cruisers, the Broadwalk is also renowned as a hangout for thousands of retirement-age snowbirds, especially from Canada, who get together for frequent dances and shows at a faded outdoor amphitheater. Despite efforts to clear out a seedy element, the area remains a haven for drunks and scam artists, so keep alert.

If you tire of the hectic diversity that defines Hollywood's Broadwalk, enjoy the natural beauty of the beach itself, which is wide and clean. There are lifeguards, showers, bathroom facilities, and public areas for picnics and parties.

A few years back, the ✪ **Fort Lauderdale Beach Promenade** underwent a $26 million renovation, and it looks fantastic. However, note that this beach is hardly in its natural state; it is across the street from an uninterrupted stretch of low- and high-rise hotels, tacky bars, and T-shirt shops. Also, on the scene is Beach Place, a megaretail and dining complex on A1A, midway between Las Olas and Sunrise boulevards (see "Shopping & Browsing," below).

Just across the road, on the sand, you will usually find hard-core volleyballers, who always welcome anyone with a good spike, and a calm ocean that embraces swimmers of all levels. The unusually clear waters are under the careful watch of some of Florida's best-looking lifeguards. Unlike at most South Florida beaches, here there are clean showers and rest rooms conveniently located along the strip.

Especially on weekends, parking along the ocean-side meters is nearly impossible to find. Try biking, skating, or hitching a ride on the water taxi instead. **"The Strip"** is located on A1A, between SE 17th Street and Sunrise Boulevard. Still somewhat popular with Spring Breakers, this area can get wild, with college kids drinking and partying on the sand.

Still known as the **HoJo's Beach** since its adjacent hotel used to be a Howard Johnson, this little-known hideaway is a perennial favorite with locals. The hotel has since changed hands but the crowd is the same. High school and college students throwing Frisbees and kicking hackey-sacks share this area with an older crowd of tourists staying at the oceanfront resort. A jetty bounds the beach on the south side, making it rather private. But keep in mind the water here gets a little choppy—a bonus for surfers and boogie boarders, but not great for swimmers. This locals' spot is located at 4660 N. Ocean Dr., in Lauderdale-by-the-Sea, a half mile north of Commercial Boulevard, on A1A.

The most popular gay beach is at **Sebastian Street,** where tanned and muscled boys dominate the scene. Another spot for men looking for men is at NE 18th Street just north of Sunrise Boulevard. More locals frequent this cruising scene.

GREAT GOLF THAT WON'T BREAK YOUR BUDGET & OTHER AFFORDABLE ACTIVITIES

BOATING   Fort Lauderdale, a boating city known as "the yachting capital of the world," provides ample opportunity for visitors to get on the water. And you don't need a fat wallet to do it. Check with your hotel to see if they have a deal with a local captain who can take you out along the **Intracoastal Waterway** or out on the open ocean. If your hotel doesn't know someone, or if they don't have their own rental boats, try **Bill's Sunrise Watersports,** 2025 E. Sunrise Blvd., Ft. Lauderdale (☎ **954/ 462-8962**). Year-round, they will outfit you with a variety of watercraft, including jet-skis, Wave Runners, 13-foot Cigarette boats, 15-foot jet boats, and 8-foot powerboats. Bill's is open daily from 9am to 6pm. Rates start at about $45 an hour, which isn't bad if you split it with three or four friends. Cheaper options include the more crowded sightseeing cruises and the water taxi (see "More Than a Boat Tour," below).

CRUISES   You can often find discount coupons for sightseeing cruises or gambling boats. Ask around or look for "Beach Bucks," a billfold-size packet of coupons good for a few dollars off these local cruises. The *Jungle Queen,* 801 Sea Breeze Blvd. (3 blocks south of Las Olas Boulevard on Fla. A1A), in the Bahia Mar Yacht Center, Ft. Lauderdale (☎ **954/462-5596**), a Mississippi River–style steamer, is one of Fort Lauderdale's best-known attractions cruising up and down the New River. All-you-can-eat dinner cruises and 3-hour sightseeing tours float visitors past Millionaires' Row, Old Fort Lauderdale, and downtown. Cruises depart nightly at 7pm and cost $24 for adults and $12 for children 12 and under. Daytime sightseeing tours are scheduled daily at 10am and 2pm and cost $11 for adults and $8 for children 10 and under.

For a shorter and slightly less expensive cruise, board the *Carrie B.* at Las Olas Blvd. and SE 5th Street behind the supermarket, just west of the shopping district (☎ **954/768-9920**). Reservations are not usually necessary; you can take this 1½ hour cruise and see Millionaires Row and naval ships while listening to an interesting tour guide explain the area. It's also the only ship that passes the cruise-ship port, Port

Everglades. Adults pay $10.50 and children under 12 pay $5.25. There's a small liquor bar with ballpark-type food. This 110-foot cruiser holds 300 passengers. Cruises leave every day at 11am, 1pm, and 3pm.

If you are feeling lucky, check out one of the several casino boats operating day cruises out of Port Everglades. Most offer blackjack, slots, and poker. **Discovery Cruise Lines** (☎ **800/937-4477**) has daily cruises to The Bahamas where you can gamble, eat, and party for 5 to 6 hours for about $120. The price includes breakfast, lunch, and dinner, but drinks cost extra.

Sea Escape (☎ **800/327-2005** or 954/453-3333) also launches daily casino cruises. But theirs don't travel more than a few miles offshore and are much cheaper. These trips "to nowhere" depart every day except Monday, from 10am until 4pm. The party cruises offer buffet meals and full casinos for about $30 a person. I'd recommend spending an additional $10 to $15 for a cabin so you can stretch out and relax in between hands. Even though the cruises don't go far from the coast, 5 or 6 hours is a long time to spend at sea, especially if the weather is rough. Evening cruises, which leave at 7:30 and return around 12:30 or 1:30am, cost a few dollars more and offer full buffet dinners and a Las Vegas–style show. Port charges are included, although you must pay a $3 departure tax. This is one of the best deals you'll find. Sea Escape also has a new 2- and 3-night cruise option, where visitors can go to Nassau, Bahamas, for as little as $199 per person with all meals included.

Also, see the box below, "More Than a Boat Tour," for details on the water taxi.

GAME PARKS   Especially great for kids, this area seems to be the home of more megaentertainment complexes than any other region in Southeast Florida. The **Grand Prix Race-O-Rama**, at 1500 NW 1st St., east of I-95 between Griffin and Sterling road exits, in Dania (☎ **954/921-1411**), is one of the originals and still the best for kids. With a massive video arcade, which is open 24 hours, five challenging miniature golf greens, go-carts for those over 4 feet 6 inches, and NASCAR racing for those over 5 feet tall, batting cages, and a huge sky coaster, this place is as exciting as it is exhausting. Plan to spend all day or night, or both. Call for prices and hours.

One of the newer additions to the scene is **Dave & Busters** at 3000 Oakwood Blvd. in Hollywood, just off the Sheridan Street exit of I-95 (☎ **954/923-5505**). This 50,000-square-foot complex caters primarily to adults; it features a full liquor bar and sit-down restaurant, as well as a more casual spot with waitress service as well. On weekends this place is packed with young adults on dates and rowdy groups of guys of all ages. An admission of $5 is charged only on Friday and Saturday after 10pm. D&B's opens weekdays at 11am and at 11:30 on weekends and usually closes by 1am.

GOLF   Most of the area's best courses are farther north, in the very expensive resorts and many private country clubs; however, don't despair—dozens of great courses are open to the public and there are ways to save money. Ask about twilight tee times. If you don't mind playing after 2 or 3pm, you can usually cut your greens fees in half. For one of Broward's best municipal challenges, try the 18-holer at the **Orangebrook Golf Course** at 400 Entrada Dr. in Hollywood (☎ **954/967-GOLF**). Built in 1937, this is one of the state's oldest courses and one of the area's best bargains. Morning and noon rates range from $17 to $32. After 2pm, you can play for less than $23, including a cart. After 3pm, prices go down even more, usually to about $15.

Some of the best courses include **Emerald Hills,** at 4100 North Hills Dr., Hollywood, just west of I-95 between Sterling Road and Sheridan Street. This beauty consistently lands on "best of" lists of golf writers throughout the country. The last and 18th hole on a two-tier green is the challenging course's signature; it's surrounded by water and is more than a bit rough. Greens fees start at $80 during the week. After

11:30 rates go down to $65. Twilight prices from Monday through Thursday are a mere $35. Weekend times are higher. Call ☎ **954/961-4000** at least 5 days in advance for tee times.

SCUBA DIVING   Although scuba diving doesn't compare to beach diving in the Caribbean islands, in Ft. Lauderdale you can see plenty of sea life at reefs just off the shore. That means you can save the expense and time of boating to your destination by walking right off the shore. Some decent reefs run north and south just about 300 yards from shore, though it can be a pain to haul your gear and swim out to the reefs. At the end of Commercial Blvd., however, many finned divers do just that. The more spectacular scenery is only accessible by boat.

If you are up for spending a little extra to see one of the county's best wreck dives, head out to the *Mercedes I.* It's a 197-foot freighter that washed up in the backyard of a Palm Beach socialite in 1984, and was sunk for divers the following year off of Pompano Beach. The artificial reef, filled with colorful sponges, spiny lobsters, and barracudas, is located 97 feet below the surface, a mile offshore between Oakland Park and Sunrise boulevards. Dozens of reputable dive outfits line the beach. Stop in to get a feel for the staff, or call **ProDive** (☎ **954/761-3413**). They head out daily for reasonable rates. Prices for a trip, including all gear, is about $75, $38 if you bring your own stuff. In Hollywood, one of the oldest and best outfits is **Diver's Unlimited** at ☎ **954/981-0156.** Prices for boat dives range from $25 to $45 without gear and drop in the summer.

If you are looking to purchase gear—anything from gloves to tanks to underwater scooters—go to **Diver's Discount** at 923 SE 20th St., just north of Port Everglades (☎ **954/523-8354**). Ask Sam Rich to show off his diving books and his incredible selection of gear, which is sold for 10% to 30% below retail prices.

SPECTATOR SPORTS   Fans can get their baseball fix at the Fort Lauderdale Stadium, 5301 NW 12th Ave. (☎ **954/938-4980**). The Baltimore Orioles now play exhibition games starting in late February; call ☎ **954/776-1921** for tickets. They cost $6 for a spot in the grandstand, $9 for reserved seats, and $12 for box seats. During the season, the spectacular 1997 World Series champs Florida Marlins play in Miami, but just south of the Dade-Broward County line at the **Pro Player Stadium.** Call Ticketmaster for tickets (☎ **305/358-5885**), which range from $2 to $40.

The **Pompano Harness Track,** 1800 SW 3rd St., Pompano Beach (☎ **954/ 972-2000**), Florida's only harness track, features horse racing and betting from October to early August. Grandstand admission is free; clubhouse admission is $2. They, like many other pari-mutuel outlets in the area, opened poker rooms in 1997.

The home of the Florida Derby, **Gulfstream Park,** 901 S. Federal Hwy., Hallandale (☎ **954/454-7000**), recently underwent a revamp that has made it one of the state's biggest and best-known race tracks. It has a popular clubhouse and is open January to mid-March from Wednesday to Monday starting at 11am.

A sort of Spanish-style indoor lacrosse, **jai-alai** was introduced to Florida in 1924 and still draws big crowds who bet on the fast-paced action. Broward's only fronton, **Dania Jai-Alai,** 301 E. Dania Beach Blvd. (at the intersection of A1A and U.S. 1; ☎ **954/920-1511** or 954/426-4330), is a great place to spend an afternoon or evening.

If ice hockey's your game, the **Florida Panthers** (☎ **954/768-1900**) are now playing in the $185-million **National Car Rental Center,** 2555 NW 137th Way, Sunrise (☎ **954/835-8000**). The arena can seat upwards of 19,000 fans.

TENNIS   There are literally hundreds of courts in Broward County and plenty are accessible to the public. Many are at resorts and hotels. If not at yours, try one of these.

Famous as the spot where Chris Evert practiced her serve in the early years, **Holiday Park,** 701 NE 12th Ave. (off Sunrise Boulevard), Ft. Lauderdale (☎ **954/ 761-5378**), has 18 clay and 3 hard courts (15 lighted). Her coach and father, James Evert, still teaches young players here, although he's quite picky about whom he'll accept. It's still a great deal; non–Fort Lauderdale residents pay $3 to $4 per hour. Reservations are accepted on weeknights, but cost an extra $3. Lights are also an extra $3 per hour and are only available on the clay courts.

Not too many people have found out about the great free courts at the **Marina Bay Resort,** 2175 S.R. 84, west of I-95 and just behind the Ramada Inn, Ft. Lauderdale (☎ **954/791-7600**). Visitors can play free on any one of nine hard courts on a first-come, first-served basis. Choose a time in the middle of the day, or expect a wait on weekends. Or, consider a night game; three courts are lighted at night.

SEEING THE SIGHTS

For an overview of Fort Lauderdale, you may want to take an informative spin around the downtown area with **South Florida Trolley Tours** (☎ **954/429-3100**). Drivers narrate the history of the area as they loop around the city's streets past all of the major (and many minor) sights. The charge for the 90-minute tour is $12 for adults, free for children 11 and under. The trolleys pick up passengers from most major hotels for six tours daily, starting at 9am. Call for current schedule. For a tour by water, see "More than a Boat Tour," below.

Bonnet House. 900 N. Birch Rd. (1 block west of the ocean, south of Sunrise Blvd.), Ft. Lauderdale. ☎ **954/563-5393.** Admission $9 adults, $8 seniors, $7 students under 18, free for children 6 and under. Tours Wed–Fri 10am–1pm, Sat–Sun noon–3pm; arrive 15 min. before the tour.

This historic 35-acre plantation home and estate survives in the middle of an otherwise highly developed beachfront condominium area and is only open by guided tour. Built in 1921, the sprawling 2-story waterfront home surrounded with formal tropical gardens is really the backdrop of a love story, which the very chatty volunteer guides will share with you if you ask. Some have actually lunched with the former resident of the house, the late Evelyn Bartlett, the wife of world-acclaimed artist Frederic Clay Bartlett. If you like quirky people, whimsical artwork, lush grounds, and very interesting details of design, you'll love this tour, which takes about 1½ hours.

✪ **Butterfly World.** Tradewinds Park South, 3600 W. Sample Rd., Coconut Creek (west of the Florida Turnpike and I-95). ☎ **954/977-4400.** Admission $10.95 adults, $6 children 4–12, free for children 3 and under. Mon–Sat 9am–5pm, Sun 1–5pm; last admission at 4pm.

One of the world's largest butterfly breeders, Butterfly World cultivates more than 150 species of these colorful and delicate insects. In the park's walk-through, screened-in aviary, visitors can see thousands of caterpillars and watch newborn butterflies emerge from their cocoons and flutter around as they learn to fly. Depending on how interested you are in these winged beauties, you may want to allow from 1 to 2 hours to tour the gardens and the well-stocked gift shop. In the new lorikeet aviary (opened limited hours) you can help hand-feed these tiny birds with cups of nectar.

✪ **Museum of Discovery & Science.** 401 SW 2nd St., Ft. Lauderdale. ☎ **954/467-6637.** Museum admission $9 adults, $8 seniors, $7 children 3–12, free for children 2 and under; combo prices $12.50 adults, $11.50 seniors, $10.50 children. Mon–Sat 10am–5pm, Sun noon–6pm. From I-95, exit on Broward Blvd. E.; continue to SW 5th Ave.; turn right; garage on right.

More Than a Boat Tour

Plan to spend at least one afternoon or evening cruising Fort Lauderdale's 300 miles of waterways the only way you can, by boat. The **Water Taxi of Fort Lauderdale** (☎ **954/467-6677**) is one of the greatest innovations for water lovers since those cool Velcro sandals. A trusty fleet of old port boats serves the dual purpose of transporting and entertaining visitors as they cruise through "The Venice of the Americas."

Each taxi operates on demand along a fairly regular route and carries up to 48 passengers. Choose a hotel on the route so that you can take advantage of this convenient and inexpensive system. For a few dollars a day, you can forego the car rental for a day or two and see the best that Lauderdale has to offer. You can be picked up at your hotel, usually within 15 minutes of calling, and then be shuttled to any of the dozens of restaurants, bars, and attractions on or near the waterfront. If you aren't sure where you want to go, ask one of the personable captains who can point out historic and fun spots along the way.

For a day cruise with the kids, pack lunch, bathing suits, sunscreen, and sunglasses and hail or call the taxi for pickup from any safe dock or seawall. Your afternoon of cruising might start with a tour of Millionaires' Row, where Lauderdale's largest yachts are dwarfed only by the homes at which they are docked. Make a stop at the Museum of Discovery and Science where you can catch an IMAX film or just enjoy the current educational exhibits. Then, if you're up for a walk, head across the 3-mile Riverwalk, a scenic palm-lined walkway along the New River, where you can enjoy your picnic lunch or try one of the restaurants dotting the way to Las Olas Boulevard. When you are ready for some shopping or a sit-down meal, reboard and head to Beach Place at Las Olas Boulevard and Cortez Street in the heart of Fort Lauderdale's most famous "strip." Stop for refreshment at Casablanca Cafe and then hit the beach.

In the evening, the water taxi is ideal for bar-hopping—no worries about parking or choosing a designated driver. Make your first stop at Shooters, where professionals, boaters, and tourists share the large lively patio for a popular happy hour from 5 to 7pm on weekdays. Right next door is Bootlegger's, featuring more than 70 beers at an outside bar. You can eat at either spot or keep your eyes on the waterway for your ride (or call for a quicker pickup). For a hard-to-beat meal, try Casablanca, a more romantic option, with piano music.

For those who want good jazz, you might want to take the taxi to the downtown section of Las Olas Boulevard. O'Hara's can always be relied on for a great mix of live jazz and blues.

Starting daily from 10am, boats usually run until midnight (until 2am on weekends), depending on the weather. The cost is $7 per person per trip, $12 round-trip, and $15 for a full day. Children under 12 ride for half price and free on Sunday. Opt for the all-day pass—it's worth it.

All establishments described above (listed under the appropriate headings elsewhere in this chapter) are used to calling the taxi for guests. Still, you may want to keep a few quarters and the phone number on hand, just in case. And, if you find yourself inland without a paddle, call **Yellow Cab** (☎ **954/565-5400**).

Children and teenagers especially love this interactive science museum that is a model of high-tech "infotainment." During the week, school groups meander through the cavernous 2-story modern building. However, most weekend nights you'll find a diverse crowd ranging from hip high school kids to 30-somethings enjoying a rock film in the Blockbuster IMAX 3D theater, which also shows short, science-related, supersize films daily. Out front, see a 52-foot-tall "Great Gravity Clock," located in the museum's atrium, the largest kinetic-energy sculpture in the state. Exhibits vary, so call for the latest details.

Stranahan House. 335 SE 6th Ave. (Las Olas Blvd. at the New River Tunnel), Ft. Lauderdale. ☎ **954/524-4736.** Admission $5 adults, $2 students and children. Wed–Sat 10am–4pm; Sun 1–4pm; the last tour begins at 3:30pm. Also accessible by water taxi.

In a town whose history isn't even as old as many of its residents, visitors may want to take a minute to see Fort Lauderdale's very oldest standing structure and a prime example of classic "Florida Frontier" architecture. Built in 1901 by "the father of Fort Lauderdale," this house once served as a trading post for Seminole trappers who came here to sell pelts. It's been a post office, town hall, and general store and now is a worthwhile little museum of South Florida pioneer life, containing turn-of-the-century furnishings and historical photos of the area, It is also the site of occasional concerts and social functions. Call for details.

SHOPPING & BROWSING

Broward County has some of Florida's best malls and some fantastic boutique areas, too. Lots of consignment shops, second-hand stores, and antique shops make for great bargains.

The best and largest concentration of these shops is clustered along Dixie Highway in Dania. Known as "Antique Row," this area has some of South Florida's best old treasures. Although many of the more upscale shops are overpriced, some of the smaller dealers offer great bargains to hagglers.

Also for bargain mavens is a strip of "fashion" stores on Hallandale Beach Boulevard's "Schmatta Row," east of Dixie Highway and the railroad tracks, where off-name brand shoes, bags, and jewelry are sold at deep discounts. Funky Hollywood Boulevard also offers some wild shops with everything from Indonesian artifacts to used and rare books to leather bustiers to handmade hats. Dozens of shops line the pedestrian-friendly strip just west of Young Circle. The art galleries are clustered along Harrison Street just east of Dixie Highway.

The area's only beachfront mall, **Beach Place,** is in Ft. Lauderdale on A1A just north of Las Olas Boulevard. Completed in 1997 at a cost of $23 million, this 100,000-square-foot giant sports the usual chains like Sunglass Hut, Limited Express, Banana Republic, and the Gap as well as lots of popular bars and restaurants.

Other more traditional malls include the upscale **Galleria at Sunrise Boulevard** near the Fort Lauderdale Beach, and Broward Mall, west of I-95 on Broward Boulevard, in Plantation.

If you are looking for unusual boutiques, especially art galleries, head to trendy **Las Olas Boulevard,** where there are literally hundreds of shops with alluring window decorations and intriguing merchandise. You'll find paintings, books, crystals, furniture, and kitchen utensils posing as modern art sculptures.

The **Fort Lauderdale Swap Shop,** 3291 W. Sunrise Blvd., Sunrise (☎ **954/791-SWAP**), is one of the world's largest flea markets. In addition to endless acres of vendors, there's a mini-amusement park, a 13-screen drive-in movie theater, weekend concerts, and even a free circus complete with elephants, horse shows, high-wire acts, and clowns.

Attention Bargain Shoppers

The well-known department store **Lord & Taylor** has a little-known clearance center where discounts on new clothing for women, kids, and men can be as big as 75%. If you can handle open dressing rooms, overstuffed racks, and surly sales help, it's a great find at 6820 N. University Dr. in Tamarac. Call ☎ **954/720-1915** to find out about specials.

The monster of all outlet malls is **Sawgrass Mills,** 12801 W. Sunrise Blvd., Sunrise (☎ **800/FL-MILLS** or 954/846-2350). Since the most recent expansion, which added more than 30 new designer outlet stores, this behemoth complex (shaped like a Florida alligator) now holds more than 275 shops and kiosks in nearly 2.3 million square feet covering 50 acres. Wear your most comfortable shoes (or buy an extra pair while you're there). Stores include Donna Karan Company Store, Levi's Outlet, Sunglass Hut, Ann Taylor Loft, and Barney's New York, all selling goods at between 20% and 80% below retail. Label-conscious shoppers are especially impressed with Off Fifth, the Saks Fifth Avenue outlet store and Last Call, the Neiman Marcus clearance center. Take I-95 north to I-595 west to the Flamingo Road exit, turn right, and drive 2 miles to Sunrise Boulevard; you will see the large complex on the left. From the Florida Turnpike, exit Sunrise Boulevard west. Parking is free. But don't forget where you parked; the lot is huge. You may want to invest in a coupon booklet ($5), which entitles you to even greater discounts at many of the mall's stores and restaurants, as well as area attractions. Books are valid for up to a year. Although they don't advertise this fact, you can usually turn in an outdated and partially used book for a new one at no charge.

ACCOMMODATIONS YOU CAN AFFORD

The Fort Lauderdale beach has a hotel or motel on nearly every block, and they range from the rundown to the luxurious.

For those who want a chain, consider the **Howard Johnson** (☎ 800/327-8578 or 954/563-2451), at 700 N. Atlantic Blvd. (on A1A, south of Sunrise Blvd.), where off-season promotional rates start at $58 and rooms in season start at $100. The **Days Inn** (☎ **800/866-6501** or 954/462-0444), at 435 N. Atlantic Blvd. (A1A), has clean ocean-side rooms for about $68 in the off-season; in season, you can get a basic room for $85 and up.

In Hollywood, where prices are generally cheaper, Howard Johnson (☎ **800/ 423-9867** or 954/925-1411) has a great location right on the beach at 2501 N. Ocean Dr. (I-95 to Sheridan Street east to A1A south). Rooms start at $59 and go up as high as $184 in season.

If you are looking for something more private or for longer than a few days, you may want to call a reservations service for help. Especially for rentals for a few weeks or months, call Florida Sunbreak (☎ **888/SUNBREAK**), Oakwood Corporate Housing (☎ **954/961-9797**), or the South Florida Hotel Network (☎ **800/ 538-3616**) for help finding condos, small inns, and lodges in any price range. Oakwood requires a minimum of 30 days stay and has more than 50 properties at any given time. A one-bedroom with weekly maid service could go for about $2,200 a month. That works out to about $75 a night. A great deal, especially considering you're getting a full apartment with a full-size kitchen. You can often find much cheaper apartments farther from the beach areas.

Most condo rentals are at least double the size of a standard hotel room and cost considerably less. In talking to several companies, I've found that rates work out to be as low as $50 a night to as high as $200. Most fall in the lower end. Even with the required 11% or 12% tax, for privacy and convenience it's still a great way to go. And don't forget that with a kitchen, you'll save on your meal budget by eating some meals at home. Parking is included in most places as well, a major savings. There are usually plenty of choices on the waterfront. But call well in advance to reserve exactly what you want.

Gay travelers will be glad to know that over the last several years many new gay-owned and -operated hotels and guest houses have opened up near the strip. The very nicest (and most expensive) is **The Royal Palms** at 2901 Terramar (☎ 800/237-PALM; www.royalpalms.com). Owned and operated by a congenial British host, this gorgeous 12-room resort was voted the number-one superior small lodging several years running by the Ft. Lauderdale Convention & Visitors Bureau. A more affordable choice and a good value is the **King Henry Arms,** at 543 Breakers Ave. (☎ 800/205-KING), with in-season singles starting at $71.

Also, check out the annual list of small lodgings compiled by the Ft. Lauderdale Convention & Visitors Bureau (☎ 954/765-4466). Many give considerable discounts for stays of over a week.

SUPER-CHEAP SLEEPS

Bermudian Waterfront Motel and Apartments. 315 N. Birch Rd., Ft. Lauderdale, FL 33304. ☎ **954/467-0467.** Fax 954/467-0467, ext. 5. 24 units, all with bathroom. A/C TV TEL. Winter $30–$65 motel rm. single or double, $65–$95 efficiency; $105–$118 apt. Off-season $21–$42 motel rm. single or double, $30–$42 efficiency; $47–$54 apt. Special weekly rates available. Extra person $10. MC, V. Free parking. From Sunrise Blvd., head east to A1A, then south to Grendada Rd., turn right.

This formerly elegant little Spanish-style building sits right on a gorgeous waterfront spot that's on the route of the efficient and fun water taxi. Besides that, what it has going for it is price, quiet, and decent-sized rooms, all with kitchenettes. The hodge-podge of secondhand furniture is comfortable and functional. All rooms have new carpeting and small tiled bathrooms, and some overlook a small tropical courtyard or the bay. The 2-story 1950s building could use some repairs, but it couldn't be more private. All rooms are quiet and well laid out. You probably won't see your fellow travelers, since there isn't any kind of lobby or common area, but they tend to be a mix of vacationing Americans and Europeans. The managers, when they're around, seem a bit harried. Still, for the money this is one of the best deals on the block, just a 2-minute walk to the ocean.

✪ **The Martindale at the Beach Resort.** 3006 Bayshore Dr. (between Sunrise and Las Olas blvds.), Ft. Lauderdale, FL 33304. ☎800/666-1841 or 954/467-1841. Fax 954/763-8109. www.florida2000.com/martindale. E-mail: ftlaud@gate.net. 18 units, all with bathroom (some with shower only). A/C TV TEL. Winter $65–$90 single or double; $115 1-bedroom apt.; $115–$175 2-bedroom apt. or penthouse for up to 4 people. Off-season $40–$60 single or double; $70 1-bedroom apt.; $80–$120 2-bedroom apt. for up to 4 people. AE, MC, V. Free parking.

One of the best little bargains on the strip, the Martindale keeps getting better. You'll walk through a pretty gate into a lushly landscaped garden that frames this simple, single-story motel-style resort. Free coffee is served in the courtyard, and the herb garden is perfect for a quiet stroll. Rooms, especially the efficiencies and apartments, are spacious and pleasantly decorated. Plus, most have at least a small fridge. For recreation you can putt a few balls on the minigolf course, swim in the small outdoor heated pool, or have a little barbecue with the gas grill. The best part is, you are steps away from Ft. Lauderdale's most popular beach and boardwalk.

Ronny Dee Resort Motel. 717 S. Ocean Blvd., Pompano Beach, FL 33062. ☎ **954/943-3020.** Fax 954/783-5112. 12 units; 24 efficiencies (rented only by the week), all with bathroom (most with shower only). A/C TV. Winter from $62 single or double; from $469 efficiency. Off-season from $32 single or double; from $225 efficiency. AE, MC, V. From I-95, exit Atlantic Blvd. E. to A1A north.

The bad news is that this family-owned motel is located on busy Fla. A1A; the good news is that it's just 100 yards from the beach and amazingly inexpensive. Popular with European guests, this 2-story yellow motel, wrapped around a central swimming pool, contains almost three dozen suburban-style wood-paneled guest rooms filled with an eclectic mix of furniture. All contain a small refrigerator, but none has a telephone; pay phones are located in a public area, near a large game room that contains a pool table, VCR, books, and other games. Ping-Pong and shuffleboard are also available.

✪ **Sea Downs (and the Bougainvillea).** 2900 N. Surf Rd., Hollywood, FL 33019. ☎ **954/923-4968.** Fax 954/923-8747. www.seadowns.com. seadowns@aol.com. 14 units, all with bathroom (some with shower only). A/C TV TEL. Winter $67–$85 efficiency, single or double; $93–$118 1-bedroom apt. and penthouse. Off-season $42–$62 efficiency, single or double; $59–$88 1-bedroom apt. Special weekly and monthly rates also available. No credit cards accepted. Free parking. From I-95, exit Sheridan St. E. to Fla. A1A south; drive a half mile to Coolidge St.; turn left.

This bargain accommodation is often booked months in advance by returning guests who want to be directly on the beach without paying a fortune. The hosts of this superclean '50s motel, Claudia and Karl Herzog, live on the premises and keep things running smoothly. They own an even less expensive property next door, the Bougainvillea. For the very best deal, choose this option, which is just half a block from the ocean. One-bedroom units here are slightly larger, bathrooms were thoroughly replaced recently, and prices are significantly lower. Guests at either spot can use the heated pool, barbecue grills, picnic area, laundry facilities, and sundeck. Besides the charming and caring owners, the best part is that all rooms have either fully-equipped kitchens or kitchenettes. The properties are also on a relatively quiet but convenient stretch of Hollywood beach.

Southern Shores Motel. 3017 Bayshore Dr., Ft. Lauderdale, FL 33304. ☎ **954/564-2904.** Fax 954/564-1785. 32 units, all with bathroom. A/C TV TEL. Winter $70 hotel rm., single or double; $86–$103 efficiency or 1-bedroom apt. Off-season $42 hotel rm. single or double; $53–$83 efficiency or 1-bedroom. AE, DC, DISC, MC, V. Free parking.

This pleasant 2-story motel is run with grace and style by Renate and Michael Flik of Germany. Since they purchased the property in late 1990s, they have been busily renovating the building and sprucing the grounds. With two fresh water pools, a grassy barbecue area, and a stellar location a block from the ocean, you couldn't ask for more for the money. Rooms are furnished with modest and generic furnishings, which are just fine. All rooms also have refrigerators, a big plus at this otherwise pricey beach location. It's on par with its neighbor The Martindale, though it has a larger and slightly nicer pool area.

The Best Hostel in Town

Floyd's Hostel & Crew House. Please call for address and directions in Ft. Lauderdale. ☎ **954/462-0631.** Fax 954/462-6881. E-mail: FECreamer@earthlink.net. 40-plus beds in 10 units, all with shared bathroom (with shower only). $13.50 single with shared bathroom; $85.50/week. No credit cards. Free daytime pickup with advanced arrangements.

Although there are a number of cheap hostels operating closer to Fort Lauderdale's renowned strip, the best place to crash is Floyd's. While it is about a mile from the beach, this well-kept lodging offers what every backpacker and international traveler wants—safety and good, warm fellow travelers. Floyd himself takes care of the guests, many of whom have come looking for work on the area's yachts. In fact, we have agreed not to list the address since Floyd insists on interviewing each prospective guest by phone before booking. Rest assured, you've found one of the area's best and safest hostels with extras like a cupboard full of complimentary staples—milk, cereal, spaghetti, rice, and generic-brand macaroni and cheese. An added bonus is that about half the rooms are reserved as no-smoking, a rarity in the hostel world. Five living room/common areas and a lovely garden patio are great places to congregate in the evening.

FOR A FEW BUCKS MORE

✪ **Banyan Marina Apartments.** 111 Isle of Venice, Ft. Lauderdale, FL 33301. ☎ **954/ 524-4430.** Fax 954/764-4870. www.banyanmarinaapts.com. E-mail: banyan-laud@ travelbase.com. 10 units, all with bathroom. A/C TV TEL. Winter $80–$175 apt., single or double. Off-season $50–$120 apt. Weekly and monthly rates available. MC, V. To get there from I-95, exit Broward Blvd. E.; cross U.S. 1 and turn right on SE 15th Ave.; at the first traffic light (Las Olas Blvd.), turn left. Turn left at the third island (Isle of Venice).

You'll feel as if your best friends left you their keys to their well-kept waterfront apartment at Peter and Dagmar Neufeldt's Banyan Marina. One of the best accommodation values in South Florida, this hidden treasure is built around a dramatic 75-year-old banyan tree and is located directly on an active waterway, halfway between Fort Lauderdale's downtown and the beach. The accommodations, one- and two-bedroom apartments, are all decorated differently. All are comfortable and spacious with full kitchens and living rooms. The best part of staying here, besides your gracious and knowledgeable hosts, is that the water taxi will find you here and take you anywhere you want to be day or night. There is also a small outdoor heated pool and a marina for those with boats.

✪ **Hollywood Beach Resort.** 101 N. Ocean Drive (at A1A and Hollywood Blvd.), Hollywood, FL 33019. ☎ **800/331-6103** or 954/921-0990. Fax 954/920-9480. 400 units (approximately 200 on rental program), all with bathroom. A/C TV TEL. Winter from $109 single or double. Off-season from $68 single or double. AE, DC, DISC, MC, V. Valet parking $8.

There is nothing cozy or quaint about this sprawling 1920s beachfront hotel, but it couldn't be better located or better priced. The two best features are that all the rooms have full kitchens and the hotel is directly on the ocean. This 8-story building, an imposing Mediterranean structure that was once a bible college, actually operates as a privately held condominium where owners can elect to put their units on a rental program. Thus the furnishings and decor vary widely (though the management does maintain certain standards). All the units I have seen are clean and modest. Larger units and those with views are significantly more expensive than studios. If the weather is bad, consider shopping at the adjacent Ocean Walk mall or hit a movie at the on-site multiplex movie theater. Also on the premises is a large outdoor pool and Jacuzzi. The many conveniences of this well-situated property make it especially popular with tour groups from Europe, South America, and Canada.

Riverside Hotel. 620 E. Las Olas Blvd., Ft. Lauderdale, FL 33301. ☎ **800/325-3280** or 954/467-0671. Fax 954/462-2148. www.riversidehotel.com. 116 units, all with bathroom. A/C TV TEL. Winter $179–$189 single or double; from $249 suite. Off-season $119–$149 single or double; from $169 suite. AE, DC, MC, V. From I-95, exit onto Broward Blvd.; turn right onto Federal Hwy. (U.S. 1), then left onto Las Olas Blvd.

Right in the thick of Ft. Lauderdale's hottest downtown area, the 6-story Riverside Hotel is one of the oldest in South Florida. Built in 1936, it looks like a Wild West movie set, complete with a second-floor wooden terrace and an enormous mural on the front facade. You are in the middle of trendy Las Olas Boulevard and on the route of the popular water taxi. On weekends the hotel is often packed with wedding guests attending ceremonies that are held outside by the small heated swimming pool. A bit nicer than the public areas that are outfitted in Mexican tile and wicker furnishings, the guest rooms upstairs are spacious and well maintained. Details like intricately tiled bathrooms and old-style furniture enhance the charm of the otherwise stark building. The best rooms face the New River, but it's hard to see the water past the parking lot and trees. The hotel does not have an abundance of services or facilities, but the central downtown location puts almost anything you could desire just steps away.

Do sample **Indigo,** a fantastic Asian/Indonesian restaurant in the hotel lobby (see "Great Deals on Dining," below). Also on the premises is a more traditional grill restaurant and a lounge.

WORTH A SPLURGE

Hyatt Regency Fort Lauderdale at Pier 66 Marina. 2301 SE 17th St. Causeway, Ft. Lauderdale, FL 33316. ☎ **800/233-1234** or 954/525-6666. Fax 954/728-3541. 396 units, all with bathroom. A/C MINIBAR TV TEL. Winter $209 single or double. Off-season $169 single or double. Year-round from $1,000 suite. AE, DC, DISC, MC, V. Valet parking $10.

The Pier 66 hotel and 142-slip marina has been hosting guests, especially boaters, since 1954. The luxurious resort attracts megayachts from all over the world, in addition to large groups and business travelers. Despite the emphasis on hosting large groups, for services and amenities this Hyatt is hard to beat. In addition to a large adjacent beach, this Hyatt also offers Spectravision movie channels, two swimming pools, a fully equipped spa, Jacuzzi, sauna, 40-person whirlpool, a jogging track, children's programs, a sundeck, two lighted clay tennis courts, water-sports equipment and boat rentals, 142-slip marina, a beauty salon, boutiques, and a shopping arcade.

Best known for its revolving rooftop lounge, the hotel also offers an American grill and a very popular waterfront cafe for dinner and lunch.

The hotel's atrium-style lobby impresses with high ceilings and marble floors. The lushly landscaped grounds add to the exotic feel of this convenient locale, situated across from the beach, and within walking distance to the best shopping and dining. Every room has a balcony; the priciest have expansive panoramas of the marina, the beach across the street, and all of Fort Lauderdale beyond. The best part is that it is serviced by the convenient water taxi.

✪ Lago Mar Resort and Club. 1700 S. Ocean Lane, Ft. Lauderdale, FL 33316. ☎ **800/255-5246** or 954/523-6511. Fax 954/524-6627. E-mail: reservations@lagomar.com. 170 units, all with bathroom. A/C TV TEL. Winter $195 single or double; from $265 suite. Off-season $90–$100 single or double; from $125 suite. AE, DC, MC, V. From Federal Hwy. (U.S. 1), turn east onto SE 17th St. Causeway; turn right onto Mayan Dr.; turn right again onto South Ocean Dr.; turn left onto Grace Dr.; then left again onto South Ocean Lane to the hotel.

After extensive renovations, this sprawling family owned resort is even better than before. Lago Mar, a casually elegant resort, occupies its own little island between Lake Mayan and the Atlantic and is very family oriented, with lots of facilities, restaurants, lounges, and supervised activities for children (especially during the winter holidays). It's also good for business travelers looking for value. Unfortunately, the word has gotten out and it has become difficult to get reservations during the season.

Most accommodations here are suites, available in a variety of configurations. The smallest suites, called "executive," are decorated in contemporary prints and are simple and comfortable. The executive suites are very large, with a king-size bed, separate dressing area, pull-out sofa, and separate tub and shower in an extralarge bathroom.

Each has a private balcony and full kitchen, or at least a microwave and a refrigerator. Ask for one of the newer units since they are generally larger and have more closet space. Definitely take advantage of the hotel's waterfront location to utilize the convenient water taxi, the outdoor pool, lagoon, beach, and sundeck. You'll also appreciate four tennis courts, miniature golf course, volleyball courts, shuffleboard, water-sports concession, men's and women's apparel shops, Laundromat, and tour desk.

BED & BREAKFASTS

These B&Bs may seem a bit higher priced than the most budget selections, but the location and personal services you get, plus free breakfast and complimentary evening extras, mean saving money at restaurants and bars.

La Casa del Mar. 3003 Granada St. (behind the Sheraton Yankee Trader Hotel on A1A), Ft. Lauderdale, FL 33304. ☎ **954/467-2037.** Fax 954/467-7439. 10 units, all with bathroom. A/C TV TEL. Winter $95–$135 single or double. Off-season $75–$95 single or double. Rates include breakfast and evening wine and cheese. Extra person $25. AE, DC, MC, V. Free parking.

Opened in 1994 by a pair of hospitable Chicagoans, Larry Ataniso and Lee Prellwitz, this charming 2-story Spanish Mediterranean–style B&B is the area's quaintest and most private. The setup is more like a motel in which each of the 10 rooms in the curved building is separate and has its own bathroom. Be sure to check in between 3pm and 6pm to take advantage of the nightly wine and cheese gathering by the outdoor pool.

The pair of 1940s buildings offers spacious guest rooms, which have remained intact over the years and have benefited from an extensive redecorating and enough refurbishing to make them clean, if not pristine. Choose the Stolen Kiss Room, based on Fragonard's painting, or a modest rendition of a Victorian room, decorated with budget reproductions and warm colors. All rooms are equipped with limited kitchenettes (you get a microwave but no range) and VCRs. At no charge, you can choose any video you like from the hosts' library. There isn't much of a view, though you're less than a block from the ocean. This unique inn attracts an eclectic mix of budget-conscious European and American vacationers.

✪ **A Little Inn by the Sea.** 4546 El Mar Dr., Lauderdale-by-the-Sea, FL 33308. ☎ **954/772-2450.** Fax 954/938-9354. 37 units, all with bathroom (some with shower only). A/C TV TEL. Winter $99–$139 single or double; $159–169 suite. Off-season $69–$89 single or double; $105–$120 suite. Rates include continental breakfast. Extra person $10. Children 11 and under stay free in parents' rm. AE, MC, V. Free self- or valet parking.

This little bed-and-breakfast by the sea is one of the most imaginatively designed inns on the Gold Coast and is recommendable for those who can do without all the services and facilities of a resort hotel. Meticulously fashioned both inside and out, the B&B is actually a pair of former motels connected by a fountain courtyard with small cafe tables. The rooms are themed with boats or birds or shells, and many come with balconies and small kitchenettes. Some rooms include a romantic mesh canopy over the bed and sofas in a tasteful sitting area. Breakfast is served in the courtyard, and guests are welcome to bring the pool furniture onto the adjacent beach.

GREAT DEALS ON DINING

Having hosted visitors for so long, Fort Lauderdale, and to some extent Hollywood as well, have some of South Florida's finest restaurants. Increasingly, ethnic restaurants are joining the legions of surf-and-turf options that dominated the area for so long. Las Olas Boulevard has dozens of eateries (so many in fact that the city has disallowed any new restaurants to open on the overcrowded 2-mile strip). Stroll along to choose from a number of good options, including **Wrapido's** at 604 East Las Olas Blvd. (☎ 954/764-4422), which sells delicious gourmet tortilla wraps.

SUPER-CHEAP EATS

Deli Den. 2889 Sterling Rd. (west of I-95), Ft. Lauderdale. ☎ **561/961-4070.** Main courses $5–$11, bagel sandwiches $1– $7.50. AE, MC, V. Daily 8am–10pm. JEWISH-STYLE DELI.

Catering to Broward's New York crowd for nearly 3 decades, this bustling deli serves the area's finest cheese blintzes, red cabbage soup, and matzo balls around. Breakfast selections include superthick French toast with bacon, sausage, or ham, plus dozens of egg specialties like minced lox, eggs, and onions or corned beef hash and eggs. All baking is done on the premises. And owners are proud to say that absolutely everything else from coleslaw to blintzes is also homemade.

✪ **East Coast Burrito Factory.** 261 E. Commercial Blvd., Ft. Lauderdale. ☎ **954/ 772-8007.** Tacos and burritos $3–$6; salads $4–$6. AE, CB, DC, DISC, MC, V. Mon–Sat 11am–9:45pm, Sun noon–7:45pm. FLORIDA/MEXICAN.

Just off of I-95, this is an oasis. A dozen wooden benches line the counter at this super Mexican diner, which serves made-to-order soft tacos, burritos, hot dogs, and salads. For a healthier spin on a burrito, try the Florito, made with black beans instead of refried beans—a uniquely Florida invention. My favorite is the "Super Veggie," stuffed with corn, salsa, mushrooms, black olives, carrots, peppers, and hearts of palm, then doused with the restaurant's own superhot chile sauce. The guacamole and various huge salads are also fantastic, especially on a sunny day on the back patio. My only complaint is that the burritos are way too big and sloppy.

Mama Mia Italian Ristorante. 1818 S. Young Circle, Hollywood. ☎ **954/923-0555.** Reservations accepted. Main courses $5–$13. AE, MC, V. Sun–Thurs 11:30am–11pm, Fri–Sat 11:30am–midnight. ITALIAN.

Mama Mia is a good, old-fashioned Italian joint that serves up authentic food at a great price. They make a fine calzone, if that's your weakness, and a great pizza with a crust so thin you can feel the cheese through the bottom. As for the toppings themselves, they're eclectic to say the least. You can choose your own or order one of the "theme pizzas" named after different regions of Italy. Be warned that you'll have plenty for the next day's lunch—portions are huge, especially the steaming plate of sausages and peppers.

Tark's. 1317 S. Federal Hwy. (at SE 13th Terrace), Dania. ☎ **954/925-TARK.** Main courses $5–$9. AE, MC, V. Sun–Thurs 11am–10pm, Fri and Sat 11am–11pm. SEAFOOD/WINGS.

This popular clam shack is little more than a big U-shaped counter with a harried waitress and a busy short-order chef who cranks out fried, steamed, and baked fish dishes. Small in size and big on atmosphere, the chowder room's business-card and neon-sign decor sets the mood for hearty eating and beer drinking. For a quieter time, try the newer outdoor seating. This budget spot offers daily specials, like 10 raw oysters on the half-shell on Thursdays for only $4.95 and 10 chicken wings on Monday for just $3.75. Appetizers include calamari rings, conch fritters, shrimp cocktail, mozzarella sticks, and clam chowder. Fried, charcoal-broiled, and blackened fish are maincourse staples, but burgers, frogs' legs, and fried alligator are also available, as are raw and steamed oysters, clam bellies, steaks, and clams. A cheap kids' menu offers chicken, shrimp, or burgers with fries and soda for less than $4.

For a Few Bucks More

Aruba Beach Cafe. 1 E. Commercial Blvd., Lauderdale-by-the-Sea. ☎ **954/776-0001.**
Reservations accepted only for parties of 10 or more. Main courses $9–$16. AE, DC, DISC,
MC, V. Daily 11am–11pm (bar stays open later). SEAFOOD/AMERICAN.

More recommendable as a spot to drink than to eat, Aruba is popular at all hours,
especially because of its very central location, directly on the beach at the end of Commercial Boulevard. The extensive menu offers salads, sandwiches, and the requisite
seafood offerings. The food is fine, but uninspired. Choose a few good appetizers like
the creamy smoked fish dip served with seasoned flat bread, the fried calamari, or a
selection from the raw bar.

☼ Casablanca Cafe. On the ocean at the corner of Fla. A1A and Alahambra St., Ft. Lauderdale. ☎ **954/764-3500.** Reservations not accepted. Main courses $8–$18. AE, DISC, DC,
MC, V. Daily 11:30am–11pm. CONTINENTAL/AMERICAN.

Although it may seem odd to sit next to a roaring fire while listening to live music in
the warm South Florida climate, at Casablanca it's a perfect complement to the stunning architecture and stupendous cooking. Everything from the warm macadamia
nut–encrusted goat-cheese salad to a filet mignon in a cognac-and-mushroom sauce
served with perfectly al dente pasta is immaculately prepared and served by a friendly
staff. Six or seven specials are included daily on the menu; the best are seafood creations with superfresh local fish or lobster.

Conca D'Oro. 1833 Tyler St. (on Young Circle), Hollywood. ☎ **954/927-6704.** Reservations not accepted. Pizzas $7–$12.50; main courses $12–$18. MC, V. Mon–Thurs
11am–11pm. Fri–Sat 11am–midnight. Sun 4pm–11pm. ITALIAN.

This bustling Italian eatery is always busy. It's not that the food is so extraordinary, but
that the portions are large, service is quick, and the attitude is straight from Brooklyn.
The pizzas, served Neapolitan (thin crust) or Sicilian style, are large and topped with
lots of cheese and a good tangy tomato sauce. Don't expect more than iceberg lettuce
in the salads, but do take advantage of the huge heroes and tasty house wines. If you
are with a group, order one or two entrees to share—you *will* have leftovers. Although
they are not always on the menu, ask for fresh mussels if they are in season. While
other appetizers are battered and fried, the young black mussels are done to perfection
in a red or white sauce. Also good is the hearty lasagna that is full of chunks of garlicky meatballs and mild sausage.

☼ Indigo. 620 East Las Olas Blvd. (in the Riverside Hotel). ☎ **954/467-0671.** Reservations
only for groups of 6 or more. Main courses $11–$19. AE, DC, MC, V. Daily 7am–11pm;
weekends until midnight or later. SOUTHEAST ASIAN/ECLECTIC.

This not-so-traditional Southeast Asian meal begins with a basket of pappadoms,
naan, and shrimp puff bread. All are delicious and easy to fill up on, especially when
spread with the tangy pineapple chutney or cucumber pickle. An impressive appetizer
is a lightly pepper-dusted seared tuna served in crispy basket of udon noodles. Look
underneath for a hidden dab of sweet apricot puree. It's fantastically rich and a good
complement to the spicy fish. A macadamia encrusted brie is astounding, served over
baby lettuce and mixed with a citrusy basil dressing. Extracrispy crostini are scattered
over the hearty dish for extra dipping advantage. Entrees run the gamut from a lean
though somewhat dry Balinese lamb to a musky smoked duckling to a rosemary-
skewered shrimp. As to be expected in Asian cuisine, vegetarians have plenty of
choices, too. In addition to a superrich grilled vegetable cassoulet au gratin and a fried
rice dish with shallots, corn and asparagus, there are pizzas baked on top of puffy naan
bread covered with such toppings as onions, shiitake mushrooms, goat cheese,
spinach, eggplant, garlic, curried tomato, and pine nuts. Particularly good is a meaty

soy and portobello mushroom combination wrapped in fluffy puff pastry served with a delicate broccoli sauce. Most all dishes are as tasty as they are interesting. Ask servers for suggestions, though. Even if they are a bit harried on weekends, they tend to be knowledgeable and honest.

✪ **Sugar Reef.** 600 N. Surf Rd. (on the Broadwalk just north of Hollywood Blvd.), Hollywood. ☎ **954/922-1119.** Reservations only for groups over 6. Main courses $12–$20; sandwiches and salads $5–$8.50. AE, DISC, MC, V. Mon 4–10:30pm, Tues–Thurs 11am–10:30pm, Fri–Sun 11am–11pm (sometimes later in winter). TROPICAL FRENCH.

A welcome addition to a strip of greasy fish joints, hot-dog stands, and bars, Sugar Reef has captured the attention of visitors and locals who appreciate superior and imaginative meals served for very reasonable prices. Chef-owner Patrick Farnault left a successful and formal restaurant in Fort Lauderdale to open this ocean-side bistro. Simple offerings might include a salmon BLT with dill mayonnaise or Jamaican-style pork loin or a burger and fries. Portions are generous but not huge. Escargot in a green curry sauce with lemongrass is a delicious twist on an old favorite, evoking memories of subtle and spicy Vietnamese dishes. More than half a dozen salads, some with cheese, chicken, or fish, are a perfect meal for beach-goers looking for something light and healthful as they enjoy the view. As is fitting for a beachside eatery, service is laid back but still professional.

Sushi Blues Cafe. 1836 S. Young Circle (east on Hollywood Blvd.), Hollywood. ☎ **954/ 929-9560.** Reservations recommended on weekends. Main courses $11–$20; nigiri sushi $1.50–$2.75 per piece. AE, MC, V. Mon–Thurs 6pm–midnight, Fri–Sat 6pm–1:30am. JAPANESE.

Live loud blues and jazz combine with pretty good sushi to make an unusual pair at this small storefront eatery located on Hollywood's largest traffic circle. There are only about 12 tables and a dozen counter stools in this relatively straightforward and unadorned sushi room. In addition to raw fish, the cafe offers some inventive specials like salmon carpaccio with caper sauce, fried soft-shell crab drizzled with a spicy sesame sauce, miso-broiled eggplant, and grilled smoked sausage with Japanese mustard. The restaurant is popular with a 20-something crowd and is packed when there's live music, Friday and Saturday nights.

✪ **Thai Spice.** 1514 E. Commercial Blvd. (east of I-95), Ft. Lauderdale. ☎ **954/771-4535.** Main courses $9–$26. AE, DC, DISC, MC, V. Mon–Thurs and Sun 11am–3pm and 5–10pm, Fri–Sat 5–11pm. THAI.

The tacky and typical decor of Thai Spice belies the authentic and delicious food turned out here. Soft-shell crab in a light and subtle chile sauce and tender shrimp cakes are fantastic and frequent specials. Regular menu items include a slightly sweet and almost buttery pad Thai with a generous serving of shrimp, chicken chunks, and scallion. Lunch specials are obscenely cheap and include all the favorites.

Topanga! 5001 N. Federal Hwy. (at Commercial Blvd.), Ft. Lauderdale. ☎ **954/771-8555.** Reservations for 5 or more suggested. Main courses $9–$13. Pastas $7–$10. AE, CB, DISC, MC, V. Mon–Thurs 11:30am– 10pm, Fri 11:30am–11pm, Sat noon–11pm, Sun noon–10pm. CALIFORNIA-STYLE GRILL/PIZZA BISTRO.

This bright and bustling restaurant is a perfect choice for a quick, relatively healthful lunch or dinner. Local businesspeople favor it in the afternoons since they can get in and out within 45 minutes or linger for hours in the pleasant sun-drenched eatery. There is even an outside terrace for those who don't mind the busy highway as a backdrop. With a large but not overwhelming menu, featuring Italian favorites like chicken marsala, pizzas, and more than a dozen pastas, this is a place that appeals to everyone (including the kids). Salads are large (like most other entrees) and can easily be shared by three. Or, ask for a half portion, which is plenty big for one or two. My favorite is a mix of fresh baby greens with large slabs of moist and spicy dolphin (mahimahi) and chunks of feta cheese, briny Greek olives, and a slightly sweet champagne vinaigrette dressing. Pizzas, too, are fresh and filling. Try the goat cheese and basil or the unusual Acapulco chicken with tequila, lime, herbs, and a side of guacamole and salsa. The daily specials like beef and veal meat loaf, seafood quesadilla, or lemon and dill salmon are usually a good bet. It's a super value and a great find in the middle of a fast-food glutted highway.

WORTH A SPLURGE

✪ **Cafe Maxx.** 2601 E. Atlantic Blvd., Pompano Beach. ☎ **954/782-0606.** Reservations recommended. Main courses $18–$32. AE, CB, DC, DISC, MC, V. Mon–Thurs 5:30–10:30pm, Fri–Sat 5:30–11pm, Sun 5:30–10pm. From I-95, exit at Atlantic Blvd. E. The restaurant is 3 lights east of Federal Hwy. INTERNATIONAL.

Every one of chef-owner Oliver Saucy's restaurants have received accolades from all who bestow them in the culinary arena. This is his best. An oak-burning grill fills the contemporary and casually formal space with enticing aromas from around the globe. The pricey à la carte offerings borrow from Italian, Asian, Creole, Cuban, and Caribbean kitchens to create exotic and delicious mixes like potato-encrusted soft-shell crab, barbecued chicken quesadilla, and pistachio-fried oysters, as well as a host of other exciting but not overwrought dishes. Consider a 5:30pm table, when you can order a few appetizers to share and a glass of wine or two without emptying your wallet. Reserve early on weekends when the most coveted seats, the cozy booths, book well in advance.

East City Grill. 505 N. Atlantic Blvd. (Fla. A1A between Las Olas and Sunrise blvds.), Ft. Lauderdale. ☎ **954/565-5569.** Reservations recommended. Main courses $13–$27. AE, DC, DISC, MC, V. Mon–Tues 11:30–3pm and 5:30–10:30 or 11pm, Wed–Fri 5:30–11pm, Sat 10am–3pm and 5:30pm–midnight, Sun 8am–3pm and 5:30–10pm. Hours vary, especially in the off-season. ASIAN-AMERICAN/SEAFOOD.

This happening spot on the beach offers an ocean-side location and a killer nouvelle-style menu. For starters consider steamed crab and goat-cheese dumplings, lots of innovative sushi dishes, or Jamaican beer-steamed prawns. A steamer bar allows you to create your own dinner with a choice of steaming broths, sauces, and sides. You must be creative to dine here. If you are and you love fresh, interesting seafood, you won't mind the wait at the stunning oak bar where you can look into the open kitchen. Otherwise, stick to the old-fashioned steak and fish houses in town.

✪ **Revolution 2029.** 2029 Harrison St., Hollywood. ☎ **954/920-4748.** Reservations suggested. Main courses $13–$24. AE, DC, DISC, MC, V. Mon (call to check, may be open for dinner), Tues–Fri 11:30am–3pm, Sun–Thurs 5–10pm, Fri–Sat 5pm–midnight. MULTI-CULTURAL.

One of the first froufrou eateries in otherwise dowdy Hollywood, Revolution attracts upscale hipsters looking for a dining "experience." While nearby South Beach has plenty of this kind of thing, Hollywood is just catching on. The menu is as modern as the sleek decor. With the best of everything from around the world, the menu varies seasonally. You may want to start with gorgeous green New Zealand mussels gently flavored with coriander, coconut curry broth, and chunks of crisp apple or a rich roasted corn chowder with sweet potato and spinach corn custard. For vegetarians, there are many great options like oven-roasted portabello mushrooms, crispy vegetable egg rolls, and almond-crusted goat cheese. Innovative dishes like tamarind grilled swordfish and port marinated pork chops are interesting but not overly fussy. The steak is one of the best in town. Introduced in 1998 and I hope still in effect by the time you are reading this is Family Night, a great bargain on some Wednesday nights. Parents spend only $20.29 for a three-course meal and kids enjoy a show and casual meal for only $5. Call for a rundown of the menu.

THE HOLLYWOOD & FORT LAUDERDALE AREA AFTER DARK

The newly hip downtown area of Hollywood is centered around Harrison Street and Young Circle (east of Dixie Highway at Hollywood Boulevard). A funky menagerie of bookstores, coffee shops, galleries, and a couple of live music joints are worth exploring. One of the latest and most welcome additions is ✪ **O'Hara's Pub and Jazz Cafe,** at 1905 Hollywood Boulevard (☎954/925-2555). Kitty Ryan, who operates another club with the same name in Ft. Lauderdale, has duplicated her successes here with a smoking jazz club that attracts superior acts from all over.

A funkier set hangs out at **Warehaus 57** just across the street (☎ 954/926-6633), where longhairs converse over killer frozen coffee drinks or glasses of jug wine. This used bookstore, clothing store, and acoustic music venue is an inviting and happening little spot. During the week, come for a game of backgammon or a cup of Joe. Folky local bands play on weekends to the delight of an eclectic crowd that comes at the generous invitation of owner Lauren Tellman (who also designs the racy and strappy leather clothing in the back). During the week she closes at 6pm, but Fridays and Saturdays she's there until at least midnight.

Sushi Blues was one of the first spots to offer live music in this neighborhood (see "Great Deals on Dining," above). Live bands play jazz, blues, or world music on Friday and Saturday, and if you have dinner there you can skip the cover (usually $10).

Also in Hollywood, just west of Young Circle at Federal Highway, is **Club M** (☎ 954/925-8396), a small local blues showcase with a bit of good jazz and electric thrown in. On busy Friday and Saturday nights when live bands perform, you'll pay a small cover.

Fort Lauderdale has hundreds of bars and clubs for every taste. There are essentially four main areas that have clusters of happening scenes you can check out for yourself. To get you started, I have highlighted the best in each neighborhood. I have also listed a few out-of-the-way spots for the more adventurous.

A fixture in Fort Lauderdale for more than 20 years, **Musician's Exchange** (☎ 954/565-1369) has been through various incarnations. This notorious live music venue now finds itself housed in a former comedy club, New York Entertainment Cafe at 1432 N. Federal Highway (between Sunrise and Oakland Park blvds.). Covers range from $6 to $20.

The waterfront bars and restaurants on the Intercoastal just south of Oakland Park Boulevard are especially recommendable for their outdoor patio bar scenes at all hours. Accessible by boat or car, **Bootlegger's,** at 3003 NE 32nd Ave. (☎ 954/563-4337), features more than 70 kinds of beers, with a featured draft of the day going for only $1. Here and next door at **Shooters,** 3033 NE 32nd Ave. (☎ 954/566-2855), you'll find nautical types, families, and young professionals mixed in with a good dose of sunburned tourists enjoying the live reggae, jazz, or Jimmy Buffettesque tunes with the gorgeous backdrop of the bay and marinas all around. If you don't have your own boat, take the water taxi to really get the feel (see box above). Both are open until 2am.

The once famous "Strip" on the waterfront just north of Las Olas was overrun with spring-breakers. Now it's been replaced with a mellower (and unfortunately more generic) scene. A newish shopping and entertainment complex called Beach Place is a sort of outdoor megamall modeled after Miami's hugely successful Bayside and Cocowalk. This block-long monster is the new home to a number of franchised bars and restaurants, like **Sloppy Joe's** (of Key West fame), **Howl at the Moon,** and

Hooters, amid the requisite Gap and Banana Republic. The view, overlooking the ocean, makes it worth a stop for a drink.

Some of the college kids' old standbys remain in the neighborhood, including the **Elbo Room** at 241 S. Atlantic Blvd., on the corner of Las Olas Boulevard and A1A (☎ **954/463-4615**). It's maintained its rowdy and divey reputation by serving up frequent drink specials and live bands. A dedicated beer-drinking, football-watching crowd mingles with young tourists. This area is also accessible by water taxi.

An older crowd hangs out after dark on Las Olas Boulevard where there are blocks and blocks of good restaurants and music clubs. One of the most happening is ✪ **O'Hara's Pub and Jazz Cafe,** at 722 E. Las Olas Blvd. (☎ **954/524-1764**). They pack 'em in until they spill onto the sidewalk of this smoky little club. Best known for presenting original jazz performers, O'Hara's also has blues and big-band music some Sunday afternoons. Call their jazz hotline (☎ **954/524-2801**) to hear the lineup for this and the newer Hollywood cafe.

Most of the alternative music scene is centered in the downtown area of Fort Lauderdale. **Squeeze** (☎ **954/522-2068**), at 2 South New River Dr. W., is located underneath the Andrew's bridge on the south side of the river. Another choice is the **Chili Pepper** (☎ **954/525-0094**) at 200 W. Broward Blvd., east of I-95. With big-name concerts as well as local band showcases, this place captures the heart and soul of the young and supercharged.

To find the heart of Fort Lauderdale's growing gay scene, head to **The Copa,** at 2800 S. Federal Hwy., east on I-595, near the airport (☎ **954/463-1507**). This big '80s-style black box has been the cornerstone of Fort Lauderdale's gay scene forever. Popular and updated shows are common on the many elevated stages surrounding a large and loud dance floor.

THE PERFORMING ARTS

Pick up *City Link,* a free weekly in newsstands around the city, the *Sun-Sentinel,* or the *Miami Herald* for current offerings of music, dance, and theater staged in Fort Lauderdale's impressive **Broward Center for the Performing Arts,** 201 SW 5th Ave. (☎ **954/462-0222**). This stunning $55 million complex contains both a 2,700-seat auditorium and a smaller 590-seat theater. The center attracts top opera, symphony, dance, and Broadway productions, as well as more modest-size shows. Or, call *Sun-Sentinel's* source line, from Fort Lauderdale (☎ **954/523-5463**), from Boca/Delray (☎ **561/496-5463**), and from Boynton Beach (☎ **561/625-5463**), for a recording of the area's happenings.

2 Boca Raton & Delray Beach

26 miles S of Palm Beach, 40 miles N of Miami

With its many mansions and waterfront condominiums, Boca Raton is the winter home to many of society's wealthy industrialists and retirees. Increasingly, the area is also attracting young families from other areas in the state that have tired of crime, corruption, and overcrowding. This planned city, known simply as "Boca" in these parts, is a bit overmanicured and glitzy for my taste, although there are certainly some great restaurants and resorts worth exploring.

Delray grew up completely separate from its southern neighbor. Named after a suburb of Detroit, this community was founded in 1894 by a midwestern postmaster who sold off 5-acre lots through Michigan newspaper ads. Because of their close proximity, Boca and Delray can easily be explored together. And budget-conscious travelers would do well to eat and sleep in more moderate Delray and dip into Boca for sightseeing and beaching only.

ESSENTIALS

Before your trip, call or write the **Palm Beach County Convention and Visitors Bureau,** 1555 Palm Beach Lakes Blvd., Suite 204, West Palm Beach, FL 33401 (☎ **800/554-PALM** or 561/471-3995; fax 561/471-3990). On weekdays from 8:30am until at least 4pm, stop by the **Boca Raton Chamber of Commerce** at 1800 N. Dixie Hwy. (4 blocks north of Glades Road), Boca Raton, FL 33432 (☎ **561/395-4433;** fax 561/392-3780; www.bocaraton.com), for information on attractions, accommodations, and events in the area. Also try the **Delray Beach Chamber of Commerce** (☎ **561/278-0424;** fax 561/278-0555; e-mail: chamber@delraybeach.com), at 64 SE 5th Ave., half a block south of Atlantic Avenue on U.S. 1, Delray Beach, FL 33483.

HITTING THE BEACHES

Thankfully, Florida had the foresight to set aside some of its most beautiful coastal areas for the public's enjoyment. Many of the area's best beaches are located in state parks and are free to pedestrians and bikers, though most do charge for parking.

The **Delray Beach Public Beach,** on Ocean Boulevard at the east end of Atlantic Avenue, is one of the area's most popular hangouts. Weekends especially attract a young crowd of active locals and tourists. Regular volleyball, Frisbee, and paddleball games make for good entertainment. For refreshments, a number of snack shops, bars, and restaurants are just across the street. Families enjoy the protection of lifeguards on the clean wide beach. Gentle waters make it a good swimming beach, too. There's limited parking at meters along Ocean Boulevard.

Spanish River Park, on North Ocean Boulevard (Fla. A1A), 2 miles north of Palmetto Park Road in Boca Raton, is a huge oceanfront park with a large grassy area, making it one of the best choices for picnicking. Facilities include picnic tables, grills, rest rooms, and a bilevel 40-foot observation tower. You can walk through tunnels under the highway to nature trails that wind through fertile grassland. Volleyball nets are ocean side and always have at least one serious game going on. The park is open from 8am until 8pm. Also, see "Scuba Diving & Snorkeling," below, for information about **Red Reef Park.**

GREAT GOLF THAT WON'T BREAK YOUR BUDGET & OTHER AFFORDABLE OUTDOOR ACTIVITIES

GOLF This area has plenty of good courses. Unfortunately, most of the best are private or are in the very expensive resorts. However, from May to October or November, about a dozen private courses open their greens to visitors staying in Palm Beach County hotels. This "Golf-A-Round" program is free or severely discounted (carts are additional), and reservations can be made through most major hotels. Ask at your hotel, or contact the Palm Beach County Convention and Visitors Bureau (☎ **561/471-3995**) for information on which clubs are available for play. You can usually get on to PGA National and the Breakers.

The semiprivate, 18-hole, par-61 course at the Boca Raton Executive Country Club, 7601 E. Country Club Blvd. (☎ **561/997-9410**), is usually open to the public. A driving range is also on the property as well as a pro shop and a restaurant. A PGA professional gives lessons, and rental clubs are available. From Yamato Road East, turn left onto Old Dixie Highway; after about a mile, turn left onto Hidden Valley Boulevard and continue straight to the club. Greens fees are $14 to $26.

The Boca Raton Municipal Golf Course, 8111 Golf Course Rd. (☎ **561/483-6100**), is located just north of Glades Road, half a mile west of the Florida Turnpike. This public 18-hole, par-72 course covers approximately 6,200 yards. There's a snack bar and a pro shop where clubs can be rented. Greens fees are $11 to $14 for 9 holes and $19 to $25 for 18 holes. Ask for special summer discount fees.

SCUBA DIVING & SNORKELING   Moray Bend, a 58-foot dive spot located about ¾ mile off Boca Inlet, is the area's most popular. It's home to three moray eels that are used to being fed by scuba divers. The reef is accessible by boat from Force E Dive Center, 877 E. Palmetto Park Rd., Boca Raton (☎ 561/368-0555). Phone for dive times. Dives cost $38 to $45 per person.

Red Reef Park, 1400 N. Fla. A1A (☎ 561/393-7974), a fully developed 67-acre oceanfront park in Boca Raton, has year-round lifeguard protection. There's good snorkeling for beginners around the rocks and reefs that lie just off the beach in 2 to 6 feet of water. There's also good swimming and a small picnic area with grills, tables, and rest rooms. The park, located a half mile north of Palmetto Park Road, is open daily from 8am to 10pm. You only pay if you drive in. It's $8 per car during the week or $10 on weekends.

TENNIS   The snazzy **Delray Beach Tennis Center,** 201 W. Atlantic Ave. (☎ 561/243-7360), has 14 lighted clay courts and 5 hard courts available by the hour. It's a great deal at $10 a day for out-of-towners. Residents pay $8.50 per day. Nonmembers can make reservations only after 3pm the day before play. The courts are open weekdays from 8am until 9pm and 6pm on Saturday and Sunday.

The 17 public lighted hard courts at **Patch Reef Park,** 2000 NW 51st St. (☎ 561/997-0881), are available by reservation. The fee for nonresidents is $5.75 per person per hour. Courts are available Monday to Saturday from 7:30am to 10pm and Sunday from 7:30am to dusk; you can phone ahead to see if a court is available. To reach the park from I-95, exit at Yamato Road West and continue past Military Trail to the park.

SEEING THE SIGHTS

Boca Raton Museum of Art. 801 W. Palmetto Park Rd. (1 mile east of I-95), Boca Raton. ☎ 561/392-2500. Admission $3 adults, $2 seniors, $1 students. Children under 12 free. Tues, Thurs, and Fri 10am–4pm, Sat–Sun noon–4pm, Wed 10am–9pm. Closed Mon and holidays. Free admission on Wed.

In addition to a relatively small but well-chosen permanent collection that's strongest in 19th-century European oils, the museum stages a wide variety of temporary exhibitions by local and international artists. Lectures and films are offered on a fairly regular basis; phone for details.

Gumbo Limbo Environmental Complex. 1801 N. Ocean Blvd. (on A1A between Spanish River Blvd. and Palmetto Park), Boca Raton. ☎ 561/338-1473. Free admission. Mon–Sat 9am–4pm, Sun noon–4pm.

Named for an indigenous hardwood tree with continuously shedding bronze bark, the 20-acre complex protects one of the few surviving coastal hammocks, or forest islands, in South Florida. Visitors can walk through the hammock, on a ⅓-mile-long elevated boardwalk that ends at a 40-foot observation tower, from which you can see the Atlantic Ocean, the Intracoastal Waterway, and much of Boca Raton. From mid-April to September, sea turtles come ashore here to lay their eggs. During this time, the center conducts turtle-watching tours and sea-turtle lectures. If you haven't seen turtles doing their thing, definitely stop in for a memorable experience.

In the museum is an impressive array of local flora and fauna, including live snakes, fish, crabs, sea turtles, and scorpions. Even city kids seem to like touching all the strange creatures here.

International Museum of Cartoon Art. 201 Plaza Real at Mizner Park, Boca Raton. ☎ 561/391-2200. www.cartoon.org. Admission $6 adults, $5 seniors, $4 students, $3 children 6–12 years old, free for members and children under 5.

Palm Beach & Boca Raton

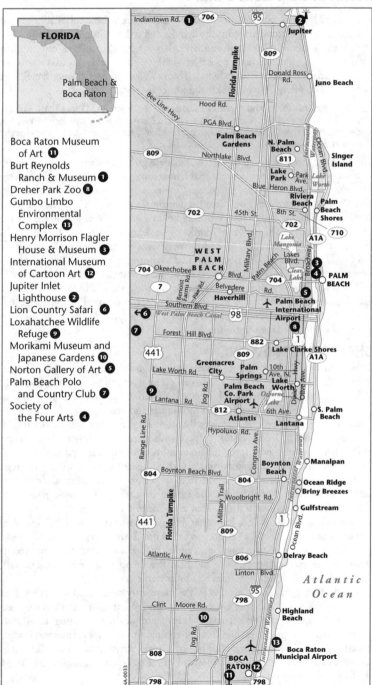

FLORIDA

Palm Beach &
Boca Raton

NA-0033

Reborn and hugely expanded after nearly 20 years of life in New York City, this extensive collection of cartoon art spans the decades and styles in its glitzy home in Mizner Park. In a gorgeous 52,000-square-foot gallery space, cartoon fans can see prints, frames, moving pictures, and books by some of the world's greatest cartoonists, including many by the museum's founder, Mort Walker (of Beetle Bailey fame). A fantastic gift shop offers posters, books, and lots of memorabilia.

✪ **Morikami Museum and Japanese Gardens.** 16869 Jog Rd., Delray Beach. ☎ **561/ 495-0233.** Museum $4.25 adults, $3.75 seniors, $2 children 6–18, free for children 5 and under, free for everyone Sun 10am–noon; gardens free. Museum Tues–Sun 10am–5pm; gardens Tues–Sat 10am–5pm. Closed major holidays.

Slip off your shoes and go into a serene Japanese garden community that dates from 1905, when Jo Sakai, an entrepreneurial farmer, came to Boca Raton to build a tropical agricultural community. The Yamato Colony, as it was known, was short-lived; by the 1920s only one tenacious colonist remained—George Sukeji Morikami. But Morikami was quite successful, eventually holding one of the largest pineapple plantations in the area. The 200-acre Morikami Museum and Japanese Gardens, which opened to the public in 1977, was Morikami's gift to Palm Beach County and the State of Florida. The park section, dedicated to the preservation of Japanese culture, is constructed to appeal to all the senses. An artificial waterfall that cascades into a koi- and carp-filled moat, a small rock garden for meditation, and a large bonsai collection that includes miniature maple, buttonwood, juniper, and Australian pine trees are all worth contemplation—and it's free. There is also a great Asian restaurant on the premises worth checking out for lunch.

SHOPPING & BROWSING

Famous in New York City for its upscale antiques and gorgeous rugs, **ABC Carpet & Home** (☎ 561/279-7777) has opened an outlet store in Delray Beach just off I-95 at 777 South Congress (between Linton and Atlantic). Look for deep discounts (usually at least 30%) on very high priced furnishings and flooring.

Mizner Park, on Federal Highway (between Palmetto Park and Glades roads) in Boca Raton (☎ 561/362-0606), is the town square of this tiny enclave, complete with clothing shops, shoe stores, restaurants, live performances, and lots of beautiful landscaping. It's really an outdoor mall, with 45 specialty shops, seven good restaurants, and a multiscreen movie house. Each shop front faces a grassy island with blue and green gazebos, potted plants, and garden benches. It's extremely popular with folks who come here just to stroll, often until late in the evening.

Town Center Mall of Boca Raton has six huge department stores including Bloomingdale's, Burdines, Lord & Taylor, and Saks Fifth Avenue. Add to that hundreds of specialty shops, an extensive food court, and a range of other restaurants, and you have got the area's most comprehensive and beautiful shopping opportunity. The mall is located on the south side of Glades Road just west of I-95.

Another great area for a stroll is in the more artsy community of Delray Beach, known by many as **Pineapple Grove.** Here, along Atlantic Avenue, especially east of Swinton Avenue, you'll find a fantastic array of antique shops, clothing stores, and art galleries shaded by palm trees and colorful awnings. A lively cafe culture and many celebrations take place on this quaint old-style main street. Pick up the "Downtown Delray Beach" map and guide at almost any of the stores on this strip, or call ☎ 561/ 278-0424 for more information.

ACCOMMODATIONS YOU CAN AFFORD

If you choose to stay in Boca or the surrounding areas, you will find some very luxurious lodgings, epitomized by the famous and often photographed pink Boca Raton

Hotel and Country Club, where deluxe suites have gone for up to $6,000 per night. But don't worry—there are plenty of affordable choices on and near the beach.

A number of national chain hotels worth considering include a moderately priced **Holiday Inn Highland Beach Oceanside** (☎ **800/234-6835** or 561/278-6241), at 2809 S. Ocean Blvd., on A1A southeast of Linton Boulevard with off-season rates as low as $69 including breakfast. The **Radisson Bridge Resort** (☎ **800/333-3333** or 561/368-9500), at 999 E. Camino Real, operates a particularly popular and affordable resort on the Intracoastal Waterway just a few blocks from the Boca Raton Resort. It books up well in advance and has a 3-day minimum stay in season.

Another good bet is the **Best Western University Inn,** 2700 N. Federal Hwy. (☎ **800/528-1234** or 561/395-5225), with in-season rates as low as $90.

Although you won't find the rows and rows of cheap hotels as in Fort Lauderdale and Hollywood, a handful of mom-and-pop motels have survived along A1A in between the towering condos of Delray Beach. Look along the beach just south of Atlantic Boulevard. Especially noteworthy is a pleasant little 2-story shingle-roofed **Bermuda Inn** at 64 S. Ocean Blvd. (☎ **561/276-5288**). Small motel rooms cost around $60 in summer months, but even in high season, rooms and the larger apartments can be had for under $100.

Even more economical options can be found in Deerfield Beach, Boca's neighbor, south of the county line. A number of beachfront efficiencies offer great deals, even in the winter months. Try the Panther Motel and Apartments, at 715 S. A1A (☎ **954/427-0700**). This clean and convenient motel has rates starting as low as $40. Although in season, you may find you have to book for a week at a time. Weekly rates in season start at $445.

In Boca, many well-priced chains are located west of I-95 at the Yamato Road exit.

If you are looking for something more private or for longer than just a few days, you may want to call a reservations service for help. Especially for rentals for a few weeks or months, call **Palm Beach Accommodations** (☎ **800/543-SWIM**).

SUPER-CHEAP SLEEPS

Boca Inn. 1801 N Federal Hwy., Boca Raton 33432. ☎ **800/442-2622** or 561/395-7500. Fax 561/391-0287. 50 units, all with bathroom. A/C TV TEL. Winter $65–$95 single or double. Off-season $35–$45 single or double. AE, MC, V.

Owned by a pleasant East Indian family, this superbudget motel is located right on busy U.S. 1 but is set back enough from the road to make it quiet. The squat, 2-story building surrounds a large pool deck with lounge furniture, vending machines, and laundry facilities. Rooms, which were renovated in 1997 and 1998, are clean but very cheaply outfitted. All have cable TV, small refrigerators, and telephones. Many have king-size beds, too. For the price this is a thoroughly decent place to crash just about half a mile from the beach. Next door is a fantastic Punjab restaurant and nearby is lots of shopping.

✪ **Ocean Lodge.** 531 N. Ocean Blvd. (just north of Palmetto Park Rd. on Fla. A1A), Boca Raton, FL 33432. ☎ **800/STAY-BOCA** or 561/395-7772. Fax 561/395-0554. 18 units, all with bathroom. A/C TV TEL. Winter $65–$80 single or double; $75–$95 efficiency. Off-season $45–$80 single or double; $55–$95 efficiency. AE, MC, V.

Situated around a small heated pool and sundeck, this 2-story little motel is a particularly well-kept accommodation in an area of run-down or overpriced options. The large rooms offer furnishings and decor that are clean but a bit impersonal. A recent do-over that added modern Formica and floral wallpaper makes this a notch above a basic motel. Ask for a room in the back since the street noise can be a bit loud especially in season. The bonus is that you are across the street from the ocean and in one of Florida's most upscale resort towns.

Riviera Palms Motel. 3960 N. Ocean Blvd. (2 miles north of Atlantic Ave.), Delray Beach, FL 33483. ☎ **561/276-3032.** 34 units, all with bathroom (motel rooms have showers only). A/C TV. Winter $50–$60 single or double; from $70 efficiency. Off-season $40 single or double; from $45 efficiency. Extra person $10. Weekly rates available. No credit cards.

The Riviera Palms offers plain, simple, and relatively inexpensive accommodations just across the street from a wide pretty beach. Behind the motel's 2-story, cream-colored exterior are large rooms filled with a mixed bag of 1950s-era furnishings. The efficiencies come with full kitchens complete with dishes and flatware. There are no phones in the rooms. A large swimming pool is surrounded by a nice courtyard with sunning lounges, patio tables, barbecue grills, and shuffleboard courts.

The Sea Breeze. 820 N. Ocean Blvd., Delray Beach, FL 33483. ☎ **561/276-7496.** 19 units, all with bathroom (some with shower only). A/C TV TEL. Winter from $70 single or double; $74–$90 studio; $109–$119 1-bedroom apt; $136–$194 2-bedroom apt. Off-season $49 single or double; $52–$59 studio; $69–$79 1-bedroom apt; $85–$127 2-bedroom apt. Extra person $15. MC, V.

The Sea Breeze has been around for a long time, but it has benefited from some work recently. The motel still isn't perfect, but its updated rooms are thoroughly recommendable. New tile floors and window treatments have been installed in every room, and many also have new furnishings that include plush comfortable chairs and sofas, glass breakfast tables, and whitewashed armoires. The studios and apartments have either a kitchenette or a full kitchen, and both have larger bathrooms than are normally found in comparable motels. There's a swimming pool on the property, as well as gas barbecue grills and laundry facilities available for guest use. Plus, it's a short walk to a nice beach.

Shore Edge Motel. 425 N. Ocean Blvd. (on Fla. A1A, north of Palmetto Park Rd.), Boca Raton, FL 33432. ☎ **561/395-4491.** Fax 561/347-8759. 16 units, all with bathroom (some with shower only). A/C TV TEL. Winter $60–$75 single or double; $80–$95 efficiency. Off-season from $45 single or double; from $55 efficiency. MC, V.

Another relic of the '50s recently spiffed up with new landscaping and some redecorating, this motel is a good choice, especially because of its location—across the street from a public beach, just north of downtown Boca Raton. It's the quintessential South Florida motel: a small, pink, single-story structure surrounding a modest swimming pool and courtyard. Although the rooms are a bit on the small side, they're very neat and clean. The higher-priced accommodations are larger and come with full kitchens.

FOR A FEW BUCKS MORE

✪ **Colony Hotel & Cabana Club.** 525 E. Atlantic Ave. (P.O. Box 970), Delray Beach, FL 33483. ☎ **800/552-2363** or 561/276-4123. Fax 561/276-0123. www.thecolonyhotel.com/florida/. E-mail: info-fla@thecolonyhotel.com. 66 units, all with bathroom (some with shower only). A/C TV TEL. Winter $145–$175 single or double. Off-season $90–$110 single or double. AE, MC, V.

This lovely 3-story hotel is located right on Delray's main commercial thoroughfare about a mile from the hotel's private beach and club. The Colony benefited from a 1996 refurbishment that brought back some of its original 1926 details, including hardwood floors and authentic furnishings. Still, the rooms are modest in size and style but comfortable and clean. The hotel is popular with families that appreciate the many planned activities at the hotel's beachfront club 1 mile away, which offers a heated saltwater swimming pool, a private beach, and putting and shuffleboard tournaments. All facilities are free for guests.

✪ **Seagate Hotel & Beach Club.** 400 S. Ocean Blvd., Delray Beach, FL 33483. ☎ **800/233-3581** or 561/276-2421. Fax 561/243-4714. 77 units, all with bathroom. A/C TV TEL. Winter $160–$290 single or double; $335–$370 2-bedroom suite. Off-season $74–$105 single or double; $136–$152 2-bedroom suite. AE, CB, DC, DISC, MC, V. From I-95, exit onto Atlantic Ave. E., turn right onto Ocean Blvd. (Fla. A1A), and continue half a mile to the hotel.

Worth it if you want to be steps from the ocean, this modest well-located hotel features generously sized rooms located in two buildings directly across the street from the beach. To make your stay more affordable and convenient, the hotel furnishes coffeemakers, fully stocked kitchens or kitchenettes, irons, large closets, and safes in each room. A recent redecorating replaced the quaint Old Florida furnishings with industrial Formica, plain blond wood, and commercial-grade carpeting. Also regretful are the tiny bathrooms with little to no counter space.

The Beach Club is located across the street, directly on the sand, where you can relax on a chaise lounge or dip into one of the heated pools. A moderately priced restaurant and bar will deliver snacks and cocktails to the beach. There's 400 feet of private beach, and special children's programs are offered during the high season. Overall, the resort is pleasant and extremely practical, especially for families. Little extras like newspapers and refreshments in the lobby make this an especially appealing option.

Spanish River Resort. 111 E. Atlantic Ave., Delray Beach, Fl 33483. ☎ **800/543-SWIM** or 561/243-7946. Fax 561/276-9634. 75 units, all with bathroom. A/C TV TEL. Winter $150–$250 studio or 1-bedrooms; $315–$350 2-bedrooms. Off-season from $85 studio or 1-bedrooms; from $200 2-bedrooms. AE, DISC, MC, V. Free 6th and 7th night with weekly booking.

An especially good value for families staying for longer than a few days, this pleasant property offers fully furnished condominiums half a block from a popular beach and walking distance to Delray's best shops, restaurants, and galleries. The 11-story Mediterranean-style building has free lighted tennis courts, a large outdoor pool, and lovely ocean-view balconies. Apartments are spacious and outfitted with fully-equipped kitchens. All units also have pullout queen-size sofa beds. The best part is there is no additional charge for extra guests. A one-bedroom unit can comfortably fit four or five people; a two-bedroom unit can easily accommodate six. Cots and roll-away beds are available at a minimum charge. Compared with many of the rundown 1950s motels in the area, this moderately priced, well-maintained tower is a real find.

WORTH A SPLURGE

✪ **Boca Raton Resort and Club.** 501 E. Camino Real Dr. (P.O. Box 5025), Boca Raton, FL 33431. ☎ **800/327-0101** or 561/395-3000. Fax 561/447-3183. 1,070 units, all with bathroom. A/C MINIBAR TV TEL. Winter packages from $320 single or double. Off-season packages from $175 single or double. AE, DC, DISC, MC, V. From I-95 north, exit onto Palmetto Park Rd. E.; turn right onto Federal Hwy. (U.S. 1), and then left onto Camino Real to the resort.

Don't gasp at the nightly rates just yet—consider that this is Boca's most historical and romantic resort and that the package rates can mean up to 30% of regular room rates and very generous add-ins.

Since 1926, this palatial hotel has been hosting the most discriminating international guests. Now with a sizable population of local sports enthusiasts who have joined the country club, and lots of conferences going on, the place is still pleasing demanding visitors. Don't worry: The huge proportions of the Spanish Moorish architecture and the sprawling grounds will ensure that you will never feel crowded or processed. And yearly renovations guarantee that you won't feel as if you are staying in a musty museum.

Compared to other destination resorts on Florida's East Coast, this superior facility is a great value with all the amenities and elegance but none of the stuffiness. In addition to its own beach, the resort also boasts extensive and outstanding facilities for tennis, golf, and anything else an active family or individual could want, including three fitness centers with brand-new equipment, more than 30 tennis courts, and two respected 18-hole golf courses. Packages, like the Romance Package that in summer costs about $220 a night, usually require a 3-day stay. It includes a gourmet dinner at one of the hotel's nine restaurants, complimentary drinks at one of the three lounges, a bottle of champagne, chocolates, a day of tennis, a day at the Beach club, a catamaran cruise or speedboat ride, T-shirts, and more.

GREAT DEALS ON DINING

The Boca Raton and Delray areas have more than their fair share of expensive fish and steak houses. Thankfully, too, there are more and more innovative and health-conscious places moving in. Mizner Park has nearly a dozen eateries, mostly pricey, but there are some well-priced options too.

SUPER-CHEAP EATS

✪ **Cornell Cafe at the Morikami Museum.** 4000 Morikami Park Rd./16869 Jog Rd. (between Yamato and Linton Blvd.), Delray Beach. ☎ **561/499-2557.** $4–$11 sushi and noodle dishes. Tues–Sun 11am–3pm and every second Sun from 10:15–noon brunch. AE, DISC, MC, V. JAPANESE.

It's a pity that this superior Japanese restaurant is open only for lunch and that it is so small. The lines on weekdays attest to its popularity, especially considering the museum is hardly in a densely populated part of town. The Chinese chef Fu Chen turns out mostly Japanese dishes. Start with seaweed salad and some dumplings and then try any of the reasonably priced entrees like teriyaki fish or tofu and eel, eggplant and garlic sauce or a variety of sushi and sushi rolls. From curry chicken to a classical Bento box, it is all *so* good. There is no need to pay the museum admission if you are passing through to dine at the quaint cafe, which has several outdoor tables overlooking the serene gardens. Second Sunday of the month is a special brunch from 10:15–11:15am at $15 per person. Make reservations in advance.

Max's Coffee Shop. 402 Plaza Real (in Mizner Park). ☎ **561/392 0454.** Reservations not accepted. Main courses $5–$13. AE, DC, DISC, MC, V. Mon–Thurs 11am–10:30pm, Fri 11am–midnight, Sat 9am–midnight, Sun 9am–10pm. DINER/AMERICAN.

For good old-fashioned comfort food in a real diner atmosphere, try this affordable and lively eatery. For a fraction of the cost of its sister restaurant next door, Max's Grill, you'll get more casual but just as fresh and well-prepared food.

Choose from favorites like meat loaf, chicken pot pie or baked macaroni and cheese. More healthful and up-to-date offerings include pastas and dozens of salads, like the sesame-seared rare tuna with cilantro vinaigrette and crunchy noodles. Fresh-baked breads and homemade soups also contribute to the overwhelming popularity of this retro diner. Great prices and a huge variety assure its success.

✪ **The Tin Muffin Café.** 364 E. Palmetto Park Rd. (between Federal Hwy. and the Intercoastal Bridge). ☎ **561/392-9446.** Sandwiches and salads $5.50–$7.50. No credit cards. Mon–Fri 11am–5pm, Sat 11am–4pm. BAKERY/SANDWICH SHOP.

Popular with the downtown lunch crowd, this excellent storefront bakery keeps them lining up for big fresh sandwiches on fresh bread, muffins, quiches, and good homemade soups like split pea or lentil. The curried chicken sandwich is stuffed with over-sized chunks of white meat doused in a creamy curry dressing and fruit. There are a few cafe tables inside and even one outside on a tiny patio. Be warned, however, that service is forgivably slow and parking is a nightmare. Try parking a few blocks away at a meter on the street.

Tom's Place. 7251 N. Federal Hwy., Boca Raton. ☎ **561/997-0920.** Reservations not accepted. Main courses $8–$15; sandwiches $5–$6; early bird special $6.95. MC, V. Tues–Fri 11:30am–10pm, Sat noon–10pm. Closed Mon. BARBECUE.

There are two important factors in a successful barbecue: the cooking and the sauce. Tom and Helen Wright's no-nonsense cook shack wins on both counts, offering flawlessly grilled meats paired with well-spiced sauces. Beef, chicken, pork, and fish are served soul-food style, with your choice of two sides like rice with gravy, collard greens, black-eyed peas, coleslaw, or mashed potatoes. Decoration is limited to signed celebrity photographs and plastic tablecloths.

FOR A FEW BUCKS MORE

Banana Boat. 739 E. Ocean Ave. (between Fla. A1A and Federal Hwy.), Boynton Beach. ☎ 561/732-9400. Main courses $12–$18; sandwiches and salads $3–$8. AE, DC, MC, V. Mon–Sat 11am–midnight, Sun 9am–midnight. AMERICAN.

Though it's more a bar than a restaurant, this Boynton Beach hot spot is crowded most nights with an eclectic crowd. Bikers hang out at the dark woodsy bar with office workers and fishers. The varied menu has lots of fried fish choices, though the best bet is a burger or sandwich, served with lots of fixings. Though more mayonnaise than fish, the fish dip is tasty and served with crackers, lettuce, carrots, celery, and superhot bottled jalapeños. You can't beat the waterfront setting and the Sunday reggae parties. Call for seasonal schedules.

Splendid Blendeds. 432 E. Atlantic Ave., Delray. ☎ 561/265-1035. Reservations recommended. Main courses $10–$17; sandwiches and salads $3–$8. AE, MC, V. Mon–Sat dinner 5:30pm–10pm, Mon–Fri lunch 11:30am–2:30pm. Closed Sun. ECLECTIC.

Loyal regulars would like to keep this storefront bistro a secret so that the lines won't get even longer on weekends. The draw here is fresh, uncomplicated seafood and pastas that are interesting without being overly ambitious. The southwestern-inspired chicken Santa Cruz is tender and juicy, served with a black-bean sauce and tangy pico de gallo. Many seafood specialties, like tuna, snapper, and shrimp dishes, are slight departures from classic recipes and seem to work most of the time. The drawback of this otherwise superb spot is the staff; they're well-meaning but easily flustered.

WORTH A SPLURGE

Fifth Avenue Grill. 821 S. Federal Hwy., Delray Beach. ☎ 561/265-0122. Additional location 4650 N. Federal Hwy., Lighthouse Point, ☎ 954/782-4433. Reservations accepted only for large parties. Main courses $16–$26. AE, DC, MC, V. Sun–Mon 11:30am–4pm and 5–11pm. STEAK HOUSE.

The old-world Fifth Avenue Grill is very popular with well-dressed seniors who come for the superb steaks, reliable service, and classic selections—onion soup, shrimp scampi, London broil, Caesar salad, and broiled local fish. This is the kind of place where they still remember to offer a touch of sherry for your conch chowder. Every main course includes unlimited house salad and is accompanied by a cheese-stuffed baked potato, fried shoestrings, or brown rice. Add to that a huge and varied wine list, and you've got a perfect night out in Delray. Everything on the predictable menu is well prepared and presented by professional servers in a dark and woodsy dining room.

✪ **La Vieille Maison.** 770 E. Palmetto Park Rd., Boca Raton. ☎ 561/391-6701 or 561/737-5677. Reservations required. Main courses $17–$40; fixed-price dinners $40 and $59. AE, CB, DC, DISC, MC, V. Daily 11:30am–2pm and 6–9:30pm (call for seating times). FRENCH.

Find an excuse to celebrate and treat yourself to this elegant dining experience that has won the loyalty of critics from far and wide. The luxurious setting, a Mediterranean-inspired home filled with a variety of antique French furnishings and paintings, gives you the feeling of walking into a friend's country manor. Begin with lobster bisque, gratin of escargots with fennel and pistachio nuts, or pan-seared foie gras—each is equally delectable. It's difficult to choose from the many enticing entrees, which range from red snapper in black- and green-olive potato crust to medaillons of beef, lamb, and venison over three sauces. You'll surely have to try at least a few of the gorgeous cheeses the waiter offers after your main course—the most extensive selection I've ever seen in this country. The lemon crepe soufflé with raspberry sauce is the dessert of choice—remember to order it early.

BOCA RATON & DELRAY AFTER DARK
THE BAR, CLUB & MUSIC SCENE

The best variety of entertainment is offered in Delray Beach where a younger and funkier set makes its home. Atlantic Avenue now boasts several venues for live music, including **The Back Room,** 16 E. Atlantic Ave. near the corner of Swinton Ave. (☎ **561/243-9110**). A reasonable cover, usually between $2 and $6, depends on who is playing. A funky decor, eclectic crowd, and excellent music almost every night make this old standby another good option for live music from jazz to big band to classic rock. Only beer and wine are served (in plastic glasses). It's open Tuesday to Saturday until 3am.

    Boston's on the Beach, at 40 S. Ocean Blvd. (☎ **561/278-3364**), is always a good choice for happy hour, Monday to Friday from 4 to 8pm, or for live reggae on Monday. A lively bar scene and good seafood on a deck overlooking the beach keep this place packed almost every night.

    Plenty of locals and visitors make a night of strolling the luxurious grounds of Mizner Park (see "Shopping & Browsing," above). After a meal, diners can shop or listen to musicians or watch performers who often are scheduled to entertain the public.

    Boca Raton's most famous dance spot, **Club Boca,** at 7000 W. Palmetto Park Rd. (☎ **561/368-3333**), which you'll hear advertised on obnoxious radio commercials, is a big, noisy warehouse out west of the highway that attracts a range of big-haired girls and macho guys. It's a fun diversion in otherwise sterile Boca and is open Thursday to Sunday until 5am.

    True to her word, Gloria Gaynor has survived; she lives on in Boca at **Polly Esther's,** 99 SE 1st Ave. (☎ **561/447-8955**). She and other disco divas can be heard blasting from the enormous sound system as the mixed young and 30-something set dances like it's Saturday night and they have the fever. Open Wednesday to Saturday. Take Palmetto Park Road East to Federal Highway; turn left onto SE 1st Avenue, where you'll see the club on the left.

THE PERFORMING ARTS

For details on upcoming events, check the *Boca News, Sun-Sentinel,* or call the Palm Beach County Cultural Council information line at ☎ **800/882-ARTS.** During business hours, a staffer can give details on current performances. After hours, a recorded message describes the week's events. The *Sun-Sentinel* also hosts a comprehensive "Source Line" for information on everything from weather to garage sales. Detailed arts information is included.

    Although the larger and more renowned venues are farther north in Palm Beach and West Palm, the southern part of Palm Beach County has its fair share of performing arts. The **Florida Symphonic Pops,** a 70-piece professional orchestra, performs jazz, swing, rock, big band, and classical music throughout Boca Raton. For nearly 50 years this ever-growing musical force has entertained audiences of every age. Call ☎ **561/393-7677** for a schedule of concerts.

    Boca's best theater company is the **Caldwell Theatre,** and it is worth checking out. Located in a strip shopping center at 7873 N. Federal Hwy., this equity showcase does well-known dramas, comedies, classics, off-Broadway hits, and new works throughout the year. Prices are reasonable (usually between $29 and $38). Full-time students will be especially interested in the little-advertised "Student Rush." Bring a valid ID and arrive at least an hour before show time to get in line. If available, tickets are sold for $5 to those who arrived earliest. Call the box office (☎ **561/241-7432**) for details.

3 Palm Beach & West Palm Beach

65 miles N of Miami, 193 miles E of Tampa

Palm Beach County encompasses cities including Boca Raton in the south to Jupiter and Tequesta in the north. But it is Palm Beach, the small island town across the Intra-coastal Waterway, that has been the traditional winter home of America's superrich—the Kennedys, the Rockefellers, the Pulitzers, the Trumps (more recently), and plenty of CEOs. Gawking at their palatial homes is the number-one tourist activity, and a stroll along Palm Beach's tony Worth Avenue is a must even for nonshoppers.

Beyond the upscale resorts and chic boutiques, it holds some surprises too, from a world-class art museum to one of the top bird-watching areas in the state. By contrast, West Palm Beach is a grittier, workday city. Recent renovations have made the metro-politan area a lively and affordable place to dine, shop, and hang out. In addition to good beaching, boating and diving, you'll find great golf and tennis throughout the county.

ESSENTIALS

GETTING THERE   If you're driving up or down the Florida coast, you'll probably reach the Palm Beach area by I-95. Exit at Belvedere Road or Okeechobee Boulevard and head east to reach the most central part of Palm Beach.

Visitors on their way to or from Orlando or Miami should take the Florida Turn-pike, a toll road with a speed limit of 65 m.p.h. But if you're watching your budget, avoid the Turnpike—tolls are high. You may pay upward of $9 from Orlando and $4 from Miami. Finally, if you're coming from Florida's west coast, you can take either S.R. 70, which runs north of Lake Okeechobee to Fort Pierce, or S.R. 80, which runs south of the lake to Palm Beach.

GETTING AROUND   Although a car is almost a necessity in this area, a recently revamped public transportation system is extremely convenient for getting to some attractions. **Palm Tran** underwent a major expansion in late 1996, increasing service to 32 routes and more than 140 buses. The fare is $1 for adults, 50¢ for children aged 3 to 18, as well as for the elderly and disabled. Free route maps are available by calling ☎ **561/233-4-BUS** from within North Palm Beach County, or ☎ **561/930-4-BUS** from South Palm Beach County. Information operators are available from 6am to 7pm, except Sunday.

In downtown West Palm free shuttles operate Monday through Friday from 9am until 4pm with plans to expand operations to evenings and weekends too. Look for the bubble gum pink minibuses throughout downtown. Call ☎ **561/833-8873** for more details.

For a more nostalgic route, consider the stately wicker chariots that run in the downtown area, especially on weekends and during special events. Rates vary according to the time of day but average $1 to $2 per block, plus a per person charge of $1. Call ☎ **561/835-8922** for pickup or information.

Among the airlines serving **Palm Beach International Airport,** at Congress Avenue and Belvedere Road (☎ **561/471-7400**), are **American** (☎ 800/433-7300),

Continental (☎ 800/525-0280), Delta (☎ 800/221-1212), Kiwi (☎ 800/538-5494), Northwest (☎ 800/225-2525), TWA (☎ 800/221-2000), United (☎ 800/241-6522), and US Airways (☎ 800/428-4322).

Amtrak (☎ 800/USA-RAIL) has a terminal in West Palm Beach, at 201 S. Tamarind Ave. (☎ 561/832-6169).

VISITOR INFORMATION   The Palm Beach County Convention and Visitors Bureau, 1555 Palm Beach Lakes Blvd., Suite 204, West Palm Beach, FL 33401 (☎ 800/554-PALM or 561/471-3995), distributes an informative brochure and will answer questions about visiting the Palm Beaches. Ask for a map as well as a copy of its *Arts and Attractions Calendar,* a day-to-day guide to art, music, stage, and other events in the county.

HITTING THE BEACHES

Public beaches are a rare commodity here in Palm Beach. Most of the island's best beaches are fronted by private estates and are therefore inaccessible to the general public. However, there are a few notable exceptions, including the newly renourished Midtown Beach on Ocean Boulevard, between Royal Palm Way and Gulfstream Road, which boasts more than 100 feet of beach that is still undeveloped and uncrowded. There are no rest rooms or concessions here, although a lifeguard is on duty until sundown. This newly widened sandy coast is now a centerpiece and a natural oasis in a town dominated by commercial glitz.

Also, about 1½ miles north, near Dunbar Street, is a popular hangout for locals who enjoy the relaxed atmosphere. Parking is available at meters along A1A. To the south is a less popular but better equipped beach at Phipps Ocean Park. On Ocean Boulevard, between the Southern Boulevard and Lake Avenue causeways, is a large and lively public beach encompassing more than 1,300 feet of groomed and guarded oceanfront. With picnic and recreation areas as well as plenty of parking, the area is especially good for families.

GREAT GOLF THAT WON'T BREAK YOUR BUDGET & OTHER AFFORDABLE OUTDOOR ACTIVITIES

In West Palm Beach, stop by the Seaside Activities Station at 400A Flagler Dr. (on the waterfront at the corner of Banyan St.) or call ☎ 561/659-4005 to arrange historic tours or sailboat, jet-ski, bicycle, kayak, water ski, and parasail rentals.

BICYCLING   Rent anything from an English single-speed to a full-tilt mountain bike at the Palm Beach Bicycle Trail Shop, 223 Sunrise Ave. (☎ 561/659-4583). Rates are $7 an hour, $18 a half day (9am to 5pm), or $24 for 24 hours; they include a basket and lock (not that it's necessary in this fortress of a town). The most scenic route is called the Lake Trail, running the length of the island along the Intracoastal Waterway. On it you'll see some of the most magnificent mansions and grounds. Enjoy the views of downtown West Palm Beach and some great wildlife.

CRUISES   The *Star of Palm Beach,* 900 E. Blue Heron Blvd., Singer Island (☎ 561/848-7827), runs regularly scheduled tours along the Intracoastal Waterway, offering visitors unobstructed views of the area's grand mansions. Daily sightseeing as well as lunch, dinner, and theme cruises are offered, some with live entertainment. They cost $10 to $30. Phone for more information and reservations.

The *Palm Beach Princess* (☎ 800/841-7447 or 561/845-7447), a small cruise ship (421 feet) offers reasonably priced casino gambling cruises out of the Port of Palm Beach (U.S. 1 between 45th Street and Blue Heron Boulevard) every day and evening. Evening cruises, which usually leave at 7pm, cost $20 to $25 and include a large buffet with average food like spaghetti and meatballs, chicken, shrimp, Greek salad, and vegetables. Best is the prime rib at the carving board. Day trips cost the same and offer slightly less food. Sunday brunch trips cost $25. A popular monthly Bahamas voyage costs $95. Call during business hours for details. Choose from craps, roulette, poker, blackjack, and slots.

GOLF   There's good golfing here, but many of the private club courses are maintained exclusively for the use of their members. Ask at your hotel, or contact the **Palm Beach County Convention and Visitors Bureau** (☎ 561/471-3995) for information on which clubs are currently available for play. In the off-season, some private courses open their greens to visitors staying in a Palm Beach County hotel. This "Golf-A-Round" program offers free greens fees (carts are additional); reservations can be made through most major hotels.

One of the state's best courses that is open to the public is **Emerald Dunes Golf Course,** 2100 Emerald Dunes Dr. in West Palm Beach (☎ 561/687-1700). Designed by Tom Fazio, this dramatic 7,006-yard, par-72 course was voted "One of the Best 10 You Can Play" by *Golf* magazine. It is located just off the Florida Turnpike at Okeechobee Boulevard. Bookings are taken up to 30 days ahead. Fees in the high season start at $125. Ask for twilight and off-season specials.

The **Palm Beach Public Golf Course,** 2345 S. Ocean Blvd. (☎ 561/547-0598), a popular public 18-hole course, is a par-54 and is open at 8am; the course is run on a first-come, first-served basis. Club rentals are available. Greens fees start at $18 per person.

POLO   What's Palm Beach without polo? See "Polo: The Sport of Kings," below, for details.

SCUBA DIVING   Year-round warm waters, barrier reefs, and plenty of wrecks make South Florida one of the world's most popular places for diving. One of the best-known artificial reefs in this area is a vintage Rolls-Royce Silver Shadow, which was sunk offshore in 1985. Mother Nature has taken her toll, however, and divers can no longer sit in the car ravaged by time and saltwater. The offshore reef is located ¾ mile east of the Florida Power and Light smokestacks, just south of the Palm Beach Inlet.

Call any of the following outfitters for gear and excursions: **The Aqua Shop,** 505 Northlake Blvd., North Palm Beach (☎ 561/848-9042); **Dixie Divers,** 1401 S. Military Trail, West Palm Beach (☎ 561/969-6688); and **Ocean Sports Scuba Center,** 1736 S. Congress Ave., West Palm Beach (☎ 561/641-1144).

TENNIS   There are literally hundreds of tennis courts in Palm Beach County. Wherever you are staying, you are bound to be within walking distance of one. In addition to the many hotel tennis courts (see "Accommodations You Can Afford," below), you can play at **Currie Park,** 2400 N. Flagler Dr., West Palm Beach (☎ 561/835-7025), a public park with three lighted hard courts. They are free and available on a first-come, first-served basis.

A WATER PLAYGROUND   On a sunny day don't miss a chance to play with the locals at the Centennial Fountain on the eastern end of Clematis Street, near Narcissus, where dozens of little kids (and a few full-grown ones) jump and play in the vertical streams of water that shoot from the ground. A computer guarantees that the jets will spout unpredictably, and a fountain guard on busy weekends assures kids are well looked after. The fountain, built to commemorate Palm Beach's 100-year anniversary in 1994, is free and operates around the clock. It's especially fun on hot summer nights when the dramatic lights make the shiny wet playground one of the best attractions in town.

Polo: The Sport of Kings

The annual ritual of "the ponies" is played out each season at the posh Palm Beach Polo and Country Club. It is one of the world's premier polo grounds and hosts some of the sport's top-rated players.

Even if you're not a sports fan, it's a blast to attend a match. Although the field is actually on the mainland in an area called Wellington, rest assured, the spectators, and many of the players, are pure Palm Beach. After all, a day at the pony grounds is one of the only good reasons to leave Palm Beach proper.

Don't worry, though—you need not be a Vanderbilt or a Kennedy to attend. Matches are open to the public and are surprisingly affordable. General admission is $6 to $10; box seats cost $18 to $26. Matches are held throughout the week. Schedules vary, but the big names usually compete on Sunday at 3:30pm from January to April.

Incidentally, the point of polo is to keep the other team from getting the ball through your goal. The fast-paced game is divided into six chukkers—like an inning in baseball—each 7 minutes long. There are 3-minute breaks between chukkers except at half-time, which lasts 10 minutes. The whole thing is narrated by a British chap who sounds as though he escaped from a Monty Python skit.

Even if you can't catch on how the game is played, you can spend your time people-watching.

The general admission seats will land you a spot on metal bleachers across the field from the boxes, where celebrity-spotting during a match is a bit difficult. If you want to mingle with the elite, splurge on the more expensive boxes for a chance to overhear great tidbits, like the one I caught recently: "Oh, I know I should be rooting for the Coca-Cola team. That's how I made all my money," whined one flamboyant heiress dressed all in gold as she cheered for the opposing team. "Still, I just can't help cheering for my friends."

Even with a ticket from the bleachers, you can still wander the grounds and soak up the whole scene. Oh dear, you're thinking, whatever will you wear? Unless, you're attending an opening game or some other special event, dress is casual. A navy or tweed blazer over jeans or khakis is a standard for men, while neat-looking jeans or a suit is the norm for ladies. On warmer days, shorts and, of course, a polo shirt are fine, too.

The fields are located at 11809 Polo Club Rd., Wellington, 10 miles west of the Forest Hill Boulevard exit of I-95. Call ☎ 561/798-7000 for a detailed schedule of events.

SEEING THE SIGHTS

Burt Reynolds' Ranch and Museum. West of the Turnpike at Indian Town and Jupiter Farms rds., Jupiter. ☎ **561/747-5390.** Admission $1. Children under 12 free. Daily 10am–4:30pm.

An old-time Florida boy, actor Burt Reynolds is northern Palm Beach's favorite celebrity. His expansive ranch property served as the backdrop for many of his and other's movies, television shows, and videos, including *B. L. Stryker* and *Smokey and the Bandit*. Though no longer opened for tours, on the 160-acre ranch there are a number of interesting buildings, production facilities, and even a chapel where Burt and Loni Anderson were married. This is a great place for kids or Burt fans. A great (and free) bonus out here is the wonderfully unstructured petting zoo where you can touch some of Burt's exotic pets, such as a 6-foot-tall blue emu, iguanas, llamas, sheep, goats, and miniature horses. Buy a handful of feed for 25¢ and have fun feeding these fascinating creatures.

✪ **Henry Morrison Flagler Museum.** 1 Whitehall Way (at Cocoanut Row), Palm Beach. ☎ **561/655-2833.** www.flagler.org. Admission $7 adults, $3 children. Tues–Sat 10am–5pm, Sun noon–5pm.

Known as the "Taj Mahal of North America," this luxurious mansion was commissioned as a gift to his third wife by the renowned Henry Flagler, a cofounder of the Standard Oil Company and builder of the Florida East Coast Railroad. The classically columned Edwardian-style mansion contains 55 rooms that include a Louis XIV music room and art gallery, a Louis XV ballroom, and 14 guest suites outfitted with original antique European furnishings. Out back, climb aboard "The Rambler," Mr. Flagler's personal railroad car. Allow at least 1½ hours to tour the stunning grounds and interior. The admission price is a true bargain considering that so many other historic homes around the country charge almost double.

✪ **Norton Museum of Art.** 1451 S. Olive Ave., West Palm Beach. ☎ **561/832-5196.** Admission $5 adults, $2 students, free for children 12 and under. Tues–Sat 10am–5pm, Sun 1–5pm. From I-95, take Belvedere Rd. (Exit 51) east to the end; then turn left onto South Olive Ave. to the museum.

Since a 1997 expansion doubled the Norton's space, the museum has gained even more prominence in the art world. It is world famous for its prestigious permanent collection and top temporary exhibitions. The museum's major collections are divided geographically. The American galleries contain major works by Edward Hopper, Georgia O'Keeffe, and Jackson Pollack. The French collection contains impressionist and postimpressionist paintings by Cézanne, Degas, Gauguin, Matisse, Monet, Picasso, Pissarro, and Renoir. And the Chinese collection contains more then 200 bronzes, jades, and ceramics as well as a collection of monumental Buddhist sculptures.

✪ **Playmobil Fun Park.** 8031 N. Military Trail, Palm Beach Gardens. ☎ **800/351-8697.** Free admission. Tues–Sun 10am–6pm. I-95 North to Palm Beach Lakes Blvd. west to Military Trail. Turn left. The park is about a mile down on the right side.

Opened in 1994, this monstrous retail outlet and play park is one of only two such parks in the world (the other one is in Germany, the company's headquarters). Housed in a replica of a castle, this indoor fantasy world is even better than FAO Schwarz. You could spend hours here and not spend a penny. The 17,000 square foot play floor is divided into age specific play areas and theme areas, including a water zone for kids to play with boats and a Victorian area with elaborately constructed doll houses. It is free, but after hours of playing with these cool plastic toys, try walking throughout the retail store without buying anything. You will find some great sales here and a small snack bar.

✪ **Society for the Four Arts.** 2 Four Arts Plaza (off Royal Palm Way), Palm Beach. ☎ **561/655-7226.** Admission varies depending on program. Gardens, library, Sunday afternoon films, art exhibitions, and gallery talks free to the public. Movies, concerts, and lectures $3–$25. Call for schedule.

Especially good for children who may be bored with the beach, this Palm Beach institution is a great place just to hang out or to enrich yourself. More than 60 years ago, the society was founded to encourage appreciation of art, music, drama, and literature, and it does a stellar job with at least three of the four (there hasn't been much drama lately), with frequent concerts, year-round art exhibitions, and weekly lectures by big names like John Updike, Gregory Hines, David Frost, and Colin Powell. Explore the well-manicured flower and sculpture gardens. Also, stop by a tremendous and little-known children's library, which includes an enormous collection of books, videos, and games for the little ones.

NATURE PRESERVES & ATTRACTIONS

✪ **Lion Country Safari.** Southern Blvd. W. at State Rd. 80, West Palm Beach. ☎ **561/ 793-1084** or 561/793-9797 for camping reservations. Admission $14.95 adults, $9.95 seniors and children 3–16, free for children under 3. Daily 9:30am–5:30pm (last vehicle admitted at 4:30pm). From I-95, exit on Southern Blvd. W. Travel 18 miles and follow signs to the attraction.

Even if you've been on an African safari, you probably haven't seen the variety of animals you'll see at this 500-acre wildlife preserve. More than 1,300 animals are divided into their indigenous regions, from the East African preserve of the Serengeti to the American West. You'll see elephants, wildebeest, ostriches, American bison, buffalo, watusi, pink flamingos, and many other more unusual species. Even the lions and elephants roam the huge grassy landscape without a cage in sight. In fact, you're the one who's confined, in your own car without an escort (no convertibles allowed). You're given a detailed informational pamphlet with photos and descriptions and are instructed to obey the 15-m.p.h. speed limit—unless you see the rhinos charge, in which case you're encouraged to floor it. To drive the loop takes just over an hour, though you could make a day of just watching the chimpanzees play on their secluded islands. Included in the admission price is Safari World, an amusement park with paddleboats, a carousel, and a nursery for baby animals born in the preserve. Picnics are encouraged and camping is available (call for reservations). Don't miss this incredible experience. Rental cars are also available for $6 per hour.

Dreher Park Zoo. 1301 Summit Blvd. (east of I-95 between Southern and Forest Hill blvds.). ☎ **561/547-WILD.** Admission $6, $5 senior citizens, $4 children 3–12, and children under 3 free. Daily 9am–5pm.

Unlike big city zoos, this intimate 23-acre park is more like a stroll in the park than an all-day excursion. It features about 500 animals representing more than 100 different species. A special monkey exhibit and petting zoo are favorites with kids. Stroller and wagon rentals are available.

SHOPPING & BROWSING

People may complain of the lack of nightlife or beaches, but no one would dare question Palm Beach's shopping opportunities. From thrift to jewels, Palm Beach has it all.

Known as the Rodeo Drive of the south, **Worth Avenue** is a window-shopper's dream. No matter what your budget, don't miss the Worth Avenue experience, and don't be put off. These days shopkeepers have learned that sometimes the most affluent shoppers wear ripped jeans or cowboy hats. Still, to fit in you might want to dress as if you were going to an elegant luncheon, not to the mall down the street. The 4 blocks between South Ocean Boulevard and Cocoanut Row—a stretch of more than 200 boutiques, posh shops, art galleries, and upscale restaurants—are home to the stores of Armani, Louis Vuitton, Cartier, Polo Ralph Lauren, and Chanel, among like company.

Victoria's Secret, Limited Express, and several other less-impressive chains have sneaked in here too, but so have a good number of unique boutiques. Stop into **Paper Treasures,** at 217 Worth Ave. (☎ **561/835-1891**); it's an autograph gallery with a priceless collection of John Hancocks like those of Joe DiMaggio, Mickey Mantle, Andrew Jackson, Abe Lincoln, Howard Hughes, and hundreds more, all displayed in beautiful frames. At **Myers Luggage,** at 313 Worth (☎ 561/832-6515), Richard Myers is happy to demonstrate his impressive assortment of toys and gifts, including a vast collection of amusing alarm clocks, spy equipment, gorilla masks, and gag gifts, along with pricey leather bags and English picnic baskets. Just off Worth Avenue, at 374 S. County Rd., is the **Church Mouse** (☎ 561/659-2154), a great consignment/thrift shop with antique furnishings and tableware. Lots of good castaway clothing and shoes are reasonably priced. This shop usually closes for 2 months during the summer. Call to be sure.

The **Palm Beach Mall,** on Palm Beach Lakes Boulevard just east of I-95 (☎ 561/686-3513), is a huge and pleasantly designed mall with tropical fountains, plants, and skylights. You will find several department stores, including JC Penney, Sears, Burdines, and Lord & Taylor, as well as hundreds of specialty boutiques and restaurants.

The **Palm Beach Outlet Center,** at 5700 Okeechobee Blvd. (3 miles west of I-95), West Palm Beach, is the most elegant outlet mall I have ever seen. Upscale clothing, luggage, and shoes at bargain prices are offered in lushly decorated surroundings. The fully enclosed mall also sports a food court.

Downtown West Palm Beach has a number of interesting boutiques along **Clematis Street.** In addition to a large and well-organized bookstore, **Clematis Street Books,** at 206 Clematis (☎ 561/832-2302), there are used-record stores, clothing shops, and a few interesting art galleries. Many new and more upscale shops are opening soon. On Saturday mornings, a fantastic **green market** sets up stalls along Narcissus, which runs perpendicular to Clematis between Flagler and Banyan streets.

ACCOMMODATIONS YOU CAN AFFORD

Staying in the Palm Beaches on a budget is a bit of a trick, since the rates are high even in the summer. This is where to find hotel rooms that rent for what some people pay as a down payment on a house. The lowest-priced rooms at "the big three"— The Breakers, the Ritz Carlton, and the Four Seasons—start at around $350 in season.

The island of Palm Beach is perhaps the most exclusive in the country. Royalty comes to winter here, and there are plenty of royally priced options to accommodate them. Happily, there exist a few special little inns that offer reasonably priced rooms in elegant settings. Surrounding the island are many more modest places to lay your straw hat. Below you'll find some fantastic options especially for the off-season when the winter snowbirds have gone.

A few of the larger hotel chains operating in Palm Beach include the **Howard Johnson Palm Beach** (☎ 800/654-2000 or 561/582-2581), at 2870 S. Ocean Blvd., which is across the street from the beach and has rooms from $60. Also beachside is the pricey **Palm Beach Hilton** (☎ 800/433-1718 or 561/586-6542), at 2842 S. Ocean Blvd. (rooms are generally over $100, but ask for midweek specials).

In general, you'll find much lower rates in West Palm Beach. The chain hotels are mostly located on the main arteries close to the highways and a short drive to the activities in downtown. They include a very well kept ✪ **Best Western** (☎ 800/331-9569 or 561/683-8810), 1800 Palm Beach Lakes Blvd., and, just down the road, a **Comfort Inn** (☎ 800/221-2222 or 561/689-6100), 1901 Palm Beach Lakes Blvd. just west of I-95.

For real budget options, you may want to check out Lake Worth, just a few miles south of West Palm Beach.

If you're looking for something for longer than just a few days, you may want to call a reservations service for help. Especially for rentals for a few weeks or months, call **Palm Beach Accommodations** (☎ 800/543-SWIM).

SUPER-CHEAP SLEEPS

Beachcomber Apartment Motel. 3024 S. Ocean Blvd., Palm Beach, FL 33480. ☎ **800/ 833-7122** or 561/585-4646. Fax 561/547-9438. 45 units, all with bathroom (shower only). A/C TV TEL. Winter $85–$150 single or double; from $115–$210 apt. Off-season $42–$80 motel rm; from $55–$120 apt. AE, DISC, MC, V. From I-95, exit 10th Ave. N., head east to Federal Hwy., and turn right. Continue to Lake Worth Ave. and turn left. Go over bridge and turn right at first traffic light (S. Ocean Dr.); the hotel is 1½ blocks on the left.

It's not just the bright-pink building that makes this 2-story motel stand out. For more than 35 years the Beachcomber has been bringing consumer sanity to pricey Palm Beach by offering a good standard of accommodation at reasonable prices. Squeezed between beachfront high-rises, the motel is located oceanfront, adjacent to Lake Worth Beach and a short drive from Worth Avenue shops and local attractions. Every room has two double beds, large closets, and distinctive green-and-white tropical-style furnishings; some have kitchenettes. The most expensive have balconies overlooking the ocean. The bathrooms are basic, and amenities are limited to towels and soap. Facilities at the motel include a coin-operated laundry, shuffleboard, a large pool, and a sundeck overlooking the Atlantic.

The Hummingbird Bed and Breakfast. 631 Lucerne Ave., Lake Worth, FL 33460. ☎ **561/582-3224.** Fax 561/540-8817. www.bbonline.com/~bbonline/. 26 units, all will have bathrooms by 1999 (some with shower only). A/C TV TEL. Winter $35 single; $65–$95 double. Off-season $29 single; $49–$75 double. DISC, MC, V. Rate includes breakfast in season.

This rough-and-tumble B&B has been undergoing some necessary rehabbing over the years—and so have many of the guests. In season, many foreigners and northerners call this downright cheap hotel home. In the slow summer months, it is more popular with transients and locals with domestic trouble. Still, it seems decent enough and safe. Request a pricier room with cooking facilities for a real deal. Located in Lake Worth just a block from the hip shopping and dining district and less than ten minutes drive from Palm Beach, you can't get this convenience for so little money anywhere else.

✪ **Lago Motor Inn.** 714 S. Dixie Hwy., Lake Worth, FL 33460. ☎ **561/585-5246.** Fax 561/547-2001. 17 units, all with bathroom. A/C TV TEL. Winter $56–$58 single, $58–$66 double. Off-season $40 single, $44–$48 double. MC, V.

This immaculate 2-story motel distinguishes itself because of its cleanliness and its price. While rooms here aren't exactly elegant, they're spacious and come with all the basics, plus small refrigerators. A small garden and pool make it especially pleasant. In the middle of an unattractive commercial strip, the motel is at least close to the bridge leading to the beach.

Mt. Vernon Motor Lodge. 310 Belvedere Rd., West Palm Beach, FL 33405. ☎ **561/ 832-0094.** Fax 561/627-3218. 46 units, all with shower but no tub. A/C TV TEL. Winter $59– $69 single or double. Off-season $49–$59 single or double. Extra person $10 in winter, $5 off-season. AE, DISC, MC, V.

It isn't the presidential palace, but it's well located and just minutes to Palm Beach. There is a good-sized pool and sundeck, too. The rooms are nearly hostel style and the smell of old food and perfume permeated the air of the one I checked out. But it's safe and inexpensive. Recent improvements (and higher rates) make it more recommendable than in years past.

✪ **ParkView Motor Lodge.** 4710 S. Dixie Hwy., West Palm Beach, FL 33405. ☎ **561/ 833-4644.** Fax 561/833-4644. 28 units, all with bathroom (some with shower only, some with tub only). A/C TV TEL. Winter $72–$88 single or double (including continental breakfast).

Off-season $46–$60 single or double (including continental breakfast). AE, DC, DISC, MC, V. Extra person $8 in winter, $5 off-season.

The best of the many hotels along shabby U.S. 1, this single-story, clean, family run spot is a real find in the Palm Beaches. There's no pool, but there are charming touches, like the colored sheets and towels in the rooms, and the bougainvillea that grows in pretty terra-cotta pots along the hallways. The nondescript rooms all have refrigerators, and the location is ideal, only 3 miles from downtown.

Shangri-La Lodge. 1700 S. Federal Hwy., Lake Worth, FL 33460. ☎ **888/303-9966** or 561/582-1700. Fax 561/582-3521. 21 units, all with bathroom (shower only). A/C TV TEL. Winter $45–$50 night single or double, $300 week. Off-season $35–$45 single or double. Free 7th night in summer. AE, CB, DC, DISC, MC, V.

This motel is situated in a strip of budget accommodations, many of which are run down and frequented by transients. This simple, 2-story property stands out not because it is gorgeous or luxurious, but because the Finnish owners have kept it clean, safe, and quiet. It's popular with European tourists looking for a good deal. Many visitors return each winter for the same value and convenience offered here. The beach is less than 2 miles away and shopping and restaurants are within walking distance. A small pool and sundeck is made private by a tall hedge. Rooms are simple, almost sparse, but with all the necessities, including a small refrigerator and coffeemaker. Microwaves are also available. A hearty European-style breakfast is served in a small coffee shop on the premises.

FOR A FEW BUCKS MORE

Heart of Palm Beach Hotel. 160 Royal Palm Way, Palm Beach, FL 33480. ☎ **800/ 523-5377** or 561/655-5600. Fax 561/832-1201. 100 units, all with bathroom. A/C TV TEL. Winter $149–$219 single or double; $275 suite. Off-season $69–$139 single or double; $175 suite. AE, CB, DC, MC, V. From I-95, exit onto Okeechobee Blvd. E. and continue over the Royal Park Bridge onto Royal Palm Way; the hotel is ahead on your right, past S. County Rd.

The centrally located Heart of Palm Beach Hotel is within walking distance of Worth Avenue's shops and just half a block from the beach. Ongoing renovations since the 1990s have improved the patio space as well as the rooms in the hotel's two buildings. Most are decorated with modest but new furnishings and fittings in a colorful contemporary style. The tiled bathrooms are small, clean, and functional. Besides the great location, another plus here is that each accommodation comes with a private balcony or patio. Choose a room on a higher floor, as those on the ground floor tend to be a bit dark. The staff is particularly outgoing and will help guests plan outings and itineraries.

There's a heated swimming pool and complimentary covered parking. A clubby restaurant serves a selection of salads, sandwiches, pastas, and cocktails. Breakfast is served in a bright dining room overlooking the gardens.

Palm Beach Hawaiian Ocean Inn. 3550 S. Ocean Blvd. (between Lantana and Lake Worth causeways), Palm Beach, FL 33480. ☎ **800/457-5631** or 561/582-5631. www.worldpub. com/hawaiian. E-mail: hawaiian@gate.net. 58 units, all with bathroom (most with showers only). A/C TV TEL. Winter $135– $145 single or double hotel rm. or efficiency; $160–$190 2-rm. suite; $230–$300 4-rm. suite. Off-season $82–$95 single or double hotel rm. or efficiency. AE, CB, DC, DISC, MC, V. Free parking on premises. Extra person over 18 $5.

Located about 7 miles south of the most exclusive shopping section of Palm Beach, this kitschy Hawaiian-style hotel has benefited from a thorough renovation completed in 1997. With oceanfront rooms, many efficiencies and large suites, the 2-story, 1960s property is recommendable for its sheer convenience. In addition to the usual amenities, all rooms have refrigerators. Efficiencies also add microwaves, coffeemakers, and toasters. Modern cherry wood furnishings and sleek new carpeting are standard throughout. A large pool deck, patio bar, and hotel restaurant serving breakfast, lunch, and dinner make this one of the most affordable full-service hotels in the area.

Palm Beach Historic Inn. 365 S. County Rd., Palm Beach, FL 33480. ☎ **561/832-4009.** Fax 561/832-6255. www.PalmBeachHistoricInn.com. E-mail: PalmBeachHistoricInn@worldnet. att.net. 13 units, all with bathroom. A/C TV TEL. Winter $125–$150 single or double; from $175 suite. Off-season $75–$95 single or double; from $100 suite. Rates include continental breakfast. Children stay free in parents' room. AE, CB, DC, DISC, MC, V.

Despite a rather abandoned look, this bed-and-breakfast is a cozy and comfortable place to stay in Palm Beach. Built in 1923, the Palm Beach Historic Inn is an area landmark located within walking distance of Worth Avenue, the beach, and several good restaurants. The small lobby is filled with antiques, books, magazines, and an old-fashioned umbrella stand, all of which add to the homey feel of this intimate bed-and-breakfast. All the rooms are on the second floor, and each is uniquely decorated and full of frills. Floral prints, sheer curtains, and the plethora of lace can sometimes be overwhelming, masking rather than complementing beautiful antique writing desks and dressers. Happily, there are also fluffy bathrobes, an abundance of towels, and plenty of good-smelling toiletries.

Palm Beach Hotel. 235 Sunrise Ave. (between County Road and Bradley Place, across the street from Publix), Palm Beach, FL 33480. ☎ **800/536-7161** or 561/659-7794. 200 units, all with bathroom (some with shower only). Winter $105–$123 studio and 1-bedroom, single, or double; $163 2-bedroom. Off-season from $75 1-bedroom, from $95 2-bedroom. AE, MC, V.

An excellent and affordable alternative right in the middle of Palm Beach's commercial section is a condo that operates as a hotel, too. This is a rare find in Palm Beach: a true bargain. Although it is not a full-service hotel, this stunning hotel/condo has the convenience of kitchenettes and large sitting areas. Perfect for visiting families, this nicely renovated property also has a pool and sundeck as well as coin laundry. All rooms are decorated differently, but the ones I saw were tasteful and clean.

Sea Lord Hotel. 2315 S. Ocean Blvd., Palm Beach, FL 33480. ☎ **561/582-1461.** 40 units, all with bathroom. A/C TV TEL. Winter $115 –$212 single or double. Off-season $58–$107 single or double. Extra person $10. DISC, MC, V.

The Sea Lord represents very good value for those who just have to stay on Florida's priciest island beach. From the outside, the aged oceanfront hotel looks as if it has been around for a while, and the dated furnishings inside concur. The rooms, however, are very clean and pleasant enough, fitted with old wood beds and bureaus, small refrigerators, and ordinary no-frills tiled bathrooms. Plans for a major overhaul were in the works at press time. The best rooms are located in the 5-story main building, and have a patio or balcony accessible via a sliding glass door. The efficiencies are larger and have fully stocked kitchens, along with the same homely furnishings and petite bathrooms that are found elsewhere on the property. Many face the sand. The least desirable rooms are in the smaller south wing and have no views. The Sea Lord's exceptionally friendly employees staff the front desk 24 hours. Beach towels and lounge chairs are always available for use on the sand or at the well-maintained heated swimming pool. A small poolside cafe serves three American-style meals daily.

WORTH A SPLURGE

✪ **The Breakers.** 1 S. County Rd., Palm Beach, FL 33480. ☎ **800/833-3141,** 888/ BREAKERS, or 561/655-6611. Fax 561/659-8403. 574 units. A/C MINIBAR TV TEL. Winter $340–$575 standard single or double; $510 deluxe single or double; from $785 suite. Off-season $160–$345 standard single or double; $275 deluxe single or double; from $500 suite. Special packages available. AE, CB, DC, DISC, MC, V. From I-95, exit onto Okeechobee Blvd. E., and turn left onto South County Rd.; the hotel is just ahead on your right.

The biggest and grandest of all of this area's resorts, this five-star historic beauty epitomizes Palm Beach luxury. It's one of only two Florida properties to win five stars from the Mobil guide and five diamonds from AAA. Though at first blush it seems out of the budget traveler's price range, great off-season rates and package deals are well worth looking into.

From the expansive manicured lawns to the elegant marble lobby, The Breakers is the place to be in Palm Beach if you want to be walking distance from all the area's most exclusive shopping and dining and be right on the beach. The lush 130-acre grounds also sport two of the island's only golf courses. (One, the Ocean Course, circa 1897, is Florida's oldest 18-hole course.) In addition, the hotel boasts a large outdoor pool, private beach, health club, bicycle rental, putting green, game rooms, supervised children's activities, children's playground, business center, 14 tennis courts, watersports concession (including scuba and sailing), croquet, shuffleboard, beach volleyball courts, beauty salon, boutiques, and shopping arcade. Three new pools, a full-service spa/fitness center, and a grand ballroom are planned for construction in 1999.

An attentive staff is as accustomed to handling steamer trunks and fur wraps as they are to sending faxes and programming VCRs. Though this 1926 palace was built for the world's most elite, it now handles more corporate clients and families with ease. While the Gatsby-esque grounds of Palm Beach's first hotel reveal a sense of history, the newly reconstructed rooms are equipped with all the modern conveniences.

Even the very smallest and cheapest rooms (called traditional or superior) are luxuriously appointed and include all the amenities you could desire. Ask for one of the few corner rooms, which (for the same price) tend to be larger and have more windows. Much pricier oceanfront suites offer huge sitting areas, closets, and luxuriously appointed sleeping quarters.

The Breakers is great for families though the formality of the lobbies and restaurants may put some off. Jackets for men are suggested, but not required, in the formal restaurants and lounge. Only hotel guests are permitted in the exclusive and Palm Beach's only oceanfront bar.

Chesterfield Hotel. 363 Cocoanut Row, Palm Beach, FL 33480. ☎ **800/243-7871** or 561/ 659-5800. Fax 561/659-6707. 65 units, all with bathroom. A/C TV TEL. Winter $269–$349 single or double; from $529 suite. Off-season $89–$169 single or double; from $219 suite. Rollaway bed $15 extra. AE, DC, DISC, MC, V. From I-95, exit onto Okeechobee Blvd. E., cross the Intracoastal Waterway, and turn right onto Cocoanut Row; the hotel is ahead on your left, just past Australian Ave.

With more charm than its expensive rivals, the intimate Chesterfield, located just 1 block from Worth Avenue, has been popular with visitors in the know since the 1920s. Behind its light stucco facade, arched windows, and colorful flags is an overly designed interior with Laura Ashley prints battling Ralph Lauren. It all creates a wonderfully authentic country-manor feel.

Guest rooms also have formal chintz and taffeta prints. Heavy wooden furniture and plush carpets give each room a warm but dark feel. Although most rooms have no view to speak of, they are comfortable and attractive. A stunning lobby library provides a quiet nook for those who may want to read at the large oak desk or borrow a book for the beach. Afternoon tea completes the illusion of being in a well-run country inn across the Atlantic. A cozy courtyard is set up with lounge chairs for sunning by the heated outdoor pool.

You may want to come for high tea in the Leopard Room, which also serves fantastic English, French, and continental favorites all day and a fantastically popular Sunday brunch. The adjacent Leopard Lounge is an area hangout in the evenings when there is usually live music, a great happy hour and no cover charge (see "The Palm Beaches After Dark," below).

BED & BREAKFASTS

✪ **Heron Cay.** 15106 Palmwood Rd., Palm Beach Gardens, FL 33410. ☎ **561/744-6315** or 561/744-2188. 4 units, 2 cottages (sleeps 6 to 8 people), all with bathroom (some with shower only). A/C. Winter $105–$180 single or double; $250 cottage. Off-season $85–$150 single or double; $200 cottage. Extra person $10. Cash or checks preferred. MC, V. Take I-95 to Donald Ross Rd. Pass Alt. A1A. Turn left on Palmwood Rd. The resort is 1 mile down on the right.

This charming little bed-and-breakfast is minutes away from the hustle and bustle of Palm Beach but is located on its own private island. All rooms open onto a wraparound second-floor balcony. For the adventurous, there's a slide from the second floor to the large tiled mosaic pool! There's also a dock for those who want to arrive by boat. The best deal going is the three-bedroom, two-bath cottage with its own pool. Another similar cottage is also available, but has no pool. Note that children are not welcome here. For a little peace and quiet in an Old Florida–style home, this is the place to be.

✪ **Hibiscus House.** 501 30th St., West Palm Beach, FL 33407. ☎ **800/203-4927** or 561/ 863-5633. Fax 561/863-5633. www.hibiscushouse.com. 8 units, all with bathroom (some with showers only). A/C TV TEL. Winter $85–$175 single or double. Off-season $65–$120 single or double. Rates include breakfast. AE, DC, MC, V. From I-95, exit onto Palm Beach Lakes Blvd. E. and continue 4 miles; turn left onto Flagler Dr., continue for about 20 blocks, then turn left onto 30th St.; the inn is 2 blocks ahead on your right.

Inexpensive bed-and-breakfasts are rare in Southeast Florida, making the Hibiscus House one of the area's firsts, a true find. Located a few miles from the coast in a quiet residential neighborhood, this 1920s-era B&B is filled with handsome antiques and tapestried in luxurious fabrics. Every room has its own private terrace or balcony. The backyard, a peaceful retreat, has been transformed into a tropical garden with a heated swimming pool and lounge chairs. Also there are plenty of pretty areas for guests to enjoy inside; one little sitting room is wrapped in glass and is stocked with playing cards and board games. Beware: Breakfast portions are enormous. The gourmet creations are as filling as they are beautiful. Ask for any special requests in advance; owners Raleigh Hill and Colin Rayer will be happy to oblige.

Tropical Gardens Bed & Breakfast. 419 32nd St., West Palm Beach, FL 33407. ☎ **800/ 736-4064** or 561/848-4064. Fax 407/842-1688. E-mail: wpbbb@aol.com. 4 units, all with bathroom (3 with shower only). A/C TV TEL. Winter $85–$125 single or double. Off-season $55–$85 single or double. Rates include large continental breakfast. Weekly rates available. AE, DC, MC, V. From I-95, take Exit 53 east (Palm Beach Lakes Blvd.) to Flagler Dr. Turn left at the stop sign (30th St.); continue to Poinsetta (1 block down); turn right. Turn left on 32nd St.

A quaint little place, the former West Palm Beach B&B is a compact and cozy home with just four individually styled, smallish guest rooms. The tropically inspired interior is decorated with plenty of knickknacks and it's a bright and clean place with lots of windows. Two of the bedrooms are located in the main house. The front room has a queen-size bed, white wicker furnishings, and a large carpet on hardwood floors. The room's bathroom is not shared, but it is a few steps down the hall, and a bathrobe is provided. Also in the main house is a cozy pink room with a tiny private bathroom with a shower and sink—no tub, and no counter space for toiletries. Because they offer more privacy than the rooms in the main house, the two cottage rooms located out back are more recommendable. Both have queen-size beds, refrigerators, microwaves, and VCRs. One has a full kitchenette. For other guests, a full kitchen is available in the main house. A continental breakfast is served each morning from 8:30 to 9:30am and a glass of wine is offered each evening. The inn has complimentary bicycles for guest use and is entirely no-smoking.

GREAT DEALS ON DINING

Palm Beach has some of the area's finest restaurants, with many classical and elegant options as well as a few more innovative choices. Dress here is slightly more formal than in most other areas of Florida: Men wear blazers, and women generally put on modest dresses when they dine out—even in the dead of summer.

SUPER-CHEAP EATS

✪ **Green's Pharmacy.** 151 N. County Rd., Palm Beach. ☎ **561/832-0304.** Breakfast $2–$5; burgers and sandwiches $3–$6. AE, MC, V. Mon–Sat 7am–6pm, Sun 7am–5pm. AMERICAN.

This neighborhood corner pharmacy offers one of the best meal deals in Palm Beach. Both breakfast and lunch are served coffee-shop style at either a Formica bar or at plain tables above a black-and-white checkerboard floor. Breakfast specials include eggs and omelettes served with home fries and bacon, sausage, or corned-beef hash. At lunch the grill serves burgers and sandwiches, as well as ice-cream sodas and milkshakes, to a loyal crowd of pastel-clad Palm Beachers.

✪ **It's in The Bag.** 423 Clematis St., West Palm Beach. ☎ **561/655-4505.** Sandwiches $3.50–$6.50. AE. Mon–Sat 10:30am–3pm. ROLLED PITA SANDWICHES/DELI.

These delicious sandwiches are the best I've had. Sort of like a pinwheel or what my Midwest friends remember as "high rollers," these rolled sandwiches are made with a large sheet of daily made, soft, thick pita, fresh-cut meats, and quality greens. With more than 30 choices, there is plenty of variety. Hummus and tabbouleh, BLT, ham and Swiss, hot tuna, chicken salad, and turkey club are just a few. Try Denya's favorite, with smoked turkey, bacon, tomato, spinach, and mayo. You can also get fresh fruit smoothies and juices. After picking up your order from the counter, sit inside in the deli-like store or at the sunny sidewalk tables.

✪ **John G's.** 10 S. Ocean Blvd., Lake Worth. ☎ **561/585-9860.** Reservations not accepted. Breakfast $3–$8.50; lunch $5–$14. No credit cards. Daily 7am–3pm. Off Fla. Turnpike, take the Lake Worth exit and head toward the ocean. AMERICAN.

This coffee shop is the most popular in the county. For decades, John G's has been attracting huge breakfast crowds; lines run out the door, or, on weekends, all the way down the block. They come for good, greasy-spoon–style food served in heaping portions right on the beachfront. This place is known for fresh and tasty fish and chips and its selection of creative omelettes and grill specials.

Montezuma. 5607 S. Dixie Hwy. (between Forest Hill and Southern blvds.), West Palm Beach. ☎ **561/586-7974.** Reservations accepted but not necessary. Main courses $2–$11. AE, DC, DISC, MC, V. Daily 9am–10pm. MEXICAN.

Up to now, 50 seats have managed to accommodate patient patrons who wait for some of the freshest burritos, tacos, mariscos, and tortillas in Palm Beach County. Thankfully, Francisco, from Mexico City, plans to expand soon. Try any of the huge egg platters for breakfast like Montezuma Chamulan, scrambled eggs with cheese and avocado, or a seafood omelette with shrimp, octopus, and squid. Eggs come with refried beans, chilaquiles, and fresh corn tortillas. Lunches are the most popular meal here when you can get huge enchiladas, salads, tacos, and enormous platters of steak, chicken, or pork dishes. Also offered is authentic tongue in green sauce.

Piccolo Mondo. 87 Via Mizner (behind Worth Ave.), Palm Beach. ☎ **581/655-9752.** Main courses $5–$8; salads and sandwiches $4.50–$5.50. MC, V. Mon–Sat 11:30–3pm. ITALIAN/CONTINENTAL.

The next best thing to room service is Piccolo Mondo. This "food boutique" offers the very best take-out and delivery menu in the city. Unfortunately it is only open for lunch. From Caesar salads to roasted veal, from lasagna to penne, from cheeseburgers and chicken salads to french fries, the entire small menu is recommendable. It is a spin-off of the popular and expensive Renato's next door. For about a third of the price, you can sample the same fare and make your own atmosphere.

Sandwiches by the Sea. 363 S. County Rd., Palm Beach. ☎ **561/655-7911.** Salads and hoagies $3.75–$5. No credit cards. Mon–Sat 9am–4pm. HOAGIES/SALADS.

Large classic hoagies, healthful salads, and pita pockets for the price of a meal at McDonald's make this little narrow take-out shop a real find in pricey Palm Beach. Breakfast choices are limited to fruit salads, muffins, breads, and croissants, but lunch choices include hearty homemade soups and overstuffed sandwiches. Choose the daily special sandwich and a large drink for about $4. Fresh white meat chicken salad and tuna are favorites. Also tempting are frozen yogurt treats, brownies, cookies, and muffins. A full selection of sodas, juices, and coffees is offered, too. This is the place to come for picnic supplies or a superbargain lunch to enjoy at a tiny counter.

TooJay's. 313 Royal Poinciana Plaza (3 miles east of I-95 off Exit 52A), Palm Beach. ☎ **561/659-7232.** Reservations not accepted. Main courses $7–$12. CB, DC, MC, V. Daily 8am–9pm. DELICATESSEN.

This simple and predictable restaurant and take-out deli is a favorite with locals and out-of-towners who want good old-fashioned deli food. So popular, in fact, that TooJay's now has more than a dozen outlets. For good cover while people-watching, choose a booth surrounded by a jungle of potted plants. The food is excellent and could hardly be fresher. All the classic sandwiches are available: hot pastrami, roast beef, turkey, chicken, chopped liver, egg salad, and more. Comfort food in the form of huge portions of stuffed cabbage, chicken pot pie, beef brisket, and sautéed onions and chicken livers is sure to satisfy.

For A Few Bucks More

✪ **Aquaterra.** 230 Sunrise Ave. (between Sunrise and Park aves.), Palm Beach. ☎ **561/366-4000.** Reservations recommended, especially on weekends. Main courses $15–$18.50; fixed-price menu 5pm–6pm $19. AE, MC, V. Tues–Sun 9:30am–2:30pm and 5–11pm, Mon 5–11pm. INNOVATIVE AMERICAN.

New York's Charlie Palmer, James Beard winner for best chef in 1997, has taken his spatula south and opened a stunning new lunch and dinner spot in Palm Beach. Slightly off the beaten track on Sunrise Avenue (across the street from the Palm Beach Hotel) but still centrally located, this fantastic restaurant is bound to please even the pickiest eaters. With nearly 20 options for bar snacks and appetizers including crispy fried oysters, beef skewers with peanut sauce, vegetable spring rolls, eggplant fritters, luscious rock shrimp pillows, and lobster salad in cold tomato consommé, the menu is simple yet diverse. A more limited selection of entrees, as the name suggests, are from the sea or land. The best choices are waterborne. Depending on the season there is mahimahi, salmon, swordfish, snapper, or tuna, all of which can be prepared to your liking: grilled, roasted, or sautéed with a complimentary array of herbs and seasonings. I favor the clean-tasting snapper grilled with caramelized lemon, olive oil, and fresh parsley. Also, an exceptional sea bass is braised table side with a subtly licorice and basil broth. Likewise, you can choose how you'd like your meats or chicken cooked. A delicate filet mignon sautéed with wild mushroom ragout is memorable. Don't skip the architecturally striking and delicious desserts. Especially good is the double caramelized banana parfait and the bittersweet chocolate torte with homemade mint ice cream.

Rhythm Cafe. 3800 S. Dixie Hwy., West Palm Beach. ☎ 561/833-3406. Reservations recommended on weekends. Main courses $10–$24. AE, DISC, MC, V. Tues–Fri 11am–3pm and 6–10pm, Sat–Sun 8am–2pm and 6–10pm. Sometimes earlier on Sun. From I-95, exit east on Southern Blvd., 1 block north of Southern Blvd. on the right. ECLECTIC AMERICAN.

This hole-in-the-wall is where those in the know come to eat some of West Palm Beach's most laid-back gourmet food. On the handwritten, photocopied menu, you will always find a fish specialty with a hefty dose of greens and garnishes. Also reliably outstanding is the sautéed medallion of beef tenderloin served on a bed of arugula with a tangy rosemary vinaigrette. Salads and soups are a great bargain since the portions are relatively large and the display usually spectacular. The kitschy decor of this tiny cafe comes complete with vinyl tablecloths and paintings by local amateurs. Young handsome waiters are attentive but not solicitous. The old drugstore where the restaurant recently relocated features an original '50s lunch counter and stools.

Testa's. 221 Royal Ponciana Way (between Flagler and A1A), Palm Beach. ☎ 561/832-0992. Reservations suggested. Main courses $7–$23. AE, DC, DISC, MC, V. Daily 7am–11pm or midnight. AMERICAN/ITALIAN.

On one of the island's ritziest streets, this large upscale diner has been serving hearty breakfasts, lunches, and dinners to a picky Palm Beach crowd since 1921. Prices aren't dirt cheap, but the selection, quality, and service make this a great choice. It's standard American fare with a number of recommendable Italian specialties thrown in, too. Known for many beef specialties, and pastas, Testa's has something for everyone. A full bar, huge selection of salads, pizzas, and a good-sized children's menu rounds out this very equitable menu. Look for discount coupons, sunset menus from 4pm until 6pm, and happy hour specials, too.

Worth A Splurge

Chuck & Harold's Cafe. 207 Royal Poinciana Way (corner of S. County Rd.), Palm Beach. ☎ 561/659-1440. Reservations recommended. Main courses $14–$28. AE, DC, DISC, MC, V. Mon–Thurs 7:30am–midnight, Fri–Sat 7:30am–1am, Sun 8am–11pm. SEAFOOD/AMERICAN.

For standard and predictable American fare, this old standby delivers. Chuck & Harold's serves good food at inflated prices. Remember, you are paying for one of the area's best people-watching perches. Sit outside and enjoy the view. Main dishes include fresh grilled or broiled fish, boiled lobster, and a small variety of straightforward homemade pasta and chicken dishes. If you happen to visit during stone crab season, order them here. The crab claws are steamed or chilled and served with a traditional honey-mustard sauce. One final hint: You might skip ordering dessert, as complimentary cookies are served at the end of each meal.

✪ Zazu. 313 Clematis St., West Palm Beach (between Olive and Dixie). ☎ 561/832-1919. Reservations suggested. Main courses $15–$23; pastas $11–$22. AE, DC, DISC, MC, V. Mon–Fri 11:30am–2:30pm and 5:30–10pm; Thurs–Sat, dinner until 11pm and nightclub until 3am. MULTICULTURAL.

This star along trendy Clematis Street has earned the loyalty of locals and visitors for its fantastically innovative cuisine and also for its lively nightlife. Most weekends feature a DJ late night and live music a few nights too. The menu is eclectic, featuring such recommendable appetizers as wild mushroom gnocchi roasted and served on top of slightly wilted greens with sweet browned caramelized onions and a classic Caesar salad with tiny rounds of Parmesan-laden pizza-bread. A varied menu of fish, chicken, beef, and veal prepared with an Italian, Southern, or Asian flare tend to work well, though a few are overwrought. Upstairs is Daddy O's, where a young attractive crowd has a raucous time, singing and dancing to whatever is going on. Arrive early (before 8pm) if you plan to get up there. Overall, the art deco decor, funky food, and lively vibe make it a fun night out for any one looking for a good time.

THE PALM BEACHES AFTER DARK
THE BAR, CAFE & MUSIC SCENE: DOWNTOWN WEST PALM BEACH

A decade-old project to revitalize downtown West Palm Beach has finally become a reality, with Clematis Street at the heart. Posh sidewalk cafes, bars, restaurants, and galleries dot the street from Flagler Drive to Rosemary Avenue, creating a prime spot for a night out, especially on weekends, when young professionals mingle with suit-clad Europeans and casually disheveled artists. Every Thursday night is a popular night out called **Clematis by Night.** Each week features a different rock, blues, or reggae band plus an art show. Vendors sell food and drinks and the street's bars and restaurants are packed. It can get a bit raucous at times, but it's always fun. Note that minors unaccompanied by their guardians are not permitted in the downtown area around Clematis Street after 10 on weeknights and after 11 on weekend nights.

Some highlights of the Strip include **Napa Valley Wine Bar** in the front of the Clematis Street Bookstore, 206 Clematis St. (☎ **561/832-5398**). This place serves a good selection of wines by the glass, coffees, and light snacks in a comfortable, slightly Bohemian setting. Quiet, artsy types whisper politely at small tables while listening to live jazz on weekends. Service is bumbling but the atmosphere is comfortable. **Sforza,** at 223 Clematis St. (☎ **561/832-8819**), is the only Italian restaurant I've ever been to that needs a bouncer at the door. On weekends this place draws crowds of yuppies and well-dressed Euros who wait to be picked to get in the elegant dining room to dance and sip expensive martinis.

If you are looking for a more casual scene, stop by ✪ **Ray's Downtown Blues,** at 519 Clematis St. (☎ **561/835-1577**), on a Thursday, Friday, or Saturday for free blues and mediocre drinks. Wednesday night is usually ladies night. Women get free drinks until midnight. This dusty little bar hosts homegrown blues bands that give it all up for the few patrons who appreciate the rough stuff.

Across the street is a long-time favorite, **Respectable Street Café,** at 518 Clematis St. (☎ **561/832-9999**). The cafe's plain storefront exterior belies its funky high-ceilinged interior decorated with large black booths, psychedelic wall murals, and a large checkerboard-tile dance floor where young hipsters dance to both live and recorded alternative music.

Just around the corner at 109 N. Olive Ave. is **Enigma** (☎ **561/832-5040**), a huge dance hall in the style of '80s New York clubs. Music varies, and the crowd represents the most outrageous Palm Beach County has to offer.

Over the bridge in Palm Beach is **E. R. Bradley's Saloon,** at 111 Bradley Pl., between Royal Poinciana Way and Sunset Ave. (☎ **561/833-3520**). Bradley's, as it is known, is about as wild as the "island" allows. Most nights a rowdy crowd of young professionals shares the old wooden tavern with hard-drinking regulars in blue blazers. Random hooting and a conga line around the block usually end with at least a couple of wannabe go-go dancers up on the bar enjoying the applause of a tipsy crowd. Check out the happy-hour buffets in the late afternoon.

A more sophisticated crowd gathers nightly at the **Leopard Lounge** in the Chesterfield Hotel (see "Accommodations You Can Afford," above). Live piano music, good conversation, and a comfortable sofa make this a perfect place to spend an evening.

THE PERFORMING ARTS

With a number of dedicated patrons and enthusiastic supporters of the arts, this area happily boasts many good venues for those craving culture. Check the *Palm Beach Post* or the *Palm Beach Daily News,* known as "the shiny sheet," for up-to-date listings and reviews. Call ☎ 800/882-ARTS for a recorded announcement of the week's events.

The **Raymond F. Kravis Center for the Performing Arts,** 701 Okeechobee Blvd., West Palm Beach (☎ 561/832-7469), is the area's largest and most active performance space. With a huge curved-glass facade and more than 2,500 seats in two lushly decorated indoor spaces, and a new outdoor amphitheater, The Kravis, as it is known, stages more than 300 performances each year. Phone for a current schedule of Palm Beach's best music, dance, and theater.

If you are in town when the **Miami City Ballet** is performing, consider yourself lucky. With a performance schedule that takes them around the state from late September to April, this critically acclaimed young company is worth catching. Call ☎ 561/833-4492.

4 Jupiter & Northern Palm Beach County

20 miles N of Palm Beach, 81 miles N of Miami

Northern Palm Beach County and its main town, Jupiter, are known primarily for pristine beaches and expansive tracts of land. The surrounding towns of Tequesta, Jupiter, Juno Beach, North Palm Beach, Palm Beach Gardens, and Singer Island are inviting for tourists who want to enjoy the many outdoor activities that make this area so popular with retirees, snowbirds, and families. Beaches and parks are clean, large, and easily accessible to the public.

ESSENTIALS

GETTING THERE   The quickest route from West Palm Beach to Jupiter is by the sometimes congested I-95. You can also take a slower but more scenic coastal route, U.S. 1 or Fla. A1A.

Since Jupiter is so close to Palm Beach, it's easy to fly into the **Palm Beach International Airport** (☎ 561/471-7420) and rent a car there. The drive should take less than half an hour.

VISITOR INFORMATION   For free maps, an arts-and-attractions calendar, and detailed trip planning guide, contact the **Palm Beach County Convention and Visitors Bureau,** 1555 Palm Beach Lakes Blvd., Suite 204, West Palm Beach, FL 33401 (☎ 800/554-PALM or 561/471-3995). Also open is a brand new visitor information center, located between I-95 and the Florida Turnpike at 8020 Indiantown Rd. in Jupiter. This center is open from 9am to 6pm daily.

HITTING THE BEACHES

The farther north you head from populated Palm Beach, the more peaceful and pristine the coast becomes. Just a few miles north of the bustle, castles and condominiums give way to wide open space and public parkland. There are dozens of recommendable spots. Following are a few of the best.

John D. MacArthur Beach, a state park, dominates a large portion of Singer Island, the barrier island just north of Palm Beach. Straddling the island from shore to shore, the park has lengthy frontage on both the Atlantic Ocean and Lake Worth Cove. The beach is great for hiking, swimming, and sunning. To reach the park from the mainland, cross the Intracoastal Waterway on Blue Heron Boulevard and turn north on Ocean Boulevard.

Jupiter Inlet meets the ocean at **Dubois Park,** a 29-acre beach that is popular with families. The shallow waters and sandy shore are perfect for kids, while adults can play in the rougher swells of the lifeguarded inlet. A footbridge leads to **Ocean Beach,** an area popular with windsurfers and surfers. There's a short fishing pier, and plenty of trees shading barbecue grills and picnic tables. Visitors can also explore the Dubois Pioneer Home, a small house situated atop a shell mound built by the Jaega Indians. The park entrance is on Dubois Road, about a mile south of the junction of U.S. 1 and Fla. A1A.

GREAT GOLF THAT WON'T BREAK YOUR BUDGET & OTHER AFFORDABLE OUTDOOR ACTIVITIES

BASEBALL   The newly built **Roger Dean Stadium,** 4751 Main Street (☎ 561/ 775-1818), hosts spring training for both the St. Louis Cardinals and the Montreal Expos, along with minor-league action from Florida's State League, The Hammerheads. Tickets range in price from $5 to $15. Baseball aficionados should call for schedules and specific ticket information.

BICYCLING   Bring your own, get one from your hotel, or rent one from **Raleigh Bicycles of Jupiter** (☎ 561/746-0585). Bicycle enthusiasts will enjoy exploring this flat and uncluttered area. North Palm Beach has hundreds of miles of smooth paved roads. Loggerhead Park in Juno Beach or A1A along the ocean has great trails for starters. You'll find many more scenic routes over the bridges and west of the highway.

BOATING & CANOEING   You can rent a boat at several outlets throughout northern Palm Beach, including **Classic Adventures,** at 2385 PGA Blvd. (at the base of the Intracoastal Bridge), Palm Beach Gardens (☎ 561/626-6771). This friendly outpost rents a variety of bow-riders that hold up to eight people for rates starting at $199 for a half day and $299 for a full day. Also fun are the Wave Runners starting at $60 an hour.

Canoe Outfitters, 9060 Indiantown Rd. (west of I-95), North Jupiter (☎ 561/ 746-7053), provides access to one of the area's most beautiful natural waterways. Canoers start at Riverbend Park along an 8-mile stretch of Intracoastal Waterway where the lush foliage supports dozens of exotic birds and reptiles. Keep your eyes open for gators that love to sunbathe on the shallow shores of the river. You'll end up tired and thoroughly wide-eyed at Jonathan Dickinson Park about 5 or 6 hours later. Eric Bailey, a local who runs the concession, will sell the environmentally minded a pamphlet for $1 that describes local flora and fauna. Trips run Wednesday to Sunday and cost $16 per person, including park charges.

CRUISES   Several sightseeing cruises offer scenic tours of the magnificent waterways that make up northern Palm Beach County. Several water taxis conduct daily narrated tours through the scenic waters. One interesting excursion departs from Panama Hatties at PGA Boulevard and the Intracoastal Waterway. Prices are $15 per person for the 1½-hour ride. Call ☎ 561/775-2628. The *Manatee Queen,* 18487 U.S. 1 (2 miles north of Jupiter Lighthouse), Blowing Rocks Marina, Jupiter (☎ 561/ 744-2191), a 40-foot catamaran with bench seating for up to 49 people, offers 2-hour tours of Jupiter Island departing daily at 2:30pm that pass Burt Reynolds's and Perry Como's mansions, among other historical and natural spots of interest. Reservations are highly recommended, especially in season; call for the current schedule of

Discovering a Remarkable Natural World: Sea Turtles & More

North Palm is well known for the giant sea turtles that lay their eggs on the county's beaches from May to August. These endangered marine animals return here annually, from as far as South America, to lay their clutch of about 115 eggs each. Nurtured by the warm sand, but preyed upon by birds and other predators, only about one or two babies from each nest survive to maturity.

Many environmentalists recommend that visitors take part in an organized turtle-watching program (rather than going on their own) to minimize disturbance to the turtles. The Jupiter Beach Resort (see "Accommodations You Can Afford," below) and the Marinelife Center of Juno Beach (see below) both sponsor free guided expeditions to the egg-laying sites from May to August. Phone for times and reservations.

Just south of Jupiter, in Juno Beach, is the **Marinelife Center of Juno Beach,** in Loggerhead Park, 14200 U.S. 1, Juno Beach (☎ **561/627-8280**). A small combination science museum and nature trail, the Marinelife Center is dedicated to the coastal ecology of northern Palm Beach County. Hands-on exhibits teach visitors about wetlands and beach areas, as well as offshore coral reefs and the local sea life. Visitors are encouraged to walk the center's sand dune nature trails, all of which are marked with interpretive signs. This is one place that you're guaranteed to see live sea turtles year-round, and during high breeding season (June and July) the center conducts narrative walks along a nearby beach. Reservations are a must. The reservation book opens on May 1 and is usually full by midmonth. Admission to the center is free, though donations are accepted. Open Tuesday to Saturday from 10am to 4pm and Sunday from noon to 3pm.

---

offerings. The cruise is wheelchair accessible. Prices start at $12.50 for adults and $10 for children and can range up to $15 for special tours. Bring your own lunch or purchase chips and sodas at the minisnack bar.

FISHING   Before you leave, send for an information-packed fishing kit with details on fish camps, charters, and tournament and tide schedules, distributed by the **West Palm Beach Fishing Club,** c/o Fish Finder, P.O. Box 468, West Palm Beach, FL 33402. The cost is $10 and is well worth it. Allow at least 4 weeks for delivery.

Once in town, several outfitters along U.S. 1 and A1A have vessels and equipment for rent if your hotel doesn't. One of the most complete facilities is the **Sailfish Marina & Resort** (☎ **561/844-1724**), 98 Lake Dr. (off Blue Heron Boulevard), Palm Beach Shores. Call for equipment, bait, guided trips, or boat rentals.

GOLF   Even if you're not lucky enough to be staying at the **PGA National Resort,** you may still be able to play on their award-winning courses. If you or someone in your group is a member of another golf or country club, have the head pro write a note on club letterhead to Jackie Rogers at PGA (see "Accommodations You Can Afford," below) or send a fax to ☎ 561/627-0155 to request a play date. Be sure the pro includes his or her PGA number and contact information. Allow at least 2 weeks for a response. Also, ask about the Golf-A-Round program, where selected private clubs open to nonmembers for free or discounted rates. Contact the Palm Beach County Convention and Visitors Bureau (☎ **561/471-3995**) for details.

Plenty of other great courses dot the area, including the **Indian Creek Golf Club,** 1800 Central Blvd., Jupiter (☎ **561/747-6262**). A well-respected 18-hole, par-70 course is situated on over 6,200 yards featuring narrow fairways and fast greens. Fees are $27 to $55, depending on the season, and include a mandatory cart. The course borders I-95.

HIKING   In an area that's not particularly known for extraordinary natural diversity, Blowing Rocks Preserve wows with a terrific hiking trail along a dramatic limestone outcropping. You won't find hills or scenic vistas, but you will see Florida's unique and varied tropical ecosystem. The well-marked mile-long trail passes oceanfront dunes, coastal strands, mangrove wetlands, and a coastal hammock. The preserve, owned and managed by the Nature Conservancy, also protects an important habitat for West Indian manatees and loggerhead turtles.

Formed over millions of years by an accumulation of marine sediments, the cliffs are a dramatic sight. At high tide, seawater crashes through the huge fissures and sends spectacular plumes high into the air. There are no beach facilities, and swimming is a bit dangerous, but I've often seen people dive and snorkel here. Fishing is also popular. Food, beverages, and pets are not permitted, and visitors must remain on designated trails. The preserve is located along South Beach Drive (Fla. A1A), north of the Jupiter inlet, about a 10-minute drive from Jupiter. From U.S. 1, head east on S.R. 707 and cross the Intracoastal Waterway to the park. Admission is free, but a $3 per person donation is requested. For more information, contact the Preserve Manager, Blowing Rocks Preserve, P.O. Box 3795, Tequesta, FL 33469 (☎ **561/575-2297**).

SCUBA DIVING & SNORKELING   Year-round, warm, clear waters make northern Palm Beach County great for both diving and snorkeling. The closest coral reef is located a quarter mile from shore and can easily be reached by boat. Three popular wrecks are clustered near each other less than a mile off shore of the Lake Worth Inlet at about 90 feet. If your hotel doesn't offer dive trips, call either **Gulf Stream Diver II,** 1030 U.S. 1, Suite 101, North Palm Beach (☎ **800/771-DIVE** or 561/627-9558), or **Seafari Dive and Surfing,** 75 E. Indiantown Rd., Suite 603, Jupiter (☎ **561/747-6115**).

TENNIS   In addition to the many hotel tennis courts (see "Accommodations You Can Afford," below), you can swing a racquet at a number of local clubs. The **Jupiter Bay Tennis Club,** 353 U.S. 1, Jupiter (☎ **561/744-9424**), has seven clay courts (three lighted) and charges $12 per person per day. Reservations are highly recommended.

More economical options are available at relatively well-maintained municipal courts. Call for locations and hours (☎ **561/966-6600**). Many are available free on a first-come, first-served basis.

A HISTORIC LIGHTHOUSE

Jupiter Inlet Lighthouse. U.S. 1 and Alt. Fla. A1A, Jupiter. ☎ **561/747-8380.** Admission $5. Sun–Wed 10am–4pm (last tour departs at 3:15pm). Children must be 4 feet or taller to climb.

Completed in 1860, this redbrick structure is the oldest extant building in Palm Beach County. Still owned and maintained by the U.S. Coast Guard, the lighthouse is now home to a small historical museum, located at its base. The Florida History Museum sponsors tours of the lighthouse, enabling visitors to explore the cramped interior, which is filled with artifacts and photographs illustrating the rich history of the area. First a 15-minute video explains the various shipwrecks, Indian wars, and other events that helped shape this region. Helpful volunteers are eager to tell colorful stories to highlight the 1-hour tour.

SHOPPING

North Palm Beach County may not have the glitzy boutiques of Worth Avenue, but it does have an impressive indoor mall, the **Gardens of the Palm Beaches,** at 3101 PGA Blvd., where you can find large department stores including Bloomingdale's, Burdine's, Macy's, and Saks Fifth Avenue, as well as more than 100 specialty shops with everything from handmade chocolates to sports equipment. A large and diverse food court and fine sit-down restaurants in this 1.3 million-square-foot facility make this shopping excursion an all-day affair. Call ☎ **561/775-7750** for store information.

ACCOMMODATIONS YOU CAN AFFORD

The northern part of Palm Beach County is much more laid-back and less crowded than the rest of the Gold Coast. Here relatively few fancy hotels or attractions are in evidence. Singer Island has the largest concentration of beachfront chains, including the **Days Inn Oceanfront Resort** (☎ **800/325-2525** or 561/848-8661), 2700 N. Ocean Dr.; the **Holiday Inn SunSpree Resort** (☎ **800/443-4077** or 561/ 848-3888), 3700 N. Ocean Dr.; and the **Quality Resort of the Palm Beaches** (☎ **800/765-5502** or 561/848-5502), 3800 N. Ocean Dr. All three have rates that average $70–$95 in the off-season.

Also notable is the very reasonably priced and recently renovated **Wellesley Inn,** at 34 Fisherman's Wharf (I-95, exit east on Indian Town Rd.; turn left before the bridge), in Jupiter (☎ **800/444-8888** or 561/575-7201). Suites, which go for about $59 in off-season months, include sofa beds, refrigerators, and microwave ovens. Though not within walking distance of the beach, the inn is located near shops and restaurants and Fla. A1A.

SUPER-CHEAP SLEEPS

✪ **Baron's Landing Hotel.** 18125 Ocean Blvd. (Fla. A1A at the corner of Love St.), Jupiter, FL 33477. ☎ **561/746-8757.** 8 efficiency/apt. units, all with bathroom (some with shower only). A/C TV. Winter from $90 single or double. Off-season from $50 single or double. No credit cards.

This charming family-run inn is a perfect little beach getaway. It's not elegant, but it's cozy. A single-story motel fronting the Intracoastal Waterway is often full in winter with snowbirds, who dock their boats at the hotel's marina for weeks or months at a time. Nearly all rooms, which are situated around a small pool, have small kitchenettes. Each unit has a hodgepodge of used furniture, and some have pull-out sofas. Considering that you're a few blocks from some of the most expensive real estate in the country, this is a good deal.

Cologne Motel. 220 U.S. 1, Tequesta/Jupiter, FL 33469. ☎ **561/746-0616.** 9 units, all with bathroom (some with shower only). A/C TV. Winter $50–$60 single or double. Off-season $45 single or double. Weekly rates available. MC, V.

The pleasant Hungarian couple who run this modest roadside motel are always busy. After they finish the landscaping and pool, they hope to add more rooms to this nine-room, 1-story little gem. The small rooms have just been updated with modest but bright bedspreads and curtains, and the newly retiled bathrooms are small but clean. The area is safe if not scenic and only about a 5-minute drive to the beach. A more direct route by foot gets you there in about 15 minutes.

FOR A FEW BUCKS MORE

Bon-Aire Yacht Club. 188 Lake Dr., Palm Beach Shores, FL 33404. ☎ **800/627-8328** or 561/844-5588. Fax 561/844-9007. www.cannonsport.com. 14 units, all with bathroom.

Winter $100 single or double, 1-bedroom apt.; $135–$155 2-bedroom apt. Off-season $75 1-bedroom apt., from $95 2-bedroom apt. AE, DC, DISC, MC, V.

A great find at the southern tip of Singer Island, this small and exclusive apartment house is located just on the lake's edge where guests enjoy a marina, barbecue grill, hammocks, and comfy lounge furniture. There is also a good-sized pool and hot tub. Plus, its just 2 blocks from the ocean. Still, the best part is that all apartments have fully stocked kitchens with stoves and ranges. The best rooms are the two-bedroom apartments, which have private sundecks. They're especially popular with boaters who dock their yachts at the adjacent marina. Take a complimentary shuttle to town or use water sports equipment.

WORTH A SPLURGE

Jupiter Beach Resort. 5 N. A1A, Jupiter, FL 33477. ☎ **800/228-8810** or 561/746-2511. Fax 561/747-3304. 176 units, all with bathroom. A/C MINIBAR TV TEL. Winter $200–$340 single or double; $310–$450 suite; $750–$1,000 penthouse. Off-season $115–$205 single or double; $135–$205 suite; $400–$600 penthouse. AE, CB, DC, DISC, MC, V. From I-95, take Exit 59A east to the end of Indiantown Rd. and then head north to Jupiter Beach Rd. The resort is on the right.

The only resort located directly on the Jupiter's beach, this unpretentious retreat is a world away from the more luxurious resorts just a few miles to the south. The lobby and public areas have a formal Caribbean motif, accented with green marble, arched doorways, and chandeliers. The simple and elegant guest rooms are furnished in a comfortable island style, and every room has a private balcony with ocean or sunset views looking out over the uncluttered beachfront. A thorough refurbishing in the mid-1990s has made this resort very popular with conventions and large groups. In fact, it is so popular that it is being gradually converted into a time-share property. Extras include kitchenettes and VCRs in suites, VCR rentals, Spectravision movie channels, an outdoor heated swimming pool, a large beach, an extensive exercise room, bicycle rental, supervised children's programs, self-service Laundromat, car-rental desk, night-lit tennis court, water-sports equipment rentals, boutique, dive shop, and summer turtle-watch programs. Excursions are available to top-rated golf courses in the area. A popular and well-run lobby restaurant serves an eclectic mix of continental, Southwestern, and Caribbean cuisine. Three other pool and beach bars serve snacks and refreshments throughout the day. The lounge features live music several nights a week.

PGA National Resort & Spa. 400 Ave. of the Champions, Palm Beach Gardens, FL 33418. ☎ **800/633-9150** or 561/627-2000. Fax 561/622-0261. 399 units, all with bathroom. A/C MINIBAR TV TEL. Winter $305–$335 single or double; from $450 suite. Off-season $119–$139 single or double; from $195 suite. Children 16 and under stay free in parents' room. Special packages regularly available. AE, DC, DISC, MC, V. From I-95, take Exit 57B (PGA Blvd.) west and continue for approximately 2 miles to the resort entrance on the left.

This rambling resort, built in 1981, is known primarily as a golf destination. With five 18-hole courses on more than 2,300 acres, golfers and other sports-minded travelers will find plenty to keep them occupied—croquet, tennis, sailing, a health and fitness center, and a top-rated Mediterranean-style spa. Constant updating has kept the grounds and buildings in like-new condition. The par-72 champion course, redesigned in 1990 by Jack Nicklaus, is the resort's most valuable asset. More than 100 sand bunkers and plenty of water on 6,400-square-foot greens keep golfers of all levels alert. Watch out for hole 16.

When you are ready to rest, you will enjoy the comfortable and spacious accommodations and good food. Ample-size guest rooms are furnished with tasteful modern furnishings and tropical prints. Bathrooms are large and thoughtfully outfitted with cushy robes, good light, and magnifying mirrors. Although you are miles from the beach, the resort has nine pools and a private lake where you can ski or sail. As for views, the best you will get is the golf course or gardens.

Six restaurants and lounges include one offering superb northern Italian cuisine, a poolside grill, and another with a surprisingly delicious spa menu.

This is the national headquarters of the PGA, so it's no surprise that there are five 18-hole tournament courses, plus the PGA National's Academy of Golf. There are also 19 clay tennis courts (12 lighted), nine swimming pools, a private beach on a 26-acre lake, water-sports equipment rentals, five tournament croquet lawns, five indoor racquetball courts, and a full-service Mediterranean spa with a full schedule of aerobics classes. Consider a day package at the spa even if you don't stay at the hotel.

GREAT DEALS ON DINING

In addition to all the national fast-food joints that line Indiantown Road and U.S. Highway 1, you'll find a number of nondescript fish restaurants serving battered-and-fried everything. A few notable exceptions are listed below.

SUPER-CHEAP EATS

✪ **Athenian Cafe.** In the Chasewood Shopping Center, 6350 Indiantown Rd., Suite 7, Jupiter. ☎ **561/744-8327.** Main courses $5–$15. Early bird specials from $5.95. AE, MC, V. Mon–Sat 11am–9pm, Sun 4–9pm during season. GREEK.

Peter Papadelis and his family have been running this pleasant storefront cafe for nearly 10 years. Tucked in the corner of a strip mall, this place is a favorite with businesspeople, who stop in for a heaping portion of rich and meaty moussaka or a flaky spinach pie made fresh by Peter himself. You could make a meal of the thick and lemony Greek soup and the large fresh antipasto. In a town replete with tourist-priced fish joints, this is a welcome alternative. Early bird specials, served until 7pm, include many Greek favorites and broiled local fish with soup or salad, rice, vegetables, pita, dessert, and coffee or tea.

Dune Dog. 775 N. Alternate Fla. A1A, Jupiter. ☎ **561/744-6667.** Main courses $2.50–$12.95. MC, V. Sun–Thurs 10am–10pm, Fri–Sat 10am–11pm.

This little outdoor hot-dog bar is a popular gathering spot in Jupiter for some of the best fish and chips and burgers anywhere. Outdoor picnic tables are set up in this roadside spot, where fresh cooked food is served all day long for a fast and thrifty meal.

Lanna Thai. In the Bluff's Square Shopping Center, 4300 S. U.S. 1 (between Indian Town Rd. and Donald Ross Rd.), Jupiter. ☎ **561/694-1443.** Main courses $8; chef's specials $9–$16. MC, V. Mon–Fri 11am–3pm and 5–10pm, Sat–Sun 5–10pm. THAI.

There are dozens of great choices at Lanna Thai, including all the old reliables like pad Thai, panang, pad king, and pad puck to pair with meat, chicken, or fish. This inauspicious storefront has a quaint, whitewashed dining room where only a dozen tables sit beneath latticework bedecked with fake plants. Come for the lunch specials that include spring rolls, soup, and fried rice for less than $6. The earnest service staff is always checking to be sure everything is all right—and it usually is.

FOR A FEW BUCKS MORE

✪ **Capt. Charlie's Reef Grill.** 12846 U.S. 1 (behind O'Brian's and French Connection), Juno Beach. ☎ **561/624-9924.** Reservations not accepted. Main courses $9–$18. MC, V. Mon–Thurs 5–9:30pm, Fri–Sat 5–10pm. Tapas/dessert Mon–Thurs 3–11pm, Fri–Sat 3pm–midnight. SEAFOOD/CARIBBEAN.

For seafood with more integrity and taste than any other in the county, come to Capt. Charlie's. The trick here is to arrive early, ahead of the crowd of local foodies. Here you'll find more than a dozen daily local-catch specials prepared any way you like. Do sample the imaginative appetizers, which include Caribbean chili, a rich chunky stew filled with fresh seafood; or a tuna spring roll big enough for two. The enormous Cuban crab cake is moist and perfectly browned without tasting fried and is served with homemade mango chutney and black beans and rice. A newly opened tapas and dessert bar features both traditional as well as tropical tapas. Sit at the bar to watch the hectic kitchen turn out perfect dishes on the 14-burner stove. Somehow the pleasant waitresses keep their cool even when the place is packed. Service is not white glove, and the ambience is early 1970s nautical. Concentrate instead on the terrific seafood and the extensive, affordable wine and beer selection—more than 30 of each from around the world.

Nick's Tomato Pie. 1697 W. Indiantown Rd. (1 mile east of I-95, Exit 59A), Jupiter. ☎ **561/744-8935.** Reservations accepted only for parties of 6 or more. Main courses $11–$19; pastas $9–$14. AE, DC, DISC, MC, V. Mon–Thurs 5–10pm, Fri–Sat 4:30–11pm, Sun 4:30–10pm. ITALIAN.

A Bennigan's-style family restaurant, Nick's is a popular attraction in otherwise food-poor Jupiter. With a huge menu of pastas, pizzas, fish, chicken, and beef, this cheery (and noisy) spot has something for everyone. On Saturday night you'll see lots of couples on dates and some families leaving with take-out bags left over from the impossibly generous portions. The homemade sausage is a delicious treat, served with sautéed onions and peppers. The pollo marsala, too, is good and authentic.

No Anchovies! 2650 PGA Blvd., Palm Beach Gardens. ☎ **561/622-7855.** Pizza and pasta $7–$13; main courses $10–$17. AE, DC, MC, V. Mon–Thurs 11:30am–2:30pm and 4:30–10:30pm, Fri–Sat 11:30am–2:30pm and 4:30–11pm, Sun 4:30–10:30pm. ITALIAN.

This large and colorful restaurant is popular with families that appreciate the large portions and reasonably priced children's specials. An equally colorful menu offers a large variety of pastas, pizzas, salads, and a variety of meat and fish specials. Mix and match your pasta with half a dozen sauces. My favorite is the thick and simple fillete de tomato over fusilli. You may also want to try some of the delicious chicken or meats prepared on the oak-burning grill.

JUPITER & NORTH PALM BEACH COUNTY AFTER DARK

If you're tired of the hotel lounge, you'll want to do what most residents and visitors to this area do—drive south to West Palm Beach's downtown scene where live music, cafes, dance clubs, and bars offer something for everyone (see "The Palm Beaches After Dark," above).

With one notable exception, there just isn't much going on here after dark. **Club Safari,** 4000 PGA Blvd. (just east of I-95), in Palm Beach Garden's Marriott Hotel (☎ **561/622-7024**), is more hip than any hotel dance club I have ever seen, although the safari theme is a bit much. Vines and potted trees surround the huge, sunken dance floor. Nearby, a large Buddha statue blows steam and smoke while waving its burly arms in front of a young gyrating crowd. There is deejay music, a large video screen, and a modest cover charge on the weekends.

The Treasure Coast

by Victoria Pesce Elliott

Over the past few years, the Treasure Coast has been attracting unprecedented numbers of new residents. Yet, it retains its small-town feel. The growth is happening at a reasonable pace, and the influx has brought with it a renewed interest in renovating the once abandoned downtown areas. The result is a batch of freshly spruced up accommodations, shops, and restaurants from Stuart to Sebastian. Along the way are miles and miles of wild rivers, state parks, and, of course, beaches.

For the purposes of this chapter, Florida's Treasure Coast runs roughly from Hobe Sound in the south to the Sebastian Inlet in the north, encompassing some of Martin, St. Lucie, and Indian River counties and all of Hutchinson Island.

In addition to a number of welcoming small communities and vast array of wildlife, the Treasure Coast also has a history as rich and colorful as its provocative nickname. For hundreds of years, Florida's east coast was a popular stopover for European explorers, many of whom arrived from Spain to fill coffers with gold and silver. Rough weather and poor navigation often took a toll on their ships. In 1715, a violent hurricane stunned the northeast coast and sank an entire fleet of Spanish ships laden with gold. Though Spanish salvagers worked for years to collect the lost treasure, much of it remained buried beneath the shifting sand. Then, builders hired to excavate the area in the 1950s and 1960s discovered centuries-old coins under their tractors.

Today, on these same beaches you'll find an occasional treasure hunter trolling the sand with a metal detector, and swimmers and sunbathers who come to enjoy the stretches of beach that extend into the horizon. The sea, especially around Sebastian Inlet, is a mecca for surfers who find some of the largest swells in the state.

Florida's largest inland lake, Lake Okeechobee, a favorite destination for anglers, lies just west of this coastal area and is covered at the end of this chapter.

ESSENTIALS
GETTING TO THE TREASURE COAST

Since virtually every town described in this chapter runs in a straight route along the Atlantic Ocean, I've given all directions below.

BY PLANE The **Palm Beach International Airport** (☎ 561/471-7420), located about 35 miles south of Stuart, is the closest gateway to this region if you're flying. See the "Getting Around" section on Palm Beach in chapter 8 for complete information. If you are traveling to the northern part of the Treasure Coast, **Melbourne International Airport,** off U.S. 1 in Melbourne (☎ **407/723-6227**), is less than 25 miles north of Sebastian and about 35 miles north of Vero Beach.

BY CAR If you're driving up or down the Florida coast, you'll probably reach the Treasure Coast via I-95. If you are heading to Stuart or Jensen Beach, take Exit 61 (Route 76/Tanner Highway) or 62 (Route 714); to Port St. Lucie or Fort Pierce, take Exit 63 or 64 (Okeechobee Road); to Vero, take Exit 68 (S.R. 60); to Sebastian, take Exit 69 (County Road).

You can also take the Florida Turnpike; this toll road is the fastest (but not the most scenic) route, especially if you're coming from Orlando. If you are heading to Stuart or Jensen Beach, take Exit 133; to Fort Pierce, take Exit 152 (Okeechobee Road); to Port St. Lucie, take Exit 142 or 152; to Vero, take Exit 193 (S.R. 60); to Sebastian, take Exit 193 to East S.R. 60 and connect to I-95 north.

If you are staying in Hutchinson Island, which runs almost the entire length of the Treasure Coast, you should check with your hotel, or see the listings below, to find the best route.

Finally, if you're coming directly from the west coast, you'll probably take S.R. 70, which runs north of Lake Okeechobee to Fort Pierce, located just up the road from Stuart.

BY RAIL Amtrak (☎ **800/USA-RAIL**) stops in West Palm Beach, at 201 S. Tamarind Ave. (☎ **800/872-7245** or 561/832-6169); and in Okeechobee at 801 N. Parrot Ave., off U.S. 441 north (no phone).

BY BUS Greyhound buses (☎ **800/231-2222**) service the area with terminals in Stuart, at 1308 S. Federal Hwy.; in Fort Pierce, at 7005 Okeechobee Rd. (☎ **561/461-3299**); and in Vero Beach, at U.S. 1 and S.R. 60 (☎ **561/562-6588**).

GETTING AROUND THE TREASURE COAST

A car is a necessity in this region. Although heavy traffic is not usually a problem here, on the smaller coastal roads, like Fla. A1A, expect to travel at a slow pace, usually between 25 and 40 miles an hour.

1 Hobe Sound, Stuart & Jensen Beach

130 miles SE of Orlando, 98 miles N of Miami

Once just a stretch of pineapple plantations, the towns of Martin County—which include Stuart, Jensen Beach, Port Salerno, and Hobe Sound—still retain much of their rural character. Dotted between citrus groves and mangroves are modest homes and an occasional high-rise condominium. Though the area sees a distinct rise in street and pedestrian traffic beginning after the Christmas holidays, the atmosphere is pure small town. Even in historic downtown Stuart—the result of a successful, ongoing restoration—expect the storefronts to be dark and the streets abandoned after 10pm.

ESSENTIALS

The **Stuart/Martin County Chamber of Commerce,** 1650 S. Kanner Hwy., Stuart, FL 34994 (☎ **800/524-9704** in Florida, or 561/287-1088; fax 561/220-3437), is the region's main source for information. The **Jensen Beach Chamber of Commerce,** 1901 NE Jensen Beach Blvd., Jensen Beach, FL 34957 (☎ **561/334-3444**), also offers visitors information about its simple beachfront town.

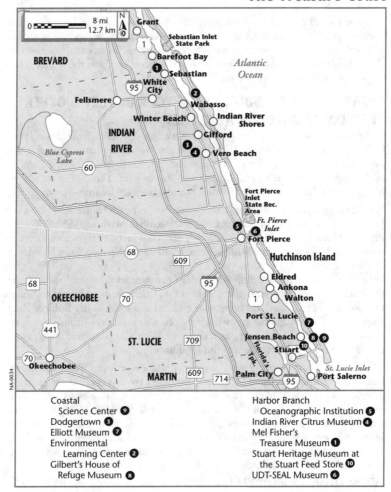

The Treasure Coast

Coastal
   Science Center **9**
Dodgertown **3**
Elliott Museum **7**
Environmental
   Learning Center **2**
Gilbert's House of
   Refuge Museum **8**

Harbor Branch
   Oceanographic Institution **5**
Indian River Citrus Museum **4**
Mel Fisher's
   Treasure Museum **1**
Stuart Heritage Museum at
   the Stuart Feed Store **10**
UDT-SEAL Museum **6**

HITTING THE BEACHES

Beaches are easily accessible throughout Hutchinson Island, the long, thin barrier island that stretches north and south from Stuart. Look for "coastal access" signs pointing the way to many public beach areas.

The best of them is ✪ **Bathtub Beach,** on North Hutchinson Island. Here, the calm waters are protected by coral reefs and visitors can explore the region on dune and river trails. Pick a secluded spot on the wide stretch of beach or enjoy marked nature trails across the street. Facilities include showers and toilets open during the day. To reach the park, head east on Ocean Boulevard (Stuart Causeway) and turn right onto MacArthur Boulevard. The beach is located about a mile ahead, on your left, just north of the Indian River Plantation. Parking is plentiful.

Also on North Hutchinson is **Jensen Beach** or **Sea Turtle Beach,** on Ocean Boulevard at NE Causeway Boulevard, on Hutchinson Island. Despite the name, this is a large, developed beach with volleyball courts, a water-sports concession, outdoor showers, a picnic area, and lots of parking.

Jaycee Park, on SE Ocean Boulevard between Hutchinson Island and the mainland, is a waterfront park that's popular with picnickers and water-sports enthusiasts. The park is divided into two sections: When you cross the Intracoastal Waterway on Ocean Boulevard, the first island you reach is the picnic area, and the second is best known for fishing and windsurfing.

GREAT GOLF THAT WON'T BREAK YOUR BUDGET & OTHER AFFORDABLE OUTDOOR ACTIVITIES

CANOEING Jonathan Dickinson State Park (see "Wildlife Exploration: From Gators to Manatees to Turtles," below) is the area's most popular for canoeing. The route winds through a variety of botanical habitats. You'll see lots of birds, and, of course, the occasional manatee. Canoes cost $6 per hour. The concession is open Monday to Friday from 9am to 5pm and Saturday and Sunday from 8am to 5pm.

FISHING Several independent charter captains operate on Hutchinson Island and Jensen Beach. One of the largest operators is the **Sailfish Marina,** 3565 SE St. Lucie Blvd., in Stuart (☎ 561/221-9456), which maintains half a dozen charter boats for fishing excursions year-round. Also on site is a bait and tackle shop and a knowledgeable and helpful staff.

In addition to the many high-priced fishing opportunities along the Treasure Coast, the Stuart and Fort Pierce areas offer plenty of land fishing from the numerous bridges that dot the bays. If you didn't bring your own rod and reel, call **Big Bob's** or **Rosemeyer's** (see "Water Sports," below). Two especially good spots include the Stuart Causeway bridge and the Jensen Beach causeway. With a little luck and patience, you can have grilled snook, trout, or red fish for dinner.

GOLF The pricey Indian River Plantation Beach Resort (see "Worth A Splurge," below) is a terrific destination for golfers, but unless you're a guest or the guest of a member, you cannot play these courses. Instead, try the **Champions Club** at Summerfield, on U.S. 1, south of Cove Road in Stuart (☎ 561/283-1500), a somewhat challenging championship course designed by Tom Fazio. This rural course, the best in the area, was built in 1994 and offers great glimpses of wildlife amid the wetlands. In winter, greens fees are around $60. Carts are mandatory. Reservations are a must and are taken 4 days in advance.

SCUBA DIVING & SNORKELING Three popular artificial reefs off Hutchinson Island provide excellent scenery for both novice and experienced divers. The *USS Rankin,* sunk in 120 feet of water in 1988, lies 7 miles east-northeast of the St. Lucie Inlet. The 58-foot-deep **Donaldson Reef** consists of a cluster of plumbing fixtures sunk in 58 feet of water. It's located due east of the Gilbert's House of Refuge Museum. The **Ernst Reef,** made from old tires, is a 60-foot dive located 4½ miles east-southeast of the St. Lucie inlet.

Deep Divers Unlimited, 6083 SE Federal Hwy. (corner of Cove Road and U.S. 1), Stuart (☎ 561/286-0078), arranges two-tank dive trips to these sites and others starting at about $37 a person. A full set of gear will cost you another $25 for the day. They can also rent gear to those wanting to explore the area's best snorkeling at Bathtub Beach (see "Hitting the Beaches," above). A natural coral reef is located so close to shore that you can swim to it.

WATER SPORTS **Big Bob's Waverunners and Boat Rentals,** 3545 NE Indian River Dr., Jensen Beach (☎ 561/225-2266), rents everything to do with the water. And while nothing is inexpensive, the rates are some of the lowest on the island. If you know how to sail, you may opt for lower-priced sailboats, for between $25 and $35 an hour. One great budget option is the 27-foot pontoon boat, which can hold up to

Wildlife Exploration: From Gators to Manatees to Turtles

One of the most scenic areas on this stretch of the coast is **Jonathan Dickinson State Park** (☎ **561/546-2771**), at 16450 S. Federal Hwy. (U.S. 1), Hobe Sound. The park is intentionally undermanaged so that it will resemble the habitat of hundreds of years ago, before Europeans started chopping, dredging, and "improving" the area. Dozens of species of Florida's unique wildlife, including alligators and manatees, live on more than 11,300 acres. Bird watchers will want to bring their books and binoculars to spot the many ospreys, woodpeckers, ibises, herons, anhingas, egrets, and even some bald eagles. Deer, reptiles, tortoises, and snakes also call this area home. There are concession areas for daytime snacks and four different scenic nature and bike trails through the scrublands and flatwoods. You can also rent canoes from the concession stand to explore the Loxahatchee River on your own. Admission is $3.25 per car of up to eight adults. Day hikers, bikers, and walkers pay $1 each. The park is open from 8am until sundown. See "Accommodations You Can Afford," below, for details on camping.

Nearby is **Hobe Sound Wildlife Refuge,** on North Beach Road off S.R. 708, at the north end of Jupiter Island (☎ **561/546-6141**). This is one of the best places to see sea turtles that nest on the shore in the summer months, especially in June and July. Because it's home to a large variety of other plant and animal species, the park is worth visiting at other times of year as well. Admission is $4 per car, and the preserve is open daily from sunrise to sunset. Exact times are posted at each entrance and change seasonally.

15 people; it costs $150 for 4 hours or $200 for the whole day. An 18-foot angler costs $120 for a half day and $175 for a full day. If you're planning to cast a rod, you'll need a fishing license too. You can pick one up next door at the bait and tackle store. Licenses are less than $10. WaveRunners are $35 a half hour and $60 an hour.

Rosemeyer's Boat Rentals, 3281 NE Indian River Dr., at Indian River Road and Jensen Beach (☎ **561/334-1000**), rents 16- to 22-foot boats. Rosemeyer's has the corner on budget WaveRunners. WaveRunners go for $35 a half-hour ride or $60 an hour, for the cheaper, smaller, older Yamahas. The newer, more stable ones are $45 a half hour. Ask for a deal from Derek (who says if you're nice, he'll treat you right). For some fun fishing on the intercoastal, consider renting a little skiff. Rates start at $89 for a half day on an 18-foot center console or $149 for a full day, and a 24-foot cuddy cabin goes for $295.

Group charters range from $50 from $150 a day with a guide. If you compare these boating rates with the $600 it would cost for a day's fishing in Miami, this is a real bargain! For diehard fishers there's a 3-day package for about $450 in an 18-footer that could hold up to four people, and you don't need to use the 3 days consecutively. Plus, with all rentals, Rosemeyer's throws in rods and reels.

SEEING THE SIGHTS

✪ **Coastal Science Center.** 890 NE Ocean Blvd. (across the street from the Elliott Museum), Hutchinson Island, Stuart. ☎ **561/225-0505.** Admission $3.50 adults, $2 children 3–12, free for children under 3. Mon–Sat 10am–5pm.

Opened by the South Florida Oceanographic Society in late 1994, this 44-acre site surrounded by coastal hammock and mangroves is its own little ecosystem and serves as an outdoor classroom, teaching visitors about the region's flora and fauna. The modest building houses saltwater tanks and wet and dry "discovery tables" with small indigenous animals. The incredibly eager volunteer staff encourages visitors to wander the lush, well-marked nature trails.

✪ Elliott Museum. 825 NE Ocean Blvd. (north of Indian River Plantation Resort), Hutchinson Island, Stuart. ☎ **561/225-1961.** Admission $6 adults, $2 children 6–13, free for children 5 and under. Daily 10am–4pm.

A treasure trove of early Americana, the Elliott Museum is a rich tribute to inventors, sports heroes, and collectors. A series of life-size dioramas depicts an apothecary, a barbershop, a blacksmith forge, a clock and watch shop, and other old-fashioned commercial enterprises. Sports lovers will appreciate the baseball memorabilia—a half million dollars' worth—including an autographed item from every player in the Baseball Hall of Fame. A gallery of patents and models of machines, invented by the museum's founder Harmon Parker Elliott and his son, provides an intriguing glimpse into the business of tinkering. Also worth exploring is the impressive collection of restored antique cars. Expect to spend at least an hour seeing the highlights.

Gilbert's House of Refuge Museum. 301 SE MacArthur Blvd. (south of Indian River Plantation resort), Hutchinson Island, Stuart. ☎ **561/225-1875.** Admission $4 adults, $2 children 6–13, free for children 5 and under. Daily 10–4pm.

Gilbert's, the oldest structure in Martin County, dates from 1875, when it functioned as one of 10 such rescue centers for shipwrecked sailors. Restored to its original condition along the rocky shores, the house now displays marine artifacts and turn-of-the-century lifesaving equipment and photographs and is worth a quick visit to get a feel for the area's early days.

Stuart Heritage Museum at the Stuart Feed Store. 161 SW Flagler Ave., Stuart. ☎ **561/220-4600.** Free admission. Tues–Sat 11am–3pm.

In 1900, when the Stuart Feed Store was the territory's most important general store, the region's inhabitants, including the Seminole, would come here from miles around to buy feed and supplies. Today the tiny, ill-kept museum is worth a quick stop to view a piece of history.

A BOAT TOUR

✪ *The Loxahatchee Queen* (☎ 800/746-1466 or 561/746-1466), a 35-foot pontoon boat in Jonathan Dickinson State Park in Hobe Sound, makes daily tours of the area's otherwise inaccessible backwater where curious alligators, manatees, eagles, and tortoises often peek out to see who's in their neighborhood. Try to catch the 2-hour tour Wednesday to Sunday, as tide permits, when it includes a stop at Trapper Nelson's home. Known as the "Wildman of Loxahatchee," Nelson lived in primitive conditions—on a remote stretch of the water in a log cabin fashioned from his own hand— which are preserved for visitors to see. Tours leave four times daily at 9am, 11am, 1pm and 3pm and cost $10 for adults, $5 for children 6 to 12, and free for children 5 and under. See "Wildlife Exploration: From Gators to Manatees to Turtles," above, for more information on the park.

SHOPPING

Downtown Stuart's historic district, along Flagler Avenue between Confusion Corner and St. Lucie Avenue, offers shoppers diversity and quality in a small old town setting. Shops offer a range of goods: antique bric-a-brac, old lamps and fixtures, books, gourmet foods, furnishings, and souvenirs.

B&A Farmer's Market, at 2885 SE Federal Highway (in front of B&A Flea market), Stuart (☎ **561/223-1570**), sells all types of locally grown produce, including the famous Indian River grapefruits and oranges, watermelons, berries, bananas, and other tropical fruits. They can arrange to have fruits and baskets shipped.

ACCOMMODATIONS YOU CAN AFFORD

Although the area boasts some beautiful beaches, the bulk of the budget hotel scene is downtown on U.S. 1, where the more competitively priced accommodations vie for business travelers.

Vacationers can take advantage of the low rates or head to the beach where there are several very recommendable hotels and inns. One of the best hotel chains in the area is the **Holiday Inn** with a recently renovated, stunning beachfront property at 3793 NE Ocean Blvd., Jensen Beach (☎ 800/992-4747 or 561/225-3000). Starting at about $155 in season, rates here are pretty steep. Holiday Inn has a less-expensive downtown location at 1209 S. Federal Hwy. (☎ 561/287-6200). Even in the height of the winter season, rates hover near $100. This simple 2-story building on a busy main road is kept in very good shape and is convenient to Stuart's downtown historic district. Just next door is a pleasant **Ramada Inn** at 1200 S. Federal Hwy. (☎ 561/287-6900). With rates in high season starting at less than $60, this is the very best deal in town.

A CHEAP SLEEP

Driftwood Motel. 4150 N.E. Indian River Dr., Jensen Beach, FL 33457. ☎ 561/334-2237. 10 units, all with bathroom (some with shower only). A/C TV TEL. Year-round $40–$75 efficiencies, single or double. MC, V.

This very basic motel has no pool or views, but it is a real bargain. And while the owners are not always gracious, they do manage to maintain a decent and very affordable, old-style motel. The good-sized rooms are especially desirable for their cooking facilities. All have fridges, stoves, and ovens as well as a small dining area. It's rough around the edges, but it's close to the water, safe, and conveniently located.

FOR A FEW BUCKS MORE

✪ **Harborfront Inn Bed & Breakfast.** 310 Atlanta Ave., Stuart, FL 34994. ☎ 800/294-1703 or 561/288-7289. Fax 561/221-0474. www.harborfrontinn.com. 6 units, all with bathroom (some with shower only). A/C TV. Year-round $80–$100 single or double; from $125 suite, $145 suite with whirlpool and outdoor spa. Off-season specials. Rates include breakfast. AE, DISC, MC, V. From I-95 take Exit 61 east to U.S. 1 north; turn left on West Ocean Blvd. and then make the first right (Atlanta Ave.). No smoking and no children.

The Harborfront Inn has the advantage of being right on the river where you can sail and ski. It consists of a series of little blue-trimmed shingled cottages within walking distance of the restaurants of downtown Stuart. Each room in this highly recommended B&B has its own private entrance making it more like a rambling inn. Also, every accommodation has a sitting area and private bathroom. The two best rooms are the bright Garden Suite, which has a queen-size bed, rattan furnishings, and a deck with river and garden views; and the Guest House, which has an extralarge bathroom with two sinks and can be rented with an adjoining full kitchen.

Breakfast is served on an enclosed porch that surrounds the inn's cozy public areas. The morning meal usually includes fresh fruit from the trees that grow on the property. Facilities include kitchenettes in cottages, VCRs in suites, a Jacuzzi and sundeck, and water-sports equipment rentals.

✪ **The Home Place.** 501 Akron Ave., Stuart, FL 34994. ☎ 561/220-9148. Fax 561/221-3265. www.homeplacebb.com. 4 units, all with bathroom (1 with private bathroom down a hall). Year-round $85–$110 single or double. Off-season and weekday specials. Rates include full breakfast. MC, V. From I-95 take Exit 61 east on S.R. 76 about 7 miles to U.S. 1.

Turn left. Continue ½ mile to West Ocean Blvd.; turn left. Turn right on Akron. No smoking and no children under 12.

Perfect for those who like the feel of a classic B&B, Home Place is as charming as it gets. Suzanne and Michael Pescitelli are the gracious owners of this historic home, and they're just the kind of innkeepers you want in a classic little bed-and-breakfast. They offer taste, style, good conversation, superb homemade sweets, wine, an always-open fridge, and a perfectly maintained inn, which is a favorite locale for weddings. They live in the adjacent building, just a few steps from the 1913 guest house and beautifully landscaped pool and Jacuzzi area. You'll be comfortable in any of the Victorian-trimmed rooms, chock-full of warm details like lace curtains, old steamer trunks, and crystal decanters. The large captain's room is a favorite for its size and big fluffy bed. While you're a few miles inland from the beach, you're only a few blocks from the quaint and rejuvenated downtown area. There isn't much in the way of grounds or amenities but there is a medium-sized pool and sundeck with lounge chairs and cushy towels.

Hutchinson Inn. 9750 S. Ocean Dr. (Fla. A1A), Jensen Beach, FL 34957. ☎ **561/ 229-2000.** A/C TV TEL. 21 units, all with bathroom. Winter from $90 single or double; $150–$225 efficiency or suite. Off-season $65 single or double; $95–$150 efficiency or suite. Rates include large continental breakfast. MC, V. From I-95 take Stuart Exit 61 east to Monterey Rd.; turn right to E. Ocean Blvd.; continue onto island and see the inn approximately 8 miles ahead on the right.

It doesn't look like much from the road—only the tennis court is visible—but you'll soon happen upon striking white gazebos dotting thick green lawns. Located directly on the beach, the Hutchinson Inn is a quiet and charming 2-story hideaway. Unfortunately, so many people know about it that it's usually booked a year in advance during high season.

The newly refurbished rooms have rattan furnishings; sofas convert into pull-out beds, and several rooms can be joined to accommodate large families. There is a good swimming beach, a large outdoor pool, one outdoor night-lit tennis court, water-sports equipment, bicycle rentals, and a self-service Laundromat. Freshly baked cookies are offered each evening before bedtime.

WORTH A SPLURGE

✪ **Indian River Plantation Marriott Resort.** 555 NE Ocean Blvd., Hutchinson Island, Stuart, FL 34996. ☎ **800/775-5936** or 561/225-3700. Fax 561/225-0003. 296 units, all with bathroom. A/C TV TEL. Winter $239–$279 single or double; from $329 suite. Off-season $119–$149 single or double; from $199 suite. AE, CB, DC, DISC, MC, V. Package and group rates available. Exit 61/Rte. 76 to Monterey Rd. take E. Ocean Blvd. over two bridges to NE Ocean Blvd.; turn right.

Purchased in summer 1997 by Marriott, this sprawling 190-acre compound offers so many diversions for active (or not-so-active) vacationers, you won't want to leave the grounds. Especially with the $8 million worth of renovations due to be completed by late 1998, Indian River is Hutchinson Island's best resort, built on the lush grounds of a former pineapple plantation between the Atlantic Ocean and the scenic Indian River. Groups especially love the resort for its family oriented activities, which include tennis, golfing, and boating. Plus, there is an extensive children's program called the Pineapple Club, offering imaginative, fun, and affordable summer-camplike activities. Sport fishing (especially for sailfish) is a big draw here, as are scuba diving and other water sports. A sampling of the amenities include four outdoor pools, a large stretch of beach, a new exercise facility, a large Jacuzzi, a decent 18-hole golf course (and access to several other pro courses), nature trails, a sundeck, 13 tennis courts, and water-sports equipment.

The grand, white lattice-and-wicker lobby is filled with a jungle of plants, and large windows overlook the hotel's swimming pool and tiki bar. Generously sized rooms, some with fully-equipped kitchens, are decorated with colorful spreads and draperies. Rooms that overlook the beach are larger and the most expensive. The standard rooms in the main building are a real value, even though it means taking a tram or long trek to the ocean. Even the most basic rooms have all the necessities—coffeemakers, hair dryers, and private terraces, plus refrigerators, irons, and full-size ironing boards.

Be sure to sign up for a "turtle watch" in the summer months to watch the large turtles crawl onto the sand to lay their eggs.

The resort's seafood restaurant is popular with locals. A less-formal restaurant serves continental breakfast, lunch, and all-day snacks. There's live music nightly in two bars.

CAMPING

There are comfortable campsites in Jonathan Dickinson State Park in Hobe Sound (see "Wildlife Exploration: From Gators to Manatees to Turtles" box, above). You can stay overnight in rustic cabins or in your tent or camper in two different sections of the park. The **River Camp** area offers the benefit of the nearby Loxahatchee River, while the **Pine Grove** site has beautiful shade trees. There are concession areas for daytime snacks and 135 campsites with showers, clean rest rooms, water, optional electricity, and an open-fire pit for cooking. Overnight rates in the winter are $18 without electricity, $20 with electricity. In the summer, rates are about $14 for four people.

For a more cushy camping experience, reserve a wood-sided cabin with a furnished kitchen, a bathroom with shower, heat and air-conditioning, and an outside grill. Bring your own linens. Cabins rent for $65 and up a night and sleep four people comfortably, six if your group is really into togetherness. Call ☎ **800/746-1466** or 561/546-2771 on Monday to Friday from 9am to 5pm well in advance to reserve a spot. A $50 key deposit is required.

GREAT DEALS ON DINING
SUPER-CHEAP EATS

✪ **Bubba's Fish Camp.** 421 S. Federal Hwy. (at the south end of the Roosevelt Bridge), Stuart. ☎ **561/220-3747.** Full meals $8–$10; seafood specials $8–$12. AE, MC, V. Daily 11am–10pm and later on weekends. Call for details on weekend breakfasts. SEAFOOD/SOUTHERN.

Owned by the same family that created the lovely B&B Home Place and just a stone's throw from there, this ultracasual spot serves up a great crawfish gumbo, corn bread, and catfish, too. After 4pm you'll find great deals on hearty Southern fare like meat loaf, baked Virginia ham with red-eye gravy, fried chicken, or pork chops. Each includes a choice of delicious side dishes. Don't miss the creamy spinach, hush puppies, and fried green tomatoes. In the style of a real old-Florida fish camp, Bubba's has given redneck a whole new meaning. Fresh and crispy onion rings are actually served on tiny bathroom plunger handles. Locals and highway travelers line up outside the screen porch to get into this rustic eatery.

✪ **Jan's Place.** 1897 Jensen Beach Blvd., Old Jensen Beach Village. ☎ **561/334-9598.** Breakfast $3–$8; lunch $5–$9. MC, V. Daily 7am–4pm (until 3pm on Sun) and Thurs 5:30–9:30pm. AMERICAN.

The wooden rafters are loaded with the weight of thousands of old photographs, blinking Christmas lights, fans, hanging lanterns, fish nets, and a 10-foot mural of swaying palms. The food is a step above diner fare and is served in generous potions. Especially for breakfast, you'll find some fresh and delicious dishes, like the Neptune Benedict, which has large chunks of shrimp, scallops, crab, and a very garlicky hollandaise. The seafood's from a can but tastes great. The large lunch menu is mostly dressed-up diner fare, but specials like blackened mahimahi can be spectacular.

✪ **Nature's Way Cafe.** 25 SW Osceola St., in the Post Office Arcade, Stuart. ☎ **561/220-7306.** Sandwiches and salads $4–$7; juices and shakes $1–$3. No credit cards. Mon–Fri 10am–4pm, Sat 11am–3pm. HEALTH FOOD.

This lovely clean and green dining room has dozens of little tables, a few bar stools, and some sidewalk seating, too. A sort of health-food deli, Nature's Way excels in putting out quick and nutritious meals like huge salads, vegetarian sandwiches, and frozen yogurts. Try some of the homemade baked goods. Sit outside on quaint Osceola Street or ask them to pack your lunch for you to take to the beach.

FOR A FEW BUCKS MORE

Black Marlin. 53 W. Osceola St., downtown Stuart. ☎ **561/286-3126.** Reservations not accepted. Salads and sandwiches $4–$8; full meals $9–$24. AE, MC, V. Mon–Thurs 5–10pm, Fri–Sat 5–11pm (the bar is open later). FLORIDA REGIONAL.

Although it sports the look and feel of an English pub, the Black Marlin offers regional flavor. The salmon BLT is typical of the dishes here—grilled salmon on a toasted bun topped with bacon, lettuce, tomato, and coleslaw. Designer pizzas are topped with shrimp, roasted red peppers, and the like. Main dishes, all of which are served with vegetables and potatoes, include lobster tail with a honey-mustard sauce, and a char-coal-grilled chicken breast served on radicchio with caramelized onions.

✪ **Conchy Joe's Seafood.** 3945 NE Indian River Dr. (half a mile from the Jensen Beach Causeway), Jensen Beach. ☎ **561/334-1130.** Reservations not accepted. Main courses $12–$20. AE, DISC, MC, V. Daily 11:30am–2:30pm and 5–10pm (happy hour 3–6pm). SEAFOOD.

Known for fresh seafood and Old Florida hospitality, Conchy Joe's enjoys an excellent reputation that's far bigger than the restaurant itself. Dining is either indoors, at red-and-white cloth-covered tables, or on a covered patio overlooking the St. Lucie River. The restaurant features a wide variety of freshly shucked shellfish and daily catch selections that are baked, broiled, or fried. Beer is the drink of choice here, though other beverages and a full bar are available. Conchy Joe's has been the most active place in Jensen Beach since it opened in 1983. The large bar is especially popular at night and during weekday happy hours from 3 until 6pm and on Wednesday evenings when a local reggae band plays good cover tunes.

WORTH A SPLURGE

Eleven Maple Street. 11 Maple St., Jensen Beach. ☎ **561/334-7714.** Reservations recommended. Main courses $15–$25. MC, V. Wed–Sun 6–10pm. Head east on Jensen Beach Blvd. and turn right after the railroad tracks. AMERICAN.

The most highly rated restaurant in Jensen Beach, Eleven Maple Street occupies a lovely little house with a white picket fence, French doors, lace curtains, and pink-clothed tables. Dining is both indoors and out, in any one of a series of cozy dining rooms or on a covered patio surrounded by gardens. Straightforward meat and fish dishes run the gamut from local seafood to game and poultry like venison and duck. Maine lobster, filet mignon, and pastas are also available, and most everything is spiced with fresh-picked herbs from the restaurant's own organic garden.

✪ **Flagler Grill.** 47 SW Flagler Ave. (just before the Roosevelt Bridge), downtown Stuart. ☎ **561/221-9517.** Reservations strongly suggested in season. Main courses $17–$23. AE, MC, V. Winter daily 5:30–10pm. Off-season Wed–Sat 5:30–9:30pm. Lounge open to 11:30. CONTEMPORARY AMERICAN.

Stuart finally can boast a restaurant that measures up. In the heart of historic downtown, this Manhattan-style bistro serves up classics with a twist. The dishes are not so unusual as to alienate the conservative pink-shirted golfers who frequent the place, yet they're fresh and light enough to quench the appetites of the more adventurous—for example, the saffron and mushroom pasta with Cajun shrimp and roasted tomatoes. The menu changes every few weeks, so see what your server recommends (ask for Victoria; she's friendly and knowledgeable). It's hard to go wrong with any of the many salads, pastas, fishes, or delectable beef choices. The desserts, too, are worth the calories.

STUART & JENSEN BEACH AFTER DARK

Local restaurants serve as the nightlife centers of Stuart and Jensen Beach. And "night" ends pretty early here, even on the weekends. The bar at the **Black Marlin** (see "Great Deals on Dining," above) is popular with local professionals and tourists alike.

No list of Jensen nightlife would be complete without mention of **Conchy Joe's Seafood** (see "Great Deals on Dining," above), one of the region's most active spots. Inside, locals chug beer and watch a large-screen TV, while outside on the waterfront patio live bands perform a few nights a week for a raucous crowd of dancers. Happy hours, weekdays from 3 to 6pm, draw large crowds with low-priced drinks and snacks. No cover.

In a strip mall just outside of downtown you'll find pickup trucks as far as the eye can see parked outside **The Rock'in Horse,** 1580 S. Federal Hwy. (U.S. 1), Stuart (☎ **561/286-1281**). It's a real locals' country-western spot that rocks—especially on Tuesday night, when ladies drink all night for $5. Bring your hat and boots for line dancing, beer drinking, and a good time in one of the only real late-night spots in town. Cover varies.

The centerpiece of Stuart's slowly expanding cultural offerings is the newly restored **Lyric Theater,** at 59 SW Flagler Ave. (☎ **561/220-1942**). This beautiful 1920s-era, 600-seat theater hosts a variety of shows and films throughout the year. Programs run the gamut from amateur plays to top-name theatrical shows, poetry readings, and concerts.

2 Port St. Lucie, Fort Pierce & North Hutchinson Island

7 miles N of Stuart

Port St. Lucie and Fort Pierce, two Old Florida towns, thrive on sportfishing. A seemingly endless row of piers juts out along the Intracoastal Waterway and the Fort Pierce Inlet for both river and ocean runs. Here visitors can also dive, snorkel, beachcomb, and sunbathe in an area that hasn't been visited by the overdevelopment that has altered its neighbors to the south and north.

Most sightseeing takes place along the main beach road. Driving along Fla. A1A on Hutchinson Island, you'll discover several secluded beach clubs interspersed with 1950s-style homes, a few small inns, grungy raw bars, and a few high-rise condominiums. Much of this island is government owned and kept undeveloped for the public's enjoyment.

ESSENTIALS

The **St. Lucie County Chamber of Commerce,** 2200 Virginia Ave., Fort Pierce, FL 34982 (☎ **561/595-9999**), is the region's main source of information. Another location is at 1626 SE Port St. Lucie Blvd., in Port St. Lucie. These are open Monday through Friday from 9am to 5pm.

HITTING THE BEACH & NATURE PRESERVE

North Hutchinson Island's beaches are the most pristine in this area. You won't find restaurants, hotels, or shopping; instead, spend your time swimming, surfing, fishing, and diving. Most of the beaches are private along this stretch of the Atlantic Ocean. Thankfully, the state has set aside some of the best areas for the public.

Fort Pierce Inlet State Recreation Area (☎ 561/468-3985 for information) is a stunning 340-acre park with almost 4,000 feet of sandy shores that was once the training ground for the original navy frogmen. A short nature trail leads through a canopy of live oaks, cabbage palms, sea grapes, and strangler figs. The western side of the area has swamps of red mangroves that are home to fiddler crabs, osprey, and a multitude of wading birds. **Jack Island State Preserve,** in the state recreation area, is popular with bird watchers and offers hiking and nature trails. Jutting out into the Indian River, the mangrove-covered peninsula contains several marked trails, varying in distance from a half mile to over 4 miles. Check out the observation tower.

The park is located at 905 Shorewinds Dr., north of Fort Pierce Inlet. To get there from I-95, take Exit 66 east (Route 68) and turn left onto U.S. 1 north; in about 2 miles, you will see signs to Fla. A1A and the North Bridge Causeway. Turn right on A1A and cross over to North Hutchinson Island. Admission is $3.25 per vehicle, and it's open daily from 8am to sunset.

Another great beach is called **Jetty Park,** in the northern part of the park. Families enjoy the large picnic areas and barbecue grills. There are rest rooms and outdoor showers, and lifeguards look after swimmers.

GREAT GOLF THAT WON'T BREAK YOUR BUDGET & OTHER AFFORDABLE OUTDOOR ACTIVITIES

FISHING   The **Fort Pierce City Marina,** 1 Ave. A, Fort Pierce (☎ 561/464-1245), has more than a dozen charter captains who keep their motors running for anglers anxious to catch a few. The price ranges from $150 per person for half-day tours, depending on the season. Charters are organized on an as-desired basis. In general, plan to arrive very early in the morning (by 6am) before all the other early birds have gotten the worms.

At the **Fort Pierce Yachting Center,** 1 Ave. A, Fort Pierce (☎ 561/464-1245), more than a dozen charter captains keep their motors running for anxious anglers who want to try to catch a few. The price can be as much as $150 per person in the busy season, but if you can get a group of four or more interested, you can usually rent a boat without a captain and save a bunch. Plus, if you catch a lot of fish, you have your dinner. Call or stop by the docks to see if it's slow. If you want to do some bottom fishing, try **The Fish Stalker** (☎ 561/464-4754), one of the best-priced boats around. It sails every day at different times. Rates are $25 to $35 for 3- to 4-hour excursions.

GOLF   This area has some of the best (and cheapest golf) on the east coast. There is a huge variety of public courses most with off season greens fees under $30.

Opened in winter 1998, the latest addition to the Treasure Coast golfing scene is the **Eagle Marsh** course designed by Tommy Fazio and located east of I-95 at 300 Jensen Beach Blvd. (☎ 561/692-3322). Situated amid marshy wetlands, pine forests, and dramatic savannas, this pristine course is one of the few in the area not surrounded by homes or condos. There is a clubhouse however, where golfers can enjoy lunch and other snacks. With 6,950 yards, this varied course is as challenging as it is gorgeous (and it's very affordable!). Off-season rates are about $30. In the height of the winter season, greens fees hover around $50.

Nearby, some of the most notable courses in Port Saint Lucie are at the **PGA Golf Club at the Reserve** (☎ 561/467-1300) at 1916 Perfect Dr. PGA's first public golf course opened in January 1996 and was designed by Tommy Fazio. The club will soon complete its fourth 18-hole course. The South Course, a classic Old Florida–style course, is set on wetlands and offers views of native wildlife. It is the most popular. Greens fees are under $60.

SPECTATOR SPORTS   The **New York Mets** hold spring training in Port St. Lucie from late February through March at the Thomas J. White Stadium, 525 NW Peacock Blvd. (☎ 561/871-2115). Tickets cost $9 to $12. During the summer, their farm team, the **Port St. Lucie Mets,** plays home games in the stadium.

SEEING THE SIGHTS

Harbor Branch Oceanographic Institution. 5600 U.S. 1 north, Fort Pierce. ☎ **800/ 333-4264** or 561/465-2400. www.hboi.edu. E-mail: tours@hboi.edu. Admission $6 adults, $4 children 3–13, free for children 5 and under. Mon–Sat 10am–4pm (tours scheduled at 10am, noon, and 2pm), Sun noon–5pm (tours scheduled at noon and 2pm). Arrive at least 20 minutes before tour.

Harbor Branch is a working nonprofit scientific institute that studies oceanic resources and welcomes visitors on regularly scheduled tours. The first stop is the J. Seward Johnson Marine Education Center, which houses institute-built submersibles that are used to conduct marine research at depths of up to 3,000 feet. A video details current research projects, and several large aquariums simulate the environments of the Indian River Lagoon and a saltwater reef. Tour goers are then shuttled by minibus to the Aqua-Culture Farming Center, a research facility containing shallow tanks growing seaweed and other oceanic plants. The new Lagoon Explorer Cruise, examining the Indian River Lagoon, departs at 10am, noon, and 2pm; cost is $15 adults, $12 children 3 to 13.

St. Lucie Historical Museum. 414 Seaway Dr., Fort Pierce. ☎ **561/462-1795.** Admission $2 adults, $1 children 6–11, free for children 5 and under. Tues–Sat 10am–4pm, Sun noon–4pm.

Fort Pierce's little historical museum displays treasures from a 1715 shipwreck, uniforms, and other objects from the 1838 Seminole War, and a re-creation of Old Fort Pierce, the garrison that gave this area its name. There's also a 1919 fire engine pumper, and an excellent collection of area photographs shot between 1880 and 1920. The 1907 Gardner House, next door, has been fully restored to give visitors a peek at local life at the turn of the century.

UDT-SEAL Museum. 3300 N. Fla. A1A, Fort Pierce. ☎ **561/595-5845.** Admission $3.25 adults, $1.25 children, free for children 6 and under. Mon–Sat 10am–4pm, Sun noon–4pm. Closed Mon in off-season.

Florida is full of unique museums, but none are more curious than the UDT-SEAL Museum, a most peculiar tribute to the secret forces of the U.S. Navy frogmen and their successors, the SEAL teams. Chronological displays trace the history of these clandestine divers and detail their most important stealthy achievements. The best exhibits are those of the intricately detailed equipment used by the navy's most elite members.

BOAT TOURS

The *Spirit of St. Joseph* Cruise Line, 424 Seaway Dr., Fort Pierce (☎ 561/ 467-BOAT), takes up to 200 passengers on guided tours of the Indian River. Most of the regularly scheduled cruises include a meal and/or entertainment, which is good because scenery in this sleepy region is relatively monotonous. Phone for fluctuating prices and tour times.

For a real deal, plan to sail on the casino cruise ship called the *Midnight Gambler* (☎ 888/777-8198). In the beginning of 1998, the company dropped the $15 admission charge in order to increase customers. The free 5-hour tour aboard the 110-foot yacht includes free parking and nightly entertainment. The food isn't great, but it is reasonably priced. A deli menu of cold sandwiches and snacks and three full bars with waitress service are offered throughout the cruise. At press time the cruises were running daily from 11am until 4:30pm and Monday through Thursday and Sunday at 7pm. Cruises leave from the Ft Pierce Marina, 1 Avenue A. Call to be sure they are sailing. The seas can be very rough at times.

ACCOMMODATIONS YOU CAN AFFORD

The Port St. Lucie mainland is pretty run-down, but there are a number of inexpensive hotel options on scenic Hutchinson Island that are both charming and well priced. Probably the best option is the **Hampton Inn** (☎ 800/426-7866 or 561/460-9855), 2831 Reynolds Dr., which is relatively new and beautifully maintained. However, if you want to be closer to the water, try the **Days Inn South Hutchinson Island,** 1920 Seaway Dr. (☎ 800/325-2525 or 561/461-8737), a small, 32-unit motel that sits along the intracoastal inlet and is simple but very well kept. Rates for standard rooms start at $60.

SUPER-CHEAP SLEEPS

Angler Motel and Apts Ft. Pierce. 1172 Seaway Dr., Ft. Pierce, S. Hutchinson Island, FL 34949. ☎ 561/466-0131. 7 units, all with bathroom (showers only). A/C TV TEL. Year-round $55–$60 single or double, $350 weekly for 1-bedroom, from $1,000 month. Dock costs $5 per night. Two-night minimum. Under 12 free. MC, V.

This tiny waterfront motel next door to the pricier Harborfront Inn is the smallest and one of the quaintest around town. Especially popular with boaters and fishers in summer who dock at the small wooden dock out back on the Ft. Pierce inlet. There is no pool but plenty of cool shade trees and bright splashes of bougainvillea. Rooms here are standard but well outfitted with fully-equipped kitchenettes. By next season there will be a small Holiday Inn next door, too. It is hoped the construction noise won't disrupt the quietude of this pleasant, affordable spot.

Dockside Harbor Light Inn. 1160 Seaway Dr., Fort Pierce, Hutchinson Island, FL 34949. ☎ 800/286-1745 or 561/468-3555. www.docksideinn.com. 65 units, all with bathroom (some with shower only) A/C TV TEL. Winter $50–$95 single or double. Off-season $43–$85 single or double. AE, DC, DISC, MC, V. Extra person $10.

Any accommodation in the Dockside Harbor Light's four angular and undistinguished buildings is a good choice, especially for boating and fishing enthusiasts. In addition to more than a dozen boat slips and two private fishing piers, the hotel offers a large pool and outdoor sundeck. The best and highest priced rooms either have waterfront balconies or small kitchenettes that contain a coffeemaker, refrigerator, oven, and toaster. In fact, more than half the rooms have at least basic cooking facilities. All but a few of the very cheapest rooms have at least refrigerators. Rooms in the Dockside building are one of the best values around; with standard rooms renting for about $50, even during the height of the fishing season, you can't do better. Though not luxurious, a thorough renovation in 1998 has made all the rooms recommendable. A Laundromat is also useful for long-term guests. Many guests enjoy the discounted weekly and monthly rates in high season.

Kiwi Motel and Apts. 1240 Seaway Dr. Ft. Pierce, FL 34949. ☎ **561/461-6645.** 10 units, all with bathroom (some with shower only). A/C TV TEL. Year-round $30–$100 single or double. Call well in advance for reservations. MC, V.

This simple and tiny 1-story charmer is popular with diving, boating, and fishing clientele—many of whom come to stay for weeks (or months) at a time in the little villas that are perfect for families or large groups. It's one of the only accommodations in the area with two-bedroom, two-bath units. It's located directly on the inlet on Hutchinson Island, so you can fish, dock or swim. There is also a small pool and spacious sundeck. Rooms are well worn but clean and comfortable. Most have kitchenettes.

FOR A FEW BUCKS MORE

Mellon Patch Inn. 3601 N. Fla. A1A, N. Hutchinson Island, FL 34949. ☎ **800/MLN-PTCH** or 561/461-5231. Fax 561/464-6463. www.sunet.net/mlnptch. 4 units, all with bathroom. A/C TV TEL. Winter $90–$120 single or double. Off-season $80–$110 single or double. Rates include breakfast. AE, DISC, MC, V. No smoking and no children.

Opened in mid-1994 by innkeepers Andrea and Arthur Mellon, the Mellon Patch offers just four bright rooms in what looks like a single-family house, each with a large bathroom and sturdy soundproof walls.

The public living room is nicer than any of the small guest rooms. It's designed with a 2-story vaulted ceiling, a fireplace, and lots of windows that overlook the Indian River. A gourmet breakfast that might include waffles topped with strawberries and pecans, chocolate-chip pancakes, or spinach soufflé is served here each morning. A public beach and free tennis courts across the street are added bonuses.

✪ **Villa Nina Island Beach Bed & Breakfast.** 3851 N. A1A, N. Hutchinson Island, FL 34949. ☎ and fax **561/467-8673.** Cellular ☎ 561/971-7095. www.gate.net/~villanin. E-mail: villnin@gate.net. 3 units, all with bathroom (two with shower only). Winter $105–$200 single or double. Off-season $95–$190 single or double. DISC, MC, V. From I-95, Exit 67 (Indrio Rd.) east to U.S. 1, turn right. Turn left (east) on S.R. A1A and proceed 3 miles to the traffic light and turn left.

This most recent addition to the B&B scene is just down the road from the Mellon Patch. Although it too is in a simple and brand-new home on the river's edge, this property provides much more privacy. Innkeepers Nina and Glenn live in the main house and have built large, fully-equipped rooms along the back, each with a private entrance and either a fully-equipped kitchen or kitchenette. The honeymoon suite in the back is the largest and brightest of all them all (and the most expensive). You can have breakfast delivered to your room or have it outside near the heated pool. You are also invited to use the bicycles to explore the quiet paths that surround the property. Or take a canoe or rowboat for river rides. Deer and other wildlife are common sights on this beautiful, 4-acre property. Night-lit tennis and basketball courts, a public beach, and nature trails are just across the street.

GREAT DEALS ON DINING

There are a number of good seafood restaurants in the Fort Pierce and St. Lucie area, but it's also easy to drive to Stuart for more diverse dining options. See section 1 of this chapter for recommendations in Stuart.

Captain's Galley. 827 N. Indian River Dr., Fort Pierce. ☎ **561/466-8495.** Reservations not accepted. Main courses $9–$12; breakfast/lunch $2–$5. MC, V. Mon–Sat 7am–2pm and 4:30–9pm, Sun 7am–12:30. DISC, MC, V. Go north on U.S. 1 to Seaway Dr.; turn right and continue over the railroad tracks. Look for one of the only buildings on left just before the bridge. SEAFOOD/AMERICAN.

Anywhere else this might be just another coffee shop. But here, just over the Intracoastal Waterway at the north end of Hutchinson Island, it's a local institution. Dressed up with printed window valances and hanging plants, the Captain's Galley is busiest at breakfast, when locals catch up over eggs, toast, and home fries. Lunch specials usually include a variety of burgers and a small selection of salads and sandwiches. And dinner is for seafood, when the Galley serves up shrimp scampi, the day's fish, or land specialties like strip steak and chicken français.

✪ **Harbortown Fish House.** 1930 Harbortown Dr., Fort Pierce. ☎ **561/466-8732.** Reservations accepted. Main courses $14–$20. AE, DISC, MC, V. Sun–Thurs 11:30am–9pm, Fri–Sat 5–10pm. SEAFOOD.

You have to drive to the end of the harbor to reach this open-air waterfront fish house. It's a rustic place with outdoor tables overlooking the port, and you might be surprised to learn that it serves the area's best and freshest seafood. The menu is posted on white boards throughout the dining room and might include jumbo shrimp cocktail or New England clam chowder. The list of main courses is long and contains both fish and meat dishes. There's angel-hair pasta with scallop- and anchovy-stuffed mushrooms, roast Muscovy duck with wild-mushroom risotto, and charcoal-grilled pepper-crusted tuna served over sautéed escarole.

✪ **P.V. Martin's.** 5150 N. Fla. N. A1A (N. Hutchinson Island), Fort Pierce. ☎ **561/ 569-0700.** Reservations recommended. Main courses $9–$20. AE, MC, V. Mon–Sat 11am–3:30pm and 5–9pm, Sun 10:30am–2:30pm and 5–8:30pm. SEAFOOD/AMERICAN.

This relatively elegant eatery with an eclectic American menu is tops in Fort Pierce. The wood floors, beamed ceilings, tiled-top tables, and rattan chairs would be nice anywhere, but here they look out through floor-to-ceiling windows, onto sweeping ocean vistas. By night a huge central stone fireplace warms the room, and on weekends there's live entertainment in the adjacent bar.

Surf-and-turf dinners run the gamut from crab-stuffed shrimp and grouper baked with bananas and almonds to Brie and asparagus-stuffed chicken breast and barbecued baby back ribs. An excellent selection of appetizers includes escargots in mushroom caps and a succulent fried soft-shell crab (available in season).

PORT ST. LUCIE/FORT PIERCE AFTER DARK

Besides a few heavy-drinking bars, waterside restaurants (see P.V. Martin's, above), and hotel lounges, the nightlife of Port St. Lucie and Fort Pierce takes place in the neighboring towns north and south of here. See sections 1 and 3 of this chapter for nearby nightspots.

3 Vero Beach & Sebastian

85 miles SE of Orlando, 130 miles N of Miami

Vero Beach and Sebastian are located at the northern tip of the Treasure Coast region in Indian River County. These two beach towns are populated with folks who knew Miami and Fort Lauderdale in the days before massive high-rises and overcrowding. They appreciate the area's small-town feel, and that's exactly the area's appeal for visitors as well: a laid-back, relaxed atmosphere, friendly people, and friendlier prices.

A crowd of well-tanned surfers from all over the state descend on the region, especially the Sebastian Inlet, to catch some of the state's biggest waves. Water-sports enthusiasts enjoy the area's fine diving, surfing, and windsurfing. Anglers are in heaven here. In spring, baseball buffs can catch some action from the Los Angeles Dodgers as they train in exhibition games.

ESSENTIALS

The **Indian River County Tourist Council,** 1216 21st St., Vero Beach, FL 32961
(☎ **561/567-3491;** fax 561/778-3181; www.vero-beach.fl.us/chamber), will send
visitors an incredibly detailed information packet on the entire county, which includes
Vero Beach, Sebastian, and Fellsmere. You'll find a detailed full-color map of the area,
a comprehensive listing of upcoming events, a hotel guide, and more.

HITTING THE BEACHES

Most of Vero's beachfront is open to the public and is almost never crowded. The best
spots are described here, but there are many others.

South Beach Park, on South Ocean Drive, at the end of Marigold Lane, is a busy,
developed, lifeguarded beach with picnic tables, rest rooms, and showers. It's known
as one of the best swimming beaches and also attracts a young crowd that plays volleyball and Frisbee. A well-laid-out nature walk takes you into beautiful secluded trails.

At the very north tip of the island, **Sebastian Inlet** has flat sandy beaches with lots
of facilities including kayak, paddleboat, and canoe rentals, a well-stocked surf shop,
picnic tables, and a snack shop. The winds seem to stir up the surf with no jetty to
stop their swells, to the delight of surfers and boarders, who get here early to catch the
big waves. Campers enjoy fully-equipped sites in a woody area. Admission to the
Sebastian Inlet State Recreation Area, 9700 South A1A, Melbourne, is $3.25 per car
and $1 for those who walk or bike in.

GREAT GOLF THAT WON'T BREAK YOUR BUDGET &
AFFORDABLE OUTDOOR ACTIVITIES

FISHING   Capt. Jack Jackson works 7 days a week out of **Vero's Tackle and
Sportshop,** 57–59 Royal Palm Point (☎ **561/567-6550**), taking anglers out on his
25-foot boat for private river excursions. Captain Jackson provides all the equipment.
Half-day jaunts on the Indian River cost $175 for two people (the minimum required
for a charter).

You can also head up to Sebastian, where **Capt. Hiram's,** 1606 Indian River Rd.
(☎ **800/797-1582** or 561/589-5433), offers private sailboat charters on the Indian
River. In addition, it runs a party boat, the *Capt. Kidd II,* which heads out daily for a
full day of bottom fishing for grouper, snapper, and more (it's usually only a half day
on Monday). The cost is $35 per person ($40 per person will get you your rod, reel,
and bait). You can bring your own lunch and beer on board, and someone will be
available to clean your fish for you. Call ahead to reserve your place.

Many other charters, guides, party boats, and tackle shops operate in this area.
Ask at your hotel for suggestions, or call the chamber of commerce for a list of local
operators.

GOLF   Hard-core golfers insist that of the dozens of courses in the area, only a
handful are worth their plot of grass.

Set on rolling hills with uncluttered views of sand dunes and sky, the **Sandridge
Golf Club** (☎ **561/770-5000**), at 5300 73rd St., Vero Beach, offers two par-72 18-
holers. The Dunes is a long course with rolling fairways, and the newer Lakes course
has lots of water. Both charge less than $50 including a cart. A small snack bar sells
beer and sandwiches. Reservations are recommended and are taken 2 days in advance.

Though less challenging, the **Sebastian Municipal Golf Course** (☎ **561/
589-6800**), at 1010 E. Airport Dr., is a good 18-hole par-72. It's scenic, well maintained, and a great bargain. Greens fees are $33 with a cart and about half that if you
want to play 9 holes after 1:30pm.

Also see "A Visit to Dodgertown," below.

SPECTATOR SPORTS   See "A Visit to Dodgertown," below.

SURFING   See **Sebastian Inlet** details under "Hitting the Beaches," above. Also consider the beach north of the **Barber Bridge** (S.R. 70), where waves are slightly gentler and the scene less competitive, and Wabasso Beach, Fla. A1A and County Road 510, a secluded area near Disney's resort where lots of high-school-age locals congregate, especially when the weather gets rough.

TENNIS   There are dozens of tennis courts around Vero Beach and Sebastian, many of which are at hotels and resorts. Check the phone book, or try **Riverside Park,** 350 Dahlia Lane, at Royal Palm Boulevard at the east end of Barber Bridge in Vero Beach (☎ **561/231-4787**). This popular park has 10 hard courts (6 lighted) that can be rented for $3 per person per hour. Reservations are accepted up to 24 hours in advance. The club also has two racquetball courts at reasonable rates in a lush park setting with nature trails and many other facilities.

SEEING THE SIGHTS

✪ **Environmental Learning Center.** 255 Live Oak Dr. (just off the 510 Causeway), Wabasso Island. ☎ **561/589-5050.** Free admission. Mon–Fri 9am–5pm, Sat 9am–noon, Sun 1–4pm.

The Indian River is not really a river at all, but a large brackish lagoon that's home to a greater variety of species than any other estuary in North America. The privately funded Environmental Learning Center was created to protect the local habitat and educate visitors about their environment. Situated on 51 island acres, the center features dozens of hands-on exhibits that are geared to both children and adults. There are live touch tanks, exhibits, and microscopes for viewing the smallest sea life close up. The best thing to do here is join one of the center's interpretive canoe trips, offered by reservation only. These cost $10 for adults and $5 for children. Phone for details.

Indian River Citrus Museum. 2140 14th Ave., Vero Beach. ☎ **561/770-2263.** Admission $1 donation. Tues–Fri 10am–4pm.

The tiny Indian River Citrus Museum exhibits artifacts relating to the history of the citrus industry, from its initial boom in the late 1800s to the present. Also, a small grove has taped information on the varieties of fruits there. The gift shop sells unique citrus-themed gift items, along with, of course, ready-to-ship fruit.

Mel Fisher's Treasure Museum. 1322 U.S. 1, Sebastian. ☎ **561/589-9874.** Admission $5 adults, $4 seniors over 55, $1.50 children 6–12, free for children 5 and under. Mon–Sat 10am–5pm, Sun noon–5pm.

Here's where you can see the treasures from the fateful fleet that went down in 1715. Though not as extensive as the museum in Key West, this exhibit is worth a look. On display are gold coins and bars and many Spanish artifacts. Also, the preservation laboratory shows how the goods are extricated, cleaned, and preserved.

A VISIT TO DODGERTOWN

Vero is the winter home of the Los Angeles Dodgers, and the town hosts the team in grand style. ✪ **Dodgertown,** the 450-acre compound at 3901 26th St. (☎ **561/ 569-4900**), encompasses two golf courses, a conference center, country club, movie theater, and recreation room. You can watch afternoon exhibition games during the winter (usually between mid-February and the end of March) in the comfortable 6,474-seat outdoor stadium. Even if the game sells out, you can catch the action from a seat on the grassy field with a $5 standing-room ticket. The stadium has never turned away an eager fan.

Even when spring training is over, you can still catch a game; the Dodger's farm team, the **Vero Beach Dodgers,** has a full season of minor-league baseball in summer.

Admission to the complex is free; tickets to games are $5 to $9. The complex is open daily from 9am to 5pm; game time is usually 1pm. From I-95 take Exit S.R. 60 east to 43rd Avenue; turn left; continue to 26th Street, and turn right.

SHOPPING

Ocean Boulevard and Cardinal Drive are Vero's two main shopping streets. Both are near the beach and lined with specialty boutiques, including antiques and home decorating shops.

If you want to send fruit back home, the local source is **Hale Indian River Groves,** 615 Beachland Blvd. (☎ **561/231-1752**), a shipper of local citrus and jams since 1947. Note that they are closed 2 to 3 months a year, usually late summer or early fall, depending on the year's crop.

The **Horizon Outlet Center,** at S.R. 60 and I-95, Vero Beach (☎ **800/866-5900** or 561/770-6171), contains more than 80 discount stores selling shoes, kitchenware, books, clothing, and other items. The mall, which added a food court and new stores in 1996, is open Monday to Saturday from 9am to 8pm and Sunday from 11am to 6pm.

The **Indian River Mall** (☎ **561/770-6255**), 6200 20th St. (S.R. 60 about 5 miles east of I-95), which opened its doors in November 1996, is a big deal in Vero Beach. This monster mall has all the big national chains, like the Gap, Structure, and Victoria's Secret, as well as several large department stores, and is open Monday through Saturday from 10am to 9pm and Sunday from noon to 6pm.

ACCOMMODATIONS YOU CAN AFFORD

Ocean Drive is dotted with a number of old, dilapidated hotels in need of renovations. Although the area is being fixed up, it's slow going. A few of the well-maintained hotels are listed below. In Vero, both the **Days Resort** (☎ **800/ 329-7466** or 561/231-2800), at 3244 Ocean Dr., and the **Holiday Inn Oceanside** (☎ **800/465-4329** or 561/231-2300), at 3384 Ocean Dr., offer oceanfront rooms and suites; rooms at the Days start at $70 in the off-season and $100 in winter months, while Holiday Inn's rooms start at $90 and jump to $130 in high season. However, the Holiday Inn is probably a better choice since it was fully remodeled in 1995, and its restaurant and lounge directly face the ocean. Also, a great spot to know, especially if you are planning to fish, is **Capt. Hiram's** (☎ **561/589-4345;** see "Fishing," above, and also "Vero Beach & Sebastian After Dark," below), where there are four clean and cozy rooms available adjacent to the restaurant and overlooking the water. Rates are between $80 and $110.

SUPER-CHEAP SLEEPS

Aquarius Resort Hotel/Motel. 3544 Ocean Dr., Vero Beach, FL 32963. ☎ **561/ 231-1133.** 28 units, all with bathroom (some with shower only). Winter $65–$115 single or double. Off-season $50–$85 single or double. Extra person $5; children 11 and under stay free in parents' unit. AE, DC, DISC, MC, V.

Hotels are a rare enough commodity in this condo-canyon, where seeing the sky is enough of a trick. Finding an inexpensive one should precipitate applause—and here it is! Just near Dodgertown in Vero Beach are two surprising facilities, the Aquarius Hotel and its sister, the Aquarius Motel. The motel is on the south end of the beach and has a swimming pool, shuffleboard courts, and a barbecue. And the best part is, there are kitchenettes in each of the 28 units. The decor is nothing spectacular—

modern Formica and dime-store prints—but the rooms are clean and well maintained. Just a few yards away is one of Vero's prettiest uncrowded beaches.

✪ **Davis House Inn.** 607 Davis St., Sebastian, FL 32958. ☎ **561/589-4114.** Fax 561/589-3108. 12 units, all with bathroom (one with shower only). Winter $69–$89 single or double. Off-season $54–$79 single or double. Rates include continental breakfast. Weekly and monthly rates available. AE, DISC, MC, V. From I-95, take Exit 69 east to Indian River Dr., turn left, go 1.25 miles to Davis St., turn left on Davis St; the inn is on the left.

Each of the dozen rooms in this contemporary, 3-story, blue-and-white bed-and-breakfast on the mainland has a private entrance and door-front parking. The rooms are large and clean, although somewhat plain, and each has a king-size bed, a pull-out sofa, and a small kitchenette, making them popular with long-term guests. The bathrooms are equally large and have plenty of counter space. There's a large wooden deck for sunbathing, a sunny second-floor breakfast room, and a self-service Laundromat. There are no views to speak of in this inland lodging, though the grounds are pretty and well kept.

FOR A FEW BUCKS MORE

Driftwood Resort. 3150 Ocean Dr., Vero Beach, FL 32963. ☎ **561/231-0550.** Fax 561/234-1981. 100 units, all with bathroom (some with shower only). A/C TV TEL. Winter $90–$210 single or double; from $170–$230 2-bedroom suite. Off-season $55–$125 double; from $130 2-bedroom suite. AE, MC, V.

Originally planned in the 1930s as a private estate by local legend Waldo Sexton, the Driftwood was opened to the public after several travelers stopped to inquire about renting a room here. Today the hotel's rooms and public areas are filled with nautical knickknacks collected by Sexton on his travels all over the world.

All the guest rooms are different. Some feature terra-cotta tile floors and lighter furniture while others have a more rustic feel with hardwoods and antiques. Each accommodation has its own bathroom and few frills. The resort, which was recently listed on the National Register of Historic Places, offers two outdoor heated pools, a sometimes narrow beach, bicycle trail, dry-cleaning services, as well as VCR and video rentals.

✪ **Islander Motel.** 3101 Ocean Dr., Vero Beach, FL 32963. ☎ **800/952-5886** or 561/231-4431. 16 units. A/C TV TEL. Winter from $89 single or double. Off-season $49–$59 single or double. Efficiencies cost $10 extra. AE, MC, V.

Resident owner Tom Collins runs one of the most comfortable and welcoming inns in the area. Well located in downtown Vero Beach, this motel is just a short walk to the beach, restaurants, and shops. Every guest room has a small refrigerator and either a king-size bed or two double beds. The accommodations are designed in a Caribbean motif with bright fabrics and white rattan furniture. There's a pool and a barbecue area in the handsomely landscaped central courtyard, along with a small walk-up cafe.

WORTH A SPLURGE

✪ **Disney's Vero Beach.** 9250 Island Grove Terrace, Vero Beach, FL 32963. ☎ **800/359-8000** or 561/234-2000. Fax 561/234-2030. 172 units, all with bathroom. A/C TV TEL. Year-round rates from $140 inn-garden view; from $160 inn-ocean view/studio; from $210 1-bedroom villa; from $280 2-bedroom villa; from $590 3-bedroom beach cottage. AE, MC, V. From I-95 take Exit 69 (512 east); turn right onto County Rd. 510 east; turn right onto S. Fla. A1A. The resort is immediately visible on the left.

Disney's megaresort opened in 1995 with much fanfare on the otherwise sleepy shores of Florida's Treasure Coast. They call it a membership-based club; as far as I can figure, it's simply a time-share. For now, nonowners are welcome. Take advantage of it while you still can—your kids will love it.

Promoters say that this is a return to "the Old Florida," but I can't imagine that it was ever quite like this—this clean, this quaint, this fun, and this convenient. This is Disney, without the rides or lines. Sign me up. The sprawling complex is designed to resemble a turn-of-the-century Florida beach community, complete with sandwashed buildings and faux-worn furniture. The beachside cottages are huge and tasteful. The villas have fully-equipped kitchens with dishwashers and microwaves.

Situated on the tip of one of the most pristine beaches on the coast, the resort takes advantage of its setting by offering truly exciting children's programs like canoe adventures, poolside miniature golf, stories around a campfire, a trip to a working cattle ranch, and stargazing from a powerful telescope. The best part is a large lagoonlike pool with a huge winding slide that elicits squeals of delight from kids and adults alike. And for younger kids, a pirate ship that squirts water is a fun way to cool off.

In addition to the pool and huge private beach, the resort offers a well-outfitted health club, a Jacuzzi, sauna, nature trails, kitchenettes, VCRs, video rentals, shuffleboard, croquet, two night-lit tennis courts, water-sports equipment, a jogging track, nine-hole miniature golf, basketball half-court, volleyball, tether ball, a large game room, extensive children's programs, conference rooms, business center, a self-service Laundromat, tour desk/guest services, gift shop, and a fully-stocked general store. Plus, guests are welcome to free coffee in the lobby each morning.

The resort offers some of the best food in the region. An elegant steak house, Sonya's, serves dinner from an eclectic, Florida-inspired menu with superb steaks, pecan-crusted salmon, and salads. In addition, a casual restaurant for lunch and dinner serves interesting pizzas, sandwiches, salads, roasted vegetables, and pastas. A picturesque lounge, which overlooks the ocean and hosts live music most nights, is popular with guests and locals alike. A poolside snack bar rounds out this resort's food and drink options.

Doubletree Guest Suites. 3500 Ocean Dr., Vero Beach, FL 32963. ☎ **800/841-5666** or 561/231-5666. Fax 561/234-4866. 55 units, all with bathroom. A/C TV TEL. Winter $210–$245 1-bedroom suite; $265–$295 2-bedroom suite. Off-season $110–$150 1-bedroom suite; $165 2-bedroom suite. AE, CB, DC, DISC, MC, V.

Vero's best all-suite hotel, part of the Doubletree chain, is located directly on the beach and is close to local restaurants and shops. First-class accommodations are located in a modern 4-story building. The guest rooms, which were renovated in late 1996, are unremarkable, but clean and attractive. What the nearly identical suites lack in character they make up for in content. The rooms are equipped with small refrigerators and coffeemakers, two phones, and modern bathrooms that include hair dryers. Two restaurants and a poolside bar are open daily for lunch, dinner, and cocktails.

CAMPING

This area is popular with campers, who can choose from nearly a dozen sites throughout Vero and Sebastian. If you aren't camping at the scenic and very popular Sebastian Inlet (see "Hitting the Beaches," above), then try the **Vero Beach KOA RV Park,** 8850 U.S. 1, Wabasso (☎ **561/589-5665**). This 120-site campground is 2 miles from the ocean and the Intracoastal Waterway and a quarter mile from the Indian River—a big draw for the crowd of regular fishing fanatics. There's running water and electricity as well as showers, a shop, and hookups for RVs. Rates range from $20 to $26 per site, and about $20 for tents. To get there, take I-95 to Exit 69 east; at U.S. 1 turn left.

Another excellent option is the **Sunshine Travel Park,** 9455 108th Ave. (County Rd. 512 and I-95, at the Sebastian/Vero border), Vero Beach, FL 32967 (☎ **800/628-7081;** fax 561/589-8244). The 300 or so sites rent for $31 to $37. Members of

Good SAM, AAA, or FMCA will get a 10% discount. This very popular RV resort has paved sites with all the hookups, and is just 15 minutes from the beach. While it's hardly in a gorgeous area, it features a heated pool, horseshoe pit, inside game room, shuffleboard, miniature golf, and a full schedule of activities. Many regulars return year after year, so be sure to book well in advance.

GREAT DEALS ON DINING

Okay, so Vero Beach isn't a culinary mecca, but the charming, Old Florida joints are actually quite good. Plenty of seaside tourist traps are worth avoiding. All the usual fast-food joints are located off of I-95 on S.R. 60.

SUPER-CHEAP EATS

Crusty's. Humiston Park, 1050 Easterlily Lane, Vero Beach. ☎ **561/231-4728.** Main courses $5–$12. AE, DISC, MC, V. Mon–Thurs 11am–10pm, Fri–Sat 11am–11pm. SNACKS/SEAFOOD.

This place is true to its name. Jutting out on its own seafront spot, it looks as if it's about to fall into the ocean. You won't find many tourists or many niceties here—it's straight-up paper and plastic—but the place serves quality seafood and beach snacks at reasonable prices. Lots of choices, like subs, pizzas, hot dogs, and salads, are carnival-priced but good. But where else can you get a "clamwich" of fried clam strips served between halves of a cornmeal bun? Everything is fresh, and the setting true Old Florida. If you want to really go for it, do the stone crab dinner for $12 (prices vary seasonally) with all the fixings—you can't beat that price.

Waldo's. In the Driftwood Resort, 3150 Ocean Dr., Vero Beach. ☎ **561/231-7091.** Reservations not necessary. Main courses $10–$13. AE, MC, V. Thurs–Sun 8am–10pm, Fri–Sat 8am–11pm. SEAFOOD/AMERICAN.

Everyone who hears that you went to Vero Beach will ask you if you went to Waldo's. The restaurant isn't famous for its food, which is good but not great. Waldo's is known for its unusual setting: Outdoor picnic tables are set as close to the ocean as you can get without getting wet. Breakfast and lunch snacks are the best bet. Sandwiches like turkey clubs, broiled chicken, or burgers served on paper plates are satisfying and hearty. Dinners are just slightly more elaborate and include Danish-style barbecued ribs and Cajun seafood kebabs.

FOR A FEW BUCKS MORE

✪ **Black Pearl.** 2855 Ocean Dr., Vero Beach. ☎ **561/234-4426.** Reservations recommended. Main courses $12–$21. AE, CB, DC, DISC, MC, V. Mon–Fri 11:30am–2:30pm and 5:30–10pm, Sat–Sun 5:30–10pm. CONTINENTAL.

It's unusual that such a small, moderately priced, and unassuming restaurant should make absolutely everything from scratch. But that's exactly what they do, and you'll be wooed by seductive smells even before you walk through the front door. There's just a single, art deco–accented dining room featuring bright prints on clean pastel walls.

The restaurant's small list of appetizers may include feta cheese and spinach fritters, chilled leek-and-watercress soup, or oysters baked with crabmeat and butter. Equally creative main courses recently included Cajun pasta (topped with shrimp, scallops, and sausage), sautéed crabmeat-stuffed veal covered with hollandaise sauce, and blackened rib-eye steak.

Ocean Grill. 1050 Sexton Plaza (by the ocean at the end of S.R. 60), Vero Beach. ☎ **561/231-5409.** Reservations accepted only for large parties. Main courses $13–$22. AE, DC, DISC, MC, V. Mon–Fri 11:30am–2:30pm and 5:45–10pm, Sat–Sun 5:45–10pm. AMERICAN.

Founded in 1941, the Ocean Grill is an institution that attracts tourists and locals alike with its simple but rich cooking and stunning locale, right on the ocean's edge.

For a dramatic experience, ask for a table along the wall of newly enlarged windows that open onto the sea. Dinners are uniformly good. Try stone crab claws when they are in season or any of the big servings of pasta or meats.

Pearl's Bistro. 56 Royal Palm Point, Vero Beach. ☎ **561/778-2950.** Reservations recommended. Main courses $9–$17. AE, MC, V. Mon–Fri 11:30am–2:30pm and 5:30–closing, Sat 11:30am–2:30pm and 6–10pm. Take U.S. 1 south to 20th St.; turn left; at Indian River Blvd. turn left again; then turn right onto Royal Palm Blvd. CARIBBEAN.

This small bistro serves one of the tastiest and best-value meals in town. The single narrow dining room is brightened with a colorful tropical mural and soothing lime walls. White chicken chili and the grilled swordfish club sandwich are two top lunch recommendations. The dinner menu includes an excellent open-face grilled-chicken burrito, steak fajita salad, and a shrimp enchilada with rice and beans.

WORTH A SPLURGE

✪ **Chez Yannick.** 1605 S. Ocean Dr., Vero Beach. ☎ **561/234-4115.** Reservations recommended. Main courses $15–$28; fixed-price dinner $18.95 in off-season only. AE, MC, V. Mon–Sat 6pm–9pm; reservations in season taken until 9pm. FRENCH/CONTINENTAL.

Fine French cooking complements the crystal and gilded decor. The nightly fixed-price dinner includes soup or salad, entree, and dessert, and is a truly outstanding value. Excellent starters include a succulent sliced duckling breast, cream of lobster soup, and hearts-of-palm salad with a slightly spicy vinaigrette. Some items, like lobster and shrimp in a cognac-dill sauce, are available as either an appetizer or an entree. Other main courses include Gorgonzola-stuffed beef tenderloin and sautéed soft-shell crabs. Desserts might include profiteroles with ice cream and chocolate or raspberry sauce, crème caramel, chocolate-mousse pie, or raspberry sorbet.

VERO BEACH & SEBASTIAN AFTER DARK

Even on weekends, this town retires relatively early. But there are a few popular spots, in addition to the many hotel lounges, that have live music and a good bar scene, especially in high season.

A mostly 30-something and younger crowd goes to **Vero's Bombay Louie's,** at 398 21st St. (☎ **561/978-0209**), where a deejay spins dance music after 9pm from Wednesday to Saturday.

In Sebastian, you'll find live music every weekend (and daily in season) at **Capt. Hiram's,** 1606 N. Indian River Dr. (☎ **561/589-4345**), a salty outdoor restaurant and bar on the Intracoastal Waterway. The feel is tacky Key West, complete with a sand floor and thatched-roof bar that locals and tourists love at all hours of the day and night.

North of the inlet, head for the tried-and-true **Sebastian Beach Inn** (or SBI to locals), 7035 S. Fla. A1A (☎ **407/728-4311**). Jazz, blues, or sometimes rock and roll starts at 9pm on Friday and Saturday. On Sunday, it's old-style reggae after 2pm.

4 A Side Trip Inland: Fishing at Lake Okeechobee

60 miles SW of West Palm Beach

Many visitors to the Treasure Coast come to fish, and they certainly get their fill off the miles of Atlantic shores and on the inland rivers. But if you want to fish freshwater and nothing else, head for "The Lake"—Lake Okeechobee, that is. The state's largest, it's chock-full of good eating fish. Only about a 1½-hour drive from the coast, it makes a great day or weekend excursion.

Two things take place in the area surrounding Lake Okeechobee: sugar production and fishing. The area, which actually encompasses five counties, is known as the bass fishing and winter vegetable capital of the state.

Okeechobee comes from the Seminole Indian word for "big water"—and big it is. The lake covers more than 467,000 acres; that's more than 730 square miles. At one time, the lake supported an enormous commercial fishing industry. Due to a commercial fishing-net ban, much of that industry has died off, leaving the sports anglers all the rich bounty of the lake.

As you approach the lake area, you'll notice a large levy surrounding its circumference. This was built after two major hurricanes, including one in 1947 that killed hundreds of area residents and cattle. In an effort to control future flooding, the Army Corps of Engineers, which had already built a cross-state waterway, constructed a series of locks and dams. The region is now safe from the threat of floods, but the ecological results of the flood control have not been as positive. The bird and wildlife population suffered dramatically, as did the southern portion of the Everglades, which relied on the down flow of water from the lake to replenish and clean the entire ecosystem.

Another threat to the region is posed by the area's largest employer, U.S. Sugar. The firm owns most of the land around Belle Glade and Clewiston, which is known as "America's Sweetest Town." Still, the area retains its rural charm and boasts the best bass fishing in the state.

ESSENTIALS

GETTING THERE   The best route is to take I-95 south to Southern Boulevard (U.S. 98 west) in West Palm Beach, which merges with S.R. 80 and S.R. 441. Follow signs for S.R. 80 west through Belle Glade to South Bay. In South Bay, turn right onto U.S. 27 north, which leads directly to Clewiston.

VISITOR INFORMATION   Contact the **Clewiston Chamber of Commerce,** 544 W. Sugarland Hwy., Clewiston, FL 33440 (☎ **941/983-7979**), for maps, business directories, and the names of numerous fishing guides throughout the area. In addition, you might contact the **Pahokee Chamber of Commerce,** 115 E. Main St., Pahokee, FL 33476 (☎ **561/924-5579;** fax 561/924-8116); they'll send a complete package of magazines, guides, and accommodations listings.

For an excellent map and brief history of the area, contact the **U.S. Army Corps of Engineers Office** of Natural Resources, 525 Ridgelawn Rd., Clewiston, FL 33440 (☎ **941/983-8101;** fax 941/983-8579). It is open weekdays from 8am to 4:30pm.

AFFORDABLE OUTDOOR ACTIVITIES

BOAT TOURS   **Captain JP's Boat Charters** (☎ **800/845-7411** or 561/924-2100) go out every day on a number of tour and dinner cruises on his 350-passenger Viking Starliner throughout the southern region of Lake Okeechobee. Most cruises leave from Pahokee or Moore Haven marina, though schedules change daily. Most cruises depart at 10am during the season and include breakfast and an all-you-can-eat buffet of salads, cheeses, and hot entrees. Prices start at $30. Call for seasonal schedules.

FISHING   See "Going After the Big One at Lake Okeechobee," below.

SKYDIVING   Besides fishing, the biggest sport in Clewiston is jumping out of planes. Because of the limited air traffic and vast areas of flat undeveloped land, this area attracts novice and expert skydivers. **Air Adventures** (☎ **800/533-6151** or 941/983-6151) operates a year-round program from the Airglades Airport. If you've never jumped before, you can go on a tandem dive, which means, as the name implies,

---

Going After the Big One at Lake Okeechobee

Fishing on the lake is a year-round affair, though the fish tend to bite a little better in the winter, perhaps for benefit of the many "snowbirds" who flock here, especially in February and March. RV camps are mobbed with fish-frenzied anglers who come down for weeks at a time for a decent catch.

You'll need a fishing license to go out with a rod and reel. It's a simple matter to apply. The chamber of commerce and most fishing shops can sign you up on the spot. The cost for non-Florida residents for 7 days is $16.50, $31.50 for the whole year.

You can rent, charter, or bring your own boat to Clewiston; just be sure to schedule your trip in advance. You don't want to show up without a reservation during the Redman Competition, for instance, which happens four times a year in the spring and winter. If you do, you'll find you can't get a room, campsite, or fishing boat because hundreds of the country's most intense bass fishers are vying for the $100,000 prize.

There are, of course, more than a few marinas where you can rent or charter boats. If it's your first time on the lake, I suggest chartering a boat with a guide who can show you the lake's most fertile spots and handle your tackle while you drink a beer and get some sun. **Roland Martin,** 920 E. Del Monte (☎ **941/983-3151**), is the one-stop spot where you can find a guide, boat, tackle, rods, bait, coolers, picnic supplies, and a choice of boats. Rates start at $40 for a half day (about 4 hours). If you've never fished these waters, consider hiring a guide. Rates, including the boat, start at $165 for a half-day. A full day costs $225 and includes all necessary equipment except bait. You'll need a license for this, too, which Roland Martin also sells. They also have boat rentals: A 16-foot johnboat is $40 for half a day, $60 for a full day with a $40 deposit. A 26-foot pontoon is $125 for a full day and $85 for half a day with a $50 deposit.

Another reputable boat-rental spot is **Angler's Marina,** 910 Okeechobee Blvd. (☎ **800/741-3141** or 941/983-BASS). Rentals for a 14-footer start at $40 for a half day, for a maximum of four people. A full day is $60. I'd opt for the 22-foot pontoon, which comes with a 50-horsepower engine and fits a max of 10 people and some more space for supplies and fish. If you want a guide, rates start at $150 (for two people) for a half day, though in the summer (June to October) when it's slow, you can usually get a cheaper deal.

---

you'll be attached to a "jumpmaster." For the first 60 seconds, the two of you free-fall, from about 12,500 feet. Then a quick pull of the chute turns your rapid descent into a gentle, balletic cruise to the ground with time to see the whole majestic lake from a privileged perspective. Dive packages start at $150 on weekdays and $165 on weekends. Group rates are available.

ACCOMMODATIONS YOU CAN AFFORD

If you aren't camping, book a room at the ✪ **Clewiston Inn,** 108 Royal Palm Ave., Clewiston (☎ **800/749-4466** or 941/983-8151). Built in 1938 by U.S. Sugar to house executives and visitors, this Southern plantation–inspired hotel is the oldest in the Lake Okeechobee region. It still hosts sugar executives and visiting sport fishers in its 52 simply decorated, nondescript, Holiday Inn–style rooms. The lounge area sports a 1945 mural depicting the animals of the region. Double rooms rent for $79 a night; bungalows for $99. All have air-conditioning, televisions, and telephones.

Another choice, especially if you're here for the fish, is **Roland Martin,** 920 E. Del Monte (☎ **800/473-6766** or 941/983-3151), the "Disney of Clewiston." This RV park offers modest motel rooms, efficiencies, condominiums, apartments, or camp-sites, with two heated pools, gift and marina shops, and a restaurant. The modern complex, dotted with prefab buildings painted in sparse white and gray, is clean and well manicured. Rooms rent for $55 to $65 and efficiencies for $70 to $85. Condos are about $130 a night with a 3-night minimum. RV sites are about $23 with TV and cable hookup.

CAMPING

In the winter, campers own the Clewiston area. Campsites are jammed with regulars who come year after year for the simple pleasures of the lake and, of course, the warm weather. Every manner of RV, from simple pop-top Volkswagens to Winnebagos to fully decked-out mobile homes, find their way to the many campsites along the lake. Also, see Roland Martin, above.

Okeechobee Landings, U.S. 27 east (☎ **941/983-4144**), is one of the best; it has every conceivable amenity included in the price of a site. More than 250 sites are sit-uated around a small lake, clubhouse, snack bar, pool, Jacuzzi, horseshoe pit, shuffle-board court, and tennis court. Full hookup includes sewer, which is not the case throughout the county. RV spots are sold to regulars. But there are usually some spots available for rental to one-time visitors. Rates are $23 a day or $350 a month, including hookup. Year-round rates for trailer rentals, which sleep two people, are $32 from Sunday to Thursday and $37 on Friday and Saturday.

GREAT DEALS ON DINING

If you aren't frying up your own catch for dinner, you can find a number of good eating spots in town. At the **Clewiston Inn** (see "Accommodations You Can Afford," above), you can get catfish, beef Stroganoff, ham hocks, fried chicken, and liver and onions in a setting as Southern as the food. The dining room is open daily from 6am to 2pm and 5 to 9pm, and entrees cost $9 to $18.

At **Julian's** (formerly Donnelly's), 842 E. Sugarland Hwy., Clewistown (☎ **941/983-8119**), in addition to the full menu of steaks and superfresh seafood, you can order alligator tail, quail, or a choice of barbecued specialties. Dinners range from $10 to $18 and include salad and vegetables. You can bring your own catch, which they'll cook however you like it, served with hush puppies, french fries, and coleslaw for just $5.95. Breakfast starts early so that the birds can get out by 5am to catch some worms. Donnelly's closes when "the fishermen are done drinking," usually Monday to Thursday by 10pm and Friday and Saturday by 11pm.

Not to be missed is the **Old South Barbecue Ranch,** 602 E. Sugarland Hwy. (☎ **941/983-7756**). You'll see signs from miles around imploring you to come to this Lake Okeechobee landmark. Go ahead; they're known for their barbecued pork, meat, and chicken, but the catfish isn't bad either. You can also get good fried gator. The place looks like a movie set from an old Western. It's open Sunday through Thursday from 11am to 9pm and Friday and Saturday from 11am to 10pm.

Southwest Florida

by Bill Goodwin

Residents of Sanibel form a "McSpoil" committee and prevent McDonald's from getting a fast-food toehold on their remarkably beautiful island. Neapolitans successfully force a referendum on development that would change the nature of their charming Olde Naples historic district. The town council in Fort Myers Beach designates a new and growing part of Estero Island as a safe haven for wildlife. And the federal government tells airboat operators to keep their noisy machines out of the pristine Everglades National Park.

If you think these recent efforts to protect both the past and the present environment make Southwest Florida one of the best parts of the state for enjoying the great outdoors and discovering remnants of Old Florida, you're right.

The region traces its nature-loving roots to inventor and amateur botanist Thomas A. Edison, who was so enamored of Southwest Florida that he spent his winters in Fort Myers from 1885 until 1931. His friend Henry Ford built his own winter home next door. The world's best tarpon fishing lured Pres. Teddy Roosevelt and his buddies to Useppa, one of literally 10,000 islands along this coast. Some of the planet's best shelling helped entice the du Ponts of Delaware to Gasparilla Island, where they founded the Nantucket-like village of Boca Grande. The unspoiled beauty of Sanibel and Captiva so entranced Pulitzer Prize–winning political cartoonist J. N. (Ding) Darling that he campaigned to preserve much of those islands in their natural states. And the millionaires who settled in Naples enacted tough zoning laws that to this day make their city one of the most alluring in Florida.

Many well-heeled individuals still are attracted to southwest Florida, making it one of the more expensive parts of the state to visit during the winter from mid-December to April. This is especially true of favorite enclaves of the rich and famous such as Boca Grande, Sanibel, Captiva, and Marco islands. During the off-season, however, even the most expensive resorts drop their room rates substantially, some drastically. And you can get some bargains in ritzy Naples even in winter—provided you book several months in advance. Consider visiting here during the "shoulder seasons" of November to mid-December and during May. The weather is warm and pleasant, rates are reduced, and most establishments that close during the slow summer season are open.

EXPLORING SOUTHWEST FLORIDA BY CAR

Most visitors who arrive by air land at **Southwest Florida International Airport** on the eastern outskirts of Fort Myers (see "Essentials" in section 1, below). From here it's less than 20 miles to Fort Myers Beach or Sanibel Island, 35 miles to Naples, or 46 miles to Marco Island. Both I-75 and U.S. 41 run north-south through the region, making for easy travel by car. This means that you can see the sights and participate in most activities easily from one base of operations. For example, you can stay in centrally located (and less expensive) Fort Myers Beach and make easy excursions into Fort Myers, Sanibel and Captiva Islands, and Naples and Marco Island. Fort Myers, Fort Myers Beach, and Sanibel and Captiva Islands are so close together—no more than 14 miles apart—that you can stay in one and pop over to one of the others for dinner. The same is true of Naples and nearby Marco Island.

EXCURSIONS TO THE EVERGLADES & KEY WEST

It's an easy excursion to Everglades City, the "back door" to Everglades National Park, which lies just 36 miles southeast of Naples. In fact, you won't be here long before you see advertisements for airboat rides in the Everglades. See chapter 7 for full details.

You can also easily make a day trip to Key West from here. During the winter season, **Cape Air** (☎ **800/352-0714**) shuttles its small planes to Key West several times a day from both Southwest Florida International Airport and Naples Municipal Airport. The same-day round-trip is about $170. **Key West Excursions** (☎ **800/ 650-KEYS,** or 941/262-3900 in Florida) makes very long day cruises to Key West from Fort Myers Beach and Naples, and the **Falcon Fleet** (☎ **941/642-1166**) does the same run from Marco Island. They all put you ashore for lunch and an afternoon look at Key West, and return late at night. There's food service and entertainment onboard. The cost is about $100 per person from Fort Myers Beach or Naples, $80 from Marco Island, including breakfast and dinner. See chapter 6 for information about Key West.

1 Fort Myers

148 miles NW of Miami, 142 miles S of Tampa, 42 miles N of Naples

It's difficult to picture this pleasant city with broad avenues along the Caloosahatchee River as a raucous cow town. But that's exactly what Fort Myers was just a few years before inventor Thomas Alva Edison came here in 1885, to regain his health after years of incessant toil and the death of his wife. Today the city's prime attractions are Seminole Lodge, the home Edison built on the banks of the Caloosahatchee, and his pal Henry Ford's digs next door. Edison planted lush tropical gardens around the two homes and royal palms in front of the properties along McGregor Boulevard, once a cow trail leading from town to the docks at Punta Rassa. Now lining McGregor Boulevard for miles, the trees give Fort Myers its nickname: The City of Palms.

Like most visitors to the area, you probably will opt to stay near the sands at nearby Fort Myers Beach or on Sanibel or Captiva Islands (see sections 2 and 3, below), but drive into Fort Myers at least to visit the Edison and Ford homes and have a riverside lunch. You also can venture inland and observe incredible numbers of wildlife in their river and swamp habitats, including those at the Babcock Ranch, largest of the surviving cattle producers and now a major game preserve.

ESSENTIALS

GETTING THERE   To reach downtown Fort Myers from I-75, take Exit 23 and follow Dr. Martin Luther King Jr. Boulevard (Fla. 82), which becomes McGregor

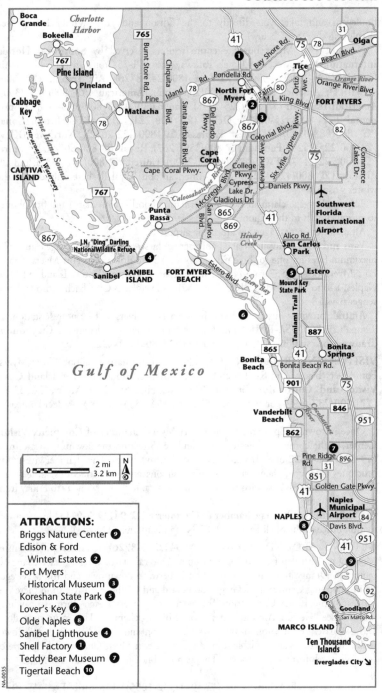

Southwest Florida

Boca Grande
Charlotte Harbor
765
Bokeelia
767
41
31
78
Olga
Beach Blvd.
Bay Shore Rd.
75
78
Tice
Orange River
Pondella Rd.
Orange River Blvd.
80
Ortiz Ave.
Pine Island
Pineland
Burnt Store Rd.
Chiquita Island Rd.
78
867
North Fort Myers
Palm
M.L. King Blvd.
FORT MYERS
Cabbage Key
Pine
Matlacha
Del Prado Pkwy.
Santa Barbara Blvd.
867
2
3
867
82
Cleveland Ave.
Colonial Blvd.
Six Mile Cypress Pkwy.
75
CAPTIVA ISLAND
Pine Island Sound
Intracoastal Waterway
767
Cape Coral
Cape Coral Pkwy.
College Pkwy.
Cypress Lake Dr.
Gladiolus Dr.
Commerce Lakes Dr.
Caloosahatchee River
McGregor Blvd.
San Carlos Blvd.
865
869
Daniels Pkwy.
41
Southwest Florida International Airport
867
Punta Rassa
Hendry Creek
Alico Rd.
San Carlos Park
J.N. "Ding" Darling National Wildlife Refuge
4
Sanibel   **SANIBEL ISLAND**
FORT MYERS BEACH
Estero Blvd.
Estero Bay
5   **Estero**
Mound Key State Park
6
Tamiami Trail
887
865
41
Bonita Springs
Bonita Beach
Bonita Beach Rd.
Gulf of Mexico
901
Cocohatchee River
Vanderbilt Beach
846
951
862
75
7
Pine Ridge Rd.
896
31
851
Golden Gate Pkwy.
41
Naples Municipal Airport
84
NAPLES
8
Davis Blvd.
951
41
9

ATTRACTIONS:
Briggs Nature Center 9
Edison & Ford
Winter Estates 2
Fort Myers
Historical Museum 3
Koreshan State Park 5
Lover's Key 6
Olde Naples 8
Sanibel Lighthouse 4
Shell Factory 1
Teddy Bear Museum 7
Tigertail Beach 10

10
Goodland
Collier Blvd.
San Marco Rd.
92
MARCO ISLAND
Ten Thousand Islands
Everglades City ↘

0   2 mi
3.2 km
N

NA-0035

Boulevard and takes you directly to the Edison and Ford Winter Estates (see "Exploring the Area," below).

Not just Fort Myers but the entire region is served by **Southwest Florida International Airport,** on Daniels Parkway east of I-75. You can get here on **Air Canada** (☎ 800/776-3000), **AirTran** (800/247-8726), **Air Transat** (☎ 800/470-1011), **America West** (☎ 800/235-9292), **American** (☎ 800/433-7300), **American Trans Air** (☎ 800/225-2995), **Canada 3000** (☎ 800/993-4378), **Continental** (☎ 800/525-0280), **Delta** (☎ 800/221-1212), **LTU International** (☎ 800/888-0200), **Midwest Express** (☎ 800/452-2022), **Northwest/KLM** (☎ 800/225-2525), **Pan Am** (☎ 800/359-7262), **Royal** (☎ 800/667-7692), **Spirit** (☎ 800/772-7117), **TWA** (☎ 800/221-2000), **United** (☎ 800/241-6522), and **US Airways** (☎ 800/428-4322). (*Note:* American and Royal fly here only during the winter season.)

The two baggage-claim areas have information booths (with maps) and free phones to various hotels in the region.

All major car-rental agencies are at the airport.

Vans and taxis are available at a booth across the street from the baggage claim. The maximum fares for one to three passengers are $24 to downtown Fort Myers, $35 to Fort Myers Beach, $37 to $44 to Sanibel Island, $56 to Captiva Island, $100 to Naples, $46 to $56 to Marco Island, and $70 to Everglades City. Each additional passenger pays $8.

Amtrak provides bus connections between Fort Myers and its nearest station, in Tampa (☎ **800/USA-RAIL**). The Amtrak buses arrive and depart the **Greyhound/Trailways** bus station, 2275 Cleveland Ave. (☎ **800/231-2222**).

VISITOR INFORMATION   For advance information about Fort Myers, Fort Myers Beach, and Sanibel and Captiva Islands, contact the **Lee Island Coast Visitor and Convention Bureau,** 2180 W. First St., Fort Myers, FL 33901 (☎ **800/237-6444** or 941/338-3500; fax 941/334-1106; www.leeislandcoast.com).

Once in town, drop by the **Greater Fort Myers Chamber of Commerce Visitor Center,** at the corner of Edwards Drive and Lee Street on the downtown waterfront (☎ **800/366-3622** or 941/332-3624; www.fortmyers.org). The chamber gives away brochures (many of them with discount coupons good at attractions, hotels, and restaurants) and sells a detailed street map of the area. It's open Monday to Friday from 8am to 4:30pm.

The **North Fort Myers Chamber of Commerce** (☎ **941/997-9111**) has an information office at the Shell Factory, 2787 N. Tamiami Trail (U.S. 41).

GETTING AROUND   LeeTran (☎ **941/275-8726**) operates public buses Monday to Saturday from 6:30am to 8pm. One-ride fares are $1 (exact change is required). Orange route no. 50 runs hourly between downtown and the McGregor Point Shopping Center, at McGregor Boulevard and Gladiolus Drive; from there you can catch the Beach Connection Trolley to Fort Myers Beach during the winter months (see "Getting Around," in section 2 of this chapter). This route runs along U.S. 41 past the Greyhound/Trailways bus station and the Edison and Bell Tower malls. System maps are available from the Greater Fort Myers Chamber of Commerce (see "Visitor Information," above). There's no public bus service to Sanibel and Captiva Islands.

For a taxi, call **Yellow Cab** (☎ **941/332-1055**), **Bluebird Taxi** (☎ **941/275-8294**), or **Admiralty Taxi** (☎ **941/275-7000**). Metered fares are $1.35 at flag fall plus $1.35 for each mile.

EXPLORING THE AREA

The easiest way to see the downtown sights is to park free at the Edison and Ford Winter Estates and either take a long walk or ride the narrated **trolley,** which makes a circuit from there to the Burroughs Home, the Fort Myers Historical Museum, and the Imaginarium. It leaves the Edison home parking lot every hour on the hour on Tuesday to Saturday from 10am to 4pm. The fare is $5 for adults, $2 for children, with free reboarding. Tickets include 50¢ off admission to the other attractions.

TOURING THE ESTATES

✪ **Edison and Ford Winter Estates.** 2350 McGregor Blvd. ☎ **941/334-3614** for a recording, or 941/334-7419. Tours of both estates $10 adults, $5 children 6–12, free for children 5 and under. Mon–Sat 9am–4pm, Sun noon–4pm (last tour daily 3:30pm). Closed Thanksgiving and Christmas.

Thomas Edison and his second wife, Mina, brought their family to this Victorian retreat, known as **Seminole Lodge,** in 1886, and wintered here until the inventor's death in 1931. Mrs. Edison gave the 14-acre estate to the city of Fort Myers in 1947, but it stands exactly as it did during Edison's lifetime.

An avid amateur botanist, Edison experimented with the exotic foliage he planted in the lush tropical gardens surrounding the mansion (he turned goldenrod into rubber and used bamboo for lightbulb filaments). Some of his lightbulbs dating from the 1920s still burn in the laboratory where he and his staff worked on some of his 1,093 inventions. The monstrous banyan tree that shades the laboratory was 4 feet tall when Harvey S. Firestone presented it to Edison in 1925; today it's the largest banyan in Florida.

A museum displays some of Edison's inventions, as well as his unique Model T Ford, a gift from friend Henry Ford. In 1916 Ford and his wife, Clara, built **Mangoes,** their bungalow-style house next door, so they could winter with the Edisons. Like Seminole Lodge, Mangoes is furnished as it appeared in the 1920s.

You must visit the homes via guided tours, which depart the visitor center every few minutes.

OTHER DOWNTOWN ATTRACTIONS

The Georgian Revival **Burroughs Home,** 2505 1st St., at Fowler Street (☎ **941/ 332-6125**), was built on the banks of the Caloosahatchee River in 1901 by cattleman John Murphy and later sold to the Burroughs family. You must take a tour in order to visit the premises; they are given on the hour Tuesday to Friday from 11am to 3pm. Admission is $3 for adults, $1 for children 6 to 12, free for children 5 and under. Park free in the Sheraton Harbor Place garage across the street.

Housed in the restored Spanish-style depot served by the Atlantic Coast Line from 1924 to 1971, the **Fort Myers Historical Museum,** 2300 Peck St., at Jackson Street (☎ **941/332-5955**), features exhibits depicting Fort Myers's history from the ancient Calusa peoples and the Spanish conquistadors to the first settlers. A replica of an 1800s "Cracker" home stands outside, as does the Esperanza—the longest and one of the last of the plush Pullman private cars. World War II buffs can see the remains of a P-39 Aircobra, which helps explain the town's role in training fighter pilots back then. Admission is $4 for adults, $2 for children 11 and under. Open Tuesday to Saturday from 9am to 4pm.

Rather than have the kids go stir crazy on a rainy day, head for the **Imaginarium,** 2000 Cranford Ave., at Martin Luther King Jr. Boulevard (☎ **941/337-3332**), an entertaining, hands-on museum in the old city water plant. A host of toylike exhibits explains such basic scientific principles as gravity and the weather. There are nature shows in the theater every hour on the half hour. Admission is $6 for adults, $5.50 for seniors, $3 for children 3 to 12. Open Tuesday to Saturday from 10am to 5pm. Closed Thanksgiving and Christmas.

A NEARBY HISTORICAL ATTRACTION

Koreshan State Historic Site. U.S. 41 at Corkscrew Rd. (15 miles south of downtown Fort Myers). ☎ **941/992-0311.** Admission $3.25 per vehicle, $1 pedestrians or bikers. Park daily 8am–sunset; settlement buildings daily 8am–5pm. From I-75, take Exit 19 and go 2 miles west to U.S. 41.

The Koreshan Unity Movement (pronounced Kor-*esh*-en), a sect led by Chicagoan Cyrus Reed Teed, established a self-sufficient settlement on these 300 acres on the narrow Estero River in 1894. They believed that humans lived *inside* the earth, and, ahead of their time, that women should have equal rights. You can visit their garden and several of their buildings, plus view photos from their archives. Nature and canoe trails wind downriver to Mound Key, an islet made of the shells discarded by the Calusa Indians (see "Great Golf That Won't Break Your Budget & Other Affordable Outdoor Activities," below). There's also a picnic and camping area (see "Accommodations You Can Afford," below).

AN OLD-FASHIONED TRAIN RIDE

The **Seminole Gulf Railway** (☎ 941/275-8487), the original railroad that ran between Fort Myers and Naples, today chugs as far south as Bonita Springs on dinner excursions and sightseeing trips, and there are occasional twilight runs and murder mystery runs. Call for the schedules, which vary from season to season. Reservations are required for the dinner trip. The trains depart Fort Myers from the Metro Mall Station, a small blue building on the western edge of the Metro Mall parking lot on Colonial Boulevard at Metro Parkway. The Bonita Springs station is on Old U.S. 41 at Pennsylvania Avenue.

SHOPPING

An institution for more than 50 years, **The Shell Factory,** 5 miles north of the Caloosahatchee River bridge on U.S. 41 (☎ 941/995-2141), carries one of the world's largest collections of shells, corals, sponges, and fossils. Entire sections are devoted to shell jewelry and shell lamps. Many items here cost under $10, some under $1. Open daily from 10am to 6pm.

Bargain hunters can browse more than 800 booths carrying antiques, crafts, fashions, and produce at **Fleamasters,** 4135 Dr. Martin Luther King Jr. Blvd. (Fla. 82), 1½ miles west of I-75 (☎ 941/334-7001). There are snack bars and entertainment, too. Open on Friday, Saturday, and Sunday from 8am to 4pm. You'll find even more old stuff at **AMTEL Fleamarket Mall,** in the old Metro Mall shopping complex at the corner of Metro Parkway and Colonial Boulevard (☎ 941-939-3132), where stalls are open Wednesday to Sunday from 9am to 5pm.

Anchored by Saks Fifth Avenue and Jacobson's, the Spanish-style **Bell Tower Shops,** Tamiami Trail (U.S. 41) at Daniels Parkway (☎ 941/489-1221), is Fort Myers's upscale mall. Open Monday to Wednesday from 10am to 7pm, Thursday to Saturday from 10am to 9pm, and Sunday from noon to 5pm. You'll find most of the familiar national stores at **Edison Mall,** Cleveland Avenue (U.S. 41) at Winkler Avenue (☎ 941/939-5464), including JC Penney, Sears, Dillards, and a two-part Burdine's. Open Monday to Saturday from 10am to 9pm, Sunday from 11:30am to 5:30pm.

Outlet shoppers will find a large Levi's store among other major-brand shops at the **Sanibel Factory Stores,** on the way to the beaches at the junction of Summerlin Road

Swamp Buggies, Alligators & Panthers

One of the easiest and most informative ways to see Southwest Florida's abundant wildlife is on a "swamp buggy" ride with ✪ **Babcock Wilderness Adventures,** on Fla. 31 about 11 miles northeast of Fort Myers (☎ **800/500-5583** for reservations, 941/338-6367 for information). Experienced naturalists lead 90-minute tours through the Babcock Ranch, the largest contiguous cattle operation east of the Mississippi River and home to countless birds and wildlife as well as domesticated bison and quarter horses. Unlike most wildlife tours in the region, this one covers five different ecosystems, from open prairie to cypress swamp.

You'll see alligators leap from a bridge into the dark-brown waters of the mysterious Telegraph Swamp when your buggy passes overhead, and you'll dismount and visit an enclosure where southern cougars stand in for their close cousins, the rare Florida panthers (which are tan, not black).

A replica of an Old Florida house built by the crew making the Sean Connery movie *Just Cause* serves as a small museum, and a restaurant serves lunch featuring—what else?—alligator bites.

Admission is $17.95 for adults, $9.95 for children 3 to 12. The tours usually leave on the hour between 9am and 3pm from November to April, from 9am to noon from May through October. Reservations are required, so call ahead.

and McGregor Boulevard (☎ **888/SHOP-333** or 941/454-1616). Open Monday to Saturday from 10am to 9pm, Sunday from 11am to 6pm.

GREAT GOLF THAT WON'T BREAK YOUR BUDGET & OTHER AFFORDABLE OUTDOOR ACTIVITIES

CANOEING & KAYAKING   The area's slow-moving rivers and quiet, island-speckled inland waters offer fine canoe and kayak ventures; you'll visit birds and manatees along the way. Two popular local venues are the winding waterways around Pine Island west of town and the Estero River south of Fort Myers. The Estero River route is an official Florida canoe trail and leads 3½ miles from U.S. 41 to Estero Bay, which is itself a state aquatic preserve. Near the mouth of the river lies **Mound Key State Archeological Site,** one of the largest Calusa shell middens. Scholars believe that this mostly artificial island is some 2,000 years old and was the capital of the Calusa chief who ruled all of South Florida when the Spanish arrived. There's no park ranger on the key, but signs explain its history.

Estero River Outfitters, at the Estero River bridge on U.S. 41 (☎ **941/992-4050**), rents canoes for $22.50 to $27.50 a day, and kayaks from $17.50 to $27.50. Open daily 7am to 6pm. Nearby, **Koreshan State Historic Site,** half a mile south of the bridge at the intersection of U.S. 41 and Corkscrew Road (☎ **941/992-0311**), rents canoes for $3 an hour, $15 per day (see "A Nearby Historical Attraction," above).

Based in Matlacha on Pine Island, the **Gulf Coast Kayak Company** (☎ **941/283-1125** or 941/283-6213) has guided nature, manatee-watching, and sunset trips, plus overnight and longer expeditions to North Captiva and Cayo Costa. Call for reservations and schedules.

CRUISES   J. C. Boat Cruises (☎ **941/334-7474**) presents a variety of year-round cruises on the Caloosahatchee River and its tributaries, including lunch and dinner voyages on the sternwheeler *Captain J.P.* The 3-hour Everglades Jungle Cruise is a good way to observe the area's wildlife, with lots of manatees to be seen from November to April. A full-day cruise goes all the way up the Caloosahatchee to Lake Okeechobee and back. The ticket office is at the downtown Fort Myers City Yacht Basin, Edwards Drive at Lee Street, opposite the chamber of commerce. Prices range from $14 to $74. Schedules change and advance reservations are strongly recommended.

Another way to see manatees and other wildlife is with **Fort Myers Manatee and Eco Tours** (☎ 941/693-1434), based at the Coastal Marine Mart on Fla. 80 just east of I-75. Cruises usually depart at 10am, noon, and 2 and 4pm, but call ahead for reservations. Fares are $12.75 for adults, $6.75 for children under 12.

The *Tropic Star* (☎ 941/283-0015) leaves the Four Winds Marina on Pine Island daily at 9:30am for Cayo Costa and Cabbage Key. Fares are $20 for adults, $12 for children 3 to 12. See "Nearby Island Hopping" in section 3, on Sanibel and Captiva Islands, for information about Cayo Costa and Cabbage Key.

The sleek, 100-foot-long yacht *Sanibel Harbour Princess* (☎ 941/644-2128) goes on dinner cruises from its base at Sanibel Harbour Resort & Spa (see "Accommodations You Can Afford," below). Prices range from $25 to $35 per person, depending on the season, but that includes a glass of champagne and buffet dinner nightly and entertainment on weekends. There's a Sunday brunch cruise during winter. Call for reservations and departure times.

GOLF   For an excellent rundown of Southwest Florida golf courses, pick up a free copy of *Golfer's Guide,* available at the visitor information centers and many hotel lobbies. See "The Active Vacation Planner" in chapter 2 for information about subscribing or ordering the current edition. And don't forget that you can call **Tee Times USA** (☎ 800/374-8633 or 888/465-3356) and book starting times at Florida courses.

Although it looks like an exclusive private enclave, the **Fort Myers Country Club,** McGregor Boulevard at Hill Avenue (☎ 941/936-2457), actually is a municipal course. Designed in 1917 by Donald Ross, it's flat and uninteresting by today's standards, but it's right in town. **Smitty's,** a steak and seafood restaurant, now occupies the fine old clubhouse. The city's other municipal course is the more challenging **Eastwood Golf Club,** on Ortiz Avenue between Colonial and Dr. Martin Luther King Jr. boulevards in the eastern suburbs (☎ 941/275-4848). Greens fees at both range from about $30 in summer to $55 during winter. Nonresidents must book tee times at least 24 hours in advance.

Other area courses open to the public include the Tom Fazio–designed **Gateway Golf & Country Club,** on Daniels Parkway east of the airport (☎ 941/561-1010); the two nationally acclaimed **Pelican's Nest** courses in Bonita Springs (☎ 941/947-4600); **Coral Oaks Golf Club** in Cape Coral (☎ 941/283-4800); **Alden Pines Country Club** on Pine Island (☎ 941/283-2179); **San Carolos Golf Club** in South Fort Myers (☎ 941/267-3131); **Bonita Springs Golf & Country Club** in Bonita Springs (☎ 941/992-2800); and **El Rio Golf Club** (☎ 941/995-2204) and **Riverbend Golf Club** (☎ 941/543-2200), both in North Fort Myers.

WATCHING THE BOYS OF SPRING

While many Major League Baseball teams have jumped around Florida for their **spring training,** the Boston Red Sox and the Minnesota Twins have worked out in Fort Myers for years. The **Boston Red Sox** play at the 6,500-seat City of Palms Park, at Edison Avenue and Broadway (☎ 941/334-4700). The **Minnesota Twins** work out at the 7,500-seat Lee County Sports Complex, on Six Mile Cypress Parkway

Fort Myers & Fort Myers Beach

Fort Myers

Edison Bridge
Caloosahatchee Bridge
Caloosahatchee River
41
45
80
Marion St.
1st St.
Edison Ave.
Michigan Ave.
Dr. Martin Luther King Jr. Blvd. 82
Palm Ave.
South St.
Fowler St.
Canal St.
Inhart Ave.
Hanson St.
Cortez Ave.
Cleveland Ave.
Broadway
Todd St.
Palmetto Ave.
Carrell Rd.
867
Winkler Ave.
Metro Pkwy.
McGregor Blvd.
41
45
884
13
14
Colonial Blvd.
869
Airport Rd.

0 .5 mi
.8 km
N

Accommodations:
Best Western
  Pink Shell Resort **17**
Budgetel Inn **13**
Courtyard by Marriott **14**
Holiday Inn **26**
Holiday Inn Central **9**
Holiday Inn
  SunSpree Resort **3**
Island House Motel **18**
Outrigger Beach Resort **25**
Palm Terrace Apartments **22**
Sandpiper Gulf Resort **23**
Sanibel Harbour
  Resort & Spa **15**

Fort Myers Beach

Bodwitch Point
Estero Pass
Hurricane Bay
San Carlos Island
Main St.
San Carlos Blvd.
Matanzas Pass
Hell Peckney Bay
Dog Key
Julies Island
865
Estero Blvd.
ESTERO ISLAND
Starvation Key
Estero Bay
Ostego Bay
Coon Key
Big Carlos Pass
Gulf of Mexico
Carlos Point
Lover's Key

0 .75 mi
1.2 km
N

Attractions:
Burroughs Home **1**
City of Palms Park **8**
Edison & Ford Winter Estates **5**
Fort Myers Historical Museum **7**
Imaginarium **6**
Lover's Key **28**

Dining:
Anthony's on the Gulf **21**
Basile's **12**
Channel Mark **16**
The Chart House **3**
Farmer's Market **10**
Greco's Italian Deli **27**
Italian Fisherman **27**
Loggerheads **27**
Matanazas Inn **19**
Oasis Restaurant **4**
Papa Mondo
  Ristorante Italiano **20**
Sasse's **11**
Shooter's Waterfront
  Cafe USA **2**
Strawberrie Corner Café
  & Ice Cream Parlor **24**

NA-0036

335

Cheap Thrills: What to See & Do for Free (or Almost) in Southwest Florida

- **Catch the "green flash" at sunset.** Like the Tampa Bay Area to the north (see chapter 11), Southwest Florida has mile after mile of beaches facing due west, thus providing glorious sunsets over the Gulf of Mexico and a chance to see the elusive "green flash" the moment the top of the sun dips below the horizon. The best places to watch for free are anywhere along Fort Myers Beach, at Blind Pass between Sanibel and Captiva Islands, from the Naples Pier, and at the public access area on Marco Island's Cresent Beach.

- **Search for oldies but goodies at Fleamasters.** Florida has numerous flea markets where bargain hunters can browse for antiques, crafts, fashions, and fresh produce. With more than 800 busy booths, Fort Myers's weekend **Fleamasters,** 4135 Dr. Martin Luther King Jr. Blvd. (☎ **941/334-7001**), is one of the biggest and best. It has snack bars and entertainment, too.

- **Canoe down a lazy river.** An official Florida canoe trail, the Estero River south of Fort Myers winds its way into Estero Bay, which is itself a state aquatic preserve. Near the mouth of the river lies Mound Key State Archeological Site, a Calusa Indian shell midden dating back some 2,000 years. **Koreshan State Historic Site,** on the river at U.S. 41 and Corkscrew Road (☎ **941/992-0311**), rents canoes for just $3 an hour, $15 per day.

- **Worship at a diamond.** With both the Boston Red Sox (☎ **941/334-4700**) and Minnesota Twins (☎ **800/338-9467** or 941/768-4270) doing their spring training here from mid-February through March, Fort Myers is a great place to see some of your favorite big league baseball stars get ready for the regular grind. Great seats close to the action cost $8 to $11, a bargain compared to what you'll pay when the boys of spring get back north.

- **Love nature on Lover's Key.** Possessed of one of Florida's best undeveloped beaches, the **Lover's Key–Carl E. Johnson State Recreation Area** south of Fort Myers Beach (☎ **941/463-4288**) is a great place to spend a day swimming, sunning, and shelling—a place where you'll find birds instead of condos as your neighbors. It costs $4 to park your car ($2 if you're the only occupant), but you can take the trolley here for 25¢ a head and pay $1 per person to get in. After that, the restrooms, showers, and tram ride through the mangroves to the deserted beach are free.

- **Walk or ride along Wildlife Drive.** The mangrove swamps, winding waterways, and uplands of Sanibel Island's J. N. (Ding) Darling National Wildlife

between Daniels and Metro parkways (☎ **800/338-9467** or 941/768-4270). Tickets to the Red Sox games cost $9 and $10; for the Twins, $8 and $11.

Fort Myers is about an hour's drive south of Charlotte County Stadium (☎ **941/625-9500**), where the **Texas Rangers** hold their spring training. To get there, take I-75 north to Exit 32, then west to the end of Toledo Blade Boulevard. Turn right there onto Fla. 776. The stadium is on the left. Tickets cost $7 to $9.

ACCOMMODATIONS YOU CAN AFFORD

As in the rest of southern Florida, room rates here are highest, and reservations essential, from mid-December to April. Even hotels and motels removed from the beach

Refuge (☎ **941/472-1100**) are great places to see alligators, raccoons, otters, and hundreds of species of birds. You can see many of the creatures from the 5-mile, one-way Wildlife Drive, which costs $4 per vehicle or $1 per pedestrian or biker. A naturalist will explain what you're seeing on a 2-hour narrated tram tour—a very good value at $8 for adults, $4 for children 12 and under.

- **Stoop for shells.** Okay, you'll have to pay a $3 toll to get here and a small fee to park your car (or lock your bike to a tree for nothing), but you can stroll Sanibel Island's world-famous shelling beaches as long as you want for free. After a few hours hunched over in the "Sanibel stoop," you're sure to go home with a prize find or two.

- **Bike on Sanibel Island.** Affluent but nature-loving Sanibel Island has one of the best networks of paved biking-blading-hiking trails in Florida. The trails end at Blind Pass, between Sanibel and Capitva, but catching a sunset here will make every pump of the pedal worth the effort. Ride your own across the 3-mile causeway from Fort Myers to the island, or rent a basic model from several Sanibel firms for $5 per hour or $15 a day.

- **Watch the millionaires from Naples Pier.** Olde Naples residents love to stroll out on their ancient pier to fish, catch a sunset, or look at Millionaires' Row, a string of magnificent mansions along the town's lovely beach. Now a state historic site, the pier is open 24 hours a day and is free, although it will cost you a few quarters to park in the nearby municipal lots.

- **Pretend you're rich on 3rd Street.** It costs not a penny to window-shop the ritzy 3rd Street district in Olde Naples. This town has industrial-strength money, but it's so Midwestern-friendly that nobody will care if you maxed your credit cards just to get here.

- **Hunker down at happy hour.** Right on the beach and facing the glorious gulf sunsets, the chickee hut bar at **Vanderbilt Inn on the Gulf,** a motel about 4 miles north of Olde Naples (☎ **800/643-8654** or 941/597-3151), cuts the price of libation during happy hour Monday to Friday from 4:30 to 8:30 and on Saturday and Sunday from 3:30 to 7:30pm. The place really fills up on Sunday, when bands play. You can almost crawl here after a day on the undeveloped beach at Delnor-Wiggins State Recreation Area, next door.

charge premium rates then. If you can't get a room at the properties mentioned below, the **Lee Island Coast Visitor and Convention Bureau** operates a free **reservation service** (☎ **800/733-7935**) covering many more accommodations in Fort Myers, Fort Myers Beach, and Sanibel and Captiva islands.

Don't be misled by our categories, which are determined by high, winter-season rates. During the off-season they drop by as much as 50% or more. All hotel bills in southwest Florida are subject to a 9% tax.

Many business travelers stay at the **Holiday Inn Central,** 2431 Cleveland Ave. (☎ **800/998-0466** or 941/332-3232), but the location near the corner of Edison Avenue is a plus for vacationers, too; it's a 2-block walk to the Boston Red Sox training facility and a longer walk or a short drive to the Edison and Ford homes. There's an outdoor pool, a 24-hour Denny's restaurant, and a tavern with live entertainment. Winter rates are $129 to $139 double, but they drop to $59 to $85 double off-season.

If you want more space and a kitchen, **Residence Inn by Marriott,** 2960 Colonial Blvd. (☎ **800/331-3131** or 941/936-0110; fax 941/936-4144), diagonally across the intersection from the Courtyard by Marriott (see below), has 78 units ranging from L-shaped suites to two-bedroom apartments. They cost from $139 to $179 during winter, from $79 to $99 off-season, but that includes continental breakfast and weekday cocktail receptions. A similar choice is **Homewood Suites Hotel,** 5255 Big Pine Way (☎ **800/225-5466** or 941/275-6000; fax 941/275-6601), a more luxurious establishment at the Bell Tower Shops complex. It charges $179 to $189 in winter, $109 off-season, including a full breakfast and an evening reception with wine, beer, and an extensive snack buffet from which you can graze a light meal. Both hotels have pools, exercise rooms, and coin laundries.

On Daniels Parkway near the airport at Exit 22 off I-75 are completely modern versions of **Hampton Inn** (☎ **800/426-7866** or 941/768-2525), **Comfort Suites** (☎ **800/435-8234** or 941/768-0005), and **Sleep Inn** (☎ **800/358-3170** or 941/561-1117).

The only true campground here is about 15 miles south of downtown Fort Myers at **Koreshan State Historic Site,** on U.S. 41 in Estero (☎ **941/992-0311;** fax 941/992-1607), which has 60 wooded sites for tents or RVs at $16 per night during winter, $10 a night off-season (see "A Nearby Historical Attraction," above, for information about the historic site). Reservations are accepted up to 11 months in advance year-round.

Super-Cheap Sleeps

Fort Myers has almost every chain motel along Cleveland Avenue (U.S. 41), in all price ranges. Among the least expensive is the local **Motel 6** (☎ **800/466-8356** or 941/656-5544; fax 941/656-6276), a converted older property just across the river in North Fort Myers. Double rooms cost just $56 in winter, $36 off-season. South of downtown are an **Econo Lodge** (☎ **800/553-2666** or 941/995-0571); a **La Quinta Inn,** 4850 S. Cleveland Ave. (☎ **800/531-5900** or 941/275-3300); a **Ramada Limited** (☎ **800/272-6232** or 941/275-1111); and a **Red Carpet Inn** (☎ **800/251-1962** or 941/9366-3229).

✪ **Budgetel Inn.** 2717 Colonial Blvd., Fort Myers, FL 33907. ☎ **800/428-3438** or 941/275-3500. Fax 941/275-5426. 122 units. A/C TV TEL. Winter $79–$89 single or double. Off-season $42–$46 single or double. Rates include continental breakfast. AE, DC, DISC, MC, V.

Like most members of the small but growing Budgetel Inn chain, this modern, 4-story establishment offers exceptional value with its large, well-equipped rooms. It's centrally situated near the Courtyard by Marriott and Residence Inn by Marriott (see above), and offers an outdoor swimming pool. Entered from exterior walkways, the comfortably furnished rooms have extras like coffeemakers, desks, and free local calls (I consider Budgetel Inns to be the poor person's Courtyard by Marriott). Complimentary juice and a Danish are left at your door before dawn.

For a Few Bucks More

✪ **Courtyard by Marriott.** 4455 Metro Pkwy. (at Colonial Blvd.), Fort Myers, FL 33901. ☎ **800/321-2211** or 941/275-8600. Fax 941/275-7087. 149 units. A/C TV TEL. Winter $129 single or double. Off-season $64 single or double. Weekend rates available. AE, DC, DISC, MC, V.

This exceptionally comfortable hotel designed for business travelers is situated out of the major traffic, 4 miles south of downtown and 10 miles north of the beach.

Surrounding a landscaped courtyard with a swimming pool, the sizable rooms all have sofas or easy chairs and rich mahogany writing tables and chests of drawers, plus extra little features like two phones and hand-basin faucets dispensing piping-hot water for tea and instant coffee (which are supplied). The marble lobby features a fireplace and dining area serving breakfast only. Other facilities include an exercise room, indoor spa pool, and guest laundry.

Holiday Inn SunSpree Resort. 2220 W. 1st St. (at Euclid Ave.), Fort Myers, FL 33901. ☎ **800/HOLIDAY** or 941/334-3434. Fax 941/334-3844. 152 units. A/C TV TEL. Winter $119–$169 single or double. Off-season $79–$129 single or double. AE, DC, DISC, MC, V.

This islandy riverside hotel is best known locally for the adjacent Shooters Waterfront Café USA, an enormously popular restaurant and bar (see "Greats Deals on Dining," below). Some of the suites are near the outdoor bar where Shooters' bands play, which can mean a bit too much entertainment for some guests' ears (others love the constant nighttime action). Rooms at the front the property, however, are far enough removed to render a quiet and convenient base from which to explore the nearby Edison and Ford Winter Estates and other downtown attractions.

The L-shaped building flanks a large courtyard with both adults' and children's pools surrounded by palms and a colorful patio. There's a fenced children's playground adjacent. Other facilities include a beauty salon with massage, an activities desk, and a small reading room off the marble-floored lobby. Shooters opens for breakfast at 7am daily, and the Oasis Restaurant is virtually across the street (see "Greats Deals on Dining," below).

WORTH A SPLURGE

✪ **Sanibel Harbour Resort & Spa.** 17260 Harbour Pointe Rd., Fort Myers, FL 33908. ☎ **800/767-7777** or 941/466-4000. Fax 941/466-2150. www.sanibel-resort.com. 240 units, 80 double condo apts. A/C MINIBAR TV TEL. Winter $270–$325 single or double; $335 suite; $320–$599 condo apt. Off-season $130–$225 single or double; $240 suite; $169–$449 condo apt. Packages available. AE, DC, DISC, MC, V. Valet parking $8, free self-parking. Take the last exit off Summerlin Rd. before the Sanibel Causeway toll plaza.

Tennis fans take note: One of Florida's best-known sports resorts, this secluded, sports-oriented complex includes a 5,000-seat stadium that has hosted Davis Cup matches in the past, and if you opt for an off-season package deal, you might even be able to afford honing your skills here yourself. It overlooks San Carlos Bay and Sanibel Island from Punta Rassa, next to the Sanibel Causeway (a complimentary shuttle takes guests to the island three times a day). A waterside cupola-topped pavilion evokes the turn-of-the-century resort that once stood on this point, but the 11-story hotel is modern and luxurious throughout, and there's a selection of fully-equipped condo apartments in two buildings next door. The more expensive rooms and some of the condos have wonderful water and island views from their balconies, including spectacular sunsets over Sanibel. This large hostelry hosts many conventions and groups, although active couples make up a sizable portion of its clientele.

The intimate Chez Le Bear leads the food outlets here, with the casual Promenade providing calorie-conscious fare for the pumping-iron set. Lounges have entertainment during the winter season, and there's a sports bar. Other amenities here include a concierge desk, room service (5am to midnight), laundry, children's activity program, state-of-the-art, 40,000-square-foot fitness center with spa, massage, and facials. Other sporting facilities include bay-side indoor and outdoor swimming pools with hot tubs and bars; 13 lighted tennis courts; jogging, fitness, and kayak trails; and a marina with boat and water-sports equipment rentals and day and sunset cruises. Except for sunset cruises, only guests can use the facilities here, and they pay extra for most activities.

GREAT DEALS ON DINING

Some Southwest Florida restaurants adjust their hours from season to season and even from year to year, so you may want to call ahead to make sure of an establishment's business hours.

Fort Myers's main commercial strip, Cleveland Avenue (U.S. 41), has most national fast-food and family chain restaurants, especially near College Parkway. There's a branch of **Mel's Diner,** an excellent regional chain, at 4820 S. Cleveland Ave., opposite Page Field (☎ 941/275-7850), offering inexpensive diner-style fare including breakfast served anytime.

SUPER-CHEAP EATS

Basile's. In the Edison Park Shopping Center, 2215-C Winkler Ave. (between Cleveland Ave. and Fowler St., opposite Edison Mall). ☎ **941/278-4600.** Reservations recommended in winter. Pastas and main courses $8–$14; early bird specials $14 (for 2 persons). MC, V. Mon–Fri 11am–10pm, Sat noon–10pm, Sun noon–9:30pm. ITALIAN.

Transplanted New Yorker Sal Basile's small dining room has a wall-size mural of an Italian scene to set the stage for food reminiscent of Little Italy. You can order the usual run of pastas, or try the veal with shrimps and scallops in a delightful cream sauce. The portions are huge and are accompanied by soup, salad, and very garlicky homemade rolls. These same monstrous meals are offered for lunch at greatly reduced prices, and complete dinners for two are served on Friday, Saturday, and Sunday for $12.95. Early birds get a choice of pastas.

The adjoining **Taste of New York** (same phone) has excellent pizza to dine in or carryout.

✪ **Farmers Market Restaurant.** 2736 Edison Ave. (at Cranford Ave.). ☎ **941/ 334-1687.** Breakfast $3–$5; sandwiches $2–$6; meals $4–$8. No credit cards. Mon–Sat 6am–8pm, Sun 6am–7pm. SOUTHERN.

The retail Farmers Market next door may be tiny, but the best of the cabbage, okra, green beans, and tomatoes end up here at this plain and simple restaurant frequented by everyone from business executives to truck drivers. The specialties of the house are smoked beef, pork barbecue, and other Southern favorites like country-fried steak, fried chicken livers and gizzards, and smoked ham hocks with a bowl of black-eyed peas. Yankees can order fried chicken, roast beef, or pork chops, and they can have hash browns instead of grits with their big breakfast.

Oasis Restaurant. In Edison-Ford Sq., 2222 McGregor Blvd. (at Euclid Ave.). ☎ **941/ 334-1566.** Breakfast $3–$6; sandwiches, burgers, and salads $4–$5.50. No credit cards. Mon–Fri 7am–3pm, Sat–Sun 8am–2pm. AMERICAN.

Near the Edison and Ford homes, Bonnie Grunberg and Tammie Shockey work hard to make their narrow storefront establishment appeal to young professionals who don't mind sitting elbow to elbow while recovering from a night at Shooters Waterfront Café USA (just behind this shopping center) with a "hangover" omelette—Italian sausage and vegetables under melted cheese. Breakfast fare is served all day here, and you can take advantage of a $1.99 eye-opening special weekdays from 7 to 9:30am. Lunches provide made-to-order Reubens, Monte Cristos, and Philly cheese steak subs, plus soups and salads.

FOR A FEW BUCKS MORE

✪ **Sasse's.** 3651 Evans Ave. (between Carrell Rd. and Winkler Ave.). ☎ **941/278-5544.** Reservations not accepted. Main courses $8–$18. No credit cards. Tues–Fri 11:30am–1:15pm, Wed–Sat 5:30–8:15pm. CONTINENTAL/ITALIAN.

In a small shopping strip near the Fort Myers Recreation Center north of the Edison Mall, this popular little spot offers one of the area's most unusual and reasonably priced dining experiences. Aromas waft from the wood-fired oven in the open kitchen, from which comes enormous slabs of pizzalike bread (served with seasoned olive oil for dipping) and the likes of log-roasted lemon chicken. The selections change daily, although you can usually count on braised lamb shank served over steamed vegetables, and veal scallopini stuffed with prosciutto, roasted peppers, and mozzarella. It's all of a quality rarely found at these prices, and the portions are so huge that most patrons carry home doggie bags (there's a $5 fee to share a single dish). The storefront setting is too cramped for romantic dining, but it's fun and the food is certainly worth putting up with the din of busily working chefs and happily chatting diners.

Shooters Waterfront Café USA. At Holiday Inn Sunspree Resort, 2220 W. 1st St. (at Euclid Ave.). ☎ **941/334-2727.** Reservations not accepted. Salads and sandwiches $6–$10; main courses $10–$16; Sun brunch $15. AE, DC, DISC, MC, V. Daily 7–10am and 11am–11pm (bar open later); Sun brunch 10am–2pm. AMERICAN.

Granted, this pub gets noisy and crowded after sunset, when it turns into Fort Myers's most popular watering hole, but the entire north wall slides open to a river-side deck, making this the most attractive spot in town for a relaxing, alfresco lunch break while seeing the sights or for watching the sun set over the Caloosahatchee. The cuisine is typically modern pub fare: a variety of pizzas, California-style pastas, grilled fish, seafood platters, steaks, and prime rib. The best bet for lunch is the reliable grouper (fried, blackened, or grilled) sandwich.

FORT MYERS AFTER DARK

For entertainment ideas and schedules, consult the daily *News-Press,* especially Friday's "Gulf Coasting" section. Also be on the lookout for "Happenings," a tabloid-size entertainment guide that is distributed free at the visitor information offices and in some hotel lobbies.

THE PERFORMING ARTS   The city's showcase performing arts venue is the $7 million **Barbara B. Mann Performing Arts Hall,** 8099 College Pkwy., at Summerlin Road (☎ **941/489-3033**), on the campus of Edison Community College. It features world-famous performers, Broadway plays, and wintertime concerts by the **Southwest Florida Symphony** (☎ 941/**433-3040** for information, or 941/481-4849 for tickets).

Originally a downtown vaudeville playhouse, the 1908-vintage **Arcade Theater,** 2267 1st St. (☎ **941/332-6688**), presents a variety of performances.

THE CLUB & BAR SCENE   Leading the bar scene, **Shooters Waterfront Café USA,** at the Holiday Inn SunSpree Resort, 2220 W. 1st St. (☎ **941/334-2727**), has live bands or a DJ spinning CDs almost every night at a riverside "chickee hut," a thatched-roof bar. National musicians often perform in the casual **Upstairs Bar & Bistro** above Peter's La Cuisine, 2224 Bay St. (☎ **941/332-2228**); recent guests have included Maria Muldaur, Matt "Guitar" Murphy, Debbie Davis, and Savoy Brown.

If you *must* watch your favorite team play back home, **Slugger's Sports Bar & Grill,** 16440 S. Tamiami Trail (U.S. 41), at Island Park Drive, about 12 miles south of downtown (☎ **941/489-0505**), is the largest such facility in the region, with nearly two dozen TV screens. Families are welcome, if they can stand the smoke (cigars are allowed in one corner).

2 Fort Myers Beach

13 miles S of Fort Myers, 28 miles N of Naples, 12 miles E of Sanibel Island

Often overshadowed by trendy Sanibel and Captiva Islands to the north and ritzy Naples to the south, down-to-earth Fort Myers Beach on Estero Island offers just as much sun and sand—and at less-expensive prices—as its affluent neighbors.

Droves of both families and young singles flock to the busy intersection of San Carlos and Estero boulevards, an area so packed with bars, beach apparel shops, restaurants, and motels that the locals call it "Times Square." The city has spiffed up Times Square lately by installing a pedestrian-only mall and improving traffic flow, and some of the establishments have been upgraded.

That Coney Island image certainly doesn't apply to the rest of Estero Island, where old-fashioned beach cottages, manicured condos, and quiet motels beckon couples and families in search of more sedate vacations. In fact, promoters of the southern end of the island say that they're not in Fort Myers Beach; they're on Estero Island. It's their way of distinguishing their part of town from congested Times Square.

The island is separated from the mainland by narrow Matanzas Pass and broad Estero Bay. While the pass is the area's largest commercial fishing port (when they say "fresh off the boat" here, they aren't kidding), the bay is an official state aquatic preserve inhabited by a host of birds as well as manatees, dolphins, and other sea life. Nature cruises go forth onto this lovely protected bay, which is dotted with islands.

A few miles south of Fort Myers Beach, a chain of pristine barrier islands includes unspoiled Lover's Key, a state park where a tractor-pulled tram runs through a mangrove forest to a lovely beach.

ESSENTIALS

GETTING THERE   From Fort Myers, take either McGregor Boulevard or Summerlin Road and turn left on San Carlos Boulevard (County Road 865). From I-75 and the airport, follow Daniels Parkway (which becomes Cypress Lake Drive after it crosses U.S. 41) due west. Turn left on Summerlin Road, then left again on San Carlos Boulevard. From Naples, take either I-75 or U.S. 41 north to Bonita Springs, then go west on Bonita Beach Road (County Road 865), which turns north into Estero Boulevard through Fort Myers Beach.

See section 1 of this chapter, on Fort Myers, for information about Southwest Florida International Airport, car-rental firms, Amtrak's trains, and Greyhound/ Trailways bus service to the area.

VISITOR INFORMATION   The **Fort Myers Beach Chamber of Commerce,** 17200 San Carlos Blvd., Fort Myers Beach, FL 33931 (☎ **800/782-9283** or 941/454-7500; fax 941/454-7910; www.coconet.com/fmbeach), provides free information, sells a detailed street map for $1, and operates a visitor welcome center on the mainland portion of San Carlos Boulevard just south of Summerlin Road. Open Monday to Friday from 8am to 6pm, Saturday from 10am to 6pm, and Sunday from 11am to 5pm.

Over at the beach, the **Tourist Information Center** on Estero Boulevard at Chapel Street (☎ **941/463-3178**) is operated by Hussey Real Estate, but it's a good source for maps and brochures as well as reservations at hotels, motels, condos, and cottages. It's open Monday to Friday from 10am to 6pm, Saturday and Sunday from 10am to 4pm.

GETTING AROUND   An alternative to heavy wintertime traffic and limited parking is the **Beach Connection Trolley,** which during winter operates daily from

8am to 8pm between Summerlin Square Shopping Center, at Summerlin Road and San Carlos Boulevard on the mainland, and Bonita Beach. The route takes it along the full length of Estero Boulevard, including Lover's Key. During the off-season it runs from Bowditch Regional Park at the north end of Estero Boulevard south to Lover's Key. It costs 25¢ per ride. Ask your hotel staff or call **LeeTran** (☎ **941/275-8726**) for schedules.

During the winter LeeTran also operates a Monday-to-Saturday beach shuttle from the parking lots at the Summerlin Square Shopping Center, Summerlin Road at San Carlos Boulevard; the Sanibel Factory Outlets, Summerlin Road at McGregor Boulevard; the McGregor Point Shopping Center, Gladiolus Drive at McGregor Boulevard; and the Main Street Park 'n' Ride Lot on San Carlos Island. The Main Street–Bowditch Park section also runs on Sunday. The shuttle fare is $1.

For a cab, call **Local Motion Taxi** (☎ **941/463-4111**).

There are no bike paths per se here, although many folks ride along the paved shoulders of Estero Boulevard. A variety of rental bikes, scooters, and in-line skates are available at **Fun Rentals,** 1901 Estero Blvd. at Ohio Avenue (☎ **941/463-8844**), and **Scooters, Inc.,** 1698 Estero Blvd. at Avenue E (☎ **941/463-1007**). Both charge about $20 a day for scooters, from $6 for 2 hours to $14 a day for scooters.

HITTING THE BEACH

A prime attraction for beachgoers is the gorgeous ✪ **Lover's Key–Carl E. Johnson State Recreation Area,** 8700 Estero Blvd. (☎ **941/463-4288**), on the totally preserved Lover's Key, south of Estero Island. Although the highway runs down the center of the island, access to this unspoiled beach from the parking lot is restricted to footpaths or a tractor-pulled tram through a bird-filled forest of mangroves and casuarinas. The beach itself is known for its multitude of shells. There are bath houses with outdoor showers, a snack shop, and canoe and kayak rentals at the parking lot. The park is open daily from 8am to 5pm. Admission is $4 per vehicle with two to eight occupants, $2 for vehicles with a single occupant, and $1 for pedestrians and bicyclists. No alcohol is allowed, nor are pets permitted on the beach or in the water (you must keep them on a leash elsewhere in the park).

On Estero Island, **Lynn Hall Memorial Park** features a fishing pier and beach right in the middle of Times Square. It has changing rooms, rest rooms, and one of the few public parking lots in the area; the meter costs 75¢ per hour, but keep it fed—there's a $32 fine if your time runs out! At the island's north end, **Bowditch Regional Park** has picnic tables, cold-water showers, and changing rooms. It has parking only for drivers with disabled permits, but it's the turnaround point for the Beach Connection Trolley.

Several beach locations are hotbeds of parasailing, Wave Runners, sailboats, and other beach activities. **Times Square,** at the intersection of San Carlos and Estero boulevards, and the **Best Western Beach Resort,** about a quarter mile north, are popular spots on Estero's busy north end. Another hotbed is on the beach in front of **Anthony's on the Gulf** restaurant and the **Junkanoo Beach Bar** in the middle beach area (see "Greats Deals on Dining," below). Down south, activities are centered around the **Holiday Inn** and the **Outrigger Beach Resort** (see "Accommodations You Can Afford," below).

AFFORDABLE OUTDOOR ACTIVITIES

BOATING & BOAT RENTALS   Powerboats are available from the **Mid Island Marina** (☎ **941/765-4371**), the **Fort Myers Beach Marina** (☎ **941/463-9552**), the **Fish Tale Marina** (☎ **941/463-3600**), the **Palm Grove Marina** (☎ **941/**

463-7333), and the **Summer Winds Marina** (☎ 941/454-6333). **Dockside Boat Rentals** (☎ 941/765-4433) rents powerboats at the Best Western Pink Shell Resort on Estero Island's northern end.

CRUISES   Two of the best environmental tours in this area are with ✪ **Calusa Coast Outfitters,** 7225 Estero Blvd., at the Fish Tale Marina behind Villa Santini shopping center (☎ 941/463-4448). Guests who go with Arden Arrington, a director of the Southwest Florida Historical Society, can listen through hydrophones as dolphins "speak" to each other, or they can go on a guided walk on historic Mound Key, the old Calusa Indian shell island at the mouth of the Estero River. Arden's 3-hour dolphin tours depart Tuesday and Thursday at 2pm and cost $28.50 for adults, $25 for seniors, $14 for kids under 13. The Mound Key trips depart Tuesday and Thursday at 10am (they involve considerable hiking at Mound Key and are not recommended for children or adults with health problems). They cost $28.50 for adults. Reservations are required for all trips, so call ahead.

Another way to see the dolphins up close is on a Wave Runner tour with **Holiday Water Sports,** which operates on the beach in front of the **Best Western Pink Shell** (☎ 941/765-4386) and the **Best Western Beach Resort** (☎ 941/463-6778), both north of Times Square. They don't do these exciting excursions all the time, so call for details.

Much easier nature excursions are on the *Island Queen* (☎ 941/765-4433), a pontoon boat that operates out of the Best Western Pink Shell Beach Resort marina on the north end of the island (see "Accommodations You Can Afford," below). It usually goes on 1½-hour nature cruises Monday, Wednesday, and Friday afternoons. Prices are $12.50 for adults, $7 for children. The *Island Queen* also has bay fishing trips Monday, Wednesday, and Friday mornings ($25 adults, $22.50 children) and shelling trips on Thursday ($25 adults, $12 children). Reservations are recommended.

A similar pontoon boat, the *Pelican Queen,* operates from **Mid Island Marina,** 4765 Estero Blvd. (☎ 941/765-4354). It has sightseeing nature cruises from 10am to 1pm Monday to Saturday, with adults paying $14, children $8.

For sailing enthusiasts, the 72-foot topsail schooner *Island Rover* (☎ 941/691-7777) has morning family cruises, afternoon sunbathing excursions, sunset sails, and moonlight cruises on the gulf from its base under the Sky Bridge on Estero Island. Prices are $15 for adults, $10 for children on the day sails, $25 per person for the sunset and moonlight trips. Soft drinks, beer, wine, and champagne are available onboard. The schedule changes by season, so call ahead for information and reservations. The *Island Rover* also is available for "boat-and-breakfast" cruises during the winter months, with rates starting at $149 double.

FISHING   Anglers can surf-cast, throw their lines off the pier at Times Square, or venture offshore on a number of charter fishing boats that dock at marinas under both ends of the Skyway Bridge. Agents have booths there to take reservations even when the boats are out.

No reservations are required on "party boats" that take groups out from December to April. The *Black Whale III* (☎ 941/765-5550) and the *Island Lady* (☎ 941/936-7470), are docked at Fisherman's Wharf, virtually under the San Carlos Island end of the Skyway Bridge. The **Miss Point Lookout III** (☎ 941/765-7786) is based at the Palm Grove Marina, on Main Street on San Carlos Island. The *Great Getaway* and *Great Getaway II* (☎ 941/466-3600) sail from the Getaway Marina on San Carlos Boulevard about half a mile north of the bridge. They all depart between 8 and 9:30am, charge between $25 and $40 per person, depending on the length of the voyage, and have air-conditioned lounges with bars.

GOLF & TENNIS   Before heading to the more challenging mainland courses, duffers can tune their game at the par 61 **Bay Beach Golf Club,** 7401 Estero Blvd. (☎ **941/463-2064**). It's open to the public daily from 7:30am to 5pm. Bay Beach Golf Club also has tennis courts available.

SCUBA DIVING & SNORKELING   Scuba diving is available at **Seahorse Scuba,** 17849 San Carlos Blvd. (☎ **941/454-3111**). Two-tank dives cost about $55. Groups of four snorkelers can go on their own excursions for $25 each, including equipment. The company also offers dive packages including bed-and-breakfast accommodation.

ACCOMMODATIONS YOU CAN AFFORD

The hostelries recommended below are removed from the crowds of Times Square, but three chain motels offer comfortable accommodations right in the center of the action: **Ramada Inn** (☎ 800/544-4592 or 941/463-6158), **Days Inn** (☎ **800/ 544-4592** or 941/463-9759), and **Howard Johnson's Motel** (☎ **800/544-4592** or 941/463-9231). The midrise **Best Western Beach Resort** (☎ 800/336-4045 or 941/ 463-6000) is a quarter mile north, just far enough to escape the noise but still have a lively beach.

Fort Myers Beach has a multitude of condominiums and cottages for rent. The Best Western Pink Shell Resort (see below) has a selection of luxurious condos and some of the most charming cottages. A number of agents offer weekly or monthly rentals, including **Hussey Real Estate** (☎ **941/463-3178;** fax 941/463-5434), which operates the "Tourist Information Center" on Estero Boulevard (see "Essentials," above), and **Bluebill Properties** (☎ **800/237-2010** or 941/463-1141), which represents properties throughout Southwest Florida. The chamber of commerce (see "Essentials," above) publishes a complete list of accommodations and rental agents.

For information about rate seasons, see "Accommodations You Can Afford" in section 1.

For campers, the somewhat cramped **Red Coconut RV Resort,** 3001 Estero Blvd. (☎ **941/463-7200;** fax 941/463-2609), has sites for RVs and tents both on the gulf side of the road and right on the beach. They cost $36 to $49 a night during winter, $24.50 to $44 off-season.

SUPER-CHEAP SLEEPS

Island House Motel. 701 Estero Blvd., Fort Myers Beach, FL 33931. ☎ **941/463-9282.** Fax 941/463-2080. 5 units. A/C TV TEL. Winter $99 single or double. Off-season $49 single or double. Weekly rates available. MC, V.

Sitting on stilts in the Old Florida fashion, but with modern furnishings, Ken and Sylvia Lachapelle's clapboard-sided establishment enjoys a quiet location directly across the boulevard from the Best Western Beach Resort and within walking distance of busy Times Square. Four of their units have screened porches; all have kitchens and ceiling fans. Ken and Sylvia maintain an open-air lounge with a small library beneath one of the units. They also have a small pool and sundeck area, a guest laundry, beach chairs, and they provide free local calls. Book as early as possible for February and March.

Palm Terrace Apartments. 3333 Estero Blvd., Fort Myers Beach, FL 33931. ☎ **800/ 320-5783** or 941/765-5783. Fax 941/765-5783. 9 apts. A/C TV TEL. Winter $82–$125 apt. Off-season $48–$80 apt. Weekly rates available. AE, DISC, MC, V.

Many European guests stay in these comfortable, well-maintained apartments about midway down the beach. The smaller, less-expensive units are on the ground level, with sliding glass doors opening to a grassy yard, but even they have cooking facilities including microwave ovens. Most units here are upstairs, with screened porches or decks overlooking a courtyard with a heated swimming pool. There's beach access across Estero Boulevard, and Anthony's on the Gulf and the Junkanoo Beach Bar are 3 short blocks away.

For a Few Bucks More

Holiday Inn. 6890 Estero Blvd., Fort Myers Beach, FL 33931. ☎ **800/465-4329** or 941/463-5711. Fax 941/463-7038. 105 units. A/C TV TEL. Winter $179–$209 single or double. Off-season $89–$139 single or double. AE, DISC, MC, V.

Built by the shifting sands, the slowly emerging Little Estero Island (actually a peninsula) has left the surf a considerable distance from this modern, 2-story motel, the center of beach activity on Estero's south end. Guests need not walk far to a courtyard swimming pool, tiki bar, and grill serving lunches and snacks. Beachfront suites are the choice accommodation here. Otherwise, you're better off paying a little more for a room facing the central courtyard rather than one looking out on the parking lots. The shops and restaurants of Villa Santini Plaza are a short walk away. With many European guests, staff here is multilingual.

The dining room serves breakfast, lunch, and dinner and has entertainment Wednesday to Sunday. Amenities include room service (7am to 9pm), laundry, free morning newspaper, outdoor pool, two lighted tennis courts, Wave Runners and parasailing, shuffleboard courts, coin laundry, and gift shop.

✪ **Outrigger Beach Resort.** 6200 Estero Blvd. (P.O. Box 271), Fort Myers Beach, FL 33931. ☎ **800/749-3131** or 941/463-3131. Fax 941/463-6577. www.outriggerfmb.com. E-mail: rooms@outriggerfmb.com. 144 units. A/C TV TEL. Winter $105–$195 single or double. Off-season $80–$135 single or double. DISC, MC, V.

The same friendly owners have maintained this clean, pleasant gulf-side motel since 1965. Their "garden efficiencies" in the original building have the feel of small cottages, with excellent ventilation through both front and rear windows and doors opening to backyard decks. Other buildings here are 2-story blocks containing motel-style rooms and efficiencies. The latter have window-style air-conditioning units but also sport front and rear jalousie windows to let in natural breezes. While some rooms have views of the parking lot, most face a courtyard with a swimming pool, a large wooden deck for sunning, and a friendly beachside tiki bar that dispenses libations until 8pm and is one of the best places here for a sunset cocktail. The Deckside Café serves inexpensive breakfasts and is open for sandwiches and snacks until 8pm. There's a coin laundry on the premises.

Sandpiper Gulf Resort. 5550 Estero Blvd., Fort Myers Beach, FL 33931. ☎ **941/463-5721.** Fax 941/463-5721, ext. 299. 63 units. A/C TV TEL. Winter $115–$145 suite. Off-season $69–$89 suite. DISC, MC, V.

The suites at this clean gulf-side motel all have living and sleeping areas, full kitchens, convertible sofas, and sundecks overlooking either the gulf or a courtyard with a heated swimming pool and hot tub. Steps lead from the bedecked pool directly to the beach. Some suites are in 2- or 3-story buildings arranged in a U with the flattened ends right on the beach; others are in the Sandpiper II, a palm-fronted high-rise with its own heated pool next door. All suites are identical, but those facing the beach are more expensive. Facilities include a coin laundry and gift shop. Restaurants are nearby.

Worth a Splurge

✪ **Best Western Pink Shell Beach Resort.** 275 Estero Blvd., Fort Myers Beach, FL 33931. ☎ **800/554-5454** or 941/463-6161. Fax 941/481-4947. 208 units. A/C TV TEL. Winter $185–$259 single or double, $239–$395 condo or cottage. Off-season $119–$155 single or double, $135–$289 condo or cottage. Packages and weekly rates available. AE, DC, DISC, MC, V.

Not to be confused with the nearby Best Western Beach Resort, this popular, family oriented establishment is quietly situated near Estero's north end; it fronts both the gulf and Matanzas Pass. It has hotel rooms, suites, one- and two-bedroom apartments, and beach cottages. Making up for a lack of luxury with lots of 1950s-style charm, the cottages are heavily booked during the winter months, so reserve early. The so-called villas here actually are spacious and luxurious apartments in one of two midrise, gulf-front buildings with lovely views of Sanibel Island from their screened balconies. The second midrise holds the hotel rooms and standard efficiencies, the least expensive units here.

The gulf beach side of the property has water-sports equipment to rent, three heated swimming pools, a kiddie pool, and a chickee hut bar serving libation and sporting entertainment at sunset time. Sailboats and nature and sightseeing cruises pick up guests at the bay-side marina, which rents boats. Facilities also include a coin laundry, store for buying victuals, lighted tennis courts, and rental bikes. Every unit has cooking facilities, but the Hungry Pelican Café, on a deck overlooking the channel, serves breakfast, lunch, and dinner.

GREAT DEALS ON DINING

The busy area around Times Square has fast-food joints to augment several local restaurants catering to the beach crowds. The pick is the **Beach Pierside Grill,** directly on the beach at the foot of Lynn Hall Memorial Pier (☎ **941/765-7800**), a lively pub that bears the bright blond wood trim and vivid fabric colors reminiscent of establishments in Miami's South Beach. It all opens onto a large beachside patio with dining at umbrella tables, outstanding sunsets, and live bands playing at night. The reasonably priced fare is a catchall of conch fritters, shrimp and fish baskets, burgers, and seafood main courses. They take reservations, a plus in this busy area. Food is served daily from 11am to 11pm, and the bar stays open till past midnight daily during summer, on weekends off-season.

Although it was closed and awaiting new owners during my recent visit, you may want to check out the **Gulf Shore Restaurant,** on the beach at 1270 Estero Blvd. (☎ **941/463-9951**). Home of the Crescent Beach Casino back in the 1920s, this old clapboard building offers splendid views of the gulf and beach. The adjacent Cottage Bar was expected to resume its role as the most infamous watering hole on the beach.

You'll find a row of national chain family restaurants at the Summerlin Square shopping center, on the mainland at San Carlos Boulevard and Summerlin Road. The beach trolley runs to Summerlin Square during the winter.

SUPER-CHEAP EATS

Greco's Italian Deli. In Villa Santini Plaza, 7205 Estero Blvd. ☎ **941/463-5634.** Subs and sandwiches $4–$5; pizzas $12–$15; ready-to-cook meals $6–$8. No credit cards. Winter Mon–Sat 8am–6pm. Off-season Mon–Sat 8am–5pm. ITALIAN.

Wonderful aromas of baking pizza, calzone, cannoli, bread, and cookies have been wafting from Greco's since 1958. Order at the counter over a deli case packed with fresh deli meats, Italian sausage, and cheeses; then devour your goodies at tables inside, out on the covered walkway, or take them to the beach for a picnic. You can also take "heat-and-eat" meals of spaghetti, lasagne, eggplant parmigiana, manicotti, and ravioli back to your hotel or condo oven. Shelves are loaded with Italian wines, pastas, butter cookies, and anisette toast.

Strawberrie Corner Café & Ice Cream Parlor. 6035 Estero Blvd. ☎ **941/463-1155.** Menu items $4–$6. No credit cards. Daily 11am–9:30pm. Closed Sept. DELI.

YOUR WILLPOWER ENDS HERE warns a sign on the front door of this bright ice-cream parlor and deli on Estero Boulevard's only sharp curve, known as Strawberry

Corner. Strawberry-print wallpaper, strawberry dolls, and photos of strawberries provide the decor, and strawberry shortcake is the house specialty. In addition, the menu offers terrific homemade soups, seafood salads, and made-to-order deli sandwiches. Each white table here is adorned with colorful fresh flowers.

FOR A FEW BUCKS MORE

Anthony's on the Gulf. 3040 Estero Blvd., on the beach at Donora Blvd. ☎ **941/ 463-2600.** Reservations not accepted. Pasta $9–$13; main courses $13–19; burgers and sandwiches $5–$7. AE, DISC, MC, V. Daily 11:30am–11pm (Sun–Thurs 11:30am–10pm off-season). ITALIAN.

Right on the beach and above the constant party in the Junkanoo Beach Bar downstairs (see "Fort Myers Beach After Dark," below), this establishment has large windows with gulf views and the appropriately named Sunset Terrace, one of the better places on the island for a day-ending cocktail or an alfresco lunch or dinner. Inside, a casual, unpretentious tropical ambience is enhanced by an old-fashioned, pole-driven ceiling fan reaching the full length of the dining room. This setting more than makes up for a somewhat less-than-inspired menu offering traditional Italian pizzas and pastas, and main courses of veal, chicken, and seafood. Sandwiches and burgers are available at all hours here.

If Italian isn't your forte, the **Beach Light Grill,** on the other side of the Junkanoo Beach Bar (☎ **941/463-6139**), offers the same beachside gulf view to go with moderately priced Florida- and Caribbean-accented cuisine.

✪ **Channel Mark.** 19001 San Carlos Blvd. (at the north end of San Carlos Island). ☎ **941/ 463-9127.** Reservations not accepted. Main courses $12–$25; sandwiches $6–$7. AE, DC, DISC, MC, V. Sun–Thurs 11am–10pm, Fri–Sat 11am–11pm. SEAFOOD.

Nestled by the "Little Bridge" leading onto San Carlos Island's northern end, every table here looks out on a maze of channel markers on Hurricane Bay. A dock with palms growing through it makes this a relaxing place for a waterside lunch. The atmosphere changes dramatically at night, with ceiling fans, potted plants, rattan chairs, well-spaced tables, and soft, indirect lighting creating a relaxed tropical ambience ideal for kindling romance. Congenial owners Mike McGuigan and Andy Welsh greet each guest and put a creative spin on their seafood dishes, such as a rich concoction of snapper smothered in a roasted macadamia-nut sauce and topped with fresh strawberry butter. Even their fried items are more innovative than your usual fare: Their renowned, delicately seasoned crab cakes are lightly breaded with cornflakes and almonds. Calorie counters can opt for shrimp or mahimahi perfectly grilled over mesquite. The adjacent lounge offers the same menu and has live entertainment on weekends.

Italian Fisherman. In Villa Santini Plaza, 7205 Estero Blvd. ☎ **941/463-5544.** Reservations not accepted. Main courses $9–$18; pasta $7–$12; pizza $10.50–$21. Early bird specials $8. AE, DC, DISC, MC, V. Sun–Thurs 4–9pm; Fri–Sat 4–9:30pm (early bird specials daily 4–6pm). ITALIAN/SEAFOOD.

Within walking distance of the Holiday Inn and other south-end accommodations, this split-level storefront establishment offers good food at reasonable prices. Lamps suspended from the ceiling add a touch of elegance, spotlighting the black booths and cafe chairs. Locals come here for the traditional Italian specialties, such as a heaping mound of shrimps and scallops surrounded by mussels and clams, all under a fra diavolo sauce rich in sweet plum tomatoes. Early bird specials feature smaller portions of the regular main courses plus soup, vegetables, and bread. You can order pizza at the adjoining **Coconuts Lounge & Eatery,** a popular local sports pub open daily from 3pm to midnight.

Loggerheads. In Villa Santini Plaza, 7205 Estero Blvd. ☎ **941/463-4644.** Reservations recommended on weekends. Sandwiches and burgers $5–$8; main courses $10–$15. AE, DISC, MC, V. Winter daily 8am–midnight. Off-season daily 11am–11pm. SEAFOOD/AMERICAN.

The motto "The Local's Nest" accurately describes this friendly storefront restaurant, where charter boat captains congregate around a big square bar on one side of the knotty pine accented dining room. The menu offers a wide range of appetizers, big salads, sandwiches, burgers, and main course options from both land and sea. Most of the main courses feature heavy cream sauces over pasta (the house specialty is scallops, spinach, artichokes, tomatoes, and bacon in a horseradish-tinged cream sauce), but you can order traditionally fried, grilled, broiled, or blackened seafood.

○ **Matanzas Inn Restaurant.** At Matanzas Marina, 416 Crescent St. (under the Skyway Bridge on Estero Island). ☎ **941/463-3838.** Reservations not accepted. Main courses $13–$18; sandwiches and light fare $6–$9. AE, DC, DISC, MC, V. Daily 11am–10pm. Closed Thanksgiving and Christmas. SEAFOOD.

Although it's in the busy Times Square tourist district, this casual, friendly, and consistent restaurant is popular with local residents who appreciate seafood fresh off the boats docking at Matanzas Marina. Dining is on a dock next to the marina or in a dark-paneled room hung with ceiling fans. The menu highlights fried, broiled, blackened, or charcoal-grilled seafood. A light-fare menu offers shrimp salad, fish sandwiches, and hamburgers.

○ **Papa Mondo Risorante Italiano.** 1821 Estero Blvd., at Ohio Ave. ☎ **941/765-9660.** Reservations recommended. Main courses $10–$16; fixed-price menu $19. AE, MC, V. Daily noon–10pm. Closed New Year's Day, Christmas, Easter. NORTHERN ITALIAN.

Brothers-in-law Andrea Mazzonetto (he's the chef) and Pasquale Riso hail from Italy, and the fare they present in their attractive dining room or out on their roadside patio is the real thing. They make everything from scratch—you can watch them producing pasta at a big machine behind a big picture window. The homemade pasta shows up in the likes of *stracci bianchi e neri ai frutti di mare,* an excellent combination of white and black pasta sautéed with fresh seafood and shaved zucchini in a white wine sauce. Ask your waiter to explain each evening's three pasta and three meat offerings (a special fixed-price menu features a sampling of all six).

FORT MYERS BEACH AFTER DARK

The area around Times Square is always active, on weekends off-season and every day during winter. In the very heart of Times Square at the foot of Lynn Hall Memorial Pier, the **Beach Pierside Grill,** 1000 Estero Blvd. (☎ 941/765-7800), has live entertainment on its beachside patio (and happy hours Monday to Friday from 3 to 6pm featuring $1 draft beers). Facing due west, **Jimmy's Beach Bar,** in the Days Inn at 1130 Estero Blvd. (☎ 941/463-9759), has live music nightly for the "best sunsets on the island" (actually you can say that of all the beachside establishments here).

Away from the maddening crowds, the **Junkanoo Beach Bar,** under Anthony's on the Gulf, 3040 Estero Blvd. (☎ 941/463-2600), attracts a more affluent crowd for its Bohemian-style parties that run from 11:30am to 1:30am daily. Live bands here specialize in reggae and other island music. The menu offers inexpensive subs, sandwiches, burgers, and pizzas, and a concessionaire rents beach cabanas and water-sports toys, making it a good place for a lively day at the beach.

Locals in the know head for **The Beached Whale,** 1249 Estero Blvd. (☎ 941/463-5505), and **The Reef,** 2601 Estero Blvd. (☎ 941/463-8414), two pubs that consistently have the best bands and the least tourists.

On the more family oriented south end of Estero Island, the **Holiday Inn,** 6890 Estero Blvd. (☎ 941/463-5711), has live music for dancing Wednesday to Saturday and a deejay on Sunday from 9pm to 1am.

On Sunday afternoons, revelers jam the docks for the famous outdoor reggae parties at **The Bridge Waterfront Restaurant,** 708 Fisherman's Wharf (☎ 941/765-0050), which is under the Sky Bridge on San Carlos Island.

3 Sanibel & Captiva Islands

14 miles W of Fort Myers, 40 miles N of Naples

Sanibel and Captiva are unique in Florida. Here you will find none of the neon signs, amusement parks, and high-rise condos that clutter most beach resorts in the state. Indeed, Sanibel's main drag, Periwinkle Way, runs under a canopy of whispery pines and gnarled oaks so thick they almost obscure the small signs for chic shops and restaurants. This wooded ambience is the work of local voters, who have saved their trees and tropical foliage, limited the size and appearance of signs, and permit no building higher than the tallest palm and no Wave Runner or other noisy beach toy within 300 yards of their gorgeous, shell-strewn beaches. Unless you fly over it, you won't realize that its southern shore is lined with hotels and condominiums. The foliage disguises the buildings that well.

Furthermore, more than half of the two islands is preserved in its natural state as wildlife refuges. Here you can ride, walk, bike, canoe, or kayak through the J. N. (Ding) Darling National Wildlife Refuge, one of Florida's best wildlife refuges.

Legend says that Ponce de León named the larger of these two barrier islands "San Ybel," after Queen Isabella of Spain. Another legend claims Captiva's name comes from the infamous pirate José Gaspar's keeping captured women here. The modern era dates from 1892, when a few farmers settled on the islands. One of them, Clarence Chadwick, started an unsuccessful key lime and copra plantation on Captiva; many of his towering coconut palms still stand, adding to that skinny island's tropical luster.

Concluding that their terrific fishing grounds could be more profitable than their sandy soil, local residents soon switched from farming to fishing camps. Affluent anglers flocked to the islands, first by private boat and then by ferry. When the Sanibel Causeway connected the islands to the mainland in 1963, the public at large began discovering their world-famous shelling beaches, wildlife, and aesthetic beauty. Nevertheless, most visitors here still fall into the affluent category. Although food prices are no more expensive here than on the mainland, room rates skyrocket from mid-December to Easter. So either visit during the off-season, or stay in Fort Myers or Fort Myers Beach during winter and make day trips to the islands.

ESSENTIALS

GETTING THERE From I-75 and the airport, follow Daniels Parkway due west, turn left on Summerlin Road (County Road 869), and proceed to the Sanibel Causeway (toll is $3 per car going to the island, free coming back). From Fort Myers, take McGregor Boulevard or Summerlin Road, which merge, to the Sanibel Causeway.

See "Getting There," in section 1, for information about air, train, and bus service. The Amoco station at 1015 Periwinkle Way, at Causeway Road, is the Sanibel agent for **Enterprise Rent-a-Car** (☎ 800/325-8007 or 941/395-3880).

VISITOR INFORMATION The **Sanibel-Captiva Islands Chamber of Commerce,** 1159 Causeway Rd., Sanibel Island, FL 33957 (☎ 941/472-1080; fax 941/472-1070; www.sanibel-captiva.org; e-mail: island@sanibel-capitva.org), maintains a

Sanibel & Captiva Islands

Accommodations:
Anchorage Inn of Sanibel **19**
Beachview Cottages **31**
Best Western Sanibel Island
  Beach Resort **30**
Brennan's Tarpon Tale Inn **23**
Holiday Inn Beach Resort **27**
Island Inn **29**
McCarthy's Marina
  & Cottages **5**
Palm View Motel **25**
South Seas Plantation Resort
  & Yacht Harbour **1**
Sundial Beach Resort **28**
'Tween Waters Inn **6**

Dining:
Bubble Room **4**
Harbor House **18**
Hungry Heron **13**
Jerry's Family Restaurant **16**
Lazy Flamingo I **20**

Lighthouse Café **22**
Mad Hatter **7**
McT's Shrimp House
  & Tavern **17**
Morgan's Forest **26**
Mucky Duck **3**
Sanibel Café **15**
Sunshine Cafe **2**
Timbers **12**

Attractions:
Bailey–Mathews
  Shell Museum **10**
Chamber of Commerce **21**
J.N. (Ding) Darling National
  Wildlife Refuge **8**
Sanibel Historical Village
  & Museum **14**
Sanibel Lighthouse **24**
Sanibel/Captiva Conservation
  Foundation **9**
Tarpon Bay Recreation **11**

visitor center on Causeway Road as you drive onto Sanibel from Fort Myers. The chamber gives away an *Island Guide* (in English, German, and Spanish) and sells a detailed street map for $2 ($3 by mail). Other books are for sale, including comprehensive shelling guides and a helpful collection of menus from the islands' restaurants. There are phones for making hotel and condo reservations. Open Monday to Saturday from 9am to 7pm, Sunday from 10am to 5pm.

GETTING AROUND   Neither Sanibel nor Captiva has public transportation. **No parking** is permitted on any street or road on Sanibel. Free beach parking is available on the Sanibel Causeway. Other municipal lots are either reserved for local residents or have a 75¢ hourly fee. Accordingly, many residents and visitors get around by bicycle (see "More Affordable Outdoor Activities," below).

   If you need a cab, call **Sanibel Taxi** (☎ **941/472-4160**).

PARKS & NATURE PRESERVES

Named for the *Des Moines Register* cartoonist who was a frequent visitor here and who started the federal Duck Stamp program, the ✪ **J. N. (Ding) Darling National Wildlife Refuge,** on Sanibel-Captiva Road (☎ **941/472-1100**), is home to alligators, raccoons, otters, and hundreds of species of birds. Occupying more than half of Sanibel Island, this 6,000-plus acres of mangrove swamps, winding waterways, and uplands has a 2-mile trail and a 5-mile, one-way **Wildlife Drive.** The visitor center shows brief videos about the refuge's inhabitants every half hour and sells a map keyed to numbered stops along the Wildlife Drive for $1. The best times for viewing the wildlife are early morning, late afternoon, and at low tide (tables are posted at the visitor center and are available at the chamber of commerce). Mosquitoes and "no-see-ums" (tiny, biting sand flies) are especially prevalent at dawn and dusk, so bring repellent.

Admission to the visitor center is free. The Wildlife Drive costs $4 per vehicle, $1 for hikers and bicyclists (free to holders of current federal Duck Stamps and National Park Service access passports). The visitor center is open from November to April, Saturday to Thursday from 9am to 5pm; off-season Saturday to Thursday from 9am to 4pm. The center is open on federal holidays from January through May, closed on holidays the rest of the year. The Wildlife Drive is open all year, Saturday to Thursday from 1 hour after sunrise to 1 hour before sunset (that is, it's closed on Friday).

If you want a naturalist to explain what you're seeing, take a 2-hour narrated **tram tour** given by **Tarpon Bay Recreation,** at the north end of Tarpon Bay Road (☎ **941/472-8900**). These are very good value at $8 for adults, $4 for children 12 and under. Schedules are seasonal, so call ahead.

Tarpon Bay Recreation also offers a variety of guided **canoe and kayak tours** in season, with an emphasis on the historical, cultural, and environmental aspects of the refuge (call for the schedule). It also rents canoes, kayaks, and small boats with electric trolling motors (see "More Affordable Outdoor Activities," below).

Almost opposite the refuge visitor center, the nonprofit **Sanibel/Captiva Conservation Foundation,** 3333 Sanibel-Captiva Rd. (☎ **941/472-2329**), maintains a nature center, native plant nursery, and 4½ miles of nature trails on 1,100 acres of wetlands along the Sanibel River. You can learn more about the islands' unusual ecosystems through environmental workshops, guided trail walks, beach walks, and a natural-history boat cruise (call for schedules). Various items are for sale, including native plants and publications about the islands' birds and other wildlife. Admission is $3 for adults, free for children 16 and under. The nature center is open in winter Monday to Saturday from 8:30am to 4pm, off-season Monday to Friday 8:30am to 3pm.

HITTING THE BEACH: SHELLING & SEA LIFE

BEACHES Sanibel has four public beach-access areas with metered parking: the eastern point around **Sanibel Lighthouse,** which has a fishing pier; **Gulfside City Park,** at the end of Algiers Lane, off Casa Ybel Road; **Tarpon Bay Road Beach,** at the south end of Tarpon Bay Road; and **Bowman's Beach,** off Sanibel-Captiva Road. **Turner Beach,** at Blind Pass between Sanibel and Captiva, is highly popular at sunset since it faces due west; there's a small free parking lot on the Captiva side, but parking on the Sanibel side is limited to holders of local permits. All except Tarpon Bay Road Beach have rest rooms. *Be forewarned:* Although nude bathing is illegal, the end of Bowman's Beach near Blind Pass often sees more than its share of bare straight and gay bodies.

Another popular beach on Captiva is at the end of Andy Rosse Lane in front of the Mucky Duck Restaurant. It's the one place here where you can rent motorized watersports equipment (see "More Affordable Outdoor Activities," below).

SHELLING Sanibel and Captiva are famous for their seashells, and local residents and visitors alike can be seen in the "Sanibel stoop" or the "Captiva crouch" while searching for some 200 species. February to April—or after any storm—are the best times of the year to look for whelks, olives, scallops, sand dollars, conch, and many other varieties. Low tide is the best time of day. The shells can be sharp, so wear Aqua Socks or old running shoes whenever you go walking on the beach.

Before you start stooping, visit the impressive ✪ **Bailey-Mathews Shell Museum,** 3075 Sanibel-Captiva Rd. (☎ **941/395-2233**), the only museum in the United States devoted solely to saltwater, freshwater, and land shells (yes, snails are included). Shells from as far away as South Africa surround a 6-foot globe in the middle of the main exhibit hall, thus showing their geographic origins. A revolving case identifies shells likely to wash up on Sanibel. Other exhibits are devoted to shells in tribal art, fossil shells found in Florida, medicinal qualities of various mollusks, the endangered Florida tree snail, and "sailor's Valentines"—shell craft made by natives of Barbados for sailors to bring home to their loved ones. The upstairs library attracts serious mala-cologists. The museum is open Tuesday to Sunday from 10am to 4pm; admission is $5 adults, $3 children 8 to 16, free for children under 8.

With so many residents and visitors scouring Sanibel, you may have better luck on the adjacent shoals and nearby islands, such as Upper Captiva and Cayo Costa (see "Nearby Island Hopping," below). **Captiva Cruises** (☎ **941/472-5300**) has shelling trips from the South Seas Plantation Resort & Yacht Harbour on Captiva daily at 9am and 1pm. They cost $35 for adults, $17.50 for children.

At least 15 charter-boat skippers also offer to take guests on shelling expeditions to these less-explored areas. Their half-day rates are about $180 for up to six people, so get up a group to go. Several operate from the **'Tween Waters Inn Marina** (☎ **941/472-5161**) on Captiva, including **Capt. Mike Fuery** (☎ **941/472-1015** or 941/994-7195 on his boat). Others are based at **Jenson's Twin Palms Marina,** on Captiva (☎ **941/472-5800**), and at the **Sanibel Marina,** on North Yachtsman Drive, off Periwinkle Way east of Causeway Boulevard (☎ **941/472-2723**). They all distribute brochures at the chamber of commerce visitor center (see "Essentials," above) and are listed in the free tourist publications found there.

Caution: Florida law prohibits taking live shells from the beaches, and federal regulations prevent them from being removed from the J. N. (Ding) Darling National Wildlife Refuge.

MORE AFFORDABLE OUTDOOR ACTIVITIES

BICYCLING, WALKING, JOGGING & IN-LINE SKATING   Paved bicycle paths follow alongside most major roads, including the entire length of Periwinkle Way and along Sanibel-Captiva Road to Blind Pass, making Sanibel a paradise for cyclists, walkers, joggers, and in-line skaters. And you can walk or bike the 5-mile, one-way nature trail through the J. N. (Ding) Darling National Wildlife Refuge.

The chamber of commerce visitor center has bike maps, as do Sanibel's rental firms: **Finnimore's Cycle Shop,** 2353 Periwinkle Way (☎ **941/472-5577**); **The Bike Rental,** 2330 Palm Ridge Rd. (☎ **941/472-2241**); **Island Moped,** 1470 Periwinkle Way (☎ **941/472-5248**); and **Tarpon Bay Recreation,** at the north end of Tarpon Bay Road (☎ **941/472-8900**). On Captiva, **Jim's Bike & Skate Rentals** on Andy Rosse Lane (☎ **941/472-1296**) rents bikes and beach equipment. Bike rates range from $5 per hour to $15 a day for basic models. Both Finnimore's and Jim's rent in-line skates.

There are no bike paths on Captiva, where trees alongside the narrow roads can make for dangerous riding.

BOATING & FISHING   On Sanibel, rental boats and charter-fishing excursions are available from **The Boat House** at the Sanibel Marina, on North Yachtsman Drive (☎ **941/472-2531**), off Periwinkle Way east of Causeway Road. **Tarpon Bay Recreation,** at the north end of Tarpon Bay Road (☎ **941/472-8900**), rents boats with electric trolling motors and tackle for fishing.

On Captiva, check with **Sweet Water Rentals** at the 'Tween Waters Inn Marina (☎ 941/472-6376), **Jenson's Twin Palms Marina** (☎ 941/472-5800), and **McCarthy's Marina** (☎ 941/472-5200), all on Captiva Road. Rental boats cost about $125 for half a day, $200 for a full day; that's about twice the price you'll pay elsewhere in Southwest Florida, including Naples.

Many **charter-fishing captains** are docked at these marinas. Half-day rates are about $200 for up to four people. The skippers leave free brochures at the chamber of commerce visitor center (see "Essentials," above), and they're listed in the free tourist publications found there.

CANOEING & KAYAKING   As noted under "Parks & Nature Preserves," above, **Tarpon Bay Recreation** (☎ 941/472-8900) has guided canoe and kayak trips in the J. N. (Ding) Darling National Wildlife Refuge. Do-it-yourselfers can rent canoes and kayaks here. They cost $20 for the first 2 hours, $5 for each additional hour. On Captiva, the **'Tween Waters Inn Marina** (☎ 941/472-5161) rents canoes and kayaks, as does **WildSide Adventures,** based at McCarthy's Marina (☎ 941/935-2925).

Naturalist, avid environmentalist, and former Sanibel mayor **Mark "Bird" Westall** (☎ 941/472-5218; fax 941/472-5128) takes visitors on guided canoe trips through the wildlife refuge and on the Sanibel River. His excursions are timed for low tide and cost $35 for adults, $15 for children under 18. He will tailor shorter trips to accommodate children or anyone else not up to 2½ to 3 hours in a canoe. On Captiva, naturalist **Brian Houston** leads kayaking trips from 'Tween Waters Inn Marina, but make your reservations at Tarpon Bay Recreation on Sanibel (☎ 941/472-8900). Brian charges $35 per person for his morning and midday trips, $25 for a shorter version leaving at 4pm. Reservations are essential with both Bird and Brian.

GOLF & TENNIS   Golfers may view a gallery of wild animals while playing the 5,600-yard, par-70, 18-hole course at the **Dunes Golf and Tennis Club,** 949 Sandcastle Rd., Sanibel (☎ 941/472-2535), whose back nine runs across a wildlife preserve. Call a day in advance for seasonal greens fees and a tee time. The Dunes also has seven tennis courts. The **South Seas Plantation Resort & Yacht Harbour** has tennis courts and a 9-hole golf course, but they're for guests only.

SAILING   If you want to learn how to sail, noted yachties Steve and Doris Colgate have a branch of their **Offshore Sailing School** at the South Seas Plantation Resort & Yacht Harbour (☎ 941/472-5111, ext. 7141). Also based on Captiva, two sailboats take guests out on the waters of Pine Island Sound: Mike McMillan's *Adventure* (☎ 941/472-7532 or 941/472-4386) and Mic Gurley's *New Moon* (☎ 941/ 395-1782). Reservations are required.

WATER SPORTS   Sanibel may prohibit motorized water-sports equipment on its beaches, but Captiva doesn't. **Yolo Watersports** (☎ 941/472-9656) offers parasailing and Wave Runner rentals on the beach in front of the Mucky Duck Restaurant, at the gulf end of Andy Rosse Lane on Captiva.

Both scuba divers and snorkelers can go along with trips offered by the **Redfish Dive Center** (☎ 941/472-3483), the **Pieces of Eight Dive Center** (☎ 941/ 472-9424), and **Captiva Dive** (☎ 941/395-2000). All rent equipment and teach diving.

MORE TO SEE & DO

The **Sanibel Historical Village & Museum,** 950 Dunlop Rd. (☎ 941/472-4648), includes the pioneer-vintage Rutland home and the 1926 versions of Bailey's General Store (complete with Red Crown gasoline pumps), the post office, and Miss Charlotta's Tea Room. Displays highlight the islands' prehistoric Calusa tribal era, old photos from pioneer days, turn-of-the-century clothing, and a variety of memorabilia. Special exhibits feature quilts in January, Valentines and old lace in February, and antique toys, dollhouses, and 200 teddy bears in December. Open Wednesday to Saturday from 10am to 4pm (and Sunday from 1 to 4pm between mid-December and Easter); closed mid-August to mid-October. Admission is by $2 donation.

At the east end of Periwinkle Way, the **Sanibel Lighthouse** has marked the entrance to San Carlos Bay since 1884. The light keepers used to live in the cottages at the base of the 94-foot tower. The now-automatic lighthouse isn't open to visitors, but the grounds and beach are.

In addition to its island trips (see "Nearby Island Hopping," below), **Captiva Cruises** (☎ 941/472-5300) goes out daily on dolphin-watching and sunset cruises from the South Seas Plantation Resort & Yacht Harbour on Captiva. These cost $17.50 for adults, $10 for children. Reservations are required.

SHOPPING

If you have no luck scouring the beaches for shells, several Sanibel shops sell thousands of them. **Sanibel Sea Shell Industries,** 905 Fitzhugh St. (☎ 941/472-1603), has one of the largest collections, with more than 10,000 shells in stock. **She Sells Sea Shells** has two locations: 1157 Periwinkle Way near Causeway Road (☎ 941/472-6991) and 2422 Periwinkle Way near the island's center (☎ 941/472-8080). Others include **Neptune's Treasures Shell Shop,** in the Tree Tops Center, 1101 Periwinkle Way opposite the Dairy Queen (☎ 941/472-3132), which also has a good collection of fossils.

You can burn up a rainy day and lots of credit at Sanibel's numerous upscale boutiques carrying expensive jewelry and apparel. Many are in **Periwinkle Place, Tahitian Gardens,** and **The Village,** the main shopping centers along Periwinkle Way. In The Village, **Toys Ahoy!** (☎ 941/472-4800) carries fascinating toys, games, and stuffed animals. In Tahitian Gardens, the **Audubon Nature Store** (☎ 941/395-2020) carries gifts and books with a wildlife theme, and **The Chesire Cat** (☎ 941/472-3545) offers nature toys and other unique items for kids.

More than a dozen Sanibel galleries feature original works of art; pick up a gallery guide at the chamber of commerce visitor center (see "Essentials," above). On Captiva, the tree-houselike **Jungle Drums,** on Andy Rosse Lane (☎ 941/395-2266), has the area's most unique collection of wildlife art.

Founded in 1899, **Bailey's General Store** is still going strong at the corner of Periwinkle Way and Tarpon Bay Road (☎ 941/472-1516), with a supermarket, deli, salad bar, hardware store, beach shop, shoe repair, and Western Union all under one roof.

ACCOMMODATIONS YOU CAN AFFORD

As I noted in the introduction to this section, Sanibel and Captiva room rates skyrocket during winter. They are highest during the shelling season, February to April, with January somewhat less expensive. But note that most rates fall during the off-season, making these otherwise expensive islands more affordable.

Since most properties on the islands are geared to 1-week family vacations, you can also save by purchasing a package deal if you're staying for 7 nights or longer. **South Seas Resorts** (☎ 800/554-5454; www.south-seas.com), which manages several expensive properties on the islands, offers a variety of discount packages during the off-season.

While modern resorts may try to re-create a South Seas island setting, there are still many Old Florida–style cottages on the two islands that really do look like they belong on Bora Bora. Some also represent good value if you can do without modern luxuries. The 32 pink clapboard structures at **Beachview Cottages,** 3325 W. Gulf Dr. (near Rabbit Road), Sanibel Island, FL 33957 (☎ **800/860-0532** or 941/472-1202; fax 941/472-4720), flank a narrow, unpaved lane running from the road to the beach and lined with coconut palms and colorful hibiscus. Winter rates here are $125 to $230 a day, but book well in advance, because this clean, well-managed property is popular. Off-season they go for $90 to $160 a day. Also, see the introduction to Captiva Island accommodations, below, for **McCarthy's Marina and Cottages.**

Sanibel also has many condominium resorts; in fact, some accommodations recommended below are condo complexes operated as hotels. **1-800-SANIBEL** is a reservations service that will book you into most properties here, including condos and cottages (☎ 800/726-4235). The largest rental agents are **Priscilla Murphy Realty,** 1177 Causeway Blvd. (P.O. Box 5), Sanibel Island, FL 33957 (☎ **800/237-6008** or 941/472-4883; fax 941/472-8995), and **VIP Vacation Rentals,** 1509 Periwinkle Way, Sanibel Island, FL 33957 (☎ **800/237-7526** or 941/472-1613; fax 941/481-8477). The chamber of commerce's *Island Guide* lists others (see "Essentials," above).

Only two chain hotels are present here, and neither is inexpensive. **Best Western Sanibel Island Beach Resort,** 3287 W. Gulf Dr. (near Rabbit Road), Sanibel Island, FL 33957 (☎ **800/554-5454** or 941/472-1700), has 45 spacious rooms, efficiencies, and apartments whose screened balconies face either the beach or a lawn festooned with palms, pink hibiscus, orange trees, a swimming pool, tennis courts, and white Adirondack chairs for lounging. Bicycles and beach equipment are complimentary. There's no restaurant on the premises, but you can dine at other nearby establishments. Winter rates range from $200 to $370 for a unit for two. Off-season they cost $145 to $250.

The **Holiday Inn Beach Resort,** 1231 Middle Gulf Dr. (at the end of Donax Street), Sanibel Island, FL 33957 (☎ **800/HOLIDAY** or 941/472-4123), is on the beach, but its rooms don't have balconies or patios. It has a tennis court, bike rentals, a gift shop, a children's playground and activities program with an environmental emphasis, and Morgan's Forest restaurant (see "Greats Deals on Dining," below). Rates range from $195 to $240 in winter, from $119 to $150 off-season.

If you can't get into one of those, try the **West Wind Inn,** 3345 W. Gulf Dr. (☎ **800/824-0476** or 941/472-1541; fax 941/472-8134), and the **Snook Motel,** 3033 W. Gulf Dr. (☎ **800/741-6166** or 941/472-1345; fax 941/472-2148), two very comfortable, on-the-beach establishments near the Best Western Sanibel Beach Resort. The West Wind Inn has a restaurant.

The islands' sole campground, the **Periwinkle Trailer Park,** 1119 Periwinkle Way, Sanibel Island (☎ **941/472-1433**), is so popular it doesn't even advertise. No other camping is permitted on either Sanibel or Captiva.

Sanibel Island
Super-Cheap Sleeps

Anchorage Inn of Sanibel. 1245 Periwinkle Way, Sanibel Island, FL 33957. ☎ **941/ 395-9688.** 12 units. A/C TV. Winter $89 single or double, $150 cottage. Off-season $59 single or double, $99 cottage. AE, DISC, MC, V.

This modest establishment is well maintained by the owners of the Holiday Inn Beach Resort (guests here can use the beach and play tennis there). Standard rooms, efficiencies, and two-room units are in low-slung buildings with broad common porches facing a central courtyard with small pool. Although these units would rent for half these rates elsewhere, they are clean and a good value for Sanibel. The three cottages are A-frame contraptions with spiral staircases to a second-story sleeping loft.

Brennan's Tarpon Tale Inn. 367 Periwinkle Way, Sanibel Island, FL 33957. ☎ **941/472-0939.** Fax 941/472-6202. www.tarpontale.com. E-mail: brennan@tarpontale.com. 5 units. A/C TV. Winter $109–$169. Off-season $69–$139. Rates include continental breakfast. DISC, MC, V.

Self-described "reformed journalists" Terry and Carlene Brennan preside over this low-slung gray building in the "Old Sanibel" neighborhood, the island's first settlement where the ferries from Fort Myers used to dock near the lighthouse. White walls and tile floors make their comfortable units bright, while French doors lead to gardens dense with sea grape, palm, and ficus trees, which provide privacy for a large outdoor hot tub. Three of their five units have separate bedrooms, while two other "deluxe studios" actually are two-bedroom suites. All have kitchens, and the Brennans deliver continental breakfast makings the night before. Newspapers, bicycles, and beach chairs and umbrellas (the gulf is about 150 yards away) are complimentary, and there's a social hour for guests twice a week. The rooms don't have phones (guests can hook their laptop computer modems into a jack in the common room), but they do have TVs and VCRs, and there's a video-rental store next door. Guests can use a coin laundry.

✪ **Palm View Motel.** 706 Donax St., Sanibel Island, FL 33957. ☎ **941/472-1606.** Fax 941/472-6733. 8 units. A/C TV. Winter $80 single or double, $105–$160 efficiency and apts. Off-season $50 single or double, $60–$95 efficiency and apts. MC, V.

In a quiet residential area less than a block from the Holiday Inn Beach Resort, Werner and Edelgard Papke's little motel is the jewel of Sanibel's few inexpensive accommodations. Originally from Germany, the Papkes have lived on the premises since 1979, keeping their grounds groomed and their units clean and very well maintained. The traditional furnishings are from the 1970s but are nonetheless comfortable. The best choices here are the spacious, well-ventilated one- and two-bedroom apartments. All units except two motel rooms have kitchens; these two rooms interconnect and are often rented together.

Worth an Off-Season Splurge

Island Inn. 3111 W. Gulf Dr., Sanibel Island, FL 33957. ☎ **800/851-5088** or 941/472-1651. Fax 941/472-0051. 56 units. A/C TV TEL. Winter $170–$280 single or double (rate includes breakfast and dinner). Off-season $95–$215 single or double (no meals). AE, DISC, MC, V.

It's difficult to get accommodations here during the peak winter season, but it's worth trying, for this classic beach resort has been in business for more than 100 years. Its original central building houses a bright, genteel dining room, a spacious lounge, and a library brightly furnished with old-style bentwood and wicker sofas and chairs. This is the kind of place where guests dress for dinner—jackets and ties recommended for men during the winter season—and seating is assigned (some guests have had the same table for years).

This main building looks out over a sandy, South Pacific–like yard to the gulf. Although neither charming in an Old Florida sense nor luxurious by today's standards, the cottages and motel rooms (with or without kitchens) are modern and comfortable and have screened porches or balconies. There's a small swimming pool, a tennis court, and a croquet area.

✪ **Sundial Beach Resort.** 1451 Middle Gulf Dr., Sanibel Island, FL 33957. ☎ **800/237-4184** or 941/472-4151. Fax 941/472-8892. 270 condo apts. A/C TV TEL. Winter $275–$575 condo apt. Off-season $145–$325 condo apt. Packages available. AE, DC, DISC, MC, V.

The largest resort on Sanibel, this popular condominium complex stars an enormous, palm-studded, beachside pool and bar area. A games area, kiddie pool, playground, a small ecology center with a touch tank, and a fine children's recreation program (parents even get a couple of nights off) make it especially attractive to families. The one-, two-, and three-bedroom condominiums have screened balconies overlooking the beach or tropically landscaped gardens. They are individually owned, so the decor varies but is always tasteful. VCRs and movies can be rented.

There are several dining options here, including the award-winning Windows on the Water dining room (glorious gulf views), Noopie's Japanese Seafood & Steakhouse, The Deli, and the poolside Crocodial's Patio Bar and Grille. The relaxing lobby lounge is popular at sunset, and a dance band plays Top 40 hits from 7 to 11pm. Extensive amenities include concierge, laundry, baby-sitting, grocery-shopping service (stocks condos before arrival), daily adult activities program, complimentary marine biology program, in-room massage. There are 12 tennis courts with pro, five swimming pools, a jogging trail, bike and boat rentals, fitness center, coin laundry, and business center. Golfing guests can play at the Dunes Golf and Tennis Club.

CAPTIVA ISLAND

There are no supercheap sleeps on exclusive Captiva, but as on Sanibel, cottages offer some of the more reasonable values. Strongly reminiscent of the genuine South Pacific is **McCarthy's Marina & Cottages,** 15041 Captiva Dr. (P.O. Box 580), Captiva Island, FL 33924 (☎ **941/472-5200;** fax 941/472-6405), where four simple houses sit in a bay-side palm and orange grove. The popular beach at the end of Andy Rosse Lane is just a block away. McCarthy's cottages range from $130 to $165 a day during winter and $85 to $115 a day off-season.

Worth an Off-Season Splurge

✪ **South Seas Plantation Resort & Yacht Harbour.** P.O. Box 194, Captiva Island, FL 33924. ☎ **800/554-5454** or 941/472-5111. Fax 941/481-4947. www.south-seas.com. 600 units. A/C TV TEL. Winter $180 single or double; to $880 apt., cottage, town house, or home. Off-season $130–$165 single or double; to $620 apt., cottage, town house, or home. Gratuity of $8 per person per day added to all bills in lieu of tipping. Packages available. AE, DC, DISC, MC, V.

Formerly Clarence Chadwick's 330-acre copra plantation, this exclusive establishment is the premier property on these two islands. It's one of the best choices in southern Florida for serious tennis buffs (18 courts with pro), and its gulf-side golf course is one of the most picturesque nine-holers anywhere. The resort occupies all of Captiva's northern third, making it ideal if you want to step from your luxury villa or condo right onto 2½ miles of gorgeous beach. There's no central focus here, for this really is a sprawling real estate development. There are no high-rise buildings, but an assortment of luxury homes and condos are so spread out along the shore that a free trolley shuttles back and forth through the mangrove forests that separate them. The great variety of accommodations include luxury villas with private pools and their own tennis courts (many are occupied exclusively by their owners; watch for famous folks wandering about). With three bedrooms or more, some units are ideal for families or couples who want to share the cost of a vacation; a variety of off-season packages offer affordable options. The least expensive (but also least inspired) units are the "Harbourside" hotel rooms at the yacht basin and marina near the island's northern tip, the jumping-off point for Captiva Cruises and Steve and Doris Colgate's Offshore Sailing School.

The resort's no-cash, charge-to-your-room policy prevents gate-crashers from dining or playing here.

Set in the plantation workers' waterside commissary, the upscale King's Crown serves gourmet-quality seafood dinners in a romantic setting. Cap'n Al's Dockside

Grill is a pleasant spot for alfresco breakfasts, lunches, and dinners while waiting to see the resident manatees surfacing in the yacht harbor. Among the amenities here are a concierge desk, room service (until 11pm), laundry, grocery-shopping service that stocks condos before arrival, babysitting and activities program for children and teenagers, 18 tennis courts (7 lighted), 9-hole golf course, two marinas (one with sailing school), 18 swimming pools (many with bars), water-sports center (arranges for parasailing, windsurfing, boat rentals, scuba diving, and more), rental bikes, boutique; golfers can also play at the Dunes Golf and Tennis Club; nature center. Outside the main gate, Chadwick's Shopping Center includes high-fashion boutiques, jewelry stores, and gift shops, all open to the public.

✪ **'Tween Waters Inn.** P.O. Box 249, Captiva Island, FL 33924. ☎ **800/223-5865** or 941/472-5161. Fax 941/472-0249. 106 units. A/C TV TEL. Winter $185–$475 single or double. Off-season $110–$350 single or double. Packages available. DISC, MC, V.

Wedged between the gulf beach and the bay on the narrowest part of Captiva, this venerable establishment was the regular haunt of cartoonist J. N. (Ding) Darling. Anne Morrow Lindbergh also spent a winter here, writing *A Gift from the Sea.* Just as Darling preserved the islands' wildlife, the 'Tween Waters has saved the cottages he stayed in. Situated in a sandy palm grove, these pink shiplap buildings capture Old Florida with simple white furniture and terrazzo floors. Some face the gulf; others, the bay. The hotel rooms and apartments are in two modern buildings (a third is expected to be open in 1998) on stilts with screened balconies facing the gulf or bay.

The Canoe Club is a bargain, with inexpensive salads, sandwiches, burgers, and pizzas; it has a bay-side deck for lunches. The Old Captiva House restaurant appears very much as it did in Ding Darling's days (his cartoons adorn the walls) and offers reasonably priced breakfasts, lunches, and seafood dinners during winter (only breakfast and dinner off-season). The popular Crow's Nest Lounge has live entertainment and provides snacks and light evening meals from 9pm to 1am.

Charter captains dock at the full-service marina (see "Hitting the Beach: Shelling & Sea Life" and "More Affordable Outdoor Activities," above). Among the amenities are rental canoes, bikes, and beach cabanas, a very large swimming pool complex complete with wood decking and a bar, 3 lighted tennis courts, and a fitness center.

GREAT DEALS ON DINING

Some restaurants here close or take long vacations during the off-season so it's wise to call ahead if you're on the islands between May and November.

SANIBEL ISLAND

The lively **Cheeburger Cheeburger,** 2413 Periwinkle Way, at Palm Ridge Road (☎ **941/472-6111**), has Sanibel's biggest and best burgers.

Many of the workers on this affluent island take their meals at **Jerry's Family Restaurant,** 1700 Periwinkle Way at Casa Ybel Road (☎ **941/472-9300**), which offers wholesome and inexpensive diner fare (ingredients come fresh from the adjacent Jerry's Supermarket). Both the restaurant and supermarket are open daily from 6am to 11pm. Breakfast is served from 6am to 4pm, and you can usually get a table quickly here (which can't be said of Sanibel's other popular breakfast spots).

Also, you'll find very reasonably priced pub fare at Sanibel's lively sports bars, such as the **Lazy Flamingo I** (see below) and the **Sanibel Grill,** 703 Tarpon Bay Rd., near Palm Ridge Road (☎ **941/472-3128**), which actually serves as the bar for the Timbers, the fine seafood restaurant next door (see below). They all have reduced-price beer and munchies during televised football games.

Super-Cheap Eats

✪ **Hungry Heron.** In Palm Ridge Place, 2330 Palm Ridge Rd. (at Periwinkle Way). ☎ **941/ 395-2300.** Reservations not accepted but call for preferred seating. Main courses $8–$15; sandwiches, burgers, snacks $4.50–$9; weekend breakfast buffet $6. AE, DISC, MC, V. Winter Mon–Fri 11am–10pm, Sat–Sun 7:30–11:30am (buffet) and 7:30–10pm. Off-season daily 11am–9pm. AMERICAN.

Ted and Jim Iannelli's tropically decorated eatery is Sanibel's most popular family restaurant. There's something for everyone on their huge, tabloid-size menu, from hot and cold appetizers and overstuffed "seawiches" to pasta and steamed shellfish. And if the 250 regular items aren't enough, there's a list of nightly specials. Seafood, steaks, and stir-fries from a sizzling skillet are popular with local residents, who bring the kids here for fun and a children's menu. Cartoons run all the time and a magician circulates among the tables from 5 to 9pm every day except Tuesday. An all-you-can-eat breakfast buffet on Saturday and Sunday in winter is an excellent value.

The Lazy Flamingo I. 1036 Periwinkle Way, near Causeway Blvd. ☎ **941/472-6939.** Reservations not accepted. Sandwiches and snacks $5–$9; main courses $11–$15. AE, DC, DISC, MC, V. Daily 11:30am–1am. SEAFOOD/PUB FARE.

T-shirts and shorts or jeans are the dress code at this very casual sport pub that always seems packed by the young and young-at-heart, who flock here for reasonably priced food, a wide choice of beers iced down in a huge box behind the bar, and sports TVs. Some of that beer is used to steam shrimp and a finger-stinging collection of oysters, clams, and spices known as "The Pot." It also serves conch fritters, conch chowder, and conch salad. The flamingo-pink menu also has an array of sandwiches, burgers, fish platters, and very spicy "Dead Parrot Wings." Fillet your own catch, and the chef will cook it to order for $6. Happy hour prices prevail whenever football games are on the TVs.

A sister institution, the **Lazy Flamingo II,** 6520 Pine Ave., at Sanibel-Captiva Road, ¼ mile south of Blind Pass (☎ **941/472-5353**), has the same menu and hours.

Lighthouse Café. In Seahorse Shops, 362 Periwinkle Way (at Buttonwood Ave., east of Causeway Rd.). ☎ **941/472-0303.** Reservations not accepted but call ahead for preferred seating. Breakfast $3–$6; main courses $8–$14. MC, V. Daily 7am–3pm and 5–9pm. Closed for dinner mid-Apr to mid-Dec. AMERICAN.

Decorated with photos and drawings of lighthouses, this casual storefront establishment appropriately near the Sanibel Lighthouse dishes up breakfast omelettes that are meals in themselves, especially the ocean frittata containing delicately seasoned scallops, crabmeat, shrimp, broccoli, fresh mushrooms, and crowned by an artichoke heart and creamy Alfredo sauce. Seafood Benedict is another unusual offering. There's also an interesting sandwich menu. Reasonably priced dinners are served during winter only.

✪ **Sanibel Café.** In the Tahitian Gardens Shops, 2007 Periwinkle Way. ☎ **941/472-5323.** Call ahead for preferred seating. Breakfast $3–$9; salads and burgers $4–$9; main courses $6–$9.50. MC, V. Daily 7am–8pm. AMERICAN.

Seashells are the theme at Lynda and Ken Boyce's pleasant cafe whose tables are museum-like glass cases containing delicate fossilized specimens from the Miocene and Pliocene epochs. Fresh-squeezed orange and grapefruit juice, Danish Havarti omelettes, and homemade muffins and biscuits highlight the breakfast menu (eggs Benedict and fruit-filled waffles are served until closing), while lunch features specialty sandwiches; among the salads served are shrimp, Greek, and chicken-and-grape versions made with a very light, fat-free dressing; and a limited list of main courses such as grilled or blackened chicken breast. Lynda and Ken even serve a sugar-free pancake syrup, but you can fatten up on Lynda's homemade red raspberry jam, apple or cherry crisps, and terrific key lime pie.

For a Few Bucks More

✪ **Harbor House.** 1244 Periwinkle Way (near Donax St.). ☎ **941/472-1242.** Reservations not required. Main courses $10–$19; early bird specials $9. AE, MC, V. Nov–May daily 11:30am–2pm and 5–9:30pm; June–Oct daily 5–9:30pm. AMERICAN.

Dating from 1948, this family-owned establishment is Sanibel's oldest seafood restaurant, and a warm, Old Florida atmosphere prevails under the beamed ceiling of its paneled dining room. The seafood selections are down-home as well, with shrimp, scallops, and freshly caught fish either broiled, fried, blackened, or bronzed (not quite blackened in order to preserve the seafood's natural flavor). Stone crab claws and Florida lobster are offered during their seasons. The early bird specials are a bargain. Made with limes from the family's own trees, the key lime pie here is an award-winner.

✪ **McT's Shrimp House & Tavern.** 1523 Periwinkle Way (at Fitzhugh St.). ☎ **941/472-3161.** Reservations not accepted. Main courses $13–$20; early bird specials $9. AE, DC, DISC, MC, V. Shrimp House daily 4:45–10pm; McT's Tavern daily 4pm–12:30am. SEAFOOD.

Shrimp reigns at this casual, Old Florida–style establishment, where you'll see a line outside at 4:15pm waiting for the early bird specials served to the first 100 persons in the door. Everyone else gets to view the daily catch displayed in a refrigerated case, including the night's shrimp ready for the chef to prepare in one of a least a dozen ways, from steamed to fried in a coconut and almonds batter. There's also grouper and swordfish, plus steaks and chicken for the land-minded, but stick to the shrimp here (see below for Timbers, which does a much better job cooking fish). With a pinball machine and a huge sports TV in the rear of the building, McT's Tavern offers an extensive choice of appetizers and light dinners.

Morgan's Forest. 1231 Middle Gulf Dr., at the Holiday Inn Beach Resort. ☎ **941/472-3351.** Reservations not accepted. Main courses $13–$23. AE, DC, DISC, MC, V. Mon–Sat 7–11am and 5–10pm, Sun 7am–noon and 5–10pm. SEAFOOD.

The kids will love dining in this miniature jungle patterned after the Rainforest Cafés elsewhere. Almost hidden among all the foliage are mechanical but lifelike moving jaguars, monkeys, birds, and a huge python entangled in vines above the bar. Squawking bird sounds, strobe-lightning bolts followed by claps of thunder, and an occasional faux fog rolling across the floor add to the Amazonian ambience. The owners of Fort Myers Beach's excellent Channel Mark are in charge here, which means that your taste buds will be as entertained as your eyes and ears. Their fine crab cakes are the pick of a menu otherwise accented with South and Central American seasonings. Order the shrimp Belize only if you're ready for a thick cream sauce and blazing hot Cajun spices. Obviously there's a children's menu.

✪ **Timbers.** 703 Tarpon Bay Rd. (at Palm Ridge Rd.). ☎ **941/472-3128.** Reservations not accepted. Main courses $13–$23; early birds get $2.50 off regular price. AE, MC, V. Winter daily 4:30–10pm; off-season daily 5–10pm. SEAFOOD/STEAK.

This casual, upstairs restaurant, with bamboo railings, oversized canvas umbrellas, and paintings of tropical scenes through faux windows, consistently has the freshest fish available. You can view the catch in the fish market out front and have the chef charcoal-grill or blacken it to order. The steaks are aged and cut on the premises. You can order a drink from the adjoining Sanibel Grill sports bar and wait for a table outside on the shopping center's porch.

Worth a Splurge

✪ **Mad Hatter.** 6467 Sanibel-Captiva Rd., at Blind Pass. ☎ **941/472-0033.** Reservations suggested. Main courses $18–$29. AE, DISC, MC, V. Mid-Dec–Apr, Tues–Sat 11:30am–2pm, daily 5–9:30pm; May–mid-Dec, Mon–Sat 5–9:30pm. INNOVATIVE/NEW AMERICAN.

Brian and Jayne Baker's popular gulf-front restaurant has only 12 tables, but each has a glorious water view that's perfect at sunset. And the food, a fantasy of New American cuisines, based on California, the Southwest, and the South, with some exotic accents, is worthy of the view. The menu changes frequently, with no dish repeated (so as not to bore their loyal local following). One recent offering was a delicious mixture of angel-hair pasta, grilled marinated shrimp, tomatoes, capers, wild mushrooms, and green olives accompanied by fresh avocado and a vegetable crepe topped with a tomato-mole sauce. Whatever they serve, you'll enjoy.

Great Picnic Fare

For picnics at Sanibel's beaches or on a canoe, **Isabella's Italian Food & Deli,** 1523 Periwinkle Way, at Fitzhugh Street (☎ **941/472-0044**), has subs, pastas, and the island's best pizza, all by carryout or delivery only (toy car collectors note the more than 400 die-cast models on display). The deli and bakery in **Bailey's General Store,** at Periwinkle Way and Tarpon Bay Road (☎ **941/472-1516**), carries a gourmet selection of breads, cheeses, and meats. **Huxter's Deli and Market,** 1203 Periwinkle Way, east of Donax Street (☎ **941/472-6988**), has sandwich fixings and "beach box" lunches to go.

CAPTIVA ISLAND

Captiva isn't an inexpensive place to dine, but you can chow down for the cost of a drink at the extensive happy hour buffet offered daily from 4:30 to 7:30pm by **Chadwick's Restaurant & Lounge,** just outside the entry to South Seas Plantation & Yacht Harbour (☎ **941/472-1511,** ext. 5181). It's also a good place for all-you-can-eat theme buffets at lunch Monday to Saturday ($9.50 per person) and at dinner nightly ($21 adults, $11 for kids 4 to 20, free for children under 4).

You can't miss the **Green Flash,** 15183 Captiva Rd. (☎ **941/472-3337**), which sits at the infamous "curve" where Captiva Road takes a sharp turn to the north. You won't see the green flash as the sun sets here, for this modern establishment looks eastward across Pine Island Sound. On the other hand, it makes for a nice view at lunch, and seeing the full moon turn the sound into glistening silver is worth having at least a late-evening drink here. The menu features continental-style seafood and other American fare.

Big deli sandwiches and picnic fare are available at the **Captiva Island Store,** Captiva Road at Andy Rosse Lane (☎ **941/472-2374**), and **C. W.'s Market and Deli,** at the entrance to the South Seas Plantation Resort & Yacht Harbour (☎ **941/ 472-5111**). The beach is a block from these stores.

Super-Cheap Eats

✪ **Sunshine Cafe.** In Captiva Village Square, Captiva Rd. at Laika Lane. ☎ **941/472-6200.** Reservations recommended. Small platters $6–$9; large platters $19–$22; sandwiches $7–$7.50. AE, DISC, MC, V. Daily 11:30am–4pm and 5–9:30pm. ECLECTIC.

This friendly, open-kitchen cafe has only 10 tables—five inside, five on the shopping center's porch—but the food is worth the close quarters. Everything except the bread is prepared on the premises. Specialties are charcoal-grilled steak and shrimp, spicy chicken breast, po-boy sandwiches, and fresh nightly pastas, but delicious daily specials usually feature fresh fish. The portions are large here, so the "small platters," such as black beans and rice, actually make a substantial meal at a reduced price. Various desserts are offered daily; the apple crisp is a winner. Anything on the menu can be ordered to carry out.

For a Few Bucks More

Mucky Duck. Andy Rosse Lane (on the gulf). ☎ **941/472-3434.** Reservations not accepted. Lunch $5–$10; dinner main courses $12–$18. AE, DISC, MC, V. Mon–Sat 11:30am–2:30pm and 5–9:30pm. SEAFOOD/PUB FARE.

A Captiva institution since 1976, this lively, British-style pub is the one place here where you can dine right by the beach. If you don't get a real seat with this great view, the humorous staff will gladly roll a fake window over to appease you. The menu offers a selection of fresh seafood items, plus English fish-and-chips, steak-and-sausage pie, and a ploughman's lunch. There's a children's menu and a vegetarian platter. No smoking is allowed inside. You can't make a reservation, but you can order drinks from the bar and bide your wait at beachside picnic tables out front (come early for sunset).

Worth a Splurge

✪ **The Bubble Room.** 15001 Captiva Rd. (at Andy Rosse Lane). ☎ **941/472-5558.** Reservations not accepted. Main courses $14–$27; lunch $6–$12. AE, DC, DISC, MC, V. Daily 11:30am–2:30pm and 5:30–10pm. Closed Christmas. STEAK/SEAFOOD.

The gaudy bubble-gum pink, yellow, purple, and green exterior of this amusing restaurant is only a prelude to the 1930s, 1940s, and 1950s Hollywood motif inside. The dining rooms are adorned with a collection of puppets, statues of great movie stars, toy trains, thousands of movie stills, and antique jukeboxes that play big band–era tunes. The menu carries on the cinematic theme: prime ribs Weismuller, Eddie Fisherman fillet of fresh grouper, and Henny Young-One boneless breast of young chicken. Both adults and children (who can dine for $7 at dinner, $3.50 at lunch) are attracted to this fun establishment. Granted, main courses are expensive, but the portions are huge, and the "Tiny Bubble" sampler (salad, choice of appetizer, and a large slice of key lime pie) will satisfy all but the heartiest appetites.

SANIBEL & CAPTIVA ISLANDS AFTER DARK

You won't find glitzy nightclubs on these family-oriented islands, but night owls have some fun places to roost at the resorts and restaurants mentioned above. Here's a brief recap.

ON SANIBEL   The Sundial Beach Resort's **Lobby Lounge,** 1451 Middle Gulf Dr. (☎ 941/472-4151), features entertainers during dinner, then live bands for dancing from 9pm on. The **Patio Lounge,** in the Jacaranda, 1223 Periwinkle Way (☎ 941/472-1771), attracts an affluent crowd of middle-agers and seniors to its live music every evening. **McT's Tavern,** 1523 Periwinkle Way (☎ 941/472-3161), has darts, video games, and a large-screen TV for sports fans. Other popular sports bars are **Legends Bar & Grille,** at Tarwinkle's Seafood Restaurant, 2447 Periwinkle Way, at Tarpon Bay Road (☎ 941/472-1366); the **Sanibel Grill,** 703 Tarpon Bay Rd. (☎ 941/472-4453); and the two **Lazy Flamingo** branches (see "Super-Cheap Eats," above).

From December to April, professional actors perform Broadway dramas and comedies Monday to Saturday at 8pm in Sanibel's state-of-the-art, 150-seat **Pirate Playhouse,** 2200 Periwinkle Way (☎ 941/472-0006). Call for the schedule and ticket prices.

Originally a one-room school built in 1896 and later housing the Pirate Playhouse before its new facility was constructed across the road, the **Old Schoolhouse Theater,** 1905 Periwinkle Way (☎ 941/472-6862), complements its neighbor by offering Broadway musicals and revues from December to April. From May to November, the

Cheeseburgers on Cabbage Key

You never know who's going to get off a boat at 100-acre Cabbage Key and walk unannounced into the funky **Cabbage Key Inn,** a rustic house built in 1938 by the son and daughter-in-law of mystery novelist Mary Roberts Rinehart. Ernest Hemingway liked to hang out here in the early days, and novelist John D. Mac-Donald was a frequent guest 30 years later. Today you could find yourself rubbing elbows at the bar with the likes of Walter Cronkite, Ted Koppel, Sean Connery, or Julia Roberts. Singer and avid yachtie Jimmy Buffett likes Cabbage Key so much that it inspired his hit song "Cheeseburger in Paradise."

A path leads from the tiny marina across a lawn dotted with coconut palms to this white clapboard house that sits atop an ancient Calusa shell mound. Guests dine in the comfort of two screened porches and seek libations in the Rinehart's's library-turned-bar, its pine-paneled walls now plastered with dollar bills left by visitors. The straight-back chairs and painted wooden tables are showing their age, but that's part of Cabbage Key's laid-back, don't-give-a-hoot charm.

In addition to the famous thick, juicy cheeseburgers so loved by Jimmy Buffett, the house specialties are fresh broiled fish and shrimp steamed in beer. Lunches range from $4 to $9; dinners are $16 to $20.

For overnight or longer, the Cabbage Key Inn has six rooms and six cottages, all with original 1920s furnishings, private baths, and air conditioners. Four of the cottages have kitchens, and one room reputedly has its own ghost. Rates are $65 single or double for rooms, $145 to $200 for cottages. Reserve well in advance for major holidays and during the tarpon season from February to May. For information or reservations, contact Cabbage Key Inn, P.O. Box 200, Pineland, FL 33945 (☎ **941/283-2278;** fax 941/283-1384).

You can get to Cabbage Key from Pine Island near Fort Myers via the inn's own launch, which leaves daily from the Mattson Marine marina, or on the *Tropic Star* (☎ **941/283-0015**), which departs the Four Winds Marina daily at 9:30am. The *Tropic Star* charges $20 for adults, $12 for children. **Captiva Cruises** (☎ **941/472-5300**) goes there daily from Captiva Island, charging $27.50 per adult, $15 for children.

Off Beach Players perform comedies and mystery plays for all ages. Call for the current schedule and prices.

For laughs, the **Sanibel Island Comedy Club,** 975 Rabbit Rd., at Sanibel-Captiva Road next to Loco's Steakhouse and Cantina (☎ **941/472-8833**), attracts national comedians by offering them a working vacation here (call for schedule).

ON CAPTIVA The **Crow's Nest Lounge,** in the 'Tween Waters Inn, on Captiva Road (☎ **941/472-5161**), is Captiva's top nightspot for dancing. **Chadwick's Lounge,** at the entrance to the South Seas Plantation Resort & Yacht Harbour (☎ **941/472-5111**), has a large dance floor and music from 9pm on.

NEARBY ISLAND HOPPING

Sanibel and Captiva are jumping-off points for island-hopping boat trips to barrier islands and keys teeming with ancient legends and Robinson Crusoe–style beaches. You don't have to get completely lost out there, however, for several islets have comfortable inns and restaurants. The trip across shallow Pine Island Sound is itself a sightseeing adventure, with playful dolphins surfing on the boats' wakes and a variety of cormorants, egrets, frigate birds, and (in winter) rare white pelicans flying above or lounging on sandbars between meals.

Captiva Cruises (☎ **941/472-5300**) has daily trips from the South Seas Plantation Resort & Yacht Harbour on Captiva. The *Lady Chadwick* goes to Cabbage Key (see box) and Useppa Island, where passengers disembark for lunch. The Island Lady goes to Boca Grande (see section 4) by way of Cayo Costa State Park. These day trips cost $27.50 per adult, $15 for children to Cabbage Key or Useppa, $35 for adults, $17.50 for children to Boca Grande or Cayo Costa. They usually leave at 10:30am. Reservations are required.

From Pine Island off Fort Myers, you can take the *Tropic Star* (☎ **941/283-0015**) to both Cabbage Key and Cayo Costa (see "Cruises" in section 1).

CAYO COSTA   You can't get any more deserted than at ✪ **Cayo Costa State Park** (pronounced *Kay*-oh *Cos*-tah), which occupies a 2,132-acre, completely unspoiled barrier island with miles of white-sand beaches, pine forests, mangrove swamps, oak-palm hammocks, and grasslands. Other than natural wildlife, the only permanent residents here are three park rangers.

Day-trippers can bring their own supplies and use a picnic area with pavilions. A tram carries visitors from the sound-side dock to the gulf beach (50¢ round-trip fare). The state maintains 12 very basic cabins and a primitive campground on the northern end of the island near Johnson Shoals, where the shelling is spectacular. Cabins cost $20 a day, and campsites are $13 a day all year. There's running water on the island but no electricity.

The park is open daily from 8am to sundown. There's an honor-system admission fee of $2 per person for day visitors. Overnight slips at the dock cost $13 a day. For more information or cabin reservations, contact **Cayo Costa State Park,** P.O. Box 1150, Boca Grande, FL 33921 (☎ **941/964-0375**). Office hours are Monday to Friday from 8am to 5pm.

4 Boca Grande

63 miles NW of Fort Myers, 105 miles NW of Naples, 50 miles SE of Sarasota

After he lost to Bill Clinton back in 1992, George Bush and first lady Barbara nursed their wounds at Boca Grande (pronounced *Grand*). They chose well, for this charming village on Gasparilla Island is definitely a president's kind of place. Legend says that the infamous pirate José Gaspar lived in style on this 7-mile-long barrier island. So did the du Pont family, which founded Boca Grande in the 1880s. They were followed by the Astors, Morgans, Vanderbilts, and other moneyed clans, who still turn the island into a Florida version of Nantucket during their winter "social season."

In addition to the warm weather, the lure was some of the world's best tarpon fishing. Descendants of the watermen who were here first—and who guided the rich and famous—still work their 1920s-vintage marinas and live on streets named Dam-If-I-Know, Dam-If-I-Care, and Dam-If-I-Will. You can see their modest homes with backyards full of old sheds, boats, and fishnets, but high hedges hide the "beach-fronter" mansions around 29th Street.

ESSENTIALS

GETTING THERE   From the north on I-75, take Exit 32 in Charlotte County, then head west to the end of Toledo Blade Boulevard. Turn right there onto Fla. 776, then left on Fla. 771 to Placida and the Boca Grande Causeway ($3.20 toll to the island, free coming back). From the south on I-75, take Exit 31 and go south on Kings Highway (Fla. 769), then an immediate left on Veterans Boulevard (Fla. 776) and left on Fla. 771 to the Boca Grande Causeway. It's about 1½ hours from Fort Myers.

Captiva Cruises (☎ 941/472-5300) has daily trips from the South Seas Plantation Resort & Yacht Harbour on Captiva to Boca Grande (see "Nearby Island Hopping" in section 3). The fare is $35 adults, $17.50 children.

VISITOR INFORMATION Contact the **Boca Grande Chamber of Commerce,** 5800 Gasparilla Rd. (P.O. Box 704), Boca Grande, FL 33921 (☎ **941/964-0568;** fax 941/964-0620; www.charlotte-online.com/bocagrande; e-mail: bgcc@ewol.com). The office is in the Courtyard Shops, on the left as you drive onto the island. You can also find information in a rack in the Theater Mall on Park Avenue in the heart of town.

GETTING AROUND **Boca Grande Taxi & Limousine** (☎ **800/771-7433** or 941/964-0455) will take you around in style, but many visitors choose to see this town on foot, or by bicycle or golf cart rented from **Island Bike 'n' Beach,** 333 Park Ave. (☎ **941/964-0711**). Bikes range from $6 an hour to $18 a day. The company also rents baby strollers, beach chairs and umbrellas, boogie boards, tennis racquets, and other items. Now a paved, 7-mile-long **bike path,** the bed of the old Charlotte Harbor and Northern Railroad runs by the depot on its way from the island's south end all the way north to the causeway.

EXPLORING THE TOWN

The pink-brick **Railroad Depot,** at the corner of Park Avenue and 4th Street, has been restored to its turn-of-the-century grandeur when it was Boca Grande's lifeline to the world. It now houses a cluster of upscale boutiques and the Loose Caboose Restaurant and Ice Cream Parlor, once visited by Katherine Hepburn (see "Greats Deals on Dining," below).

You can stand on the railway platform and see numerous high-end **boutiques** and **art galleries** along 4th Street and Railroad and Park avenues. Across the street, **Fugate's** has been selling everything from rain slickers to wedding gowns since 1916.

Banyan Street (actually 2nd Street) is canopied with tangled banyan trees and is one of the prettiest places for a stroll. Nearby, **St. Andrew's Episcopal Church** and the **First Baptist Church,** both at Gilchrist and 4th streets, and the **United Methodist Church,** at Gilchrist and 3rd streets, all date from the town's early years.

The **Johann Fust Community Library,** at Gasparilla Road and 10th Street (☎ **941/964-2488**), contains 12,000 volumes and the extraordinary **Du Pont Shell Collection,** all gathered by Henry Francis du Pont during nearly 50 years of combing the island's beaches. The library has a lovely interior garden and outdoor reading room. Open December to April, Monday to Friday from 10am to noon and 4 to 6pm; the rest of the year, Monday to Friday from 4 to 6pm.

At the south end of the island, the **Boca Grande Lighthouse** began marking the pass into Charlotte Harbor in 1890 (the steel tower on Gulf Boulevard served as the light from 1966 to 1986, when the old building was restored). **Gasparilla Island State Recreation Area** around the lighthouse is open daily from 8am to sunset.

AFFORDABLE OUTDOOR ACTIVITIES

By far the biggest event here is the chamber of commerce–sponsored **World's Richest Tarpon Tournament,** usually the second week in July, when anglers try to reel in $100,000. Charter fishing is available through **Boca Grande Charter Booking Services,** located at Miller's Marina on Harbor Drive (☎ **941/964-2232**). **Miller's Marina** (☎ **941/964-2283**) also has backwater nature tours and parasailing during the winter season. You can rent boats there and at **Whidden's Marina** (☎ **941/**

964-2878), also on Harbor Drive. The **Boca Grande Pass Marina** (☎ 941/ 964-0607), on the south end of the island at the old phosphate port (now an oil trans-shipment facility), also is a base for charter fishing boats.

Beach access is limited by the expensive homes along the gulf, but there's a **public beach** just south of town on Gulf Boulevard. **Gasparilla Island State Recreation Area** has a small beach park just south of the village and a lovely strip of sand on the island's south end. The area is open daily from 8am to sunset. Admission is $2 per vehicle.

Also near the south end, **Sun Chaser Watersports,** on the beach at South Beach restaurant (☎ 941/769-2142), rents ocean kayaks and Windsurfers.

Boca Grande Ferry Service (☎ 941/964-1100 or 941/964-0607) takes passengers out to Cayo Costa, Cabbage Key, and other islands. It departs at 10:30am daily from the Boca Grande Pass Marina on the island's south end. Fares are $16 to $20, depending on the destination. Reservations are required. See "Nearby Island Hopping" in section 3 of this chapter, on Sanibel and Captiva Islands, for information about Cayo Costa and Cabbage Key.

ACCOMMODATIONS YOU CAN AFFORD

The only way to stay on the beach here is to rent a condo or a house. One example is **Sundown Colony,** a group of 28 spacious, 2-story, two-bedroom/two-bath town homes right on the beach a mile south of town. Rates range from $945 to $1,800 a week, depending on the season. It's one of several rental properties managed by **Boca Grande Real Estate,** P.O. Box 686, Boca Grande, FL 33921 (☎ 800/881-2622 or 941/964-0338; fax 941/964-2301).

Innlet on the Waterfront. 12th St. (at E. Railroad Ave.; P.O. Box 248), Boca Grande, FL 33921. ☎ **941/964-2294.** Fax 941/964-0382. 32 units. A/C TV TEL. Winter $95–$135 double. Off-season $85–$115 double. MC, V.

This motel has a large veranda across the back, from which guests can view Boca Grande Bayou, the creeklike waterway forming the town's eastern boundary. The efficiencies, opening to the veranda and equipped with kitchens, are more expensive than the standard motel units. There's a swimming pool and marina on the premises, but no restaurant.

GREAT DEALS ON DINING
SUPER-CHEAP EATS

✪ **Jam's Italian Restaurant.** Railroad Ave. at 5th St. ☎ **941/964-2002.** Pizzas $5–$14; pastas $5.50–$10; sandwiches $3–$6. AE, MC, V. Mon–Thurs 11am–9pm, Fri–Sat 11am–10pm, Sun noon–9pm. ITALIAN.

Although President Bush usually hobnobbed at the Gasparilla Inn when he was here, he did join his White House staffers once at their hangout in this pleasant Italian restaurant, whose motto is "More food for less lira." Neither the food nor the value has changed since they scarfed down tons of excellent pizza and pasta while watching ball games on three TVs. Jam's even has a White House plaque to prove the staffers were here.

Loons on a Limb. 3rd St. at Railway Ave. ☎ **941/964-0155.** Reservations recommended for dinner. Breakfast $4.50–$8; main courses $11–$20. No credit cards. Winter daily 7:30–11:30am and 6–9pm. Off-season daily 7:30–11:30am. Closed Aug, Thanksgiving, and Christmas. SEAFOOD/THAI/CREOLE.

Owned and operated by Boca Grande natives, "The Loon" is famous for both eggs Benedict and grits, which speaks reams about this town's split personality. It's one of the few places on the island serving breakfast. Talented chef Michael Perlov usually prepares a chalkboard dinner menu from October to May, featuring seafood prepared in Creole and Thai fashions. Photos and paintings of wild birds share the tongue-in-groove walls with a stuffed deer's head.

Loose Caboose. Park Rd. at 3rd St., in the Railroad Depot. ☎ **941/964-0440.** Reservations not accepted. Salads and sandwiches $3.50–$10; main courses $6.50–$14. MC, V. Winter daily 9am–9pm. Off-season daily 9am–6pm. Closed Thanksgiving and Christmas. AMERICAN.

Everyone from actress Katherine Hepburn to local bank clerks who can't afford to live on the island flocks here for good yet inexpensive fare. You can dine inside the old Railroad Depot or outside under its soaring brick arches. Tops here are warm Oriental salads and sandwiches composed with Black Forest ham and brie, but you can order a variety of fare from nachos to baskets of fried oysters or shrimp. A limited dinner menu is offered during the winter season.

FOR A FEW BUCKS MORE

South Beach. 777 Gulf Blvd. (south end of island). ☎ **941/964-0765.** Reservations recommended. Main courses $12–$22. AE, DISC, MC, V. Daily 11am–10pm. Bar open until 2am. SEAFOOD.

The only place on Gasparilla where you can dine or have a sunset cocktail by the gulf, this casual establishment has a covered patio with plastic chairs and tables right by the white sand. Patrons also have a view of the beach through the window walls of the dining room, whose solid walls bear a jungly mural and works by local artists. The regular menu features the usual assortment of shrimp, grouper, and broiled mahimahi, but the specials such as stone crab claws or pompano are your best bets. Wednesday usually is all-you-can-eat shrimp night ($19), while Friday offers a stuffing of fish ($17). Bands make music on the patio on weekends during the winter season.

GREAT PICNIC FARE

For picnic fixings, go to the village's sole grocery, **Hudson's,** on Park Avenue between 4th and 5th streets opposite the Railroad Depot (☎ **941/964-2570**). It's open Monday to Saturday from 8am to 5:30pm.

5 Naples

42 miles S of Fort Myers, 106 miles W of Miami, 185 miles S of Tampa

Because its wealthy residents are accustomed to the very best, Naples is easily Southwest Florida's most sophisticated city. Indeed, its boutiques and galleries would upstage those in Palm Beach or Beverly Hills. And yet Naples has an easygoing friendliness to all comers, and it offers some surprisingly affordable places to stay within easy reach of its long, magnificent beach and pricey resorts.

Naples began in 1886, when a group of 12 Kentuckians and Ohioans bought 8,700 acres, laid out a town, and started selling lots. They built a pier and the 16-room Naples Hotel, whose first guest was President Grover Cleveland's sister Rose. She and other notables soon built a line of beach homes known as "Millionaires' Row." Known today as Olde Naples and carefully protected by its modern residents, their original settlement still retains the air of that time a century ago.

Even the newer sections of Naples have their charm, thanks to Ohio manufacturer Henry B. Watkins Sr. In 1946, Watkins and his partners bought the old hotel and all the town's undeveloped land and laid out the Naples Plan, which created the environmentally conscious city you see today. While strict zoning laws preserve the old part of town, the Naples Plan blends development with the natural environment along the town's 10 miles of beachfront.

ESSENTIALS

GETTING THERE   From Miami, U.S. 41 (the Tamiami Trail) leads through the Everglades to Naples. A faster route from Miami and Fort Lauderdale is via I-75 ("Alligator Alley"), which will also bring you south from Tampa and Fort Myers. From I-75, take Immokalee Road (Exit 17) for Vanderbilt Beach, Pine Ridge Road (Exit 16) for the Pelican Bay area north of downtown, or Davis Boulevard (Exit 15) for downtown.

Most visitors arrive at the **Southwest Florida International Airport,** 35 miles north of Naples (see "Getting There" under "Essentials," in section 1, on Fort Myers). **Naples Municipal Airport,** on North Road off Airport–Pulling Road (☎ **941/ 643-6875**), is served by **American Eagle** (☎ **800/433-7300**) and **US Airways Express** (☎ **800/428-4322**). Taxis await all flights outside the small terminal building.

VISITOR INFORMATION   The **Naples Area Chamber of Commerce** maintains a visitor center at 895 5th Ave. South (at U.S. 41), Naples, FL 34102 (☎ **941/ 262-6141**; fax 941/262-8374; www.naples-online.com), which has a host of free information and phones for making hotel reservations. It sells a detailed street map for $2. By mail, they will send a complete Naples vacation packet for $7 ($12 to Canada, $25 outside North America) and the street map for $3. The visitor center is open Monday to Friday from 9am to 5pm, Saturday and Sunday from 10am to 3pm.

You can get on-the-street information at **kiosks** in the Marketplace at Tin City on U.S. 41 at the Gordon River Bridge, and on 3rd Street South at 12 Avenue South in Olde Naples.

GETTING AROUND   The **Naples Trolley** (☎ **941/262-7300**) clangs around 25 stops between the Marketplace at Tin City in Olde Naples and Vanderbilt Beach on Monday to Saturday from 8:30am to 5:15pm and on Sunday from 10:15am to 5:15pm. Daily fares are $12 for adults, $5 for children 3 to 12, free for children under 3, with free reboarding. You can buy tickets from the driver or at the Naples Trolley Depot and Welcome Center, 1010 6th Ave. S. (2 blocks west of Tin City), and at the chamber of commerce visitor center. Schedules are available in brochure racks in the lobbies of most hotels and motels.

For taxis, call **Yellow Cab** (☎ **941/262-1312**), **Maxi Taxi** (☎ **941/262-8977**), or **Naples Taxi** (☎ **941/775-0505**). Fares are $1.75 for the first tenth of a mile, 30¢ for each two-tenths of a mile thereafter.

The Naples Area Chamber of Commerce (see above) distributes an area bicycle route map. Rent a bike from **The Bike Route,** 655 N. Tamiami Trail (☎ **941/ 262-8373**). For scooters, call **Good Times Rental,** 1947 Davis Blvd. (☎ **941/ 775-7529**).

HITTING THE BEACH

Access to Olde Naples's gorgeous white-sand beach is at the gulf end of each avenue, although parking in the neighborhood can be precious. Try the metered lots on 12th Avenue South near the **Naples Pier,** the town's most popular beaching spot. Families gather on the beach north of the pier, while local teens congregate on the south side. There's a food concessionaire on the pier.

Also popular with families, lovely **Lowdermilk Park,** on Millionaires' Row at Gulf Shore Boulevard and North Banyan Boulevard, has a pavilion, rest rooms, showers, a refreshment counter, professional-quality volleyball courts (the area's best players practice here), a duck pond, and picnic tables. There's metered parking, so bring quarters. A few blocks farther north is another metered parking lot with beach access beside the Naples Beach Hotel & Golf Resort, 851 Gulf Shore Blvd. N., at Golf Drive.

Nature lovers head to the Pelican Bay development north of the historic district and the popular ✪ **Clam Pass County Park** (☎ 941/353-0404). A tram takes you along a 3,000-foot boardwalk winding through mangrove swamps and across a back bay to a beach of fine white sand. It's a strange sight, what with high-rise condos standing beyond the mangrove-bordered backwaters, but this actually is a miniature wilderness. Some 6 miles of canoe and kayak trails—with multitudes of birds and an occasional alligator—run from Clam Pass into the winding streams. The beach pavilion here has a snack bar, rest rooms (foot showers only), picnic tables, and beach equipment rentals, including one- and two-person kayaks and 12-foot canoes. Admission and the tram are free, but there's a $3-per-vehicle fee in the parking lot at the end of Seagate Drive. You can push, but not ride, bicycles on the boardwalk.

At Vanderbilt Beach, about 4 miles north of Olde Naples, the **Delnor-Wiggins State Recreation Area,** at the west end of Bluebill Avenue–111th Ave. N. (☎ 941/597-6196), has been listed among America's top 10 stretches of sand by "Dr. Beach." It has bathhouses, a boat ramp, and the area's best picnic facilities. Fishing from the beach is excellent here. The area is open daily from 8am to sunset. Admission is $2 per vehicle with one occupant, $4 for vehicles with two to eight occupants, $1 for pedestrians and bikers.

GREAT GOLF THAT WON'T BREAK YOUR BUDGET & OTHER AFFORDABLE OUTDOOR ACTIVITIES

BOATING & BOAT RENTALS   Powerboat rentals are available from **Club Nautico,** at the Boat Haven Marina, 1484 E. Tamiami Trail (☎ 941/774-0100), on the east bank of the Gordon River behind Kelly's Fish House; the **Port-O-Call Marina,** 550 Port of Call Way (☎ 941/774-0479); the **Parkshore Marina,** 4310 Gulf Shore Blvd. N. (☎ 941/434-6964), in the Village Shops at Venetian Bay; the **Brookside Marina,** 2023 Davis Blvd. (☎ 941/774-9100); and the **Cove Marina,** 860 12th Ave. S. (☎ 941/263-7250), at the City Docks.

Sailing enthusiasts can line up a charter with **Sailboats Unlimited,** at the City Docks on 12th Avenue South (☎ 941/262-0139).

CRUISES   The Gordon River and Naples Bay from the U.S. 41 bridge on 5th Avenue South to the gulf are prime territory for sightseeing, dolphin-watching, and sunset cruises. The double-decked *Double Sunshine* (☎ 941/263-4949) sallies forth onto the river and bay daily from Tin City, where it has a ticket office. The 1½-hour cruises usually leave at 10am, noon, 2pm, and an hour before sunset. They cost $15 per adult, $10 for children under 12.

The *Sweet Liberty* (☎ 941/793-3525), a 53-foot sailing catamaran, makes morning shelling cruises to Keewaydin Island, a private wildlife sanctuary south of Olde Naples. The vessel then spends the afternoon sightseeing and the evening on sunset cruises on Naples Bay before docking at Boat Haven Marina on the east side of the Gordon River Bridge. Shelling cruises cost $25 for adults, $10 for children; sightseeing and sunset cruises cost $20 for adults, $10 for children.

For a good deal more luxury, the 83-foot *Naples Princess* (☎ 800/728-2970 or 941/649-2275) has narrated breakfast, lunch, and sunset dinner cruises from Olde Naples Seaport, 10th Avenue South at 10th Street South. These usually leave at 9am, noon, and sunset. With extensive continental breakfast and sandwich lunch buffets, the two daytime cruises are excellent values at $20 and $25 per person. Call for schedule and prices of sunset cruises.

FISHING   The locals like to fish from the **Naples Pier** (see "Exploring the Town," below). The pier has tables on which to clean your catch, but watch out for the ever-present pelicans, who are master thieves. You can buy tackle and bait from the local marinas (see "Boating & Boat Rentals," above).

The least expensive way for singles, couples, and small families to fish without paying for an entire boat is on the 34-foot *Lady Brett* (☎ 941/263-4949), which makes two daily trips from Tin City for $45 per person. Rod, reel, bait, and fishing license are included, but bring your own drinks and lunch. A number of charter boats are based at the marinas mentioned under "Boating & Boat Rentals," above; call or visit them for booking information and prices.

GOLF   Most of Naples's excellent golf courses are private clubs, but the area also has a few of America's best public golf courses, including the ✪ **Lely Flamingo Island Club** and the **Lely Mustang Golf Club,** both on U.S. 41 between Naples and Marco Island (☎ 800/388-GOLF or 941/793-2223). The Lely Flamingo course was designed by Robert Trent Jones Sr., and its hourglass fairways and fingerlike bunkers present many challenges. Designed by Lee Trevino, the new Lely Mustang course is more forgiving but still fun. Former PGA Tour player Paul Trittler has his golf school at these courses. You'll pay a price here in winter, when 18-hole fees are about $135 at Lely Flamingo and $148 at Lely Mustang, including cart and range balls, but they drop progressively after Easter to about $40 and $48, respectively, in the muggy summer months.

Boyne South, on U.S. 41 between Fla. 931 and Fla. 92 (☎ 941/732-5108), is another winner, with lots of wildlife inhabiting its many lakes (a 16-foot alligator reportedly resides near the 17th hole). There's a driving range, practice facility, and restaurant, and instruction is available. Wintertime fees are $70, but off-season they drop to $35 or less. Tee times are taken 4 days in advance.

Another local favorite is the player-friendly **Hibiscus Golf Club,** half a mile east of U.S. 41 off Rattlesnake Hammock Road in East Naples (☎ 941/774-0088). There's a pro shop and a teaching professional on hand. Fees are about $70 in winter, including cart, dropping to about $25 in summer.

In Old Naples, nonguests can sign up to play at **Naples Beach Hotel & Golf Club** (see "Accommodations You Can Afford," below).

In Golden Gate, west of I-75, the **Quality Inn Golf & Country Club,** 4100 Golden Gate Pkwy. (☎ 800/228-5151 or 941/455-1010), has an 18-hole course and 153 rooms, suites, and efficiencies.

SCUBA DIVING   The **Under Seas Dive Academy,** 998 6th Ave. S., in Olde Naples (☎ 941/262-0707), takes divers into the gulf, teaches diver-certification courses, and rents water-sports equipment. So does Kevin Sweeney's **SCUBA-d-ventures,** 971 Creech Rd., at Tamiami Trail (☎ 941/434-7477).

TENNIS   In Olde Naples, the city's **Cambier Park Tennis Center,** 755 8th Ave. S., at 9th Street South (☎ 941/434-4694), offers 12 lighted clay courts. It's one of the few public tennis facilities anywhere to match those found at luxury resorts. Play costs $6 for 90 minutes. It's open Monday to Friday from 8am to 10pm, Saturday and Sunday from 8am to 5pm. Book with the pro in the middle of the courts. There's a children's playground next to the courts.

Nonguests can play at the **Naples Beach Hotel & Golf Club,** 851 Gulf Shore Blvd. N. (☎ 941/261-2222), for $9.50 an hour, but call ahead to reserve court time.

Dedicated buffs can play to their hearts' content on the 11 clay and 5 hard courts at **World Tennis Center Resort & Club,** 4800 Airport–Pulling Rd., at Pine Ridge Road (☎ 800/292-6663 or 941/263-1900; fax 941/649-7855), but you must stay in one of the 72 two-bedroom condominiums here to use them. There's a restaurant, swimming pool, and sauna on the premises.

WATER SPORTS   Good Times Rental, 1947 Davis Blvd. (☎ 941/775-7529), rents Wave Runners, Windsurfers, skim boards, canoes, snorkeling gear, rafts, and other beach equipment. Hobie Cats and Windsurfers can also be rented on the beach at the **Naples Beach Hotel & Golf Club,** 851 Gulf Shore Blvd. N. (☎ 941/261-2222), and at **Clam Pass County Park,** at the end of Seagate Drive (☎ 941/353-0404). See "Hitting the Beach," above, for more about Clam Pass County Park.

EXPLORING THE TOWN

Old Naples is a great place to stroll and do some window shopping, and during the winter you can take evening horse-drawn carriage rides with the **Naples Horse & Carriage Co.** (☎ 941/649-1210). Prices begin at $30 per person for a 30-minute ride. The carriages can hold up to four adults.

OLDE NAPLES

Its history may only date from 1886, but **Olde Naples** still has the charm of that Victorian era. The heart of the district lies below 5th Avenue South (that's where U.S. 41 takes a 45° turn). The town docks are on the bay side, the glorious beach along the gulf. Laid out on a grid, the tree-lined streets run between many houses—some dating from the town's beginning—and along Millionaires' Row between Gulf Shore Boulevard and the beach. With these gorgeous homes virtually hidden in the palms and casuarinas, the Olde Naples beach seems a century removed from the high-rise condos found farther north.

The **Naples Pier,** at the gulf end of 12th Avenue South, is a focal point of the neighborhood. Built in 1888 to let steamers land potential real-estate customers, the original 600-foot-long, T-shaped structure was destroyed by hurricanes and damaged by fire. Local residents have rebuilt it because they like strolling its length to catch fantastic gulf sunsets and to get a glimpse of Millionaires' Row from its gulf side. The pier is now a state historic site. It's free and open 24 hours a day, but parking in the nearby metered lots is restricted between 11pm and 7am.

Nearby, **Palm Cottage,** 137 12th Ave. S., between 1st Street and Gordon Drive (☎ 941/261-8164), was built in 1885 by one of Naples's founders, *Louisville Courier-Journal* publisher Walter Haldeman, as a winter retreat for his chief editorial writer. After World War II, its socialite owners hosted many galas attended by Hollywood stars such as Hedy Lamarr, Gary Cooper, and Robert Montgomery. One of the few remaining Southwest Florida houses built of tabbie mortar (made by burning shells), Palm Cottage today is the home of the Naples Historical Society, which maintains it as a museum filled with authentic furniture, paintings, photographs, and other memorabilia. Tours are given during winter, Monday to Friday from 1 to 4pm. Adult admission is by $5 donation; free for children.

Near the Gordon River Bridge on 5th Avenue South, the old corrugated waterfront warehouses are now a shopping-and-dining complex known as the **Marketplace at Tin City,** which tourists throng to and local residents assiduously avoid during the winter months.

MUSEUMS & ZOOS

Caribbean Gardens. 1590 Goodlette-Frank Rd. (at Fleischman Blvd.). ☎ **941/262-5409.** Admission $13.95 adults, $8.95 children 4–15, free for children 3 and under. Daily 9:30am–5:30pm (last admission at 4:30pm). Closed Easter, Thanksgiving, and Christmas.

A family favorite formerly known as "Jungle Larry's," for noted animal trainer and owner Larry Tetzlaff, this zoo features a variety of animals and birds, including a fascinating community of primates living free on their own island. You can see them on a safari through the spectacular tropical gardens. Many visitors are captivated by the Big Cat Show, in which lions and tigers are put through their paces by Larry's son, David Tetzlaff, himself a talented trainer. Big Cat show times vary, so call for the schedule. You can also see three of the world's 40 golden tigers here. For kids, there's a petting farm, elephant rides, and a playground. The Canyon Cafe serves snacks, and there are picnic facilities on the premises.

✪ **Teddy Bear Museum.** 2511 Pine Ridge Rd. (at Airport–Pulling Rd.). ☎ **800/681-2327** or 941/598-2711. Admission $6 adults, $4 seniors, $2 children 4 to 12, free for children under 4. Winter Mon and Wed–Sat 10am–5pm, Sun 1–5pm. Off-season Wed–Sat 10am–5pm, Sun 1–5pm. Closed New Year's Day, July 4, Thanksgiving, and Christmas.

Another family favorite, this entertaining museum contains 3,000-plus examples of stuffed teddy bears from around the world. They're cleverly displayed descending from the rafters in hot-air balloons, attending board meetings, sipping afternoon tea, celebrating a wedding, even doing bear things like hibernating. There's a gift shop where you can buy your own bears.

PARKS & NATURE PRESERVES

You don't have to go far east of Naples to reach the magnificent Everglades, much of it protected by Everglades National Park and Big Cypress National Preserve. See chapter 7 for full details on activities in and near the national park. Other nearby nature preserves are described in section 6 of this chapter, on Marco Island.

One of the largest private preserves is the ✪ **Corkscrew Swamp Sanctuary** (☎ **941/348-9151**), 16 miles northeast of Naples off Immokalee Road (County Road 846). Maintained by the National Audubon Society, this 11,000-acre wilderness is home to countless wood storks that nest high in the cypress trees from November to April. Wading birds also are best seen in winter, when the swamp is likely to be dry (they don't nest when water levels are high). The birds congregate around pools near a boardwalk that leads 2 miles through the largest bald cypress forest with some of the oldest trees in the country. Ferns and orchids also flourish. Admission is $6.50 for adults, $5 for full-time college students, $3 for children 6 to 18, and free for children 5 and under. The sanctuary is open December to April, daily from 7am to 5pm; May to November, daily from 8am to 5pm. To reach the sanctuary, take Exit 17 off I-75 and go east on Immokalee Road (County Road 846).

About a 30-minute drive away, the **Corkscrew Marsh Trail System,** on Corkscrew Road south of Fla. 82, consists of a 5-mile loop through mostly pine forests managed jointly by the Corkscrew Regional Ecosystem Watershed Trust and the South Florida Water Management District. Only hikers are allowed to use these trails, which are free but have no drinking water or rest rooms.

You can also experience Southwest Florida's abundant natural life without leaving town at **The Conservancy's Naples Nature Center,** 14th Avenue North, east of Goodlette-Frank Road (☎ **941/262-0304**), one of two preserves operated by The Conservancy of Southwest Florida (see the Briggs Nature Center in section 6). There are nature trails, an aviary with bald eagles and other birds, and electric boat rides through a mangrove forest to observe wildlife (you can also rent canoes and kayaks and see it by yourself). A nature store carries interesting gift items. The trails and boat rides are included in the admission of $5 for adults, $2 for children 3 to 12, free for children under 3. Canoe and kayak rentals are $13 for 2 hours, $5 for each additional hour. The center is open year-round Monday to Saturday from 9am to 4:30pm, and also on Sunday from 1 to 5pm from January through March.

SHOPPING

Two blocks of **3rd Street South,** at Broad Avenue, is the Rodeo Drive of Naples. This glitzy collection of jewelers, clothiers, and art galleries may be too rich for many budgets, but the window shopping here is unmatched. Be sure to pick up a free brochure, which lists the merchants and has a map of the area, from the chamber of commerce visitors center (see "Essentials," above).

Nearby, the **5th Avenue South** shopping area, between 3rd and 9th Streets South, is longer and a bit less chic, with stockbrokerages and real-estate offices thrown into the mix of boutiques and antique dealers. Both areas have several bistros and other dining spots. Also in Olde Naples, the **Old Marine Marketplace at Tin City,** 1200 5th Ave. S., at the Gordon River, has 50 boutiques selling everything from souvenirs to avant-garde resort wear and imported statuary. There are more boutiques in the **Dockside Boardwalk,** half a block west on 6th Avenue South.

Even the malls in Naples have their charms. The **Village at Venetian Bay,** 4200 Gulf Shore Blvd., at Park Shore Drive, evokes images of its Italian namesake, with 50 canal-side shops featuring high-fashion men's and women's clothiers and fine-art galleries. Ornate Mediterranean architecture and a tropical waterfall highlight the open-air **Waterside Shops at Pelican Bay,** Seagate Drive at North Tamiami Trail (U.S. 41), where the anchor stores are Saks Fifth Avenue and Jacobson's. There's a huge Barnes & Noble bookstore across Seagate Drive.

Coastland Center, on North Tamiami Trail (U.S. 41) between Fleischman Boulevard and Golden Gate Parkway, is the regular mall here, but it's a monster (you'll walk nearly a mile from end to end). Burdine's, Dillards, and JC Penney anchor most of the familiar national chains.

Discount shoppers can head to **Coral Isle Factory Outlets,** on Fla. 951 about a mile south of U.S. 41 on the way to Marco Island, although it's smaller and less promising than the Sanibel Factory Outlets in Fort Myers (see "Shopping" in section 1). You'll find the usual clothiers here, plus outlets for Villeroy & Bosh, Mikasa, and Coach Leathers.

ACCOMMODATIONS YOU CAN AFFORD

Most Naples establishments offer weekly and monthly rates during winter, especially the town's many condominium complexes, including the Park Shore Resort (see below). One of the biggest condo-rental agents here is **Bluebill Properties,** 26201 Hickory Blvd., Bonita Springs, FL 33923 (☎ **800/237-2010** or 941/597-1102; fax 941/597-7175).

Even the national chain motels in Naples tend to be of higher quality and better value than their counterparts elsewhere in Southwest Florida. Within walking distance of the historic district, the **Comfort Inn on the Bay,** 1221 5th Ave. S. (☎ **800/ 228-5150** or 941/649-5800), enjoys a picturesque setting on Naples Bay. Known for its poolside tiki bar, the **Howard Johnson Resort Lodge,** 221 9th St. S. (☎ **800/ 654-2000** or 941/262-6181), also is within walking distance of Olde Naples.

SUPER-CHEAP SLEEPS

Lighthouse Inn Motel. 9140 Gulf Shore Dr. North, Naples, FL 34108. ☎ **941/597-3345.** Fax 941/597-5541. 15 units. A/C TV. Winter $90 single or double, $95 efficiency, $105 apt. Off-season $40 single or double, $49 efficiency, $59 apt. MC, V.

A relic from decades gone by, Judy and Buzz Dugan's spotlessly clean, 2-story motel sits across the street from other more expensive properties on Vanderbilt Beach and within walking distance of the Ritz-Carlton Naples. The efficiencies and apartments are simple, with freshly painted cinder-block walls and small kitchens. The one kitchenless room has a small fridge and coffeemaker. Most guests take advantage of weekly and monthly rates in winter, when it's heavily booked. Buzz's Lighthouse Café next door is a pleasant place for an inexpensive, dockside breakfast, lunch, or dinner.

✪ Olde Naples Inn & Suites. 801 3rd St. S., Naples, FL 34102. ☎ **800/637-6036** or 941/262-5194. Fax 941/262-4876. www.bestof.net/naples/hotels/oldenaplesinn. 60 units. A/C TV TEL. Winter $99–$179 single or double. Off-season $55–$92 single or double. Rates include continental breakfast. AE, DC, DISC, MC, V.

In the heart of Olde Naples, this dated but extraordinarily well-maintained apartment hotel is just 2 blocks from the beach and 4 blocks from the 3rd Street South shopping area (which more than makes up for the lack of an on-site restaurant). Its eclectic combination of rooms, efficiencies, and one- and two-bedroom suites are in three buildings occupying about 60% of a city block, but the tropical landscaping makes it seem smaller. Some of the bath and kitchen fixtures apparently date from the 1950s, but otherwise the units are comfortably furnished, immaculately maintained, and breezy. There are two heated swimming pools, laundry facilities, and off-street parking.

Stoney's Courtyard Inn. 2630 N. Tamiami Trial (U.S. 41), Naples, FL 34103. ☎ **800/ 432-3870** or 941/261-3870. Fax 941/261-4932. 76 units. A/C TV TEL. Winter $90–$105 single or double; $125 suite. Off-season $45–$60 single or double; $70–$105 suite. Rates include continental breakfast. AE, DISC, MC, V.

If you can't get into one of the apartment hotels, this pleasant, locally-owned motel is the next best bargain in town. It does indeed have a courtyard, with tropical foliage and a genuine thatch pavilion next to a heated swimming pool. The rooms facing this scene are worth an additional $5 per night over those on the parking lot side. All open to external walkways, and most are of standard motel configuration, with two double beds, a spacious dressing area with an open closet, an armoire for the cable TV, and a combination bath. Restaurants are nearby on U.S. 41.

✪ Tides Inn of Naples. 1801 Gulf Shore Blvd. N., Naples, FL 34102. ☎ **800/438-8763** or 941/262-6196. Fax 941/262-3055. 35 units. A/C TV TEL. Winter $105–$235 single or double. Off-season $65–$130 single or double. AE, MC, V.

There's a very good reason why this immaculate 2-story motel stays heavily booked during the winter months: It's right on the beach, just one door removed from the Edgewater Beach Hotel, and on the edge of Millionaires' Row and Olde Naples. Comfortable suites and efficiencies, all tropically furnished and decorated, have screened balconies or patios angled to face the beach across a courtyard with coconut palms and heated swimming pool. (Motel rooms have no balcony or patio and overlook the parking lot.) In winter, the suites and efficiencies must be reserved for at least a month; otherwise, ask for a room and pray for a cancellation. It's certainly worth a try, for you can't stay anywhere else on a Naples beach for these rates.

FOR A FEW BUCKS MORE

Inn by the Sea. 287 11th Ave. S., Naples, FL 34102. ☎ **941/649-4124.** 5 units. A/C. Winter $149–$189 single or double. Off-season $94–$114 single or double. Rates include continental breakfast. AE, DISC, MC, V.

Listed in the National Register of Historic Places, this bed-and-breakfast 2 blocks from the beach in the heart of Olde Naples was built in 1937 as a boardinghouse by Alice Bowling, one of Naples's first schoolteachers and a grocer and entrepreneur to boot. Owned and operated by Peggy Cormier, the Federal-style house still has much of its original pine floors, matching pine or cypress woodwork, and exterior pinkish galvanized shingles. Comfy wicker furniture and ceiling fans add to the Old Florida ambience. Two of the five rooms have separate sitting areas. Bikes are provided, and guests are served oranges from the backyard tree. Note that children 13 and under are not accepted.

Inn of Naples. 4055 N. Tamiami Trail (U.S. 41), Naples, FL 34103. ☎ **800/237-8858** or 941/649-5500. Fax 941/430-0422. 100 units. A/C MINIBAR TV TEL. Winter $138–$176 single or double; $176–$275 suite. Off-season $69–$126 single or double; $126–$176 suite. Rates include continental breakfast. AE, DC, DISC, MC, V.

Many business travelers who can't afford the Ritz-Carlton like to stay at this comfortable, semielegant establishment near Park Shore Drive and Pelican Bay. The 5-story Spanish-style building with red-tile roof and arches contains guest rooms and suites furnished with oak and pine furniture. All are equipped with easy chairs or love seats, writing desks, two telephones, VCRs, refrigerators as well as minibars, and spacious baths with separate dressing areas. Each unit also has a balcony, although some are postage-stamp size and close to noisy external air-conditioning units. The inn's presidential suite is a 1,200-square-foot apartment called the Grand Mizner.

There's an exercise room for burning off the calories ingested at an Italian restaurant that serves lunch and dinner, either indoors or in a screened patio next to a heated, terra-cotta–lined swimming pool and whirlpool, both surrounded by colorful bougainvillea and other tropical foliage.

Park Shore Resort. 600 Neapolitan Way, Naples, FL 34103. ☎ **800/548-2077** or 941/263-2222. Fax 941/262-0946. 156 condos. A/C TV TEL. Winter $204–$224. Off-season $91–$154. AE, DC, DISC, MC, V.

A good bet if you want a kitchen and more space than a hotel room, these attractive one- and two-bedroom condos surround an artificial lagoon with waterfalls cascading on its own island. Guests can walk across a bridge to the artificial island, where they can swim in the heated pool, order from the bar, and barbecue.

The Island Club restaurant serves lunch, dinner, and Sunday brunch, and there are plenty of other restaurants nearby. Amenities include children's activities program; daily maid service; complimentary shuttle to the beach daily at 11am and 2:30pm; tennis, racquetball, volleyball, basketball, and shuffleboard courts; whirlpool; laundry room.

Vanderbilt Inn on the Gulf. 11000 Gulf Shore Dr., Naples, FL 34108. ☎ **800/643-8654** or 941/597-3151. Fax 941/597-3099. 163 units. A/C TV TEL. Winter $180–$295 single or double. Off-season $95–$160 single or double. (Highest rates for beachfront units.) Weekly rates available. AE, DC, DISC, MC, V.

Cheerful tropical decor in the accommodations and public areas sets the tempo for a casual, fun vacation at this motel. It's located 4 miles north of Olde Naples on Vanderbilt Beach, where guests can go parasailing and rent boats and water-sports equipment. About half the rooms face a beachside courtyard with a kidney-shaped, heated swimming pool surrounded by a brick terrace and tropical grounds. The other rooms face the exterior parking lots. Although the rooms are entered from exterior walkways, their big windows are darkly tinted to provide privacy. All rooms have refrigerators, and 16 also have cooking facilities.

A thatch-roofed Chickee Bar and Restaurant serves alfresco lunches and dinners and draws a crowd for sunset happy hour Monday to Friday from 4:30 to 8:30pm and on Saturday and Sunday when bands play from 3:30 to 7:30pm. Also popular for lunch, the Seabreeze Lounge turns lively on Saturday night when its band cranks up. The Jasmine Court serves breakfast and romantic candlelit dinners (early bird specials from 5 to 7pm, and guests 12 and under dine free when accompanied by adults). Other amenities here include concierge; limited room service; babysitting; outdoor heated pool, kid's pool, bicycle rentals, and coin laundry.

Saving Money: Naples's Apartment Hotels

While Naples has some of the most expensive resorts in the region, it also has some surprisingly reasonable rates, particularly at several older but very well-maintained "apartment motels" in the historic district within a few blocks of the beach. Although dated by today's standards, most are clean and comfortable, and many have been upgraded over the years to include modern kitchens and air-conditioning (the old louvered windows and doors, however, let in plenty of fresh air during the pleasant winter months). They are very popular from mid-December to mid-April, when many guests stay a month or more, so book as early as possible.

One of the best is the **Olde Naples Inn & Suites,** where rooms cost as little as $55 off-season (see the listing under "Super-Cheap Sleeps," above). Others include the **Beachcomber Club,** 290 5th Ave. S. (☎ 800/634-1311 or 941/262-8112); **Flamingo Apartment Motel,** 383 6th Ave. S. (☎ 941/261-7017; fax 941/261-7769); **Mahalo Apartment Motel,** 441 8th Ave. S. (☎ 941/261-6332; fax 941/263-0182); **Neptune Apartment Hotel,** 651 3rd Ave. S. (☎ 941/262-6126; fax 941/263-6126); **Suntide Apartment Motel,** 649 10th Ave. S. (☎ 941/261-8131); and **Tropical Apartments,** 745 4th Ave. S. (☎ 941/262-1011).

WORTH A SPLURGE

✪ **Naples Beach Hotel & Golf Club.** 851 Gulf Shore Blvd., Naples, FL 33940. ☎ **800/237-7600** or 941/261-2222. Fax 941/261-7380. 315 units. A/C TV TEL. Winter $205–$315 single or double; $280–$435 suite. Off-season $95–$170 single or double; $140–$240 suite. Packages available. AE, DC, DISC, MC, V.

Although Henry B. Watkins Sr. bought the Naples Hotel along with the town's undeveloped land in 1946, he soon replaced that turn-of-the-century building with this charming establishment, still owned and operated by his family. The beachside setting on Millionaires' Row in Olde Naples couldn't be better for carrying on the hallowed, friendly, and relaxed Old Florida ambience Watkins installed a half century ago. The least expensive units here, in fact, are in the Old Florida Wing, a 2-story relic from 1948 but recently spiffed up during a $10 million overhaul (they are a very good deal in summer at $95 for a double). The old wing's comfortable rooms and suites open to long, railing-enclosed porches with views across a manicured lawn to the gulf. Other accommodations here are more modern and spacious, but all have lots of bright colors and old-style accents.

Since the resort predates the strict historic district zoning laws, it has Olde Naples's only two restaurants and bars directly on the beach. HB's on the Gulf is a casual spot for an alfresco, beachside lunch or dinner. Wedged between the beach and an Olympic-size pool, the Sunset Beach Bar is one of the region's most famous beachside "chickee" bars and is always crammed as the sun sets over the gulf. It's especially active on Sunday afternoon during the winter season, when live bands perform. Inside the main building but facing the gulf, the semicircular Everglades Dining Room emphasizes traditional Florida cuisine, offers an excellent breakfast buffet to guests and nonguests alike (a genuine all-you-can-eat bargain at $7 a head for continental, $9.50 for hot foods), and has live entertainment and dancing Tuesday to Saturday night in winter. Off the lobby, the Seminole Store offers inexpensive pastries, pizzas, salads, and sandwiches in addition to a wide range of Florida products. Complimentary afternoon tea is served in the lobby lounge.

Among the amenities here: concierge, turndown, complimentary newspaper, laundry, activities desk, supervised children's program with its own playroom, 18-hole par-72 championship golf course, 6 tennis courts, Olympic-size swimming pool, sailboat and other water-sports equipment rentals at the beach, gift shop, beauty salon.

GREAT DEALS ON DINING

Many first-time visitors opt to have a lunch or dinner at the Marketplace at Tin City, on the Gordon River at 5th Avenue South, where the **Riverwalk Fish & Ale House** (☎ 941/262-2734) and **Merriman's Wharf** (☎ 941/261-1811) specialize in moderately priced seafood and steaks.

You'll find budget-priced fast-food and family-style restaurants along U.S. 41, including a branch of **Mel's Diner**, 3650 Tamiami Trail North (☎ 941/643-9898).

SUPER-CHEAP EATS

Dock at Crayton Cove. 12th Ave. S. (at the City Dock in Olde Naples). ☎ **941/263-9940.** Reservations not accepted. Main courses $13–$19; sandwiches $5–$10.50. AE, DISC, MC, V. Mon–Sat 11:30am–1am, Sun noon–midnight. SEAFOOD.

Located right on the City Dock, this lively pub is the best place in town for an open-air meal or a cool drink while watching the boats go back and forth across Naples Bay. The chow emphasizes well-prepared local seafood, from hearty chowders by the mug to grilled swordfish, with Jamaican-style jerk shrimp thrown in for spice. The main courses aren't cheap, but on the light side, there's grilled seafood Caesar salad and a good selection of sandwiches, hot dogs, and other pub-style fare, plus a raw bar that is open daily from 3 to 6pm. Unlike its sister establishment, the tourist-frequented Riverwalk Fish House at Tin City, "The Dock" is highly popular with local residents, who regularly socialize at the bar during happy hours daily from 4 to 7pm and from 9pm to midnight. If you're here on the second Saturday in May, the "Great Dock Canoe Race" draws thousands of onlookers.

✪ **First Watch.** In Gulf Shore Square, 1400 Gulf Shore Blvd. (at Banyan Rd.). ☎ **941/434-0005.** Most items $3.50–$6.50. AE, DISC, MC, V. Daily 7am–2:30pm. AMERICAN.

Just like its sibling in Sarasota, this corner shop with big louvered shutters to temper the morning sun is one of Naples's favorite spots for breakfast, late brunch, or a midday meal. This is anything but a diner, however. Instead you get classical music and widely spaced tables topped with pitchers of lemon-tinged ice water. A young staff provides quick and friendly service. The menu leans heavily on healthy selections, but you can get your cholesterol from a sizzling skillet of fried eggs served over layers of potatoes, vegetables, and melted cheese. Lunch features large salads, sandwiches, and quesadillas. In addition to the dining room, there's additional seating in the shopping center's courtyard.

Old Naples Pub. 255 13th Ave. S. (between 3rd and 4th sts. S., behind Thalheimer's Jewelers). ☎ **941/649-8200.** Salads, sandwiches, and burgers $5–$9; main courses $13. Mon–Sat 11am–11pm, bar open until midnight; Sun noon–10pm, bar open until 11pm. AMERICAN.

You would never guess that the person sitting next to you at the bar is very, very rich, so relaxed is this small, somewhat cramped pub in the middle of the 3rd Street South shops. Diners fortunately find more room at tables on the shopping center's patio. Inside, the pine-paneled walls are hung with trophy fish, a dart board, and old newspaper clippings about Naples. The menu features very good pub fare, including homemade soups, nachos, red beans and rice, burgers, and sandwiches ranging from charcoal-grilled bratwurst to fried grouper. Only two main courses are offered: platters with either New York strip steak or grilled tuna. You can catch live entertainment here Monday to Saturday evenings and jazz on Sunday from 5 to 8pm.

✪ **Silver Spoon Café.** In the Waterside Shops at Pelican Bay, 5395 N. Tamiami Trail (at Seagate Dr.). ☎ **941/591-2123.** Reservations not accepted, but call ahead for preferred seating. Main courses $8.50–$14; pizza and pasta $7–$10; soups, salads, and sandwiches $6–$8.50. AE, DC, DISC, MC, V. Sun–Thurs 11am–10pm, Fri–Sat 11am–11pm. AMERICAN/ITALIAN.

Befitting the swanky Waterside Shops complex, this chic bistro flaunts sophisticated black-and-white high-tech decor and has large window walls overlooking the mall action. Thick sandwiches are served with either french fries, spicy pecan rice, or black beans. The tomato-dill soup and the gourmet pizzas and pasta dishes are popular, especially with the after-theater crowds from the nearby Philharmonic Center for the Arts, and the less-expensive main courses such as orange Dijon chicken are both tasty and an excellent value. Matron shoppers love to do lunch here, so come early or be prepared for a wait.

FOR A FEW BUCKS MORE

✪ **Bistro 821.** 821 5th Ave. S. (between 8th and 9th sts. S.). ☎ **941/261-5821.** Reservations recommended. Main courses $10–$23. AE, DC, MC, V. Sun–Thurs 5–10pm; Fri–Sat 5–10:30pm. MEDITERRANEAN.

One of several chic bistros near the eastern end of the 5th Avenue South shopping strip, this popular, noisy bistro began the trend toward Mediterranean restaurants here (see Terra, below). A bench covered in bright print fabric runs down one side of this storefront to a bar and open kitchen in the rear. Although the quarters are too close for private conversations, small spotlights hanging from the ceiling romantically illuminate each table. The house specialty is rotisserie chicken, and a daily risotto leads a menu featuring penne pasta in a vodka sauce, and a seasonal vegetable plate with herb couscous. There's sidewalk dining here, too.

Michelbob's Rib Capital of Florida. 371 Airport–Pulling Rd. (at Progress Ave.). ☎ **941/643-7427.** Reservations not accepted. Sandwiches $3.50–$6.50; platters $8–$19. AE, DC, MC, V. Winter Mon–Thurs 11am–9pm, Fri–Sat 11am–10pm, Sun 8am–1:30pm (brunch) and 1:30–9pm. Off-season Mon–Sat 11am–9pm, Sun 8:30am–1:30pm (brunch) and 1:30–9pm. BARBECUE.

The name says it all about this barnlike establishment, winner of more than 20 national and international cook-offs for the best ribs and barbecue sauces. The big specialty is baby back ribs, imported from Denmark (where the hogs are reputedly tulip-fed). Sliced pork or beef platters and sandwiches are also offered but don't match the ribs. There's a children's menu and an extensive Sunday brunch buffet. The smoke aroma comes from the barbecue pit, not from cigarettes or cigars, since no smoking is permitted.

Terra. 1300 3rd St. S. (actually on 13th Ave. S.). ☎ **941/262-5550.** Reservations recommended. Pizzas and sandwiches $6.50–$12.50; main courses $10.50–$27. AE, DC, DISC, MC, V. Daily 11:30am–10pm (bar until 11:30pm). MEDITERRANEAN.

This elegant yet casual restaurant in the heart of the 3rd Street South shopping district has muted lighting, a few antiques and paintings, and green-and-black woven rattan chairs at oak tables inlaid with terra-cotta tiles. A pianist lends romance as you enjoy Mediterranean dishes such as lamb shank osso buco, tasty wild mushroom lasagne, a risotto of the day, and personal-size pizzas. Italian panini sandwiches, including a lamb shank version accompanied by ratatouille, are served at both lunch and dinner, so you don't necessarily have to spend a fortune here.

Tommy Bahama's Tropical Café. 1220 3rd St. S. (at 12th Ave. S.). ☎ **941/643-6889.** Sandwiches $6–$9; main courses $12–$22. AE, DC, MC, V. Daily 11am–10pm. CARIBBEAN.

You walk through a thatch gateway into this lively, island-style pub—an incongruous sight in the middle of the staid 3rd Street South shopping enclave. Diners gather on a large front patio under shade trees or inside, where a large back-wall mural creates a Polynesian scene. There's an open kitchen and serving bar on one side of the dining room, a real bar dispensing drinks on the other. In between, round-backed cane chairs and classic ceiling fans add to the exotic mood. Although the Caribbean cuisine doesn't quite live up to the ambience, you'll have too much fun here to care if it's not gourmet. If a meal doesn't appeal, a blackened red-snapper sandwich is served at all hours. The restaurant is an offshoot of Tommy Bahama's tropical clothing store next door.

GREAT PICNIC FARE

Naples's beaches are ideal for picnics. In Olde Naples, you can get freshly baked breads and pastries, prepacked gourmet sandwiches, and fruit plates at **Tony's Off Third,** 1300 3rd St. S. (☎ 941/262-7999). It's also a fine place for coffee while window shopping on 3rd Avenue South. The **Pelicatessen,** in the Waterside Shops at Pelican Bay, Seagate Drive at North Tamiami Trail (☎ 941/597-3003), offers imported cheeses, freshly sliced meats, unusual salads, and shelves of gourmet items. Buy there and take it to Clam Pass County Park, at the end of Seagate Drive.

NAPLES AFTER DARK

For entertainment ideas, check the *Naples Daily News,* especially the "Neapolitan" section in Friday's edition.

THE PERFORMING ARTS   The impressive **Philharmonic Center for the Arts,** 5833 Pelican Bay Blvd., at West Boulevard (☎ 941/597-1900), is the home of the Naples Philharmonic, but its year-round schedule is filled with cultural events such as performances by the Bolshoi Ballet, concerts by celebrated artists and internationally known orchestras, and Broadway plays and shows aimed at children and families. Call "The Phil" for a copy of its seasonal calendar.

THE BAR & CLUB SCENE   Much of Naples's nightlife centers on the hotels and restaurants mentioned above. The beachside "chickee hut" bar at the **Naples Beach Hotel & Golf Club** (☎ 941/261-2222) is always popular and has live entertainment many nights and is *the* place to go on Sunday afternoon and early evening. So is the beachside bar at the **Vanderbilt Inn on the Gulf** (☎ 941/597-3151). If it hasn't changed it name or character, the Club Zanzibar in the **Registry Resort** (☎ 941/597-3232) has deejay music for listening and dancing. Among the restaurants, the **Bay-side Seafood Grille & Bar** (☎ 941/649-5552) has pianists or jazz musicians. Since their schedules vary by season, it's always best to call ahead.

The **Olde Naples Pub,** 255 13th Ave. S. (☎ 941/649-8200), in the 3rd Street South shopping area, has a pianist Monday to Saturday evening and jazz in the courtyard on Sunday from 5 to 8pm. See "Greats Deals on Dining," above.

The **Old Marine Marketplace at Tin City,** the restored waterfront warehouses on 5th Avenue South on the west side of the Gordon River, comes alive during the winter when visitors flock to its shops and the **Riverwalk Fish & Ale House** (☎ 941/262-2734), which has live entertainment during the season.

6 Marco Island

15 miles SE of Naples, 53 miles S of Fort Myers, 100 miles W of Miami

Capt. William Collier would hardly recognize Marco Island if he were to come back from the grave today. No relation to Collier County founder Barron Collier, the captain settled his family on the north end of this largest of Florida's Ten Thousand Islands back in 1871. He traded pelts with the Native Americans, caught and smoked fish to sell to Key West and Cuba, and charged fishermen and other guests $2 a day for a room in his home. By 1896, he was doing such a roaring tourist business that he built a proper inn.

His Old Marco Inn still stands (it's now a fine restaurant), along with a few other turn-of-the-century buildings. But Captain Collier would be shocked to come across the high-rise bridge to the island and see it now sliced by artificial canals and virtually covered by resorts, condos, shops, restaurants, and winter homes. These are the products of an extensive real-estate development begun in 1965, which means that Marco lacks any of the charm found in Naples and on Sanibel and Capitva islands. Much of the sales effort here was aimed at the northeastern states, so the island smacks more of New York and Massachusetts rather than the laid-back midwestern style of its neighbors.

Marco's year-round population of some 10,000 swells to more than 30,000 during the winter season. Most of this multitude are retirees coming south for the winter, families on vacation, and groups convening at the island's three big resort hotels. While here, they enjoy Marco's crescent-shaped beach, the nearby waterways running through a maze of small islands, excellent boating and fishing, and the island's proximity to thousands of acres of wildlife preserves.

ESSENTIALS

GETTING THERE   From either I-75 or U.S. 41, take Fla. 951 south directly to Marco Island.

See the Fort Myers and Naples sections, earlier in this chapter, for information about the **Southwest Florida International Airport** and the **Naples Municipal Airport,** respectively, and about Amtrak's train service and Greyhound/Trailways buses to those cities.

VISITOR INFORMATION   The **Marco Island Area Chamber of Commerce,** 1102 N. Collier Blvd., Marco Island, FL 34145 (☎ **800/788-6272** or 941/394-7549; fax 941/394-3061; www.marco-island-florida.com/chamber; e-mail: chamber@marco-island-florida.com), provides free information about the island. There's a message board and phone outside for making hotel reservations even when the office is closed. The chamber is open Monday to Friday from 9am to 4pm, and on Saturday from 10am to 3pm during winter.

GETTING AROUND   Starting and ending at the Marriott resort, **Marco Island Trolley Tours** (☎ **941/394-1600**) makes four complete loops around the island daily from 10am to 3:15pm on Monday to Saturday. The conductors sell tickets and render an informative narration about the island's history. Daily fare is $10 for adults, $4 for children 11 and under, with free reboarding.

For a cab, call **A-Action Taxi** (☎ **941/394-4400**), **Classic Taxi** (☎ **941/394-1888**), or **A-Ok Taxi** (☎ **941/394-1113**).

Depending on the type, rental bicycles cost $10 to $20 a day at **Beach Sports,** 571 S. Collier Blvd. (☎ **941/642-4282**), opposite the Hilton, and at **Scootertown,**

842 Bald Eagle Dr. (☎ 941/394-8400), north of North Collier Boulevard near Old Marco. Scooters cost $45 a day.

HITTING THE BEACH & OTHER AFFORDABLE OUTDOOR ACTIVITIES

BEACHES   The sugar-white Crescent Beach curves for 3½ miles down the entire western shore of Marco Island. Its southern 2 miles are fronted by an unending row of high-rise condos and hotels, but the northern 1½ miles are preserved in **Tigertail Public Beach** (☎ 941/642-8414). A sandbar offshore here creates a shallow lagoon safe for swimming and perfect for learning to windsurf. There are rest rooms, cold-water outdoor showers, a children's playground, and volleyball nets. Tigertail Beach Rentals gives windsurfing lessons, conducts pontoon-boat nature and shelling tours, and rents cabanas, chairs, umbrellas, sailboats, windsurfers, kayaks, water tricycles, and other toys. A display illustrates the shells you'll find lying on the beach. **Todd's at Tigertail** (☎ 941/394-8828) has a fully screened patio where it serves inexpensive hot dogs, sandwiches, salads, and other snacks daily from 10am to 4pm. The park is at the end of Hernando Drive. It's open daily from dawn to dusk. There's no admission charge to the beach, but parking in the lot costs $3 per vehicle.

The beaches in front of the Marriott, Hilton, and Radisson resorts have parasailing, windsurfing, and other water-sports activities, all for a fee. In addition, **Beach Sports,** 571 S. Collier Blvd. (☎ 941/642-4282), opposite the Hilton, rents windsurfers, snorkeling gear, skim boards, fishing gear, tennis racquets, and a wide range of other equipment, including beach baby strollers. Beach Sports also has a scuba-dive operation charging $60 to $80 per dive, depending on depth, and teaching novice to advance courses.

If you're not staying at the big resorts, Collier County maintains a $3-per-vehicle parking lot and access to the developed beach on the southern end of the island, on Swallow Avenue at South Collier Boulevard.

OUTDOOR ACTIVITIES   A single source of information and the easiest way to book backcountry fishing, shelling, sightseeing, and sunset excursions through the beautiful inland waterways is through **Sea Excursions** (☎ 941/642-6400). Per person prices are about $20 for sightseeing, $25 for shelling, $35 for fishing, and $25 for sunset cruises. Reservations are required.

Or you can arrange it yourself at **Factory Bay Marina,** on North Bald Eagle Drive (☎ 941/642-6717), the island's major center for boating, fishing, and cruising. Here you can rent powerboats, take airboat rides, and charter fishing boats with captains. A half day of deep sea fishing on the party boat *Marco Cat* costs $45 for adults, $35 for children under 12, including license, bait, and tackle. You can go on 1½-hour airboat tours through the Ten Thousand Islands on the *Marco Eagle* or the *Marco Flyer* for $20 adults, $10 children under 12. The pontoon boat *Curve Ball* has 2-hour shelling excursions to remote beaches for $25 adults, $18 for children 8 to 16, $12 for kids under 8. It also runs sunset cruises. Call the marina for schedules and reservations.

Pier 81 Marina, also on Bald Eagle Drive (☎ 941/642-7881), is home base to the *Rosie* (☎ 941/394-7673), an old-fashioned, 105-foot-long paddlewheeler that has year-round sightseeing, lunch buffet, and dinner cruises. Call for its prices and seasonal schedule.

Naples's Lely and Boyne South golf courses are a short drive away (see "Great Golf That Won't Break Your Budget & Other Affordable Outdoor Activities" in section 5, above). The closest public courses are the **Marco Shores Golf Club,** 1450 Mainsail Dr. (☎ 941/394-2581), and **Marriott's Golf Club at Marco** (☎ 941/353-7061), both in the marshlands off Fla. 951 north of the island. A sign at the Marriott's course ominously warns: PLEASE DON'T DISTURB THE ALLIGATORS. Fees range from about $115 in winter down to $75 in summer.

Tennis courts are at the **Marco Island YMCA** (☎ **941/394-3144**) and the **Collier County Racquet Club** (☎ **941/394-5454**), both on San Marco Road, and at the **Tommie Barfield Elementary School,** Trinidad Avenue and Kirkwood Street (☎ **941/394-2611**).

PARKS & NATURE PRESERVES

Many species of birds inhabit ✪ **Collier Seminole State Park,** 20200 E. Tamiami Trail, Naples, FL 34114 (☎ **941/394-3397**), an inviting, 6,423-acre preserve on the edge of Big Cypress Swamp, 12 miles east of Marco Island on U.S. 41 just east of Fla. 92. Given to the state by Barron Collier, it offers fishing, boating, picnicking, canoeing over a 13-mile loop with a primitive campsite, observing nature along 6 miles of hiking trails (open during dry periods) and a 1-mile nature walk, and regular tent and RV camping (see "Accommodations You Can Afford," below). A "walking" dredge used to build the Tamiami Trail in the 1920s sits just inside the park entrance. Housed in a replica of a Seminole Wars–era log fort, an interpretive center has information about the park, and there are ranger-led programs from December to April. Narrated boat tours wander through the winding waterways daily from 9:30am to 3:30pm. Canoes can be rented, but the park has only four camping sites along the canoe trails. Admission to the park is $3.25 per vehicle, $1 for pedestrians and bikers. The boat tours cost $8.50 for adults, $5.50 for children 6 to 12, free for children 5 and under. Canoes rent for $3 per hour, $15 a day. The park is open daily from 8am to sundown.

Operated by The Conservancy and part of the Rookery Bay National Estuarine Research Reserve, the **Briggs Nature Center,** on Shell Island Road, off Fla. 951 between U.S. 41 and Marco Island (☎ **941/775-8569**), has a half-mile boardwalk through a pristine example of Florida's disappearing scrub lands, home to the threatened scrub jays and gopher tortoises. Rangers lead a variety of nature excursions (call for the seasonal schedule), and there's a self-guided canoe trail and canoes for rent during winter ($13 for the first 2 hours, $5 for each additional hour). During winter, the *Sea Queen* has three nature cruises daily on the bay ($20 per person). The center is open Monday to Friday from 9am to 4:30pm year-round, Saturday from 9am to 4:30pm October to May, and Sunday from 1 to 5pm January to March. The interpretive center and a butterfly garden (27 varieties) are free. Admission to the boardwalk is $3 for adults, $1 for children 3 to 12, free for children under 3. For more information, contact **The Conservancy of Southwest Florida,** 1450 Merrihue Dr., Naples, FL 34102 (☎ **941/262-0304;** fax 941/262-0672).

ACCOMMODATIONS YOU CAN AFFORD

There are no chain hotels on Marco Island other than the large, high-rise **Marco Island Hilton Beach Resort,** 560 S. Collier Blvd., Marco Island, FL 34145 (☎ **800/443-4550** or 941/394-5000; fax 941/394-8410); the **Marco Island Marriott Resort & Golf Club,** 400 S. Collier Blvd., Marco Island, FL 34145 (☎ **800/438-4373** or 941/394-2511; fax 941/642-2628), and the **Radisson Suite Beach Resort,** 600 S. Collier Blvd., Marco Island, FL 34145 (☎ **800/992-0651** or 941/394-4100; fax 941/394-0262). None inexpensive, they stand in a row along Cresent Beach on the island's southwestern corner.

On the other hand, Marco is loaded with condominium resorts. The **Paramount Suite Hotel,** 901 S. Collier Blvd., Marco Island, FL 34145 (☎ **800/323-8860** or 941/394-8860; fax 941/394-3040), on the inland side of the boulevard but near the big resorts, has 47 one- and two-bedroom units. Daily rates range from $145 to $186 in winter, $109 to $159 off-season.

Rental agents representing house and condo owners include **Century 21 First Southern Trust** (☎ **800/255-9487** or 941/394-7658; fax 941/394-0004; e-mail cent21sst@aol.com) and **Marco Beach Rentals** (☎ **800/423-7809** or 941/642-5400).

As elsewhere in South Florida, the high season here is from mid-December to mid-April. Rates drop precipitously in the off-season.

There's no campground in the developed part of Marco Island. **Collier Seminole State Park,** 20200 E. Tamiami Trail, Naples, FL 34114 (☎ **941/394-3397;** fax 941/394-5113), 12 miles east via Fla. 92, has 130 tent and RV sites laid out in circles and shaded by palms and live oaks. It has hot showers and a screened, open-air lounge. From December through April, sites cost $16 with electricity, $14 without. Off-season rates are $10.75 with electricity, $8.50 without. Reservations are accepted up to 11 months in advance. No pets are allowed in the campground.

SUPER-CHEAP SLEEPS

✪ **Boat House Motel.** 1180 Edington Place, Marco Island, FL 34148. ☎ **941/642-2400.** Fax 941/642-2435. www.theboathousemotel.com. 20 units, 3 condo apts., 2 cottages. A/C TV TEL. Winter $75–$149 double; $125–$200 apt. or cottage. Off-season $55–$75 double; $75–$135 apt. or cottage. MC, V.

One of the best bargains in these parts, this comfortable little motel sits beside the Marco River in Old Marco, on the island's northern end. The rooms are in a 2-story, lime-green-and-white building ending at a wooden dock. Here there's a small heated swimming pool with lounge furniture, picnic tables, and barbecue grills. Two rooms on the end have their own decks, and all open to tiny courtyards. Bright paint, ceiling fans, and louvered doors add a tropical ambience throughout. The one-bedroom condos next door open to a riverside dock, upon which is built a two-bedroom cottage named "The Gazebo," whose peaked roof is supported by umbrella-like spokes from a central pole. Facilities include a guest laundry, small library, and bicycle rentals. Olde Marco restaurants are a short stroll away.

GREAT DEALS ON DINING

For inexpensive fare, head for the Town Center Mall, at the corner of North Collier Boulevard and Bald Eagle Drive, where you'll find three good choices: **Susie's Diner** (☎ **941/642-6633**) is popular with the locals for breakfasts and especially for Susie's inexpensive full-meal lunch specials. She's open Monday to Saturday from 6:30am to 2:30pm and Sunday from 6:30am to 1pm (for breakfast only). **Breakfast Plus** (☎ **941/642-6900**) has eye-openers ranging from bacon and eggs to kippers to latkes. It's open daily from 7am to 2:30pm.

The island's popular sports bars also offer inexpensive pub fare to go with their multitudinous TVs. Most popular is **Rookie's Bar & Grill,** in Mission de San Marco Plaza at the corner of South Collier Boulevard and Winterberry Drive (☎ **941/394-6400**). Others are the **Crazy Flamingo,** in the Town Center Mall, North Collier Boulevard at Bald Eagle Drive (☎ **941/642-9600**); and the **Sand Bar,** on Bald Eagle Drive north of North Collier Boulevard (☎ **941/642-3625**).

SUPER-CHEAP EATS

Kahuna Restaurant. 1035 N. Collier Blvd., in Town Center. ☎ **941/394-4300.** Reservations not accepted. Sandwiches and burgers $3–$7; main courses $6–$11. MC, V. Daily 11am–9pm. AMERICAN.

Advertising itself as the "Island's Family Restaurant," Kahuna certainly is the least expensive choice here for dinner. The decor is plain and simple, with a mix of coral-colored booths and round tables under black ceiling fans. The burgers are some of Marco's best (there's a condiment bar with a variety of fixings). Main courses include several fried seafood selections, sautéed crab cakes, and charcoal-grilled tuna, but your best bet should be a nightly special such as salmon in a light dill sauce. Don't expect gourmet dining here, but the quality is fine for the price.

FOR A FEW BUCKS MORE

Little Bar & Restaurant. Harbor Place (County Rd. 892), Goodland. ☎ **941/394-5663.** Reservations recommended for dinner. Main courses $13–$17; early bird specials $8–$10. DISC, MC, V. Daily 11:30am–10pm (bar until 2am). Early bird specials 5–6pm. Closed Aug. SEAFOOD.

This very casual waterfront establishment is located in the heart of Goodland, an Old Florida fishing village on the eastern edge of Marco Island, some seven miles (and at least 30 years) removed from the heavily developed western end of the island. One dining room here actually was the interior of the *Star of the Everglades,* a boat that took presidents Truman and Eisenhower around and appeared in the Burl Ives movie *Winds Across the Everglades.* Other rooms possess antique bits and pieces from various buildings in the Chicago area, including an old pipe organ. A screened porch beside Goodland's fishing boat harbor is this area's most popular spot for lunches featuring seafood and other sandwiches. Daily specials from a nightly chalkboard might include Everglades frogs' legs.

✪ **Kretch's.** 527 Bald Eagle Dr. (south of N. Collier Blvd.). ☎ **941/394-3433.** Reservations recommended in winter. Main courses $13–$23. DC, MC, V. Mon–Fri 11am–3pm and 5–9pm, Sat–Sun 5–9pm. Closed Mon off-season and Easter, July 4, Thanksgiving, and Christmas. SEAFOOD/CONTINENTAL.

Noted pastry chef Bruce Kretschmer has created a sinfully rich seafood strudel by combining shrimp, crab, scallops, cheeses, cream, and broccoli in a flaky Bavarian pastry and serving it all under a lobster sauce. Cholesterol counters can choose from broiled or charcoal-grilled fish, shrimp, Florida lobster tail, steaks, or lamb chops. Bruce's popular "Mexican Friday" lunches feature delicious tacos and other inexpensive, south-of-the-border selections. Sunday is home-cooking night during winter, with chicken and dumplings, Yankee pot roast, and braised lamb shanks.

Snook Inn. 1215 Bald Eagle Dr. (at Palm St.), Old Marco. ☎ **941/394-3313.** Reservations not accepted. Main courses $11–$19; sandwiches $8–$10. AE, DC, DISC, MC, V. Daily 11am–10pm. SEAFOOD.

The choice seats at this Old Florida establishment are in an enclosed dock right beside the scenic Marco River. Although seafood is the specialty, tasty steaks, chicken, burgers, and sandwiches are among the choices. The dockside Chickee Bar is a fun place, especially during sunset happy hour Monday to Friday from 4 to 6pm. The bar really rocks when live entertainment is featured during the winter season. Call for free shuttle service from anywhere on Marco Island.

MARCO ISLAND AFTER DARK

It's not after dark, but one of the biggest parties in Florida takes place every Sunday afternoon at ✪ **Stan's Idle Hour Seafood Restaurant,** on County Rd. 892 in Goodland (☎ **941/394-3041**), where Owner Stan Gober, an Ernest Hemingway look-alike, host fires up the barbecue grills, bands crank up country music for dancing the "Buzzard Lope," and men compete to see who has the best legs. Stan's Goodland

Mullet Festival, always the weekend before the Super Bowl, is the mother of all parties.

Over on the developed part of the island, everyone turns out for outdoor entertainment at the **Mission San Marco Plaza** shopping center, South Collier Boulevard at Winterberry Drive, every Tuesday night year-round.

The lounges in the **Marriott and Hilton resorts** (see "Accommodations You Can Afford," above) provide pianists every evening. The **Olde Marco Inn** and the **Snook Inn** have live entertainment nightly during the winter season (see "Greats Deals on Dining," above). The schedules vary by season, so call ahead.

One of the most lively local spots is **La Casita Mexican Restaurant,** in the Shops of Marco, San Marco Road at Barfield Drive (☎ **941/642-7600**), where owners Frankie Ray and Maryellen play a variety of Mexican, Irish, popular, and traditional music Monday to Saturday. On Sunday, 1950s and 1960s dance music is highlighted.

Another choice is **Alan's Hideaway Piano Bar,** 23 Front St. (☎ **941/642-0770**), where owner Alan Bogdan plays.

The Tampa Bay Area 11

by Bill Goodwin

Many families visiting Orlando's theme parks eventually drive an hour west on I-4 to another major kiddie attraction, Busch Gardens Tampa Bay. But this area shouldn't be a mere side trip from Disney World, for Florida's central west coast is an exciting destination unto itself.

At the head of the bay, the city of Tampa is the commercial center of Florida's west coast—the country's eleventh busiest seaport and a center of banking, high-tech manufacturing, and cigar making (half a billion drugstore stogies a year). Downtown Tampa may roll up its sidewalks after dark, but you can come here during the day to see the sea life at the Florida Aquarium and stroll through the Henry B. Plant Museum, housed in an ornate, Moorish-style hotel built a century ago to lure tourists to Tampa. A trolley will take you on a short ride to Ybor City, the historic Cuban enclave that is now an exciting entertainment and dining venue. And out in the suburbs, Busch Gardens may be best known for its scintillating rides, but it's also one of the world's largest zoos.

Two bridges and a causeway will whisk you westward across the bay to the Pinellas Peninsula, one of Florida's most densely packed urban areas. Over here on the bay front, lovely downtown St. Petersburg is famous for wintering seniors, a shopping and dining complex built way out on a pier, and the world's largest collection of Salvador Dalí's surrealist paintings.

Keep driving west and you'll come to a line of barrier islands where St. Pete Beach, Treasure Island, Clearwater Beach, and other gulf-side communities boast 28 miles of sunshine, surf, and white sand. Yes, they're lined with resorts and condos of every description and price, but parks on each end preserve two of the nation's finest beaches.

Drive north up the coast, and you'll go back in time at the old Greek sponge enclave of Tarpon Springs, one of Florida's most attractive small towns, and at Weeki Wachee Springs, a tourist attraction where "mermaids" have been entertaining underwater for half a century.

Heading south, the Sunshine Skyway will take you soaring 175 feet above the bay to Bradenton, Sarasota, and another chain of barrier islands. One of Florida's cultural centers, affluent Sarasota is the gateway to St. Armands and Longboat keys, two playgrounds of the rich and famous, and to Lido and Siesta keys, attractive to families of more modest means. Even more reasonably priced is Anna Maria Island, off the riverfront town of Bradenton. You might say the bridge from Longboat to Anna Maria goes from one price range to another.

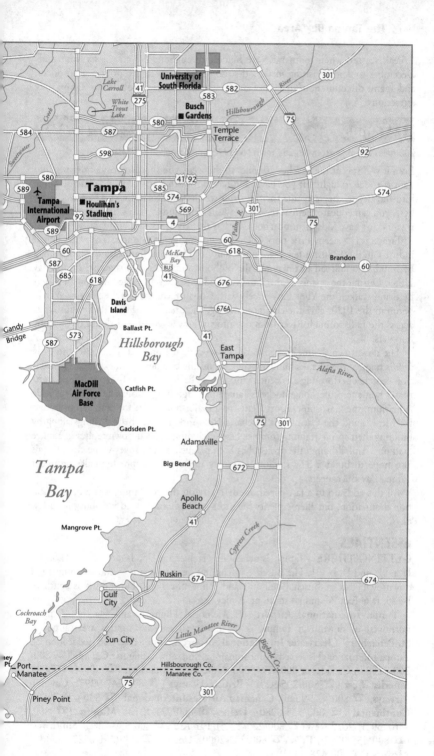

Peak season, when room rates are highest throughout the area, lasts from mid-December to April. Visiting in the off-season is one way to get around steep prices, and many discount hotel packages then include admission to various Tampa Bay attractions.

1 Tampa

200 miles SW of Jacksonville, 254 miles NW of Miami, 63 miles N of Sarasota

Even if you stay at the beaches 20 miles to the west, you should consider driving into Tampa to see its sights. If you have children in tow, they will *demand* that you come into the city so they can ride the rides and see the animals at Busch Gardens. While here, you can educate them at the Florida Aquarium and the city's fine museums. And if you don't have kids, historic Ybor City has the bay area's liveliest nightlife.

Tampa was a sleepy little port when Cuban immigrants founded Ybor City's cigar industry in the 1880s. A few years later Henry B. Plant put Tampa on the tourist map by building a railroad to town and the bulbous minarets over his garish Tampa Bay Hotel. During the Spanish American War, Teddy Roosevelt trained his Rough Riders here and walked the Ybor City streets with Cuban revolutionary José Martí. A land boom in the 1920s gave the city its charming, Victorian-style Hyde Park suburb, just across the Hillsborough River from downtown, now a gentrified redoubt of the baby boomers.

The downtown skyline we see today, however, is the product of a 1980s and early 1990s boom, when banks built skyscrapers and the city put up an expansive convention center, a performing arts center, and the Ice Palace, a 20,000-seat bay-front arena that is home to professional hockey's Tampa Bay Lightning. Alongside the new Florida Aquarium, the Garrison Seaport Center is a major home port for cruise ships bound for Mexico and the Caribbean. Baseball's New York Yankees helped things along by building their spring training complex here, including a scaled-down replica of Yankee Stadium. And although the project has been plagued by controversy, the city officials also hope to build a new stadium to satisfy the owners of pro football's resurgent Tampa Bay Buccaneers.

All this adds up to a fast-paced, modern city on the go. Tampa isn't a beach vacation destination, but there's plenty here to keep both adults and kids busy for a few days.

ESSENTIALS

GETTING THERE Tampa is accessible via I-275, I-75, I-4, U.S. 19, U.S. 41, U.S. 92, and U.S. 301. The Busch Gardens area lies between I-75 and I-275 north of downtown; exit at Busch Boulevard and follow the signs. Downtown is south of I-275; take Exit 26 and go south on Ashley Street.

Tampa International Airport, off Memorial Highway and Fla. 60, 5 miles northwest of downtown Tampa, is the major air gateway to this area, although **St. Petersburg–Clearwater International Airport** has limited service (see section 2). Tampa International is served by most major airlines, including **Air Canada** (☎ 800/268-7240 in Canada, or 800/776-3000 in the U.S.), **American** (☎ 800/433-7300), **America West** (☎ 800/235-9292), **British Airways** (☎ 800/247-9297), **Cayman Airways** (☎ 800/422-9626), **Canadian Airlines International** (☎ 800/426-7000), **Continental** (☎ 800/525-0280), **Delta** (☎ 800/221-1212), **Midway** (☎ 800/446-4392), **Northwest** (☎ 800/225-2525), **Pan Am** (☎ 800/359-7262), **Southwest** (☎ 800/435-9792), **TWA** (☎ 800/221-2000), **United** (☎ 800/241-6522), and **US Airways** (☎ 800/428-4322).

All of the major car-rental firms have booths at or near the airport.

The Limo (☎ 813/396-3730 in Tampa, or 800/282-6817 or 813/572-1111 in St. Petersburg) and **Red Line Limo** (☎ 800/359-5466 or 813/535-3391) operate van services between the airport and hotels throughout the Tampa Bay area. Fares for one person vary considerably depending on where you're going (some hotels have special rates). One passenger will pay at least $6 to Tampa's West Shore area or downtown Tampa, $13 to Busch Gardens or Clearwater Beach, and $17 to downtown St. Petersburg. **Taxis** are plentiful at the airport; the ride to downtown Tampa takes about 15 minutes and costs $11 to $14. In addition, the **Hillsborough Area Regional Transit Authority/HARTline** (☎ 813/254-HART) operates service between the airport and downtown on its local no. 31 bus from 6am and 8:15pm. Look for the HARTline bus sign outside each airline terminal; the fare is $1.15 (exact change required).

Amtrak trains arrive downtown at the **Tampa Amtrak Station,** 601 Nebraska Ave. N. (☎ 800/USA-RAIL).

VISITOR INFORMATION   Contact the **Tampa/Hillsborough Convention and Visitors Association (THCVA),** 400 N. Tampa St., Tampa, FL 33602-4706 (☎ 800/44-TAMPA or 813/223-2752; fax 813/229-6616; www.thcva.com) for advance information. Once you're downtown, head to the THCVA's visitors information center at the corner of Ashley and Madison streets. Be sure to check the display racks for brochures and maps, which contain discount coupons to Adventure Island, Busch Gardens, and other area attractions as well as restaurants and hotels. Open Monday to Saturday from 9am to 5pm.

Near Busch Gardens, the **Tampa Bay Visitor Information Center,** 3601 E. Busch Blvd., at N. Ednam Place (☎ 813/985-3601), is a privately owned operation (see Swiss Chalet Tours under "Organized Tours," below), but it offers free brochures about attractions in Tampa and sells discounted tickets to many attractions. You may be able to both save about $2 a head and avoid waiting in long Busch Gardens ticket lines by buying here, and the staff gives expert advice about how to get the most out of your visit.

GETTING AROUND   Like most other Florida destinations, it's virtually impossible to see Tampa's major sights and enjoy the best restaurants without a car. Nevertheless, the **Tampa-Ybor Trolley** connects downtown, Harbour Island, the Florida Aquarium, the Garrison Seaport Center, and Ybor City daily from 9am to 4pm, with additional service between downtown and the aquarium daily from 7:30 to 9am and from 4 to 5:30pm. The fare is 25¢ per person. Get a route map at the visitor information center (see above), or call HARTline at ☎ 813/224-4278 for information. The 18 stops are marked with green and orange signs.

There's little reason to go to Harbour Island unless you're staying there, but the **Harbour Island People Mover,** an automated tram on elevated tracks, runs between the third level of the Fort Brooke Parking Garage, on Whiting Street at Franklin Street, and Harbour Island continuously Monday to Saturday from 7am to midnight and Sunday from 8am to midnight (there's a shuttle bus off-hours). The fare is 25¢ each way.

The **Hillsborough Area Regional Transit/HARTline** (☎ 813/254-HART) provides regularly scheduled bus service between downtown Tampa and the suburbs. Fares are $1.15 for local rides, $1.50 for express routes; correct change is required. Pick up a route map at the visitor information center (see above).

Taxis in Tampa don't normally cruise the streets for fares, but they do line up at public loading places, such as hotels, the performing arts center, and bus and train depots. If you need a taxi, call **Tampa Bay Cab** (☎ 813/251-5555), **Yellow Cab**

(☎ **813/253-0121**), or **United Cab** (☎ **813/253-2424**). Fares are 95¢ at flag fall plus $1.50 for each mile.

EXPLORING THE THEME & ANIMAL PARKS

Adventure Island. 10001 McKinley Dr. (between Busch Blvd. and Bougainvillea Ave.). ☎ **813/987-5600.** Admission $22.95 adults, $20.95 children 3–9, plus tax. Free for children 2 and under. *Note:* Prices keep increasing, so expect to pay slightly more. Seasonal passes available. Mid-Feb to Labor Day, daily 10am–5pm; Sept–Oct, Fri–Sun 10am–5pm (extended hours in summer and on holidays). Closed Nov–mid-Feb. Take exit 33 off I-275, go east on Busch Blvd. for 2 miles, turn left onto McKinley Dr. (N. 40th St.), and entry is on right.

If the summer heat gets to you before one of Tampa's famous thunderstorms brings late afternoon relief, you can take a waterlogged break at this 36-acre outdoor water theme park near Busch Gardens Tampa Bay (see below). In fact, you can frolic here even during the cooler days of spring and fall, when the water is heated. The Key West Rapids, Tampa Typhoon, Gulf Scream, and other exciting water rides will drench the teens, while other calmer rides are geared for kids. There are places to picnic and sunbathe, a games arcade, a volleyball complex, and an outdoor cafe. If you forget to bring your own, a surf shop sells bathing suits, towels, and suntan lotion.

⭐ **Busch Gardens Tampa Bay.** 3000 E. Busch Blvd. (at McKinley Drive/N. 40th St.). ☎ **813/987-5283.** Admission $37.95 adults, $31.95 children 3 to 9, plus tax. Free for children 2 and under. *Note:* Prices keep increasing, so expect to pay slightly more. Seasonal passes available. Parking $4 cars, $3 motorbikes, $5 campers and trailers. Take I-275 north of downtown to Busch Blvd. (Exit 33), and go east 2 miles. From I-75, take Exit 54 and follow Fowler Ave. and the signs west.

Although its thrill rides, live entertainment, shops, restaurants, and games get most of the ink, this venerable theme park (it predates Disney World) ranks among the top zoos in the country. This is a great place for the kids to see in person all those wild beasts they've watched on the Discovery Channel. The animals, several thousand of them, live in naturalistic environments and help carry out an overall "Dark Continent" of Africa theme.

The park is divided into several areas, each with its own theme, animals, live entertainment, thrill rides, kiddie attractions, dining, and shopping. A monorail train will take you from one to another. A Skyride cable car soars over the park, offering a bird's-eye view of the beasts (but not much else).

Allow at least a day here, and arrive early—but try not to come when it's raining, since some rides may not operate and you won't get a rain check for admission on another day. You can avoid waiting in long lines and save a few dollars by buying your tickets in advance at the **Tampa Bay Visitor Information Center** (see "Essentials," above). Also, some off-season hotel packages include discounted admission.

Bring comfortable shoes, and remember, you may get wet on some of the rides, so wear appropriate clothing. You can exchange foreign currency in the park, and interpreters are available.

As soon as you're through the turnstiles, pick up a copy of a park map and the day's activity schedule, which tells what's showing and when at the park's 14 entertainment venues. Then take a few minutes to carefully plan your time.

Just past the main gate you'll come to **Morocco,** a walled city with exotic architecture, craft demonstrations, a sultan's tent with snake charmers, and an exhibit featuring alligators and turtles. The Moroccan Palace Theater features "Hollywood Live on Ice," which many families consider to be the park's best entertainment. Here you can also attend "American Jukebox," a song and dance show, in the Marrakesh Theater, or a live TV show in the Tangiers Theater.

After watching the snake charmers in Morocco, walk eastward to the main Skyride and monorail station and **Crown Colony,** home of a team of Anheuser-Busch's big-footed Clydesdale horses, the park's hospitality center, and Questor, a flight-simulator adventure ride.

From here, take the monorail train to **Egypt,** which mirrors that country's culture and history, including a replica of King Tutankhamen's tomb. Adults and older kids can ride Montu, the tallest and longest inverted roller coaster in the world with seven upside-down loops, one of them barely missing a crocodile pit. Youngsters can dig for their own ancient treasures in a sand area. Everyone can join comedian Martin Short, who plays a shady Egyptian tour guide in Akbar's Adventure Tours, a wacky simulator that transports one and all across Egypt via camel, biplane, and mine car.

From Egypt, walk under the monorail and out onto the **Serengeti Plain,** where glass walls separate you from lions, hippos, crocodiles, hyenas, meerkats, and vultures among more than 500 African animals roaming freely on an 80-acre natural grassy veldt.

After you've seen them close-up, get back on the monorail and ride across the plain and around the park to **Nairobi,** where you can see gorillas and chimpanzees in the Myombe Reserve, replicating their natural tropical habitat. Nairobi also has a baby animal nursery, a petting zoo, turtle and reptile displays, an elephant exhibit, and Nocturnal Mountain, a simulated environment that allows you to observe animals that are active in the dark.

From Nairobi, walk into **Timbuktu,** evoking an ancient desert trading center with African craftspeople at work. Here you'll find several rides, including a train for kids, one through a sandstorm, another on swinging boats, and Scorpion, a 360° roller coaster. Plan to have lunch here at Das Festhaus, a 1,000-seat, air-conditioned German festival hall featuring a lively musical show (be sure to arrive at least 15 minutes before show time). The kids will enjoy the Dolphin Theater, with performing porpoises, otters, and sea lions.

After lunch, head to **The Congo,** highlighted by rare white Bengal tigers living on Claw Island. The Congo also is home to Kumba, the largest and fastest roller coaster in the southeastern United States, and the Python, which twists and turns for 1,200 feet. You will get drenched (and refreshed on a hot day) by riding the Congo River Rapids. There are bumper cars and kiddie rides here, too.

From The Congo, walk south into **Stanleyville,** a prototype African village, with a shopping bazaar, orangutans living on an island, and the Stanleyville Theater, featuring a troupe of Russian acrobats. Two more water rides are here: the Tanganyika Tidal Wave and Stanley Falls. Serving ribs and chicken, the Stanleyville Smokehouse has some of the best chow here. This also is a good place to board the monorail for a sightseeing ride all the way around the park and back, since you'll avoid the crowds waiting to board elsewhere.

From Stanleyville, the next stop is **Land of the Dragons,** where the younger set can easily spend an entire day enjoying a variety of play elements in a fairy-tale setting, plus just-for-kids rides. The area is dominated by Dumphrey, a whimsical dragon that interacts with visitors and guides children around a 3-story tree house with winding stairways, tall towers, stepping stones, illuminated water geysers, and an echo chamber.

The last stop is **Bird Gardens,** the park's original core, offering rich foliage, lagoons, and a free-flight aviary for hundreds of exotic birds, including golden and American bald eagles. Catch the Bird Show here.

You can finish your visit back at the hospitality center in Crown Colony, where adults can imbibe some of Anheuser-Busch's famous beers (there's a limit of two free mugs per seating).

Tampa Attractions

Adventure Island 3
Busch Gardens 4
Florida Aquarium/
    Garrison Seaport
    Center 12
Henry B. Plant
    Museum 9
Houlihan's Stadium 8
Lowry Park Zoo 5
Museum of African-
    American Art 13
Museum of Science
    and Industry 2
N.Y. Yankees Spring
    Training Complex 7
Seminole Indian
    Casino 6
Tampa Bay Downs 1
Tampa Museum
    of Art 14
University of Tampa 9
Visitor Information
    Center 15
Ybor City
    Brewing Co. 11
Ybor City State
    Museum 10

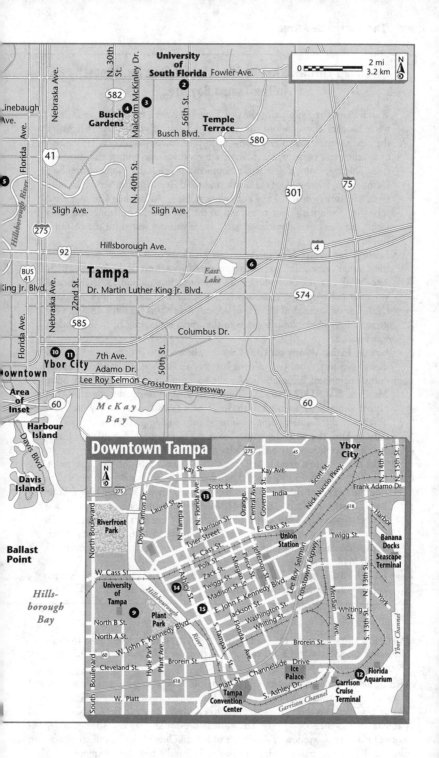

Cheap Thrills: What to See & Do for Free (or Almost) in the Tampa Bay Area

- **Watch the setting sun paint the sky.** Facing due west, the St. Pete and Clearwater beaches offer glorious sunsets over the gulf. If you're staying right on the beach, watch the colorful show from your balcony or patio. For the rest of us, the area's many public beaches are good vantage points, and most are free. The two with the least development to spoil the moment are Fort Desoto Park, south of St. Pete Beach, and Sand Key Park, just across the inlet from Clearwater Beach. They both close at dark, but by then you may have seen the "green flash" just as the top of the sun hits the horizon. And don't forget the area's many beachside bars, where you can watch for the cost of a drink.

- **Learn a lot about African American art.** One of four such museums in the United States, Tampa's **Museum of African-American Art** (☎ 813/272-2466) charges just $3 for adults, less for seniors and kids, to examine the works of more than 80 artists, including sculptures and paintings depicting the history, culture, and lifestyle of African Americans from the 1800s to the present. Special emphasis is given to the works emanating from the Harlem Renaissance.

- **Get the inside skinny on Ybor City.** The best way to get the inside story on Tampa's historic Ybor City district is on a free 1½-hour walking tour led by enthusiastic local volunteers under the sponsorship of the **Ybor City State Museum** (☎ 813/247-6323). Tours start at the information desk in Ybor Square shopping center, on 13th Street between 8th and 9th avenues, and cover over three dozen points of interest before ending at the museum. January to April the tours depart on Tuesday, Thursday, and Saturday at 11am; May to December, only on Thursday and Saturday.

- **Take the ferry to a great beach.** You'll have to pay admission to Honeymoon Island State Recreation Area and another $6 for adults or $3.50 per kid to ride the ferry, but that's a small price to pay to reach **Caladesi Island State Park,** north of Clearwater (☎ 813/469-5942), and one of Florida's best beaches—a lovely, relatively secluded stretch of fine soft sand edged in sea grass and palmettos. You might even see dolphins cavorting offshore, or perhaps rattlesnakes, black racers, raccoons, armadillos, or rabbits from the park's nature trail.

- **Help birds to mend.** You can visit more than 500 sea and land birds recuperating at the **Suncoast Seabird Sanctuary** in Indian Shores (☎ 813/

✪ **Florida Aquarium.** 701 Channelside Dr. ☎ **813/273-4000.** Admission $10.95 adults, $9.95 seniors, $5.95 children 3–12, free for children under 3. Parking $3. Daily 9:30am–5pm. Closed Thanksgiving and Christmas.

Visitors here are introduced to more than 5,300 aquatic animals and plants that call Florida home. Various exhibits allow you to follow the pristine springs of the Florida Wetlands Gallery, go through a mangrove forest in the Bays and Beaches Gallery, and stand amazed at the Coral Reefs. The most impressive display is a 43-foot-wide, 14-foot-tall panoramic window with schools of fish and lots of sharks and stingrays. You can watch a diver twice a day. There's a half-million-dollar "Explore a Shore"

391-6211), the nation's largest wild-bird hospital. Cormorants, white herons, birds of prey, ubiquitous brown pelicans: They're all here. Down Sarasota way, the **Pelican Man's Bird Sanctuary** (☎ 941/388-4444) treats more than 5,000 injured birds and other wildlife each year. Admission is free to both, but you'll want to make a donation.

- **Poke through a dusty museum dedicated to sponges.** The highlight of any stroll along the carnival-like Sponge Docks in Tarpon Springs is the rickety **Spongeorama** (☎ 813/943-9509), a dusty museum dedicated to sponges and sponge divers. You can buy a wide variety of fresh-from-the-gulf sponges here and watch a 30-minute video about sponge-diving. Admission is free. The docks also have a host of inexpensive restaurants featuring authentic Greek cuisine brought here by the town's sponge-diving settlers.

- **Play great golf on the cheap.** A round of golf in southern Florida can cost $70 and up in winter, but Sarasota's municipal **Bobby Jones Golf Complex** (☎ 941/365-GOLF) has two 18-hole championship layouts and a 9-hole executive course. But get this: Greens fees range from just $25 to $31, including cart rental.

- **Find out what the Big Top bought.** Adults pay $8 or $9 to get in, but you'll have three "rings" to visit at the **Ringling Museums** in Sarasota (☎ 941/359-5700, or 941/351-1660 for recorded information), which house the phenomenal collections of circus master John Ringling. A pink Italian Renaissance villa is filled with more than 500 years of European and American art, including one of the world's most important collections of grand 17th-century Baroque paintings. The Ringling's 30-room winter residence displays their personal mementos. And the Circus Galleries are devoted to memorabilia from The Greatest Show on Earth.

- **Hide your plastic at St. Armand's Circle.** Don't bring your credit cards, but by all means do some window-shopping on Sarasota's St. Armand's Circle, the lushly landscaped home to more than 150 international boutiques, gift shops, and galleries rivaling those in Palm Beach and on Naples's 3rd Avenue South. Plan to take a break at lunch, when the otherwise expensive restaurants here offer some good deals.

playground to educate the kids, a deep-water exhibit, and a tank housing moray eels. The Cafe Ray serves snacks and light meals.

Lowry Park Zoo. 7530 North Blvd. ☎ **813/932-0245.** Admission $7.50 adults, $6.50 seniors, $4.95 children 3–11, free for children 2 and under. Daily 9:30am–5pm. Closed Thanksgiving and Christmas. Take I-275 to Sligh Ave. (Exit 31) and follow the signs.

Watching the 2,000-pound manatees, the Komodo dragons, and the red pandas makes this a worthwhile excursion after the kids have seen the plains of Africa at Busch Gardens. With lots of greenery, bubbling brooks, and cascading waterfalls, this 24-acre zoo displays animals in settings similar to their natural habitats. Other major exhibits include a Florida wildlife display, an Asian Domain, a Primate World, an Aquatic Center, a free-flight aviary with a birds of prey show, a children's petting zoo and hands-on Discovery Center, and an endangered species carrousel ride. There are plenty of food outlets here, including an on-site McDonald's.

VISITING THE MUSEUMS

Henry B. Plant Museum. 401 W. Kennedy Blvd. (between Hyde Park and Magnolia aves.). ☎ 813/254-1891. Free admission; suggested donation, $3 adults, $1 children 12 and under. Tues–Sat 10am–4pm, Sun noon–4pm. Take Fla. 60 west of downtown.

You can't miss the 13 silver minarets and distinctive Moorish architecture—it's modeled after the Alhambra in Spain—that make this National Historic Landmark a focal point of the Tampa skyline. Originally built in 1891 as the 511-room Tampa Bay Hotel by railroad tycoon Henry B. Plant, it's filled with art and furnishings from Europe and the Orient. Other exhibits focus on the history of the original railroad resort, Florida's early tourist industry, and the hotel's role as a staging point for Teddy Roosevelt's Rough Riders during the Spanish-American War.

✪ **Museum of African-American Art.** 1308 N. Marion St. (entry and parking lot face N. Florida Ave. between Scott and Laurel sts.), downtown. ☎ 813/272-2466. Admission $3 adults, $2 seniors and children grades K–12. Tues–Fri 10am–4:30pm, Sat 10am–5pm. Take Exit 26 off I-275.

Recently renovated to the tune of $200,000, the museum is touted as the first of its kind in Florida and one of four in the United States. It's the home of the Barnett-Aden collection, considered the state's foremost collection of African American art. More than 80 artists are represented in the display, which includes sculptures and paintings that depict the history, culture, and lifestyle of African Americans from the 1800s to the present, with special emphasis on the works of artists active during the Harlem renaissance.

Museum of Science and Industry (MOSI). 4801 E. Fowler Ave. (at N. 50th St.). ☎ 813/987-6300. www.tampatrib.com/mosi. Admission $11 adults; $9 seniors, college students with identification, and children 13–18; $7 children 2–12; free for children under 2. MOSIMAX tickets $6 adults; $5 seniors, college students, and children 3–18; $4 kids 2–12. Combination tickets available. Free parking. Daily 9am–5pm or later. From downtown, take I-275 north, then Fowler Ave. east 2 miles to museum on right.

A great place to take the kids on a rainy day, MOSI is the largest science center in the Southeast and has more than 450 interactive exhibits. Guests can step into the Gulf Hurricane and experience gale-force winds, defy the laws of gravity in the unique *Challenger* space experience, or cruise the mysterious world of microbes in LifeLab. The Amazing You allows visitors to explore the body, Our Florida focuses on environmental factors, and Our Place in the Universe introduces them to space, flight, and beyond. You can also watch stunning movies in MOSIMAX, Florida's first IMAX dome theater.

Tampa Museum of Art. 600 N. Ashley St. (at Twiggs St.), downtown. ☎ 813/274-8130. Admission $5 adults, $4 seniors and students with identification, $3 children 6–18, free for children 5 and under, by donation for everyone Wed 5–9pm and Sat 10am–noon. Mon–Tues and Thurs–Sat 10am–5pm, Wed 10am–9pm, Sun 1–5pm. Take I-275 to Exit 25 (Ashley St.).

Located on the east bank of the Hillsborough River next to the round NationsBank building (locals facetiously call it the "Beer Can") and just south of the Tampa Bay Performing Arts Center, this fine-arts complex offers eight galleries with changing exhibits ranging from classical antiquities to contemporary Florida art. There's also a 7-acre riverfront park and sculpture garden. Museum tours are offered on Wednesday and Saturday at 1pm and on Sunday at 2pm.

YBOR CITY

On the northeast edge of downtown, Tampa's historic Latin Quarter is famous for cigars and Columbia, the largest Spanish restaurant in the world (see "Great Deals on Dining," below). It takes its present name from Don Vicente Martinez Ybor, a Spanish cigar maker who arrived here in 1886 via Cuba and Key West. Soon his and other Tampa factories were producing more than 300,000 hand-rolled stogies a day.

It may not be the cigar capital of the world anymore, but "Ybor" is the happening part of Tampa, a cross between New Orleans's Bourbon Street, Washington's George-town, and New York's SoHo. By day, you can stroll past the art galleries, boutiques, and trendy new restaurants and cafes that line 7th Avenue East. At night, when good food and great music dominate the scene, streets will be bustling until 4am. Unique shops offer a wide assortment of goodies, from silk boxer shorts to unique tattoos. Dozens of outstanding nightclubs and dance clubs have waiting lines out the door. Live-music offerings run the gamut from jazz and blues to indie rock. There are lots of police around in the wee hours, but be as cautious here as you would exploring any big city at night.

✪ **Ybor City Walking Tours** are an ideal way to check out the highlights of this historic district. Free 1½-hour tours are sponsored by the Ybor City State Museum (see below) and are led by enthusiastic local volunteers. Tours start at the information desk in Ybor Square shopping center, on 13th Street between 8th and 9th avenues, and cover more than three dozen points of interest before ending at the Ybor City State Museum. January to April the tours depart on Tuesday, Thursday, and Saturday at 11am; May to December, only on Thursday and Saturday.

Cigar smokers will enjoy a stroll through the **Ybor City State Museum,** 1818 9th Ave., between 18th and 19th streets (☎ **813/247-6323**), housed in the former Fer-lita Bakery (1896–1973). You can take a self-guided tour around the museum to see a collection of cigar labels, cigar memorabilia, and works by local artisans. Admission is $2 per person, including a 30-minute guided tour of **La Casita,** a renovated cigar worker's cottage adjacent to the museum; it's furnished as it was at the turn of the century. The museum is open Tuesday to Saturday from 9am to noon and 1 to 5pm (La Casita, from 10am to 3pm).

Another interesting stop here is the **Ybor City Brewing Company,** 2205 N. 20th St., facing Palm Avenue (☎ **813/242-9222**). Housed in a 100-year-old, 3-story former cigar factory, this microbrewery produces Ybor Gold and other brews, none with preservatives. Admission of $2 per person includes a tour of the brewery and taste of the end result. Open Tuesday to Saturday from 11am to 3pm.

ORGANIZED TOURS

Swiss Chalet Tours, 3601 E. Busch Blvd. (☎ **813/985-3601**), opposite Busch Gardens in the privately run Tampa Bay Visitor Information Center (see "Essentials," above), operates guided bus tours of Tampa, Ybor City, and environs. The 4-hour half-day tours are given daily; they cost $35 for adults and $25 for children. The 8-hour full-day tours are given on Tuesday and Friday, and cost $60 for adults and $50 for children. Reservations are required at least 24 hours in advance; passengers are picked up at major hotels and various other points in the Tampa/St. Petersburg area. Tours can also be booked to Sarasota, Bradenton, and other regional destinations.

GREAT GOLF THAT WON'T BREAK YOUR BUDGET & OTHER AFFORDABLE OUTDOOR ACTIVITIES

Tampa Outdoor Adventures (☎ **800/44-TAMPA,** ext. 6, or 813/223-2752) is a one-stop source of information and reservations for a variety of recreational activities in the Tampa area, from ballooning to yachting. In addition, try these contacts directly:

BIKING, IN-LINE SKATING & JOGGING   Bayshore Boulevard, a 7-mile promenade, is famous for its sidewalk right on the shores of Hillsborough Bay. Reputed to be the world's longest continuous sidewalk, it's a favorite for runners, joggers, walkers, and in-line skaters. The route goes from the western edge of downtown in a southward direction, passing stately old homes of Hyde Park, a few high-rise condos, retirement communities, and houses of worship, ending at Ballast Point Park. The view from the promenade across the bay to the downtown skyline is unmatched here (Bayshore Boulevard also is great for a drive).

Rent bicycles and in-line skates at **Blades & Bikes,** in a pink-and-blue shop at 201-A W. Platt St., at South Parker Street (☎ 813/251-0780), a block west of the northern end of Bayshore Boulevard. Prices for both bikes and blades range from $8 for 1 hour to $20 for all day. Hours are Monday to Friday from 10am to 7pm, Saturday from 9am to 7pm, and Sunday from 10am to 5pm.

CANOEING   You can paddle downstream along a 20-mile stretch of the Hillsborough River amid 16,000 acres of rural lands in Wilderness Park, the largest regional park in Hillsborough County. **Canoe Escape,** 9335 E. Fowler Ave. (☎ 813/986-2067), rents canoes for $13 per person or $26 per craft. The company also has 2- to 6-hour guided trips. Open Monday to Friday from 9am to 5pm and Saturday and Sunday from 8am to 6pm.

FISHING   There's good freshwater fishing for trout in **Lake Thonotosassa,** east of the city, or for bass along the **Hillsborough River.** Pier fishing on Hillsborough Bay is also available from **Ballast Point Park,** 5300 Interbay Blvd. (☎ 813/831-9585). Ballast Point Park is at the southern end of Bayshore Boulevard and has a terrific view back across the bay to downtown.

Light Tackle Fishing Expeditions (☎ 813/963-1930) offers sportfishing trips for tarpon, redfish, cobia, trout, and snook. Prices start at $50 per person.

GOLF   Tampa has three municipal golf courses where you can play for a relative pittance—just $26 to $34—when compared to the privately owned courses here and elsewhere in Florida. The **Babe Zaharias Municipal Golf Course,** 11412 Forest Hills Dr., north of Lowry Park (☎ 813/631-4374), is an 18-hole, par-70 course with a pro shop, putting greens, and a driving range. It's the shortest of the municipal courses, but small greens and narrow fairways present ample challenges. Water presents obstacles on 12 of the 18 holes at **Rocky Point Municipal Golf Course,** 4151 Dana Shores Dr. (☎ 813/673-4316), located between the airport and the bay. It's a par-71 course with a pro shop, practice range, and putting greens. On the Hillsborough River in north Tampa, the **Rogers Park Municipal Golf Course,** 7910 N. 30th St. (☎ 813/673-4396), is an 18-hole, par-72 championship course with a lighted driving and practice range. They all are open daily from 7am to dusk, and lessons and club rentals are available.

Another inexpensive place to play is the **University of South Florida Golf Course,** Fletcher Avenue and 46th Street (☎ 813/632-6893), just north of the USF campus. This 18-hole, par-71 course is nicknamed "The Claw" because of its challenging layout. It offers lessons and club rentals. Greens fees range from about $19 to $25, or $25 to $35 with a cart, depending on the season and time of day. It's open daily from 7am to dusk.

Other courses open to the public include the **Hall of Fame Golf Club,** just south of the airport at 2222 N. Westshore Blvd. (☎ 813/876-4913), an 18-hole, par-72 affair with a driving range; **Persimmon Hill Golf Club,** 5109 Hamey Rd. (☎ 813/

623-6962); **Silver Dollar Trap & Golf Club,** 17000 Patterson Rd., Odessa (☎ **813/ 920-3884**); and **Westchase Golf Club,** 1307 Radcliff Dr. (☎ **813/854-2331**).

You can book starting times and get information about these and the area's other courses by calling **Tee Times USA** (☎ **800/374-8633**).

If you want to do some serious work on your game, the **Arnold Palmer Golf Academy World Headquarters** is at the renowned Saddlebrook Resort, 5700 Saddlebrook Way, Wesley Chapel, FL 33543 (☎ **800/729-8383** or 813/973-1111; fax 813/ 973-4504), 12 miles north of Tampa. There are 2-, 3-, and 5-day programs available for adults and juniors ranging from $248 to $320 per person per night—a relative bargain since it includes double occupancy accommodations, breakfast, daily instruction, 18 holes of golf daily, cart and greens fees, and nightly club storage and cleaning. You have to stay at the resort or enroll in the golf program to play at Saddlebrook.

SPECTATOR SPORTS National Football League fans can catch the improving **Tampa Bay Buccaneers** at Houlihan's Stadium, 4201 N. Dale Mabry Hwy., at Dr. Martin Luther King Jr. Blvd. (☎ **813/872-BUCS**). Their season runs from September through December, and tickets range from $20 to $30.

You can also watch two of the nation's better college football teams in the **Outback Bowl** on New Year's Day (☎ **813/874-BOWL**).

The Arena Football League's **Tampa Bay Storm** play in the 20,000-seat Ice Palace, downtown between the Tampa Convention Center and the Florida Aquarium, from May through July (☎ **813/276-7300**). Tickets cost $12 to $18.

The National Hockey League's **Tampa Bay Lightning** also play in the Ice Palace, beginning every October (☎ **813/229-8800**). Tickets range from $17.50 to $75.

New York Yankees fans can watch the Boys in Blue during baseball spring training from mid-February through March at Legends Field, opposite Houlihan's Stadium (☎ **813/875-7753**). A scaled-down replica of Yankee Stadium, it's the largest spring-training facility in Florida, with a 10,000-seat capacity. Tickets range from $6 to $10. The club's minor league team, the **Tampa Yankees** (same phone), plays at Legends Field from April to September. Tickets are $3 for adults, $2 for kids.

The only oval thoroughbred race course on Florida's west coast, ✪ **Tampa Bay Downs,** 11225 Racetrack Rd., Oldsmar (☎ **800/200-4434** in Florida, or 813/ 855-4401), is the home of the Tampa Bay Derby. Races are held from December to May, and the track presents simulcasts year-round. Call for post times. Admission is $1.50 to the grandstand, $3 to the clubhouse. Parking costs $1.

Professional players volley the lethal *pelota* at the **Tampa Jai-Alai Fronton,** 5125 S. Dale Mabry Hwy., near Gandy Blvd. (☎ **813/831-1411**). Admission is $1 to $4 and parking is $1 or free. It's open year-round, with games Monday to Saturday beginning at 6:45pm, and matinees on Monday, Wednesday, Friday, and Saturday beginning at noon.

TENNIS The **City of Tampa Tennis Complex,** at Hillsborough Community College, 3901 Tampa Bay Blvd. (☎ **813/348-1173**), across from Houlihan's Stadium, is the largest public complex in Tampa, with 16 hard courts and 12 clay courts. It also has four racquetball courts, a pro shop, locker rooms, showers, and lessons. Reservations are recommended. Prices range from $2.50 to $5 per person per hour. It's open Monday to Thursday from 8am to 9pm, Friday from 8am to 7pm, and Saturday and Sunday from 8am to 6pm.

On the water and overlooking Harbour Island, the **Sandra W. Freedman Tennis Complex,** in Marjorie Park, 59 Columbia Dr., Davis Island (☎ **813/259-1664**), has eight clay courts. Reservations are required. The price is $5 per person per hour and it's open Monday to Friday from 8am to 9pm and Saturday and Sunday from 8am to 6pm.

Beginners to highly skilled players can sharpen their games at the **Phil Green Tennis Program,** located at the Saddlebrook Resort, 5700 Saddlebrook Way, Wesley Chapel (☎ 800/729-8383 or 813/973-1111). Packages start at $372 person for 2 days, or $816 person for 6 days, double occupancy, including tennis instruction, unlimited playing time, video analysis, agility exercises, fitness center, and accommodations at the Saddlebrook Resort for 5 days and 6 nights. You must be a member or a guest to play here.

SHOPPING

Hyde Park and Ybor City are two areas of Tampa worth some window shopping, perhaps sandwiched around lunch at one of their fine restaurants (see "Great Deals on Dining," below).

✪ **Old Hyde Park Village,** 1507 W. Swann Ave., at South Dakoka Avenue (☎ 813/251-3500), is a terrific alternative to cookie-cutter suburban malls. Walk around little shops in the sunshine and check out Hyde Park, one of the city's oldest and most historic neighborhoods at the same time. The cluster of 50 upscale shops and boutiques is set in a village layout. The selection includes Williams-Sonoma, Pottery Barn, Banana Republic, Brooks Brothers, Crabtree & Evelyn, Godiva Chocolatier, Laura Ashley, Polo Ralph Lauren, and Talbots, to name a few. There's a free parking garage on South Oregon Avenue behind Jacobson's department store. The shops are open Monday to Wednesday and Saturday from 10am to 6pm, Thursday and Friday from 10am to 9pm, and Sunday from noon to 5pm.

Ybor City, along East 7th Avenue East between 14th and 22nd streets, has several shops worth browsing. **Adam's Ybor City Hats,** 1621 E. 7th Ave. East(☎ 813/229-2850), has a mind-boggling inventory of more than 18,000 hats of every description. **La France,** 1612 E. 7th Ave. (☎ 813/248-1381), has racks upon racks of vintage clothing and funky costumes. Named after the Irish monk who became the patron saint of gardeners, **St. Fiacre's Herb Shop,** 1807 N. 16th St. (☎ 813/248-1234), stocks a wide array of fresh herbs, herbal products, fragrances, exotic teas, T-shirts, herbal gift baskets, and books.

Cigar aficionados can stock up at **El Sol,** 1728 E. 7th Ave. (☎ 813/247-5554), the city's oldest cigar store, and at **Metropolitan Cigars & Wine,** 2014 E. 7th Ave. (☎ 813/248-3304).

You can watch an artisan rolling stogies at **Tampa Rico Cigar Co.,** one of the shops in **Ybor Square,** 1901 13th St., at 8th Avenue (☎ 813/247-4497), a shopping complex that is listed on the National Register of Historic Places. The three brick buildings date from 1886 and once comprised the largest cigar factory in the world. Today it's primarily notable for several small shops selling an amazing variety of collectibles.

The main mall in the city is **West Shore Plaza,** on Kennedy Boulevard where it turns into Memorial Highway (Fla. 60). Burdine's, JC Penney, and Dillards are the anchors. **University Mall** is nearest Busch Gardens, on Fowler Avenue just east of I-275. Burdine's, Dillards, JC Penney, and Sears are the biggies both there and at **Brandon TownCenter,** at I-4 and Fla. 60 in the eastern suburb of Brandon, where most stores have unusually large amounts of floor space, and hence, more merchandise from which to choose.

If you want to stock up on fresh Florida fruits and vegetables, head to **Whaley's Markets,** 533 S. Howard Ave., at DeLeon, northwest of Hyde Park (☎ 813/254-2904). This purveyor of gourmet foods has a terrific selection of marmalades and other local foods, including picnic items and deli sandwiches. They'll ship your citrus home. Open Monday to Saturday from 7am to 9pm and Sunday from 7am to 8pm.

ACCOMMODATIONS YOU CAN AFFORD

The accommodations listed below are near Busch Gardens and convenient to Adventure Island, Lowry Park Zoo, and the Museum of Science and Industry (MOSI). None of the hotels downtown or in the Westshore area south of the airport (all geared to business travelers) is inexpensive. Your best bet, therefore, is to stay out near the theme parks and drive into downtown to visit the Florida Aquarium, the Museum of African-American Art, the Tampa Museum of Art, the Henry B. Plant Museum, the Tampa Bay Performing Arts Center, scenic Bayshore Boulevard, and the dining and shopping opportunities in the Hyde Park historic district. At night, you can drive to Ybor City's restaurants and nightlife.

The high season in Tampa generally is January to April, but you won't find as large an increase here as at the beach resorts. Most hotels offer discounted package rates in the summer and weekend specials all year, dropping their rates by as much as 50%. Hotels often combine tickets to major attractions like Busch Gardens in their packages, so always ask about special deals.

Hillsborough River State Park, 15402 U.S. 301 North, Thonotosassa, FL 33592 (☎ **813/986-1020**), offers 118 campsites year-round, plus fishing, canoeing, and boating.

Hillsborough County adds 12% tax to your hotel room bill.

SUPER-CHEAP SLEEPS

Budgetel Inn. 9202 N. 30th St. (at Busch Blvd.), Tampa, FL 33612. ☎ **800/428-3438** or 813/930-6900. Fax 813/930-0563. 150 units. AC TV TEL. Winter $77 single or double. Off-season $57 single or double. Rates include continental breakfast. AE, DC, DISC, MC, V.

Fake banana trees and a parrot cage welcome guests to the terra-cotta–floored lobby of this comfortable and convenient member of a fine chain of budget-conscious motels. All rooms are spacious and have ceiling fans, bright wood furniture with tropical trim, desks, phones with long cords, and coffeemakers (a container with Danish pastries or a blueberry muffin and juice is hung on your doorknob before dawn). Rooms with king beds also have recliners. Outside, a courtyard with an unheated swimming pool has plenty of space for sunning. There's a game room and coin laundry, and local telephone calls are free. There's no restaurant on the premises, but plenty are nearby.

Days Inn Maingate. 2901 E. Busch Blvd. (at N. 30th St.), Tampa, FL 33612. ☎ **800/DAYS-INN** or 813/933-6471. Fax 813/931-0261. 175 units. Winter $64 single or double. Off-season $42–$52 single or double. AE, DC, DISC, MC, V.

Although it's completely surrounded by a black-top parking lot and is less appealing than the Budgetel Inn across the street, this 2-story, glass-and-steel motel is convenient for families on a budget. There's an outdoor swimming pool, and a Denny's and a Taco Bell are both on the premises.

Red Roof Inn. 2307 E. Busch Blvd. (between 22nd and 26th sts.), Tampa, FL 33612. ☎ **800/THE-ROOF** or 813/932-0073. Fax 813/933-5689. 108 units. A/C TV TEL. Winter $69 single or double. Off-season $45 single or double. AE, DC, DISC, MC, V.

Less than a mile from Busch Gardens, this 2-story, soft gray with red trim building is away from the road in a well-landscaped grassy setting. Most of the rooms are done up in bright colors. An outdoor pool and whirlpool are in the center of the complex.

FOR A FEW BUCKS MORE

Best Western Resort Tampa at Busch Gardens. 820 E. Busch Blvd. (at I-275), Tampa, FL 33612. ☎ **800/288-4011** or 813/933-4011. Fax 813/932-1784. 255 units. A/C TV TEL. Winter $99 single or double. Off-season $59 single or double. AE, DC, DISC, MC, V.

Right at the Busch Boulevard exit off I-275, this motel is fine for families on a budget. The lobby leads to an enclosed skylit atrium-style courtyard with fountains, street-lights, benches, a pool, and tropical foliage. Guest rooms in this wing open to walk-ways facing the indoor atrium or the parking lots. Newer units are in a 4-story annex. They all have standard furnishings and coffeemakers.

The Palm Grill Restaurant off the lobby features a variety of dishes, while the Bull Pen Sports Bar offers pub fare and libation until 11pm nightly. Services include a concierge desk, secretarial services, valet laundry, limited room service, and courtesy transport to Busch Gardens. There are indoor and outdoor heated swimming pools, two whirlpools, a sauna, four lighted tennis courts, exercise and game rooms, a coin-operated laundry, and a gift shop.

✪ **Quality Suites Hotel—USF Near Busch Gardens.** 3001 University Center Dr., Tampa, FL 33612. ☎ **800/786-7446** or 813/971-8930. Fax 813/971-8935. 150 units. A/C TV TEL. Winter $99–$159 suite. Off-season $89–$139 suite. Rates include full breakfast buffet and evening cocktail reception. AE, DC, DISC, MC, V.

Actually on North 30th Street, between Busch Boulevard and Fletcher Avenue, this hacienda-style all-suite hotel sits about a mile from the Busch Gardens entrance and is the pick of the hotels in this area. The complex encloses a lushly tropical courtyard surrounding a heated pool, hot tub, covered games area, and outdoor seating for Ruzik's Roost, a beach-bar type grill serving a complimentary breakfast buffet plus lunch and dinner (it can get noisy on this end of the courtyard, so ask for a suite away from the action). Opening to this pleasant vista, each suite has two TVs, and a sepa-rate bedroom with built-in armoire and well-lit mirrored vanity area. Living/dining rooms have a sofa bed, La-Z-Boy recliner, wet bar, coffeemaker, microwave, and stereo/VCR unit. Facilities also include a 24-hour gift shop/food store, VCR rentals, whirlpool, meeting rooms, and coin-operated laundry.

GREAT DEALS ON DINING

I have organized the restaurants below by geographic area: near Busch Gardens, in or near Hyde Park (just across the Hillsborough River from downtown), and in Ybor City (on the northeastern edge of downtown).

NEAR BUSCH GARDENS

You'll find the national fast-food and family restaurants east of I-275 on Busch Boule-vard and along Fletcher Avenue near University Mall.

✪ **Mel's Hot Dogs.** 4136 E. Busch Blvd., at 42nd St. ☎ **813/985-8000.** Main courses $3–$6.50. No credit cards. Daily 11am–9pm. AMERICAN.

Catering to everyone from businesspeople on a lunch break to hungry families craving inexpensive all-beef hot dogs, this red-and-white cottage offers everything from "bagel-dogs" and corn dogs to a bacon-cheddar Reuben. All choices are served on a poppy seed bun and most come with french fries and a choice of coleslaw or baked beans. Even the decor is dedicated to wieners: The walls and windows are lined with hot-dog memorabilia. And just in case hot-dog mania hasn't won you over, there are a few alternative choices (sausages, chicken breast, and beef and veggie burgers).

Shells. 11010 N. 30th St. (between Busch Blvd. and Fowler Ave.). ☎ **813/977-8456.** Reser-vations not accepted. Main courses $6–$17. AE, DISC, MC, V. Mon–Thurs 11:30am–10pm, Fri–Sat 11:30am–11pm, Sun noon–10pm. SEAFOOD.

You'll see Shells restaurants in many parts of Florida, and with good reason, for this casual, award-winning chain consistently provides excellent value, especially if you have a family to feed. They all have the same menu and prices and are particularly known for their spicy Jack Daniel's Buffalo shrimp and scallop appetizers. Main courses range from the usual fried seafood platters to pastas and charcoal-grilled shrimp, fish, steaks, and chicken. I counted 21 tender, bite-size shrimp in a light, garlic-tinged cream sauce and served over linguine, a bargain for $9.50, and 30 of them perfectly charcoal-grilled on a skewer and served with saffron rice and steamed vegetables for $11. There's a children's menu.

HYDE PARK
Super-Cheap Eats
Cactus Club. In Old Hyde Park shopping complex, 1601 Snow Ave. (south of Swan St.). ☎ 813/251-4089. Reservations not accepted. Main courses $6.50–$15. AE, DC, MC, V. Mon–Thurs 11am–11pm, Fri–Sat 11am–midnight, Sun 11am–10:30pm. AMERICAN SOUTH-WEST.

Watch all the shoppers go by at Old Hyde Park from this fun and casual cafe with a southwestern accent. Dine inside or outside on tacos, enchiladas, chili, sizzling fajitas, hickory-smoked baby back ribs, Jamaican jerk chicken, guacamole/green-chile burgers, quesadillas, sandwiches, smoked chicken salad, and more. It's always packed at lunchtime—get here early.

The Colonnade. 3401 Bayshore Blvd. (at W. Julia St.). ☎ **813/839-7558.** Reservations accepted only for large parties. Main courses $8–$18. AE, DC, DISC, MC, V. Sun–Thurs 11am–10pm, Fri–Sat 11am–11pm. AMERICAN/SEAFOOD.

Locals have been flocking to this rough-hewn, shiplap place since 1935, primarily for the great view of Hillsborough Bay across Bayshore Boulevard. The food is a bit on the Red Lobsterish side, but get here early or wait for a window table; the view is worth it. Fresh seafood is the specialty: grouper prepared seven ways, crab-stuffed flounder, Maryland-style crab cakes, even wild Florida alligator as an appetizer. Prime rib, steaks, and chicken are also available.

Four Green Fields. 205 W. Platt St. (between Parker St. and Plant Ave.). ☎ **813/254-4444.** Reservations accepted. Sandwiches $6; main courses $8.50–$14. AE, MC, V. Mon–Sat 11am–2am, Sun noon–2am. IRISH/AMERICAN.

This thatched-roof pub may be surrounded by palm trees instead of potato fields, but it still offers the ambience and tastes of Ireland just across the bridge from the downtown convention center. Staffed by genuine Irish immigrants, the large room with a square bar in the center smells of Irish ale. The Gaelic stew is predictably bland, but the salads and sandwiches are passable. The crowd usually is young, especially for live Irish music on Thursday, Friday, and Saturday nights.

SideBern's. 2208 W. Morrison Ave. (at S. Howard St.). ☎ 813/258-2233. Reservations not accepted. Sandwiches and salads $4–$7.50; desserts $4–$5.50. AE, DC, DISC, MC, V. Sun and Tues–Thurs 6–11pm, Fri–Sat 6pm–1am. SANDWICHES/SALADS/DESSERTS.

The owners of Bern's Steakhouse (see "Worth a Splurge," below) opened this informal outlet to accommodate everyone who wanted to partake of their gourmet goodies but couldn't fit into the dessert rooms at the main restaurant. Their most popular desserts are offered at this sophisticated bistro, whose cathedral ceiling covers an open kitchen (wonderful aromas) and cherry-wood tables and chairs. Banana cheesecake is a consistent winner, as is the chocolate pâté served with Curaçao, raspberry, or rum sauce. Sandwiches are served on a choice of regular wheat, focaccia, or roasted garlic potato bread. Tops among these features a tender, perfectly charcoal-grilled tenderloin steak accompanied by baked-potato salad, lettuce, tomato, a huge slice of onion, and shaved cucumber salad—a meal in itself. Top-notch coffees are roasted on the premises.

For a Few Bucks More
✪ **Lauro Ristorante Italiano.** 3915 Henderson Blvd. (2 blocks west of Dale Mabry Hwy., between Watrous and Neptune aves.). ☎ **813/281-2100.** Reservations recommended.

Tampa Accommodations & Dining

Accommodations:

Best Western Resort Tampa **1**
Budgetel Inn **2**
Days Inn Maingate **3**
Days Inn–Rocky Point **7**
Quality Suites Hotel–
   USF near Busch Gardens **5**

Dining:

Bern's Steak House **9**
Cactus Club **10**
Cafe Creole & Oyster Bar **17**
Carmine's Restaurant & Bar **18**
The Colonnade **12**
The Columbia **19**
Four Green Fields **14**
Frankie's Patio Bar & Grill **16**
Lauro Ristorante Italiano **7**
Mel's Hot Dogs **6**
Mise en Place **13**
Ovo Cafe **15**
Selena's **11**
Shells **4**
SideBern's **8**

Main courses $10–$25. AE, DC, DISC, MC, V. Mon–Fri 11:30am–2pm and 5:30–10pm, Sat 5:30–11pm. ITALIAN.

Known for creating extraordinary sauces and pastas, chef/owner Lauro Medeglia is a native Italian who cooks his home fare with love. Though his restaurant is off the beaten track, it's worth the detour. Classical decor and soft music have made it one of Tampa's favorite places to "pop the question," and smartly attired waiters render efficient yet friendly and unobtrusive service. Try the caprese, putanesca, gnocchi, or agnolotti.

Selena's. In Old Hyde Park shopping complex, 1623 Snow Ave. (south of Swan St.). ☎ **813/ 251-2116.** Reservations recommended. Main courses $10–$18. AE, MC, V. Mon–Thurs 11am–10pm, Fri–Sat 11am–11pm, Sun 11am–9pm. LOUISIANA.

This charming restaurant seems straight out of New Orleans. Sit in the plant-filled Patio Room, the eclectic Queen Anne Room, or watch the world go by at the outdoor cafe. Local seafoods, especially grouper and shrimp, top the menu at dinner, with many of the dishes served Louisiana style (to exercise your taste buds, try the rustic crab cakes with Cajun spices or the "voodoo" shrimp Creole). The vegetarian broccoli, cauliflower, and mushrooms over linguine has justifiably won awards. Other choices include pastas, chicken, steaks, and apricot-glazed quail. At night, jazz sounds enliven the proceedings, as musical groups perform in the upstairs lounge.

Worth a Splurge

Bern's Steak House. 1208 S. Howard Ave. (at Marjory Ave.). ☎ **813/251-2421.** Reservations required. Main courses $19–$35. AE, DC, DISC, MC, V. Daily 5–11pm. Closed Christmas. AMERICAN.

The exterior of this famous steak house looks like a factory built almost under the Lee Roy Selmon Crosstown Expressway. Inside, however, you'll find eight ornate dining rooms with themes like Rhône, Burgundy, and Irish Rebellion. They set an appropriately dark atmosphere for meat lovers, for here you order and pay for charcoal-grilled steaks (beef or buffalo) according to the thickness and weight. They come with onion soup, salad, baked potato, garlic toast, onion rings, and vegetables grown in Bern's own organic garden. The phone book–size wine list offers more than 7,000 selections.

The big surprise here are the dessert quarters upstairs, where 50 romantic booths paneled in aged California redwood can privately seat from two to 12 guests. Each of these little chambers is equipped with a phone for placing your order and a closed-circuit TV for watching and listening to a resident pianist. The dessert menu offers almost 100 delicious selections, plus some 1,400 after-dinner drinks. It's possible to reserve a booth for dessert only, but preference is given to those who dine. You can get some of the same sweet things nearby at SideBern's (see above).

✪ **Mise en Place.** In Grand Central Place, 442 W. Kennedy Blvd. (at S. Magnolia Ave., opposite the University of Tampa). ☎ **813/254-5373.** Reservations accepted only for parties of 6 or more. Main courses $13–$21. AE, DC, DISC, MC, V. Mon–Fri 11am–3pm, Tues–Thurs 5:30–10pm, Fri–Sat 5:30–11pm. INTERNATIONAL.

Look around at all those happy, stylish people soaking up the trendy ambience and you'll know why chef Marty Blitz and his wife, Marianne, are the culinary darlings of Tampa. They continue to present the freshest of ingredients, with a creative international menu that changes daily. Main courses often include such choices as roast duck with Jamaica wild-strawberry sauce, grilled swordfish with trimelon mint salsa, or Ethiopian lentil stew served with steamed *injera* bread. There's valet parking at the rear of the building on Grand Central Place.

After dinner you can wander next door into **442,** an upscale bar with live jazz and blues.

YBOR CITY

Super-Cheap Eats

✪ **Carmine's Restaurant & Bar.** 1802 E. 7th Ave. (at 18th St). ☎ **813/248-3834.** Reservations not accepted. Sandwiches $4–$7; main courses $5–$16 (most $7–$8). No credit cards. Mon–Tues 9am–10pm, Wed–Thurs 9am–midnight, Fri–Sat 9am–3am, Sun 9am–6pm. CUBAN/ITALIAN/AMERICAN.

Bright blue poles hold up an ancient pressed-tin ceiling above this noisy corner cafe, one of Ybor's most popular hangouts. A great variety of patrons gather at a stainless steel–topped bar or sit at an eclectic collection of chairs and tables that appear to have been gathered at a long series of yard sales. For lunch or dinner, you can order a genuine Cuban sandwich—smoked ham, roast pork, Genoa salami, Swiss cheese, pickles, salad dressing, mustard, lettuce, and tomato on a crispy submarine roll. There's a vegetarian version, too, and the combination half sandwich and bowl of Spanish soup made with sausages, potatoes, and garbanzo beans makes a hearty meal for just $4. Main courses are led by Cuban-style roast pork, thin-cut pork chops with mushroom sauce, spaghetti with a blue crab tomato sauce, and a few seafood and chicken platters.

Frankie's Patio Bar & Grill. 1905 E. 7th Ave. (between 19th and 20th sts.). ☎ **813/ 249-3337.** Reservations accepted only for large parties. Main courses $8–$14; sandwiches $4.25–$6.50. AE, MC, V. Mon–Tues 11am–3pm, Wed–Thurs 11am–1am, Fri–Sat 11am–3am. INTERNATIONAL.

Known mostly as a venue for outstanding musical acts, this Ybor City attraction is also fun at lunch and dinner. With exposed industrial pipes, the large 3-story restaurant stands out from the usual Spanish-themed, 19th-century architecture of Ybor City. There's seating indoors, on a large outdoor patio, or on an open-air balcony overlooking the action on the street. It's a fun atmosphere, and the food blends Cuban, American, Creole, and Italian influences. Live jazz, blues, reggae, and rock add to the atmosphere Wednesday to Saturday.

For a Few Bucks More

✪ **Cafe Creole and Oyster Bar.** 1330 9th Ave. (at Avenida de Republica de Cuba/14th St.). ☎ **813/247-6283.** Reservations not accepted but call for preferred seating. Main courses $9–$17. AE, DC, DISC, MC, V. Mon–Thurs 11:30am–10pm, Fri 11:30am–11:30pm, Sat 5–11:30pm. CREOLE/CAJUN.

Resembling a turn-of-the-century railway station, this brick building dates from 1896 and was originally known as El Pasaje, the home of the Cherokee Club, a gentlemen's hotel and private club with a casino and a decor rich in stained-glass windows, wrought-iron balconies, Spanish murals, and marble bathrooms. Specialties include exceptionally prepared Louisiana crab cakes, oysters, blackened grouper, and jambalaya. If you're new to cuisine to the bayou, try the Creole sampler. Dine inside or out.

✪ **Columbia.** 2117 E. 7th Ave. (between 21st and 22nd sts). ☎ **813/248-4961.** Reservations recommended. Main courses $12–$23. AE, DC, DISC, MC, V. Mon–Thurs 11am–10pm, Fri–Sat 11am–11pm, Sun noon–9pm. SPANISH.

Dating from 1905, this hand-painted tile building occupies an entire city block in the heart of Ybor City. Tourists flock here to soak up the ambience and so do the locals because it's so much fun to clap along during fire-belching floor shows in the main dining room. You can't help coming back time after time for the famous Spanish bean soup and original "1905" salad. The paella à la valenciana is outstanding, with more than a dozen ingredients from gulf grouper and gulf pink shrimp to calamari, mussels, clams, chicken, and pork. The decor throughout is graced with hand-painted tiles, wrought-iron chandeliers, dark woods, rich red fabrics, and stained-glass windows. You can breathe your own fumes in the Cigar Bar.

Ovo Cafe. 1901 E. 7th Ave. (at 19th St.). ☎ **813/248-6979.** Reservations not accepted. Main courses $8–$15. AE, MC, V. Mon–Tues 11am–4pm, Wed–Sat 11am–2am, Sun 11am–10pm. INTERNATIONAL.

This cafe, popular with the business set by day and the club crowd at night, is Tampa's answer to New York's SoHo. You'll find a blend of good food, eclectic art, and pleasing surroundings. Locals love the "ménage à trois" omelettes at breakfast. The fresh Ovo's chicken feta salad is a great lunch choice. An eclectic menu includes pierogies, smoked tuna sandwiches, and shrimp bisque soup. The big surprise is finding Dom Perignon on the menu, as well as root-beer floats made with Absolut vodka.

TAMPA AFTER DARK

The Tampa/Hillsborough Arts Council maintains an **Artsline** (☎ **813/229-ARTS**), a 24-hour information service providing the latest on current and upcoming cultural events. Racks in many restaurants and bars have copies of *Weekly Planet, Focus,* and *Accent on Tampa Bay,* three free publications detailing what's going on in the entire bay area. And you can check the "Baylife" and "Friday Extra" sections of the *Tampa Tribune* and the Friday "Weekend" section of the *St. Petersburg Times.* The visitor center usually has copies of the week's newspaper sections (see "Essentials," above). And be on the lookout for the slick bimonthly magazine *Event Guide Tampa Bay,* which gives a rundown on what's going on.

THE CLUB & MUSIC SCENE Ybor City is Tampa's favorite nighttime venue by far. All you have to do is stroll along 7th Avenue East between 15th and 20th streets to find a club or bar to your liking. The avenue is packed with people of every possible age and description on Friday and Saturday from 9pm to 3am, but you'll also find something going on from Tuesday to Thursday and even on Sunday. You don't need addresses or phone numbers; your ears will guide you along 7th Avenue East.

Starting at 15th Street and heading east, you'll come first to **The Masquerade,** with retro and old wave bands on Friday to Sunday. The body-pierced 20-something crowd gets primed at **Club Hedo** and **Cherry's** before dancing at **The Rubb** across the avenue. Between 16th and 17th streets, the **Blue Shark** features the blues (and refuses to sell alcoholic beverages to anyone who appears to be intoxicated).

Between 17th and 18th streets, you'll smell the cigar smoke coming from the sidewalk tables of the **Green Iguana Bar & Grill,** a refined establishment frequented by young professionals. The **Irish Pub** is just that, while **Fat Tuesday** has a large dance floor and long bar. Between 18th and 19th streets, you'll see **Harpo's** and **The Polyester Patio,** which don't extract a cover charge. Keep going across 19th Street to **The Beach Club,** the kind of noisy joint that advertises "no panties" on Thursday. Upstairs over Bubba's is one of Ybor's best clubs, **Blues Ship Café on Top,** which features live blues, jazz, and reggae. And last but not least is the warehouselike ✪ **Frankie's Patio Bar & Grill,** known for its reasonably priced food as well as its outstanding musical acts (see "Great Deals on Dining," above). Across the avenue, country meets city at **Spurs in Ybor,** a country-and-western joint.

Lastly, comedy-lovers can get their laughs at **Key West on 7th,** between 20th and 21st streets.

Although not in the heart of Ybor's bar scene, the ✪ **Jazz Cellar,** on 9th Avenue East between 13th Street and Avenida de Republica de Cuba (14th Street), features contemporary jazz, rhythm and blues, and just plain blues. This basement establishment is on the north side of Ybor Square. Call ☎ **813/248-1862** for reservations.

Elsewhere in town, you can lose your life savings playing bingo, poker, and the video slot machines at the **Seminole Indian Casino,** 5223 N. Orient Rd., at Hillsborough Road east of the city (☎ **800/282-7016** or 813/621-1302). It's open 24 hours every day of the year.

THE PERFORMING ARTS With a prime downtown location on 9 acres along the east bank of the Hillsborough River, the huge **Tampa Bay Performing Arts Center,** 1010 N. MacInnes Pl. (☎ **800/955-1045** or 813/229-STAR), is the largest performing arts venue south of the Kennedy Center in Washington, D.C. Accordingly, this four-theater complex is the focal point of Tampa's performing arts scene, presenting a wide range of Broadway plays, classical and pop concerts, operas, cabarets, improv, and special events.

A sightseeing attraction in its own right, the restored ✪ **Tampa Theatre,** 711 Franklin St. (☎ **813/223-8981**), dates from 1926 and is on the National Register of Historic Places. It presents a varied program of classic, foreign, and alternative films, as well as concerts and special events.

The 74,301-seat **Houlihan's Stadium,** 4201 N. Dale Mabry Hwy. (☎ **813/ 673-4300**), is frequently the site of headliner concerts. The **USF Sun Dome,** 4202 E. Fowler Ave. (☎ **813/974-3111**), on the University of South Florida campus, hosts major concerts by touring pop stars, rock bands, jazz groups, and other contemporary artists.

2 St. Petersburg

20 miles SW of Tampa, 289 miles NW of Miami, 84 miles SW of Orlando

On the western shore of the bay, St. Petersburg stands in contrast to Tampa, much like San Francisco compares to Oakland in California. While Tampa is the area's business, industrial, and shipping center, St. Petersburg was conceived and built almost a century ago primarily for tourists and wintering snowbirds. Here you'll find one of the most picturesque and pleasant downtowns of any city in Florida, with a waterfront promenade and the famous, pyramid-shaped Pier offering great views across the bay, plus quality museums, interesting shops, and fine restaurants.

Away from downtown, the city pretty much consists of strip malls dividing residential neighborhoods, but plan at least to have a look around the charming bay-front area. If you don't do anything else, go out on The Pier and take a pleasant stroll along Bayshore Drive.

All is not completely happy in this urban paradise, however, for St. Petersburg was rocked by riots after a white police officer shot and killed a black motorist in late 1996. Although the city soon quieted down and was still peaceful at presstime, it's a good idea to avoid the area south of I-175 and east of I-275.

ESSENTIALS

GETTING THERE To reach downtown from Tampa, take I-275 or the Gandy Causeway (U.S. 92) across the bay, then I-275 south to I-375 east to the waterfront. From Sarasota and Bradenton, take I-275 north across the towering Sunshine Skyway ($2 toll) to I-175 or I-375 east. From points north, take congested U.S. 19 straight to downtown.

Tampa International Airport, approximately 16 miles northeast of St. Petersburg, is the prime gateway for the area (see "Getting There" in section 1, above). **St. Petersburg–Clearwater International Airport,** on Roosevelt Boulevard (Fla. 686) about 10 miles north of downtown St. Petersburg (☎ **813/535-7600**), primarily handles charter flights, although limited regular service is provided by two commuter carriers, **American Trans Air** (☎ 800/225-2995) and **SunJet** (☎ 800/478-6538). **Sky America** (☎ 800/368-2307) flies from here to Key West. Incidentally, St. Petersburg–Clearwater International was the birthplace of commercial aviation, since the world's first scheduled carrier, the St. Petersburg–Tampa Airboat Line, took off from here in 1914.

All major car-rental firms are represented at the airports.

The Limo (☎ 800/282-6817 or 813/572-1111) and **Red Line Limo** (☎ 800/359-5466 or 813/535-3391) offer 24-hour van service between both Tampa International or St. Petersburg–Clearwater airports and any St. Petersburg area destination or hotel. The flat-rate, one-way fare is about $13 from the Tampa airport and $11.50 from the St. Petersburg–Clearwater airport to any St. Pete or gulf beach destination. **Yellow Cab Taxis** (☎ 813/821-7777) line up outside baggage-claim areas. Average fare from the Tampa airport to St. Petersburg or any of the gulf beaches is about $25 to $35 per taxi (one or more passengers). The fare from the St. Petersburg–Clearwater airport is approximately $15 to $20.

Amtrak (☎ 800/USA-RAIL for reservations) has rail service to Tampa (see "Getting There" in section 1).

VISITOR INFORMATION   For advance information about both St. Petersburg and the beaches, contact the **St. Petersburg/Clearwater Area Convention & Visitors Bureau,** 14450 46th St. N., Clearwater, FL 34622 (☎ 800/345-6710, or 813/464-7200 for advance hotel reservations; fax 813/464-7222; www.stpete-clearwater.com). The office is south of Roosevelt Boulevard (Fla. 686) opposite St. Petersburg–Clearwater International Airport.

A wealth of information is also available from the **St. Petersburg Area Chamber of Commerce,** 100 2nd Ave. N. (at 1st Street), St. Petersburg, FL 33701 (☎ 813/821-4069; fax 813/895-6326; www.stpete.com). This downtown main office and visitor center is open Monday to Friday from 8am to 5pm. Ask for a copy of the chamber's visitor guide, which lists hotels, motels, condominiums, and other accommodations.

The chamber also operates the **Suncoast Welcome Center,** on Ulmerton Road at Exit 18 southbound off I-275 (there's no exit here for northbound traffic).

Also downtown, there are **walk-in information centers** on the first level of The Pier and in the lobby of the Florida International Museum (see "Seeing the Top Attractions," below).

CITY LAYOUT   St. Petersburg's **downtown** is laid out according to a grid system, with streets running north-south and avenues running east-west. **Central Avenue** is the dividing line for north and south addresses. "Northeast" avenues—those designated NE—lie east of 1st Street North. With the exception of Central Avenue, most streets and avenues downtown are one way.

GETTING AROUND   You can see everything on the free **Looper: the Downtown Trolley** (☎ 813/571-3440), which runs out to the end of The Pier and past all of the downtown attractions every 30 minutes from 11am to 5pm daily except Thanksgiving and Christmas.

The **Pinellas Suncoast Transit Authority/PSTA** (☎ 813/530-9911) operates regular bus service throughout Pinellas County. The fare is $1.

If you need a cab, call **Yellow Cab** (☎ 813/821-7777) or **Independent Cab** (☎ 813/327-3444).

Pierside Rentals, on The Pier (☎ 813/822-8697), rents bicycles for $5 an hour, $20 a day, or $50 a week.

SEEING THE TOP ATTRACTIONS

Florida International Museum. 100 2nd St. N. (between 1st and 2nd aves. N.). ☎ **800/777-9882** or 813/822-3693. www.floridamuseum.org. Admission $13.95 adults, $12.95 seniors, $5.95 children. Daily 9am–6pm (or later depending of special exhibits).

This facility attracted 600,000 visitors from around the world in 1995 when it opened its first exhibition, called "Treasures of the Czars," and the success has continued (its recent exhibit on the *Titanic* was a smash hit). Call to see what's scheduled during your visit. The museum is housed in the former Maas Brothers Department Store, long an area landmark. Tickets should be reserved and purchased in advance to be sure of a specific time. Each visitor is equipped with an audio guide as part of the admission price; allow at least 2 hours to tour a major exhibition.

Museum of Fine Arts. 255 Beach Dr. NE (at 3rd Ave. N.). ☎ **813/896-2667.** Admission Tues–Sat $6 adults, $5 seniors, $2 students. Free admission on Sun. Tues–Sat 10am–5pm, Sun 1–5pm; winter, third Thurs of each month 10am–9pm.

Resembling a Mediterranean villa on the waterfront, this museum houses a permanent collection of European, American, pre-Colombian, and Far Eastern art, with works by such artists as Fragonard, Monet, Renoir, Cézanne, and Gauguin. Other highlights include period rooms with antiques and historical furnishings, plus a gallery of Steuben crystal, a new decorative-arts gallery, and world-class rotating exhibits.

The Pier. 800 2nd Ave. NE. ☎ **813/821-6164.** www.stpete-pier.com. Free admission to all the public areas and decks; donations welcome at the aquarium. Valet parking $5, self-parking $3. Pier Mon–Sat 10am–9pm, Sun 11am–6pm. Aquarium Mon–Sat 10am–8pm, Sun noon–6pm. Restaurant hours vary.

Walk or ride out on The Pier and enjoy this festive waterfront dining and shopping complex overlooking Tampa Bay. Originally built as a railroad pier in 1889, today it's capped by a spaceshiplike inverted pyramid offering five levels of shops and restaurants, plus an aquarium, tourist information desk, observation deck, catwalks for fishing, boat docks, a small bay-side beach, miniature golf, boat and water-sports rentals, sightseeing boats, and a food court. You can rent boats and go on cruises from here (see "Great Golf That Won't Break Your Budget & Other Affordable Outdoor Activities," below), and from November to April climb aboard the **HMS Bounty,** a replica of the famous vessel built in 1960 for the Marlon Brando version of *Mutiny on the Bounty* (30-minute tours of the ship cost $5 for adults, $4 for seniors, and $3 for kids 5 to 17; call ☎ 813/896-5668 for more information). A free trolley service operates between The Pier and the parking lots on shore.

✪ Salvador Dalí Museum. 1000 3rd St. S. (near 11th Ave. S.). ☎ **813/823-3767.** Admission $8 adults, $7 seniors, $4 students, free for children 9 and under. Mon–Wed 9:30am–5:30pm, Thurs 9:30am–8pm, Fri–Sat 9:30am–5:30pm, Sun noon–5pm. Closed Thanksgiving and Christmas.

Located on Tampa Bay south of The Pier, this starkly modern museum houses the world's largest collection of works by the renowned Spanish surrealist. Valued at over $150 million, it includes 94 oil paintings, more than 100 watercolors and drawings, and 1,300 graphics, plus posters, photos, sculptures, objets d'art, and a 5,000-volume library on Dalí and surrealism. There also are special exhibits of works by other famous artists.

MORE ATTRACTIONS

Great Explorations: The Hands On Museum. 1120 4th St. S. (at 11th Ave. S.). ☎ **813/821-8885.** Admission $5, free for children 2 and under. Mon–Sat 10am–5pm, Sun noon–5pm.

With a variety of hands-on exhibits, this museum is great for a rainy day or for kids who've overdosed on the sun and need to cool off inside. They can explore a long, dark tunnel; measure their strength, flexibility, and fitness; paint a work of art with sunlight; and play a melody with a sweep of the hand.

St. Petersburg Museum of History. 335 2nd Ave. NE. ☎ **813/894-1052.** Admission $4 adults, $3.50 seniors, $1.50 children 7–17, free for children 6 and under. Mon–Sat 10am–5pm, Sun 1–5pm.

Located at the foot of The Pier, this museum features a permanent interactive exhibition chronicling St. Petersburg's history, ranging from prehistoric artifacts to documents, clothing, and photographs. There are also computer stations where you can "flip through the past." Walk-through exhibits include a replica of the Benoist airboat, which made the world's first scheduled commercial flight from St. Petersburg in 1914.

Sunken Gardens. 1825 4th St. N. (between 18th and 19th aves. NE). ☎ **813/896-3186.** Admission $14 adults, $8 children 3–11, free for children 2 and under. Daily 9:30am–5pm.

One of the city's oldest attractions, this 7-acre tropical garden park dating from 1935 is a holdover from Florida's early tourist days. It contains a vast array of 5,000 plants, flowers, and trees, and there are bird and alligator shows.

GREAT GOLF THAT WON'T BREAK YOUR BUDGET & OTHER AFFORDABLE OUTDOOR ACTIVITIES

You can get up-to-the-minute recorded information about the city's sports and recreational activities by calling the **Leisure Line** (☎ 813/893-7500).

BIKING With miles of flat terrain, the St. Petersburg area is ideal for bikers, in-line skaters, and hikers. The **Pinellas Trail** is especially good, since it follows an abandoned railroad bed 47 miles from St. Petersburg north to Tarpon Springs. The St. Pete trailhead is on 34th Street South (U.S. 19) between 8th and Fairfield avenues south. It's packed on the weekends. Free strip maps of the trail are available at the St. Petersburg Area Chamber of Commerce (see "Visitor Information," above).

It's a long way from the trailhead, but you can rent bikes from **Pierside Rentals** on The Pier (see "Getting Around," above, and "Boat Rentals," below).

BOAT RENTALS On The Pier, **Pierside Rentals** (☎ 813/363-0000) rents Wave Runners and jet boats. Prices for Wave Runners begin at $45 for an hour; for jet boats, from $55 per hour. Open daily from 9am to dusk.

CRUISES The *Caribbean Queen* (☎ 813/895-BOAT) departs from The Pier and offers 1-hour sightseeing and dolphin-watching cruises around Tampa Bay. Sailings are daily at 1, 3, and 5pm; they cost $10 for adults, $8 for seniors and juniors 12 to 17, $5 for children 3 to 11, and free for children 2 and under.

GOLF One of the nation's top 50 municipal courses, the **Mangrove Bay Golf Course,** 875 62nd Ave. NE (☎ 813/893-7797), hugs the inlets of Old Tampa Bay and offers 18-hole, par-72 play. Facilities include a driving range; lessons and golf-club rental are also available. Fees are about $22, $32 including a cart in winter, slightly lower off-season. Open daily from 6:30am to 6pm.

The city also operates the challenging, par-3 **Twin Brooks Golf Course,** 3800 22nd Ave. S. (☎ 813/893-7445).

In Largo, the **Bardmoor Golf Club,** 7919 Bardmoor Blvd. (☎ 813/397-0483), is often the venue for major tournaments. Lakes punctuate 17 of the 18 holes on this par-72 championship course. Lessons and rental clubs are available, as is a Tom Fazio–designed practice range. Call the clubhouse for seasonal greens fees. Open daily from 7am to dusk.

Downtown St. Petersburg

Accommodations:
Bay Gables Bed & Breakfast **4**
Mansion House Bed & Breakfast **3**
The Heritage/Holiday Inn **7**

Dining:
Apropos **12**
Bay Gables Tea Room **5**
Fourth Street Shrimp Store **1**
Garden Bistro **14**
Keystone Club **6**
Nick's on the Water **10**

Attractions:
Florida International Museum **13**
Museum of Fine Arts **8**
The Pier **11**
Salvador Dalí Museum **15**
Great Explorations **16**
St. Petersburg Museum of History **9**
Sunken Gardens **2**

Adjacent to the St. Petersburg–Clearwater airport, the **Airco Flite Golf Course,** 3650 Roosevelt Blvd., Clearwater (☎ **813/573-4653**), is a championship 18-hole, par-72 course with a driving range. Golf club rentals are also available. Greens fees including cart range from $25 to $35 in winter, about $20 off-season. Open daily from 7am to 6pm.

Call **Tee Times USA** (☎ **800/374-8633**) to reserve times at these and other area courses.

If you want to take up golf or sharpen your game, TV "Golf Doctor" Joe Quinzi hosts his **Quinzi Golf Academy** (☎ **813/725-1999**), at Safety Harbor Resort and Spa (see "Accommodations You Can Afford," below). His school offers personalized instruction and clinics for up to six players.

SAILING   The **Annapolis Sailing School,** 6800 Sunshine Skyway Lane S. (☎ **800/638-9192** or 813/867-8102), almost at the foot of the Sunshine Skyway bridge, can teach you to sail or perfect your sailing skills. Various courses are offered at this branch of the famous Maryland-based school, lasting 2, 5, or 8 days. Prices range from $250 to $2,215 per person, depending on season and length of course.

The school is based at the **Holiday Inn SunSpree Resort,** 6800 Sunshine Skyway Lane S., St. Petersburg, FL 33711 (☎ **800/227-8045** or 813/867-1151), a recently renovated motel where doubles range from $89 to $159 in winter, $69 to $129 off-season.

SPECTATOR SPORTS   St. Petersburg has always been a baseball town, and **Tropicana Field,** a 45,000-seat domed stadium alongside I-175 between 9th and 16th streets south, is the home of the **Tampa Bay Devil Rays,** the area's expansion team which began American League play 1998. The season runs from April through September. Call ☎ **813/898-RAYS** for schedule and ticket information. The Devil Rays move outdoors to Al Lang Stadium, on 2nd Avenue South at 1st Street South (☎ **813/822-3384**), for their spring training games from mid-February through March. Tickets to the spring games range from $3 to $12.

The **Philadelphia Phillies** play their spring-training season at Jack Russell Stadium, 800 Phillies Dr., in nearby Clearwater (☎ **813/442-8496**). Admission is $8 to $9. Their minor league **Clearwater Phillies** play in the stadium from April to September. Grant Field, 373 Douglas Ave. in Dunedin (☎ **813/733-0429**), is the winter home of the **Toronto Blue Jays.**

SHOPPING

The Pier, at the end of 2nd Avenue NE (☎ **813/821-6164**), houses more than a dozen boutiques and craft shops, but nearby Beach Drive, running along the waterfront, is one of the most fashionable downtown strolling and shopping venues. Here you'll find the **Glass Canvas Gallery,** at 4th Avenue NE (☎ **813/821-6767**), featuring a dazzling array of glass sculpture, tableware, art, and craft items by 250 local, national, and international artists. Also at 4th Avenue NE, **P. Buckley Moss** (☎ **813/894-2899**), is a museum-grade store carrying the works of the individualistic artist best known for her portrayal of the Amish and the Mennonites. The works include paintings, graphics, figurines, and collector dolls. **Red Cloud,** between 1st and 2nd avenues (☎ **813/821-5824**), is an oasis for Native American crafts, from jewelry and headdresses to sculpture and art.

Central Avenue is another shopping area, featuring the **Gas Plant Antique Arcade,** between 12th and 13th streets (☎ **813/895-0368**), the largest antique mall on Florida's west coast, with more than 100 dealers displaying their wares. The **Florida Craftsmen Gallery,** at 5th Street (☎ **813/821-7391**), is a showcase for the works of more than 150 Florida artisans and craftspeople: jewelry, ceramics, woodwork, fiber works, glassware, paper creations, and metalwork. And **Haslam's,** between 20th and 21st streets west (☎ **813/822-8616**), claims to be Florida's largest bookstore, with more than 300,000 new and used volumes.

In the suburbs, outlet shoppers can browse Corning Revere, Linens 'N Things, BonWorth, Dress Barn, Van Heusen, Bugle Boy, L'eggs, Bass Shoes, T. J. Maxx, and more at the air-conditioned **Bay Area Outlet Mall,** at the intersection of U.S. 19 and East Bay Drive (☎ **813/535-2337**), west of St. Petersburg–Clearwater International Airport.

ACCOMMODATIONS YOU CAN AFFORD

Ask the **St. Petersburg Area Chamber of Commerce** (see "Essentials," above) for a copy of its visitor guide, which lists a wide range of hotels, motels, condominiums, and other accommodations. In addition, the St. Petersburg/Clearwater Convention & Visitors Bureau has a free **reservations service** (☎ **800/345-6710**).

You'll find plenty of chain motels along U.S. 19.

With regard to prices, the high season is from January to April. The hotel tax rate in Pinellas County is 11%.

SUPER-CHEAP SLEEPS

Bay Gables Bed & Breakfast. 136 4th Ave. NE (between Beach Dr. and 1st St. N), St. Petersburg, FL 33701. ☎ **800/822-8803** or 813/822-8855. Fax 813/824-7223. 9 units, all with bathroom. A/C. $85–$135 single or double. Rates include continental breakfast. MC, V.

You can walk to The Pier from this charming B&B, which was built in the 1930s. It overlooks a flower-filled garden with a gazebo and faces a fanciful Victorian-style house whose first floor is a tearoom/restaurant (see "Great Deals on Dining," below). The guest rooms have been furnished with ceiling fans and Victorian pieces, including some canopy beds. All units have bathrooms with claw-foot tubs and modern showers; half of the rooms have a porch, while the rest have a separate sitting room and kitchenette. Continental breakfast is served in the common room, on the garden deck, or in the gazebo. This is a professionally managed operation; the owners don't live on the premises.

✪ **Heritage/Holiday Inn.** 234 3rd Ave. N. (between 2nd and 3rd sts.), St. Petersburg, FL 33701. ☎ **800/283-7829** or 813/822-4814. Fax 813/823-1644. 71 units. A/C TV TEL. Winter $86–$107 single or double. Off-season $58–$74 single or double. Rates include continental breakfast. AE, DC, DISC, MC, V.

No ordinary Holiday Inn, the Heritage dates from the early 1920s and is the closest thing to a Southern mansion you'll find in the heart of downtown. With a sweeping veranda, French doors, and tropical courtyard, it attracts an eclectic clientele, from young families to seniors. The furnishings include period antiques. There's a heated swimming pool and a whirlpool in a small tropical courtyard between the main building and the Heritage Grill next door, one of the area's most popular restaurants.

FOR A FEW BUCKS MORE

Mansion House Bed & Breakfast. 105 5th Ave. NE (at 1st St. N.), St. Petersburg, FL 33701. ☎ **800/274-7520** or 813/821-9391. Fax 813/821-9391 (same as phone). www. mansionbandb.com. 6 units, all with bathroom. A/C. Winter $110–$150 single or double. Off-season $95–$130 single or double. Rates include full breakfast. AE, MC, V.

This 2-story, shingle-and-stucco house was built in 1904 by a local doctor and extensively renovated in 1991. Sporting a faux fireplace adorned with hand-painted tiles, the comfortable living room opens to a sunroom, off which a small screened porch provides mosquito-free lounging and the only place where guests can smoke here. There's another front parlor upstairs with a TV. Tall, old-fashioned windows let lots of light into the attractive guest rooms. The "Pembrooke" room actually is upstairs over the carriage house; it has its own refrigerator, phone, TV, and four-poster bed with mosquito net. In an unusual architectural twist, the "Harlech" room has a toilet and hand basin in one converted closet, a shower in another. Proprietors Rob and Rosie Ray serve a full breakfast in two formal dining rooms and keep fruit bowls and snacks available at all hours. There's a whirlpool bath in its own screened hut in the backyard.

A NEARBY SPA WITH GOOD PACKAGE DEALS

Safety Harbor Resort and Spa. 105 N. Bayshore Dr., Safety Harbor, FL 34695. ☎ **800/ BEST-SPA** or 813/726-1161. Fax 813/726-4268. www.south-seas.com. 192 units. Winter $159–$179 single or double. Off-season $109–$145 single or double. Packages from $209 per person single occupancy, $134 per person double occupancy. AE, DC, DISC, MC, V.

Sanibel Island's excellent South Seas Resorts Company (see chapter 10) recently gave a much-needed face-lift and upgrading to this tranquil, waterfront retreat on Old Tampa Bay. The full-service spa, the only one in Florida with mineral springs, offers pampering from massages to hydrotherapy and a full menu of fitness classes from boxing to yoga. The resort sits on 22 waterfront acres in the sleepy town of Safety Harbor, north of St. Petersburg. Guests have been enjoying the curative mineral waters for more than 50 years and the water-fitness programs receive acclaim every year. The least-expensive way to enjoy all this is via the spa's basic fitness package, which includes accommodation, meals, and unlimited use of spa facilities, fitness classes, and daytime tennis; a 2-night minimum stay is required.

Nutritious meals emphasizing American fusion cuisine use lots of Florida ingredients in both the Spa Dining Room and the resort's Cafe, which is open to the public for lunch and dinner. Amenities include concierge, limited room service, laundry, valet parking, Clarins Skin Institute, spa salon, natural mineral springs, fitness center, and the Phil Green tennis and Quinzi golf academies (see "Great Golf That Won't Break Your Budget & Other Affordable Outdoor Activities," above).

GREAT DEALS ON DINING

Don't overlook the food court at **The Pier,** where the inexpensive chow is accompanied by a very rich but quite free view of the bay. Among the stalls, **Alessi Deli** is a good bet for salads, pastries, and coffee. Upstairs there's a branch of Tampa's famous **Columbia restaurant** (see "Great Deals on Dining" in section 1, above).

SUPER-CHEAP EATS

Apropos. 300 2nd Ave. NE (at Bayshore Dr.). ☎ **813/823-8934.** Reservations accepted only for dinner. Breakfast $3.50–$6; lunch $5–$9; dinner main courses $9–$16. DC, MC, V. Tues–Sat 7:30–10:30am and 11am–3pm; Thurs–Sun 6–10pm (Sun brunch 8:30am–2pm). AMERICAN.

Sitting at the foot of The Pier, Apropros is a fine place to breakfast before your tour of downtown, perhaps with a brie and bacon omelette, or a seasonal fruit plate, or just plain eggs. At lunch, the view through the masts in the adjacent marina sets the scene for the likes of shrimp and artichoke salad with a sherry mayonnaise dressing. And at dinner, you can choose from a blackboard offering the chef 's nightly nouveau cuisine selections. You'll find as many locals here as tourists.

Bay Gables Tea Room & Garden. 136 4th Ave. NE (between Beach Dr. and 1st St. N.). ☎ **813/822-0044.** Reservations recommended for lunch, required for afternoon tea. Main courses $6–$12 plus 18% service charge. MC, V. Mon–Sat 11am–2pm, afternoon tea at 3pm; Sun brunch 10am–2pm. AMERICAN.

Set in the beautifully restored 1910 Victorian Bay Gables Bed & Breakfast (see "Accommodations You Can Afford," above), replete with Old Florida antiques and frilly trimmings, this spot less than 2 blocks from the bay front caters mostly to the midday shopping crowd. Meals are served on heirloom china and silver in the cozy atmosphere of three small rooms and a tiny porch upstairs or on a wraparound ground-floor veranda. The menu is simple but freshly prepared, featuring salads, quiches, soups, and finger sandwiches.

○ **Fourth Street Shrimp Store.** 1006 4th St. N. (at 10th Ave. N.). ☎ **813/822-0325.** Reservations not accepted. Sandwiches $2.50–$6; main courses $4–$12. MC, V. Sun–Thurs 11am–9pm, Fri–Sat 11am–10pm. SEAFOOD.

If you're anywhere in the area, don't miss at least driving by to see the color-ful, cartoonlike mural on the outside of this eclectic establishment just north of downtown. On first impression it looks like graffiti, but it's actually a gigantic drawing of people eating. Inside, it gets even better, with paraphernalia and murals on two walls making the dining room seem like a warehouse with windows looking out on an early 19th-century seaport (one painted sailor permanently peers in to see what you're eating). You'll pass a seafood market counter when you enter, from which comes the fresh namesake shrimp, the star here. You can also pick from grouper, clam strips, catfish, or oysters fried, broiled, or steamed, all served in heaping portions. This is the best and certainly the most interesting bargain in town.

Nick's on the Water. On The Pier, east end of 2nd Ave. NE. ☎ **813/898-5800.** Reserva-tions recommended for dinner. Main courses $8–$18. AE, DC, MC, V. Sun–Thurs 11:30am–10pm, Fri–Sat 11:30am–11pm. ITALIAN/SEAFOOD.

Located on the main level of The Pier, this informal restaurant offers expansive views of downtown St. Petersburg and the bay-front marina. The menu features a variety of Italian choices, including Nick's tortellini, but the specialty of the house is wood-fired fish, meats, and pizza. The veal dishes also are a big hit, especially the française, with sautéed medaillons.

FOR A FEW BUCKS MORE

Garden Bistro. 217 Central Ave. ☎ **813/896-3800.** Reservations recommended for dinner. Main courses $10–$16. AE, MC, V. Daily noon–2pm and 5pm–2am. MEDITERRANEAN.

A popular hot spot with those in the know, this lively restaurant combines European ambience with Moroccan cuisine. Choice seats are under huge shade trees in the garden, screened from the street by a trellis fence. Inside, the decor blends the Amer-ican Southwest with the Mediterranean, with arches, a 19th-century tiled floor, modern local art, and lots of flowers and plants. The creative menu features couscous, a daily tajine (a traditional Moroccan stew), pastas such as wild mushrooms with strips of roast duck, and smoked salmon in a light cream sauce. On Friday and Saturday, live jazz adds to the ambience from 9pm to 1am.

Keystone Club. 320 4th St. N. (between 3rd and 4th aves. N.). ☎ **813/822-6600.** Reser-vations recommended. Main courses $11–$23; early bird specials $7.50–$12. AE, DC, DISC, MC, V. Mon–Fri 11am–2:30pm and 5–10pm, Sat 4–10pm, Sun 4–9pm. Early bird specials winter only Mon–Fri 4:30–5:30pm, Sat–Sun 4–5:30pm. STEAKS/PRIME RIB.

Resembling an exclusive men's club, this cozy restaurant's forest-green walls accented by dark wood and etched glass create an atmosphere that's reminiscent of a Manhattan-style chophouse. But women are also welcome to partake of the beef, which is king here. Specialties include roast prime rib, New York strip steak, and filet mignon. Seafood also makes an appearance, with fresh lobster and grouper at market price. During winter, "sunset" early bird specials include lunch-size portions, a bev-erage, and dessert.

ST. PETERSBURG AFTER DARK

Good sources of nightlife information are the Friday "Weekend" section of the *St. Petersburg Times,* the "Baylife" and "Friday Extra" sections of the *Tampa Tribune,* and the *Weekly Planet,* a tabloid available at the visitor information offices and in many hotel and restaurant lobbies. The bimonthly magazine *Event Guide Tampa Bay* gives a rundown on what's going on.

THE CLUB & MUSIC SCENE A historic attraction as well as an entertainment venue, the Moorish-style **Coliseum Ballroom,** 535 4th Ave. N. (☎ **813/892-5202**), has been hosting dancing, big bands, boxing, and other events since 1924 (it even made an appearance in the 1985 movie *Cocoon*). An acquaintance of mine said it's fun to watch the town's many seniors doing the jitterbug just like it was 1945 again! Call for the schedule and prices.

A much younger set heads to the casual, downtown **Big Catch,** 9 1st St. NE (☎ **813/821-6444**), featuring live and danceable rock and Top 40 hits, as well as darts, pool, and hoops. North of downtown, the **Ringside Cafe,** 2742 4th St. N. (☎ **813/894-8465**), in a renovated boxing gymnasium, is an informal neighborhood cafe with a decided sports motif. The music focuses on jazz and blues (and sometimes reggae).

PERFORMING ARTS VENUES **Tropicana Field,** 1 Stadium Dr. (☎ **813/ 825-3100**), has a capacity of 50,000 for major concerts, but also hosts a variety of smaller events when the Devil Rays aren't playing baseball.

The **Bayfront Center,** 400 1st St. S. (☎ **813/892-5767,** or 813/892-5700 for recorded information), houses the 8,100-seat Bayfront Arena and the 2,000-seat Mahaffey Theater. The schedule includes a variety of concerts, Broadway shows, big bands, ice shows, and circus performances.

3 The St. Pete & Clearwater Beaches

If you're looking for sun and sand, you'll find plenty of both on the 28 miles of slim barrier islands that skirt the gulf shore of the Pinellas Peninsula. With some one million visitors coming here every year, don't be surprised if you have lots of company. But you'll also discover quieter neighborhoods geared to families, and this area has some of the nation's finest beaches, which are protected from development by parks and nature preserves.

At the southern end of the strip, St. Pete Beach is the granddaddy of the area's resorts. In fact, visitors started coming here nearly a century ago, and they haven't quit. Today St. Pete Beach is heavily developed and often overcrowded during the winter season. If you like high-rises and mile-a-minute action, St. Pete Beach is for you. But even here, Pass-a-Grille, on the island's southern end, is a quiet residential enclave with eclectic shops and a fine public beach.

A more gentle lifestyle begins just to the north on 3½-mile-long Treasure Island. From there, you cross famous John's Pass to Sand Key, a 12-mile island occupied primarily by residential Madeira Beach, Redington Beach, North Redington Beach, Redington Shores, Indian Shores, Indian Rocks Beach, and Belleair Beach. Finally the road crosses a soaring bridge to Clearwater Beach, whose silky sands attract active families and couples.

If you like your great outdoors unfettered by development, the jewels here are Fort Desoto Park, down below St. Pete Beach at the mouth of Tampa Bay, and Caladesi Island State Park, north of Clearwater Beach. They are consistently rated among America's top beaches. And Sand Key Park, looking at Clearwater Beach from the southern shores of Little Pass, is one of Florida's finest local beach parks.

ESSENTIALS

GETTING THERE   To reach St. Pete Beach and Treasure Island from I-275, take Exit 4 and follow the Pinellas Bayway (Fla. 682) west (50¢ toll). For Indian Rocks Beach, take Exit 18 and follow Ulmerton Road due west to the gulf. For the Redington beaches, take Exit 15 and follow Gandy and Park boulevards (Fla. 694) due west (Park Boulevard also is known as 74th Avenue North). For Clearwater Beach, take the Courtney Campbell Causeway (Fla. 60) west from Tampa; the causeway becomes Gulf-to-Bay Boulevard (also Fla. 60), which leads straight west into Clearwater.

See "Getting There" in sections 1 and 2 for information about flights to, and transportation from, Tampa International and St. Petersburg–Clearwater International airports.

VISITOR INFORMATION   See "Visitor Information" in section 2 for the St. Petersburg/Clearwater Area Convention & Visitors Bureau and the St. Petersburg Area Chamber of Commerce. You can get information specific to the beaches from the **Gulf Beaches of Tampa Bay Chamber of Commerce,** 6990 Gulf Blvd. (at 70th Avenue), St. Pete Beach, FL 33706 (☎ **800/944-1847** or 813/360-6957; fax 813/360-2233). The main office is open Monday to Friday from 9am to 5pm. The chamber also has welcome centers at 501 150th Ave. in Madeira Beach (☎ **813/391-7373**); at 105 5th Ave. in Indian Rocks Beach (☎ **813/595-4575**); and at 152 108th Ave. in Treasure Island (☎ **813/367-4529**).

If you're going to be here for more than a week, the chamber sells a **dining and entertainment coupon book** for $30. It could more than pay for itself if you use it religiously at the restaurants, attractions, and other establishments it advertises.

For advance information about Clearwater Beach, contact the **Greater Clearwater Chamber of Commerce,** 128 N. Osceola Ave. (P.O. Box 2457), Clearwater, FL 34615 (☎ **813/461-0011**).

GETTING AROUND   **BATS City Transit** (☎ 813/367-3086) offers bus service along the St. Pete Beach strip. The fare is $1.

Treasure Island Transit System (☎ 813/547-4575) runs buses along the Treasure Island strip. The fare is $1.

The **Jolley Trolley** (☎ 813/445-1200), operated in conjunction with the City of Clearwater, provides service in the Clearwater Beach area, from downtown to the beaches as far south as Sand Key. It also goes to the Belleview Mido resort. The ride costs 25¢.

Along the beach, the major cab company is **BATS Taxi** (☎ 813/367-3702).

Water Taxis operate along the bay side of the islands Tuesday to Sunday from 11am to 1am (☎ 813/323-8294). It's best to call for reservations. Rides cost $5 per person one way, or you can buy an all-day pass for $15 per person.

You can rent bicycles and scooters in St. Pete Beach from **Beach Cyclist Sports Center,** 7517 Blind Pass Rd. (☎ 813/367-5001), and **Cycle & Scooter Services,** 7116-A Gulf Blvd. In Clearwater Beach, contact **Transportation Station,** 652 Gulf-view Blvd. (☎ **813/443-3188).** See "Great Golf That Won't Break Your Budget & Other Affordable Outdoor Activities," below, for more information.

HITTING THE BEACH

This entire stretch of coast is one long beach, but since hotels, condominiums, and private homes occupy much of it, you may want to sun and swim at one of the area's public parks. The very best are described below, but there's also the fine **Pass-a-Grille Public Beach,** on the southern end of St. Pete Beach, where you can watch the boats going in and out of Pass-a-Grille Channel. This and all other Pinellas County public beaches have metered parking lots, so bring a supply of quarters.

Clearwater Public Beach has beach volleyball, water-sports rentals, lifeguards, rest rooms, showers, and concessions. The swimming is excellent, and there's a children's playground and a pier for fishing. Gated municipal parking lots here cost $1 per hour or $7 a day. The lots are right across the street from Clearwater Beach Marina, a prime base for boating, cruises, and other waterborne activities (see "Great Golf That Won't Break Your Budget & Other Affordable Outdoor Activities," below).

HONEYMOON ISLAND & CALADESI ISLAND STATE PARK

Occupying a 3½-mile island north of Clearwater Beach, ✪ **Caladesi Island State Park** boasts a lovely, relatively secluded beach with fine soft sand edged in sea grass and palmettos. Dolphins cavort in the waters offshore. In the park itself, there's a nature trail, and you might see one of the rattlesnakes, black racers, raccoons, armadillos, or rabbits that live here. A concession stand, ranger station, and bathhouses (with rest rooms and showers) are available. Caladesi Island is accessible only by ferry from **Honeymoon Island State Recreation Area**, which is connected by Causeway Boulevard to Dunedin, north of Clearwater. (Honeymoon Island isn't great for swimming, but it has its own rugged beauty and a fascinating nature trail.) You'll first have to pay the admission to Honeymoon Island: $4 per vehicle with two to eight occupants, $2 per single-occupant vehicle, $1 for pedestrians and bicyclists. Beginning daily at 10am, the ferry departs Honeymoon Island every hour on winter weekdays, every 30 minutes on summer weekdays, and every 30 minutes on weekends year-round. Rides cost $6 for adults and $3.50 for kids. The two parks are open daily from 8am to sunset. The two islands are administered by **Gulf Islands Geopark,** 1 Causeway Blvd., Dunedin, FL 34698 (☎ **813/469-5942**).

FORT DESOTO PARK

South of St. Pete Beach at the very mouth of Tampa Bay, this group of five connected barrier islands has been set aside by Pinellas County as a 900-acre bird, animal, and plant sanctuary. Besides the stunning white-sugar sand beach (where you can watch the manatees and dolphins play offshore), there's a Spanish-American War–era fort, great fishing from piers, a large playground for kids, and 4 miles of trails winding through the park for in-line skaters, bicyclists, and joggers.

Sitting on an island by themselves, the park's 230 campsites all have water and electricity hookups, but they usually are sold out, especially on weekends. Sites cost $18.76 a night. To make reservations, you must appear *in person* and pay for your site no more than 30 days in advance at the campground office, at 631 Chestnut St. in Clearwater, or at 150 5th St. North in downtown St. Petersburg. You must camp here at least 2 nights, but you can stay no more than 14 nights. The park is open from 8am to dusk, although campers and persons fishing from the piers can stay later. Admission is free. To get here, take the Pinellas Byway (50¢ toll) east from St. Pete Beach and follow Fla. 679 (35¢ toll) and the signs south to the park. For more information, contact the park at 3500 Pinellas Bayway, Tierra Verde, FL 33715 (☎ **813/866-2662**).

SAND KEY PARK

This fine county park on the northern tip of Sand Key facing Clearwater Beach sports a wide beach and gentle surf and is relatively off the beaten path in this commercial area. It's great to get out of the hotel for a morning walk or jog here. Open 8am to dark. Admission is free, but the parking lot has meters. For more information, call ☎ **813/464-3347**.

OTHER AFFORDABLE OUTDOOR ACTIVITIES

BICYCLING & IN-LINE SKATING With miles of flat terrain and paved roads, the beach area is ideal for bikers and in-line skaters, and the 47-mile-long Pinellas Trail runs close by on the mainland (see "Great Golf That Won't Break Your Budget & Other Affordable Outdoor Activities" in section 2, above). In St. Pete Beach, you can rent bicycles, skates, and scooters from **Beach Cyclist Sports Center,** 7517 Blind Pass Rd. (☎ 813/367-5001), and **Cycle & Scooter Services,** 7116-A Gulf Blvd. In Clearwater Beach, contact **Transportation Station,** 652 Gulf-view Blvd. (☎ 813/ 443-3188). Bikes and skates at all three range from about $5 per hour to $20 a day; scooters, about $13 a hour to $40 per day.

BOATING, FISHING & OTHER WATER SPORTS You can indulge in para-sailing, boating, deep-sea fishing, wave running, sightseeing, dolphin-watching, water-skiing, and just about any other waterborne diversion your heart could desire here. All you have to do is head to one of two beach locations: **Hubbard's Marina,** at John's Pass Village and Boardwalk (☎ 813/393-1947), in Madeira Beach on the southern tip of Sand Key; or **Clearwater Beach Marina,** at Coronado Drive and Causeway Boulevard (☎ 800/772-4479 or 813/461-3133), which is at the beach end of the causeway leading to downtown Clearwater. Agents in booths there will give you the schedules and prices, answer any questions you have, and make reservations if neces-sary. Go in the early morning to set up today's activities, or in the afternoon to book tomorrow's.

CRUISES The **Shell Key Shuttle,** Merry Pier, 801 Pass-a-Grille Way in south-ern St. Pete Beach (☎ 813/360-1348), uses a 57-passenger catamaran to shuttle out to Shell Island, one of Florida's last completely undeveloped barrier islands. It's great for bird watchers, who could spot a remarkable 88 different species, including some of North America's rarest shorebirds. Boats leave daily at 10am, noon, and 2pm, plus 4pm in summer. Prices are $10 for adults, $5 for children 12 and under. The ride takes 15 minutes, and you can return on any shuttle you wish. Depart-ing Hubbard's Marina at John's Pass Village and Boardwalk in Madeira Beach, **Shell Island Adventure** (☎ 813/399-9633) has a 5-hour daily trip to the island, including a barbecue lunch, for $27 adults, $15 for kids, and you can rent beach chairs, umbrellas, snorkeling gear, and other equipment once you get there.

   Captain Memo's Pirate Cruise, at Clearwater Beach Marina (☎ 813/446-2587), sails the *Pirate's Ransom,* an authentic reproduction of a pirate ship, on 2-hour day-time "pirate cruises" as well as sunset and evening champagne cruises. Cruises operate year-round, daily at 10am and 2, 4:30, and 7pm. For adults, daytime or sun-set cruises cost $27; evening cruises, $30; both daytime and evening cruises cost $20 for seniors and juniors 13 to 17, $17 for children 2 to 12, free for children under 2.

   Two paddle-wheel riverboats operate here: The *Show Queen* has lunch, sunset dinner, and Sunday brunch cruises from Clearwater Beach Marina (☎ 813/ 461-3113). The *Starlite Princess* does likewise from 3400 Pasadena Ave. S. (☎ 813/ 462-2628), at the eastern side of the Corey Causeway linking St. Pete Beach to the mainland. Call for schedules and prices.

ATTRACTIONS ON LAND

Clearwater Marine Aquarium. 249 Windward Passage, Clearwater. ☎ 813/447-0980. Admission $6.75 adults, $4.25 children 3–11, free for children 2 and under. Mon–Fri 9am–5pm, Sat 9am–4pm, Sun 11am–4pm. The aquarium is off the causeway between Clearwater and Clearwater Beach; follow the signs.

This little jewel of an aquarium on Clearwater Harbor is very low key and friendly; it's dedicated to the rescue and rehabilitation of marine mammals and sea turtles. Exhibits include dolphins, otters, sea turtles, sharks, stingrays, mangroves, and sea grass.

✪ **John's Pass Village and Boardwalk.** 12901 Gulf Blvd. (at John's Pass), Madeira Beach. ☎ **800/944-1847** or 813/397-1511. Free admission. Shops and activities, daily 9am–6pm or later.

Casual and charming, this Old Florida fishing village on John's Pass consists of a string of simple wooden structures topped by tin roofs and connected by a 1,000-foot board-walk. Most of the buildings have been converted into shops, art galleries, restaurants, and saloons. The focal point is the boardwalk and marina, where many water sports are available for visitors (see "Great Golf That Won't Break Your Budget & Other Affordable Outdoor Activities," above).

✪ **Suncoast Seabird Sanctuary.** 18328 Gulf Blvd., Indian Shores. ☎ **813/391-6211.** Free admission, donations welcome. Daily 9am–dusk. Free tours Wed and Sun 2pm.

At any one time there are usually more than 500 sea and land birds living at the sanctuary, from cormorants, white herons, and birds of prey to the ubiquitous brown pelican. The nation's largest wild-bird hospital, dedicated to the rescue, repair, recuperation, and release of sick and injured wild birds, is also here.

The Tampa Bay Holocaust Memorial and Educational Research Center. 55 5th St. S., at Duhme Rd. (113th St. N), Madeira Beach. ☎ **813/821-8261.** Admission $6 donation adults, $5 seniors. Mon–Fri 10am–4pm, Sun noon–4pm.

Situated on the mainland grounds of the Jewish Community Center of Pinellas County, this thought-provoking museum has exhibits about the Holocaust, including a boxcar used to transport human cargo to the Auschwitz death camp in Poland. Its main focus, however, is to promote tolerance and understanding in the present. It was founded by Walter P. Loebenberg, a local businessman who escaped Nazi Germany in 1939 and fought with the U.S. Army in World War II.

SHOPPING

In addition to being a sightseeing attraction here, **John's Pass Village and Boardwalk,** on John's Pass in Madeira Beach, just north of Treasure Island (☎ 813/391-7373), is the key shopping venue on the beaches. The houses of this old fishermen's village have been converted into more than 60 shops selling everything from antiques and beach-wear to every souvenir you can imagine. There are also several art galleries, including the **Bronze Lady,** the world's largest single dealer of works, especially paintings of circus clowns, by the late comedian-artist Red Skelton. The shops here are open daily from 9am to 6pm or later.

If you're in the market for some one-of-a-kind hand-hammered jewelry, try **Evander Preston Contemporary Jewelry,** 106 8th Ave., Pass-a-Grille (☎ 813/ 367-7894), a unique gallery/workshop housed in a 75-year-old building within Pass-a-Grille's small business district. Open Monday to Saturday from 10am to 5:30pm.

Among the shops in St. Pete Beach's Corey Landings Area, the town's original business strip along 75th Street east of Gulf Boulevard, **The Shell Store** (☎ 813/ 360-0586) specializes in corals and shells, with an on-premises minimuseum illustrating how they live and grow. There's a good selection of shell home decorations, shell hobbyist supplies, shell art, planters, and jewelry. Open Monday to Saturday from 9:30am to 5pm.

St. Pete & Clearwater Beaches

Accommodations:
Beach Haven **11**
Best Western Sea
    Stone Resort **22**
Captain's Quarters Inn **5**
Clearwater Beach Hotel **16**
Colonial Gateway Inn **6**
Days Inn Island
    Beach Resort **7**
Great Heron Inn **3**
Island's End Resort **14**
Palm Pavilion Inn **15**
Pelican—East & West **1**
Sun West Beach Motel **21**
TradeWinds Resort **9**

Dining:
Bob Heilman's
    Beachcomber **18**
Bubby's Bistro
    & Wine Bar **19**
Crabby Bill's **12**
Frenchy's Cafe **17**
Guppy's **2**
Hurricane **13**
Internet Outpost Cafe **10**
Lobster Pot **4**
Seafood & Sunsets
    at Julie's **20**
Skidder's **8**

On the mainland in Clearwater, the ✪ **Senior Citizen Craft Center Gift Shop,** 940 Court St. (☎ 813/442-4266), is one of the area's most unique gift shops—an outlet for the work of some 400 local senior citizens. You'll find knitwear, crochet work, woodwork, stained glass, clocks, scrimshaw, jewelry, pottery, tile work, ceramics, and hand-painted clothing. It's off the beaten tourist track but well worth a visit. Open Monday to Friday from 10am to 4pm, but it's staffed by volunteers, so call ahead.

ACCOMMODATIONS YOU CAN AFFORD

St. Pete Beach has national chain hotels and motels of every name and description along Gulf Boulevard. For even more choices, the **St. Petersburg Area Chamber of Commerce** lists a wide range of hotels, motels, condominiums, and other accommodations in its annual visitor guide (see "Essentials" in section 2). You can also use the St. Petersburg/Clearwater Convention & Visitors Bureau's free **reservations service** (☎ 800/345-6710).

As is the case throughout Florida, there are at least as many rental condominiums here as there are hotel rooms. Many of them are in high-rise buildings right on the beach. Among several local rental agents, **Excell Vacation Condos,** 14955 Gulf Blvd., Madeira Beach, FL 33708 (☎ 800/733-4004 or 813/391-5512; fax 813/393-8885; www.islandtime.com/vacation), and **JC Resort Management,** 17200 Gulf Blvd., North Redington Beach, FL 33708 (☎ 800/535-7776 or 813/397-0441; fax 813/ 397-8894; www.jcresort.com), have many from which to choose.

With regard to prices, high season runs from January to April. Ask about special discounted packages in the summer. Any time of year, though, it's wise to make reservations early. The hotel tax in Pinellas County is 11%.

I have organized accommodations geographically, starting with the congested St. Pete Beach area on the south end of the strip, then the mostly residential Indian Rocks Beach area, then the relatively quiet but still busy Clearwater Beach at the north.

ST. PETE BEACH AREA
Super-Cheap Sleeps

✪ **Beach Haven.** 4980 Gulf Blvd. (at 50th Ave.), St. Pete Beach, FL 33706. ☎ **813/ 367-8642.** Fax 813/360-8202. 18 units. A/C TV TEL. Winter $75–$125 single or double. Off-season $50–$108 single or double. MC, V.

Nestled on the beach between two high-rise condos, these low-slung, pink-with-white-trim structures look from the outside like the early 1950s motel they once were. But Jone and Millard Gamble (they also own the charming Island's End Resort, below) have replaced the innards and installed bright tile floors, vertical blinds, pastel tropical furniture, and many modern amenities, including TVs, VCRs, refrigerators, and coffeemakers. Five of the original quarters remain as motel rooms (with shower-only bathrooms), but the Gambles linked the others to make 12 one-bedroom and 1 two-bedroom units. The choice is the one-bedroom unit with sliding glass doors opening to a deck shaded by a sprawling Brazilian pepper tree. There's an outdoor heated pool surrounded by a white picket fence, plus a sunning deck with lounge furniture by the beach. You don't get maid service on Sunday or holidays, and the rooms and bathrooms are 1950s smallish, but every unit here is bright, airy, and comfortable. Complimentary coffee and tea are served to all guests 2 days a week, and they can use barbecue grills and a coin laundry. This is the heart of the hotel district, so lots of restaurants are just steps away.

Captain's Quarters Inn. 10035 Gulf Blvd. (between 100th and 101st aves.), Treasure Island, FL 33706. ☎ **800/526-9547** or 813/360-1659. Fax 813/363-3074. 9 units. A/C TV TEL. Winter $70–$100 double. Off-season $55–$75 double. Weekly rates available. MC, V.

This nautically themed property is a real find, offering well-kept accommodations on the gulf at inland rates. All but one of the units sit on 100 yards of beach, an ideal vantage point for sunset-watching. Six units are efficiencies (two of them on the beach) with minikitchens including microwave oven, coffeemaker, and wet bar or sink. There's also a bay-side cottage with separate bedroom and a full kitchen. Facilities include an outdoor solar-heated freshwater swimming pool, a sundeck, guest barbecues, and a library. Small pets are accepted.

✪ **Island's End Resort.** 1 Pass-a-Grille Way (at 1st Ave.), St. Pete Beach, FL 33706. ☎ **813/ 360-5023.** Fax 813/367-7890. 6 cottages. A/C TV TEL. Dec 15 to June 1, $82–$175. Off-season $61–$175. Weekly rates available. MC, V.

A wonderful respite from the maddening crowd, and a great bargain to boot, this little all-cottage hideaway sits right on the southern tip of St. Pete Beach, smack-dab on Pass-a-Grille, where the Gulf of Mexico meets Tampa Bay. You can step from the six contemporary cottages right onto the beach. And since the island curves sharply here, nothing blocks your view of the emerald bay. If you prefer to swim directly in the gulf or grab a brilliant sunset, the Pass-a-Grille public beach is virtually next door. Linked to each other by boardwalks, the comfortable one- or three-bedroom cottages have dining areas, living rooms, VCRs, and kitchens; the one three-bedroom unit also has its own private pool. Facilities include a fishing dock, patios, decks, barbecues, and hammocks. Owners Jone and Millard Gamble are no fools: They live at this shady, idyllic setting.

For a Few Bucks More

Colonial Gateway Inn. 6300 Gulf Blvd. (at 63rd Ave.), St. Pete Beach, FL 33706. ☎ **800/ 237-8918** or 813/367-2711. Fax 813/367-7068. 200 units. A/C TV TEL. Winter $97–$123 single or double. Off-season $73–$115 single or double. Efficiencies $10 more. AE, DC, DISC, MC, V.

On the beachfront, this U-shaped complex of 1- and 2-story units is a favorite with families. The rooms, most of which face the pool and a central landscaped courtyard, are contemporary, with light woods and beach tones. About half the units are efficiencies with kitchenettes.

On the premises is a branch of the very good Shells seafood restaurant (see "Great Deals on Dining" in section 1, above). Bambooz Lounge and the Swigwam beach bar offer light refreshments. Facilities include an outdoor heated swimming pool with an expansive concrete deck, a kiddie pool, shuffleboard, and a game room. The watersports shack here offers parasailing equipment rentals and also services the Days Inn Island Beach Resort next door (see below).

Days Inn Island Beach Resort. 6200 Gulf Blvd. (at 62nd Ave.), St. Pete Beach, FL 33706. ☎ **800/544-4222** or 813/367-1902. Fax 813/367-4422. 102 units. A/C TV TEL. Winter $118–$148 single or double. Off-season $78–$108 single or double. AE, DC, DISC, MC, V.

Two long, gray buildings flank a courtyard with heated swimming pool at this beachside property popular with young families. Furnished in dark woods and rich tones, guest rooms have picture-window views most of the courtyard. All units have refrigerators and coffeemakers, and about half have kitchenettes. Inside the building, Players Bar & Grille has sports TVs, pizzas, pub fare, and free hot snacks from noon to 7pm daily. Outside, Jimmy B.'s beach bar is a fine place for a sunset cocktail (happy hour runs from noon to 7:30pm) and evening entertainment, including beachside bonfires on Saturdays in winter. Facilities include two outdoor heated swimming pools, volleyball, horseshoes, shuffleboard, and a game room.

Worth a Splurge

TradeWinds Resort. 5500 Gulf Blvd. (at 55th Ave.), St. Pete Beach, FL 33706. ☎ **800/ 237-0707** or 813/367-6461. Fax 813/360-3848. 377 units. A/C TV TEL. Winter $195–$221 single or double. Off-season $135–$180 single or double. Discount packages available in summer and fall. Valet parking $3–$6; free self-parking. AE, DC, DISC, MC, V.

Don't be dismayed by the outward appearance of this 6- and 7-story, concrete-and-steel monstrosity, for underneath and beside it runs a maze of brick walkways, patios, and lily ponds connected by a quarter mile of streams. It all gives surprising charm to this employee-owned hotel. The guest units, which look out on the gulf or the 18 acres of grounds, have up-to-date kitchens or kitchenettes, contemporary furnishings, and private balconies. The children's program and summer packages are a big hit with families from around the world, attracting lots of Europeans.

The top spot for lunch or dinner is the Palm Court, with an Italian-bistro atmosphere; for dinner, there's also Bermudas, a casual family spot. Other food outlets include the Fountain Square Deli, Pizza Hut, and Tropic Treats. Bars include Reflections piano lounge; B. R. Cuda's, with live entertainment and dancing; and the Flying Bridge, a Florida cracker-house–style beachside bar floating on one of the lily ponds.

With the employees having a stake in the profits as well as the tips, you should get good service here. There is room service, valet parking, laundry, babysitting, children's program. Amenities include 4 heated swimming pools, whirlpools, sauna, fitness center, four tennis courts, racquetball, croquet, water-sports rentals, gas grills, guest laundry, video-game room, gift shops, full-service hair salon with massage and tanning.

INDIAN ROCKS BEACH AREA

Super-Cheap Sleeps

Great Heron Inn. 68 Gulf Blvd. (south of 1st Ave.), Indian Rocks Beach, FL 33785. ☎ **813/ 595-2589.** Fax 813/596-7309. 16 units. A/C TV TEL. Winter $85–$88 single or double. Off-season $59–$63 single or double. Weekly and monthly rates available. DISC, MC, V. Hotel is 4 blocks south of Fla. 688.

Formerly known as Alpaugh's Gulf Beach Apartments but now owned and operated by transplanted Michiganers Ralph and Teena Hickerson, this family-oriented motel sits at the narrowest section of Indian Rocks Beach, facing the gulf on one side and its own Intracoastal Waterway dock on the other. The buildings flank a central courtyard with a heated pool. The rooms offer modern furnishings, and each unit has a full kitchen and dining area. Facilities include coin-operated laundry and picnic tables. There's a boat dock across the boulevard.

✪ **Pelican—East & West.** 108 21st Ave. (at Gulf Blvd.), Indian Rocks Beach, FL 33785. ☎ **813/595-9741.** 8 units. A/C TV. Winter $50–$75 single or double. Off-season $40–$60 single or double. Weekly rates available. MC, V.

"PDIP" (Perfect Day in Paradise) is the motto at Mike and Carol McGlaughlin's motel complex, which offers a choice of two settings. Their lowest rates are at Pelican East, in a residential setting 500 feet from the beach, where four suites each have a bedroom and a separate kitchen. You'll pay more at Pelican West, but it's directly on the beachfront. The four beachside apartments each have a living room, bedroom, kitchen, patio, and unbeatable views of the gulf. You don't get phones in your rooms here or a swimming pool to splash around in, but it's clean and modern in all other respects.

CLEARWATER BEACH
Super-Cheap Sleeps

Palm Pavilion Inn. 18 Bay Esplanade (at Mandalay Ave.), Clearwater Beach, FL 33767. ☎ **800/433-PALM** or 813/446-6777. 28 units. A/C TV TEL. Winter $82–$117 single or double. Off-season $56–$81 single or double. AE, DISC, MC, V.

Just north of the tourist area, this quiet beachfront spot is removed from the bustle yet within easy walking distance of all the action. The 3-story art deco building is artfully trimmed in pink and blue. The lobby area and guest rooms, also art deco in design, feature rounded light-wood and rattan furnishings, bright sea-toned fabrics, photographs from the 1920s to 1950s eras, and vertical blinds. Rooms in the front of the house face the gulf, while those in back face the bay. Four efficiencies have kitchenettes. Facilities include a rooftop sundeck, beach access, heated swimming pool, complimentary coffee, and beach chair and umbrella rentals. By the beach, the Palm Pavillion Grill & Bar is a fine place to catch the sunset and some live entertainment Tuesday to Sunday nights during winter, on weekends off-season. Lighted tennis courts and an athletic center are across the street.

✪ **Sun West Beach Motel.** 409 Hamden Dr. (at Bayside Dr.), Clearwater Beach, FL 33767. ☎ **813/442-5008.** Fax 813/461-1395. www.clearwaterbeach.com/SUNWEST/sunwest. E-mail: sunwest@mail.gte.net. 14 units. A/C TV TEL. $40–$61 single or double; $48–$79 efficiency. MC, V.

Overlooking the bay and yet only a 2-block walk from the beach, this well-maintained 1-story motel has a heated pool, fishing/boating dock, sundeck, shuffleboard court, and guest laundry. All units, which face either the bay, the pool, or the sundeck, have contemporary resort-style furnishings. The four motel rooms have small refrigerators and the 10 efficiencies have kitchens.

For a Few Bucks More

Best Western Sea Stone Resort. 445 Hamden Dr. (at Coronado Dr.), Clearwater Beach, FL 33767. ☎ **800/444-1919,** 800/528-1234, or 813/441-1722. Fax 813/449-1580. 108 units. A/C TV TEL. Winter $103–$201 single or double. Off-season $72–$140 single or double. AE, DC, DISC, MC, V.

Located just across the street from the beach in Clearwater's busy south end, the Sea Stone Suites is a 6-story building of classic Key West–style architecture containing 43 one-bedroom suites, each with a kitchenette and a living room. Their living room windows look across external walkways to the harbor. A few steps away, the older 5-story Gulfview Wing offers 65 bedrooms. The furnishings are bright and airy, with pastel tones, light woods, and sea scenes on the walls. The on-site Marker 5 Restaurant serves breakfast only. There's valet laundry service, newspaper delivery, and complimentary coffee in the lobby. Facilities include a heated outdoor swimming pool, whirlpool, boat dock, coin-operated laundry, and meeting rooms.

✪ **Clearwater Beach Hotel.** 500 Mandalay Ave. (at Belmont St.), Clearwater Beach, FL 33767. ☎ **800/292-2295** or 813/441-2425. Fax 813/449-2083. 157 units. A/C TV TEL. Winter $105–$185 single or double. Off-season $98–$118 single or double. AE, DC, MC, V.

Besides the great beach location, you'll enjoy easy access to many nearby shops and restaurants from this Old Florida–style hotel. It's been owned and operated by the same family for more than 40 years and attracts an older clientele. Directly on the gulf, the complex consists of a 6-story main building and 2- and 3-story wings. Rooms and rates vary according to location—bay view or gulf view, poolside or beachfront. Some rooms have balconies. The dining room is romantic at sunset and offers great views of the gulf, while the nautically themed lounge has entertainment nightly. A bar provides snacks and libations beside an outdoor heated swimming pool. There's valet laundry and parking, and limited room service.

GREAT DEALS ON DINING

St. Pete Beach and Clearwater Beach both have a wide selection of national chain fast-food and family restaurants along their main drags.

As with the accommodations above, I have grouped the restaurants by geographic area: St. Pete Beach, including Pass-a-Grille; Indian Rocks Beach, including Madeira Beach, Redington Beach, North Redington Beach, Redington Shores, and Indian Shores; and finally, Clearwater Beach.

ST. PETE BEACH AREA
Super-Cheap Eats

✪ **Crabby Bill's.** 5100 Gulf Blvd. (at 51st Ave.), St. Pete Beach. ☎ **813/360-8858.** Reservations not accepted. Sandwiches $4–$6; main courses $6–$18. AE, MC, V. Mon–Thurs 11am–10pm, Fri–Sat 11am–11pm, Sun noon–10pm. SEAFOOD.

The least-expensive gulf-side dining here, this member of a small local chain sits right on the beach in the heart of the hotel district. It's a great place to bring the kids, especially after 5:30pm Tuesday, when they eat free and are entertained by games and contests. There's a small al fresco area off one of the two bars here, but big glass windows enclose the large dining room. They offer fine water views from picnic tables equipped with rolls of paper towels and buckets of saltine crackers to accompany the Alaskan, snow, golden, and stone crabs that are the big draws here. The crustaceans fall into the moderate price category, but most other main courses, such as fried clam strips or a combo broiled fish platter, are inexpensive. The creamy smoked fish spread is a delicious appetizer, and you'll get enough to whet the appetites at least two persons for just $4.

Internet Outpost Cafe. 7400 Gulf Blvd. (at Corey Ave./75th Ave.), St. Pete Beach. ☎ **813/360-7806.** Reservations not accepted. Coffee and pastries $1–$2; sandwiches $5. AE, MC, V. Mon 6–10pm, Tues–Thurs 10am–10pm, Fri–Sat 10am–midnight, Sun 11am–6pm. PASTRIES/SANDWICHES.

If you left your laptop at home and can't stand not getting your e-mail or surfing the Net any longer, head for this cozy coffee emporium with nine computer terminals, all with fast connections to the Internet ($2 for 15 minutes access time). You can also lounge in the sofas and wing chairs while sipping your coffee, kill a rainy afternoon playing chess, or listen to live music on Friday and Saturday evenings. In addition to coffees, teas, and pastries, the fare includes freshly made chicken salad, Cuban, spicy turkey, and other sandwiches.

Hurricane. 807 Gulf Way (at 9th Ave.), Pass-a-Grille. ☎ **813/360-9558.** Reservations not accepted. Salads and sandwiches $2.50–$9; main courses $7–$17. MC, V. Daily 8am–1am (breakfast Mon–Fri 8–11am, Sat–Sun 8am–noon). SEAFOOD.

A longtime institution across the street from Pass-a-Grille Public Beach, this three-level gray Victorian building with white gingerbread trim is a great place to toast the sunset, especially on the rooftop. It's more beach bar than fine restaurant, but the grouper sandwiches are a big hit, and there's always fresh fish to be broiled or fried and shrimp and crab to be steamed. You can dine inside the knotty-pine paneled dining room or on the sidewalk terrace, where bathers from across Gulf Way are welcome (there's a walk-up bar for beach libation). The joint jumps at night when one level turns into a virtual dance hall.

Skidder's Restaurant. 5799 Gulf Blvd. (at 60th Ave.), St. Pete Beach. ☎ **813/360-1029.**
Reservations not accepted. Breakfast $3–$6; sandwiches and burgers $3–$7; pizza $5.50–$15;
main courses $8–$15. AE, DC, DISC, MC, V. Daily 7am–9pm. ITALIAN/GREEK/AMERICAN.

A local favorite, this inexpensive family restaurant in the hotel district offers a full
range of breakfast fare plus pizzas (available to eat here or carry out), burgers and sandwiches, big salads, gyro and souvlaki platters, and Italian-style veal and chicken dishes
(sautéed in wine with artichokes is a house specialty). Divided by cut-glass panels, the
dining room has ceiling fans rotating over gray tables and booths.

INDIAN ROCKS BEACH AREA
Super-Cheap Eats
You'll find a bay-front edition of **Shells,** the fine and inexpensive local seafood chain,
opposite the Lobster Pot on Gulf Boulevard at 178th Avenue in Redington Shores
(☎ **813/393-8990**). See "Great Deals on Dining" in section 1, above, for more information about Shells' menu and prices, which are the same at all branches.

For a Few Bucks More
✪ **Guppy's.** 1701 Gulf Blvd. (at 17th Ave.), Indian Rocks Beach. ☎ **813/593-2032.** Reser-
vations not accepted. Sandwiches $5–$7; main courses $9–$20. AE, DC, DISC, MC, V. Sun–
Thurs 11:30am–10:30pm; Fri–Sat 11:30am–11:30pm. SEAFOOD.

Locals love this small bar and grill across from Indian Rocks Public Beach because they
know they'll always get terrific chow (it's associated with the excellent Lobster Pot,
mentioned below). You won't soon forget the salmon coated with potatoes and lightly
fried to brown, then baked with a creamy leek and garlic sauce; it's fattening, yes, but
also a bargain at $9. Another good choice is lightly cooked tuna (only slightly more
done than sushi) finished with a peppercorn sauce. The atmosphere is casual beach
friendly, with a fun bar in the rear. Scotty's famous upside-down apple-walnut pie
topped with ice cream will require a little extra work on the weights tomorrow. You
can dine outside on a patio beside the main road.

Worth a Splurge
✪ **Lobster Pot.** 17814 Gulf Blvd. (at 178th Ave.), Redington Shores. ☎ **813/391-8592.**
www.beachdirectory.com. Reservations recommended. Main courses $14.50–$29.50. AE, DC,
MC, V. Mon–Thurs 4:30–10pm, Fri–Sat 4:30–11pm, Sun 4–10pm. SEAFOOD.

Step into this weathered-looking restaurant near the beach and owner Eugen
Fuhrmann will tell you to get ready to experience the finest seafood in the area. The
prices are high, but the variety of lobster dishes is amazing. The lobster américaine is
flambéed in brandy with garlic, and the bouillabaisse is as authentic as any you'd find
in the south of France. In addition to lobster, there's a wide selection of grouper,
snapper, salmon, swordfish, shrimp, scallops, crab, and Dover sole, prepared simply or
with elaborate sauces. There's no ordinary children's menu here: It features half a
Maine lobster and a petite filet mignon.

CLEARWATER BEACH
Super-Cheap Eats
Frenchy's Cafe. 41 Baymont St. ☎ **813/446-3607.** Reservations not accepted. Main
courses $5–$15. AE, MC, V. Mon–Thurs 11:30am–11pm, Fri–Sat 11:30am–midnight, Sun
noon–11pm. SEAFOOD.

Always popular with locals and visitors in the know, this casual cafe makes the best
grouper sandwiches in the area, and has all the awards to prove it. They're fresh, thick,
juicy, and always delicious. The atmosphere is pure Florida casual style, and there's
always a wait.

For more casual fare directly on the beach, **Frenchy's Rockaway Grill,** at 7 Rockaway St. (☎ **813/446-4844**), has a wonderful outdoor setting.

✪ **Seafood & Sunsets at Julie's.** 351 S. Gulfview Blvd. (at 5th St.), Clearwater Beach. ☎ **813/441-2548.** Reservations recommended. Main courses $8–$15. AE, MC, V. Daily 11am–10pm. SEAFOOD.

A Key West–style tradition takes over Julie Nichols's place at dusk as both locals and visitors gather to toast the sunset over the beach across the street. The best seats are in the tiny upstairs dining room. Check out the seafood menu featuring mahimahi charcoal-broiled with sour cream, fresh Florida grouper, and Mike Macy's stuffed flounder.

For a Few Bucks More

✪ **Bob Heilman's Beachcomber.** 447 Mandalay Ave. (at Papaya St.). ☎ **813/442-4144.** Reservations recommended. Main courses $12–$24. AE, DC, DISC, MC, V. Mon–Sat 11:30am–11pm, Sun noon–10pm. AMERICAN.

In a restaurant row opposite the beach, this nautically attired establishment has been popular for more than 45 years. It's a classy bistro, with a pianist adding to an elegant but relaxed ambience. The menu presents a variety of fresh seafood, beef, veal, and lamb selections. The "back-to-the-farm" fried chicken, from an original 1910 Heilman family recipe, is incredible.

Bubby's Bistro & Wine Bar. 447 Mandalay Ave. (at Papaya St., behind Bob Heilman's Beachcomber). ☎ **813/446-9463.** Reservations not accepted. Sandwiches and pizzas $6–$12; main courses $10–$17. AE, DC, DISC, MC, V. Daily 5pm–midnight. AMERICAN.

Bob and Sherri Heilman opened this dark, very urban bistro behind their popular restaurant in 1993, and it's been a local hit ever since. The wine-cellar theme is amply justified by the real thing: a walk-in closet with several thousand bottles kept at a constant 55°F. Walk through and pick your vintage, then listen to jazz while you dine inside at tall, bar-height tables or outside on a covered patio. The chef specializes in gourmet pizzas on homemade focaccia crust (as a tasty appetizer), plus charcoal-grilled veal chops, filet mignon, fresh fish, and monstrous pork chops with caramelized Granny Smith apples and a Mount Vernon mustard sauce. Everything's served à la carte here, so watch your credit card. On the other hand, there's an affordable sandwich menu featuring the likes of bronzed grouper and chicken with a spicy Jack cheese.

THE BEACHES AFTER DARK

If you haven't already found it during your sightseeing and shopping excursions, the restored fishing community of **John's Pass Village and Boardwalk,** on Gulf Boulevard at John's Pass in Madeira Beach, has plenty of restaurants, bars, and shops to keep you occupied after the sun sets. Elsewhere, the nightlife scene at the beach revolves around rocking bars that pump out the music until 2am.

Down south in Pass-a-Grille, there's the popular, always lively **Hurricane lounge,** on Gulf Way at 9th Avenue opposite the public beach (see "Great Deals on Dining," above).

On Treasure Island, **Beach Nutts,** on West Gulf Boulevard at 96th Ave. (☎ 813/367-7427), is perched atop a stilt foundation like a wooden beach cottage on the Gulf of Mexico. The music ranges from Top 40 to reggae and rock. **Manhattans,** Gulf Boulevard at 116th Avenue (☎ 813/363-1500), offers a variety of live music, from country to contemporary and classic rock. Up on the northern tip of Treasure Island, **Gators on the Pass** (☎ 813/367-8951) claims to have the world's longest waterfront bar, with a huge deck overlooking the waters of John's Pass. The complex also includes a no-smoking sports bar and a 3-story tower with a top-level observation deck for panoramic views of the Gulf of Mexico. There's live music, from acoustic and blues to rock, most nights.

In Clearwater Beach, the **Palm Pavilion Grill & Bar,** on the beach at 18 Bay Esplanade (☎ 813/446-6777), has live music Tuesday through Sunday nights during winter, on weekends off-season. Nearby, **Frenchy's Rockaway Grill,** at 7 Rockaway St. (☎ 813/446-4844), is another popular hangout.

If you're into laughs, **Coconuts Comedy Club,** at the Howard Johnson motel, Gulf Boulevard at 61st Avenue in St. Pete Beach (☎ 813/360-5653), has an ever-changing program of live stand-up funny men and women. Call for the schedule, performers, and prices.

For a more highbrow evening, go to the Clearwater mainland and the 2,200-seat **Ruth Eckerd Hall,** 1111 McMullen-Booth Rd. (☎ 813/791-7400), which hosts a varied program of Broadway shows, ballet, drama, symphonic works, popular music, jazz, and country music.

4 Tarpon Springs

30 miles N of St. Petersburg, 23 miles W of Tampa, 13 miles N of Clearwater

One of Florida's most fascinating small towns, Tarpon Springs calls itself the "Sponge Capital of the World." That's because Greek immigrants from the Dodecanese Islands settled here in the late 19th century to harvest sponges, which grew in abundance offshore. By the 1930s Tarpon Springs was producing more sponges than any other place in the world. A blight ruined the business in the 1940s, but the descendants of those early immigrants stayed on. Today they comprise about a third of the population, making Tarpon Springs a center of transplanted Greek culture.

Although sponges still arrive at the historic Sponge Docks on Dodecanese Boulevard, the town's mainstays today are commercial fishing and tourism. With a lively, carnival-like atmosphere, the docks are a great place to spend an afternoon or early evening, poking your head into shops selling sponges and other souvenirs while Greek music comes from the dozen or so family restaurants purveying authentic Aegean cuisine. You can also venture offshore from here, for booths on the docks hawk sightseeing and fishing cruises.

Just south of the docks, restored Victorian homes facing the winding creek known as Spring Bayou make this one of the most picturesque towns in the state.

ESSENTIALS

GETTING THERE   From Tampa or St. Petersburg, take U.S. 19 north and turn left on Tarpon Avenue (County Road 582). From Clearwater Beach, take Alt. U.S. 19 north through Dunedin. The center of the historic downtown district is at the intersection of Pinellas Avenue (Alt. U.S. 19) and Tarpon Avenue. To reach the Sponge Docks, go 10 blocks north on Pinellas Avenue and turn left at Pappas' Restaurant onto Dodecanese Boulevard.

VISITOR INFORMATION   The **Tarpon Springs Chamber of Commerce** (☎ 813/937-6109) has an information office on Dodecanese Boulevard at the Spong Docks. Open Tuesday to Saturday from 10:30am to 4:30pm, Sunday from 11am to 5pm.

EXPLORING THE TOWN

Two areas are worth visiting here. You'll first come to the **Tarpon Springs Downtown Historic District,** with its turn-of-the-century commercial buildings along Tarpon Avenue and Pinellas Avenue (Alt. U.S. 19). The **Tarpon Springs Cultural Center,** on

Pinellas Avenue a block south of Tarpon Avenue, explains the town's history and has visitor information. On Tarpon Avenue west of Pinellas Avenue, you'll come to the Victorian homes overlooking **Spring Bayou.** This creekside area makes for a delightfully picturesque stroll.

The carnival-like **Sponge Docks** line Dodecanese Boulevard, which is peppered with shops, restaurants, and fishing and sightseeing boats pulling at their mooring lines along the riverside boardwalk. Poke your head into the old rickety warehouse that is now home to the ✪ **Spongeorama** (☎ 813/943-9509), a dusty museum dedicated to sponges and sponge divers. You can buy a wide variety of sponges here (they'll ship them home) and watch a 30-minute video about sponge-diving that is played several times a day. Admission is free. The Spongeorama is open daily from 10am to 5pm. In the **Coral Sea Aquarium,** at the western end of the boulevard (☎ **813/938-5378**), a scuba diver feeds sharks at 11:30am and 1, 2:30, and 4pm. The aquarium is open daily from 10am to 5pm. Admission is $4 adults, $3.25 seniors, $2 for children 3 to 11, free for kids under 3.

You also can **cruise** down the Anclote River to watch sponge divers at work, go fishing on a party boat, or perhaps have lunch or dinner afloat. Booths along the docks sell tickets for a variety of these excursions. Make your reservations as soon as you get here, then go sightseeing ashore while you wait for the next boat to shove off.

Bikers, in-line skaters, hikers, and joggers can come right through downtown on the **Pinellas Trail,** which runs along Safford Avenue and crosses Tarpon Avenue two blocks east of Pinellas Avenue (see "Great Golf That Won't Break Your Budget & Other Affordable Outdoor Activities," in section 2, above).

ACCOMMODATIONS YOU CAN AFFORD

In addition to the establishments listed below, there are national chain motels on busy U.S. 19, including the **Holiday Inn Hotel & Suites,** 38724 U.S. 19 North (☎ 800/ HOLIDAY or 813/934-5781); **Days Inn Tarpon Springs,** 40050 U.S. 19 (☎ 800/ DAYS-INN or 813/934-0859); and the **Best Western Tahitian Resort,** 2337 U.S. 19 North in Holiday (☎ 800/931-0333 or 813/937-4121).

SUPER-CHEAP SLEEPS

Spring Bayou Inn. 32 W. Tarpon Ave., Tarpon Springs, FL 34688. ☎ and fax **813/ 938-9333.** 5 units, 3 with bathroom. Winter $60–$110 single or double. Off-season $54–$99 single or double. Weekly rates available. No credit cards. House is in the block west of Pinellas Ave. (Alt. U.S. 19).

Built around the turn of the century, this historic district bed-and-breakfast is virtually across Pinellas Avenue from downtown and within a mile of the Sponge Docks. The large, comfortable home reflects an elegance of the past without giving up modern-day conveniences. Enjoy a complimentary cup of tea or glass of wine in the afternoon and complimentary breakfast in the morning. The best room has a king-size bed, sitting area, private bathroom, and balcony.

WORTH A SPLURGE FOR GOLFERS

The Westin Innisbrook Resort. 36750 U.S. 19 (P.O. Box 1088), Tarpon Springs, FL 34688. ☎ **800/456-2000** or 813/942-2000. Fax 813/942-5577. 1,000 units. Winter $195–$370 single or double. Off-season $135–$360 single or double. Golf packages available. AE, DC, DISC, MC, V.

Golf Digest, Golf magazine, and others pick this as one of the country's best places to play (provided you stay here, of course). The 1,000-acre resort has 90 holes on championship courses that are more like the rolling links of the Carolinas than the usually flat courses found in Florida. Each December, the most famous course, the Copper-

Mermaids & Manatees

Drive north of Clearwater for an hour on congested U.S. 19, and you'll come to one of Florida's original tourist attractions, the famous **Weeki Wachee Spring** (☎ **800/678-9335** or 352/596-2062). "Mermaids" have been putting on acrobatic swimming shows behind 4-inch-thick windows here every day since 1947. It's a sight to see them doing their dances in waters that come from one of America's most prolific freshwater springs, which pour some 170 million gallons of 72°F water a day into the river. The show combines elements of Hans Christian Andersen's fairy tales with the real story of Pocahontas. Admission is $16.95 for adults, $12.95 for children 3 to 10, plus tax. Kids under 3 get in free. The springs are open daily from 9am to 4pm in winter, to 5pm the rest of the year.

There's more than mermaids at Weeki Wachee Spring, for you can take a Wilderness River Cruise across the Weeki Wachee River, visit the Animal Forest Petting Zoo, take in the live Exotic Birds of Prey show, and send the kids on flume and bumper-boat rides at **Buccaneer Bay** water park (☎ **352/596-2062**). Buccanner Bay is open from March to Labor Day, daily from 10am to 5pm. Admission is $11.95 for adults, $9.95 for kids 3 to 10.

If you decide to stay overnight here, there's a **Holiday Inn** across U.S. 19 from the springs (☎ **800/678-9335** or 352/596-2062).

From Weeki Wachee, travel 21 miles north to the **Homosassa State Wildlife Park,** on U.S. 19 in Homosassa Springs (☎ **352/628-5343**). The highlight here is a floating observatory where visitors can "walk" underwater and watch manatees in a rehabilitation facility, as well as thousands of fresh and saltwater fish. You'll also see deer, bears, bobcats, otters, egrets, and flamingos along unspoiled nature trails. The park is open daily from 9am to 5:30pm. Admission is $7.95 for adults and $4.95 for children 3 to 12, which includes a 30-minute narrated boat ride.

About 7 miles north of Homosassa Springs, some 300 manatees spend the winter in Crystal River, and you can swim, snorkel, or scuba with them in the warm-water natural spring of Kings Bay. **American Pro Diving Center,** 821 S.E. Hwy. 19, Crystal River, FL 34429 (☎ **800/291-DIVE** or 352/563-0041), offers daily dive and snorkel tours. Early mornings are the best time to see the manatees, so try to take the 7am departure. The trips range from $21.50 to $50 per person. Call for the schedule and reservations.

You can stay in Crystal River at hotels that have their own dive shops and marinas, such as the 142-room **Plantation Inn and Golf Resort,** at 9301 W. Ft. Island Trail (☎ **800/632-6262** or 352/795-4211), or the 100-room **Best Western Crystal River Resort,** at 614 NW U.S. 19 (☎ **800/435-4409** or 352/795-3171).

During mid-February you can enjoy the Crystal River Chamber's **Florida Manatee Festival,** with a seafood festival, golf tournament, art show, concerts, and manatee displays.

For more information about the area, contact the **Nature Coast Chamber at Crystal River,** 28 NW Hwy. 19, Crystal River, FL 34425 (☎ **352/795-3149;** fax 352/795-4260). The chamber's visitor center is open Monday to Thursday from 8:30am to 5pm, Friday from 8:30am to 4pm.

head, hosts the JC Penny Classic, a major stop on the PGA circuit. Innisbrook has the largest resort-owned and -operated golf school in North America, and the Nick Bollettieri Tennis Academy here boasts 11 clay and 4 Laykold courts. There's even a children's program to take care of the kids. The spacious quarters actually are privately owned homes and apartments spread all over the premises, so there are no focal points here except the building where you check in and the golf and tennis clubhouses.

GREAT DEALS ON DINING

Your Tarpon Springs experience will be incomplete without taking a Greek meal here. In addition to Hellas Restaurant & Bakery listed below, you'll find about a dozen other family owned restaurants along the lively Sponge Docks, all of them clean, inviting, and serving authentic, inexpensive Greek fare.

If you're shopping or sightseeing downtown, or biking on the Pinellas Trail as it runs along Safford Avenue, you can stop into **Yours Truly Gourmet Café,** 150 Tarpon Ave. (☎ 813/934-1770), a bistro-style restaurant with a winding wrought-iron staircase lending a quaint Bourbon Street feel. Dinner-size salads and new American–style seafood are the specialties here (check out the famous french-fried shrimp with cherry sauce).

SUPER-CHEAP EATS

✪ **Hellas Restaurant & Bakery.** Sponge Docks, 785 Dodecanese Blvd. ☎ 813/943-2400. Reservations not accepted. Sandwiches and salads $4–$6; main courses $7–$14. AE, DISC, MC, V. Daily 11am–10pm. GREEK.

The lovely hand-painted tile tables on the street-side patio here make fine spots from which to watch the action on the Sponge Docks while sampling authentic Aegean cuisine. If you like feta cheese, you'll enjoy the pungent Greek-style shrimp or scallops. If not, opt for the perfectly panfried grouper or any of the Aegean standbys: moussaka, pastitsio, dolmades, or one of the largest gyro sandwiches in town. The bakery supplies baklava, galactombouriko (egg custard), and other desserts from the old country. With Greek cuisine, Greek music, and a Greek-looking (if not Greek-accented) waiter, it's easy to imagine yourself quay side on Mykonos.

Pappas' Restaurant. Sponge Docks, 10 Dodecanese Blvd. (at Pinellas Ave./Alt. U.S. 19). ☎ 813/937-5101. Reservations not accepted. Main courses $8.50–$26. AE, MC, V. Sun–Thurs 11:30am–10:30pm, Fri–Sat 11:30am–11:30pm. SEAFOOD.

Although it offers a few Greek-style salads and main courses, Pappas is famous statewide for its fresh American-style seafood—shrimp, grouper, red snapper, and even stone crab claws in season—most of it right off the boat. The family-run restaurant has been operating on the banks of the Anclote River since 1925 when it was founded by Louis Pappamichaelopoulus of Sparta, Greece. You get nice river views from the tall windows of this modern building. Downstairs, you can poke through several shops, including one selling hand-rolled cigars.

5 Sarasota

52 miles S of Tampa, 150 miles SW of Orlando, 225 miles NW of Miami

One of Florida's cultural centers, sophisticated Sarasota is far enough away from Tampa Bay to have an identity very much its own. In fact, many snowbirds spend their winters here because there's so much to keep them stimulated and entertained, including the very fine Asolo Center for the Performing Arts and the Van Wezel Performing Arts Hall. Like affluent Naples down in Southwest Florida, it also has an extensive array of first-class resorts, restaurants, and upscale boutiques.

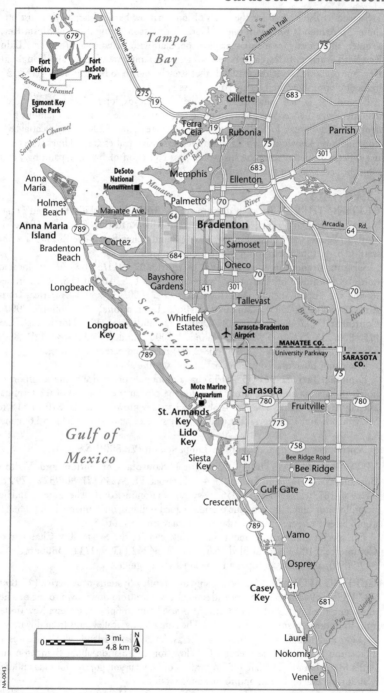

Sarasota & Bradenton

Sarasota is also known for the series of long, narrow barrier islands lying just off-shore: **St. Armands Key,** with one of Florida's ritziest shopping districts; **Siesta Key,** a quiet and mostly residential enclave popular with artisans and writers; **Lido Key,** with a string of affordable hotels attractive to family vacationers; and **Longboat Key,** one of Florida's wealthiest islands that stretches north to Bradenton. Together, 35 miles of gloriously white beaches fringe these keys.

Legend has it that Sarasota was named after the explorer Hernando de Soto's daughter, Sara (hence, Sara-sota). In more recent times, the town's most famous resident was circus legend John Ringling, who came here in the 1920s, built a palatial bay-front mansion known as Ca'd'Zan, acquired extensive real estate holdings, erected a magnificent museum to house his world-class collection of Baroque paintings, and built the causeway out to St. Armands and Lido keys.

ESSENTIALS

GETTING THERE   To reach downtown, St. Armands Key, Lido Key, and Long-boat Key, take Exit 39 off I-75 and follow Fruitville Road (Fla. 780) west. To reach southern Sarasota and Siesta Key, take Exit 38 and follow Bee Ridge Road (Fla. 758) west. U.S. 41 runs north-south through downtown.

Sarasota-Bradenton International Airport (☎ **941/359-2770**) is located north of downtown off University Parkway between U.S. 41 and U.S. 301. Airlines serving the airport include **American Eagle** (☎ 800/433-7300), **America Trans Air** (☎ 800/225-2995), **Canadian Airlines International** (☎ 800/426-7000), **Continental** (☎ 800/525-0280), **Delta** (☎ 800/221-1212), **Northwest/KLM** (☎ 800/225-2525), **TWA** (☎ 800/221-2000), and **US Airways** (☎ 800/428-4322). **Sky America** (☎ 800/368-2307) flies from here to Key West.

The major car-rental companies have booths at the airport.

Diplomat Taxi (☎ **941/355-5155**) has a monopoly on service from the airport to hotels in Sarasota and Bradenton. Look for the cabs at the west end of the terminal outside baggage claim. The fare is about $9 to downtown Sarasota, $10 to $15 to St. Armands and Lido keys, $14 to $21 to Siesta Key, and $14 to $35 to Longboat Key.

Amtrak has bus connections to its Tampa station (☎ **800/USA-RAIL**).

VISITOR INFORMATION   Contact the **Sarasota Convention and Visitors Bureau,** 655 N. Tamiami Trail (U.S. 41), Sarasota, FL 34236 (☎ **800/522-9799** or 941/957-1877; fax 941/951-2956; www.sarasota/online.com). The bureau and its helpful visitor center are in a blue pagoda-shaped building on Tamiami Trail (U.S. 41) at 6th Street. They're open Monday to Saturday from 9am to 5pm.

For specific information about Siesta Key, contact the **Siesta Key Chamber of Commerce,** 5100-B Ocean Blvd., Sarasota, FL 34242 (☎ **941/349-3800;** fax 941/349-9699), and ask for a copy of its biennial visitor guide.

GETTING AROUND   A private company, **Trolley Systems of America** (☎ **800/787-6554** or 941/346-3115), provides regular service from downtown to the beaches and along the keys Tuesday to Saturday from 9:30am to 6pm. The Siesta Key Trolley runs from downtown out to Siesta Key. The Anna Maria Trolley runs from downtown to Lido and Longboat keys north as far as Anna Maria Island, with pick ups in Bradenton twice a day (see section 6, below, for information about Bradenton and Anna Maria Island). The fare is $5 regardless of how far you go, free for kids under 3. Call for the exact schedule and to make reservations.

Sarasota County Area Transit (SCAT) (☎ **941/316-1234**) provides regularly scheduled bus service Monday to Saturday from about 7am to 6pm. The Sarasota Convention and Visitor Bureau distributes route maps (see "Visitor Information," above). Route number 4 runs between downtown and St. Armands and Lido Keys; number 18, downtown and Longboat Key; and number 11, downtown and Siesta Key. The standard fare is 50¢; exact change is required. The main downtown transfer station is at 1st Street and Lemon Avenue.

Taxi companies include **Diplomat Taxi** (☎ 941/355-5155), **Green Cab Taxi** (☎ 941/922-6666), and **Yellow Cab of Sarasota** (☎ 941/955-3341).

HITTING THE BEACH

Much of the area's 35 miles of beaches are occupied by hotels and condominium complexes, but there are excellent public beaches here, too—and they're free. After you've driven the length of Longboat Key and admired the luxurious homes and condos blocking access to the beach, take a right off St. Armands Circle onto Lido Key and **North Lido Beach.** Unfortunately recent storms have robbed most of the sand here, but the south end of the island is occupied by **South Lido Beach Park,** with plenty of shade making it a good spot for picnics and walks.

Sarasota's most popular beach is **Siesta Key Public Beach,** with a picnic area, 700-car parking lot, and crowds of families. More secluded and quiet is **Turtle Beach,** at Siesta Key's south end. It has shelters, boat ramps, picnic tables, and volleyball nets.

GREAT GOLF THAT WON'T BREAK YOUR BUDGET & OTHER AFFORDABLE OUTDOOR ACTIVITIES

BICYCLING & IN-LINE SKATING   You can bike and skate from downtown to Lido and Longboat keys, since paved walkways/bike paths run alongside the John Ringling Causeway and then up Longboat. Narrow streets make Siesta Key less appealing. You can rent bikes and blades at **Sarasota Bicycle Center,** 4084 Bee Ridge Rd. just east of downtown (☎ 941/377-4505), and at **Siesta Sports Rentals,** 6551 Midnight Pass Rd. on Siesta Key (☎ 941/346-1797). **C. B.'s Saltwater Outfitters,** 1249 Stickney Point Rd., at the Siesta Key side of the Stickney Point Bridge (☎ 941/349-4400), rents bicycles.

BOAT RENTALS   **All Watersports,** in the Boatyard Shopping Village, on the mainland end of Stickney Point Bridge (☎ 941/921-2754), rents personal watercraft such as Wave Runners, jet boats, and jet-skis, as well as speedboats, runabouts, and b   o   w   - riders. At the island end of the bridge, **C. B.'s Saltwater Outfitters,** 1249 Stickney Point Rd. (☎ 941/349-4400), and **Siesta Key Boat Rentals,** 1265 Old Stickney Point Rd. (☎ 941/349-8880), both rent runabouts, pontoon boats, and other craft. Bait and tackle are available at the marinas.

CRUISES   From October to May, you can head over to Marina Jack's Marina, U.S. 41 at Island Park Circle for 2-hour sightseeing and sunset cruises around Sarasota's waterways aboard the 65-foot, two-deck *Le Barge* (☎ 941/366-6116). The cruises run Tuesday to Sunday, with the sightseeing cruise ($16 per person) leaving at 2pm. The sunset cruises ($15 adults, $5 for kids under 13) change with the time of sunset. Snacks and libation are available for an extra charge. Call for reservations.

FISHING   Charter fishing boats dock at most marinas here. The **Flying Fish Fleet,** downtown at Marina Jack's Marina, U.S. 41 at Island Park Circle (☎ 941/366-3373), offers party boat charter-fishing excursions, with bait and tackle furnished. Prices for half-day trips are $28; all-day voyages are $40. Seniors and children pay less. Call for the schedule. You can also charter a 39-foot custom sportfishing boat; 4-hour trips cost about $300.

GOLF The **Bobby Jones Golf Complex,** 1000 Circus Blvd. (☎ 941/365-GOLF), is Sarasota's only municipal facility, but it has two 18-hole championship layouts—the American (par 71) and British (par 72) courses—and the 9-hole Gillespie executive course (par 30). Tee times are assigned 3 days in advance. Greens fees range from $25 to $31, including cart rental.

You can also tune your game at the public **Village Green Golf Club,** 3500 Pembroke Dr., near Bee Ridge and Beneva roads (☎ 941/925-2755), whose executive-length 18 holes can be parred in 58.

The semiprivate **Rolling Green Golf Club,** 4501 Tuttle Ave. (☎ 941/355-6620), is an 18-hole, par-72 course. Facilities include a driving range, rental clubs, and lessons. Tee times are assigned 2 days in advance. Prices, including cart, are about $40 in winter, $25 off-season.

Also semiprivate, the **Sarasota Golf Club,** 7820 N. Leewynn Dr. (☎ 941/371-2431), is an 18-hole, par-72 course. Facilities include a driving range, lessons, club rentals, restaurant, lounge, and golf shop. Fees, including carts, are about $42 in winter, $25 off-season.

If you have reciprocal privileges, **University Park Country Club,** west of I-75 on University Parkway (☎ 813/359-9999), is Sarasota's only nationally ranked course.

SAILING The 41-foot, 12-passenger sailboat *Enterprise,* docked at Marina Jack's Marina, U.S. 41 at Island Park Circle (☎ 941/951-1833), cruises the waters of both Sarasota Bay and the Gulf of Mexico. Half-day cruises cost $35; the sunset cruise, $20. Departure times vary, and reservations are required.

Based on Siesta Key, **Siesta Sailing** (☎ 888/539-7245 or 941/346-7245) has half-day, full-day, and 2-day cruises on three boats, ranging from $50 to $225 per person, respectively. Reservations are essential.

If you'd like more room on deck for sunning, **Fat Cat Cruises** (☎ 941/362-7564) has 2-hour catamaran cruises in the bay waters off Siesta and Lido keys. Call for reservations and prices.

SPECTATOR SPORTS **Ed Smith Stadium,** 2700 12th St., at Tuttle Avenue (☎ 941/954-4101 or 941/954-7699), is the winter home of the **Cincinnati Reds,** who hold spring training here in February and March. East of downtown, the stadium seats 7,500 fans. Admission is $5 to $10.

The **Sarasota Polo Club,** 8201 Polo Club Lane, Sarasota (☎ 941/359-0000), midway between Sarasota and Bradenton, is the site of weekly polo matches from November through March, on Sunday afternoons. Call for the schedule of matches and admission fees.

TENNIS The **Colony Beach & Tennis Resort,** one of the country's finest playing-and-practicing facilities is the big draw here for tennis players who can afford it. The rest of us can play at **Payne Park Tennis Center,** 2050 Adams Lane (☎ 941/364-4605), a downtown public facility with nine Har-Tru tennis courts, available for play on a first-come, first-served basis. The price is $4.50 per person per hour. It's open daily from 8am to 9pm.

WATER SPORTS The downtown center for jet-skiing, wave running, sailing, and other water-sports activities is **O'Leary's,** in the Island Park Marina, U.S. 41 and Island Park Circle (☎ 941/953-7505). It's open daily from 8am to 8pm.

On Siesta Key, **Sweet Water Kayaks,** 5263 Ocean Blvd., Suite 7 (☎ 941/346-1179), rents fully-equipped single and double sea kayaks for use in the gulf bays and Intracoastal Waterway. One-person models go for $35 for 2 hours or $60 a day per day, while tandems cost $50 for 2 hours or $60 a day. They also teach 2-hour beginners sea kayaking courses for $45 per person. It's open daily from 10am to 6pm.

Also on Siesta Key, **Siesta Sports Rentals,** 6551 Midnight Pass Rd. (☎ **813/ 346-1797**), rents kayaks and sailboats, plus beach chairs and umbrellas.

You can soar above the bay with **Siesta Parasail,** based at C.B.'s Saltwater Outfitters at the western end of the Stickney Point Bridge (☎ **941/349-1900**).

EXPLORING THE AREA
MUSEUMS & ART GALLERIES

Cars & Music of Yesterday Museum. 5500 N. Tamiami Trail (at University Pkwy.). ☎ **941/355-6228.** Admission $9 adults, $5 children 6–12, free for children under 6. Daily 9am–6pm. Take U.S. 41 north of downtown; museum is 2 blocks west of the airport.

View more than 80 classic and antique autos, from Rolls-Royces and Pierce Arrows to the four cars used personally by circus czar John Ringling. In addition, there are more than 1,200 antique music boxes, from tiny music boxes to a huge 30-foot Belgian organ. Check out the Penny Arcade with antique games, and grab a cone at the ice cream and sandwich shop.

✪ Ringling Museums. Bayshore Rd. at N. Tamiami Trail (U.S. 41). ☎ **941/359-5700**, or 941/351-1660 for recorded information. Admission $9 adults, $8 seniors, free for children 12 and under. Daily 10am–5:30pm. From downtown, take U.S. 41 north to University Parkway and follow signs to museum.

This is a huge 60-acre site—showman John Ringling collected art on a grand scale. The **John and Mable Ringling Museum of Art,** housed in a pink Italian Renaissance villa, is filled with more than 500 years of European and American art, including one of the world's most important collections of grand 17th-century Baroque paintings. The old master collection also includes five world-renowned tapestry cartoons by Peter Paul Rubens and his studio. The museum houses collections of decorative arts and traveling exhibits. The Ringlings' 30-room winter residence **Ca'd'Zan** (House of John), built in 1925 and modeled after a Venetian palace, is on display and filled with personal mementos. The grounds also include **Circus Galleries,** a building devoted to circus memorabilia including parade wagons, calliopes, costumes, and colorful posters; and the historic **Asolo Theater,** a 19th-century Italian court playhouse; plus a classical courtyard, rose garden, restaurant, and shops.

Sarasota Visual Art Center. 707 N. Tamiami Trail (at 6th St.). ☎ **941/365-2032.** Free admission. Mon–Fri 10am–4pm, Sat–Sun 1–4pm.

Sarasota is home to more than 40 art galleries and exhibition spaces, all open to the public year-round. A convenient artistic starting point is this downtown community art center, next to the Sarasota Convention and Visitors Bureau. It contains three galleries and a small sculpture garden, presenting the area's largest display of art by national and local artists, from paintings and pottery to sculpture, cartoons, jewelry, and enamelware. There are also art demonstrations and special events.

PARKS, NATURE PRESERVES & GARDENS

The peaceful **✪ Marie Selby Botanical Gardens,** South Palm Avenue, at U.S. 41 (☎ **941/366-5731;** www.selby.org), on the bay just south of downtown, is said to be the only botanical garden in the world specializing in the preservation, study, and research of epiphytic plants ("air plants"), such as orchids, pineapples, and ferns. It's home to more than 20,000 exotic plants, including more than 6,000 orchids, as well as a bamboo pavilion, butterfly and hummingbird garden, medicinal plant garden, waterfall garden, cactus and succulent garden, fernery, hibiscus garden, palm grove, two tropical food gardens, and a native shore-plant community. Admission is $8 for adults, $4 for children 6 to 11, free for children 5 and under accompanied by an adult. Open daily from 10am to 5pm.

Between downtown and the airport, the 10-acre **Sarasota Jungle Gardens,** 37–01 Bayshore Rd. (☎ 941/355-5305), features lush tropical vegetation, cool jungle trails, tropical plants, exotic waterfowl, and reptiles in natural habitats. In addition, there are bird shows, reptile shows, a petting zoo, and a shell and butterfly museum. Admission is $9 for adults, $8 seniors, $5 for children 4 to 12, free for children 3 and under. Open daily from 9am to 5pm except Christmas. From downtown, take U.S. 41 north to Myrtle Street, turn left, and go 2 blocks.

On City Island, at the southern end of Longboat Key, kids love the ✪ **Mote Marine Aquarium,** 1600 Thompson Pkwy. (☎ 800/691-MOTE or 941/388-4441) because they get to touch cool stuff like a stingray (minus the stinger, of course) and watch sharks in the shark tank. Part of the noted Mote Marine Laboratory complex, this facility focuses on the marine life of the Sarasota area and nearby gulf waters, including a manatee exhibit. The kids won't believe all the sea horse babies that come from the dad's pouch (one of Mother Nature's strange-but-true surprises). There are also many research-in-progress exhibits, and you can go on 1-hour, 45-minute environmental tours abroad a boat named the *Explorer* daily or on tropical sunset cruises daily (call ahead for times, reservations, and prices). Admission is $8 for adults, $6 for children 4 to 17, free for children 3 and under. Open daily from 10am to 5pm. From St. Armands Circle, go north toward Longboat Key; the aquarium is at the foot of the Lido-Longboat bridge.

On the aquarium grounds, **Pelican Man's Bird Sanctuary,** 1708 Thompson Pkwy. (☎ 941/388-4444), is a sanctuary and rehabilitation center where more than 5,000 injured birds and other wildlife are treated each year. The sanctuary is home to about 30 species of birds. There's a gift shop with many bird-oriented items for sale. Admission is free, but donations are encouraged. Open daily from 10am to 5pm. From St. Armands Circle go north toward Longboat Key and follow the signs.

In the country, the **Myakka River State Park,** on Fla. 72 about 9 miles east of I-75, is one of Florida's largest, covering more than 35,000 acres of wetlands, prairies, and dense woodlands along the Myakka River. It's an outstanding wildlife sanctuary and breeding ground, home to hundreds of species of plants and animals, including alligators. Get an overview of the entire park via a 1-hour tram tour (during the winter) or a 1-hour airboat ride (year-round). Admission is $1 per person or $4 per car with two to eight occupants. **Myakka Wildlife & Nature Tours** (☎ 941/365-0100) has nature excursions through the park by boat and tram. These cost $7 for adults, $3 for children 12 and under. Call for the schedules, which change seasonally. The park is open daily from 8am to sunset. For more information, contact the headquarters at 13207 S.R. 72, Sarasota, FL 34241 (☎ 941/361-6511).

Near Myakka, you can see the famous **Lippizzan Stallions** do their dancing show at the Ottomar Herrmann training grounds, on Singletary Road (☎ 941/322-1501). They perform at 3pm Thursday and Friday, at 10am Saturday from January to March. Call for ticket prices.

SHOPPING

Visitors come from all over the world to shop, or at least browse, at ✪ **St. Armands Circle,** on St. Armands Key just inside Lido Key. Wander around this outdoor circle of more than 150 international boutiques, gift shops, galleries, restaurants, and nightspots, all surrounded by lush landscaping, patios, and antiques. Pick up a map at the Sarasota Convention and Visitors Bureau (see "Essentials," above). Many shops here are comparable to those in Palm Beach and on Naples's 3rd Avenue South, so check your credit-card limits—or resort to some great window shopping. I love to poke through **Global Navigator** (☎ 813/388-4515), a travel equipment and apparel shop that reminds me of Banana Republic when it carried really cool stuff.

Downtown, the **Burns Court** and **Herald Square** historic districts, centered on Pineapple Avenue south of Ringling Boulevard, have a trove of upscale boutiques and art galleries worth exploring. Nearby, **Main Street** is more pedestrian, but it boasts a few art galleries and the **Main Bookshop** (☎ **941/366-7653**), the city's largest and most interesting bookstore for browsers and shoppers alike (open daily from 9am to 11pm). You can pick from the freshest of Florida's fruits and vegetables at the downtown **farmer's market,** from 7am to noon on Saturday on Lemon Avenue between Main and 1st streets.

Sarasota Square Mall, 8201 S. Tamiami Trail, at Beneva Road (☎ **941/ 922-9600**), south of downtown, is the area's largest enclosed mall. **Sarasota Outlet Mall,** on University Parkway just west of I-75 (☎ **941/359-2050**), has about 40 of the better-known factory stores, but you'll find a much wider selection at Gulf Coast Factory Shops in Bradenton (see "Shopping" in section 6, below).

ACCOMMODATIONS YOU CAN AFFORD

In addition to the chain hotels listed below, you'll find the **Comfort Inn** (☎ **800/ 228-5150** or 941/355-7091), **Days Inn Airport** (☎ **800/329-7466** or 941/ 355-9271), and **Hampton Inn** (☎ **800/336-9335** or 941/351-7734) standing side by side on Tamiami Trail (U.S. 41) between 47th Street and Mecca Drive, just south of the airport and near the Ringling Museums and the Asolo Center for the Performing Arts. All are of recent vintage and thoroughly modern.

A new **Courtyard by Marriott** (☎ **800/321-2211** or 941/355-3337) and a **Sleep Inn** (☎ **800/627-5447** or 941/359-8558) are nearby on University Parkway opposite the airport.

With the beaches here virtually lined with condominiums, it's not surprising that the Resort at Longboat Key Club, the Colony Beach & Tennis Resort, and the Crescent View Beach Club actually are all condo projects operated as hotels. A good starting point in finding other options is the annual visitors guide published by the Sarasota Convention and Visitors Bureau (see "Essentials," above). It lists and briefly describes all the projects as well as the real estate agents who represent individual owners who rent their properties out. Among the agencies requiring stays of less than a month are **Argus Property Management,** 1200 Siesta Bay-side, Sarasota, FL 34242 (☎ **800/237-2252** or 941/346-3499; fax 941/349-6156; www.argusmgmt. com); **Longboat Accommodations,** 4030 Gulf of Mexico Drive, Longboat Key, FL 34228 (☎ **800/237-9505** or 941/383-9505; fax 941/383-1830; www.longboatkey. com); and **Michael Saunders & Company,** 100 S. Washington Blvd., Sarasota, FL 34236 (☎ **800/881-2222** or 941/951-6668; www.michaelsaunders.com).

The hotels below are organized by geographic region: on the mainland, on Lido Key, on Longboat Key, and on Siesta Key. Some of the Longboat Key hotels mentioned below actually are in Manatee County, about halfway between Bradenton and downtown Sarasota.

In terms of prices, the high season here is from January to April. The best bargains are found May to September. Rates are usually higher along the beaches at all times, so bargain hunters should stick to the downtown area and commute to the beach. The hotel tax here is 9%.

ON THE MAINLAND
Super-Cheap Sleeps
On U.S. 41 north between downtown and the airport, the local **Knights Inn** (☎ **800/43-5644** or 941/355-8867) and **Super 8 Motel** (☎ **800/800-8000** or 941/ 355-9326) were recently renovated and offer clean, comfortable, and inexpensive motel rooms.

Southland Inn Motel. 2229 N. Tamiami Trail (U.S. 41), Sarasota, FL 34234. ☎ **941/954-5775.** Fax 941/364-8329. 31 units. Winter $75–$125 single or double. Off-season $39 single or double. Weekly rates available. MC, V.

One of several older mom-and-pop motels on busy U.S. 41 a few minutes north of downtown, this 2-story complex has an outdoor pool and a guest laundry. More than half the units are efficiencies or apartments with kitchens, but they usually are rented on a weekly basis during winter. Summer rates can be lower based on availability, but call ahead to get the best prices.

Wellesley Inn & Suites. 1803 N. Tamiami Trail (U.S. 41, at 18th St.), Sarasota, FL 34234. ☎ **800/444-8888** or 941/366-5128. Fax 941/953-4322. 106 units. A/C TV TEL. Winter $110 single or double; $140 suite. Off-season $44 single or double; $60–$70 suite. Rates include continental breakfast. AE, DC, DISC, MC, V.

The closest chain motel to downtown, this 4-story hotel with an impressive portico overlooks a marina and boatyard, but you won't have a balcony from which to enjoy the view. The bedrooms are spacious, with light woods, pastel tones, and coffeemakers. Suites have microwave ovens and refrigerators, which you can request for the rooms. There's laundry service, an outdoor heated swimming pool, and complimentary airport shuttle.

For a Few Bucks More

Best Western Midtown. 1425 S. Tamiami Trail (U.S. 41, at Prospect St.), Sarasota, FL 34239. ☎ **800/722-8227,** 800/528-1234, or 941/955-9841. Fax 941/954-8948. 100 units. A/C TV TEL. Winter $96–$106 single or double. Off-season $66–$82 single or double. Rates include continental breakfast. AE, DC, DISC, MC, V.

Location is the buzzword here, for this modern L-shaped 2- and 3-story hotel is 2 miles in either direction from the main causeways leading to the keys. Although positioned next to the Midtown Plaza shopping center, it's set back from the busy main road. Tropical palms and plantings surround a heated outdoor swimming pool and sundeck. Guests can graze a buffet-style breakfast, and there's a guest laundry. The rooms are modern and cheery, with light woods and Florida pastel tones. Some of them have kitchenettes.

LIDO KEY
For a Few Bucks More

✪ **Half Moon Beach Club.** 2050 Ben Franklin Dr. (at Taft Dr.), Sarasota, FL 34236. ☎ **800/358-3245** or 941/388-3694. Fax 941/388-1938. 85 units. A/C MINIBAR TV TEL. Winter $115–$225 single or double. Off-season $85–$159 single or double. AE, DC, DISC, MC, V.

Near the south end of Lido, this 2-story art deco–style hotel is right on the beach and less than half a block from South Lido Beach Park. The front of the building forms a circle around a small but very attractive courtyard with a heated pool and sunning area. From there, guests take a hallway through a motel-style block of rooms to the beach, where they can rent cabanas and order libation to be delivered from the bar inside. The spacious guest rooms are furnished with light woods, refrigerators, and coffeemakers, and some have kitchenettes with microwave ovens. Facilities include Seagrapes, an indoor/outdoor restaurant; an outdoor heated swimming pool; volleyball; a gulf-front sundeck; a coin laundry; and bike and video rentals. Complimentary newspapers are delivered to the rooms each morning.

SIESTA KEY
Super-Cheap Sleeps

✪ **Best Western Siesta Beach Resort.** 5311 Ocean Blvd. (at Calle Miramar), Sarasota, FL 34242. ☎ **800/223-5786** or 941/349-3211. Fax 941/349-7915. 53 units. A/C TV TEL.

Winter $120 single or double, $159–$220 suites. Off-season $59 single or double, $85–$120 suites. Weekly rates available. AE, DC, DISC, MC, V.

In Siesta Village on the northern end of the key, this older but very well-maintained motel has two buildings across the street from each other. It offers standard hotel rooms and one- and two-bedroom suites, all decorated in pastel tones with light woods. The suites have kitchenettes. Facilities include a heated swimming pool, whirlpool, and guest laundry. Public beach access is across the street, and Siesta Key Public Beach is about half a mile away.

Gulf Sun Motel. 6722 Midnight Pass Rd. (at Sarasota Circle), Sarasota, FL 34242. ☎ **800/653-6753** or 941/349-2442. Fax 941/349-7141. 17 units. A/C TV TEL. Winter $90 single or double, $115–$125 efficiency. Off-season $50 single or double, $65–$75 efficiency. DISC, MC, V.

In Siesta Key's midsection business district, this 1-story, 1960s motel with red Spanish tile roof is clean and within a 2-block walk of Crescent Beach. The bedrooms have standard furnishings with queen-size beds and refrigerators. All but two units here are efficiencies with kitchens. A swimming pool is set in the motel's roadside lawn.

For a Few Bucks More

Crescent View Beach Club. 6512 Midnight Pass Rd. (at Old Stickney Point Rd.), Sarasota, FL 34242. ☎ **800/344-7171** or 941/349-2000. Fax 941/349-9748. 26 units. A/C TV TEL. Winter $190–$350 efficiency or suite for 2. Off-season $120–$260 efficiency or suite for 2. AE, DISC, MC, V.

Located in the business district where Stickney Point Bridge comes onto Siesta Key in its midsection, this 4-story condo resort offers one- and two-bedroom suites facing the beach and gulf as well as efficiencies overlooking the pool or garden. All units are decorated in tropical tones with rattan furnishings; each has a living/dining area and a balcony. The smaller units have kitchenettes with microwave ovens and coffeemakers; the condo suites have completely outfitted kitchens with dishwashers. There's a guest laundry on the premises.

✪ **Turtle Beach Resort.** 9049 Midnight Pass Rd., Sarasota, FL 34242. ☎ **941/349-4554.** Fax 941/918-0203. 5 cottages. A/C TV TEL. Winter $1,200–$1,700 per week single or double. Off-season $125–$200 per day single or double. AE, DC, DISC, MC, V.

On Siesta Key's south end near Turtle Beach, this intimate little bay-side charmer began life years ago as a traditional Old Florida fishing camp. In the early 1990s, owners Gail and Dave Rubinfeld renovated the small clapboard cottages and turned them into this comfortable inn. With an eye to romance, they gave each cozy unit a patio with its own whirlpool shielded from view by a high wooden fence.

The cottages are done in Victorian, Southwest, Key West, country French, or traditional American country cottage decor. The living room of the American country model sits, docklike, right on the bay (it's justifiably the honeymoon cottage), and the Southwest model looks across the bay-side pool to the water. There's no restaurant on the grounds, but Ophelia's on the Bay seafood restaurant next door was once the old fishing camp's dining room, and two units have kitchens (all have microwave ovens and coffeemakers). The complex is tightly packed, but heavy tropical foliage provides privacy. Guests can use fishing poles and paddleboats. No smoking is allowed inside, but the Rubinfelds do take pets (10% extra charge). Winter rentals are by the week, but you might be able to get a few nights if there's a vacancy.

GREAT DEALS ON DINING

The restaurants below are organized geographically: on the mainland, on St. Armands Key (next to Lido Key), and on Siesta Key. You can also drive up to the north end of

Longboat Key to Moore's Stone Crab, which is just across the bridge on Bradenton Beach (see "Great Deals on Dining" in section 6, below).

The Tamiami Trail (U.S. 41) has most of the national chain fast-food and family restaurants, especially in the area around Sarasota Square Mall south of downtown.

ON THE MAINLAND
Super-Cheap Eats
First Watch. 1395 Main St. (at Central and Pineapple aves.). ☎ **941/954-1395.** Reservations not accepted. Breakfast $3–$6; sandwiches and salads, $4–$6.50. AE, DISC, MC, V. Daily 7am–2:30pm. AMERICAN.

Like its sister establishment in Naples (see section 5 in chapter 10), this bright dining room with natural wood Windsor chairs at oak-trimmed tables is *the* downtown place for breakfast or lunch (it's usually packed on weekend mornings, so be prepared to wait). Traditional breakfast offerings range widely, from bacon-and-eggs and omelettes to a skillet layered with eggs and vegetables. There are several healthy choices, too, such as oatmeal cooked with cinnamon and apples. Lunch adds sandwiches on fresh bread and creative salads, including a tasty white-meat chicken version with raisins and crunchy water chestnuts.

Patrick's. 1400 Main St. (at Pineapple and Central aves.). ☎ **941/952-1170.** Reservations not accepted. Sandwiches and burgers $5.50–$7; main courses $11–$15. AE, MC, V. Daily 11am–midnight (Sun brunch 11am–3pm). AMERICAN.

With a semicircular facade, this informal, polished-oak and brass-rail brasserie offers wide-windowed views of downtown's main intersection. The decor also boasts hanging plants and ceiling fans, plus a unique collection of sports memorabilia. The menu offers a range of pub fare: steaks and chops, burgers, seafood, pastas, salads, sandwiches, and omelettes, plus veal piccata, francese, or marsala; broiled salmon with dill-hollandaise sauce; and sesame chicken.

✪ **Yoder's.** 3434 Bahia Vista St. (west of Bahia Rd.). ☎ **941/955-7771.** Reservations not accepted. Breakfast $2–46; sandwiches and burgers $3–$6; main courses $6.50–$12. No credit cards. Mon–Sat 6am–8pm. AMISH/AMERICAN.

It's worth driving about 3 miles east of downtown to check out this good-value, award-winning eatery operated by an Amish family (both Sarasota and Bradenton have sizable Amish communities). Evoking the Pennsylvania Dutch country, the simple dining room displays handcrafts, photos, and paintings celebrating the Amish way. The menu emphasizes plain, made-from-scratch cooking such as home-style meat loaf, baked and southern-fried chicken, country-smoked ham, and fried fillet of flounder. Burgers, salads, soups, and sandwiches are also available. Leave room for traditional shoo-fly pie. There's neither alcohol nor smoking here. They don't take credit cards, but there's an ATM near the entrance.

For a Few Bucks More
Cafe of the Arts. 5230 N. Tamiami Trail (near University Pkwy.). ☎ **941/351-4304.** Reservations recommended for dinner. Main courses $11–$20. AE, DISC, MC, V. Mon–Fri 11am–3pm and 5–9pm, Sat–Sun 9am–3pm and 5–9pm. FRENCH.

Warm and soothing hospitality with a European flair welcomes you to Alain Taulere's cafe-bakery-wine bar. Across from the Ringling museum complex, this gathering place offers an artsy ambience with photos of entertainers and scenes of Europe on the walls. Dinner dishes range from heart-healthy vegetable platters to rack of lamb dijonnais. Don't leave until you sample the chocolate eclair or strawberry mousse. Breakfast is served Saturday and Sunday.

Coasters Marina Bar & Restaurant. In Sarasota Boat Yard Shopping Village, 1500 Stickney Point Rd. (east end of Stickney Point Rd. Bridge). ☎ **941/923-4848.** Reservations recommended. Main courses $13–$17. AE, DC, DISC, MC, V. Sun–Thurs 11:30am–10pm, Fri–Sat 11:30am–10:30pm (bar to 1:30am). SEAFOOD.

On the bay in a quaint, New England–style shopping complex and marina, this casual restaurant offers great water views and fresh seafood selections like grouper, snapper, swordfish, and mahimahi. The indoor brasserie-style dining room leads to an outdoor sundeck and waterfront patio. There's a children's menu and entertainment Thursday to Saturday during winter.

Marina Jack. In Island Park, Bayfront at Central Ave. ☎ **941/365-4232.** Reservations recommended. Main courses $9–$22. MC, V. Dining room, daily noon–3pm and 5–10pm; lounge, daily noon–10pm. SEAFOOD/CONTINENTAL.

Be sure to make reservations before you go to this longtime favorite. It has spectacular water vistas and a carefree "on vacation" attitude. Overlooking the waterfront with a wraparound 270° view of Sarasota Bay and Siesta and Lido keys, this restaurant is synonymous with seafood. The menu offers fresh native fish such as grouper, red snapper, swordfish, tuna, and dolphin, prepared charcoal-grilled, pan-seared, blackened, or sautéed. In addition, there are half a dozen shrimp selections, crab-stuffed roughy, and Caribbean lobster, as well as steaks, chicken, and pastas. The dining room closes daily from 3 to 5pm, but the Deep Six Lounge continues serving a snack menu.

If you prefer to dine on the bay rather than beside it, the paddle-wheel sightseeing boat *Marina Jack II* (☎ 941/366-9255) offers dinner cruises from October to August. Call for information and reservations.

Nick's on the Water. In Sarasota Quay, Tamiami Trail at Fruitville Rd. ☎ **941/954-3839.** Reservations recommended. Main courses $10–$18. AE, DISC, MC, V. Winter Sun–Thurs 11:30am–10pm, Fri–Sat 11:30am–11pm. Off-season Sun–Thurs 11:30am–9pm, Fri–Sat 11:30am–10pm. ITALIAN/SEAFOOD.

In the Sarasota Quay waterfront dining, shopping, and entertainment complex a block north of the John Ringling Causeway, this indoor/outdoor spot is really two restaurants. One is a terrace overlooking the marina; the other, an indoor wine bar with a winery ambience. The menu offers pizzas and pastas as well as such traditional Italian dishes as veal or chicken prepared parmigiana, marsala, or Française style, and shrimp scampi or fra diavolo. There are sports TVs in the bar and live entertainment Thursday to Saturday nights.

Worth a Splurge

Bijou Cafe. 1287 1st St. (at Pineapple Ave.). ☎ **941/366-8111.** Reservations recommended. Main courses $17–$23. AE, DC, MC, V. Mon–Thurs 11:30am–2pm and 5–9:30pm, Fri 11:30am–2pm and 5–10:30pm, Sat 5–10:30pm, Sun 5–9:30pm. Closed Sun June–Dec. INTERNATIONAL.

Locals always recommend the award-winning cuisine at this charming cafe in the heart of the theater district. Menu highlights include the likes of prime veal Louisville (with crushed pecans and bourbon-pear sauce), sautéed red snapper, and New Orleans crab cakes. Watching your weight? You may request a "fit and trim" menu. The outstanding wine list has been recognized by *Wine Spectator* magazine.

✪ **Michael's on East.** 1212 East Ave. S. (between Bahia and Prospect sts.). ☎ **941/366-0007.** Reservations recommended. Main courses $14.50–$26. AE, DC, MC, V. Winter Mon–Fri 11:30am–2pm, daily 5:30–10pm. Off-season Mon–Fri 11:30am–2pm, Mon–Sat 6–10pm. CREATIVE INTERNATIONAL.

At the rear of the Midtown Plaza shopping center on U.S. 41 south of downtown, this chic art deco bistro is one of the top places here for fine dining. Huge cut-glass walls create three intimate dining areas, one with a black marble bar for pre- or after-dinner drinks. Prepared with fresh ingredients and a creative flair, the offerings here will tempt your taste buds. A heart of palm salad with mangoes, stone crab meat, and a brazil nut dressing is an exciting starter. From there, you can progress to spicy Louisiana-style crab cakes, seared Chilean sea bass with a roasted garlic and lemon sauce, or perhaps duckling served with a Bartlett pear relish.

ST. ARMANDS KEY
Super-Cheap Eats
The Buttery. 470 John Ringling Blvd. (1 block off St. Armands Circle). ☎ **941/388-1523.** Reservations not accepted. Breakfast $4–$8; sandwiches $5.50–$6.50; main courses $8–$10 at dinner. AE, DISC, MC, V. Daily 6:30am–11pm. AMERICAN/DINER.

On the John Ringling Boulevard spoke of St. Armands Circle, this plain, informal diner is the only inexpensive place to eat in this affluent area. It offers standard breakfast and lunch choices as well as mesquite-grilled breast of chicken, Jamaican jerk chicken, fish and chips, grilled grouper, and an 8-ounce rib-eye steak at dinner. You can order breakfast anytime.

For a Few Bucks More
Charley's Crab. 420 St. Armands Circle (between John Ringling Blvd. and Blvd. of the Presidents). ☎ **941/388-3964.** Reservations recommended. Main courses $13.50–$20; dinner sandwiches $7–$10.50. AE, MC, V. Mon–Thurs 11:30am–10pm, Fri–Sat 11:30am–10:30pm, Sun noon–10pm. SEAFOOD.

A favorite for people-watching, Charley's is popular not just for crab cakes and crab fettuccine (with mushrooms and basil in a shrimp sauce) but for a full range of seafood dishes. Alfresco diners fill sidewalk tables early at lunch and dinner as shoppers stroll past. A pianist adds to the lively outdoor atmosphere. Large windows in the comfortable indoor dining room give a great view of the passing parade as well.

Columbia. St. Armands Circle (between John Ringling Blvd. and John Ringling Pkwy.). ☎ **941/388-3987.** Reservations recommended. Main courses $14–$22. Early bird specials $10–$14. AE, DC, DISC, MC, V. Mon–Sat 11am–11pm, Sun noon–10pm. Early bird specials daily 4–6pm. SPANISH.

Like the original Columbia in Tampa's Ybor City (see "Great Deals on Dining" in section 1, above), this one is a culinary tour de force of Spanish specialties. You can dine outside or inside, where old-world decor combines graciousness with New World efficiency and impeccable service. If you can't decide what to order, try the paella à la valenciana prepared with grouper, shrimp, calamari, mussels, clams, chicken, and lean pork. All main dishes include Cuban bread and rice or potato. The early bird specials are good values for pretheater dining. The Patio Lounge is one of the liveliest spots here for evening entertainment from Thursday to Sunday.

Hemingway's. 325 John Ringling Blvd. (½ block off St. Armands Circle). ☎ **941/ 388-3948.** Reservations recommended. Main courses $12–$22; dinner sandwiches $8–$12. AE, DC, DISC, MC, V. Sun–Thurs 11:30am–10pm, Fri–Sat 11:30am–11pm. FLORIDIAN/ CARIBBEAN.

For a casual spot with an eclectic "Floribbean" menu and a large bar with a friendly, laid-back Key West ambience, take the elevator or climb the winding stairs to this above-the-mob second-floor hideaway. Hemingway's is charming and comfortable in the best Old Florida tradition. The decor features a mix of green floral booths and tables with rattan chairs. You might start with gator bits or conch fritters, then choose from a evenly distributed mix of seafood, barbecued ribs, and other meats. Mariner's shrimp is a healthy winner: They're perfectly charcoal-grilled, basted with a light teriyaki sauce, and served over rice with fresh asparagus and baby carrots.

Worth a Splurge

✪ **Cafe l'Europe.** 431 St. Armands Circle (at John Ringling Blvd.). ☎ **941/388-4415.** Reservations recommended. Main courses $18–$26. Pretheater dinner $55 per couple. AE, DC, MC, V. Daily 11am–4pm and 5–10pm (pretheater dinner, daily 5–6:15pm). CONTINENTAL.

As its name implies, a European atmosphere prevails at this consistently excellent restaurant, with a decor of brick walls and arches, dark woods, brass fixtures, pink linens, and hanging plants. The menu offers selections ranging from bouillabaisse Marseilles (with lobster, snapper, shrimp, and clams) to veal and portobello napoleon with fresh tomato, garlic, and herb sauce over bow-tie pasta. A fine value, the fixed-price, pretheater dinner includes a bottle of wine.

SIESTA KEY
Super-Cheap Eats

Turtles. 8875 Midnight Pass Rd. (at Turtle Beach Rd.). ☎ **941/346-2207.** Reservations not accepted. Salads and sandwiches $6–$9; main courses $9–$15; early bird specials $8. AE, DC, DISC, MC, V. Winter daily 11:30am–11pm. Off-season daily 11:30am–9:30pm. Early bird specials daily 4–6pm. AMERICAN.

With tropical overtones and breathtaking water vistas across from Turtle Beach, this informal restaurant on Little Sarasota Bay has tables both indoors and on an outside deck at which to try dishes such as snapper New Orleans, Florida-style blue crab cakes, or steak under a Jack Daniels whiskey sauce. There's a selection of pastas and platters to devour. The early bird specials include a medium-sized fish portion.

SARASOTA AFTER DARK

The cultural capital of Florida's west coast, Sarasota is home to a host of performing arts, especially during the winter season. To get the latest update on what's happening any time of year, call the city's 24-hour Artsline (☎ **941/365-ARTS**).

THE PERFORMING ARTS   Designated as the State Theater of Florida in 1965, the ✪ **Asolo Center for the Performing Arts,** 5555 N. Tamiami Trail (U.S. 41), at the Ringling museum complex (☎ **941/351-8000**), is home to the Asolo Theatre Company and the Conservatory for Professional Actor Training. The main stage, the 487-seat Harold E. and Ethel M. Mertz Theatre, is an attraction in itself—the former Dumferline Opera House, originally constructed in Scotland in 1900 and transferred piece by piece to Sarasota in 1987. In 1994–95 the 161-seat Asolo Conservatory Theatre was added as a smaller venue for experimental and alternative offerings. The season runs from December to mid-June for the main stage and from November to May for the smaller theater. Ticket prices range from $5 to $39.

Free guided tours of the center are offered Wednesday to Saturday from 10 to 11:30am, except from June to August and during technical rehearsals between plays; call for tour times.

Downtown, the lavender, seashell-shaped **Van Wezel Performing Arts Hall,** 777 N. Tamiami Trail (U.S. 41), at 9th Street (☎ **941/953-3366**), is visible for miles on the bay-front skyline. It offers excellent visual and acoustic conditions, with year-round programs ranging from symphony and jazz concerts, opera, musical comedy, and choral productions to ballet and international productions. It's the home of the Florida West Coast Symphony, the Jazz Club of Sarasota, the Sarasota Ballet of Florida, and the Sarasota Concert Band.

Downtown Sarasota's theater district is home to the **Florida Studio Theatre,** 1241 N. Palm Ave., at Cocoanut Avenue (☎ **941/366-9796**), which has contemporary performances from December to August, including a New Play Festival in May. **The Opera House,** 61 N. Pineapple Ave., between Main and 1st streets (☎ **941/953-7030**), hosts the Sarasota Opera in February and March, while the Sarasota Ballet and other companies take the stage the rest of the year. Next door to The Opera House, the **Golden Apple Dinner Theatre,** 25 N. Pineapple Ave. (☎ **941/366-5454**), presents cocktails, dinner, and a professional Broadway-style show year-round. The professional, nonequity **Theatre Works,** 1247 1st St., at Cocoanut Ave. (☎ **941/952-9170**), presents musical revues and other works all year.

THE CLUB & MUSIC SCENE   You can find plenty of music to dance to at **Sarasota Quay,** the downtown waterfront dining-shopping-entertainment complex on Tamiami Trail (U.S. 41) a block north of John Ringling Causeway. Just walk around this brick building and your ears will take you to the action. The laser sound-and-light crowd gathers at **In Extremis** (☎ **941/954-2008**), where a high-energy deejay spins Top 40 tunes. **Downunder Jazz Bar** (☎ **941/951-2467**) offers contemporary jazz. Michael's Seafood Grill turns into **Anthony's After Dark** rocking disco at 10:30pm. And the Vineyard at **Nick's on the Water** restaurant offers live entertainment on weekends and sports TV all week.

Over on St. Armands Circle, the Patio Lounge in the Columbia Restaurant (☎ **941/388-3987**) is one of the liveliest spots along the beach strip, featuring live, high-energy dance music on Tuesday to Sunday evenings.

You laughing types can get yours at **Coconuts Comedy Club,** 8440 N. Tamiami Trail (U.S. 41), north of downtown (☎ **941/351-8225**). Open Thursday to Saturday nights.

6 Bradenton & Anna Maria Island

26 miles S of St. Petersburg, 41 miles SW of Tampa, 15 miles N of Sarasota

Visitors often overlook Bradenton as they speed south on their way to Sarasota and beyond. But if you stop, you'll thoroughly enjoy this pleasant town on the Manatee River, and especially **Anna Maria Island,** northernmost in the chain of barrier islands stretching from Tampa Bay to Sarasota. Anna Maria claims 7½ miles of white-sand beaches—but no glitzy resorts, just a lot of casual island getaways. The island's communities—Bradenton Beach, Holmes Beach, and Anna Maria—are popular with family vacationers and seniors, offering a variety of public beaches, fishing piers, bungalows, and low-rise motels. You can have a very relaxing beach vacation here without the high-rises, bustle, and out-of-sight prices found elsewhere.

Bradenton and Manatee County also own the northern half of Longboat Key, connected by bridge to Anna Maria Island. Most of the Longboat resorts are closer to Sarasota than to Bradenton, so I have included them in section 5 of this chapter. On the northern tip of Longboat, the little fishing village of Longbeach was established in 1885 and still has some remnants of Old Florida.

Although mainland Bradenton has been touched by urban sprawl in recent years, the town maintains links with the past through its historic Old Main Street, many Spanish-style buildings, and historic parks and sites. Compared to affluent Sarasota, its southern neighbor, Bradenton is a working-class community synonymous with the sweet aroma of fresh oranges. As the home of Tropicana, this city of 40,000 people is a major producer of orange juice and citrus products.

ESSENTIALS

GETTING THERE   From Tampa, take I-75 south. From St. Petersburg, go south across the Sunshine Skyway on I-275, then follow U.S. 19 and U.S. 41 south. The easiest way from I-75 into downtown Bradenton is to take Exit 43 and follow U.S. 301 south across the Manatee River.

Bradenton shares **Sarasota-Bradenton International Airport** with Sarasota (see "Essentials" in section 5, above). **Diplomat Taxi** (☎ 941/355-5155) charges about $20 to downtown Bradenton, $30 to Bradenton Beach, and $35 to Anna Maria Island.

VISITOR INFORMATION   For a packet of information about Bradenton, Anna Maria Island, and surrounding Manatee County, contact the **Greater Bradenton Area Convention and Visitors Bureau,** P.O. Box 1000, Bradenton, FL 34206 (☎ 800/ 4-MANATEE or 941/729-9177; fax 941/729-1820; www.floridaislandbeaches.org).

For maps, brochures, and specific information, call or drop by the **Manatee County Tourist Information Center,** on U.S. 301 just west of Exit 43 off I-75 (☎ 941/729-7040). Open daily except holidays from 8:30am to 5:30pm, it has a volunteer staff on hand to answer your questions.

GETTING AROUND   Based in Sarasota (see section 5, above), **Trolley Systems of America** (☎ 800/787-6554 or 941/346-3115) provides service along Anna Maria Island Tuesday to Saturday, with pick ups in Bradenton twice a day. The fare is $5, free for kids under 3. Call for the exact schedules and to make reservations.

Manatee County Area Transit, known locally as **Manatee CAT** (☎ 941/ 749-7116), operates scheduled public bus service throughout the area. The basic fare is $1, with exact change required. Route number 5 goes out Cortez Avenue to Anna Maria Island. From downtown, take route number 4 to Blake Hospital and transfer there to route number 5.

Taxi companies in Bradenton include **Bruce's Taxi** (☎ 941/755-6070), **Checker Cab** (☎ 941/751-3181), and **Yellow Cab** (☎ 941/748-4800).

HITTING THE BEACH

There are four public beaches on Anna Maria Island, all with rest rooms, picnic areas, lifeguards, and free parking. The largest and best is **Coquina Beach,** which occupies the southern mile of the island below Bradenton Beach. It has both gulf and bay sides, is sheltered by whispering Australian pines, and has large parking lots. **Cortez Beach** is in Bradenton Beach, just north of Coquina Beach. In the island's center, **Manatee County Public Beach** is at Gulf Drive. **Holmes Beach** is at the west end of Manatee Avenue (Fla. 64). **Anna Maria Bayfront Park** is on Bay Boulevard at the northwest end of the island, fronting both the bay and the Gulf of Mexico.

GREAT GOLF THAT WON'T BREAK YOUR BUDGET & OTHER AFFORDABLE OUTDOOR ACTIVITIES

BIKING & IN-LINE SKATING   The flat terrain makes for good in-line skating and fine if not challenging bike riding. **Native Rentals,** 5302 Marina Dr. in Holmes Beach (☎ 941/778-7757), rents both, with bikes starting at $3 an hour or $9 per day, skates for $4 an hour or $15 a day. The office is behind the BP service station on Gulf Drive in the Holmes Beach business district. Open Monday to Saturday from 7am to 7pm, Sunday from 9am to 5pm.

BOATING & FISHING   When Florida's ban on net fishing devastated its traditional business, the village of Cortez on the east side of the Cortez Bridge aimed for another catch: tourist dollars. Here you can rent boats, go deep-sea fishing, and take a sightseeing cruise on the bay, all provided by the **Cortez Fleet,** 4330 127th St. W. (☎ 941/794-1223). The rental part of the business has ski and pontoon boats, Wave Runners, and other equipment, ranging in price from $45 an hour for Wave Runners to $155 for a day's use of a pontoon boat. Party boat deep-sea fishing voyages range from 4 hours to 9 hours, with prices starting at $25 for adults, $22 for seniors, and $12.50 for children. Call for the schedules, which can change from day to day.

On Anna Maria Island, you can rent boats from **Bradenton Beach Marina,** 402 Church Ave. (☎ **941/778-2288**); **Captain's Marina,** 5501 Marina Dr., Holmes Beach (☎ **941/778-1977**); and **Five O'Clock Marina,** 412 Pine Ave., (☎ **941/778-5577**). On northern Longboat Key, **Cannons Marina,** 6040 Gulf of Mexico Dr. (☎ **941/383-1311**), also rents boats. Several deep-sea fishing charter boats are based at these marinas.

You also can fish from **Anna Maria City Pier,** on the north end of Anna Maria Island, and at the **Bradenton Beach City Pier,** at Cortez Road. Both are free of charge.

CRUISES The *Miss Cortez XI* (☎ **941/794-1223**), operated by the Cortez Fleet (see "Boating & Fishing," above), makes sightseeing cruises to **Egmont Key State Park,** on historic Egmont Key 3 miles off the northern end of Anna Maria Island at the mouth of Tampa Bay. This uninhabited island is the site of a lighthouse, of now-crumbling Fort Dade (built in 1900 during the Spanish-American War but abandoned long ago), and of threatened gopher tortoises. Sea turtles come ashore here to nest. You can go snorkeling and shelling here, so bring your swimsuit and gear. This cruise costs $14 for adults, $8 for children 14 and under. Call for the schedules and reservations, which are recommended.

You can also get to Egmont Key on a 30-foot sloop-rigged sailboat with **Spice Sailing Charters** (☎ **941/778-3240**), based at the Galati Yacht Basin on Bay Boulevard on northern Anna Maria Island. The company also has sunset cruises. Call for schedule, prices, and reservations, which are required.

That paddlewheeler you see going up and down the bay is the *Seafood Shack Showboat,* operated by the Seafood Shack restaurant, 4110 127th St. W., in Cortez (☎ **800/299-5048** or 941/794-5048). It has afternoon and sunset cruises to Sarasota Bay, Tampa Bay, and as far away as the Sunshine Skyway. Prices range from $11.22 to $14.95 for adults, $10.28 to $14.02 for seniors, and $4.67 to $5.61 for children 4 to 11. The *Showboat* goes to a different destination each day, so call for the schedule.

Open-air, eight-passenger craft are operated by **Manatee Airboat Tours,** Perico Harbour Marina, Manatee Avenue (U.S. 64) (☎ **941/730-1011**). The ride lasts 55 minutes, with departures year-round. Rides cost $12 for adults, $10 for children. Call for schedule and reservations.

You can also skim across the bays with **Sun Hovercraft Rides,** 12507 Cortez Rd., Cortez (☎ **941/792-1290**). They run from Tuesday to Sunday. Call for times, prices, and reservations.

GOLF The city and county operate several municipal courses where you can play without breaking your budget.

Locals say they prefer the county's 18-hole, par-72 **Buffalo Creek Golf Course,** on the north side of the river at 8100 Erie Rd. in Palmetto (☎ **941/776-2611**). At well over 7,000 yards, it's the longest in the area, and lots of water and alligators will keep you entertained. Wintertime greens fees are about $34 with cart, $24 without. They drop to about $18 and $16, respectively, during summer.

You'll pay the same at **Manatee County Golf Course,** 5290 66th St. W. (☎ **941/792-6773**), an 18-hole, par-72 course on the southern rim of the city. Both county courses require that tee times be set up at least 2 days in advance.

Also open to the public, the city's **River Run Golf Links,** 1801 27th St. E. (☎ **941/747-6331**), set beside the Braden River, is an 18-hole, par-70 course with lots of water in its layout. Winter fees here are about $26 with cart, $17 walking. They're about $16 riding, $8 walking in summer. A 2-day advance notice is required for tee times here, too.

Other courses include the **Palma Sola Golf Club,** 3807 75th St. W. (☎ 941/792-7476), just north of Fla. 684 and east of Palma Sola Bay, with an 18-hole, par-72 course and the same 2-day advance booking requirement.

Situated just off U.S. 41, the **Heather Hills Golf Club,** 101 Cortez Rd. W. (☎ 941/755-8888), operates an 18-hole, par-61 executive course on a first-come, first-served basis. There's a driving range and clubs can be rented. It's open daily from 6:30am until dark.

Bradenton also is home to the well-known **David Leadbetter Golf Academy,** 1414 69th Ave. (at U.S. 41) (☎ 800/424-3542 or 941/739-2483), a part of the Nick Bollettieri Sports Academy (see "Tennis," below). Presided over by one of golf's leading instructors, this facility offers practice tee instruction, video analysis, and scoring strategy, as well as general tuition. Prices start at $150.

SPECTATOR SPORTS   The **Pittsburgh Pirates** do their February-through-March spring training at 6,562-seat **McKechnie Field,** 9th Street West and 17th Avenue West (☎ 941/748-4610), south of downtown. Admission ranges from $5.50 to $8.50.

TENNIS   The **Nick Bollettieri Sports Academy,** 5500 34th St. W. (☎ 800/872-6425 or 941/755-1000), is one of the world's largest tennis-training facilities, with more than 70 championship courts and a pro shop. It's open year-round, and reservations are required for all activities. One-day instructional programs cost $163 for adults, $155 for juniors age 8 to 18. Overnight packages start at $285 for adults, $185 for juniors. The academy also has training courses in soccer, baseball, and football.

The municipal **Walton Racquet Center,** 5502 33rd Ave. Dr. W. (☎ 941/742-5973), has eight clay and eight hard tennis courts plus eight racquetball courts. It's open Monday to Thursday from 7am to 9:30pm, on Friday from 7:30am to 5:45pm, and on Saturday and Sunday from 7am to 1pm. Prices are $2.50 per person for 1½ hours on the hard courts, $4.50 on the clay courts, and $3 for racquetball.

EXPLORING THE AREA

On weekends, you can see the sights of rural Manatee County northwest of Bradenton on a 1¼-hour narrated sightseeing tour aboard a 1950s diesel-engine train operated by the **Florida Gulf Coast Railroad,** 83rd Street East, off U.S. 301 in Parrish (☎ 941/722-4272). The schedule and fares are seasonal, so call before driving out here.

Art League of Manatee County. 209 9th St. W. (Business U.S. 41, at 3rd Ave. W.). ☎ 941/746-2862. Free admission. Mon–Fri 9am–4:30pm.

Bradenton's downtown cultural hub, this gallery offers an ever-changing program of art exhibits, shows, courses, workshops, and craft demonstrations.

✪ **DeSoto National Memorial.** DeSoto Memorial Hwy. (north end of 75th St. W.). ☎ 941/792-0458. Free admission. Daily 9am–5pm. Take Manatee Ave. (Fla. 64) west to 75th St. W. and turn right; follow the road to its end and the entrance to the park.

Nestled on the Manatee River west of downtown, this park re-creates the look and atmosphere from when Spanish explorer Hernando de Soto landed here in 1539. It includes a restoration of de Soto's original campsite and a scenic half-mile nature trail that circles a mangrove jungle and leads to the ruins of one of the first settlements of the area. From December to March, park employees dress in 16th-century costumes and portray the way the early settlers lived, including demonstrations of cooking and musket firing.

Gamble Plantation. 3708 Patten Ave., Ellenton. ☎ **941/723-4536.** Admission free. Tours $3 adults, $1.50 children 6–12, free for children under 6. Thurs–Mon 9am–5pm; guided tours given at 9:30 and 10:30am, and 1, 2, 3, and 4pm. Take U.S. 301 north of downtown to Ellenton; the site is on the left at the juncture of U.S. 301 and Ellenton-Gillette Rd. (Fla. 683).

Situated northeast of downtown Bradenton, this is the oldest structure on the southwestern coast of Florida, and a fine example of an antebellum plantation home. Built over a 6-year period in the late 1840s by Maj. Robert Gamble, it was constructed primarily of "tabby mortar" (a mixture of oyster shells, sand, molasses, and water), with 10 rooms, verandas on three sides, 18 exterior columns, and eight fireplaces. It's maintained as a state historic site and includes a fine collection of 19th-century furnishings. Entrance to the house is by tour only, although the grounds may be explored on your own.

Manatee Village Historical Park. 6th Ave. E. and 15th St. E. ☎ **941/749-7165.** Free admission; donations welcome. Mon–Fri 9am–4:30pm, Sun 1:30–4:30pm. Call for Sat hours. Closed Sun in July–Aug. From downtown, go east on 6th Ave. E. through a merger with Manatee Ave., then right on 15th St. E.

A tree-shaded park with a courtyard of hand-laid bricks, this national historic site features restored buildings from the city of Bradenton and the surrounding county. It contains the Manatee County Court House, dating from 1860 and the oldest structure of its kind still standing on the south Florida mainland; a Methodist church built in 1887; a typical "Cracker Gothic" house built in 1912; and the Wiggins General Store, dating to 1903 and full of local memorabilia from swamp root and grub dust to louse powder, as well as antique furnishings and an art gallery.

✪ South Florida Museum, Bishop Planetarium, and Parker Manatee Aquarium. 201 10th St. W. (on the riverfront, at Barcarrota Blvd.). ☎ **941/746-4131.** Admission $6 adults, $5 seniors, $3.50 children 5–12, free for children 4 and under. Jan–Apr and July, Mon–Sat 10am–5pm, Sun noon–5pm. May–June and Aug–Dec, Tues–Sat 10am–5pm, Sun noon–6pm. From U.S. 41, take Manatee Ave. west to 10th St. W. and turn right.

The star at this downtown complex is "Snooty," the oldest manatee born in captivity (1948) and Manatee County's official mascot. Snooty and a friend acquired in 1998 live in the Parker Manatee Aquarium. The South Florida Museum tells the story of Florida's history, from prehistoric times to the present, including a Native American collection with life-size dioramas and a Spanish courtyard containing replicas of 16th-century buildings. The Bishop Planetarium features a 50-foot hemispherical dome that arcs above a seating area, for laser light and educational star shows.

SHOPPING

For discount shopping, the focal point of the Bradenton area is the **Gulf Coast Factory Shops,** on U.S. 301 at exit 43 off I-75 in Ellenton (☎ **941/723-1150**), about a 15-minute drive northeast of downtown (turn left at the first stoplight east of I-75). This Spanish-style, coral stucco outdoor center has more than 100 factory and outlet stores, including a Saks Off Fifth Avenue (I found mostly leftovers from the main stores), Coach Leather, Liz Claiborne, Bass Shoes, Corning Revere, Jockey, Levi's, Nike, Ann Taylor, Donna Karan, Jones New York, Geoffrey Beene, Van Heusen, Maidenform, Royal Doulton, Sony, and Bose. Shops are open Monday to Saturday from 10am to 9pm and Sunday from 11am to 6pm.

ACCOMMODATIONS YOU CAN AFFORD

The Bradenton Area Convention and Visitors Bureau (see "Essentials," above) operates a free **reservation service** (☎ 800/4-MANATEE, and its annual visitor guide lists all of Manatee County's accommodations, including condominium complexes. **A Paradise Rental Management,** 5201 Gulf Dr., Holmes Beach, FL 34217 (☎ **800/ 237-2252** or 941/778-4800; fax 941/778-7090; www.manatee-online.com/ aparadise), represents a number of condo complexes with weekly rates ranging from $500 off-season to $1,950 a week during winter.

Except for those near I-75 east of the city, Bradenton has few national chain motels. On the other hand, those on U.S. 41 and University Parkway near the Sarasota-Bradenton International Airport are about halfway between downtown and Sarasota. On Longboat Key, the Hilton and Holiday Inn are equally convenient to Anna Maria Island and Bradenton. See "Accommodations You Can Afford," in section 5, for details about nearby Sarasota accommodations. The high season here is January to April. Hotel tax is 9% in Manatee County.

ON THE MAINLAND

Super-Cheap Sleeps

Five Oaks Bed and Breakfast Inn. 1102 Riverside Dr. (at 11th Ave. W.), Palmetto, FL 34221. ☎ **941/723-1236.** 4 units. A/C TEL. Year-round $75–$110 double. Rates include breakfast. AE, MC, V. Go north across river on 9th St. W. (Business U.S. 41), take first left on Riverside Dr., and go 3 blocks to house on right.

Known for its full Southern-style breakfast, this Victorian inn sits on the north shore of the Manatee River directly opposite downtown, surrounded by palm trees, oaks, and gardens overlooking the water. Guests enjoy use of a parlor with a fireplace, and an enclosed wraparound solarium/sunporch or formal dining room filled with wicker and rattan furnishings. Those in search of total quiet will enjoy it here, since kids are not welcome, and the rooms don't have televisions.

For a Few Bucks More

✪ **Holiday Inn Riverfront.** 100 Riverfront Dr. W. (at 3rd St. W.), Bradenton, FL 34205. ☎ **800/HOLIDAY** or 941/747-3727. Fax 941/746-4289. 153 units. A/C TV TEL. Winter $119–$139 single or double. Off-season $89–$109 single or double. Golf packages available. AE, DC, DISC, MC, V. From U.S. 41, go west on Manatee Ave. (Fla. 64) and turn right on 3rd St. W. to hotel on left.

This 5-story Spanish hacienda-style structure overlooking the Manatee River is Bradenton's prime commercial hotel. The highlight is a remarkable riverside landscaped courtyard with fountains and tropical trees. Inside, the public areas reflect an Iberian ambience, with dark wood trim, tile floors, and high-beamed ceilings. The bedrooms are contemporary, with standard hotel furnishings augmented by coffeemakers, irons and boards, and hair dryers. Those above the ground floor have balconies and views of the river or the courtyard. Facilities include a Spanish-themed restaurant, a nautical-style lounge, heated outdoor swimming pool, exercise room, and gift shop. There's laundry and room service and weekday complimentary newspaper delivery.

✪ **Park Inn Club and Breakfast.** 4450 47th St. W. (at 44th Ave./Cortez Rd.), Bradenton, FL 34210. ☎ **800/437-PARK** or 941/795-4633. Fax 941/795-0808. 130 units. A/C TV TEL. Winter $109–$139 single or double. Off-season $79–$109 single or double. Rates include continental breakfast and evening cocktails. Golf packages available. AE, DC, DISC, MC, V. From I-75, take Exit 41 and follow Fla. 70 west 6½ miles, turn right on U.S. 41 north, left on 44th Ave. W. (Fla. 684) to 47th St. W., and hotel is on left.

Families will find this busy Cortez Road/44th Avenue location to be convenient, for there are ample chain restaurants and a multiscreen cinema in the adjacent shopping centers. And you can't get lost driving to Bradenton Beach, a straight-line, 6-mile trip west on Cortez Road. The 3-story contemporary building is wrapped around a central courtyard with a patio and swimming pool. The guest rooms are spacious, and the suites have whirlpools. All bathrooms here have hair dryers, phones, and TV speakers. Facilities include a courtyard pool and a lounge in which guests are served breakfast and complimentary cocktails each evening. Guests get free use of Gold's Gym next door.

ANNA MARIA ISLAND

Anna Maria's lone chain motel is the moderately priced **Econo Lodge Surfside,** 2502 Gulf Dr. N. (at 25th St. N.), Bradenton Beach, FL 34217 (☎ **800/55-ECONO** or 941/778-6671; fax 941/778-0360). Recently remodeled, this beachfront facility has 18 suites and 36 spacious rooms in its main 3-story building, plus 18 rooms in another one-story building on the beach and five more across the street (the least expensive).

Super-Cheap Sleeps

✪ **Catalina Beach Resort.** 1325 Gulf Dr. N. (at 14th St. N.), Bradenton Beach, FL 34217. ☎ **941/778-6611.** Fax 941/778-6748. 35 units. A/C TV TEL. Winter $81 single or double; $112–$184 suite. Off-season $49–$57 single or double; $69–$125 suite. Weekly rates available. AE, DC, DISC, MC, V.

In a shady spot across Gulf Drive from the beach, 10 short blocks north of the Cortez Bridge, this 2-story Spanish-style motel offers exceptional value. Its well-kept units have modern furnishings and bright Florida colors. Most of them are one- and two-bedroom suites with kitchenettes. Facilities include a restaurant, outdoor solar-heated swimming pool, barbecue grills, shuffleboard courts, guest laundry, fishing and boating dock, and water-sports rentals.

For a Few Bucks More

✪ **Harrington House.** 5626 Gulf Dr. (at 55th St.), Holmes Beach, FL 34217. ☎ **941/778-5444.** Fax 941/778-0527. www.harhousebb.com. 12 units, all with bathroom. A/C TV. Winter $149–$225 single or double. Off-season $109–$225 single or double. MC, V.

Flowers will be everywhere and a private beach awaiting when you arrive at this bed-and-breakfast, the best romantic lovers' getaway hereabouts. In a tree-shaded setting on the beach overlooking the Gulf of Mexico, this 3-story clapboard house was built in 1925 and exudes an Old Florida ambience. The eight bedrooms are individually decorated with antique, wicker, or rattan furnishings. Some units have four-poster or brass beds, and the higher-priced rooms have French doors leading to balconies overlooking the gulf. In addition to the bedrooms in the main house, four rooms are available in the adjacent Beach House, a remodeled 1920s captain's home updated. All guests enjoy use of the high-ceilinged living room with fireplace, an outdoor pool, patio, and complimentary use of bicycles, kayaks, and other sports equipment.

GREAT DEALS ON DINING
ON THE MAINLAND
Super-Cheap Eats

✪ **Miller's Dutch Kitchen.** 3401 14th St. W. (U.S. 41, at 34th Ave. W.). ☎ **941/746-8253.** Reservations not accepted. Sandwiches $2.50–$5; main courses $6.25–$13. MC, V. Mon–Sat 11am–8pm. Closed Christmas. AMERICAN.

There's a charming treat waiting inside this modern, nondescript brick building among the auto dealers on busy U.S. 41, for its Pennsylvania Dutch country dining room is surrounded by a balcony, around whose edge chugs a model train. Over the balcony railing you'll see quilts and other handcrafts, all products of Bradenton's Amish community and all very much for sale. Although plain, the food here is as fresh as it gets. The regular American items such as fried shrimp, stuffed flounder, and barbecued pork ribs are augmented by daily Amish specialties such as cabbage rolls and Dutch casserole (noodles, peas, cheese, potatoes, beef, mushrooms, and chicken soup with croutons). Leave room for dessert: You can choose from 30 types of homemade pies. No smoking and no alcohol here.

For a Few Bucks More

Twin Dolphin Marina Grill. On The Pier, 1200 1st Ave. W. (north end of 12th St. W.). ☎ **941/748-8087.** Reservations recommended on weekends. Main courses $12–$32. AE, DC, DISC, MC, V. Sun–Thurs 11:30am–10pm, Fri–Sat 11:30am–11pm. FLORIBBEAN.

With commanding views of the Manatee River, this restaurant is *the* place to dine downtown. It's housed in a stately Spanish-style landmark building at the foot of 12th Street (Old Main Street) on Memorial Pier. The menu offers the day's fresh catch either grilled, broiled, blackened, bronzed, or jerked Jamaican-style. Florida lobster tails are served fried in a light tempura sauce, or you can opt for crab cakes, shrimp à la Provençal, or sushi-quality yellowfin tuna glazed with a teriyaki sauce. Lighter fare is available outside at **Flipper's Dockside Patio Grill,** a tropical-style bar by the river.

ANNA MARIA ISLAND
Super-Cheap Eats

✪ **Gulf Drive Café.** 900 Gulf Dr. N. (at 9th St.), Bradenton Beach. ☎ **941/778-1919.** Reservations not accepted. Breakfast $2.25–$5.25; sandwiches and burgers $4–$5.25; main courses $6–$11. DISC, MC, V. Daily 7am–9:30pm. SEAFOOD.

Locals flock to this bright gulf-side cafe for the best bargains on the beach. With big windows, bentwood cafe chairs with colorful cushions, and lots of hanging plants and ceiling fans, the coral and green dining room opens to a beach-side patio with tables shaded by a trellis. The breakfast fare is led by sweet Belgian waffles, which are available all day. You can also order salads, sandwiches, and burgers anytime here, with quiche du jour, Mediterranean seafood pasta, and regular seafood platters joining the show at 4pm.

For a Few Bucks More

The Beachhouse. 200 Gulf Dr. N. (at Cortez Rd.), Bradenton Beach. ☎ **941/779-2222.** Reservations not accepted on patio, but call for preferred seating inside. Sandwiches $6.50–$9; main courses $10–$19. AE, DC, DISC, MC, V. Daily 11:30am–10:30pm. AMERICAN.

This large, lively place sits right on Bradenton Beach with a huge open deck and a covered pavilion facing out to the gulf. Even inside, wide windows let in the view. Owned by Ed Chiles, son of the current Florida governor, the Beachhouse offers daily fresh fish specials, including the signature beechnut grouper (with nutty crust in citrus-butter sauce). There's also a good variety of fare, including seafood salads and pastas, crab cakes, fish-and-chips, and broiled steaks. Local musicians play out on the patio most afternoons and evenings.

Rotten Ralph's. 902 S. Bay Blvd., Anna Maria. ☎ **941/778-3953.** Reservations not accepted. Sandwiches and burgers $4–$8; main courses $11–$17. DC, DISC, MC, V. Daily 11am–9pm. From Gulf Dr., turn toward the bay on Pine Ave., then right at a dead end to the end of Bay Blvd. SEAFOOD.

On the north end of the island overlooking Bimini Bay, this casual Old Florida–style restaurant has both indoor and outdoor seating. The menu offers many seafood choices from scallops and shrimp to crab cakes, snow crab, oysters, and grouper. Other choices include Danish baby back ribs and Anna Maria chicken (marinated and grilled with a honey-mustard sauce).

✪ **Sandbar.** 100 Spring Ave. (east of Gulf Dr.), Anna Maria. ☎ **941/778-0444.** Reservations not accepted on deck; call for preferred seating in the main restaurant. Snacks $6–$9; main courses $12–$18. AE, DC, DISC, MC, V. Dining room daily 11:30am–3pm and 4–10pm; deck daily 11:30am–10pm. SEAFOOD.

Sitting on the site of the former Pavilion, built in 1913 when people from Tampa and St. Pete took the ferry here, this popular restaurant is perched right on the beach overlooking the gulf. The air-conditioned, knotty-pine dining room offers several preparations of seafood (stuffed grouper, crab cakes over a roasted pepper sauce, fried shrimp) as well as steaks and chicken. But the real action here is under the umbrellas on the lively beachside deck, where a menu of sandwiches, salads, and a few platters is served all day and night. Live music makes a party on the deck Monday to Friday nights and on Saturday and Sunday from 1 to 10pm. The inside bar is one of the few I've seen in Florida with no sports TVs.

Seafood Shack. 4110 127th St. W. (east end of Cortez Bridge), Cortez. ☎ **941/794-1235.** Reservations not accepted. Main courses $10–$24. AE, DISC, MC, V. Sun–Thurs 11:30am–9pm, Fri–Sat 11:30am–10pm. Cross Cortez Bridge (Fla. 684) and take first left. SEAFOOD.

A tradition since 1972, this large, informal seafood restaurant sits on the Cortez village waterfront, on the mainland but close enough to Anna Maria Island to be a popular beach dining spot. The menu offers many different seafood combinations and at least six different shrimp dishes (from scampi to stuffed), but the "Shack specialty" is sautéed frogs' legs. Downstairs, the publike **Marina Grill** offers snacks, burgers, fried seafood baskets, and main courses for less than $10.

The cruising paddlewheeler *Seafood Shack Showboat* is docked beside the restaurant (see "Great Golf That Won't Break Your Budget & Other Affordable Outdoor Activities," above). Cruise tickets get you dinner discounts in the restaurant.

Worth a Splurge

✪ **Beach Bistro.** 6600 Gulf Dr. N. (at 66th St.), Holmes Beach. ☎ **941/778-6444.** Reservations recommended. Main courses $19–$29. AE, DC, DISC, MC, V. Daily 5:30–10pm. INTERNATIONAL.

Winner of a Golden Spoon award as one of Florida's 20 best restaurants, this small, 12-table culinary oasis is Anna Maria Island's top place for fine dining. It sits right beside the beach, offering wide-windowed views of the gulf waters. A romantic ambience and overall elegance is enhanced by crisp linens, sparkling crystal, and fresh flowers on every table. Check out the nightly specials, such as Bistro bouillabaisse made with premium fish, shrimp, scallops, and squid. Regular offerings include grouper Picasso finished with fresh fruits and berries.

LONGBOAT KEY

✪ **Moore's Stone Crab.** 800 Broadway (at Bay-side Dr). ☎ **941/383-1748.** Reservations not accepted. Sandwiches and salads $6–$10; main courses $10–$22. DISC, MC, V. Winter daily 11:30am–9:30pm. Off-season Mon–Fri 5–10pm, Sat–Sun 11:30am–10pm. SEAFOOD.

In Longbeach, the old fishing village on the north end of Longboat Key, this popular bay-front restaurant began in 1967 as an offshoot of a family seafood business established 40 years earlier. From the outside, in fact, it still looks a little like a packing house, but the view of the bay dotted with mangrove islands makes a fine complement to stone crabs fresh from the family's own traps from October to March. Otherwise, the menu offers every imaginable seafood, most of it fried or broiled. Sandwiches and salads are served all day.

BRADENTON AFTER DARK

Locals and visitors alike head south to neighboring Sarasota for their culture (see "Sarasota After Dark" in section 5). Meantime, the action here is at beach restaurants and pubs.

Live bands lend a party atmosphere to the gulf-side deck at the **Sandbar** restaurant every night and from 1pm on weekends (see "Great Deals on Dining," above). The elegant **Cafe Robar,** at the corner of Gulf Drive and Pine Avenue in Anna Maria (☎ **941/778-6969**), offers piano music and a sing-along bar on Tuesday to Sunday evenings. **D. Coy Ducks Bar & Grille,** in the Island Shopping Center at Marina Drive and 54th Street in Holmes Beach (☎ **941/778-5888**), has a varied program of live Dixieland bands, jazz pianists, and guitarists.

12 Walt Disney World & Orlando

by Mary Meehan

Flying over 43 square miles of scrub brush and swampland just south of a sleepy Southern town, Walt Disney saw what he needed to make a whole new world. Orlando, where the biggest tourist draw up until then had been a downtown fountain, would never be the same. As the millennium approaches, it seems at least one full-scale theme park is opening every year, and visitors have never had more options.

Walt's world now claims four distinct parks, two entertainment districts, enough hotels to house a small city and several such smaller attractions as water parks and putt-putt courses. Universal Studios Florida is rapidly expanding, adding a nighttime entertainment destination, CityWalk, in 1998. A second park, Islands of Adventure, opens in 1999. Universal, The Sequel, showcases stomach-churning thrill rides and many attractions with Baby Boomer appeal, like Cat in the Hat and Spider Man. The one-two punch of both parks could give The Mouse some serious competition.

Sea World is also growing, albeit at a slower pace; a major renovation in 1997 updated its 1970s look. Sea World has also added its most expensive attraction yet, a roller coaster called Journey to Atlantis.

And as if that wasn't enough competition, after years of cowering to "The Mouse," Universal and other non-Disney attractions have banded together to offer special packages and discounts. These "Flex Passes" offer visitors the choice of several parks for one flat price and is a direct assault on Disney's multiday pass system. (See "Coupons, Passes & Other Tips for Saving Your Orlan-dough," below).

Of course, Disney, too, is going about its ever-expanding business, having entered the cruise market and opening yet another theme park, Animal Kingdom.

The bottom line is, with so many tourist attractions vying for your time, and a hypercommercial atmosphere that could burn a serious hole in your wallet, advance planning is a must. Coming to Orlando, it's easy to get overwhelmed by the urge to do everything in the (Disney) world and then some. But, to borrow a phrase from my New York in-laws, *fugedaboudit*. As your guide, I'm telling your right now: The typical 2-week stay isn't long enough to hit everything.

But hey, don't panic. I've done it all so you won't have to. I've inspected every restaurant, every hotel, every inch of every park. If I do my job, and you do a little preplanning, you'll be able to actually relax enough so that you won't need an extra few days off to recover from your vacation.

PACKAGE TOURS

Frankly, the number and diversity of package tours to Orlando are staggering. But significant savings are available for those willing to do the research. Best bet: stop at a sizable travel agency and pick up brochures from several companies. Pore over them at home, comparing offerings to find the optimum package for your trip. Also obtain the Walt Disney World Vacations brochure (☎ **407/934-7639**), which lists the company's own packages. Try to find a package that meets rather than exceeds your needs; there's no sense in paying for elements you won't use.

Since 1996, Universal Studios has offered its own packages through **Universal City Travel Company** (☎ **800/224-3838**). These packages highlight Universal Studios and offer special VIP access to the park-and-rides, and discounts to other parks. Universal City Travel also offers trips that include stays at beach hotels before or after the theme-park trips. These excursions are billed as "an alternative resort experience."

American Express Vacations (☎ **800/241-1700**) is also officially authorized to use Disney resorts in its packages. Additional airline package sources include **American Airlines' Fly Away Vacations** (☎ **800/32l-2l2l**), **Continental Vacations** (☎ **800/634-5555**), and **USAir Vacations** (☎ **800/455-0123**). Most **hotels** listed below also offer packages; inquire when you call. Also check with your **travel agent.**

1 Orientation

WHEN SHOULD I GO?

Orlando's busiest seasons are whenever kids are out of school—summer (early June to about August 20), holiday weekends, Christmas season (mid-December to mid-January), and Easter. Obviously, the whole experience is more enjoyable when the crowds are thinnest and the weather most temperate. The best times to go are from the week after Labor Day until Thanksgiving, from the week after Thanksgiving until mid-December, and the 6 weeks before and after school spring vacations. The worst time is summer, when the crowds are large and the weather is hot and humid. Because of a large influx of international visitors, Orlando doesn't have a traditional high and low season.

ARRIVING

BY PLANE As I mentioned, the **Orlando International Airport,** which handles more than 26 million passengers a year, is in the midst of a billion-dollar expansion project. With more terminals being added, you'll soon have even more options for flying. **Delta** (☎ 800/221-1212) has the most flights, more than 25%, into Orlando International Airport. It offers service from 200 cities and has a Fantastic Flyer program for kids. Delta Express offers direct service from 14 cities and also has the Fantastic Flyer program for kids. Other carriers include **Air Jamaica** (☎ 800/523-5585), **America West** (☎ 800/235-9292), **American** (☎ 800/433-7300), **American Trans Air** (☎ 800/293-6194), **British Airways** (☎ 800/247-9297), **Canadian Airlines** (☎ 800/426-3838), **Continental** (☎ 800/231-0856), **Midway** (☎ 800/446-4392), **Northwest** (☎ 800/225-2525), **Southwest** (☎ 800/435-9792), **SunJet** (☎ 800/4-SUNJET), **Transbrasil** (☎ 800/872-3153), **TWA** (☎ 800/221-2000), **United** (☎ 800/241-6522), **US Airways** (☎ 800/428-4322), and **Virgin Atlantic** (☎ 800/862-8621).

The airport is 25 miles from Walt Disney World (WDW). **Mears Transportation Group** (☎ 407/423-5566) shuttle vans ply the route from the airport (board outside baggage claim) to all Disney resorts and "official" hotels as well as most other area hostelries. Their comfortable, air-conditioned vehicles operate around the clock, departing every 15 to 25 minutes in either direction. Rates vary with your destination. The round-trip cost for adults is $21 between the airport and downtown Orlando or International Drive, $25 for Walt Disney World/Lake Buena Vista or Kissimmee/ U.S. 192. Children 4 to 11 are charged $14 for the Orlando route and $17 for the Walt Disney World route; children 3 and under ride free.

BY CAR   Orlando is 436 miles from Atlanta, 1,312 miles from Boston, 1,120 miles from Chicago, 1,170 miles from Dallas, 1,105 miles from New York City, and 230 miles from Miami. All major car-rental companies are located at or near the airport.

From northern points, take I-75 south to the Florida Turnpike to I-4, which runs right through the city. If you're taking I-95 south, you'll intersect with I-4 near Daytona Beach.

American Automobile Association (AAA) (☎ 800/336-4357) and some other automobile club members can call local offices for maps and optimum driving directions.

BY TRAIN   **Amtrak** trains (☎ 800/872-7245) pull into stations at 1400 Sligh Blvd., between Columbia and Miller streets in downtown Orlando (about 23 miles from Walt Disney World), and 111 Dakin Ave., at Thurman Street in Kissimmee (about 15 miles from Walt Disney World). There is also a stop in Winter Park, about 10 miles north of downtown Orlando, at 150 W. Morse Blvd. and in Sanford, about 23 miles northeast of downtown Orlando. The Sanford station, located at 600 Persimmon Ave., is also the end terminal for the Auto Train.

For details about bus transportation from the Orlando Amtrak station, call ☎ 407/841-8240. A taxi from the downtown Orlando Amtrak station to Walt Disney World–area hotels is about $42.

There may be some restrictions on travel dates for discounted fares, mostly around very busy holiday times. Amtrak (☎ 800/321-8684) also offers money-saving packages with your train fare, including hotel accommodations (some at WDW resorts), car rentals, tours, and more. Zoned fares, available for 45 days to U.S. residents, range from about $400 during peak season (January through May and July through mid-September) to about $320 during off-peak season (June and mid-September through December).

Amtrak's **Auto Train** offers the convenience of having a car in Florida without driving it there. The Auto Train begins in Lorton, Virginia, in the afternoon and ends up at Sanford, Florida (about 23 miles northeast of Orlando), the next morning. Reserve early for the lowest fares. Call ☎ 800/USA-RAIL for details.

BY BUS   **Greyhound** buses (☎ 800/231-2222) connect the entire country with Orlando. They pull into terminals at 555 N. Magruder Blvd., a few miles west of downtown Orlando (☎ 407/292-3422), and 16 N. Orlando Ave. in Kissimmee, about 14 miles from Walt Disney World (☎ 407/847-3911). There is van transport from the Kissimmee terminal to most area hotels and motels. From Orlando, you can call a **Mears shuttle van** (☎ 407/423-5566), which will cost $12 to $13 one way to a Disney-area hotel, $8 for children 4 to 11, free for children 3 and under (round-trip fares are less). For the return trip, call from your hotel 24 hours in advance. A **taxi** to Disney-area hotels will cost about $40. Greyhound's fare structure tends to be complex, but the good news is that when you call to make a reservation, the agent will always give you the lowest-fare options. Once again, advance-purchase fares booked 3 to 21 days before travel represent vast savings.

The Orlando Area/Walt Disney World Orientation

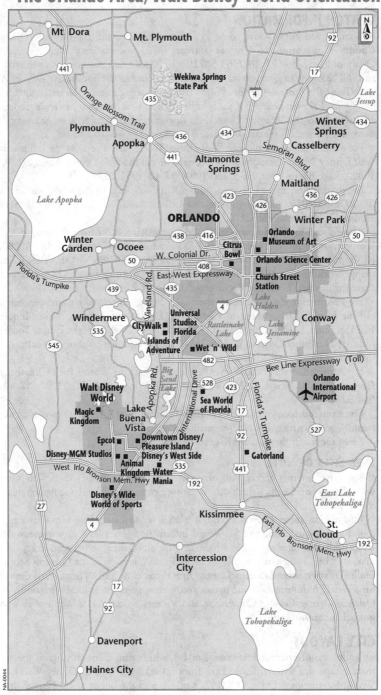

VISITOR INFORMATION

As soon as you know you're going to Orlando, write or call the **Orlando/Orange County Convention & Visitors Bureau,** 8723 International Dr., Suite 101, Orlando, FL 32819 (☎ **407/363-5871**). The bureau can answer all your questions and will be happy to send you maps, brochures (including the informative *Official Visitors Guide,* the *African-American Visitors Guide,* the area guide to local restaurants, and the *Official Accommodations Guide*). The packet, which should arrive in about 3 weeks, includes the "Magicard," good for discounts of 10% to 50% on accommodations, attractions, car rentals, and more.

For general information about Walt Disney World, and a copy of the informative Walt Disney World Vacations brochure, write or call the Walt Disney World Co., Box 10000, Lake Buena Vista, FL 32830-1000 (☎ **407/934-7639**).

For information about Universal Studios, CityWalk, and Islands of Adventure, call ☎ **407/393-8080.** You can also write to Universal Studios Florida, 1000 Universal Studios Dr., Orlando, FL 32816.

Also contact the **Kissimmee–St. Cloud Convention & Visitors Bureau,** 1925 E. Irlo Bronson Memorial Hwy. (U.S. 192), Kissimmee, FL 34744, or P.O. Box 422007, Kissimmee, FL 34742-2007 (☎ **800/327-9159** or 407/847-5000). They'll send maps, brochures, discount coupon books, and the *Kissimmee–St. Cloud Vacation Guide,* which details the area's accommodations and attractions.

For information about the entire state, including Orlando and Kissimmee, write or call the **Florida Department of Commerce,** Division of Tourism, Visitor Inquiry, 126 Van Buren St., Tallahassee, FL 32399-2000. You can also call the Florida Tourism Industry Marketing Corp. at ☎ **888/735-2872** for information about the entire state including Orlando and Kissimmee.

For information about the Winter Park area, contact the **Winter Park Chamber of Commerce,** 150 New York Ave., P.O. Box 280, Winter Park, FL 32790 (☎ **407/644-8281**).

Once you touch down in town, **Orlando International Airport** is thoroughly user-friendly, with centrally located information kiosks.

All of the major theme parks have stores in the airport.

WEB SITES OF NOTE

If you have Internet access, you can visit Walt Disney World's own Web site at **www.disneyworld.com,** which has extensive, entertaining, and regularly updated information.

Information about Universal Studios Islands of Adventure and CityWalk can be found at **www.usf.com,** and Sea World information is available at **www.seaworld. com.** Both sites offer maps and a basic description of rides, shows, and ticket information. The city newspaper, *The Orlando Sentinel,* also produces Orlando Sentinel Online at **www.orlandosentinel.com.** Once there, click into "Theme Park Central" for a variety of information and updates on what is going on at local attractions. The Orlando/Orange County Convention and Visitors Bureau has a Web site at **www. goflorida.com/orlando.**

CITY LAYOUT

Orlando's major artery is Interstate 4 or I-4, which runs diagonally across the state from Tampa to Daytona Beach. Exits from I-4 take you to Walt Disney World, Sea World, International Drive, U.S. 192, Kissimmee, Lake Buena Vista, Church Street Station, downtown Orlando, and Winter Park. The Florida Turnpike crosses I-4 and links up with I-75 to the north. U.S. 192, a major east-west artery, stretches from Kissimmee (along a major motel strip) to U.S. 27, crossing I-4 near the Walt Disney

World entrance road. Farther north, a toll road called the Beeline Expressway (Fla. 528) goes east from I-4 past Orlando International Airport to Cape Canaveral.

Walt Disney World property is bounded roughly by I-4 and Fla. 535 to the east (the latter also north), World Drive (the entrance road) to the west, and U.S. 192 to the south. Epcot Center Drive (Fla. 536, the south end of International Drive) and Buena Vista Drive cut across the complex in a more or less east-west direction; the two roads cross at Bonnet Creek Parkway. Excellent highways and explicit signs make it very easy to find your way around.

Note: The Disney parks are actually much closer to Kissimmee than to downtown Orlando.

NEIGHBORHOODS IN BRIEF

Walt Disney World (WDW)   A city unto itself, Walt Disney World (WDW) sprawls over more than 26,000 acres containing theme parks, resorts, hotels, shops, restaurants, and recreational facilities galore. *Downtown Disney* was a term coined in 1997 to put the shopping at Disney's Village Marketplace and the clubs and restaurants at Pleasure Island and Disney's West Side under one name.

Lake Buena Vista   This area centers on a hotel village/marketplace owned and operated by Walt Disney World on the eastern edge of Disney property that since 1997 has been tagged Downtown Disney. However, while Disney owns all the real estate, many of the hotels, and some shops and restaurants here, are independently owned. Lake Buena Vista is a charming area of manicured lawns and verdant thoroughfares with traffic islands shaded by towering oak trees. The lovely scenery is kind of hard to see over the tour buses, however. This is a very busy part of town so expect long waits at restaurants during peak season. (The Rainforest Cafe, for example, has had waits of 4 hours!)

Celebration   Imagine living in a Disney world. Disney tries to re-create its squeaky-clean, completely controlled magic in this town, the first residential area ever to receive the special Disney touch. Located on 4,900 acres in northwest Osceola County, Celebration will eventually have about 8,000 residents living in Disney-designed homes and attending a Disney-run school. The average sale price of a home is over $240,000, with some reportedly selling for up to $900,000. Celebration's downtown is, however, designed for the tourist trade, being architecturally interesting with some first-rate shops and restaurants.

Kissimmee   South of the Disney parks, Kissimmee centers on U.S. 192/Irlo Bronson Memorial Highway, a somewhat tacky strip, as archetypal of American cities as Main Street. U.S. 192 is lined with budget motels, lesser attractions like Gatorland, and every fast-food restaurant you can name. Kissimmee is still, in many ways, true to its cowboy routes and there are some wide open spaces to explore if you are in the mood for a ride in the country.

International Drive (Fla. 536)   Can you say *tourist mecca?* This area extends 7 to 10 miles north of the Disney parks between Fla. 535 and the Florida Turnpike. From bungee jumping to ice-skating and dozens of theme restaurants and T-shirt shops, this is the tourist strip in Central Florida. It contains numerous hotels, restaurants, shopping centers, and the Orange County Convention Center, and it offers easy access to Sea World and Universal Studios. The place is already packed but, somehow, developers manage year after year to find space for just one more attraction.

Note: Locally, this road is always referred to as I-Drive.

Downtown Orlando   No, Downtown Disney is not *really* Downtown. To get to the real thing you have to travel on I-4 East, reaching a burgeoning Sunbelt metropolis that is 17 miles northeast of Walt Disney World. It includes the entertainment/ shopping complex Church Street Station and the Orlando Science Center, a recently completed multimillion-dollar complex, which is the largest in the Southeast. Hundreds of clubs, shops, and restaurants are located in the heart of the city, one of the fastest growing in the country. Dozens of antique shops line "Antique Row" on Orange Avenue near Lake Ivanhoe. The free downtown bus system, called Lymmo, makes it easy to park in one place and travel throughout downtown, including the Orlando Arena and Bob Carr Centre for the Performing Arts. Art exhibits at both City Hall and the courthouse reflect the diverse work of Florida artists.

Winter Park   Just north of downtown Orlando, Winter Park is the place many of Central Florida's old-money families call home. As the name implies, it began as a haven for Yankees traveling away from the cold. Today, it's home to Park Avenue, a collection of upscale shops and restaurants along an original cobblestoned street that is frequented by local "ladies who lunch." With the main attractions being shopping, dining, and several small museums, Winter Park is definitely a grown-up diversion.

GETTING AROUND

BY CAR   Though you can get to and around Walt Disney World and other major attractions without a car, it's always handy to have one. All major companies are represented in Orlando and maintain desks at the airport. I was quoted the lowest rates by **Value Rent-A-Car** (☎ 800/GO-VALUE), which also offered excellent service and 24-hour pick up and return. Some other handy phone numbers: **Alamo** (☎ 800/ 327-9633), **Avis** (☎ 800/331-1212), **Budget** (☎ 800/527-0700), **Dollar** (☎ 800/ 800-4000), **Hertz** (☎ 800/654-3131), and **Thrifty** (☎ 800/367-2277).

BY BUS   Disney shuttle buses serve all Disney resorts and "official" hotels, offering unlimited complimentary transportation via bus, monorail, ferry, and/or water taxi to all four parks from 2 hours before opening until 2 hours after closing; they also go to Disney Village Marketplace, Typhoon Lagoon, Pleasure Island, Fort Wilderness, and other Disney resorts. Disney hostelries offer transportation to other area attractions as well, though it's not complimentary. Almost all area hotels and motels also offer transportation to WDW; some are free. The going rate when you pay is $10 to $14 a day, which means if you are traveling with your family you could easily rent a car for the same price.

When deciding whether to rent a car, consider your needs. You can get around the WDW properties on the Disney transportation. It can take a great deal of time, especially if you are staying at the lower-priced resorts, which are farther from the theme parks. Also keep in mind if you are planning to explore the rest of the Orlando area.

The **Mears Transportation Group** (☎ 407/423-5566) operates buses to all major attractions, including Cypress Gardens, Kennedy Space Center, Universal Studios Florida, Sea World, Busch Gardens (in Tampa), and Church Street Station, among others. Call for details.

BY TAXI   Taxis line up in front of major hotels, and at smaller hostelries the front desk will be happy to call you a cab. Or call **Yellow Cab** (☎ 407/699-9999). The charge is $2.75 for the first mile, $1.50 per mile thereafter.

FAST FACTS: Walt Disney World & Orlando

Babysitters   Most Orlando hotels offer babysitting services. If yours doesn't, call **KinderCare** (☎ 407/827-5444); 24-hour advance notice is required.

Convention Center   The **Orange County Convention/Civic Center** is located at 9800 International Dr. (☎ **407/345-9800**).

Doctors & Dentists   There are basic first-aid centers in all the major parks. Tourists have encountered ill-trained doctors making calls in hotels. You can get a reputable referral from **Ask-A-Nurse,** a free service operated by a local hospital chain. In **Kissimmee** call ☎ **407/870-1700;** in **Orlando** call ☎ **407/897-1700.**

Walk-in medical clinics are available, with a visit usually costing under $50. Prescriptions are extra. **Centra-Care,** operated by locally run Florida Hospital, is a reputable medical facility with more than a dozen locations throughout the Orlando area. Several walk-in clinics have popped up in recent years. Not all are created equal. Opt for Centra-Care. For information, and the nearest location, call ☎ **407/660-8118.**

To find a dentist, call **Dental Referral Service** (☎ **800/917-6453**). They can tell you the nearest dentist who meets your needs. Operators are on duty from 5:30am to 6pm daily. Check the yellow pages for 24-hour emergency services.

Emergencies   Dial ☎ **911** to contact the police or fire department or to call an ambulance.

Hospitals   **Sand Lake Hospital,** 9400 Turkey Lake Rd., is about 2 miles south of Sand Lake Road (☎ **407/351-8550**). From the WDW area, take I-4 east to Exit 29, turn left at the exit onto Sand Lake Road, and make a left on Turkey Lake Road. The hospital is 2 miles up on your right.

Kennels   All the major theme parks offer animal-boarding facilities at reasonable fees. At Walt Disney World, there are kennels at Fort Wilderness, Epcot, the Magic Kingdom, and Disney–MGM Studios.

Lost Children   Every theme park has a designated spot for parents to meet up with lost children. Find out where it is when you enter any park. Show your children what uniformed park personnel look like and tell them to someone dressed in that way if they get lost. Young children should have name tags.

Pharmacies (Late-Night)   **Walgreens Drug Store,** 1003 W. Vine St. (U.S. 192), just east of Bermuda Avenue (☎ **407/847-5252**), operates a 24-hour pharmacy. There is an **Eckherd's Drug Store** at 7324 International Dr. (☎ **407/345-0491** open 24-hours a day. There is also a 24-hour Eckherd's store at 1306 Bermuda Ave. (☎ 407/847-5174). Many K-mart stores also have pharmacies. All should carry generic brands, so don't forget to ask.

Photography   Two-hour film processing is available at all major theme parks—look for the photo express sign. Local store chains, such as Eckherd's and Walgreens, offer film developing, usually available for pickup the next day. There are often half-off coupons printed in fliers available in these stores. Some offer deals where you don't pay for prints you don't want, which can save considerable money if you are taking a lot of pictures. (And who doesn't on vacation?) You can also buy film and rent or buy 35mm, disc, and video cameras in most parks. As with everything else, prices go up when you are in the theme parks. It's better to purchase these items ahead of time. Buying a multi-pack of film before you come, usually available buy three rolls get one free, is a good idea.

Caution: If you're flying, put your film in the tray to bypass X-ray machines to avoid damage. Keeping film in the trunk of the car, especially in the Florida heat, can ruin your pictures.

Taxes The hotel tax in both Orlando and Kissimmee is 11%, which includes the 6% state sales tax that's charged on all goods except most grocery store items and medicines.

Tourist Information See "Visitor Information" under "Orientation," earlier in this chapter.

Weather Call ☎ 407/851-7510 for a recorded weather forecast.

2 Accommodations You Can Afford, in & Around the Parks

It's important to reserve as far in advance as possible—the minute you've decided on the dates of your trip. The average hotel rate for the Orlando metro area is about $81, and increasing at about 10% a year. Overall room rates are lowest in July, August, and September; they're highest in January, February and March. And remember to factor in the 11% hotel tax.

HOW TO SAVE MONEY BY STAYING WITH MICKEY Many people assume that motels outside the Disney parks will cost you less than staying on WDW premises, where the lowest basic rate is $74 to $89 and the most expensive suite can run thousands of dollars a night.

But don't forget that if you don't have a car, you'll need to add the cost (as high as $14 per person per day) of hotel shuttle buses to and from Walt Disney World parks to your expenses. In recent years even some of the low- to moderate-priced hotels have started offering free shuttle service. Disney-owned hostelries and "official" hotels offer complimentary transportation to and from WDW parks. In general, however, the lower the room rate, the farther away from the theme parks and the longer it takes to travel. You will have to weigh time against cost to determine whether to rent a car.

In or out of Walt Disney World, if you book your hotel as part of a package (details below) you'll likely enjoy big savings. Ask about special discounts for students, government employees, senior citizens, military, AAA, and/or corporate clients.

There are 15 Disney-owned properties (hotels, resorts, villas, wilderness homes, and campsites) and nine privately owned "official" hotels. All of those within our price range are described below. In addition to their proximity to the parks, there are a number of advantages to staying at a Disney property or "official" hotel. Even the budget choices offer extensive resort facilities, not to mention accommodations and landscaping more typically found at luxury properties. At all Disney resorts and official hotels, benefits include:

- **Unlimited complimentary transportation** via bus, monorail, ferry, and/or water taxi to/from all four parks from 2 hours before opening until 2 hours after closing. Unlimited complimentary transport is also provided to/from Disney Village Marketplace, Typhoon Lagoon, Pleasure Island, Fort Wilderness, and other Disney resorts. This free transport can not only save money, but also means you're guaranteed admission to all parks, even during peak times when the parking lots sometimes fill up.
- **Free parking** at WDW parking lots (other visitors pay $6 a day).
- **Reduced-price children's menus** in almost all restaurants, and character breakfasts and/or dinners at most resorts.
- A **guest services desk** where you can purchase tickets to all WDW theme parks and attractions and obtain general information.

- **Use of**—and in some cases, complimentary transport to—the **Disney-owned golf courses** and preferred tee times at them (these can be booked up to 30 days in advance).
- "Surprise Mornings" where select **rides are open early** to resort guests.
- Access to most recreational facilities at other Disney resorts.
- Service by the **Mears airport shuttle.**

Additional perks at Disney-owned hotels, resorts, villas, and campgrounds (but not at "official" hotels) charge privileges throughout Walt Disney World; early admission to Epcot and Disney–MGM Studios on specific days; and dining and show reservations (including Epcot restaurants) can be made through the hotel.

Walt Disney World Central Reservations Office   To reserve a room at Disney hotels, resorts, and villas, "official" hotels, and Fort Wilderness homes and campsites, contact **Central Reservations Operations (CRO),** P.O. Box 10100, Lake Buena Vista, FL 32830-0100 (☎ **407/W-DISNEY [934-7639]**), open Monday to Friday from 8am to 10pm and on Saturday and Sunday from 9am to 6pm. Have your dates and credit or charge card ready when you call. WDW doesn't have an 800 number. If you have an on-line service, or if your local library has Internet access, it may save you money to surf the Web site yourself to check out room rates and options before going through the whole operation on your dime. Click on **resorts & spas,** not resort reservations, at **www.disneyworld.com** to explore options. (Click on **resort reservations** to actually make reservations.)

The CRO can recommend accommodations that will suit your specific needs as to price, location, and facilities. It can also give you information about various park ticket options and reservations for you at dinner shows and character breakfasts.

When you call the CRO, be sure to inquire about the numerous package plans, which include meals, tickets, recreation, and other features. The right package can save you both money and time, and is helpful in computing the cost of your vacation in advance. Be sure to ask if any special discounts are being offered at the time of your trip.

THE DISNEY RESORTS

The latest "All-Star" resort set to open is the **All-Star Movie Resort.** Scheduled to open in 1999, the decor will be dominated by giant images from *101 Dalmatians, Toy Story,* and *Fantasia,* along with other Disney classics. And, from the people who brought you a snow-themed water park, a hockey-rink themed swimming pool.

SUPER-CHEAP SLEEPS

Disney's All-Star Music Resort. 1801 W. Buena Vista Dr. (at World Dr. and Osceola Pkwy.; P.O. Box 10000), Lake Buena Vista, FL 32830-1000. ☎ **407/W-DISNEY** (934-7639) or 407/ 939-6000. Fax 407/354-1866. 1,920 units. A/C TV TEL. $74–$89 double. Children 17 and under stay free in parents' room. AE, MC, V. Free parking.

Though the unbeatable combination of rock-bottom rates and extensive facilities at Disney's All-Star Music and Sports resorts (see below) is very attractive to families, there is one caveat: The rooms are small (a mere 260 square feet). They're ideal for single adults or couples traveling with one child; larger families had best be into togetherness. Set amid pristine pine forests, this Disney hostelry is part of a 246-acre complex that also includes the adjacent All-Star Sports Resort (see below). Its 10 buildings are musically themed around country, jazz, rock, calypso, and Broadway show tunes. The calypso building, for instance, has a palm-fringed roof frieze and balconies adorned with tropical birds and musical notes, while a convoy of 18-wheelers travels around the country building, which comes adorned with fiddles and banjos. Oversize

Walt Disney World Attractions & Accommodations

MAGIC KINGDOM RESORT AREA
Disney's Contemporary Resort
Disney's Fort Wilderness
Resort & Campground
Disney's Grand Floridian Beach Resort
Disney's Polynesian Resort
Disney's Wilderness Lodge

EPCOT RESORT AREA
Disney's All-Star Music Resort
Disney's All-Star Sports Resort
Disney's Beach Club Resort
Disney's BoardWalk
Disney's Caribbean Beach Resort

DOWNTOWN DISNEY RESORT AREA
Disney Institute Villas
Disney's Dixie Landings Resort
Disney's Port Orleans Resort
Doubletree Guest Suites Resort
Courtyard by Marriott

DISNEY'S
ANIMAL KINGDOM

Disney's Coronado Springs Resort

Disney's All-Star Sports Resort

Disney's All-Star Music Resort

DISNEY'S BLIZZARD BEACH

WALT DISNEY WORLD INTERNATIONAL SPORTS COMPLEX

Walt Disney World Dolphin
Walt Disney World Swan
DISNEY'S FANTASIA GARDENS MINIATURE GOLF

Disney's Yacht Club Resort
Disney's Beach Club Resort

Epcot Main Entrance / Toll Plaza

Epcot Parking
Bus Transportation

EPCOT

Disney's BoardWalk
Exxon Gas Station

Disney's Caribbean Beach Resort

DISNEY-MGM STUDIOS
Studio Main Entrance / Toll Plaza

Guest Parking
Handicap Parking
Bus Transportation

West Buena Vista Dr.

World Dr.

Osceola Pkwy.

Reedy Creek

Sea Breeze Dr.

Cayman Way

Bonnet Creek

Buena Vista Dr.

Epcot Center Dr.

Epcot Resort Blvd.

Bonnet Creek Pkwy.

Orleans Resort

Orleans Dr.

Community Dr.

Disney's Old Key West Resort

DISNEY'S INSTITUTE & VILLAS AT THE DISNEY INSTITUTE

Oak Ln.

LAKE BUENA VISTA GOLF CLUB

DISNEY'S WEST SIDE
DISNEY'S TYPHOON LAGOON

DISNEY VILLAGE MARKETPLACE
PLEASURE ISLAND
AMC THEATRES
Planet Hollywood

Team Disney

Exxon Gas Station

Buena Vista Dr.

Casting Center

SunTrust Building

The Hilton
Grosvenor Resort

Buena Vista Palace
Travelodge Hotel

Doubletree Guest Suites Resort

Hotel Royal Plaza
Courtyard Marriott

Black Lake

Hotel Plaza Blvd.

Vista

Exit 27
← I-4 to Orlando

535

To Kissimmee

536

To Orlando Int'l Airport →

Exit 26B
To: EPCOT
DOWNTOWN DISNEY

4

Exit 25B
To:
MAGIC KINGDOM PARK
DISNEY-MGM STUDIOS
DISNEY'S FORT WILDERNESS RESORT & CAMPGROUND

I-4 to Tampa

192

U.S. 192 to Kissimmee →

CELEBRATION

↖ U.S. 192 to U.S. 27

192

471

Plan Ahead: How to Enjoy the Parks Without Getting Fleeced

It's easy to get seduced by the ever-happy goodwill of these fantasylands—and pretty soon you start to think that paying 15 bucks for a hamburger actually *makes sense*. But by keeping a level head, doing a little advance planning, and following these simple tips, you can maximize your park experience without the usual wallet drain.

1. **Bring a cooler,** or if you're flying, invest in an inexpensive disposable cooler once you arrive. Grocery stores and discount drug stores tend to be a little more expensive in tourist areas, but whatever you buy will still be cheaper than anything in the parks. Fill it with snacks, lunch basics, sodas, bottled water and other drinks, and you will save you a bundle in the long run.

2. Before traveling to Orlando, **buy inexpensive rain ponchos** for the entire family. All major parks include water rides and believe me, it is *miserable* to walk around wet all day, even in the summer. They will also come in handy during summer storms, which can arrive quickly and violently. Something you can buy at home for $3 will cost $6 in the parks.

3. **Pack for the park.** As a frequent (and thrifty) theme-park visitor, I've learned how to easily make it through the whole day on a slim budget. Get a refreezeable ice pack—you can freeze one in an ice bucket or cooler overnight. Wrap it is a washcloth and put it in a plastic bag to keep things dry. If Mom and Dad each carry a normal-sized backpack you can bring enough snacks, juice, water, and soda to allow you to splurge a little during your sit-down meal.

4. **Reconsider stroller rental.** This is one expenditure that can really add up—especially given that most of the time your buggy will be parked outside of rides and attractions, while you are inside. If you'd like forgo the rental cost, consider investing in an inexpensive model that is lightweight and easy to carry. You could always use a spare at home. But whatever you decide, *don't* bring your Cadillac of kiddie carriers; it could get stolen.

5. **Drink up.** Some Disney resorts offer "bottomless souvenir cups" that allow you unlimited drinks at the hotel food courts. It's worth the cost, especially if you consume a lot of coffee or soda.

icons in the public areas—such as 3-story cowboy boots or a walk-through jukebox—are lit by neon and fiber optics at night. The attractive rooms have musically themed bedspreads, paintings, and wallpaper borders. In-room safes are a plus. There's a cheerful food court with an adjoining bar. Among the amenities are room service (serves pizza only), babysitting, and a guest-services desk. Other features include two vast swimming pools, kiddie pool, playground, coin-op washers/dryers, large retail shop, car-rental desk, and video-game arcade.

Disney's All-Star Sports Resort. 1701 W. Buena Vista Dr. (at World Dr. and Osceola Pkwy.; P.O. Box 10000), Lake Buena Vista, FL 32830-1000. ☎ **407/W-DISNEY** (934-7639) or 407/939-5000. Fax 407/354-1866. 1,920 units. A/C TV TEL. $74–$89 single or double. Children 17 and under stay free in parents' room. AE, MC, V. Free parking.

Adjacent to and sharing facilities with the above-described All-Star Music Resort, this 82-acre hostelry is elaborately sports themed. The rooms are housed in buildings designed around football, baseball, basketball, tennis, and surfing motifs. For instance, the turquoise surf buildings have waves along their rooflines, surfboards mounted on the exterior walls, and pink fish swimming along the balcony railings.

The immense public-area icons include tennis ball–can stairways and 4-story football helmets and whistles. The cheerful rooms feature sports-action-motif bedspreads, paintings, and wallpaper borders; in-room safes are among your amenities. As noted above, however, the rooms here are small. There's a brightly decorated food court with an adjoining bar. Again, amenities include room service (pizza only), babysitting, and guest-services desk. There are also two vast outdoor swimming pools (one surfing themed with two 38-foot shark fins, the other shaped like a baseball diamond with an "outfield" sundeck), kiddie pool, playground, coin-op washers/dryers, shops, car-rental service, and video-game arcade.

FOR A FEW BUCKS MORE

Disney's Dixie Landings Resort. 1251 Dixie Dr. (off Bonnet Creek Pkwy.; P.O. Box 10000), Lake Buena Vista, FL 32830-1000. ☎ **407/W-DISNEY** (934-7639) or 407/934-6000. Fax 407/934-5777. 2,048 units. A/C TV TEL. $119–$154 room for up to 4. AE, MC, V. Free parking.

Low rates, extensive child-oriented facilities, and a food court make the Dixie Landings popular with families, even though the rooms are midsized and the bathrooms rather small. Adults traveling alone might prefer a more sedate setting since there are plenty of children. Nestled on the banks of the "mighty Sassagoula River" and dotted with bayous, it shares its 325-acre site with the Port Orleans Resort (described below). It includes Ol' Man Island, a woodsy 3½-acre recreation area containing an immense swimming pool with waterfalls cascading from a broken bridge and a water slide, a playground, children's wading pool, whirlpool, and fishin' hole (rent bait and poles and angle for catfish and bass). The accommodations areas, themed after the Louisiana countryside, are divided into "parishes," with rooms housed in stately colonnaded plantation homes or rural Cajun-style dwellings fronted by brick courtyards. **Boatwright's Dining Hall,** housed in a replica of an 1800s boat-building factory, serves American/Cajun fare at breakfast and dinner. The Cotton Co-op lounge airs Monday night football games and offers entertainment (singers and comedians) Tuesday to Saturday nights. A food court and pool bar round out the facilities.

Amenities include six large outdoor swimming pools (one with a water slide), a 1.7-mile riverfront jogging/biking path, Fulton's General Store, room service (pizza only), guest-services desk, babysitting, boat transport (to Port Orleans, Village Marketplace, and Pleasure Island on Disney's West Side), coin-op washers/dryers, video-game arcade, car-rental desk, and bicycle and boat rental.

Disney's Port Orleans Resort. 2201 Orleans Dr. (off Bonnet Creek Pkwy.; P.O. Box 10000), Lake Buena Vista, FL 32830-1000. ☎ **407/W-DISNEY** (934-7639) or 407/934-5000. Fax 407/934-5353. 1,008 units. A/C TV TEL. $95–$129 room for up to 4. AE, MC, V. Free parking.

This beautiful resort, themed after turn-of-the-century New Orleans, shares a site on the banks of the Sassagoula with Dixie Landings, described above. Its identical room rates and comparable facilities make it, too, a good bet for families. The midsized rooms, with small bathrooms, are housed in pastel buildings with shuttered windows and lacy wrought-iron balconies; they're fronted by lovely flower gardens opening onto fountained courtyards. Cherry-wood furnishings, swagged draperies, and walls hung with botanical prints make for pretty interiors. And the landscaping throughout the property is especially nice, with stately oaks, formal boxwood hedges, azaleas, and fragrant jasmine. **Bonfamille's Café** is open for breakfast and dinner, the latter featuring Creole specialties. **Scat Cat's Club,** a cocktail lounge off the lobby, airs Monday-night football and features family oriented live entertainment. A food court and pool bar round out the facilities. The larger-than-Olympic-size Doubloon Lagoon swimming pool is surmounted by an enormous water slide. And again here, amenities

The Disney Institute: The Mouse Grows Up

The Disney Institute is an exciting concept designed for adults and older children (10 and up). Designed to resemble a small town with a village green and architecture evocative of barns, mills, and country houses, it sprawls over 265 acres of lakes, streams, and woodlands.

The institute enables guests to custom-design Walt Disney World vacations that focus on interactive programs in dozens of diverse areas. It's a great one-day adventure for couples, seniors, or adult children traveling with older parents. Not only is it a nice physical rest from trekking through the theme parks, but classes are small, so it offers a chance to spend real face-to-face time together. For example, my mom and I enjoyed a morning learning Oriental cooking and an afternoon engrossed in an introduction to animation. We left with recipes from the cooking class and a tape of our first (and probably last) short film.

The institute's resort-style public areas and accommodations (bungalows and one- and two-bedroom townhouses) are gorgeous. An elegant on-premises restaurant called **Seasons** features menus and cuisines that change nightly. Among the extensive sporting facilities are an 18-hole/par-72 championship golf course, tennis courts, and swimming pools.

Nightly performances and recitals take place in a 1,150-seat open-air amphitheater and a 250-seat performance center, and films are screened weeknights in a state-of-the-art movie theater. A counselor-supervised youth center, comfortably appointed with couches, videos and games, offers a full roster of daytime programs and activities for children 10 to 13 as well as evening activities for teens.

The institute is adjacent to the Disney Village Marketplace at 1960 N. Magnolia Way. Package rates range from 3-night stays for around $600 to 7-night stays for about $2,000. A good bet for the budget-minded is a single day, at around $100, that includes programs and classes but not accommodations. Single-day visitors should allow plenty of time to find their bungalow classroom—the signs can be confusing and we were misdirected several times by employees during our visit. But once you find what your looking for, you'll be glad you made the effort. For further information on programs and rates, call ☎ **800/4-WONDER** or 407/827-4800.

abound; among them whirlpool, kiddie pool, coin-op washers/dryers, video-game arcade, bicycle and boat rental, car-rental service, 1.7-mile riverfront jogging path, shops, room service (pizza only), guest-services desk, babysitting, boat transport (to Dixie Landings, Village Marketplace, and Pleasure Island on Disney's West Side).

WORTH A SPLURGE

✪ **Disney's BoardWalk.** 2101 N. Epcot Resorts Blvd. (off Buena Vista Dr.; P.O. Box 10000), Lake Buena Vista, FL 32830-1000. ☎ **407/W-DISNEY** (934-7639) or 407/939-5100 (407/939-6200 for villas). Fax 407/354-1866. 378 units, 532 villas. A/C TV TEL. $249–$450 double; $415–$1,200 suites; $210–$780 villas, depending on view and season. Children 17 and under stay free in parents' room. AE, MC, V. Free self- and valet parking.

It's true that even in good-value season, a room here could go for $260. But the property's proximity to nightclubs, restaurants, and shopping makes it a splendid choice for singles or young married couples.

The BoardWalk, occupying 45 acres along the shores of Lake Crescent, takes its theme from the plush mid-Atlantic Victorian seaside resorts of the 1920s and 1930s.

A large deck with rocking chairs overlooks a village green and the lake beyond, and the stunning 70-foot lobby has a working fireplace. With shingled rooftops surrounding private courtyards and New England–style flower gardens, the property connects to a quarter-mile boardwalk complete with shops, restaurants, and street performers. There's plenty to do here once the sun goes down, making it a good choice for singles and couples without children. The B&B-style accommodations are just gorgeous and may include a brass or four-poster bed. All have safes, irons and ironing boards, and hair dryers; refrigerators are available. The villas, though pricey, might be a good choice for large families or groups; they offer kitchenettes or full kitchens and washers/dryers, and some contain whirlpool tubs. Within walking distance are Epcot and the Yacht and Beach clubs.

Dining options include the upscale **Flying Fish Café** for steak and seafood; **Spoodle's,** a casual spot serving Mediterranean fare; **the Big River Grille and Brewing Works** (featuring handcrafted beers and ales); **ESPN Club,** a sports bar; a bakery and an espresso shop. There are also several cocktail lounges, a sing-along bar, a 1920s-style dance hall, and a carousel-themed pool bar.

Among the amenities are concierge, room service (24 hours), baby-sitting, boat transport (to MGM, Epcot, and Epcot resorts), guest-services desk, a large outdoor swimming pool with water slide, two additional secluded pools, kiddie pool, whirlpool, two tennis courts, 2-mile jogging path, playground, extensively-equipped health club, two video-game arcades, Community Hall (for games, crafts, recreational equipment rentals, videotapes and books), and Harbour Club (a counselor-supervised child-care activity center).

✪ **Disney's Wilderness Lodge.** 901 West Timberline Dr. (on the southwest shore of Bay Lake just east of the Magic Kingdom; P.O. Box 10000), Lake Buena Vista, FL 32830-1000. ☎ 407/W-DISNEY (934-7639) or 407/824-3200. Fax 407/354-1866. 728 units. A/C TV TEL. $165–$245 double, depending on view and season; $280–$315 junior suite; $540–$665 suite. Extra person $15. AE, MC, V. Free self- and valet parking.

The geyser out back, bubbling creek, mammoth stone hearth in the lobby, and bunk beds for the kids are just a few reasons this is one of my favorite Walt Disney World (WDW) resorts. The main dining room, with a sweeping view of 340-acre Bay Lake, might even inspire some romance. Reminiscent of rustic turn-of-the-century national park lodges, this 56-acre resort is surrounded by towering oak and pine forests. Wilderness Lodge has the advantage of feeling removed from the rest of WDW, but consequently is one of the more difficult places to access via the WDW transportation system. The 5-minute geyser shows take place in the meadow periodically throughout the day, and nightly electric water pageants can be viewed from the shores of Bay Lake. The courtyard-view rooms are a good value during slow times, which makes this another good family choice—kids will love the sandy lakefront beach, immense serpentine swimming pool, and funky wild-West decor, while parents are sure to go for the tranquil setting and fine dining.

The modestly sized guest rooms—with patios or balconies overlooking the lake, woodlands, or meadow scenery—are furnished in Mission style and adorned with tribal friezes and landscape paintings of the Northwest. In-room safes are a plus. Steak, seafood, and game specialties are served at the lodgelike **Artist Point** restaurant, overlooking Bay Lake. Amenities include a swimming pool (see above), kiddie pool with water slide, spa pools, boat rental, bicycle rental, 2-mile jogging/bike trail, video-game arcade, Cub's Den (a supervised activity center for children 4 to 12), room service, guest-services desk, babysitting, boat transport to the Magic Kingdom and Contemporary Resort, and bus transport to MGM, Epcot, and other park areas.

A Disney Campground/Wilderness Homes

Disney's Fort Wilderness Resort and Campground. 3520 N. Fort Wilderness Trail (P.O. Box 10000), Lake Buena Vista, FL 32830-1000. ☎ **407/W-DISNEY** (934-7639) or 407/824-2900. Fax 407/354-1866. 784 campsites, 408 wilderness homes. A/C TV TEL (homes only). $35–$54 campsite, depending on season, location, number of people, size, and extent of hookup; $180–$215 wilderness home. AE, MC, V. Free self-parking.

This woodsy 780-acre camping resort—shaded by towering pines and cypress trees and crossed by fish-filled streams, lakes, and canals—is ideal for family vacations. Though it's a tad less central than other Disney hostelries, its abundance of on-premises facilities more than compensate. Secluded campsites offer 110/220-volt outlets, barbecue grills, picnic tables, and children's play areas. There are also wilderness homes—rustic one-bedroom cabins with pine interiors that accommodate up to six people. These have cozy living rooms with Murphy beds, fully equipped eat-in kitchens, picnic tables, and barbecue grills. Guests here enjoy extensive recreational facilities ranging from a riding stable to a nightly campfire program hosted by Chip 'n' Dale. The rustic log-beamed Trails End offers buffet meals, and the cozy Crockett's Tavern features Texas fare. During summer, guests enjoy a dazzling electrical water pageant from the beach, nightly at 9:45pm. And the rambunctious *Hoop-Dee-Doo Musical Revue* takes place in Pioneer Hall nightly.

Other extras include a guest-services desk, babysitting, and boat transport to the Magic Kingdom and the Contemporary Resort. Among the amenities are a comfort station in each campground area (with rest rooms, private showers, ice machines, phones, and laundry rooms), two large swimming pools, a white-sand beach, horseback riding, petting farm, pony rides, fishing, three sand volleyball courts, ballfields, shuffleboard, bike rentals, boat rental, 1½-mile nature trail, 2.3-mile jogging path, two tennis courts, two 18-hole championship golf courses, shops, kennel, and two video-game arcades.

AN "OFFICIAL" HOTEL AT LAKE BUENA VISTA

Properties designated "official" Walt Disney World hotels are located on and around Hotel Plaza Boulevard. Guests at these hotels enjoy many privileges (see "How to Save Money by Staying with Mickey," above). The location is a big advantage—close to the Disney parks and within walking distance of the Disney Village Marketplace, Crossroads Shops and restaurants, Pleasure Island, and Disney's West Side. (This area has been dubbed Downtown Disney.)

One difference between "official" hotels and actual Disney resorts is that the former generally have less relentless themes; decide for yourself if that's a plus or a minus. *Note:* Only one "official" hotel meets our budget, and you can make reservations there through **Central Reservations Operations** at ☎ **407/W-DISNEY** (934-7639); see details above.

Courtyard by Marriott. 1805 Hotel Plaza Blvd. (between Lake Buena Vista Dr. and Apopka-Vineland Rd./Fla. 535), Lake Buena Vista, FL 32830. ☎ **800/223-9930** or **407/828-8888.** Fax 407/827-4623. 333 units. A/C TV TEL. $89–$149 double, depending on view and season. AE, CB, DC, DISC, JCB, MC, V. Free parking. From I-4, take Exit 27.

Though it's a little on the pricey side for this book, Courtyard offers quite a bit. Guests enjoy many of the privileges associated with staying at an "official hotel." Courtyard is a moderately priced link in the Marriott chain; prices are lower because services are limited. But don't envision a spartan, no-frills atmosphere. This property was recently renovated to the tune of $4.5 million, and it's looking great. The attractive rooms, most with balconies, have in-room safes, coffeemakers, pay-movie options, and Nintendo; refrigerators are available on request. A full-service restaurant serves American fare at all meals and provides room service. There's also a lobby cocktail lounge, a pool-side bar (in season), and an on-premises deli featuring pizza and frozen yogurt. The guest services desk sells tickets and arranges transport to all nearby attractions. Other facilities include two swimming pools, a whirlpool, a kiddie pool, boat rental at nearby Disney Village Marina, a playground, car rental, an exercise room, shops, coin-op washers/dryers, and a video-game arcade.

OTHER LAKE BUENA VISTA AREA HOTELS

The hotels in this section are all within a few minutes' drive of the Walt Disney World (WDW) parks.

FOR A FEW BUCKS MORE

Comfort Inn. 8442 Palm Pkwy. (between Fla. 535 and I-4), Lake Buena Vista, FL 32830. ☎ **800/999-7300** or 407/239-7300. Fax 407/239-7740. 640 units. A/C TV TEL. $35–$85 for rm. with up to 4 people. AE, CB, DC, DISC, MC, V. Free parking. From I-4 east, take Exit 27; turn north on 535, then turn right at second traffic light onto Palm Parkway.

This is an ideally located, large, and attractively landscaped property with two small artificial lakes amid expanses of manicured lawn and lush greenery. It offers free trans-port to WDW parks, which are just 2 miles away. In-room safes are among the ameni-ties in the immaculate guest rooms. The Boardwalk Buffet serves reasonably priced buffet meals at breakfast and dinner; kids 11 and under eat free. A bar/lounge adjoins, and complimentary tea and coffee are served in the lobby every afternoon. The guest-services desk sells tickets (most of them discounted) and provides transport to all nearby theme parks, dinner shows, and the airport. On-premises facilities include two swimming pools, coin-op washers/dryers, a gift shop, and a video-game arcade. Pets are permitted.

WORTH A SPLURGE FOR THE FAMILY

Holiday Inn Sunspree Resort Lake Buena Vista. 13351 Fla. 535 (between State Road 536 and I-4), Lake Buena Vista, FL 32821. ☎ **800/FON-MAXX** or 407/239-4500. Fax 407/239-7713. www.kidsuites.com. E-mail: Max@kidsuites.com. 507 units. A/C TV TEL. $77–$169 room for up to 4 people, depending on season. AE, CB, DC, DISC, JCB, MC, V. Free parking. From I-4 east, take Exit 27; turn left at traffic light, and it's the first hotel on the left—look for the pink buildings.

Less than a mile from WDW, this family friendly hotel combines a chain's affordable dependability while catering to children in a big way. Kids "check in" at their own pint-size desk; receive a free fun bag containing a video-game token coupon, a lol-lipop, and a small gift; and get a personal welcome from animated raccoon mascots, Max and Maxine. Camp Holiday activities—magic shows, clowns, sing-alongs, arts and crafts, and much more—are available at a minimal charge for kids 2 to 12. And parents can arrange (by reservation) for Max to come tuck a child into bed. The pretty, family sized rooms have kitchenettes with refrigerators, microwave ovens, and cof-feemakers. And if you're renting a second room for the children, "kidsuites" here—themed as igloos, space capsules, Noah's Ark, and so on—sleep up to three. Amenities include VCRs (tapes can be rented), hair dryers, and safes. Maxine's serves all meals, including steak and seafood dinners. Max's CyberArcade boasts video games, other family diversions and airs sports on large-screen TV. Kids 12 and under eat all meals free, either in a hotel restaurant with their parents or in Kid's Kottage, a cheerful facility where movies and cartoons are shown and dinner includes a make-your-own-sundae bar. Handicapped-accessible rooms are available. Among the amenities are free shuttle service to WDW and other parks, room service, a guest-services desk (that sells tickets to all nearby attractions), large swimming pool, two whirlpools, kiddie pool,

① Family-Friendly Hotels

Days Inns *(see p. 479)*   At 4104 and 4125 W. Irlo Bronson Memorial Hwy., good basic service and a central location make these good bets for families. There is a swimming pool on the property, but more importantly, there are restaurants, shops, and movie theaters within walking distance.

Disney-Owned Resorts & Official Hotels *(see p. 469)*   These offer many advantages for kids, including proximity to Walt Disney World parks, complimentary transportation between the hotel and the parks, and reduced-price children's menus and Disney character appearances in hotel restaurants. Extensive facilities might include lakefront beaches, boating, bike rentals, playgrounds, video-game arcades, swimming pools with waterfalls and slides, and/or organized children's activities.

Disney's Fort Wilderness Resort and Campground *(see p. 476)*   All of the above and more is offered here, including nightly campfire programs with Chip 'n' Dale, trail rides, pony rides, and a petting farm—and you get to go camping.

Holiday Inn Sunspree Resort Lake Buena Vista *(see p. 477)*   This Holiday Inn has a special check-in desk for kids and on-premises mascots to welcome them. Rooms are equipped with kitchenettes, and there are themed "kidsuites" available. Kids under 12 eat free in their own restaurant, where movies and cartoons are shown. Numerous organized children's activities are free.

playground, coin-op washers/dryers, shops, video-game arcade, and Camp Holiday (a supervised child-care/activity center for children 2 to 12).

Note: The **Holiday Inn Hotel & Suites**, Main Gate East, 5678 West Irlo Bronson Hwy., Kissimmee, FL 34746 (☎ **800/FON-KIDS** or 407/396-4488), offers similar services and accepts pets.

Riu Orlando Hotel. 8688 Palm Pkwy. (between Fla. 535 and I-4), Lake Buena Vista, FL 32830. ☎ **800/WYNDHAM** or 407/239-8500. Fax 407/239-8591. 167 units A/C TV TEL. $80–$175 double, depending on season. Children 17 and under stay free in parents' room. AE, CB, DC, DISC, MC, V. Free self-parking. From I-4 east, take Exit 27, turning north on 535. Turn right at second traffic light and onto Palm Parkway.

Taken over by new management in 1997, this 6-story property still has a location on a pleasant tree-lined street and overlooks a lake out back—a big plus. The presence of Crossroads Shopping Center and Walt Disney World Village Marketplace put dozens of shops, services, and restaurants within easy walking distance. The family-friendly rooms come with coffeemakers and tea and coffee (a nice touch), Nintendo, hair dryers, irons and ironing boards. The Garden Cafe serves American fare at breakfast and dinner, and has an outdoor poolside seating area and an adjoining bar/lounge. Room service, baby-sitting, and a complimentary daily newspaper are available, and the guest-services desk sells tickets (many of them discounted) and arranges transport (free shuttles) to all nearby attractions. On premises are a nice-size swimming pool and whirlpool, coin-op washers/dryers, an exercise room, a business center, and a small video-game arcade.

ON U.S. 192/KISSIMMEE

This very American stretch of highway dotted with fast-food eateries isn't what you'd call scenic, but it does contain many inexpensive accommodations that are within 1 to 8 miles of WDW parks. All the hostelries listed below are clean, safe, and well run.

There are also two branches of the rock-bottom budget **Motel 6** (☎ **800/ 4-MOTEL6**) in Kissimmee on U.S. 192; the one at 7455 W. Irlo Bronson Memorial Hwy. (☎ 407/396-6422) is a tad nicer because it has been recently renovated. The other branch is at 5731 W. Irlo Bronson Memorial Hwy. (☎ 407/396-6333).

A system of highway markers have been recently erected along Irlo Bronson Highway to help tourists better find their way. These tall markers by the side of the road are aptly dubbed, "Marker" along with a number. For example, a property may be located between Marker 15 and Marker 16. The marker designations are included below.

SUPER-CHEAP SLEEPS

Comfort Inn Maingate. 7571 W. Irlo Bronson Memorial Hwy. (U.S. 192, between Reedy Creek Blvd. and Sherbeth Rd.), Kissimmee, FL 34747. ☎ **800/221-2222** or 407/396-7500. Fax 407/396-7497. 281 units. A/C TV TEL. $32–$98 double, depending on season; garden rooms $6–$10 extra. AE, CB, DC, DISC, JCB, MC, V. Free parking. From I-4, take Exit 25B. Go west on 192, about 1 mile, near Marker 6.

Just 1 mile from the WDW parks, this Comfort Inn houses clean, spiffy-looking standard motel accommodations. Most upscale are the garden rooms, facing a lawn with a gazebo; they're equipped with small refrigerators, coffeemakers, and hair dryers. A restaurant on the premises serves low-priced meals, kids eat free. A comfortable bar/lounge adjoins. There's also a Waffle House right across the street. The guest-services desk sells tickets to Disney and other parks (most of them discounted) and the hotel provides transport to all nearby attractions and the airport; a round-trip to WDW parks costs $7 per person round trip. Also on hand are an outdoor swimming pool, a playground, coin-op washers/dryers, and a small video-game arcade.

Days Inn. 4104 and 4125 W. Irlo Bronson Memorial Hwy. (U.S. 192, at Hoagland Blvd. N. or Marker 15), Kissimmee, FL 34741. ☎ **800/647-0010**, 800/DAYS-INN, or 407/846-4714. Fax 407/932-2699. www.daysinn.com. 220 units. A/C TV TEL. $29–$59 rm. for up to 4, depending on season; $37–$63 efficiency; $55–$75 Jacuzzi rm. (for 1 or 2 people). Rates include continental breakfast. Rates may be higher during major events, such a bike week or big conventions. AE, CB, DC, DISC, MC, V. Free parking. From I-4, take Exit 25A, then turn right; the hotel is 6 miles on right.

Offering good value for your hotel dollar, these two Days Inns—on either side of U.S. 192—share facilities, including two swimming pools, coin-op washers and dryers, and a video-game arcade. Several restaurants (which deliver food), a large shopping mall with a 12-theater movie house, and a supermarket are within close walking distance.

The rooms at both locations are clean and attractive standard motel units. The best bets are the efficiency units with fully-equipped kitchenettes at no. 4104. On the other hand, at no. 4125 you can ask for a room with a large Jacuzzi, a refrigerator, and a microwave oven. All accommodations offer pay-movie options and in-room safes, and both locations serve free coffee, juice, and doughnuts in their lobbies each morning. Guest services at no. 4104 sells tickets (many of them discounted) and arranges transport to all nearby attractions, including WDW parks. A big plus: Round-trip transport to WDW parks is free. Airport transfers can be arranged.

Days Inn, Eastgate. 5245 W. Irlo Bronson Memorial Hwy. (U.S. 192, between Poinciana and Polynesian Isle blvds., or near Marker 12), Kissimmee, FL 34746. ☎ **800/329-7468** or 407/ 396-7700. Fax 407/396-0293. 200 units. A/C TV TEL. $39–$79 rm. for up to 4, depending on view and season. Rates may be higher during major events. AE, DC, DISC, MC, V. Free parking. From I-4, take Exit 25A; it's about 3.5 miles on 192.

This 2-story pink stucco Days Inn forms an attractively landscaped courtyard around a large swimming pool. Families will appreciate the picnic tables and a children's play area on the lawn. The rooms are nicely decorated. Lucille's Cafe serves buffet break-fasts, and the comfy Half Time Lounge, where sporting events are aired on a large-screen TV, has a pool table and dart boards. Other facilities include a video-game room, coin-op washers/dryers, and a gift shop. Guest services sells tickets to all WDW parks and nearby attractions (many of them discounted) and offers transportation to/from them and the airport. Round-trip transport to WDW parks is $7.

Econo Lodge Maingate East. 4311 W. Irlo Bronson Memorial Hwy. (U.S. 192), between Hoagland Blvd. and Fla. 535, marker 15. Across the street from Medieval Times. ☎ **800/ENJOY-FL** or 407/396-7100. www.enjoyfloridahotels.com. A/C TV TEL. $49.95–$54.95 single or double. From I-4, take Exit 25A.

This property is set well back from the highway to prevent disturbance from traffic noise (although ask for a room away from the balconies). A new lobby has been added but the same standard of service and cleanliness continues. All in all, a good bargain. Shuttles are free to WDW parks, and transportation is available to other parks. There's also a heated swimming pool.

Howard Johnson Express Inn. 4836 W. Irlo Bronson Hwy. (between markers 11 and 12), Kissimmee, FL. ☎ **800/952-5464** or 407/396-4762. Fax 407/396-4866. 131 units. A/C TV TEL. $39.95–$66 doubles and suites. From I-4, take Exit 25A; it's 3.5 miles on right. Free parking.

As a lakefront property, this is one of the more scenic Kissimmee offerings. You can have picnics by the lake or rent jet-skis for about $60 an hour. The pink-and-blue buildings contain clean, comfortable rooms, and some of the suites contain in-room Jacuzzis, microwave ovens, and refrigerators. A large heated swimming pool and a video-game room are added pluses, as is the free shuttle to the WDW parks. Trans-portation to other attractions can be arranged for a fee.

Magic Castle. 5055 W. Irlo Bronson Memorial Hwy. (U.S. 192, near Marker 11 between Poin-ciana Blvd. and Fla. 535), Kissimmee, FL 34746. ☎ **800/446-5669** or 407/396-2212. Fax 407/396-0253. www.daysinn.com. 107 units. A/C TV TEL. $35.95–$61.95 rm. for up to 4. Rates include continental breakfast. AE, DC, DISC, MC, V. Free self-parking. From I-4, take Exit 25A; it's about 3.5 miles on the left, next to the Olive Garden.

The owner has discontinued his affiliation with Ramada Inn, but this 3-story stucco building continues to provide adequate accommodations at a good price. The standard-sized rooms are equipped with cable TV (with Disney Channel and HBO movies), safes, and refrigerators.

Facilities include an outdoor swimming pool and coin-op washers/dryers. Conti-nental breakfast is served in the lobby each morning. Shuttle service to WDW parks is available for $9 per person, round-trip. It'll cost about $12 or $14 to get to other parks. Pets are accepted ($6 per night).

Ramada Inn. 4559 W. Irlo Bronson Memorial Hwy. (U.S. 192, between Siesta Lago Dr. and Bass Rd./Old Vineland Rd. or markers 13 and 14), Kissimmee, FL 34746. ☎ **800/544-5712** or 407/396-1212. Fax 407/396-7926. 114 units. A/C TV TEL. $29.95–$59.95 rm. for up to 4. AE, DC, DISC, MC, V. From I-4, take Exit 25A; it's about 5 miles on left, across from Jungle-land. Free self-parking.

This Ramada offers standard motel rooms, a little on the small side, with cable TV and safes; refrigerators and microwaves are available on request for $8 a night. Facili-ties include coin-op washers/dryers, a swimming pool, a children's playground, and picnic tables. The 1950s-style Hollywood Diner—which has an adjoining bar/lounge—serves American fare at all meals. Shuttle service to WDW parks is avail-able for $10 per person, round-trip. Pets are accepted ($6 per night). Children stay and eat free.

Super 8 Motel (formerly Colonial Motor Lodge). 1815 W. Vine St. (between Bermuda and Thacker aves.), Kissimmee, FL 34741. ☎ **800/325-4348** or 407/847-6121. A/C TV TEL. $29.95–$59.95 single, depending on season. Rates include free continental breakfast. AE, DC, DISC, MC, V.

This facility was completed, renovated, and expanded in 1998 and includes basic rooms with laundry facilities and cable TV. Suites are available that sleep six, but mostly you'll find standard motel rooms and two-bedroom apartments featuring fully-equipped kitchens. The surroundings ain't pretty, but the small rooms are clean and the price is right. If you need a morning jolt, you'll find coffee in lobby.

FOR A FEW BUCKS MORE

✪ **Holiday Inn Hotel & Suites.** 5678 Irlo Bronson Hwy. (U.S. 192, between I-4 and Poinciana Blvd.), Kissimmee, FL 34746. ☎ **800/FON-KIDS** or 407/396-4488. Fax 407/396-8915. 614 units. A/C TV TEL. $75–$105 rm. for up to 4; $99–$195 1-bedroom suite with kitchenette. Inquire about packages. AE, CB, DC, DISC, JCB, MC, V. Free parking.

Just 3 miles from the entrance to the Magic Kingdom, this attractively landscaped 23-acre property offers identical facilities to the Holiday Inn Sunspree Resort Lake Buena Vista (described above), including its own Camp Holiday and all the kid-pleaser features. There's even a small merry-go-round in the lobby. The accommodations are in 2-story motel-style buildings enclosing courtyard swimming pools. Pets are permitted.

The **Vineyard Cafe** serves breakfast and dinner, the latter featuring steak and seafood. There's also a food court and a pool bar proffering frozen tropical drinks. Kids 12 and under eat all meals free, either in a hotel restaurant with their parents or in the Gingerbread House, a cheerful facility where movies and cartoons are shown on a large-screen TV and dinner includes a make-your-own-sundae bar.

Room service and baby-sitting are available, and the guest-services desk sells tickets to all nearby attractions (including WDW parks) and arranges the free scheduled transport to WDW parks (there's a charge for transport to other nearby attractions), telephone grocery shopping, and the Mears airport shuttle. Facilities include two Olympic-size swimming pools, two whirlpools, a kiddie pool, a playground, two tennis courts, sand volleyball, a basketball court, coin-op washers/dryers, shops, car rental, two video-game arcades, and Camp Holiday, a supervised child care/activity center for children ages 3 to 12.

Howard Johnson Maingate East. 6051 W. Irlo Bronson Memorial Hwy. (U.S. 192, just east of I-4 between markers 8 and 9), Kissimmee, FL 34747. ☎ **800/288-4678** or 407/396-1748. Fax 407/649-8642. 367 units. A/C TV TEL. $75–$100 double. Children 18 and under stay free in parents' room. Inquire about packages. AE, CB, DC, DISC, JCB, MC, V. Free self-parking. From I-4, take Exit 25A; it's 1 mile on the left.

Just 2 miles from WDW parks—and offering free transport to and from the Disney parks—it maintains a special guest-services phone number (☎ **800/TOUR-FLA**) that you can call in advance of your trip to arrange attractions tickets, paid transportation, car rental, and other vacation needs. The accommodations here are nicely decorated; amenities include cable TV (with pay-movie options and Nintendo) and safes. The efficiency units have fully-equipped kitchenettes with small refrigerators, two-burner stoves, and sinks.

Among the facilities are a medium-size outdoor swimming pool, a whirlpool, a kiddie pool, a children's playground, coin-op washers/dryers, a video-game arcade, a car-rental desk, and a pool table. Adjoining the property is the large water park, **Watermania** (see Larson's Lodge Main Gate, below), and an IHOP where kids 11 and under with an adult eat free. On premises, a pool bar serves light fare and drinks, and coffee and tea are served each morning in the lobby. Guest services sells tickets to all Disney parks and nearby attractions (some discounted), and offers transportation to/ from them and the airport.

✪ **Larson's Lodge Main Gate.** 6075 W. Irlo Bronson Memorial Hwy. (U.S. 192, just east of I-4 between markers 8 and 9, Kissimmee, FL 34747. ☎ **800/327-9074** or 407/396-6100. Fax 407/396-6965. 128 units. A/C TV TEL. $59–$79 double. All units have microwave and refrigerator. Children under 18 stay free in parents' room. Inquire about packages. AE, CB, DC, DISC, MC, V. Free parking. Take I-4 to Exit 27; it's on the left, across from the old-fashioned water tower at the Celebration entrance and behind Watermania.

With a water park (Watermania) next door, a playground, poolside picnic tables, barbecue grills, and a cheerful on-site Shoney's restaurant, Larson's Lodge is a good choice for families. Accommodations are equipped with refrigerators, microwave ovens, and safes. There are also efficiency units with fully-equipped kitchenettes. A supermarket is just a few minutes away by car.

The guest-services desk can arrange transport to other nearby attractions and the airport. Round-trip to WDW parks is $10. On-premises facilities include a large heated swimming pool and whirlpool, shops, coin-op washers/dryers, and a video-game arcade. Guests enjoy a free newspaper and coffee in the lobby each morning. Pets are permitted.

Quality Inn on Lake Cecile. 4944 W. Irlo Bronson Memorial Hwy. (between markers 5 and 6), Kissimmee, FL 34746. ☎ **800/228-1828** or 407/396-4455. 200 units. A/C TV TEL. $59–$79 double. Rates include extended continental breakfast. AE, CB, DC, DISC, JCB, MC, V. Free parking. From I-4, take Exit 25A. About 3 miles from exit.

Located on the banks of beautiful 223-acre Lake Cecile, the lakefront property gives this property an edge over the competition. You can rent jet-skis or water skis. There is a food court and scheduled transportation to the WDW parks. Rooms are small but clean and comfortable. It's ideal for young singles or young couples looking for a bargain.

INTERNATIONAL DRIVE AREA

Hotels and resorts listed here are 7 to 10 miles north of the Walt Disney World parks (a quick freeway trip) and close to Universal Studios Florida and Sea World. International Drive hostelries tend to be somewhat less kid-oriented than hotels in other areas.

SUPER-CHEAP SLEEPS

Fairfield Inn by Marriott. 8342 Jamaican Court (off International Dr. between the Beeline Expy. and Sand Lake Rd.), Orlando, FL 32819. ☎ **800/228-2800** or 407/363-1944. Fax 407/363-1944. www.marriott.com. 134 units. A/C TV TEL. $45–$79 rm. for up to 4. Rates include continental breakfast. AE, CB, DC, DISC, JCB, MC, V. Free parking. From I-4, take Exit 29 (Sand Lake Rd.); go east 1 block, and turn right on International Dr. Turn right on Jamaican Court. The hotel is on the right.

I love this inn's quiet and safe location in a secluded area off International Drive. It nestles in Jamaican Court, a neatly landscaped complex of hotels and restaurants (that means a number of eateries are within walking distance). The spiffy-looking rooms offer cable TV with HBO, and the phones are equipped with 25-foot cords and modem jacks. Daily newspapers and local calls are free, as is the continental breakfast served in the lobby each morning.

The guest-services desk sells tickets (most of them discounted) and can arrange transport to all nearby theme parks and attractions and the airport; round-trip to

WDW parks is $10. A small outdoor swimming pool and video-game room are on the premises, and the lobby has a microwave oven for guest use.

FOR A FEW BUCKS MORE

Country Hearth Inn. 9861 International Dr. (between the Beeline Expy. and Sand Lake Rd.), Orlando, FL 32819. ☎ **800/447-1890** or 407/352-0008. Fax 407/352-5449. 150 units. A/C TV TEL. $59–$139 double, depending on view and season. Children 17 and under stay free in parents' room. Rates include continental breakfast. AE, CB, DC, DISC, MC, V. Free self-parking. From I-4, take Sand Lake Road exit, then go east to International Drive.

Though it doesn't offer much in the way of resort facilities, the Country Hearth Inn's low rates, great location, and newly renovated rooms make this an appealing choice. Centered on a white-trimmed octagonal building crowned by a windowed cupola, the inn evokes 19th-century Florida—the leisurely era of riverboat travel and gracious plantations. Ceiling fans whir slowly over verandas and balconies furnished with wicker rocking chairs, and a charmingly landscaped courtyard with neat lawns and flower beds encompasses a large free-form swimming pool backed by verdant woodlands and a wide canal. In-room amenities include cable TV (with HBO and Spectravision movie options), coffeemakers, phones with modem jacks, ceiling fans, safes, and small refrigerators.

The elegant Country Parlor, in the balustraded Victorian lobby, serves moderately priced American fare at all meals; a pianist entertains at Sunday champagne brunches. The Front Porch Lounge, a popular gathering spot for locals, features happy hour buffets Monday to Friday from 5:30 to 7pm. Room service is available.

The guest-services desk sells tickets (many of them discounted) and arranges transport to all nearby attractions (including WDW parks), baby-sitting, and the Mears airport shuttle. Shuttle service to theme parks ranges from $5 to $15.

WORTH A SPLURGE

Orlando Marriott. 8001 International Dr. (at Sand Lake Rd.), Orlando, FL 32819. ☎ **800/421-8001** or 407/351-2420. Fax 407/351-5611. www.marriott.com. 1,078 units. A/C TV TEL. $99–$300 double. Children 17 and under stay free in parents' room. AE, DC, DISC, MC, V. Free self-parking. From I-4 east, take Exit 29; turn right at traffic light at end of ramp; the hotel is to the right of the next traffic light.

The verdant 48-acre grounds feature neatly manicured lawns and flower beds with fern gullies, lush tropical foliage, and serene lagoons. This hostelry offers a feeling of plush resort seclusion that's all the more appealing because you're actually in the heart of a busy area, with proximity to many great restaurants. And the rates are very reasonable in light of the facilities you'll enjoy here. The accommodations, housed in pale pink stucco bilevel villas, are attractively decorated in resort mode; half have balconies or patios, and about a fifth contain full kitchens. All offer pay-movie stations and safes; many are also equipped with hair dryers, electric shoe-shine machines, and irons and ironing boards. The tropical Grove specializes in steaks, prime rib, and seafood. The Chelsea Cafe serves American fare at all meals. A club called Illusions features a deejay spinning Top 40 tunes, as well as blackjack, a pool table, and darts. Fast food is available, plus a cozy lobby bar and several poolside bars. Amenities include room service, babysitting, guest-services desk (which sells tickets, many of them discounted, and arranges transportation to/from WDW parks and all other nearby attractions), 24-hour free tram service around the property, and Mears airport shuttle. Round-trip fare to WDW parks is $8.

3 Great Deals on Dining, Both Inside the Parks & Out

IN WALT DISNEY WORLD

Since many Orlando visitors spend most of their time in the Walt Disney World area, I've focused on the best and most reasonably priced choices throughout that vast enchanted empire. Also listed are some worthwhile budget establishments beyond the realm. Throughout Walt Disney World, look for **Mickey's Value Meals** (complete fixed-price meals that are quite reasonably priced) and, even better value, attractively priced **Family Meals** that serve four.

Note that all Walt Disney World restaurants have no-smoking interiors (you can smoke on patios and terraces); that Magic Kingdom restaurants serve no alcoholic beverages, but liquor is available at Epcot and Disney–MGM eateries and elsewhere in the WDW complex; and all sit-down restaurants in Walt Disney World take American Express, MasterCard, Visa, and the Disney Card.

Of course, there are plenty of other places to eat in Orlando. International Drive is packed with a variety of budget eateries and downtown Orlando also has a variety of great, and relatively inexpensive, eateries. Parents will be pleased to see that just about every restaurant in town offers a low-priced children's menu and usually provides some kind of kid's activity as well. The down side of restaurants that cater to kids is that they're noisy; if you're looking for a quiet meal, head for restaurants in the International Drive area, which are farther from the Disney parks.

See also the listings for dinner shows in "Walt Disney World & Orlando After Dark," later in this chapter.

EPCOT

Though an ethnic meal at one of the World Showcase pavilions is a traditional part of the Epcot experience, most of the major restaurants here are not only expensive, but overpriced for the value received. Below you'll find the best strategies for getting the most out of Epcot's fancier restaurants, along with many lower-priced walk-in eateries throughout the park.

World Showcase

These restaurants are arranged geographically, beginning at the Canada pavilion and proceeding counterclockwise around the World Showcase Lagoon.

CANADA   Located in the Victorian Hôtel du Canada in the castlelike ambience of **Le Cellier Steakhouse,** this is a good choice for families. Diners sit in tapestried chairs under vaulted stone arches. There are no reservations needed for this self-service cafeteria. Regional dishes include Cheddar-cheese soup, carved pemeal bacon (a pork loin with a light cornmeal crust), French Canadian tourtière, maple-syrup pie, and Canadian beers. Meals cost $10 per person.

UNITED KINGDOM   The Tudor-beamed **Rose & Crown,** entered via a cozy pub with a pungent aroma of ale, is evocative of Victorian England. The outdoor seating overlooking the lagoon is a good place to watch IllumiNations. The menu features traditional items—smoked salmon with Stilton cheese, prime rib, Yorkshire pudding, and sherry trifle. Wash it all down with a pint of Irish lager beer, Bass ale, or Guinness stout. Lunch entrees are $9 to $15; dinner is $10 to $30. Traditional afternoon tea is served daily at 3:30pm; the cost is $9.95. Another option here is bar fare (sausage rolls, Cornish pasties, a Stilton cheese and fruit plate), all under $4.50. If the pub is too crowded, as it can be in peak season, you can grab some suitably tasty fish-and-chips sold from a nearby outdoor cart yet cooked inside the Rose & Crown.

FRANCE   Traditional cafe fare—quiche Lorraine, salade niçoise and French onion soup—are available throughout the day at **Au Petit Café,** a sidewalk bistro adjacent to Chefs de France on an awninged terrace overlooking the lagoon. Desserts and wines are also available. No reservations are required. Entrees are under $10.

And the **Pâtisserie/Boulangerie,** its interior redolent of croissants and pastries baking in the oven, offers tempting desserts plus French coffees and wines.

MOROCCO   Although not exactly a budget eatery, the Restaurant Marrakesh offers great value for the price, the food is top notch, and the belly dancers and other entertainment make it both dinner and show. The palatial ✪ **Restaurant Marrakesh** features exquisitely carved archways, hand-set mosaic tile work, and a beamed ceiling painted with Moorish motifs. Belly dancers perform while you dine on lamb couscous, braised tagine of chicken, or shish kebab. The Moroccan *diffa* (traditional feast), which lets you sample a variety of dishes, is recommended. This exotic restaurant perhaps best captures the international-experience spirit of Epcot. A meal will cost $21 to $40 per person; the Moroccan *diffa* is $29.95 for two at lunch, $53.90 for two at dinner. Call ahead for priority seating.

JAPAN   Adjoining the teppanyaki rooms is a U-shaped **tempura counter** where you can also order some sushi and sashimi items. Meals will cost between $10 and $20 for lunch and $21 to $40 for dinner. No reservations are required for counter seating.

But for me, the gem of this complex is a peaceful plant-filled **cocktail lounge** with large windows overlooking the lagoon—a very pleasant setting for appetizers and sake. Menu items are $3.95 to $8.25, and no reservations are required. A window seat here is a great venue to view IllumiNations.

Finally, housed in a replica of the 16th-century Katsura Imperial Villa in Kyoto is **Yakitori House,** a bamboo-roofed cafeteria serving Japanese snack-fare items all under $7, and full children's meals for under $5. Umbrella tables on a terrace overlooking a rock waterfall are a plus.

AMERICAN ADVENTURE   The **Liberty Tree Tavern** replicates an 18th-century pub, with low-beamed ceilings and a vast brick fireplace hung with copper pots. Main courses range from New England pot roast with mashed potatoes and vegetables to a traditional roast turkey dinner with all the trimmings, and there's apple crisp topped with vanilla ice cream for dessert. I prefer the food here to King Stefan's (below), and this restaurant is also more likely to be able to seat large parties.

GERMANY   Lit by street lamps, the **Biergarten** simulates a Bavarian village courtyard at Oktoberfest with autumnal trees, a working water wheel, and geranium-filled flower boxes adorning Tudor-style houses. Entertainment might be an oompah band and/or a strolling accordionist. Guests are encouraged to dance or sing along. All-you-can-eat buffet meals featuring traditional fare (sauerbraten, spaetzle with gravy, sauerkraut with salads) are offered at lunch and dinner. Beverages and desserts are extra. Lunch buffet is $10.95 for adults, $5.50 children 3 to 11; dinner is $15.75 for adults, $6.99 children.

Sommerfest is a cafeteria with indoor seating and courtyard tables overlooking a fountain. You can purchase bratwurst sandwiches with sauerkraut, goulash soup, and desserts such as apple strudel. All items are under $7.

CHINA   At the open-air **Lotus Blossom Cafe,** a pleasant self-service eatery, you can order typical Cantonese fare: egg rolls, pork-fried rice, sweet-and-sour chicken, stir-fried chicken, and vegetables served over noodles. Chinese beer and wine are options. Nothing is more than $8.

NORWAY   **Akershus** re-creates a 14th-century castle fortress that stands in Oslo's harbor. Its pristine white stone interior, with Gothic stone archways creating intimate

How to Arrange Priority Seating
at Walt Disney World Restaurants

Priority seating is similar to a reservation. It means that you get the next table available when you arrive at a restaurant, but a table is not kept empty pending your arrival. You can arrange priority seating up to 60 days in advance at almost all full-service Magic Kingdom, Epcot, Disney–MGM Studios, resort, and Disney Village restaurants—as well as character meals and shows throughout the complex—by calling ☎ **407/WDW-DINE.** Nighttime shows can actually be booked as far in advance as you wish. Exceptions to this format are noted in the listings below.

Since this priority-seating phone number was instituted in 1994, it has become much more difficult to obtain a table by just showing up. So I strongly advise you to avoid disappointment by calling ahead. Remember that guests at Disney resorts and "official" hotels can make restaurant reservations through guest-services or concierge desks.

However, if you don't reserve in advance, you can take your chances reserving in the parks themselves:

At Epcot: Make reservations at the WorldKey interactive terminals at Guest Relations in Innoventions East, at WorldKey Information Service Satellites located on the main concourse to World Showcase and at Germany in World Showcase, or at the restaurants themselves.

At the Magic Kingdom: Reserve at the restaurants themselves.

At Disney–MGM Studios: Make reservations at the Hollywood Junction Station on Sunset Boulevard or at the restaurants themselves.

---

dining niches, is softly lit by gas lamps, candelabra chandeliers, and flickering sconces. The meal is an immense smorgasbord of traditional dishes—smoked pork with honey mustard, strips of venison in cream sauce, gravlax in mustard sauce, an array of Norwegian breads and cheeses, and much more. Norwegian beer and aquavit complement a list of French and California wines. The lunch buffet costs $11.95 for adults, $5.25 for children 4 to 9, free for children 3 and under; the dinner buffet is $18.95 for adults, $7.95 for children. There are also nonsmorgasbord children's meals for $4.75.

MEXICO   The setting for the ✪ **San Angel Inn** is a hacienda courtyard amid dense jungle foliage in the shadow of a crumbling Yucatán pyramid. It's nighttime: The tables are candlelit (even at lunch) and the lighting is very low. The Popocatepetl volcano erupts in the distance, spewing molten lava, and you can hear the sounds of faraway birds. Thunder, lightning, and swiftly moving clouds add a dramatic note, but the overall ambience is soothing and, important during the summer, cool. Order an appetizer of *queso fundido* (melted cheese with Mexican pork sausage, served with homemade corn or flour tortillas), and follow it up with an entree of *filete ranchero* (grilled tenderloin of beef served over corn tortillas with sauce ranchero, poblano pepper strips, Monterey Jack cheese, onions, and refried beans). Combination platters are also an option at both meals. The margaritas here are as good as they get. Meals cost $10 to $20 per person. A special vegetarian menu is available.

The **Cantina de San Angel,** a cafeteria with outdoor seating at umbrella tables overlooking the lagoon, offers affordable tacos, burritos, and combination plates, along with frozen margaritas; a complete children's meal is under $5.

Future World

These restaurants are arranged geographically, with listings beginning at Innoventions (the section to the right as you enter the park) and proceeding counterclockwise.

INNOVENTIONS WEST   If you haven't had breakfast, a good first stop in Epcot is the **Fountain View Espresso & Bakery,** a circular facility (to the right of the Spaceship Earth globe) with indoor and outdoor seating overlooking a beautiful splashing fountain. It offers sophisticated European patisserie fare, plus fresh-baked bagels and muffins. Later in the day, come by for gourmet coffees (spiked with liqueurs if you wish) and wines.

Adjoining the Fountain View is **Pasta Piazza Ristorante,** a vast cheerful cafeteria with an exhibition pasta kitchen (all the pasta here is homemade). Its breakfasts (served until 11am; under $7) are more in the traditional American mode than those at Fountain Views and include French toast and cheese omelettes with Canadian bacon and fried potatoes. At lunch and dinner there are pizzas and Italian dishes such as pasta with meat sauce. A Mickey's Value Meal of chicken Parmesan served over spinach pasta with salad and a soft drink is under $10. Fresh-baked desserts run the gamut from a cannoli to Heath Bar cheesecake. Wine and beer are available.

INNOVENTIONS EAST   The Innoventions building (to the left of the Spaceship Earth globe) houses the **Electric Umbrella,** another spacious cafeteria with seating under colorful electric umbrellas lit by twinkling lights; there's also outdoor seating. Light American fare is featured: chili, fries, burgers, sandwiches, and salads (all under $10), which you can enhance from an extensive toppings bar. Wine and beer are available, and fresh-baked desserts include chocolate cream or peanut butter pie. Mickey's Value Meal here is a chicken fajita sandwich with fries and a beverage for under $8.

THE LAND   This pavilion's Garden Grill is the setting for the character meals described below. It also houses a lower-level food court (a good choice for family dining) called the **Sunshine Season Food Fair,** where vendors proffer an array of low-priced items—barbecued chicken and ribs, immense cinnamon rolls, stuffed baked potatoes, sandwiches, oven-fresh cakes and pastries, ice cream, and more.

WONDERS OF LIFE   This health- and fitness-oriented pavilion houses a cafeteria called **Pure and Simple,** where you might purchase fruit smoothies, fresh fruit, nonfat yogurt shakes, a bran-and-grain waffle topped with fruit sauce, or even a sub on multi-grain bread stuffed with turkey pastrami, turkey ham, sliced turkey breast, and low-fat mozzarella. Adults can eat here for under $10.

THE MAGIC KINGDOM

The full-service restaurants in the Magic Kingdom are almost ridiculously expensive, charging $8 to $10 even for burgers and sandwiches. Fortunately, there are dozens of fast-food eateries, almost all of them with pleasant outdoor tables. The listings below are arranged geographically, proceeding counterclockwise from Cinderella Castle. *Remember:* No alcoholic beverages are served in Magic Kingdom restaurants.

TOMORROWLAND   The major facility here is **Cosmic Ray's Starlight Cafe,** an enormous facility. If you sit indoors, you'll likely be entertained by a group that plays music and cracks Disney-scripted jokes. Keep in mind, that will notch up the noise level a bit. You can opt for a quieter terrace with alfresco seating at umbrella tables. Best deal here is the Family Meal: a whole rotisserie chicken, 16 ounces of rice and beans, 16 ounces of potato salad, and four corn muffins for under $20. An individual serving of the above is $5 to $7, depending on what part of the chicken you choose.

Other choices here (most of them $6 or less) include burgers, soups, sandwiches, subs, and salads. There's ice cream and fresh fruit for dessert.

Another possibility is the equally vast **Plaza Pavilion,** which, in addition to indoor seating, has a covered outdoor terrace overlooking the lagoon. Its menu is similar to the above. Mickey's Value Meal here is a 6-inch pepperoni pizza with salad and a soft drink for under $8.

For a quick meal, pick up a smoked turkey leg—a WDW specialty that you can gnaw on like Henry the Eighth—at the **Lunching Pad** for under $5. Top it off with a sundae or soft ice creams from the nearby **Aunt Gravity's Galactic Goodies.**

FANTASYLAND   The **Pinocchio Village Haus,** a large cafeteria, has a charming alpine-castle/storybook-themed interior and outdoor seating at umbrella tables, some of them overlooking the fountained waters of It's a Small World. Items such as chicken with pasta salad, burgers and fries, and smoked turkey subs are under $10. Finish up with soft ice cream or a sundae from **Mrs. Potts' Cupboard** nearby.

LIBERTY SQUARE   The **Columbia Harbor House,** a pleasant cafeteria, has a New England interior with a nautical decor, and the food is more or less of the same genre. Items such as New England clam chowder, fried fish, fried chicken strips, seafood-pasta salad, and a smoked-turkey sandwich are all under $10, and there's apple pie for dessert.

Sleepy Hollow, with outdoor tables only, may be the park's best venue for vegetarian fare. You can order sandwiches on pita or Norwegian potato bread here stuffed with avocado, sprouts, Havarti cheese, jalapeños, sesame seeds, cucumber, tomato, and spinach. Other choices include a feta-cheese salad with tahini dressing, tabbouleh salad, vegetarian chili, and peanut butter roll-ups with fresh fruit. All items are under $8.

In the mood for a light but satisfying meal? I'm partial to the **baked- and sweet-potato cart** in Liberty Square and the adjacent fresh fruit and juice stand.

FRONTIERLAND   Best choice here is the **Diamond Horseshoe Saloon Revue** (details below in section 5). The food's not much, but you can enjoy it while watching a show in air-conditioned comfort.

The **Pecos Bill Cafe,** a large cafeteria adjacent to Adventureland, has a rustic interior with a vast stone fireplace. The fare (all items are under $6) consists of burgers, hot dogs, salads, sandwiches, and chili, which you can enhance at an extensive toppings bar. Mickey's Value Meal here is a barbecued chicken sandwich served with fries or grapes and a soft drink for under $10. There are brownies for dessert.

I also like **Aunt Polly's Landing** on Tom Sawyer's Island, reached via a short raft trip across the Rivers of America. With its outdoor tables on a porch overlooking the water, it provides a tranquil respite from park hyperactivity. The inexpensive light fare includes sandwiches and soft drinks. And you can relax over refreshing lemonade while the kids explore the island's dark caves and abandoned mines. It's open for lunch only.

ADVENTURELAND   The major facility here is **El Pirata y El Perico,** a cafeteria with covered seating on a Mexican-style Saltillo-tile patio. The fare includes nachos, tacos, chili, salads, and hot dogs; it's served up in hearty portions. Everything is under $8.

Juices, frozen yogurt, and iced cappuccino are available from the **Sunshine Tree Terrace,** a thatch-roofed structure topped by tiki gods holding flaming torches; it offers outdoor seating at umbrella tables.

DISNEY–MGM STUDIOS

There are more than a dozen eateries in this Hollywood-themed park with names like the Studio Commissary and Starring Rolls Bakery. The best food is at:

The **Hollywood Brown Derby,** modeled after the famed Los Angeles celebrity haunt where Louella Parsons and Hedda Hopper held court, mirrors its defunct West Coast counterpart with interior palm trees and mahogany-wainscoted walls hung with more than 1,500 caricatures (from Barbara Stanwyck to Rin Tin Tin). The Derby's signature dish is the Cobb salad, invented by owner Bob Cobb in the 1930s. It's not for everyone. You might try champagne-flavored oyster-Brie soup, followed by baked grouper meunière served atop pasta, and a dessert of grapefruit cake with vanilla icing (another house specialty). Lunch ranges from $10 to $20 per person; dinner, $21 to $40.

The **50s Prime-Time Cafe** places diners in a time warp/sitcom psychodrama. The eating areas look like homey 1950s kitchens, wherein black-and-white TV sets air clips of shows like *My Little Margie* and *Topper.* The service staff greets diners like family ("Hi Sis, I'll go tell Mom you're home"), and may threaten you with no dessert if you don't eat your veggies or report you to Mom for resting your elbows on the table. The food—meat loaf with mashed potatoes, Granny's pot roast, Dad's chili, and such—isn't all that great, but the place is fun anyway. Desserts include banana splits and S'mores. Meals average between $10 and $20 for lunch, $21 to $40 for dinner.

Toy Story Pizza Planet, located in the Muppets Courtyard, offers what the name implies along with salads, espresso, and cappuccino. The food is not exactly gourmet, but meals are under $10 per person and kids of all ages will love the many games and diversions. This is a boisterous family eatery.

ANIMAL KINGDOM

The **RainForest Cafe** here, just like the one in Disney Village Marketplace, is a big draw for sit-down eating. While perhaps worth a splurge, it's certainly out of our budget price range. Less expensive options include **Tuskers House** in Africa, which serves rotisserie, grilled, and fried chicken and salads. The **Restaurantorsaurus** is—yep, you guessed it—in DinoLand U.S.A. It serves hamburgers, hot dogs, and authentic McDonald's fries and Chicken McNuggets. The meals at both restaurants will run between $10 and $20 per person.

AT DISNEY RESORTS
SUPER-CHEAP EATS

The Colonel's Cotton Mill. At Disney's Dixie Landings Resort, 1251 Dixie Dr. (off Bonnet Creek Pkwy.). ☎ **407/934-6000.** Reservations not accepted. All items under $10. AE, MC, V. Daily 7am–11pm (bakery opens at 6am; pizza served to midnight). AMERICAN.

This rustic food court centers on a rotating 32-foot water wheel. Five shops sell fresh-baked goods (including some New Orleans specialties), pizza, calzones, fresh fruit, tacos and nachos, sandwiches, burgers, and more. Entrees such as spit-roasted chicken or barbecued ribs served with red beans and rice, a vegetable, and a corn muffin are in the $8 range.

Dixie Landings' sibling property, **Disney's Port Orleans Resort,** at 2201 Orleans Dr. (☎ **407/934-5000**), has a similar food court, the festive Mardi Gras-themed **Sassagoula Floatworks and Food Factory.** New Orleans specialties here include beignets at breakfast, baked potatoes stuffed with andouille sausage, and blackened chicken in creole sauce. Other fare is American.

Intermission Food Court. At Disney's All-Star Music Resort, 180I W. Buena Vista Dr. (at World Dr. and Osceola Pkwy.). ☎ **407/939-6000.** Reservations not accepted. All items under $10. AE, MC, V. Daily 7am–11pm (bakery opens at 6am; pizza served to midnight). AMERICAN.

This cheerful food court, adorned with music paraphernalia and memorabilia, has stations ranging from fresh-baked goods and pizza to chicken pot pie and meatball subs. There is a barbecued beef, chicken, or pork dinner for under $10. Or for the same price you can have a prime rib dinner with baked potato and vegetable. Wine and beer are available, and kids can adjourn to a vast video-game arcade while Mom and Dad linger over coffee. All-you-can-eat buffet breakfasts are another option here and are under $7 for those 9 and older and under $5 for children.

There's a similar food court operation at the adjoining All-Star Sports resort.

Old Port Royale. At Disney's Caribbean Beach Resort, 900 Cayman Way (off Buena Vista Dr.). ☎ **407/934-3400.** Reservations not accepted. All items under $10. AE, MC, V. Daily 7am–11pm (bakery opens at 6am; pizza served to midnight). AMERICAN.

This festive Caribbean food court, entered via a Jamaican-style straw market, has all the usual food-court offerings, supplemented by such items as jerk chicken and Jamaican beef patties. Wine and beer are available. From 7 to 11:30am daily, an extensive breakfast—scrambled eggs, French toast, potatoes, bacon and sausage, grits, fresh fruit, and biscuits—is under $7 for adults, under $5 for children 10 and under. Kids will enjoy a large video-game arcade on the premises and a room where Disney movies and cartoons are aired.

FOR A FEW BUCKS MORE

Boatwright's Dining Hall. In Disney's Dixie Landings Resort, 1251 Dixie Dr. (off Bonnet Creek Pkwy.). ☎ **407/WDW-DINE** for priority seating. Breakfast items under $8; sandwiches under $10; main courses $10–$20. AE, MC, V. Daily 7–11:30am and 5–10pm. AMERICAN/ CAJUN.

Boatwright's is themed to look like an 1800s boatbuilding factory, complete with the wooden hull of a Louisiana fishing boat suspended from its lofty beamed ceiling. Kids will enjoy the wooden toolboxes on every table that serve condiments.

The Cajun breakfasts offer intriguing possibilities. French toast here is made with sourdough/sweet-potato baguette tossed in rich egg custard, deep-fried, and coated with cinnamon sugar. Another option: a pan of sautéed crayfish, mushrooms, green onions, and tomatoes in mustard-cream sauce. Dinner here might consist of an appetizer of deep-fried bacon-wrapped oysters and scallops, followed by an entree of rich bouillabaisse redolent of oaken cognac or a medley of blackened seafood served over brown-buttered pasta in creamy garlic sauce. For dessert, there's homemade fruit cobbler topped with vanilla ice cream and smothered in whipped cream.

Bonfamille's Cafe. In Disney's Port Orleans Resort, 2201 Orleans Dr. (off Bonnet Creek Pkwy.). ☎ **407/WDW-DINE** for priority seating. Breakfast items $5–$10; main courses $10– $20. AE, MC, V. Daily 7–11:30am and 5–10pm. AMERICAN/CREOLE.

Named for a character in *The Aristocats,* the charming Bonfamille's is patterned after a French Quarter courtyard, and Dixieland jazz plays softly in the background. During breakfast it's light and sunny; evenings, candle lamps provide soft lighting.

The Louisiana-style breakfasts range from fresh hot beignets and café au lait to a skillet of crayfish and andouille sausage topped with zesty creole sauce and melted sharp Cheddar. A typical dinner here is an appetizer of chicken wings tossed in spicy Louisiana hot sauce, followed by grilled Atlantic salmon with spicy pecan butter, and a dessert of Bourbon Street pudding with strawberry and caramel-bourbon sauces. After dinner, families can head over to the hotel's Scat Cats Lounge where

ⓘ Family-Friendly Restaurants

Keep in mind that almost all Walt Disney World restaurants offer very inexpensive kids' meals (usually $4), as do most restaurants in this very child-oriented town. Themes that appeal to youngsters and place mats with puzzles and pictures to color are also the norm. Of course, all the character meals described in this chapter delight the kids. Some other notables:

50's Prime-Time Cafe *(see p. 489)*   Also at Disney–MGM Studios, this highly themed restaurant re-creates the world of 1950s sitcoms, with TV sets airing old shows visible from every table. Homey food, such as meat loaf and mashed potatoes, is also of that era.

Mickey's Tropical Luau *(see p. 493)*   Not just a meal but a Polynesian floor show featuring Minnie, Mickey, Pluto, and Goofy along with a cast of South Sea Islanders. You'll find it at Disney's Polynesian Resort in Luau Cove. (It hosts character breakfasts, too.)

'Ohana *(see p. 491)*   Centering on an 18-foot fire-pit grill, 'Ohana, at Disney's Polynesian Resort, is a sumptuous island feast enhanced by storytellers, hula-hoop contests, and lots of audience participation.

Hoop-Dee-Doo Musical Revue *(see p. 538)*   I've never met anyone who didn't have a great time at this whoopin' and hollerin' country-music dinner show in Fort Wilderness's Pioneer Hall. A less-expensive variation on the same theme is the **Diamond Horseshoe Saloon Revue** in the Magic Kingdom's Frontierland *(see p. 488)*.

RainForest Cafe *(see p. 489)*   Monkeys screech in the background, waterfalls drop near your table, you sit atop zebra or rhinoceros legs—perfect for kids.

Planet Hollywood *(see p. 492)*   Kids love all the action and excitement—a fiber-optic ceiling, video walls, hundreds of movie costumes and props on display, and the elusive possibility that they'll actually see someone famous. Long waits in line to get in, however.

entertainment—sing-alongs and live music with lots of audience participation—is featured most nights.

WORTH A SPLURGE

✪ **Cape May Café.** At Disney's Beach Club Resort, 1800 Epcot Resorts Blvd. ☎ **407/ WDW-DINE** (939-3463) for priority seating. Dinner $19.95 for adults, $9.50 children 3–11; character breakfast $14.95 adults, $8.50 children 3–11. AE, MC, V. Daily 5:30–9:30pm. Free valet and self-parking. CLAMBAKE BUFFET.

A hearty 19th-century–style New England clambake is featured here nightly. Sand sculptures and furled striped beach umbrellas create the ambience of an upscale seaside resort. Aromatic New England chowder, steamed clams and mussels, corn on the cob, chicken, lobster, and red-skin potatoes are cooked up in a crackling rockweed steamer pit that serves as the restaurant's centerpiece. And these traditional clambake offerings are supplemented by dozens of salads, hot dishes (barbecued pork ribs, smoked sausage, pastas), and a wide array of oven-fresh baked goods.

'Ohana. At Disney's Polynesian Resort, 1600 Seven Seas Dr. ☎ **407/WDW-DINE** (939-3463)) for priority seating. Buffet $20.95 adults, $8.95 children 3–11, free for children 3 and under. AE, MC, V. Daily 5–10pm. Transportation to WDW resorts. Free parking. PACIFIC RIM.

You'll be welcomed here with warm island hospitality by a server who addresses you as "cousin." The setting is South Seas exotic, with thatched roofing and tapa-cloth tenting overhead, carved Polynesian columns, and an open kitchen centering on a wood-burning 18-foot fire-pit grill.

Soon after you're seated, a lazy Susan arrives laden with steamed dumplings in soy-sesame oil, napa cabbage slaw with honey mustard, black-bean and corn relish, and several tangy sauces. And course succeeds course in rapid succession (ask your server to slow the pace if it's too fast). The feast includes salad; fresh-baked herbed focaccia; grilled chicken, smoky pork sausage, marinated turkey breast, mesquite-seasoned beef, teriyaki ribs, and jumbo shrimp; stir-fry noodles and vegetables; fresh pineapple with caramel sauce; soft drinks; and coffee. Passion-fruit crème brûlée is extra, but worth it. A full bar offers tropical drinks, including nonalcoholic ones for kids.

AT DOWNTOWN DISNEY
SUPER-CHEAP EATS

Portobello Yacht Club. Pleasure Island. ☎ **407/934-8888.** Reservations strongly recommended. Lunch main courses $7.95–$8.95; pizzas $6.95–$8.95. AE, MC, V. Daily 11:30am–midnight. Valet parking $5; free self-parking. NORTHERN ITALIAN.

Dinner here would be out of our budget range, but lunch is reasonable and the pizzas, which are prepared in an exhibition kitchen, can be ordered with toppings such as mozzarella, provolone, and sun-dried tomatoes. It's a tasty deal.

Wolfgang Puck's Cafe. Disney's West Side. ☎ **407/WDW-DINE** (939-3463). Reservations recommended. Daily 11am–midnight. Main courses $8.95–$18.95. AE, MC, V. CALIFORNIA CUISINE.

Avant-garde chef Wolfgang Puck brings his West Coast creations to the heart of Florida. Your budget will pretty much be limited to the gourmet pizzas, which come with thin, crispy crusts and the predictable exotic toppings. You can dine inside or eat on a lovely outdoor patio.

FOR A FEW BUCKS MORE

Planet Hollywood. 1506 E. Buena Vista Dr., Pleasure Island. ☎ **407/827-7827.** Reservations not accepted. Main courses $7.50–$18.95 (most under $13). AE, DC, MC, V. Daily 11am–2am. AMERICAN WITH INTERNATIONAL INFLUENCES.

Planet Hollywood crashed meteor-like into the Pleasure Island solar system in 1994 with a lavish opening-night party. The lines can still be long, although the increased competition of Disney's West Side may soon make this both quiet and affordable. Inside the globelike building is a show-business museum with more than 300 items ranging from Peter O'Toole's *Lawrence of Arabia* costume to the front end of the bus from the movie *Speed*.

Video clips from films and TV play while you dine. The big surprise amid all the special effects is that the food is quite good, and, if you select carefully, pretty inexpensive. You can opt to nosh on a selection of appetizers; easily affordable are burgers and sandwiches served with fries, immense salads, pizzas, and pastas. Beverages run the gamut from chocolate malts to exotic specialty drinks. Try Arnold's mother's apple strudel, topped with nutmeg ice cream for dessert.

MEALS WITH DISNEY CHARACTERS

Especially for the 10 and under set, it's a thrill to dine in a restaurant where costumed Disney characters show up to greet the customers, sign autographs, pose in family photos, and interact with little kids. Make reservations as far in advance as possible for these very popular meals. The breakfast prices are all around $15 for adults and $8 for children; at dinner $20 for adults, $9 for children 3 to 11, free for children 2 and under. Prices vary from location to location but you will often have to take what is available, especially if you don't make reservations far in advance. It's best to make reservations when you book your hotel. For reservations to any of the character breakfasts call ☎ **407/WDW-DINE** (939-3463). *Note:* On selected days, Disney resort guests can arrive earlier at some of the below-listed character breakfasts.

Artist Point. At Disney's Wilderness Lodge, 901 Timberline Dr. Breakfast with Pocahontas and friends. Daily 7:30–11am.

In a rustic lodgelike dining room with a beamed ceiling supported by tree-trunk beams and large windows providing scenic lake views, Pocahontas and friends host all-you-can-eat buffet breakfasts.

Cape May Café. At Disney's Beach Club Resort, 1800 Epcot Resorts Blvd. Daily 7:30–11am.

The Cape May Café, a delightful New England–themed dining room, serves lavish buffet character breakfasts with Admiral Goofy and his crew—Chip 'n' Dale and Pluto (exact characters may vary)—as hosts.

Chef Mickey's. At Disney's Contemporary Resort, 4600 N. World Dr. Daily 7:30–11:30am and 5–9:30pm.

The whimsical Chef Mickey's is the setting for buffet character breakfasts and dinners. On hand to meet, greet, and mingle with guests are Mickey and various pals. Chef Mickey's ✪ **prime rib buffet dinners** include a make-your-own-sundae bar.

✪ Garden Grill. In The Land pavilion at Epcot. Daily 8:30am–8pm.

This is a revolving restaurant with seating in comfortable semicircular booths. As you dine, your table travels past desert, prairie, farmland, and rain-forest environments. There's a "momma's-in-the-kitchen" theme here: You'll be given a straw hat at the entrance, and the just-folks service staff speaks in country lingo. Hearty family-style meals are hosted by Mickey, Minnie, and Chip 'n' Dale. Extensive American breakfasts, lunches, and dinners include several entrees (roast chicken, farm-raised fish, and hickory-smoked steak), smashed potatoes, vegetables, squaw bread and biscuits, salad, beverage, and dessert.

King Stefan's Banquet Hall. In Cinderella's Castle in the Magic Kingdom. Daily 8–10am.

This Gothic castle—the focal point of the park—serves up character breakfast buffets daily. Hosts vary, but Cinderella always puts in an appearance. This is one of the most popular character meals in the park, so reserve far in advance. It's a great way to start your day in the Magic Kingdom.

✪ Liberty Tree Tavern. In Liberty Square in the Magic Kingdom. Daily 4pm to park closing.

This Williamsburg-like 18th-century pub offers character dinners hosted by Mickey, Goofy, Pluto, Chip 'n' Dale, and Tigger (some or all of them). Meals, served family style, consist of salad, roast chicken, marinated flank steak, trail sausages, homemade mashed potatoes, rice pilaf, vegetables, and a dessert of warm apple crisp with vanilla ice cream.

✪ Luau Cove. At Disney's Polynesian Resort, 1600 Seven Seas Dr. Daily 7:30–10:30am; dinner at 4:30pm.

Luau Cove, an exotic open-air facility, is the setting for an island-themed character show called Mickey's Tropical Luau. It's an abbreviated version of the Polynesian Luau Dinner Show described later in this chapter in section 14, featuring Polynesian dancers along with Mickey, Minnie, Pluto, and Goofy. Your set-price meal includes honey-roasted chicken, vegetables, glazed cinnamon bread, and an ice-cream sundae. Guests are presented with shell leis upon entering.

The Polynesian also hosts Minnie's Menehune Character Breakfast in the Polynesian-themed 'Ohana (described above). Traditional breakfast foods are prepared on an 18-foot fire pit and served family style. Minnie, Goofy, and Chip 'n' Dale appear, and there are children's parades with Polynesian musical instruments.

✪ **1900 Park Fare.** At Disney's Grand Floridian Beach Resort, 4001 Grand Floridian Way. ☎ **407/WDW-DINE** (939-3463). Daily 7:30–11:30am and 5:30–9pm.

This exquisitely elegant (and expensive) Disney resort hosts character meals in the festive exposition-themed 1900 Park Fare. Big Bertha—a French band organ that plays pipes, drums, bells, cymbals, castanets, and xylophone—provides music. Mary Poppins, Winnie the Pooh, Goofy, Pluto, Chip 'n' Dale, and Minnie Mouse appear at the elaborate buffet breakfasts. Mickey and Minnie appear at nightly buffets featuring prime rib, stuffed pork loin, fresh fish, and more.

Soundstage Restaurant. At Disney–MGM Studios, adjacent to the Magic of Disney Animation. ☎ **407/WDW-DINE** (939-3463). Daily 8:30–10:30am and 11:30am–3:30pm.

A vast buffet meal is set out in this warehouse-motif restaurant decorated with movie props and posters, and selected characters from the movies *Aladdin* and *Pocahontas* sign autographs as favorite tunes from both Disney hits play in the background.

Watercress Café. At the Buena Vista Palace, 1900 Buena Vista Dr. ☎ **407/827-2727.** Reservations not accepted. Sun 8–10:30am.

The plant-filled Watercress Café, with large windows overlooking Lake Buena Vista, is the setting for Sunday-morning character breakfasts featuring Minnie, Goofy, and Pluto. Both à la carte and buffet meals are offered. Since reservations are not accepted, arrive early to avoid a wait.

IN THE LAKE BUENA VISTA AREA

There are a number of good choices in this area outside Walt Disney World, but adjacent to the Disney theme parks.

SUPER-CHEAP EATS

Chili's. 12172 Apopka-Vineland Rd. (just north of Fla. 535/Palm Pkwy.). ☎ **407/239-6688.** Reservations not accepted, but you can call ahead from your hotel when you leave to get on a waiting list. Main courses $5.25–$11. AE, CB, DC, DISC, MC, V. Sun–Thurs 11am–midnight, Fri–Sat 11am–1am. SOUTHWESTERN.

This Texas-based chain has always been a good choice for family dining, especially this branch, where children's books and toys are provided for youngsters. Adults, on the other hand, might appreciate the bar area, where sporting events are aired on four TV monitors and all drinks are priced two-for-one during an extended daily happy hour (11am to 7pm). Its rustic/whimsical interior is appealing, with exposed brick and painted walls and upside-down copper kettles serving as hanging lamps over ceramic-tiled tables.

Chili is, of course, a specialty here. I like it on a half-pound chili cheeseburger served with home-style fries. Other possibilities include battered fried farm-raised catfish with fries and corn on the cob, heaping platters of steak or chicken fajitas, grilled baby back ribs, and salads. Save room for dessert: a chocolate brownie topped with vanilla ice cream and hot fudge. Several low-fat items are specified on the menu.

Romano's Macaroni Grill. 12148 Apopka-Vineland Rd. (just north of Fla. 535/Palm Pkwy.). ☎ **407/239-6676** for priority seating. Main courses $4.95–$8.25 at lunch, $6.95–$15.95 at dinner (most under $10). AE, CB, DC, DISC, MC, V. Sun–Thurs 11am–10pm, Fri–Sat 11am–11pm. NORTHERN ITALIAN.

Though Orlando friends had raved about the Macaroni Grill, I didn't really expect much from a chain restaurant. Upon entering, I was favorably impressed by its cheerful interior and the welcoming glow from the exhibition kitchen, where white-hatted chefs were tending an oak-burning pizza oven. Food, Chianti, flowers, and desserts were aesthetically arrayed on counters.

But the big surprise was the food. Everything was made from the freshest ingredients, and the quality of cuisine would have been notable at three times the price. The thin-crusted pizzas—such as the Mediterranea, topped with fresh tomato sauce, shrimp, and feta and mozzarella cheeses—were scrumptious, as was a dish of bow-tie pasta tossed with grilled chicken, pancetta, and red and green onions in Asiago-cream sauce. Equally good was the sautéed chicken with mushrooms, artichoke hearts, capers, and pancetta in lemon butter. There were fresh-baked foccacia and ciabatta (a crusty country loaf) for sopping up sauces or dipping in extra-virgin olive oil. And the desserts—especially an apple-custard torte with hazelnut crust and caramel topping—kept to the same lofty standard. There's a full bar, premium wines are sold by the glass, and a children's menu offers an entree and beverage for under $5. Bravo Romano!

FOR A FEW BUCKS MORE

Pebbles. In the Crossroads Shopping Center, 12551 Fla. 535, in Lake Buena Vista. ☎ **407/827-1111.** Reservations not accepted. Sandwiches and salads $4.95–$8.50; main courses mostly $7.95–$15.95. AE, CB, DC, DISC, MC, V. Daily 11am–1am. CALIFORNIA-STYLE AMERICAN.

Pebbles is one of Orlando's most popular restaurants, especially with a young yuppie crowd. The multilevel dining room centers on a sunken bar, and wooden shutters and windowed enclosures create a warren of intimate dining areas in the large space with its tropical greenery and garden-party ambience.

The same menu is offered throughout the day, supplemented by specials. Start off with a "lite bite" of creamy baked chèvre served atop chunky tomato sauce with hot garlic bread. Pebbles offers the option of a casual meal—perhaps a Cheddar burger on toasted brioche or a Caesar salad tossed with grilled chicken. More serious entrees are available, but they're pricier. Dessert of choice: the gold brick sundae—a scoop of vanilla ice cream encased in a candylike chocolate/almond shell and served atop caramel sauce with fresh strawberries. There's a full bar, and many premium wines are offered by the glass.

INTERNATIONAL DRIVE & VICINITY

Some of the best area restaurants outside Walt Disney World are along International Drive, within about 10 minutes of WDW parks by car.

SUPER-CHEAP EATS

Flipper's. In the Kirkman Shoppes strip mall, 4774 S. Kirkman Rd. (just north of Conroy Rd.). ☎ **407/521-0607.** Reservations not accepted. Main courses $4.25–$6.95; subs $2.95–$5.95; pizzas $6.95–$14.95. No credit cards. Mon–Thurs 11:30am–midnight, Fri 11:30am–1am, Sat 4pm–1am, Sun 4pm–midnight. PIZZERIA.

A casual shopping-center eatery with neon beer signs adorning its walls, Flipper's offers a good variety of fresh-made pizzas. Three people can easily dine on the $9.95 16-inch pizza bianca (my favorite) topped with olive oil, fresh garlic, oregano, and Romano, ricotta, and mozzarella cheeses. There's a choice of about 25 toppings. Other options here are calzones, hearty subs, and pastas such as baked ziti tossed with

A Cut Above Fast Food

Family restaurants such as Denny's, Perkins, and Shoney's, all offer pleasant surroundings and quite good but really inexpensive fare. Menus are vast and varied, and there are rock-bottom rates for seniors and children. All have convenient Lake Buena Vista locations reachable via Exit 27 off I-4; check your phone book for other sites around town.

You'll find a 24-hour **Denny's** at 12375 Apopka-Vineland Rd., between Hotel Plaza Boulevard and Fla. 535/Palm Parkway (☎ **407/239-7900**). It offers specials such as a prime rib dinner with baked potato and Dijon horseradish for under $8. You can add soup or salad for $1. And there are full lunch specials for around $5. A wide choice of desserts includes sundaes with homemade ice cream. Wine and beer are available.

A 24-hour **Perkins** can be found in the Crossroads of Lake Buena Vista Shopping Center, 12259 Fla. 535 (☎ **407/827-1060**). Here, from 11am to 11pm, you can enjoy specials such as grilled Cajun chicken ($7) or a 9-ounce charcoal-broiled strip steak ($9) served with two side dishes—perhaps red-skin potatoes and sugar snap peas.

A highlight of **Shoney's**, at 12204 Apopka-Vineland Rd., between Lake Ave. and Fla. 535/Palm Parkway (☎ **407/239-5416**), is its lavish daily $5 breakfast buffet ($3 for kids 11 and under). For that price, you can help yourself to unlimited quantities of scrambled eggs, breakfast meats, sausage gravy, hash browns, grits, sautéed mushrooms, buttermilk biscuits, muffins, pancakes, Belgian waffles, fresh fruits, cinnamon rolls, doughnuts, dry cereal, and more. Seniors 55 and over enjoy this morning feast for $3 every Tuesday. Shoney's also features a great seafood buffet for $9 every Friday and Saturday night from 4 to 10pm. Other nights there's a country-style buffet ($6.90 for adults, $4 for children). No alcoholic beverages are served here. Shoney's is open daily from 6am to midnight.

---

chicken and feta cheese in fresh tomato sauce and topped with provolone cheese. Beer and wine are available.

✪ **Le Peep.** In the Kirkman Oaks Shopping Center, 4666 Kirkman Rd. (just east of Conroy Rd.). ☎ **407/291-4580.** Reservations accepted only for parties of 6 or more. Main courses $2–$6.25. AE, DC, DISC, MC, V. Mon–Fri 6:30am–2:30pm, Sat–Sun 7am–2:30pm. AMERICAN.

Le Peep is one of Orlando's best-kept secrets (90% of its devoted clientele is local)—a delightful, inexpensive restaurant serving huge portions of scrumptious food. It has a gardenlike interior, and, weather permitting, you can sit at umbrella tables on the patio.

Le Peep is open for breakfast/brunch and lunch only, and everything on its menu is prepared from scratch—even the orange juice is fresh squeezed. There are all kinds of yummy egg dishes served sizzling in skillets, including southwestern fare such as scrambled eggs, green chiles, onions, and diced chicken wrapped in flour tortillas and topped with chile verde sauce and melted Cheddar. Other choices are eggs Benedict, seafood crepes, cheese blintzes topped with fresh fruits and sour cream, fabulous French toast, and pancakes. Other options include sandwiches, burgers, salads, and stuffed baked potatoes. There's key lime pie for dessert. No alcoholic beverages are served.

PR's. In the Kirkman Shoppes strip mall, 4750 S. Kirkman Rd. (just north of Conroy Rd.). ☎ **407/293-8226.** Reservations accepted only for parties of 8 or more. Main courses $5.50–$12.25 (most under $9); lunch specials (served Mon–Sat to 4pm) $3.25–$5.25. AE, DC, MC, V. Mon–Thurs 11am–10pm, Fri–Sat 11am–11pm, Sun noon–10pm. MEXICAN.

In the same shopping center as Flipper's (see above), PR's is a lively local hangout with a funky Margaritaville interior and rock music always playing in the background. It has exposed metal beams, a corrugated-tin warehouse ceiling, and model trains going round and round on an overhead track. A vast terra-cotta–topped horseshoe bar— above which sporting events are aired—is the hub of the action.

People come for good times and humongous portions of freshly made Mexican food. Start off with a platter of jalapeño peppers, breaded, stuffed with cheeses, lightly fried, and served with chili con queso. Main dishes include hearty combination platters, fajitas, and specialties such as green chiles stuffed with blackened chicken, lightly fried, and topped with a spicy cream sauce and Monterey jack cheese, served with rice and beans. The margaritas are made from scratch, and there's a good selection of Mexican beers.

FOR A FEW BUCKS MORE

B-Line Diner. In the Peabody Orlando Hotel, 9801 International Dr. ☎ **407/345-4460.** Reservations not accepted. Main courses $3.25–$8.25 at breakfast, $6.95–$10.95 at lunch, $6.95–$17.95 at dinner. AE, CB, DC, DISC, JCB, MC, V. Daily 24 hours. AMERICAN/ INTERNATIONAL.

This popular local eatery is of the nouvelle art deco diner genre, which is to say that it's an idealized version of America's ubiquitous roadside establishments. A jukebox plays oldies tunes. The seasonally varying menu offers sophisticated versions of diner food such as honey-ginger buffalo wings or a ham-and-cheese sandwich on a baguette. Other items have no relation to traditional diner fare. Portions are hearty. A glass display case here is filled with scrumptious fresh-baked desserts: everything from banana-cream pie to white-chocolate/Grand Marnier mousse cake. Ice-cream sundaes are also options. There's a full bar.

✪ **Cafe Tu Tu Tango.** 8625 International Dr. (just west of the Mercado). ☎ **407/ 248-2222.** Reservations not accepted. Tapas (tasting portions) $3.75–$7.95. AE, DISC, MC, V. Daily 11:30am–2am. INTERNATIONAL TAPAS.

Though one might question the need for yet one more themed experience outside the parks, this zany restaurant is a welcome respite from Orlando's predictable "chain gang." For one thing, there's an ongoing performance-art experience taking place while you dine: An elegantly dressed couple might tango past your table, or a magician demonstrate his tricks tableside. In addition, there's a studio area where artists are creating pottery, paintings, and jewelry.

Tu Tu's colorful ambience is a lot of fun, but its food is the real draw. The larger your party, the more dishes you can sample; two full plates will sate most appetites. My favorites include Cajun egg rolls and pepper-crusted seared tuna sashimi with crispy rice noodles and cold spinach in a sesame-soy vinaigrette. International wines can be ordered by the glass or bottle. There are great desserts here, too, such as creamy almond/amaretto flan and rich guava cheesecake with strawberry sauce.

Enzo's. In the Marketplace Shopping Center, 7600 Dr. Phillips Blvd. (off Sand Lake Rd. just west of I-4). ☎ **407/351-1187.** Reservations not accepted. Panini (sandwiches) $4.75– $5.95; main courses $4.50–$6.95 at lunch, $8.50–$12.75 at dinner. AE, CB, DC, DISC, MC, V. Mon–Thurs 11:30am–10pm, Fri–Sat 11:30am–11pm. ITALIAN.

Upon entering this charming little restaurant and Italian charcuterie, you'll walk past display cases filled with antipasti, deli meats, pâté, and cheeses; and shelves stocked with homemade pastas and other fancy foodstuffs. And if that's not enough to whet your appetite, you'll also glimpse chefs tending a pizza oven in an exhibition kitchen. The dining area is cheerful and inviting. Enzo's is a casual kind of place, very popular locally.

Pretty much the same menu is available throughout the day. Families troop in for pizzas—either the traditional American kind or Napoli pies with more sophisticated toppings and crisp, delicate crusts. Until 4:30pm you can also opt for panini (sandwiches on crusty Italian bread) with fillings such as Italian sausage, grilled onions, and peppers. Homemade pastas include fat bucatini tossed with mushrooms, fresh-grated Parmesan, prosciutto, bacon, and peas in a robust sauce. And Enzo's most fabulous entree is pollo alla cecco (roast breast of free-range chicken with rosemary potatoes and an Italian version of ratatouille). Beer and wine are available. For dessert, try zuccotto (Italian sponge cake soaked in Grand Marnier, layered with fresh fruit and crème anglaise, and topped with chocolate shavings). In busy seasons, arrive off-hours to avoid a wait.

WORTH A SPLURGE

✪ **Ming Court.** 9188 International Dr. (between Sand Lake Rd. and the Beeline Expy.). ☎ **407/351-9988.** Reservations recommended. Dim sum items mostly $1.95–$2.50; main courses $4.50–$7.95 at lunch, $12.50–$19.95 at dinner. AE, CB, DC, DISC, JCB, MC, V. Daily 11am–2:30pm and 4:30pm–midnight. CHINESE REGIONAL.

I was thrilled to find haute-cuisine Chinese fare in Orlando on a par with fine Chinese restaurants in New York and California. The Ming Court is fronted by a serpentine "cloud wall" crowned by engraved sea-green Chinese tiles (it's a celestial symbol; you dine above the clouds here, like the gods). Glass-walled terrace rooms overlook lotus ponds filled with colorful koi, and a plant-filled area under a lofty skylight ceiling evokes a starlit Ming Dynasty courtyard. A musician plays classical Chinese music on a *zheng* (a long zither) at dinner.

The menu offers specialties from diverse regions of China. Begin by ordering a variety of appetizers such as crispy wontons stuffed with vegetables and cream cheese, and wok-smoked shiitake mushrooms topped with sautéed scallions. The entrees will open up new culinary vistas to even the most sophisticated diners. Lightly battered deep-fried chicken breast is served with a delicate lemon-tangerine sauce. And crispy stir-fried jumbo Szechuan shrimp is enhanced by a light fresh tomato sauce nuanced with sake. At lunch, you can order dim sum items in addition to menu offerings. There's an extensive wine list, and, as a concession to Western palates, the Ming Court features sumptuous desserts such as a moist cake layered with Mandarin oranges, key lime, and fresh whipped cream in orange-vanilla sauce.

Wild Jacks. 7364 International Dr. (between Sand Lake Rd. and Carrier Dr.). ☎ **407/352-4407.** Reservations not accepted. Main courses $9.45–$17.95. AE, CB, DC, DISC, JCB, MC, V. Daily 4:30–11pm. STEAK/BARBECUE.

This exuberantly Western upscale steak and barbecue restaurant whimsically combines honky-tonk and haute elements in its decor. There's an exhibition kitchen with an open-pit grill and a copper bar with an iced beer well. The appetizers here are first rate: skewers of tangy barbecued shrimp served over Texas rice studded with corn kernels and red and green peppers or miniature tacos filled with smoked chicken and cheeses. The best main choice is the smoked brisket barbecue, served with salad, warm molasses bread and honey, and your choice of two side dishes—take the jalapeño mashed potatoes and grilled corn on the cob. For dessert, there's peach cobbler topped with vanilla ice cream sprinkled with cinnamon.

4 Tips for Visiting Walt Disney World Attractions

Walt Disney World encompasses the Magic Kingdom; Animal Kingdom; Epcot; Disney–MGM Studios; Pleasure Island; the Walt Disney Village Marketplace and Disney's West Side, a lakeside enclave of shops and restaurants; Disney's West Side, three water parks (Typhoon Lagoon, River Country, and Blizzard Beach). Discovery Island, a nature preserve and aviary, closed with the opening of Animal Kingdom.

TIPS FOR PLANNING YOUR TRIP

Planning is essential. Unless you're staying for considerably more than a week, you can't possibly experience all the rides, shows, and attractions here, not to mention the vast array of recreational facilities. You'll only wear yourself to a frazzle trying—it's better to follow a relaxed itinerary, including leisurely meals and recreational activities, than to make a demanding job out of trying to see everything.

Read the *Vacations* guide and the detailed descriptions in this book, and plan your visit to include all shows and attractions that interest you. It's a good idea to make a daily itinerary, putting these in some kind of sensible geographical sequence so you're not zigzagging all over the place. Familiarize yourself in advance with the layout of each park. Schedule in sit-down shows, recreational activities (a boat ride or swim late in the afternoon can be wonderfully refreshing), and at least some unhurried meals. My suggested itineraries are given below.

INFORMATION   Call or write the **Walt Disney World Co.,** P.O. Box 10000, Lake Buena Vista, FL 32830-1000 (☎ **407/934-7639**), for a copy of the very informative *Walt Disney World Vacations,* an invaluable planning aid. Once you've arrived in town, guest-services and concierge desks in all area hotels—especially Disney properties and "official" hotels—have **up-to-the-minute information** about what's going on in the parks. If your hotel doesn't have this information, call ☎**407/824-4321.**

There are also **information locations** in each park—at City Hall in the Magic Kingdom, at Innoventions East near the World Key terminals in Epcot, and the Guest Services Building in Disney–MGM Studios.

BUY TICKETS IN ADVANCE   You can purchase multi-day passes (see details below) before your trip by calling **Ticket Mail Order** (☎ **407/934-7639**). Allow 21 days for processing your request, and include a $2 postage and handling charge. Of course, you can always purchase tickets at any of the parks, but why stand in an avoidable line? *Note:* One-day tickets can be purchased only at park entrances.

ARRIVE EARLY   Always arrive at the parks a good 30 to 45 minutes before opening time, thus avoiding a traffic jam entering the park and a long line at the gate. Early arrival also lets you experience one or two major attractions before big lines form. In high season the parking lots sometimes fill up and you may even have to wait to get in. The longest lines in all parks are between 11am and 4pm.

PARKING   Parking, which is free to guests at WDW resorts, costs $6 per day no matter how many parks you visit. **Be sure to note your parking location before leaving your car.** There are special lots for travelers with disabilities at each park (call ☎ 407/824-4321 for details). Don't worry about parking far from the entrance gates; trams constantly ply the route.

WHEN YOU ARRIVE IN THE PARKS   Upon entering any of the four major Disney parks, you'll be given an **entertainment schedule** and a comprehensive **park guide map,** which contains a map of the park and lists all attractions, shops, shows, and restaurants. If by some fluke you haven't obtained these, they're available at the information locations mentioned above. If you lose one during the day, many shops have extra copies behind the cash register. If you've formulated an itinerary before arrival, you already know the major shows (check show schedules for additional ideas) you want to see during the day and what arrangements you need to make. If you haven't done this, use your early arrival time, while waiting for the park to open, to figure out which shows to attend, and, where necessary, make reservations for them as soon as the gates swing open. Plan, but remember to be flexible. If you miss the 12:15 show, there is almost always another one. You dictate your schedule. Don't let your schedule dictate you.

LEAVING THE PARKS   If you leave any of the parks and plan to return later in the day, be sure to get your hand stamped on exiting. If you are park hopping, remember to also keep your paper pass.

BEST DAYS TO VISIT   The busiest days at the Magic Kingdom, Animal Kingdom, and Epcot are Monday to Wednesday; at Disney–MGM Studios, Thursday and Friday. Surprisingly, weekends are the least busy at all parks. In peak seasons, especially, arrange your visits accordingly.

THE EASY WAY   Staying at Disney resorts and "official" hotels simplifies many of the above tasks and procedures. See the full list of perks for Disney and "official" hotel guests under "Accommodations You Can Afford, in & Around the Parks," earlier in this chapter.

OPERATING HOURS   Hours of operation vary somewhat throughout the year. The **Magic Kingdom** and **Disney–MGM Studios** are generally open from 9am to 7pm, with extended hours, sometimes as late as midnight, during major holidays and the summer months. **Animal Kingdom** is open from 8am to 5pm.

Epcot hours are generally from 9am to 9pm, with Future World open from 9am to 7pm and World Showcase from 11am to 9pm—once again with extended holiday hours.

Typhoon Lagoon and **Blizzard Beach** are open from 10am to 5pm most of the year (with extended hours during some holidays), 9am to 8pm in summer.

River Country is open from 10am to 5pm most of the year (with extended hours during some holidays), 10am to 7pm in summer.

Note: Epcot and MGM sometimes open a half hour or more before the posted time. Keep in mind, too, that Disney-resort guests enjoy early admission to all three major parks on designated days.

TICKETS   There are several ticket options. Most people get the best value from 4- and 5-day passes. All passes offer unlimited use of the WDW transportation system. The prices quoted here do no include sales tax, and they are, of course, subject to change.

Adult prices are paid by anyone over 10 years of age. **Children's rates** are for ages 3 to 9; children 2 and under are admitted free.

A **1-day, one-park ticket for the Magic Kingdom, Animal Kingdom, Epcot, or Disney–MGM Studios** is $42 for adults, $34 for children. A **1-day ticket to Typhoon Lagoon or Blizzard Beach** is $25.95 for adults, $20.50 for children. A **1-day ticket to River Country** is $15.95 for adults, $12.50 for children. A **1-day ticket to Pleasure Island** is $18.95 for adults.

The **Four-Day Value Pass** provides single-day admission to Magic Kingdom, MGM Studios, Animal Kingdom, and Epcot. Unlike the park hopper, with this pass you are restricted to one park a day. Adults pay $149, children $119.

The **5-Day Park-Hopper Pass** provides unlimited admission to the Magic Kingdom, Animal Kingdom, Epcot, and Disney–MGM Studios on any 5 days; you can visit any combination of parks on any given day. It also includes admission to Typhoon Lagoon, River Country, Blizzard Beach, and Pleasure Island for a period of 7 days beginning the first date stamped. Adults pay $189; children $151.

The **All-in-One Hopper Pass** comes in both 6-day ($249 adults, $199 children) and 7-day ($274 adults, $219 children) versions.

If you're staying at any Walt Disney World resort or "official" hotel, you're also eligible for a money-saving **Be Our Guest Pass** priced according to length of stay. It also offers special perks.

If you plan on visiting Walt Disney World more than once during the year, inquire about a money-saving annual pass.

BEHIND THE SCENES: SPECIAL TOURS IN WALT DISNEY WORLD

In addition to the greenhouse tour described below in Epcot's Land pavilion, the Disney parks offer a number of walking tours and learning programs. Call ☎ **407/WDW-TOUR** (407/939-8687) for more information. These include:

- The 3-hour **Hidden Treasures of the World Showcase** focuses on the architecture and entertainment offerings of Epcot's international pavilions; it's $25 per person.
- **Gardens of the World,** a 3-hour tour of the extraordinary landscaping at Epcot led by a Disney horticulturist, costs $25 per person.
- The 4-hour **Keys to the Kingdom** provides an orientation to the Magic Kingdom and a glimpse into the high-tech operational systems behind the magic; it costs $45 per person.
- There are also **learning programs** (☎ **407/363-6000**) on subjects ranging from animation to international cultures. Call for details.

SUGGESTED ITINERARIES

You won't see all the attractions at any of the parks in a single day, especially during peak season when lines are very long. Read through the descriptions, decide which are musts for you, and try to get to them. My favorite rides and attractions are starred. I stress once more: It's more enjoyable to keep a relaxed pace than to race around like a maniac trying to do it all.

ONE DAY IN THE MAGIC KINGDOM Get to the park well before opening time, tickets in hand. When the gates open, make a dash for Extra"TERROR"estrial Alien Encounter in Tomorrowland, which, as the newest major attraction, will have very long lines later in the day.

Then hightail it to Frontierland and ride Splash Mountain, another biggie, before long lines form there. (There is limited shade in the waiting lines and it can also get hot in the afternoon.) When you come off, it will still be early enough to beat the lines at one more major attraction; head over to Adventureland and do Pirates of the Caribbean.

Then relax and take it slow. Complete whatever else interests you in Adventureland. Then walk over to Frontierland and enjoy the attractions there until lunchtime. Have lunch while taking in the 12:15 or 1:30pm show at the Diamond Horseshoe Saloon Revue (they don't take reservations, so arrive early).

After lunch, continue visiting Frontierland attractions as desired, or proceed to the Hall of Presidents and the Haunted Mansion in Liberty Square. By 2:30pm (earlier in

Coupons, Passes & Other Tips for Saving Your Orlan-dough

- **One Day, One Park.** When buying multiday tickets from Disney, stick with the Value Pass over the Park Hopper. Both options allow visits to multiple parks, but with the Park Hopper, you're paying for the privilege to go from park to park during a single day. This takes considerable effort and time, and can be difficult if you're traveling with children. It's better to stick to one park per day.
- **It's Not Just Disney Anymore.** Universal Studios Florida, Sea World, and Wet 'n' Wild have joined together to fight Disney's multipark pass system. With the **Flex Pass,** you'll pay one price to visit any of the participating non-Disney parks during either a 7- or 10-day period. A 7-day, three-park pass is $99.95 for ages 10 to adult or $82.95 for children under 10. A 10-day, four-park pass that includes Busch Gardens in Tampa sells for $129.95 for adults and $107 children. (Children under 2 are free.) You can purchase a Flex Pass at any participating park.
- **Coupons, Coupons Everywhere.** For less than $40, you can purchase the coupon book **Entertainment 99,** which can save you money on dining, car rentals, hotels, and tickets to smaller attractions, such as the Orlando Science Center and Ripley's Believe It or Not. There are lots of coupons for eateries on International Drive and the tourist populated areas. There is even a discount card that can be used for a free entree at several fine-dining establishments. You won't find big discounts on the major parks, although there are sometimes dollars-off coupons that will add up for large families. If you're driving into the area, the book is also helpful, because the Orlando edition also includes some Daytona Beach establishments. For information call ☎ **800/374-4464.**
- **Extra! Extra! Local Newspaper Saves You Money.** There's no shortage of golf courses in the Orlando area; the best way to find a good deal is to look in the sports section of the *Orlando Sentinel* for discount coupons and otherwise unadvertised specials. The Friday "Calendar" section of the *Orlando Sentinel* also sometimes includes two-for-one dinner special coupons and other entertainment discounts to entertainment. It will also list cultural events and concerts throughout central Florida, some of which are free or have a nominal admission charge.

peak seasons), you should snag a seat on the curb in Liberty Square along the parade route. After the parade, continue around the park taking in Fantasyland and Tomorrowland attractions. If SpectroMagic is on during your stay, don't miss it.

If you have little kids (age 8 and under) in your party, start your day instead by taking the WDW Railroad from Main Street to Mickey's Toon Town to see the show. Work your way through Fantasyland until lunch, once again at the Diamond Horseshoe. After lunch, visit the Country Bear Jamboree in Frontierland and proceed to Adventureland for the Jungle Cruise, Swiss Family Treehouse, and Tropical Serenade. Once again, stop in good time to get parade seats (in Frontierland). Little kids need to sit right up front to see everything. That's a long enough day for most young children, and your best plan is to go back to your hotel for a nap or swim. If, however, you wish to continue, return to Frontierland and/or Fantasyland for the rides you didn't complete earlier.

IF YOU CAN SPEND ONLY 1 DAY AT EPCOT   Epcot really requires at least 2 days, so this is a highlight tour. As above, arrive early, tickets in hand. If you haven't already made lunch reservations in advance by calling ☎ **407/WDW-DINE,** make your first stop at the WorldKey terminals in Innoventions East. I suggest a 1pm lunch at the San Angel Inn Restaurant in the Mexico pavilion. If you don't like Mexican food, move up one pavilion to Norway and reserve for the buffet at Akershus. You can make dinner reservations at the same time. Plan dinner for about 7pm, which will allow you time to eat and find a good viewing spot for IllumiNations (usually at 9pm, but check your schedule).

Spend no more than an hour exploring Innoventions East. Then move on to the Universe of Energy show. Continue to the Wonders of Life Pavilion where must-sees include Body Wars, Cranium Command, and The Making of Me.

If time allows—it will depend on line waits at attractions—take in the show at Horizons before heading into World Showcase for lunch in the Mexico pavilion. At lunch, check your show schedule and decide which shows to incorporate into your day.

Then walk around the lagoon, visiting highlight attractions: *Wonders of China, The American Adventure, Impressions de France,* and *O Canada,* allowing yourself some time for browsing and shopping. After dinner, stay on for IllumiNations.

A word about Epcot dining: Sit-down meals at World Showcase Pavilions and the Living Seas are a pleasant but pricey part of the Epcot experience. There are plenty of less-expensive eateries throughout the park, including ethnic ones with cafe seating in many World Showcase Pavilions. And since these don't require reservations, you're not tied down to specific mealtimes. See your *Epcot Guidemap* for details.

IF YOU CAN SPEND 2 DAYS AT EPCOT   Ignore the 1-day itinerary above, and begin your day by making all necessary restaurant reservations—once again for lunch in Mexico or Norway at about 1pm. Make reservations for Day 2 at the same time.

Skip Innoventions East for now, and work your way thoroughly through the Universe of Energy, Wonders of Life, Horizons, and World of Motion pavilions, keeping your lunch reservation time in mind. After lunch, walk clockwise around the lagoon, visiting each foreign pavilion and taking in as many shows as you like (consult your show schedule and try to keep pace as well as possible). Leave IllumiNations for your second day's visit.

Begin your second day exploring Innoventions East, and proceed counterclockwise, taking in Spaceship Earth, Innoventions West, the Living Seas (its Coral Reef restaurant is a good choice for lunch), and all the other pavilions on the west side of the park. Cap your Epcot visit with IllumiNations.

A DAY AT DISNEY–MGM STUDIOS THEME PARK   Since show times change frequently here, it's impossible to really give you a workable itinerary. Upon entering the park, if you haven't already made dining arrangements, stop at the Hollywood Brown Derby and make reservations for lunch. Or you might want to conserve touring time by having a light lunch at a casual eatery and saving the Derby for a relaxing dinner.

Make a beeline for the Twilight Zone Tower of Terror. While you're waiting in line, plan the rest of your schedule, being sure to include these not-to-be-missed attractions: the Magic of Disney Animation, the Great Movie Ride, Jim Henson's Muppet Vision 3-D. In the back lot there are usually shows attached to Disney movie releases, such as *The Voyage Of The Little Mermaid, The Spirit of Pocahontas,* and *Beauty and the*

Beast. These shows do fill up but since there are several performance times during the day you are sure to get a seat.

Time for more? Do Superstar Television, the Indiana Jones Epic Stunt Spectacular, Star Tours, Inside the Magic, and the Backstage Studio Tour. In peak seasons stay on for the fireworks.

There is an afternoon parade in this park but it is not nearly as spectacular as its Magic Kingdom counterpart. If you have children and their favorite movie provides the parade theme, you may have to go. Otherwise, skip the parade and enjoy shorter lines at the attractions and restaurants.

IF YOU HAVE 1 DAY IN ANIMAL KINGDOM For the best chance of seeing the animals, arrive about 30 minutes before the gates open at 8am. Although not as packed with attractions as other WDW parks, the size of Animal Kingdom means a considerable amount of travel time once you pass through those opening gates. Don't linger in the Oasis area or around the Tree of Life—head directly to the back of the park to be first in line for Kilimanjaro Safari. You'll see the animals before the heat of the day; this is when they are most active (and before the lines become impossibly long).

Work your way back through Africa, visit Gorilla Falls and, if you have children, take the train to Conservation Station. (If not, go back to Safari Village.) Head back to Safari Village, tour the Tree of Life, watch *It's Tough to Be a Bug* and eat lunch. If the weather is not oppressively hot, you may want hit up one of the food carts for a snack and enjoy some of the street performers or African storytellers. If you want to sit down to eat, dine at Tuskers Restaurant.

After lunch, if you have children, visit Camp Minnie-Mickey, greet some characters, and visit Grandmother Willow's cove. After that head to Dinoland to play in the Boneyard, watch *Journey into the Jungle Book* and, if the little ones are tall enough, ride Countdown to Extinction. Adults will probably want to postpone Camp Minnie-Mickey and go straight to Dinoland. Wind up the day with the last Lion King show in Camp Minnie-Mickey before heading out through Oasis.

End the day with a leisurely stroll through the animal habitats in Oasis. If you want to dine at the RainForest Cafe, go make reservations, making sure you can get back into the park, and then, while you are waiting, explore the Oasis.

5 The Magic Kingdom

Centered around Cinderella Castle, the Magic Kingdom occupies about 100 acres, with 45 major attractions and numerous restaurants and shops in seven themed sections or "lands." From the parking lot, you have to take a short monorail or ferry ride to the entrance. During peak attendance times, arrive at the Magic Kingdom an hour before opening time to avoid long lines at these conveyances.

Upon entering the park, consult your *Magic Kingdom Guidemap* to get your bearings. Also consult your entertainment schedule to see what's on for the day.

If you have questions, most park employees are very knowledgeable, and City Hall, on your left as you enter, is both an information center and, along with Mickey's Toon Town, a likely place to meet up with costumed characters. There's a stroller-rental shop just after the turnstiles to your right, and the Kodak Camera Center, near Town Square, supplies all conceivable photographic needs, including camera and Camcorder rentals and 2-hour film developing. (Of course, all these items are considerably more expensive than if you shop before you enter the park.)

MAIN STREET, U.S.A.

Designed to replicate a typical turn-of-the-century American street (albeit one that culminates in a 13th-century castle), this is the gateway to the Kingdom. Don't dawdle on Main Street when you enter the park; leave it for the end of the day when you're heading back to your hotel.

WALT DISNEY WORLD RAILROAD & OTHER MAIN STREET VEHICLES
You can board an authentic 1928 steam-powered railroad here for a 15-minute journey clockwise around the perimeter of the park. There are stations in Frontierland and Mickey's Starland. There are also horse-drawn trolleys, horseless carriages, jitneys, omnibuses, and fire engines plying the short route along Main Street from Town Square to Cinderella Castle.

MAIN STREET CINEMA   The Main Street Cinema is an air-conditioned hexagonal theater where vintage black-and-white Disney cartoons (including *Steamboat Willie* from 1928, in which Mickey and Minnie debuted) are aired continually on two screens. Viewers have to watch these standing—there are no seats.

CINDERELLA CASTLE   At the end of Main Street, in the center of the park, you'll come to a fairyland castle, 180 feet high and housing a restaurant (King Stefan's Banquet Hall) and shops. Cinderella herself, dressed for the ball, often makes appearances in the lobby area. Don't linger here; save it for the end of the day.

ADVENTURELAND

Cross a bridge to your left and stroll into an exotic jungle of lush tropical foliage, thatch-roofed huts, and carved totems. Amid dense vines and stands of palm and bamboo, drums are beating and swashbuckling adventures are taking place.

SWISS FAMILY TREEHOUSE   This attraction is based on the 1960 Disney movie version of Johann Wyss's *Swiss Family Robinson,* about a shipwrecked family who created an ingenious dwelling in the branches of a sprawling banyan tree. Using materials and furnishings salvaged from their downed ship, the Robinsons created bedrooms, a kitchen, a library, and a living room. Visitors ascend the 50-foot tree for a close-up look into these rooms. Note the Rube Goldberg rope-and-bucket device with bamboo chutes that dips water from a stream and carries it to treetop chambers.

✪ **JUNGLE CRUISE**   What a cruise! In the course of about 10 minutes, your boat sails through an African veldt in the Congo, an Amazon rain forest, the Mekong River in Southeast Asia, and along the Nile. You'll see lavish scenery, cascading waterfalls, and lush foliage (most of it real), including dozens of audio-animatronic birds and animals—elephants, zebras, lions, giraffes, crocodiles, tigers, even fluttering butterflies. On the shore you'll pass an Asian temple cave guarded by snakes and a jungle camp taken over by apes. But the adventures aren't all on shore. Passengers are menaced by everything from water-spouting elephants to fierce warriors who attack with spears.

PIRATES OF THE CARIBBEAN   You'll proceed through a long grottolike passageway to board a boat into a pitch-black cave where elaborate scenery and hundreds of audio-animatronic figures (including lifelike dogs, cats, chickens, and donkeys) depict a pirate raid on a Caribbean town. Passengers view tableaux of fierce-looking pirates swigging rum, looting, and plundering. This might be scary for kids under 5.

TROPICAL SERENADE   In a large hexagonal Polynesian-style dwelling, 250 tropical birds, chanting totem poles, and singing flowers whistle, tweet, and warble songs

The Magic Kingdom

MAIN STREET, U.S.A.:
Main Street Cinema ③
Main Street Vehicles ②
Walt Disney World Railroad ①

ADVENTURELAND:
Jungle Cruise ④
Pirates of the Caribbean ⑤
Swiss Family Treehouse ⑦
Tropical Serenade with the
  Enchanted Tiki Birds ⑥

FRONTIERLAND:
Big Thunder Mountain
  Railroad ⑭
Country Bear Jamboree ⑧
The Diamond Horseshoe
  Saloon Revue ⑩
Frontierland Shootin'
  Arcade ⑨
Splash Mountain ⑫
Tom Sawyer Island ⑪
Walt Disney World Railroad ⑬

LIBERTY SQUARE:
The Hall of Presidents ⑯
The Haunted Mansion ⑱
Liberty Square Riverboat ⑮
Mike Fink Keelboats ⑰

FANTASYLAND:
Castle Forecourt Stage ⑲
Cinderella's Castle ⑳
Cinderella's Golden
  Carousel ㉑

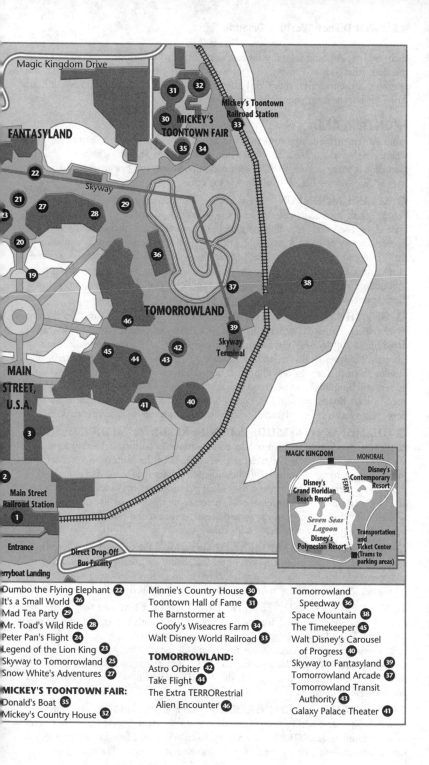

Magic Kingdom Drive

FANTASYLAND

MICKEY'S
TOONTOWN FAIR

Mickey's Toontown
Railroad Station

Skyway

TOMORROWLAND

Skyway
Terminal

MAIN
STREET,
U.S.A.

Main Street
Railroad Station

Entrance

Direct Drop-Off
Bus Facility

Ferryboat Landing

MAGIC KINGDOM   MONORAIL

Disney's
Contemporary
Resort

Disney's
Grand Floridian
Beach Resort

Seven Seas
Lagoon

Disney's
Polynesian Resort

Transportation
and
Ticket Center
(Trams to
parking areas)

such as "Let's All Sing Like the Birdies Sing." Highlights include a thunderstorm in the dark (the gods are angry!), a light show over the fountain, and, of course, the famous "in the tiki, tiki, tiki, tiki, tiki room" song. You'll find yourself singing it all day. This is a must for young children.

FRONTIERLAND

From Adventureland, step into the wild and woolly past of the American frontier, where rough-and-tumble architecture runs to log cabins and rustic saloons, and the landscape is southwestern scrubby with mesquite, yucca, and prickly pear. Across the river is Tom Sawyer Island, reachable via log rafts.

✪ **SPLASH MOUNTAIN**   Themed after Walt Disney's 1946 film *Song of the South,* Splash Mountain takes you on an enchanting journey in a hollowed-out log craft along the canals of a flooded mountain, past tableaux of backwoods swamps, bayous, spooky caves, and waterfalls. The longest of the Disney rides, its a mixture of thrill ride and themed show. Your log craft twists, turns, and splashes—sometimes plummeting in total darkness—culminating in a thrilling 5-story splashdown from mountaintop to briar-filled pond at 40 miles per hour! *Note:* You will get wet, so if you have a poncho, wear it.

✪ **BIG THUNDER MOUNTAIN RAILROAD**   This mining-disaster-themed roller coaster—its thrills deriving from hairpin turns and descents in the dark—is situated in a 200-foot-high red-stone mountain with 2,780 feet of track winding through windswept canyons and bat-filled caves. You'll board a runaway train that careens through the ribs of a dinosaur, under a thundering waterfall, past spewing geysers and bubbling mud pots, and over a bottomless volcanic pool. Riders are threatened by flash floods, earthquakes, rickety bridges, and avalanches. Because of the outdoor twists and turns and lantern lighting, this is a fun ride to take after dark.

✪ **DIAMOND HORSESHOE SALOON REVUE & MEDICINE SHOW** Here's an opportunity to sit down in air-conditioned comfort and enjoy a rousing Western revue. The "theater" is a re-creation of a turn-of-the-century saloon. Marshall John Charles sings and banters with the audience, Jingles the Piano Man plays honky-tonk tunes, there's a magic act, and dance hall girls do a spirited cancan—all with lots of humor and audience participation. There are seven shows daily; plan on going around lunchtime so you can eat during the show. The menu features deli or peanut butter and jelly sandwiches served with chips.

✪ **COUNTRY BEAR JAMBOREE**   I've always loved the Country Bear Jamboree, a 15-minute show featuring a troupe of fiddlin', banjo strummin', harmonica playin' audio-animatronic bears belting out rollicking country tunes and crooning plaintive love songs. A special holiday show plays throughout the Christmas season each year.

TOM SAWYER ISLAND   Board Huck Finn's raft for a 1-minute float across the river to the densely forested Tom Sawyer Island, where kids can explore the narrow passages of Injun Joe's Cave (complete with scary sound effects), a walk-through windmill, a serpentine abandoned mine, or Fort Sam Clemens. Narrow winding tree-lined paths create an authentic backwoods island feel. You might combine this attraction with a fried-chicken lunch at Aunt Polly's restaurant, which has outdoor tables on a porch overlooking the river.

FRONTIERLAND SHOOTIN' ARCADE   Combining state-of-the-art electronics with a traditional shooting-gallery format, this vast arcade presents an array of targets in a three-dimensional 1850s gold-mining town scenario. Electronic firing mechanisms loaded with infrared bullets are concealed in genuine Hawkins 54-caliber buffalo rifles. When you hit a target, elaborate sound and motion gags are set off. You get 25 shots for 50¢.

LIBERTY SQUARE

Serving as a transitional area between Frontierland and Fantasyland, Liberty Square evokes 18th-century America with Georgian architecture and Colonial Williamsburg-type shops. You might encounter a fife-and-drum corps marching along Liberty Square's cobblestone streets.

THE HALL OF PRESIDENTS   In this redbrick colonial hall, all American presidents—from George Washington to Bill Clinton (who recorded the voice for his character)—are represented by audio-animatronic figures. They dramatize important events in the nation's history, from the signing of the Constitution through the space age. The show begins with a film, projected on an 1808 screen, about the importance of the Constitution. Maya Angelou narrates.

✪ **THE HAUNTED MANSION**   Its eerie ambience enhanced by inky darkness, weird music, and mysterious screams and rappings, this mansion is replete with spooky effects: a ghostly banquet and ball, a graveyard band, a suit of armor that comes alive, luminous spiders, a talking head in a crystal ball, and much more. At the end of the ride, a ghost joins you in your car. The experience is more amusing than terrifying, so you can take most small children inside.

BOAT RIDES   A steam-powered sternwheeler called the ***Richard F. Irvine*** and two **Mike Fink Keel Boats** (the *Bertha Mae* and the *Gullywhumper*) depart (the latter summers and holidays only) from Liberty Square for scenic cruises along the Rivers of America. Both ply the identical route and make a restful interlude for foot-weary parkgoers.

FANTASYLAND

The attractions in this happy "land"—themed after such Disney film classics as *Snow White* and *Peter Pan*—are especially popular with young visitors. If your kids are 8 or under, you might want to make it your first stop in the Magic Kingdom.

LEGEND OF THE LION KING   This stage spectacular based on Disney's blockbuster motion-picture musical combines animation, movie footage, sophisticated puppetry, and high-tech special effects.

SNOW WHITE'S ADVENTURES   This attraction used to focus only on the more sinister elements of Grimm's fairy tale—most notably the evil queen and the cackling toothless witch—leaving small children screaming in terror. It's been toned down now, with Snow White appearing in a number of pleasant scenes—at the castle courtyard wishing well, in the dwarfs' cottage, and riding off with the prince to live "happily ever after." Even so, this could be scary for kids under 7.

MAD TEA PARTY   This is a traditional amusement park ride à la Disney with an *Alice in Wonderland* theme. Riders sit in oversize pink teacups on saucers that careen around a circular platform. Believe it or not, this can be a pretty wild ride or a tame one—it depends on how much you spin, a factor under your control via a wheel in the cup.

MR. TOAD'S WILD RIDE   This ride is based on the 1949 Disney film *The Adventures of Ichabod and Mr. Toad,* which was itself based on the classic children's book *The Wind in the Willows.* Riders navigate a series of dark rooms, hurtling into solid objects (a fireplace, a bookcase, a haystack) and through barn doors into a coop of squawking chickens. They're menaced by snorting bulls and an oncoming locomotive in a pitch-black tunnel, and are sent to jail (for car theft), to hell (complete with pitchfork-wielding demons), and through a fiery volcano.

CINDERELLA'S GOLDEN CAROUSEL   It's a beauty, built by Italian wood carvers in the Victorian tradition in 1917 and refurbished by Disney artists who added scenes from the Cinderella story. The band organ plays such Disney classics as "When You Wish Upon a Star."

DUMBO, THE FLYING ELEPHANT   This is a very tame kiddie ride in which the cars—baby elephants (Dumbos)—go around and around in a circle gently rising and dipping.

IT'S A SMALL WORLD   You know the song—and if you don't, you will. It plays continually as you sail "around the world" through vast rooms designed to represent different countries. They're inhabited by appropriately costumed audio-animatronic dolls and animals, all singing in tiny voices. This cast of thousands includes Chinese acrobats, Russian kazatski dancers, Indian snake charmers, Arabs on magic carpets, African drummers, a Venetian gondolier, and Australian koalas. Cute. Very cute.

PETER PAN'S FLIGHT   Riding in Captain Hook's ship, passengers career through dark passages while experiencing the story of *Peter Pan.* The adventure begins in the Darlings' nursery, and includes a flight over nighttime London to Never-Never-Land, where riders encounter mermaids, Indians, a ticking crocodile, the lost boys, Tinker-bell, Hook, Smee, and the rest—all to the movie music "You Can Fly, You Can Fly, You Can Fly." It's fun.

SKYWAY   Its entrance close to Peter Pan's Flight, the Skyway is an aerial tramway to Tomorrowland, which makes continuous round-trips throughout the day.

MICKEY'S TOONTOWN FAIR

Head off those cries of "where's Mickey" by taking the kids to this 2-acre replacement for Mickey's Starland that was unveiled during the 25th anniversary celebration in 1996. Toontown Fair offers kids a chance to meet their favorite Disney characters including Mickey, Minnie, Donald Duck, and Goofy. Set in a whimsical collection of candy-striped tents harking back to those turn-of-the-century county fairs, highlights include the Toontown Hall of Fame, animated shorts hosted by the stars, and both Mickey's and Minnie's country houses. Everything is brightly colored and kid-friendly in the best Disney tradition; there is even a kid-sized roller coaster. Toontown Fair has its own stop on the WDW Railroad.

TOMORROWLAND

This land focuses on the future—most notably, space travel and exploration. In 1994, the Disney people decided that Tomorrowland (originally designed in the 1970s) was beginning to look like "Yesterdayland." It has now been revamped to reflect the future as a galactic, science fiction–inspired community inhabited by humans, aliens, and robots. A vast state-of-the-art video-game arcade has also been added.

✪ **EXTRA "TERROR" ESTRIAL ALIEN ENCOUNTER**   Director George Lucas contributed his space-age vision to this major new Tomorrowland attraction. The action begins at the Interplanetary Convention Center where a mysterious corporation called X-S Tech is marketing an interplanetary "teletransporter" to Earthlings. In order to demonstrate it, X-S technicians try to teleport their sinister corporation head, Chairman Clench, to Earth. But the machine malfunctions, sending him to a distant planet instead and inadvertently teleporting a fearsome man-eating extraterrestrial to Earth. Lots of high-tech special effects here, from the alien's breath on your neck to a mist of alien slime.

THE TIMEKEEPER   This Jules Verne/H. G. Wells–inspired multimedia presentation combines Circle-Vision and IMAX footage with audio-animatronics. It's hosted by Timekeeper, a mad scientist robot and his assistant, 9-EYE, a flying female camera-headed droid and time machine test pilot. In an unpredictable jet-speed escapade, the audience visits medieval battlefields in Scotland, watches Leonardo at work, and floats in a hot-air balloon above Moscow's Red Square. There are many other adventures. Timekeeper also throttles his calendar forward, to the 300th anniversary of the French Revolution in 2089.

✪ **SPACE MOUNTAIN**   Space Mountain entertains visitors in its long lines with space-age music, meteorites, shooting stars, and space debris whizzing about overhead. These "illusioneering" effects, enhanced by appropriate audio, continue during the ride itself, which is a cosmic roller coaster in the inky starlit blackness of outer space. Your rocket climbs high before racing through a serpentine complex of aerial galaxies, making thrilling hairpin turns and rapid plunges. If you can, grab that very first seat for a truly thrilling ride. (Though it feels like you're going at breakneck speed, your car actually never goes faster than 28 miles per hour.)

DREAMFLIGHT   The history and wonder of aviation, from barnstorming to space shuttles, is captured in this whimsical fly through adventure. High-tech special effects and 70mm live-action film footage add dramatic 3-D–style verisimilitude. Guests travel from a futuristic airport up a hillside to witness a flying circus, parachutists, and other stunt flyers; the action moves on to the ocean-hopping age of commercial flight, and finally your vehicle is pulled into a giant jet engine and sent into outer space at a simulated speed of 300 miles per hour.

WALT DISNEY'S CAROUSEL OF PROGRESS   This 22-minute show in a revolving theater features an audio-animatronic family in various tableaux demonstrating a century of development (beginning in 1900) in electric gadgetry and contraptions from Victrolas to virtual reality.

SKYWAY   Its Tomorrowland entrance just west of Space Mountain, this aerial tramway to Fantasyland makes continuous round-trips throughout the day.

TOMORROWLAND TRANSIT AUTHORITY   A futuristic means of transportation, these small five-car trains have no engines. They work by electromagnets, emit no pollution, and use little power. Narrated by a computer guide named Horack I, TTA offers an overhead look at Tomorrowland, including a pretty good preview of Space Mountain. If you're only in the Magic Kingdom for 1 day, this can be skipped.

GRAND PRIX RACEWAY   This is a great thrill for kids (including teens still waiting to get their driver's license) who get to put the pedal to the metal, steer, and *vroom* down a speedway in an actual gas-powered sports car. Maximum speed on the 4-minute drive around the track is about 7 miles per hour, and kids have to be 4 feet 4 inches tall to drive alone.

ASTRO ORBITER   This is a tame, typical amusement park ride. The "rockets" are on arms attached to "the center of the galaxy," and they move up and down while orbiting spinning planets.

PARADES, FIREWORKS & MORE

You'll get an *Entertainment Show Schedule* when you enter the park, which lists all kinds of special goings-on for the day. These include concerts (everything from steel drums to barbershop quartets), encounters with Disney characters, holiday events, and the three major happenings listed below.

THE 3 O'CLOCK PARADE You haven't really seen a parade until you've seen one at Walt Disney World. This spectacular daily event kicks off at 3pm year-round on Main Street and meanders through Liberty Square and Frontierland. The route is outlined on your *Entertainment Show Schedule*.

The only problem: Even in slow seasons, you have to snag a seat along the curb a good half hour before it begins, and earlier during peak travel times. (That's a long time to sit on a hard curb; consider packing inflatable pillows.)

But the parade is worth a little discomfort. In addition to Mickey and all his Disney pals, there are elaborate floats, stunning costumes, special effects, and a captivating cavalcade of dancers, singers, and other talented performers. Great music, too.

✪ **SPECTROMAGIC** Along a darkened parade route (the same one as above), 72,000 watts of dazzling high-tech lighting effects (including holography) create a glowing array of pixies and peacocks, sea horses and winged horses, flower gardens and fountains. Roger Rabbit is the eccentric conductor of an orchestra producing a rainbow of musical notes that waft magically into the night air. There are dancing ostriches from *Fantasia*, whirling electric butterflies, bejewelled coaches, luminescent ElectroMen atop spinning whirlyballs, and, of course, Mickey, surrounded by a sparkling confetti of light. And the music and choreography are on a par with the technology.

Once again, very early arrival is essential to get a seat on the curb. SpectroMagic takes place nightly in summer, on selected nights during Christmas and Easter vacation times, and during other special celebrations. Consult your *Entertainment Show Schedule* for details.

✪ **FIREWORKS** Like SpectroMagic, Fantasy in the Sky Fireworks, immediately preceded by Tinker Bell's magical flight from Cinderella's Castle, take place nightly in summer, on selected nights during Christmas and Easter vacation times, and during other special celebrations. Consult your *Entertainment Show Schedule* for details. Suggested viewing areas are Liberty Square, Frontierland, and Mickey's Starland.

6 Epcot

Ever growing, Epcot today occupies 260 acres so stunningly landscaped as to be worth visiting for its botanical beauty alone. There are two major sections, Future World and World Showcase.

Epcot is huge, and walking around it can be exhausting (some say Epcot's acronym stands for "Every Person Comes Out Tired"). Don't try to do it all in 1 day. Conserve energy by taking launches across the lagoon from the edge of Future World to Germany or Morocco. There are also double-decker buses circling the World Showcase Promenade and making stops at Norway, Italy, France, and Canada.

Unlike the Magic Kingdom, Epcot's parking lot is right at the gate. If you don't get them in the parking lot or at the gate, stop by the Innoventions East information center when you come in to pick up an *Epcot Guidemap* and entertainment schedule, and, if you so desire, make reservations for lunch or dinner. Many Epcot restaurants are described in the "Dining" section, earlier in this chapter.

Strollers can be rented to your left at the Future World entrance plaza and in World Showcase at the International Gateway between the United Kingdom and France.

FUTURE WORLD

The northern section of Epcot (where you enter the park) comprises Future World, centered on a giant geosphere known as Spaceship Earth. Future World's 10 themed areas, sponsored by major corporations, focus on discovery, scientific achievements,

WORLD SHOWCASE

THE AMERICAN
ADVENTURE

ITALY

JAPAN

MOROCCO

GERMANY

American Gardens
Theatre

Refreshment
Outpost

FRANCE

Boat Dock

Boat
Dock

World Showcase Lagoon

Stroller &
Wheelchair
Rental

IllumiNations
(nightly)

INTERNATIONAL
GATEWAY

CHINA

UNITED
KINGDOM

NORWAY

Boat
Dock

WORLD
SHOWCASE
PLAZA

Boat
Dock

MEXICO

Disney
Traders

Port of
Entry

CANADA

JOURNEY INTO
IMAGINATION

WORLD
OF
MOTION

INNOVENTIONS

HORIZONS

THE
LAND

WONDERS
OF LIFE

EARTH
STATION

THE
LIVING
SEAS

SPACESHIP
EARTH

UNIVERSE OF
ENERGY

Stroller &
Wheelchair
Rental

Lost & Found

Guest
Relations
Window

Pet Care
Kennel

ENTRANCE PLAZA
Monorail Station

Bus
Information

Taxi Pickup

FUTURE WORLD

NA-0047

and tomorrow's technologies in areas running the gamut from energy to undersea exploration.

✪ **SPACESHIP EARTH** This massive, silvery geosphere symbolizes Epcot, so it is a must-do. But long lines can be avoided by saving it until later in the day when you can, more than likely, simply walk on in. Inside, a show takes visitors on a 15-minute journey through the history of communications. You board time-machine vehicles to the distant past, where an audio-animatronic Cro-Magnon shaman recounts the story of a hunt while others record it on cave walls. You advance thousands of years to ancient Egypt, where hieroglyphics adorn temple walls and writing is recorded on papyrus scrolls. You'll progress through the Phoenician and Greek alphabets, and the Guttenburg printing press and the Renaissance. Technologies develop at a rapid pace, through the telegraph, telephone, radio, movies, and TV. It's but a short step to the age of electronic communications. You are catapulted into outer space to see "Spaceship Earth" from a new perspective, returning for a finale that places the audience amid interactive global networks. High-tech special effects, animated sets, and laser beams create an exciting experience.

INNOVENTIONS The pair of crescent-shaped buildings to your right and left just beyond Spaceship Earth house a constantly evolving 100,000-square-foot exhibit that showcases cutting-edge technologies and future products. Leading manufacturers sponsor ever-changing exhibit areas here. Visitors get a chance to preview virtual reality, check out electric cars, experience interactive television, and try out more than 200 new computer programs and games. Kids will be thrilled to preview new Sega video games. It is a chance to feel, hear, and see the future, hands-on.

The **virtual reality offerings**—from swimming with the sharks at the Vivid Group pod to a walking tour of St. Peter's Basilica by ENEL—are the latest high-tech wonders and a chance to experience what you have been reading about in science magazines.

There are several **show areas:** You can be interviewed by Jay Leno on TV. Sky Cyberguy takes you on a tour of the future of wireless communication. The Honeywell's Home Automation at the House of Innoventions Tour visits the computer-controlled abode of the future. The computer literate will find this a fascinating place to play. The technologically challenged will find it less rewarding.

The 2-story **Discovery Center,** located on the right side of Innoventions, includes an information resource area where guests can get answers to all their questions about Epcot attractions in particular and Walt Disney World in general. The Discovery Center also houses several shops including Field Trips, which features educational products and software.

✪ **THE LIVING SEAS** This pavilion contains the world's sixth "ocean," a 5.7-million-gallon saltwater aquarium (including a complete coral reef) inhabited by more than 4,000 sea creatures—sharks, barracudas, parrot fish, rays, and dolphins among them. A 2½-minute multimedia preshow about today's ocean technology is followed by a 7-minute film demonstrating the formation of the earth and seas as a means to support life.

After the film, visitors enter hydrolators for a rapid descent to the ocean floor. Upon arrival, they board Seacabs that wind around a 400-foot-long tunnel to enjoy stunning close-up views of ocean denizens in a natural coral-reef habitat. The ride concludes in the Seabase Concourse, which is the visitor center of **Seabase Alpha,** a prototype ocean-research facility of the future. Here, informational modules focus on practical resources grown in controllable undersea environments, marine mammals, the study of oceanography from space, and life in a coral-reef community. You can step into a diver's JIM Suit and use controls to complete diving tasks, and expand your knowledge of oceanography via interactive computers.

Note: Via a program called **Epcot DiveQuest,** certified divers can participate in a program that includes a 30- to 40-minute scuba dive in the Living Seas aquarium; for details, call ☎ **407/WDW-TOUR.**

THE LAND This largest of Future World's pavilions highlights humankind's relation to food and nature.

Living with the Land: A 13-minute boat ride takes you through three ecological environments (a rain forest, an African desert, and windswept American plains), each populated by appropriate audio-animatronic denizens. New farming methods and experiments—ranging from hydroponics to plants growing in simulated martian soil!—are showcased in real gardens. If you'd like a more serious overview, take a 45-minute guided walking tour of the growing areas, offered daily. Sign up at the Green Thumb Emporium shop near the entrance to Food Rocks. The cost is $5 for adults, $3 for children 3 to 9, free for children 2 and under. It's not, by the way, really geared to children.

Circle of Life: Combining spectacular live-action footage with animation, this 15-minute, 70mm motion picture based on *The Lion King* is a cautionary environmental tale.

Food Rocks: Audio-animatronic rock performers deliver an entertaining message about nutrition here.

✪ JOURNEY INTO IMAGINATION In this terrific pavilion, even the fountains are magical, with arching streams of water that leap into the air like glass rods. Its major attractions are:

Honey I Shrunk the Audience: This 3-D attraction is based on the Disney hit *Honey I Shrunk the Kids* films. The audience, after being menaced by hundreds of mice and a 3-D cat, is shrunk and given a good shaking by a gigantic 5-year-old. Dramatic 3-D action is enhanced by vibrating seats and creepy tactile effects. Finally, everyone returns to proper size—everyone but the family dog, which creates the final, not altogether pleasant, special effect (I won't reveal it).

Journey into Imagination Ride: Visitors board moving cars for a 14-minute ride. After a simulated flight across the nighttime sky, you enter the "Imaginarium," where whimsical tableaux featuring audio-animatronic characters explore creativity in the fine arts, performing arts, literature, science, and technology. The ride culminates at Image Works.

Image Works: Here you'll find dozens of hands-on electronic devices and interactive computers. You can activate musical instruments by stepping on hexagons of colored light, participate in a TV drama, draw patterns with laser beams, and conduct an electronic philharmonic orchestra.

TEST TRACK Called a mix of General Motors engineering and Disney imagineering, the newest Epcot attraction has guests in the driver's seat to experience the rigors of automobile testing. During a preshow—essentially a GM commercial—guests will learn how the company works to promote automotive safety, reliability, and performance. Then they'll board full-scale six-passenger test cars and travel on what appears to be an actual roadway, accelerating on long straight-aways, hugging hairpin turns, climbing steep hills, and braking abruptly—often in less-than-perfect road conditions. The ride will culminate with a terrifying high-speed outdoor run along the track's steeply banked "speed loop" that extends far beyond the pavilion facility. Cars will go at a top speed of 65 miles per hour. This was formerly World of Motion.

HORIZONS   The theme of this pavilion is the future, which presents an unending series of new horizons. You board gondolas for a 15-minute journey into the next millennium. The first tableau honors visionaries of past centuries (like Jules Verne) and looks at outdated visions of the future and classic sci-fi movies. You ascend to an area where an IMAX film projected on two 80-foot-high screens presents a kaleidoscope of brilliant micro and macro images—growing crystals, colonies in space, a space shuttle launching, DNA molecules, and a computer chip. You then travel to 21st-century cityscapes, desert farms, floating cities under the ocean's surface, and outer space colonies populated by audio-animatronic denizens. For the return to 20th-century earth, you can select one of three futuristic transportation systems: a personal spacecraft, a desert Hovercraft, or a minisubmarine.

⚙ **WONDERS OF LIFE**   Housed in a vast geodesic dome fronted by a 75-foot replica of a DNA molecule, this pavilion offers some of Future World's most engaging shows and attractions.

The Making of Me: Starring Martin Short, this captivating 15-minute motion picture combines live action with animation and spectacular in-utero photography to create the sweetest introduction imaginable to the facts of life. Don't miss it, although the presentation may prompt some questions from young children.

Body Wars: You're miniaturized to the size of a single cell for a medical rescue mission inside the immune system of a human body. Your objective: to save a miniaturized immunologist who has been accidentally swept into the bloodstream. This motion-simulator ride takes you on a wild journey through gale-force winds (in the lungs) and pounding heart chambers.

Cranium Command: In this hilarious multimedia attraction, Buzzy, an audio-animatronic brain-pilot-in-training, is charged with the seemingly impossible task of controlling the brain of a typical 12-year-old boy. The boy's body parts are played by Charles Grodin, Jon Lovitz, Bob Goldthwait, Kevin Nealon and Dana Carvey (as Hans and Franz), and George Wendt. It's another must-see attraction.

There are large areas filled with fitness-related shows, exhibits, and participatory activities, including a film called *Goofy About Health;* Coach's Corner, where your tennis, golf, or baseball swing is analyzed by experts; and the Sensory Funhouse, where you can test your perceptions.

UNIVERSE OF ENERGY   This 32-minute ride-through attraction—with visitors seated in solar-powered "traveling theater" cars—aims to better our understanding of America's energy problems. Recently refurbished, it's called **Ellen's Energy Adventure** and features comedian and television sitcom star Ellen DeGeneres as an energy expert tutored to be a *Jeopardy* contestant by Bill Nye, the Science Guy. On a massive screen in Theater I, an animated motion picture depicts the earth's molten beginnings, its cooling process, and the formation of fossil fuels. You move from Theater I to travel back 275 million years into an eerie storm-wracked landscape of the Mesozoic era, a time of violent geological activity. Here you're menaced by giant audio-animatronic dragonflies, pterodactyls, dinosaurs, earthquakes, and streams of molten lava before entering a steam-filled tunnel deep through the bowels of the volcano to emerge back in the 20th century in Theater II. In this new setting, which looks like a NASA Mission Control room, a 70mm film projected on a massive 210-foot wraparound screen depicts the challenges of the world's increasing energy demands and the emerging technologies that will help meet them. Your moving seats now return to Theater I where swirling special effects herald a film about how energy impacts our lives. It all ends on an upbeat note, with a vision of an energy-abundant future and Ellen as a new *Jeopardy* champion.

WORLD SHOWCASE

Surrounding a 40-acre lagoon at the park's southern end is World Showcase, a permanent community of 11 miniaturized nations, all with indigenous landmark architecture, landscaping, background music, restaurants, and shops. The cultural facets of each nation are explored in art exhibits, dance performances, innovative rides, films, and attractions. Employees in each pavilion are natives of the country represented.

✪ **CANADA**   Our neighbors to the north are represented by diverse architecture ranging from a mansard-roofed replica of Ottawa's Château Laurier (here called the Hôtel du Canada) to a rustic stone building modeled after a famous landmark near Niagara Falls. A Native American village signifies the culture of the Northwest, while the Canadian wilderness is reflected by a steep mountain (a Canadian Rocky), a waterfall cascading into a white-water stream, and a "forest" of evergreens, stately cedars, maples, and birch trees. Don't miss the stunning floral displays inspired by the Butchart Gardens in Victoria, British Columbia. The pavilion's highlight attraction is *O Canada!,* a dazzling 18-minute, 360° Circle-Vision film that reveals Canada's scenic splendor. Canada pavilion shops carry everything from soapstone carvings and snowshoes to rabbit-skin caps and heavy knitted sweaters—and, of course, maple syrup.

UNITED KINGDOM   Centered on Brittania Square—a formal London-style park, complete with copper-roofed gazebo bandstand and a statue of the Bard—the U.K. pavilion evokes Merry Olde England. Four centuries of architecture are represented along quaint cobblestone streets, troubadours and minstrels entertain in front of a traditional British pub, and a formal garden replicates the landscaping of 16th- and 17th-century palaces. High Street and Tudor Lane shops display a broad sampling of British merchandise, including toy soldiers, Paddington bears, Scottish tartans, and shortbreads. A tea shop occupies a replica of Anne Hathaway's thatch-roofed 16th-century cottage in Stratford-upon-Avon.

✪ **FRANCE**   This pavilion is entered via a replica of the beautiful cast-iron Pont des Arts footbridge over the Seine. It leads to a park inspired by Seurat's painting **A Sunday Afternoon on the Island of La Grande Jatte.** A one-tenth replica of the Eiffel Tower looms above the *grands boulevards.* The highlight attraction is *Impressions de France.* Shown in a palatial (mercifully sit-down) theater à la Fontainebleau, this 18-minute film is a scenic journey through diverse French landscapes projected on a vast 200° wraparound screen. Emporia in the covered shopping arcade have interiors ranging from a turn-of-the-century bibliothèque to a French château. Merchandise includes French art prints, cookbooks, wines (there's a tasting counter), fancy French foodstuffs, Limoges boxes, Madeline and Babar books and dolls, perfumes, and original letters of famous Frenchmen ranging from Jean Cocteau to Napoléon. Another marketplace revives the defunct Les Halles, where Parisians used to sip onion soup in the wee hours. The heavenly aroma of a boulangerie penetrates the atmosphere, and mimes, jugglers, and strolling chanteurs entertain.

MOROCCO   This exotic pavilion is heralded by a replica of the Koutoubia Minaret, the prayer tower of a 12th-century mosque in Marrakesh. The Medina (old city), entered via a replica of an arched gateway in Fez, leads to Fez House (a traditional Moroccan home) and the narrow winding streets of the *souk,* a bustling marketplace where all manner of authentic handcrafted merchandise—pottery, Berber and Rabat carpets, ornate silver boxes, straw baskets, and prayer rugs—is on display. There are weaving demonstrations in the *souk* throughout the day. The Medina's rectangular courtyard centers on a replica of the ornately tiled Najjarine Fountain in Fez, the setting for musical entertainment. The pavilion's Royal Gallery contains an ever-changing exhibit of Moroccan art, and the Center of Tourism offers a continuous three-screen slide show.

JAPAN   Heralded by a flaming-red *torii* (gate of honor) on the banks of the lagoon, and the graceful blue-roofed Goju No To pagoda (inspired by a shrine built at Nara in A.D. 700), this pavilion focuses on Japan's ancient culture. In a traditional Japanese garden, trees and flowering shrubs frame a contemplative setting of pebbled footpaths, rustic bridges, waterfalls, exquisite rock landscaping, and a pond of golden koi. The **Yakitori House** is based on the renowned 16th-century Katsura Imperial Villa in Kyoto, considered by many to be the crowning achievement of Japanese architecture. Exhibits ranging from 18th-century Bunraki puppets to samurai armor are on display in the moated White Heron Castle, a replica of the Shirasagi-Jo, a 17th-century fortress overlooking the city of Himeji. And the **Mitsukoshi Department Store** (Japan's answer to Macy's) is housed in a replica of the Shishinden (Hall of Ceremonies) of the Gosho Imperial Palace built in Kyoto in A.D. 794. It sells lacquerware, kimonos, kites, fans, dolls, samurai swords, bonsai trees, and Japanese foods—even modern electronics. In the courtyard, artisans demonstrate the ancient arts of *anesaiku* (shaping brown rice candy into dragons, unicorns, and dolphins), *sumi-e* (calligraphy), and *origami* (paper folding). Be sure to include a show of traditional Japanese music and dance at this pavilion in your schedule. It's one of the best in the World Showcase.

✪ **AMERICAN ADVENTURE**   Housed in a vast Georgian-style structure, the American Adventure is a 29-minute dramatization of U.S. history using a 72-foot rear-projection screen, rousing music, and a large cast of lifelike audio-animatronic figures, including narrators Mark Twain and Ben Franklin. The "adventure" begins with the voyage of the *Mayflower* and encompasses major historic events. You view Jefferson writing the Declaration of Independence, the expansion of the frontier, Mathew Brady photographing a family about to be divided by the Civil War, the stock market crash of 1929, the attack on Pearl Harbor, and the Eagle heading toward the moon. While waiting for the show to begin, you'll be entertained by the Voices of Liberty Singers performing American folk songs in the Main Hall. A shop called Heritage Manor Gifts sells signed presidential photographs, needlepoint samplers, quilts, Davy Crockett hats, books on American history, classic political campaign buttons, and vintage newspapers.

ITALY   One of the prettiest World Showcase pavilions, Italy lures visitors over an arched stone footbridge to a replica of the Venetian Doge's Palace. Other architectural highlights include the 83-foot campanile (bell tower) of St. Mark's Square, Venetian bridges, and a central piazza enclosing a version of Bernini's Neptune Fountain. A garden wall suggests a backdrop of provincial countryside, and Mediterranean citrus, olive trees, cypress, and pine frame a formal garden. Gondolas are moored on the lagoon. Shops here carry Perugina chocolates, kitchenware, cameo and filigree jewelry, Murano and Venetian glass, alabaster figurines, and inlaid wooden music boxes. A troupe of street actors performs a contemporary version of 16th-century commedia dell'arte in the piazza.

GERMANY   Enclosed by towered castle walls, this festive pavilion is centered on a cobblestone *platz* (plaza) with pots of colorful flowers girding a fountain statue of St. George and the Dragon. An adjacent clock tower is embellished with whimsical glockenspiel figures that herald each hour with quaint melodies. The pavilion's outdoor biergarten—where it's Oktoberfest all year long—was inspired by medieval

Rothenberg. Shops here carry cuckoo clocks, cowbells, Alpine hats, German wines (there's a tasting counter), toys (including an extensive selection of beautiful German dolls and teddy bears), and books. An artisan demonstrates the molding and painting of Hummel figures; another paints exquisite detailed scenes on eggs.

✪ **CHINA**   Bounded by a serpentine wall that snakes around its outer perimeter, the China pavilion is entered via a vast ceremonial gate inspired by the Temple of Heaven in Beijing. Passing through the gate, you'll see a half-size replica of this ornate red-and-gold circular temple, built in 1420 during the Ming Dynasty. Gardens simulate those in Suzhou, with miniature waterfalls, fragrant lotus ponds, groves of bamboo, and weeping mulberry trees. The highlight attraction here is *Wonders of China,* a 20-minute, 360° Circle-Vision film that explores 6,000 years of dynastic and Communist rule and the breathtaking diversity of the Chinese landscape. Adjacent to the theater, an art gallery houses changing exhibits of Chinese art. A bustling marketplace offers an array of merchandise including silk robes, jade figures, cloisonné vases, dolls, fans, and wind chimes. Artisans here demonstrate calligraphy.

NORWAY   Centered on a picturesque cobblestone courtyard, this pavilion evokes ancient Norway. A *stavekirke* (stave church), styled after the 13th-century Gol Church of Hallingdal, houses changing exhibits. A replica of Oslo's 14th-century Akershus Castle, next to a cascading woodland waterfall, is the setting for the pavilion's featured restaurant. Other buildings simulate the red-roofed cottages of Bergen and the timber-sided farm buildings of the Nordic woodlands. There's a two-part attraction here. **Maelstrom,** a boat ride in a dragon-headed Viking vessel, traverses Norway's fjords and mythical forests to the music of *Peer Gynt*—an exciting journey during which you'll be menaced by polar bears prowling the shore and trolls that cast a spell on the boat. The watercraft crashes through a narrow gorge and spins into the North Sea where a violent storm is in progress. But the storm abates, and passengers disembark safely in a 10th-century Viking village to view the 70mm film *Norway,* which documents a thousand years of history. Shops feature hand-knit wool hats and sweaters, toys (there's a Lego table where kids can play while you shop), wood carvings, Scandinavian foods, pewter ware, and jewelry.

MEXICO   You'll hear the music of marimba and mariachi bands as you approach the festive showcase of Mexico, fronted by a towering Mayan pyramid modeled on the Aztec Temple of Quetzalcoatl (God of Life). Upon entering the pavilion, you'll find yourself in a museum of pre-Colombian art and artifacts. Down a ramp is a small lagoon, the setting for **El Rio del Tiempo,** where visitors board boats for 8-minute cruises through Mexico's past and present. Shops in and around the Plaza de Los Amigos (a "moonlit" Mexican *mercado*) display an array of leather goods, baskets, sombreros, piñatas, pottery, jewelry, serapes, colorful papier-mâché birds, and blown-glass objects (an artisan gives demonstrations). La Casa de Vacaciones, sponsored by the Mexican Tourist Office, provides travel information.

SHOWS & SPECTACULARS

As at the Magic Kingdom, check your show schedule upon entering the park and plan to attend many of the below-listed performances.

WORLD SHOWCASE PAVILION SHOWS   These international entertainments make up an important part of the Epcot experience. There are Chinese lion dancers and acrobats, German oompah bands, Caledonian bagpipers, Italian "living statues" and stilt walkers, colonial fife-and-drum groups, Moroccan belly dancers, and much more. Don't miss the Voices of Liberty Singers at American Adventure and the traditional music and dance displays in Japan.

✪ **ILLUMINATIONS**   A backdrop of classical music by international composers, high-tech lighting effects, darting laser beams, fireworks, and rainbow-lit dancing fountains combine to create this awesome 16½-minute Epcot spectacular, presented nightly. Each nation is highlighted in turn—colorful kites fly over Japan, the giant Rockies loom over Canada, a gingerbread house rises in Germany, and so on. Don't miss it! Find a seat around the lagoon about a half hour before show time.

RHYTHMS OF THE WORLD   Varied international cultural performances take place at the America Gardens Theater in World Showcase.

7 Disney–MGM Studios

Disney–MGM Studios offers exciting movie and TV-themed shows and behind-the-scenes "reel-life" adventures. Its main streets include Hollywood Boulevard and Sunset Boulevard, with art deco movie sets evocative of Hollywood's glamorous golden age. There's also a New York street lined with Gotham landmarks (the Empire State, Flatiron, and Chrysler buildings) and typical New York characters including peddlers hawking knock-off watches. More important, this is a working movie and TV studio, where shows are in production even as you tour the premises.

Arrive at the park early, tickets in hand. Unlike the Magic Kingdom and Epcot, MGM's 110 acres of attractions can pretty much be seen in 1 day. The parking lot is right at the gate, although trams do run. Pay attention to your parking location, which is not as distinctly marked as in the Magic Kingdom.

If you don't get a *Disney–MGM Studios Guidemap* and **entertainment schedule** when you enter the park, you can pick one up at **Guest Services** (MGM's information center). First thing to do is check show times and work out an entertainment schedule based on highlight attractions and geographical proximity. My favorite MGM restaurants are described in the "Dining" section of this chapter. **Strollers** can be rented at Oscar's Super Service inside the main entrance. Note the "Character Spotlight" on the back of the guide map. This tells you the time and location that Disney characters will appear and be available for autographs.

✪ **THE TWILIGHT ZONE TOWER OF TERROR**   A thrilling journey to another dimension! Legend has it that during a violent storm on Halloween night in 1939, lightning struck the Hollywood Tower Hotel, causing an entire wing, along with an elevator full of people, to disappear. Rod Serling is about to introduce you to those who disappeared as you become the star in a special episode of *The Twilight Zone.* After various spooky adventures, the ride ends in a dramatic climax: a terrifying 13-story fitful, free-fall plunge into *The Twilight Zone!* The best thrill ride at Disney with a "preshow" so authentic that maintenance crews kept fixing leaking pipes designed to drip as part of the ambience.

THE MAGIC OF DISNEY ANIMATION   You'll see Disney characters come alive at the stroke of a brush or pencil as you tour actual glass-walled animation studios and watch artists at work. The tour also includes entertaining video talks by animators and a grand finale of magical moments from Disney classics. This popular attraction should be visited early in the morning; long lines form later in the day.

DISNEY–MGM STUDIO BACK LOT TOUR   This 25-minute tram tour takes you behind the scenes for a close-up look at the vehicles, props, costumes, sets, and special effects used in your favorite movies and TV shows. You'll see real costumers stitching away in wardrobe, the house facade of television's *The Golden Girls,* even carpenters building sets. Most of the sets are pretty dated or from short-lived shows you've probably never seen. Things pick up considerably once the tram ventures into **Catastrophe Canyon,** where an earthquake causes canyon walls to rumble and riders are threatened by a raging fire, massive explosions, torrents of rain, and flash floods! Then you're taken behind the scenes to see how filmmakers use special effects to create such disasters. After the tram tour, visit **Studio Showcase,** a changing walk-through display of sets and props from popular and classic movies.

✪ **BACKSTAGE PASS TO 101 DALMATIANS**   Have a "De Vil" of a good time spotting Cruella and the other stars of Disney's live-action remake of the animated classic. The stark, eerie sets from Cruella's movie are among the top attractions during this short tour. Wizzer, the most fluid of the canine actors, is featured in a film about the dog's life of a four-pawed star. Taking a cue from Universal, where you Ride the Movies, the special effects show allows one lucky, usually tall and male, spectator to ride in the movies by re-creating Jeff Daniels's runaway bike scene. Real Dalmatians are also on display. But don't call PETA yet. The pups pull only 2-hour shifts and are treated better, one employee grumbled, than most of the two-legged "cast" members.

Note: Nearby "making of" shows are usually updated and changed as new movies come out. At press time, it featured props and secrets about *Flubber,* starring Robin Williams, but that will likely change. Check your park schedule for information.

✪ **VOYAGE OF** *THE LITTLE MERMAID*   Hazy light, creating an underwater effect in the reef-walled theater, helps set the mood for this charming musical spectacular based on the Disney feature film. The show combines live performers with more than 100 puppets, movie clips, and innovative special effects. It all has a happy ending, as most of the young audience knows it will—they've seen the movie.

✪ **THEATER OF THE STARS**   This 1,500-seat covered amphitheater is currently presenting a live Broadway-style production of *Beauty and the Beast,* based on the Disney movie version. Sets and costumes are lavish, production numbers spectacular. Arrive early to get a good seat. Also catch the *Hunchback of Notre Dame* stage show at the nearby theater.

Note: Disney often changes shows to tie in with recent movies. Some other Disney release may be highlighted during this show by the time of your visit.

✪ **JIM HENSON'S MUPPET VISION 3-D**   Disney has slightly revamped this longtime favorite. The film still stars Kermit and Miss Piggy, and combines Jim Henson's puppets with Disney audio-animatronics and special-effects wizardry, 70mm film, and cutting-edge 3-D technology. The coming-at-you action includes flying Muppets, cream pies, cannonballs, fiber-optic fireworks, bubble showers, even an actual spray of water. Statler and Waldorf critique the action (which includes numerous mishaps and disasters) from a mezzanine balcony. Kids in the first row interact with the characters. In the preshow area, guests view a hilarious Muppet video on overhead monitors and see an array of Muppet movie props.

STAR TOURS   A wild galactic journey based on the *Star Wars* trilogy (George Lucas collaborated on its conception), this action-packed adventure uses dramatic film footage and flight-simulator technology to transform the theater into a vehicle careening through space. The spaceship lurches out of control, and passengers experience sudden drops, violent crashes, and oncoming laser blasts. The harrowing ride ends safely, and you exit into a *Star Wars* merchandise shop. A good thrill, with generally short lines.

✪ **THE GREAT MOVIE RIDE**   Film footage and audio-animatronic replicas of movie stars take you on a nostalgic journey through some of the most famous scenes in movie history. The action is enhanced by dramatic special effects, and your tram is always hijacked en route by outlaws or gangsters. The setting for this attraction is a full-scale reproduction of Hollywood's famous Mann's Chinese Theatre, complete with hand- and footprints of the stars out front.

✪ ABC SOUND STUDIO ONE SATURDAY MORNING   Scream. Wave your hands. Making a little noise is likely to help get you from the audience onto the stage where you will then take part in creating the sound effects to go along with the video. The real stars are the tourists trying to make it all happen like the professionals. Volunteer. You're on vacation. You'll *probably* never see these people again. If you can't muster the gumption to go on stage, the postshow, Soundworks, provides the opportunity for a little joyful noise on interactive computers and away from the madding crowd.

SUPERSTAR TELEVISION   This 30-minute show takes guests through a broadcast day that spans TV history. During the preshow, "casting directors" choose volunteers from the audience to reenact 15 famous television scenes (arrive early if you want to snag a role and *wave that hand!*). The broadcast day begins with a 1955 black-and-white *Today* show featuring Dave Garroway and continues through *Late Night with David Letterman,* including scenes from a classic *I Love Lucy* episode (the candy factory), *General Hospital, Bonanza, Gilligan's Island, Cheers,* and *The Golden Girls,* among others. Real footage is mixed with live action, and though occasionally a star is born, there's plenty of fun watching amateur actors freeze up, flub lines, and otherwise deviate from the script.

GOOSEBUMPS HORRORLAND FRIGHT SHOW   Shows throughout the day from around 9:30am to 4pm Monday through Saturday help the scary characters in the R. L. Stine book series come to life.

✪ INDIANA JONES EPIC STUNT SPECTACULAR   Visitors get an inside look at the world of movie stunts in this dramatic 30-minute show, which re-creates major scenes from the Indiana Jones series. The show opens on an elaborate Mayan temple backdrop. Indiana Jones crashes dramatically onto the set via a rope, and, as he searches with a torch for the golden idol, he encounters booby traps, fire and steam, and spears popping up from the ground, before being chased by a vast rolling boulder! The set is dismantled to reveal a colorful Cairo marketplace where a sword fight ensues, and the action includes jumps from high places, virtuoso bullwhip maneuvers, lots of gunfire, and a truck bursting into flame. An explosive finale takes place in a desert scenario. Throughout, guests get to see how elaborate stunts are pulled off and wonder how close the actors really do come to peril. (Here it is—another chance to be part of the fun. Arrive early and sit near the stage for your shot at short-lived stardom. Go ahead, you're running out of chances—*and this time you get to wear a turban.*)

PARADES, SHOWS, FIREWORKS & MORE   A parade celebrating *Mulan,* Disney's 36th full-length animated feature, has replaced the Hercules parade at Disney–MGM. The short parade is based on the movie's story line: A young, high-spirited girl saves her father's life by disguising herself as a man and joining the Chinese army in his place. The parade will be performed daily along Hollywood Boulevard. It in no way matches the size and scope of the parades in the Magic Kingdom so, unless you're a big fan of the movie, this might be a good time to drop in on the Tower of Terror while the lines are short. The parade takes place daily; check your entertainment schedule for route and times.

The **✪ Sorcery in the Sky** fireworks show is presented nightly during summer and peak seasons. Check your entertainment schedule to see if it's on.

The **Visiting Celebrity** program features frequent appearances by stars such as Betty White, Burt Reynolds, Joan Collins, Leonard Nimoy, and Billy Dee Williams.

They visit attractions, record their handprints in front of the Chinese Theater, and appear at question-and-answer sessions with park guests. Check your entertainment schedule to see if it's on.

A movie set replica serves as a playground in the *Honey, I Shrunk the Kids* **Movie Set Adventure.** Outside props include 30-foot blades of grass, giant Legos, and a sliding pond made from an immense film reel.

Centering on a gleaming 14½-foot bronze Emmy, the **Academy of Television Arts & Sciences Hall of Fame Plaza,** adjacent to SuperStar Television, honors TV legends. Bronze sculptures of Carol Burnett, Sid Caesar, Red Skelton, Milton Berle, and other television luminaries are displayed.

8 Animal Kingdom

Disney's fourth major park combines animals, elaborate landscapes, and rides to create yet another reason not to venture outside of the Disney world. Michael Eisner says it's the next best thing to going to Africa and it is certainly interesting to see how Disney integrates the wonders of nature with the magic of make-believe, but don't cancel that safari vacation just yet.

Opened in spring 1998, Animal Kingdom is divided into five "regions": **The Oasis,** a main entryway; **Safari Village,** a shopping area/entertainment area; **Africa,** the main animal viewing area which is dedicated to the wildlife in Africa today; **Dinoland,** focusing on issues of extinction; and **Camp Minnie-Mickey,** the kids equivalent of ToonTown in the Magic Kingdom.

The park covers more than 500 acres, nearly twice the size of Epcot. At the heart of it all is a 14-story **Tree of Life,** an intricately carved free-form representation of animals hand-crafted by Disney artists. This impressive landmark is nearly as tall and as imposing as the silver golf-ball dome, also known as Spaceship Earth, that has come to best symbolize Epcot.

A sixth section of the park, **Asia,** is expected to open late in 1999. And **Safari Lodge,** a jungle-themed hotel adjacent to the 100-acre savannah, should be open by the end of 2000.

THE OASIS

Basically the garden entrance to the park, the painstaking designed landscaped sets with streams, grottoes and waterfalls, sets the tone for the rest of the park.

SAFARI VILLAGE

Like Cinderella's Castle in the Magic Kingdom and the silver, golf-ball dome in Epcot, the 14-story **Tree of Life** located here is the park's central landmark. It is an intricately carved free-form representation of animals hand-crafted by Disney artists. Teams of artists worked for months creating the various sculptures and it is worth a leisurely stroll. One of the creators says he expects it to become one of the most photographed works of art in the world.

IT'S TOUGH TO BE A BUG!   The creepy-crawly special effects of this tour of a bug's life will keep you on the edge of your seat. It's fun for the family, but not for the arachna-phobic. Located inside the Tree of Life in a 430-seat theater.

DISCOVERY RIVER BOATS   Rolling along the river may be just the thing to give adults an overview of what they are going to see. This is a leisurely tour of the many attractions and gives you a good idea of what you put at the top of your list. Children, however, may find it hard to keep still if they've just entered the park, so you may want to save this for later in the day, when your feet need a rest.

THE GARDEN PATH   A leisurely stroll—are you detecting a theme here?—through the root system of The Tree of Life. This soft landscape is filled with otters, flamingos, tamarinds, lemurs, tortoises, and colorful ducks, storks, cranes, and cockatoos.

DINOLAND U.S.A.

Enter by passing under "Olden Gate Bridge," a 40-foot tall Brachiosaurus reassembled from excavated fossils, and you'll come upon a world filled with a series of wooden cabins and national-park like structures that give the land a nostalgic look from the '50s and '60s.

JOURNEY INTO JUNGLE BOOK   He's still the King of the Swingers, the Jungle VIP; Mowgli and friends party in Theater in the Wild and relive the adventures of Mowgli, the man-child abandoned as a baby and raised by wolves. When Mowgli's life is threatened by a fierce Bengal tiger, a wise and caring panther attempts to guide the boy back to the "man-village" where he rightfully belongs.

COUNTDOWN TO EXTINCTION   This ride is along the lines of *Star Wars* and *Body Wars,* stationary seating that bobs and weaves in front of a special-effects screen. It's got nothing on Back to the Future, but is a bit of a thrill. One minute you're entering the Dino Institute to study creatures that roamed the earth long ago; the next you're hurtling back 65 million years to rescue the last dinosaur from extinction. Along the way you dip and soar, avoiding asteroids and snarling dinos while speeding toward a happy ending.

CRETACEOUS TRAIL   Wander—there's that word again—back in time as you stroll down a path filled with living plants and animal species that have survived since the age of the dinosaur. You'll encounter a Chinese alligator, Florida soft-shelled turtle, and red-legged seriama. Along the way, you'll discover the evolution of a dig site.

THE BONEYARD   Kids love the chance to slip, slither, slide, and crawl through this giant playground and dig site. Discover the remains of triceratops, T-rex, and other vanished giants. You can even dig up the bones of a woolly mammoth in the dig site.

CONSERVATION STATION   This offers a behind-the-scene look at how Disney cares for animals inside the park. It includes the **Affection Section,** where you can cuddle with some friendly animals, explore their private habitats and learn how they are cared for and fed. Check out **Eco Heroes,** interactive videos that connect you to endangered animal information as well as world-famous biologists and conservationists, and **Song of the Rainforest,** which surrounds you with the sounds of the endangered wildlife of that deep jungle. But unless you are into doing a little research on your vacation, skip **Eco Web,** a computer link to conservation organizations worldwide.

CAMP MINNIE-MICKEY

Join your favorite Disney characters "on vacation" in Camp Minnie-Mickey, an entire land that recreates a kid-friendly Adirondack resort.

COLORS OF THE WIND   Pocahontas and Grandmother Willow and some new creatures from the forest perform in stage show at Grandmother Willow's Grove, a cozy 350-seat theater.

FESTIVAL OF THE LION KING   Arrive early for this popular attraction that regularly draws enough people to fill the 1,000-seat pavilion. Based loosely on the animated movie, this stage show combines the pageantry of a parade with a tribal celebration. In an interesting switch, the audience is seated in the center of the theater as the action moves around them.

CHARACTER GREETING PAVILIONS   This is a must for people traveling with children. A variety of Disney characters, from Winnie the Pooh to Timon and Baloo, greet you. Mickey, in recognition of his star status, can be found in his own pavilion.

AFRICA

Enter through the town of Harambe, a realistic representation of an African coastal village poised on the edge of the 21st century. Whitewashed structures built of coral stone and thatched with reed by craftsmen brought over from Africa surround a central marketplace rich with local wares and colors.

GORILLA FALLS EXPLORATION TRAIL   There are no visible barriers between you and the animals as you watch a troop of African gorillas emerging from the reeds. Bathed in lush jungle foliage, this entire area is filled with exotic East African animals that range from toothy reptiles to brightly colored birds. Don't forget to visit the underwater hippo-viewing area and a savanna overlook.

KILIMANJARO SAFARI   This is one of the few "rides" in the park. Essentially, you board a very big truck for a very bumpy ride through the faux African landscape. The vehicle is open, so open you can get thwacked in the face with foliage, and the animals sometimes wander in very close. But the whole experience is hit or miss. The lions are difficult to see, and poacher-fighting story line doesn't add much to the whole experience. In fact, the poacher looks like a refugee from an old Tommorrowland exhibit. If you have small children, you'll need to wrangle a seat on the end so they will be able to see out the sides of the car.

It does get bumpy and those with heart, back, and neck problems, and expectant mothers should skip it. In an early version of the ride, Disney, in its long-standing tradition of whacking maternal figures, killed off the mother elephant. There was even a fake carcass visible from the trucks. This plan was (wisely) changed after they discovered the dead mother upset young children.

9 Other Walt Disney World Attractions

TYPHOON LAGOON

Located off Lake Buena Vista Drive halfway between Walt Disney World Village and Disney–MGM Studios, this is the ultimate in water theme parks. Its fantasy setting is a palm-fringed tropical island village of ramshackle tin-roofed structures, strewn with wreckage left by a legendary "great typhoon." A storm-stranded fishing boat dangles precariously atop the 95-foot-high Mount Mayday, the steep setting for several major park attractions. Every half hour, the boat's smokestack erupts, shooting a 50-foot geyser of water into the air.

In summer, arrive no later than 9am to avoid long lines; the park is often filled to capacity by 10am and closed to later arrivals. Beach towels and lockers can be obtained for a minimal fee, and all beach accessories can be purchased at Singapore Sal's. Light fare is available at two restaurants, and there are picnic tables. Guests are not permitted to bring their own floatation devices into the park. But it makes sense to purchase sunscreen and snacks before entering the park for those on a budget.

Many of the above-mentioned attractions require that guests be at least 4 feet tall. But the Ketchakiddie Creek section of the park is a kiddie area exclusively for those *under* 4 feet. An innovative water playground, it has bubbling fountains to frolic in, water minislides, a pint-sized white-water tubing adventure, spouting whales, and squirting seals.

BLIZZARD BEACH

✪ **Blizzard Beach** is Disney's newest, and zaniest, water park—a 66-acre "ski resort" in the midst of a tropical lagoon. The park centers on a 90-foot snow-capped mountain (Mt. Gushmore), which swimmers ascend via chair lifts, and the on-premises restaurant resembles a ski lodge.

It's located on World Drive just north of the All-Star Sports and Music resorts. Arrive at or before park opening to avoid long lines and to be sure you get in. Beach towels and lockers are available for a small charge, and you can buy beach accessories at the Beach Haus, but it's less expensive to bring your own.

A nice-size sandy beach below Mt. Gushmore offers Tike's Peak, a scaled-down kiddie version of Mt. Gushmore attractions; Melt-Away-Bay, a 1-acre free-form wave pool fed by melting-snow waterfalls; Cross Country Creek, where inner tubers can float in a lazy circle around the entire park; and Ski Patrol Training Camp, which is designed for preteens.

RIVER COUNTRY

One of the many recreational facilities at the Fort Wilderness Resort campground, this water minipark is themed after Tom Sawyer's swimming hole. Kids can scramble over artificial boulders that double as diving platforms for a 330,000-gallon clear-water pool. Two 16-foot water slides also provide access to the pool. Attractions on the adjacent Bay Lake, which is equipped with ropes and ships' booms for climbing, include a pair of flumes. There are poolside and beachside areas for sunning and picnicking, plus a 350-yard boardwalk nature trail. Beach towels and lockers can be obtained for a minimal fee. Light fare is available at Pop's Place.

To get here, take a launch from the dock near the entrance to the Magic Kingdom or a bus from its Transportation and Ticket Center.

10 Universal Studios Florida & Islands of Adventure

Universal Studios Florida (1000 Universal Studios Plaza; ☎ **407/363-8000;** www. usf.com) bills itself as the "No. 1 Movie Studio and Theme Park in the World." It is a working motion-picture and television production studio, although most of the production goes on inside at the Nickelodeon sound stages. But remember cable's *The Swamp Thing* or the short-lived *SeaQuest?* Those television series were shot on the property. Occasionally visitors will come upon an actual working shoot. But every day you will amble amid reel history in the form of some 40 actual sets displayed along "Hollywood Boulevard" and "Rodeo Drive." On hand to greet visitors are Hanna-Barbera characters (Yogi Bear, Scooby Doo, Fred Flintstone, and others) and a talented group of actors representing Universal stars from Harpo Marx to the Blues Brothers.

A 1-day ticket costs $42 for ages 10 and over, $34 for children 3 to 9; a 2-day ticket is $62 for ages 10 and over, $52 for children 3 to 9; an annual pass (admission for a full year) is $80 for ages 10 and over, $65 for children 3 to 9; children 2 and under enter free. Parking costs $6 per vehicle, $7 for RVs and trailers. Universal also offers a multi-park pass in conjunction with Sea World, Wet 'n Wild, and Busch Gardens; for details, see "Coupons, Passes & Other Tips for Saving Your Orlandough," above.

The park is open 365 days a year from 9am; closing hours vary seasonally. Call before you go. To get there, take I-4 east, making a left on Sand Lake Road, then a right onto Turkey Lake Road, and follow the signs.

UNIVERSAL STUDIOS ATTRACTIONS

Rides and attractions use cutting-edge technology—such as OMNIMAX 70mm film projected on 7-story screens—to create terrific special effects. While waiting in line, you'll be entertained by excellent preshows, better even than those at *that other theme park.* Universal, as a whole, takes itself less seriously than the Mouse That Roared and the atmosphere is peppered by subtle reminders that in the competitive 90s it is *not* a small world after all.

CITYWALK   The 12-acre entertainment complex could easily be renamed theme-restaurant heaven. Not only is it home to the world's largest Hard Rock Cafe—the grande dame of all theme restaurants—but also the NASCAR Cafe, the Motown Cafe, and Marvel Mania, a theme send-up of villains and superheroes. CityWalk, which opened in 1998, also contains a hearty dose of Cajun spice with Pat O'Brien's, a re-creation of the joint in New Orleans, and Emeril's of New Orleans, featuring the creole-based cuisine of chef Emeril Lagasse. If that's not enough to keep you busy, there is the Down Beat Jazz Hall of Fame, a tribute to reggae artist Bob Marley, and a 5,000-seat Cineplex Odeon Megaplex.

Finally, celebrity hounds may catch a live taping involving one of their favorite stars at the E! Entertainment Television Production Center.

A DAY IN THE PARK WITH BARNEY   Set in a parklike theater-in-the-round, this musical show—starring the popular purple one, Baby Bop, and BJ—uses song, dance, and interactive play to deliver an environmental message. For young children, this could be the highlight of the day.

TERMINATOR 2: 3-D BATTLE ACROSS TIME   He's back, at least in Orlando. This is billed as "the quintessential sight and sound experience for the 21st century!" Jim Cameron, the same director who made *The Terminator* and *Titanic* has overseen this production. It features the Big Man himself (Arrhnaldd), along with other original cast members, and combines 70mm 3-D film (using three 23-by-50-foot screens) with live stage action and thrilling technical effects.

JAWS   Did you really think it was safe to go back into the water? As your boat heads out to the open seas, an ominous dorsal fin appears on the horizon. What follows is a series of terrifying attacks from a 3-ton, 32-foot-long great white shark that tries to sink its teeth into passengers. And there's more trouble ahead. The boat is surrounded by a 30-foot wall of flame, caused from burning fuel that lets you truly feel the heat. I won't tell you how it ends, but let's just say, blackened shark, anyone? (The effects are more startling after dark.)

E. T. ADVENTURE   Visitors are given a passport to E. T.'s planet, which needs his healing powers to rejuvenate it. You'll soar with E. T. on a mission to save his ailing planet, through the forest and into space, aboard a star-bound bicycle—all to the accompaniment of that familiar movie theme music. A cool wooded forest serves to create one of the most pleasant waits for any ride in Central Florida. This is a wait worth the ride.

✪ BACK TO THE FUTURE   Visitors blast through the space-time continuum, plummeting into volcanic tunnels ablaze with molten lava, colliding with Ice Age glaciers, thundering through caves and canyons, and are briefly swallowed by a dinosaur, in a spectacular multisensory adventure. You twist, you turn, you dip and dive and feel like you are really flying. Stick to seats in the back of the car to avoid ruining the illusion by glimpsing your neighbors careening hydraulically in the next bay.

✪ **KONGFRONTATION** It's the last thing the Big Apple needed. King Kong is back! As you stand in line in a replica of a grungy, graffiti-scarred New York subway station, CBS newsman Roland Smith reports on Kong's terrifying rampage. Everyone must evacuate to Roosevelt Island, so it's all aboard the tram. Cars collide and hydrants explode below, police helicopters hover overhead putting you directly in the line of fire, the tram malfunctions, and, of course, you encounter Kong—32 feet tall and 13,000 pounds. He emits banana breath in your face and menaces passengers, dangling the tram over the East River. A great thrill—or just another day in New York.

✪ **EARTHQUAKE, THE BIG ONE** You board a BART train in San Francisco for a peaceful subway ride, but just as you pull into the Embarcadero station there's an earthquake—the big one, 8.3 on the Richter scale! As you sit helplessly trapped, vast slabs of concrete collapse around you, a propane truck bursts into flames, a runaway train comes hurtling at you, and the station floods (60,000 gallons of water cascade down the steps).

TWISTER Visitors from the twister-prone Midwest may find this recreation a little too close to the real thing. An ominous funnel cloud, 5 stories tall, is created by 2 million cubic feet of air per minute. The freight-train fills the theater, cars, signs, and trucks fly about as the audience watches just 20 feet away. The windy version of Earthquake.

NICKELODEON STUDIOS TOUR You'll tour the soundstages where Nick shows are produced, view concept pilots, visit the kitchen where Gak and green slime are made, play typical show games, and try out new Sega video games. There's lots of audience participation, and a volunteer will get slimed.

WILD, WILD, WILD WEST SHOW Stunt people demonstrate falls from 3-story balconies, gun and whip fights, dynamite explosions, and other oater staples. This is a well-performed, lively show that is especially popular with foreign visitors with celluloid visions of the American West. Kids, do not try this at home.

BEETLEJUICE GRAVEYARD REVUE Dracula, Wolfman, the Phantom of the Opera, Frankenstein and his bride, and Beetlejuice put on a funky and very funny rock musical with pyrotechnic special effects and MTV-style choreography. Loud and lively enough to scare some small children.

THE FUNTASTIC WORLD OF HANNA-BARBERA This motion-simulator ride takes guests careening through the universe in a spaceship piloted by Yogi Bear to rescue Elroy Jetson. Before this wild ride, you'll learn about how cartoons are created. After it, in an interactive area, you can experiment with animation sound effects— boing! plop! splash!—and color in your own cartoons. This is a great place for kids of all ages to take some time and play.

ADDITIONAL ATTRACTIONS

Other park attractions include the Gory, Gruesome & Grotesque Horror Makeup Show for a behind-the-scenes look at the transformation scenes from movies like *The Fly* and *The Exorcist;* a tribute to Lucille Ball, America's queen of comedy; Fievel's Playland, an innovative Western-themed playground based on the Spielberg movie *An American Tail;* and *Hercules & Zena, Wizards of the Screen,* which puts you on the set with the buff gladiators as the audience battles to make the sound effects match the videos. Alfred Hitchcock's 3-D Theatre, a tribute to the "master of suspense" in which Tony Perkins narrates a reenactment of the famous shower scene from *Psycho;* and *The Birds,* as if it weren't scary enough, becomes an in-your-face 3-D movie.

Descendants of Lassie, Benji, Mr. Ed, and other animal superstars perform their famous pet tricks in the Animal Actors Show. During Screen Test Home Video Adventure, a director, crew, and team of "cinemagicians" put visitors on the screen in an exciting video production. And Dynamite Nights Stuntacular, a nightly show, combines death-defying stunts with a breathtaking display of fireworks.

More than 25 shops in the park sell everything from Lucy collectibles to Bates Motel towels, and restaurants run the gamut from Mel's Drive-In (of *American Graffiti* fame) to the Hard Rock Cafe to Schwab's.

ISLANDS OF ADVENTURE

Universal's second park is scheduled to open in 1999 with a vibrantly colored, cleverly themed collection of fast, fun rides for kids of all ages. With Stephen Spielberg as a creative consultant, Islands promises to have some of the most thrilling and technologically advanced rides and attractions ever made.

Divided into five areas, **Seuss Landing, Toon Lagoon, Lost Continent, Marvel Super Hero Island,** and **Jurassic Park,** this park offers the biggest concentration of thrill rides and coasters of any park in the area. Park hours and ticket prices had not been released at press time but should be similar to Universal Studios Florida (see above). For information on-line, go to www.usf.com.

Seuss Landing

This 10-acre island is the only place in the world where Dr. Suess's famous books are brought to life.

CAT IN THE HAT   Six-passenger couches travel through 18 show scenes past animatronic characters. The highlight is a revolving 24-foot tunnel that alters your perceptions and leaves your head spinning.

ONE FISH, TWO FISH, RED FISH, BLUE FISH   The point here is to avoid getting sprayed as you guide your fish through the ride taking directions from a Seussian rhyme. Of course, if the kids are driving, bring a raincoat. Special adaptations are available for travelers with disabilities to enjoy the fire from their chair.

CARO-SEUSS-EL   Go in and out, up and down on one of seven characters from the world of Seuss, including the elephant-birds from Horton Hatches an Egg.

SYLVESTER MCMONKEY MCBEAN'S VERY UNUSUAL DRIVING MACHINES   The name is almost as long as the ride, but children will love steering along an elevated track through Seuss Landing.

IF I RAN THE ZOO   This interactive playland for kids of all ages includes everything from flying water snakes to a chance to tickle the toes of a Seussian animal. A nice place to let the kids burn off some excited energy.

Marvel Super Hero Island

Thrill junkies will love the twisting, turning and stomach churning rides based on characters from Marvel Comics.

THE SPIDER-MAN ADVENTURE   Combines moving rides with 3-D action and special effects taking guests on a tour of the Daily Bugle where Peter Parker suddenly encounters evil villains and becomes Spider-Man. The high-tech ride, similar to Back to the Future, includes a simulated 400-foot drop that feels an awful lot like the real thing.

INCREDIBLE HULK COASTER   Blasting from zero to 40 mph in two seconds, you spin upside down 100 feet from the ground, feeling weightless. Coaster lovers will love the two-minute and 15-second ride that includes seven roll-overs and two deep drops.

DR. DOOM'S FEARFALL   You are in for a rush as you drop, with feet dangling, down one of two, 200-foot steel towers. Similar to the Tower of Terror at Disney, but with the added thrill of hanging free.

TOON LAGOON

More than 150 life-sized sculpted cartoon images let you know you have entered this section dedicated to your favorites from the Sunday funnies.

DUDLEY DO-RIGHT'S RIPSAW FALLS   This water ride, touted as first to send riders plummeting below the water surface, takes you around a 400,000-gallon lagoon, culminating in a 75-foot drop at 50 miles per hour. *Note:* You will get wet. Very wet.

POPEYE & BLUTO'S BILGE RAT BARGES   Whirling 12-person rafts bump and churn their way through a white-water ride encountering some scary creatures along the way, including the twirling octopus boat wash. *Note:* You can get completely soaked.

COMIC STRIP LANE   Beetle Bailey, Hagar the Horrible, and Dagwood and Blondie are highlighted in this lively jaunt through some beloved comic strips.

JURASSIC PARK

Okay, stay with me here. This is the theme park creation based on a movie featuring a theme park creation that might become a movie. Yes, you'll find the basics from Stephen Spielberg's wildly successful movies, and some of the high-tech wizardry, all incorporated in a lushly landscaped tropical locale.

JURASSIC PARK RIVER ADVENTURE   Come face to face with the living, breathing inhabitants of Jurassic Park. Dinosaurs 5-stories high come within inches of the ride where tyrannosauruses decide you look like a tasty morsel. To escape you take an 85-foot plunge, straight down the fastest, steepest water descent ever built.

TRICERATOPS ENCOUNTER   Pet a "living" dinosaur and learn from the trainers about the care and feeding of the 24-foot long, 10-foot-high triceratops. The creature's responses to touch include realistic blinks and muscle flinches.

DISCOVERY CENTER   An interactive discovery center within the celebrated gates of Jurassic Park's Visitors Center, where guests will find a variety of entertaining and educational opportunities. This is a good place to play in the air-conditioning with lots of stuff kids of all ages can touch and enjoy.

PTERANODON FLYERS   Get a bird's-eye view of the Jurassic Park compound soaring on the backs of these gentle flying creatures.

CAMP JURASSIC   A play area with everything from lava pits with undiscovered dinosaur bones to a rain forest. Watch out for the spitters.

LOST CONTINENT

Although they kind of mixed their millennia—the age-old Greek gods with a medieval forest—Universal has done a good job creating a foreboding mood in this section of the park. Among the highlights are **Escape from the Lost City,** similar to Universal's Earthquake ride, where you're stuck in the middle of a battle between the gods Poseidon (lots of water) and Zeus (lots of fire and heat); **Deuling Dragons,** a 60mph roller coaster that has you dangling from the seat—the thing is, there are two coasters, and the tracks intertwine; and **The 8th Voyage of Sinbad,** which takes you on a journey with the mythical traveler (expect lots of pyrotechnics; it may be too intense for small children).

11 Sea World

This popular 200-plus-acre marine-life park (7007 Sea World Dr.; ☎ 407/351-3600; www.seaworld.com), explores the mysteries of the deep in a format that combines entertainment with wildlife-conservation awareness. Bell-bottoms and Marcia Brady prints may be all the rage in fashion, but Sea World of Florida has updated its 1970s look.

A second phase is in the works, so visitors may encounter some dust.

But it is worth visiting this beautifully landscaped park, centering on a 17-acre lagoon, including flamingo and pelican ponds and a lush tropical rain forest. Shamu, a killer whale, is the star of the park along with his expanding family, including several baby whales. The pace is much more laid back than either Universal or Disney and is a good way to end a long week of trudging through the other parks. Be sure to budget some extra money to buy smelt to feed the animals—the close encounters offered at many wading and feeding pools are the real attraction here and more than half the fun. Sea World can't compete with the high-tech wonders abounding elsewhere, but where else can you discover that a stingray feels like crushed velvet or learn the song of a seal?

A 1-day ticket costs $42 for ages 10 and over, $34 for children 3 to 9; children 2 and under enter free. Parking costs $5 per vehicle, $7 for RVs and trailers. Sea World also offers a multi-park pass in conjunction with Universal Studios, Wet 'n Wild, and Busch Gardens; for details, see "Coupons, Passes & Other Tips for Saving Your Orlandough," above.

The park is open from 9am to 7pm 365 days a year, later during summer and holidays when there are additional shows at night. Call before you go. To get there, take I-4 to the Bee Line Expressway (Fla. 528) and follow the signs.

MAJOR ATTRACTIONS

✪ **WILD ARCTIC**   Enveloping guests in the beauty, exhilaration, and danger of a polar expedition, Wild Arctic combines a high-definition adventure film with flight-simulator technology to evoke breathtaking Arctic panoramas. After a hazardous flight over the frozen north, visitors emerge at a remote research base—home to four polar bears (including star residents and polar twins Klondike and Snow), seals, walruses, and white beluga whales.

✪ **JOURNEY TO ATLANTIS**   This is the park's first, true thrill ride. Taking a cue from Disney Imagineerers, Sea World has created a storyline to go with the ride, something about Greek fisherman and ancient Sirens in a battle over good and evil. (A "media horde" is somehow involved.) But what really matters is the promise of "two of the steepest, wettest, fastest drops to be found in any theme park."

The bottom line is a wild ride with 60-foot drops and the promise of "lugelike curves." Journey to Atlantis breaks from Sea World's "edu-tainment" formula that seemed to stress equal measures of learning and fun. No hidden lesson here, just a splashy thrill.

✪ **MERMAIDS, MYTHS & MONSTERS**   This nighttime multimedia spectacular is a must-see, featuring fireworks and hologram-like imagery against a towering 60-foot screen of illuminated water. King Neptune rises majestically from the deep, as do terrifying sea serpents, storm-tossed ships, and frolicking mermaids. Not quite the Disney fireworks, but an interesting show worth waiting for.

TERRORS OF THE DEEP This exhibit houses 220 specimens of venomous and otherwise scary sea creatures in a tropical reef habitat. Immense acrylic tunnels provide close encounters with slithery eels, three dozen sharks, barracudas, lionfish, and poisonous pufferfish. A theatrical presentation focusing on sharks puts across the message that pollution and uncontrolled commercial fishing make humankind the ultimate "terror of the deep."

✪ **MANATEES: THE LAST GENERATION?** Today the Florida manatee is in danger of extinction, with as few as 2,000 remaining. Underwater viewing stations, innovative cinema techniques, and interactive displays combine to create an exciting format for teaching visitors about the manatee and its fragile ecosystem. Also on display here are hundreds of other native fish as well as alligators, turtles, and shorebirds.

✪ **KEY WEST AT SEA WORLD** It's not quite the way Ernest Hemingway saw it, but this 5-acre paved paradise dotted with palms, hibiscus, and bougainvillea is set in a Caribbean village offering island cuisine, street vendors, and entertainers. The attraction comprises three naturalistic animal habitats: Stingray Lagoon, where visitors enjoy hands-on encounters with harmless southern diamond and cownose rays; Dolphin Cove, a massive habitat for bottlenose dolphins set up for visitor interaction; and Sea Turtle Point, home to threatened and endangered species such as green, loggerhead, and hawksbill sea turtles. Shortly after opening, dolphins showed their intelligence by realizing how easy humans are to tease. They'd routinely swim just out of arms' reach but discovered that there are advantages to coming in a little closer—namely smelt.

KEY WEST DOLPHIN FEST At the Whale and Dolphin Stadium, a big partially covered open-air stadium, whales and Atlantic bottlenose dolphins perform flips and high jumps, swim at high speeds, twirl, swim on their backs, and give rides to trainers—all to the accompaniment of calypso music. The tricks are impressive, but go before the show-stopping behemoth, Shamu, puts these little mammals to shame.

BAYWATCH NIGHTS Actors and stunt drivers re-create some of the high-powered drama of the most popular syndicated television show in the world. Sorry, no Pamela Sue Anderson (is she still Lee?) look-alikes.

SHAMU: WORLD FOCUS Sea World trainers develop close relationships with killer whales, and in this partly covered open-air stadium, they direct performances that are extensions of natural cetacean behaviors—twirling, waving tails and fins, rotating while swimming, and splashing the audience. Splash zones are clearly marked. Sit in the upper tiers if you don't want to get soaked. The evening show here, called "Shamu: Night Magic," uses rock music and special lighting effects. There is no reason to attend both shows, unless you really like whales. The tricks are much the same. I'd opt for the evening show, taking advantage of shorter lines as others flock to the stadium in the afternoon. If you do decide on the afternoon show, arrive at least 30 minutes early. The stadium does fill up.

Shamu: Close Up!, an adjoining exhibit, lets you get close up to killer whales and talk to trainers; don't miss the underwater viewing area here and a chance to see a mother whale with her offspring. Talk about a big baby!

✪ **PENGUIN ENCOUNTER** This display of hundreds of penguins and alcids (including adorable babies) native to the Antarctic and Arctic regions also serves as a living laboratory for protecting and preserving polar life. On a moving walkway, you'll view six different penguin species congregating on rocks, nesting, and swimming underwater. There's an additional area for puffins and murres (flying Arctic cousins of penguins).

HOTEL CLYDE & SEAMORE   Two sea lions, along with a cast of otters and walruses, appear in this fishy *Fawlty Towers* comedy with a conservation theme.

SWIM WITH THE DOLPHINS   Visitors can also take a DIP: Dolphin Interactive Program. Sea World has expanded this program that allows eight people a chance to frolic with some of Flipper's friends. You pay $125 for roughly 20 minutes of hand-to-fin contact (the cost includes park admission; annual pass holders pay less). The rest of the time is spent learning about how to interact with the dolphin and wrestling your body in and out of those tricky wet suits. (There is no graceful way to get into or out of a wet suit.) Interestingly enough, you don't have to be able to swim.

Beginning in October there will be both an 8am and a 10:30am session. Make reservations, accepted only through fax or mail, at least 6 weeks in advance. Children under 13 cannot participate, but can observe for $39.95 if they accompany a paid participant. That rule applies to all observers. For information call ☎ **407/363-2380.** Call ahead for information.

The park's other attractions include Pacific Point Preserve, a 2½-acre naturalistic setting that duplicates the rocky northern Pacific Coast home of California sea lions and harbor and fur seals; Tropical Reef, a tide pool of touchables, such as sea anemones, starfish, sea cucumbers, and sea urchins, plus a 160,000-gallon coral-reef aquarium, home to 1,000 brightly hued tropical fish displayed in 17 vignettes of undersea life; and Shamu's Happy Harbor, an innovative 3-acre play area that has a 4-story net tower with a 35-foot crow's-nest lookout, water cannons, remote-controlled vehicles, and a water maze—one of the most extensive play areas at any park. Bring extra clothes for the tots.

A Hawaiian dance troupe entertains in an outdoor facility at Hawaiian Village; if you care to join in, grass skirts and leis are available. You can ascend 400 feet to the top of the Sea World Sky Tower for a revolving 360° panorama of the park and beyond (there's an extra charge of $3 per person for this activity). And at the 5.5-acre Anheuser-Busch Hospitality Center you can try free samples of Anheuser-Busch beers and snacks and stroll through the stables to watch the famous Budweiser Clydesdale horses being groomed (Anheuser-Busch owns Sea World).

The Aloha! Polynesian Luau Dinner and Show, a musical revue featuring South Seas food, song, and fire dancing, takes place nightly at 6:30pm. Park admission is not required. The cost is $35.95 for adults, $25.95 for children 8 to 12, $15.95 for children 3 to 7, and free for children 2 and under. Reservations are required (☎ **800/ 227-8048** or 407/363-2559).

Visitors can take 90-minute behind-the-scenes tours of the park's breeding, research, and training facilities and/or attend a 45-minute presentation about Sea World's animal behavior and training techniques. The cost for either tour is $5.95 for ages 10 and over, $4.95 for children 3 to 9, and free for children 2 and under.

12 More Area Attractions

KISSIMMEE

Kissimmee's sights are closest to the Walt Disney World area—about a 10- to 15-minute drive.

Splendid China. Formosa Gardens Blvd., off W. Irlo Bronson Memorial Hwy. (U.S. 192, between Entry Point Blvd./Sherbeth Rd. and Black Lake Rd.). ☎ **407/396-7111.** Admission $26.99 adults, $16.99 children 5–12, free for children 4 and under. Daily from 9:30am; closing hours vary seasonally (call ahead). Free parking.

This 76-acre outdoor attraction features more than 60 miniaturized replicas of China's most noted artificial and natural wonders, spanning 5,000 years of history and culture.

Park highlights include a half-mile-long copy of the 4,200-mile Great Wall, the Forbidden City's 9,999-room Imperial Palace, Tibet's sacred Potala Palace, the massive Leshan Buddha, carved out of a mountainside between A.D. 713 and A.D. 803, the Stone Forest of Yunan, and the Mongolian mausoleum of Genghis Khan. Live shows (acrobats, martial-arts demonstrations, storytelling, dance, puppetry, and more) take place throughout the day; check your entertainment schedule. There's recorded commentary at each attraction.

Free trams circle the park, stopping at major attractions for pickup and drop-off. The 2-hour guided walking tours, departing several times a day, cost $5.35 per person (children 11 and under are free), and 1-hour golf-cart tours ($45 per six-person cart including guide) depart every half hour. This attraction can be explored in several hours.

INTERNATIONAL DRIVE

Like Kissimmee's attractions, these are about a 10- to 15-minute drive from the Disney area.

Ripley's Believe It or Not! Museum. 8201 International Dr. (1½ blocks south of Sand Lake Rd.). ☎ **407/345-0501.** Admission $10.55 adults, $7.37 children 4–12, free for children 3 and under. Daily 10am–midnight.

It's always fun to peruse a Ripley collection of oddities, curiosities, and fascinating artifacts from faraway places. Among the hundreds of items and mannequins on display here are a 1,069-pound man, a five-legged cow, a mosaic of the Mona Lisa created from 1,426 pieces of toast, torture devices from the Spanish Inquisition, a Tibetan flute made from human bones, a shrunken head, and statues of Ubangi women with wooden plates in their lips.

Wet 'n Wild. 6200 International Dr. (at Republic Dr.). ☎ **800/992-WILD** or 407/351-WILD. Admission $23.95 adults, $18.95 children 3–9, free for children 2 and under. Open daily; hours vary seasonally (call before you go). Free parking. Take I-4 east to Exit 30A and follow the signs.

When temperatures soar, head for this 25-acre water park and cool off by jumping waves, careening down steep flumes, and running rapids. Among the highlights: Fuji Flyer (a 6-story toboggan ride along 450 feet of banked curves); The Surge (one of the longest, fastest multipassenger tube rides in the Southeast); Bomb Bay (enter a bomb-like casing 76 feet in the air for a speedy vertical flight straight down to a target pool); Black Hole (step into a spaceship and board a two-person raft for a 30-second, 500-foot, twisting, turning, reentry through total darkness propelled by a 1,000-gallon-a-minute blast of water!); Raging Rapids, a simulated white-water tubing adventure with a waterfall plunge; and Lazy River, a leisurely float trip. There are additional flumes, a vast wave pool, a large and innovative children's water playground, a sunbathing area, and a picnic area.

Food concessions are located throughout the park, lockers and towels can be rented, and you can purchase beach accessories at the gift shop. It's easy to spend the whole day here, if you remember the sunscreen. *Note:* Wet 'n Wild also offers a discounted multi-park pass in conjunction with Sea World, Universal Studios, and Busch Gardens; for details, see "Coupons, Passes & Other Tips for Saving Your Orlan-dough," above.

ORLANDO

All the following Orlando attractions are in close proximity to each other, making for a pleasant day's excursion. Loch Haven Park is about 35 minutes by car from the Disney area. You can probably also incorporate some Winter Park sights into the same day.

✪ Orlando Science Center. 777 E. Princeton St. (between Orange and Mills aves.), in Loch Haven Park. ☎ **407/896-7151** (press 4). Basic admission $8 adults, $6.50 children 3–11, free for children 2 and under. Additional charges for CineDome movies and planetarium shows. Mon–Thurs 9am–5pm, Fri–Sat 9am–9pm, Sun noon–5pm. Closed Thanksgiving and Christmas. Take I-4 east to Exit 43 (Princeton St.). It is the building with the large, shiny silver dome.

A $44 million expansion completed in 1997 made the Orlando Science Center the largest center of its kind in the southeastern United States. The exhibits are state-of-the-art and geared toward encouraging kids to have fun while learning. This is the kind of museum where kids are encouraged to touch. The CineDome projects images onto an 8-story domed screen with a powerful audio system generating more than 28,000 watts of sound. Families can easily spend half a day touring the 10 exhibit halls.

✪ Harry P. Leu Gardens. 1920 N. Forest Ave. (between Nebraska St. and Corrine Dr.). ☎ **407/246-2620.** Admission $3 adults, $1 children 6–16, free for children 5 and under. Gardens, daily 9am–5pm; Leu House tours, Sun–Mon 1–3:30pm, Tues–Sat 10am–3:30pm. Closed Christmas. Take I-4 east to Exit 43 (Princeton St.), follow Princeton St. east, make a right on Mills Ave., turn left on Virginia Dr., and look for the gardens on your left.

At this delightful 50-acre botanical garden on the shores of Lake Rowena, meandering paths lead through forests of giant camphors, moss-draped oaks, palms, cycads, and camellias. Exquisite formal rose gardens display 75 varieties. Free 20-minute tours of the Leu House, built in 1888, take place on the hour and half hour. The house is a veritable decorative arts museum filled with Victorian, Empire, and Chippendale pieces. It takes about 2 hours to see the house and gardens.

Orange County Historical Museum. 812 E. Rollins St. (between Orange and Mills aves.), in Loch Haven Park. ☎ **407/897-6350.** Admission $2 adults, $1.50 seniors 65 and over, $1 children 6–12, free for children 5 and under; Mon admission is by donation. Mon–Sat 9am–5pm, Sun noon–5pm. Closed New Year's Day, Martin Luther King Day, Memorial Day, July 4, Labor Day, Thanksgiving, and Christmas. Take I-4 east to Exit 43 (Princeton St.) and follow the signs to Loch Haven Park.

This museum focuses on Central Florida history, beginning with prehistoric cultures that existed here 12,000 years ago. Other exhibits include displays of Seminole pottery and clothing, items from a pioneer kitchen, artifacts from an 1892 courthouse, a chronicle of the citrus industry, and re-creations of a turn-of-the-century country store, a Victorian parlor, and the old *Orlando Sentinel* composing room. Also on the premises is Fire Station No. 3, a restored 1926 firehouse.

Orlando Museum of Art. 2416 N. Mills Ave. (off U.S. 17/92), in Loch Haven Park. ☎ **407/896-4231.** Admission $4 adults, $2 children 4–11, free for children 3 and under. Museum Tues–Sat 9am–5pm, Sun noon–5pm; Art Encounter Tues–Fri and Sun noon–5pm, Sat 10am–5pm. Closed New Year's Day, Memorial Day, July 4, Labor Day, Thanksgiving, and Christmas. Free parking. Take I-4 east to Exit 43 (Princeton St.) and follow the signs to Loch Haven Park.

Also undergoing a multimillion-dollar expansion, the museum displays its permanent collection of 19th- and 20th-century American art, pre-Columbian art, and African art on a rotating basis. These holdings are augmented by long-term loans focusing on Mayan archaeology and arts of the African sub-Saharan region. "Art Encounter" is an interactive hands-on area for children. At this writing, a 31,000-square-foot expansion is underway, which will allow for major exhibitions.

13 Outdoor Activities & Spectator Sports

The **Walt Disney World recreational facilities** (☎ **407/824-4321**) listed below are all open to the public, no matter where you're staying. Call for further information about WDW recreational facilities.

BIKING Bike rentals (single- and multispeed bikes for adults, tandems, and children's bikes) are available from the **Bike Barn** (☎ **407/824-2742**) at Fort Wilderness Resort and Campground. Rates are $5 per hour, $12 per day, $18 overnight. Both Fort Wilderness and Disney's Village Resort offer good bike trails.

BOATING At the **Walt Disney World Village Marketplace Marina** (☎ **407/828-2204**) you can rent Water Sprites, canopy boats, and 20-foot pontoon boats.

The **Bike Barn** at Fort Wilderness (☎ **407/824-2742**) rents canoes and pedal boats ($6 per half hour, $10 per hour).

FISHING Fishing excursions on Lake Buena Vista, mainly for largemouth bass, can be arranged up to 14 days in advance by calling ☎ **407/824-2621.** No license is required. The fee is $137.50 for up to five people for 2 hours, and rates include gear and guide.

You can also rent cane poles and rods and reels at the Bike Barn (☎ **407/824-2742**) to fish in Fort Wilderness canals. No license is required.

GOLF Like most of Florida, Orlando is a golfer's paradise. Within a 45-minute drive of downtown are 123 courses designed by Arnold Palmer, Jack Nicklaus, Tom Fazio, Pete Dye, Robert Trent Jones, and other major players.

Consider calling **Golfpac** (☎ **800/327-0878** or 407/260-2288), an organization that packages golf vacations (with accommodations and other features) and pre-arranges tee times at more than 40 Orlando-area courses. The further in advance you call (I'm talking months here), the better your options.

The most famous local courses include the legendary **Arnold Palmer's Bay Hill Club,** 9000 Bay Hill Blvd. (☎ **800/523-5999** or 407/876-2429), site of the Bay Hill Invitational. Its 18th hole, nicknamed the Devil's Bathtub, is supposed to be the toughest par-4 on the tour.

Walt Disney World Resorts (☎ **407/824-2270**) offer 99 holes of golf; they operate five championship 18-hole, par-72 golf courses and one 9-hole, par-36 walking course. All are open to the general public and offer pro shops, equipment rentals, and instruction. For tee times and information, call up to 7 days in advance (up to 30 days for Disney resort and "official-hotel" guests). The most famous hazard is a sand trap on the Magnolia Course's sixth hole in the shape of Mickey Mouse. Call ☎ **407/W-DISNEY** (934-7639) for information about golf packages.

Also notable are two beautifully landscaped facilities: the award-winning 45-hole, par-72 Jack Nicklaus–designed course at the **Villas of Grand Cypress** (☎ **800/835-7377** or 407/239-4700) and the 18-hole, par-71 Joe Lee–designed championship course at the **Marriott Orlando World Center** (☎ **800/621-0638** or 407/239-4200).

The **Falcon's Fire Golf Club,** 3200 Seralago Blvd., in Kissimmee (☎ **407/239-5445**), a challenging Ree Jones course, has 136 bunkers and water on 10 holes.

South of Kissimmee, in Haines City, is the **Grenelefe Golf & Tennis Resort** (☎ **800/237-9549** or 941/422-7511), with three championship courses. It's the home of the Wally Armstrong Golf School, and annually hosts U.S. Seniors Open and U.S. Women's Open qualifiers.

HAYRIDES   The hay wagon departs from Pioneer Hall at Fort Wilderness nightly at 7 and 9:30pm for hour-long old-fashioned hayrides with singing, jokes, and games. The cost is $6 for adults, $4 for children 3 to 10, free for children 2 and under; children under 12 must be accompanied by an adult. No reservations—it's first-come, first-served.

HORSEBACK RIDING   Disney's Fort Wilderness Resort and Campground offers 45-minute scenic guided-tour **trail rides** (☎ 407/824-2832) daily, with four to six rides per day. The cost is $17 per person. Children must be at least 9 years old. Call for information and reservations up to 5 days in advance.

TENNIS   There are 17 lighted tennis courts located throughout the Disney properties. Most are free and available on a first-come, first-served basis. If you're willing to pay for court time, courts can be reserved up to several months in advance at the **Contemporary** (☎ 407/824-3578) or the **Grand Floridian** (☎ 407/824-2435). Both charge $12 per hour; you can also reserve lesson times with resident pros. There's a large pro shop at the Contemporary where equipment can be rented.

SPECTATOR SPORTS

Disney's Wide World of Sports, at Walt Disney World (☎ 407/363-6600), is a massive complex offering everything from basketball to gymnastics and soccer. It's also the spring training site of the Atlanta Braves and the Harlem Globetrotters. Ticket prices vary. There is also the NFL experience, where you can try out your gridiron gifts in such physical tests as the Quarterback Challenge and kicking extra points.

The Orlando **Centroplex** administers six public sports and entertainment facilities in the downtown area. These include three major sporting arenas: the Florida Citrus Bowl, the Orlando Arena, and Tinker Field.

The **Florida Citrus Bowl,** 1 Citrus Bowl Place, at West Church and Tampa streets (☎ 407/896-2442 for information, or 407/839-3900 to charge tickets), seats 70,000 people for major sporting events including the annual CompUSA Florida Citrus Bowl game, college football games, and NFL preseason games. Parking is $5. Take I-4 east to the East-West Expressway and head west to U.S. 441, make a left on Church Street, and follow the signs.

The **Orlando Magic** play at the **Orlando Arena,** 600 W. Amelia St., between I-4 and Parramore Avenue (☎ 407/849-2020 for information, or 407/839-3900 to charge tickets). Tickets to Magic games (about $13 to $50) usually have to be acquired far in advance. There are generally about 1,000 tickets available for sale before each game. Single tickets are often available when the Magic goes against low-profile NBA competitions, such as the Timberwolves. Parking at the arena costs $5 (for up-to-the-minute parking information, tune your car radio to 1620 AM). Take I-4 east to Amelia Avenue, turn left at the traffic light at the bottom of the off-ramp, and follow the signs. Call to find out about other sporting events when you're in town. Orlando is also home to several other professional teams, including the **Predators,** an arena football team, and the **Solar Bears,** an ice hockey team.

Spring training for the **Houston Astros** begins in late February, with exhibition games through March or early April at the **Osceola County Stadium,** 1000 Bill Beck Blvd., in Kissimmee (☎ 407/933-2520). Tickets are $6, $8, and $10. Call for details and tickets.

The **Bay Hill Invitational Golf Tournament** is held in mid-March at Arnold Palmer's Bay Hill Club, 9000 Bay Hill Blvd. (☎ 407/876-2888 for details). And another stop on the PGA tour is October's **Walt Disney World Oldsmobile**

Golf Classic (☎ **407/824-4321**). Daily ticket prices range from $8 to $15. Call for details.

14 Walt Disney World & Orlando After Dark

My hat's off to those of you who, after a long day of traipsing around amusement parks, still have the energy to venture out at night in search of entertainment. You'll find plenty to do. And this being kids' world, many evening shows inside the parks are geared to families. There is adult entertainment at Pleasure Island, CityWalk, and in downtown Orlando at Church Street Station where there are many bars and restaurants that normally cater to locals.

Check the **"Calendar"** section of Friday's *Orlando Sentinel* for up-to-the-minute details on local clubs, visiting performers, concerts, and events. (Also check out the *Orlando Sentinel Online* at **www.oso.aol.com**. It has hundreds of listings. The *Orlando Weekly* is a free magazine circulated through boxes in Central Florida and highlighting more offbeat and, often, up-to-date performers and performances.

Tickets to many performances are handled by **Ticketmaster** (☎ **407/839-3900** to charge tickets).

WALT DISNEY WORLD DINNER SHOWS

Other nighttime park options include SpectroMagic, fireworks, and IllumiNations (see sections 5 to 9 in this chapter for details).

Hoop-Dee-Doo Musical Revue. Disney's Fort Wilderness Resort and Campground, 3520 N. Fort Wilderness Trail. ☎ **407/WDW-DINE** (939-3463). Reservations required. Admission $37 adults, $19.50 children 3–11; taxes and gratuities extra. Show times daily at 5, 7:15, and 9:30pm. Free parking.

Fort Wilderness's rustic log-beamed Pioneer Hall is the setting for this 2-hour down-home musical revue. It's a high-energy show, with 1890s costumes, corny vaudeville jokes, rousing songs, and lots of good-natured audience participation. During the show, you'll chow down on an all-you-can-eat barbecue dinner including a big slab of strawberry shortcake for dessert. Beverages are included. If you catch an early show, stick around for the Electrical Water Pageant at 9:45pm, which can be viewed from the Fort Wilderness Beach.

Polynesian Luau Dinner Show. At Disney's Polynesian Resort, 1600 Seven Seas Dr. ☎ **407/WDW-DINE** (939-3463). Reservations required. Admission $38 adults, $19.50 children 3–11, free for children 2 and under; taxes and gratuities extra. Show times daily at 6:45 and 9:30pm. Free valet and self-parking.

This delightful 2-hour dinner show features a colorfully costumed cast of entertainers from New Zealand, Tahiti, Hawaii, and Samoa performing authentic hula, warrior, ceremonial, love, and fire dances on a flower-bedecked stage. There's even a Hawaiian/Polynesian fashion show. It all takes place in a heated open-air theater (dress for the weather). The meal, served family style, includes a big platter of fresh island fruits, half a barbecued chicken, vegetables, cinnamon bread, beverages, and a tropical ice-cream sundae. There's also a 4:30pm version daily (see "Meals with Disney Characters," above).

ENTERTAINMENT COMPLEXES: PLEASURE ISLAND & CHURCH STREET STATION, CITYWALK & DISNEY'S WEST SIDE

Pleasure Island. In Walt Disney World, adjacent to Walt Disney World Village. ☎ **407/ 934-7781.** Free before 7pm, $19.03 after 7pm (admission included in the 5-Day World-

Hopper Pass). Clubs daily 7pm–2am; shops daily 11am–2am. Valet parking $5, free self-parking.

This Walt Disney World theme park is a 6-acre complex of nightclubs, restaurants, shops, and movie theaters; for a single admission price, you can enjoy a night of club-hopping until the wee hours. The park is designed to suggest an abandoned waterfront industrial district with clubs in "converted" ramshackle lofts, factories, and warehouses, but the streets are festive with brightly colored lights and balloons. You'll be given a map and show schedule when you enter the park; take a look at it and plan your evening around shows that interest you. You can feel perfectly secure sending your teenage kids here for the evening, though they must be 18 to get in unless accompanied by a parent or legal guardian.

The on-premises clubs come and go. At this writing they include the **Island Jazz Company,** a big barnlike club featuring contemporary and traditional live jazz. **Mannequins Dance Palace** is a high-energy dance club with a large rotating dance floor and a deejay playing contemporary tunes at an ear-splitting decibel level (you must be 21 to get in). The **Neon Armadillo Music Saloon** features live country bands nightly; dancers whirl around the floor doing the Texas two-step or cotton-eyed Joe (lessons are given Sunday from 7 to 8pm). Sometimes stars come in and take the stage. You can order Southwestern fare.

The most unusual of Pleasure Island's clubs, and my personal favorite, is the **Adventurers Club,** chock-full of artifacts ranging from early aviation photos to shrunken heads. In the eerie Mask Room, more than 100 masks move their eyes, jeer, and make odd pronouncements. Improvisational comedy shows take place throughout the evening in the main salon, and there are diverse 20-minute cabaret shows in the library. You could easily hang out here all night sipping potent tropical drinks in the library and at the bar.

The **Comedy Warehouse,** another of my favorites, has a rustic interior with tiered seating. A very talented troupe performs improvisational comedy based on audience suggestions. There are five shows a night, and bar drinks are available. Arrive early.

Live bands play classic rock at the **Rock & Roll Beach Club.** There are bars on all three floors. The first level contains the dance floor; the second and third levels offer air hockey, pool tables, basketball machines, pinball, video games, darts, and a pizza and beer stand. There's also **8 Trax,** a 1970s-style club with about 50 TV monitors airing shows and videos over the dance floor. A deejay plays disco music, and guests play Twister.

In addition, live bands, including occasional big-name groups, play the **West End Plaza** outdoor stage and the **Hub Stage;** check your schedule for show times. You can star in your own music video at **SuperStar Studios.** There are carnival games, a video-game arcade, a Velcro wall, and an Orbitron (originally developed for NASA, it lets you experience weightlessness). And every night features a midnight **New Year's Eve celebration** with fireworks and confetti. **Shops and eateries** are found throughout the park, including **Planet Hollywood** (see "Great Deals on Dining, Both Inside the Parks & Out," earlier in this chapter).

In 1997, Disney added Disney's West Side, a collection of clubs, restaurants, and shops targeting adult visitors. It includes the 1,500-seat Dan Aykroyd–conceived **House of Blues;** an expanded 24-screen movie complex; a **Wolfgang Puck's Cafe,** serving his uniquely California cuisine; **Bongos,** a restaurant created by Miami's favorite Home Girl, Gloria Estefan, featuring Latin American entertainment; a performing arts theater; and more. A lushly tropical **RainForest Cafe** has already opened in the Disney Village Marketplace, replete with indoor waterfalls, thunder, lightning, and tropical birds.

Church Street Station. 129 W. Church St. (off I-4 between Garland and Orange aves.), in downtown Orlando. ☎ **407/422-2434.** Free before 5pm, $16.95 after 5pm; always free to restaurants, the Exchange Shopping Emporium, and the Midway game area. Clubs, daily until 2am; shops, daily until 11pm. Valet parking at Church St. and Garland Ave. $6; several parking lots are nearby (call for specifics). Take I-4 east to Exit 38 (Anderson St.), stay in the left lane, and follow the blue signs. Most hotels offer transportation to and from Church St. (and if you'll be drinking, I certainly advise it).

Though not part of Walt Disney World, Church Street Station in downtown Orlando operates on a principle similar to Pleasure Island. Occupying a cobblestone city block lined with turn-of-the-century buildings, it, too, is a shopping/dining/nightclub complex offering an evening of diverse entertainment for a single admission price. There are 20 live shows nightly; consult your show schedule upon entering.

Stunning interiors are the rule here. It's worth coming by just to check out the magnificent woodwork, stained glass, and thousands of authentic antiques. The shopping is pretty good, also.

Highlights include **Rosie O'Grady's Good Time Emporium,** an 1890s antique-filled saloon, where Dixieland bands, banjo players, singing waiters, and cancan dancers entertain nightly. Light fare is available. Adjoining Rosie's, **Apple Annie's Courtyard** evokes a Victorian tropical garden. Patrons sip potent tropical drinks while listening to folk and bluegrass music.

The plush interior of **Lili Marlene's Aviator's Pub & Restaurant** is embellished with World War I memorabilia, stained-glass transoms, and accoutrements from an 1850 Rothschild townhouse in Paris. The menu features premium aged steaks, prime rib, and fresh seafood. The whimsical **Phineas Phogg's Balloon Works,** with hot-air balloons and airplanes over the dance floor, is a high-energy club playing loud, pulsating music. Every Wednesday from 6:30 to 7:30pm beers cost just 5¢ here. No one under 21 is admitted.

The stunning trilevel **Cheyenne Saloon and Opera House** is constructed of golden oak lumber from a century-old Ohio barn. Quality western art is displayed throughout, including many oil paintings and 11 Remington sculptures. Balcony seating, in restored church pews, overlooks the stage, the setting for entertainment ranging from country bands to clogging exhibitions.

The **Orchid Garden Ballroom,** with ornate white wrought-iron arches and Victorian lighting fixtures suspended from an elaborate oak-paneled ceiling, is the setting for an oldies dance club. A deejay plays rock 'n' roll classics interspersed with live bands. As the evening progresses, so do the musical decades. Brick columns, oak paneling, and a gorgeous antique oak-and-mahogany bar characterize **Crackers Oyster Bar,** a cozy late 1800s–style dining room. Fresh Florida seafood is featured, along with more than 50 imported beers.

In addition, the 87,000-square-foot **Exchange** houses the carnival-like **Commander Ragtime's Midway of Fun, Food and Games,** including an enormous video-game arcade, a food court, and over 50 specialty shops. You can rent a **horse-drawn carriage** out front for a drive around the downtown area and Lake Eola, and **hot-air balloon flights** can be arranged (☎ 407/841-8787).

MAJOR CONCERT HALLS & AUDITORIUMS

Three large entertainment facilities, administered by the Orlando Centroplex, host most big-name performers playing the Orlando area.

The **Florida Citrus Bowl,** 1610 W. Church St., at Tampa Street (☎ **407/849-2020** for information, or 407/839-3900 to charge tickets), with 70,000 seats, is the largest. This is the setting for major rock concerts and headliners. To reach the

Citrus Bowl, take I-4 east to the East-West Expressway and head west to U.S. 441; make a left on Church Street, and follow the signs. Parking is $5.

The 17,500-seat **Orlando Arena,** at 600 W. Amelia St., between I-4 and Parramore Avenue (☎ **407/849-2020** for information, or 407/839-3900 to charge tickets), also hosts major performers in addition to an array of family-oriented entertainment: the circus every January, ice-skating, and more. To reach the arena, take I-4 east to Amelia Avenue, turn left at the traffic light at the bottom of the off-ramp, and follow the signs. Parking is $5.

The area's major cultural venue is the **Bob Carr Performing Arts Centre,** 401 W. Livingston St., between I-4 and Parramore Avenue (☎ **407/849-2020** for information, or 407/839-3900 to charge tickets). Concert prices vary with performers; ballet tickets are $15 to $35; opera tickets $12 to $45; the Broadway Series $24.50 to $46.50. This 2,500-seat facility is home to the **Orlando Opera Company** and the **Southern Ballet Theater,** both of which have October-to-May seasons. The **Orlando Broadway Series** (September to May) features original-cast Broadway shows. Also featured at the Bob Carr are concerts and comedy shows. To get here, take I-4 east to Amelia Avenue, turn left at the traffic light at the bottom of the off-ramp, and follow the signs. Parking is $5.

15 A Side Trip to Cypress Gardens

Founded in 1936, **Cypress Gardens** came into being as a 16-acre public garden along the banks of Lake Eloise, with cypress-wood-block pathways and thousands of tropical and subtropical plants. It's located on Fla. 540 at Cypress Gardens Boulevard (40 miles southwest of Walt Disney World), in Winter Haven (☎ **800/282-2123** or 941/ 324-2111).

Today it has grown to over 200 acres, with ponds and lagoons, waterfalls, classic Italian fountains, topiary, bronze sculptures, manicured lawns, and ancient cypress trees shrouded in Spanish moss. All this forms a backdrop to ever-changing floral displays of 8,000 varieties of plants from more than 90 countries. Southern belles in Scarlett O'Hara costumes stroll the grounds or sit on benches under parasols in idyllic tree-shaded nooks.

Strolling the grounds is, of course, the main attraction (there are more than 2 miles of winding botanical paths, and half the park's acreage is devoted to floral displays), but this being Central Florida, it's not the only one. Several shows are scheduled throughout the day (check your schedule upon entering the park). The world-famous **Greatest American Ski Team** performs on Lake Eloise in a show augmented by an awesome hang-gliding display. The breathtaking **ice skating show** is the Russian answer to America's Ice Capades. **Variété Internationale** features specialty acts from all over the world. An enchanting exhibit called **Wings of Wonder** surrounds visitors with more than 1,000 brightly colored free-flying butterflies in a 5,500-square-foot Victorian-style glass conservatory. **Electric boats** navigate a maze of lushly landscaped canals in the original botanical gardens area. You can ascend 153 feet to the **Island in the Sky** for a panoramic vista of the gardens and a beautiful chain of Central Florida lakes. **Carousel Cove,** with eight kiddie rides and arcade games, centers on an ornate turn-of-the-century–style carousel. It adjoins another kid pleaser, **Cypress Junction,** an elaborately landscaped model railroad that travels over 1,100 feet of track with up to 20 trains moving at one time. **Cypress Roots,** a museum of park memorabilia, displays photographs of famous visitors (Elvis on water-skis, Tiny Tim tiptoeing through the roses) and airs ongoing showings of *Easy to Love* starring Esther Williams (it was filmed here). Wind up your visit with a relaxing 30-minute narrated **pontoon cruise** on scenic Lake Eloise, past virgin forest, bulrushes, and beautiful shoreline homes (there's a $4 per person charge). Bring your binoculars; on a recent visit two bald eagles were spotted nesting in the trees.

Restaurants are on the premises, as is a picnic area. Admission is $29.50 for ages 10 and over, $24.50 for seniors, $19.50 for children 3 to 9, free for children 2 and under. It's open daily from 9:30am to 5:30pm, with extended hours during peak seasons. To get there, take I-4 west to U.S. 27 south, and proceed west to State Route 540; parking is free.

Northwest Florida: The Panhandle

by Bill Goodwin

13

If you like beaches, you'll love Florida's northwestern Panhandle. Thanks to quartz washed down from the Appalachian Mountains, the beaches here consist of dazzlingly white sand that is so talcumlike it actually squeaks when you walk across it. And walk across it you can, for some 100 miles of these incomparable sands are protected in state parks and the gorgeous Gulf Islands National Seashore.

Pensacola, Fort Walton Beach, Destin, and Panama City Beach have long been summertime beach meccas for families, couples, and singles from the adjoining states of Alabama and Georgia. Their demand for inexpensive lodging and meals make prices here among the most reasonable in the state, and their tastes put Southern specialties like turnip greens and cheese grits on many menus. And thanks to the Panhandle's proximity to their home states, this entire area has the languid charm of the Deep South.

But there's more here than beaches and southerners. Offshore, you'll find abundant marine life swimming over the gulf's natural sandbar system, which makes for good snorkeling and scuba diving. Championship catches of grouper, amberjack, snapper, mackerel, cobia, sailfish, wahoo, tuna, and blue marlin have made Destin one of the world's fishing capitals. In the interior near Pensacola, the Blackwater, Shoal, and Yellow Rivers teem with bass, bream, catfish, and largemouth bass, and also offer some of Florida's best canoeing and kayaking adventures.

The area also is steeped in history. Rivaling St. Augustine as Florida's oldest town, picturesque Pensacola carefully preserves a heritage derived from Spanish, French, English, and American conquest. Famous for its oysters, Apalachicola saw the invention of the air conditioner, a moment of great historical note in Florida. And Tallahassee, seat of state government since 1824, has a host of 19th-century buildings and homes, including the Old State Capitol.

EXPLORING NORTHWEST FLORIDA BY CAR

Both I-10 and U.S. 98 link Tallahassee and Pensacola, some 200 miles apart. The fastest route is I-10, but all you'll see is a huge pine forest divided by two strips of concrete. Plan to take U.S. 98, a scenic excursion in itself. This highway is particularly beautiful as it literally skirts the bay east of Apalachicola and the gulf west of Port St. Joe. There's another lovely stretch along skinny Okaloosa Island and across the high-rise bridge between Fort Walton Beach and Destin. From the bridge you'll see the brilliant color of the gulf and immediately understand why they call this the Emerald Coast.

1 Pensacola

191 miles W of Tallahassee, 354 miles W of Jacksonville

Native Americans left pottery shards and artifacts in the coastal dunes here centuries before Tristan de Luna arrived with a band of Spanish colonists in 1559. Although his settlement lasted only 2 years, modern Pensacolans claim that de Luna made their town the oldest in North America. Pensacola actually dates its permanence from a Spanish colony established here in 1698, however, St. Augustine wins this friendly feud, having been permanently settled in 1565.

France, Great Britain, the United States, and the Confederacy subsequently captured this strategically important deepwater port, leaving Pensacola with a charming blend of Old Spanish brickwork, colonial French balconies reminiscent of New Orleans, and magnificent Victorian mansions built by British and American lumber barons.

West of town, the magnificent National Museum of Naval Aviation at the U.S. Naval Air Station celebrates the storied past of naval pilots who trained at Pensacola. Based here, the Blue Angels demonstrate the high-tech present with thrilling exhibitions of precision flying in the navy's fastest fighters.

Also on the Naval Station, historic Fort Barrancas looks across the bay to Perdido Key and Santa Rosa Island, which reach out like narrow pinchers to form the harbor. Out there, powdery white-sand beaches beckon sun-and-surf lovers to their spectacular gulf shores, which include Pensacola Beach, a small family-oriented resort, and most of Florida's share of Gulf Islands National Seashore, home of historic Fort Pickens.

ESSENTIALS

GETTING THERE   From the east or west, take I-10, U.S. 90, or U.S. 98. From I-10, Exit 4 puts you on I-110, which terminates in downtown Pensacola. From I-65 in Alabama, take Exit 69 and follow Ala. 113 south to Flomaton near the Alabama-Florida line, then U.S. 29 south to Pensacola.

ASA (☎ 800/282-3424), **Continental** (☎ 800/525-0280), **Delta** (☎ 800/221-1212), **Northwest** (☎ 800/225-2525), and **US Airways** (☎ 800/428-4322) serve **Pensacola Regional Airport,** on 12th Avenue at Airport Road.

The major car-rental firms have booths at the airport, and taxis wait outside the modern terminal. Fares are approximately $11 to downtown, $15 to Gulf Breeze, and $20 to Pensacola Beach.

The **Amtrak** transcontinental *Sunset Limited* stops in Pensacola at 980 E. Heinberg St. (☎ **800/USA-RAIL** for information and reservations).

VISITOR INFORMATION   The **Pensacola Visitor Information Center,** 1401 E. Gregory St., Pensacola, FL 32501 (☎ **800/874-1234** or 850/434-1234; fax 850/432-8211; www.visitpensacola.com), gives away helpful information about the Greater Pensacola area, including maps of self-guided tours of the historic districts, and sells a detailed street map of the area. The office is at the mainland end of the Pensacola Bay Bridge and is open Monday to Friday from 8am to 5pm, and Saturday and Sunday from 8am to 4pm April through September, 9am to 4pm October to March.

For information specific to the beach, contact the **Pensacola Beach Chamber of Commerce,** 735 Pensacola Beach Blvd. (P.O. Box 1174), Pensacola Beach, FL 32561 (☎ **800/635-4803** or 850/932-1500; fax 850/932-1551; www.pensacolabeach.com).

The Panhandle

The chamber's offices and visitor center are on the right-hand side as you drive onto Santa Rosa Island across the Bob Sikes Bridge. They're open daily from 9am to 5pm.

GETTING AROUND   To see the historic sights in town, park at the Pensacola visitor center (see above) and take the **Five Flags Trolley** (☎ 850/436-9383). The one-way East Bay (Blue) Line runs Monday to Friday from 9am to 4pm between the visitor center and downtown. The Palafox (Red) Line runs Monday to Friday from 7am to 6pm north-south along Palafox Street between the waterfront and North Hill Preservation District. Both pass through Historic Pensacola Village. The 25¢ fare includes a transfer between the two lines. The visitor center has free route maps.

Escambia County Area Transit System (ECAT) runs **buses** around town Monday to Saturday from 6am to 6pm. The base fare is $1. Call ☎ 850/463-9383, ext. 611, for schedules. The ECAT buses don't go to Gulf Breeze or the beach, but a free **Island Trolley** operates along the full length of Pensacola Beach from May to September on Friday, Saturday, and Sunday from 10am to 3am. One route runs parallel to the beach on Via de Luna and Fort Pickens Road. A second runs along Pensacola Beach Boulevard from the Bob Sikes Bridge to the Via de Luna/Fort Pickens Road intersection.

If you need a cab, call **Airport Express Taxi** (☎ 850/572-5555), **Crosstown Cab** (☎ 850/456-TAXI), **Pensacola Red & Gold Taxi** (☎ 850/505-0025), or **Yellow Cab** (☎ 850/433-3333).

TIME   Pensacola is in the **central time zone**, 1 hour behind Miami, Orlando, and Tallahassee.

HITTING THE BEACH

Stretching eastward 47 miles, from the entrance to Pensacola Bay to Fort Walton Beach, skinny **Santa Rosa Island** is home to the resorts, condominiums, cottages, restaurants, and shops of **Pensacola Beach,** the area's prime vacation spot. This relatively small and low-key resort began life a century ago as the site of a beach pavilion, or "casino" as such facilities were called back then, and the heart of town—at the intersection of Pensacola Beach Boulevard, Via de Luna, and Fort Pickens Road—is still known as **Casino Beach.** At the base of the town's water tank, this lively area sports restaurants, snack bars, a games arcade for kids, a minigolf course, public rest rooms, walk-up beach bars with live bands blaring away, an indoor sports bar, and an outdoor concert pavilion with summertime entertainment. And the shops, restaurants, and bars of **Quietwater Boardwalk** are just across the road on the bay side of the island. If you want an active beach vacation, it's all here in one compact zone.

One reason Pensacola Beach is so small is that most of Santa Rosa Island is included in the ✪ **Gulf Islands National Seashore.** Jumping from island to island from Mississippi to Florida, this magnificent preserve includes mile after mile of undeveloped white-sand beach and rolling dunes covered with sea grass and sea oats. Established in 1971, the national seashore is a protected environment for more than 280 species of birds. Visitors enjoy swimming, boating, fishing, scuba diving, camping, and ranger-guided fort tours and nature hikes.

✪ **Fort Pickens,** built in the 1830s to team with Fort Barrancas in guarding Pensacola's harbor entrance, stands silent guard in the dunes at the western end of Santa Rosa. This huge brick structure saw combat during the Civil War, but it's famous today as the prison home of Apache medicine man Geronimo from 1886 to 1888. A small museum features displays about Geronimo, coastal defenses, and the seashore's ecology. The fort and museum are open April to October, daily from 9:30am to 5pm; November to March, daily from 8:30am to 4pm. Both are closed on Christmas.

Seven-day admission permits to the Fort Pickens area are $6 per vehicle, $3 per

Legend
- North Hill Preservation District
- Palafox Historic District
- Seville Historic District

NA-0049

pedestrian or bicyclist, free for holders of National Park Service passports. For more information, contact the **Gulf Islands National Seashore** at 1801 Gulf Breeze Pkwy., Gulf Breeze, FL 32561 (☎ 850/934-2600).

NATURE PRESERVES & ZOOS

A former federal tree plantation, the Gulf Islands National Seashore's 1,378-acre **Naval Live Oaks Area,** on U.S. 98 a mile east of Gulf Breeze (☎ 850/934-2600), is a place of primitive beauty. Nature trails lead through the oaks and pines to picnic areas and a beach; pick up a map at the headquarters building, which has a small museum and a gorgeous view through the pines to Santa Rosa Sound. Picnic areas and trails are open from 8am to sunset all year except Christmas. The visitor center is open April to October, daily from 8:30am to 5pm; November to March, daily from 8:30am to 4:30pm. Admission is free.

The Zoo, on U.S. 98 about 10 miles east of Gulf Breeze, 15 miles east of Pensacola (☎ 850/932-2229), has more than 700 exotic animals—including white tigers, rhinos, and gorillas—on 50 acres of landscaped habitats. Japanese gardens, elephant shows, a giraffe feeding tower, and a petting farm make for a fun visit. A Safari Line train chugs through a 30-acre wildlife preserve with free-ranging herds. Admission is $9.75 adults, $8.75 seniors, $5.75 children 3 to 11, free for children 2 and under. Open during summer daily from 9am to 5pm; off-season, daily from 9am to 4pm. It's also open from 6 to 9pm from the day after Thanksgiving until January 4 for a holiday lights festival, when proceeds go to charity. Closed Thanksgiving and Christmas days.

GREAT GOLF THAT WON'T BREAK YOUR BUDGET & OTHER AFFORDABLE OUTDOOR ACTIVITIES

CANOEING & KAYAKING Less than 20 miles northeast of Pensacola via U.S. 90, the little town of Milton is the official "Canoe Capital of Florida" (by an act of the state legislature, no less). It's a well-earned title, for the nearby Blackwater River, Cold-water River, Sweetwater Creek, and Juniper Creek are all perfect for canoeing, kayaking, tubing, rafting, and paddleboating.

The Blackwater is considered one of the world's purest sand-bottom rivers. It has retained a primordial, backwoods beauty, thanks in large part to Florida's largest state forest (183,000 acres of oak, pine, and juniper) and **J Blackwater River State Park,** 7720 Deaton Bridge Rd., Holt, FL 32564 (☎ 850/953-5363), where you can closely observe plant life and wildlife along nature trails. The park has facilities for fishing, picnicking, and camping. Admission is $2 per day per vehicle with up to eight occupants. Campsites cost $8 per night ($10 with electricity), and discounts for stays of 7 days or longer are available.

Adventures Unlimited, Rte. 6, Box 283, Milton (☎ **800/239-6864** or 850/623-9197), is a year-round resort with canoeing, kayaking, rafting, camping, a high- and low-challenge course, and paddleboating expeditions in the state park and surrounding rivers. Special arrangements are made for novices. Canoes rent from at $13 per person, kayaks from $17, and inner tubes for $9. The company also has 14 cottages on the Coldwater River ranging from $39 to $109 a night. Campsites cost $15 a night.

Blackwater Canoe Rental, 10274 Pond Rd., Milton (☎ **800/967-6789** or 850/623-0235), also rents canoes, kayaks, floats, tubes, and camping equipment. It has day trips by canoe, kayak, or inner tubes ranging from $9 to $19 per person and overnight excursions ranging from $19 to $28 per person. Tents, sleeping bags, and coolers are available for rent.

FISHING Red snapper, grouper, mackerel, tuna, and billfish are abundant in these waters. Anglers congregate along the **Pensacola Bay Bridge Fishing Pier** (it's on the old bridge). The **Bob Sikes Bridge Fishing Pier** also is on the old bridge.

Fishing charter services are offered by **Scuba Shack/Charter Boat** *Wet Dream,* 719 S. Palafox St., in Pensacola (☎ 850/433-4319); *Hooligan* **Charters** (☎ 850/968-1898) and *Rocky Top* **Charters** (☎ 850/432-7536), both at Pitt Slip Marina off East Main Street in Pensacola; and *Lo-Baby* **Charters,** 38 High-point Dr., in Gulf Breeze (☎ 850/934-5285). At Pensacola Beach, choose from *Chulamar* (☎ 850/434-6977), *Lively One* (☎ 850/932-5071), *Boss Lady* (☎ 850/932-0305 or 850/477-4033), *Entertainer* (☎ 850/932-0305), *Exodus* (☎ 850/626-2545 or 850/932-0305), and *Lady Kady* (☎ 850/932-2065 or 850/932-0305). Expect to pay between $300 and $750 for one to four passengers, depending on length of trip. You may be able to save by driving to Destin, where party boats charge less per person (see "Great Golf That Won't Break Your Budget & Other Affordable Outdoor Activities" in section 2, below). Sightseeing and evening cruises here go for about $50 per person.

GOLF The Pensacola area has its share of Northwest Florida's numerous championship golf courses. Look for free copies of *Gulf Coast Tee Time,* an annual directory describing all of them, at the visitor information offices and in many hotel lobbies (see "The Active Vacation Planner" in chapter 2 for information about ordering copies). Reasonably priced golf packages can be arranged through many local hotels and motels.

Among this region's best courses is **Marcus Pointe,** on Marcus Pointe Boulevard off North W Street (☎ **800/362-7287** or 850/484-9770), which has hosted the Nike Tour, the American Amateur Classic, and the Pensacola Open. *Golf Digest* magazine has described the wide-ranging, 18-hole course as a "great value," and it is: Greens fees with cart are about $40 to $49, depending on the season.

The Moors, on Avalon Boulevard north of I-10 (☎ **800/727-1010** or 850/995-4653), also has greeted the Nike Tour and is home to the Emerald Coast Classic, a PGA seniors event. Pot bunkers here make you think you're playing in Scotland. Greens fees here are about $30 without cart. The Moors also has a lodge with eight luxury rooms.

Others worth considering are **Scenic Hills,** on U.S. 90 northwest of town (☎ **850/476-9611**), whose rolling fairways are unique for this mostly flat area; the 36-hole **Tiger Point,** 1255 Country Club Rd. east of Gulf Breeze by Santa Rosa Sound (☎ **850/932-1330**), overlooking the water (the fifth-hole green of the East Course actually sits all by itself on an island); **Hidden Creek,** 3070 PGA Blvd., in Navarre between Gulf Breeze and Fort Walton Beach (☎ **850/939-4604**); **Creekside Golf Course,** 2355 W. Michigan Ave. (☎ **850/944-7969**); and **Osceola Municipal Golf Course,** 300 Tonawanda, off Mobile Highway (☎ **850/456-2761**).

In addition, the **Perdido Bay Golf Resort,** 1 Doug Ford Dr., near Perdido Key (☎ **800/874-5355** or 850/492-1223), has accommodations available for visiting golfers. It was home of the PGA Pensacola Open from 1978 to 1987.

WATER SPORTS Visibility in the waters around Pensacola can range from 30 to 50 feet inshore to 100 feet 25 miles offshore. Although the bottom is sandy and it's too far north for coral, the battleship USS *Massachusetts,* submerged in 30 feet of water 3 miles offshore, is one of some 35 artificial reefs where you can spot loggerhead turtles and other creatures.

Scuba Shack, 711 S. Palafox St. (☎ **850/433-4319**), is Pensacola's oldest dive shop, offering sales, rentals, classes, and diving and fishing charters on the *Wet Dream,* moored behind the office. **Dive Pros,** 7203 U.S. 98 west (☎ **850/456-8845**), with a branch in Gulf Breeze (☎ **850/934-8845**), offers rentals, all levels of instruction, and diving excursions. The *Chulamar* at Pensacola Beach (☎ **850/434-6977**) and the *Lo-Baby,* in Gulf Breeze (☎ **850/934-5285**), both make arrangements for diving excursions.

Kirk Newkirk's **Key Sailing Center,** 500 Quietwater Beach Rd., on the Quiet-water Beach Boardwalk (☎ **850/932-5550**), rents Hobie Cats, pontoon boats, Wave Runners, jet-skis, and windsurfing boards. So does **Bonifay Water Sports** next door (☎ **850/932-0633**) and **Radical Rides,** 444 Pensacola Beach Blvd., near the Bob Sikes Bridge (☎ **850/934-9743**).

EXPLORING HISTORIC PENSACOLA

Civil War Soldiers Museum. 108 S. Palafox St. (south of Romana St.). ☎ **850/469-1900.** Admission $5 adults, $2 children 6–12, free for children 5 and under. Mon–Sat 10am–4:30pm. Closed New Year's Day, Thanksgiving, and Christmas.

Founded by Dr. Norman Haines Jr., a local physician who grew up discovering Civil War relics in Sharpsburg, Maryland, this storefront museum in the heart of the Palafox

Street business district emphasizes how ordinary soldiers lived during that bloody conflict. The doctor's collection of military medical equipment and treatment methods is especially informative. A 23-minute video tells of Pensacola's role during the Civil War. The museum's bookstore carries more than 600 titles about the war.

✪ **Historic Pensacola Village.** 205 E. Zarragossa St. (east of Tarragona St.). ☎ **850/ 444-8905.** Admission $6 adults, $5 seniors, $2.50 children 4–16, free for children 3 and under. Tues–Sat 10am–4pm. Guided tours Mon–Sat 11am and 1pm. Closed state holidays.

Bounded by Government, Tarragona, Adams, and Alcaniz streets, this original part of Pensacola resembles a shady English colonial town—albeit with Spanish street names—complete with town green and **Christ Church,** built in 1823 and resembling Bruton Parrish in Williamsburg, Virginia. It has some of Florida's oldest homes (now owned and preserved by the state), along with charming boutiques and interesting restaurants. During summer, costumed characters go about their daily chores and demonstrate old crafts, and University of Florida archaeologists unearth the old Spanish commanding officer's compound at Zarragossa and Tarragona streets. Among the landmarks to visit are the Museum of Industry, the Museum of Commerce, the French Creole–style Charles Lavalle House, the elegant Victorian Dorr House, the French Colonial–Creole Quina House, and St. Michael's Cemetery (land was deeded by the king of Spain).

Another fascinating site is the **Julee Cottage Black History Museum,** 204 Zarragossa St. Built around 1790, this small house was owned by Julee Panton, a freed slave who ran her own business, invested in real estate, and loaned money to slaves so they could buy their freedom. Today the museum recalls her life and deeds, as well as the achievements of other African Americans with Pensacola associations.

Across Tarragona Street, the **Pensacola City of Five Flags Exhibit,** in the J. Earle Bowden Building, 120 E. Church St., traces the city's history from Spanish colonial times to the present. Of special interest is the archaeological section, where you can see one of the oldest coins ever found in North America, minted between 1471 and 1474.

Start your tour by buying tickets at **Tivoli House,** 205 E. Zarragossa St., just east of Tarragona Street, where you can get free maps and brochures and purchase audio driving tapes of the city's three historic districts for $5. Admission to the village includes the T. T. Wentworth, Jr., Florida State Museum (see below), where you also can buy tickets.

Adjacent to the village, Pensacola's **Vietnam Memorial,** on Bayfront Parkway at 9th Avenue, is known as the "Wall South," since it is a three-quarters-size replica of the national Vietnam Veterans Memorial in Washington, D.C. Look for the Huey helicopter atop the wall.

✪ **National Museum of Naval Aviation.** Radford Blvd., U.S. Naval Air Station. ☎ **850/ 452-3604.** Free admission. IMAX movies $4.50 adults, $4 seniors and children under 13. Daily 9am–5pm; guided tours daily at 9:30am, 11am, 1, and 2:30pm; IMAX films on the hour daily 10am–4pm. Closed New Year's Day, Thanksgiving, and Christmas.

The U.S. Navy and Marine Corps have trained at the sprawling U.S. Naval Air Station since they began flying airplanes early in this century. Celebrating their heroics, this truly remarkable museum has more than 100 aircraft dating from the 1920s to the space age. There's even a torpedo bomber flown by former president George Bush during World War II. Both children and adults can sit at the controls of a jet trainer. You can almost feel the tug of gravity while watching the Blue Angels and other naval aviators soaring about the skies in *The Magic of Flight,* a stunning IMAX film shown on a screen six times the size of the average cinema.

Fort Barrancas (☎ 850/934-2600) also is definitely worth a visit while you're at the naval station. On Taylor Road near the museum, this imposing brick structure overlooks the deepwater pass into Pensacola Bay. The Spanish built the water battery in 1797. Linked to the battery by a tunnel, the incredibly intricate brickwork of the upper section was constructed by American troops between 1839 and 1844. Entry is by a drawbridge across a dry moat, and an interior scarp gallery goes all the way around the inside of the fort. Meticulously restored and operated by the National Park Service as part of Gulf Islands National Seashore, it's open from April to October, daily from 9:30am to 5pm; November through March, Wednesday to Sunday from 10:30am to 4pm. Guided tour schedules change from season to season, so call for the latest information. Admission is free.

The **Pensacola Lighthouse,** opposite the museum entrance on Radford Boulevard, has guided ships to the harbor entrance since 1825. The lighthouse is not open to the public, but you can drive right up to it. The nearby **Lighthouse Point Restaurant** (☎ 850/452-3251) offers bountiful, all-you-can-eat luncheon buffets and magnificent bay views for just $5.50 per person; it's open Monday to Friday from 10:30am to 2pm, and reservations are not required.

The naval station is southwest of downtown Pensacola. Enter either at the Main Gate at the south end of Navy Boulevard (Fla. 295) or at the Back Gate on Blue Angel Parkway (Fla. 173). No passes are required.

Pensacola Museum of Art. 407 S. Jefferson St. (at Main St.). ☎ 850/432-6247. Admission free Tues; other days, $2 adults, $1 active-duty military and students, free for kids under 6. Tues–Fri 10am–5pm, Sat 10am–4pm, Sun 1–4pm.

Housed in what was the city jail from 1906 to 1954, this museum showcases permanent art and sculpture collections as well as art on loan, from tribal art to classic European pieces to avant-garde modern works.

T. T. Wentworth, Jr., Florida State Museum. 330 S. Jefferson St. (at Church St.). ☎ 850/444-8586. Admission $6 adults, $5 seniors and military, $2.50 children 4–16, children 3 and under free (includes Historic Pensacola Village). Tues–Sat 10am to 4pm.

The classic yellow brick building houses exhibits of western Florida's history and has a special hands-on Discovery Museum for children on the third floor.

HISTORIC DISTRICTS

In addition to Historic Pensacola Village in the Seville Historic District (see above), the city has two other preservation areas worth a stroll. The Pensacola Visitor Information Center provides free walking-tour maps, and you can buy an audiotape driving tour for $5 at Tivoli House in Historic Pensacola Village (see above).

PALAFOX HISTORIC DISTRICT   Running up Palafox Street from the water to Wright Street, the Palafox Historic District is also the downtown business district. Beautiful Spanish Renaissance- and Mediterranean-style buildings stand from the early days, including the ornate Saenger Theatre. In 1821 Gen. Andrew Jackson formally accepted Florida into the United States during a ceremony in Plaza Ferdinand VII, now a National Historic Landmark. His statue commemorates the event.

The Palafox district is home to the **Pensacola Museum of Art,** in the old city jail, and the **T. T. Wentworth, Jr., Florida State Museum** (see "Exploring Historic Pensacola," above).

NORTH HILL PRESERVATION DISTRICT   Another entry in the National Register of Historic Places, the North Hill Preservation District covers the 50 square blocks north of the Palafox Historic District bounded by Wright, Blount,

Palafox, and Reus streets. Descendants of Spanish nobility, timber barons, British merchants, French Creoles, buccaneers, and Civil War soldiers still live in some of the more than 500 homes. They are not open to the public, but are a bonanza for anyone interested in architecture. In 1863 Union troops erected a fort in Lee Square, at Palafox and Gadsden streets. It later was dedicated to the Confederacy, complete with a 50-foot-high obelisk and sculpture based on John Elder's painting *After Appomattox.*

SHOPPING

Sightseeing and shopping can be combined in Pensacola's Palafox and Seville historic districts, where many shops are housed in renovated centuries-old buildings. The **Quayside Art Gallery,** on Plaza Ferdinand at the corner of Zarragossa and Jefferson streets (☎ 850/438-2363), is the largest cooperative gallery in the Southeast. More than 100 artists display their works here, and the friendly staff will direct you to other nearby galleries.

North T Street between West Cervantes Street and West Fairfield Drive has so many antique dealers and small flea markets that it's known as **Antique Alley.** Others have booths in the **Ninth Avenue Antique Mall,** 380 N. 9th Ave. between Gregory and Strong streets (☎ 850/438-3961). Get a complete list of local antique dealers from the Pensacola Visitor Information Center (see "Essentials," above).

Browsers will enjoy poking through the 400 dealer spaces covering 45 acres at the **Flea Market,** on U.S. 98, opposite the zoo about 10 miles east of Gulf Breeze (☎ 850/934-1971). It's open on Saturday and Sunday from 9am to 5pm. Admission is free.

ACCOMMODATIONS YOU CAN AFFORD

The high season at all of the Northwest Florida beaches runs from Easter to Labor Day, and hotel or motel reservations are essential during this time. Room rates are highest during school vacation from mid-May to mid-August, and premiums are charged at Easter, Memorial Day, July 4, and Labor Day. There's another high-priced peak in March, when thousands of raucous college students invade during spring break. Economical times to visit are April (except Easter) and September—the weather's warm, most establishments are open, and room rates are significantly lower than during summer. The least expensive rates come during winter, but many attractions and some restaurants may be closed then.

The Pensacola Visitor Information Center (see "Essentials," above) publishes a complete list of rental condominiums and cottages. Among the leading rental agents are **Gulf Coast Accommodations,** 400 Quietwater Beach Rd., Box 12, Pensacola Beach, FL 32561 (☎ 800/239-4334 or 850/932-9788; fax 850/932-3449; www. innisfree.com/gca); **JME Management,** 22A Via de Luna, Pensacola Beach, FL 32562 (☎ 800/554-3695 or 850/932-0775; fax 850/932-0787); and **Tristan Realty,** P.O. Box 1611, Gulf Breeze, FL 32562 (☎ 800/445-9931 or 850/932-7363; fax 850/932-8361; www.pcola.com/tristan/).

For camping, the **Fort Pickens Area** of Gulf Islands National Seashore (☎ 800/365-2267 for reservations, or 850/934-2621 for recorded information) has 200 sites (135 with electricity) in a pine forest about 7 miles west of Pensacola Beach on the bay side of Santa Rosa Island. Nature trails lead from the camp through Blackbird Marsh and to the beach. A small store sells provisions. Sites cost $15 a night without power, $20 a night with it. Golden Age and Golden Access cardholders get a 50% discount. You can make reservations up to 5 months in advance.

Escambia County adds 11½% to all hotel and campground bills.

The accommodations listed below are arranged by geographic area: downtown Pensacola and Pensacola Beach.

PENSACOLA

The University Mall complex at I-10 and Davis Highway, about 5 miles north of downtown, has a host of chain motels, including **Residence Inn by Marriott** (☎ 800/331-3131 or 850/479-1000), in which all rooms and apartments have kitchens and fireplaces, and **Fairfield Inn by Marriott,** 7325 N. Davis Hwy. (☎ 800/331-3131 or 850/484-8001). The recently renovated **Motel 6–North** (☎ 800/466-8356 or 850/476-5386) is within walking distance on the north side of I-10. There's an ample supply of inexpensive restaurants on Plantation Road and in the adjacent mall.

Super-Cheap Sleeps

Seville Inn. 223 E. Garden St. (between Alcaniz and Manresa sts.), Pensacola, FL 32501. ☎ **800/277-7275** or 850/433-8331. Fax 850/432-6849. 120 units. A/C TV TEL. Summer $69–$79 single or double. Winter $39–$44 single or double. Rates include continental breakfast. AE, DC, MC, V.

This dated but clean 2-story motel is conveniently located at the edge of the Seville Historic District, across the street from the Civic Center, and about 4 blocks from the Saenger Theatre. An outdoor swimming pool is open during the warm months. Guests receive complimentary local phone calls, and passes to the Pensacola Greyhound track and Seville Quarter entertainment complex (see "Pensacola After Dark," below).

For a Few Bucks More

New World Landing. 600 S. Palafox St. (at Pine St.), Pensacola, FL 32501. ☎ **850/432-4111.** Fax 850/432-6836. 15 units. A/C TV TEL. $85 single or double; $130 suite. AE, DC, MC, V.

Near the scenic bay and in the historic district, this urban version of a comfortable country inn is enhanced by flower gardens and fountains. From the colonial-style lobby, a grand staircase leads to high-ceilinged and spacious rooms artistically decorated with antiques. The rooms depict aspects of Pensacola's rich history: Four flaunt Spanish decor, four are very chic French style, four portray early Americana, and four focus on old England.

The adjoining New World Landing Restaurant and pub recalls the city's colorful historic past, honoring Spain with a Barcelona Room, spotlighting French history in a Marseilles Room, and giving tribute to the city itself in the Pensacola Room. Fresh seafood in wine or butter sauce is a specialty, but the menu also features excellent steaks, prime rib of beef, veal, and more. Lunch is served Monday to Friday; dinner, Tuesday to Saturday.

Pensacola Grand Hotel. 200 E. Gregory St. (at Alcaniz St.), Pensacola, FL 32501. ☎ **800/348-3336** or 850/433-3336. Fax 850/432-7572. 212 units. A/C TV TEL. $90–$100 single or double; $204–$408 suite. Weekend rates available. AE, DC, DISC, MC, V.

Opposite the Civic Center in the Seville Historic District near the southern end of I-110, this unique hotel has turned the historic L&N Railroad Depot into a grand lobby with bar, restaurants, lounges, meeting rooms, and a cozy library. You'll see such turn-of-the-century accoutrements as an ornate railroad clock, original oak stair rails, imported marble, ceramic mosaic tile floors, and old-fashioned carved furniture. The plush L&N Lobby Bar and the 1912 Restaurant capture this railroad ambience. A 2-story glass Galleria links the depot to a modern 15-story tower, whose rooms and suites are popular with business travelers and groups. Facilities include a fitness center and outdoor pool.

PENSACOLA BEACH

If you don't need a room right on the beach and don't mind hunting for a parking spot once you get there during the summer, you can save by staying on U.S. 98 in Gulf Breeze, a short ride across the Bob Sykes Bridge to Pensacola Beach. The pick here is the **Holiday Inn-Bay Beach,** 51 Gulf Breeze Pkwy. (☎ **800/HOLIDAY** or 850/ 932-2214; fax 904/932-0932), which sits on a small beach with a grand view of Pensacola across the bay. There's a pool in a grassy bay-side courtyard, plus the very good Bon Appetit Cafe. Double rooms range from $70 to $100 during summer, $60 to $80 off-season. For basic accommodations, try the **Gulf Coast Inn Motel,** 843 Gulf Breeze Pkwy. (☎ **850/932-2222**), an older but clean establishment where doubles cost $38 to $48 in summer, $30 to $40 off-season.

Super-Cheap Sleeps

❂ **Five Flags Inn.** 299 Fort Pickens Rd., Pensacola Beach, FL 32561. ☎ **850/932-3586.** Fax 850/934-0257. 49 units. A/C TV TEL. Summer $85 single or double. Off-season $49–$69 single or double. Packages available. AE, DISC, MC, V.

This friendly motel between the Holiday Inn and The Dunes may look like a jail from the road, but don't be fooled. Big picture windows look out to the swimming pool and gorgeous white-sand beach, which comes right up to the property. Although the accommodations are small, the rates are a bargain for well-furnished, gulf-front rooms.

For a Few Bucks More

Best Western Pensacola Beach. 16 Via de Luna Dr., Pensacola Beach, FL 32561. ☎ **800/ 934-3301** or 850/934-3300. Fax 850/934-9780. 122 units. A/C TV TEL. Summer $119–$139 single or double. Off-season $59–$109 single or double. Golf packages available. Rates include continental breakfast. AE, DC, DISC, MC, V.

On the gulf front, this casual hotel is notable for bright, clean, and extraspacious accommodations, complete with refrigerators, coffeemakers, microwaves, and wet bars. Outside corridors lead to all rooms. Although none has its own balcony or patio, units facing the beach have great views; the less-expensive "inland" rooms don't. Two swimming pools, the Cabana Bar, and a children's playground are on the beach. Chan's Market Café (see "Great Deals on Dining," below) sits in the parking lot.

Clarion Suites Resort & Convention Center. 20 Via de Luna Dr., Pensacola Beach, FL 32561. ☎ **800/874-5303** or 850/932-4300. Fax 850/934-9112. 86 units. A/C TV TEL. Summer $110–$161 up to 4 persons. Off-season $67–$123 up to 4 persons. Rates include continental breakfast. AE, DC, DISC, MC, V.

Built to resemble a village of cottages, this tin-roofed, pastel-sided beachfront resort offers one-bedroom suites that can accommodate four people. The attractively decorated accommodations include a living room with a dining area, bathroom (39 bilevel loft suites have 1½ baths), kitchen, and private entrance. The living rooms and bedrooms each have their own TVs and telephones. There's no restaurant, but complimentary continental breakfast is served daily in the lobby, and eateries are within walking distance. Facilities include a swimming pool, fitness center, children's play area, beach pavilion, coin laundry, and conference rooms.

The Dunes. 333 Fort Pickens Rd., Pensacola Beach, FL 32561. ☎ **800/83-DUNES** or 850/932-3536. Fax 850/932-7088. 76 units. A/C TV TEL. Summer $115–$145 single or double; $230–$275 suite. Off-season $70–$90 single or double; $195–$245 suite. Packages available. AE, DISC, MC, V.

This 8-story tower has spacious rooms, all with balconies with gorgeous gulf or bay vistas. They come equipped with coffeemakers and hair dryers, and the penthouse suites have their own Jacuzzis. The small but pleasant Gulf Front Cafe serves breakfast, lunch, and dinner. The kids can participate in the supervised children's program from May to Labor Day. The hotel will even take care of the kids so Mom and Dad can take Saturday night off. Facilities also include a heated swimming pool, jogging trail, bike path, and volleyball area. There's an undeveloped dune preserve next door.

Hampton Inn Pensacola Beach. 2 Via de Luna, Pensacola Beach, FL 32561. ☎ **800/ 320-8108** or 850/932-6800. Fax 850/932-6833. 181 units. A/C TV TEL. Summer $99–$139 single or double. Off-season $65–$109 single or double. Rates include continental breakfast. AE, DC, DISC, MC, V.

Opened in 1995, this pastel, 4-story hotel sits right by the gulf next to Casino Beach. The bright lobby opens to a wooden sundeck with beachside swimming pools on either side (one is heated). Half the oversize rooms have balconies overlooking the gulf; these are more expensive than rooms on the bay side, which have nice views but no outside sitting areas. Each unit is equipped with a refrigerator, microwave oven, and wet bar. There's no restaurant on the premises, but Chan's Gulfside Café and Surf-side Saloon is next door. Guests have their own coin laundry. Local calls are free to guests, and the TVs carry HBO.

Holiday Inn Pensacola Beach. 165 Fort Pickens Rd., Pensacola Beach, FL 32561. ☎ **800/ 465-4329** or 850/932-5361. Fax 850/932-7121. 150 units. A/C TV TEL. Summer $105–$130 single or double. Off-season $65–$110 single or double. Senior citizen discounts. AE, DC, DISC, MC, V.

This 9-story establishment boasts terrific views from its brightly furnished upper-floor rooms and Penthouse Lounge. It's one of the oldest hotels in the area, which means the rooms aren't as large as at other new properties, such as the Hampton Inn; there's adequate space for a king-size bed, but rooms with two double beds are relatively cramped. They all have private balconies, however, with the most expensive rooms facing directly onto the gulf. The Penthouse Lounge serves dinners and has summer-time entertainment. Facilities include a lobby bar looking out to a beachside heated swimming pool.

GREAT DEALS ON DINING
PENSACOLA

Housed in the 1879-vintage Moreno Cottage, **Mr. P's Sandwich Shop,** 221 E. Zarragossa St., (☎ **850/433-0294**), opposite Old Christ Church is a good place to stop for inexpensive soups, salads, quiches, and sandwiches while touring Historic Pensacola Village. Open Monday to Saturday from 11am to 2pm.

Other low-priced options here include two branches of **Barnhill's Country Buffet,** one on North Davis Highway and Olive Road north of I-10 (☎ **850/477-5465**), and a second on U.S. 98 at Oriole Drive 3 miles east of Gulf Breeze (☎ 850/932-0403). Both offer a cornucopia of fried chicken and fish, baked ham, roast beef, a tasty pot roast, boiled cabbage and collard greens, old-fashioned 'Nilla Wafer banana pudding, and other Southern fare. Adults pay $5.59 a head at lunch, while kids 12 and under are charged 40¢ times their age. At dinner, the prices jump to $7 and 45¢. Both Barn-hill's are open Sunday to Thursday from 10:45am to 8pm, Friday and Saturday from 10:45am to 8:30pm (to 8:30 and 9pm, respectively, in summer). MasterCard and Visa are accepted.

Super-Cheap Eats

✪ **Hopkins' Boarding House.** 900 N. Spring St. (at Strong St.). ☎ **850/438-3979.** Reservations not accepted. Breakfast $3.50; full meals $7. No credit cards. Tues–Sun 7–9:30am, 11:15am–2pm, and 5:15–7:30pm; Sun noon–2pm. SOUTHERN.

There's a delicious peek into the past when you dine at this Victorian boarding house in the heart of the North Hill Preservation District. Outside, ancient trees shade a wraparound porch with old-fashioned rocking chairs in which to await the next available place at the large dining tables inside. You could be seated next to the mayor or a mechanic, for everyone in town dines here, and everyone eats family style. Platters are piled high with seasonal Southern-style vegetables from nearby farms. Tuesday is famous as Fried Chicken Day, and you're likely to be served fried fish on Friday. Every Yankee should sample the piping-hot grits that accompany each bountiful breakfast. In true boardinghouse fashion, guests bus their own dishes and pay the one price when they're finished eating.

Marina Oyster Barn. 505 Bayou Blvd. (on Bayou Texar). ☎ **850/433-0511.** Reservations not accepted. Sandwiches $2.50–$5.50; main courses $5.50–$12; lunch specials $3.75–$5.50. AE, DISC, MC, V. Tues–Sat 11am–9pm (lunch specials 11am–2pm). Go east on Cervantes St. across the Bayou Texar Bridge, then left at the stoplight on Perry Ave., and left again to the end of Strong St. SEAFOOD.

Exuding the ambience of the quickly vanishing Old Florida fish camps, this plain but clean restaurant at the Johnson-Rooks Marina has been a favorite with seafood lovers since 1969, for both its view and its down-home-style seafood. Served raw, steamed, fried, or Rockefeller, freshly shucked oysters are the main feature; but the seafood salad here is first rate, and the fish, shrimp, and oysters are breaded with cornmeal in true Southern fashion. The daily luncheon specials give you a light meal at a bargain price.

For a Few Bucks More

McGuire's Irish Pub & Brewery. 600 E. Gregory St. (between 11th and 12th aves.). ☎ **850/433-6789.** Reservations not accepted. Snacks, burgers, and sandwiches $7.50–$8; meals $13–$25. AE, DC, DISC, MC, V. Mon–Sat 11am–2am, Sun 11am–3pm (brunch) and 3pm–1am. AMERICAN/IRISH.

Every day is St. Patrick's Day here, with corned beef and cabbage, Irish stew, and such hybrids as an scampi o'fettucini (shrimp in Alfredo sauce). Supersize hamburgers, tender steak, grilled fish, beer-batter shrimp, barbecued ribs, prime rib, hearty bean soup, and salads are also on the menu. You can watch the house beer being brewed in copper kettles and dine in a cellarlike room with 8,000 bottles of wine on display. You can leave an autographed dollar bill; more than 125,000 of them line the bar's walls and ceilings (bucks from famous folks are framed near the entrance). Live music is offered most nights.

Skopelos on the Bay. 670 Scenic Hwy. (U.S. 90 east, at E. Cervantes St.). ☎ **850/432-6565.** Reservations recommended. Main courses $13–$19. AE, DISC, MC, V. Tues–Sat 5–10:30pm. SEAFOOD/STEAKS/GREEK.

Perched on a bluff overlooking the bay, Skopelos is famous hereabouts for its great views and creative seafood dishes, such as the scamp Cervantes, a sautéed fillet of scamp topped with crabmeat. Other seafood selections range from broiled scallops to Mediterranean-style grouper prepared with a sauce of tomato and roasted eggplant. The menu also features charcoal-grilled steaks and chicken and roast leg of lamb. Befitting the owner's Greek heritage, roast lamb is served with moussaka, dolmades, titopita, and spanakopita.

Worth a Splurge

✪ **Jamie's.** 424 E. Zarragossa St. (between Alcaniz and Florida Blanca). ☎ **850/434-2911.** Reservations recommended at both lunch and dinner. Main courses $18–$23. AE, DISC, MC, V. Mon 6–10pm, Tues–Sat 11:30am–2:30pm and 6–10pm. CONTINENTAL/AMERICAN.

Occupying a restored Victorian home in Historic Pensacola Village, the town's classiest and most romantic restaurant enhances the dining experience with glowing fireplaces, soft candlelight, gleaming antiques, and subdued background music. The menu changes regularly to include such creative dishes as veal Oscar with a Cajun-spiced hollandaise sauce giving it a distinct Louisiana twist. The menu includes Jamie's recommended wines for each course.

PENSACOLA BEACH
Super-Cheap Eats

✪ **Chan's Market Café.** 16 Via de Luna. ☎ **850/932-8454.** Breakfast/lunch/snacks $3–$7; dinner $4–$7. AE, DISC, MC, V. Daily 7am–9pm. AMERICAN.

The aroma of cappuccino and pastries in the oven permeates this pleasant little cafe and bakery, which shares quarters with a liquor store in the parking lot of the Best Western Pensacola Beach. It's the best place on the beach for a breakfast of freshly baked croissants or bagels. Lunches and dinners feature economical ($4 to $7) white-plate specials of such favorites as meat loaf, rotisserie chicken, pot roast, and grilled fish, all served with a choice of Southern-style veggies. Or you can order a heaping sandwich made with one of Chan's large, flaky croissants.

For a Few Bucks More

Chan's Gulfside Café & Surfside Saloon. 2½ Via de Luna (at Fort Pickens Rd.). ☎ **850/932-3525.** Reservations recommended upstairs, not accepted downstairs. Upstairs main courses $17–$23. Downstairs sandwiches and burgers $6–$9, main courses $10–$18. AE, DC, DISC, MC, V. Upstairs Sun–Thurs 5:30–10pm, Fri–Sat 5:30–11pm. Downstairs daily 11am–2am (to 11pm off-season). SEAFOOD.

Offering Pensacola Beach's only gulf-front dining, this modern complex on Casino Beach offers two lively dining choices. The upstairs Florida Room is more formal yet still relaxed, with blond wood and widely spaced tables enjoying terrific views of the beach and gulf. Cuisine here features mesquite-fired tuna, grouper, and shrimp, plus the likes of coconut shrimp, triggerfish with Rockefeller spinach, and grouper Lyonnaise. The downstairs pub is completely informal, with a long bar where fans can sample an extensive collection of beers from microbreweries while watching their favorite teams on several TVs. Although not of the same quality, many of the same wood-grilled items are offered down here, along with pub-style fare such as pastas, salads, burgers, sandwiches, pastas, and baskets full of fried seafood or chicken. The pub opens to a beachside patio, which has outdoor dining and live entertainment during summer.

Flounder's Chowder and Ale House. 800 Quietwater Beach Rd. (at Via de Luna and Fort Pickens Rd.). ☎ **850/932-2003.** Reservations not accepted. Main courses $15–$18; burgers and sandwiches $7–$8. AE, DC, DISC, MC, V. Mon–Sat 11am–2am (to 11pm in winter), Sun 11am–2pm (brunch) and 2pm–2am (to 11pm in winter). SEAFOOD.

From Cajun to Florentine, you can order flounder in many different preparations at this publike establishment, whose decor features stained-glass windows from an old New York convent and confessional-booth walls from a New Orleans church. Bookshelves give a cozy, studious feel to one dining room, but Flounder's lively atmosphere is more accurately captured by the glass walls of another dining area; these face a popular beachside bar where patrons boogie to live reggae bands during the summer season. Burgers, salads, and sandwiches are offered all day, and there's a children's menu. A glass of champagne accompanies a sumptuous bay-side Sunday brunch.

Jubilee Restaurant & Entertainment Complex. 400 Quietwater Beach Rd. (Via de Luna at Fort Pickens Rd.), on Quietwater Beach Boardwalk. ☎ **850/934-3108.** Reservations not required. Topside main courses $16–$22; Beachside Café sandwiches and salads $6–$8, main courses $10–$17. AE, DC, DISC, MC, V. Beachside Café Mon–Sat 11am–11pm, Sun 10am–11pm; Topside daily 6–10pm (Sun brunch 9am–2pm). SEAFOOD/CAJUN/AMERICAN.

At this beachside restaurant complex, complete with Capt'n Fun's Beach Bar, most dining is very casual, even in the elegant, near-gourmet Topside Restaurant. Up there, where you'll get a bird's-eye view of the sound, the chef excels in the preparation of local fish and shellfish, especially with Louisiana flavors. There's a larger difference in quality than price downstairs in the pub-style Beachside Café, opening to a sound-side dock and offering a varied menu of fish, pastas, sandwiches, salads, and barbecue pork, shrimp, and oysters. The J-Sweet Coffee & Dessert Room has homemade sweets and gourmet coffees. On summer evenings there are live bands for dancing under the stars and indoor entertainment year-round.

PENSACOLA AFTER DARK

THE CLUB & BAR SCENE   Pensacola's downtown entertainment center is at ✪ **Seville Quarter,** 130 E. Government St., at Jefferson Street (☎ 850/434-6211), in the Seville Historic District. This restored antique brick complex with New Orleans–style wrought-iron balconies is actually a collection of pubs and restaurants whose names capture the ambience: Rosie O'Grady's Goodtime Emporium, Lili Marlene's Aviator's Pub, Apple Annie's Courtyard, End o' the Alley Bar, Phineas Phogg's Balloon Works (a dance hall, not a balloon shop), and Fast Eddie's Billiard Parlor (which has electronic games for kids, too). The pubs all serve up libations, food, and live entertainment from Dixieland jazz to country and western. Get a monthly calendar at the information booth next to Rosie O'Grady's. Open daily from 11am to 2am.

Every night is party time at **McGuire's Irish Pub & Brewery,** 600 E. Gregory St. (☎ 850/433-6789), the city's popular Irish pub, brewery, and eatery (see "Great Deals on Dining," above). Irish bands appear nightly during summer, on Saturday and Sunday the rest of the year. For live laughs, the **Coconuts Comedy Club,** in the Holiday Inn, University Mall, 7200 Plantation Rd. (☎ 850/484-NUTS), features comedians from Thursday to Saturday. Doors open at 7:30pm, with the first performance usually at 8:30pm. Cover charge is $4 on Thursday, $6 on Friday and Saturday.

Nightlife at the beach centers around **Quietwater Boardwalk,** Via de Luna at Fort Pickens Road (no phone), a shopping/dining complex on Santa Rosa Sound. Jubilee's Beachside Café and Entertainment Complex heads the list. The Sun Ray Taco Shop offers live bands nightly during the summer, on weekends off-season, and a no-name sports bar keeps the TVs going. With the lively Flounder's Beach and Reggae Bar just a few steps away, it's easy to bar-hop until you find a band and crowd to your liking. Across Via de Luna at Casino Beach, **The Dock** (☎ 850/934-3316) and **Chan's Gulfside Saloon** next door (☎ 850/932-3525) both have beachside live bands nightly during summer, on weekends off-season. You can catch all the games here at **Sidelines Sports Bar & Restaurant** (☎ 850/934-3660). See "Great Deals on Dining," above, for details about Chan's, Jubilee's, and Flounder's.

Over on Perdido Key, about 15 miles west of downtown Pensacola, the **Flora-Bama Lounge,** on Fla. 292 at the Florida-Alabama line (☎ 850/492-0611), is almost a shrine to country music. This slapped-together gulf-side pub is famous for its special jam sessions from noon until way past midnight on Saturday and Sunday. Flora-Bama is the prime sponsor and a key venue for the Frank Brown International Songwriters' Festival during the first week of November. If you've never attended an Interstate Mullet Toss, catch the fun here during the last weekend of April. The raw oyster bar is popular all the time. Take in the great gulf views from the Deck Bar. It's open daily from 8:30am to 2:30am.

THE PERFORMING ARTS   Pensacola has a surprisingly sophisticated array of entertainment choices for such a relatively small city. For a schedule of upcoming events, get a copy of *Vision,* a bimonthly newsletter published by the Arts Council of Northwest Florida, P.O. Box 731, Pensacola, FL 32594 (☎ 850/432-9906). Also pick up *Sneak Preview,* a calendar of events at the Pensacola Civic Center and the Saenger Theater. Both publications are available at the Pensacola Visitor Information Center (see "Essentials," above). Tickets for all major performances can be purchased by phone from **Ticketmaster** (☎ **800/488-5252** or 850/433-6311).

The highlight venue here is the ornate **Saenger Theater,** 118 S. Palafox St., near Romano Street (☎ **850/444-7686**), a painstakingly restored masterpiece of Spanish Baroque architecture. The variety of presentations include the local opera company and symphony orchestra, Broadway musicals, and touring performers. The 10,000-seat **Pensacola Civic Center,** 201 E. Gregory St., at Alcaniz Street (☎ **850/433-6311**), hosts a variety of entertainment. Call ahead for the current schedule.

2 Fort Walton Beach & Destin

40 miles E of Pensacola, 160 miles W of Tallahassee

At the outbreak of the Civil War in 1861, a small Confederate contingent set up camp on Santa Rosa Sound to guard the eastern approaches to Pensacola. The Rebels beat a hasty retreat when Yankee troops shelled their position from Okaloosa Island, but the name they gave their little outpost has remained to this day: Fort Walton.

Back then the only settlement in these parts was Destin, a tiny fishing village east of Fort Walton and separated from it by East Pass, which lets broad, beautiful Choctowhatchee Bay flow into the Gulf of Mexico. And even though the U.S. government established sprawling Eglin Air Force Base here in the 1930s, Fort Walton had just 90 residents as late as 1940.

But then came World War II, and Eglin grew into a major U.S. Army Air Corps training base. When Okaloosa Island became popular with Alabamians and Georgians after the war, Fort Walton officially added "Beach" to its name. Although summertime tourism dominates Okaloosa Island, mainland Fort Walton Beach still relies on the U.S. Air Force for its year-round living.

On a picturesque harbor and world famous for its fishing, Destin stands in contrast to its neighbor. No longer a sleepy village, Destin today is Northwest Florida's fastest growing vacation destination. It has multitudes of high-rise condominiums, the huge Sandestin luxury resort, several excellent golf courses, and some of Northwest Florida's best restaurants and lively nightspots. By and large, it attracts a generally more affluent crowd than does the more down-to-earth Fort Walton Beach.

To the east of Destin, development in the beaches of southern Walton County has been slower and more controlled, with cottages nestled among sand dunes and sea oats. Walton County is home both to charming DeFuniak Springs and the village of Seaside. While DeFuniak Springs is a genuine Victorian town nestled around an inland lake, Seaside was built on a lovely stretch of beach in the 1980s—but with Victorian architecture that makes it look a century older. Seaside's gulf-side honeymoon cottages make for one of Florida's most romantic retreats, and the village has interesting shops and art galleries, delightful restaurants, a stamp-size post office, and a resident population of artists, writers, and other creative folks who permit no cars in their pleasant little enclave.

ESSENTIALS

GETTING THERE   From east or west, take I-10 or U.S. 98. For Fort Walton Beach, exit I-10 at Crestview and follow Fla. 85 south for 24 miles. For Destin and the beaches of southern Walton County, exit I-10 at DeFuniak Springs and follow U.S. 331 south to Santa Rosa Beach. You can avoid the beach traffic between there and Destin by leaving U.S. 331 at Freeport and taking Fla. 20 west to Villa Tasso, then

Fla. 293 across the Mid Bay Bridge ($2 toll). From the north, take U.S. 331 south through Alabama.

Flights arriving at and departing from **Okaloosa County Air Terminal** actually use the field at Eglin Air Force Base. The terminal is on Fla. 85 north of Fort Walton Beach and is served by **American Eagle** (☎ 800/433-7300), **Delta Connection/ASA** (☎ 800/221-1212), **Northwest/KLM** (☎ 800/225-2525), and **US Airways Express** (☎ 800/428-4322). The major car-rental firms are here, or you can take a taxi or limousine that's waiting outside the modern terminal. Fares are based on a zone system: to Fort Walton Beach, $10 to $14; to Destin, $20 to $22; and to Sandestin, $28 to $30.

The *Sunset Limited* transcontinental service on **Amtrak** (☎ 800/USA-RAIL) stops at Crestview, 26 miles north of Fort Walton Beach.

VISITOR INFORMATION For advance information about both Fort Walton Beach and Destin, contact the **Emerald Coast Convention and Visitors Bureau,** P.O. Box 609, Fort Walton Beach, FL 32549 (☎ 800/322-3319 or 850/651-7131; fax 850/651-7149; www.destin-fwb.com). The bureau shares quarters with the **Okaloosa County Visitors Welcome Center** in a tin-roofed, beachside building on Miracle Strip Parkway (U.S. 98) on Okaloosa Island at the eastern edge of Fort Walton Beach. Stop there for brochures, maps, and other information, especially the *Insider,* a free tabloid with an excellent listing of restaurants and attractions. The welcome center is open during summer daily from 8am to 5pm. Off-season hours are Monday to Friday from 8am to 5pm, Saturday and Sunday from 10am to 4pm.

The **Destin Area Chamber of Commerce,** P.O. Box 8, Destin, FL 32541 (☎ 850/837-6241; fax 850/654-5612; www.destinfl.com/chamber), gives away brochures and sells maps of the area. The chamber has resided at 1021 U.S. 98 East, opposite the Holiday Inn in Destin, but it expects to move in 1999, so call for the new location. Open Monday to Friday from 9am to 5pm all year.

For information about the Beaches of South Walton, contact the **South Walton Tourist Development Council,** P.O. Box 1248, Santa Rosa Beach, FL 32459 (☎ 800/822-6877 or 850/267-1216; fax 850/267-3943; www.beachesofsouthwalton. com). Its **visitor center** is at the intersection of U.S. 98 and U.S. 331 in Santa Rosa Beach (☎ 850/267-3511). Open daily 8:30am to 4:30pm, later in summer.

GETTING AROUND For a cab in Fort Walton Beach, call **Charter Taxis** (☎ 850/863-5466), **Crosstown Taxi** (☎ 850/244-7303), **JC's Cab** (☎ 850/865-0578), **Veterans Cab Co.** (☎ 850/243-1403), **Yellow Cab** (☎ 850/244-3600), or **Checker Cab** (☎ 850/244-4491). In Destin, call **Destin Taxi** (☎ 850/654-5700). Fares are based on a zone system rather than meters, with a $3 minimum. Trips within Fort Walton Beach or Destin should range from $3 to $5.

STREET ADDRESSES Don't worry if you're confused by the street addresses here, for even many local residents don't fully comprehend the post office's naming and numbering system. This is especially true of addresses along U.S. 98, which runs east-west through the area.

In Fort Walton Beach, U.S. 98 is known as the "Miracle Strip Parkway," with "southwest" and "southeast" addresses on the mainland and "east" addresses on Okaloosa Island.

In Destin, U.S. 98 is officially known as "Hwy. 98 East" from the Destin Bridge to Airport Road, and street numbers get progressively higher as you head east from the bridge. The post office calls U.S. 98 the "Emerald Coast Parkway" east of Airport Road, although locals still say a place is on "98 East." To add to the confusion, "Old Hwy. 98 East" is a short spur from Airport Road to the western side of Henderson

Beach State Recreation Area, and "Scenic Hwy. 98 East" runs along the beach from the eastern side of Henderson Beach to Sandestin.

In south Walton County, U.S. 98 is known as the Emerald Coast Parkway, but the street numbering system changes completely once you pass the county line.

In other words, call and ask for directions if you're not sure how to find an establishment here.

TIME   The area is in the **central time zone,** an hour behind Miami, Orlando, and Tallahassee.

HITTING THE BEACH

FORT WALTON BEACH   Do your loafing on the white sands of **Okaloosa Island,** joined to the mainland by the high-rise Brooks Bridge over Santa Rosa Sound. Most resort hotels and amusement parks are grouped around the Gulfarium on U.S. 98 east of the bridge. Here you'll find **The Boardwalk,** a collection of tin-roofed beachside buildings between the Gulfarium and the Ramada Inn, that has a games arcade for the kids, the Soggy Dollar Saloon for adults, and covered picnic areas, a summertime snack bar, and Harpoon Hanna's restaurant (see "Great Deals on Dining," below). Just to the east, you can use the free facilities at **Beasley Park,** home of the Okaloosa County Visitor Welcome Center.

Across U.S. 98, the **Okaloosa Area, Gulf Islands National Seashore** has picnic areas and sailboats for rent on Choctawhatchee Bay, plus access to the gulf. Admission to this part of the national seashore is free.

DESTIN   The 208-acre ✪ **Henderson Beach State Recreation Area,** east of Destin Harbor on U.S. 98, allows easy access to swimming, sunning, surf fishing, picnicking, and seabird watching. There are rest rooms, outdoor showers, and surf chairs for disabled persons. The area is open daily from 8am to sunset. Admission is $2 per vehicle, $1 for pedestrians and cyclists. Several good restaurants are just outside the park's western boundary. Campsites will be opened here sometime in 1999. For more information, contact the area at 1700 Emerald Coast Pkwy., Destin, FL 32541 (☎ 850/837-7550).

The **James W. Lee Park,** Destin and Sandestin on Scenic Hwy. 98, has a long white-sand beach overlooked by covered picnic tables, an ice-cream parlor, and **The Crab Trap Restaurant** (☎ **850/654-2822**), whose moderately priced snacks and seafood make it a fine spot for lunch with a view or dinner with a sunset.

SOUTHERN WALTON COUNTY   Sporting perhaps the finest stretch of white sand on the gulf, ✪ **Grayton Beach State Recreation Area,** on County Road 30A, also has 356 acres of pine forests surrounding scenic Western Lake. There's a boat ramp and campground with electric hookups on the lake (see "Accommodations You Can Afford," below). Get a self-guided tour leaflet for the nature trail at the main gate. It's open daily from 8am to sunset. Admission is $3.25 per vehicle with up to eight occupants, $1 per pedestrian or bicyclist. For more information, contact the area at 357 Main Park Rd., Santa Rosa Beach, FL 32459 (☎ **850/231-4210**).

Seaside has free public parking along County Road 30A and is a good spot for a day at the beach, a stroll or bike ride around the quaint village, and a tasty meal at one of its restaurants.

GREAT GOLF THAT WON'T BREAK YOUR BUDGET & OTHER AFFORDABLE OUTDOOR ACTIVITIES

BOATING & BOAT RENTALS   Powerboat lovers can get their thrills during the summer season on the *Sea Blaster* (☎ **850/837-1136** or 850/664-7872), one of the world's largest speedboats. It roars out every 2 hours from 11am to 5pm from AJ's Seafood & Oyster Bar on Destin Harbor. Rides cost $12 for adults, $7 for children 12 and under.

Pontoon boats are highly popular for use on the back bays and on Sunday afternoon floating parties in East Pass. Several companies rent them, including **Best Boat Rentals** (☎ 850/664-7872) on Okaloosa Island in Fort Walton Beach and **Adventure Pontoon Rentals** (☎ 850/837-3041), **B&J Boat Rentals** (☎ 850/243-4488), and **Premier Powerboat Rentals** (☎ 850/837-7755), all on Destin Harbor. Expect to pay about $70 for a half day, $120 for all day. Premier Powerboat Rentals also has speedboats for rent, ranging from $120 for a half day to $190 for all day.

Hobie Cats, Wave Runners, jet boats, jet-skis, and fishing craft rentals are available from many marinas, as well as from several beachfront resorts. **Paradise Water Sports** (☎ 850/664-7872) rents equipment and offers parasailing rides at seven locations along U.S. 98, and **Boogies** (☎ 850/654-4497) is at the east end of the Destin Bridge.

CRUISES The *Emerald Magic* (☎ 850/837-1293) and the *Southern Star* (☎ 850/837-7741) have daily dolphin and sunset cruises from June through August, by arrangement the rest of the year. The *Emerald Magic* is operated by Moody's, on U.S. 98 at Destin Harbor (see "Fishing," below), while the *Southern Star* docks in Destin at the Harbor Walk Marina, behind the Lucky Snapper Restaurant. Expect to pay about $15 for adults, $12 for seniors, and $5 for children, depending on the cruise.

If you want to learn to sail, **Sailing South** (☎ 850/837-7245), on U.S. 98 at Destin Harbor, teaches 2-day basic courses for $220 per person. It also charters 24-foot boats to qualified sailors, and it has a 72-foot schooner available for crewed charters. If you can't sail and don't want to learn, you can go out on the 54-foot schooners *Nathaniel Bowditch* (☎ 850/650-8787), *Flying Eagle* (☎ 850/837-4986 or 850/837-3700), or *Blackbeard* (☎ 850/837-2793), all of which have afternoon and sunset trips for about $25 per person.

On Okaloosa Island, **Leeside Bareboat Sailing,** at the Leeside Motel, 1352 U.S. 98 east (☎ 850/244-5454), rents 25- and 30-foot Catalina sloops bareboat (you do the skippering) at prices ranging from $95 per half day to $450 for three days.

FISHING Billing itself as the "World's Luckiest Fishing Village," Destin has Florida's largest charter-boat fleet, with more than 140 vessels based at the marinas lining the north shore of Destin Harbor, on U.S. 98 east of the Destin Bridge. Arranging a trip is as easy as walking along the Destin Harbor waterfront, where you will find the booking booths of several agents, such as **Pelican Charters** (☎ 850/837-2343), **Harbor Cove Charters** (☎ 850/837-2222), and **Fishermen's Charter Service** (☎ 850/654-4665). They all can arrange for you to fish until your heart's content. Rates for private charters range from about $360 to $900 per boat, depending on length of voyage.

A less-expensive way to try your luck is on a larger group-oriented party boat such as those operated by **Moody's,** at 194 U.S. 98 east on Destin Harbor (☎ 850/837-1293). Moody's charges $30 per person for its morning runs (the best fishing) and $25 for afternoon trips. Children 8 to 12 and nonfishing sightseers are charged half price. Other party boats are the *Emmanuel* (☎ 850/837-6313), the *Lady Eventhia* (☎ 850/837-6212), and three craft operated by **Capt. Duke's Boat Service** (☎ 850/837-6152), all based at **Destin Harbor.**

You don't have to go to sea to fish from the catwalk of the 3,000-foot **Destin Bridge** over East Pass. The marinas and bait shops at Destin Harbor can provide gear, bait, information, and a fishing license.

GOLF The area takes great pride in having more than 250 holes of golf. For advance information on all area courses, contact the **Emerald Coast Golf Association,** P.O. Box 304, Destin, FL 32540 (☎ 850/654-7086). Also look for *Gulf Coast Tee Time,* the free annual directory published in Pensacola (see "Golf" under "Great Golf That Won't Break Your Budget & Other Affordable Outdoor Activitie" in section 1, above). And be sure to inquire if your choice of accommodations here offers golf packages, which can represent significant savings.

On the mainland, nonresidents are welcome to play at the city-owned **Fort Walton Beach Golf Club,** on Lewis Turner Boulevard (County Road 189) north of town (☎ 850/862-3314 or 850/862-0933). The club has two 18-hole courses—the **Pines** (☎ 850/833-9529) and the **Oaks** (☎ 850/833-9530)—plus a pro shop. Greens fees at both courses are about $26.50 year-round, including a cart.

In Destin, scenic **Indian Bayou Golf and Country Club,** off Airport Road (☎ 850/837-6191), has three 9-hole courses with large greens and wide fairways. They look easy, but watch out for water hazards and strategically placed hidden bunkers! Fees with a cart range from $45 to $65, including cart.

In southern Walton County, **The Resort at Sandestin,** on U.S. 98 east (☎ 850/267-8211 for tee times), is the largest facility here (see "Accommodations You Can Afford," below). Its 63 holes are spread over three outstanding championship courses: Baytowne, Burnt Pine, and Links. The Baytowne and Links courses overlook Choctawhatchee Bay. Fees for 18 holes are about $66 from mid-February through October, about $48 the rest of the year.

Scenery is on display at **Emerald Bay Golf Club,** 2 miles east of the Mid-Bay Bridge on U.S. 98 (☎ 850/837-5197). Some of the 27 championship holes here run along Choctawhatchee Bay, so water adds both beauty and challenges to the otherwise wide and forgiving fairways. Greens fees range between $60 and $75, with cart.

In southern Walton County, the semiprivate **Santa Rosa Golf & Beach Club,** off County Road 30A in Dune Allen Beach (☎ 850/267-2229 or 850/654-7888), offers a challenging 18-hole course through tall pines looking out to vistas of the gulf. The club has a pro shop, beachside restaurant, lounge, and tennis courts. The **Seascape Resort & Conference Center,** 100 Seascape Dr. (☎ 850/837-9181), off County Road 30A, features a Joe Lee–designed 18-hole course winding through woods and around lakes, with a premium placed on accuracy rather than power. The center also has tennis courts, accommodations, restaurant, bar, and pro shop.

In Niceville, a 20-minute drive north via the Mid Bay Bridge, nonguests may play golf (four 9-hole courses) or tennis (21 courts) at the **Bluewater Bay Resort** (☎ 850/897-3613), which also has condos for rent.

Call ahead for reservations and current fees at all these clubs.

SCUBA DIVING & OTHER WATER SPORTS At least a dozen dive shops are located along the beaches. Considered one of the best, **Scuba Tech Diving Charters** has two locations in Destin: at 301 U.S. 98 east in Destin Harbor (☎ 850/837-2822) and at 10004 U.S. 98 east (☎ 850/837-1933), about a half mile west of the Sandestin Beach Resort. Reef or wreck dives start at $45 to $85, depending on length. Open-water courses cost about $225; resort courses, $75. **Fantasea,** at the foot of the Destin Bridge, 1 U.S. 98 east (☎ 800/326-2732 or 850/837-6943), and the **Aquanaut Scuba Center,** 24 U.S. 98 east (☎ 850/837-0359), are other local operators.

The three diving operators and **Kokomo Snorkeling Adventures,** 500 U.S. 98 east in Destin (☎ 850/837-9029), all take snorkelers on excursions into the Gulf of Mexico and Choctawhatchee Bay for $20 per person, including gear.

TENNIS **The Resort at Sandestin,** U.S. 98 east (☎ 850/837-2121), has 16 courts open to the public, including hard, clay, and grass. *Tennis* magazine rated it one of the nation's top 50 tennis resorts and the only ranked resort with natural grass courts.

EXPLORING THE AREA

Gulfarium. 1010 Miracle Strip Pkwy. (U.S. 98) on Okaloosa Island. ☎ **850/244-5169.** Admission $15 adults, $13 seniors, $10.70 children 4–11, free for children 3 and under. Daily 9am through last show; shows daily at 10am, noon, 2, and 4pm; additional shows at 6 and 8pm in summer.

One of the nation's original marine parks features ongoing shows with dolphins, California sea lions, Peruvian penguins, loggerhead turtles, dolphins, sharks, sting rays, moray eels, and alligators. Among the fascinating exhibits is the Living Sea, with special windows that provide viewing of undersea life. During one of the shows, a scuba diver explains the sea life while swimming among them. A gift shop offers an extensive collection of marine-oriented souvenirs.

Indian Temple Mound and Museum. 139 Miracle Strip Pkwy., on the mainland. ☎ **850/833-9595.** Park free; museum $2 adults, $1 children 6–17, free for children 5 and under. Park daily dawn–dusk. Museum Oct–May, Mon–Fri 11am–4pm, Sat 9am–4pm; June–Sept, Mon–Sat 9am–5pm (summer hours may vary, so call ahead).

This ceremonial mound, one of the largest ever discovered, dates back to A.D. 1200. The museum, located next to it, showcases ceramic artifacts from southeastern Native American tribes. The largest such collection, it contains more than 6,000 items. Exhibits depict the lifestyles of the four tribes that lived in the Choctawhatchee Bay region for 10,000 years.

✪ **U.S. Air Force Armament Museum.** At Eglin Air Force Base, Eglin Pkwy. (Fla. 85), 5 miles north of downtown. ☎ **850/882-4062.** Free admission. Daily 9:30am–4:30pm. Closed New Year's Day, Thanksgiving, and Christmas.

Located on the world's largest air force base (more than 700 square miles), this fascinating museum traces military developments from World War II through the Korean and Vietnam wars to the Persian Gulf War. On display are 28 reconnaissance, fighter, and bomber planes, including the SR-71 Blackbird spy plane. Also exhibited are war films, photographs, rockets, bombs, and missiles. The base itself is home to the world's largest environmental test chamber, in the McKinley Climatic Laboratory, and to the 33rd Tactical Fighter Wing, the "Top Guns" of Desert Storm. World War II's historic Doolittle's Tokyo Raiders trained here.

✪ **Eden State Gardens.** County Rd. 395, Point Washington. ☎ **850/231-4214.** Grounds and gardens $2 per vehicle; mansion tours $1.50 adults, 50¢ children 12 and under. Grounds and gardens daily 8am–5pm; mansion tours on the hour Thurs–Mon 9am–4pm.

Evoking images from *Gone With the Wind*, the magnificent 1895 Greek Revival–style Wesley Mansion has been lovingly restored and richly furnished. It stands overlooking scenic Choctawhatchee Bay and is surrounded by immense moss-draped oak trees and the Eden Gardens, resplendent with camellias, azaleas, and other typical Southern flowers. Picnicking is allowed on the plantation grounds. The gardens and mansion are north of Seagrove Beach in southern Walton County.

SHOPPING

The major shopping attractions here are two well-stocked manufacturers' outlet malls. By far the best is **J Silver Sands Factory Stores,** on U.S. 98 between Destin and Sandestin. One of the largest outlet malls in Florida, this one has the upscale likes of

Anne Klein, Donna Karan, J. Crew, Jones New York, Brooks Brothers, Hartman Luggage, Coach leathers, Bose electronics, and so many more you'll have to drive from one end to the other to spot your favorite brands. There's even a food court with a branch of Harbor Docks Restaurant (see "Great Deals on Dining," below). On the Fort Walton Beach mainland, you'll find a limited selection of factory stores on U.S. 98 in the **Brooks Bridge 98 Center,** at the northern end of the Brooks Bridge, and at **Bayview 98 Center,** about 1 mile to the west.

Over at the Sandestin Beach Resort on U.S. 98, you can window-shop in **The Market at Sandestin,** where 28 shops purvey expensive clothing, gifts, and Godiva chocolates.

ACCOMMODATIONS YOU CAN AFFORD

The area has a vast supply of condos and cottages for rent. One good-value example is Venus Condos, listed below. The tourist information offices (see "Essentials," above) will provide lists of others for rent. The largest rental agent is **Abbott Realty Services,** 3500 Emerald Coast Pkwy., Destin, FL 32541 (☎ **800/336-4853** or 850/837-4853; fax 850/654-2937; www.abbott-resorts.com). It publishes a magazine-size annual brochure picturing and describing its many accommodations throughout the area.

For campers, **Grayton Beach State Recreation Area,** 357 Main Park Rd., Santa Rosa Beach (☎ **850/231-4210**), which actually is on County Road 30A, offers hookups for RVs as well as primitive sites in a beautiful 356-acre setting. Campfire interpretive programs are available to campers (call for the current schedule). Sites cost $14 from March to September, $8 from October to February. You can reserve sites up to 11 months in advance by contacting the park.

Camping on the Gulf Holiday Travel Park, 10005 W. Emerald Coast Pkwy. (U.S. 98), Destin (☎ **850/837-6334**), just west of the Sandestin Beach Resort, is the area's largest and oldest campground and the only one with sites directly on the beach. During summer, campsites cost $50 on the beach, $30 inland; off-season, they go for $28 and $23, respectively. Reserve your summertime site well in advance.

State and local governments add 9% to all hotel and campground bills.

FORT WALTON BEACH

Among the chain motels here, the moderately priced **Rodeway Inn,** 866 Santa Rosa Blvd. (☎ **800/458-8552** or 850/243-3114), and **Days Inn & Suites Gulfside Resort,** 573 Santa Rosa Blvd. (☎ **800/DAYS-INN** or 850/244-8686), are right on Okaloosa Island's beach.

Super-Cheap Sleeps

Marina Motel. 1345 E. Miracle Strip Pkwy. (U.S. 98), Fort Walton Beach, FL 32548. ☎ **800/ 237-7021** or 850/244-1129. Fax 850/243-6063. 38 units. A/C TV TEL. Summer $58–$66 single or double; $95 apt. Off-season $39–$56 single or double; $60–$75 apt. AE, DC, DISC, MC, V.

This family-operated motel may be rather pedestrian-looking, but it makes up for a lack of charm with clean, comfortable rooms and a location directly across U.S. 98 from the magnificent public beach at Beasley Park. A low-slung, brick-fronted motel block holds most of the rooms. Other units are in 2-story stucco structures near a marina whose 560-foot pier is home to charter-fishing boats. Two one-bedroom apartments at the end of the complex overlook the marina and bay. All units here have refrigerators and microwaves; 16 have full kitchens. If traffic is too busy to cross U.S. 98 to the beach, you can sun at the motel's little bay-side beach or take a dip in its roadside pool. There's also a guest laundry.

Cheap Thrills: What to See & Do for Free (or Almost) in Northwest Florida

- **Hit a powdery beach.** Admission is free to most of 100-plus miles of powdery, snow-white beaches that make this area special, but a few bucks will let you into the Gulf Islands National Seashore at Pensacola, the Henderson Beach and Grayton Beach state recreation areas at Destin, the St. Andrews State Recreation Area at Panama City Beach, and the St. Joseph Peninsula and St. George Island state parks near Apalachicola. You won't soon forget the time you spend on these protected sands and dunes, all consistently ranked among the nation's finest beaches.
- **Stroll through Florida's second oldest town.** You'll have to pay to go into its homes and museums, but you can walk the streets of Historic Pensacola Village (☎ 850/444-8905) for free. Built in 1823, the village boasts some of Florida's oldest homes, along with charming boutiques and interesting restaurants. During summer, costumed characters go about their daily chores and demonstrate old crafts, and archaeologists unearth the old Spanish commanding officer's compound.
- **Visit the Blue Angels and top guns.** Next to the Smithsonian Institution's National Air and Space Museum in Washington, D.C., the next best places to see our nation's warplanes on display are at the National Museum of Naval Aviation in Pensacola (☎ 850/452-3604) and at the U.S. Air Force Armament Museum in Fort Walton Beach (☎ 850/882-4062). Admission to both is free. The IMAX films shown at the naval museum will make you believe you're flying in a Blue Angel's cockpit (there's a charge for the films). Near the Pensacola museum and also free, historic **Fort Barrancas** (☎ 850/934-2600) dates from 1797, when the Spanish built its water battery. The incredibly intricate brickwork of the upper section was laid by American troops between 1839 and 1844.
- **Get away from it all on Shell Island.** The round-trip boat fare costs $7.50 for adults, $5.50 for kids 11 and under, but the ride over to Shell Island, off Panama City Beach (☎ 850/233-5140), will take to you to an uninhabited natural preserve that's great for shelling, swimming, suntanning, or just relaxing. Bring chairs, beach gear, coolers, food, and beverages. The boat shuttles from April to October between the island and St. Andrews State Recreation Area.
- **Celebrate the air conditioner.** Without air-conditioning, Florida would be an uncomfortable place to live or visit during its hot, humid summers. In the late 1800s, Doctor John Gorrie of Apalachicola invented a cooling machine to keep his malaria patients comfortable. It was a moment of great note in

For a Few Bucks More

Four Points Sheraton. 1325 E. Miracle Strip Pkwy. (U.S. 98), Fort Walton Beach, FL 32548. ☎ **800/874-8104** or 850/243-8116. Fax 850/244-3064. 229 units. A/C TV TEL. Summer $99–$150 single or double. Off-season $60–$115 single or double. Rates include full breakfast. AE, DC, DISC, MC, V.

Florida's history, duly celebrated by his home town's **John Gorrie State Museum** (☎ 850/653-9347). For $1, you can see a working replica of his device, the prototype of the air-conditioning units that make Florida summers bearable today.

- **Look down on the capital and out to the gulf.** State legislators meet in Tallahassee's $43 million skyscraper New Capitol Building (☎ 850/487-1902) from March to May, but you can take the elevators to the 22nd-floor observatory any day and look down over all of the capital—and on a clear day all the way to the Gulf of Mexico, some 20 miles away. Also free are guided tours of the building and the Old Capitol, directly in front of the skyscraper. With its majestic dome, old building has been restored to its original 19th century beauty and has an eight-room exhibit portraying Florida's political history.

- **Learn about black history and art.** Florida A&M University in Tallahassee is one of the country's leading all-black colleges, and it's a wonderful place to learn about African American history and see some of that community's major works of art. Housed in a columned library built by Andrew Carnegie in 1908, the Black Archives Research Center and Museum (☎ 850/561-2603) displays one of the nation's most extensive collections of African American artifacts and historical materials, while The Florida A&M University Art Gallery (☎ 850/599-3161) focuses on works by African American artists, with a wide variety of paintings, sculptures, and more. Admission is free to both.

- **Take in the camellias and azaleas at Maclay State Gardens.** It'll cost a few bucks to get through the gate, but you won't find many places as naturally magnificent in springtime as Maclay State Gardens, on the northeastern outskirts of Tallahassee (☎ 850/487-4556). The more than 300 acres here feature more than 200 varieties of flowers, with 28 acres devoted exclusively to azaleas and camellias. This floral wonderland surrounds the beautifully restored 1923 home of New York financier Alfred B. Maclay and his wife, Louise. The blooming season is January to April, with the peak about mid-March. The park also offers nature trails, canoe rentals, boating, picnicking, swimming, and fishing.

- **See where Johnny Weissmuller played Tarzan.** Wakulla Springs, 15 miles south of Tallahassee, is so jungly that some of the 1930s Tarzan movies starring Johnny Weissmuller were filmed here. Today they are within the 2,860 acres of **Edward Ball Wakulla Springs State Park** (☎ 850/922-3632), which means you'll have to pay a few dollars to get in. You can also pay $4.50 for adults, half price for children, to take glass-bottom-boat sightseeing and wildlife-observation tours. You can swim in the lake formed by the springs, but watch for alligators!

This beachfront resort sports very spacious rooms decorated with vivid, tropical colors. The older wings here surround a lush tropical courtyard with a South Pacific–style bar adjacent to a heated swimming pool and whirlpool. A cut-out in the new, 7-story gulf-side building covers a second swimming pool and allows access to the beach. Rooms have refrigerators, microwave ovens, and coffeemakers, and some also have kitchenettes. Dining is in the Plantation Grill dining room and in Dempsey's Grill and Bar, which, along with the beach bar, provides entertainment during summer. There's an exercise room and coin laundry.

Radisson Beach Resort. 1110 Santa Rosa Blvd. (at U.S. 98), Fort Walton Beach, FL 32548. ☎ **800/732-4853** or 850/243-9181. Fax 850/664-7652. 188 units. A/C TV TEL. Summer $125–$160 single or double. Off-season $70–$145 single or double. Packages available. AE, DC, DISC, MC, V.

A glass-enclosed elevator climbs up through a soaring, lean-to atrium lobby to rooms with spectacular gulf views from a 6-story building at this resort (which until a recent upgrading was the Holiday Inn Fort Walton Beach). Less expensive rooms are in 2-story buildings flanking a courtyard surrounding a pool and open on one end to the beach. A lobby cafe serves breakfast, lunch, and dinner, and an atrium bar has nightly entertainment during summer. Facilities here include three outdoor pools (one under a glass roof), a children's playground, a beach bar and barbecue area, two lighted tennis courts, an exercise room, a gift shop, and a convention center.

Ramada Plaza Beach Resort. 1500 E. Miracle Strip Pkwy. (U.S. 98), Fort Walton Beach, FL 32548. ☎ **800/874-8962** or 850/243-9161. Fax 850/243-2391. www.ramadafwb.com. 353 units. A/C TV TEL. Summer $110–$150 single or double; $235–$300 suite. Off-season $65–$85 single or double; $135–$160 suite. AE, DC, DISC, MC, V.

Considered Fort Walton Beach's prime hotel, this big resort with a gaudy, Vegas-style gold facade boasts one of the most beautiful swimming pool/patio areas anywhere, with waterfalls cascading over lofty rocks and a romantic grotto bar, all surrounded by thick tropical foliage. Unfortunately all this is cut off from the beach by a 6-story block of hotel rooms. The tastefully furnished rooms in this building have gulf or courtyard views, but the less-expensive units in a 2-story structure next door overlook a parking lot.

On-site dining options include the casual Pelican's Roost, which features seafood favorites year-round, and a barbecue shack near the pool. The family-oriented Lobster House serves moderately priced seafood in summer. The Boardwalk beach pavilion and restaurants are next door (see "Great Deals on Dining," below). For entertainment, there's dancing in Bubble's Lounge. Facilities here include three swimming pools (one indoors), a children's pool, a health spa, three whirlpools, and a gift shop.

✪ **Venus Condos.** 885 Santa Rosa Blvd., Fort Walton Beach, FL 32548. ☎ **800/476-1885** or 850/243-0885. Fax 850/664-5221. 45 units. A/C TV TEL. Summer $105–$170 apt. Off-season $50–$125 apt. Weekly and monthly rates available. DISC, MC, V.

Offering considerably more space than a hotel would at these rates, this pleasant, 3-story enclave on western Okaloosa Island is immaculately maintained. Each of the one-, two-, and three-bedroom units has a long living-dining-kitchen room, with a rear door leading to a balcony or patio. Facilities include a guest laundry and a grassy courtyard with palm trees, swimming pool, and large barbecue pit. A lighted tennis court destroyed by Hurricane Opal should be rebuilt by the time you arrive. The beach is a short walk across the dunes.

DESTIN
Super-Cheap Sleeps
The local **Motel 6,** 405 U.S. 98 East (☎ 800/466-8356 or 850/837-0007; fax 850/837-5325), sitting across the highway from the harbor, was a Comfort Inn until 1997. Then the Motel 6 chain bought it and renovated the rooms, which in this case means they removed rather than added some amenities. Nevertheless, the units were spiffed up, and they are generally larger than at many other members of this cut-rate

chain. There's an outdoor swimming pool on premises. Summertime rates had not been set at press time. Off-season, rooms cost about $37 single, $40 double.

For a Few Bucks More

Best Western SummerPlace Inn. 14047 Emerald Coast Pkwy. (U.S. 98, at Airport Rd.), Destin, FL 33541. ☎ **800/BEACH-99** or 850/650-8003. Fax 850/650-8004. 72 units. A/C TV TEL. Summer $120–$170 single or double. Off-season $60–$100 single or double. Rates include continental breakfast and local telephone calls. AE, DC, DISC, MC, V.

Across U.S. 98 from the Hampton Inn Destin (see below), this 4-story, Spanish motif building opened in 1997, offering innlike rooms and suites decorated with wildlife prints. All units have refrigerators and coffeemakers, and a few suites have Jacuzzis in their living rooms. Gulfside units have balconies; those facing the bay do not. Doors open from an indoor pool, whirlpool, and exercise equipment to an outdoor pool. Amenities include a coin laundry, small business center, a video-games arcade. A complimentary shuttle runs to the beach—handy, since otherwise you'd have to negotiate your way across busy U.S. 98 to reach the gulf. There are three restaurants next door, and those on Old Hwy. 98 East are a short walk away.

Hampton Inn Destin. 1625 Hwy. 98 East (at Old Hwy. 98 and Airport Rd.), Destin, FL 32541. ☎ **800/HAMPTON** or 850/654-2677. Fax 850/654-0745. 104 units. A/C TV TEL. Summer $135–$150 single or double, $160–$180 suite. Off-season $59–$79 single or double, $85–$110 suite. Rates include continental breakfast. AE, DC, DISC, MC, V.

This pink, 2-story building sits at the junction of the new and old U.S. 98s, about 100 yards west of Henderson Beach State Recreation Area (see "Hitting the Beach," above) and near a covey of restaurants just outside the recreation area and another bunch of them across U.S. 98. There's beach access through a line of condos sitting across the old highway, which means you don't have to fight the traffic on U.S. 98 to reach the gulf. External corridors lead to the standard motel-style rooms and suites with two rooms and kitchenettes. A gazebo-like sitting area offers shade next to a heated outdoor pool.

Holiday Inn of Destin. 1020 Hwy. 98 East (P.O. Box 577), Destin, FL 32541. ☎ **800/HOLIDAY** or 850/837-6181. Fax 850/837-1523. 233 units. A/C TV TEL. Summer $130–$165 single or double. Off-season $75–$105 single or double. Packages available. AE, DC, DISC, MC, V.

Most of the nicely furnished rooms in this gulf-front resort are in a round high-rise building. Get one facing south or east because a tall condo next door blocks southwest-facing units from enjoying the spectacular gulf views. The rooms in an older, 4-story building are more spacious than those in the tower. Some of these older units open to an enclosed "Holidome," a fountained lobby sporting a comfortable mezzanine lounge with indoor pool, billiard, Ping-Pong, and Foosball tables. The tropically attired Destin Cafe in the lobby serves breakfast, lunch, and dinner. Children can play in their own pool or in a video-game arcade (there's a summertime activities program for them). Adults can use a whirlpool, sauna, and exercise room, or spend money at the gift shop.

Worth a Splurge

✪ **Henderson Park Inn.** 2700 Scenic Hwy. 98 East (P.O. Box 30), Destin, FL 32540. ☎ **800/336-4853** or 850/837-4853. Fax 850/654-0405. 35 units. A/C TV TEL. Summer $180–$279 single or double. Off-season $114–$223 single or double. Rates include buffet breakfast. Packages and weekly rates available. AE, DISC, MC, V.

At the end of Old U.S. 98 on the undeveloped eastern edge of the Henderson Beach State Recreation Area, this shingle-sided, Cape Hatteras–style bed-and-breakfast is a romantic, get-away-from-it-all escape for adults only (no children are accepted).

Individually decorated in a Victorian theme, the rooms have high ceilings, fireplaces, Queen Anne furniture, and gulf views from private balconies. Some have canopy beds. The main building (15 rooms are in a separate shingle-sided structure next door) sports a beachside veranda complete with old-fashioned rocking chairs to sit in and admire the glorious sunsets.

All rates include daily Southern-style buffet breakfast and beer and wine at the nightly before-dinner social hour in The Veranda Restaurant, which opens to the wrap-around porch of the main building. Reservations are recommended for The Veranda's gourmet-style dinners. Amenities include a heated swimming pool, beachside sundeck, complimentary beach umbrellas and chairs, beach gazebo, and nightly turndown.

SOUTHERN WALTON COUNTY

If you want to stay near The Resort at Sandestin (see below) without paying its prices, there's a modern **Sleep Inn** a mile west at 5000 Emerald Coast Pkwy./U.S. 98 (☎ **800/627-5337** or 850/654-7022).

Super-Cheap Sleeps

A Highlands House Bed & Breakfast. 4193 W. County Rd. 30A (P.O. Box 1189), Santa Rosa Beach, FL 32459. ☎ **850/267-0110.** Fax 850/267-3602. 7 units, all with bathroom. A/C. Mar–Nov, $70–$135 single or double; Dec–Feb, $70–$135 single or double. Rates include full breakfast. Extra person $20. Children 10 and under stay free in parents' room. DISC, MC, V.

Beautifully situated in Dune Allen Beach, this B&B was built by innkeepers Joan and Ray Robins in the style of luxurious 18th-century plantation homes in the South Carolina low country, where they once lived. Although the house isn't directly on the beach, a path leads along a streambed to the sands. The Robinses furnished their dream inn with four-poster rice beds, comfy wingback chairs, and antique accoutrements. The most expensive rooms have French doors that open to an extrawide porch with wicker furniture and a view of the gulf. One unit has a fireplace; another, a whirlpool tub. The less-expensive models are in an old but modernized house to the rear of the main building. The delicious breakfasts often include brandy-battered French toast heaped with strawberries and cream.

Worth a Splurge for Golf & Tennis Players

✪ **The Resort at Sandestin.** 9300 Hwy. 98 West, Destin, FL 32541. ☎ **800/277-0800** or 850/267-8000 in the U.S., 800/933-7846 in Canada. Fax 850/267-8222. 175 units, 400 condo apts. Summer $145–$215 single or double; $195–$676 condo apt. Off-season $75–$185 single or double; $90–$475 condo apt. Packages available. Rates include health club, bicycle, boogie board, canoe, and kayak use, 1 hour tennis daily, discounts on other amenities. AE, DC, DISC, MC, V.

One of Florida's best sports-oriented resorts, this luxurious real estate development sprawls over 2,300 acres complete with a spectacular beach 5 miles west of Destin. An array of handsomely decorated accommodations overlook the gulf or Choctawhatchee Bay, the golf fairways, lagoons, or a nature preserve. The hotel rooms are in the Inn at Sandestin, on the bay. All the other accommodations—junior suites, condominium apartments, villas, and three-bedroom penthouses—are spread over the property and come complete with kitchen, living room, and patio or balcony. Most amenities are a short walk or bike or tram ride away, and a tunnel runs under U.S. 98 to connect Sandestin's gulf and bay areas.

The Sunset Bay Café offers breakfast, lunch, and dinner by the bay, but the dining delight here is the romantic **Elephant Walk** (☎ 850/267-4800), located on the gulf. There's a story here: In 1890 a tea planter in Ceylon named John Whiley tried to prevent damage to his trees by building a huge home across an elephant herd's path to the river. When the thirsty stampede reduced his house to ruins, Whiley vowed never to return. He roamed for 30 years, buying treasures in all four corners of the world. Then he discovered Northwest Florida and settled here. His eclectic purchases are displayed in this lovely building designed to evoke his Ceylon mansion. The candlelit dining room features entirely different, gourmet-quality choices for dinner each evening.

Among the many amenities here are a shuttle tram around the resort; arrangements for deep-sea fishing and other outside activities; summer children's program for ages 3 to 13; rental bikes, boats, and water-sports equipment; fishing and charter boats based at Baytowne Marina; fully-equipped sports spa and health center; nine swimming pools; three wading pools; children's playground; conference center; 63 holes of championship golf; Golf Learning Center with Tom Stickney; outstanding Bayside Tennis Center with clinic and hard, Rubico, and grass courts.

SEASIDE

If you decide to rent a home or romantic honeymoon cottage in this quaint village, contact the **Seaside Cottage Rental Agency,** P.O. Box 4730, Seaside, FL 32459 (☎ **800/277-8696** or 850/231-1320; fax 850/231-2219; www.seasidefl.com). It has some 240 cottages in its rental inventory, from one to six bedrooms. The beachside honeymoon cottages are a favorite getaway for newlyweds or anyone else looking for a romantic escape.

✪ **Josephine's French Country Inn at Seaside.** County Rd. 30A (P.O. Box 4767), Seaside, FL 32459. ☎ **800/848-1840** or 850/231-1940. Fax 850/231-2446. www.josephinesfl.com. 9 units, all with bathroom. A/C TV TEL. $130–$215 single or double. Rates include gourmet breakfast. Weekly rates available. AE, MC, V.

With its six large Tuscan columns reminiscent of an elegant Virginia mansion, Josephine's is an elegant country inn, with mahogany four-poster beds, lace comforters, rich furnishings, and marble bathtubs. Most guest rooms also have fireplaces. Conveniences like wet bars, microwaves, coffeemakers, and small refrigerators are neatly incorporated into the design so they don't conflict with the nostalgic charm. Sumptuous breakfasts are served either in-room (beside the fireplace or on your private veranda) or in the gracious dining room. The Guest House offers four suites, two with gulf views. Each has a fireplace, kitchen, and full bathroom. No smoking or pets are allowed inside. Guests can use the house bicycles for free.

With rich mahogany furniture and a wealth of period accoutrements, the dining room here is one of the region's finest places for a gourmet romantic dinner. Glowing with candlelight, this intimate room seats only 22 people. Josephine's Maryland-style crab cakes are consistently delicious.

Seaside Motor Court. County Rd. 30A (P.O. Box 4730), Seaside, FL 32459. ☎ **800/277-8696** or 850/231-1320. Fax 850/231-2219. www.seasidefl.com. 6 units. A/C TV TEL. $125–$250 single or double. AE, DC, DISC, MC, V.

Reminiscent of the 1-story motels of the 1940s, this establishment in the center of things has standard rooms furnished with tasteful decor. Although they lack the usual porches and furbelows of Seaside's architecture, the motel rooms are perfect for an overnight stay. The more expensive units have refrigerators, coffeemakers, and a separate bedroom.

GREAT DEALS ON DINING

Except for the strip on Okaloosa Island, a plethora of national fast-food and family chain restaurants line U.S. 98.

FORT WALTON BEACH

Super-Cheap Eats

Two good inexpensive choices are on the mainland a few minutes drive from the beach. One is **Barnhill's Country Buffet,** 431 Mary Ester Cutoff, opposite Santa Rosa Mall (☎ 850/243-1103), a member of the chain I described in Pensacola (see "Great Deals on Dining" in section 1). It has the same hours and prices as the Pensacola branches.

The other is **Mary's Kitchen,** offering the best barbecue in these parts, at 575-D N. Beal Pkwy., in the small shopping center at the corner of Mary Esther Cutoff (☎ 850/863-1141). Beef and pork are slowly smoked in a brick pit that sits in the middle of the dining room here. Ask for the sauce on the side, then apply as much or as little as suits your taste. Sandwiches cost $2 to $5, while barbecue platters go for $5.50 to $6.50. Open Monday to Friday from 11am to 8pm. No credit cards.

✪ **Magnolia Grill.** In Brooks Bridge 98 Center, 255 SE Miracle Strip Pkwy. (U.S. 98), on the mainland at north end of Brooks Bridge. ☎ **850/302-0266.** Reservations accepted. Sandwiches and salads $3–$6.25. Main courses $8–$14. AE, MC, V. Mon–Sat 11am–9pm. SEAFOOD/CAJUN/ITALIAN.

Don't think this is just another shopping center restaurant, for the Magnolia Grill is the province of Tom Rice, an accomplished local chef who honed his skills at several other establishments before opening his own here in 1996. Upon first impression, the decor resembles a diner with an old-fashioned ice-cream parlor, but look again. Tom and wife, Peggy, scoured every attic in town for an amazing collection of 1940s to 1960s memorabilia. Every table has an old radio or portable typewriter, and the walls sport a collection of photos that show Fort Walton Beach a half century ago. You may not notice, but the divider down the center of the room actually is the art deco sign salvaged from Eloise Shop, once an elegant ladies' clothier here. Tom also has resurrected some favorite old local recipes, including a scintillating asparagus mold served under a horseradish sauce, and J.S.'s Famous Warm Cuban Sandwich. Otherwise, his seafood, Cajun, and Italian fare shows the fine touch he has developed over the years.

For a Few Bucks More

✪ **Caffè Italia.** 189 Brooks St., on the mainland in the block west of Brooks Bridge. ☎ **850/664-0035.** Reservations recommended in winter. Pizza and pasta $5.50–$13; main courses $13–$16. AE, DC, DISC, MC, V. Tues–Sun 11am–10pm. Closed Thanksgiving and Christmas. NORTHERN ITALIAN.

Nada Eckhardt is from Croatia, but she met her American husband, Jim, while working at a restaurant named Caffè Italia in northern Italy. The Eckhardts duplicated that establishment in this 1925 Sears & Roebuck mail order house tucked away on the waterfront. You can dine on the patio with a view of the sound through sprawling live oak trees (one table is set romantically under its own gazebo), or inside, where Nada has installed floral tablecloths and photos from the old country. Her menu is limited to excellent pizzas, pasta dishes such as tortellini with mushrooms and peas in Alfredo sauce, northern Italian risotto with either asparagus or smoked salmon, and meat and seafood dishes to fit the season. Don't expect to make a full meal by ordering only a pasta here, for meals are served in the authentic Italian fashion, with a small portion of pasta preceding the seafood or meat course. On the other hand, you can quickly fill up on the seasoned, pizza-dough breadsticks served with olive oil for dipping. The cappuccino here is absolutely first rate, as are the genuine Italian desserts.

Harpoon Hanna's at the Boardwalk. 1450 E. Miracle Strip Pkwy. ☎ **850/243-5500.** Reservations accepted. Sandwiches and burgers $6–$9; main courses $9–$17. AE, DISC, MC, V. Summer daily 11am–11pm. Off-season Mon–Sat 11am–9pm, Sun noon–9pm. SEAFOOD.

Don't expect fine cuisine here, but this is the one place in Fort Walton Beach where you can have lunch or dinner right beside the beach. Part of the Boardwalk complex and built to look like an old-fashioned beach pavilion, it has big windows that swing up to let in gulf breezes. A deck is used for alfresco dining in good weather, and the outdoor Ship's Deck Bar is a great spot to catch a sunset. The menu features such items as coconut shrimp and blackened, fried, broiled, sautéed, or grilled fish. There's a children's menu. The restaurant's snack menu is available next door at the Soggy Dollar Saloon, which has live entertainment during the summer.

✪ **Staff's Seafood Restaurant.** 24 SW Miracle Strip Pkwy. (U.S. 98), on the mainland. ☎ **850/243-3526.** Reservations not necessary. Main courses $12–$27. AE, DISC, MC, V. Summer daily 5–11pm. Off-season Mon–Thurs 5–9:30pm, Fri–Sat 5–10pm. SEAFOOD/ STEAKS.

Considered the first Emerald Coast restaurant, Staff's started as a hotel in 1913 and moved to this barnlike building in 1931. Among the display of memorabilia are an old-fashioned phonograph lamp and a 1914 cash register. All main courses are served with heaping baskets of hot, home-baked wheat bread from a secret 70-year-old recipe. One of the most popular main dishes is the "seafood skillet," sizzling with broiled grouper, shrimp, scallops, and crabmeat drenched in butter and sprinkled with cheese. The tangy seafood gumbo also has gained fame for this casual, historic restaurant. In addition to the bread, main courses are accompanied by salad and dessert.

DESTIN

If you didn't catch a fish to be grilled at Fisherman's Wharf (see below), you can buy one to brag about from **Sexton's Seafood,** 602 Hwy. 98 East opposite Destin Harbor (☎ **805/837-3040**). It's the best market here.

Super-Cheap Eats

✪ **Callahan's Island Restaurant & Deli.** 950 Gulf Shore Dr. (2 blocks south of U.S. 98). ☎ **850/837-6328.** Main courses $6–$14; sandwiches and burgers $3.50–$6. DISC, MC, V. Summer Mon–Thurs 10am–9pm, Fri 10am–10pm, Sat 8:30am–9pm. Off-season Mon–Thurs 8:30am–9pm, Fri 10am–9pm, Sat 8am–10:30am. STEAKS/DELI.

The best place in the area for picnic fare, this family-operated deli offers burgers, excellent Reubens, and other made-to-order sandwiches, pastas, and nightly specials such as charcoal-grilled chicken, grilled pork chops, and teriyaki-style stir-fry. A long refrigerator case across the rear holds a variety of top-grade cheeses, deli meats, steaks, and chops (choose your own cut, and the chef will charcoal-grill it to order). Tables and booths are set up garden fashion, adding an outdoorsy ambience to this pleasant storefront establishment. Locals like to do lunch here. Breakfast is served only on Saturday morning.

Donut Hole. 635 U.S. 98 East, Destin. ☎ **850/837-8824.** Reservations not accepted. Breakfast $3.50–$7; sandwiches, salads, burgers $3.50–$5.50; meals $6.75. No credit cards. Summer daily 24 hours. Off-season daily 6am–10pm. Daily specials year-round 11am–8pm. Closed 2 weeks in December. SOUTHERN/AMERICAN.

Having spent his early career as a traveling salesman based in Texas, owner Bill Chandler designed this very popular establishment to be "the restaurant I couldn't find when I was on the road." Available around the clock during summer, his breakfasts highlight freshly baked doughnuts and other pastries. Daily special meals feature Southern favorites such as meat loaf, country-style steak, crispy fried chicken, salmon patties, and chicken and dumplings, all cooked on the premises using fresh vegetables and other top-quality ingredients.

There's a Donut Hole II Café and Bakery (☎ 850/267-3239) on U.S. 98 east in southern Walton County 2½ miles east of the Sandestin Beach Resort. It's known more for its bakery than meals. Open daily from 6am to 7pm.

Harry T's Boat House. 320 U.S. 98 east, Destin Harbor. ☎ **850/654-4800.** Reservations not accepted. Main courses $6.50–$17; sandwiches and burgers $7–$9.50. AE, MC, V. Summer Mon–Sat 11am–2am, Sun 10am–2am. Off-season Mon–Sat 11am–11pm, Sun 10am–11pm. Sun brunch year-round 10am–2pm. AMERICAN.

The family of trapeze artist "Flying Harry T" Baben opened this lively, fun restaurant on the ground floor of Destin Harbor's tallest building to honor his memory. Standing guard is a stuffed Stretch, Harry's beloved giraffe. Other decor features circus memorabilia and relics from the luxury cruise ship *Thracia,* which sank off the Emerald Coast in 1927; Harry T was presented with the ship's salvaged furnishings and fixtures for personally leading the heroic rescue of its 2,000 passengers.

The tabloid-style menu offers a wide range of such taste-tempters as chimichangas, Cajun-style burgers, blackened grouper sandwich, and buffalo wings. Kids eat for 99¢ until 7pm. Both the dining room and the downstairs lounge (with live entertainment Friday and Saturday nights) enjoy harbor views.

✪ **June's Dunes.** 1780 Old Hwy. 98 East. ☎ **850/654-0455.** Breakfast $2–$4; sandwiches and burgers $2–$4. No credit cards. Daily 5:30am–2pm. Closed Thanksgiving week. AMERICAN.

Locals love to eat at the rustic picnic tables of this red wooden structure, where June Decker has served beachside breakfasts and lunches since 1951. June's menu is chalked on a board over the counter of her screened-in kitchen. Give her your order and pick up your food when she calls your name. Breakfasts include waffles, French toast, fruit plates, and biscuits with sausage gravy. Lunches feature sandwiches, burgers (for $2, believe it or not), and German and Polish sausages with sauerkraut. June's little establishment is just west of the Henderson Beach State Recreation Area. Windows along three walls let in gulf breezes and lovely beach views.

✪ **Scampi's.** 1741 Old Hwy. 98 East. ☎ **850/837-7686.** Reservations not accepted. Main courses $8–$14; seafood buffet $15 adults, $7 children 8–12, $4 children 4–7, free for children under 4. AE, DC, DISC, MC, V. Daily 4:30–9:30pm. Closed mid-Oct to mid-Feb. SEAFOOD.

Constructed from the historic pilings of the old Destin Bridge, this two-level restaurant is especially popular for the bountiful seafood buffet bargain priced at $8 to $10 for adults, $7 for children 8 to 12, $4 for children 7 and under. An entire baked fish is the star of this veritable groaning board. For starters, the regular menu has just-shucked oysters, and a steaming hot bowl of piquant seafood gumbo is almost a meal in itself. Just about any piscine preference will be satisfied in this casual, friendly restaurant. The lengthy bar and cocktail lounge are a local rendezvous. This place lies near the Back Porch, reviewed below.

For a Few Bucks More

AJ's Seafood & Oyster Bar. 116 Hwy. 98 East, Destin Harbor. ☎ **850/837-1913.** Reservations not accepted. Main courses $12–$19; sandwiches and salads $5.50–$8. AE, DISC, MC, V. Summer daily 11am–midnight (bar until 2am). Off-season daily 11am–10pm. SEAFOOD.

Jimmy Buffet tunes set the tone at this fun, tiki-topped establishment on the picturesque Destin Harbor docks, where fishing boats unload their daily catches right into the kitchen. Obviously, the best items here are grilled or fried fish, but raw or steamed Apalachicola oysters also lead the bill of fare. You can sample a bit of everything with a "run of the kitchen" seafood patter. AJ's is most famous for its top-side Club Bimimi, featuring reggae music and limbo contests every summer evening (you may want to have dinner elsewhere if you're not in the partying mood). At lunch, picnic tables on the covered dock make a fine venue with a view across the harbor to the gulf.

Back Porch. 1740 Old Hwy. 98 East. ☎ **850/837-2022.** Reservations not accepted. Main courses $11–$18; sandwiches, burgers, and pastas $6.50–$8. AE, DC, DISC, MC, V. Summer daily 11am–11pm. Off-season daily 11am–10pm. From U.S. 98, turn toward the beach at the Hampton Inn. SEAFOOD.

A cedar-shingled seafood shack whose long porch offers glorious beach and gulf views, this popular, casual restaurant originated charcoal-grilled amberjack, which you'll now see on menus throughout Florida. Other fish and seafood, as well as chicken and juicy hamburgers, also come from the coals. Monthly specials feature crab, lobster, and seasonal fish. Come early, order a rum-laden Key Lime Freeze, and enjoy the sunset. The Back Porch sits with a number of other restaurants (see above for Scampi's and June's Dunes) near the western boundary of the Henderson Beach State Recreation Area.

Fisherman's Wharf. 210D Hwy. 98 East, Destin Harbor. ☎ **850/654-4766.** Reservations not accepted. Sandwiches and burgers $6.50–$9; main courses $14–19; cook-your-catch $8. AE, DC, DISC, MC, V. Summer daily 11am–11pm (deck bar open later). Off-season daily 11am–9pm. SEAFOOD.

Have that fish you caught filleted, bring it here, and the chef will charcoal-grill it at this atmospheric restaurant next to the charter fleet marina. If you had no luck, and didn't stop by Sexton's Seafood on the way here to buy a few fillets (see above), you can select from the restaurant's fresh-off-the-boat catch for grilling, broiling, frying, or blackening. Charcoal-grilling is the house specialty—my triggerfish fillet was white and flaky but still moist. All main courses come with a trip to a central salad bar and rice pilaf, baked potato, or roasted vegetables. Although this building dates from 1996, it evokes an Old Florida fish camp, with rough-hewed wood walls and double-hung windows looking out to a large harborside deck, a venue during the summer season for two libation bars, an oyster bar, and live music.

Harbor Docks. 538 U.S. 98 East, Destin Harbor. ☎ **850/837-2506.** Reservations not accepted. Main courses $14–$20; burgers and sandwiches $8.50–$10. AE, DC, DISC, MC, V. Daily 4:30am–10:30am and 11am–11pm. Closed for breakfast Thanksgiving–Feb 14. SEAFOOD/SUSHI.

The harbor views are spectacular from indoors or outdoors at this casual, somewhat rustic establishment whose splendid hand-carved wood-and-marble bar dates from 1890. Specialties include a sautéed daily catch served with artichoke hearts. Appetizers on the dinner menu might feature smoked yellowfin tuna with mustard sauce and shrimp nachos, and sushi is offered daily from 5:30 to 10pm. Hearty fishermen's breakfasts are cooked by the owners of the Silver Sands, a popular local haunt that burned down. At night, frequent live entertainment keeps the action going on the outdoor deck.

McGuire's Irish Pub & Brewery. 33 Hwy. 98 East, Destin Harbor (in Harborwalk Center near Destin Bridge). ☎ **850/650-0000.** Reservations not accepted. Snacks, burgers, and sandwiches $7.50–$8; meals $13–$25. AE, DC, DISC, MC, V. Mon–Sat 11am–2am, Sun 11am–1am (brunch 11am–3pm). AMERICAN/IRISH.

Like Pensacola's original McGuire's (see "Great Deals on Dining" in section 1, above), this younger sibling sports thousands of dollar bills stuck on the ceilings and walls, plus Notre Dame University football schedules, a prominent logo of the Boston

Celtics pro basketball team, and more memorabilia recalling Irish American lore. This is Destin's most popular hangout, and many patrons congregate at the big oak bar in the center of the dining room, especially when live entertainment starts nightly at 9pm. If you're here to dine, you can opt for a table on either side of the bar or up on a rooftop deck. Dining here is almost secondary to the see-and-be-seen scene, but you can order corned beef and cabbage, Irish stew, scampi o'fettucini (shrimp in Alfredo sauce), big salads, supersize hamburgers, steaks, and various seafood offerings.

Worth a Splurge

✪ Marina Cafe. 404 Hwy. 98 East, Destin Harbor. ☎ **850/837-7960.** Reservations recommended. Main courses $16–$23; pizza and pasta $8–$17. AE, DC, DISC, MC, V. Daily 5–10pm. Closed Jan. ITALIAN/NEW AMERICAN.

Destin's finest restaurant provides a classy atmosphere with soft candlelight, subdued music, and formally attired waiters. The outdoor balconied deck overlooks Destin Harbor and is the setting for drinks and appetizers. Inside, window walls provide the same view. The creative chef prepares pizzas and pastas with a special flair, with an emphasis on light, spicy fare. Menu highlights include a fettucini combined with andouille sausage, shrimp, crawfish tails, and a piquant tomato-cream sauce.

SOUTHERN WALTON COUNTY
Super-Cheap Eats

Buster's Oyster Bar and Seafood Restaurant. 125 Poinciana Blvd., in Delchamps Plaza, U.S. 98 at Scenic Hwy. 98. ☎ **850/837-4399.** Reservations not accepted. Main courses $10–$14; sandwiches and burgers $5.50–$7. AE, DC, DISC, MC, V. Summer daily 11am–11pm. Off-season daily 11am–10pm. SEAFOOD.

Shingles, plants, and wood make this local favorite seem not at all like a shopping-center restaurant, 1 mile west of The Resort at Sandestin. Buster claims that more than five million oysters have been shucked here, and with good reason, since they go for $1.59 a dozen during his daily 5 to 6pm happy hour. Buster also likes to add something outrageous to his tabloid-style menu, such as "a toasted sea spider sandwich" (aka soft-shell crab). Fried, broiled, steamed, or blacked fish and seafood dinners are prepared to order. Kids have their own menu.

Chan's Market Café. 5494 U.S. 98 East, in the Market at The Resort at Sandestin. ☎ **850/837-1334.** Reservations not accepted. Breakfast $3–$7; sandwiches and salads $3.50–$7; meals $5–$8. DISC, MC, V. Mar to Labor Day, daily 7am–9pm; Labor Day to Feb, daily 7am–6pm. AMERICAN.

The inexpensive prices and good food at this red-and-black-accented cafe draw scores of families vacationing at The Resort at Sandestin. A wide array of offerings include freshly baked croissants and bagels at breakfast or deli sandwiches at lunch, charcoal-grilled chicken and burgers, and meals featuring amberjack or yellowfin tuna grilled over coals. During the off-season, "white-plate" specials of meat loaf, chicken Parmesan, and roast turkey with dressing are good values at $4 to $6. Seating is both indoors and, in good weather, outside on a shaded veranda beside a pond filled with lily pads. An outdoor oyster bar is open from March to Labor Day.

Worth a Splurge

✪ Criolla's. 170 E. County Rd. 30A, ¼ mile east of County Rd. 283, Grayton Beach. ☎ **850/267-1267.** Reservations recommended. Main courses $15–$25. DISC, MC, V. Apr–Sept, Mon–Sat 6–10pm; Feb–Mar and Oct–Nov, Tues–Sat 6–9:30pm. Closed Dec–Jan. LOUISIANA CREOLE/CARIBBEAN.

One of Florida's finest restaurants, this charming establishment derives its name from the archaic word *criollo*, signifying persons of pure Spanish descent born in the New World. The attractive decor, combining New Orleans with the Caribbean, features potted palms, whirling ceiling fans, and tropical island paintings. Seasonal menus carry out the theme, always offering Creole and Caribbean selections. Many fish dishes carry the wonderful aroma of smoke from a wood-fired grill. An "Island Hopper" menu offers gourmet appetizers, main courses, and homemade sweets at fixed prices.

✪ **Lake Place Restaurant.** 5960 County Rd. 30A, Dune Allen Beach. ☎ **850/267-2871.** Reservations required in summer, recommended off-season. Main courses $17–$27. AE, DISC, MC. V. Tues–Sat 5:30–9pm. SEAFOOD.

Owners Richard and Evalee Grenamyer scour the markets each morning for fresh fish, which they serve at this rustic plank building on the shores of picturesque Lake Allen. You can order the daily catch crispy fried, sautéed with white wine and roasted garlic sauce, or herb-crusted with jumbo crabmeat and butter sauce. If the day's specials don't appeal, fresh salmon is prepared on a seasoned cedar plank. Landlubbers can choose from steaks, lamb and pork chops, and free-range chicken. An excellent wine list changes daily to complement each evening's special dishes.

SEASIDE

✪ **Bud and Alley's.** County Rd. 30A, in the beachside shops. ☎ **850/231-5900.** Reservations recommended. Sandwiches $8; main courses $16–$27.50. MC, V. Summer Wed–Mon 11:30am–3pm and 6–9:30pm. Off-season Wed–Mon 11:30–3pm and 5:30–9pm. Closed Jan. SEAFOOD/STEAKS/MEDITERRANEAN.

Seaside's first restaurant is still number one to its steady patrons. The freshest of seafoods can be selected from seasonal menus featuring an innovative selection of Basque, Italian, Louisianan, and Floridian dishes prepared by owners and accomplished chefs Scott Witcoski and Dave Raushkolb. You can dine indoors or outdoors, on the screened porch, or under an open-air gazebo where you hear the waves splashing against the white sands. Opening at 3pm except during winter, a roof deck offers a variety of tapas as appetizers or light meals. Jazz is usually in the spotlight on weekends. On New Year's Eve, everyone in town and from miles around celebrates at Bud and Alley's. Call ahead to see if a noted guest chef is cooking or a special wine-tasting dinner is scheduled (there's an extensive list here). No smoking.

Shades. Town Sq. and Markets. ☎ **850/231-1950.** Reservations not accepted. Main courses $14–$17; sandwiches and burgers $5–$9. AE, DISC, MC, V. Summer daily 8–10am and 11am–10pm. Off-season daily 8–10am and 11am–9pm. AMERICAN.

In another life this was a rustic house built in the early 1900s in the small town of Chattahoochee. It was moved to Seaside's Town Square some 70 years later and reborn as this quaint restaurant, which doubles as Seaside's community pub. Stacked-high sandwiches, hot wings, and hamburgers are popular for lunch. At dinner, the bountiful fried seafood platter is a big favorite. Dine inside or on the porch in warm weather.

FORT WALTON BEACH & DESTIN AFTER DARK

Most resorts spotlight live entertainment during the summer season, including the Radisson Beach Resort and the Ramada Beach Resort in Fort Walton Beach, and the Sandestin Hilton and The Resort at Sandestin in southern Walton County (see "Accommodations You Can Afford," above). It's a good idea to inquire ahead to make sure what's scheduled, especially during the slow season from October through February.

FORT WALTON BEACH Country music and dancing fans will find a home at the **Seagull,** on Miracle Strip Parkway (U.S. 98) opposite the Gulfarium (☎ **850/243-3413**). The generations of air force pilots who have hung out here call it the

"Dirty Gull." Its main rival for the country set is the **High Tide Oyster Bar,** at Okaloosa Island off the Brooks Bridge (☎ **850/244-2624**). Over at the Boardwalk on U.S. 98 east, the **Soggy Dollar Saloon** (☎ **850/243-5500**) has live music on weekends.

The young beach set is attracted to rock and reggae in Shanty Town, on the east side of Brooks Bridge, where **Hoser's,** 1225 Santa Rosa Blvd. (☎ **850/664-6113**), is the liveliest pub (its name mirrors a fire-fighting motif).

DESTIN Twenty-somethings are attracted to the dance club, rowdy saloon, Jimmy Buffet–style reggae bar, and sports TV and billiards parlor all under one roof at the acclaimed **Nightown,** 140 Palmetto St. (☎ **850/837-6448**), near the harbor on the inland side of U.S. 98 east. One admission of $3 to $7 covers it all. Not far away, the **Fish Heads** pub, at 414 U.S. 98 east (☎ **850/837-4848**), features the "Big Red Snapper," a lethal mixture of rum and vodka. Nearby, **Hogs Breath Destin,** 541 Hwy. 98 East (☎ **850/837-5991**), is another lively pub with bands playing beach music.

Several Destin restaurants offer entertainment nightly during summer, on weekends off-season. The dockside **AJ's Club Bimini,** 116 U.S. 98 east (☎ **850/837-1913**), has live reggae under a big thatch-roofed deck. A somewhat older, if not more sober, crowd gathers for entertainment at the big harborside deck at **Fisherman's Wharf,** on U.S. 98 east (☎ **850/654-4766**); at **The Deck,** on U.S. 98 east at the Harbor Docks restaurant, overlooking the harbor (☎ **850/837-2506**); at **Harry T's Boat House** (☎ **850/654-6555**), also on the harbor; and for Irish tunes nightly year-round at **McGuire's Irish Pub & Brewery** (☎ **850/650-0000**), in the Harborwalk Shops on U.S. 98 just east of the Destin Bridge. See "Great Deals on Dining," above, for details about the restaurants. The **Grande Isle Sky Bar,** above Grazti Italian Restaurant, 1771 Old Hwy. 98 (☎ **850/837-7475**), draws the after-dinner crowd from the Back Porch and Scampi's restaurants, both adjacent.

Out toward Sandestin, **Fuddrucker's Beachside Bar & Grill,** 20001 Hwy. 98 East (☎ **850/654-4200**), opposite the Henderson Beach State Recreation Area, offers double the fun with two summertime stages, one on the bay-side deck, the other in the Down Under Bar. There's another Fudrucker's at 108 Santa Rosa Blvd. on Okaloosa Island in Fort Walton Beach (☎ **850/243-3833**).

3 Panama City Beach

100 miles E of Pensacola, 100 miles SW of Tallahassee

Ask O. J. Simpson what the Panhandle's main attraction is, and he'll probably tell you Panama City Beach. This was, after all, the first place outside southern California he visited after he was acquitted of murder. Simpson still had some money when he came here to see his then-girlfriend's family and to play a little golf.

He was one of an increasing number of upscale visitors who are changing the image of this 22-mile stretch of gorgeous white sand. Panama City Beach has long been known as the centerpiece of the "redneck Riviera," since it's a summertime mecca for millions of low- and moderate-income vacationers from nearby southern states. It still has a seemingly unending strip of bars, amusement parks, and old-fashioned motels. But this lively and crowded destination now also has luxury resorts and condominiums to go along with its great beaches, golf courses, fishing, boating, and fresh seafood.

Panama City Beach is also the most seasonal resort in Northwest Florida, as many restaurants, attractions, and even some hotels close between October and spring break in March. On the other hand, spring break is a big deal here; MTV even sets up shop in Panama City Beach for its annual beach-party broadcasts.

ESSENTIALS

GETTING THERE   Interstate 10 runs east-west, 45 miles to the north. From I-10, take U.S. 231 south to Panama City, or Fla. 77 south to the beach. U.S. 98, the gulf-hugging east-west artery, runs through both Panama City Beach and nearby Panama City.

ASA (☎ 800/292-3424), **Delta Connection** (☎ 800/221-1212), **Northwest Airlink** (☎ 800/225-2525), and **US Airways Express** (☎ 800/428-4322) fly into Panama City/Bay County International Airport, on Airport Road, north of St. Andrews Boulevard, in Panama City.

The major car-rental firms have booths at the airport. You can take a taxi to your hotel (see "Getting Around," below). Taxi fares from the airport to the beach range from about $12 to $25.

The *Sunset Limited* transcontinental service on **Amtrak** (☎ 800/USA-RAIL) stops at Chipley, 45 miles north of Panama City.

VISITOR INFORMATION   For advance information, contact the **Panama City Beach Convention & Visitors Bureau,** P.O. Box 9473, Panama City Beach, FL 32407 (☎ 800/PC-BEACH or 850/233-6503; www.travelfile.com/get?pcbeach). It operates the **James I. Lark, Sr., Visitors Information Center,** on the beach at 12015 Front Beach Rd. opposite the Miracle Strip Amusement Park.

You can buy detailed maps at **Alvin's Island Tropical Department Store,** across the street from the visitor center.

GETTING AROUND   Call **AAA Taxi** (☎ 850/785-0533), **Yellow Cab** (☎ 850/763-4691), or **Deluxe Coach Service** (☎ 800/763-0211 or 850/763-0211). Fares are on a zone system rather than meters. Local fares in Panama City Beach will range from $4.50 to $9.

TIME   The Panama City area is in the **central time zone,** 1 hour behind Miami, Orlando, and Tallahassee.

HITTING THE BEACH

A nearly unbroken strand of fine white sand fronts all the 22 miles of Panama City Beach, but the highlight for many here is ✪ **St. Andrews State Recreation Area,** 4607 State Park Lane, at the east end of the beach (☎ 850/233-5140). With more than 1,000 acres of dazzling white sand and dunes, this preserved wilderness demonstrates what the area looked like before motels and condominiums lined the beach. Lacy, golden sea oats sway in the refreshing gulf breezes, and fragrant rosemary grows wild. Picnic areas are on both the gulf beach and Grand Lagoon. Rest rooms and open-air showers are available for beachgoers. For anglers, there are jetties and a boat ramp. A nature trail reveals wading birds and perhaps an alligator or two. And drive carefully here, for the area is home to foxes, coyotes, and a herd of deer. Overnight camping is permitted (see "Accommodations You Can Afford," below). On display is a historic turpentine still formerly used by lumbermen to make turpentine and rosin, both important for caulking the old wooden ships. Admission is $4 per car with two to eight occupants, $2 for single-occupant vehicles, and $1 for pedestrians and cyclists. The area is open daily from 8am to sunset.

A few hundred yards across an inlet from St. Andrews State Recreation Area sits pristine ✪ **Shell Island,** a 7½-mile-long, 1-mile-wide barrier island. This uninhabited natural preserve is great for shelling and also fun for swimming, suntanning, or just relaxing. Visitors can bring chairs, beach gear, coolers, food, and beverages. The island is accessible only by boat. A **ferry shuttle** (☎ 850/233-5140) runs from April to October between St. Andrews State Recreation Area and the island every 30 minutes: daily from 9am to 5pm in summer, weekends from 10am to 3pm in spring and fall. Fares are $7.50 for adults, $5.50 for children 11 and under, plus admission fees to the state recreation area (see above). A special snorkel package costs $16.95, including shuttle ride and equipment, and a 3-hour "ecosnorkel" tour for $24.95 departs twice daily.

Several cruise boats go to Shell Island. The glass-bottom *Capt. Anderson III* cruises there from Capt. Anderson's Marina, 5500 N. Lagoon Dr., at Thomas Drive (☎ 850/234-3435). The *Island Queen* paddle wheeler departs from the pier at Marriott's Bay Point Resort Village, 4200 Marriott Dr., off Jan Cooley Road (☎ 850/234-3307, ext. 1816). The *Island Star* and *Island Runner* (☎ 850/235-2809) both leave from Hathaway Marina, on U.S. 98 at the west end of Hathaway Bridge. All of these boats charge about $10 for adults, $5 for children. The *Miss Ashely* (☎ 850/785-4878) has all-day shelling, swimming, and snorkeling trips for about $18 adults, $7.50 children, including food and soft drinks.

The more adventurous can take the 2½-hour tours offered by **Shell Island Wave Runner Tours** (☎ 850/785-4878), at the east end of Hathaway Bridge. The trips cost about $70 for single boats, $80 for doubles. Reservations are required, so call ahead. Or you can paddle over to the island with **Shell Island Kayaks,** based at St. Andrews State Recreation Area (☎ 850/235-4004). Full-day rentals are $35 for a single, $45 for a tandem.

The *Glass Bottom Boat* (☎ 850/234-8944) stops at Shell Island as part of its "sea school" trips from Treasure Island Marina, 3605 Thomas Dr. at Grand Lagoon (see "Cruises," under "Great Golf That Won't Break Your Budget & Other Affordable Outdoor Activities," below).

GREAT GOLF THAT WON'T BREAK YOUR BUDGET & OTHER AFFORDABLE OUTDOOR ACTIVITIES

BOATING   A variety of rental boats are available at the marinas near the Thomas Drive bridge over Grand Lagoon. These include the **Capt. Davis Queen Fleet,** based at Capt. Anderson's Marina, 5500 N. Lagoon Dr. (☎ 800/874-2415, or 850/234-3435 from nearby states); the **Panama City Boat Yard,** 5323 N. Lagoon Dr. (☎ 850/234-3386); the **Passport Marina,** 5325 N. Lagoon Dr. (☎ 850/234-5609); the **Port Lagoon Yacht Basin,** 5201 N. Lagoon Dr. (☎ 850/234-0142); the **Pirates Cove Marina,** 3901 Thomas Dr. (☎ 850/234-3839); and the **Treasure Island Marina,** 3605 Thomas Dr. (☎ 850/234-6533).

You can put to gulf under sail with **Bombay Sailing Charters** (☎ 850/234-7794), which charges $25 per person for half-day trips, $20 for sunset or moonlight cruises. **Port to Port Sailing Charters** (☎ 850/230-0830) rents Sunfish and regular sailboats, with or without captain.

Many resorts and hotels provide beach toys for their guests' use. Wave Runners, jet boats, inflatables, and other equipment can be rented from **Panama City Beach Sports** (☎ 850/234-0067), **Raging Rentals** (☎ 850/234-6775), and **Lagoon Rentals** (☎ 850/234-7245).

CRUISES   One of the most comprehensive outings here is aboard the *Glass Bottom Boat,* based at Treasure Island Marina, 3605 Thomas Dr., at Grand Lagoon (☎ 850/234-8944). Its 3-hour, narrated "sea school" cruise includes underwater viewing, dolphin-watching, bird-feeding, and a 1-hour stop for swimming at Shell

Island. Along the way, the crew picks up and rebaits a crab trap and explains the creatures brought up in a shrimp net. The boat has a snack bar and air-conditioned cabin. The trips cost about $14 for adults and $8 for children. This same company operates a **Super Shelling Safari,** on which guests are taken to the eastern end of Shell Island to scavenge in the shallow water for shells (wear your bathing suit). Call for cruise times, exact prices, and reservations.

The **Capt. Davis Queen Fleet,** based at Capt. Anderson's Marina, 5500 N. Lagoon Dr. (☎ 800/874-2415 from neighboring states, or 850/234-3435 in Florida), has daily sightseeing trips, nature cruises, dolphin-watching and bird-feeding excursions, and dinner-dance cruises during the summer season. So do the *Island Star* and *Island Runner* (☎ 850/235-2809), both at the Hathaway Marina on U.S. 98 at the west end of Hathaway Bridge. The 32-foot *AquaStar* (☎ 850/230-2800) has dolphin-watching cruises to the shallow waters off Shell Island, where larger boats can't go.

FISHING   You can cast your line from the concrete **Dan Russell Municipal Pier,** which unlike other piers in the area, withstood Hurricane Opal in 1995.

A relatively inexpensive way for novices to try their luck fishing is with **Capt. Anderson's Deep Sea Fishing,** at Capt. Anderson's Marina on Thomas Drive at Grand Lagoon (☎ 800/874-2415 or 850/234-5940). The captain's party-boat trips last from 5 to 12 hours, with prices ranging from about $30 to $50 per person, including bait and tackle. Observers can go along for half price.

More expensive are the charter-fishing boats that depart daily from March to November from the marinas mentioned in "Boating," above.

GOLF   Thirty-six holes of championship golf are offered at **Marriott's Bay Point Resort Village,** 4200 Marriott Dr., off Jan Cooley Road (☎ 850/234-3307), where the Bruce Devlin–designed Lagoon Legends and the Club Meadows courses offer 36 holes of championship play—Lagoon Legends is rated as one of the country's most difficult. Both have clubhouses, putting greens, driving ranges, clinics, and private instruction. Greens fees with cart range from about $50 in summer to $80 in winter, depending on day of the week. See "Accommodations You Can Afford," below.

The **Edgewater Beach Resort,** 11212 U.S. 98A (☎ 850/235-4044), also has a 9-hole resort course.

O. J. Simpson made the rounds at **The Hombre,** 120 Coyote Pass, 3 miles west of the Hathaway Bridge off Panama City Beach Parkway/U.S. 98 (☎ 850/234-3573), a par-72 championship course and home to the Nike Panama City Beach Classic. Fifteen of its 18 holes have water hazards (the unforgiving 7th hole sits on an island). Greens fees are about $65 in summer, $60 in winter, including cart.

The championship course at the semiprivate **Holiday Golf Club,** 100 Fairway Blvd. (☎ 850/234-1800), sports lake-line fairways and elevated greens. Greens fees with cart are about $45 in summer, $35 in winter. You can play at night here on a lighted 9-hole, par-29 executive course.

The least expensive place to play here is the flat and forgiving **Signal Hill,** 9516 N. Thomas Dr. (☎ 850/234-3218), where you'll pay about $20 to walk 18 holes in summer, $13 in winter. Add about $10 per person for a cart.

SCUBA DIVING & SNORKELING   Although the area is too far north for extensive coral formations, more than 50 artificial reefs and shipwrecks in the gulf waters off Panama City attract a wide variety of sea life. Local operators include **Hydrospace Dive Shop,** 6422 W. Hwy. 98 (☎ 850/234-3036); the **Panama City Dive Center,** 4823 Thomas Dr. (☎ 850/235-3390); **Emerald Coast Divers,** 5121 Thomas Dr. (☎ 800/945-DIVE or 850/233-3355); **West End Dive Center,** 17320 Panama City Beach Pkwy. (☎ 850/235-7873); and **Pete's Scuba Center,** 9007 Front Beach Rd.

(☎ **800/401-DIVE** or 850/230-8006). These companies lead dives, teach courses, and take snorkelers to the grass flats off Shell Island.

EXPLORING THE AREA

Gulf World. 15412 Front Beach Rd. (at Hill Ave.), Panama City Beach. ☎ **850/234-5271.** Admission $16 adults, $9.55 children 5–12, free for children 4 and under. Summer daily 9am–7pm. Off-season Tues–Sun 9am–3pm. Closed Thanksgiving and 3 days at Christmas.

This landscaped tropical garden and marine showcase features shows with talented dolphins, sea lions, penguins, and more. Not to be upstaged, parrots perform daily, too. Sea turtles, alligators, and other critters also call Gulf World home. Scuba demonstrations, shark feedings, and underwater shows keep the crowds entertained.

Museum of Man in the Sea. 17314 Panama City Beach Pkwy. (at Heather Dr., west of Fla. 79), Panama City Beach. ☎ **850/235-4101.** Admission $5 adults, $2.50 children 6–16, free for children 5 and under. Daily 9am–5pm. Closed New Year's Day, Thanksgiving, and Christmas.

Owned by the Institute of Diving, this unusual museum exhibits relics from the first days of scuba diving, historical displays of the underwater world dating from 1500, and treasures recovered from sunken ships, including Spanish treasure galleons. Hands-on exhibits include experiments on water and air pressure, light refraction, and why diving bells work. Both kids and adults can climb through a submarine, see live sea animals in a pool, and look out of a diving helmet. Videos and aquariums explain the sea life found in St. Andrew Bay.

ZooWorld Zoological & Botanical Park. 9008 Front Beach Rd. (near Moylan Dr.), Panama City Beach. ☎ **850/230-1243.** Admission $8.95 adults, $7.95 seniors, $6.50 children 3–11, free for children under 3. Daily 9am–sunset. Closed Christmas.

The largest captive alligator in Florida ("Mr. Bubba") lives in a re-created pine forest habitat at this educational and entertaining zoo. The facility is an active participant in the Species Survival Plan, which helps protect endangered species with specific breeding and housing programs. Other guests here include rare and endangered animals as well as orangutans and other primates, big cats, more reptiles, and other creatures. Activities also include a walk through an aviary, a bat exhibit, and a petting zoo.

AMUSEMENT PARKS

An exciting, 105-foot-high roller coaster is just one of the 30 rides at the **Miracle Strip Amusement Park,** 12000 Front Beach Rd., at Alf Coleman Road (☎ 850/234-5810). Little ones will love the traditional carousel. The 9 acres of fun include nonstop live entertainment and tons of junk food. Hours and prices change from year to year, so call for the latest. It's closed from Labor Day to mid-March.

Adjoining the amusement park, the **Shipwreck Island Water Park** (☎ 850/234-0368) offers a variety of water-related fun, including the 1,600-foot winding Lazy River for tubing and a daring 35-mph Speed Slide. The Tad Pole Hole is exclusively for young kids. Lounge chairs, umbrellas, and inner tubes are free, and lifeguards are on duty. Admission is less than $20. Open June to mid-August; call for hours.

SHOPPING

An attraction in itself is the main branch of **Alvin's Island Tropical Department Store,** 12010 Front Beach Rd. (☎ 850/234-3048), opposite the James I. Lark, Sr., Visitors Information Center. It not only sells a wide range of beach gear and apparel, it also has cages containing colorful parrots, tanks with small sharks, and an enclosure with alligators. The sharks are fed at 11am daily; the gators get theirs at 4pm (the older ones are too lethargic to eat during the cool winter months).

The **African Curio Shoppe,** 8730 Thomas Dr., at Joan Road (☎ **800/235-1351** or 850/235-1288), is another fascinating place to browse for stuffed animal heads and woodcarvings, soapstone sculptures, leather bags, and other handcrafts from Africa. Open daily 9:30am to 9:30pm in summer, Wednesday to Saturday 9am to 6pm off-season.

ACCOMMODATIONS YOU CAN AFFORD

There are literally scores of motels along the beach here, ranging from small mom-and-pop operations to sizable members of national chains. The annual guide distributed by the Panama City Beach Convention & Visitors Bureau has a complete list (see "Essentials," above). Among the beachside chain motels, you'll find the **Best Western Casa Loma** (☎ **800/528-1234** or 850/234-1100), the **Days Inn Beach** (☎ **800/ 329-7466** or 850/233-3333), and the **Ramada Inn Beach & Convention Center** (☎ **800/228-3344** or 850/234-1700). The somewhat less expensive **Best Western Del Coronado** (☎ **800/528-1234** or 850/234-1600) is open from March to September.

Panama City Beach also abounds with condominium complexes, such as the Edgewater Beach Resort listed below. Although it's not on the beach, the **Inn at St. Thomas Square,** 8730 Thomas Dr., Panama City Beach, FL 32408 (☎ **800/ 874-8600** or 850/234-0349; fax 850/235-8104), has charm and enjoys a quiet location. The complex consists of some units above the small St. Thomas Square shopping center, at Thomas Drive and Joan Road, but highly preferable are the Spanish-style, town-house–looking apartments set along the skinny upper arm of Grand Lagoon. There's a pool and tennis court on the premises. Rates range from $85 for efficiencies to $165 for three-bedroom apartments in summer. Off-season they go for $55 to $99, respectively. The complex is managed by Basic Management Inc., which also has some beachfront units to rent, obviously at higher rates.

Among the many other agencies offering condominium apartments are **St. Andrew Bay Resort Management,** 726 Thomas Dr., Panama City Beach, FL 32408 (☎ **800/ 621-2462** or 850/235-4075; fax 850/233-2833; www.sabre1.net); and **Condo World,** 8815A Thomas Dr. (P.O. Box 9456), Panama City Beach, FL 32408 (☎ **800/ 232-6636** or 850/234-5564; fax 850/233-6725; www.condoworld-pcb-fla.com).

This area has two of the Panhandle's finest campgrounds, both with sites right beside the water. ✪ **St. Andrews State Recreation Area,** 4607 State Park Lane, Panama City Beach (☎ **850/233-5140**), one of this area's major attractions (see "Hitting the Beach," above), has RV and tent sites beautifully situated in a pine forest right on the shores of Grand Lagoon. Rates from March to September are $17 to $19 for waterfront sites, $15 to $17 for others. They drop to $8 to $12 from October to February. Reservations are required, up to 11 months in advance. No pets are allowed.

You can bring your pet, but not your tent, to **Magnolia Beach RV Park,** 7800 Magnolia Beach Rd., Panama City Beach (☎ **850/235-1581**), with great views of Panama City from an idyllic setting under magnolias and moss-draped oaks on the shores of St. Andrew Bay. Rates are $20 to $24 a night in summer, $16 to $19 off-season. The park is 2 miles from Marriott's Bay Point Resort Village. Take Magnolia Beach Road off Thomas Drive and go straight to the camp.

Bay County adds 3.5% tax to all hotel and campground bills, bringing the total add-on tax to 9.5% .

SUPER-CHEAP SLEEPS

Flamingo Motel. 15525 Front Beach Rd., Panama City Beach, FL 32413. ☎ **800/ 828-0400** or 850/234-2232. 67 units. A/C TV TEL. Summer $66–$119 single or double. Off-season $32–$74 single or double. AE, DISC, MC, V.

Evoking Key West, this well-maintained, family-owned motel takes great pride in its gorgeous tropical garden surrounding a heated swimming pool and a large sundeck overlooking the gulf. The brightly decorated rooms have either full kitchens or refrigerators and microwave ovens. They can sleep two to six people, some in separate bedrooms. Kitchenette rooms in a 2-story motel block across the road are less appealing but will accommodate six to eight. Budget-conscious families can opt for the low-priced rooms, accommodating two to four. Some units have shower-only bathrooms. The Dan Russell fishing pier is only half a mile away, Gulf World is within walking distance, and Shuckums Oyster Pub & Seafood Grill is across the road (see "Great Deals on Dining," below). Forget spending spring break here unless you're a family or couple.

Next door, the midrise **Flamingo Towers** was due to open in 1998, with 49 junior suites, all sporting balconies facing the gulf. The complex will have its own pool and hot tub.

Georgian Terrace. 14415 Front Beach Rd., Panama City Beach, FL 32413. ☎ **850/ 234-2144** or 850/234-8413. 28 units. A/C TV TEL. Summer $69–$109 single or double. Off-season $43–$89 single or double. AE, DISC, MC, V.

Right on the beach, Karen Grant's two-level motel offers clean, quiet, and cozy apartments. Opening to the beach, cheerfully decorated, and lined with knotty pine, they all have full kitchens separated by room dividers. The homey decor is extended to each unit's private enclosed sunporch. A greenhouse-enclosed heated pool area with lush tropical plantings and attractive lounge chairs make this place a good pick off-season. There's a rare stretch of undeveloped beach almost next door.

Sunset Inn. 8109 Surf Dr., Panama City Beach, FL 32408. ☎ and fax **850/234-7370.** 62 units. A/C TV TEL. Summer $55–$155 single or double. Off-season $35–$110 single or double. Weekly and monthly rates available. AE, DISC, MC, V.

This very well-maintained establishment off Thomas Drive near the east end of the beach is right on the gulf but away from the crowds. The beachside units accommodate families in one- and two-bedroom apartments with kitchens, while across the street stand an older block of efficiencies and a new building with tropically furnished one- and two-bedroom condos (the most expensive units here). The inn sports a large heated swimming pool and a spacious sundeck with steps leading down to the beach.

FOR A FEW BUCKS MORE

Edgewater Beach Resort. 11212 Front Beach Rd. (P.O. Box 9850), Panama City Beach, FL 32407. ☎ **800/874-8686** or 850/235-4044. Fax 850/233-7599. 510 units. Summer $105– $358 condo. Off-season $57–$144 condo. Weekly rates and maid service available. DC, DISC, MC, V.

One of the Panhandle's largest condominium resorts, this sports-oriented facility enjoys a beautiful beachfront location and 110 tropically landscaped acres. Units in five gulf-side towers enjoy commanding views of the emerald gulf and gorgeous sunsets from their private balconies. A pedestrian overpass leads across Front Beach Road to low-rise apartments and town homes fringing ponds and the fairways of the resort's own nine-hole golf course. A daytime shuttle runs around the resort to three swimming pools, whirlpools, 12 tennis courts (6 lighted), and the 18-hole Hombre Golf Club a quarter mile north.

Food outlets here serve all three meals, and the Shoppes at Edgewater restaurants are across the road.

Holiday Inn SunSpree Resort. 11127 Front Beach Rd., Panama City Beach, FL 32407. ☎ **800/633-0266** or 850/234-1111. Fax 850/235-0888. 342 units. A/C TV TEL. Summer $149–$259 single or double. Off-season $59–$129 single or double. Weekly and monthly rates available. AE, DC, DISC, MC, V.

One building removed from the Edgewater Beach Resort and across the road from the Shoppes at Edgewater, this 15-story hotel is designed in an arch, with all rooms having balconies looking directly down on a foot-shaped swimming pool and wooden sundeck beside the beach. The hotel has won architectural awards for its dramatic lobby with a waterfall and the Fountain of Wishes (coins go to charity). The attractive, spacious guest rooms feature full-size ice-making refrigerators, microwave ovens, and two spacious vanity areas with their own lavatory sinks.

There's a poolside grill for lunches, while the lobby restaurant under a skylight dome features good breakfasts, lunches, and dinners at moderate prices. There's a Pizza Hut outlet for carryout pies. The lively Starlight Lounge serves drinks until late and usually offers entertainment during the peak summer season. The lobby bar has sports TVs, and there's poolside entertainment during summer evenings. Facilities include a swimming pool, sundeck, whirlpool, exercise and game rooms, gift shop, and children's playground.

Worth a Splurge for Golfers

✪ **Marriott's Bay Point Resort Village.** 4200 Marriott Dr., Panama City Beach, FL 32408. ☎ **800/874-7105** or 850/234-3307. Fax 850/233-1308. 355 units. A/C TV TEL. Summer $119–$169 single or double. Off-season $99–$129 single or double. Packages available. From Thomas Dr., take Magnolia Beach Rd. and follow the signs for 3 miles. AE, DC, DISC, MC, V.

Not only is this luxurious vacation miniworld ranked among the nation's top 25 golf and tennis resorts, it's an extraordinarily good value for Florida. Although guests pay extra for most activities, its room rates are among the top steals in the state. That's because the property is not beside the gulf; instead, it's the centerpiece of a real estate development sprawling over 1,100 landscaped acres on a peninsula bordered by St. Andrew Bay and Grand Lagoon. Situated beside the lagoon, the luxurious, vivid-coral stucco hotel is surrounded by gardens, palm trees, oaks, and magnolias. From the glamorous 3-story lobby, window walls look out to scenic water views and four swimming pools (one in its own glass-enclosed building). Furnished in dark woods, the Marriottesque rooms are spacious and luxurious.

You won't go hungry here, for the Bay View Restaurant in the hotel serves breakfast, lunch, and dinner featuring moderately price buffets. Outlets in the Lagoon Legends pro shop next door serve breakfast, snacks, and light meals at lunch. Snacks and libations also are proffered from March to October on the long pier in front of the hotel, where day-long beach parties go on during summer. Sports fans will find TVs going nonstop in the English-style bar off the lobby.

The highlights for duffers are the Lagoon Legends and the Club Meadows golf courses (see "Great Golf That Won't Break Your Budget & Other Affordable Outdoor Activities," above). The Bay Point Tennis Center has 12 clay courts (4 lighted), a tennis shop, clinics, and lessons. Water sports here are at Grand Lagoon beach, reached by the hotel's long pier, where both guests and nonguests can rent Wave Runners and boats, and go waterskiing and parasailing during the season. The *Island Queen* paddle wheeler departs the pier for sunset cruises and excursions to Shell Island. Guests can burn off the calories at two health clubs and excess money at the Bay Town Shops, which have a deli and dry cleaner. Over at the marina, the Bay Point Billfish Invitational in July is one of the world's richest. Rent a bike or scooter at the front desk to get around this widespread resort.

Great Deals on Dining

Except for fast-food joints, there aren't many national chain family restaurants in Panama City Beach (you'll find those along 15th and 23rd streets over in Panama City). There is one local chain worth a meal: the **Montego Bay Seafood Houses,** which offer a wide range of munchies, sandwiches, burgers, and seafood main courses, most in the inexpensive category. Branches are at the "curve" on Thomas Drive (☎ **850/234-8687**); at the intersection of Thomas Drive and Middle and Front Beach roads (☎ 850/236-3585); and in the Shoppes at Edgewater, Front Beach Drive at Beckrich Road (☎ 850/233-6033).

Pay attention to the restaurant hours here, for some places are closed during the winter months.

SUPER-CHEAP EATS

✪ Billy's Steamed Seafood Restaurant. 3000 Thomas Dr. (between Grand Lagoon and Magnolia Beach Rd.). ☎ **850/235-2349.** Reservations not accepted. Sandwiches $2.50–$5; seafood $6.50–$18. AE, MC, V. Summer Sun–Thurs 11am–9:30pm, Fri–Sat 11am–10pm. Off-season daily 11am–9pm. Closed Nov–Feb. SEAFOOD.

More a lively raw bar than a restaurant, Billy and Eloise Poole's casual spot is famous for serving the best crabs in town. These are hard-shell blue crabs prepared Maryland style: steamed with lots of spicy Old Bay Seasoning. Unlike the crab houses in Baltimore, however, Billy and Eloise remove the top shell, clean out the "mustard" (intestines), and cut the crabs in two for you: All you have to do is "pick" the meat. The staff will demonstrate how to do that. Other steamed morsels include shrimp (also with spicy seasoning), oysters, crabs, and lobster served with corn on the cob and garlic bread. Order anything from the briny deep here, but pass over other items. If you're in town during the off-season, check to see if the Pooles have an all-you-can-eat crab feast scheduled.

Cajun Inn. In the Shoppes at Edgewater, 477 Beckrich Rd., at Front Beach Rd. ☎ **850/235-9987.** Reservations not accepted. Main courses $8–$15; sandwiches $4–$6. AE, DC, DISC, MC, V. Daily 11am–10pm. LOUISIANA CAJUN.

Almost hidden away in the "elbow" of the Shoppes at Edgewater, next to a multiscreen cinema, this cozy, family-owned restaurant with high-backed wooden booths and Mardi Gras decor brings the Big Easy to the gulf. Offerings include jambalaya, seafood étouffée, peppered shrimp or crayfish, and Cajun-style blackened fish. Po' boys (over-stuffed hoagie sandwiches of fried oysters or fried shrimp) are a lunchtime specialty. You won't get gourmet New Orleans cuisine at these prices, but your tongue will have plenty of spice to savor. Dine inside, or outside on the shopping center walkway.

Shuckums Oyster Pub & Seafood Grill. 15614 Front Beach Rd. (at Powell Adams Dr.). ☎ **850/235-3214.** Reservations not accepted. Main courses $11–$14; burgers and sandwiches $6–$10. DISC, MC, V. Summer daily 11am–2am. Off-season Sun–Thurs 11am–9pm, Sat–Sun 11am–midnight. SEAFOOD.

"We shuck 'em, you suck 'em" is the motto of this noisy, lively, and smoky pub, which became famous when comedian Martin Short tried unsuccessfully to shuck oysters here during the making of an MTV spring-break special. The original bar is virtually papered over with dollar bills signed by old and young patrons who have been flocking here since 1967. The obvious specialty is fresh Apalachicola oysters, served raw, steamed, or baked with a variety of toppings. Otherwise, the menu consists of pub fare and mediocre seafood main courses.

FOR A FEW BUCKS MORE

Boar's Head Restaurant. 17290 Front Beach Rd. (just west of Fla. 79). ☎ **850/234-6628.** Reservations accepted. Main courses $14–$21.50. AE, DC, DISC, MC, V. Summer daily 4:30–10pm. Off-season Sun–Thurs 4:30–9pm, Fri–Sat 4:30–10pm. STEAKS/SEAFOOD.

An institution here since 1978, this shingle-roofed establishment appears from the road to be a South Seas resort. Inside, its impressive beamed ceiling, stone walls, and fireplaces create a warm, almost English tavern atmosphere suitable to the house specialties: tender, marbled prime rib of beef and perfectly cooked steaks. Beef eaters don't have the Boar's Head to themselves, however, for the coals are also used to give a charred flavor to shrimp and tuna. Other cooking styles are offered too, including a combination of lobster, shrimp, and scallops in a cream sauce over angel-hair pasta. And venison, quail, and other game find their way here during winter. An extensive wine list has won awards, and a cozy tavern to one side has live music, usually Wednesday to Saturday evenings.

✪ **Canopies.** 4423 W. Hwy. 98, Panama City (1 mile east of Hathaway Bridge on U.S. 98). ☎ **850/872-8444.** Reservations recommended. Main courses $14–$25. Early bird specials $10. AE, DISC, MC, V. Daily 5–10pm. Early bird specials daily 5–6pm. Closed Thanksgiving and Christmas. SEAFOOD/STEAKS.

This area's most elegant restaurant and purveyor of its finest cuisine occupies a 1910-vintage gray clapboard house with a magnificent view of St. Andrew Bay. Dining is on an enclosed veranda, but the dark, cozy bar in the old living room invites before- or after-dinner drinks. The menu changes every week or two, but consistent favorites are a creamy she-crab soup under a flaky croissant dome; grilled tuna, salmon, or grouper with a trio of sauces; sautéed grouper with lump crabmeat in a sherry-butter sauce; and sushi-quality yellowfin tuna in a sherry-soy sauce and served over a haystack of leeks. Landlubbers can partake of award-winning beef, veal, lamb, pork, and game dishes. White chocolate mousse is among several gourmet dessert and coffee creations to top off these delicious meals.

Capt. Anderson's Restaurant. 5551 N. Lagoon Dr. (at Thomas Dr.). ☎ **850/234-2225.** Reservations not accepted. Main courses $10–$35. AE, DC, DISC, MC, V. Mon–Sat 4–10pm (or later, depending on crowds). Closed Nov–Jan. SEAFOOD.

Overlooking Grand Lagoon, this famous restaurant attracts early diners who come to watch the fishing fleet unload the catch of the day at the busy marina. It's so popular, in fact, that you may have to wait 2 hours for a table during the peak summer months, either in the air-conditioned lounge or admiring the views from the open-air top deck. The Captain's menu is noted for grilled local fish, crabmeat-stuffed jumbo shrimp, and a heaped-high seafood platter. A Greek salad accompanies dinner. If this is your first time at Panama City Beach, don't miss the local atmosphere at Capt. Anderson's.

✪ **Hamilton's Seafood Restaurant & Lounge.** 5711 N. Lagoon Dr. (at Thomas Dr.). ☎ **850/234-1255.** Reservations not accepted. Main courses $13–$18. AE, DISC, MC, V. Sun–Thurs 4–10pm, Fri–Sat 4–11pm. Closed 1 day a week off-season (call ahead). SEAFOOD.

Proprietor Steve Stevens continues in the tradition of his noted Biloxi, Mississippi, restaurateur father. His attractive blond-wood and knotty-pine restaurant lies on Grand Lagoon. His baked oysters Hamilton appetizer—a rich combination of oysters, shrimp, and crabmeat—almost left me too full for a main course. Several other dishes are unique to Hamilton's, such as spicy snapper étouffée and a Greek-accented shrimp Cristo. Mesquite-grilled fish and steaks are also house specialties, and vegetarians can order a coal-fired vegetable kebab served over angel-hair pasta. A Lagoon Saloon makes the wait for a table go by quickly, and you can choose from an extensive selection of well-chosen California and French wines.

✪ **Marina Grill.** 6426 U.S. 98 west (at the west end of Hathaway Bridge). ☎ **850/233-0008.** Reservations not accepted. Main courses $13–$17. AE, DISC, MC, V. Sun–Thurs 11am–10pm, Fri–Sat 11am–11pm. LOUISIANA/SEAFOOD.

Ships' lanterns, knotty pine, and big windows looking to the boats moored in Hathaway Landing Marina give this spot an appropriately nautical ambience, perfect for enjoying the area's best New Orleans–style seafood and Cajun dishes. Some items, such as jambalaya pasta with shrimp and andouille sausage, will be familiar to anyone who has been to New Orleans, but other dishes are more creative. One example is the fried grouper brochette, which should be attacked only if you have a hearty appetite and a slim waistline. Doesn't sound that unusual? But wait. These morsels of grouper, green pepper, and onion are first dashed with Cajun spices, battered, and fried together, then served smothered with a rich garlic-butter sauce containing fresh diced tomatoes and green onions. Although the grouper taste gets totally lost in all this, it's an absolutely terrific concoction. Grilled and sautéed local seafood is also available. The big thatch roof of Hathaway's Landing waterside pub is next door.

SPECIAL DINING EXPERIENCES

You've got to see the **Treasure Ship,** at Treasure Island Marina, 3605 S. Thomas Dr., at Grand Lagoon (☎ **850/234-8881**), to believe it. This amazing 2 acres of ship space claims to be the world's largest land-based Spanish galleon, a replica of the three-masted sailing ships that carried loot from the New World to Spain in the 16th and 17th centuries. You can get anything from an ice-cream cone to peel-it-yourself shrimp to a sophisticated dinner in various dining rooms and eateries. The restaurants and bars open daily at 4:30pm; closed from October through December.

Lady Anderson **dinner-dance cruises** are a romantic evening escape; they're available from March through October. Boarding is at Capt. Anderson's Marina, 5550 N. Lagoon Dr. (☎ **850/234-5940**), at 6:30pm Monday to Saturday, with the cruises lasting from 7 to 10pm. Buffet dinners are featured, followed by live music for dancing. Tickets cost $32.50 for adults, $20 for children 11 and under (tips included). This triple-decker fun boat is so popular that reservations must be made well in advance.

PANAMA CITY & PANAMA CITY BEACH AFTER DARK

The Breakers, 12627 Front Beach Rd. (☎ **850/234-6060**), is the area's premier supper club, with unsurpassed gulf views and music for dining and dancing. Open daily at 4pm during summer, Monday to Saturday during the off-season. The beachfront **Harpoon Harry's Waterfront Cafe** is part of the same complex.

Romantic lounges with both live entertainment and dancing are at the **Treasure Ship,** 3605 S. Thomas Dr. (☎ **850/234-8881**), and the **Boar's Head,** 17290 Front Beach Rd. (☎ **850/234-6628**). See "Great Deals on Dining," above, for more information.

Hathaway's Landing, on U.S. 98 at the west end of the Hathaway Bridge (☎ **850/230-0409**), has one of the largest thatch pavilions in Florida, under which live entertainment takes place nightly and on Saturday and Sunday afternoons from March to September. The emphasis is on Jimmy Buffet–style music, reggae, and some country and western. Away from the beach, it draws lots of customers over 30 years old.

The 20-something crowd likes to boogie all night at beach clubs such as **Schooners,** 5121 Gulf Dr. (☎ **850/235-9074**), where every table has a gulf view; **Spinnaker's,** on the beach at 8795 Thomas Dr. (☎ **850/234-7882**); and **Club La Vella,** one of Florida's largest nightclubs (it's a bikini contest kind of place), also on the beach at 8813 Thomas Dr. (☎ **850/234-3866**). They often stay open until 4am in summer while their bands play on. **Pineapple Willie's Lounge,** beachside at 9900 S. Thomas Dr. (☎ **850/235-0928**), is open from 11am until 2am, serving very good ribs (basted with Jack Daniels whisky) and spotlighting live entertainment during summer and a host of sports TVs all year.

THE PERFORMING ARTS   The Rader family and a cast of 20 perform year-round in the ✪ **Ocean Opry Show,** 8400 Front Beach Rd., Panama City Beach (☎ **850/234-5464**), the area's answer to the Grand Ole Opry. Popcorn, hot dogs, and soft drinks are sold at the theater. There's a show every night at 8pm during the summer, less frequently off-season. Admission is $18 for adults, $9 for children ($20 to $30 when stars like Roy Clarke, George Jones, and Glen Campbell are in town). The box office opens at 9am Monday to Saturday, and reservations are recommended.

Across the Hathaway Bridge, downtown Panama City has a lively arts scene, with several galleries in its small downtown area and the **Martin Theater,** Harrison Avenue at 4th Street (☎ **850/736-8080**), a grand cinema that has been renovated and converted to host dramas and musicals staged by the Martin Ensemble (an excellent local repertory company) and performances by touring artists. Also on the downtown waterfront at the end of Harrison Avenue, the **Marina Civic Center** (☎ **850/763-4696**) hosts a variety of performances by nationally known troupes and artists throughout the year. Call for a schedule and ticket prices.

4 Apalachicola

65 miles E of Panama City, 80 miles W of Tallahassee

Sometimes called Florida's Last Frontier, Apalachicola makes a fascinating day trip from Panama City Beach or Tallahassee for many visitors, as well as a destination in its own right. The long, gorgeous beaches here are among the nation's best, and the bays and estuaries, justifiably famous for Apalachichola oysters, are great for fishing and boating. And if you love nature, the area also is rich in wildlife preserves.

The charming little town of Apalachicola (pop. 2,600) was a major seaport during autumns from 1827 to 1861, when plantations in Alabama and Georgia shipped tons of cotton down the Apalachicola River to the gulf. The town had a racetrack, an opera house, and a civic center that hosted balls, socials, and gambling. The population shrank during the mosquito-infested summer months, however, when yellow fever and malaria epidemics struck. It was during one of these outbreaks that Dr. John Gorrie of Apalachicola tried to develop a method of cooling his patients' rooms. In doing so, he invented the forerunner of the air conditioner—a device that made Florida tourism possible and life a whole lot more bearable for locals.

Apalachicola has traditionally made its living primarily from the gulf and the lagoonlike bay that lies behind a chain of offshore barrier islands. Today Apalachicola produces the bulk of Florida's oyster crop, and shrimping and fishing are major industries. The town also has been discovered by a number of urban expatriates, who have moved here, restored old homes, and opened interesting antique and gift shops. (Do you know of any other town this size where you can buy Crabtree & Evelyn products?) They'll be glad to see you.

ESSENTIALS

GETTING THERE   Apalachicola is about 65 miles east of Panama City via U.S. 98, and about 80 miles west of Tallahassee via U.S. 319 and U.S. 98. From I-10, take Exit 21 at Marianna, then follow Fla. 71 south to Port St. Joe, and U.S. 98 east to Apalachicola.

VISITOR INFORMATION   The **Apalachicola Bay Chamber of Commerce,** 99 Market St., Apalachicola, FL 32320 (☎ **850/653-9419;** fax 850/653-8219; www.homtown.com/apalachicola; e-mail: chamber1@digitalexp.com), supplies information about the area from its office on Market Street (U.S. 98) between Avenue D and

Avenue E. The chamber is open Monday to Friday from 9:30am to 4pm, Saturday from 10am to 3pm.

TIME   The town is in the **eastern time zone,** like Orlando, Miami, and Tallahassee (it's 1 hour ahead of Panama City Beach and the rest of the Panhandle). Many shops are closed on Wednesday afternoon, when Apalachicolans go fishing.

BEACHES, PARKS & WILDLIFE REFUGES

Countless terns, snowy plover, black skimmers, and other birds nest along the dunes and 9 miles of beaches (which some experts consider to be among America's best) at **J St. George Island State Park,** on the island's eastern end (☎ 850/927-2111). The wildlife can be viewed from a hiking trail and observation platform. The park has picnic areas, rest rooms, showers, a boat launch, and a campground with electric hookups. Entry to the park costs $2 for a vehicle with one occupant, $4 for vehicles with up to eight occupants, and $1 for pedestrians and bicyclists.

The beaches are even longer at ✪ **St. Joseph Peninsula State Park,** at the end of County Road 30E, about 26 miles west of Apalachicola (☎ 850/227-1327). The peninsula is populated by cottages and a few shops around Cape San Blas, but beyond the park entrance it's totally preserved. Facilities include picnic areas, a marina with a boat ramp, campgrounds with electricity, and eight remote cabins. Entry fees are $3.25 per vehicle with up to eight occupants, $1 for pedestrians and bicyclists.

Both state parks are open daily from 8am to sunset.

There are no facilities at the **St. Vincent National Wildlife Refuge** (☎ 850/653-8808), southwest of Apalachicola. This 12,358-acre barrier island has been left in its natural state by the U.S. Fish and Wildlife Service, but visitors are welcome to walk through its pine forests, marshlands, ponds, dunes, and beaches. In addition to native species like the bald eagle and alligators, the island is home to a small herd of sambar deer from Southeast Asia. Red wolves are bred here for reintroduction to other wildlife areas. Access is by boat only, usually from Indian Pass, 21 miles west of Apalachicola via U.S. 98 and County Roads 30A and 30B. The chamber of commerce (see "Essentials," above) will arrange to have a boat captain take you over, and some cruise operators go there (see "Cruises," below). The refuge headquarters, at the north end of Market Street in town, has exhibits of wetland flora and fauna. It's open Monday to Friday from 8am to 4:30pm. The rangers conduct managed hunts for deer and wild hogs from November to January.

The huge **Apalachicola National Forest** begins a few miles northeast of town. It has a host of facilities, including canoeing and mountain-bike trails. See section 5 of this chapter, on Tallahassee, for details.

AFFORDABLE OUTDOOR ACTIVITIES

CRUISES   Jeanni McMillan of ✪ **Jeanni's Journeys** (☎ 850/927-3259) takes guests on narrated nature cruises to the barrier islands and on canoe and kayak trips in the creeks and streams of the Apalachicola River basin. She also has night hikes with blue crab netting, shelling excursions, and fishing and scalloping trips, plus excursions tailored exclusively for children. Prices range from $30 to $75 per person. Reservations are required, so call her to find what she's offering when you'll be in town. Jeannie also rents canoes, kayaks, sailboats, and sailboards.

Other cruise operators to contact are **Eco Ventures** (☎ 850/653-2593), which goes out in the motorized, covered-deck *Osprey* Tuesday to Saturday from 5 to 7pm, earlier in winter; **Capt. Tom's Adventures in Paradise** (☎ 850/653-8463), offering a variety of barrier island trip and backwater canoeing; and **Captain Tony Charters**

(☎ 850/653-3560), which has sightseeing trips and excursions to St. Vincent Island. Contact them in advance for schedules and reservations.

The *Governor Stone,* an 1877-vintage Gulf Coast schooner, makes cruises on Apalachicola Bay each day during the summer months, less frequently off-season. This fine old craft has seen duty as a cargo freighter, oyster buyer, sponge boat, and U.S. Merchant Marine training vessel. It departs from the Rainbow Inn dock on Water Street, but book in advance at the Maritime Museum at 268 Water St., north of Avenue F (☎ 850/653-8700 for schedule and reservations); reservations are recommended. The cruises cost $20 for adults, $10 for children 12 and under.

FISHING Fishing is excellent in these waters, where trout, redfish, flounder, tarpon, shark, drum, and others abound. The chamber of commerce (see "Essentials," above) can help arrange charters on the local boats, many of which dock at the Rainbow Inn on Water Street. For guides, contact **Professional Guide Service** (☎ 850/670-8834) or **Boss Guide Services** (☎ 850/653-8139).

EXPLORING THE TOWN

Start your visit by picking up a map and a self-guided tour brochure from the chamber of commerce (see "Essentials," above) and then stroll around Apalachicola's waterfront, business district, and Victorian-era homes.

Along Water Street, several tin warehouses evoke the town's seafaring days of the late 1800s, as does the 1840s-era **Sponge Exchange** at Commerce Street and Avenue E. A highlight of the residential area, centered around Gorrie Square at Avenue D and 6th Street, is the Greek Revival–style **Trinity Episcopal Church,** built in New York and shipped here in 1837. At the water end of 6th Street, Battery Park has a children's playground. A number of excellent art galleries and gift shops are grouped on Market Street, Avenue D, and Commerce Street.

The showpiece at the **J John Gorrie State Museum,** Avenue D at 6th Street (☎ 850/653-9347), is a display replica of Doctor Gorrie's cooling machine, a prototype of today's air conditioner. Open Thursday to Monday from 9am to 5pm. Closed New Year's Day, Thanksgiving, and Christmas. Admission is $1, free for children 6 and under.

There's a small **Maritime Museum** at 268 Water St., north of Avenue F. It's usually open Tuesday to Saturday from 1 to 4pm. Admission is free.

It's only open Saturdays from 1 to 4pm, but the **Raney House Museum,** on Market Street, at Avenue F (no phone), shows what life was like when Apalachicola was a booming cotton port. The stately house was built in 1838, and the Apalachicola Area Historical Society has furnished it with 19th-century pieces. Admission is by $2 donation.

The **Estuarine Walk,** at the north end of Market Street on the grounds of the Apalachicola National Estuarine Research Reserve (☎ 850/653-8063), contains aquariums full of fish and turtles and displays of various other estuarine life. Open Monday to Friday from 8am to 5pm. Admission is free.

ACCOMMODATIONS YOU CAN AFFORD

Outside the state park, the dunes of St. George Island are virtually lined with beach cottages and a few condominiums. These are available on a weekly or monthly basis. Among the rental agents are **Anchor Realty & Mortgage Co.,** 212 Franklin Blvd., St. George Island, FL 32328 (☎ 800/824-0416 or 850/927-2625; www. fla-beach.com); **Gulf Coast Vacation Rentals,** 45 E. 1st St. (HCR Box 90), St. George Island, FL 32328 (☎ 800/367-1680 or 850/927-2596); and **Sun Coast**

Vacation Property Management, HCR Box 2, St. George Island, FL 32328
(☎ **800/341-2021** or 850/927-2282).

At **St. George Island State Park,** summertime camping fees are $14.84 per night
for a campsite with electricity, $12.72 without, including tax. Off-season they go for
$10.60 and $8.48, respectively. Primitive camping (take everything with you, including water) costs $3 a night per adult, $2 for children. For more information, contact
the park at 1900 E. Gulf Beach Dr., St. George Island, FL 32328 (☎ **850/ 927-2111**).

Campsites at **St. Joseph Peninsula State Park** cost $15 a night from March 1 to
October 31, $8 a night the rest of the year. Cabins rent for $70 a night during
summer, $55 a night off-season, with minimum stays of 5 nights during summer,
2 nights off-season. You can contact the park at 8899 Cape San Blas Rd., Port St. Joe,
FL 32456 (☎ **850/227-1327**).

SUPER-CHEAP SLEEPS

✪ **Gibson Inn.** 51 Ave. C, Apalachicola, FL 32320. ☎ **850/653-2191.** Fax 850/653-3521.
30 units. A/C TV TEL. $65–$80 single or double; $75–$115 suite. AE, MC, V.

Built in 1907 as a seaman's hotel and gorgeously restored in 1985, this cupola-topped
inn is such a brilliant example of Victorian architecture that it's listed on the National
Register of Historic Inns. No two guest rooms are alike (some still have the original
sinks in the sleeping area), but all are richly furnished with period reproductions.
Nonguests are welcome to wander upstairs and peek into unoccupied rooms (whose
doors are left open). Room and dining reservations are advised, especially on weekends, and rooms should be booked well in advance in summer—and as much as
5 years ahead for the seafood festival in November. Grab a drink from the bar and relax
in one of the high-back rockers on the old-fashioned veranda. The dining room serves
excellent seafood and is open to all comers, so don't expect this to be private like a
bed-and-breakfast; instead, you'll find yourself in a reborn, absolutely charming turn-
of-the-century hotel.

Rainbow Inn. 123 Water St., Apalachicola, FL 32320. ☎ **850/653-8139.** Fax 850/
653-2018. 27 units. A/C TV TEL. Summer $69–$129 double. Off-season $59–$109 double.
AE, DC, DISC, MC, V.

This 2-story motel's rough-hewn exterior timbers make it look like one of the neighboring waterfront warehouses. And there's absolutely nothing fancy here, except views
of Apalachicola Bay from the rooms. Those on the second floor have their own balconies with views. All are furnished with bright fabrics and have light paneled walls.
The most expensive unit is a suite with kitchen and Jacuzzi. Caroline's Restaurant
serves breakfast, lunch, and seafood dinners, and the Roseate Spoonbill Cocktail
Lounge, over the restaurant, is a popular local watering hole with a grand view and
music on an outdoor deck on weekends.

FOR A FEW BUCKS MORE

✪ **Coombs House Inn.** 80 6th St., Apalachicola, FL 32320. ☎ **850/653-9199.** Fax 850/
653-2785. 18 units. A/C TV TEL. $89–$129 single or double. Rates include continental breakfast. AE, MC, V.

This large house in the historic district was built in 1905 by a lumber baron, and it
shows: Polished black cypress paneling lines the entire central hallway and grand
parlor. The house had gone to seed by the early 1990s, when noted interior designer
Lynn Wilson bought it and completely restored it, furnishing it throughout with Victorian reproductions. Each of the 10 rooms in the main house is tastefully decorated;
outstanding is the Coombs Suite, with bay windows, sofa, four-poster bed, and its
own whirlpool. Less grand but still impressive are eight rooms in another restored
Victorian (the "Annex") half a block away. One of these rooms has a whirlpool tub and

bidet. One room in each house is equipped for disabled guests. A major truck route, U.S. 98 runs along the north side of both houses; request a south room to escape the periodic road noise. Guests can use the house bikes for free.

GREAT DEALS ON DINING

Townsfolk still plop down on the round stools at the marble-topped counter to order Coca-Colas and milkshakes at the **Old Time Soda Fountain & Luncheonette,** 93 Market St. (☎ 850/653-2006). This 1950s relic was once the town drugstore. It's open Monday to Saturday from 10am to 5pm.

Local sweet tooths also find satisfaction at **Delores Sweet Shoppe,** 29 Ave. E, at Commerce St. (☎ 850/653-9081), where Delores Roux's cookies, brownies, cakes, and key lime pies are famous hereabouts. She also serves sandwiches and chili for lunch. Open Monday to Friday from 9am to 5pm.

Apalachicola Seafood Grill & Steakhouse. 100 Market St. (at Ave. E/U.S. 98). ☎ **904/653-9510.** Reservations recommended in summer. Salads and sandwiches $6–$7; main courses $8–$15. AE, DISC, MC, V. Mon–Sat 11:30am–9pm. SEAFOOD/STEAKS.

With cafe curtains bedecking its storefront windows, this establishment from the outside looks like the typical small-town diner it once was, but the sophisticated restaurant offers Apalachicola-style gumbo and oyster stew; sautéed smoked oysters; meal-size salads and sandwiches; and charcoal-grilled grouper, yellowfin tuna, and salmon. The "basic meals" for $10 or less feature southern-style fried oysters, fish, scallops, and shrimp accompanied by potatoes and daily vegetable.

✪ **The Boss Oyster.** 125 Water St. ☎ **850/653-9364.** Reservations not accepted. Main courses $10–$23; sandwiches $6–$8. AE, DC, DISC, MC, V. Sun–Thurs noon–9pm, Fri–Sat 2–10pm. SEAFOOD.

You've probably heard about the aphrodisiacal properties of Apalachicola oysters. Well, this rustic, dockside eatery is a good place to see if it's true. The bivalves are served raw, steamed, or under a dozen toppings ranging from capers to crabmeat. They'll even steam three dozen of them and let you do the shucking. Steamed crabs and shrimp and fried seafood platters also are offered, as are delicious po-boy sandwiches with fried oysters or shrimp. Dine inside or at picnic tables on a screened dockside porch. Everyone in town eats here, from bankers to watermen.

✪ **Chef Eddie's Magnolia Grill.** Ave. E (U.S. 98; at 11th St.). ☎ **850/653-8000.** Reservations recommended. Main courses $12–$24. MC, V. Mon–Sat 6–10pm. Closed 2½ weeks starting weekend after Thanksgiving. SEAFOOD/SOUTHERN.

One of the top places to dine in Northwest Florida, Boston-bred owner/chef Eddie Cass's pleasant restaurant occupies a small bungalow built in the 1880s and still in possession of the original black cypress paneling in its central hallway. Eddie has turned the old living room into the dining quarters, where he offers nightly specials emphasizing fresh local seafood and New Orleans–style sauces. He received more than 2,000 orders for his spicy seafood gumbo at a recent Florida Seafood Festival, and you will long remember his snapper or mahimahi Pontchartrain, with cream and artichoke hearts. Eddie and his wife, Bettye, do not allow smoking inside the house.

5 Tallahassee

163 miles W of Jacksonville, 191 miles E of Pensacola, 250 miles NW of Orlando

Tallahassee was selected as Florida's capital in 1824 because it was halfway between St. Augustine and Pensacola, then the state's major cities. That location puts it almost in Georgia; in fact, Tallahassee has more in common with Macon than with Miami.

There's more Old South ambience here than anywhere else you're likely to visit in Florida. You'll find lovingly restored antebellum mansions, towering pine and sprawling live oak trees, richly scented magnolia blossoms, and colorful springtime azaleas. Tradition and history are important here, and you can visit many lovingly restored 19th-century homes and buildings, including the 1845 Old Capitol.

That's not to say you won't find the modern era in this extraordinarily pleasant small city, beginning with the New Capitol Building towering 22 stories over downtown. And usually sleepy Tallahassee takes on a very lively persona when the legislature is in session and when the powerful football teams of Florida State University and Florida A&M University take to the gridiron.

You'll think you're in an enormous forest, since local residents need permits to cut down trees. Majestic, moss-draped live oaks form virtual tunnels along Tallahassee's five official Canopy Roads, which are lined with historic plantations, ancient Native American settlement sites and mounds, gorgeous gardens, quiet parks with picnic areas, and beautiful lakes and streams.

Given its mild climate, state parks, federal forests, and wildlife refuges, the Tallahassee area is a popular destination for outdoor activities: boating and canoeing, golf and tennis, biking, and hiking. The nearby Apalachicola National Forest is a virtual gold mine of outdoor recreational pursuits. If you're more inclined to give your credit cards a workout, the nearby town of Havana is Florida's antiquing capital.

ESSENTIALS

GETTING THERE The **Tallahassee Regional Airport,** 10 miles southwest of downtown on Southeast Capital Circle, is served by **ASA** (☎ **800/282-3424**), **Delta** (☎ **800/221-1212**), **Gulf Stream International** (☎ **800/992-8532**), and **US Airways** (☎ **800/428-4322**).

The major car-rental agencies have booths at the airport. You can take a taxi to downtown for about $10 to $15. There was no shuttle bus service at press time.

From east and west, highway access is via I-10 and U.S. 90. From the north and south, it's U.S. 27 and U.S. 319.

The **Amtrak** transcontinental train *Sunset Limited* stops in Tallahassee at 918½ Railroad Ave. (☎ **800/USA-RAIL**).

VISITOR INFORMATION For information in advance, contact the **Tallahassee Area Convention and Visitors Bureau,** 200 W. College Ave. (P.O. Box 1369), Tallahassee, FL 32302 (☎ **800/628-2866** or 850/413-9200; fax 850/487-4621; www.co. leon.fl.us/cvb/homepage).

Your first stop in town should be the **Tallahassee Area Visitor Information Center** (same phone numbers as the bureau), in the West Plaza foyer of the New Capitol Building, just inside the Duval Street entrance. The staff here dispenses free street and public transportation maps, brochures, and pamphlets outlining tours of the historic districts and the Canopy Roads. The **Florida Welcome Center** in the same foyer has information about the entire state. Both are open Monday to Friday 8am to 5pm, weekends 9am to 3pm.

GETTING AROUND Built like an old-time streetcar, the free **Old Town Trolley** (☎ **850/891-5200**) is the best way to see the sights of historic downtown Tallahassee. You can get on or off at any point between Adams Street Commons, at the corner of Jefferson and Adams streets, and the Governor's Mansion. The trolley runs Monday to Friday every 10 minutes between 7am and 6pm.

TALTRAN provides city **bus** service from its downtown terminal at Tennessee and Adams streets (☎ **850/891-5200**). The fare is $1. Both the ticket booth there and the

Tallahassee

Tallahassee Area Visitor Information Center in the New Capitol Building have route maps and schedules for the Old Town Trolley and TALTRAN buses.

For taxi service, call **Yellow Cab** (☎ 850/580-8080) or **City Taxi** (☎ 850/ 562-4222).

TIME Tallahassee is in the **eastern time zone,** like Orlando, Miami, and Apalachicola. It's 1 hour ahead of the rest of the Panhandle.

EXPLORING THE CITY
THE CAPITOL COMPLEX

After stopping by the visitor information center on the first-floor foyer of the New Capitol, proceed to tour the rest of Florida's capitol complex, on South Monroe Street at Apalachee Parkway. It dominates the downtown area and should be the start of your sightseeing here.

The **New Capitol Building,** a $43 million skyscraper, was built in 1977 to replace the 1845-vintage Old Capitol. State legislators meet here from March to May. The chambers of the House and the Senate have public viewing galleries. For a spectacular view, take the elevators to the 22nd-floor **observatory,** where on a clear day you can see all the way to the Gulf of Mexico. The New Capitol is open Monday to Friday from 8am to 5pm (closed major holidays). **Guided tours** (☎ 850/413-9200) are scheduled on the hour, Monday to Friday from 9 to 11am and 1 to 3pm, and on Saturday, Sunday, and holidays from 9am to 3pm.

Directly in front of the skyscraper is the strikingly white **J Old Capitol** (☎ 850/ 487-1902). With its majestic dome, this "Pearl of Capitol Hill" has been restored to its original beauty. An eight-room exhibit portrays Florida's political history. Turn-of-the-century furnishings, cotton gins, and other artifacts are also of interest. The Old Capitol is open Monday to Friday from 9am to 4:30pm, Saturday from 10am to 4:30pm, and Sunday and holidays from noon to 4:30pm. Admission is free to both the old and new capitols.

Facing the Old Capitol across Monroe Street are the twin granite towers of the **Vietnam Veterans Memorial,** honoring Florida's Vietnam vets.

The Old Town Trolley will take you to the lovely Georgian-style **Governor's Mansion,** north of the capitol at Adams and Brevard streets (☎ 850/488-4661). Enhanced by a portico patterned after Andrew Jackson's columned antebellum home, the Hermitage, and surrounded by giant magnolia trees and landscaped lawns, the mansion is furnished with 18th- and 19th-century antiques and such collectibles as the hollowware from the battleship USS *Florida*. Tours are given when the legislature is in session from March to May. Call for a schedule and reservations.

Adjacent to the Governor's Mansion, **The Grove** was home to Ellen Call Long, known as "The Tallahassee Girl," the first child born after Tallahassee was settled.

HISTORIC DISTRICTS

While modern buildings have made inroads in downtown, Tallahassee makes an ongoing effort to preserve many of its historic homes and buildings. Many of them are concentrated in three historic districts within an easy walk north of the capitol complex. The information center in the New Capitol (see "Essentials," above) distributes free walking-tour brochures covering the three areas. Taken together, they're about 4 miles long and should take half a day. Most interesting is the Park Avenue District, 3 blocks north of the capitol, which you can see in about 1 hour.

Tours of Tallahassee (☎ 850/513-1230) has 2-hour walking tours around the Capitol complex and nearby historic districts Monday to Saturday at 10am, 1pm, and

3pm. These cost $6 for adults, $4 for children 5 and up. The company also has van tours of the area, which cost $20 or adults, $20 for children, free for children under 5. Call ahead for van tour schedules and reservations.

ADAMS STREET COMMONS   This 1-block winding brick and landscaped area along Adams Street begins on the north side of the capitol complex. It retains an old-fashioned town-square atmosphere. Restored buildings include the Governor's Club, a 1900s Masonic lodge, and Gallie's Hall, where Florida's first five African American college students received their Florida A&M University diplomas in 1892. Restaurants, shops, and Gallie Alley are also here. Adams Street crosses Park Avenue 3 blocks north of the capitol.

PARK AVENUE HISTORIC DISTRICT   The 7 blocks of Park Avenue between Martin Luther King Jr. Boulevard and North Meridian Street are a lovely promenade of beautiful trees, gardens, and outstanding old mansions. This broad avenue with a shady median strip lined with moss-bearded live oaks was originally named 200 Foot Street and then McCarty Street, but was renamed Park Avenue to satisfy a snobbish Anglophile society matron who didn't want an Irish name imprinted on her son's wedding invitations.

Several Park Avenue historic homes are open to the public, including the **Knott House Museum,** at Calhoun Street (see "Museums & Art Galleries," below). **The Columns,** at Duval Street, was built in the 1830s and is the city's oldest surviving building (it's home of the Tallahassee Chamber of Commerce). **The First Presbyterian Church,** at Adams Street, built in 1838, is the city's oldest church and has been an important African American historic site since slaves were welcome to worship here without their masters' consent. **The Walker Library,** between Monroe and Calhoun streets, was one of Florida's first libraries, dating from 1903 (it's home to Springtime Tallahassee, which sponsors the city's top special event). Just north of Park Avenue on Gadsden Street, the **Meginnis-Monroe House** contains the Lemoyne Art Gallery (see "Museums & Art Galleries," below).

At Martin Luther King Jr. Boulevard, the adjacent **Old City Cemetery and Episcopal Cemetery** contain the graves of Prince Achille Murat, Napoleon's nephew, and Princess Catherine Murat, his wife and George Washington's grand-niece. Also buried here are two governors and numerous Confederate and Union soldiers who died at the Battle of Natural Bridge during the Civil War. The cemeteries are important to African American history since a number of slaves and the first black Florida A&M graduates are interred here. The visitor information center in the New Capitol has a cemetery walking-tour brochure.

CALHOUN STREET HISTORIC DISTRICT   Affectionately called "Gold Dust Street" in the old days, the three blocks of Calhoun Street between Tennessee and Georgia streets, and running east on Virginia Street to Leon High School, sport elaborate homes built by prominent citizens between 1830 and 1880. A highlight here is the **Brokaw-McDougall House,** in front of Leon High School at the eastern end of Virginia Street, which was built in 1856.

MUSEUMS & ART GALLERIES

Black Archives Research Center and Museum. On the Florida A&M University campus, at Martin Luther King Jr. Blvd. and Gamble St. ☎ **850/561-2603.** Free admission. Mon–Fri 9am–4pm. Closed major holidays. Parking lot next to building.

Housed in the columned library built by Andrew Carnegie in 1908, this fascinating research center and museum displays one of the nation's most extensive collections of African American artifacts as well as such treasures as a 500-piece Ethiopian cross collection. The archives contain one of the world's largest collections on African American history. Visitors here can listen to tapes of gospel music and of elderly people reminiscing about the past. Florida Agricultural and Mechanical University (FAMU) was founded in 1887, primarily as a black institution. Today it's acclaimed for its business, engineering, and pharmacy schools.

The Florida A&M University Art Gallery. In Foster-Tanner Art Building, between Osceola and Gamble sts., off Martin Luther King Jr. Blvd. ☎ **850/599-3161.** Free admission. Mon–Sat 9am–5pm.

The focus in this gallery is on works by African American artists, with a wide variety of paintings, sculptures, and more. Exhibits change five times between September and May with local, national, and international artists in the limelight.

Florida State University Museum of Fine Arts. 250 Fine Arts Building, at Copeland and Call sts., on the FSU campus. ☎ **850/644-6836.** Free admission. Sept–Apr Mon–Fri 10am–4pm, Sat–Sun 1–4pm. May–July Mon–Fri 10am–4pm. Closed Aug.

A permanent art collection here features 16th-century Dutch paintings, 20th-century American paintings, Japanese prints, pre-Colombian artifacts, and much more. Touring exhibits are displayed every few weeks.

Knott House Museum ("The House That Rhymes"). 301 E. Park Ave. (at Calhoun St.). ☎ **850/922-2459.** Admission free (donations encouraged). Wed–Fri 1–4pm, Sat 10am–4pm.

Adorned by a columned portico, this stately 1843 mansion is furnished with Victorian elegance and boasts the nation's largest collection of 19th-century gilt-framed mirrors. The most unusual feature is the eccentric rhymes written by Mrs. Knott and attached by satin ribbons to tables, chairs, and lamps. Her poems comment upon 19th-century women's issues, plus the social, economic, and political events of the era. The house is in the Park Avenue Historic District and is listed in the National Register of Historic Places. It's preserved as it looked in 1928, when the Knott family left it and all of its contents to the city. The museum gift shop carries Victorian greeting cards, paper dolls, tin toy replicas, reprints of historic newspapers, and other nostalgic items.

Lemoyne Art Gallery. 125 N. Gadsden St. (between Park Ave. and Call St.). ☎ **850/222-8800.** Free admission except $1 during Christmas season. Tues–Sat 10am–5pm, Sun 2–5pm. Closed New Year's Day, last 2 weeks in July, Thanksgiving, Christmas Day.

This restored 1852 antebellum home is listed in the National Register of Historic Places and is a lovely setting for fine art. Known as the **Meginnis-Monroe House,** the gallery itself is named in honor of Jacques LeMoyne, a member of a French expedition to Florida in 1564. Commissioned to depict the natives' dwellings and map the sea coast, LeMoyne was the first artist known to have visited North America. Exhibits here include permanent displays by local artists, traveling exhibits, sculpture, pottery, and photography—everything from the traditional to the avant-garde. The gardens, with an old-fashioned gazebo, are spectacular during the Christmas holiday season. Programs of classical music are combined with visual arts during the year; check in advance for the current schedule.

Museum of Florida History. In the R. A. Gray Building, 500 S. Bronough St. (at Pensacola St.). ☎ **850/488-1484.** Free admission. Mon–Fri 9am–4:30pm, Sat 10am–4:30pm, Sun and holidays noon–4:30pm. Closed Thanksgiving and Christmas.

An 11-foot-tall mastodon greets you at the official state history museum, which takes you back 12,000 years to the first Native Americans to live in Florida (mastodons were very much alive back then). Ancient artifacts from Native American tribes are exhibited, plus such relics from Florida's past as 16th- and 17th-century sunken Spanish galleon treasures and a reconstructed steamboat. Inquire about guided tours and special exhibits. There's an interesting museum gift shop.

ARCHAEOLOGICAL SITES

De Soto Historical Site. 1022 de Soto Park Dr. (off Lafayette St.). ☎ **850/922-6007.** Free admission. Grounds daily 8am–5pm (mansion closed to the public).

During the winter of 1539 Spanish conquistador Hernando de Soto, his troops, and friars set up an encampment here before continuing their ill-fated search for gold. It's believed the friars celebrated the first Christmas mass in North America. An archaeologist searching for Spanish mission ruins discovered the de Soto encampment site in 1986. Rare copper coins, armor fragments, and a preserved pig's jaw have been unearthed. Former Gov. John Martin had no idea de Soto had camped here when he built his English hunting lodge mansion at the site in the 1930s. A colorful living-history time trail with exhibits and speakers is presented in January. Call for the date and program schedule.

Lake Jackson Mounds State Archaeological Site. 3600 Indian Mounds Rd. (off N. Monroe St., north of I-10). ☎ **850/922-6007.** Free admission. Daily 8am–sunset.

Artifacts discovered on this 18-acre excavation have revealed that native tribes settled on the shores of Lake Jackson (still one of the nation's best bass-fishing spots) centuries ago. A ceremonial complex flourished here around A.D. 1200, which includes six earth temple mounds and a burial mound. Part of the village and plaza area and two of the largest mounds are within the state site. The largest mound is 36 feet high with a base that measures 278 by 312 feet.

Mission San Luís. 2020 Mission Rd. (between W. Tennessee and Tharpe sts.). ☎ **850/487-3711.** Free admission. Mon–Fri 9am–4:30pm, Sat 10am–4:30pm, Sun noon–4:30pm. Closed Thanksgiving and Christmas. From downtown, take Tennessee St. (U.S. 90) west, turn right on White Dr., then right on Mission Rd. to the entrance.

A Spanish Franciscan mission named San Luís was set up in 1656 on this hilltop, already a principal village of the Apalachee Indians. From then until 1704 it served as the capital of a chain of Spanish missions in Northwest Florida. The mission complex included a tribal council house, a Franciscan church, a Spanish fort, and residential areas. Although there are no visible remains from this period, the first of two 17th-century reconstructions was completed in 1996. Interpretive displays are located across the 60-acre site and inside the visitor center. Call for information about archaeological excavations and living-history programs.

TRAVELING THE CANOPY ROADS

Graced by canopies of live oaks draped with Spanish moss, St. Augustine, Miccousukee, Meridian, Old Bainbridge, and Centerville roads are the five official Canopy Roads leading out of Tallahassee. Driving is slow on these winding, two-lane country roads (the locals only reluctantly are turning some limited sections of them into four-lane highways), some of them canopied for as much as 20 miles. Take along a picnic lunch, since there are few places to eat along these tranquil byways.

The visitor information center in the New Capitol provides a useful driving guide map of the Canopy Roads and Leon County's country lanes (see "Essentials," above).

If you have time for only one, take **Old Bainbridge Road,** which leads to the Lake Jackson Mounds State Archaeological Site in the northwest suburbs and on to Havana, Florida's antiquing capital 12 miles north of Tallahassee (see "Shopping," below).

PARKS & NATURE PRESERVES

In 1923 New York financier Alfred B. Maclay and his wife, Louise, began planting the floral wonderland of **Maclay State Gardens,** which surrounded their winter home on Lake Hall, 3540 Thomasville Rd. (U.S. 319), north of I-10 (☎ **850/487-4556**). After her husband's death in 1944, Louise Maclay continued his dream of an ornamental garden to delight the public. In 1953 the land was bequeathed to the state of Florida. The more than 300 acres of flowers feature at least 200 varieties; 28 acres are devoted exclusively to azaleas and camellias. The beautifully restored home contains a camellia information center, and the surrounding park offers nature trails, canoe rentals, boating, picnicking, swimming, and fishing. The high blooming season is January to April, with the peak about mid-March. Admission to the park is $3.25 per vehicle with up to eight passengers, $1 for pedestrians and cyclists. Admission to the gardens during the blooming season from January to April is $3 for adults, $1.50 for children 11 and under; the gardens are free from May to December. The park and gardens are open daily from 8am to sunset. The Maclay House is open from January to April only, daily from 9am to 5pm.

Beyond the house and gardens, the state park also includes Lake Overstreet, around which wind 5½ miles of hiking, biking, and horseback riding trails, making this a major venue for those outdoor activities.

SHOPPING

Antique hounds flock to the little village of ✪ **Havana,** 12 miles northwest of I-10 on U.S. 27. Havana used to make its living from shade tobacco, and when that industry went into decline in the 1960s, the town went with it. Things turned around 20 years later, however, when Havana began opening art galleries and antique, handcraft, and collectible shops. Today these are housed in lovingly restored, turn-of-the-century brick buildings along Havana's commercial streets. Just drive into town on Main Street (U.S. 27), turn left on 7th Avenue, find a parking place, and start browsing. You'll have plenty of company on weekends. After shopping, stick around and have a humongous steak at the nearby Nicholson Farmhouse (see "Great Deals on Dining," below).

Bradley's Country Store, about 8 miles north of I-10 on Centerville Road (☎ **850/893-1647**), sells more than 80,000 pounds of homemade sausage per year, both over the counter and from mail orders. You can also buy coarse-ground grits, country-milled cornmeal, hogshead cheese, liver pudding, cracklings, and specially cured hams. In the National Register of Historic Places, the friendly store is also a sightseeing attraction with self-guided tours. Open Monday to Friday from 9am to 6pm, Saturday from 9am to 5pm.

GREAT GOLF THAT WON'T BREAK YOUR BUDGET & OTHER AFFORDABLE OUTDOOR ACTIVITIES

BIKING & IN-LINE SKATING   The 16-mile **Tallahassee–St. Marks Historic Railroad State Trail** is the city's most popular bike route. Constructed with the financial assistance of wealthy Panhandle cotton-plantation owners and merchants, this was Florida's oldest railroad, functioning from 1837 to 1984. Cotton and other products were transported to St. Marks (see "Side Trips from Tallahassee," below) for shipment to other cities. In recent years the tracks were removed and 16 miles of the historic trail were improved for joggers, hikers, bicyclists, and horseback riders. A paved parking lot is at the north entrance, on Woodville Highway (Fla. 363) just south of Southeast Capital Circle.

Rental bikes and in-line skates are available at the north entrance from **About Bikes** (☎ **850/656-0001**). Bike-rental rates are $9 for 2 hours, $16 for 4 hours, $35 for 24 hours, and various rates for families and groups. Guide maps and refreshments are also on hand. The shop is open April through October, Monday to Friday from 2 to 8pm, Saturday and Sunday from 9am to 5pm. Hours from November through March are Monday to Friday from noon to 6pm, Saturday and Sunday from 9am to 5pm.

The **Apalachicola National Forest** also has extensive biking trails (see "Side Trips from Tallahassee," below), and there are 5½ miles of trails at **Maclay State Gardens** (see "Parks & Nature Preserves," above).

GOLF   Play golf at outstanding Hilaman Park, 2737 Blair Stone Rd., where the **Hilaman Park Municipal Golf Course** features 18 holes (par-72), a driving range, racquetball, squash courts, and a swimming pool. Rental equipment is at the club, and there's a restaurant, too (☎ **850/891-3935** for information and fees). Compared to most courses in Florida, greens fees are a steal: $25 on weekdays, $30 on weekends, including cart (they're just $12.36 and $17.04, respectively, if you walk). The park also includes the **Jake Gaither Municipal Golf Course,** at Bragg and Pasco streets (☎ **850/891-3942**), with a 9-hole, par-35 fairway and a pro shop. The Gaither course was recently renovated, so call for fees.

The leading golf course is at the **Killearn Country Club and Inn** (☎ **800/476-4101** or 850/893-2186), which once hosted the Sprint Classic. Moss-draped oaks enhance the beautiful 27-hole championship course, which is for members and hotel guests only (see "Accommodations You Can Afford," below).

SPECTATOR SPORTS   Tallahassee succumbs to football frenzy whenever the perennially powerful Seminoles of **Florida State University** take to the gridiron. Hollywood star Burt Reynolds, who played defensive back for the 'Noles in 1957, can easily get tickets; the rest of us should call ☎ **850/644-1830** well in advance. Even when the Seminoles play on the road, everything except Tallahassee's many sport bars comes to a stop while fans watch the games on TV.

The **Florida A&M University** Rattlers are cheered on by the school's high-stepping, world-famous Marching 100 Band. Call ☎ **850/599-3230** for FAMU schedules and tickets.

Both FSU and FAMU have seasonal basketball, baseball, tennis, and track schedules. Call the numbers above for information.

Ice-hockey fans can watch the **Tallahassee Tiger Sharks** compete in the East Coast Hockey League from October to March. Games are played in the Tallahassee–Leon County Civic Center, 505 W. Pensacola St. (☎ **800/322-3602,** or 850/222-0400 for schedules and ticket information).

ACCOMMODATIONS YOU CAN AFFORD

There is no high or low season here, but every hotel and motel for miles around is completely booked during FSU and FAMU football weekends from September to November, and again at graduation in May. Reserve well in advance or you may have to stay 60 miles or more from the city. For the schedules, call FSU or FAMU (see "Spectator Sports," above).

Except for the special weekends, rates at Tallahassee's hotels and motels are less than you'll pay at the beaches. Accordingly, the inexpensive establishments here offer much better quality accommodations than you'll find for the same price at the resort areas.

Most hotels are concentrated in three areas: downtown Tallahassee, north of downtown along North Monroe Street at Exit 29 off I-10, and along Apalachee Parkway east of downtown.

North Monroe Street at I-10 has most of the national chain motels catering to the highway traffic. On Apalachee Parkway east of the Capitol, the choices are **Best Western Pride Inn & Suites** (☎ 800/827-7390 or 850/656-6312), **Days Inn** (☎ 800/235-2525 or 850/224-2181), **La Quinta Inn** (☎ 800/531-5900 or 850/878-5099), **Motel 6** (☎ 800/466-8356 or 850/87-6171), and **Ramada Inn** (☎ 800/721-9890 or 850/877-3171).

Tax on all hotel and campground bills is 10% in Leon County.

SUPER-CHEAP SLEEPS

Cabot Lodge North. 2735 N. Monroe St., Tallahassee, FL 32303. ☎ **800/223-1964** or 850/386-8880. Fax 850/386-4254. 160 units. A/C TV TEL. $66–$78 single or double. Rates include continental breakfast and evening reception. AE, DC, DISC, MC, V.

A clapboard plantation-style house with a tin roof and a partially screened wraparound porch provides Southern country charm to distinguish this friendly motel from its nearby competitors. Guests can sit and relax in straight-back rockers on the porch or on comfy sofas and easy chairs by a fireplace in the living room. Although the guest rooms in the 2-story motel buildings out back don't hold up their end of the atmosphere factor, they're still quite satisfactory at these rates, and they give quick access to the outdoor swimming pool. Guests can graze at a continental breakfast buffet, drink coffee all day, and partake in free evening cocktails.

Riedel House Bed & Breakfast. 1412 Fairway Dr., Tallahassee, FL 32301. ☎ **850/222-8569.** 3 units, all with bathroom. A/C. $75 single or double (higher on special weekends). Rates include breakfast. No credit cards.

Surrounded by majestic live oaks, pines, magnolias, and flowers, this white-brick, Federal-style, 2-story home was built in 1937 for the Cary D. Landis family (he was a former Florida attorney general). The present owner and innkeeper is talented artist and art teacher Carolyn Riedel. A spiral staircase leads from the beautiful foyer to her art gallery and spacious guest rooms, each adorned with period furniture and antiques. Carolyn serves an extensive continental breakfast in the dining room overlooking terraced gardens. Located in the prestigious Capitol Country Club area, the Riedel House is within walking distance of public tennis courts and the club's golf course.

FOR A FEW BUCKS MORE

✪ **Courtyard by Marriott.** 1018 Apalachee Pkwy., Tallahassee, FL 32301. ☎ **800/321-2211** or 850/222-8822. Fax 850/561-0354. 154 units. A/C TV TEL. $104 single or double Sun–Thurs, $59 single or double Fri–Sat. AE, DC, DISC, MC, V.

Just a mile east of the Old Capitol, this comfortable member of the business traveler-oriented chain encloses a landscaped courtyard with a swimming pool and gazebo. About half the rooms face the courtyard; the others face parking lots. They are a bit cramped for families but ideal for singles and couples. All have sofas or easy chairs and rich mahogany writing tables and chests of drawers, plus features like two phones with modem ports, voice mail, and hand-basin faucets dispensing piping-hot water for tea and instant coffee (which are supplied). Other facilities include an exercise room and indoor spa pool. The marble-floored lobby features a lounge with fireplace and a dining area open for a breakfast buffet only. An Olive Garden, Bennigan's, and several other restaurants are within walking distance or a short drive away. The Parkway Shopping Center is also across the road.

DoubleTree Hotel. 101 S. Adams St., Tallahassee, FL 32301. ☎ **800/222-TREE** or 850/224-5000. Fax 850/513-9516. 251 units. A/C TV TEL. $79–$129 single or double; $175–$300 suite. AE, DC, DISC, MC, V.

Formerly the Holiday Inn Capitol Plaza, this 16-story hotel is one of the tallest buildings in town. Just 2 blocks from the Capitol Building at Park Avenue, it usually is booked solid during legislative sessions from March through May. Politicians and lobbyists, who love the spacious guest rooms, have power lunches at Jacob's on the Plaza, the hotel's Southern-accented restaurant. Amenities include room service, an exercise room, golf privileges, same-day laundry service, and complimentary airport transportation. There's an outdoor swimming pool, a gift shop, parking garage, and convention facilities.

✪ **Radisson Hotel.** 415 N. Monroe St. (at Virginia St.), Tallahassee, FL 32301. ☎ **800/333-3333** or 850/224-6000 (latter also is fax). 116 units. A/C TV TEL. $106 single or double; $150–$197 suite. AE, DC, DISC, MC, V.

About half a mile north of the Capitol, this 7-story establishment is Tallahassee's second most elegant hotel (behind the Governor's Inn), with an innlike lobby with reproduction antiques and cheerfully decorated guest rooms. The master suites come equipped with whirlpool baths, wet bars, concierge, and turndown services. There's a fitness facility with a sauna, and the hotel provides business services and complimentary airport transportation. The pleasant Plantation Dining Room is open daily for breakfast, lunch, and dinner.

Killearn Country Club and Inn. 100 Tyron Circle, Tallahassee, FL 32308. ☎ **800/476-4101** or 850/893-2186. Fax 850/893-8267. 39 units. A/C TV TEL. $80 single or double. Golf packages available. AE, DISC, MC, V.

Located in upscale Killearn Estates between Thomasville and Centerville roads north of I-10, this country club is home to Tallahassee's leading 18-hole golf course, which house guests can play for $30 Monday to Friday and $40 on weekends, making this one of the region's best golf-resort bargains. The rooms and suites have sitting areas and dressing rooms; some have wet bars, and some open to central living rooms (which lobbyists turn into hospitality areas to influence legislators from March to May). Each unit is individually decorated and has a balcony overlooking the woodland-bordered golf course. The club also offers 8 tennis courts, plus racquetball and handball courts. The swimming pool is Olympic size, and there's an exercise facility and miles of surrounding roads for jogging. Moderate prices prevail in the classy, beamed-ceilinged Oak View restaurant.

✪ **Quality Inn & Suites.** 2020 Apalachee Pkwy., Tallahassee, FL 32301. ☎ **800/228-5151** or 850/877-4437. Fax 850/878-9964. 100 units. A/C TV TEL. $62–$81 single or double; $67–$72 suite. Rates include continental breakfast. AE, DC, DISC, MC, V.

In contrast to most every Quality Inn I've ever seen, there's real charm here. In fact, an almost English country inn atmosphere prevails in the classy, marble-lined lobby and spacious guest rooms, which are furnished with sofas, reclining wing chairs, two doubles or a king-size bed, desks, and coffeemakers. Complimentary continental breakfasts are served in a ground-level lounge with views of the inn's swimming pool. Guests can partake in a free work-night wine bar. There's a pool on the premises, and guests receive passes to the nearby YMCA. Several fast-food and family style restaurants are within a short walk.

Worth a Splurge

✪ **Governors Inn.** 209 S. Adams St., Tallahassee, FL 32301. ☎ **800/342-7717** in Florida, or 850/681-6855. Fax 850/222-3105. 40 units. A/C TV TEL. $119–$129 single or double; $139–$219 suite. Rates include continental breakfast and evening cocktails. AE, DC, DISC, MC, V.

Just half a block from the Old Capitol, this elegant, richly furnished hotel was once a livery stable on historic Adams Commons. Part of the building's original architecture has been preserved, including the impressive beams. The guest rooms are distinctive, with four-poster beds, black-oak writing desks, rock-maple armoires, and antique accoutrements. The suites, each one named for a Florida governor, are sumptuous, some with a whirlpool bath or a loft bedroom with wood-burning fireplace. Among the amenities are comfy robes.

Complimentary continental breakfast and afternoon cocktails are presented in the pine-paneled Florida Room. Services include valet parking, nightly turndown, newspapers delivered daily to rooms, same-day laundry service, shoe shine, room service, airport transportation, and health club privileges.

GREAT DEALS ON DINING

Numerous budget-priced fast-food and family chain restaurants lie along Apalachee Parkway and North Monroe Street.

SUPER-CHEAP EATS

✪ **Bahn Thai.** 1319 S. Monroe St. (near Oakland Ave.). ☎ 850/224-4765. Reservations accepted. Main courses $5.75–$15. Lunch buffet $5.25. DISC, MC, V. Mon–Thurs 11am–2:30pm and 5–10pm, Fri 11am–2:30pm and 5–10:30pm, Sat 5–10:30pm. THAI/CANTONESE.

Lamoi (Sue) Snyder and progeny have been serving the spicy cuisine of her native Thailand at this storefront since 1979. In deference to local Southerners, who may never have sampled anything spicier than cheese grits, much of her menu is devoted to mild Cantonese-style Chinese dishes. More adventurous diners flock here to order such authentic tongue-burners as yon voon-sen, a combination of shrimp, chicken, bean threads, onions, lemongrass, ground peanuts, and the obligatory chili peppers. Sue's specialty, however, is her deliciously sweet, ginger-hinted version of Penang curry. You can ask her to turn down the heat in her other Thai dishes. Come at lunch and sample it all from the all-you-can-eat buffet, a real bargain.

Barnacle Bill's Seafood Restaurant. 1830 N. Monroe St. (north of Tharpe St.). ☎ 850/385-8734. Reservations not accepted. Main courses $8–$17 (most $9); sandwiches and salads $5–$8. AE, MC, V. Daily 11am–11pm. SEAFOOD.

There's always plenty of action at this noisy, very casual spot, with sports TVs over an enormous tile-topped raw bar in the middle of the room. Freshly shucked Apalachicola oysters are the feature at the bar, but the menu offers a mélange of seafood to please the palates of the singles, couples, and families who flock here. The cooking is simple (often done by FSU students working part-time jobs), but the ingredients are the freshest available. The young staff is accomplished at charcoal-grilling mahimahi, tuna, amberjack, and grouper. Skillet dishes combine shrimp, oysters, or scallops with vegetables and kielbasa sausage, but order one only if you like the strong smoked flavor of kielbasa. For a smoked sensation you definitely will enjoy, try the mahimahi and amberjack cured on the premises. Carbohydrate lovers can order a half pound of their favorite seafood served with Alfredo or scampi sauce over linguine. During summer, guests can sit at outdoor tables under a lean-to tent. Bands play in the Half Shell Lounge every weekend.

Food Glorious Food. 1950 Thomasville Rd., at Bradford Rd. in the Betton Place Shops. ☎ 850/224-9974. Reservations not required. Most items $6.25–$12.50. AE, DISC, MC, V. Mon–Sat 11am–8pm. AMERICAN/INTERNATIONAL.

Very unusual and very healthy sandwiches, salads, and pastas make this deli/cafe the talk of the town. Items displayed in a cold case change daily and could include such treats as Mexican lasagna, a tasty dish of layered baked polenta with piquantly spiced chicken, tomato-chili sauce, and a topping of Monterey Jack cheese. There's always gazpacho, salad, a daily quiche, and plenty of tempting pastries and cookies. You can get it to go or dine at a few tables inside or, in good weather, on the outside courtyard.

Mom and Dad's Italian Restaurant. 4175 Apalachee Pkwy. (2 miles east of Capital Circle). ☎ **850/877-4518.** Reservations not accepted. Main courses $7.50–$16. AE, DC, DISC, MC, V. Tues–Thurs 5–10pm, Fri–Sat 5–11pm. ITALIAN.

Diane Violante and Gary McLean have been making their own pastas and baking Italian breads at this popular, aroma-filled trattoria since 1963. Diane is a native of Abruzzo, Italy, so her specialty is "spaghetti à la Bruzzi"—a casserole of vermicelli, sautéed mushrooms, and tomato meat sauce topped with mozzarella and Parmesan cheeses. Diane, Gary, and their son, Gene, ensure that all plates are piled high, making the drive out here well worth the time.

FOR A FEW BUCKS MORE

Anthony's. 1950 Thomasville Rd., at Bradford Rd. in the Betton Place Shops. ☎ **850/ 224-1447.** Reservations recommended. Main courses $11–$15. AE, MC, V. Mon–Sat 5:30– 10pm, Sun 5:30–9pm. ITALIAN.

Locals come to see and be seen at Dick Anthony's elegantly relaxed trattoria. Among his specialties are pesce Venezia, spinach fettuccine tossed in a cream sauce with scallops, crabmeat, and fish. Chicken piccata and chicken San Marino are also favorites, and Dick's thick, juicy steaks are always popular with beef eaters. A wall-size wine cupboard features choices from Italy and the United States by the bottle or glass. Espresso pie leads the dessert menu.

✪ **Chez Pierre.** 1215 Thomasville Rd. (at 6th Ave.) ☎ **850/222-0936.** Reservations recommended. Lunch $5.50–$11; main courses $12–$22. AE, DC, MC, V. Mon–Sat 11am– 2:30pm and 5:30–10pm. FRENCH.

You become an instant Francophile in Florida at this chic restaurant in a beautifully restored 1920s brick home a few blocks north of the intersection of North Monroe Street and Thomasville Road. French-born chef Eric Favier and his American wife and partner Karen Cooley offer traditional French cuisine either inside the house—the walls are adorned with changing works by local artists—or outside on a large deck nearly shaded by live oaks draped with Spanish moss. Eric offers daily specials to take advantage of fresh produce, but his constant winners are chicken crepes, a version of provincial ratatouille, half a roasted chicken with a different sauce each day, Bretagne-style fresh mussels, and crab cakes with a luscious mustard sauce. French table wines are moderately priced, and California house wines are also served. Live music accompanies dining Thursday to Saturday nights, and you can take a horse-drawn carriage ride Friday and Saturday evenings. No smoking except on the front porch, where stogies and brandy can be enjoyed while lounging in wicker chairs. Book as early as possible for Bastille Day (July 14), which sees a humongous party here.

Silver Slipper. 531 Scotty's Lane (1 block south of the Tallahassee Mall behind Scotty's Hardware). ☎ **850/386-9366.** Reservations recommended. Main courses $11–$29. AE, DC, DISC, MC, V. Mon–Sat 5–11pm. STEAK/SEAFOOD.

The oldest family-operated restaurant in Florida, the Silver Slipper has served thick, tender, juicy Black Angus steaks to every president from Kennedy to Bush (they got a Christmas card from Clinton). From the award-winning menu you can also select seafood dishes, lamb, and veal. Although steaks and tender prime rib draw the crowds, a dozen bacon-wrapped big shrimp or bits of Black Angus beef are the culinary stars here. Featuring live entertainment on Tuesday to Saturday, the cocktail lounge is a favorite haunt of politicians and lobbyists. It's open until midnight on Monday to Thursday, until 2am on Friday and Saturday. Private, curtained booths are available in the dining room.

The Wharf. 4141 Apalachee Pkwy. (2 miles east of Capital Circle). ☎ **850/656-2332.** Reservations not accepted. Main courses $9–$24 (most $11–$16). AE, DC, DISC, MC, V. Sun–Thurs 4–9pm, Fri–Sat 4–10pm. SEAFOOD.

With or without children, local residents drive out in droves to this rough-hewn establishment evoking the ambience of an Old Florida fishing camp. The basic fried, broiled, or blackened dinners here are in the old-time tradition too, with flounder or the day's fresh catch served with their heads off but their bones left very much intact. Accompanied by a salad or coleslaw, potatoes or cheese grits, these filling main courses are a bargain at $9. If you don't feel up to dissecting your catch, you can choose shrimp or scallops for a few dollars more. The menu also offers shrimp Creole, seafood au gratin, and a selection of seafood pastas. Several dining rooms—most divided by skinny aquariums built into the walls—make The Wharf seem smaller and more intimate than a 400-seat restaurant. Sweet tooths are satisfied by homemade desserts such as an anything-but-ordinary bread pudding. There's also a kid's menu here. Mom and Dad's Italian Restaurant (see above) is next door and is a bit easier to see from Apalachee Parkway.

NEARBY DINING

✪ **Nicholson Farmhouse.** Fla. 12, 3½ miles west of Havana. ☎ **850/539-5931.** Reservations recommended. Main courses $10–$25. AE, DISC, MC, V. Tues–Sat 4–10pm. STEAKS.

This quaint cottage was built in 1828 by Dr. Malcolm Nicholson and is now on the National Register of Historic Places. Longing for a place where he could order a 32-ounce steak, the doctor's great-great-grandson, Paul Nicholson, turned the old house into a restaurant in 1988. His casual, very informal operation has been so successful that he has added two turn-of-the-century farmhouses and made extra dining space of the smokehouse and other outbuildings. At least an inch thick and aged on the premises, Paul's tender steaks are charcoal-grilled to perfection. Grilled chicken breasts, boneless pork chops, shrimp, and fish are also offered. Each table gets a bowl of boiled peanuts as munchies. There's a children's menu. Nonalcoholic beverages are served, and you may bring your own wine or spirits. Guests can take mule-drawn wagon rides around the farm Thursday to Saturday. This is the most popular weekend dining spot in the area, so make reservations well in advance for FSU football and graduation weekends.

TALLAHASSEE AFTER DARK

Check the "Limelight" section of Friday's *Tallahassee Democrat* for what's playing.

As a college town, Tallahassee has numerous pubs and nightclubs with live dance music, not to mention a multitude of sports bars. A good place to pick up copies of the *Break* and other entertainment tabloids with news about what's going on is **Barnacle Bill's Seafood Emporium,** which is also one of several restaurants featuring entertainment. Others include **Chez Pierre** and the **Silver Slipper** (see "Great Deals on Dining," above).

For laughs, Dooley's Down Under pub becomes the **Comedy Zone,** a weekend comedy club in the Ramada Inn, 2900 N. Monroe St., at I-10 (☎ **850/386-1027**). Call for schedule and reservations.

The major performing-arts venue is the **Tallahassee–Leon County Civic Center,** 505 W. Pensacola St. (☎ **800/322-3602** or 850/222-0400), which features a

Broadway series, concerts, and sporting events including FSU collegiate basketball and Tiger Sharks pro hockey. Special concerts are presented by the **Tallahassee Symphony Orchestra** at FSU Ruby Diamond Auditorium, College Avenue and Copeland Street (☎ 850/224-0462). The **FSU Mainstage/School of Theatre,** Fine Arts Building, Call and Copeland streets (☎ 850/644-6500), presents excellent productions from classic dramas to comedies.

SIDE TRIPS FROM TALLAHASSEE

The following excursions generally are on the way to Apalachicola, so if you're headed that way, plan to make a detour or two.

WAKULLA SPRINGS

The world's largest and deepest freshwater spring is 15 miles south of Tallahassee in the 2,860-acre ✪ **Edward Ball Wakulla Springs State Park** (☎ 850/922-3632). Edward Ball, a financier who administered the DuPont estate, turned the springs into a preservation area. Divers have mapped an underwater cave system extending more than 6,000 feet back from the spring's mouth. Wakulla has been known to dispense an amazing 14,325 gallons of water per second at certain times. Mastodon bones, including those of Herman, now in Tallahassee's Museum of Florida History, were found in the caves. The 1930s Tarzan movies starring Johnny Weissmuller were filmed here.

A free orientation movie is offered at the park's theater. You can hike or bike along the nature trails, and swimming is allowed, but only in designated areas. It's important to observe swimming rules since alligators are present. Glass-bottom-boat sight-seeing and wildlife-observation tours are offered daily: from 9:45am to 5pm during daylight saving time, 9:15am to 4:30pm the rest of the year. They cost $4.50 for adults, half price for children.

Entrance fees to the park are $3.25 per vehicle with up to eight passengers, $1 for pedestrians and bicyclists. The park is open daily from 8am to dusk.

The park entrance is just east of the junction of Fla. 61 and Fla. 267.

Accommodations You Can Afford

Wakulla Springs Lodge. 550 Wakulla Springs Dr., Wakulla Springs, FL 32305. ☎ **850/224-5950.** Fax 850/561-7251. 28 units. A/C TV TEL. $65–$90 single or double; from $250 suite. MC, V.

On the grounds of Edward Ball Wakulla Springs State Park, the lodge is distinctive for its magnificent Spanish architecture and ornate old-world furnishings, such as rare Spanish tiles, black-granite tables, marble floors, and ceiling beams painted with Florida scenes by a German artist (supposedly Kaiser Wilhelm's court painter). The high-ceilinged guest rooms are simple by today's standards but are beautifully furnished and have marble bathrooms.

You don't have to be a lodge guest to dine in the lovely Ball Room, enhanced by an immense fireplace and arched windows looking onto the springs. Very reasonably priced meals feature Southern cuisine. The coffee shop provides snacks and light meals (there's a 60-foot-long marble drugstore-style counter for old-fashioned ice-cream sodas).

THE ST. MARKS AREA

Rich history lives in the area around the little village of **St. Marks,** 18 miles south of the capital at the end of both Fla. 363 and the Tallahassee–St. Marks Historic Railroad State Trail (see "Great Golf That Won't Break Your Budget & Other Affordable Outdoor Activities," above).

After marching overland from Tampa Bay in 1528, the Spanish conquistador Panfilo de Narvaez and 300 men arrived at this strategic point at the confluence of the St. Marks and Wakulla rivers near the Gulf of Mexico. Since their only avenue back to Spain was by sea, they built and launched the first ships made by Europeans in the New World. Some 11 years later, Hernando de Soto and his 600 men arrived here after following Narvaez's route from Tampa. They marked the harbor entrance by hanging banners in the trees, then moved inland. Two wooden forts were built here, one in 1679 and one in 1718, and a stone version was begun in 1739. The fort shifted among Spanish, British, and Native American hands until Gen. Andrew Jackson took it away from the Spanish in 1819.

Parts of the old Spanish bastion wall and Confederate earthworks built during the Civil War are in the **San Marcos de Apalache State Historic Site,** reached by turning right at the end of Fla. 363 in St. Marks and following the paved road. A museum built on the foundation of the old marine hospital holds exhibits and artifacts covering the area's history. The site is open Thursday to Monday from 9am to 5pm; closed New Year's Day, Thanksgiving, and Christmas. Admission to the site is free; admission to the museum costs $1, free for children 6 and under. For more information, contact the site at P.O. Box 27, St. Marks, FL 32355 (☎ 850/925-6216).

De Soto's men marked the harbor entrance in what is now the **St. Marks Lighthouse and National Wildlife Refuge,** P.O. Box 68, St. Marks, FL 32355 (☎ 850/925-6121). Operated by the U.S. Fish and Wildlife Service, this 65,000-acre preserve occupies much of the coast from the Aucilla River east of St. Marks to the Ochlockonee River west of Panacea, and is home to more species of birds than anyplace else in Florida except the Everglades. The visitor center is off U.S. 98 about 2 miles east of St. Marks (turn south at Newport on Lighthouse Road/County Road 59). Stop there for self-guided-tour maps of the roads and hiking trails through the preserve. Built of limestone blocks 4 feet thick at the base, the 80-foot-tall St. Marks Lighthouse has marked the harbor entrance since 1842. The nearby beach is a popular crabbing spot.

Admission to the refuge is $4 per vehicle. The refuge is open daily from sunrise to sunset; the visitor center, Monday to Friday from 8am to 4:15pm, and Saturday and Sunday from 10am to 5pm (closed all federal holidays). Contact the refuge for information about seasonal tours and hunting.

In 1865, during the final weeks of the Civil War, Federal troops landed at the lighthouse and launched a surprise attack on Tallahassee. The Confederates quickly assembled an impromptu army of wounded soldiers, old men, and boys as young as 14. This ragtag bunch fought the Federal regulars for 5 days at what is now the **Natural Bridge State Historic Site.** Surprisingly, the old men and boys won. As a result, Tallahassee remained the only Confederate state capital east of the Mississippi never to fall into Yankee hands. The historic site is on County Road 2192, 6 miles east of Woodville on the St. Marks River, halfway between Tallahassee and St. Marks. Follow the signs from Fla. 363 and go to the end of the pavement. It's open daily from 8am to sunset and admission is free. For more information, contact the San Marcos de Apalache State Historic Site (see above).

APALACHICOLA NATIONAL FOREST

The largest of Florida's three national forests, this huge preserve encompasses 600,000 acres stretching from Tallahassee's outskirts southward to the Gulf Coast and westward some 70 miles to the Apalachicola River. Included are a variety of woodlands, rivers, streams, lakes, and caves populated by a host of wildlife. There are picnic facilities with sheltered tables and grills, canoe and mountain-bike trails, campgrounds with tent and

RV sites, and a number of other facilities, some of them especially designed for the physically disabled.

The **Leon Sinks Area** is closest to Tallahassee, 5½ miles south of Southeast Capital Circle on U.S. 319 near the Leon-Wakulla County line. Nature trails and boardwalks lead from one sinkhole (a lake formed when water erodes the underlying limestone) to another. The trails are open daily from 8am to 8pm.

A necessary stop before heading into this wilderness is the **Wakulla Area Ranger Station,** Rte. 6, Box 7860, Crawfordville, FL 32327 (☎ **850/926-3561**), which provides information about the forest and its facilities and sells topographical and canoe trail maps. The station is on U.S. 319 about 20 miles south of Tallahassee and 5 miles north of Crawfordville. It's open Monday to Thursday from 8am to 5pm and Friday from 8am to 4pm.

14 Northeast Florida

by Bill Goodwin

Known as the "First Coast," Northeast Florida traces its history from 1513, when Juan Ponce de León happened upon these sandy shores. In 1565 the Spanish established a colony at St. Augustine, making it the country's oldest permanent settlement. (No, it wasn't Jamestown in 1607 or the Pilgrims at Plymouth Rock in 1620.)

Those early colonists would feel right at home in present-day St. Augustine, where the streets of the restored Old City look like they did in Spanish times. For us modern mortals, St. Augustine offers a rich look back to when the settlers struggled to establish a life in a new and unfamiliar world.

But they surely would be astonished at what they'd see elsewhere in Northeast Florida.

Their eyes would pop open with disbelief at Cape Canaveral, to the south, where rockets blast off at the Kennedy Space Center. In nearby Cocoa Beach, they would see another peculiarly modern curiosity: surfers. In Daytona Beach, they'd be stunned by the deafening roar of the stock cars and motorbikes that make this beach town the "World Center of Racing."

Heading north along the coast, they would marvel at sprawling Jacksonville, Florida's largest metropolis and a thriving exemplar of what we call the New South. And up on the Georgia border, they would cross a bridge to Amelia Island, where exclusive resorts take full advantage of 13 miles of beautiful beaches. Amelia's Victorian-era town, Fernandina Beach, would seem modern to them; to us, it's a quaint and historic retreat.

1 Cocoa Beach, Cape Canaveral & the Kennedy Space Center

46 miles SE of Orlando, 186 miles N of Miami, 65 miles S of Daytona

Known as "The Space Coast" after its most famous occupant, the NASA space program, the area around Cape Canaveral was once a sleepy place where city dwellers escaped the crowds from the exploding urban centers of Miami and Jacksonville. Now, the region has grown to accommodate its own crowds, especially hordes of tourists who come to visit the Kennedy Space Center and enjoy 72 miles of beaches, plus fishing, surfing, golfing, and tennis.

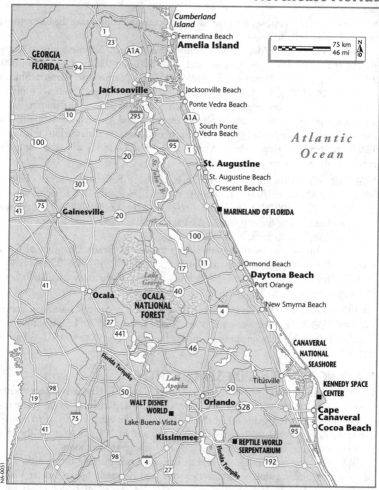

I Dream of Jeannie fans will recognize this as the home of television's most famous astronaut, Maj. Anthony Nelson, who lived with his bottle-dwelling Jeannie in Cocoa Beach.

Thanks to NASA, this also is a prime destination for nature lovers. The space agency originally took over much more land than it has needed to launch its rockets. Rather than sell off the unused portions, it turned them over to the Cape Canaveral National Seashore and the Merritt Island National Wildlife Refuge, which have preserved them in their pristine natural states.

ESSENTIALS

GETTING THERE   Most people who visit the space center stay in nearby Cocoa Beach; dozens of beachfront hotels and restaurants make it a convenient home base. If you're driving from north or south, take I-95 to Fla. 520 east (the Merritt Island Causeway). You'll cross the Indian River and Banana River before hitting Fla. A1A, the north-south artery running along the Atlantic Ocean and connecting the beach towns from Sebastian Inlet to Port Canaveral.

The nearest airport is **Melbourne International Airport,** 22 miles south of Cocoa Beach, which is served by **Continental** (☎ 800/525-0280), **Delta** (☎ 800/221-1212), and **US Airways** (☎ 800/428-4322). **Melbourne Airport Shuttle** (☎ 407/724-1600) takes passengers to the Cocoa Beach hotels, about a 45-minute ride, for $20 for the first person, $10 for each additional person. The shuttle desk is located in the baggage claim area. **Orlando International Airport,** about 35 miles to the southwest, is a larger hub with more flight options (see "Orientation" in chapter 12). From there, the **Cocoa Beach Shuttle** (☎ 407/784-3831) will take you to the beach for about $20 per person.

VISITOR INFORMATION   For information about the area, contact the **Florida Space Coast Office of Tourism,** 8810 Astronaut Blvd., Suite 102, Cape Canaveral, FL 32920 (☎ 800/872-1969 or 407/868-1126; fax 407/868-1193; www.space-coast.com). The office is on Fla. A1A at Central Boulevard and is open Monday to Friday from 8am to 5pm.

You can also get specific information from the **Cocoa Beach Chamber of Commerce,** 400 Fortenberry Rd., Merritt Island, FL 32952 (☎ 407/459-2200; fax 407/459-2232). The chamber is between Plumosa Street and Merritt Square Mall. Open Monday to Friday from 9am to 5pm.

GETTING AROUND   A car is essential in this area. The **Space Coast Area Transit** (☎ 407/633-1878) does operate buses, but routes tend to be circuitous and therefore extremely time-consuming. The fare for riders aged 18 to 60 is $1. All others pay 50¢.

TOURING THE KENNEDY SPACE CENTER

Nearly 60 million people have visited NASA's ✪ **John F. Kennedy Space Center** since it opened to the public in 1963. Whether you're a space buff or not, you're sure to appreciate the sheer grandeur of the facilities and the achievement of technology displayed here. Astronauts departed Earth at this site in 1969 en route to the most famous "small step" in history: humankind's first voyage to the moon.

All visitors who want to see more than the two roads running through the space center are required to stop at the privately operated **Kennedy Space Center Visitor Center,** on NASA Parkway half a mile west of Fla. 3 (☎ 407/452-2121; www.ksvisitor.com). You can get here from Titusville on the mainland via the NASA Parkway Causeway (Fla. 405), or from Cape Canaveral and Cocoa Beach via Fla. 3. All other space center roads are closed to the public. From Orlando, take the Bee Line Expressway (Fla. 528) east, and where the road divides, go left on Fla. 407, make a right on Fla. 405, and follow the signs. Parking is free.

The center is open from 9am to dusk every day except Christmas and some launch days, but arrive early and pick up a schedule of events and a map to help plan your day. The offerings can be confusing, but a knowledgeable and helpful staff is on duty to answer questions and give advice. You'll need at least a full day to see and do everything.

The best way to get an overview of the area, and the only way to see actual working facilities, is by taking a **bus tour.** Two main tours are offered; each departs the visitor center every 15 minutes starting at 9:45am, with the last tour leaving late in the afternoon (call for details). The tours will take at least 2 hours, depending on how interested you are in hanging out at the stops along the way. Buses run continuously, so you can reboard as you wish.

The best of the two is the **Kennedy Space Center Tour,** which visits facilities now in use, including the Complex 39 Space Shuttle launch pads and the massive Vehicle Assembly Building where shuttles are prepared for launch. The tour includes the impressive Apollo/Saturn V Center, a $37 million, 100,000-square-foot exhibit that includes the most powerful rocket ever launched by the United States, the 363-foot-tall Saturn V. Videos, artifacts, photos, and interactive exhibits bring the history of the Apollo program to life.

The **Cape Canaveral Tour** is more historical and stops at the Cape Canaveral Air Station, where America's first satellites and astronauts were launched into space. Other stops include the launch pads currently used for unmanned launches, the original site of Mission Control, and the Air Force Space Museum.

For the same price as the longer tours, you can take the **Saturn Express Tour.** This scenic 15-minute drive to the new Apollo/Saturn V Center (described above) is a worthwhile abbreviated trip if you are short of time or have no patience for lengthy bus tours.

Back at the visitor center, rockets, interactive exhibits, and IMAX movies will both inform you and keep you entertained. Not-to-be-missed, the 3-D IMAX movie **L-5: First City in Space** depicts future life among the stars. Two other IMAX films are also shown on the 5½-story-high screens every day: the 37-minute **Dream Is Alive,** giving an insider's view of the Space Shuttle program with in-flight footage shot by astronauts on various missions; and **Destiny in Space,** a Leonard Nimoy–narrated odyssey of the universe with exterior shots of shuttle flights.

Several dining venues in the visitor center will keep you fed and refreshed during your day here.

Admission to the visitor center is free, but tickets for the **bus tours** cost $10 for adults, $7 for children 3 to 11, free for children 2 and under. The regular **IMAX films** cost $6 for adults, $4 for children 3 to 11, free for children under 3. The 3-D IMAX movie costs $7 for adults and $5 for children. If you have a full day here, a **Mission Pass** is a better deal. It includes a bus tour and any two IMAX movies. These cost $23 for adults, $16 for kids 3 to 11, free for children under 3.

If you'd like to **see a launch,** call ☎ 407/867-4636 for a schedule of upcoming take-offs and ☎ 407/452-2121 for ticket information. At press time, tickets cost $10 to see the launch, $15 for the launch and an IMAX movie, and you were required to buy them in person at the visitors center up to 5 days before a launch. They were sold on a first-come, first-served basis.

OTHER ASTRONAUT ATTRACTIONS

An homage to our space voyagers, the **Astronaut Hall of Fame,** 6225 Vectorspace Blvd. (at the mainland end of NASA Causeway/Fla. 405), Titusville (☎ **407/ 269-6100**), has artifacts from the space program. You'll also find several interactive exhibits, such as a flight simulator and a G Force Trainer that subjects you to four times the pull of gravity. A full-size replica of a space shuttle holds a theater with a multimedia presentation. Admission is $13.95 for adults, $9.95 for children 6 to 12, free for kids under 6. Open daily from 9am to 5pm.

The **Astronaut Memorial Planetarium and Observatory,** 1519 Clearlake Rd., Cocoa (☎ **407/634-3732**), south of Fla. 528, has its own International Hall of Space Explorers, but its big attractions are sound and light shows in the planetarium. The building is open Tuesday, Friday, and Saturday from 6:30 to 9pm on a regular basis, but call for the show schedule. Admission to the building is free; shows cost $4 for adults, $3 for seniors and students, and $2 for kids 12 and under.

BEACHES & WILDLIFE REFUGES

To the north of the Kennedy Space Center, ✪ **Canaveral National Seashore** is a protected 13-mile stretch of barrier island beach backed by cabbage palms, sea grapes, palmettos, marshes, and Mosquito Lagoon. This is a great area for watching herons, egrets, ibis, willets, sanderlings, turnstones, terns, and other birds; and giant sea turtles nest here from May to August. You might also glimpse dolphins and manatees in Mosquito Lagoon. Canoeists can paddle along a marked trail through the marshes of Shipyard Island, and you can go backcountry camping here from November through April (permits required).

The southern access gate and ranger station is east of Titusville on Fla. 402, just east of Fla. 3. A paved road leads from there to undeveloped ✪ **Playalinda Beach,** one of Florida's most beautiful. Nude sunbathing has long been a tradition here (at least for those willing to walk a few miles to the more deserted areas), though it's now officially illegal. The main visitor center is at Apollo Beach, at the north end of the island, accessible via Fla. A1A south from New Smyrna Beach. Admission fees are $5 per motor vehicle, $1 for pedestrians or bicyclists. For more information, contact the seashore at 308 Julia St., Titusville, FL 32796 (☎ **407/267-1110**).

Its neighbor to the south and west is the 140,000-acre **Merritt Island National Wildlife Refuge,** home to hundreds of species of shorebirds, waterfowl, reptiles, alligators, and mammals, many of them endangered. Stop and pick up a map and other information at the visitors center, on Fla. 402 about 4 miles east of Titusville (it's on the way to Playalinda Beach). You can see some of nature's creatures from the 6-mile-long Black Point Wildlife Drive, or you can hike one of three nature trails through the hammocks and marshes. The visitors center is open Monday to Friday from 8:30am to 4:30pm, Saturday and Sunday from 9am to 5pm (closed Sunday from May through October). Admission is free. For more information, contact the refuge at P.O. Box 6504, Titusville, FL 32782 (☎ **407/861-0667**).

Other beach areas here include **Port Canaveral Beach,** which boasts bike paths, campsites, wide beaches, parks, and dozens of shops and restaurants.

The beach at ✪ **Cocoa Beach Pier,** on Meade Avenue east of Fla. A1A (☎ **407/783-7549**), is also a popular spot, especially for surfers. Appearing rustic and slapped-together, the pier was built in 1962 and shortly thereafter became the East Coast's surfing capital. It has 842 feet of fishing, shopping, and food and drinks overlooking a wide, sandy beach (see "Great Deals on Dining," below).

GREAT GOLF THAT WON'T BREAK YOUR BUDGET & OTHER AFFORDABLE OUTDOOR ACTIVITIES

CRUISES **Port Canaveral** is where a handful of the major Caribbean-bound cruise ships depart, including the *Disney Magic* and *Disney Wonder.* You can go on day trips under sail with **Tradewinds Sail Charters,** at the Port Canaveral Seaport (☎ **888/635-1895** or 407/635-1898; fax 407/456-5770; www.yourlink.net/tradewinds). Many cruises are offered, from a 2-hour port excursion ($35 per person) to weekend getaways to Daytona Beach ($275 per person) to a week's cruise to The Bahamas ($500 per person).

ECOTOURS Call **Funday Discovery Tours** (☎ **407/725-0796**) to arrange back-country kayaking, airboat rides, horseback tours, and bird-watching expeditions. Prices range from $39 to $69 for adults, $19 to $49 for children 6 to 12.

FISHING Whether you choose freshwater, shore, or deep-sea fishing, Brevard County has endless opportunities to cast a line. **Mosquito Lagoon** and **Eddy Creek** to the north are where you'll find trout and redfish. The **Indian River** and **Banana River** also yield trout and redfish as well as snook, ladyfish, and black drum. Bass fishers enjoy a region in the west called **Farm 13/Stick Marsh** with more than 20,000 acres of freshwater angling. Head to Port Canaveral for offshore catches like snapper and grouper. Many beachside accommodations arrange fishing charters and the port is lined with charter boats. For private outings, call **Dominics Guide Service** (☎ **800/BASS-909** or 407/242-892), one of the oldest licensed guides in the area.

You can go deep-sea fishing on the *Miss Cape Canaveral,* an 85-foot party boat docked at 670 Glen Cheek Dr., on the south dock in Port Canaveral (☎ **407/783-5274,** or 407/648-2211 in Orlando). The day-long voyages leave daily at 8am and cost $55 per person, including breakfast, lunch, unlimited beer and soft drinks, gear, bait, and license.

GOLF You can read about Northeast Florida's best courses in the free *Golfer's Guide,* available at the tourist information offices and in many hotel lobbies. See "The Active Vacation Planner," in chapter 2, for information about ordering copies.

In Cocoa Beach, the municipal **Cocoa Beach Country Club,** 500 Tom Warringer Blvd. (☎ **407/868-3351**), has 27 holes of championship golf and 10 lighted tennis courts set on acres of natural woodland, rivers, and lakes. Greens fees are about $38 in winter, dropping to about $32 in summer, including cart.

On Merritt Island south of the Kennedy Space Center, **The Savannahs at Sykes Creek,** 3915 Savannahs Trial (☎ **407/455-1377**), has 18 holes over 6,636 yards bordered by hardwood forests, lakes, and savannas inhabited by a host of wildlife. You'll have to hit over a lake to reach the seventh hole. Fees with cart are $35 in winter, less in summer.

The best nearby course is the Gary Player-designed **Baytree National Golf Club,** 8010 N. Wickham Rd., half a mile east of I-95 in Melbourne (☎ **407/259-9060**). Challenging marshy holes are flanked by towering palms. This par-72 course has 7,043 yards with a unique red-shale waste area. Fees are $85 in winter, dropping to about $50 in summer, including cart.

In Melbourne Beach, the expanded executive course at **Spessard Holland Golf Club,** 2374 Oak St. (☎ **407/952-4530**), lies between the Atlantic and the bays, making it one of the area's most scenic. The par-67 course covers 5,130 yards, with six holes of no more than 191 yards presenting opportunities for holes-in-one. Winter fees here are $32 with cart, less in summer.

SURFING   Rip through some totally awesome waves at the **Cocoa Beach Pier** area or down south at the **Sebastian Inlet.** Get outfitted at Ron Jon Surf Shop (see "Shopping" below). Or, call **Cocoa Beach Surfing School,** 301 N. Atlantic Ave., at Desperados Restaurant (☎ **407/452-0854**). They offer equipment and lessons for beginners or pros at area beaches. Bring a towel, flip-flops, and sunscreen, and a lot of nerve.

SPECTATOR SPORTS   The Boys of Spring here take the form of Miami's **Florida Marlins,** who play their spring training baseball games from mid-February through March at the Space Coast Stadium, 5800 Stadium Pkwy., off I-95 Exit 73 in Melbourne (☎ **407/633-9200**). Tickets range from $5 to $12.

SHOPPING

If you haven't already been lured by the hundreds of billboards along the highway beckoning you to the 24-hour surf shop, once you drive through Cocoa Beach, you'll definitely notice the glaringly original building that houses the **Ron Jon Surf Shop,** at 4151 N. Atlantic Ave. (☎ **407/799-8888**), set beside Fla. A1A a block from the beach. It's a Hollywood version of art deco gone wild with tropical colors, lights, and towering sand sculptures of famous sports heroes. Inside you'll find souvenirs of every description and everything you need to make you look like a surfer. The shop also rents beach bikes, boogie boards, surfboards, scuba diving gear, and in-line skates by the hour, day, or week, and they give scuba lessons. They even have a cafe (more like a fast-food burger joint).

The **Merritt Square Mall,** at 777 E. Merritt Island Causeway, has more than 100 stores including Florida's own department store, Burdine's, and many specialty shops as well as a 12-screen movie theater.

Bargain hunters can dig through the wares of hundreds of merchants at **Frontenac Flea Market,** open Friday through Sunday from 8am until 4pm. It's located at 5605 U.S. 1 midway between Cocoa and Titusville.

ACCOMMODATIONS YOU CAN AFFORD

If you want to combine your space center visit with some beaching, your best bet is to locate in Cocoa Beach, about a half-hour drive south.

The area has a plethora of rental condominiums and cottages. **King Rentals,** 320 N. Atlantic Ave., Cocoa Beach, FL 32930 (☎ **888/295-0934** or 407/784-5046; www.kingrentals.com), has a wide selection in its inventory.

Given the proximity of Orlando and the generally warm weather all year, there is little if any seasonal fluctuation in room rates here.

You'll pay a 4% hotel tax on top of the Florida sales tax here.

SUPER-CHEAP SLEEPS

Comfort Inn & Suite Resort. 3901 N. Atlantic Ave. (Fla. A1A, at Brevard Lane), Cocoa Beach, FL 32931. ☎ **800/247-2221** or 407/783-2221. Fax 407/783-0461. 144 units. A/C TV TEL. $55–$87 single or double; $61–$135 suite. AE, DC, DISC, MC, V.

Half a block from the beach and a block from the congestion around Ron Jon Surf Shop (see "Shopping," above), this resort was born in the 1960s as a 1-story motel enclosing a courtyard, which today sports a pool, whirlpool, bar with snacks, and volleyball and shuffleboard courts. Long since updated, the older rooms are medium size and have doors opening to the courtyard and to the surrounding parking lots. Those in the south wing have cathedral ceilings which lend an almost cottagelike ambience. Newer one-bedroom suites are in their own midrise building at the beach end of the courtyard. The resort has a lounge but no restaurant (fast-food outlets sit across Atlantic Avenue).

Econo Lodge. 1275 N. Atlantic Ave. (Fla. A1A, at Holiday Lane), Cocoa Beach, FL 32931. ☎ **800/553-2666** or 407/783-2252. Fax 407/783-4485. 128 units. A/C TV TEL. $39–$75 single or double. AE, DC, DISC, MC, V. Pets accepted.

Across the avenue from the Holiday Inn Cocoa Beach (see below), this Econo Lodge is more charming than most members of this budget-priced chain. About half of its spacious rooms face a tropical courtyard with an L-shaped swimming pool whose bottom displays the names of the seven original astronauts. A poolside tiki hut serves libation and other refreshments, and there's a Chinese restaurant on the premises. Some units have kitchenettes.

Holiday Inn Cocoa Beach. 1300 N. Atlantic Ave. (Fla. A1A, at Holiday Lane), Cocoa Beach, FL 32931. ☎ **800/226-6587** or 407/783-2271. Fax 407/783-8878. 515 units. A/C TV TEL. $69–$99 single or double. AE, DC, DISC, MC, V.

Set on 30 beachside acres, this sprawling complex offers a wide variety of hotel rooms, efficiencies, and cottagelike villas in several buildings flanking a central courtyard with tropical foliage and eight tennis courts. A large heated pool sits to one side, and guests can use sports equipment at the beach. Dining outlets include Willard's Restaurant, specializing in buffets, and the Oceanside Cafe by the beach. There's a volleyball court, whirlpool, concierge desk, beauty salon, coin-op laundry, and gift shop. A convention center draws groups here.

FOR A FEW BUCKS MORE

Cocoa Beach Hilton. 1550 N. Atlantic Ave., Cocoa Beach, FL 32931. ☎ **800/526-2609** or 407/799-0003. Fax 407/799-0344. 298 units. A/C TV TEL. Winter $129–$149 single or double; from $300 suite. Off-season $119–$129 single or double; from $200 suite. AE, DC, DISC, MC, V. Free parking.

True, there isn't much competition, but a recent upgrading has made this Hilton more upscale than the other chains represented here. No doubt you will run into a crew of name-tagged conventioneers, since it's especially popular with large groups. Rooms are a decent size, most have at least some view of the ocean, and all have coffeemakers, irons and ironing boards, and hair dryers. The best part is that you're right on the beach and can rent water and sports equipment. Other diversions include a game room, weight room, and a modestly sized outdoor heated pool surrounded by a sundeck. An ocean-side restaurant and bar serves food and drinks, and room service is available until 10pm. Laundry, dry cleaning, and complimentary weekday newspaper delivery are convenient extras.

Radisson Resort at the Port. 8701 Astronaut Blvd. (Fla. A1A, at Central Blvd.), Cape Canaveral, FL 32920. ☎ **800/333-3333** or 407/784-0000. Fax 407/784-3737. 200 units. A/C TV TEL. $119 single or double. AE, DC, DISC, MC, V. Free parking.

Although it's not on the beach, this resort complex is the closest major hotel to Port Canaveral, making it a handy base if you're visiting the space center or waiting to board one of the cruise ships based here. If you don't feel like driving a mile to the beach, relax at the lushly landscaped deck area where there's an outdoor heated pool (with a waterfall cascading over fake rocks) and a separate kids' pool. A large health club, whirlpool, and night-lit tennis courts are also on the premises. The hotel caters to a business crowd, which means lots of convenient services and facilities such as room service, laundry and dry cleaning, baby-sitting, express checkout, courtesy van to Port Canaveral, a conference desk, car-rental desk, and beauty salon.

GREAT DEALS ON DINING

On the **Cocoa Beach Pier,** at the beach end of Meade Avenue, the view down the coast overwhelms the seafood offerings at **The Pier House Restaurant** (☎ 407/783-7549), a favorite haunt of astronauts on break (open daily from 5 to 10pm). So is the adjacent **Marlins Good Times Bar & Grill** (same phone), where inexpensive pub fare is offered daily from 11am until the last patron crawls home. Even if you don't dine on the pier, the outdoor, tin-roofed **Mai Tiki Bar** is a fine place to have a drink while watching the surfers or a sunset.

Cocoa Beach has more fast-food chains than you could ask for along Fla. A1A and Fla. 520, a profusion of bars serving bar snacks, Chinese restaurants, and barbecue joints. The best dining choices here, however, are on Cocoa Beach about 3 miles south of the Fla. 520 causeway.

SUPER-CHEAP EATS

Rusty's Seafood & Oyster Bar. 2 S. Atlantic Ave. (Fla. A1A, at Minuteman Causeway Rd.), Cocoa Beach. ☎ **407/783-2401.** Reservations not accepted. Sandwiches and salads $3–$8; main courses $5–$15. AE, DC, DISC, MC, V. Daily 11am–2am. SEAFOOD/PUB FARE.

Adjacent to and part of Bernard's Surf (see below), this lively sports bar with indoor and outdoor seating offers inexpensive chow ranging from very spicy seafood gumbo to a pot of seafood that will give two normal persons their fill of steamed oysters, clams, shrimp, crab legs, potatoes, and corn on the cob. Daily happy hours from 3 to 6pm see oysters (raw or steamed) and spicy Buffalo wings go for 25¢ each.

FOR A FEW BUCKS MORE

Bernard's Surf. 2 South Atlantic Ave. (at Minuteman Causeway Rd.), Cocoa Beach. ☎ **407/783-2401.** Main courses $15–$25; early bird specials (4–6:30pm) $8–$11. AE, DC, DISC, MC, V. Mon–Sat 11am–11pm, Sun 5–10pm. SEAFOOD/STEAKS.

This Florida institution has been serving standard steak and seafood fare in a large and elegant setting since 1948. Photos on the wall testify to the claim that many astronauts come here to celebrate their landings. House specials like the filet mignon served with sautéed mushrooms and béarnaise sauce are your best bets. Grilled swordfish and other fish are always good choices, too. A warm loaf of fresh bread is irresistible served with roasted whole garlic.

WORTH A SPLURGE

✪ **The Mango Tree.** 118 N. Atlantic Ave. (Fla. A1A, between N. 1st and N. 2nd sts.), Cocoa Beach. ☎ **407/799-0513.** Reservations recommended. Main courses $13–$29. AE, MC, V. Tues–Sun 6–9pm. CONTINENTAL.

Gourmet seafood, pastas, and chicken are served in a plantation-home atmosphere with elegant furnishings in this stucco house, now the finest dining venue here. A waterfall splashing into a Japanese koi pond provides a pleasing backdrop out in the lush tropical gardens. The chef does his daily spin on fresh tuna fillets, but you can chose from roast Long Island duckling, tournedos with peppercorn mushroom sauce, and other excellent offerings drawing their inspiration from the continent.

THE SPACE COAST AFTER DARK

For a rundown of current performances and exhibits, call the **Brevard Cultural Alliance's Arts Line** (☎ 407/690-6819). For live music, walk out on the **Cocoa Beach Pier,** on Meade Avenue at the beach, where **Marlins Good Times Bar & Grill** (☎ 407/783-7549) has bands on weekends, more often during the winter season, and the al fresco **Mai Tiki Bar** is a great place to hang out over a cold beer.

2 Daytona Beach

54 miles NE of Orlando, 251 miles N of Miami, 78 miles S of Jacksonville

Daytona Beach is a town with many personalities. It is at once the "World's Most Famous Beach," the "World Center of Racing," and a mecca for spring breakers. It has been a destination for racing enthusiasts since the days when cars were called "horseless carriages" and raced on the hard-packed sand beach. One thing is for sure: Daytonans still love their cars. Recent debate over the environmental impact of unrestricted driving on the beach caused an uproar from citizens who couldn't imagine it any other way. As it worked out, they can still drive on the sand, but not in areas where sea turtles are nesting.

Today, hundreds of thousands of race enthusiasts come to the home of the National Association for Stock Car Auto Racing (NASCAR) for the Daytona 500, the Pepsi 400, and other races throughout the year. The Speedway is home to Daytona USA, a state-of-the-art motor-sports entertainment attraction worth a visit even by nonracing fans.

Daytona Beach Shores even provides a drive-in church where a dedicated following flocks to hear Sunday morning sermons from speakers hooked to their car windows.

But you don't have to be a car aficionado to enjoy Daytona. It has 23 miles of sandy beach, an active nightlife, surprisingly good museums, and good shopping options. Be sure to check the "Florida Calendar of Events," in chapter 2, to know when the town belongs to college students during spring break, hundreds of thousands of leather-clad motorcycle buffs during Bike Week, or racing enthusiasts for big competitions. Don't bother trying to find a hotel room, drive the highways, or enjoy a peaceful vacation at those times. You won't be able to.

ESSENTIALS

GETTING THERE   If you're driving from north or south, take I-95 and head east on International Speedway Boulevard (U.S. 92). From Tampa or Orlando, take I-4 east and follow the Daytona Beach signs to I-95 north to U.S. 92. From northwestern Florida, take I-10 east to I-95 south to U.S. 92.

Continental (☎ 800/525-0280) and **Delta** (☎ 800/221-1212) fly into **Daytona Beach International Airport,** 4 miles inland from the beach near the speedway.

All major car-rental agencies operate from airport. But why not rent a Harley? This is Daytona, after all. Call **American Road Collection** (☎ 888-RENT-HD3 or 904/238-1999). Rates start at about $100 a day, twice that amount during biker events.

Call **Yellow Cab Co.** (☎ 904/255-5555). The ride from the airport to most beach hotels runs between $10 and $15.

Daytona-Orlando Transit Service (DOTS) (☎ 800/231-1965 or 904/257-5411) provides van transportation to or from Orlando International Airport. The fare is $26 for adults one way, $46 round-trip; children 11 and under are charged half. The service brings passengers to the company's terminal at 1598 N. Nova Rd., at 11th Street (LPGA Boulevard) or, for an additional fee, to beach hotels.

VISITOR INFORMATION The **Daytona Beach Area Convention & Visitors Bureau,** 126 E. Orange Ave. (P.O. Box 910), Daytona Beach, FL 32115 (☎ **800/ 854-1234** or 904/255-0415; fax 904/255-5478; www.daytonabeach-tourism.com), can help you with information on attractions, accommodations, dining, and events. The office is on the mainland just west of the Memorial Bridge. The information area of the lobby is open daily from 9am to 7pm; office hours are Monday to Friday from 9am to 5pm. The bureau also maintains a branch at Daytona USA, 1801 W. International Speedway Blvd.

GETTING AROUND Although it's primarily a driver's town, **VOTRAN,** Volusia County's public transit system (☎ **904/761-7700**), runs a **trolley** along Atlantic Avenue on the beach, Monday to Saturday from noon to midnight. Fares are 75¢ for adults, 35¢ for seniors and children 6 to 17, free for kids under 6 riding with an adult. Voltran also runs **buses** throughout downtown and the beaches Monday through Saturday until 7:30pm and on Sunday until 7pm.

A VISIT TO THE WORLD CENTER OF RACING

Opened in 1959 with the first Daytona 500, the 480-acre ✪ **Daytona International Speedway complex,** at 1801 W. International Speedway Blvd. (U.S. 92 at Bill France Boulevard; P.O. Box 2801), Daytona Beach, FL 32120-2801 (☎ **904/253-RACE** for tickets, or 904/254-2700 for information), is certainly the keynote of the city's fame. It presents about nine weekends of major racing events annually, featuring stock cars, sports cars, motorcycles, and go-carts, and is also used for automobile testing. Its grandstands seat more than 120,000.

Big events sell out months in advance (tickets to the Daytona 500 in February are gone as early as a year ahead of time), so get yours, and reserve your accommodations, well before your trip.

To learn more about racing, head for the **World Center of Racing Visitors' Center** at the east end of the Speedway and NASCAR office complex. Open daily from 9am to 5pm, the center is also the departure site for entertaining 25-minute guided tram tours of the facility. Admission is $5, free for children 6 and under. Tours depart daily every 30 minutes between 9:30am and 4pm, except during races and special events.

On the Speedway grounds, the phenomenally popular 50,000-square-foot ✪ **Daytona USA** (☎ **904/947-6800**) is a state-of-the-art interactive motor-sports entertainment attraction presenting the history, color, and excitement of stock-car, go-cart, and motorcycle racing in Daytona. Bring your video camera. There are lots of colorful photo-ops here. Visitors can participate in a pit stop on a NASCAR Winston Cup stock car, see the actual winning Daytona 500 car still covered in track dust, talk via video with favorite competitors, and play radio or television announcer by calling the finish of a race. The highlight of the attraction is the action-packed IMAX film that puts you in the winner's seat of a Daytona 500 race. Allow at least 3½ hours to enjoy this new theme attraction, which is open daily except Christmas from 9am to 6pm. Admission for adults is $12, seniors pay $10, children 6 to 12 pay $6, and children 5 and under are free. Discounted combination tickets are available for those who also want to take the tour of the facilities.

HITTING THE BEACH

The beach near the **Adam's Mark** and **Main Street Pier,** popular with families, is the hub of activity, with concessions, the city's famous **Boardwalk,** and a small amusement park. Couples seeking greater privacy usually prefer the northern or southern extremities of the beach. Especially peaceful is **Ponce Inlet** at the very southern tip of the island where there is precious little commerce or traffic to disturb the silence. Surfers and bikers congregate near the **Main Street** and **Sun Glow piers.**

Daytona Beach

Accommodations:
Acapulco Inn 19
Adam's Mark Daytona
  Beach Resort 2A
Beach House 20
Breakers Beach
  Oceanfront Motel 3
Capri Motel 1
Captain's Quarters
  All Suite Inn 25
Coquina Inn 11
Days Inn 16
Daytona Beach
  Hilton 18
Daytona Beach
  Hostel 5
Live Oak Inn 10
Pierside Inn 24
Pierside Motel 23
Talisman Oceanfront
  Resort Lodge 21
Tropical Manor
  Motel 17

Dining:
Anna's Italian
  Trattoria 2
Aunt Catfish's 22
The Cellar 7
The Chart House 27
Down the Hatch 27
McK's Tavern 6
Shells 4
Sophie Kay's Waterfall
  Restaurant 21

Attractions:
Daytona International
  Speedway 13
Halifax Historical
  Museum 8
Mark Martin's Klassix
  Auto Museum 14
Museum of Arts
  and Sciences 12
Ponce de León Inlet
  Lighthouse 26
Tiny Cruise Line 9

621

Cheap Thrills: What to See & Do for Free (or Almost) in Northeast Florida

- **Take a giant leap for mankind at Cape Canaveral.** You can see some of the exhibits at the visitors center of the ✪ **John F. Kennedy Space Center** in Cape Canaveral (☎ **407/452-2121**) for free, but bus tours of the complex are well worth the $10 for adults, $7 for children 3 to 11 (they're free for children 2 and under). You'll visit the facilities now in use, including the Complex 39 Space Shuttle launch pads and the massive Vehicle Assembly Building. Also on the tour are the impressive Apollo/Saturn V Center, where you can see the most powerful rocket ever launched by the United States, and the original pads where the moonwalkers were launched into space.

- **Contemplate skinny dipping at Playalinda Beach.** It isn't legal anymore, but you'll feel like stripping it all off on beautiful and deserted **Playalinda Beach,** in the Canaveral National Seashore (☎ **407/267-1110**), a protected 13-mile stretch of barrier island beach backed by cabbage palms, sea grapes, palmettos, marshes, and Mosquito Lagoon. The seashore and the adjacent **Merritt Island National Wildlife Refuge** (☎ **407/861-0667**) also are great places to see herons, egrets, ibis, and other birds, plus giant sea turtles nesting from May to August.

- **Vroom around Daytona International Speedway.** You can't really drive your own race car around Daytona Beach's world center of racing, but the next best thing is action-packed IMAX film *Daytona USA* (☎ **904/947-6800**). You'll think you're in the winner's seat of the Daytona 500. You also can participate in a pit stop on a NASCAR Winston Cup stock car, see the actual winning car still covered in track dust, talk via video with favorite competitors, and play radio or television announcer by calling the finish of a race. Compared to admissions to other Florida theme parks, Daytona USA charges a reasonable $12 for adults, $10 for seniors, and $6 for children 6 to 12. Kids 5 and under get in free.

- **Buy a radar frog at Dunn's.** Pres. Bill Clinton bought a "radar frog" when he visited **Dunn Toys & Hobbies** in Daytona Beach (☎ **904/253-3644**). These motion-sensitive toys, which "ribbit" when you walk by, are part of what is one of the country's largest selection of toys, games, art supplies, puzzles, model kits, costumes, collectibles, and other diversions for kids of all ages. The president also ate a strawberry ice-cream cone from the store's old-fashioned soda fountain/coffee shop, which offers incredibly cheap sandwiches, bagels, hot dogs, soups, salads, and pastries. The tiny storefront cafe is packed on Friday nights for its family sing-alongs, puppet shows, or theater

You can drive and park directly on the sand along most of Daytona Beach's 500-foot-wide beaches, but watch for signs warning of sea turtles nesting. There's a $5 access fee, although in some areas like Ponce Inlet, the fee is waived in winter.

If Daytona's beaches aren't enough, you can venture south. **New Smyrna Beach** has 7 miles of hard-packed white sand, a quiet historic downtown, an active arts community, and excellent accommodations. **Flagler Beach** to the north is another pristine beach for those looking for solitude and natural beauty away from the condos and hotels.

performances. The show and a simple kid-friendly dinner like pizza and dessert cost just $5 adults, $3 for kids under 12.

- **Relive the past in America's oldest city.** Older than either Jamestown or Plymouth Rock, St. Augustine's restored Spanish Quarter offers a look back to America's very beginnings. You'll have to pay a few dollars to enter sites such as the nation's oldest store and oldest jail, but you can freely stroll these narrow streets for hours, poking your head into antique shops, peering into lush yards surrounding ancient buildings, and watching the boats out on the Matanzas River. Or for $12 adults, $5 children, you an ride around town all day on a trolley, train, or horse-drawn carriage.

- **Quaff a couple of brews in Jacksonville.** It's a chilly 45°F in the fermenting vaults at Jacksonville's pungent-smelling **Anheuser-Busch Brewery** (☎ **904/751-8118),** but guided tours are free, and you get two gratis beers (or soft drinks) when you're done walking through the facility. Call ahead to see if Anheuser-Busch's famous Clydesdale horses are visiting the brewery while you're here.

- **Stroll along a lazy river.** City leaders have developed appealing, parklike commercial complexes on the banks of the broad, slow-moving St. Johns River. On the north stands **Jacksonville Landing** (☎ **904/353-1188**), a 6-acre dining/shopping/entertainment center with a small maritime museum, more than 65 shops, about half a dozen full-service restaurants, and an inexpensive food court with indoor and outdoor seating overlooking the river. The Landing is the scene of special events such as arts festivals and free outdoor rock, blues, country, and jazz concerts. On the opposite shore, you can stroll along the 1.2-mile wooden zigzag boardwalk of the Southbank Riverwalk.

- **Visit a new breed of national park.** Jacksonville's Timucuan Ecological and Historic Preserve is not your usual national park. For one thing, it's a vast, intriguing system of sites on both sides of the St. Johns River. And for another, admission is free. The prime attraction is the **Fort Carolina National Memorial** (☎ **904/641-7155**), the site of a 16th-century French Huguenot settlement wiped out by the Spanish who landed at St. Augustine. On the north side of the river, the **Zephaniah Kingsley Plantation** (☎ **904/ 251-3537**) was an early 19th-century manse owned by Zephaniah Kingsley, a white man who married a Senegalese woman he once owned and then moved his family to Haiti to escape racism at home.

GREAT GOLF THAT WON'T BREAK YOUR BUDGET & OTHER AFFORDABLE OUTDOOR ACTIVITIES

CRUISES   Take a leisurely cruise on the Halifax River aboard the 14-passenger, 25-foot *Fancy,* a replica of the old fantail launches used at the turn of the century. It's operated by **A Tiny Cruise Line River Excursions,** 425 S. Beach St., at Halifax Harbor (☎ **904/226-2343**). Captain Jim regales passengers with river lore and points out dolphins, manatees, herons, diving cormorants, pelicans, egrets, osprey, oyster beds, and other natural phenomena during the morning cruise. Cruises are $8.75 to $14 for adults, $5.50 to $7.50 for children 4 to 12, free for children 3 and under. Weather permitting, cruises depart year-round (with a brief hiatus during the holidays), Monday through Saturday at 11:30am. A 1-hour tour of riverfront homes is at 2pm and of historic downtown at 3:30pm; there are no Monday cruises in winter months. Call for reservations. Romantic sunset cruises are also available.

Water Wheels of Daytona (☎ 407/255-2400) uses one vehicle for combined land-and-river tours: It's an amphibious "duck" that crawls into the river at the Riverfront Parking Lot, International Speedway Boulevard and Beach Streets. Call for schedule and prices.

FISHING   The easiest and least-expensive way to fish offshore for marlin, sailfish, king mackerel, grouper, red snapper, and more is with the **Critter Fleet,** 4950 S. Peninsula Dr., Ponce Inlet (☎ 800/338-0850 or 904/767-7676), which operates two party boats. One goes on all-day trips ($50 adults, $30 kids under 12), while the other makes morning and afternoon voyages ($30 adults, $20 kids under 12). The fares include rod, reel, and bait.

Deep-sea charter fishing boats dock at **Sea Love Marina,** 4884 Front St., Ponce Inlet (☎ 904/767-3406).

Save the cost of a boat and fish with the locals from the **Main Street Pier,** at the ocean end of Main Street near the Adam's Mark (☎ 904/253-1212). Admission to the pier is $1 for adults, 50¢ for kids. Bait and fishing gear are available, and no license is required.

GOLF   There are more than a dozen excellent courses within 25 minutes of the beach, and most hotels can arrange starting times for you. **Golf Daytona Beach,** 126 E. Orange Ave., Daytona Beach, FL 32114 (☎ 800/881-7065 or 904/ 239-7065; fax 904/239-0064; www.golf-daytona.com), publishes an annual brochure describing the major courses. It's available at the tourist information offices (see "Essentials," above).

Daytona's best known course is the **LPGA International,** 300 Championship Dr. (☎ 904/274-5742), one of the nation's top-rated links for women golfers. Designed by Rees Jones, the 7,088-yard, 18-hole course boasts five sets of tees and a number of challenging holes. A second 18-hole course designed by Lloyd Clifton is due to be on line by 1999. Just down the street from the Ladies Professional Golf Association headquarters, this center for professional and amateur women golfers has workshops and teaching programs, and the pro shop carries a great selection of ladies' equipment and clothing. Greens fees with a cart are usually about $75, less in summer.

Another Lloyd Clifton–designed course, the centrally located 18-hole, par-72 **Indigo Lakes Golf Course,** 2620 W. International Speedway Blvd. (☎ 904/ 254-3607), has flat fairways and large bunkered Bermuda greens. Fees here are about $55 in winter, including a cart, less in summer.

The semiprivate South Course at **Pelican Bay Country Club,** 550 Sea Duck Dr. (☎ 904/788-6494), is one of the area's favorites, with fast greens to test your putting skills. With-cart fees are $40 in winter, less in summer (no walking allowed). The North Course here is for members only.

The city's prime municipal course is the **Daytona Beach Country Club,** 600 Wilder Blvd. (☎ 904/258-3119), which has 36 holes. Winter fees here are $18 to walk, $26.50 to share a cart. They drop $3 in summer.

HORSEBACK RIDING   **Shenandoah Stables,** 1759 Tomoka Farms Rd., off U.S. 92 (☎ 904/257-1444), offers daily trail rides and lessons. Call for prices and schedules.

WATER SPORTS   For jet-ski rentals, contact **Daytona High Performance–MBI**, 925 Sickler Dr., at the Seabreeze Bridge (☎ **904/257-5276**). Additional water-sports equipment, as well as bicycles, beach buggies, and mopeds, can be rented along the beach in front of major hotels. A good place to look is in front of the **Adam's Mark,** on the beach at 100 N. Atlantic Ave.

MUSEUMS

✪ **Halifax Historical Museum.** 252 S. Beach St. (just north of Orange Ave.). ☎ **904/ 255-6976.** Admission $3 adults, $1 children 11 and under; free for everyone Sat. Tues–Sat 10am–4pm.

This local history museum is housed in a former bank and is worth seeing just for the 1912 neoclassical architectural details. A mural of Old Florida wildlife graces one wall, the stained-glass ceiling reflects the sunlight, and across the room, an old gold metal teller's window still stands. Its eclectic collection includes Native American artifacts, more than 10,000 historic photographs, possessions of past residents (such as a ball gown worn at Lincoln's inauguration), and, of course, model cars.

Mark Martin's Klassix Auto Museum. 2909 W. International Speedway Blvd., at Tomoka Farms Rd., just west of I-95. ☎ **904/252-3800.** Admission $8.50 adults, $4.25 children 7–12, free for children under 7. Daily 9am–6pm.

This museum showcases Corvettes—a model from every year since 1953. Also on display are collector cars (including cars from the movie *Days of Thunder*), and historic Daytona vehicles from all motor sports. A 1950s-style soda shop and gift shop are on the premises.

Museum of Arts and Sciences. 1040 Museum Blvd. (off Nova Rd./Fla. 5A). ☎ **904/ 255-0285.** Museum $4 adults, $1 children and students with ID, free for children 5 and under; planetarium shows, $2. Tues–Fri 9am–4pm, Sat–Sun noon–5pm. Take International Speedway Blvd. west, make a left on Nova Rd. (Fla. 5A), and look for a sign on your right.

Most impressive in this eclectic collection are the Cuban works—mostly paintings acquired in 1956, when Cuban dictator Fulgencio Batista donated his private collection to the city. One highlight is a portrait of Eva ("Evita") Perón, said to be the only existing painting completed while she was alive. Other exhibits include "Masterworks of American Art," a gallery dedicated to the prehistory of Florida, and "Africa: Life and Ritual."

Ponce de León Inlet Lighthouse & Museum. 4931 S. Peninsula Dr., Ponce Inlet. ☎ **904/ 761-1821.** Admission $4 adults, $1 children 11 and under. May–Aug, daily 10am–8pm; Sept–Apr, daily 10am–4pm (last admission an hour before closing). Follow Atlantic Ave. south, make a right on Beach St., and follow the signs.

If you are in the area, this 175-foot lighthouse—the second tallest in the United States—is worth a quick stop. Built in the 1880s and restored in the 1970s, this brick-and-granite sentinel's beacon is visible for 16 nautical miles. The head lighthouse keeper's cottage now houses a museum of exhibits of maritime artifacts. The first-assistant keeper's house is furnished to reflect turn-of-the-century occupancy. A concise 12-minute video details the structure's history. Outside, you can walk around the tugboat *F. D. Russell,* now sitting high and dry in the sand.

SHOPPING

Daytona Beach's main riverside drag, Beach Street, is one of the only areas in town where people actually stroll. The street is wide and inviting, with decorative wrought-iron archways and fancy brickwork overlooking the Halifax River.

Today, between Bay Street and Orange Avenue, Beach Street offers more than a dozen antique shops, a magic shop, an excellent historical museum (see "Museums" above), several good cafes, and the world famous **Dunn Toys & Hobbies** (see box below), which has an antiques mall upstairs.

Cycle fans should stop at the **Harley Davidson Store,** 290 Beach St., at Dr. Mary McLeod Bethune Boulevard, a 20,000 square-foot retail store and new diner serving breakfast and lunch (☎ 904/253-2453). It's one of the largest dealerships in the country. In addition to hundreds of gleaming new and used Hogs, you'll find as much fringy leather as you've ever seen in one place.

The **Daytona Flea Market,** on Tomoka Farms Road at the junction of I-95 and U.S. 92, a mile west of the Speedway (☎ 904/252-1999), is huge, with 1,000 covered outdoor booths plus 100 antique vendors in an air-conditioned building. Open year-round Friday through Sunday from 8am to 5pm. Admission and parking are free.

ACCOMMODATIONS YOU CAN AFFORD

Room rates here are highest from the day after Christmas all the way to Labor Day, and many of them skyrocket during major events at the Speedway, during bikers' gatherings, and whenever college students are on break (see "Florida Calendar of Events," in chapter 2). Daytona Beach hotels fill to the bursting point during these periods, and even if you can find a room, there's often a minimum-stay requirement. Avoid these periods or be prepared to pay at least double the regular rate.

In addition to the listings below, there are dozens of hotels and motels along Atlantic Avenue, many of them family owned and operated. The Daytona Beach Area Convention & Visitors Bureau (see "Essentials," above), distributes a list of superior small lodgings. None of these properties have more than 75 rooms, and all have been inspected for cleanliness, quality, comfort, privacy, and safety.

Among the other chain motels here, one of the better options is the **Days Inn,** 1909 S. Atlantic Ave., at Flamingo Ave., in Daytona Beach (☎ 800/224-5056 or 904/255-4492), a 9-story beachfront hotel with a swimming pool/kiddie pool and a sundeck overlooking the beach. The **Ramada Inn Surfside,** 3125 S. Atlantic Ave. (☎ 800/255-3838 or 904/788-1000), also boasts a prime beachfront location. Families will appreciate its efficiency units with fully equipped eat-in kitchens and, in summer, free children's activities. Facilities include a large swimming pool, oceanfront picnic tables, and more. All rooms at these two properties have ocean views and balconies. In addition, there are three oceanfront **Howard Johnsons** from which to choose (☎ 800/446-4656).

In addition to the 6% state sales tax, Daytona levies a 4% tax on hotel bills.

AT THE BEACHES
Super-Cheap Sleeps

In addition to the accommodations listed below, you can stay at the **Daytona Beach Hostel,** 140 S. Atlantic Ave. (Fla. A1A, at International Speedway Blvd.), Daytona Beach, FL 32118 (☎ 904/258-6937; fax 904/258-6541), which has 33 rooms for singles or couples and 12 rooms with four or five dorm beds in each. The rooms cost about $25 off-season but jump to $65 to $100 during peak periods such as spring break and Race Week. Dorm beds cost from $13.35 to $16.50. This no-frills hostel draws a young European clientele.

✪ **Beach House.** 3221 S. Atlantic Ave. (at Esmerlda St., half a mile north of Dunlawton Ave.), Daytona Beach, FL 32118. ☎ **800/647-3448** or 904/788-7107. Fax 904/760-3672.

Toys to Enjoy: A "Dunn" Deal

Since 1905, the Dunns have been selling toys in downtown Daytona. Back then they owned a hardware store with a small toy department upstairs. Now this 18,000 square-foot emporium, **Dunn Toys & Hobbies,** 166 S. Beach St. (☎ **904/253-3644**), carries one of the country's largest selection of toys, games, art supplies, puzzles, model kits, costumes, collectibles, and other diversions for kids of all ages.

In fact, one of the store's most illustrious visitors was President Clinton, who stopped by during his 1996 campaign. "Yeah, it was incredible," said Wes Dunn, the store's fifth-generation Dunn owner. "I was really honored."

You can buy one of the "Radar Frogs" (a motion-sensitive toy that "ribbits" when you walk by) like the one Clinton brought back to the White House with him. The store is still adorned with photos of the historic visit. The president ate a strawberry ice-cream cone from the store's old-fashioned soda fountain/coffee shop—where, by the way, you can get incredibly cheap sandwiches, bagels, hot dogs, soups, salads, and pastries. They serve a great soup and sandwich or salad combo for $3. The homemade chicken salad, with fresh apple chunks and all white meat, is fantastic.

But, perhaps the best offerings at Dunn's are the family activities. On Friday night, the tiny storefront cafe is packed to capacity with families enjoying sing-alongs, puppet shows, or theater performances with a simple kid-friendly dinner like macaroni and cheese or pizza, and of course, dessert. The cost is minimal: $5 for adults and $3 for kids under 12. It fills up early, so call for reservations. Wednesday at 3pm is the gathering spot for moms and dads who come out with the children for free puppet performances, storytelling, and crafts.

Of course, while you're there you won't be able to help buying some souvenirs to take home, and you can browse through **Dunn's Antique Mall,** on the second floor.

The store and cafe is open Monday through Saturday from 9am until 6pm. Friday night, they're open until 8pm.

---

11 units. A/C TV TEL. $28–$59 single or double; $50–$69 ocean-view suite. Weekly rates available. AE, DISC, MC, V.

You'll know as soon as you see its nicely landscaped exterior that owners Pat and Barbara Welsh care about this place. And inside, the furnishings and appointments are excellent for a property in this price range. All accommodations have front lawns with umbrella tables overlooking the ocean, and all but two have full kitchens. There are barbecue grills and a heated swimming pool.

Breakers Beach Oceanfront Motel. 27 S. Ocean Ave. (between Harvey and Main sts.), Daytona Beach, FL 32118. ☎ **800/441-8459** or 904/252-0863. Fax 904/238-1247. 21 units. A/C TV TEL. $42–$85 single or double. Weekly and monthly rates available. AE, DC, DISC, MC, V. Free parking.

This is a friendly, just-folks kind of place, where guests (many of them repeat visitors) socialize with each other and affable owners Tom and Virginia Brown. The location is very central—right at the boardwalk and the Main Street Pier (where you can fish without a license; bait and tackle are available). The rooms aren't fancy, but they're clean and well maintained. Especially desirable are the oceanfront efficiencies with full kitchens, though all rooms have small refrigerators. Facilities include a picnic area with barbecue grills, a swimming pool, and coin-op washers and dryers.

Capri Motel. 832 N. Atlantic Ave. (between Riverview and Jessamine blvds.), Daytona Beach, FL 32118. ☎ **800/874-1820** or 904/252-2555. Fax 904/255-7378. 24 units. A/C TV TEL. $35–$75 single or double. AE, DC, DISC, MC, V. Free parking.

A large pool with a 60-foot water slide, a kiddie pool, barbecue grills, a video-game room, a coin-op laundry, and a year-round roster of planned activities for all ages make this a good choice for families, especially since all accommodations here offer full eat-in kitchens or kitchenettes.

Pierside Inn. 3703 S. Atlantic Ave. (4 blocks south of Dunlawton Ave.), Daytona Beach, FL 32127. ☎ **800/728-4650** or 904/767-4650. Fax 904/756-5532. 37 units. A/C TV TEL. $35–$85 single or double; $50–$100 suite. Weekly and monthly rates available. DISC, MC, V. Free parking.

A beachfront location adjacent to the Sunglow Pier (where bait and tackle are available) makes this a great choice if you like to fish. And its very large, homey rooms—all with fully-equipped kitchens, dining areas, patios or balconies, and cable TV (with HBO and Disney channels)—will also appeal to families. The two-bedroom suites have full living rooms and furnished wooden decks. Services here include a gratis newspaper daily, and free coffee each morning. Among the facilities are a lounge with a pool table, a nice-size swimming pool and kiddie pool, a sundeck, a shuffleboard court, a putting green, and coin-op washers and dryers.

Pierside Motel. 3710 S. Atlantic Ave. (4 blocks south of Dunlawton Ave.), Daytona Beach, FL 32127. ☎ **800/728-4650** or 904/767-4650. Fax 904/756-5532. 11 units. A/C TV TEL. $27–$37 single or double; $32–$42 efficiency; $57–$67 apt. Weekly and monthly rates available. DISC, MC, V. Free parking.

This well-run hostelry, under the same ownership as the Pierside Inn (see above), charges considerably lower rates because it's across the street from the beach rather than right on it. Fronted by a neat rock garden with a gazebo, it's rather appealing, and most of its accommodations offer full kitchens. Guests can use all the facilities across the street.

Talisman Oceanfront Resort Lodge. 3411 S. Atlantic Ave. (at Seaway Ave., just north of Dunlawton Ave.), Daytona Beach, FL 32118. ☎ **800/881-3411** or 904/761-0511. Fax 904/756-2076. 9 units, 41 efficiencies. A/C TV TEL. $40–$48 single or double; $45–$75 efficiency. Weekly and monthly rates available. AE, DISC, MC, V. Free parking.

Many of this beachfront property's accommodations offer balconies or patios and ocean views. It isn't a fancy place, but it is homey, clean, and well maintained. Owners Frank and Monica Vitale are usually on the premises. The accommodations are spacious, especially the pleasant two-room apartments with living rooms and full kitchens; all the efficiencies have kitchenettes, and even the motel rooms feature refrigerators. Facilities include a coffee shop, a video-game room, barbecue grills, and coin-op washers and dryers. The beachfront swimming pool has a large sundeck with expanses of palm-fringed lawn.

Tropical Manor Motel. 2237 S. Atlantic Ave. (at Bonner Ave.), Daytona Beach, FL. ☎ **800/253-4920** or 904/252-4920. 71 units. A/C TV TEL. Winter $33–$43 single or double; $34–$100 efficiency/suite; $95–$135 3-bedroom suite. High season $52–$63 single or double; $54–$127 efficiency/suite; $165–$237 3-bedroom suite. AE, DC, DISC, MC, V.

This Caribbean-tinted beachfront motel wins points for its unique and colorful murals, pleasant staff/owners, and meticulous upkeep. Located square in the middle of Daytona's nicest beach, these funky accommodations also offer sundecks, umbrella-covered tables, lounge areas, a large heated pool, water slide, shuffleboard court, cookout area, heated kiddie pool, and two gazebos—all surrounded by lush tropical foliage. The rooms are not large or particularly fancy, but many come with cable TV, kitchens, and ocean views. Especially good for families are the two- and three-bedroom suites.

For a Few Bucks More

✪ **Acapulco Inn.** 2505 S. Atlantic Ave. (between Dundee Rd. and Seaspray St.), Daytona Beach, FL 32118. ☎ **800/874-7420,** 800/245-3580, or 904/761-2210. Fax 904/253-9935 or 904/761-2216. 133 units. A/C TV TEL. $50–$100 single or double; $54–$124 efficiency. Monthly rates and packages available. AE, DC, DISC, MC, V.

This Mayan-themed, midrise hotel is one of five beachfront hostelries managed by Oceans Eleven Resorts (the first toll-free and fax numbers given above go to Oceans Eleven's central reservations desk) and is a great choice for families. It's especially popular with Canadian snowbirds, who return year after year for the warm hospitality, clean ocean-view rooms with balconies, and organized activities like Bingo, bridge, and mah-jongg. All of the 42 hotel rooms have small refrigerators, and 91 efficiencies have fully-equipped eat-in kitchens.

A large dining room overlooks the ocean, serving American fare at breakfast and lunch; a comfortable lounge adjoins. Facilities include a heated oceanfront swimming pool, two whirlpools, a kiddie pool, a picnic area, a coin-op laundry, and a video-game room. An on-staff PGA pro helps guests plan golf vacations and will arrange lessons and tee times.

Captain's Quarters All Suite Inn. 3711 S. Atlantic Ave. (half a mile south of Dunlawton Ave.), Daytona Beach, FL 32127. ☎ **800/332-3119** or 904/767-3119. Fax 904/767-0883. 27 units. A/C TV TEL. $85–$100 single or double; $140–$165 oceanfront penthouse suite. Lower rates available for extended stays. AE, DISC, MC, V.

A great choice down on the quiet southern part of Daytona Beach, this 5-story beachfront inn has spacious suites, all with ocean or river views and large living/dining-room areas, balconies, and fully-equipped kitchens. The country-look bedrooms have French doors that open onto balconies or patios with wooden rockers. Each is equipped with two cable TVs and VCRs (movies can be rented). The penthouse suite has a fireplace, a spa tub, and a big picture window overlooking the ocean. On-premises facilities include a heated swimming pool, a sundeck with love-seat swings and barbecue grills, and coin-op washer/dryers. The restaurant, which has an outdoor deck overlooking the ocean, is open for breakfast and lunch except on Tuesday. Newspapers are complimentary.

Worth a Splurge

Adam's Mark Daytona Beach Resort. 100 N. Atlantic Ave. (between Earl St. and Auditorium Blvd.), Daytona Beach, FL 32118. ☎ **800/872-9269** or 904/254-8200. Fax 904/253-0275. 413 units. A/C MINIBAR TV TEL. $99–$179 single or double; $159–$400 suite. AE, DC, DISC, MC, V. Valet parking $8; free self-parking in lot across the street.

This is Daytona's most central beachfront hotel—and one of its most luxurious—designed so that every room has an ocean view. Although the lobby and common areas are more elegantly detailed, guest rooms are not as spacious or well laid out as the less-expensive and quieter Hilton further south (see below). It's right at the band shell, and, in season, its beach and boardwalk concessions offer parasailing, bicycle rentals, motorized four-wheelers, surfboards, boogie boards, cabanas, and umbrellas.

The hotel's premier dining room features steak and seafood dinners. Another facility, with picture windows overlooking the beach and umbrella tables outside, serves all meals. There's also a complex of small beachfront restaurants and bars with outdoor cafe seating. The sophisticated lounge offers piano bar or other live music nightly. Amenities include concierge, room service, dry cleaning and laundry, self-service Laundromat, free newspapers in executive-level rooms, baby-sitting, secretarial services, express checkout, indoor/outdoor heated swimming pool and kiddie pool, beach, health club, two whirlpools, steam and sauna, bicycle rental, children's center, business center, conference rooms, sundeck, water-sports equipment, sand volleyball court, playground, gift shops.

○ **Daytona Beach Hilton Oceanfront Resort.** 2637 S. Atlantic Ave. (between Florida Shores Blvd. and Richard's Lane), Daytona Beach, FL 32118. ☎ **800/525-7350** or 904/767-7350. Fax 904/760-3651. 218 units. A/C TV TEL. $89–$150 river-view single or double; $124–$189 oceanfront single or double; from $250 suite. AE, DC, DISC, MC, V.

The best hotel choice here, the Hilton welcomes guests in an elegant terra-cotta–tiled lobby with comfortable seating areas, a fountain, and potted palms. The large guest rooms here are grouped in pairs and can be joined to form a suite; one of each pair has a balcony, the other does not. All have ocean and/or river views and major convenient extras like safes, coffeemakers, irons, full-size ironing boards, hair dryers, and small refrigerators. The hotel also has a small fitness room, unisex hair salon, and gift shop. Daily newspapers are complimentary. Kids appreciate the video-game room with pool table and the kiddie pool on the beautiful oceanfront sundeck where you can often see seagulls drinking from the large heated pool. A surprisingly good lobby restaurant—one of Daytona's most beautiful—serves all meals; patio dining is an option. A comfy bar/lounge with game tables adjoins; it's the setting for nightly entertainment. In summer, reggae bands play near the poolside bar.

BED-AND-BREAKFASTS ON THE MAINLAND

○ **Coquina Inn.** 544 S. Palmetto Ave. (at Cedar St.), Daytona Beach, FL 32114. ☎ **800/805-7533** or 904/254-4969. Fax 904/254-4969. 4 units. A/C TV. $80–$110 single or double ($175–$200 single or double during special events). Rates include full breakfast. AE, MC, V. Free parking.

This charming coquina and cream-stucco house was built in 1912 in the Old Daytona historic section, just south of the Beach Street business district. It sits on a tranquil shady street half a block west of the Halifax River, about a 5-minute drive to the beaches. Innkeepers Joe Witek and Craig Heidel serve breakfast on fine china in their crystal-chandeliered dining room, and complimentary tea and sherry are available in the parlor throughout the day. A sitting room outfitted in a mishmash of antiques is a tranquil spot to enjoy the fireplace and a selection of books and magazines. Each of the guest rooms is decorated differently. In the sunny Hibiscus Room, French doors lead to a private plant-filled balcony (with Jacuzzi) overlooking an ancient live oak draped with Spanish moss. It and the next-door Jasmine Room (it has a fireplace) can be combined to create a two-bedroom/two-bath suite. All rooms have cable TVs. Beach cruiser bikes are available at no charge. New in 1997 were two octagonal wooden decks, one with a large whirlpool under a Victorian gazebo, and a gift shop. There is no smoking inside, and children 11 and under are not accepted.

Live Oak Inn. 444-448 S. Beach St. (at Loomis Ave.), Daytona Beach, FL 32114. ☎ **888/881-4664** or 904/252-4667. Fax 904/239-0068. 12 units. A/C TV TEL. $80–$150 single or double. Rates include extended continental breakfast. AE, MC, V. Free parking.

Facing the river and occupying two adjoining restored 19th-century houses with a front lawn enclosed by a white picket fence, this B&B is surrounded by centuries-old live oaks. An inviting front porch with white wicker rocking chairs faces the street and a marina beyond. The guest rooms—seven with private sun porches or balconies—are delightfully decorated, with area rugs strewn on polished oak floors and wood-bladed fans whirring slowly overhead. Yours might be furnished with an Eastlake bed, or perhaps you'll get a Victorian sleigh bed with a patchwork quilt and a private plant-filled sun porch furnished with Adirondack chairs. The rooms look out on the Halifax Harbor Marina or a garden, and all are equipped with remote-control cable TVs, VCRs, and Victorian soaking tubs or Jacuzzis. Breakfast is served on an enclosed porch with lace-curtained windows. No smoking is permitted in the house, and children 9 and under are not accepted.

GREAT DEALS ON DINING

Perhaps as a concession to the spring-break crowd, Daytona Beach has a profusion of fast-food places that line the major thoroughfares, especially along International Speedway Boulevard, near the racetrack. You'll find many old and new restaurants on and around Beach Street. An old favorite is the little diner inside **Dunn's Toy Store** (see "Toys to Enjoy: A 'Dunn' Deal," above). Also check out the **Main Street Pier,** where a casual oceanfront restaurant serves burgers and chicken wings and lots of beer.

AT THE BEACHES
Super-Cheap Eats

The local branch of **Shells,** the excellent and inexpensive seafood chain, is at 200 N. Atlantic Ave., between 5th Avenue and International Speedway Boulevard (☎ **904/ 258-0007**). See "Great Deals on Dining" in the Tampa section of chapter 11 for details.

Down the Hatch. 4894 Front St., Ponce Inlet. ☎ **904/761-4831.** Reservations not accepted; call ahead for priority seating. Breakfast $2–$5; main courses $8–$15; early bird menu (served 11:30am–5pm) $5–$7. Kids' menu available. AE, MC, V. Daily 7am–10pm. Take Atlantic Ave. south, make a right on Beach St., and follow the signs. SEAFOOD.

Occupying a 50-year-old fish camp on the Halifax River, Down the Hatch serves up fresh fish and seafood (note its shrimp boat docked outside). You can start your day here with a bagel or a country-style breakfast while taking in the scenic views of boats and shorebirds through the big picture windows—you might even see dolphins frolicking. At night, arrive early to catch the sunset over the river, and also to beat the crowd at this very popular place. In summer, light fare is served outside on an awninged wooden deck. Portions are large.

For a Few Bucks More

✪ **Anna's Italian Trattoria.** 304 Seabreeze Blvd. (at Peninsula Dr.). ☎ **904/239-9624.** Reservations recommended. Main courses $9–$17. AE, DISC, MC, V. Mon–Sat 5–10pm. ITALIAN.

The Triani family lends a warm, friendly air to this simple yet comfortable trattoria. Many of the pastas are homemade, but a star here is risotto alla Anna, an Italian version of Spanish paella. Portions are hearty; main courses come with soup or salad and a side dish of angel-hair pasta or a vegetable. There's a good selection of Italian wines to complement your meal. Everything is cooked to order, so allow plenty of time. Free parking is available in a lot on Seabreeze Boulevard across Peninsula Drive.

Sophie Kay's Waterfall Restaurant. 3516 S. Atlantic Ave. (at Raymond Ave.). ☎ **904/ 756-4444.** Reservations recommended. Main courses $7–$24; early bird menu (served 4–6:30pm) $8–$10. AE, DC, DISC, MC, V. Mon–Thurs 4–10pm, Fri–Sat 4–11pm, Sun noon–10pm. (Bar serves light fare, Sun–Thurs until midnight, Fri–Sat until 1am.) CONTINENTAL.

Longtime Daytona restaurateur, cookbook author, and local television personality Sophie Kay has created a faux-tropical atmosphere with romantic details like a rock waterfall that cascades into a goldfish pond, full-size palm trees, candles, and soft piano music. Oysters Rockefeller (bubbling with cheese) or shrimp scampi make excellent starters. Sophie's chef has a great hand with pasta, and the primavera linguine in delicate white-wine sauce is perfection. Also very good is the baked seafood served en papillote in a creamy lobster béchamel sauce. Many people come here for filet mignon, roast prime rib au jus with creamy horseradish sauce, or surf-and-turf combinations. For dessert, don't pass up Sophie's delicious twice-baked cheesecake on a buttery graham-cracker crust. After dinner, adjourn to the piano bar for cocktails.

ON THE MAINLAND
Super-Cheap Eats
✪ **Aunt Catfish's.** 4009 Halifax Dr. (at the west end of the Port Orange Bridge). ☎ **904/ 767-4768.** Reservations not accepted, but call ahead for priority seating. Main courses $8–$15; early bird dinners (served noon–6:30pm) $8–$11. Sun brunch $10 adults, $6 for children 4–12, free for children 3 and under. Reduced prices for children and seniors. AE, DC, DISC, MC, V. Mon–Sat 11:30am–9:30pm, Sun 9am–2pm (brunch) and 2–9:30pm. Closed Christmas Day. SOUTHERN/SEAFOOD.

This country-cozy Southern restaurant represents one of the best values I've ever encountered. The homey setting is appealing; in daytime, ask for a window seat overlooking the Halifax River. The food is great and there's plenty of it. For one thing, all main courses include hush puppies, a chunk of watermelon, unbelievably yummy hot cinnamon rolls, a side dish, and unlimited helpings from an extensive salad bar. The Florida cracker sampler platter gives you a wide range of flavors—a spit-roasted quarter chicken with cranberry-orange relish, crab cakes served in hollandaise sauce, fried shrimp, and fried catfish fingerlings. The lightly breaded fried oysters are also yummy. There's a full bar, though you might prefer fresh-squeezed lemonade. The lavish Sunday brunch buffet will tempt you to overindulge.

The Cellar. 220 Magnolia Ave. (between Palmetto and Ridgewood aves.). ☎ **904/ 258-0011.** Reservations accepted only for large parties. Soups, salads, sandwiches $6–$7. AE, DC, DISC, MC, V. Mon–Fri 11am–3pm. AMERICAN.

An excellent place for lunch while you're touring downtown, this tea room occupies the basement of a National Historic Register Victorian home built in 1907 for Pres. Warren G. Harding. It couldn't be more charming, with low ceilings, fresh flowers on every table, and backlit stained-glass windows. In the warm months there's outdoor seating at umbrella tables on a covered garden patio. A small but varied menu includes soups, salads, sandwiches, fresh seafood, chicken, and pastas.

McK's Tavern. 218 S. Beach St. (between Magnolia St. and Ivy Lane). ☎ **904/238-3321.** Reservations not accepted. Main courses $8–$14, salads and sandwiches $4–$7. AE, MC, V. Mon–Sat 11am–3am, Sun 4pm–3am. IRISH/AMERICAN.

Especially worth knowing about because it serves food until three in the morning, this upscale Irish tavern has a highly eclectic menu. The pub fare includes vegetarian burritos and a few main courses of steaks, chicken, and "Mumzy's" meat loaf. Club sandwiches and burgers round out the large and reasonably priced selection. The food is not exceptional, but it's perfectly acceptable, especially once you've had a few Bass ales. The service is sometimes rushed, but usually pleasant.

Worth a Splurge
✪ **The Chart House.** 1100 Marina Point Dr. (off Beach St. south of business district). ☎ **904/255-9022.** Reservations recommended. Main courses $16–$25. AE, DC, DISC, MC, V. Sun–Thurs 5–9:30pm, Fri–Sat 5–10:30pm. SEAFOOD/STEAKS/PRIME RIB.

Locals head for this member of the upscale chain when they want to celebrate a special occasion. The setting is stunning—under a soaring teepee roof and with big windows looking out to water views on three sides. The menu is led by gargantuan cuts of tender prime rib, but the daily fresh catch dishes and perfectly grilled steaks also draw the locals for special-occasion dinners. Caviar stars over on the bountiful salad bar.

DAYTONA BEACH AFTER DARK

THE PERFORMING ARTS   Check the Friday edition of the Daytona Beach *News-Journal* for weekly listings of upcoming events, or call the **Peabody Auditorium,** 600 Auditorium Blvd., between Noble Street and Wild Olive Avenue (☎ **904/ 255-1314**), the city's major venue for high-brow performances.

They may look like them, but that's not Elvis Presley, Elton John, or Dolly Parton making music at **Legends in Concert,** in the Coliseum Theater, 176 N. Beach St. on the downtown waterfront (☎ **904/258-1500**). No, these are look-alikes doing very close imitations of a host of music's big names. The curtain rises on this Las Vegas–style revue Tuesday to Thursday at 8pm, Friday and Saturday at 6 and 9pm, and Sunday at 6pm, with matinees Tuesday, Wednesday, and Sunday at 2pm. Tickets are $19.95 adults, $16.95 seniors, and $9.95 for kids under 15, plus tax. Not all of the "stars" appear at once, so call to see who'll be on stage.

You might just see a real country music star at the **Daytona Opry,** 2400 Ridgewood Ave., South Daytona (☎ **904/756-6779**), whose shows usually are Monday to Saturday at 7pm, with a matinee Sunday at 2pm (but call to make sure). Tickets are $17.95 adults, $10.95 kids under 12.

Under the city auspices, the **Oceanfront Bandshell** (☎ **904/258-3169**), on the boardwalk next to the Adam's Mark Hotel, hosts a series of free big-band concerts at the band shell every Sunday night from early June to Labor Day. It's also the scene of raucous spring-break concerts.

THE CLUB & BAR SCENE   In addition to the following, the piano bar at **Sophie Kay's Waterfall Restaurant** (see "Great Deals on Dining," above) and the sophisticated **Clocktower Lounge** at the Adam's Mark (see "Accommodations You Can Afford," above) are worth a visit. Especially during biker festivities, Main Street is a happening area where dozens of bars and restaurants catering to the leather set are in full swing.

A popular beachfront bar for more than 40 years, **Ocean Deck,** 127 S. Ocean Ave., next to the Mayan Inn (☎ **904/253-5224**), is packed with a mix of locals and tourists, young and old, who come for live music and cheap drinks. Often reggae or ska bands will play after 9:30pm. Park across Ocean Avenue at the beach and surf shop, Reggae Republic (under the same ownership).

A typical spring-break party spot, **Razzles,** 611 Seabreeze Blvd., between Grandview and South Atlantic avenues (☎ **904/257-6236**), plays Top 40 tunes and high-energy music until 3am nightly. There's plenty to keep you occupied if you're not dancing—10 pool tables, a blackjack table, air hockey, electronic darts, pinball, and video games. The crowd is young—18 and up—and the scene is wild.

3 St. Augustine: America's First City

105 miles NE of Orlando, 302 miles N of Miami, 39 miles S of Jacksonville

With its 17th-century fort, horse-drawn carriages clip-clopping along narrow streets, old city gates, and reconstructed 18th-century Spanish Quarter, St. Augustine seems more like a picturesque European village than a modern American city. This is an exceptionally charming town, complete with palm-lined ocean beaches, excellent restaurants, an active nightlife, and shopping bargains—but its primary lure is historic.

This is, after all, the oldest permanent European settlement in the United States. The Spaniard Juan Ponce de León, who later undertook a Quixotic quest for the Fountain of Youth, sighted this coast in 1513, landed somewhere between present-day Jacksonville and Cape Canaveral, and named it "La Florida." Spain concentrated its efforts on Florida's west coast until 1562, when a group of French Huguenots settled near the mouth of the St. Johns River, near present-day Jacksonville. Three years later, a Spanish force under Pedro Menéndez de Avilés arrived on the scene, wiped out the Huguenot men (de Avilés spared their women and children), and established a settlement on the harbor he named "St. Augustín."

The colony survived attacks by pirates, Indians, and the British over the next 2 centuries. The Treaty of Paris ending the French and Indian War ceded the town to Britain in 1763, but the British gave it back 20 years later. The United States took control when it acquired Florida from Spain in 1821.

Notwithstanding today's tourist attraction here, Ponce de León never did find his elusive Fountain of Youth.

ESSENTIALS

GETTING THERE   St. Augustine is about equidistant (a 1-hour drive) from airports in Jacksonville and Daytona Beach.

If you're coming from north or south, take I-95 to a St. Augustine exit to U.S. 1 (Exits 92 to 95 are for St. Augustine; ask when you reserve accommodations which is closest). From Orlando and points southwest, take I-10 to I-95 south to U.S. 1.

VISITOR INFORMATION   Before you go, contact the **St. Johns County Visitors and Convention Bureau,** 88 Riberia St., Suite 250, St. Augustine, FL 32084 (☎ **800/OLD-CITY** or 904/829-1711, fax 904/829-6149; www.oldcity.com), and request the *Visitor's Guide,* detailing attractions, events, restaurants, accommodations, shopping, and more.

Your Web browser can also go to the advertiser-supported **www.staugustine.com**.

Upon arrival, stop first at the **St. Augustine Visitor Information Center,** 10 Castillo Dr., at San Marco Avenue opposite the Castillo de San Marcos National Monument (☎ **904/825-1000**). There are numerous ways to see the city, depending on your interest and time, and this is the best place to make your plans. And you can park all day in the visitor center lots for $3. You can view a free visitor information video, pick up brochures, and obtain tickets for sightseeing trains and trolleys, which include discount admissions to the attractions (see "Getting Around," below). The center is open daily from 8:30am to 7:30pm from Memorial Day to Labor Day, until 6:30pm from April to Memorial Day and the day after Labor Day to the end of October, and until 5:30pm from November to March. It and most area attractions are closed on Christmas.

In the historic district, there's a small **information kiosk** on St. George St. at Cathedral Place. It's open daily from 9am to 5pm except Christmas.

Over on St. Augustine Beach, there's a walk-in visitors information center at the **St. Johns County Fishing Pier,** 350 A1A Beach Blvd., St. Augustine Beach, FL 32084 (☎ **904/471-1596**). It's open daily from 8:30am to 5pm.

GETTING AROUND   There are a number of **parking lots** in the historic district, though they're sometimes crowded and difficult to find. Your best bet is to park at the visitor information center ($3 a day) and to walk from there or take a trolley or train. Otherwise, you'll have to carry a pocketful of quarters to feed the meters in the other lots.

Sightseeing trolleys, trains, and horse-drawn carriages are the easiest way to get around. The trolleys and trains follow 7-mile routes, stopping at the visitors center and

St. Augustine

Accommodations:
Carriage Way Bed and Breakfast **13**
Casa de Solana **23**
Casa de Sueños **12**
Casablanca Inn **20**
Kenwood Inn **24**
La Fiesta Oceanside Inn **27**
Monterey Inn **17**
Radisson Ponce de León Golf & Conference Resort **1**
Westcott House **25**

Dining:
Bunnery Café **19**
Fiddler's Green **2**
Gypsy Cab Co. **28**
La Parisienne **16**
Raintree **8**
Saltwater Cowboys **29**
Schmagel's Bagels **18**
The Spanish Bakery **14**
Sunset Grill **30**

Attractions:
Authentic Old Jail **4**
Castillo de San Marcos National Monument **10**
Florida Heritage Museum **3**
Fountain of Youth **6**
Lightner Museum **21**
Mission of Nombre de Dios **7**
Oldest House **26**
Oldest Store Museum **22**
Oldest Wooden Schoolhouse **11**
Ripley's Believe It Or Not! Museum **9**
St. Augustine Alligator Farm **31**
Spanish Quarter Museum **15**
Tragedy in U.S. History Museum **5**

0   5 km
     3 mi

N

at or near most attractions. You can buy tickets at the visitors center or from the drivers.

St. Augustine Historical Tours (☎ 800/397-4071 or 904/829-3800), operates the green-and-white, open-air trolleys between 8:30am and 5pm daily (last trolley departs at 4:30pm). You can park your car at the headquarters (the Old Jail and Florida Heritage Museum), which are also stops on the tour. There are 25 stops, including Sebastian Winery, one of the few vintners in Florida. For the price of your ticket you can get off at any stop, visit the attractions, and step aboard the next vehicle that comes along. Several trolleys make a continuous circuit along the route throughout the day; you won't ever have to wait more than 15 or 20 minutes. If you don't get off at any attractions, it takes about an hour and a half to complete the tour.

St. Augustine Sightseeing Trains (☎ 800/226-6545 or 904/829-6545), is almost identical to the above, but takes a different route and makes 20 stops leaving out the Old Jail and Florida Heritage Museum. Rumor has it that an old feud keeps the owner from promoting his competitor across the street. Its vehicles are red-and-blue open-air trains.

Both companies charge $12 for adults, $5 for children 6 to 12, free for children 5 and under.

You may also want to see the sights from the back of a horse-drawn carriage. **Colee's Carriage Tours** (☎ 904/829-2818) has been showing people around town since 1877. The carriages line up at the bay front, just south of the fort. Slow-paced, entertainingly narrated 1-hour rides past major landmarks and attractions are offered from 8am to midnight. The cost is $12 per adult, $5 for children 5 to 11, free for children 4 and under; hotel and restaurant pickup is available for an additional charge.

For more personalized tours, call **Tour St. Augustine** (☎ 800/797-3778 or 904/471-9010), which offers guided walking tours around the historical area and nightly ghost tours.

SEEING THE HISTORIC SIGHTS

✪ **Authentic Old Jail.** 167 San Marco Ave. (at Williams St.). ☎ **904/829-3800.** Admission $4.25 adults, $3.25 children 6–12, free for children 5 and under. Daily 8:30am–5pm.

You can do the tour of this compact Victorian prison in less than half an hour, but you'll learn lots while you're there. The brick structure was built in 1890 and it served the county until 1953. The sheriff and his wife raised their children upstairs and used the same kitchen facilities to prepare the inmates' meals and their own. Downstairs are a maximum-security cell where murderers and horse thieves were confined; a cell housing prisoners condemned to hang (they could see the gallows being constructed from their window); and a grim solitary-confinement cell—pitch-dark with no windows, bed, or mattress. There's a restaurant here serving inexpensive lunch fare.

Castillo de San Marcos National Monument. 1 E. Castillo Dr. (at San Marco Ave.). ☎ **904/829-6506.** Admission $4 adults, free for children 16 and under with an adult. Daily 8:45am–4:45pm. Metered parking.

America's oldest and best-preserved masonry fortification, which took 23 years (1672–95) to build, is stellar in design, with a double drawbridge entrance over a 40-foot dry moat. Diamond-shaped bastions in each corner, which enabled cannons to set up a deadly crossfire, contained domed sentry towers. The seemingly indestructible Castillo was never captured in battle, and its coquina walls did not crumble when pounded by enemy artillery or violent storms throughout more than 300 years.

Today the old storerooms house exhibits documenting the history of the fort, a national monument since 1924. Also, visitors can tour the vaulted powder magazine, a dank prison cell, the chapel, and guard rooms. A self-guided tour map and brochure are provided at the ticket booth. In addition, subject to staff availability, 20- to 30-minute ranger talks are given several times a day, and there are occasional living-history presentations and cannon firings (call for times before you go).

Florida Heritage Museum. In the Old Jail, 167 San Marco Ave. (at Williams St.). ☎ **904/829-3800.** Admission $4.25 adults, $3.25 children 6–12, free for children 5 and under. Daily 8:30am–5pm.

History buffs will appreciate the information-packed museum documenting 400 years of Florida's past, focusing on the colorful life of Henry Flagler, the Civil War, and the Seminole Wars. A replica of a Spanish galleon filled with weapons, pottery, and treasures complements display cases filled with actual gold, silver, and jewelry recovered by treasure hunters. A typical wattle-and-daub hut of a Timucuan in a forest setting illustrates the lifestyle of St. Augustine's first residents. There's also an extraordinary collection of toys and dolls, mostly from the 1870s to the 1920s.

Fountain of Youth. 11 Magnolia Ave. (at Williams St.). ☎ **800/356-8222** or 904/829-3168. Admission $4.75 adults, $3.75 seniors, $1.75 children 6–12, free for children 5 and under. Daily 9am–5pm.

Never mind that Juan Ponce de León never did find the Fountain of Youth, this 25-acre archaeological park bills itself as North America's first historic site. It offers hokey 45-minute guided tours beginning with a planetarium show about 16th-century celestial navigation, during which the audience experiences a hurricane at sea. The famed fountain itself is located in the Springhouse along with a coquina stone cross believed to date from Ponce de León's ostensible visit in 1513. Visitors get to sample the sulfury and not very tasty spring water from a paper cup. Please let us know if it works!

⭐ **Lightner Museum.** 75 King St. (at Granada St.). ☎ **904/824-2874.** Admission $6 adults, $2 college students with ID and children 12–18, free for children 11 and under. Daily 9am–5pm.

Henry Flagler's opulent Spanish Renaissance–style Alcazar Hotel, built in 1889, closed during the Depression and stayed vacant until Chicago publishing magnate Otto C. Lightner bought the building in 1948 to house his vast collection of Victoriana. The building is an attraction in itself and makes a gorgeous museum, centering on an open palm courtyard with an arched stone bridge spanning a fish pond. The first floor houses a Victorian village, with shop fronts representing emporia selling period wares. A Victorian Science and Industry Room displays shells, rocks, minerals, and Native American artifacts in beautiful turn-of-the-century cases. Other exhibits include stuffed birds, an Egyptian mummy, steam engine models, and amazing examples of Victorian glassblowing. And a room of automated musical instruments is best seen during the daily concerts of period music at 11am and 2pm.

Mission of Nombre de Dios. San Marco Ave. and Old Mission Rd. ☎ **904/824-2809.** Free admission; donations appreciated. Daily 7am–6pm.

This serene setting overlooking the Intracoastal Waterway is believed to be the site of the first permanent mission in the United States, founded in 1565. The mission is a popular destination of religious pilgrimages. Whatever your beliefs, it's a beautiful tree-shaded spot, ideal for quiet meditation.

⭐ **The Oldest House.** 14 St. Francis St. (at Charlotte St.). ☎ **904/824-2872.** Admission $5 adults, $4.50 seniors 55 and over, $3 students, free for children 6 and under; $12 families. Daily 9am–5pm; tours depart on the hour and half hour (last tour at 4:30pm).

Archaeological surveys indicate that a dwelling stood on this site as early as the beginning of the 17th century. What you see today, called the Gonzáles-Alvarez House (for two of its prominent owners), evolved from a two-room coquina dwelling built between 1702 and 1727. The rooms are furnished to evoke various historical eras.

Admission also entitles you to explore the adjacent **Manucy Museum of St. Augustine History,** where artifacts, maps, and photographs document the town's history from its origins through the Flagler era.

The Oldest Store Museum. 4 Artillery Lane (between St. George and Aviles sts. behind Trinity Episcopal Church). ☎ **904/829-9729.** Admission $5 adults, $1.50 children 6–12, free for children 5 and under. Mon–Sat 9am–5pm, Sun noon–5pm (in summer, Sun 10am–5pm).

The C&F Hamblen General Store was St. Augustine's one-stop shopping center from 1835 to 1960, and the museum on its premises today replicates the emporium at the turn of the century. On display are more than 100,000 items sold here in that era, many of them gleaned from the store's attic. They include high-button shoes, butter churns, spinning wheels, 1890s bathing suits, barrels of dill pickles (you can purchase one), and medicines that were 90% alcohol. Some 19th-century brand-name products shown here are still available today, among them Hershey's chocolate, Coca-Cola, Ivory soap, and Campbell's soups. It all makes for fascinating browsing.

The Oldest Wooden Schoolhouse in the U.S.A. 14 St. George St. (between Orange and Cuna sts.). ☎ **800/428-0222** or 904/824-0192. Admission $2 adults, $1.50 for seniors 55 and over, $1 children 6–12, free for children 5 and under. Daily 9am–5pm.

This red-cedar and cypress structure, held together by wooden pegs and handmade nails, is more than 2 centuries old, with hand-wrought beams still intact. The classroom is re-created today using animated pupils and teacher, complete with a dunce and a below-stairs "dungeon" for unruly children. The last class was held here in 1864. You can park in the pay lot on the corner of Orange Street and Avenida Menendez.

✪ **Spanish Quarter Village.** Entrance at 33 St. George St. (between Cuna and Orange sts.). ☎ **904/825-6830.** Admission to all exhibit buildings $5 adults, $4.50 seniors, $2.50 students 6–18, free for children 5 and under; $10 per family. Daily 9am–5pm.

This 2-block area south of the City Gate is St. Augustine's most comprehensive historic section, where the city's colonial architecture and landscape have been re-created. Interpreters in 18th-century attire are on hand to help you envision the life of early inhabitants. Candlelight tours are offered at dusk on weekends during spring. About 90% of the buildings in the area are reconstructions, with houses named for prominent occupants. The Spanish Colonial–style **Florencia House** serves as the museum entrance and store.

The St. Augustine Lighthouse and Museum. 81 Lighthouse Ave. (off Fla. A1A east of the Bridge of Lions). ☎ **904/829-0745.** Admission to lighthouse and museum $4 adults, $3 seniors, $2 children 7–11, free for kids under 7. Museum only $2.50 adults, $1.75 seniors, free for kids under 12. Museum daily 9am–5pm. Lighthouse daily 9:30am–4:30pm.

This 165-foot tall structure was built in 1875 to replace the old Spanish lighthouse which had stood at the inlet since 1565. Sitting in a shady grove of live oaks, the lightkeeper's Victorian cottage was destroyed by fire in 1970 but meticulously reconstructed by the local Junior League. It now houses a museum explaining the history of both the lighthouse and the area. You should be in reasonable physical condition to climb the 219 steps to the top of the lighthouse, where you can see 19 nautical miles on a clear day. Children must be 7 years old and at least 4 feet tall to make the ascent.

OTHER ENTERTAINING ATTRACTIONS

3-D World. 28 San Marco Ave. (at Castillo Dr.). ☎ **904/824-1220.** Admission $9 per person. Daily 10am–10pm.

Put on your Polaroid glasses and take a 3-D underwater plunge in The Bahamas at one of two movie theaters here. The second screen shows *Escape from Capt. Nemo,* an action adventure. One of the other of the 45-minute productions begins every 15- to 20 minutes. It's a good place to park the kids when they tire of walking through old buildings.

Ripley's Believe It or Not! Museum. 19 San Marco Ave. (at Castillo Dr.). ☎ **800/ 584-2956** or 904/824-1606. www.ripleys.com. Admission $8.50 adults, $5.50 seniors, $7 teens 13–18, $4.50 children 5–12, free for children 4 and under. Daily 9am–10pm. Free parking.

Housed in a converted 1887 Moorish Revival residence—complete with battlements, massive chimneys, and rose windows—this immense display comprises hundreds of oddities collected by Robert Ripley and enhanced by later additions. Like the Ripley's in a dozen other U.S. cities, the exhibits run a wide gamut, from a Haitian voodoo doll owned by Papa Doc Duvalier to letters carved on a pencil with a chain saw by Ray "Wild Mountain Man" Murphy. This retro freak show is augmented by videos, photos, and film including footage of amazing people tricks, like the man who made a habit of banging nails into wood planks with his hands and pulling them out with his teeth. If you don't mind your kids being exposed to this kind of bizzaro, Ripley's is a good place to take them for all or part of an evening.

✪ **St. Augustine Alligator Farm and Zoological Park.** 999 Anastasia Blvd. (Fla. A1A), at Old Quarry Rd. ☎ **904/824-3337.** Admission $10.95 adults, $9.95 seniors 65 and over, $6.95 children 3–10, free for children under 3. June–Labor Day, daily 9am–6pm; Labor Day– May, daily 9am–5pm. Free parking.

You can't leave Florida without seeing at least one real live gator, and there are more than 1,000 of them on display at this century-old attraction. In fact, it houses the world's most complete collection of crocodilians, a category that includes alligators, crocodiles, caiman, and gavial. Other creatures living here include geckos, prehensile-tailed skinks, lizards, snakes, tortoises, spider monkeys, and exotic birds. There are ponds filled with a variety of ducks, geese, and swans, as well as a petting zoo with pygmy goats, potbellied pigs, miniature horses, mouflon sheep, and deer. Entertaining (and educational) 20-minute alligator and reptile shows take place hourly throughout the day, and spring through fall you can often see narrated feedings. If you're into this kind of thing, allow at least 2 hours to tour the extensive and well-maintained facilities.

NEARBY PORPOISE SHOWS

Marineland of Florida. 9507 Ocean Shore Blvd. (Fla. A1A), Marineland (18 miles south of St. Augustine). ☎ **904/471-1111.** Admission $14.95 adults, $9.95 for children 13–18, $7.95 children 3–12, free for children 2 and under. Daily 9am–5:30pm.

If you haven't seen porpoises jumping out of a big tank elsewhere in Florida, you can at this beachfront marine life park on the Atlantic Ocean. This is the first place to successfully maintain the animals in an oceanarium. Today Marineland features porpoise shows in a vast saltwater oceanarium as well as displays of other marine animals. A second oceanarium is home to marine specimens representing more than 125 species; the 35,000-gallon Wonders of the Spring aquarium holds native Florida species.

HITTING THE BEACH

There are several places to find sand and sea, but the 1,800-acre **Anastasia State Recreation Area,** on Anastasia Boulevard (Fla. A1A) across the Bridge of Lions and just past the Alligator Farm, has 4 miles of sandy beach bordered by picturesque dunes, as well as a lagoon flanked by tidal marshes. Also available are shaded picnic areas with grills, rest rooms, windsurfing, sailing and canoeing (on a saltwater lagoon), a nature trail, and saltwater fishing (for bluefish, pompano, and whiting from the surf; sea trout, redfish, and flounder—a license is required for out-of-state residents). In summer, you can rent chairs, beach umbrellas, and surfboards. There's good bird watching here too, especially in spring and fall; pick up a brochure at the entrance. Admission is $3.25 per vehicle and $1 for bicyclists and pedestrians. The day-use area is open daily from 8am to sunset.

Anastasia is one of Florida's most popular state facilities for **camping,** with its 139 wooded sites in high demand all year. They have picnic tables, grills, and electricity and rent for $14 to $18 a night. Campsite reservations are required: Make them up to 11 months in advance by writing or calling **Anastasia State Recreation Area,** 1340A A1A South, St. Augustine, FL 32084 (☎ **904/461-2033**).

To reach **St. Augustine Beach,** take the Bridge of Lions to Fla. A1A and proceed south past the Alligator Farm to Dondanville Road, where you can park right on the beach.

North of town, you can reach **Vilano Beach** by taking the Vilano Bridge and making a left on Fla. A1A; there's a parking lot at Surfside Ramp (on your right shortly after your turn onto A1A). You can park on the beach at Vilano too, but beware of soft sand. A few miles farther north along Fla. A1A, you'll come to a parking area with covered picnic tables and grills. It's a popular beach for fishing, but the surf is too rough for swimming.

All St. Augustine beaches charge a fee of $3 per car at official access points from Memorial Day to Labor Day; the rest of the year you can park free, but there are no lifeguards on duty and no toilet facilities on the beach.

GREAT GOLF THAT WON'T BREAK YOUR BUDGET & OTHER AFFORDABLE OUTDOOR ACTIVITIES

For additional outdoor options, contact the St. Johns County Visitors and Convention Bureau (see "Essentials," above) and ask them to send you a copy of their "Outdoor Recreation Guide."

CRUISES The Usina family has been running **St. Augustine Scenic Cruises** (☎ **800/542-8316** or 904/824-1806) on Matanzas Bay since the turn of the century. They offer 75-minute narrated tours aboard open-air sightseeing boats departing from the Municipal Marina just south of the Bridge of Lions. You can sometimes spot dolphins, brown pelicans, cormorants, and kingfishers. Snacks, soft drinks, beer, and wine are sold onboard. Weather permitting, departures normally are at 11am, 1, 2:45, and 4:30pm daily except Christmas, with an additional tour at 6:15pm from April 1 to May 21 and Labor Day to October 15; May 22 to Labor Day there are two additional tours, at 6:45 and 8:30pm. Call ahead—schedules can change. Fares are $9.50 adults, $8 seniors, $6.50 juniors ages 13 to 18, $4.50 children 4 to 12, free for children under 4. If you're driving, allow extra time to find a parking space on the street.

FISHING See **Anastasia State Recreation Area** under "Hitting the Beach," above, for information about surf casting. You can also cast your line off **St. Johns County Fishing Pier,** on the north end of St. Augustine Beach (☎ **904/461-0119**). The pier is open 24 hours daily and has a bait shop with rental equipment that is open from 6am to 10pm. Admission to the pier is $2 adults, $1 children.

For full-, half-day, and overnight **deep-sea fishing** excursions (for snapper, grouper, porgy, amberjack, sea bass, and other species), contact the **Sea Love Marina,** 250 Vilano Rd. (Fla. A1A north), at the eastern end of the Vilano Beach Bridge (☎ **904/**

824-3328). Full-day trips on the party boat *Sea Love II* cost $45; half-day trips, $30. No license is required, and rod, reel, bait, and tackle are supplied. Bring your own food and drink.

GOLF   The PGA Tour's world headquarters and the area's best golf resorts are in Ponte Vedra about a half-hour's drive north on Fla. A1A, closer to Jacksonville than St. Augustine (see "Great Golf That Won't Break Your Budget & Other Affordable Outdoor Activities," in section 4, below, for details). There are only a few courses in St. Augustine, including those at the **Radissons Ponce de León Resort** (see "Accommodations You Can Afford," below) and the **St. Augustine Shores Golf Club,** 707 Shores Blvd., off U.S. 1 (☎ **904/794-4653**). The latter is a par-70 course featuring 18 holes, lots of water, a lighted driving range and putting green, and a restaurant and lounge. Greens fees are $25.50 to $29.50, including cart, less in the summer months.

SAILING   You can rent sailboats, go on a variety of cruises, or learn to sail with **St. Augustine Sailing,** 3076 Harbor Dr. (☎ **800/683-7245** or 904/829-0648). Call for details, prices, and reservations.

WATER SPORTS   Jet-skis and surfing and windsurfing equipment can be rented at **Surf Station,** 1020 Anastasia Blvd. (Fla. A1A), a block south of the Alligator Farm (☎ **904/471-9463**); **Raging Water Sports,** at the Conch House Marina Resort, 57 Comares Ave. (☎ **904/829-5001**), which is off Anastasia Ave. (Fla. A1A) halfway between the Bridge of Lions and the Alligator Farm; and **Watersports of St. Augustine,** at Sea Love Marina, 250 Vilano Rd. (Fla. A1A north), at the eastern end of the Vilano Beach Bridge (☎ **904/823-8963**).

SHOPPING

The winding streets of the historic district are home to dozens of **antique stores** and **art galleries** stocked full of original paintings, sculptures, bric-a-brac, fine furnishings, china, and other treasures. Brick-lined Aviles Street, 1 block from the river, has an especially good mix of shops for browsing, as does St. George Street south of the visitor center. The Alcazar Court at the Lightner Museum has a good selection of antique shops (see "Seeing the Historic Sights," above). The visitor center has complete lists of art galleries and antique shops, the latter published by **The Antique Dealers Association of St. Augustine,** 60 Cuna St., St. Augustine, FL 32084 (no phone).

Chocoholics will find their version of heaven at **Whetstone Chocolates,** 2 Coke Rd. (Fla. 312), between U.S. 1 and the Mickler O'Connell Bridge (☎ **904/825-1700**). Free tours of the store and factory usually take place Monday to Saturday from 10am to 5:30pm, but call to make sure of the factory's schedule.

The biggest shopping draw here is the **St. Augustine Outlet Mall,** on Fla. 16 about ¼ mile west of I-95 at Exit 95 (☎ **904/825-1555**), about a 10-minute drive from downtown. Among the 95-plus stores are outlets by Laura Ashley, Sunglass Hut, Levi's, Adolfo II, Mikasa, Brooks Brothers, Coach, and more than a dozen shoe manufacturers. It's open until 9pm Monday through Saturday, 6pm on Sunday.

ACCOMMODATIONS YOU CAN AFFORD

If you're going to be here for a week or longer, consider ✪ **Villas on the Bay,** 105 Marine St., between San Salvador and St. Francis sts. (☎ **904/826-0575;** fax 904/826-1892; www.thevillas.com), whose nine one- and two-bedroom suites occupy a building that served as a Civil War military hospital. The spacious suites are furnished with antiques and Victoriana and have private balconies sporting spectacular bay views, rocking chairs, and/or hammocks. Most also have double Jacuzzi tubs. Rates range from $550 to $750 a week. Out at the beach, the **Ocean Gallery,** 4600 Fla. A1A

South, between Dondonville Rd. and Trade Winds Lane (☎ **800/940-6665** or 904/ 471-6663; fax 904/471-5994), has about 200 condo apartments in its rental inventory. The complex is set on 44 attractively landscaped acres with gardens, lakes, and lagoons. They range from $375 to $985 a week, depending on size, season, and view.

Almost all accommodations increase prices on weekends when the town is most crowded with visitors. St. Johns County charges a 9% tax on hotel bills.

The best **camping** here is at Anastasia State Recreation Area (see "Hitting the Beach," above), but reserve your site as early as possible.

IN ST. AUGUSTINE

St. Augustine is known for its many colorful and popular bed-and-breakfasts in restored historic homes. Most don't take young children or allow smoking inside the house. Check before booking. All the B&Bs listed below are within walking distance of the historic district, or right in it. They all provide free parking.

There are plenty of moderate and inexpensive motels and hotels here, including several along Ponce de Léon Boulevard (U.S. 1) at or near the Fla. 16 intersection north of the historic district. The pick is the **Quality Inn Alhambra,** 2700 Ponce de León Blvd., at Fla. 16 (☎ **800/223-4153** or 904/824-2883), a well-run family-owned property with large, attractively decorated rooms, some with Jacuzzis. There's a large swimming pool and whirlpool. Rooms range from $59 to $125 double. Among the budget-priced motels, the **Super 8,** 3552 N. Ponce de León Blvd., between Rambla and Fairbanks streets (☎ **800/800-8000** or 904/824-6399), has attractively landscaped grounds with a palm-fringed lawn surrounding a swimming pool. The upstairs units with peaked beamed ceilings are especially appealing. Doubles range from $35 to $43.

Closer to the historic district, the 2-story stucco **Comfort Inn,** 1111 Ponce de León Blvd., at Old Mission Rd (☎ **800/575-5288** or 904/824-5554), has large suites with double-sink dressing rooms and parlor areas with extra TVs and pull-out sofas, making them ideal for families. Doubles range from $42 to $99, depending on their size and time of year.

Super-Cheap Sleeps

Carriage Way Bed and Breakfast. 70 Cuna St. (between Cordova and Spanish sts.), St. Augustine, FL 32084. ☎ **800/908-9832** or 904/829-2467. Fax 904/826-1461. 9 units. A/C TEL. $69–$130 single or double. Rates include full breakfast. AE, DISC, MC, V.

Occupying an 1883 Victorian wood-frame house fronted by roses and hibiscus, the Carriage Way is like coming to an old friend's house. It is not fancy or formal, but is comfortable and well worn. Rooms are furnished with simple antique reproductions, including many four-poster beds. One room even retains its original fireplace. A console TV, books, magazines, and games are provided in a homey parlor. The energetic and hospitable owners/hosts Bill and Diane Johnson, who live on the premises, offer many extras: old one-speed bicycles, decanters of red wine and sherry on a buffet table in the hallway, and a refrigerator stocked with beer and soft drinks.

Monterey Inn. 16 Avenida Menendez (between Cuna and Hypolita sts.), St. Augustine, FL 32084. ☎ **904/824-4482.** Fax 904/829-8854. 59 units. A/C TV TEL. Winter Sun–Thurs $32– $69 single or double. Summer $49–$150 single or double. AE, DISC, MC, V.

For the price, you can't find a better choice this close to the attractions and nightlife of Old Town, and you couldn't ask for a more well-kept though modest place to spend the night. Three generations of the Six family have run this simple 2-story motel overlooking the Matanzas Bay. With renovations constantly in the works, you'll find the 1960s building and grounds always clean and functional. Rooms are not especially spacious but they are comfortable. A small swimming pool, pleasant staff, and free coffee each morning are just some of the extras at this superaffordable and convenient spot.

For a Few Bucks More

Casa de Sueños. 20 Cordova St. (at Saragossa St.), St. Augustine, FL 32084. ☎ **800/ 824-0804** or 904/824-0887. Fax 800/735-7534 or 904/825-0074. www.oldcity.com/suenos. E-mail: suenos@aug.com. 6 units. A/C TV TEL. $95–$165 single or double; $145–$185 suite. Rates include full breakfast. AE, DISC, MC, V.

Casa de Sueños offers small and thoughtfully decorated rooms in a turn-of-the-century house that was later transformed into the Mediterranean style you see today. When innkeepers Sandy and Ray Tool renovated the space in 1993, they updated again with faux antiques and many modern conveniences, including some whirlpools, dimmer switches on the lights, ceiling fans, hand-held shower attachments, and Touch-Tone phones with modem jacks. In the downstairs parlor you'll find a CD/cassette/record player, TV, VCR, books, magazines, games, and a small refrigerator stocked with beer and soft drinks. A fax and copy machine are available, too.

Besides your hosts and fellow guests, you'll meet Spice, an endearing Golden Lab that likes attention, and Holly, a folksy guitarist who entertains on weekend social hours and on Sunday morning. If you are into this kind of campy thing, you'll love the very popular Casa de Sueños. Breakfasts are superb here, and huge. When it is offered, the strawberry-covered French toast is especially delicious. You'll always appreciate fresh-baked breads, muffins, or biscuits. Services include nightly turndown with a chocolate and complimentary daily newspapers.

✪ **Casablanca Inn on the Bay.** 24 Avenida Menendez (between Hypolita and Treasury sts.), St. Augustine, FL 32084. ☎ **800/826-2626** or 904/829-0928. Fax 904/826-1892. 19 units. A/C. $89–$199 single or double. Rates include full breakfast. AE, DISC, MC, V.

This 1914 Mediterranean-style white stucco house faces the bay, although only a few of the rooms actually offer views. The most stunning are the two second-floor suites whose bay-front balconies have generously sized hammocks and private porches. The furnishings—a mix of turn-of-the-century American oak, European, and Victorian pieces—are of a higher quality than those at many other inns. Unique touches in each room might include glass figurines, oil paintings, or rare books. One modern convenience is a cassette player with a small selection of classical tapes. This may be appreciated, especially if you are on a ground-floor room that unfortunately suffers from the noise of the street and next-door bar and grill.

Guests can use the microwave and refrigerator in the kitchen and help themselves to complimentary beer, wine, soft drinks, chocolates, and fresh-baked cookies at all hours; hors d'oeuvres are served every afternoon; and weekend visitors get free champagne. Breakfast can be enjoyed alfresco on the porch or in a glass-enclosed conservatory. Ask to use the house bicycles to tour the city.

✪ **Kenwood Inn.** 38 Marine St. (at Bridge St.), St. Augustine, FL 32084. ☎ **904/ 824-2116.** Fax 904/824-1689. 14 units. A/C. $85–$115 single or double; $150 3-room suite for 1 or 2. Rates include continental breakfast. Extra person $10. DISC, MC, V.

Somewhere between a B&B and a cozy inn, the Kenwood is one of Old Town's best accommodations. This Victorian wood-frame house with graceful verandas has served as a boardinghouse or inn since the late 19th century. Rooms are larger and more private than most other accommodations in converted single-family homes. Everything from the carpeting to the linens to the china is first class. It's unusual also because of its relatively large outdoor space, which includes an outdoor swimming pool, a lushly landscaped sundeck, and a secluded garden courtyard (complete with a fish pond and neat flower bed under a sprawling pecan tree). Complimentary sherry, tea, and coffee are offered throughout the day.

✪ **Radisson Ponce de León Golf & Conference Resort.** 4000 U.S. Hwy. 1 north, St. Augustine, FL 32095. ☎ **800/333-3333** or 904/824-2821. Fax 904/824-8254. 193 units. A/C TV TEL. $99–$149 single or double; $119–$159 minisuite. Golf, family, and other packages available. AE, DC, DISC, MC, V. Free parking.

Located just a 5-minute drive from historic Old Town, this 400-acre resort has been a St. Augustine tradition since Henry Flagler built it in 1916. Pres. Warren G. Harding came here in 1921 to relax before his inauguration. In addition to the impressive Donald Ross–designed par-72 course, the resort features an 18-hole putting green next to the large outdoor swimming pool. Also on the grounds, amid the palms, magnolias, and centuries-old live oaks and clumps of saw grass, are six night-lit tennis courts, a sand volleyball court, shuffleboard, croquet, bocci, basketball, and horseshoes.

Many of the rooms and suites feature furnished patios or balconies overlooking the golf course, and coffeemakers. The minisuites, ideal for families, have small sitting rooms separated from sleeping areas by trellises.

A golf-side restaurant serves continental meals. On weekend evenings you can join conferences unwinding in the lounge for live piano entertainment in a cozy bar overlooking the greens.

Westcott House. 146 Avenida Menendez (between Bridge and Francis sts.), St. Augustine, FL 32084. ☎ **904/824-4301.** Fax 904/824-4301. 9 units. A/C TV TEL. Sun–Thurs $95–$175 single or double; Fri–Sat $150–$175 single or double. Rates include continental breakfast. AE, DISC, MC, V. Parking is on the street or free in a nearby lot.

Overlooking Matanzas Bay on the edge of historic Old Town, this 2-story, woodframe house offers rare opportunities for an uncluttered view from the porch, secondstory veranda, and a shady courtyard. The rooms—some with bay windows and/or working fireplaces—are exquisitely furnished and immaculate; everything here just gleams! Yours might have authentic Victorian furnishings and a brass bed made up with a white quilt and lace dust ruffle, with extras like hair dryers and terry bathrobes. Complimentary fresh fruit and brandy are available all day in the parlor of one of the town's most well-kept inns.

Worth a Splurge

Casa de Solana. 21 Aviles St. (at Cadiz St.), St. Augustine, FL 32084. ☎ **904/824-3555.** Fax 904/824-3316. 4 units. A/C TV. $125–$145 single or double. Rates include full breakfast. AE, DISC, MC, V.

Built in 1763 on a narrow cobbled street, this charming colonial house is the seventh oldest in the city. In the mid-1800s, its coquina-stone exterior was covered over with the pale-pink stucco you see today. The house also sports a lovely walled garden planted with jasmine and trumpet vines. The rooms are nicely decorated with an eclectic mix of antique pieces. Yours might have a four-poster, brass, art deco, or mahogany bed. A welcoming decanter of sherry awaits your arrival in the room. Three suites have full living rooms (the fourth has a small parlor), and one has a balcony. Hostess Faye McMurry's homemade breakfasts always include delicious fresh-baked muffins. There's a baby grand in the dining room, scene of occasional impromptu nighttime sing-alongs.

AT THE BEACHES

St. Augustine Beach has its share of chain motels, all on A1A Beach Boulevard (Fla. A1A). They include the **Best Western Ocean Inn** (☎ **800/528-1234** or

904/471-8010); **Days Inn Beach** (☎ **800/DAYS-INN** or 904/461-4774); **Econo Lodge** (☎ **800/446-6900** or 904/471-2330); a 1997-vintage **Hampton Inn** (☎ **800/426-7866**); **Holiday Inn Beachside** (☎ **800/626-7263** or 904/471-2555), with a popular tiki bar; **Howard Johnson Resort Hotel** (☎ **800/752-4037** or 904/471-2575); and **Ramada Limited** (☎ **800/2-RAMADA** or 904/471-1440).

La Fiesta Oceanside Inn. 810 A1A Beach Blvd. (Fla. A1A), St. Augustine Beach, FL 32084. ☎ **800/852-6390** or 904/471-2220. Fax 904/471-0186. 36 units. A/C TV TEL. $49–$159 single or double. DISC, MC, V.

Housed in 2-story tan stucco buildings with Spanish-style terra-cotta roofs, La Fiesta is attractive from the road. Inside, the generic Formica and wood-outfitted rooms are average chain motel-like, but a new block under construction at press time should add suites with more charm. The location couldn't be better, since you are directly on the beach and close to the best dining and drinking spots. Some rooms have wet bars, small refrigerators, double-size tubs, and king-size beds. A cafe serves breakfast daily. Other facilities include coin-op washer/dryers, a boardwalk over the dunes, a children's playground, a swimming pool, an 18-hole beachfront miniature golf course, and a picnic area with a barbecue grill.

GREAT DEALS ON DINING

In a town as heavily touristed as St. Augustine, there are, of course, a fair number of "tourist trap" restaurants. But on the whole, the food in St. Augustine, even at the popular eateries, is fairly priced and of good quality. For good late-night bites, see A1A Ale Works and Ann O'Malley's in "St. Augustine After Dark," below.

IN ST. AUGUSTINE
Super-Cheap Eats
Bunnery Café. 35 Hypolita St. (east of St. George St.). ☎ **904/829-6166.** Reservations not accepted. Everything under $4. No credit cards. Daily 9am–5:30pm. BAKERY.

Alluring aromas waft from the Bunnery, a bakery and cafe in the heart of the historic district. It's lovely to come here for breakfast. Arrive weary from a day of sightseeing, plop yourself into a chair on the arcaded terra-cotta patio, and indulge in a fresh-baked cinnamon roll, pecan sticky bun, or strawberry and cream-cheese croissant accompanied by a big cup of cappuccino.

Schmagel's Bagels. 69 Hypolita St. (at Cordova St.). ☎ **904/824-4444.** Bagels and sandwiches $4–$5. No credit cards. Mon–Sat 7:30am–3pm, Sun 8:30am–2pm. BAGEL SANDWICHES.

Yes, bagels have made it to St. Augustine, and Schmagel's makes them almost like the real plump New York ones. They come in 12 varieties—everything from cinnamon-raisin to blueberry. A variety of toppings include the traditional lox and cream cheese to a BLT. For breakfast you can also get bacon and eggs, homemade soups, and fresh-baked fruit muffins.

The Spanish Bakery. 42½ St. George St. (between Cuna and Orange sts.). ☎ **904/471-3046.** Reservations not accepted. Lunch specials $3; cookies and rolls 40¢–50¢ each. No credit cards. Daily 9:30am–3pm. Closed Thanksgiving and Christmas. COLONIAL.

Occupying a reconstructed 17th century kitchen building, this little family-operated establishment bakes almond, lemon, and cinnamon cookies using recipes from the Spanish colonial period, when a lack of refrigeration limited the use of milk and eggs. A couple of these crunchy morsels, eaten at the picnic tables outside, make a fine snack while you're touring the historic district. Or you can have lunch here, choosing from daily specials such as spicy Spanish-style chili over rice served with soup, a small loaf of freshly baked bread, and a drink.

For a Few Bucks More

✪ **Gypsy Cab Co.** 828 Anastasia Blvd. (Fla. A1A, at Ingram St., east of Bridge of Lions). ☎ **904/824-8244.** Reservations not accepted. Main courses $9–$17; sandwiches and salads $5–$7. AE, DC, DISC, MC, V. Mon and Wed–Thurs 11am–10pm, Tues 4:30–10pm, Fri–Sat 11am–11pm, Sun 10:30am–10pm. NEW AMERICAN.

Billing itself as a temple of "urban cuisine," this high-energy establishment with bright and art-filled dining rooms offers the likes of Shrimp Buena Vista, a concoction featuring gulf shrimp, linguine, Canadian bacon, green peas, and onions in a white-wine sauce. It is delicious. Salads and sandwiches are also excellent. Since the menu changes daily, it is tough to give recommendations, although the black-bean soup, which is a constant, is worth a try if you want something hearty. Park free behind the building, not in Trader Jack's lot next door.

✪ **La Parisienne.** 60 Hypolita St. (between Spanish and Cordova sts.). ☎ **904/829-0055.** Reservations recommended. Main courses $9–$24. AE, DISC, MC, V. Thurs–Tues 11am–3pm; Thurs–Sun 5–9pm. TRADITIONAL FRENCH.

La Parisienne will remind you of Paris. The lovely dining room has a rough-hewn beamed pine ceiling, lace-curtained windows, and ladderback chairs. Begin with escargot in a garlic cream sauce, then go on to a classic steak au poivre and roast rack of lamb coated with Dijon mustard and fresh garlic. The lunch menu offers traditional bistro fare, such as quiche Lorraine, croque monsieur, and salad niçoise. At afternoon tea, you might enjoy oven-fresh chocolate eclairs, praline ganaches, or fruit tarts.

✪ **Raintree.** 102 San Marco Ave. (at Bernard St.). ☎ **904/824-7211.** Reservations recommended. Main courses $12–$20; early dinner selections (served 5–6pm except holidays and special events) $9–$13; full children's dinners $7. AE, MC, V. Sun–Fri 5–9:30pm, Sat 5–10pm. Courtesy car provides transportation from/to downtown hotels. CONTINENTAL/AMERICAN.

Occupying an 1879 Victorian house, this is one of St. Augustine's most romantic yet casual restaurants. Bamboo furnishings, dozens of plants and ficus trees, and an awning create an indoor-garden setting, and cut-crystal lamps cast a soft glow. When the weather is warm, you might opt for after-dinner drinks or a selection of coffees and desserts on the open-air porch, balcony, or lushly planted brick patio. To start, you might try veal-stuffed mushrooms or a blue-crab cake with a spicy horseradish sauce. Duck and lamb dishes are tasty and served with light but delicious fruit-based condiments. More serious main courses include fresh fish (perhaps grouper with sautéed mushrooms in a white-wine/Dijon-mustard cream sauce), beef Wellington, and filet mignon béarnaise. An extensive dessert and coffee cart tempts with a variety of hot crepes and an exemplary crème brûlée. The list of more than 300 vintages has won *Wine Spectator* awards.

AT THE BEACHES

✪ **Fiddler's Green.** 2750 Anahma Dr. (at Ferrell Rd.), Vilano Beach. ☎ **904/824-8897.** Reservations recommended Sun–Fri, not accepted Sat. Main courses $9–$17. AE, CB, DC, DISC, MC, V. Sun–Thurs 5–9pm, Fri–Sat 5–10pm; Closed Mon Nov–Dec. Take Fla. A1A north across the Vilano Bridge and bear right to Vilano Beach. FLORIDIAN/SEAFOOD.

Situated right on the Atlantic, the shiplike Fiddler's Green is appropriately entered via a kind of gangplank. Inside, rustic elegance is achieved with two blazing coquina stone fireplaces and a profusion of hanging plants. Start your meal with crunchy-peppery conch fritters (ask for tarragon tartar and pepper sauce with them) or a platter of oysters "Rockefiddler" with oven-browned Cheddar topping. For a main course I like fish

Matanzas—fresh catch of the day (perhaps red snapper) pan-blackened with a mélange of spices and served with drawn butter.

Salt Water Cowboy's. 299 Dondanville Rd. (off Fla. A1A), St. Augustine Beach. ☎ **904/ 471-2332.** Reservations not accepted, so arrive early to avoid a wait. Main courses $9–$15. AE, DC, DISC, MC, V. Jan–Oct daily 5–10pm.; Nov–Dec Sun–Thurs 5–9pm, Fri–Sat 5–10pm. Follow A1A Beach Blvd. south; just past the restaurant's billboard make a right onto Dondanville Rd. at the traffic light. SEAFOOD/BARBECUE.

Arrive early for dinner at Salt Water Cowboy's—not only to beat the crowd but to enjoy a spectacular view of the sun setting over a saltwater marsh. Designed to resemble a turn-of-the-century fish camp, this rambling restaurant has a rustic candlelit interior and a mix of dining areas ranging from intimate booths to an outdoor plant-filled deck shaded by live oaks and lit by tiki torches. Order up a half-dozen oysters or perhaps some gator bits while you peruse the menu. For openers, there's a very rich and creamy chowder with big chunks of clam, potato, and celery. A main course of fork-tender baby back ribs is a great choice. Another winner: oysters, scallops, or shrimp fried in light cornmeal batter.

Sunset Grille. 421 A1A Beach Blvd. (Fla. A1A at 15th St.), St. Augustine Beach. ☎ **904/ 471-5555.** Reservations not accepted. Main courses $8–$16. DISC, MC, V. Mon–Fri 11am– 10pm (limited late-night menu served until midnight), Sat–Sun 7am–10pm. AMERICAN.

This casual Key West–style sports bar is a kick-back kind of place with half a dozen TVs and a mixture of music blaring from loud speakers. You can escape the noise in a small dining room to the rear, but what's the point? The action take precedence over the food here. Sunday afternoon a live band plays oldies and the place is mobbed. At lunch or dinner you can dine on sandwiches, burritos, or burgers. A more substantial dinner might consist of blackened chicken or grilled fresh fish or shrimp, with most main courses priced under $10. The windows latch up and have stools outside so the beach crowd (the ocean is across the street) can eat and drink in bathing attire.

ST. AUGUSTINE AFTER DARK

Especially on weekends, the Old Town is full of strollers and partiers making the rounds to the dozens of active bars, clubs, and restaurants. For up-to-date details on what's happening in town, check the local daily, the *St. Augustine Record,* or the more irreverent *Folio Weekly.*

Ann O'Malley's, 23 Orange St., near the Old City Gate (☎ **904/825-4040**), is the quintessential Irish pub open every day and night until 1am. Besides the selection of ales, stouts, and drafts, this is one of the only spots in town to grab a late-night bite. Granted, the deli-meat sandwiches and salads are nothing to write home about, but they're fresh and cheap.

The best-looking crowd in town can be found at the **A1A Ale Works,** 1 King St., at Avenida Menendez (☎ **904/829-2977**). Twenty-something hipsters and middle-age partiers mingle at this handsome, New Orleans–style microbrewery and restaurant. Thursday through Saturday nights downstairs, you'll find live music, often in the form of an acoustic guitarist and singer performing light rock and R&B tunes on a crowded window-front stage.

Popular with locals, **Mill Top Tavern,** 19½ St. George St., at the Fort (☎ **904/ 829-2329**), is a warm and rustic tavern housed in a 19th-century mill building (the waterwheel is still outside). Weather permitting, it's an open-air space. There's music every day from 1pm until 1am.

One of St. Augustine's most famous nighttime hangouts is **Scarlett O'Hara's** at 70 Hypolita St., at Cordova Street (☎ **904/824-6535**). A catacomb of cozy rooms with working fireplaces in a rambling 19th-century wood-frame house is the setting for live rock, jazz, and R&B bands nightly from 9:30pm. And though there's no dance floor, people get up and dance wherever. Sporting events are aired on a large-screen TV in a tropically themed oyster bar. Park in a lot across Cordova Street.

If you're looking for a real bikers' hangout, **Trade Winds Tropical Lounge,** at 124 Charlotte St., between Cathedral Place and Treasury Street (☎ **904/829-9336**), is the place. It often features live local bands playing a mix of Southern rock, oldies, folk, country, and blues.

Out at St. Augustine Beach, a casual and happening beach club, **Cafe Iguana,** 321 A1A Beach Blvd. (☎ **904/471-7797**), hosts retro music, semifunny comedians, and a sloppy dance scene Tuesday through Saturday nights. Several nights will find local live music and various contests. Especially popular is Friday's Happy Hour from 4:30 to 8pm and Wednesday's ladies' night.

Also at the beach is **Panama Hattie's Saloon,** 361 A1A Beach Blvd. (☎ **904/ 471-2255**), a funky and very popular beach bar with a rustic interior housing bars and dance floors on two levels. The older crowd hangs downstairs where on Friday and Saturday nights there are oldies bands while upstairs on the beach deck a deejay plays Top 40 tunes.

4 Jacksonville

36 miles S of Georgia, 134 miles NE of Orlando, 340 miles N of Miami

Once infamous for its smelly paper mills, the sprawling metropolis of "Jax" is now one of the insurance and banking capitals of the South and home to many Fortune 500 companies. Accordingly, its tourism facilities cater to the business travelers who make up more than 70% of the city's visitors. The result is a downtown that is a vibrant center of activity on weekdays, but virtually deserted in the evenings and weekends.

Development is rampant throughout Duval County, with hotels, restaurants, attractions, and clubs rapidly springing up, especially in suburban areas near the interstate highways. Nevertheless, there are shady older neighborhoods to explore, 20 miles of Atlantic Ocean beaches upon which to sun and swim, many championship golf courses to play, and an abundance of beautiful and historic national and state parks to roam.

Although it claims to be the capital of Florida's historic "First Coast," Jacksonville dates its beginnings from an early 1800s settlement named Cowford—because cattle crossed the St. Johns River here. Cowford changed its name to Jacksonville in 1822 to honor Gen. Andrew Jackson, the provisional governor who forced Spain to cede Florida to the United States 2 years earlier.

ESSENTIALS

GETTING THERE   I-95 and I-10 intersect in downtown Jacksonville. I-295 bypasses the city to the west.

Jacksonville International Airport is on the city's north side, about 12 miles from downtown. It's served by **Air South** (☎ 800/247-7688), **AirTran** (☎ 800/ AIR-TRAN), **American** (☎ 800/433-7300), **Continental** (☎ 800/525-0280), **Delta** (☎ 800/221-1212), **Midway** (☎ 800/446-4392), **Northwest** (☎ 800/ 225-2525), **Southwest** (☎ 800/435-9792), **TWA** (☎ 800/221-2000), **United** (☎ 800/241-6522), and **US Airways** (☎ 800/428-4322). The **First Coast Information Booth,** on the lower level by the baggage area (☎ **904/741-4902**), is open daily from 9am to 10pm. **Gator City Taxi** (☎ **904/741-0008**) provides transportation to and from the airport. Fares are about $20 to downtown, $40 to $45 to beach hotels, $55 to $65 to the St. Augustine area.

Jacksonville

To Airport ↑

Oceanway ❶

Eastport Rd. ❷

Heckscher Dr. 105

Fort George Island ❹
Mayport ❺

University Blvd.
Ft. Caroline Rd.
Mill Cove
❸

Arlington 9A

Monument Rd.
Kings Rd

Atlantic Ocean

Intracoastal Waterway

Atlantic Beach A1A

Area of Inset

St. Johns River

Roosevelt Blvd.
Phillips Hwy.
San Jose Rd.
Old St. Augustine Rd.
Southside Blvd.
St. Johns Bluff Rd.

Atlantic Blvd.
Neptune Beach ❻
❼
Beach Blvd. ❽ ❾
❿
Jacksonville Beach

J.T. Butler Blvd. 202

A1A

Yukon ⑰

Baymeadows Rd.

Jacksonville Naval Air Station

Buckman Bridge

Sunbeam Rd.

Duval County

St. Johns County

Downtown Jacksonville

Edison St.

Water St. ⓫
Jacksonville Landing

Bay St.
Newnan

Price
Dora
Jackson
Stonewall
Magnolia
Riverside Ave.

Acosta Bridge
Main St. Bridge

The Riverwalk ⓬

Edison St.
Chelsea
Rosselle
Peninsular Ave.

St. Johns River

St. Johns River Park and Marina

Gulf Life Dr.
90 Alvarez
Prudential Dr.

Fuller Warren Bridge

River City Brewing Co. ⓭

Dellwood Ave.

Stockton St.
Osceola St.
Copeland St.
Goodwin St.
College Park

College St.
Post St.
Barrs St.
Park St.
Gilmore
Fisk St.
Oak
May
Lomax St.
Margaret St.
Riverside
Standish Pl.

Plantation Manor House ⑯

Riverside Ave.

⓯ ⓮

King St.
James St.
Cherry St.
Mallory
211 ⑰
Willowbranch Terrace

⑱
⑲

Attractions:
Anheuser-Busch Brewery ❶
Cummer Museum of Art & Gardens ⑲
Fort Caroline National Memorial ❸
Jacksonville Zoo ❷
Timucan Ecological and
   Historic Preserve ❸ & ❹
Zephaniah Kingsley Plantation ❹

Accommodations:
Comfort Inn Oceanfront ❼
House on Cherry Street ⑰
Jacksonville Hilton & Towers ⓬
Omni Jacksonville Hotel ⓫
Plantation Manor House ⑯
The San Marco Point House ⓮
Sea Horse Oceanfront Inn ❻

Dining:
Biscotti's ⑱
Café Carmon ⓯
The Homestead ❿
Island Grille ❾
Old Siam ❽
River City Brewing Co. ⓭
Singleton's Seafood Shack ❺

NA-0045

649

There's an **Amtrak** station in Jacksonville at 3570 Clifford Lane, off U.S. 1, just north of 45th Street (☎ **800/USA-RAIL**).

VISITOR INFORMATION   Contact the **Jacksonville and the Beaches Convention & Visitors Bureau,** 3 Independent Dr., Jacksonville, FL 32202 (☎ **800/ 733-2668** or 904/798-9148; fax 904/789-9103; e-mail: jaxflcvb@jax-inter.net), for maps, brochures, calendars, and advice. In the Chamber of Commerce Building across Water Street from Jacksonville Landing, the office is open Monday to Friday from 8am to 5pm.

GETTING AROUND   You're better off having a car if you want to explore this vast area. You can hail a **taxi** downtown if you spot one, although it is usually best to call **Gator City Taxi** (☎ **904/355-8294**) for a pickup. Fares are $1.25 when the meter drops, and 25¢ for each ⅛ mile thereafter. The **Jacksonville Transportation Authority** (☎ **904/630-3100**) provides local **bus service** 7 days a week, with most buses running between 4:30am and 12:30am. The fare is 60¢ for adults, free for seniors and children shorter than 42 inches accompanied by an adult. A bus to the beach costs $1.10 each way.

The **St. Johns River Ferry** (☎ **904/241-9969**) shuttles vehicles across the river at Mayport daily from 6:20am to 10:15pm. It shortens the trip between the Jacksonville beaches and Amelia Island, but call before driving out here to make sure it's running. One-way fare is $2.50 per vehicle.

EXPLORING THE AREA

Anheuser-Busch Brewery. 111 Busch Dr. ☎ **904/751-8118.** Free admission. Mon–Sat 9am–4pm. Guided tours depart on the hour. Take I-95 north to Busch Dr. (exit 125), go east to brewery on left.

If you're into beer, you may appreciate the free and informative 30-minute tour of these monstrous and pungent-smelling facilities where Budweiser, Bud Light, Michelob, Busch, and O'Doul's are brewed. The best part is the conclusion of the tour, when you can quaff two free glasses of beer (or soft drinks) in the hospitality center. Bring a sweater, since you'll pass through 45° chambers where stainless-steel vaults hold the fermenting ale. You can take the guided tour, show yourself around, or head straight to the bar and extensive gift shop. Call ahead to see if the Anheuser-Busch Clydesdale horses are visiting.

✪ **Cummer Museum of Art & Gardens.** 829 Riverside Ave. (between Post and Fisk sts.). ☎ **904/356-6857.** Admission $5 adults; $3 seniors over 65, students, and military; $1 children under 5; free for everyone Tues after 4pm. Tues and Thurs 10am–9pm, Wed and Fri–Sat 10am–5pm, Sun 2–5pm.

Built on the grounds of a private Tudor mansion, this modestly-sized but outstanding museum is worth a visit for anyone who appreciates the visual arts. The permanent collection encompasses works from 2000 B.C. to the present. It's especially rich in American impressionist paintings, and includes an impressive collection of 18th-century porcelain and 18th- and early 19th-century Japanese Netsuke ivory carvings. Don't miss the stunning Italian and English gardens set on the scenic St. Johns River.

Jacksonville Landing. 2 Independent Dr. (between Main and Pearl sts.), on the St. Johns River. ☎ **904/353-1188.** Free admission. Parking $4.80 maximum daily charge. Mon–Thurs 10am–8pm, Fri–Sat 10am–9pm, Sun noon–5:30pm; bars and restaurants may be open later. From I-95, take Exit 107 downtown to Main St., go over the Blue Bridge, turn left at Bay St., then go 2 blocks and make a left on Laura St., which dead-ends at the Landing. Parking lot is on east side of complex.

This 6-acre dining/shopping/entertainment complex on the waterfront has more than 65 shops, including some of the mall regulars. Diners can choose from about half a dozen full-service restaurants plus a food court with indoor and outdoor seating overlooking the river. Also on the premises are a couple of bars and a small maritime museum. The Landing is the scene of numerous special events ranging from arts festivals to baseball-card shows. From March to the end of December there are free outdoor rock, blues, country, and jazz concerts every Friday and Saturday night. Call to find out what's going on at the Landing during your stay.

✪ **Jacksonville Zoo.** 8605 Zoo Rd. ☎ **904/757-4462** or 904/757-4463. Admission $6.50 adults, $4.50 seniors 65 and over, $4 children 3–12, free for children 2 and under; shows are free. Daily 9am–5pm (Memorial Day through Labor Day, Fri–Sat until 8pm). Take I-95 north to Hecksher Dr. (Exit 124A) and follow the signs.

In the midst of a 10-year expansion plan, the Jacksonville Zoo is well on its way to becoming one of the country's best. The main exhibits are centered around an extensive and growing collection of African wildlife including lions, impalas, ostriches, rhinos, elephants, antelopes, Nile crocodiles, cheetah, Kirk's dik-diks, monkeys, and South African crested porcupines. You'll enter the 73-acre park through the authentic thatched roof built in 1995 by 24 Zulu craftsmen. Whether you go on foot or by tram, allow at least 2 hours to tour this vast and lush zoo, just south of the airport. When you arrive, ask about current animal shows and special events. Strollers and wheelchairs are available for rent.

Southbank Riverwalk. On the south bank of the St. Johns River, flanking Main Street Bridge between San Marco Blvd. and Ferry St. ☎ **904/396-4900.** Take I-95 north to the Prudential Dr. exit, make a right, and follow the signs.

This 1.2-mile wooden zigzag boardwalk bordering the St. Johns River is filled with joggers, tourists, and folks sitting on benches watching the riverboats and shorebirds. The downtown skyline across the river is reflected on the water. The **Friendship Fountain,** at the west end, is, at 200 feet in diameter, the nation's largest self-contained fountain; it's especially beautiful at night when illuminated by 265 colored lights. Farther along, you'll pass military memorials and the **Museum of Science & History of Jacksonville,** at Museum Circle and San Marco Boulevard (☎ **904/396-7062**), an interactive children's museum focusing on science and the history of northeast Florida (admission $6 adults, $4 kids 3 to 12). The Riverwalk is the scene of seafood fests, parties, parades, and arts and crafts festivals. Food vendors, picnic tables, and restaurants line the route.

THE TIMUCUAN ECOLOGICAL & HISTORIC PRESERVE: A NEW BREED OF NATIONAL PARK

Named after the native people who inhabited Central and North Florida some 1,000 years before European settlers arrived, the **Timucuan Ecological and Historic Preserve** offers visitors an opportunity to explore untouched wilderness, historical buildings, and informative exhibits on the area's natural history. This 46,000-acre preserve is not your average national park. Besides the enormous size, it's is unusual in that it hasn't been hacked off from the rest of the community and drawn within arbitrary boundaries. The result is a vast, intriguing system of sites joined by rural roads alongside tumble-down fish camps, trailer parks, strip malls, condominiums, and stately old homes.

South of the River

The prime attractions are on the south bank of the St. Johns River between downtown and the beaches. Your starting point here his the ✪ **Fort Caroline National**

Memorial, on Ft. Caroline Road (☎ **904/641-7155**), which serves park headquarters. This was the site of the 16th-century French Huguenot settlement that was wiped out by the Spanish who landed at St. Augustine. This two-thirds–size replica shows you what the original was like. You can see archaeological artifacts and two very well-produced half-hour videos highlighting the area. The fort and all other park facilities are open daily from 9am to 5pm except Christmas. Admission is free.

The fort sits at the northwestern edge of the 600-acre **Theodore Roosevelt Area,** a beautiful wood- and marshland rich in history and undisturbed since the Civil War. On a 2-mile hike along a centuries-old park trail, you'll see a wide variety of birds, wildflowers, and a maritime hammock forest. Bring binoculars if you have them, since such birds as the endangered wood stork, great and snowy egrets, osprey, hawks, and painted buntings make their home here in spring and summer. On the ground, you might catch sight of a gray fox or furry raccoon. You may also want to bring a blanket and picnic basket to spread out under the ancient oak trees that shade the banks of the St. Johns River, where recreational and commercial boats still ply the wide and winding waters. After the trail crosses Hammock Creek, you're in ancient Timucuan country, where their ancestors lived as far back as 500 B.C. Farther along is the site of a cabin in the wilderness that belonged to reclusive brothers Willie and Saxon Browne, who lived without the modern conveniences of indoor plumbing or electricity until the last brother's death in 1960. If you're here on a weekend, take the 1½-hour guided tours of the fort and Theodore Roosevelt Area, offered every Saturday and Sunday at 1pm (when weather and staffing permit); park rangers provide a wealth of fascinating information about history, flora, and fauna. Call the fort for details and schedules.

About half a mile east of the fort is the **Ribault Monument** on St. Johns Bluff, erected in 1924 to commemorate the arrival in 1562 of French Huguenot Jean Ribault, who died defending Fort Caroline from the Spanish. It's worth a stop just for the dramatic view of the area.

To get here from downtown, take Atlantic Boulevard (Fla. 10) east, make a left on Monument Road, and turn right on Fort Caroline Road; the Theodore Roosevelt Area is entered from Mt. Pleasant Road, about 1 mile southeast of the fort; look for an inconspicuous sign on your left that says "trailhead parking" and follow the narrow dirt road to the parking lot.

North of the River

On the north side of the river, history buffs also will appreciate the ✪ **Zephaniah Kingsley Plantation,** at 11676 Palmetto Ave. on Fort George Island (☎ **904/ 251-3537**). A winding 3-mile road runs under a canopy of trees with dense tropical foliage on either side to the remains of this 19th-century plantation owned by Zephaniah Kingsley, a white man who held some seemingly contradictory views on race. Although he owned more than 200 slaves, he believed that "the coloured race were superior to us, physically and morally." He married a Senegalese woman (one of his former slaves) and ultimately moved his family to Haiti in 1837 to escape what he called the "spirit of intolerant injustice" at home. The National Park Service maintains the well-preserved 2-story residence, kitchen house, barn/carriage house, and remnants of 23 slave cabins built of "tabby mortar"—oyster shell and sand. A self-guided tour is the best way to see it all; clear and informative signs tell the history of this former citrus, cotton, and sugar-cane farm, and of the workers who built it. Allot about an hour. A well-stocked book and gift shop will keep you even longer. Rangers sometimes offer interpretive programs.

To get here from I-95, take Heckscher Drive (Fla. 105) east and follow the signs. From Fort Caroline, take Fla. 9A north over the St. Johns River to Hecksher Drive east. The plantation is about 12 miles east of Fla. 9A, on the left.

HITTING THE BEACH

Fish, swim, snorkel, sail, sunbathe, or stroll on the sand dunes along Jacksonville's beaches—they're just a 20- to 30-minute drive from downtown via Atlantic, Beach, or J. Turner Butler boulevards. At 4th Avenue North you'll find free beach parking and rest rooms. **Jacksonville Beach** is probably the liveliest of the bunch, with beach concessions, rental shops, and a fishing pier. This is also the most popular local surfing beach. **Atlantic Beach,** further north, has great nightlife and restaurants along the Atlantic. To the south, the ritzy enclave of **Ponte Vedra Beach** is actually in St. Johns County (St. Augustine), but it's so much closer to Jacksonville that I've included it in this chapter. Here you'll find the Marriott at Sawgrass Resort and the Ponte Vedra Inn & Club, both with outstanding golf courses.

GREAT GOLF THAT WON'T BREAK YOUR BUDGET & OTHER AFFORDABLE OUTDOOR ACTIVITIES

BIKES, BALLOONS, BOATS & SKY-DIVING   A one-stop outfitter for all kinds of outdoor fun is **Outdoor Adventures** (☎ 904/393-9030), offering kayaking and canoeing, ballooning, bicycle trips, and other outdoor adventures, both day trips and longer camping trips. Call for schedules, prices, and reservations. If you want to learn to sky-dive, **Blue Sky Adventures** (☎ 904/272-4864) offers parachute training.

FISHING/CRUISING   You can go **fishing** for whiting, mackerel, flounder, bluefish, catfish, and more off the **Jacksonville Beach Fishing Pier,** just south of Beach Boulevard at 6th Avenue (☎ 904/246-6001). No license is required, and rods, reels, and bait can be rented on the premises. The pier is open daily: from 6am to 11pm Memorial Day to Labor Day, until 9pm the rest of the year. It costs $4 for adults to fish the pier, $2 for children 8 and under and seniors over 60.

Another option is to fish for red snapper, grouper, sea bass, small sharks, amberjack, and more, 15 to 30 miles offshore in the Atlantic Ocean aboard the *King Neptune,* a 65-foot air-conditioned deep-sea fishing boat. It departs at 8am daily from 4378 Ocean St., a half mile south of the Mayport Ferry (☎ 904/246-7575). The price is $40 per person, including all bait and tackle. You don't need a license, but reservations are required. The boat usually returns by 5pm.

GOLF   Golfers passing through this area will be glad to know that Jacksonville offers a great variety of public golf courses, many of which are rated tops in the country. Of course the most famous course is TPC course at the Marriott Sawgrass, in Ponte Vedra, located in the next county and open only to resort guests. Top courses open to the public include the semiprivate **Cimarrone,** at 2690 Cimarrone Blvd. (☎ 904/287-2000), a fast and watery course with affordable greens fees ranging from $30 to $50; and the public **Golf Club of Jacksonville,** at 10440 Tournament Lane (☎ 904/779-0800), which is managed by the PGA Tour. It's a great bargain, with rates ranging from $28 to $39.

On your way out the beach, the semiprivate **Windsor Parke Golf Club,** at 4747 Hodges Blvd., at J. Turner Butler Boulevard (☎ 904/223-GOLF), is one of the most challenging and scenic courses in Jacksonville. Designed by Arthur Hill, the 6,740 yards of green are surrounded by towering pines and lots of water. After it opened in 1991, *Golf Digest* rated it the best new course in the Southeast. Fees are usually less than $45 and include a cart—even on the weekends. Nonmembers should call 4 or 5 days in advance for tee times.

Scheduled to open in 1998, the **World Golf Village,** on 240 acres in St. Johns County, off I-95 and Golf Parkway (☎ 904/273-3350), brings together the biggest golf organizations, professionals, and duffers from around the world. The centerpiece is the **World Golf Hall of Fame,** a 75,000-square-foot museum paying tribute to golf's finest.

For a review of other options in northeast Florida, call ☎ **800/555-0807** to request a copy of *Florida Golf Vacations.* And be on the lookout for the free *Golfer's Guide* in the visitors centers and hotel lobbies (see "The Active Vacation Planner," in chapter 2, for information about ordering copies).

HORSEBACK RIDING For a scenic ride along the sand and dunes, call **Sawgrass Stables,** 23900 Marsh Landing Pkwy., off Fla. A1A in Ponte Vedra Beach (☎ **904/ 285-3791**). Rates start at $35 for a supervised ride. Lessons are also available.

SPECTATOR SPORTS The 73,000-seat **Alltel Municipal Stadium,** 1 Stadium Place, at East Duval and Haines streets (☎ **904/630-3901** for information, or 904/353-3309 to charge tickets), hosts the annual Florida-Georgia football game every October, other college football games September to December, motor-sports events, and the National Football League's **Jacksonville Jaguars** (☎ **904/633-6000** for ticket information). One of the stadium's biggest draws is the **Toyota Gator Bowl,** usually on New Year's Day (see "Florida Calendar of Events," in chapter 2).

Adjacent to the stadium, and under the same auspices, is the 10,600-seat **Jacksonville Veterans Memorial Coliseum,** 1145 E. Adams St. (☎ **904/630-3900** for information, or 904/353-3309 to charge tickets), home of **Jacksonville Lizards** East Coast Hockey team, and a venue for NHL exhibition games, Division I college basketball games, ice-skating exhibitions, wrestling matches, and various family shows.

Jax has yet to get a big league baseball team, but you can see **Jacksonville Suns**, a Detroit Tigers affiliate, play their Class AA minor league games from April to early September at Wolfson Park, 1201 E. Duval St. (☎ **904/358-2842**). Tickets range from $4 to $7.

TENNIS As home to the International Association of Tennis Professionals, Jacksonville also abounds in high-quality tennis courts, including the notable facilities at the Ponte Vedra Beach and Amelia Island resorts (see "Accommodations You Can Afford," below and in section 5). In the city, **Southside Park,** 1541 Hendricks Ave., off Atlantic Boulevard (☎ **904/399-1761**), has six city-run Har-Tru courts for daytime play and six asphalt-base courts lit for night play. There's no charge to play. There are additional city courts (14 clay, two Har-Tru, and a practice wall, all lit for night play) at **Boone Park,** 3730 Park St., just east of Roosevelt Boulevard (☎ **904/ 384-8687**). There's a small charge here. Both locations are open daily year-round and offer lessons from resident tennis pros. Call for hours, and make reservations a day or two in advance.

WATER & ENTERTAINMENT PARK **Adventure Landing,** 1944 Beach Blvd., at 20th St., Jacksonville Beach (☎ **904/246-4386**), is a pirate theme park with all kinds of fun activities for kids and adults. A giant water park, open March through September, is a great way to cool off. Or, you can try your hand in the huge arcade with video games, laser tag, virtual reality machines, and carnival-style games. Outside you can ride the go-carts or bumper boats, play miniature golf, and take some swings in the batting cages. Admission to the water park is about $16 for adults, $13 for children under 48 inches, free for children 3 and under. There are separate charges for activities.

SHOPPING & BROWSING

Jacksonville has shopping opportunities galore, including Jacksonville Landing (see "Exploring the Area," above), an upscale mall, **The Avenues Mall,** south of town at 10300 Southside Blvd., as well as a number of flea markets, including the **Beach**

Boulevard Flea and Farmer's Market, on Beach Boulevard (Fla. 90) (☎ **904/ 645-5961**). More than 600 vendors show up daily, from 9am to 5pm, to sell their wares in a partially covered facility.

The **San Marco Square** shopping district, at San Marco Boulevard and Atlantic boulevards south of downtown, is a quaint shopping district in the middle of a stunning residential area. Shops in meticulously refashioned Mediterranean revival buildings sell antiques and home furnishings as well as clothing, books, and records.

Another worthwhile neighborhood to explore is the **Avondale/Riverside** historic district southwest of downtown along St. Johns Avenue between Talbot Avenue and Boone Park, on the north bank of the river. More than 60 boutiques, antique stores, art galleries, shoe stores, and cafes line the wide, tree-lined avenue.

Nearby, the younger set hangs out at **Five Points,** on Park Street where used record stores, vintage clothiers, coffee shops, smoke shops, and funky art galleries stay open late.

Like St. Augustine, Jacksonville is a mecca for chocoholics, particularly **Peterbrooke Chocolatier Production Center,** 1470 San Marco Blvd., in the San Marco Square neighborhood (☎ **904/398-4812**). If you've never tried chocolate-covered popcorn or pretzels, this is the place. Open Monday to Friday from 10am to 5pm.

ACCOMMODATIONS YOU CAN AFFORD

I've arranged the accommodations listed below geographically, in and around downtown first, followed by the beach scene. The suburbs have dozens more from which to choose, especially along I-95. Many are clustered south of downtown in the **Southpoint** (Exit 101, J. Turner Butler Boulevard/Fla. 202) and **Baymeadows** (Exit 101, Baymeadows Road/Fla. 152) suburban areas. These locales have a multitude of chain restaurants, and you can hop on the highways and zoom to the beach or downtown—although you aren't really at either one if you stay out here. Tops is the **Jacksonville Marriott at Southpoint,** 4670 Salisbury Rd. (☎ **800/228-9290** or 904/296-2222), among the area's best all-around hotels. Also here are a comfortable and inexpensive **Budgetel Inn,** 3199 Hartley Rd. (☎ **800/428-3488** or 904/268-9999) and a **Motel 6,** at 8285 Dix Ellis Trail (☎ **800/4-MOTEL-6** or 904/731-8400).

For a complete list of lodging, contact the Jacksonville and the Beaches Convention & Visitors Bureau (see "Essentials," above).

Note that rates in the downtown hotels are higher midweek when rooms are in demand by business travelers. Beach accommodations are somewhat less expensive in the cold months from December through March.

IN JACKSONVILLE
Super-Cheap Sleeps
The House on Cherry Street. 1844 Cherry St. (on the St. Johns River), Jacksonville, FL 32205. ☎ **904/384-1999.** Fax 904/384-5013. 4 units, all with bathroom. A/C TV. $79–$99 single or double. Rates include continental breakfast. AE, MC, V.

This colonial-style wood-frame house, nestled in a tree-shaded cul-de-sac on the St. Johns River, is ideal for a romantic B&B vacation (no small children are accepted). French doors open to a delightful screened-in back porch furnished with rocking chairs; it overlooks an expanse of tree-shaded lawn (where guests play croquet) leading to the river. You might select the Rose or Duck rooms, both with canopied four-poster beds and river views. Ducks are rather a theme here, with hundreds of antique decoys on display. All accommodations offer adjacent sitting rooms, ceiling fans, and are supplied with fresh flowers, books, and magazines. Complimentary wine and hot and cold hors d'oeuvres are presented daily at 6pm on the patio or in the dining room. An upstairs refrigerator is stocked with free soft drinks and beer, and there are bicycles for guest use. Genial owner/hosts Carol and Merrill Anderson keep a gentle pet greyhound—formerly a racing dog—named Streak, but don't bring your own pet. No smoking is permitted.

The San Marco Point House. 1709 River Rd. (between Riviera and Laverne sts.), Jacksonville, FL 32207. ☎ **904/396-1448.** Fax 904/396-7760. sanmarcopt@aol.com. 5 units, all with bathroom. A/C TV TEL. $75–$100 single or double. Rates include full breakfast. AE, MC, V.

Within hailing distance of trendy restaurants in the San Marco Square neighborhood and half a block from a promenade along the river, this Sears Craftsman bungalow was built in 1921. Downstairs has two sitting rooms, one with a fireplace, the other with French doors opening to a side patio. But wait until you see the African lion skin, snarling head and all, lying on the floor of the small lounge at the top of the stairs. No, neither Owner Todd Kemp nor innkeeper Linda Olsvasky are big-game hunters; it and the other stuffed trophies in this Hemingwayesque room were purchased at estate sales. The guest rooms in the house are adorned with an eclectic mix of furnishings, including some antiques, and all have little sitting alcoves backed by bay windows. More private is the one room in a small cottage in the backyard.

For a Few Bucks More

✪ **Plantation Manor Inn.** 1630 Copeland St. (between Oak and Park sts.), Jacksonville, FL 32204. ☎ **904/384-4630.** Fax 904/387-0960. 9 units. A/C TV TEL. $95–$150 single or double. Rates include full breakfast. AE, DC, MC, V.

The setting for many weddings and special events, this 3-story plantation-style home in the historic Riverside district is just 10 minutes from downtown. Its homey interior, outfitted with a mix of thrift-store antiques, features glossy pine floors and gorgeous cypress paneling, wainscoting, and carved moldings. Breakfast, including fresh-baked muffins and breads, is served in a lovely dining room with a working fireplace. When the sun is shining, take the morning meal on an enclosed brick patio, a delightful setting with ivy-covered walls, flower beds, and garden furnishings under the shade of a massive oak tree. The patio also contains a lap pool and whirlpool spa. On the second floor you can enjoy a big wraparound porch with seating amid potted geraniums, hibiscus, and bougainvillea.

Good Weekend Deals

Jacksonville Hilton & Towers. 1201 Riverplace Blvd. (at Main St. on Southbank Riverwalk), Jacksonville, FL 32207. ☎ **800/HILTONS** or 904/393-8800. Fax 904/398-5570. 310 units. A/C TV TEL. $89–$149 single or double; $114–174 suite. Lowest rates on weekends. AE, DC, DISC, MC, V. Valet parking $5; free self-parking.

Once known as the Jacksonville Hotel, this 10-story Hilton opened in 1997 after extensive renovation. Featured is the Elvis Room, where "the King" purportedly stayed half a dozen times between 1955 and 1976. It and the other units have dark wood furniture, two phones with data ports, irons and boards, hairdryers, and balconies overlooking the river. A branch of Ruth's Chris Steakhouse offers expensive but extraordinarily tender beef, while a lobby cafe with open kitchen feeds the rest of us. There's an outdoor pool and an exercise room for keeping fit. If you're here on a weekend, you can take advantage of the hotel's lowest rates.

Omni Jacksonville Hotel. 245 Water St. (across from Jacksonville Landing between Pearl and Hogan sts.), Jacksonville, FL 32202. ☎ **800/THE-OMNI** or 904/355-OMNI. Fax 904/791-4809. 354 units. A/C MINIBAR TV TEL. $79–$199 single or double; $300–$500 suite. Lowest rates on weekends. AE, DC, DISC, MC, V. Valet parking $8; self-parking $6.

Jacksonville's best downtown digs is directly across the street from Jacksonville Landing and caters primarily to a corporate clientele that fills the gleaming marble lobby and meeting facilities during the week. The spacious guest rooms, thoroughly renovated in 1995, have blond-wood furnishings, plenty of lighting, and all the practical necessities you could ask for, including a reasonably priced minibar, a writing desk, two phones with voice mail, data ports, hair dryers, a fully-prepped coffee pot, large closets, and an iron and ironing board. Dining options in the hotel include a reasonably priced room serving continental cuisine as well as an extensive room service menu until 11pm. Sports-minded guests will appreciate the jogging and walking maps provided in each room, the outdoor swimming pool, and the well-equipped but closet-sized exercise room. Like the Hilton (see above), the Omni charges its lowest rates on weekends.

AT THE BEACHES

A dozen modest hotels line Jacksonville Beach's 1st Street, along the Atlantic Ocean, including a **Holiday Inn Sunspree** (☎ **800/HOLIDAY** or 904/249-9071), where all rooms come with refrigerators, microwaves, and coffee pots; **Days Inn Oceanfront Resort** (☎ **800/321-2037** or 904/249-7924); and **Ramada Resort** (☎ **800/ 2-RAMADA** or 904/241-5333).

Comfort Inn Oceanfront. 1515 N. 1st St. (2 blocks east of Fla. A1A), Jacksonville Beach, FL 32250. ☎ **800/654-8776** or 904/241-2311. Fax 904/249-3830. 180 units. A/C TV TEL. $79–$129 single or double; $140–$175 suite. Rates include continental breakfast. AE, DC, DISC, MC, V.

One of the best-priced options on the beachfront, this Comfort Inn offers rooms with balconies or screened patios. Microwave and/or refrigerator units are available for an extra charge. An especially good deal here is a honeymoon suite with whirlpool tub and living-room area. Continental breakfast and light fare are served in a small poolside dining room. An oceanfront lounge features live music for dancing on weekend nights from April to Labor Day. There's a large pool with rock waterfalls and a palm-fringed sundeck, secluded grotto whirlpool, small fitness room, gift/sundries shop, and multicourt sand volleyball park.

Sea Horse Oceanfront Inn. 120 Atlantic Blvd. (between Ocean Blvd. and the beach), Neptune Beach, FL 32266. ☎ **800/881-2330** or 904/246-2175. Fax 904/246-4256. 38 units. A/C TV TEL. $69–$109 single or double; $175–$250 penthouse suite for up to 6 people. AE, DC, DISC, MC, V.

All the rooms at this well-run beachfront property offer ocean views from balconies or patios. Families will appreciate the six units here with fully-equipped kitchenettes, not to mention a nice-size oceanfront pool, volleyball, shuffleboard, picnic tables, and a barbecue grill. And young couples will enjoy proximity to some of Jacksonville's top nightspots. If you have a large family or group, consider the vast and lovely third-floor penthouse—it has a big living room and dining area, a full kitchen, a separate bedroom as well as sofa beds, and a huge balcony furnished with a dining table and chaises lounges. A coffee shop adjoins the motel, and many other restaurants are within easy walking distance, as is a launderette.

GREAT DEALS ON DINING

Once a town where any dish other than Southern fried chicken or catfish was considered exotic, Jacksonville's dining scene is evolving into culinary diversity. The convention and visitors bureau's annual guide (see "Essentials," above) contains a complete list of restaurants, which now includes a handful of sushi bars, one or two authentic

Mexican eateries, a few Jewish delis, and some Cuban diners. The area even has half a dozen Thai restaurants, such as Old Siam, listed below.

IN JACKSONVILLE
Super-Cheap Eats

Don't forget that **Jacksonville Landing** on the downtown riverfront has several full-service restaurants and an inexpensive food court with outdoor seating (see "Exploring the Area," above).

✪ **Biscotti's.** 3556 St. Johns Ave. (between Talbot and Ingleside aves. in the Avondale section). ☎ **904/387-2060.** Reservations not accepted. Sandwiches and salads $5–$7; pastas and pizzas $7–$10; nightly fish special from $12. AE, DC, DISC, MC, V. Tues–Thurs 7am–10pm, Fri 7am–midnight, Sat 8am–midnight, Sun 8am–3pm. CALIFORNIA/ECLECTIC.

This brick-walled little neighborhood gem might have come out of New York's East Village, San Francisco's downtown, or Washington's Georgetown. A young and hip wait staff is pleasant and well informed. Daily specials, like pan-seared salmon or pork loin, are always fresh and beautifully presented. The huge and inventive salads are especially good: Try the Oriental version with chicken breast, orange slices, roasted peppers, and creamy sesame dressing. Pizzas, too, are served with wonderfully exotic and delicious toppings—ever try guacamole and black beans on your slice? On warm days choose a seat outside for great people-watching.

✪ **Cafe Carmon.** 1986 San Marco Blvd. (between Carlo St. and Naldo Ave.). ☎ **904/399-4488.** Reservations not accepted. Sandwiches $7–$8.50; main courses $7–$15. AE, DC, DISC, MC, V. Mon–Thurs 11am–11pm, Fri–Sat 11am–midnight, Sun 11am–9pm. FLORIDA CAFE.

A short drive from the Southbank Riverwalk, this comfy and casual restaurant is located in the heart of the San Marco Square shopping and dining district. In the daytime it's a mecca for shoppers and professionals; most nights the place is jammed with an after-theater crowd dropping in for cappuccinos and delectable desserts. The inside is sparsely decorated in black-and-white tile; the brick patio out front offers cafe seating. At lunch or dinner, you can order delicious salads, such as sautéed goat cheese with sun-dried tomatoes, toasted hazelnuts, cilantro, and mixed greens in a tangy vinaigrette. Generous-sized dinner options include a grilled, sautéed, or blackened fresh catch (often grouper) prepared Provençal, in beurre blanc sauce, or with pineapple salsa. Great lunch fare here, too.

For a Few Bucks More

River City Brewing Company. 835 Museum Circle (on Southbank Riverwalk). ☎ **904/398-2299.** Reservations only for parties of 8 or more. Main courses $14–$24; Sun brunch buffet $16 adults, $13 seniors, $8 children 3–12. AE, DC, DISC, MC, V. Mon–Thurs 11am–3pm and 5–10pm, Fri–Sat 11am–3pm and 5–11pm, Sun 10:30am–2:30pm and 5–10pm. (Lounges and terrace open for light fare Sun–Tues until midnight, Wed–Sat until 2am.) CALIFORNIA/LOUISIANA.

Occupying a prime location on the south bank of the St. Johns River, this gorgeous restaurant and microbrewery is an excellent choice for lunch or dinner. Its glass walls provide most tables with dramatic waterfront and skyline views. Or for an even better vantage point, sit outside on the enormous covered deck. Some weekends you'll hear live bands performing on the riverside stage.

Some guests find the home-brews to be bitter, but all rave about the super pastas, steaks, and seafood. Appetizers, too, are excellent. The crab cakes are delicately sautéed and served with a mix of baby greens and a tangy mango salsa. Pot stickers filled with morsels of shrimp and vegetables are also sautéed and seasoned with an Asian flair. For a main course, try the Cajun chicken linguine with mushrooms and ham in a spicy cream sauce.

Sunday brunch brings incredible buffets with fresh fruits and vegetables, bagels with smoked salmon and cream cheese, French toast, dozens of salads, and a carving station with honey-baked ham and prime rib. There is also a selection of decadent desserts.

AT THE BEACHES
Super-Cheap Eats

✪ **The Homestead.** 1712 Beach Blvd. (next to Adventure Landing, between 15th and 19th sts.), Jacksonville Beach. ☎ **904/249-5240.** Reservations only for large parties. Full dinners $7–$14. AE, DISC, MC, V. Mon–Fri 11am–4pm, daily 4:30pm–midnight. SOUTHERN.

This Jacksonville institution is usually packed with regulars waiting for a table in this log-cabinesque restaurant that has been serving big eaters since 1947. There's a good reason for the greasy atmosphere, for the big draw here is Southern fried chicken served in a skillet with homemade buttermilk biscuits and fresh honey, coleslaw, black-eyed peas, rice and gravy, creamed peas, and a choice of daily vegetables. Other favorites, like the saucer-sized chicken dumpling, is served with thick gravy and all the fixings. The narrow 50-foot-long copper-topped bar is a popular hangout for the local beach drinkers and the major nighttime haunt of celebrity golfers during Tournament Players Club championship games.

Old Siam. 1716 N. 3rd St. (Fla. A1A, in Holiday Plaza shopping center, between 16th and 17th aves. N), Jacksonville Beach. ☎ **904/247-7763.** Reservations only for parties of 6 or more. Main courses $8–$16. AE, MC, V. Mon–Tues 5–10pm, Wed–Thurs 11:30am–2:30pm and 5–10pm, Fri–Sat 5–11pm, Sun 5–9:30pm. THAI.

The best of the area's Thai restaurants, Pam Souvannasoth's trendy little enclave serves fine cuisine from his homeland and a good selection of wines to match its spicy yet subtle flavors. Pam's signature dish is his seafood special: shrimp, sea scallops, mussels, squid, and crab claws in a red chili sauce accented with sweet basil. The chilis in his "Number 3" spice level (out of 6) touched my tongue but did not overwhelm the other seasonings. Standard favorites like Pad Thai are light and perfectly balanced with sweet and slightly sour fish sauce.

For a Few Bucks More

✪ **Island Grille.** 981 N. 1st St. (at 9th Ave.), Jacksonville Beach. ☎ **904/241-1881.** Reservations recommended. Main courses $14–$17; main-course salads $9–$11. AE, DC, DISC, MC, V. Mar–Oct daily 11:30am–10pm; Nov–Feb Mon–Tues 4:30–10pm, Wed–Thurs 11:30am–10pm, Fri–Sat 11:30am–11pm, Sun 11:30am–10pm. (Bar open to 1:30am.) FLORIBBEAN/CONTINENTAL.

This is one of the area's most popular dining venues, especially in summer when the beach crowd vies for seats on the huge oceanfront deck. The Island Grille serves a varied menu with lots of innovative seafood as well as basic offerings like shrimp scampi, New York strip steak, pasta primavera, and even burgers. The many salads including one topped with tuna tataki are delicious and large. The appetizers here are so good you might just graze; they range from Bahamian conch fritters served with spicy pink rémoulade to escargots served in mushroom caps. You can enjoy good live music Wednesday through Saturday evenings.

✪ **Singleton's Seafood Shack.** 4728 Ocean St. (Fla. A1A, at St. Johns River Ferry landing), Mayport. ☎ **904/246-4442.** Full dinners $9–$13; sandwiches and salads $2–$6. DISC, MC, V. Sun–Thurs 10am–9pm, Fri–Sat 10am–10pm. SEAFOOD.

Capt. Ray Singleton has been serving fresh catches from this wooden shack since 1969. Locals swear this is the best fish camp in Jacksonville; a taste of any of the fresh catches like the blackened mahimahi or Cajun shrimp will confirm it. Unlike most other rustic fish houses in Florida's northeast that tend to overbatter and overfry everything that comes into the kitchen, Singleton's offers a variety of preparations for every imaginable kind of seafood. Of course, the fried standbys like conch fritters, shrimp, clam strips, and calamari are available, too. Along with your entree—try the grouper or cobia with mushroom and wine sauce—your Styrofoam plate will come stacked with a choice of side items like black beans and rice, coleslaw, fries, and hush puppies. You can also choose from a selection of chicken. Just off the water-side patio, check out the captain's model boat "museum," a wood shop filled with his finely carved ships.

JACKSONVILLE AFTER DARK

"Where do you take a date in Jacksonville?" goes an old local joke. The answer: "St. Augustine." Those who lament the lack of a nightlife remember when there really wasn't much to do after dusk unless you drove down to the Old City. These days, options beyond leaving town or lounging at the hotel bar are increasing. In addition to the spots recommended below, check listings in the weekend section of Friday's *Florida-Times Union,* or *Folio Weekly,* the free local alternative paper, available at restaurants, hotels, and all over town.

THE BAR SCENE   On the downtown riverfront, **Jacksonville Landing** has free outdoor rock, blues, country, and jazz concerts every Friday and Saturday night except during winter (see "Exploring the Area," above), and you'll have several libation options here, including a lively **Hooters** (☎ **904/356-5400**). The downtown post-teen crowd hangs at **Moto Lounge,** 214 W. Adams St. (☎ **904/355-6686**), where local and regional bands perform.

In the Avondale neighborhood, **Partners,** 3585 St. Johns Ave. at Ingleside Ave. (☎ **904/387-3585**), has a mellow, piano-bar ambience, innovative American food, and live jazz Wednesday to Saturday nights, making it a local favorite.

In the southern suburbs, an older crowd gathers at **T-Birds,** 9039 Southside Blvd. between Baymeadows Road and Phillips Highway (☎ **904/363-3399**), where a deejay spins dance music and good-time rock 'n' roll Tuesday to Saturday until 2am. Occasionally, former headliners you haven't heard from in years—such as the Little River Band, Starship, Kansas, and ELO—appear. Also big here is happy hour, featuring a lavish complimentary buffet and drink specials from 5 to 7:30pm weeknights.

Out at Neptune Beach, one of the more popular spots is **Ragtime Tavern and Taproom,** 207 Atlantic Blvd. (☎ **904/241-7877**). This beach bar and restaurant features local groups playing live jazz and blues Thursday to Sunday nights. Weekends, especially, the place is really jumping and the crowd is young, but it's lively rather than rowdy. Ragtime brews its own beer. It's open nightly until at least 12:30am. Across the street is the **Sun Dog Diner,** at 207 Atlantic Blvd. (☎ **904/241-8221**), with nightly acoustic music and decent diner food.

The favorite pub in Jacksonville Beach, **Sloppy Joe's,** 200 N. 1st St. (☎ **904/270-1767**), is an off-shoot of the Key West institution.

THE PERFORMING ARTS   With the 73,000-seat **Alltell Stadium,** at East Duval and Haines streets (☎ **904/630-3900**), the 10,600-seat **Jacksonville Veterans Memorial Coliseum,** 1145 E. Adams St. (☎ **904/630-3900** for information, or 904/353-3309 to charge tickets), and the 3,200-seat **Florida Times Union Center for the Performing Arts,** 300 Water St., between Hogan and Pearl streets (☎ **904/630-3900**), Jacksonville has plenty of seats for concerts, touring Broadway shows, dance companies, and big-name performers. Check the local papers mentioned above for current offerings, or call the *Times-Union*'s automated information service for up-to-date schedules (☎ **904/355-1500,** ext. 7450).

5 Amelia Island

32 miles NE of Jacksonville, 192 miles NE of Orlando, 372 miles N of Miami.

Exclusive and beautiful Amelia Island is a charming getaway about a 45-minute drive northeast of downtown Jacksonville. Sitting at the Georgia line, this pristine barrier island has 13 beautiful miles of beachfront and offers world-class tennis and golfing at two of Florida's most luxurious resorts. Yes, it has two paper mills and small seaport, but the island's bay-side town of **Fernandina Beach** also boasts a 50-block area of gorgeous Victorian and Queen Anne homes listed in the National Register of Historic Places.

The town's Victorian district dates from the late 19th century, when island's timber, phosphate, and naval stores industries boomed. The 1970s and '80s saw another economic explosion, as real estate developers built condos, cottages, and the two big resorts that now dominate the southern end of the island. In recent years, Fernandina Beach has seen another big boom, this time in bed-and-breakfast establishments.

ESSENTIALS

GETTING THERE   The island is served by **Jacksonville International Airport** (see "Essentials" in section 4, above). The scenic drive here from downtown Jacksonville is via Heckscher Drive (Fla. 105) and Fla. A1A; from the beaches, via Fla. A1A north and the St. John's River Ferry. The fast, four-lane way is via I-95 north and the Buccaneer Trail (Fla. A1A) east.

VISITOR INFORMATION   For advance information, contact the **Amelia Island–Fernandina Beach–Yulee Chamber of Commerce,** 102 Centre St. (P.O. Box 472), Fernandina Beach, FL 32035 (☎ **800/2-AMELIA** or 904/261-3248; fax 904/261-6997; www.goflorida.com/amelia-island). The chamber's visitor information center, in the old train station at the bay end of Centre Street, is open Monday to Friday from 9am to 5pm.

GETTING AROUND   There's no public transportation on this 13-mile-long island, so you'll need a vehicle. The **Old Towne Carriage Company** (☎ **904/277-1555**) offers narrated, horse-drawn carriage tours of Fernandina Beach's historic district, leaving from the waterfront on Centre Street. They close for 2 months during the winter when the horses are put out to pasture. Rides cost $15 for adults, $7.50 for kids under 13.

HITTING THE BEACH

Wrapping around the island's northern end and backed by rolling dunes, the exquisite white-sand beach at **Fort Clinch State Park** is one of the area's most beautiful and is filled with shells and driftwood. Also, the best part is that the coast curves here, which gives the feeling of being in a private cove. The park entrance is on Atlantic Avenue, just east of Fletcher Avenue; wooden boardwalks lead from the parking area to the sands. At the western end of the beach, a jetty and a pier jutting into Cumberland South are popular with anglers. Entrance fees are $3.25 per vehicle with up to eight occupants, $1 for pedestrians and bicyclists. There are 62 campsites available at $20.62 per night with electricity, $18.53 without. You can reserve a site up to 11 months in advance (a very good idea in summer) by contacting the park at 2601 Atlantic Ave., Fernandina Beach, FL 32034 (☎ **904/277-7274**).

Main Beach, on North Fletcher Avenue (Fla. A1A) and Trout Street, is the center of activity, with good swimming, rest rooms, picnic shelters, showers, a food concession, a playground, and more. There's lots of free parking, and this area is popular with families.

Pets on leashes are allowed on all the island's public beaches.

AFFORDABLE OUTDOOR ACTIVITIES
BOATING, FISHING, SAILING & KAYAKING   The **Amelia Island Charter Boat Association** (☎ 904/261-2870) can help arrange deep-sea fishing charters, party-boat excursions, sailing trips, sightseeing cruises, and more.

Voyager Adventures, based at Fernandina Harbor Marina, 3977 1st Ave. (☎ 904/ 321-1244; fax 904/321-2505), has several cruises aboard the *Voyager,* a 100-foot replica of a 19th-century gaff-rigged packet schooner. A prime destination is Cumberland Island, across the sound in Georgia (remember when John F. Kennedy Jr. was married over there without a single paparazzi present?). Also based at the marina, **Windward Sailing School** (☎ 904/261-9125) will teach you to skipper your boat. Call these companies for details, prices, and reservations.

Kayak Amelia (☎ 904/321-0697; www.kayakamelia.com) has learning and advanced-level trips on the back bays. Half-day trips cost $50 per person; sunset paddles on Friday, $25 per person.

GOLF & TENNIS   If you're not staying in a resort with golf and tennis facilities, try the 27-hole **Fernandina Municipal Golf Course** (☎ 904/277-7370) and the two tennis courts at the municipal park in Fernandina Beach at Atlantic Avenue and 11th Street.

HORSEBACK RIDING   **Seahorse Stables,** 7500 Fla. A1A (☎ 904/261-4878), is open daily and can arrange horseback riding on the beach at the south end of the island for $35. Reservations are required.

SCENIC CRUISES   Departing from the city marina on Front Street in Fernandina Beach, the sleek *Good Times Too* (☎ 904/277-8482) goes cruising on the inland waterways hereabouts. Call for schedule and prices.

SCUBA DIVING   **Aqua Explorers Dive Center,** 2856 Sadler Rd. (☎ 904/ 261-5989), open Monday to Saturday from 10am to 6pm, teaches certification courses, arranges charters, and sells and rents equipment.

SHOPPING
Stroll down **Centre Street** in downtown Fernandina Beach, with its vintage storefronts and charming boutiques. Quality antiques, consignment shops, and bookstores line the wide boulevard ending at the marina. On the south end of the island, **Palmetto Walk,** under a canopy of live oaks, is another good shopping bet. The chamber of commerce has complete lists and descriptions of the island's many up-scale stores (see "Essentials," above).

ACCOMMODATIONS YOU CAN AFFORD
I don't know for sure, but Fernandina Beach may have more bed-and-breakfast inns than the rest of Florida combined. Indeed, more than two dozen of the town's charming Victorian and Queen Anne houses have been restored and turned into B&Bs, and apparently they all stay busy, at least on weekends. Industry veteran David Caples, who holds seminars nationwide for wannabe innkeepers, is based here at the Elizabeth Pointe Lodge (see below). For a complete list, contact the chamber of commerce (see "Essentials," above), or check out the Web site of the **Amelia Island Bed**

& Breakfast Association at **www.ameliaislandinns.com** (the association does not have an address or phone number).

Also, a number of agencies will book vacation properties ranging from affordable cottages to magnificent mansions. Contact **Amelia Island Lodging Systems**, 584 S. Fletcher Ave., Fernandina Beach, FL 32034 (☎ **800/872-8531** or 904/261-4148; fax 904/261-9200), which even has a lighthouse for rent. Or try **Amelia Island Resort Rentals,** 5012 First Coast Hwy. (P.O. Box 6159), Amelia Island, FL 32035 (☎ **800/ 874-8679** or 904/261-9444; fax 904/261-9479; www.amelia.com).

The island has two chain motels: a **Hampton Inn** (☎ **800/HAMPTON** or 904/ 321-1111) and a **Shoney's Inn** (☎ **800/222-2222** or 904/277-2300), both on Sadler Road a block from the beach.

Your best **camping** option here is Fort Clinch State Park (see "Hitting the Beach," above).

SUPER-CHEAP SLEEPS

✪ **Beachside Motel Inn.** 3172 S. Fletcher Ave. (Fla. A1A, south of Simmons Rd.), Fernandina Beach, FL 32034. ☎ **904/261-4236.** Fax 904/261-8336. 20 units. A/C TV TEL. $65–$103 single or double; $79–$139 efficiency. Weekly discounts available. AE, MC, V.

The only motel beside the beach here, this inexpensive property is clean and well maintained by resident owners Jerry and Joy Knight. The white-and-blue 2-story 1970s stucco building sits on a beautiful stretch of public but uncluttered beach. The rooms, many with ocean views, are spacious and furnished with standard motel furnishings. Many long-term visitors return each season to stay in the efficiencies with fully-equipped kitchens. An outdoor pool is surrounded by lounge chairs and a spacious deck overlooking the ocean. The hotel is convenient to lots of sports activities and good restaurants (the Surf Restaurant and its outdoor pub is directly across the road). Room rates include free coffee each morning and a selection of store-bought breakfast rolls, doughnuts, and pastries.

WORTH A SPLURGE

Elizabeth Pointe Lodge. 98 S. Fletcher Dr. (just south of Atlantic Ave.), Fernandina Beach, FL 32034. ☎ **800/772-3359** or 904/277-4851. Fax 904/277-6500. 24 units, 1 cottage. A/C TV TEL. $125–$195 single or double; $215 cottage. Rates include buffet breakfast and evening social hour. Packages available. AE, DISC, MC, V.

Sitting right on the beach, this 3-story, Nantucket-style shingle-sided building's Victorian appearance belies the fact that it was built in 1991 by B&B guru David Caples. Big paned windows look out from the comfy lounge (with library and fireplace) and dining room to an expansive front porch and the surf beyond. Antiques and reproductions, handmade quilts, and other touches lend the 20 rooms in the main building a turn-of-the-century cottage ambience. They all have oversize bathtubs (some with Jacuzzi jets), robes, irons, and ironing boards. Four other rooms are in the Harris Lodge next door, and there's the two-bedroom, two-bath Mills Cottage for rent. The main house's dining room provides breakfast, a light-fare lunch and dinner menu, and 24-hour room service.

Fairbanks House. 227 South 7th St. (between Beech and Cedar sts.), Fernandina Beach, Amelia Island, FL 32034. ☎ **800/261-4838** or 904-277-0500. Fax 904/277-3103. 9 units, 3 detached cottages. A/C TV TEL. $125–$225 single or double; $175 cottage. Rates include full breakfast. AE, DISC, MC, V.

With all the amenities and almost as much privacy of a first-class hotel in a superbly refurbished 1885 Italianate home, the Fairbanks House is a top B&B choice for those looking to be pampered. Many rooms and all the cottages offer private entrances for guests who prefer not to walk through the main house. Room no. 3, in the back of the house on the main floor, is one of the finest rooms, with a private entrance, a large sitting room, a plush king-size bed, period antiques, porcelain, oil paintings, and fresh flowers. Occupying the entire top floor, the two-bedroom Tower Suite has plenty of room to spread out, plus 360° views and its own Jacuzzi. Note that Fairbanks is the only B&B on the island with a pool. No smoking indoors.

GREAT DEALS ON DINING

In addition to Shakespeare's Kitchen (see below), you'll find several restaurants, pubs, and snack shops along Centre Street, between the bay and 8th Street (Fla. A1A), in Fernandina Beach's old town.

SUPER-CHEAP EATS

✪ **Shakespeare's Kitchen.** Upstairs at 316 Centre St. (between 3rd and 4th sts.). ☎ 904/277-2076. Sandwiches and salads $6–$8; dinner main courses $10–$13. DISC, MC, V. Mon–Sat 8–10:30am and 11:30am–3pm, Thurs–Sat 6–10pm, Sun 10am–2pm. SANDWICHES/SALADS.

A tiny and sunny dining room hidden on the second floor of a store on Centre Street, Linda Harter's seedsy-weedsy spot provides hearty and healthy breakfasts, homemade sandwiches like roasted bell peppers and goat cheese on rustic white bread, and salads such as blackened chicken and pasta. Linda serves her sandwiches with a side such as pasta salad with fresh herbs and field greens, making for a substantial portion. Dinner sees a few main courses added to the mix, usually pastas. You can wash it down with a glass of perfumed Hawaiian iced tea. A loyal following of young professionals and shoppers chows down at the small antique tables inside or at wrought-iron versions out on a rooftop deck.

WORTH A SPLURGE

✪ **Beech Street Grill.** 801 Beech St. (at 8th St./Fla. A1A), Fernandina Beach. ☎ 904/277-3662. Reservations strongly suggested. Main courses $17–$25; pastas $12–$17. AE, DC, DISC, MC, V. Daily 6–10pm. REGIONAL NEW AMERICAN.

Surpassed only by The Grill in the Ritz-Carlton as the island's best restaurant, the Beech Street Grill pleases all palates with a large menu of fish, chicken, and meat choices including seasonal game like roasted venison loin in a black currant sauce with sweet potato and onion hash. Nightly fish specialties are always exceptional, but be sure to ask the price, since some can be higher than printed menu options. A Parmesan-encrusted grouper with a tropical fruit salsa is superb. When available, seared tuna is always perfect, too. The dense and tasty crab cakes or the chewy steamed dumplings are great choices for starters, as is the huge mixed green salad with mustard-basil vinaigrette and toasted pecans and blue cheese. Housed in a century-old landmark home and a newer addition adjacent to the original building, three dining rooms offer large tables in a lively atmosphere. Attentive and knowledgeable waiters serve the showy plates with efficiency and grace.

Cafe Atlantis. 22 S. 4th St. (½ block south of Centre St.). ☎ 904/277-0042. Reservations suggested. Main courses $17–$22. AE, DC, DISC, MC, V. Daily 5:30–9:30pm. ECLECTIC/NEW WORLD.

Chef/owner Brian Batsel, who left a cooking position at the Ritz-Carlton and who earlier broke in his Southwestern cuisine spurs at the notable Red Sage in Washington, D.C., expands his range here to include Asian-inspired salads, Caribbean pork and chicken dishes, Spanish seafood stews, and local seafood specialties to create a thoroughly exciting menu. Offered on a bitter chilly January night, the black-bean soup with cilantro and a cream garnish was rich and tasty, if a little tame. Ask for hot sauce; you'll get the real thing, a bright orange scotch bonnet pepper puree with a real kick.

AMELIA ISLAND AFTER DARK

This romantic island goes to bed early. If you tire of the lounges in the island's resorts, check out the **Palace Saloon,** 117 Centre St., at 2nd St. (☎ **904/261-6320**). It claims to be Florida's oldest watering hole (open since 1878). Complete with a pressed-tin ceiling and a mahogany bar, it once hosted the Carnegies and the du Ponts; now, a lively bar and an adjacent pool bar and stage area are often packed. Some nights you'll find live local blues or rock.

Appendix

AIRLINES

Air Canada
☎ 800/776-3000
www.aircanada.ca

American Airlines
☎ 800/433-7300
www.americanair.com

British Airways
☎ 800/247-9297
☎ 0345/222-111 in Britain
www.british-airways.com

Canadian Airlines International
☎ 800/426-7000
www.cdnair.ca

Continental Airlines
☎ 800/525-0280
www.flycontinental.com

Delta Air Lines
☎ 800/221-1212
www.delta-air.com

Kiwi International Air Lines
☎ 800/538-5494
www.jetkiwi.com

Midway Airlines
☎ 800/446-4392

Northwest Airlines
☎ 800/225-2525
www.nwa.com

Southwest Airlines
☎ 800/435-9792
www.iflyswa.com

Tower Air
☎ 800/34-TOWER (800/348-6937) outside New York
(☎ 718/553-8500 in New York)
www.towerair.com

Trans World Airlines (TWA)
☎ 800/221-2000
www.twa.com

United Airlines
☎ 800/241-6522
www.ual.com

USAirways
☎ 800/428-4322
www.usair.com

Virgin Atlantic Airways
☎ 800/862-8621 in Continental U.S.
☎ 0293/747-747 in Britain
www.fly.virgin.com

CAR RENTAL AGENCIES
Advantage
☎ 800/777-5500
www.arac.com

Alamo
☎ 800/327-9633
www.goalamo.com

Avis
☎ 800/331-1212 in the Continental U.S.
☎ 800/TRY-AVIS in Canada
www.avis.com

Budget
☎ 800/527-0700
www.budgetrentacar.com

Dollar
☎ 800/800-4000
www.dollarcar.com

Enterprise
☎ 800/325-8007
www.pickenterprise.com

Hertz
☎ 800/654-3131
www.hertz.com

National
☎ 800/CAR-RENT
www.nationalcar.com

Payless
☎ 800/PAYLESS
www.paylesscar.com

Rent-A-Wreck
☎ 800/535-1391
rent-a-wreck.com

Thrifty
☎ 800/367-2277
www.thrifty.com

Value
☎ 800/327-2501
www.go-value.com

MAJOR HOTEL & MOTEL CHAINS

Best Western International
☎ 800/528-1234
www.bestwestern.com

Clarion Hotels
☎ 800/CLARION
www.hotelchoice.com/cgi-bin/res/webres?clarion.html

Comfort Inns
☎ 800/228-5150
www.hotelchoice.com/cgi-bin/res/webres?comfort.html

Courtyard by Marriott
☎ 800/321-2211
www.courtyard.com

Days Inn
☎ 800/325-2525
www.daysinn.com

Doubletree Hotels
☎ 800/222-TREE
www.doubletreehotels.com

Econo Lodges
☎ 800/55-ECONO
www.hotelchoice.com/cgi-bin/res/webres?econo.html

Fairfield Inn by Marriott
☎ 800/228-2800
www.fairfieldinn.com

Hampton Inn
☎ 800/HAMPTON
www.hampton-inn.com

Hilton Hotels
☎ 800/HILTONS
www.hilton.com

Holiday Inn
☎ 800/HOLIDAY
www.holiday-inn.com

Howard Johnson
☎ 800/654-2000
www.hojo.com/hojo.html

Hyatt Hotels & Resorts
☎ 800/228-9000
www.hyatt.com

ITT Sheraton
☎ 800/325-3535
www.sheraton.com

Marriott Hotels
☎ 800/228-9290
www.marriott.com

Motel 6
☎ 800/4-MOTEL6 (800/466-8536)

Quality Inns
☎ 800/228-5151
www.hotelchoice.com/cgi-bin/res/webres?quality.html

Radisson Hotels International
☎ 800/333-3333
www.radisson.com

Ramada Inns
☎ 800/2-RAMADA
www.ramada.com

Red Carpet Inns
☎ 800/251-1962

Red Lion Hotels & Inns
☎ 800/547-8010
www.travelweb.com

Red Roof Inns
☎ 800/843-7663
www.redroof.com

Residence Inn by Marriott
☎ 800/331-3131
www.residenceinn.com

Rodeway Inns
☎ 800/228-2000
www.hotelchoice.com/cgi-bin/res/webres?rodeway.html

Super 8 Motels
☎ 800/800-8000
www.super8motels.com

Travelodge
☎ 800/255-3050

Vagabond Inns
☎ 800/522-1555
www.vagabondinns.com

Wyndham Hotels and Resorts
☎ 800/822-4200 in Continental U.S. and Canada
www.wyndham.com

Index

Save $15 on a Weekly Rental

Terms and Conditions:

Offer valid on an Intermediate (Group C) through a Full Size 4-Door (Group E) car. Dollars off applies to the cost of the total rental with a minimum of 5 days. Coupon must be surrendered at time of rental; one per rental. An advance reservation is required. May not be used in conjunction with any other coupon, promotion or offer. Coupon valid at participating Avis locations in the contiguous U.S. Offer may not be available on all rates at all times. Cars subject to availability. Taxes, local government surcharges, vehicle licensing fee no higher than $1.85/day in CA, airport recoupment fee up to 12% at some locations and optional items, such as LDW, additional driver fee and fuel service are extra. Renter must meet Avis age, driver and credit require-ments. Minimum age is 25 but may vary by location. Rental must begin by 9/30/2000.

Rental Sales Agent Instructions
At checkout:
In CPN, enter **MULA067**
Complete this information:

RA #: _____

Rental location: _____
Attach to coupon tape.

AVIS®

We try harder.

COUPON # MULA067

©1998 Wizard Co., Inc.

FROMMER'S® COMPLETE TRAVEL GUIDES
(Comprehensive guides with selections in all price ranges—from deluxe to budget)

Alaska
Amsterdam
Arizona
Atlanta
Australia
Austria
Bahamas
Barcelona, Madrid & Seville
Belgium, Holland &
 Luxembourg
Bermuda
Boston
Budapest & the Best of
 Hungary
California
Canada
Cancún, Cozumel & the
 Yucatán
Cape Cod, Nantucket &
 Martha's Vineyard
Caribbean
Caribbean Cruises &
 Ports of Call
Caribbean Ports of Call
Carolinas & Georgia
Chicago
China
Colorado
Costa Rica
Denver, Boulder &
 Colorado Springs
England
Europe
Florida

France
Germany
Greece
Hawaii
Hong Kong
Honolulu, Waikiki & Oahu
Ireland
Israel
Italy
Jamaica & Barbados
Japan
Las Vegas
London
Los Angeles
Maryland & Delaware
Maui
Mexico
Miami & the Keys
Montana & Wyoming
Montréal & Québec City
Munich & the Bavarian Alps
Nashville & Memphis
Nepal
New England
New Mexico
New Orleans
New York City
Nova Scotia, New
 Brunswick &
 Prince Edward Island
Oregon
Paris
Philadelphia & the Amish
 Country

Portugal
Prague & the Best of the
 Czech Republic
Provence & the Riviera
Puerto Rico
Rome
San Antonio & Austin
San Diego
San Francisco
Santa Fe, Taos &
 Albuquerque
Scandinavia
Scotland
Seattle & Portland
Singapore & Malaysia
South Pacific
Spain
Switzerland
Thailand
Tokyo
Toronto
Tuscany & Umbria
USA
Utah
Vancouver & Victoria
Vermont, New Hampshire &
 Maine
Vienna & the Danube Valley
Virgin Islands
Virginia
Walt Disney World &
 Orlando
Washington, D.C.
Washington State

FROMMER'S® DOLLAR-A-DAY GUIDES
(The ultimate guides to comfortable low-cost travel)

Australia from $50 a Day
California from $60 a Day
Caribbean from $60 a Day
England from $60 a Day
Europe from $50 a Day
Florida from $60 a Day
Greece from $50 a Day
Hawaii from $60 a Day
Ireland from $50 a Day

Israel from $45 a Day
Italy from $50 a Day
London from $70 a Day
New York from $75 a Day
New Zealand from $50 a Day
Paris from $70 a Day
San Francisco from $60 a Day
Washington, D.C., from
 $60 a Day

FROMMER'S® MEMORABLE WALKS

Chicago
London

New York
Paris

San Francisco

FROMMER'S® PORTABLE GUIDES

Acapulco, Ixtapa/
    Zihuatanejo
Bahamas
California Wine
    Country
Charleston & Savannah
Chicago

Dublin
Las Vegas
London
Maine Coast
New Orleans
New York City
Paris

Puerto Vallarta, Manzanillo
    & Guadalajara
San Francisco
Sydney
Tampa Bay & St. Petersburg
Venice
Washington, D.C.

FROMMER'S® NATIONAL PARK GUIDES

Grand Canyon
National Parks of the American West
Yellowstone & Grand Teton

Yosemite & Sequoia/
    Kings Canyon
Zion & Bryce Canyon

THE COMPLETE IDIOT'S TRAVEL GUIDES
(The ultimate user-friendly trip planners)

Cruise Vacations
Planning Your Trip to Europe
Hawaii

Las Vegas
Mexico's Beach Resorts
New Orleans

New York City
San Francisco
Walt Disney World

SPECIAL-INTEREST TITLES

The Civil War Trust's Official Guide to
    the Civil War Discovery Trail
Frommer's Caribbean Hideaways
Israel Past & Present
New York City with Kids
New York Times Weekends
Outside Magazine's Adventure Guide
    to New England
Outside Magazine's Adventure Guide
    to Northern California

Outside Magazine's Adventure Guide
    to the Pacific Northwest
Outside Magazine's Guide to Family Vacations
Places Rated Almanac
Retirement Places Rated
Washington, D.C., with Kids
Wonderful Weekends from Boston
Wonderful Weekends from New York City
Wonderful Weekends from San Francisco
Wonderful Weekends from Los Angeles

THE UNOFFICIAL GUIDES®
(Get the unbiased truth from these candid, value-conscious guides)

Atlanta
Branson, Missouri
Chicago
Cruises
Disneyland

Florida with Kids
The Great Smoky
    & Blue Ridge
    Mountains
Las Vegas

Miami & the Keys
Mini-Mickey
New Orleans
New York City
San Francisco

Skiing in the West
Walt Disney World
Walt Disney World
    Companion
Washington, D.C.

FROMMER'S® IRREVERENT GUIDES
(Wickedly honest guides for sophisticated travelers)

Amsterdam
Boston
Chicago

London
Manhattan

New Orleans
Paris

San Francisco
Walt Disney World
Washington, D.C.

FROMMER'S® DRIVING TOURS

America
Britain
California

Florida
France
Germany

Ireland
Italy
New England

Scotland
Spain
Western Europe

www.frommers.com

Arthur Frommer's OUTSPOKEN ENCYCLOPEDIA OF TRAVEL

You've Read our Books, Now Visit our Website...

With more than 6,000 pages of the most up-to-date travel bargains and information from the name you trust the most, Arthur Frommer's Outspoken Encyclopedia of Travel brings you all the information you need to plan your next trip.

Register to Win free tickets, accommodations and more!

Arthur Frommer's Daily Newsletter

Bookmark the daily newsletter to read about the hottest travel news and bargains in the industry or subscribe and receive it daily on your own desktop.

Hot Spot of the Month

Check out the Hot Spot each month to get the best information and hottest deals for your favorite vacation destinations.

200 Foreign & Domestic Destinations

Choose from more than 200 destinations and get the latest information on accommodations, airfare, restaurants, and more.

Frommer's Travel Guides

Shop our online bookstore and choose from more than 200 current Frommer's travel guides. Secure transactions guaranteed!

Bookmark www.frommers.com for the most up-to-date travel bargains and information—updated daily!

WHEREVER YOU TRAVEL, *H*ELP IS NEVER FAR AWAY.

From planning your trip to providing travel assistance along the way, American Express® Travel Service Offices are always there to help.

Florida

American Express Travel Service
32 Miracle Mile
Coral Gables
305/446-3381

American Express Travel Service
330 Biscayne Boulevard
Miami
305/358-7350

American Express Travel Service
3312-14 N.E. 32nd Street
Fort Lauderdale
954/565-9481

American Express Travel Service
2 West Church Street, Suite 1
Orlando
407/843-0004

American Express Travel Service
9908 Baymeadows Road
Jacksonville
904/642-1701

American Express Travel Service
1343 Main Street, Suite 501
Sarasota
941/365-2520

American Express Travel Service
Epcot Center
Walt Disney World Resort
Lake Buena Vista
407/827-7500

American Express Travel Service
One Tampa City Center
Tampa
813/273-0310

Travel

http://www.americanexpress.com/travel

**American Express Travel Service Offices are located throughout Florida.
For the office nearest you, call 1-800-AXP-3429.**